EVIDENCE

EVIDENCE

SECOND EDITION

DECLAN McGRATH
LL.B., LL.M., ATTORNEY-AT-LAW, SENIOR COUNSEL

With a contribution from

EMILY EGAN McGRATH
LL.B. LL.M., BARRISTER-AT-LAW

ROUND HALL

THOMSON REUTERS

Published in 2014 by
Thomson Reuters (Professional) Ireland Limited
(Registered in Ireland, Company No. 80867.
Registered Office and address for service:
43 Fitzwilliam Place, Dublin 2, Ireland)
trading as Round Hall

Typeset by
Gough Typesetting Services
Dublin

Printed and bound in the UK by
CPI Group (UK) Ltd, Croydon, CR0 4YY

ISBN 978-0-41403-505-8

A catalogue record for this book
is available from the British Library

To my father

FOREWORD

In the history of Irish law, the law of evidence has been ubiquitous but perhaps unloved. It is, after all, the operating system upon which all litigation runs and is present, if sometimes unobserved, in every single case, large or small, heard on any day in any Irish court. It is, however, a complex and eclectic mixture of logic, pragmatism, experience and observations upon human nature, and increasingly, conceptions of fairness as to the circumstances in which evidence is obtained. It also tends to function best when unobserved. On those occasions when the law of evidence becomes an issue to be addressed, it is essentially negative in character. A dispute only arises when one party seeks to exclude a piece of information which the other party considers helpful to resolving the issue in the case. Perhaps for these reasons, the law of evidence has always been seen as an area of the law which could benefit from a comprehensive review and reorganisation.

In his foreword to the first edition of this work, the then Chief Justice, Mr Justice Keane, observed that the law was "in serious need of clarification or even radical reform". This was not the first Benthamite call for reform. In April 1940, the members of the Statistical Society of Ireland, an influential group comprising senior civil servants, academics and members of professions and others, heard a paper on *Desirable Ameliorations of the Law* delivered by James Creed Meredith, a former President of the Society, a former President of the Supreme Court of the Dáil Courts, a Kantian scholar, a published author, and not least, a judge of the Irish Supreme Court at the time of the lecture. Foremost among the areas for reform identified by him was the whole law of evidence, which in his view required to be brought up to date. He considered the main defect in the "theory and statement of our inherited law of evidence is its negative character". Among the audience that evening, and an enthusiastic respondent to the paper, was T.C. Kingsmill Moore, SC, himself a future Supreme Court Judge, and who would make his own significant contribution to the development of the law in this area in his thoughtful judgments in *The People (Attorney General) v. Casey (No.2)* [1963] I.R. 33, and *The People (Attorney General) v. O'Brien* [1965] I.R. 142.

The first programme for law reform announced by the Department of Justice in 1962 contained a proposal for the codification of the entire law of evidence. A similar proposal was contained in the first programme for law reform of the newly established Law Reform Commission in 1975. That body addressed the hearsay rule in a working paper in 1980, and in a full report in 1988, The Commission's third programme for law reform produced reports on documentary evidence, expert evidence, and again, hearsay. Most of these reports express a desire for more radical reform. Despite these efforts, comprehensive reform seems very far away, not least because agreement as to the unsatisfactory nature of the present law may mask significant disagreement about the nature of the defects, and the reforms to be desired.

It seems possible that further developments of the law of evidence, whether by statutory intervention or by judicial decision, will continue to be incremental, and by molecular rather than molar movements, although even that may be attended by controversy. Whether the law develops by incremental steps or radical leaps, two things appear necessary: first, a comprehensive survey of the law as it exists and second, a thoughtful analysis of the law as a guide for future decisions and legislative reform. These are tasks that require both practical knowledge and academic skills. Declan McGrath is ideally placed to carry out this work combining as he does, a strong academic background in study, research and teaching, with a wide and demanding practice as a barrister. Perhaps the most striking and welcome feature of this book is the fact that the law of evidence is presented and discussed by reference to a wealth of modern Irish case law, which is carefully collected, lucidly analysed, and occasionally thoughtfully criticised. It is not so long ago that the law of evidence was taught and practised through English text books with only occasional reference to major landmark Irish cases, themselves often treated as subcategories of constitutional law. That gap in Irish legal practice and education is comprehensively and admirably addressed in the present volume.

It seems unavoidable that students, teachers, practitioners, judges and law reformers will continue to struggle with the law of evidence in the years to come. But whether their task is the resolution of individual cases, the elucidation of principle, the reform of the statute book or the answering of exam questions, I have no doubt that they will find in the second edition of this book, an authoritative and indispensable guide.

Donal O'Donnell
24 November 2014

FOREWORD TO THE FIRST EDITION

"There is in truth no one theory which will account for the decisions. Within a single exception are found refinements and qualifications inconsistent with the reason upon which the exception itself is built. In short, a picture of the ... rule with its exceptions would resemble an old-fashioned crazy quilt made of patches cut from a group of paintings by cubists, futurists and surrealists."[1]

The learned authors in that passage were discussing the rule against hearsay. But their metaphor could also stand as a description of our law of evidence in general. So much so indeed that, when the Law Reform Commission many years ago first addressed possible reforms in the law, it was simply the immensity of the task involved that persuaded them not to advocate, in the short term at least, a wholesale codification of the law.

The absence of such a code makes it all the more important that judges, practitioners and students should have available to them reliable and comprehensive textbooks on the Irish law of evidence. This book by Declan McGrath is not the first such work, but I have no doubt that its generous scope and length and the erudition and industry which have gone into its compilation will earn it a ready welcome in all branches of the legal profession. The need for such a work is all the more pressing given the wide and significant differences that have emerged in recent decades between the law in Ireland and the neighbouring jurisdictions. Since the law of evidence constitutes the essential framework within which all adversarial litigation is conducted within our system—and its principles cannot be wholly disregarded even by the many tribunals which are now a feature of Irish life—a practitioner who ventures on the conduct of a case armed only with one of the standard English works, splendid as some of them are, may be courting disaster.

The reasons for those divergences between Irish and English law in this area are well known but will bear restating. Although the law of evidence is in the main judge-made, there have been radical interventions by the legislature in recent times and these are fully and helpfully outlined by Mr McGrath. It is sufficient to point to the provisions of the Criminal Evidence Act 1992 which have in criminal cases removed the shadow of the House of Lord's decision in *Myers v DPP* [1965] A.C. 1001, by enabling documents to be proved by a person other than the author in carefully defined circumstances. Similarly, in cases concerning the welfare of children, there has been the welcome relaxation of the strict requirements of the common law effected by Part III of the Children Act 1997.

It is, however, the influence of the Constitution which has most profoundly reshaped our common law rules of evidence. It is a feature of Mr McGrath's work that he lays emphasis on the extent to which some of the major principles of the law of evidence, such as the right to silence, the privilege against self-incrimination and the right to cross-examine are nowadays anchored in the constitutional guarantees of a trial in due course of law in criminal cases and of fair procedures in all proceedings affecting the rights of individuals. A study of what he has to say, however, inevitably conveys the impression that in some areas the law is seriously in need of clarification or even radical reform.

This is particularly of concern when one views the state of our law as to the reception of evidence which has been allegedly obtained in breach of a person's constitutional rights. One can resist the proposition that in the case of what the law has sometimes called "real evidence", such as illegal drugs found in a house, courts should not be

obliged to decide the case without regard to the existence of such evidence, however
it has been obtained. But there is surely room, in the case of trivial and unintended
infringements of a person's constitutional rights, for a process of balancing against
the need to uphold the rights of particular individuals the interest of the public in the
prosecution of serious crime.

I have no doubt that Mr McGrath's scholarly but extremely practical work will
find a place on the bookshelves of all lawyers concerned with the application of the
law of evidence. I wish it every success.

Ronan Keane
8 November 2004

PREFACE

In the decade since the first edition of this text was written, the law of evidence in this jurisdiction has undergone significant development. Although there have been some significant legislative interventions, including Part 3 of the Criminal Justice Act 2006 and s.34 of the Criminal Procedure Act 2010, the bulk of the development has occurred by way of judicial decision, impelled in some areas by the ever increasing influence of the jurisprudence of the European Court of Human Rights. The landmark decision of the Supreme Court in *People (DPP) v Gormley and White* [2014] IESC 17, in relation to the right of access to a lawyer is a particularly noteworthy example. I have attempted to provide an analysis of these developments while also referring to relevant comparative material.

Such has been the volume of case law in this and other jurisdictions to review, that I had to persuade my wife, Emily, to go beyond the usual limits of spousal support and share the writing burden by updating the Privilege chapter. I am very grateful to her for doing so. I should also mention our children, Maedbh and Eoin, who left me in relative peace to work on the book.

I was very fortunate to have the able assistance of Aoife Beirne BL who was responsible for most of the research as well as reviewing the proofs. Special thanks are due to her because, without her assistance, this edition would not have been published. Acknowledgment is also due to Donough Cassidy who assisted with the research in relation to a number of chapters.

Finally, I would like to thank all of the staff at Thomson Reuters Round Hall for their encouragement and support, including, in particular, Frieda Donohue, Martin McCann and Alana Gerring.

Declan McGrath
18 November 2014

TABLE OF CONTENTS

TABLE OF CASES

TABLE OF LEGISLATION

BUNREACHT NA hÉIREANN

IRELAND – STATUTES

IRELAND – STATUTORY INSTRUMENTS

EUROPEAN UNION

UNITED KINGDOM – STATUTES

UNITED KINGDOM – STATUTORY INSTRUMENTS

AUSTRALIA

CANADA

NEW ZEALAND

SOUTH AFRICA

UNITED STATES

INTERNATIONAL AND EUROPEAN CONVENTIONS

CHAPTER 1

RELEVANCE AND ADMISSIBILITY

A. Introduction

1–01   In civil or in criminal proceedings, a court can only determine the issues before it on the basis of evidence[1] adduced in that case.[2] In order for evidence to be admissible before the tribunal of fact, it must, firstly, be relevant to the issues to be determined. However, even if relevant, the evidence will not be admitted if it falls to be excluded pursuant to any of the many exclusionary rules of evidence which are discussed in later chapters. Further, even if evidence is relevant and would not be excluded pursuant to any of those specific exclusionary rules, a trial court retains a residual discretion to exclude any evidence, the prejudicial effect of which exceeds its probative value.

B. Relevance

1. Introduction

1–02   Evidence can only be admitted in civil or criminal proceedings if it is relevant to the issues in the proceedings.[3] As Fennelly J observed in the criminal context in *People (DPP) v Ferris*[4]:

---

[1]   An assertion by counsel as to the existence of a disputed fact does not constitute evidence (*KA v Health Service Executive* [2012] IEHC 288 at [23], [2012] 1 IR 794 at 801). *A fortiori*, a question asked by counsel based on the existence of fact cannot be regarded as evidence of the existence of that fact (*People (DPP) v Connolly* [2003] 2 IR 1 at 5; *People (DPP) v Murphy* [2005] IECCA 1 at [70], [2005] 2 IR 125 at 149). A trial judge, as part of his or her duty to guide and instruct a jury as to what constitutes evidence on which they are entitled to rely, can point out that questions and material put by counsel in cross-examination do not constitute evidence (*People (DPP) v Boyce* [2005] IECCA 143; *People (DPP) v C.C. (No.2)* [2012] IECCA 86 at [41]; *People (DPP) v MJ* [2014] IECCA 21 at [73]).

[2]   *DPP v Corcoran,* unreported, High Court, 22 June 1999. See also *People (DPP) v Mackin* [2010] IECCA 81, [2011] 4 IR 506 where it was held that evidence taken on commission in Northern Ireland pursuant to s.11 of the Criminal Law (Jurisdiction) Act 1976 was not evidence taken as part of the trial and, thus, could not be relied on without being proved in evidence at the trial.

[3]   *People (DPP) v O'Callaghan* [2001] 1 IR 584 at 589, [2001] 2 ILRM 184 at 189; *People (DPP) v Shortt (No.1)* [2002] 2 IR 686 at 693; *People (DPP) v Ferris* [2008] 1 IR 1 at 6; *People (DPP) v Fahy* [2007] IECCA 102 at [11], [2008] 2 IR 292 at 298; *People (DPP) v McGrath* [2013] IECCA 12 at 13; *People (DPP) v MJ* [2014] IECCA 21 at [18]. See also *R. v Corbett* [1988] 1 SCR 670 at 715; *R. v Graat* [1982] 2 SCR 819 at 835; *R. v Morris* [1983] 2 SCR 190 at 201, (1983) 7 CCC (3d) 97; *Wilson v R.* (1970) 123 CLR 334 at 337; *R. v Fox* [1973] NZLR 458 at 463.

[4]   [2008] 1 IR 1 at 6.

"The common law has acted on one fundamental principle of proof since early modern times and since the abandonment of the primitive methods of proof of Saxon times. This rule has operated for centuries and is that the only evidence which is admissible at a criminal trial whether for or against the guilt of the accused is evidence which is relevant. This means evidence which tends to prove or disprove whether the accused committed the act with which he is charged."[5]

1–03   Thus, as emphasised by Hardiman J in *People (DPP) v Shortt (No.1)*,[6] relevance is a pre-condition to admissibility:

"All evidence must be relevant to a matter in issue as the first condition of admissibility. There are exceptions to the admissibility of relevant evidence, but irrelevant evidence is never admissible…"[7]

1–04   The onus is on the party tendering the evidence to establish its relevance[8] and evidence which does not satisfy this prerequisite is absolutely inadmissible.[9]

2. Concept of Relevance

1–05   A number of explanations of the concept of relevance have been advanced. The classic definition is considered to be that of Stephen[10] who said that it means that:

"… any two facts to which it is applied are so related to each other that according to the common course of events one either taken by itself or in connection with other facts proves or renders probable the past, present or future existence or non-existence of the other."[11]

1–06   A simpler and more practical definition is that given by Lord Simon in *DPP v Kilbourne*,[12] where he said that evidence is relevant "if it is logically probative or disprobative of some matter which requires proof … evidence which makes the matter which requires proof more or less probable."[13] An even pithier explanation was given by O'Donnell J in *Galway City Council v Samuel Kingston Construction Ltd*[14] who said that "evidence is relevant to an issue when if accepted it would tend to prove or disprove it".[15] Evidence may be relevant not only where it tends to prove or disprove

---

5   [2008] 1 IR 1 at 6.
6   [2002] 2 IR 686 at 692.
7   See also *People (DPP) v O'Callaghan* [2001] 1 IR 584 at 588, [2001] 2 ILRM 184 at 189, where Hardiman J stated that "relevance is the first and most basic requirement of admissibility". Similarly, in *People (DPP) v MJ* [2014] IECCA 21 at [18], it was emphasised that: "it is a necessary precondition to the admissibility of any piece of evidence in a criminal trial (or for that matter in a civil action), that it be relevant; evidence which is irrelevant is not admissible."
8   See *Sterling Manson v O'Donnell*, unreported, High Court, 27 January 2000.
9   *People (DPP) v Shortt (No.1)* [2002] 2 IR 686 at 693; *R. v Byrne* [2002] Crim LR 487. See Montrose, "Basic Concepts of the Law of Evidence" (1954) 70 LQR 527 and Choo, "The Notion of Relevance and Defence Evidence" [1993] Crim LR 114.
10   *Digest of the Law of Evidence* (12th ed., McMillan & Co. Ltd., London, 1907), Art.1.
11   This passage was quoted with approval by Charleton J in *Condron v ACC Bank plc* [2012] IEHC 395 at [14], [2013] 1 ILRM 113 at 121. In *R. v Kearley* [1992] 2 AC 228 at 263, [1992] 2 All ER 345 at 370, Lord Oliver stated that relevance could not be better defined.
12   [1973] AC 729 at 756, [1973] 1 All ER 440 at 461.
13   This test of relevance was endorsed by Lord Bingham in *O'Brien v Chief Constable of South Wales Police* [2005] 2 AC 534 at 540, [2005] 2 WLR 1038 at 1040. See to similar effect, *per* Kingsmill Moore J in *People (AG) v O'Brien* [1965] IR 142 at 151, who stated that evidence is relevant "if it is logically probative".
14   [2010] IESC 18 at [50], [2010] 3 IR 95 at 115.
15   A similar formulation was used by the Court of Criminal Appeal in the criminal context in *People (DPP) v MJ* [2014] IECCA 21 at [18]: "'relevance' at least in a general sense, will be established where the evidence tends to prove or disprove, or … renders it more or less probable, that the

a fact in issue, but also where it tends to prove or disprove a fact from which the existence or non-existence of a fact in issue may be inferred.[16]

3. Determination of Relevance

1–07 It is obvious from the foregoing definitions of relevance that the touchstone of the concept is logic and the key question for a court is whether a particular item of evidence is logically probative or disprobative of a fact in issue. However, the determination of relevance is not confined to the application of logic alone, which needs to be tempered by considerations of experience and common sense. As Watt JA explained in the Canadian decision of *R v Luciano*[17]: "An item of evidence is relevant if it renders the fact it seeks to establish slightly more or less probable than it (the fact) would be without the evidence, through the application of everyday experience and common sense."[18]

1–08 An example of a case where an unduly narrow view of relevance was adopted, and the remorseless application of logic in determining relevance led to a result which was at variance with experience and common sense, is furnished by *R v Kearley*.[19] The police found drugs in the accused's flat, but not in sufficient quantities to raise the inference that he was a dealer. The police remained there for several hours and intercepted 10 telephone calls in which the callers asked to speak to the defendant and asked for drugs. Seven people called to the flat, also asking for the defendant and asking to be supplied with drugs. At the defendant's trial for possession with the intent to supply, the officers gave evidence of these conversations. However, a majority of the House of Lords held that evidence of the requests made by the callers and visitors was irrelevant because it could only be evidence of the state of mind or belief of those making the requests, which was not a relevant issue at the trial, the issue being whether the defendant intended to supply drugs:

> "Each of those requests was, of course, evidence of the state of mind of the person making the request. He wished to be supplied with drugs and thought that the appellant would so supply him. It was not evidence of the fact that the appellant had supplied or could or would supply the person making the request."[20]

1–09 It made no difference that there was a large number of such requests all made

accused person did or did not commit the act in question". *Cf.* Rule 401(a) of the US Federal Rules of Evidence which states that evidence is relevant if: "it has any tendency to make a fact more or less probable than it would be without the evidence" and s.55(1) of the Australian Evidence Act 1995 which provides that: "The evidence that is relevant in a proceeding is evidence that, if it were accepted, could rationally affect (directly or indirectly) the assessment of the probability of the existence of a fact in issue in the proceeding."

16   *Presho v Doohan* [2009] IEHC 619 at [28], [2011] 3 IR 524 at 530; *Condron v ACC Bank plc* [2012] IEHC 395 at [14], [2013] 1 ILRM 113 at 121.

17   [2011] ONCA 89 at [204].

18   See also *per* Dickson J in *R. v Graat* [1982] 2 SCR 819 at 835: "Admissibility is determined, first, by asking whether the evidence sought to be admitted is relevant. This is a matter of applying logic and experience to the circumstances of the particular case." To similar effect, Lord Steyn said in *A (No.2)* [2001] 2 Cr App R 351 at 362: "[to] be relevant evidence need merely have some tendency in logic and common sense to advance the proposition in issue". *Cf.* the comments of Hardiman J in *Bradley v Independent Star Newspapers* [2011] IESC 17 at [69], [2011] 3 IR 96 at 118, [2012] 2 ILRM 26 at 44 and of Charleton J in *Condron v ACC Bank plc* [2012] IEHC 395 at [13], [2013] 1 ILRM 113 at 120.

19   [1992] 2 AC 228; [1992] 2 All ER 345.

20   [1992] 2 AC 228 at 253, [1992] 2 All ER 345 at 362 (*per* Lord Ackner).

at the same place on the same day. The minority agreed with the majority as to the irrelevance of the calls if offered merely as evidence of belief on the part of the callers but took the view that the large number of telephone calls and visitors implied that "the appellant had established a market as a drug dealer by supplying or offering to supply drugs and was thus attracting customers".[21] Therefore, "the existence of a substantial body of potential customers provides some evidence which a jury could take into account in deciding whether the accused had an intent to supply".[22]

1-10   When a similar issue arose for decision in *People (DPP) v Timmons*,[23] the Court of Criminal Appeal adopted a more common sense approach to relevance along the lines advocated by the minority in *Kearley* (although that decision was not considered). In that case, the accused was charged of conspiracy to possess a controlled drug for the purposes of sale or supply. During a search of the house where the accused was living, the Gardaí found two mobile phones (acknowledged by the accused to be his) from which they had retrieved text messages querying whether drugs were available. In circumstances where the defence of the accused was that of innocent association with his alleged co-conspirators and he denied any knowledge of the drugs that had been found, the Court of Criminal Appeal considered that these texts were relevant to the nature of the offence charged and the issues to be decided. Also relevant and of probative value was evidence of the finding of a notebook in a bedroom which the evidence suggested was that of the accused which contained entries in relation to the supply of drugs.[24]

1-11   It should be noted that the determination of relevance may also be influenced by considerations of public policy so that evidence that would seem to be relevant applying logic and common sense may be deemed not to be relevant because of pragmatic or policy considerations. A good example can be seen in *Hart v Lancashire & Yorkshire Railway Co.*,[25] where it was held that evidence that after an accident the defendants to a negligence action had altered and improved their practice was not relevant to the question as to whether the accident was caused by their negligence. Bramwell B observed that: "Because the world gets wiser as its gets older, it was not therefore foolish before".[26] Although not explicitly stated, this decision can be justified by public policy considerations; if such evidence was considered to be relevant and could be admitted, it would act as a powerful disincentive to persons taking such remedial measures.[27]

---

[21]   [1992] 2 AC 228 at 253, [1992] 2 All ER 345 at 349 (*per* Lord Griffiths).

[22]   [1992] 2 AC 228 at 279, 1992] 2 All ER 345 at 383 (*per* Lord Browne-Wilkinson).

[23]   [2011] IECCA 13.

[24]   See also *People (DPP) v Kearney* [2010] IECCA 112, where it was held that the trial judge had been correct to admit evidence at the trial of the accused for the murder of his wife that the deceased had kept a diary recording that she was committed to pursuing a separation because, even though this related to the state of mind of the deceased only, it was relevant to the issue of motive.

[25]   (1869) 21 LT 261.

[26]   (1869) 21 LT 261 at 263.

[27]   Evidence of what are sometimes referred to as "subsequent remedial measures" was also excluded in *Versloot Dreding BV v HDI Gerling Industrie Versicherung AG* [2014] EWHC 1666 and *Independent Broadcasting Authority v BICC Construction Ltd* [1995] PNLR 179. However, such evidence has been held to be admissible in Australia (*State Electricity Commission of Victoria v Gray* [1951] VLR 104; *Anderson v Morris Wools Pty Ltd* [1965] Qd R 65) and Canada (*Canadian Pacific Railway v Calgary (City)* (1966) 58 WWR 124, 59 DLR (2d) 642; *Sandhu (Litigation Guardian of) v Wellington Place Apartments* [2008] ONCA 215, 291 DLR (4th) 220; *Prosser v 20 Vic Management* [2009] ABQB 177, 8 Alta LR (5th) 68).

1–12   Evidence may also be found to be irrelevant, or insufficiently relevant to be admissible, if its admission would or might give rise to collateral issues which would distract the tribunal of fact from the main issue and lengthen the proceedings.[28] In *Browne v Tribune Newspapers Plc.*[29] the plaintiff was a detective superintendent in the Garda Síochána who unsuccessfully brought libel proceedings against the defendant on foot of a newspaper article dealing with the circumstances surrounding a shooting incident. On appeal, it was held that trial judge had erred in permitting counsel for the defendant to cross-examine the plaintiff during the trial in order to elicit from him the fact that he had recovered a substantial sum as a result of four previous libel actions and was not, therefore, as he attempted to characterise himself, a reluctant litigant. Keane CJ, delivering the judgment of the Court, pointed out that cross-examination as to actions for defamation brought by the plaintiff in the past in respect of other unrelated publications was clearly not relevant to the issues of justification, fair comment, the meaning to be attributed to the words complained of, or the identification of the plaintiff. It could, therefore, only be relevant, if at all, to the issue of damages. However, he was of the view that permitting cross-examination of this nature would involve the Court in trying collateral issues. It would, he said, be necessary to permit the plaintiff, in order to correct any damaging impression in the mind of the jury arising from the recovery of damages in earlier proceedings, to give details as to the precise nature of the defamation on the previous occasion, the course that the proceedings had taken, whether any apology had been offered, and the nature of the trial. The defendant would, in turn, be entitled to call rebutting evidence, and the Court would find itself in the position of having to conduct a virtual trial within a trial on this issue. The Chief Justice regarded it as:

> "remarkable that the Court would be obliged to try collateral issues of this nature simply in order to determine whether, in the event of the plea of justification failing, the plaintiff's damages should be reduced because of his readiness to bring defamation proceedings in the past".[30]

1–13   It is also important to note that the concept of relevance is very contextual in nature. As stated by Doherty JA in the Canadian decision of *R v Pilon*[31]: "Relevance is assessed by reference to the material issues in a particular case and in the context of the entirety of the evidence and the positions of the parties". The determination of whether a particular item of evidence is relevant is, thus, crucially dependent upon the issues that arise in proceedings and the facts that are in issue. A good example can be seen in *People (AG) v O'Neill*,[32] where the accused had been charged with manslaughter arising out of a car accident. Evidence was led by the prosecution that the accused had spent an hour in a pub on the evening of the accident and had consumed a shandy and two glasses of ale. No suggestion was made, however, that his driving had been impaired by alcohol. Although it might be thought that such evidence would be relevant to show

---

[28]   *Browne v Tribune Newspapers Plc* [2001] 1 IR 521; *Agassiz v London Tramway Co.* (1872) 21 W.R. 199; *CJM (No.2) v HM Advocate* [2013] HCJAC 22. *Cf.* the comments of Rolfe B in *AG v Hitchcock* (1847) 1 Exch. 91 at 105, in relation to the rule that answers given by a witness under cross-examination concerning collateral matters must be treated as final: "if we lived for a thousand years instead of about sixty or seventy, and every case was of sufficient importance, it might be possible, and perhaps proper ... to raise every possible inquiry as to the truth of statements made. ... In fact mankind finds it to be impossible."

[29]   [2001] 1 IR 521.

[30]   [2001] 1 IR 521 at 531.

[31]   [2009] ONCA 248, 243 CCC (3d) 109 at [33].

[32]   [1964] Ir Jur Rep 1. But see *People (AG) v Moore* [1964] Ir Jur Rep 6 and *R v Pleydell* [2005] EWCA Crim 1447.

that the accused's driving ability was impaired, it was held by the Court of Criminal Appeal that this evidence was "wholly irrelevant to any of the issues at trial"[33] because the prosecution was not suggesting that the accused's driving had been affected by alcohol, and, therefore, should not have been admitted.[34] The prosecution sought to justify its admission on the basis that it was tendered in order to trace the movements of the accused prior to the accident, but the Court was satisfied that those movements were themselves irrelevant.[35]

1–14   A similar approach was adopted in *People (DPP) v Cahill*,[36] where the trial judge ruled that the prosecution could call evidence to disprove an alibi although an application for leave to adduce evidence in support of the alibi (which would have been required) had not been made by the second accused. The Court of Criminal Appeal accepted the submission advanced on behalf of the second accused that the prosecution should not have been permitted to lead this evidence. It agreed that the evidence had no probative force whatever in the absence of an application for leave to adduce evidence in support of the alibi and could only have been prejudicial to the second accused.

1–15   It follows from the ambulatory nature of the concept of relevance that a determination by a trial judge in relation to relevance of a particular item of evidence is not immutable and may require review in the course of a trial depending on how the issues in the case develop. This was pointed out in *People (DPP) v O'Callaghan*[37] where Hardiman J noted that "circumstances may arise in the course of a trial in which evidence of the nature in question here, or any *prima facie* irrelevant evidence, might become relevant".

1–16   Finally, it should be noted that the assessment of the relevance of evidence does not involve an assessment of its cogency or weight.[38] As explained in section E below, this is a matter for the tribunal of fact if the evidence is admitted.

4. Circumstantial Evidence

1–17   The relevance or irrelevance of direct evidence of facts in issue in proceedings will generally be readily apparent, but more difficult questions may arise in relation to the relevance of circumstantial evidence, *i.e.* any fact from the existence of which the judge or jury may infer the existence or non-existence of a fact in issue.[39] The classic example of such evidence given in *People (DPP) v Lafferty*[40] is the testimony of a witness at a trial for murder that he saw the accused carrying a blood-stained knife at the door of the house in which the deceased was found mortally wounded.[41]

---

33 [1964] Ir Jur Rep 1 at 4.
34 *Cf. R. v Sandhu* [1997] Crim LR 288; [1997] JPL 853 (evidence of *mens rea* irrelevant and inadmissible in prosecution for an offence of strict liability).
35 See also *R. v Treacy* [1944] 2 All ER 229.
36 [2001] 3 IR 494.
37 [2001] 1 IR 584 at 598.
38 *People (DPP) v MJ* [2014] IECCA 21 at [19] and [41].
39 *People (DPP) v Lafferty*, unreported, Court of Criminal Appeal, 22 February 2000, p.21.
40 Unreported, Court of Criminal Appeal, 22 February 2000.
41 See *AG v Edwards* [1935] IR 500, where the court refused to set aside a verdict of murder in circumstances where death was admitted, but the finding that the death was caused by violence or deliberate criminal neglect was based on circumstantial evidence. Similarly, in *People (AG) v*

1–18   In *Thomas v Jones*,[42]Atkin LJ gave what is regarded as an authoritative explanation of the operation of circumstantial evidence as follows:

> "Evidence of independent facts, each of them in itself insufficient to prove the main fact, may yet, either by their cumulative weight or still more by their connection of one with the other as links in a chain, prove the principal fact to be established."[43]

1–19   Thus, circumstantial evidence consists of a number of items of oral, documentary or real evidence that, when taken together, tend to establish a fact in issue.[44] As such, the relevance and probative force of an item of circumstantial evidence falls to be considered, not in isolation, but in tandem with the other evidence, direct and circumstantial in the proceedings.[45] It follows that it is not an objection to the admissibility of an item of circumstantial evidence that it does not, of itself, prove or tend to prove a fact in issue.[46]

1–20   In *People (DPP) v Nevin*,[47] the Court of Criminal Appeal rejected the submission that a conviction on the basis of circumstantial evidence requires the abandonment of the presumption of innocence:

> "Without ever abandoning the presumption of innocence, the prosecution in proceeding against the applicant on the murder charge is perfectly entitled to rely on any piece of evidence which might be suspicious or uncannily coincidental and such items of evidence cannot just be viewed in isolation of each other. It is the combined effect of the circumstantial evidence which is of importance even though, in respect of each item of such circumstantial evidence, the jury has to consider whether it accepts it or not and also has to consider whether an inference suggested to be drawn from it is warranted or not."

1–21   There are numerous items of circumstantial evidence which may be relevant because they permit the tribunal of fact to make inferences as to the existence or non-existence of facts in issue. It would be difficult to categorise all of them but some of the more common examples include: (i) evidence that establishes motive;[48] (ii)

Kirwan [1943] IR 279 at 298, it was held that in the absence of direct evidence, the fact of death and the identification of the limbless body with the person alleged to have been murdered were properly proved by circumstantial evidence. This evidence included evidence as to the duration and locality of the burial, the fact that no other person had gone missing in the locality, and that the sack buried with the body was connected to the accused.

[42] [1921] 1 KB 22, [1920] All ER 462.
[43] [1921] 1 KB 22 at 48. This explanation was quoted with approval by Edwards J in *The Leopardstown Club Ltd v Templeville Developments Ltd* [2010] IEHC 152 at [5.3]. See, to similar effect, the explanation of Pollock CB in *R. v Exall* (1866) 4 F & F 922 at 929 that: "One strand of the cord might be insufficient to sustain the weight, but three stranded together might be of sufficient strength. Thus it may be in circumstantial evidence—there may be a combination of circumstances, no one of which would raise a reasonable conviction or more than a mere suspicion; but the three taken together may create a conclusion of guilt with as much certainty as human affairs can require or admit of." The analogy of strands in a rope was also used by the Court of Criminal Appeal in *People (DPP) v Boyle* [2010] IECCA 3 at [34], [2010] 1 IR 787 at 798.
[44] *Per* Learned Hand J in *United States v Pugliese* (1946) 153 F 2d 497 at 500: "Most convictions result from the cumulation of bits of proof which, taken singly would not be enough in the mind of a fair minded person. All that is necessary, and all that is possible, is that each bit may have enough rational connection with the issue to be considered a factor contributing to an answer."
[45] See *O'Brien v Derwin* [2009] IEHC 2 at [12].
[46] *People (DPP) v Egan* [2010] IECCA 28 at [11], [2010] 3 IR 561 at 566 (evidence of semen stained cloth found in the accused's car relevant to establish that a sexual act had taken place and because it was consistent with the complainant's account of what had occurred).
[47] [2003] 3 IR 321 at 347.
[48] *People (DPP) v Kearney* [2009] IECCA 112 at [14]-[15]; *People (DPP) v Nevin* [2003] 3 IR 321 at 344; *AG v Joyce* [1929] IR 526 at 539; *Toppin v Feron* (1909) 43 ILTR 190; *R. v Palmer*

evidence of opportunity to commit the offence[49]; (iii) evidence as to the state of mind
of the accused at the time the offence took place[50]; (iv) the commission of preparatory
acts[51]; (v) the possession of items that could be used to commit the offence[52]; (vi)
evidence of identification,[53] fingerprints,[54] DNA,[55] mobile phone records[56] or tracker
dogs[57] establishing presence at a place or connection to an object; (vii) evidence of
the commission of similar acts at a point close in time to the commission of the *actus
reus* of an offence[58]; (viii) adverse inferences in civil cases drawn from a failure to call
evidence that a party could reasonably have been expected to call[59] or from a failure to
discover relevant documents in the possession of a related person[60]; (ix) lies told by an
accused where the tribunal of fact is satisfied that the motive for lying is realisation of
guilt and a fear of the truth[61]; (x) differing versions of events given by an accused[62]; and
(xi) evidence forming part of the *res gestae, i.e.* a fact that is relevant to a fact in issue
because it throws light on it by reason of proximity in time, place or circumstance.[63]

(1856) 5 E & B 1024; *Russell v Hawes* (1863) 3 F & F 322. This evidence is relevant on the
basis explained by Lord Atkinson in *R. v Ball* [1911] AC 47 at 68, that: "it is more probable that
men are killed by those that have some motive for killing them than by those who have not".
Applying the same reasoning, evidence of lack of motive may also be admissible to show that a
person is less likely to have committed a particular act (*People (DPP) v Nevin* [2003] 2 IR 321
at 344; *R. v Grant* (1865) 4 F & F 322).

49 *People (DPP) v Boyce* [2005] IECCA 143 (evidence that the accused was a local person living
locally relevant to charges of sexual offences against a complainant who described the perpetrator
as a local person with a local accent); *R. v Ball* [1911] AC 47; [1908-10] All ER 111 (evidence
that brother and sister shared bed relevant on charge of incest).
50 *People (DPP) v O'Reilly* [2009] IECCA 18 (evidence of emails sent by accused charged with
murdering his wife admissible to demonstrate that his state of mind concerning the breakdown
of relations in the marriage).
51 *R. v Palmer* (1856) 5 E. & B. 1024 (purchase of poison by person accused of murder).
52 See *People (DPP) v Boyle* [2010] IECCA 3 at [38], [2010] 1 IR 787 at 799.
53 *People (DPP) v McGinley* [2013] IECCA 7 at [24]–[29].
54 See *People (DPP) v Ryan,* unreported, Court of Criminal Appeal, 30 November 1992; *People
(DPP) v White* [2011] IECCA 78; *R. v Buckley* [1999] All ER (D) 1521.
55 See *People (DPP) v Allen* [2003] 4 IR 295. For a discussion of some of the issues arising in
relation to the admission of DNA evidence, see *People (DPP) v Boyce* [2005] IECCA 143, [2008]
IESC 62, [2009] 2 IR 124, [2009] 1 ILRM 253.
56 *People (DPP) v Murphy* [2005] IECCA 1, [2005] 2 IR 125; *Byrne v Judges of the Circuit Court*
[2013] IEHC 396.
57 See *R. v Montgomery* [1966] NI 120; *R. v Pieterson* [1975] 1 WLR 293; *R. v Haas* (1962) 25
DLR (2d) 172; *R. v Lindsay* [1964] NZLR 748.
58 See *People (DPP) v Lafferty,* unreported, Court of Criminal Appeal, 22 February 2000, where it
was held that evidence as to the manner in which a car was being driven a relatively short time
before an accident was admissible as circumstantial evidence in a prosecution for dangerous
driving causing death. See also *Beresford v St. Albans Justices* (1905) 22 T.L.R. 1; *Hallet v Warren*
(1929) 93 J.P. 225 and *R. v Horvath* [1972] VR 533. *Cf.* the presumption of continuance of life
discussed in Chap.2.
59 *Dunne v Coombe Women and Infants University Hospital* [2013] IEHC 58 at [197]; *Walsh v
Sligo County Council* [2010] IEHC 437 at [306], [2011] 2 IR 260 at 378; *Smart Mobile Ltd v
Commission for Communications Regulation* [2006] IEHC 338; *Fyffes plc v DCC plc* [2005]
IEHC 477 at [199], [2009] 2 IR 417 at 508; *Quinn v Mid Western Health Board* [2005] IESC 19
at [63-64], [2005] 4 IR 1 at 24; *Crofter Properties Ltd v Genport Ltd* [2002] 4 IR 73 at 85; *Doran
v Cosgrave* [1999] IESC 74. See further the discussion of these authorities in Chap.3.
60 *Thema International Fund plc v HSBC Institutional Trust Services (Ireland) Ltd* [2013] IESC 3
at [7.3].
61 *People (DPP) v Goulding* [2010] IECCA 85 at [19]; *R. v Lucas* [1981] QB 720, [1981] 2 All ER
1008.
62 *People (DPP) v Boyle* [2010] IECCA 3 at [38], [2010] 1 IR 787 at 799.
63 *People (DPP) v O'Callaghan* [2001] 1 IR 584 at 588, [2001] 2 ILRM 184 at 189 (*per* Hardiman

1–22   In *DPP v Kilbourne*,[64] it was explained that circumstantial evidence "works by cumulatively, in geometrical progression, eliminating other possibilities". If the circumstantial evidence is effective to eliminate all other possibilities consistent with the innocence of the accused, then it can provide sufficient evidence of the guilt of the accused. An example can be seen in *People (DPP) v Kearney*[65] where the accused had been convicted of the murder of his wife who had died at their home from strangulation in circumstances where there was no indication of forced entry to the house or theft and her death had been made to look like a suicide. The case against the accused was based solely on circumstantial evidence which was criticised on appeal on the basis that it was insufficient to exclude the possibility that some third party had entered the house and killed the deceased shortly after the accused left for work. However, the Court of Criminal Appeal considered the circumstantial evidence to be compelling "such as to exclude every other reasonable possibility in the case" and regarded the possibility that an unknown intruder, with no apparent motive, had entered the house and murdered the deceased as "so remote and unlikely as to be off any scale of either probability or possibility".[66]

1–23   In order to ground a conviction where the case against the accused rests entirely on circumstantial evidence, such evidence must be consistent with the guilt of the accused and must be inconsistent with any rational hypothesis consistent with innocence.[67] It is common practice to instruct the jury in those terms and as to how they should approach and weigh circumstantial evidence.[68] The instruction in that regard may be conveniently linked to a charge in relation to the burden of proof and the obligation on the jury where there are two or more inferences open is to draw the

---

J) endorsing the definition of *res gestae* contained in Tapper (ed.), *Cross and Tapper on Evidence* 9th edn (London: Butterworths, 1999), p.29. Hardiman J in *O'Callaghan* was very critical of the concept of *res gestae* endorsing the criticisms of it by Stone, "Res Gestae Reagitata" (1939) 55 LQR 66 at 67 ("the lurking place of a motley crowd of conceptions in mutual conflict and reciprocating chaos") and the infamous statement of Lord Blackburn (quoted in *Cross and Tapper on Evidence* (above), p.30, n.10) that: "If you wish to tender inadmissible evidence, say it is part of the res gestae". The learned judge concluded by stating that: "The term is merely an expression of the general proposition that there is no universal formula for all kinds of relevancy. This proposition is not elucidated by the use of this Latin term which, unlike others, has no virtue of precision or historical connotation." Interestingly, notwithstanding those criticisms, the concept of *res gestae* was invoked as the basis for the admissibility of certain evidence in *DPP v Byrne* [2002] 2 ILRM 68, [2002] 2 IR 397.

[64]   [1973] AC 729 at 758, [1973] 1 All ER 440 at 462.

[65]   [2009] IECCA 112.

[66]   [2009] IECCA 112 at [29].

[67]   *People (AG) v McMahon* [1946] IR 267 at 272. *Cf. People (DPP) v Madden* [1977] IR 336 at 349, where O'Higgins CJ stated that the test to be applied in relation to circumstantial evidence was whether "such evidence was inconsistent with any credible explanation other than the guilt" of the accused.

[68]   See the charge which was approved by the Court of Criminal Appeal in *People (DPP) v Nevin* [2003] 3 IR 321. See also *People (DPP) v White* [2011] IECCA 78, where criticisms of the charge in relation to circumstantial evidence were rejected by the Court of Criminal Appeal. The courts in the UK have held that there is no requirement for a special or additional direction where the evidence against an accused is wholly or partly circumstantial: *McGreevy v DPP* [1973] 1 All ER 503, [1973] 1 WLR 276; *R v P (JM)* [2007] EWCA Crim 3216; *R v Marcus* [2013] NICA 60 at [33]. The Canadian courts have also rejected the argument that a special warning must be given to the jury in a case where circumstantial evidence is relied on: *R. v Cooper* [1978] SCR 860 at 865–866.

inference most favourable to the accused unless that contended for by the prosecution has been proved beyond a reasonable doubt.[69]

1–24   A trial judge should be very careful in his or her instruction not to overstate the status or weight to be attached to circumstantial evidence. In *People (DPP) v Cahill*[70] it was held that the trial judge had done just that and mis-directed the jury by instructing them that circumstantial evidence "is evidence of surrounding circumstances which by undesigned coincidence is capable of proving a proposition with the accuracy of mathematics".[71] The Court of Criminal Appeal in that case indicated that the proper direction to give in respect of circumstantial evidence is that derived from the judgment of Pollock CB in *R. v Exall*[72] that: "There may be a combination of circumstances, no one of which would raise a reasonable conviction or more than a mere suspicion; but…taken together, may create a conclusion of guilt…with as much certainty as human affairs can require or admit of."[73] However, it appears from *People (DPP) v Nevin*[74] that there is no obligation on a trial judge to review in his or her charge each individual item of circumstantial evidence or to summarise all the arguments made by defence counsel in relation thereto.

C. Admissibility

1. Introduction

1–25   As noted above, it is a fundamental prerequisite that evidence be relevant in order to be admitted. The corollary is that all relevant evidence is admissible unless specifically excluded by one of the exclusionary rules.[75] There are a number of such exclusionary rules including the rule against hearsay, the rule against the admission of non-expert opinion and the rule against the admission of misconduct evidence, and

---

[69]   In *People (DPP) v Rattigan* [2013] IECCA 13 at [37], the Court of Criminal Appeal upheld as "perfectly adequate" the instruction of the trial judge in relation to circumstantial evidence in the following terms: "If two or more inferences are reasonably made and you have to decide which to draw, you might draw the inference most favourable to the accused unless satisfied beyond a reasonable doubt that the inference for which the prosecution contend is the appropriate one to draw. In a situation where a case depends entirely on circumstantial evidence, the jury may indeed properly convict but they can only do so in a certain situation where it is not the case that the circumstances established were merely consistent with guilt, but over and above that, that the circumstances established are inconclusive with any other rational conclusion other than the person in charge was guilty."

[70]   [2001] 3 IR 494.

[71]   [2001] 3 IR 494 at 510–511. This impugned direction was based on a passage from Sandes, *Criminal Law and Procedure in the Republic of Ireland* 3rd edn (London: Sweet & Maxwell, 1951), p.177, where he states: "Circumstantial evidence is very often the best evidence that the nature of the case permits of. It is evidence of surrounding circumstances which, by undesigned coincidence, is capable of proving a proposition with the accuracy of mathematics." That passage was also quoted by the trial judge as part of her charge in relation to circumstantial evidence in *People (DPP) v Nevin* [2003] 3 IR 321, but in a conclusion that is very difficult to reconcile with *Cahill*, her directions on this point were described by the Court of Criminal Appeal as "most appropriate" (at 349).

[72]   (1866) 4 F & F 922 at 929.

[73]   *People (DPP) v Cahill* [2001] 3 IR 494 at 510 (quoting Pollock C.B. in *R. v Exall* (1866) 4 F & F 922).

[74]   [2003] 3 IR 321 at 350–351.

[75]   *R. v Donnelly* [1986] 4 NIJB 32 at 56.

these are dealt with in detail in later chapters. In addition, as will be seen below, a trial judge enjoys a general discretion to exclude relevant evidence where its probative value is outweighed by its prejudicial effect.

1–26 It is no longer the case that evidence, which is relevant and otherwise admissible, can be excluded on the basis that there may be available more probative or reliable evidence. The "best evidence rule", which was an important principle in the early days of the development of the law of evidence,[76] dictated that a party was required to adduce the best evidence available but it has fallen into desuetude and has no continuing vitality in Irish law as an independent rule of admissibility.[77]

1–27 It should be noted that the rules in relation to the admissibility of evidence apply whether a party seeks to adduce the evidence by way of evidence-in-chief or by way of cross-examination and inadmissible evidence cannot be made admissible by its use in cross-examination.[78] Therefore, a trial judge will disallow a line of questioning that is directed towards eliciting inadmissible evidence.[79]

1–28 The onus of establishing that evidence is admissible rests on the party that wishes to adduce the evidence. That party also bears the onus of proving any facts required to be proved in order to establish the admissibility of the evidence.[80]

2. Time at which the Admissibility of Evidence is to be Determined

1–29 The traditional view of a criminal trial is that it is unitary and indivisible in character.[81] Accordingly, the admissibility of evidence falls to be determined by the trial judge in the course of a trial and the courts have generally resisted attempts to have the issue of admissibility of evidence determined in advance of the commencement of a trial.

1–30 In *AG v McCabe*,[82] the Court of Criminal Appeal held that a *voir dire* should be held at the point at which the admissibility of evidence is challenged, and rejected as unsupported by authority the proposition that the admissibility of evidence could be challenged prospectively before the hearing of the case had begun.[83] However, in

---

[76] In *Omychund v Barker* (1744) 1 Atk. 21 at 49, Lord Hardwicke declared that "the judges and sages of the law have laid it down that there is but one general rule of evidence, the best that the nature of the case will permit". The best evidence rule provided part of the doctrinal underpinnings of the hearsay rule (see *Dascalu v Minister for Justice*, unreported, High Court, 4 November 1999) and of the rules in relation to the receivability into evidence of documents (*Martin v Quinn* [1980] IR 244 at 249; *Primor plc v Stokes Kennedy Crowley* [1996] 2 IR 459 at 518; *The Leopardstown Club Ltd v Templeville Developments Ltd* [2010] IEHC 152 at [5.17]).

[77] *Hussey v Twomey* [2009] IESC 1 at [31], [2009] 3 IR 293 at 306, *sub nom. Hussey v MIBI* [2009] 1 ILRM 321 at 332–333. See also *per* Henchy J in *Martin v Quinn* [1980] IR 244 at 249.

[78] *The Leopardstown Club Ltd v Templeville Developments Ltd* [2010] IEHC 152 at [6.9].

[79] *Donohue v Killeen* [2013] IEHC 22.

[80] *Weir v DPP* [2008] IEHC 268 at [14]; *Cf. People (DPP) v Dillon* [2003] 1 ILRM 531.

[81] This principle was most vividly expressed by Ó Dálaigh CJ in *People (AG) v McGlynn* [1967] IR 232 at 239, who said that: "The nature of a criminal trial by jury is that once it starts, it continues right through until discharge or verdict. It has the unity and continuity of a play." See also *DPP v Special Criminal Court* [1999] 1 IR 60 at 89, *Blanchfield v Harnett* [2002] 3 IR 207 at 224 and *People (DPP) v Mackin* [2010] IECCA 81 at [21], [2011] 4 IR 506 at 513.

[82] [1927] IR 129.

[83] An exception applies where the prosecution propose to tender misconduct evidence in a trial involving multiple complaints. If an application is made by the accused for separate trials, the

People (DPP) v McCann,[84] the Court indicated that it might be better for issues of the admissibility of certain items of evidence such as confessions to be decided at the outset of a case.[85] In that case, the trial of the applicant had lasted 48 days and challenges to the admissibility of various items of evidence had necessitated such frequent withdrawals of the jury that the judge expressed his concern about the hardship this had caused them. This prompted the Court to state that:

> "Consideration should be given to the introduction of a system whereby contests on the admissibility of evidence—when clearly foreseen by prosecution and defence—could be resolved at the outset of the trial so that, as far as practicable, a jury may hear all the relevant and admissible evidence in a coherent and uninterrupted progression and without the need for the jury to withdraw to their room, or otherwise absent themselves from the courtroom, for protracted periods of time."[86]

1–31   A similar suggestion was mooted in *People (DPP) v Quinn*,[87] with the Court stating that perhaps the time had come to "introduce a system that will be more efficient and more conducive to the proper administration of justice so that just verdicts are returned".[88] Again, in *Cruise v O'Donnell*,[89] Hardiman J lamented the inefficiencies caused by the need to send juries out for potentially long periods while issues as to the admissibility of evidence were dealt with in the course of a trial and expressed the view that, disposing of evidential issues before the jury is sworn would assist and emphasise, rather than detract from the unity and continuity of a criminal trial.[90]

1–32   However, there is currently no legislative provision for such a procedure, apart from s.34 of the Criminal Procedure Act 2010 dealing with the admissibility of expert evidence adduced by an accused.[91] In *Cruise v O'Donnell*,[92] the Supreme Court rejected the proposition that an application pursuant to section 4E of the Criminal Procedure Act 1967[93] to dismiss charges on the basis that there is not a sufficient case to put the accused on trial could be used to determine the admissibility of evidence unless the question of admissibility was clear and did not involve the resolution of

---

admissibility of the misconduct evidence ought to be determined by the trial judge at that juncture: *People (DPP) v LG* [2003] 2 IR 517 at 524–525; *People (DPP) v BK* [2000] 2 IR 199 at 208; *DPP v Boardman* [1975] AC 421 at 459.

84   [1998] 4 IR 397.

85   In England and Wales, legislative provision is made for what are known as preparatory hearings in the course of which a judge may determine issues as to the admissibility of evidence (see Malek (ed.), *Phipson on Evidence* 18th edn, paras 10-21–10-22.

86   [1998] 4 IR 397 at 415 (*per* O'Flaherty J).

87   Unreported, Court of Criminal Appeal, *ex tempore*, 23 March 1998.

88   Unreported, Court of Criminal Appeal, *ex tempore*, 23 March 1998 at 4. See Goldberg, "*Voir dire*: Disrupting the Jury" (2000) 2 (2) P. & P. 10.

89   [2007] IESC 67, [2008] 3 IR 230, [2008] 2 ILRM 187.

90   [2007] IESC 67 at [29], [2008] 3 IR 230 at 240, [2008] 2 ILRM 187 at 196. The *Final Report of the Balance in the Criminal Law Group* (2007) at pp.174–175, was also critical of the current position: "We consider that the present arrangement whereby a jury is sworn in before any admissibility issue is determined is illogical and inconvenient on a number of levels and only explicable by historical considerations which no longer apply. It involves the jury waiting in the jury room for long periods, or being sent away, and increases the chance of jurors becoming unavailable during a long trial. We consider that all admissibility issues on which issue has been joined by the defence statement should be determined prior to the swearing in of a jury. On balance – and particularly to avoid the danger of running the case twice – we suggest that this should be done on the first day or days of the trial."

91   See further Chap.6.

92   [2007] IESC 67, [2008] 3 IR 230, [2008] ILRM 187.

93   As inserted by s.9 of the Criminal Justice Act 1999.

any conflicts of fact or the tendering of evidence going beyond that contained in the book of evidence. In *People (DPP) v Jagutis*,[94] the decision in *Cruise* was applied in the context of evidence obtained in foot of a search warrant and it was held by the Court of Criminal Appeal that, while an application pursuant to section 4E could, in an appropriate case, be a proper vehicle for a determination of whether unconstitutionally obtained evidence is plainly inadmissible, having regard to the nature of the inquiry which the Court is required to conduct in respect of illegally obtained evidence, it was unlikely that such an application could be the proper vehicle for the determination of the inadmissibility of illegally obtained evidence.[95]

1–33 In a series of decisions, it has also been held that it is not appropriate to seek an anticipatory determination as to the admissibility of evidence by means of an application for relief by way of judicial review.[96] In *Byrne v Grey*,[97] Hamilton P exercised his discretion to refuse to grant an order of certiorari to quash a search warrant in circumstances where the warrant had been executed and was spent and the purpose of seeking that relief was to seek to have rendered inadmissible the evidence obtained on foot of it. That decision was followed in *Blanchfield v Harnett*[98] which concerned a challenge to the validity of orders obtained pursuant to the Bankers' Books Evidence Act 1879. It was held by the Supreme Court that a trial judge had sufficient power to adjudicate on the legality of measures taken to extract, collect or gather evidence so that he or she could rule on the admissibility of the evidence obtained, thereby obviating the need to apply for relief by way of judicial review to quash the relevant orders.

1–34 A marked lack of enthusiasm for determining the admissibility of evidence in advance of trial is also evident in the civil sphere. Although it was held in *Director of Corporate Enforcement v Bailey*[99] that portions of affidavits that contained clearly inadmissible evidence could be struck out in advance of a trial on affidavit, the courts will be slow to entertain a pre-emptive application to rule out evidence as inadmissible where a plenary trial is to take place. In *Condron v ACC Bank plc*,[100] Charleton J expressed the view that the trial judge is in the best position to ascertain the real issues in the case and considered that it would be rare that he or she, in advance of the trial, with access to affidavit evidence only and limited papers, would be in a position to make an informed decision. He considered that the determination of admissibility of evidence on foot of a pre-trial motion would interfere with the discretion of the trial judge to run the trial in a way that best enabled admissible evidence to be called and justice to be done. He concluded that the burden of excluding evidence as to fact in advance of a trial is a heavy one which had not been discharged in the case before him.[101]

---

[94] [2013] IECCA 4.
[95] [2013] IECCA 4 at [4.11]. As to the difference between the exclusionary rules applied in respect of unconstitutionally obtained evidence and illegally obtained evidence, see Chap.7.
[96] *Byrne v Grey* [1988] IR 31; *Berkeley v Edwards* [1988] IR 217; *Carlton v DPP (No.2)* [2000] 3 IR 269 at 280, *TH v DPP* [2004] IEHC 76 at [63]; *McCormack v DPP* [2007] IEHC 123 at [13], [2008] 1 ILRM 49 at 56; *McNulty v DPP* [2009] IESC 12 at [13], [2009] 3 IR 572 at 576.
[97] [1988] IR 31 at 41.
[98] [2001] 1 ILRM 193 (H.C.), [2002] 3 IR 207 (S.C.).
[99] [2007] IEHC 365, [2008] 2 ILRM 13, [2011] IESC 24, [2011] 3 IR 278.
[100] [2012] IEHC 395, [2013] 1 ILRM 113.
[101] This decision was approved and applied by Kelly J in *Bank of Ireland v O'Donnell* [2012] IEHC 475. See also *Wilkinson v West Coast Capital* [2005] EWHC 1606, [2005] All ER (D) 321.

3. *Voir Dire*

1–35   The admissibility of evidence is a matter of law for the trial judge to decide.[102] It may be possible for this determination to be made without hearing any evidence[103] but the admissibility of evidence will often turn on matters of fact as, for example, where an accused challenges the admission of his or her confession on the grounds that it is involuntary or was obtained in breach of his or her constitutional rights. Where this is the case, the proper procedure in a jury trial, as laid down in *State v Treanor*,[104] is for the trial judge to conduct a "trial within a trial" in the absence of the jury, also known as a *voir dire*.[105]

1–36   During the *voir dire*, witnesses will be called by the party seeking to adduce the disputed evidence to give whatever testimony is necessary to ground its admission. Those witnesses will then be subject to cross-examination and the party seeking to exclude the evidence may, in turn, call witnesses who will also be exposed to cross-examination. If it is relevant to the admissibility of the evidence at issue, evidence can be adduced during the *voir dire* and considered by the trial judge that would not be inadmissible before the jury.[106]

1–37   After hearing all the evidence, the trial judge will decide whether to admit or exclude the disputed evidence.[107] If the trial judge decides to exclude the evidence,

---

[102] *R. v Colclough* (1882) 10 LR Ir 241 at 257; *People (DPP) v Boyce* [2005] IECCA 143; *R. v Mohan* [1994] 2 SCR 9 at 20; (1994) 114 DLR 419 at 427.

[103] *R v Kematch* [2010] MBCA 18 at [43].

[104] [1924] 2 IR 193. This was the first decision of the Court of Criminal Appeal that had been established by the Courts of Justice Act 1924 (No.10 of 1924). See also *People (AG) v O'Brien* (1969) 1 Frewen 343, 346–347, where the Court of Criminal Appeal affirmed that the correct course of action where there was an objection to the admissibility of evidence was for that objection to be heard and determined in the absence of the jury.

[105] The *voir dire* procedure prescribed in *Treanor* was applied without question until the decision of the Supreme Court in *People (DPP) v Lynch* [1982] IR 64. A majority of the Court pointed out that, under Art. 38.1, the determination of issues of fact was within the province of the jury. The view was, therefore, taken that where matters of fact arose in relation to the admissibility of evidence, these were for the jury and not the judge to resolve. However, the decision in *Lynch* was not followed in the later case of *People (DPP) v Conroy* [1986] IR 460 which also involved a disputed confession. Finlay CJ said that *Lynch* involved a departure from previously accepted practice and he did not believe that the right to trial by jury involved a right to have issues of fact arising with regard to the admissibility of evidence tried by a jury. He drew attention to the constitutional and practical difficulties attendant upon the procedure laid down in *Lynch*. The constitutional right to trial in due course of law, guaranteed by Art.38.1, meant that a person has the right to be tried by a jury from whose knowledge is excluded any evidence of guilt which is inadmissible at law. Even if the jury was warned not to take such evidence into account when deciding whether the accused was guilty, it would be unreal to expect it not to do so, and therefore there was a real risk of injustice. Apart from the impugned evidence itself, it was likely that evidence would be led in seeking to establish its admissibility or inadmissibility which would be of an inculpatory nature or prejudicial to the accused. For the foregoing reasons, Finlay CJ concluded that the interests of justice in criminal trials with a jury would be best served by a return to the traditional *voir dire* procedure. For an example of where such evidence was led as part of a *voir dire* and may have been relied on by the Special Criminal Court to convict the accused, see *People (DPP) v Murphy* [2005] IECCA 1 at [67], [2005] 2 IR 125 at 148.

[106] *People (DPP) v AD* [2012] IESC 33 at [52], [2012] 2 IR 332 at 349. An example might be evidence in relation to the formation of a suspicion or opinion by a garda (*cf. DPP v Cash* [2010] IESC 1, [2010] 1 IR 609, [2010] 1 ILRM 389; *DPP v McDonnell* [2014] IEHC 35).

[107] Where the ruling is a significant one, reasons for it should be given: *R v Woodard* [2009] MBCA 42, 245 CCC (3d) 522, 240 Man R (2d) 24 at [25].

then no reference to it will be made in front of the jury. If, on the other hand, the trial judge decides to admit the evidence, it should be adduced without any reference being made by trial judge to the *voir dire* or his or her ruling on admissibility lest the jury form the impression that the evidence has some form of curial endorsement.[108] It should be noted that evidence that is admitted in the course of a *voir dire* does not form part of the evidence in the case[109] and any of that evidence that it is proposed to rely in the proceedings will have to re-adduced before the jury following the conclusion of the *voir dire*.

1–38 When evidence is admitted following a *voir dire*, it is open to the accused to challenge the veracity and reliability of that evidence in front of the jury[110] even if that involves a re-run of the cross-examination that took place during the *voir dire*.[111] However, an accused will not be permitted to revisit the question of the admissibility of the evidence or to engage in cross-examination directed to facts that underpinned the decision of the trial judge to admit the evidence in order to invite the jury to reach a different conclusion.[112]

1–39 While a determination of inadmissibility reached following a *voir dire* is generally treated as final, it is not irreversible. In *People (DPP) v Collins*,[113] the Court of Criminal Appeal rejected the proposition that once a trial judge has decided, following a *voir dire*, to rule out evidence, he or she cannot subsequently revisit and reverse that ruling. One circumstance where this might be appropriate is where the evidence at trial departs significantly from that given in the course of the *voir dire*.[114]

4. The Effect of a Determination of Inadmissibility

1–40 If an item of evidence is held to be inadmissible, then a trial judge has no discretion to admit it.[115] Such evidence is absolutely inadmissible and cannot be admitted for any purpose such as undermining the credibility of a witness.[116]

5. Failure to Object to Inadmissible Evidence

1–41 Evidence that could be excluded as inadmissible is frequently admitted because

---

[108] *People (DPP) v McDonagh* [2010] IECCA 127 at [24]–[25], [2012] 1 IR 49 at 57; *Mitchell v R.* [1998] AC 695.
[109] *People (DPP) v Murphy* [2005] IECCA 1 at [65]–[67], [2005] 2 IR 125 at 148; *R v Dela Cruz* [2007] MBCA 55, (2007) 220 CCC (3d) 272, 214 Man R (2d) 160 at [28].
[110] *R. v Corr* [1968] NI 193 at 208; *Sparks v R.* [1964] AC 964 at 983, [1964] 1 All ER 727 at 736; *R v Mushtaq* [2005] UKHL 25 at [38], [2005] 1 WLR 1513 at 1528. In *People (AG) v Ainscough* [1960] IR 136 at 140, it was held that a trial was rendered unsatisfactory by the failure of a trial judge to remind an unrepresented accused of his entitlement to challenge a confession again in front of the jury that had been admitted following a *voir dire*.
[111] As pointed out by Finlay CJ in *People (DPP) v Conroy* [1986] IR 460 at 472, one of the disadvantages of the *voir dire* procedure is that the witnesses will be well prepared for the line of cross-examination involved.
[112] *People (DPP) v Boyce* [2005] IECCA 143.
[113] [2011] IECCA 64 at [27].
[114] *R v Farrah* [2011] MBCA 49 at [23].
[115] *People (DPP) v Meleady (No.3)* [2001] 4 IR 16; *Myers v DPP* [1965] AC 1001 at 1024, [1964] 2 All ER 881 at 887.
[116] *R. v Treacy* [1944] 2 All ER 229 at 236.

the opposing party does not object or waives any objection to its admission.[117] If this is the position, then the party by virtue of an express representation or implied representation by conduct, will generally be estopped from later complaining about, or appealing on the basis of, the admission of that evidence.[118] However, a party may be permitted to belatedly challenge the admissibility of evidence already admitted where the interests of justice so require.[119] It has been held that, given the adversarial character of proceedings, absent exceptional circumstances, it is not for the trial judge of his or her own motion, to exclude evidence.[120]

6. Conditional Admissibility

1–42   As noted above, the question of relevance is very contextual in nature and it can sometimes be difficult to determine whether a particular item of evidence is relevant at the point at which it is sought to be adduced. In such circumstances, a trial judge may decide to admit the evidence on a conditional basis, *i.e. de bene esse*, whereby it will be taken into account if, in light of the evidence subsequently adduced, it is determined to be relevant. However, given the difficulties that may arise where the jury are exposed to evidence on a *de bene esse* basis that is not subsequently admitted,[121] the safer course of action in the case of a trial by jury is for the trial judge to refuse to admit the evidence but to afford a party the opportunity to have it admitted at a later point in the proceedings if it transpires to be relevant.[122]

7. Admission for a Specific Purpose

1–43   In general, if evidence is admitted, then the tribunal of fact can rely on it in determining any fact in issue in the proceedings even if was adduced to prove another fact.[123] However, evidence may sometimes be admissible for a specific and limited purpose only.[124] For example, under the hearsay rule, out-of-court statements are generally inadmissible to prove the truth of their contents. However, such a statement is admissible to prove the fact that it was made. Where such evidence is admitted, the trial judge should warn the jury of the limited purpose for which the evidence has been admitted.[125] Whether the jury will in practice draw such a distinction is open

---

[117] See, for example, *The Leopardstown Club Ltd v Templeville Developments Ltd* [2010] IEHC 152 at [6.9], in the civil context, and *People (DPP) v Small* [2011] IECCA 4 and *R v Park* (1981) 59 CCC (2d) 385 at 393, in the criminal context.

[118] See *Mapp v Gilhooley* [1991] 2 IR 253 at 262-263.

[119] *R v Gundy* [2008] ONCA 284, 231 CCC (3d) 26 at [22].

[120] *People (DPP) v Doherty* [2009] IECCA 17. But see *R v Hook* (1994) *Times,* 11 November 1994.

[121] See *O'Sullivan v Conroy*, unreported, High Court, 31 July 1997, where the applicant argued, on the basis of the decision in *People (DPP) v Conroy* [1986] IR 460, that the procedure of receiving evidence *de bene esse* was constitutionally impermissible. Barr J did not find it necessary to deal with this submission on the facts but expressed doubt as to whether the principle enunciated in *Conroy* that the jury should not be exposed to evidence of guilt which is inadmissible at law would extend to conditional admissibility.

[122] *Cf. People (DPP) v O'Callaghan* [2001] 1 IR 584, [2001] 2 ILRM 184.

[123] *Bradley v Independent Star Newspapers* [2011] IESC 17 at [32] and [143], [2011] 3 IR 96 at 109 and 135, [2012] 2 ILRM 26 at 36 and 59.

[124] As recognised by Hardiman J in *Irish Bank Resolution Corporation Ltd v Quinn Investments Sweden AB* [2012] IESC 51 (at p.32 of his judgment).

[125] [2012] IESC 51 at p.32 of the judgment of Hardiman J; *People (DPP) v McGrath* [2013] IECCA 12 at 13. See also *R v Norman* [2006] EWCA Crim 1662; *R v White* [2011] 1 SCR 433.

to question but the view is taken that this risk is outweighed by the benefit of the admission of the evidence.[126]

8. The Consequences of the Introduction of Inadmissible Evidence

1–44 The consequences of the introduction of inadmissible evidence in proceedings will depend on a variety of factors including whether any objection was raised at the time,[127] the importance of the evidence in the context of the proceedings[128] and whether the tribunal of fact consists of a jury or a judge sitting alone. In the case of a trial by jury, it may be possible for the trial judge to cure any prejudice arising by giving appropriate directions to the jury.[129] However, in some cases, there may be a risk that any attempt by the judge to undo the damage done by the introduction of inadmissible evidence by way of a direction to ignore that evidence may be counterproductive by drawing the jury's attention to that evidence.[130]

1–45 If the inadmissible evidence is so prejudicial that it creates "a real and substantial risk of an unfair trial",[131] which cannot be avoided by any directions that might be given to the jury, then it will be necessary to discharge the jury.[132] However, the discharge of a jury has been characterised as "a very extreme remedy"[133] and "an extreme step, to be taken only in exceptional circumstances".[134] As was made clear by O'Flaherty J in

---

[126] *Willis v Bernard* (1832) 8 Bing. 376 at 383.
[127] See *AG v O'Sullivan* [1930] IR 552 at 559; *People (AG) v Coughlan* (1968) 1 Frewen 325; *People (DPP) v Moloney*, Court of Criminal Appeal, 2 March 1992; *People (DPP) v Cronin* [2003] 3 IR 377 at 390–392; *People (DPP) v Fahy* [2007] IECCA 102 at [13], [2008] 2 IR 292 at 299.
[128] *People (DPP) v Hardiman* [2011] IECCA 69 at [12].
[129] *People (DPP) v Fahy* [2007] IECCA 102 at [13], [2008] 2 IR 292 at 299. For examples of such directions, see *People (DPP) v Lavery*, Court of Criminal Appeal, 19 March 2002 (reference to IRA); *People (DPP) v Doyle*, unreported, Court of Criminal Appeal, 22 March 2002 (prejudicial evidence of previous acts of violence by accused); *People (DPP) v Kavanagh*, unreported, Court of Criminal Appeal, *ex tempore*, 7 July 1997 (inadmissible misconduct evidence); *People (DPP) v Barr*, unreported, Court of Criminal Appeal, 21 July 1992 (inadmissible DNA evidence); *People (DPP) v Diemling*, unreported, Court of Criminal Appeal, 4 May 1992 (reference to membership of the SAS); *People (DPP) v Cunningham* [2007] IECCA 49 (reference to recognition evidence that had been ruled inadmissible); *People (DPP) v Cleary* [2009] IECCA 142 (suggestion that accused who was charged with dangerous driving causing death may have been racing); *People (DPP) v Freiberg* [2010] IECCA 33 at [39] (hearsay evidence); *People (DPP) v O'Sullivan* [2013] IECCA 18 (reference to target sheet by witness which was not entered into evidence). For the position in England and Wales, see *R v Sammon* [2011] EWCA Crim 1199.
[130] *People (DPP) v Fahy* [2007] IECCA 102 at [13], [2008] 2 IR 292 at 299; *People (DPP) v Kelly* [2006] IECCA 2 at [40], [2006] 4 IR 273 at 286.
[131] This test was stated by Keane CJ in *Murtagh v Ireland*, unreported, Supreme Court, February 5, 2004, p.6, in the context of a civil case but would appear to be equally applicable to criminal cases.
[132] *People (DPP) v Fahy* [2007] IECCA 102 at [13], [2008] 2 IR 292 at 299. See, *e.g. People (DPP) v Marley* [1985] ILRM 17 (evidence that accused had been acquitted of murder); *People (DPP) v G*, unreported, Court of Criminal Appeal, 13 November 1992 (inadmissible evidence of complaint of sexual assault); *People (DPP) v Brophy* [1992] ILRM 709 (inadmissible evidence of complaint of sexual assault). If the circumstances are such as would have warranted the discharge of the jury and this did not occur, then a conviction is likely to be quashed on appeal: *People (DPP) v McDermott*, Court of Criminal Appeal, 17 June 2002.
[133] *People (DPP) v Brophy* [1992] ILRM 709 at 716 (*per* O'Flaherty J).
[134] *People (DPP) v O'Sullivan* [2013] IECCA 18 at [88].

Dawson v Irish Brokers' Association,[135] the courts will only countenance the discharge of the jury where this is very clearly necessary:

> "Once again it is necessary to reiterate, as this court is doing with increasing frequency, that the question of having a jury discharged because something is said in opening a case or some inadmissible evidence gets in should be a remedy of the very last resort and only to be accomplished in the most extreme circumstances. Juries are much more robust and conscientious than is often thought. They are quite capable of accepting a trial judge's ruling that something is irrelevant, or should not have been given before them. ..."[136]

1–46   If a trial judge decides not to discharge the jury by reason of the introduction of inadmissible evidence, this decision will only be overturned on appeal if the Court of Criminal Appeal is satisfied that there "is a real and substantial risk of an unfair trial".[137] When applying that test, the Court will not lightly interfere with the exercise by the trial judge of his or her discretion[138] in circumstances where he or she is in a good position to evaluate the significance of what occurred in the context of the trial as a whole,[139] including the risk of prejudice to the accused.[140] But this test will be satisfied where the Court of Criminal Appeal is satisfied that the evidence was highly prejudicial and that there was a risk that any attempt to ameliorate the damage done could have been counterproductive.[141]

1–47   An even more robust approach is adopted in the case of a judge or judges sitting alone. Judges, by reason of their training and experience, are thought to be capable of excluding inadmissible evidence from their minds and, thus, it would appear that it will only be extreme cases that they will be required to discharge themselves.[142]

1–48   It should also be noted that the introduction of inadmissible evidence before a jury may render rebuttal evidence admissible.[143] For example, in *People (DPP) v Nevin*,[144] the Court of Criminal Appeal held that the trial judge had correctly admitted testimony from family members of the deceased to rebut surprise evidence given by the accused that the deceased had been a member of the IRA.

---

[135] [1998] IESC 39.

[136] This passage was approved in the criminal context by the Court of Criminal Appeal in *People (DPP) v Cleary* [2009] IECCA 142 at [8] and was paraphrased in *People (DPP) v Fahy* [2007] IECCA 102 at [13], [2008] 2 IR 292 at 299. See also *People (DPP) v Doyle*, unreported, Court of Criminal Appeal, 22 March 2002, p.10, and *Murtagh v Ireland*, unreported, Supreme Court, 5 February 2004, p.6, where the decision of the trial judge to discharge the jury was described as "a disproportionate reaction in the circumstances".

[137] *People (DPP) v Cleary* [2009] IECCA 142 at [7].

[138] *People (DPP) v McGartland*, unreported, Court of Criminal Appeal, *ex tempore*, 20 January 2003 at [7]; *People (DPP) v Kenny* [2006] IECCA 137 at [7].

[139] *People (DPP) v Cleary* [2009] IECCA 142 at [7–8]; *People (DPP) v O'Sullivan* [2013] IECCA 18 at [88].

[140] See *People (DPP) v JEM* [2001] 4 IR 385 at 398–399.

[141] *People (DPP) v Fahy* [2007] IECCA 102, [2008] 2 IR 292.

[142] See *People (DPP) v McMahon* [1984] ILRM 461. *Cf. People (DPP) v Healy* (1984) 3 Frewen 11.

[143] *People (DPP) v Nevin* [2003] 3 IR 321 at 351. Some other common law jurisdictions have also recognised a limited discretion to introduce rebuttal evidence, which may itself be inadmissible, where irrelevant evidence has been admitted by the other side without objection. For the Canadian approach, see *R v Rosik* [1971] 2 CCC (2d) 351; *R. v Gowland* (1978) 45 CCC 303; *R. v Rhodes* (1981) 59 CCC 426 and, generally, Bryant, Lederman and Fuerst, *Sopinka, Lederman & Bryant: The Law of Evidence in Canada* 4th edn (Lexis Nexis, 2014), § 2.93. For the position in New South Wales, see *R. v Taylor* [1967] 2 NSWR 278.

[144] [2003] 3 IR 321 at 351–352.

D. Discretion to Exclude Relevant Evidence

1–49 In *People (AG) v O'Brien*,[145] Walsh J stated that "the primary purpose of the rules of evidence is to ensure a fair trial of the person accused". It is, thus, well established that a trial judge, as part of his or her function to ensure that an accused receives a fair trial, has a discretion to exclude evidence if, in his or her opinion, its probative value is outweighed by its prejudicial effect.[146] As Geoghegan J stated in *People (DPP) v Meleady (No.3)*[147]:

> "A judge, as part of his inherent power, has an overriding duty in every case to ensure that the accused receives a fair trial and always has discretion to exclude otherwise admissible prosecution evidence if, in his opinion, its prejudicial effect, in the minds of the jury outweighs its true probative value."[148]

1–50 The exercise of this discretion can be seen in *People (AG) v O'Neill*.[149] The defendant had been convicted of manslaughter arising out of a car accident and it was held by the Court of Criminal Appeal that evidence that he had been in a pub on the evening of the accident and had consumed alcohol was irrelevant in the absence of a suggestion by the prosecution that his driving had been affected by alcohol. The Court went on to point out that such evidence could be highly prejudicial to an accused and held that, even if relevant, the trial judge should have exercised his discretion to exclude it unless he was satisfied that its probative value outweighed its prejudicial effect.[150]

1–51 A more recent example of where the exercise of the discretion was considered can be seen in *People (DPP) v Carney*.[151] The accused had been convicted of the murder of his partner. He admitted that, in the course of an argument, he had put his hands around her neck and squeezed and that her face turned blue, at which point he realised she was dead. He maintained that he had not intended to kill or seriously injure her. On appeal, it was contended that the trial judge had erred in admitting photographs of the deceased into evidence, which showed the marks on her neck and face and the colour of her face. The accused argued that these photographs should not have been admitted because they were highly prejudicial and their admission was not necessary because the accused had conceded that the deceased's face had turned blue. However, the prosecution submitted that the photographs were relevant to support the evidence of the pathologist and to rebut the assertion by the accused that he had not intended to kill

---

[145] [1965] IR 142 at 167.
[146] See *People (AG) v O'Neill* [1964] Ir Jur Rep 1; *People (AG) v O'Brien* [1965] IR 142 at 159 (*per* Kingsmill Moore J); *People (DPP) v Coddington*, unreported, Court of Criminal Appeal, 31 May 2001; *People (DPP) v Meleady (No.3)* [2001] 4 IR 16; *Blanchfield v Harnett* [2002] 3 IR 207 at 219; *People (DPP) v Murphy*, Court of Criminal Appeal, 8 July 2003; *People (DPP) v Flynn*, unreported, Court of Criminal Appeal, 30 July 2003; *People (DPP) v Kavanagh* [2008] IECCA 100; *People (DPP) v Carney* [2011] IECCA 53; *People (DPP) v Kearney* [2012] IECCA 1 at [8]; *People (DPP) v Timmons* [2011] IECCA 13 at [18]. In England and Wales, a similar discretion was recognised in *R. v Sang* [1980] AC 402, [1979] 2 All ER 1222 but has been largely superseded by s.78 of the Police and Criminal Evidence Act 1984 (see Malek (ed.), *Phipson on Evidence* 18th edn, para.39). An equivalent discretion is also provided for in Rule 403 of the US Federal Rules of Evidence (see Broun (ed.), *McCormick on Evidence* 7th edn, Vol. II, p.778). For the Canadian approach, see *Thompson Newspapers Inc. v Canada* [1990] SCR 425 at 559–560 and, for an example of the approach adopted in Australia, see *R v DG* [2010] VSCA 173.
[147] [2001] 4 IR 16.
[148] [2001] 4 IR 16 at 31.
[149] [1964] Ir Jur Rep 1.
[150] *Cf. People (AG) v Moore* [1964] Ir Jur Rep 6 and *People (AG) v Regan* [1975] IR 367.
[151] [2011] IECCA 53.

or seriously injure the deceased and that they were sufficiently necessary, material and probative to outweigh any prejudicial effect. The Court of Criminal Appeal summarised the principles governing the exercise of this discretion as follows:

> "A discretion exists in the trial judge to exclude material, such as the photographs in the present case, although otherwise admissible, if the evidence is either of little probative value but is prejudicial, or if it is of greater probative value but nevertheless its prejudice outweighs its true probative value. Where its prejudicial effect outweighs its true probative value, that discretion should be exercised in a manner which best guarantees the fairness of the trial for the accused."[152]

1–52   The Court was satisfied that, although there might be a practice that photographs which were merely "prurient or distressing, or even inflammatory" were not adduced in evidence, there was no general principle that they were to be excluded.[153] Instead, it was a matter for the trial judge to exercise his or her discretion judicially, having considered the nature of the evidence and its probative value and prejudicial effect. In this case, the trial judge took the view that the photographs were not particularly shocking, were illustrative of the evidence that would be given by the pathologist and were admissible so that the prosecution could "put flesh on the bones of their case". The Court of Criminal Appeal concluded that the trial judge had exercised his discretion to admit the photographs appropriately, judicially and for stated valid reasons.[154] The Court also declined to interfere with the decision of the trial judge to admit into evidence as relevant and probative certain answers given by the accused when interviewed by the gardaí in which he acknowledged that the deceased would have known that he was killing her.

1–53   The difficulties in deciding whether the prejudicial effect of evidence exceeds its probative value can be seen in *People (DPP) v Coddington*.[155] The applicant had been convicted of possession of a controlled drug for the purpose of supply and, on appeal, argued that the trial judge had erred in admitting evidence of the finding of a large sum of cash hidden in two locations at his residence. He argued that the prejudicial effect of this evidence outweighed its probative value, pointing out that it was common knowledge that drug dealers have large amounts of cash. However, the Court of Criminal Appeal took the view that this was actually a reason why the finding of a substantial sum of cash in a case such as this might have sufficient probative value to be admissible. The Court was, thus, satisfied that the evidence was not so prejudicial as to outweigh its probative value and that the trial judge had exercised his discretion correctly to admit it. The conclusion of the Court on the facts is unremarkable but it does illustrate the circularity which is often involved in the application of this balancing test of probative value and prejudicial effect. This is because the basis of the probative value of evidence, *i.e.* the unlikelihood of coincidence that a person who was accused

---

152   [2011] IECCA 53 at [7–8].
153   [2011] IECCA 53 at [9].
154   [2011] IECCA 53 at [10]. A similar conclusion in relation to the admission of photographs of the victim of a homicide was reached in *People (DPP) v Barnes* [2006] IECCA 165 at [95], [2007] 3 IR 130 at 158 and *People (DPP) v Hussain* [2014] IECCA 26 at [7.1]–[7.2] but without any consideration of the weighing of the probative value or prejudicial effect of such evidence.
155   Unreported, Court of Criminal Appeal, 31 May 2001. *Cf.* the line of English authorities dealing with the admission of evidence of possession of sums of money on charges of possession of drugs with intention to supply which include: *R. v Blatt* [1994] Crim LR 592; *R. v Wright* [1994] Crim LR 55; *R. v Morris* [1983] 2 SCR 190, (1983) 7 CCC (3d) 97; *R. v Gordon* [1995] 2 Cr App R 61; *R. v Halpin* [1996] Crim LR 112 and *R. v Guney* [1998] 2 Cr App R 242.

of being a drug dealer should happen to have large amounts of cash concealed at his home, is also the source of its prejudicial effect.

1–54 In *DPP v McCutcheon*,[156] it was held that, if circumstances arise which require a District Judge to exercise his or her discretion as to whether or not to admit relevant probative evidence, he or she must be sufficiently informed of the nature and substance of the intended evidence in order to weigh its possible value and prejudicial effect.[157]

1–55 Given that the purpose of this discretion is to ensure that an accused receives a fair trial, there would appear to be little scope for it to operate in civil cases heard by a judge but, as a matter of principle, there does not seem to be any reason why it should not be applied in a civil case to be heard by a jury.[158]

E. Weight

1–56 If evidence is admitted, the weight to be attributed to it is a matter for the tribunal of fact[159] and will depend on its assessment of the probative value or persuasiveness of the evidence.[160] This may in turn depend on the tribunal of fact's assessment of the credibility of the witness giving the evidence.[161] In *Clayton v Cashman*,[162] Peart J provided a very useful enumeration of the factors that may be considered when assessing the credibility of a witness, which include: (i) the consistency of the witness's evidence with what is agreed, or clearly shown by other evidence to have occurred; (ii) the internal consistency of the witness's evidence; (iii) consistency with what the witness has said on other occasions; (iv) the credibility of the witness generally; and (v) the demeanour of the witness.[163] In the criminal context, in *People (DPP) v McKevitt*,[164] the

---

[156] [1986] ILRM 433.

[157] Ó Caoimh J cited this *dicta* with approval in *DPP v Clifford*, unreported, High Court, 22 July 2002, where it was held that the trial judge had erred in withdrawing the case from the jury, as he had failed to address what the requirements of justice were in the particular circumstances.

[158] See the comments of Charleton J in *Condron v ACC Bank plc* [2012] IEHC 395 at [11], [2013] 1 ILRM 113 at 119, that "the issue of prejudicial effect of evidence before a professional judge, as opposed to a jury, is not likely to have any real impact".

[159] *People (AG) v Williams* [1940] IR 195 at 205; *People (DPP) v Boyce* [2005] IECCA 143.

[160] *F. McK. v G.W.D. (Proceeds of crime outside State)* [2004] IESC 31 at [47], [2004] 2 IR 470 at 485, [2004] 2 ILRM 419 at 433.

[161] In *People (DPP) v Collins*, unreported, Court of Criminal Appeal, 22 April 2002, it was held that the assessment of the credibility of a witness and the weight to be attached to his or her evidence is manifestly within the province of a jury in a criminal trial.

[162] *Clayton v Cashman* [2006] IEHC 360 at 31.

[163] Although considerable weight may be attributed by the tribunal of fact to the demeanour of a witness, it should be careful not to over-estimate it. As Lord Atkins cautioned in *Lek v Mathews* (1926) 25 Lloyd's Rep 525 at 543: "The lynx-eyed judge who can discern the truth teller from the liar by looking at him is more often found in fiction or in appellate judgments than on the bench." For that reason, the same judge stated in *Société d'Avances Commerciales v Merchants Marine Insurance Co.* (1924) 20 Lloyd's Rep 140 at 152 that: "an ounce of intrinsic merit or demerit in the evidence, that is to say, the value of the comparison of the evidence with known facts is worth pounds of demeanour". That statement was quoted by O'Donnell J in *People (DPP) v C.C. (No.2)* [2012] IECCA 86 at [18] who said that it was an observation borne of lengthy experience and regarded it as "significant that those with the greatest experience of judging the credibility of witnesses have the least faith in the capacity of any person to simply observe the witness giving evidence and determine if he or she is telling the truth".

[164] Unreported, Special Criminal Court, 6 August 2002 (judgment not available). See the judgment

Special Criminal Court identified a somewhat overlapping list of criteria for evaluating the credibility of a witness: (i) his knowledge of the facts to which he testified, (ii) his disinterestedness; (iii) his integrity; (iv) his veracity; (v); being bound to speak the truth by such an oath as he deems to be obligatory; (vi) the court's overall opinion of the witness; (vii) any evidence of corroboration; and (viii) general.

1–57   It should be noted that, even if evidence is not challenged, the tribunal of fact is not obliged to accept and act on it. It is the duty of the court to weigh and evaluate the evidence and decide whether to accept it.[165] Thus, in the case of oral evidence, even if a witness is not cross-examined in relation to a particular matter, the tribunal of fact is entitled to assess the credibility of the witness and decide whether to accept or reject the evidence of the witness in relation to that matter.[166]

---

of the Court of Criminal Appeal at [2005] IECCA 139 and of the Supreme Court at [2008] IESC 51, [2009] ILRM 401 at 417 and [2009] 1 IR 525 at 542.

[165] *Lopes v Minister for Justice, Equality and Law Reform* [2014] IESC 21 at [7.8]. *Cf. Koulibaly v Minister for Justice, Equality and Law Reform* [2004] IESC 50 at 9 (court not obliged to accept evidence on affidavit not challenged by cross-examination).

[166] *Lopes v Minister for Justice, Equality and Law Reform* [2014] IESC 21 at [7.8]; *Stanley v Kieran* [2011] IESC 19 at [40]–[41].

THE BURDEN OF PROOF

A. Introduction

2–01   This chapter deals with the rules and principles relating to the allocation and discharge of the burden of proof in criminal and civil proceedings. However, it is necessary, at the outset, to clarify that this phrase actually encompasses two distinct concepts, the "legal burden" and the "evidential burden". It is very important to distinguish them because much of the analysis that follows is predicated on a clear distinction being drawn between the two.[1]

1. The Legal Burden

2–02   The "legal burden"[2] is a burden of proof properly so called and is the burden fixed by law on a party to satisfy the tribunal of fact as to the existence or non-existence of a fact or matter. Where the legal burden is borne by a party in relation to an issue, he or she is required to persuade the tribunal of fact to the criminal or civil standard of proof, as appropriate, in relation to that issue. If the party fails to discharge this burden, then he or she will lose on that issue. It can be seen, therefore, that the legal burden allocates the risk of failure in proceedings. It is important to note that the legal burden is issue specific and, given that a case will often involve more than one issue, the legal burden on different issues may be distributed between the parties to the proceedings.

2–03   The standard of proof required to discharge the legal burden depends on whether the proceedings are criminal or civil and, in criminal cases, on the identity of the party fixed with the legal burden. In civil cases, the standard of proof is proof on a balance of probabilities and that is also the standard that has to be met where the accused bears a legal burden in criminal proceedings. However, the prosecution can only discharge its legal burden by proving a matter beyond a reasonable doubt.

---

[1]   There has been considerable judicial and academic debate about the appropriate labels and types of burdens that may be imposed on parties. The concepts of the "legal burden" and the "evidential burden" are utilised in this chapter because they are the terms used by Costello J in his seminal decision in *O'Leary v Attorney General* [1993] 1 IR 102 at 109, [1991] ILRM 454 at 460. They have also gained judicial currency in subsequent decisions.

[2]   This has also been described on occasion as "the probative burden" (*DPP v Morgan* [1976] AC 182 at 217, [1975] 2 All ER 347 at 364 (*per* Lord Simon)), "the persuasive burden" (*Hardy v Ireland* [1994] 2 IR 550 at 559 (*per* Flood J)) and "the risk of non-persuasion" (*Hutch v Dublin Corporation* [1993] 3 IR 551 at 558 (*per* McCarthy J)).

2. The Evidential Burden

2–04 The "evidential burden"[3] is the burden borne by a party of adducing sufficient evidence to satisfy the trial judge that an issue should be left to the tribunal of fact. The evidential burden performs what is effectively a filtering function and involves a determination of whether a party could possibly succeed in relation to an issue.

2–05 The evidential burden is discharged when the party on whom it is placed adduces sufficient evidence to prevent the trial judge withdrawing the issue from the tribunal of fact. What constitutes sufficient evidence depends on whether the case is civil or criminal and on which party bears the burden. In civil proceedings, the burden will be discharged when a party makes out a *prima facie* case, *i.e.* when the evidence adduced is such that the tribunal of fact would be entitled to make a finding in favour of that party. A *prima facie* case is also what is required of the prosecution in criminal proceedings, but the accused will generally discharge an evidential burden borne by him or her in relation to an issue if the evidence on the issue might leave the jury in a reasonable doubt.

3. Presumptions

2–06 The distribution of the legal and evidential burden in respect of issues in proceedings is often dictated by presumptions, most of them statutory in origin. They are frequently used to make it easier for one party to discharge the burden of proof on it in respect of an issue or to relieve it of the obligation to establish a particular fact or matter.[4] Of particular importance in that regard are mandatory presumptions, which require the tribunal of fact, upon proof of one fact, known as the basic fact, to infer the existence of another fact, known as the presumed fact. These presumptions are rebuttable and the quantum of evidence required to rebut the presumption gives rise to two discrete sub-categories: (a) mandatory legal presumptions, which place a legal burden on a party to rebut the existence of the presumed fact; and (b) mandatory evidential presumptions, which place an evidential burden on a party to adduce evidence as to the non-existence of the presumed fact. The categories of presumptions are discussed further below.

B. Criminal Cases

1. Introduction

2–07 In criminal cases, the general rule is that the prosecution bears the legal burden of proving every fact necessary to establish the guilt of the accused. However, as will be seen below, there are a number of circumstances where a legal burden may be placed on an accused. Given that the incidence of the evidential burden in relation to an issue usually coincides with that of the legal burden, the evidential burden is generally borne by the prosecution. However, there are also exceptions where it will

---

3   This is generally referred to in the United States as the "burden of producing evidence" (see Broun (ed.), *McCormick on Evidence* 4th edn, (Thomson Reuters, 2013), § 336.
4   See the explanation of the role and operation of presumptions given by McKechnie J in *Sweeney v Fahy* [2014] IESC 50 at [37]–[50].

be borne by an accused, most notably where he or she raises a defence which is more than a mere denial of the prosecution case.

2. The Presumption of Innocence

2–08   The presumption of innocence is the principle underlying two fundamental rules with regard to the burden of proof in criminal cases: (a) the rule that the prosecution bears the legal burden of proving all the elements of an offence necessary to establish the guilt of an accused[5]; and (b) the rule that the guilt of the accused must be proved by the prosecution beyond a reasonable doubt.[6]

2–09   In *R. v Oakes*,[7] Dickson CJC explained the basis for the presumption of innocence as follows:

> "The presumption of innocence is a hallowed principle lying at the very heart of criminal law... [It] protects the fundamental liberty and human dignity of any and every person accused by the State of criminal conduct. An individual charged with an offence faces grave social and personal consequences, including potential loss of physical liberty, subjection to social stigma and ostracism from the community, as well as other social, psychological and economic harms. In light of the gravity of these consequences, the presumption of innocence is crucial. It ensures that until the State proves an accused's guilt beyond all reasonable doubt, he or she is innocent. This is essential in a society committed to fairness and social justice. The presumption of innocence confirms our faith in humankind; it reflects our belief that individuals are decent and law-abiding members of the community until proven otherwise."[8]

2–10   Similar reasons were advanced by Brennan J in *Re Winship*[9]:

> "The requirement of proof beyond a reasonable doubt has this vital role in our criminal procedure for cogent reasons. The accused during a criminal prosecution has at stake interests of immense importance, both because of the possibility that he may lose his liberty upon conviction and because of the certainty that he would be stigmatized by the conviction. Accordingly, a society that values the good name and freedom of every individual should not condemn a man for commission of a crime when there is reasonable doubt about his guilt."[10]

2–11   It can be seen, therefore, that the principal justification for the presumption of innocence is that it allocates the risk of adjudicative error to the prosecution and, thus, reduces the risk of a wrongful conviction.[11] If a person is wrongfully convicted, the serious consequences are borne by him or her alone, whereas, if a guilty person is

---

[5]   *People (DPP) v DO'T.* [2003] 4 IR 286 at 290; *R. v Oakes* [1986] 1 SCR 103 at 121, (1986) 26 DLR (4th) 200 at 214.

[6]   *People (DPP) v DO'T.* [2003] 4 IR 286 at 291; *R. v Oakes* [1986] 1 SCR 103 at 121, (1986) 26 DLR (4th) 200 at 214; *In re Winship* (1970) 397 US 358 at 363–364. See also Stephen, *History of the Criminal Law* (1883), vol. 1, p.438, who stated that: "the presumption of innocence is otherwise stated by saying the prisoner is entitled to the benefit of every reasonable doubt". On the presumption of innocence generally, see: Hamilton, *The Presumption of Innocence and Irish Criminal Law: Whittling the Golden Thread* (Irish Academic Press, 2007); Hamilton, "Threats to the Presumption of Innocence in Irish Criminal Law: An Assessment" (2011) E & P 81; Naughton, "How the presumption of innocence renders the innocent vulnerable to wrongful convictions" (2011) 2 (1) IJLS 40.

[7]   [1986] 1 SCR 103, (1986) 26 DLR (4th) 200.

[8]   [1986] 1 SCR 103 at 119–120, (1986) 26 DLR (4th) 200 at 212–213. See also *per* Dickson CJC in *R. v Holmes* [1988] 1 SCR 914 at 933.

[9]   (1970) 397 US 358.

[10]   (1970) 397 US 358 at 363–364.

[11]   See *per* Brennan J in *Speiser v Randall* (1958) 357 US 513 at 525–256; *per* Harlan J in *In re Winship* (1970) 397 US 358 at 370–371.

wrongfully acquitted, the consequences of that error are borne by society as a whole.[12] Furthermore, wrongful convictions have the potential to seriously undermine the moral basis of, and confidence in, the criminal justice system.[13] It is for these reasons that "the law holds that it is better that ten guilty persons escape than that one innocent suffer".[14] The presumption of innocence is also explicable in terms of the disparity in power and resources between the State and the accused[15] and constitutes a safeguard against abuse by the State of its superior power.[16] Finally, there is, as articulated in *Oakes*, a normative justification for the presumption based on a faith in humanity.

2–12   The presumption of innocence is a principle of considerable antiquity.[17] Lord Sankey LC, in an oft quoted passage, stated in *Woolmington v DPP*[18] that:

> "Throughout the web of the English criminal law one golden thread is always to be seen, that it is the duty of the prosecution to prove the prisoner's guilt. ... No matter what the charge or where the trial, the principle that the prosecution must prove the guilt of the prisoner is part of the common law of England and no attempt to whittle it down can be entertained."[19]

2–13   This statement of principle has been endorsed on numerous occasions in this jurisdiction[20] and in *McGowan v Carville*,[21] Murnaghan J declared that it was:

> "a cardinal principle of the administration of the criminal law in this country, which has often been stated, and cannot be too often re-stated, that there is no onus on a person charged with an offence to prove his innocence, the onus at all times being on the State to prove his guilt."

---

12   See *per* Harlan J in *In re Winship* (1970) 397 US 358 at 372: "I view the requirement of proof beyond a reasonable doubt in a criminal case as bottomed on a fundamental value determination of our society that it is far worse to convict an innocent man than to let a guilty man go free."

13   In *In re Winship* (1970) 397 US 358 at 364, Brennan J stated that: "use of the reasonable doubt standard is indispensable to command the respect and confidence of the community in applications of the criminal law. It is critical that the moral force of the criminal law not be diluted by a standard of proof that leaves people in doubt whether innocent men are being condemned."

14   Blackstone, *Commentaries on the Laws of England*, vol. 2, c.27, p.358. See to similar effect, Sir Matthew Hale, *Pleas of the Crown* (1678), vol. 2, p.290: "it is better five guilty persons should escape unpunished than one innocent person should die" and *per* Quigley J in *Gillet v Nissan* (1975) 3 WWR 520 at 534: "it is better that 99 guilty men go free than one innocent man be convicted".

15   Ashworth, *Principles of Criminal Law* 2nd edn (Oxford, 1995) at p.81.

16   In *In re Winship* (1970) 397 US 358 at 364, Brennan J stated: "It is also important in our free society that every individual going about his ordinary affairs have confidence that his government cannot adjudge him guilty of a criminal offense without convincing a proper factfinder of his guilt with utmost certainty."

17   The history of the presumption is traced in *Coffin v United States* (1895) 156 US 432 at 453 ff., where White J demonstrated that it could be traced back to Roman law and, possibly, to the laws of ancient Greece.

18   [1935] AC 462, [1935] All ER 1.

19   [1935] AC 462 at 481, [1935] All ER 1 at 8. It should be noted that, as acknowledged by the Privy Council in *Jayasena v R.* [1970] AC 618 at 625, [1970] 1 All ER 219 at 222, this "golden thread" was not as universal in application as the Lord Chancellor indicated and there was a considerable body of pre-*Woolmington* authority that placed the legal burden in respect of particular defences on an accused. For a discussion of the status and application of the principle in English law, see Ashworth and Blake, "The Presumption of Innocence in English Criminal Law" [1996] Crim LR 306; Ho, "The Presumption of Innocence as a Human Right" in Roberts and Hunter (eds) *Criminal Evidence and Human Rights: Reimagining Common Law Procedural Traditions* (Oxford: Hart Publishing, 2012), pp.259–81; Hamer, "A Dynamic Reconstruction of the Presumption of Innocence" (2011) 31 OJLS 417.

20   See, *e.g. People (AG) v McMahon* [1946] IR 267 at 273; *People (AG) v Oglesby* [1966] IR 162 at 165.

21   [1960] IR 330 at 345.

2–14   It is not surprising, therefore, that the presumption of innocence has been held to be a constitutionally required constituent of a trial in due course of law.[22] In *O'Leary v AG*,[23] Costello J pointed out that the presumption of innocence had been an integral part of the common law tradition before the enactment of the Constitution and, furthermore, was enshrined in numerous international instruments.[24] He thus accepted the plaintiff's contention that it was constitutionally protected:

> "I have little difficulty in … construing the Constitution as conferring on every accused in every criminal trial a constitutionally protected right to the presumption of innocence….The Constitution of course contains no express reference to the presumption but it does provide in Article 38.1 that 'no person shall be tried on any criminal charge save in due course of law.' It seems to me that it has been for so long a fundamental postulate of every criminal trial in this country that the accused was presumed to be innocent of the offence with which he was charged that a criminal trial held otherwise than in accordance with this presumption would, *prima facie*, be one which was not held in due course of law."[25]

2–15   His conclusion on this point was upheld by the Supreme Court, with O'Flaherty J declaring that the presumption of innocence was a necessary ingredient of a trial in due course of law as protected by Art.38(1).[26]

2–16   The importance of the presumption of innocence was re-iterated in *People (DPP) v DO'T*.[27] Hardiman J, delivering the judgment of the Court of Criminal Appeal, referred to the decision of Costello J in *O'Leary* as authority that "the presumption of innocence is a vital, constitutionally guaranteed, right of a person accused in a criminal trial" and went on to point out that the presumption of innocence "is not only a right in itself: it is the basis of other aspects of a trial in due course of law at common law".[28]

---

[22]   *O'Leary v AG* [1993] 1 IR 102 at 107, [1991] ILRM 454 at 458-459, [1995] 1 IR 254 at 259, [1995] ILRM 259 at 267; *Hardy v Ireland* [1994] 2 IR 550 at 564–565; *Phipps v Hogan*, unreported, High Court, 27 May 2004, at 9; *McNally v Ireland* [2009] IEHC 753 at [176], [2011] 4 IR 431 at 473, [2011] 1 ILRM 40 at 77.

[23]   [1993] 1 IR 102, [1991] ILRM 454.

[24]   He referred to Art.11 of the United Nations Universal Declaration of Human Rights 1948 ("Everyone charged with a penal offence has the right to be presumed innocent until proved guilty according to law…"); Art.6(2) of the European Convention on Human Rights ("Everyone charged with a criminal offence shall be presumed innocent until proved guilty according to law."); Art.8(2) of the American Convention on Human Rights 1969 ("Every person accused of a criminal offence has the right to be presumed innocent so long as his guilt has not been proven according to law."); and Art.7 of the African Charter on Human Rights and Peoples' Rights (every individual has "the right to be presumed innocent until proven guilty by a competent Court or tribunal"). Although not mentioned by Costello J, it might be noted that the presumption of innocence is also constitutionally protected in a number of other common law countries. See, *e.g.* Art.11(d) of the Canadian Charter of Rights and Freedoms (a person charged with an offence has the right "to be presumed innocent until proven guilty according to law in a fair and public hearing by an independent and impartial tribunal"); s.25(c) of the New Zealand Bill of Rights Act 1990 (one of the minimum rights of a person charged with an offence, in relation to the determination of the charge is the "right to be presumed innocent until proved guilty according to law"); *Estelle v Williams* (1976) 425 US 501 at 503 (*per* Burger CJ) ("The presumption of innocence, although not articulated in the Constitution, is a basic component of a fair trial under our system of criminal justice."). See generally, Stumer, *The Presumption of Innocence: Evidential and Human Rights Perspectives* (Oxford: Hart Publishing, 2010).

[25]   [1993] 1 IR 102 at 107, [1991] ILRM 454 at 458–459.

[26]   [1995] 1 IR 254 at 259, [1995] ILRM 259 at 267.

[27]   [2003] 4 IR 286.

[28]   [2003] 4 IR 286 at 290.

3. Allocation of the Legal Burden

2–17   As noted above, the general rule is that the prosecution bears the legal burden of proving every fact necessary to establish the guilt of the accused.[29] This obligation may involve the proof of a negative[30] if this is an ingredient of the offence in question such as the absence of consent in a rape or assault case. This obligation also extends to proof of any procedural conditions, such as limitation periods, which must be satisfied before a prosecution can be brought[31] and to proof of any facts required to be proved to ground the admissibility of any evidence that the prosecution wishes to adduce.[32]

2–18   Apart from proving the ingredients of an offence, the prosecution also bears the legal burden of "negativing every supposition consistent with the innocence of the accused."[33] Thus, where a defence is raised by the accused (other than insanity), and he or she adduces sufficient evidence to satisfy the evidential burden and get the issue before the jury, the legal burden is on the prosecution to disprove that defence.[34] In *People (AG) v Quinn*,[35] Walsh J explained, in the context of the defence of self-defence, that:

> "When the evidence in a case, whether it be the evidence offered by the prosecution or by the defence, discloses a possible defence of self-defence the onus remains throughout upon the prosecution to establish that the accused is guilty of the offence charged. The onus is never upon the accused to raise a doubt in the minds of the jury. In such case the burden rests on the prosecution to negative the possible defence of self-defence which has arisen and if, having considered the whole of the evidence, the jury is either convinced of the innocence of the prisoner or left in doubt whether or not he was acting in necessary self-defence they must acquit."[36]

2–19   It was, however, acknowledged by Costello J in *O'Leary v Attorney General*[37] that the right to the presumption of innocence protected by Art. 38.1 is not absolute[38] and there are three exceptions where the prosecution is relieved of the obligation to prove every fact necessary to establish the guilt of the accused and/or where a legal burden is placed on the accused: (a) statutory exceptions; (b) insanity; and (c) the peculiar knowledge principle.

---

[29] *AG (McLoughlin) v Rhatigan* (1966) 100 ILTR 37; *Minister for Supplies v Brady & Co.* (1943) 77 ILTR 91; *People (AG) v Dwyer* [1972] IR 416; *Crosby v Delap*, unreported, High Court, 31 January 1992; *People (DPP) v O'Neill*, unreported, Court of Criminal Appeal, 24 July 1995; *DPP v Crimmins*, unreported, High Court, 8 June 2000; *Weir v DPP* [2008] IEHC 268 at [10]; *People (DPP) v Smyth* [2010] IECCA 34 at [15], [2010] 3 IR 688 at 694, [2011] 1 ILRM 81 at 86.

[30] *McGowan v Carville* [1960] IR 330 at 350–351 (*per* Maguire CJ).

[31] See *People (AG) v Curran* [1949] Ir Jur Rep 27 and *DPP v Hussey*, unreported, High Court, 20 October 1987.

[32] *People (DPP) v Dillon* [2003] 1 ILRM 531 at 539.

[33] *Per* Maguire P in *People (AG) v McMahon* [1946] IR 267 at 273.

[34] *People (AG) v Quinn* [1965] IR 366 at 383; *People (AG) v Dwyer* [1972] IR 416; *People (DPP) v Kavanagh*, unreported, Court of Criminal Appeal, 18 May 1999 at 2–3; *People (DPP) v Kelly* [2000] 2 IR 1 at 12; *People (DPP) v Ceka* [2004] IECCA 25, at 14; *People (DPP) v Kelly* [2011] IECCA 25 at 11; *R. v Gill* (1963) 47 Cr App R 166 at 172.

[35] [1965] IR 366.

[36] [1965] IR 366 at 382.

[37] [1993] 1 IR 102 at 110, [1991] ILRM 454 at 461.

[38] *Cf. Abbey Films v AG* [1951] IR 159 at 170; *Woolmington v DPP* [1935] AC 462 at 481, [1935] All ER 1 at 8.

(a) Statutory exceptions

2–20 The legislature may, by statutory provision, abridge the presumption of innocence by relieving the prosecution of the obligation to prove every fact necessary to establish the guilt of the accused. As Charleton J pointed out in *People (DPP) v Smyth*[39]:

> "It is for the Oireachtas, in each case, to set the parameters of proof in a criminal charge; to decide whether there should be a reversed burden of proof in respect of any element of a crime; and to indicate expressly, or by implication, the nature of the burden of proof that it to be discharged by the defence."

2–21 Many such provisions take the form of mandatory legal or evidential presumptions but, as noted below, there are a variety of ways by which this can be achieved and a careful analysis of each statutory provision is required in order to ascertain its effect. Although Charleton J in the passage set out above contemplated that a statutory provision could be found to have impliedly placed a burden of proof on an accused and there is a line of UK case law to this effect,[40] the balance of authority is against the proposition that there can be implied statutory exceptions to the general principle that the prosecution bears the burden of proof.[41]

2–22 As noted above, the presumption of innocence has the object and effect of ensuring that an accused can only be convicted of an offence where his or her guilt of the offence charged has been proven beyond a reasonable doubt.[42] Accordingly, a question potentially arises in relation to the constitutional validity of any statutory provision that trenches on that fundamental principle. The principles to be applied in this regard have been considered in a number of Canadian decisions, which have developed a sophisticated jurisprudence in this area.[43] In summary, it has been held that

---

[39] [2010] IECCA 34 at [14], [2010] 3 IR 688 at 694, [2011] 1 ILRM 81 at 86.

[40] In *R. v Hunt* [1987] AC 352, [1987] 1 All ER 1, it was held that there could be implied statutory exceptions to the principle that the prosecution bore the burden of proof in respect of every element of an offence, but subsequent cases such as *R(P) v Liverpool Magistrates' Court* [2006] EWHC 887 indicate a reluctance to do this and only in clear cases.

[41] *DPP v Rostas* [2012] IEHC 19 at [14]. See also *Dunne v PJ Construction Ltd Co. Ltd* [1989] ILRM 803 at 805 (courts will not reverse the usual rules governing the onus of proof unless this is clearly mandated by the terms of a statute) and *Crosby v Delap*, unreported, High Court, 31 January 1992 (Johnson J took the view that because s.2(2)(d) of the Casual Trading Act 1980 did not expressly place the burden of proof on the accused, it remained on the prosecution).

[42] *R. v Oakes* [1986] 1 SCR 103 at 121, (1986) 26 DLR (4th) 200 at 214; *R. v Vaillancourt* [1987] 2 SCR 636 at 654, (1987) 47 DLR (4th) 399 at 415.

[43] See *R. v Oakes* [1986] 1 SCR 103, (1986) 26 DLR (4th) 200; *R. v Vaillancourt* [1987] 2 SCR 636, (1987) 47 DLR (4th) 399; *R. v Whyte* [1988] 2 SCR 3, (1988) 51 DLR (4th) 481; *R. v Chaulk* [1990] 3 SCR 1303; *R. v Keegstra* [1990] 3 SCR 697; *R. v Downey* [1992] 2 SCR 10, (1992) 90 DLR (4th) 448; *R v Osolin* [1993] 4 SCR 595; *R. v Laba* [1994] 3 SCR 965, (1994) 120 DLR (4th) 175; *R v B(D)* [2008] 2 SCR 3; *R v St-Onge Lamoureux* [2012] 3 SCR 187. See further, Bryant, Lederman and Fuerst, *Sopinka, Lederman & Bryant: The Law of Evidence in Canada* 4th edn (Lexis Nexis, 2014), § 4.66 – 4.106; Delisle, "When Do Evidential Burdens Violate s.11(d)" (1992) 13 CR (4th) 161; D. Tanovich, "The Unravelling of the Golden Thread: The Supreme Court's Compromise of the Presumption of Innocence" (1993) 35 Crim LQ 194; Stuart, "A Welcome New Approach to Section 1 Justification in Criminal Cases" (1995) 34 CR (4th) 399; Trakman, Hamilton and Gation, "*R. v Oakes* 1986–1997: Back to the Drawing Board" (1998) 36 Osg. Hall LJ 83; McLachlin, "Charter Myths" (1999) 33 UBCLR 23; Newman, "The Limitation of Rights; A Comparative Evolution and Ideology of the Oakes and Sparrows Tests" (1999) 62 Sask LR 543. The Canadian cases are examined and compared with the Irish decisions in *O'Leary* and *Hardy* in an excellent article by Ní Raifeartaigh, "Reversing the Burden of Proof in a Criminal Trial: Canadian and Irish Perspectives on the Presumption of Innocence" (1995) 5 ICLJ 135.

the presumption of innocence dictates two distinct though interlinked concomitant rules with regard to the burden of proof: (a) the prosecution bear the legal burden of proving every fact essential to establish the guilt of the accused; and (b) the prosecution are required to prove the guilt of the accused beyond a reasonable doubt. Thus, a breach of the presumption of innocence will arise, not only where a statutory provision places a legal burden on the accused, but also where it relieves the prosecution of the obligation of proving any fact necessary to establish the guilt of an accused. This will usually be accomplished by means of a mandatory presumption and, even if a provision is interpreted as a mandatory evidential presumption which merely requires an accused to adduce evidence to rebut the presumed fact, it will violate the presumption of innocence where the presumed fact is an ingredient of the offence.[44] If a provision relieves the prosecution of the obligation to prove a constituent element of an offence and/or places a legal burden on an accused, the constitutionality of that provision should be tested in accordance with the proportionality test that has been developed by the Canadian courts, and which is also applied by the European Court of Human Rights when considering whether there has been a breach of Art.6(2) of the European Convention on Human Rights.[45] As will be seen below, the proportionality test is now a well recognised part of Irish constitutional analysis.

2–23   In this jurisdiction, the seminal authority with regard to the principles applicable in determining the constitutionality of provisions that abridge the presumption of innocence by relieving the prosecution of the obligation to prove every fact necessary to establish the guilt of the accused and/or placing a legal burden on the accused is *O'Leary v Attorney General*.[46] The plaintiff in *O'Leary* had been convicted of membership of an unlawful organisation[47] and challenged the constitutionality of s.24 of the Offences Against the State Act 1939 and s.3(2) of the Offences Against the State (Amendment) Act 1972. In considering whether these provisions contravened what he accepted to be the constitutionally protected principle of the presumption of innocence, Costello J in the High Court made a number of observations. First, he pointed out that there were a number of statutes which have the effect of shifting the burden of proof from the prosecution to the accused and, because the wording of each differed, it was important to carefully analyse the nature and effect of the provision. Secondly, he distinguished between the legal and evidential burden and stated that it was the placing of a legal, as opposed to an evidential, burden which involved the possibility of a breach of an accused's constitutional rights. This was because the placing of an evidential burden on an accused did not affect the incidence of the legal burden of proof, which remained on the prosecution to prove the guilt of the accused beyond a reasonable doubt.[48] He

---

[44]   *Cf.* the Canadian decisions of *Boyle v R.* (1983) 148 DLR (3d) 69; *R. v Vaillancourt* [1987] 2 SCR 636, (1987) 47 DLR (4th) 399; *R. v Downey* [1992] 2 SCR 10, (1992) 90 DLR (4th) 449; *R. v Osolin* [1993] 4 SCR 595; (1993) 109 DLR (4th) 478; *R. v Audet* [1996] 2 SCR 171, (1996) 135 DLR (4th) 20; *R. v McDonnell* [1997] 1 SCR 948, (1997) 145 DLR (4th) 577. See further, Delisle, "When do Evidential Burdens Violate Section 11(d)?" (1992) 13 CR (4th) 161. See also the US decisions of *Tot v United States* (1943) 319 US 463; *Leary v United States* (1969) 395 US 6; *Ulster County Court v Allen* (1979) 442 US 140; *Francis v Franklin* (1985) 471 US 307.

[45]   See *Salabiaku v France* (1991) 13 EHRR 379; *Janosevic v Sweden* (2004) 38 EHRR 22.

[46]   [1993] 1 IR 102, [1991] ILRM 454 (HC); [1995] 1 IR 254, [1995] 2 ILRM 259 (SC).

[47]   Contrary to s.21 of the Offences Against the State Act 1939 (as amended by s.2 of the Criminal Law (Jurisdiction) Act 1976).

[48]   *Cf. R. v Oakes* [1986] 1 SCR 103 at 132–133, (1986) 26 DLR (4th) 200 at 222, where it was held that a statutory provision which places a legal burden on an accused in relation to an important element of an offence violates the presumption of innocence protected by s.11(d) of the Canadian

went on to posit the following test of whether a statute has the effect of shifting a legal or evidential burden:

> "if the effect of the statute is that the court *must* convict an accused should he or she fail to adduce exculpatory evidence then its effect is to shift the legal burden of proof ... whereas if its effect is that notwithstanding its terms the accused *may* be acquitted even though he calls no evidence because the statute has not discharged the prosecution from establishing the accused's guilt beyond a reasonable doubt then no constitutional invalidity could arise."[49]

2–24　Thirdly, he stated that a statute was not unconstitutional merely because its effect was that the failure of an accused to adduce exculpatory evidence must result in a conviction if the statute thereby gave legal effect to an inference which it was reasonable to draw from the facts established. In that situation, the presumption of innocence was rebutted not by the statute but by the inference.[50] Fourthly, he held that the presumption of innocence was not an absolute right but could be abridged in certain circumstances. He then went on to examine the provisions in question.

2–25　Section 3(2) of the 1972 Act provides that where a garda officer, not below the rank of Chief Superintendent, in giving evidence in proceedings related to an offence under s.21 of the 1939 Act, states that he believes that the accused was at a material time a member of an unlawful organisation, the statement is evidence that he or she was then such a member. Costello J rejected the contention that this provision infringed the presumption of innocence. All that it did was to render admissible the non-expert opinion evidence of the Garda which would otherwise be inadmissible. Such evidence, if admitted, had to be weighed and considered and did not place a legal burden on the accused because the court could still hold that the prosecution had not proved its case beyond a reasonable doubt.[51]

2–26　Next for consideration was s.24 of the 1939 Act. This section provides that proof of possession by an accused of an incriminating document is evidence, without more, until the contrary is proved, that the accused is a member of an unlawful organisation. Costello J considered the drafting of the section and reached the conclusion that it did not infringe the rights of the plaintiff because it merely shifted an evidential burden onto an accused. The section did not impose an obligation on an accused to give evidence in order to avoid conviction and, thus, only shifted an evidential burden onto

---

Charter of Fundamental Rights and Freedoms. This is because the placing of a legal burden on an accused imposes on obligation on him or her to disprove, on a balance of probabilities, an essential element of an offence thus raising the possibility that an accused could be convicted despite the existence of a reasonable doubt.

[49]　[1993] 1 IR 102 at 109, [1991] ILRM 454 at 460–461. He did, however, acknowledge that it might not be desirable or possible to lay down any hard and fast rule for the construction of statutes involving the shifting of a burden of proof.

[50]　He gave s.27A of the Firearms Act 1964 (inserted by s.8 of the Criminal Law (Jurisdiction) Act 1976) as an example of such a provision. Section 27A provides: "A person who has a firearm or ammunition in his possession or under his control in such circumstances as to give rise to a reasonable inference that he has not got it in his possession or under his control for a lawful purpose shall, unless he has it in his possession or under his control for a lawful purpose, be guilty of an offence. ..."

[51]　His decision on this point was endorsed by McMahon J in *Redmond v Ireland* [2009] IEHC 201, [2009] 2 ILRM 419 at 432, 436 and in *People (DPP) v Donnelly* [2012] IECCA 78 at [24]. This analysis was also approved and applied in relation to s.8 of the Proceeds of Crime Act 1996 by Fennelly J in *FMcK. v GWD (Proceeds of crime outside State)* [2004] IESC 31 at [47], [2004] 2 IR 470 at 485-6, [2004] 2 ILRM 419 at 433.

an accused. The ideas of "possession"[52] and "an incriminating document"[53] were widely drafted and, as such, the strength of the inference to be drawn would vary with the circumstances. The section did not prevent the court from evaluating the evidence or require it to convict in the absence of exculpatory evidence. Costello J, therefore, concluded:

> "As actually drafted it seems to me that the court may evaluate and assess the significance of the evidence of possession and if it has a reasonable doubt as to the accused's guilt of membership of an unlawful organisation it must dismiss the charge, even in the absence of exculpatory evidence. If this is so then the section does not infringe an accused's right to the presumption of innocence."[54]

2–27 The plaintiff appealed unsuccessfully to the Supreme Court in respect of the constitutionality of s.24. Delivering the decision of the Court, O'Flaherty J pointed out that s.24 merely provides that possession of an incriminating document is *evidence* of membership of an unlawful organisation. It is not proof and its probative value can be undermined in a number of ways, including cross-examination. He concluded, therefore, that the effect of the section was merely that proof of possession of an incriminating document would satisfy the evidential burden on the prosecution, entitling but not requiring a jury to convict. He went on to stress that:

> "Courts, whether comprising a judge sitting with a jury or a judge or judges only, will not act as automatons in the assessment of evidence. With a statutory provision setting out what is to be regarded as evidence—and whether it is called a presumption or not is of no moment[55] —the court must always approach its task in a responsible manner and have proper regard to the paramount place that the presumption of innocence occupies in any criminal trial."[56]

2–28 The constitutionality of provisions that abridge the presumption of innocence was also considered in *Hardy v Ireland*,[57] which was decided in the interval between the High Court and Supreme Court decisions in *O'Leary*. At issue in that case was s.4(1) of the Explosive Substances Act 1883 which provides that:

> "Any person who ... knowingly has in his possession or under his control any explosive substance, under such circumstances as to give rise to a reasonable suspicion that he ... does not have it in his possession or under his control for a lawful object, shall, unless he can show that he ... had it in his possession or under his control for a lawful object, be guilty of felony. ...'"

2–29 The contention that this section places a legal burden on an accused and was, therefore, unconstitutional was rejected in the High Court by Flood J, who took the view that the section merely cast an evidential burden on the accused and, thus, the legal burden remained at all times upon the State.

---

[52]   Section 24 applies where an incriminating document is found on a person charged with the offence of membership of an unlawful organisation, or in his possession, or in premises owned or occupied by him or under his control.

[53]   Section 2 of the Offences Against the State Act 1939 defines an incriminating document as "a document of whatsoever date, or bearing no date, issued by or emanating from an unlawful organisation or appearing to be so issued or so to emanate or purporting or appearing to aid or abet any such organisation or calculated to promote the formation of an unlawful organisation."

[54]   [1993] 1 IR 102 at 113, [1991] ILRM 454 at 463.

[55]   This statement can hardly be taken at face value because, as Costello J pointed out in the High Court, it is important to consider carefully the drafting of an impugned provision in order to assess its precise effect.

[56]   [1995] 1 IR 254 at 266, [1995] 2 ILRM 259 at 269. See also *Rock v Ireland* [1997] 3 IR 484, [1998] 2 ILRM 35 where the decision in *O'Leary* was followed.

[57]   [1994] 2 IR 550.

2–30 His decision was upheld by the Supreme Court, but varying approaches were adopted by the members of the Court. Hederman J (with whom O'Flaherty and Blayney JJ concurred) agreed with the submissions on behalf of the State that the section did not interfere with the incidence of the legal burden, which remained on the prosecution throughout the case. The section merely enabled the State to discharge its evidential burden and establish a *prima facie* case against the accused, which could then be rebutted in a number of ways including cross-examination, submissions, or by giving evidence. A minority of the Court adopted a different analysis. Egan J examined the wording of the section and opined that it clearly placed a legal burden upon the accused to bring himself within the saving clause.[58] If he did not do so, then he would be convicted. However, he noted that the Constitution did not absolutely prohibit the shifting of the legal burden and he was satisfied that the section passed constitutional muster. Murphy J was also of the view that the section placed a legal burden on the accused[59] and that it was not inconsistent with Art.38.1.

2–31 It is difficult to extract guiding principles from the decision in *Hardy* because the judgments are brief and the submissions of the plaintiff were dismissed in a somewhat cursory fashion. Having regard to the drafting of s.4(1), and in particular the use of the word "show" which is a synonym for "prove" or "establish", the conclusion of the minority that, as a matter of statutory interpretation, the section placed a legal burden on an accused is more persuasive. However, given that statutory provisions which place legal burdens upon an accused are *prima facie* unconstitutional,[60] it is understandable that the majority should approach a reverse onus provision on the basis that it should be interpreted as placing an evidential burden on an accused only, unless it is absolutely clear that the legislature intends to place a legal burden on him or her.[61]

2–32 The approach in *Hardy* was applied in *McNulty v Ireland*,[62] which concerned a challenge to the constitutionality of s.41(3) of the Criminal Justice Act 1999. Section 41(1) of that Act makes it an offence for a person to harm, threaten, menace or otherwise intimidate or put in fear a person assisting an investigation by An Garda Síochána of an offence or who is a witness or potential witness or a juror or potential juror or a member of his or her family with the intention of thereby causing the investigation or the course of justice to be obstructed, perverted or interfered with. Subsection (3) provides that proof to the satisfaction of the court that the accused committed the *actus reus* is evidence that the act was done with the requisite *mens rea*. Gilligan J rejected the contention that this subsection reversed the onus of proof and infringed the presumption of innocence, holding that it did not make the evidence of intention conclusive or oblige the trial judge to accept the evidence or draw any inferences. On the contrary, the subsection conferred a discretion on the court and it was for the court to evaluate and assess the significance of the evidence before it. Accordingly, the

---

[58] See *R. v Oakes* [1986] 1 SCR 103 at 116–118, (1986) 26 DLR (4th) 200 at 210–212, where the contention that s.8 of the Narcotic Control Act 1970, which provides that an accused will be convicted of the offence of trafficking in narcotics if he "fails to establish that he was not in possession of the narcotic for the purpose of trafficking", placed an evidential burden only on an accused was rejected by the Canadian Supreme Court.

[59] Citing the decisions of *R. v Fegan* [1972] NI 80 and *R. v Berry* [1985] 1 AC 246, [1984] 3 All ER 1008 in support of this conclusion.

[60] *O'Leary v AG* [1993] 1 IR 102 at 107, [1991] ILRM 454 at 459.

[61] A similar approach to the interpretation of reverse onus provisions was been adopted in Hong Kong in *HKSAR v Lam Kwong Wai* [2006] NKCFA 84.

[62] [2013] IEHC 357.

burden of proof remained on the prosecution to prove the guilt of the accused beyond a reasonable doubt and the subsection merely provided that the accused might have an evidential burden to displace where there was *prima facie* evidence pointing to his guilt.

2–33   The constitutionality of reverse onus provisions was revisited by MacMenamin J in *McNally v Ireland*.[63] At issue in that case was the constitutionality of s.99 of the Charities Act 2009, which makes it an offence to sell a Mass card other than pursuant to an arrangement with a recognised person and provides in subs.(2) that, in proceedings for an offence under the section, "it shall be presumed, until the contrary is proved on a balance of probabilities, that the sale of the Mass card to which the alleged offence relates was not done pursuant to an arrangement with a recognised person". The plaintiff contended that this reverse onus provision, which clearly places the legal burden on an accused, infringed Art.38.1. MacMenamin J held that the constitutionality of the section should be tested using a proportionality analysis which he summarised as follows[64]:

> "I would identify the following principles as being applicable to the applicable test of proportionality: (a) the necessity to establish whether the means it employs to achieve its aim correspond to the importance of the aim; (b) whether the means adopted are necessary for the achievement of the objective; (c) whether the means actually becomes the end in itself; (d) whether the objective can be attained by other methods which may be more conveniently applied; (e) whether the method chosen is the least restrictive and the disadvantage caused is least disproportionate to the aim; and (f) whether the means may be rationally connected to the objective and not be arbitrary, unfair or based on irrational considerations."

2–34   Applying those criteria, he noted that it was not disputed that reasonable consumers could be deluded by misrepresentation and by bogus Mass cards and the genuineness of the signatures on Mass cards or that whether a Mass would actually be said was not susceptible to verification. Whether or not the existence of an arrangement with a recognised person and, thus, the authenticity, verification and charitable object of a donation, could be considered to be peculiarly within the knowledge of an accused, he believed that they would be easily provable for an accused whereas proof of the existence of an arrangement with a recognised person would be an impossibility for a prosecutor. He, therefore, concluded that the reverse onus provision satisfied the test of proportionality[65]:

> "Accordingly, it may be seen that there is a rational connection between the means and the objective of the legislation. It is minimally intrusive into the constitutional rights of a potential accused. It is an attenuated intrusion into the right to trial in due course of law. No other means have been suggested to attain the object. The subsection does not "create" guilt. It provides a framework within which the existence of the offence may be proved or disproved. Absent such a legislative framework the existence of an offence would be simply not susceptible to proof in any practical sense, as an onus would lie on the prosecution to negative literally thousands of possible avenues which might be called in aid as constituting 'validation' or 'authentication'."

2–35   The proper interpretation and application of a reverse onus provision also arose for consideration in *People (DPP) v Smyth*.[66] In that case, the accused had been convicted of possession of cannabis for the purpose of sale or supply contrary to s.15A of the Misuse of Drugs Act 1977. Section 29(2)(a) of the Misuse of Drugs Act 1977 provides that, in any proceedings for possession of a controlled drug, it is a defence

---

[63]   [2009] IEHC 753, [2011] 4 IR 431, [2011] 1 ILRM 40.

[64]   [2009] IEHC 753 at [183], [2011] 4 IR 431 at 474, [2011] 1 ILRM 40 at 78.

[65]   [2009] IEHC 753 at [187], [2011] 4 IR 431 at 475–476, [2011] 1 ILRM 40 at 79.

[66]   [2010] IECCA 34, [2010] 3 IR 688, [2011] 1 ILRM 81. See O'Dunlaing and Donnelly at (2010) 20(3) ICLJ 92.

for an accused to prove that he did not know and had no reasonable grounds for suspecting that what he had in his possession was a controlled drug or that he was in possession of a controlled drug. On appeal, it was argued that the trial judge had erred in the charge that he had given as to the onus of proof in relation to this defence, as he had suggested that the accused had to satisfy the jury beyond a reasonable doubt that the defence was made out. The Court of Criminal Appeal had no difficulty in finding that this charge was erroneous and that it was no part of the reversed burden of proof carried by the accused for them to prove beyond a reasonable doubt that they did not know and had no reasonable grounds for suspecting that what was in their possession was a controlled drug. In providing guidance as to the correct charge to be given, the Court took, as its starting point, the guarantee of a trial in due course of law in Art.38.1, with Charleton J explaining that[67]:

> "The fundamental principle of our criminal justice system is that an accused should not be convicted unless it is proven beyond reasonable doubt that the accused committed the offence. The legal presumption that the accused is innocent, until his guilt is proven to that standard, operates to ensure objectivity within the system. It is a matter for the Oireachtas to decide whether on a particular element of the offence an evidential burden of proof should be cast on an accused person. Of itself, this does not infringe the constitutional principle that the accused should be presumed to be innocent until found guilty. Reasons of policy may perhaps require that any reversed element of proof cast on the accused should be discharged as a probability. That should either be stated in the legislation or be a matter of necessary inference therefrom. The construction of a criminal statute requires the court to presume that the core elements of an offence must be proven beyond reasonable doubt; otherwise the accused must be acquitted. A special defence, beyond the core elements of the offence, may carry a different burden; insanity and diminished responsibility are examples of such a defence which casts a probability burden on the accused. Where, however, in relation to an element of the offence itself, as opposed to a defence, a burden is cast upon the accused, the necessary inference that the accused must discharge that burden on the balance of probability is not easily made. The court notes that bearing the burden of proving a defence as a probability could have the effect that in respect of an element of the offence an accused person might raise a doubt as to his guilt, but not establish it as a probability. This might lead to a situation where the charge was not proven as to each element of the offence beyond reasonable doubt, but nonetheless the accused could be convicted. That would not be right. Proof of a guilty mind is integral to proof of a true criminal offence, in distinction to a regulatory offence. In s.29 of the Misuse of Drugs Act 1977, as amended, the normal burden of proving the mental element of possession of a controlled drug is removed from the prosecution and the accused is required to prove that it did not exist."

2–36   Accordingly, the Court went on to hold that the effect of s.29 was to place what was described as "an evidential burden of proof" on an accused[68]:

> "In consequence, the court considers that an evidential burden of proof is cast on the accused by s. 29 of the Misuse of Drugs Act 1977, as amended, which is discharged when the accused proves the existence of a reasonable doubt that he did not know, and had no reasonable ground for suspecting that what he had in his possession was a controlled drug. This is not a burden merely of adducing evidence. It is legal burden discharged on the lowest standard of proof, namely that of proving a reasonable doubt. This has consequences for the trial of charges based on possession of a controlled drug. The prosecution must prove possession as against the accused. They must also prove that the substance in question was a controlled drug as defined in the Misuse of Drugs Act 1977, as amended. Regulations may need to be proven by handing in an official copy of them. These elements must be proven by the prosecution beyond all reasonable doubt. A burden is then cast on the accused to make out a reasonable doubt in accordance with s. 29. This may be done by pointing to a weakness in the prosecution case, by reference to a statement made to the gardaí, or by the accused himself giving evidence.

---

[67]   [2010] IECCA 34 at [20], [2010] 3 IR 688 at 696, [2011] 1 ILRM 81 at 87–88.
[68]   [2010] IECCA 34 at [21], [2010] 3 IR 688 at 696–697, [2011] 1 ILRM 81 at 88.

Because this is a legal burden of proof, the decisions as to what evidence on that issue will be sufficient so as to raise a reasonable doubt are for the accused. He must decide if he has put sufficient evidence by way of proof to raise a reasonable doubt before the jury."

2–37   The terminology used in this decision and, in particular, the distinctions drawn between "the burden of proof", "the burden of adducing evidence", a "legal burden of proof" and an "evidential burden of proof" is somewhat confusing, but it seems reasonably clear that the effect of the decision is to hold that s.29 casts an evidential burden only on an accused. This is how it was interpreted subsequently by the Court of Criminal Appeal in *People (DPP) v PJ Carey (Contractors) Ltd*,[69] where the same approach was adopted to the application of s.50 of the Safety Health and Welfare at Work Act 1989. Such an approach is to be welcomed because it avoids the risk of an accused being convicted notwithstanding the existence of a reasonable doubt as to his or her guilt.[70]

2–38   A further gloss on the approach to be adopted to reverse onus provisions emerges from the decision of the Court of Criminal Appeal in *People (DPP) v Egan*.[71] The accused had been convicted of the offence of a sexual act with a child under the age of 17 years contrary to s.3(1) of the Criminal Law (Sexual Offences) Act 2006. Section 3(5) of that Act provides that:

"It shall be a defence to proceedings for an offence under this section for the defendant to prove that he or she honestly believed that, at the time of the alleged commission of the offence, the child against whom the offence is alleged to have been committed had attained the age of 17 years."[72]

2–39   On appeal, the accused contended that the trial judge had erred in how he had instructed the jury as to the effect of this section and the burden that was thereby placed on an accused to raise the defence of self-defence. The Court of Criminal Appeal stated that there were three possible approaches to the interpretation of this subsection: (1) it placed an evidential burden on the accused, which could be discharged upon the whole of the evidence and, once discharged, the legal burden reverted to the prosecution to disprove the defence beyond a reasonable doubt; (2) it placed a legal burden on the accused, whereby he had to establish this defence by reference to some evidence in the case, and it could be discharged by the accused establishing a reasonable doubt in the mind of the jury; or (3) it placed a legal burden on the accused to establish this defence on a balance of probabilities. The trial judge had instructed the jury in accordance with the second approach and the Court of Criminal Appeal held that the appeal on this ground must fail because, even if the first approach (which was most favourable to the accused) was adopted, the evidence did not support the availability of this defence and the trial judge had not been asked to and had not ruled that the defence could be raised. However, the Court went to express the view, *obiter*, that the first approach was

---

[69]   [2011] IECCA 63 at 14.
[70]   In England, the Criminal Law Revision Committee, *Eleventh Report* (1972), HMSO, Cmnd 4991, para.140, was "strongly of the opinion that, both on principle and for the sake of clarity and convenience in practice, burdens on the defence should be evidential only". This was also the view of the Canadian Law Reform Commission, *Recodifying Criminal Law* (Report No.31) (Law Reform Commission, Ottawa, 1987) at p.4. See also Dennis, "Reverse Onuses and the Presumption of Innocence: In Search of Principle" [2005] Crim LR 901.
[71]   [2010] IECCA 28, [2010] 3 IR 561.
[72]   This defence of honest belief was introduced following the decision of the Supreme Court in *CC v Ireland* [2006] IESC 33, [2006] 4 IR 1. See Prendergast, "The Constitutionality of Strict Liability in Criminal Law" (2011) DULJ 285.

not correct and that the section placed a legal burden on the accused, which could be discharged on the basis of any of the evidence given in the case.[73] The Court flagged that it might be the case that the section, correctly interpreted, placed a heavier burden on an accused, namely to prove on the balance of probabilities that he had the requisite honest belief, but expressly refrained from expressing a view on this point.[74]

2–40   As noted above, there are a variety of legislative provisions by which the prosecution may be relieved of the obligation to prove every element necessary to establish the commission of an offence by an accused and a careful analysis of each statutory provision is required in order to ascertain its effect and, in particular, whether it casts a legal or evidential burden on an accused. Accordingly, each decision interpreting such a provision turns, to some extent at least, on the wording of the particular provision at issue. That said, there seems to be an emerging consensus. In *Hardy v Ireland*,[75] the view of the majority of the Supreme Court was that the effect of the use of the term "show" in s.4(1) of the Explosive Substances Act 1883 did no more than to place an evidential burden on an accused. Consistent with that approach, in *DPP v Byrne*,[76] Murray J interpreted s.50(8) of the Road Traffic Act 1961,[77] which provides that in a prosecution for an offence under the section "it shall be presumed that the defendant intended to drive or attempt to drive the vehicle concerned unless he shows the contrary", as imposing an obligation on the defendant "to show to the contrary so as to raise a reasonable doubt in the mind of the trial judge".[78] In effect, where possible, what would appear on the basis of the language used to be a mandatory legal presumption will be interpreted as a mandatory evidential presumption. The rationale for this approach was explained by McKechnie J in *Sweeney v Fahy*[79]:

> "As made clear in both *Hardy* and *O'Leary,* the proper construction of s.4 of the 1883 Act and s.24 of the 1939 Act, given the constitutional context in which such provisions arise, is to regard them as evidentially focused, thus leaving untouched the legal burden with regard to the guilt and innocence of the accused.
>
>   Although *Hardy* and *O'Leary* dealt with specific statutory provisions, I have no doubt but that, unless clearly mandated by its specific wording, all such presumptions should likewise be construed; if necessary the double construction rule should be invoked: *McDonald v Bord na gCon* [1965] IR 217. Otherwise constitutional issues will arise."

2–41   The decision of the Court of Criminal Appeal in *People (DPP) v Smyth*[80] that the term "prove" in s.29 of the Misuse of Drugs Act 1977 places an evidential burden, rather than a legal burden on an accused, is consistent with that approach. However, it is important to note that it departs from orthodoxy in one significant respect. As will be seen below, the traditional approach of the Irish courts has been that, if an evidential burden is placed on an accused, this is discharged if the accused can merely

---

[73]   The Court's decision on this point is consistent with that of the minority in *Hardy v Ireland* [1994] 2 IR 550.

[74]   [2010] IECCA 28 at [37], [2010] 3 IR 561 at 575.

[75]   [1994] 2 IR 550.

[76]   [2002] 2 ILRM 68, [2002] 2 IR 397 at 408.

[77]   As inserted by s.11 of the Road Traffic Act 1994.

[78]   But see *DPP v Corcoran*, unreported, High Court, 22 June 1999 and *DPP v Bourke* [2005] IEHC 327 where it was held that the formula "until the contrary is shown" as used in s.21(1) of the Road Traffic Act 1994 shifted the onus of proof to the accused. This would seem to suggest that this subsection has the effect of placing a legal burden and not merely an evidential burden on the accused but it is not clear if this is the import of that holding.

[79]   [2014] IESC 50 at [43]–[44].

[80]   [2010] IECCA 34, [2010] 3 IR 688, [2011] 1 ILRM 81. See (2012) 30(5) ILT 64.

point to evidence in the case which might leave the jury with a reasonable doubt.[81] However, by drawing a distinction between a "burden of adducing evidence" and an "evidential burden of proof", the decision in *Smyth* suggests some form of enhanced obligation whereby an accused bearing an evidential burden in respect of a defence or constituent of an offence is required to establish the existence of a reasonable doubt, rather than simply identifying evidence that might leave the jury with a reasonable doubt on the issue. The emergence of this higher threshold may be driven, at least in part, by a concern that the bar has been set too low in respect of the discharge of an evidential burden in respect of defences such as provocation and self-defence,[82] so that merely requiring an accused to discharge an evidential burden in accordance with the traditional approach would open the door to the raising of unmeritorious defences.

2–42   The caveat should also be entered that it is apparent from the decision in *Egan* that a statutory provision requiring an accused to "prove" some matter by way of defence will not automatically be interpreted as placing an evidential burden only on an accused which can be discharged by raising a reasonable doubt. Depending on the nature of the defence and the statutory context, it may be interpreted as placing a legal burden on an accused requiring him or her to establish a defence on the balance of probabilities.[83] Such a provision will have to run the gauntlet of constitutional scrutiny, but the decisions in *O'Leary*, *Hardy* and *McNally* suggest that the proportionality test should be surmountable in most cases.

(b) Insanity

2–43   At common law, it was well established that the legal burden of proving insanity rested upon the accused raising that defence.[84] In *R. v Stokes*,[85] Rolfe B stated:

> "If the prisoner seeks to excuse himself upon the plea of insanity, it is for him to make it clear that he was insane at the time of committing the offence charged. The onus rests on him, and the jury must be satisfied that he actually was insane. If the matter is left in doubt, it will be their duty to convict him; for every man must be presumed to be responsible for his acts until the contrary is clearly shown."[86]

2–44   This exception to the general principle that the burden of proof rests on the prosecution was based on the inherent unlikelihood of a defective mental state, the

---

[81]   *Hardy v Ireland* [1994] 2 IR 550 at 560; *Bratty v AG for Northern Ireland* [1961] 3 All ER 523 at 530.

[82]   See *People (DPP) v Clarke* [1995] 1 ILRM 355, discussed below, where O'Hanlon J left the issue of self-defence to the jury despite his view that it was only theoretically open to them to acquit on this ground.

[83]   See also the *obiter* views of McKechnie J in *Sweeney v Fahy* [2014] IESC 50 at [46]: "As the shifting of the evidential burden in the context under discussion does not relate to the question of guilt or innocence, there is therefore no question of the standard of proof being that of beyond a reasonable doubt. The standard in my view should not exceed the civil standard, which standard Egan and Murphy JJ applied in *Hardy*. In fact I am not even convinced that contrary proof to such level is required. It may be that evidence, of a credible and plausible nature, which creates a reasonable doubt, would be sufficient to negative a presumption."

[84]   *M'Naghten's Case* (1843) 10 Cl & Fin 200; *R. v Stokes* (1848) 3 Car & K 185; *Attorney General v Boylan* [1937] IR 449; *People (AG) v Fennell (No.1)* [1940] IR 445; *People (AG) v Quinn* [1965] IR 366 at 383; *People (DPP) v O'Mahony* [1985] IR 517.

[85]   (1848) 3 Car & K 185.

[86]   (1848) 3 Car & K 185 at 188.

difficulty of rebutting this defence and on the fear of feigned insanity.[87] As Charleton J explained in *People (DPP) v Smyth*[88]:

> "Sound reasons of policy may indicate that a defence should be proven by the accused as a probability. One reason arises in relation to the special defence of insanity. A person who is found to have committed an intentional killing, for instance, and who might make out a plea of insanity on the basis of merely raising a reasonable doubt would, if not insane, be in danger of being discharged almost immediately by the Central Mental Hospital."

2–45   Provision for the return of a special verdict to the effect that an accused is not guilty by reason of insanity is now made in s.5 of the Criminal Law (Insanity) Act 2006.[89] This section stipulates that the tribunal of fact should return such a verdict if it finds that the accused committed the act alleged against him or her and, having regard evidence relating to the mental condition of the accused given by a consultant psychiatrist, it finds that: (a) the accused was suffering at the time from a mental disorder; and (b) the mental disorder was such that the accused ought not to be held responsible for the act alleged by reason of the fact that he or she did not know the nature and quality of the act, or did not know that what he or she was doing was wrong, or was unable to refrain from committing the act. This section is silent as to the allocation of the burden of proof in relation to this issue but the Court of Criminal Appeal in *People (DPP) v Smyth*[90] indicated, *obiter*, that this remained on the accused.[91] In the case of the defence of diminished responsibility to a charge of murder, which was introduced by s.6 of that Act, it is expressly provided in subs.(2) that it is for the defence to establish that the person is, by virtue of that section, not liable to be convicted.

2–46   In *R. v Chaulk*,[92] the Canadian Supreme Court considered the compatibility with the guarantee of the presumption of innocence in s.11(d) of the Canadian Charter of Rights and Freedoms with a section of the Criminal Code that stipulated that an accused was presumed to be sane "until the contrary is proved". A majority of the Court held that this section infringed the presumption of innocence but that it satisfied the proportionality test. However, this conclusion has been criticised[93] and it should be noted that a contrary conclusion was reached in *Davis v United States*,[94] where it was held by the United States Supreme Court that an accused is entitled to be acquitted if there is a reasonable doubt as to his capacity to commit the offence charged.

(c) The peculiar knowledge principle

2–47   There is a long established principle,[95] of uncertain parameters, that where a matter lies within the peculiar knowledge of the accused, the prosecution is not required to prove it.[96]

---

[87]   See *R. v Chaulk* [1990] 3 SCR 1303 and *Davis v United States* (1895) 160 US 469.

[88]   [2010] IECCA 34 at [14], [2010] 3 IR 688 at 694, [2011] 1 ILRM 81 at 86.

[89]   As amended by s.5 of the Criminal Law (Insanity) Act 2010.

[90]   [2010] IECCA 34 at [14]–[17], [2010] 3 IR 688 at 694–695, [2011] 1 ILRM 81 at 86-87.

[91]   See also *People (DPP) v Tomkins* [2012] IECCA 140 at [27] where counsel for the accused accepted that the accused bore the burden of proof in respect of the defence of insanity.

[92]   [1990] 3 SCR 1203.

[93]   Jones, "Insanity, Automatism and the Burden of Proof on the Accused" (1995) 111 LQR 475.

[94]   (1895) 160 US 469.

[95]   Bennion ([1988] Crim LR 31) traces the origin of the peculiar knowledge label to the judgment of Bayley J in *R. v Turner* (1816) 5 M&S 206 at 211.

[96]   The Irish authorities on the peculiar knowledge principle include *Attorney General v Duff* [1941]

2–48 An example of the application of the principle can be seen in *Minister for Industry and Commerce v Steele*.[97] The accused was charged with offences in relation to the sale of pork sausages pursuant to the Emergency Powers (Pork Sausages and Sausage Meat) (Maximum Prices) Order 1943. Under art.2 of the Order, "pork sausages" were defined as sausages of which not less than 65 per cent of the meat content consists of pork. It was argued by the accused that, in accordance with the general rule as to the allocation of the legal burden, the onus of proof was on the prosecution to prove that the sausages were "pork sausages" within the meaning of art.2. However, the complainant contended that because this was a matter peculiarly within the knowledge of the accused, the onus of proof on this issue rested on the accused. The President of the Circuit Court found as a matter of fact that it was not possible to prove by analysis what proportion of the meat content of the sausages consisted of pork and, thus, only the accused was in a position to give evidence on this matter. The Supreme Court accepted the argument that the onus of proof lay on the accused because the matter was peculiarly within his knowledge. Murnaghan J pointed out that to hold otherwise would be to render the Order a mere "*brutum fulmen*"[98] because it would be impossible to convict the accused of the offences in question.

2–49 Subsequent decisions have, however, sought to restrict the application of this principle. In *McGowan v Carville*,[99] the accused was charged with driving a vehicle without a licence contrary to s.22(1) of the Road Traffic Act 1933. He had been stopped by the complainant garda while driving a van. He failed to produce his licence when requested to do so by the complainant but stated that he would do so at a specified Garda Station. At the hearing of the complaint, no evidence was given as to whether the accused had produced his driving licence at the Garda station and the District Justice dismissed the complaint, taking the view that the onus was on the complainant to prove that the accused had no driving licence and that he had failed to discharge the onus. This decision was upheld by both the High Court and the Supreme Court.

2–50 In the High Court, Davitt P refused to accede to the argument of counsel for the complainant that there was a general principle that, where the doing of an act is unlawful unless it is done under lawful authority, and the existence of such authority is a fact which is peculiarly within the knowledge of the person charged with doing the act unlawfully, then the onus of proving the authority rests upon the person charged. He was of opinion that the principle that the burden of proof rested on the prosecution in relation to every essential element of the offence charged should have as few exceptions as possible.[100] He acknowledged that the principle that the burden of proof rested on the prosecution, if applied strictly and literally, would, in some circumstances, render it impossible, or virtually impossible, to administer criminal justice.[101] However, he was of opinion that the word "peculiarly" as used in the proposition should mean "exclusively" or "almost exclusively" if the proposition was not to be open to grave objection. Turning to the facts of the case before him, he took the view that, on the

---

IR 406; *Minister for Industry and Commerce v Steele* [1952] IR 304; *Buchanan v Moore* [1963] NI 194; *McGowan v Carville* [1960] IR 330; and *AG v Shorten* [1961] IR 304.
[97] [1952] IR 304.
[98] [1952] IR 304 at 315.
[99] [1960] IR 330.
[100] [1960] IR 330 at 336–337.
[101] [1960] IR 330 at 336.

proper construction of s.22(1), the legislature had not intended to place the onus of proof with regard to the possession of a licence upon the accused.

2–51 The judgment of Murnaghan J in the Supreme Court contains a resounding affirmation of the importance of the presumption of innocence. He stated that it was "a cardinal principle of the administration of the criminal law"[102] and that "the Courts should steadfastly refuse to allow any unnecessary exception to the principle".[103] However, he recognised that the courts must "be careful to see that justice not only is done but shall appear to be done"[104] and thus, try to adopt a realistic and reasonable attitude. He considered that, where the existence or otherwise of lawful authority is in issue, it may not always be possible for the prosecution to prove affirmatively and beyond reasonable doubt the fact of the non-existence of such lawful authority. In such cases, where sufficient evidence of the fact of non-existence of such lawful authority has been given, the onus of proving the contrary shifts to the accused. In considering the amount of evidence necessary to shift the burden of proof in such a case, he held that the judge should have regard to the opportunities of knowledge of the parties with respect to the fact to be proved.

2–52 A reluctance to employ the peculiar knowledge principle was also evident in *Attorney General v Shorten*.[105] The accused was charged with having made a declaration that his car had not been used by him or with his consent during a certain period, knowing that declaration to be false or misleading. At the hearing of the charge, evidence was given that, during the period in question, the car was seen being driven along the public road but that the driver could not be identified. The accused, when interviewed concerning the incident, had said that he had no explanation to offer since he believed the declaration to be true. Davitt P was of the opinion that the District Justice had been wrong to hold that the burden of proof had shifted to the accused in the circumstances. He seems to have applied the restrictive interpretation of peculiar knowledge, to mean "exclusively" or "almost exclusively", that he had canvassed in *McGowan v Carville*.[106] Given that the owner of a car which is not taxed does not normally take any special precautions to see that nobody uses it, and because there were bound to be opportunities for someone, whether a member of his household or not, to use it without his knowledge, the learned judge was unwilling to hold that the prosecution had discharged the evidential burden placed upon it so as to shift the burden of proof to the accused. Davitt P went on to express considerable unhappiness with the peculiar knowledge principle:

> "I find it very hard to regard resort to the 'peculiar knowledge' principle, even in its modified form, or to any similar principle, as other than attempts to whittle down the principle of the presumption of innocence."[107]

2–53 The precise nature and effect of the peculiar knowledge principle is difficult to ascertain. In *Steele*, it seems to have been applied so as to effectively reverse the onus of proof and place a legal burden on the defendant to disprove the matter categorised as being within his peculiar knowledge. However, in *McGowan v Carville* and *Attorney General v Shorten*, a more diluted application of the principle is evident whereby

---

[102] [1960] IR 330 at 345.
[103] [1960] IR 330 at 346.
[104] [1960] IR 330 at 346.
[105] [1961] IR 304.
[106] [1960] IR 330 at 336.
[107] [1961] IR 304 at 310.

the prosecution is required to discharge an evidential burden in respect of the matter within the peculiar knowledge of the accused so that the evidence adduced will, in the absence of rebutting evidence from the accused, suffice to discharge the legal burden on the prosecution. In effect, the failure of the accused to call evidence in relation to the matter that is regarded as being within his or her peculiar knowledge will give rise to an inference adverse to the accused in relation to that matter which, when coupled with the evidence adduced by the prosecution in satisfaction of the evidential burden, serves to discharge the legal burden upon it.[108]

2–54 It is submitted that, whatever its precise ambit, the peculiar knowledge principle is flawed in principle and should be abandoned, at least insofar as it might be used to place a legal burden on an accused. First, the principle clearly violates the presumption of innocence and, on this ground alone, should be rejected. It is open to the legislature (subject to constitutional scrutiny) to place a legal or evidential burden on an accused on the basis that a particular matter is within the peculiar knowledge of the accused.[109] If it has not done so, then the courts should not interfere with the default allocation of the burden of proof which is grounded on the presumption of innocence. Secondly, the principle is open to constitutional objection on the basis that it has the effect, in many cases, of forcing an accused to give evidence thus undermining his or her right not to testify[110] because the only effective way of discharging the evidential burden placed on the accused may be for him or her to give evidence. Finally, the principle is inherently illogical. As Davitt P pointed out in *McGowan v Carville*,[111] many offences require an act to be done with a particular intent and such intent could certainly be said to be peculiarly within an accused's own knowledge. However, it could hardly be contended that the onus of disproving such intent rests on an accused. Accordingly, it is difficult, if not impossible, to apply the principle on any sort of consistent and principled basis.

2–55 Notwithstanding these criticisms, the continuing vitality of the peculiar knowledge principle was affirmed by White J in *DPP v Rostas*.[112] In that case, the accused had been charged with begging in a public place contrary to s.2 of the Criminal Justice (Public Order) Act 2011 and a case was stated by the District Judge as to whether the prosecution was required to adduce evidence to show that the accused did not have a licence, permit or authorisation permitting him to beg, or whether the accused bore the burden of adducing evidence in this regard. White J considered *McGowan v Carville* to still constitute good law and concluded that the peculiar knowledge principle had been restricted but not abolished. Applying that decision, he went on to hold that the

---

[108] *Cf. per* Flood J in *Hardy v Ireland* [1994] 2 IR 550 at 559, who stated that what is shifted to an accused by the operation of the peculiar knowledge principle is an obligation to raise a doubt of substance in relation to the prosecution case. See also the detailed discussion of the principle by Davitt P in *McGowan v Carville* [1960] IR 330.

[109] See, *e.g.* s.18(2) of the School Attendance Act 1926 which places the burden of proof in relation to a number of defences to a prosecution for non-attendance of children at school on an accused parent, including the defence that the children are receiving a suitable elementary education in some manner other than by attending school. In *DPP v Best* [2000] 2 IR 171, Denham J commented that: "This transfer of the burden of proof is appropriate given that the relevant matters are within the special knowledge of the parents. The State, as guardian of the common good, must protect the child's right to a certain minimum education and parents who choose not to avail of the State education system must prove that their children are receiving the required education."

[110] This, as explained in Chap.12, is a constitutionally protected element of the general right not to be compelled to incriminate oneself.

[111] [1960] IR 330 at 337.

[112] [2012] IEHC 19. See O'Dunlaing [2012] 22(2) ICLJ 60.

issue of licence, permit or authorisation was not a matter of legal defence and that the prosecution were obliged to lead some evidence to establish a *prima facie* case that the begging took place without authorisation. Only then would the burden of proof transfer to the accused to establish a reasonable doubt as to the legality of the begging. Although the learned judge referred to the "burden of proof" shifting to the accused, it seems reasonably clear that what he envisaged shifting is an evidential burden only and not the legal burden.

4. Discharge of the Legal Burden

(a) By the prosecution

2–56   The standard of proof required of the prosecution to discharge the legal burden is proof beyond a reasonable doubt.[113] This standard was discussed by Denning J in *Miller v Minister for Pensions*[114] who said that the evidence:

> "need not reach certainty, but it must carry a high degree of probability. Proof beyond a reasonable doubt does not mean beyond the shadow of a doubt. The law would fail to protect the community if it admitted fanciful possibilities to deflect the course of justice. If the evidence is so strong against a man as to leave only a remote possibility in his favour, which can be dismissed with the sentence 'of course it is possible but not in the least probable' the case is proved beyond a reasonable doubt, but nothing short of that will suffice."[115]

2–57   It is important to note that, although this standard of proof applies in all criminal proceedings, the stringency of its application will depend on the nature of the case and, in particular, the seriousness of the charge and the consequences of a conviction. As Denning LJ noted in *Bater v Bater*[116]:

> "It is true that by our law there is a higher standard of proof in criminal cases than in civil cases, but this is subject to the qualification that there is no absolute standard in either case. In criminal cases the charge must be proved beyond reasonable doubt, but there may be degrees of proof within that standard. Many great judges have said that, in proportion as the crime is enormous, so ought the proof to be clear."[117]

2–58   Thus, even though the same standard of proof applies to a summary prosecution for assault as to a prosecution on indictment for murder, it will be more difficult to satisfy the tribunal of fact that the guilt of the accused has been proved beyond a reasonable doubt in the case of the latter.

2–59   Whether the prosecution has discharged the legal burden upon it to prove the guilt of the accused beyond a reasonable doubt is decided by the tribunal of fact at the end of the case after both parties have adduced evidence. It necessarily follows that this decision will be based upon all the evidence adduced in the case, including that adduced by the accused.[118]

---

[113] As noted above, this standard of proof is constitutionally required: *R. v Oakes* [1986] 1 SCR 103 at 121; (1986) 26 DLR (4th) 200 at 214; *In re Winship* (1970) 397 US 358 at 363–364.

[114] [1947] 2 All ER 372.

[115] [1947] 2 All ER 372 at 373–374. *Cf. Devane v Murphy* [1958] Ir Jur Rep 73 at 74, where Deale J held, in the context of a charge of dangerous driving, that where other innocent explanations exist, and one of such explanations is equally probably the true one, then the prosecution fails.

[116] [1950] 2 All ER 458.

[117] [1950] 2 All ER 458 at 459.

[118] See *People (DPP) v Byrne*, unreported, Court of Criminal Appeal, 7 June 2000.

(b) By the accused

2–60 Where the defence bears the legal burden, it is discharged by proof on the balance of probabilities.[119] In *Convening Authority v Doyle*,[120] the Courts-Martial Appeal Court endorsed as correct the decision of the English Court of Criminal Appeal in *R. v Carr-Briant*[121] that:

> "in any case where, either by statute or at common law, some matter is presumed against an accused person 'unless the contrary is proved', the jury should be directed that it is for them to decide whether the contrary is proved, that the burden of proof required is less than that required at the hands of the prosecution in proving the case beyond a reasonable doubt, and that the burden may be discharged by evidence satisfying the jury of the probability of that which the accused is called upon to establish."[122]

2–61 This standard of proof has been applied in relation to the defence of insanity in a number of decisions.[123]

2–62 An accused can discharge this standard of proof by cross-examination of prosecution witnesses, by calling witnesses or by giving evidence himself or herself but it is important to note that, because the accused enjoys a constitutionally protected right not to testify, there is no obligation on him or her to give evidence.[124]

5. Allocation of the Evidential Burden

2–63 In general, the incidence of the legal burden and the evidential burden coincide. Accordingly, the prosecution will usually bear the evidential burden. However, an accused may be fixed with an evidential burden in a variety of circumstances: (a) where a statutory provision places a legal burden on an accused by means of a reverse onus provision or a mandatory legal presumption; (b) where a statutory provision contains a mandatory evidential presumption or otherwise places an evidential burden on an accused; (c) where the peculiar knowledge principle applies; (d) where the accused raises a defence that is more than a mere denial of the prosecution case; and (e) s.78 of the County Officers and Courts (Ireland) Act 1877. As the first three of these circumstances are discussed elsewhere in this chapter, only the later two will be examined here.

(a) Where the accused raises a defence

2–64 In a series of decisions, it has been held that an accused bears an evidential

---

[119] *Convening Authority v Doyle* [1996] 2 ILRM 213; *Syon v Hewitt* [2006] IEHC 376 at [75], [2008] 1 IR 168 at 196; *R. v Carr-Briant* [1943] 1 KB 607; *R. v Daniel* [2003] 1 Cr App R 6.
[120] [1996] 2 ILRM 213.
[121] [1943] 1 KB 607.
[122] [1943] 1 KB 607 at 612.
[123] *People (DPP) v O'Mahony* [1985] IR 517 at 522; *Sodeman v R.* [1936] 2 All ER 1138, (1936) 55 CLR 192. See also *People (DPP) v Tomkins* [2012] IECCA 140 at [27] where it was accepted by the defence that this was the standard to be met and it had not been met in the circumstances of that case. The decisions of *Attorney General v Boylan* [1937] IR 449 and *People (AG) v Fennell (No.1)* [1940] IR 445, to the effect that the standard of proof required is proof beyond a reasonable doubt, can no longer be considered to be good law on this point.
[124] *People (DPP) v P(P)M* [2010] IECCA 61 at [9].

burden to raise the affirmative defences of self-defence,[125] provocation,[126] duress,[127] automatism,[128] and accident.[129] There is also strong authority for the broader proposition that an accused bears an evidential burden to raise any defence that is more than a mere denial of the prosecution case. In *DPP v Collins*,[130] the accused had been convicted of an offence of driving while intoxicated contrary to s.49(2) of the Road Traffic Act 1961. He argued that his conviction was invalidated by the presence of an unspecified white substance in the containers in which the blood specimens were put. However, it was held that the mere assertion that this substance might have affected the result of the blood test was not enough because the accused bore an evidential burden in respect of this defence:

> "Where, as in this case, the prosecution have adduced evidence showing the existence of all the elements necessary for the commission of the offence, and the defence wish to controvert or cast the necessary doubt on the prosecution case by suggesting the existence of a factor which would justify an acquittal, the evidential burden as to that factor passes to the defence."[131]

2–65 The placing of an evidential burden on the accused in relation to such a defence is designed to act as a filter to prevent unmeritorious defences being raised and put to the jury. It also means that the prosecution does not have to rebut every possible defence which might be raised, thus shortening the trial and simplifying the issues involved.[132] If an accused discharges the evidential burden to raise a defence, then the prosecution will be given the opportunity to call rebutting evidence.[133]

(b) Section 78 of the County Officers and Courts (Ireland) Act 1877

2–66 The general rule that an accused bears an evidential burden to raise a defence is given statutory form in summary prosecutions by s.78 of the County Officers and Courts (Ireland) Act 1877[134] which provides that:

> "In all cases of summary jurisdiction any exception, exemption, proviso, qualification, or excuse, whether it does or does not accompany the description of the offence complained of,

---

[125] *People (AG) v Quinn* [1965] IR 366; *People (AG) v Dwyer* [1972] IR 416; *People (AG) v Byrne* [1974] IR 1; *People (DPP) v Clarke* [1994] 3 IR 289; [1995] 1 ILRM 355; *R. v Lobell* [1957] 1 All ER 734. In *People (DPP) v Barnes* [2006] IECCA 165 at [83], [2007] 3 IR 130 at 155, Hardiman J, in an *obiter dictum*, was prepared to countenance the possibility that, where a defence of self-defence was raised by a burglar who killed a householder, he might bear the legal burden of establishing that defence because, having killed the householder, he had put himself in the position where he had exclusive knowledge of cause of the householder's death.

[126] *People (DPP) v McEoin* [1978] IR 27; *People (DPP) v Kelly* [2000] 2 IR 1 at 11; *People (DPP) v Davis* [2001] 1 IR 146 at 155; *People (DPP) v Ceka* [2004] IECCA 25; *Mancini v DPP* [1941] 3 All ER 272.

[127] *People (DPP) v Kavanagh*, unreported, Court of Criminal Appeal, 18 May 1999.

[128] *Bratty v AG for Northern Ireland* [1963] AC 386, [1961] 3 All ER 523; *R. v Burgess* [1991] QB 92; *R. v Falconer* (1990) 171 CLR 30.

[129] *Bratty v AG for Northern Ireland* [1963] AC 386, [1961] 3 All ER 523.

[130] [1981] ILRM 447.

[131] [1981] ILRM 447 at 453 (*per* Henchy J). The decision in *Collins* on this point was followed in *DPP v Spaight*, unreported, High Court, 27 January 1981; *DPP v Smyth* [1987] ILRM 570 at 573; and *DPP v Morrissey*, unreported, High Court, 15 December 1998.

[132] *Cf.* the comments of O'Flaherty J in *DPP v McCormack* [1999] 1 ILRM 398 at 400: "there is I think a certain mythology abroad that some onus rests on the prosecution to prove cases to an impossible extent so as to exclude every hypothesis that might occur to the most ingenious mind. That is not the law."

[133] *DPP v Collins* [1981] ILRM 447 at 453; *DPP v Nash* [2011] IEHC 418 at [24].

[134] 40 & 41 Vict., c.56. See, further, Smith, "The Presumption of Innocence" (1987) 38 NILQ 223.

may be proved by the defendant, but need not be specified or negatived in the information or complaint, and if so specified or negatived no proof in relation to the matters so specified or negatived shall be required from the complainant, unless evidence shall be given by the defendant concerning the same."

2–67 Section 78 is predicated on the assumption that offences and the exceptions thereto are readily distinguishable. However, this is not always the case and, sometimes, what appears to be an exception to the definition of an offence is in reality part of the definition of the offence. This problem was adverted to in *R. (Sheahan) v Justices of Cork*[135] where Gibson J proposed the following test:

"Does the statute make the act described an offence subject to particular exceptions, qualifications, etc., which where applicable, make the *prima facie* offence an innocent act? Or does the statute make an act, *prima facie* innocent, an offence when done under certain conditions? In the former case the exception need not be negatived; in the latter, words of exception may constitute the gist of the offence."[136]

2–68 A good example of an act, *prima facie* innocent, which is made an offence when done under certain conditions, is the offence of driving without a licence. In *McGowan v Carville*,[137] the test in *Sheahan* was applied to s.22(1) of the Road Traffic Act 1933 which made it an offence for any person to drive a mechanically propelled vehicle unless he or she held a driving licence. Murnaghan J stated that the gist of the offence created by the section was driving a vehicle without a licence and not the driving of a vehicle *simpliciter*. The driving of a motor vehicle was *prima facie* a lawful act and, thus, s.78 had no application.[138]

2–69 The application of the test in *Sheahan* led to the opposite conclusion in *McCarthy v Murphy*.[139] The accused was charged with, *inter alia*, permitting persons to be on his licensed premises after hours contrary to s.62 of the Intoxicating Liquor Act 1962.[140] A number of exceptions were set out in s.17 of the Intoxicating Liquor Act 1927[141] and one of the questions in the case stated to the High Court was who bore the onus of proving the application of these exceptions. Keane J held that the act of permitting a person to be on licensed premises during prohibited hours was clearly treated by the legislature as an offence, subject to particular exceptions, which, where applicable, made the *prima facie* offence an innocent act.[142] It followed, applying s.78, that the onus of proving the exception rested on the accused.[143]

2–70 What is implicit in the foregoing decisions, and has been made explicit in some English decisions,[144] is that the question of whether s.78 applies is not purely a question of statutory interpretation but involves policy considerations including, in particular, an assessment of the moral quality of the act involved.

---

[135] [1907] 2 IR 5.

[136] [1907] 2 IR 5 at 11.

[137] [1960] IR 330.

[138] See also *Bridgett v Dowd* [1961] IR 313 where the decision in *McGowan* on this point was distinguished.

[139] [1981] ILRM 213.

[140] No.21 of 1962.

[141] No.15 of 1927.

[142] [1981] ILRM 213 at 218.

[143] See also *AG v Duff* [1941] IR 406 and *Bridgett v Dowd* [1961] IR 313.

[144] See, *e.g. Nimmo v Alexander Cowan & Sons Ltd* [1968] AC 107 at 135, [1967] 3 All ER 187 at 203, where Lord Pearson stated that it is necessary to look at the substance and effect of an enactment, as well as its form, in order to ascertain whether it contains an excuse or qualification.

2–71 Although the decisions in relation to s.78 might seem to indicate that the section casts a legal burden on an accused,[145] it is submitted that the proper construction of the section, which merely requires "evidence" to be given by the accused, is that it places an evidential burden only on an accused.[146] This conclusion is bolstered by reference to the constitutional status of the presumption of innocence which, as noted above, renders statutes that place a legal burden on an accused *prima facie* unconstitutional.[147] It seems unlikely that s.78, which is a provision of general application in all summary prosecutions, would withstand constitutional challenge if it was construed as placing a legal burden on an accused and the courts will avoid that construction where an interpretation that it places an evidential burden only on an accused is open.

6. Discharging the Evidential Burden

(a) By the prosecution

2–72 The evidential burden borne by the prosecution will be discharged, and a case will be left to the jury, when the prosecution has "adduced sufficient evidence to raise a *prima facie* case against the accused."[148] The prosecution will have made out a *prima facie* case where there is evidence upon which the tribunal of fact (properly charged in the case of a jury) could reasonably find the accused guilty.[149] In assessing this, the court will take the prosecution case at its highest point.[150] The question of whether the prosecution has discharged its evidential burden will generally arise in the context of an application to withdraw a case from the jury and the principles to be applied to such an application are considered below.

(b) By the accused

2–73 The quantum of evidence required for an accused to discharge an evidential burden borne by him or her depends on whether the accused bears an evidential burden only or an evidential and legal burden.

2–74 Where an evidential burden only is borne by an accused, it will be discharged

---

[145] In *Bridgett v Dowd* [1961] IR 313 at 322, Davitt P spoke of the accused having to *prove* the facts necessary to establish the defence raised and in *McCarthy v Murphy* [1981] ILRM 213 at 218, Keane J also referred to the onus placed on an accused by s.78 as being one of proving the application of the exception. It should also be noted that the English equivalent of s.78 has been interpreted as clearly placing a legal burden on an accused (*Gatland v Metropolitan Police Commissioner* [1968] 2 QB 279, [1968] 2 All ER 100; *R. v Edwards* [1975] QB 27, [1974] 2 All ER 1085). The legislative history of s.78, which replaced s.20(1) of the Petty Sessions (Ireland) Act 1851, lends support to the argument that the section was intended to cast a legal burden on an accused. See, further, Smith, "The Presumption of Innocence" (1987) 38 NILQ 223 at pp.227ff.
[146] *Cf.* the interpretation placed on s.24 of the Offences Against the State Act 1939 by the Supreme Court in *O'Leary v AG* [1995] 1 IR 254, [1995] 2 ILRM 259.
[147] *O'Leary v AG* [1993] 1 IR 102 at 107, [1991] ILRM 454 at 459.
[148] *DPP v Collins* [1981] ILRM 447 at 452. See also *DPP v Smyth* [1987] ILRM 570 at 574; *DPP v Morrissey,* unreported, High Court, December 15, 1998.
[149] *People (DPP) v Ceka* [2004] IECCA 25; *DPP v Smyth* [1987] ILRM 570 at 574. *Cf. People (DPP) v Connolly* [2011] IESC 6 at [34], [2011] 1 IR 755 at 764, [2012] 1 ILRM 170 at 178.
[150] *People (DPP) v Gilligan* [1992] ILRM 769 at 772–773; *People (DPP) v M,* unreported, Court of Criminal Appeal, 15 February 2001; *People (DPP) v Cagney* [2004] IECCA 10 at 19; *R. v Galbraith* [1981] 2 All ER 1060 at 1062, [1981] 1 WLR 1039 at 1042.

where the evidence adduced in the case, whether led by the prosecution or the accused,[151] discloses "a doubt of substance",[152] *i.e.* evidence which might leave a jury in reasonable doubt.[153] In general, trial judges take a generous attitude and, if a defence is raised by an accused, will readily find this burden to have been discharged. For example, in *People (DPP) v Clarke*,[154] O'Hanlon J left the issue of self-defence to the jury despite his view that it was only theoretically open to the jury to acquit on this ground.[155] However, the courts have emphasised that it is not sufficient to merely assert a hypothetical or to suggest the existence of a possible defence; there must be an evidential foundation for the defence.[156] As Charleton J observed in *People (DPP) v Smyth*[157]: "Criminal trials would be chaotic were the accused entitled to run any potential defence which might be hypothetically open on the facts of the prosecution case." Thus, a mere suggestion of a defence advanced but not accepted in cross-examination will not suffice.[158]

2–75   The principles applicable in determining whether an accused has discharged his or her evidential burden to raise a defence were outlined in the context of the defence of provocation in *People (DPP) v Davis*.[159] Delivering the judgment of the Court of Criminal Appeal, Hardiman J emphasised that an accused bears an evidential burden to raise the defence and that it will not automatically be left to the jury simply because it is asserted:

> "We entirely accept that the burden on the defendant is not a heavy one but it necessarily involves being able to point to evidence of some sort suggesting the presence of all the elements of provocation ... the burden which rests with the accused is to produce or indicate evidence suggesting the presence of the various elements of the defence. This can be produced either through direct evidence or by inference on the evidence as a whole, but before leaving the issue to a jury the judge must satisfy himself that an issue of substance, as distinct from a contrived issue, or a vague possibility, has been raised."[160]

2–76   The Court went on to state that the determination of this preliminary issue, as to whether there is sufficient evidence of the defence such that the issue can be left to the jury, is one to be determined by the trial judge on the basis of an assessment of the evidence. In making this determination, the trial judge has to bear in mind that questions as to the credibility of evidence, as opposed to its existence, are for the jury and not for him. He or she also has to bear in mind that, before provocation becomes an issue in the case fit to be left to the jury's determination, there must be

---

[151]   *People (AG) v Quinn* [1965] IR 366 at 382–383; *People (DPP) v Curran* [2011] IECCA 95 at [34], [2011] 3 IR 785 at 805; *DPP v Ennis* [2011] IESC 46 at 11.
[152]   *Hardy v Ireland* [1994] 2 IR 550 at 560 (*per* Flood J).
[153]   *Bratty v AG for Northern Ireland* [1961] 3 All ER 523 at 530.
[154]   [1995] 1 ILRM 355.
[155]   *Cf. People (DPP) v Halligan*, unreported, Court of Criminal Appeal, 13 July 1998, where the determination of the trial judge that there was no evidence of provocation fit to be considered by the jury was upheld on appeal.
[156]   *DPP v Collins* [1981] ILRM 447 at 452–453; *DPP v Smyth* [1987] ILRM 570 at 573; *DPP v Morrissey*, unreported, High Court, 15 December 1998 at 8.
[157]   [2010] IECCA 34 at [15], [2010] 3 IR 688 at 694, [2011] 1 ILRM 81 at 86.
[158]   *DPP v Bourke* [2005] IEHC 327 at [8].
[159]   [2001] 1 IR 146. *Cf. People (DPP) v McDonagh* [2001] 3 IR 201 at 207.
[160]   [2001] 1 IR 146 at 156. See also *People (DPP) v O'Carroll* [2004] IECCA 16, [2004] 3 IR 521 (principles laid down in *Davis* applied in context of defence of self-defence); *People (DPP) v Ceka* [2004] IECCA 25, unreported, Court of Criminal Appeal, 28 July 2004 at 14 (defence has to satisfy a test of the existence of a body of apparently credible evidence to justify leaving the matter to the jury). *Cf. R. v Gill* (1963) 47 Cr App R 166 at 172 and *Jaysena v R.* [1970] AC 618 at 623, [1970] 1 All ER 219 at 221.

evidence (direct or inferential) suggesting the presence of all the elements required for the defence. In this regard, it was suggested that a useful approach might be for the judge to consider whether or not a jury would be perverse in finding, on the evidence available, that there had been provocation. In the instant case, the Court was of the view that the evidence fell far short of meeting the requirements for permitting the issue of provocation to go to the jury.

2–77 A higher standard is imposed where an accused bears both the legal and evidential burden, as where he or she raises the defence of insanity. In that case, the evidential burden is discharged by evidence which might satisfy the jury of the probability of that which the accused is called upon to establish.[161]

2–78 It is apparent from the decision in *People (DPP) v Smyth*[162] that a higher standard will also have to be met where a statutory provision places an evidential burden on an accused, in which case it is not sufficient to merely identify evidence which might possibly leave the jury with a reasonable doubt; the accused has to establish the existence of a reasonable doubt in respect of the matter. In that case, it held that this burden may be satisfied by pointing to a weakness in the prosecution case, by reference to a statement made to gardaí or by the accused himself or herself giving evidence.[163]

7. Application for a Direction

2–79 The trial judge has a duty to withdraw a case or charge from the jury or to direct them that they must acquit where the prosecution has failed to discharge its evidential burden and make out a *prima facie* case.[164] In *People (DPP) v O'Shea*,[165] Finlay P explained that:

> "One of the functions of a trial judge in a criminal trial is to reach a decision at the conclusion of the evidence tendered on behalf of the prosecution as to whether there is evidence which if accepted by a jury could as a matter of law lead to a conviction. This may frequently occur in practice in cases where there is a gap in the evidence tendered on behalf of the prosecution and where some vital link in the chain of proof is missing.[166] It also arises in my view, however, and not infrequently, in cases where an apparent link in the chain of proof is so tenuous that it would clearly be perverse for a jury properly directed as to the onus of proof upon the prosecution to act upon it."[167]

2–80 The starting point for a consideration of the principles governing the withdrawal of a case from the jury[168] is the decision in *R. v Galbraith*,[169] where the English Court of Appeal considered the two schools of thought which existed at the time as to the proper approach to be adopted by a judge where a submission of no case to answer

---

[161] *R. v Carr-Briant* [1943] 2 All ER 156.
[162] [2010] IECCA 34, [2010] 3 IR 688, [2011] 1 ILRM 81.
[163] [2010] IECCA 34 at [21], [2010] 3 IR 688 at 697, [2011] 1 ILRM 81 at 88.
[164] See *People (DPP) v Reid* [2004] IECCA 3 at [9]. It is clear from the decision in *DPP v Independent Newspapers* [2009] IESC 20, [2009] 3 IR 598, [2009] 2 ILRM 199 that the position is the same when the High Court hears a motion for relief in respect of an allegation of criminal contempt.
[165] [1983] ILRM 592.
[166] *Cf. Attorney General v Armitage* (1928) 62 ILTR 174 at 176 (conviction quashed where prosecution had failed to call evidence in relation to essential fact).
[167] [1983] ILRM 592 at 594.
[168] Although this application is generally made at the close of the prosecution case, it can also be made at the close of the entirety of the evidence and the same principles will apply: *People (DPP) v Daly* [2009] IECCA 90 at [8].
[169] [1981] 1 WLR 1039, [1981] 2 All ER 1060.

was made at the conclusion of the prosecution case. The first was that the judge should stop the case if, in his or her view, it would be unsafe or unsatisfactory for the jury to convict, such as where the judge thought that the main witnesses for the prosecution were not telling the truth. The second was that the judge should only do so if there was no evidence on which a jury properly directed could convict. The Court of Appeal emphasised that a balance had to be struck between "on the one hand a usurpation by the judge of the jury's functions and on the other the danger of an unjust conviction".[170] It, therefore, preferred the second of the two schools of thought, endorsing the views of Widgery CJ in *R. v Barker*[171] that:

> "It cannot be too clearly stated that the judge's obligation to stop the case is an obligation which is concerned primarily with those cases where the necessary minimum evidence to establish the facts of the crime has not been called. It is not the judge's job to weigh the evidence, decide who is telling the truth, and to stop the case merely because he thinks the witness is lying. To do that is to usurp the function of the jury."[172]

2–81   In a passage that has been repeatedly cited by the Irish courts, Lord Lane CJ laid down the principles which should be applied by a trial judge in dealing with an application for a direction or a submission of no case to answer:

> "(1) If there is no evidence that the crime alleged has been committed by the defendant, there is no difficulty. The judge will of course stop the case. (2) The difficulty arises where there is some evidence but it is of a tenuous character, for example because of inherent weakness or vagueness or because it is inconsistent with other evidence. (a) Where the judge comes to the conclusion that the Crown's evidence, taken at its highest, is such that a jury properly directed could not properly convict on it, it is his duty, on a submission being made, to stop the case. (b) Where however, the Crown's evidence is such that its strength or weakness depends on the view to be taken of a witness's reliability, or other matters which are generally speaking within the province of the jury and where on one possible view of the facts there is evidence on which a jury could properly come to the conclusion that the defendant is guilty, then the judge should allow the matter to be tried by the jury. ... There will of course, as always in this branch of the law, be borderline cases. They can safely be left to the discretion of the judge."[173]

2–82   A gloss was subsequently placed on the *Galbraith* principles in *R. v Shippey*.[174] The defendants were charged with rape and the prosecution case against them was based effectively on the uncorroborated evidence of the complainant. At the conclusion of the prosecution case, a submission of no case to answer was made. While the defence conceded that there was undoubtedly some evidence that showed that the alleged offences had been committed, it was argued that the evidence was so inherently weak and inconsistent that no jury properly directed could convict. For its part, the prosecution conceded that there were weaknesses and inconsistencies in the evidence. However, it was argued that, consistent with *Galbraith*, it was a matter for the jury to assess its strength or weaknesses. Taking the evidence at its highest, it was submitted that it could not be said that a jury properly directed could not properly convict.

2–83   Turner J rejected the proposition that the effect of *Galbraith* was that, if there are parts of the evidence which go to support the charge, then no matter what the state of the rest of the evidence, that is enough to leave the matter to the jury. He stated that taking the prosecution case at its highest "did not mean picking out the plums and

---

170   [1981] 1 WLR 1039 at 1040, [1981] 2 All ER 1060 at 1061.
171   (1977) 65 Cr App R 287.
172   (1977) 65 Cr App R 287 at 288.
173   [1981] 1 WLR 1039 at 1042, [1981] 2 All ER 1060 at 1062.
174   [1988] Crim LR 767.

leaving the duff behind";[175] it was necessary to assess the evidence as a whole. He emphasised that it was not a sufficient basis for the withdrawal of the case from the jury that there were issues as to the credibility of individual witnesses or evidential inconsistencies between their evidence. On the other hand, if the evidence was self-contradictory or contained such inherent weaknesses that it lacked a foundation in reason and common sense, it might be regarded as so tenuous and weak as to justify withdrawal from the jury. Having examined the evidence before him, he was satisfied that parts of the complainant's evidence were "incredible" and were wholly inconsistent with the allegation of rape.[176] He was, therefore, satisfied that the submission of no case to answer should be allowed and he withdrew the case from the jury.

2–84 The principles in *Galbraith* were approved as representing the law in this jurisdiction by Flood J in *People (DPP) v Barnwell*,[177] who linked them to the cardinal rule that the prosecution bears the onus of proof in a criminal trial. Applying them to the case before him, the learned judge was satisfied that there were serious inconsistencies and a clear conflict of evidence within the evidence adduced by the prosecution which rendered it "tenuous in the extreme". In the circumstances, he had no doubt but that the case should be withdrawn from the jury. Subsequently, in *People (DPP) v Nolan*,[178] Herbert J emphasised that, in order for a case to be withdrawn from the jury in accordance with principle 2(a) laid down by Lord Lane CJ in *Galbraith*, there must be something, as clearly was the case in *Barnwell*, going beyond questions of credibility; there must be no basis on which the jury could properly find the accused guilty.

2–85 The principles in *Galbraith* were also endorsed by the Court of Criminal Appeal in *People (DPP) v M*.[179] The applicant sought leave to appeal his conviction on a charge of sexual assault on the ground that the trial judge had erred in refusing to withdraw the case from the jury because of the inconsistent versions of the incident given by the complainant both during and prior to the trial. Having examined the transcript of the evidence, the Court was satisfied that although different descriptive terms had been used by the complainant in her evidence and there were inconsistencies, the complainant remained consistent in the basic story that she told. Furthermore, the inconsistencies in the case went to issues of credibility and reliability and these, as issues of fact, were for the jury to determine. The Court was, thus, satisfied that the trial judge had not erred in refusing to withdraw the counts of sexual assault from the jury:

> "If there is no evidence that an element of the crime alleged had been committed, the situation would be clear. The judge would have to stop the trial. However, that is not the situation here. If a judge comes to the conclusion that the prosecution evidence taken at its highest is such that a jury properly directed could not properly convict, it is his duty to stop the trial. However, that is not the case here. Here there is lengthy evidence from the complainant in which there are some inconsistencies. These inconsistencies are matters which go to the issues of reliability and credibility and thus, in the circumstances, are solely matters for the jury. The learned trial judge therefore was correct in letting the trial proceed. These are matters quintessentially for the jury to decide. However, if the inconsistencies were such as to render it unfair to proceed with the trial then the judge in the exercise of his or her discretion should stop the trial."[180]

---

[175] [1988] Crim LR 767.
[176] [1988] Crim LR 767 at 768.
[177] Unreported, Central Criminal Court, 24 January 1997.
[178] Unreported, Central Criminal Court, 27 November 2001.
[179] Unreported, Court of Criminal Appeal, 15 February 2001.
[180] Unreported, Court of Criminal Appeal, 15 February 2001 at 15.

2–86   In *People (DPP) v Leacy*,[181] Geoghegan J approved the following summary of the *Galbraith* principles as developed in subsequent cases contained in *Blackstone's Criminal Practice*:

> "(a) If there is no evidence to prove an essential element of the offence a submission must obviously succeed.
> (b) If there is some evidence which - taken at face value - establishes each essential element, then the case should normally be left to the jury. The judge does, however, have a residual duty to consider whether the evidence is inherently weak or tenuous. If it is so weak that no reasonable jury properly directed could convict on it, then a submission should be upheld. Weakness may arise from the sheer improbability of what the witness is saying, from internal inconsistencies in the evidence or from its being of a type which the accumulated experience of the courts has shown to be of doubtful value (especially in identification evidence cases, ...)
> (c) The question of whether a witness is lying is nearly always one for the jury, but there may be exceptional cases (such as *Shippey*) where the inconsistencies (whether in the witness's evidence viewed by itself or between him and other prosecution witnesses) are so great that any reasonable tribunal would be forced to the conclusion that the witnesses is untruthful. In such a case (and in the absence of other evidence capable of founding a case) the judge shall withdraw the case from the jury."

2–87   More recently, in *People (DPP) v AD*,[182] the Supreme Court subscribed to the consensus that the test to be applied on an application for a direction was that laid down in *Galbraith*, with the question in that case being whether the trial judge had actually applied that test by asking whether a jury would be perverse in convicting.

2–88   It can be seen from the foregoing authorities that a submission of no case to answer will not be successful merely because the defence can identify inconsistencies, even serious inconsistencies, in the prosecution case, provided that there is evidence that supports the charges.[183] However, if it is possible to point to inherent conflicts in the prosecution case, of a kind which render the evidence adduced tenuous or incapable of belief, or which cast serious doubt on whether the defendant committed the alleged offences, then the trial judge is under a duty to withdraw the case from the jury.[184]

2–89   In *DPP v Buckley*,[185] Charleton J noted that the issue before the trial judge at direction stage on the close of the prosecution case, whether sitting with a jury or as the sole tribunal of fact, is whether the prosecution has adduced sufficient evidence which might enable a safe conviction to occur on a full consideration of that evidence by the tribunal of fact. He summarised the approach to be adopted to an application for a direction as follows[186]:

> "The test to be applied, therefore, revolves around whether the tribunal of fact, be it judge or jury, on full consideration and having heard speeches or submissions on both sides, could properly convict on the evidence. It is the trial judge's duty, at that point, to stop the trial if that evidence is absent. The trial judge must bear in mind, however, that it is the fundamental duty of the jury, or the trial judge as tribunal of fact, to decide facts and, in that regard, to

---

[181] Unreported, Court of Criminal Appeal, 3 July 2002.
[182] [2012] IESC 33 at [59]–[60], [2012] 2 IR 332 at 351.
[183] See *People (DPP) v Hourigan* [2004] IECCA 7; *People (DPP) v O'Reilly* [2009] IECCA 30; *People (DPP) v McManus* [2011] IEHC 32; *People (DPP) v Walsh* [2011] IECCA 101; *People (DPP) v MJ* [2014] IECCA 21.
[184] *People (DPP) v Morrissey*, unreported, Court of Criminal Appeal, 10 July 1998; *People (DPP) v M.*, unreported, Court of Criminal Appeal, 15 February 2001.
[185] [2007] IEHC 150, [2007] 3 IR 745.
[186] [2007] IEHC 150 at [8], [2007] 3 IR 745 at 750.

apply reason and commonsense to the evidence. It is their task to weigh the importance of the individual pieces of evidence in determining the issue as to whether the prosecution have discharged the burden and standard of proof. It is not the function of the trial judge at direction stage to weigh the evidence. His or her function, at that stage, is to see whether the requisite proofs to establish the case have been adduced in evidence, bearing in mind that there can be cases where an apparent link in the chain of proof is so tenuous that it would clearly be perverse for a properly directed jury to act upon it."

2–90 Having quoted the *Galbraith* principles, he went on to reiterate that issues as to the absence of evidence are part of the trial judge's function at the direction stage, but issues as to the credibility are not.[187]

2–91 An example of where a gap in the evidence adduced by the prosecution was identified which should have led to the withdrawal of the case from the jury can be seen in *People (DPP) v Connolly*.[188] The accused had been charged with two counts of possession of drugs, including possession of drugs with a market value of €13,000 or more contrary to s.15A of the Misuse of Drugs Act 1977 (as amended) which carries a presumptive minimum sentence of 10 years. When stopped by Gardaí, the accused told them that there was ten kilos of amphetamines in the car and, when they searched the car, they found 10 packs filled with white powder weighing close to 10 kilos. At the trial, a forensic scientist gave evidence on behalf of the prosecution that, consistent with accredited laboratory procedures, she had analysed 5 of 10 packs found in the accused's car and had established that they contained amphetamine but not the quantity. Using a statistical model for sampling, she could say with 100 per cent certainty that 5 of the packs contained amphetamine and with 99 per cent certainty that at least 7 of the packs did so. She was unable to state what the percentage content of amphetamine was in the packs tested but gave evidence that amphetamine purities generally fell between 10 per cent and 40 per cent. An application for a direction was made on the basis that there was insufficient evidence to establish the amphetamine content of the packs so as to exclude the possibility that the content could have been as low as 1 per cent, in which case the value of the drugs would not have exceeded the statutory threshold in s.15A. On appeal, it was held that the trial judge had erred in not granting that application. Delivering the judgment of the Supreme Court, Fennelly J explained that probability was not enough and, even if uncommon, the evidence of the forensic scientist did not go so far as to exclude the very real possibility that the percentage of amphetamine content in the drugs could have been as low as 1 per cent. While he noted that it is the totality of the evidence before the jury which is important and accepted that, looking at all the circumstances, there was every reason to suspect that the drugs had a significant amphetamine content, he concluded nonetheless that there was a gap in the prosecution evidence so that the case should have been withdrawn from the jury.

2–92 Given that a trial judge is required to review the totality of the evidence for the purpose of ruling on an application for a direction[189] and will have the benefit of having seen the witnesses give evidence,[190] and is exercising a discretion albeit one

---

[187] [2007] IEHC 150 at [89, [2007] 3 IR 745 at 751.
[188] [2011] IESC 6, [2011] 1 IR 755, [2012] 1 ILRM 170.
[189] It would appear that the obligation to give reasons for this ruling is limited: *McCann v Halpin* [2014] IEHC 276 at [18].
[190] In *R. v Cameron* [2001] EWCA 562, the English Court of Appeal emphasised that the decision in relation to a submission of no case to answer is a matter for the trial judge who has the advantage of seeing and assessing the prosecution witnesses.

that has to be exercised judicially,[191] if he or she refuses to withdraw the case from the jury, it will be difficult to overturn that decision on appeal.[192]

8. Charge to the Jury

2–93   In every case tried before a jury, the judge is obliged to instruct the jury as to the burden and standard of proof.[193] There are a number of elements to this instruction which are required to be addressed by the trial judge as follows: (a) the jury must be told of the presumption of innocence and instructed that, because of this presumption, they cannot convict the accused unless his or her guilt is proved by the prosecution beyond a reasonable doubt; (b) the jury should be given some guidance as to the standard of proof beyond a reasonable doubt; and (c) the jury should be instructed as to the proper approach where a defence is raised by the accused. Although, for ease of exposition, the required charge to the jury is examined below by reference to its discrete elements, it is important to emphasise that the Court of Criminal Appeal has resisted attempts at calcification of the charge into a ritualistic formula[194] and, further, in dealing with any challenge to the charge of a trial judge, the Court will have regard to the terms of the charge as a whole.[195]

(a) Instruction as to the presumption of innocence

2–94   In *People (DPP) v DO'T.*,[196] the importance of instructing the jury as to the

---

[191]   *People (DPP) v Dundon* [2008] IECCA 14 at [9].
[192]   Appeals against the refusal of a trial judge to grant a direction were unsuccessful in, *inter alia*, *People (DPP) v M.* unreported, Court of Criminal Appeal, 15 February 2001; *People (DPP) v Leacy*, unreported, Court of Criminal Appeal, 3 July 2002; *People (DPP) v RB*, unreported, Court of Criminal Appeal, 12 February 2003; *People (DPP) v Hourigan* [2004] IECCA 7; *People (DPP) v Murphy* [2005] IECCA 1, [2005] 2 IR 125; *People (DPP) v Costa* [2008] IECCA 1; *People (DPP) v Dundon* [2008] IECCA 14; *People (DPP) v AD* [2008] IECCA 101; *People (DPP) v O'Reilly* [2009] IECCA 30; *People (DPP) v Daly* [2009] IECCA 90; *People (DPP) v Creed* [2009] IECCA 95; *People (DPP) v Quigley* [2009] IECCA 106; *People (DPP) v Kearney* [2009] IECCA 112, *People (DPP) v Pauliukonis* [2009] IECCA 130; *People (DPP) v Boyle* [2010] IECCA 3, [2010] 1 IR 787; *People (DPP) v Goulding* [2010] IECCA 85; *People (DPP) v Timmons* [2011] IECCA 13; *People (DPP) v McManus* [2011] IECCA 32; *People (DPP) v White* [2011] IECCA 78; *People (DPP) v Walsh* [2011] IECCA 101; *People (DPP) v Bolger* [2013] IECCA 6; *People (DPP) v McGinley* [2013] IECCA 7; [2014] IECCA 21. An appeal against the refusal of a direction was, however, successful in *People (DPP) v Morrissey*, unreported, Court of Criminal Appeal, 10 July 1998; *People (DPP) v Higginbotham*, unreported, Court of Criminal Appeal, 17 November 2000; *People (DPP) v M*, unreported, Court of Criminal Appeal, 15 February 2001; *People (DPP) v Connolly* [2011] IESC 6, [2011] 1 IR 755, [2012] 1 ILRM 170; *People (DPP) v PJ Carey (Contractors) Ltd* [2011] IECCA 63, [2012] 1 IR 234 and *People (DPP) v Callaghan* [2013] IECCA 46.
[193]   He is not relieved of this obligation by the explanation to the jury by counsel of these matters (*Attorney General v O'Connor* [1935] Ir Jur Rep 1).
[194]   *People (DPP) v LG* [2003] 2 IR 517 at 532; *People (DPP) v DO'S* [2004] IECCA 23 at [10]. *Cf. R. v Allan* [1969]1 All ER 91, where the use of a precise formula was deprecated. However, in *Ferguson v R.* [1979] 1 All ER 877, Lord Scarman took the view that although the law did not require a particular formula, judges were wise, as a general rule, to adopt one.
[195]   *People (AG) v Casey* [1938] Ir Jur Rep 56 at 57; *People (AG) v Duggan* [1958] IR 116 at 124–125; *People (AG) v Sykes* [1958] IR 355 at 356; *Convening Authority v Byrne*, unreported, Courts-Martial Appeal Court, *ex tempore*, 2 November 1998 at 5; *People (DPP) v Kiely*, unreported, Court of Criminal Appeal, 21 March 2001 at 25; *People (DPP) v D.O'S* [2004] IECCA 23; *People (DPP) v Curran* [2011] IECCA 95 at [32], [2011] 3 IR 785 at 803–804.
[196]   [2003] 4 IR 286.

presumption of innocence was emphasised by the Court of Criminal Appeal. Hardiman J pointed to the constitutional status of the presumption and stated:

> "The presumption of innocence ... is not only a right in itself: it is the basis of other aspects of a trial in due course of law at common law. The rule that, generally speaking, the prosecution bears the burden of proving all the elements of the offence necessary to establish guilt is a corollary of the presumption. To state the incidence of the burden of proof without indicating its basis in the presumption is to risk understating its importance and perhaps relegating it to the status of a mere technical rule.... It is therefore important that the presumption itself should be explained as an essential feature of the criminal trial. The prosecution's burden of proof, the corollary of the presumption, should be itself separately explained."[197]

2–95   In that case, the trial judge did not refer to the presumption of innocence at all in his initial charge but, after requisitions were raised, he recharged the jury to the effect that "there is a presumption of innocence and it's a very serious presumption". It was held, however, that this reference was not sufficient to discharge his duty to charge the jury in relation to the presumption of innocence because it did not contain "a statement that the presumption is that every accused person is innocent until a jury is satisfied to the contrary to the appropriate standard and that this presumption is the basic, constitutionally guaranteed, condition of a trial in due course of law."[198] Hardiman J went on to reiterate the importance of a specific instruction as to the presumption of innocence:

> "Due to the fundamental importance of the presumption of innocence, these shortcomings are a serious matter for the integrity of the trial. It is of course essential that the jury should understand that the onus of proof is on the prosecution and that they should understand the standard of proof. These things should be presented, not as arbitrary rules, but as the corollary of the basic principle of the presumption of innocence, which is a constitutional and universally recognised human right. The trial process, including the jury's role in it, has to be presented as one grounded in principle, and that principle is one of high constitutional significance."[199]

2–96   Thus, a trial judge is required to instruct the jury in clear terms as to: (i) the presumption of innocence and its importance as a fundamental principle; and (ii) that the corollaries of that principle are that the burden of proof is on the prosecution to prove the guilt of the accused and that the standard of proof that has to be met by

---

[197] [2003] 4 IR 286 at 290–291. A challenge to the charge as to the burden on proof on the basis that this obligation had not been complied with was rejected in *People (DPP) v Piotrowski* [2014] IECCA 17. *Cf. Coffin v United States* (1895) 156 US 432, where it was held that a trial judge had been incorrect to refuse to charge the jury as to the presumption of innocence even though he fully explained that the case against the accused had to be proved beyond a reasonable doubt. By way of contrast, the Australian courts have held there there is no requirement that a trial judge make express reference to the presumption of innocence (*Tulic v R* [1999] FCA 1120; *Momcilovic v R* [2011] HCA 34).
[198] [2003] 4 IR 286 at 292.
[199] [2003] 4 IR 286 at 293.

the prosecution is proof beyond a reasonable doubt.[200] Whether the trial judge has adequately done this will be assessed on the basis of the judge's charge as a whole.[201]

2–97 Applying these principles, a trial judge is required to instruct the jury that the prosecution has to prove its case beyond a reasonable doubt and that if the jury entertain any reasonable doubt as to the guilt of the accused, they must give him or her the benefit of that doubt.[202] However, it was held in *People (DPP) v White*[203] that it is not a necessary component to the charge that the trial judge instructs the jury that the prosecution are required to "negative every supposition consistent with the innocence of the accused".[204]

2–98 It is clear that any charge by a trial judge that dilutes the presumption of innocence or the obligation of the prosecution to prove the guilt of an accused beyond a reasonable doubt will be a misdirection. So, for example, in *People (DPP) v Cremin*,[205] it was held that the trial judge had erred in instructing the jury that, although the onus was on the prosecution to prove the guilt of the accused and this onus never shifted to the accused, this did not mean that doubt on any one matter entitled the accused to be acquitted. The Court of Criminal Appeal thought it probable that what the trial judge meant to convey was that doubt on a peripheral matter, a matter which is not in any sense an essential ingredient in the charge, would not prevent the jury from arriving at a verdict of guilty. However, this was not what he had said and his charge in this regard was capable of leaving the jury under the mistaken impression that a doubt, even in respect of an essential aspect of the case, would not entitle the accused to an acquittal.[206] It is not, however, a misdirection for a trial judge to instruct a jury that, if

---

[200] It would appear that there is no scope for a trial judge to use any formula other than that of proof beyond a reasonable doubt. In *People (AG) v Byrne* [1974] IR 1 at 4, Kenny J, delivering the judgment of the Court of Criminal Appeal, criticised the charge of the trial judge wherein he had told the jury that they had to be "satisfied" of the guilt of the accused as an "unfortunate" departure from the "time-honoured formula" of telling the jury that the prosecution is required to prove the guilt of the accused beyond a reasonable doubt which he regarded as the best way of indicating the degree of proof required. In *People (DPP) v DO'T.* [2003] 4 IR 268 at 291, the Court of Criminal Appeal went further and took the view that the standard of proof beyond a reasonable doubt is a corollary of the presumption of innocence and, thus, constitutionally required. See also *People (DPP) v Cotter*, unreported, Court of Criminal Appeal, 28 June 1999, where it was held that the trial judge had been correct to instruct the jury that the standard of proof was not, as they had been told by counsel for the accused, "moral certitude" but rather proof beyond a reasonable doubt.

[201] *People (DPP) v White* [2011] IECCA 78 at [40]; *People (DPP) v Piotrowski* [2014] IECCA 17 at [3.1]–[3.3].

[202] *Attorney General v O'Connor* [1935] Ir Jur Rep 1 at 2; *People (DPP) v C* [2001] 3 IR 345 at 357. See also *People (DPP) v Hourigan* [2004] IECCA 7 at [15]–[16], where the trial judge instructed the jury, that if they were not satisfied beyond a reasonable doubt that the particular accused was involved in a joint enterprise, "then he is entitled to a verdict of not guilty in his favour and he walks free", a phrase which was described as "unfortunate" given its common connotation of an unworthy escape from the consequences of one's acts but the use of which was not, on its own, a sufficient ground to quash the verdict of the jury.

[203] [2011] IECCA 78 at [38]–[39].

[204] This was the formula used by Maguire P in *People (AG) v McMahon* [1946] IR 267 at 273.

[205] Unreported, Court of Criminal Appeal, *ex tempore*, 10 May 1999.

[206] See also *People (DPP) v DO'T.* [2003] 4 IR 286 at 292–293, where the charge of the trial judge was criticised on the basis that he had instructed the jury that the onus of proof was on the prosecution "where there is a difference". Hardiman J emphasised that the burden of proof is on the prosecution throughout the trial and not merely "where there is a difference".

the prosecution has satisfied them beyond a reasonable doubt that the accused is guilty and that there is no basis for an acquittal, they are obliged to convict.[207]

2–99 It is not open to a trial judge to instruct a jury or give them the impression that they are required to choose between the evidence adduced by the prosecution and that adduced by the defence[208] or that, if they disbelieve the evidence of the accused or the evidence called on his behalf, they are entitled to convict.[209] This is because such an instruction gives the jury the impression that the issue which they have to try is whether they accept or reject the explanation given by the accused,[210] whereas the question of whether the prosecution has discharged the legal burden "is distinct from, and is not necessarily to be determined by, the truth, or the probability, or the reasonableness, in the estimation of the jury, of the story told by the accused".[211] The proper direction to give the jury, where there is a conflict of evidence between the prosecution witnesses and the accused or witnesses on behalf of the defence, is that the burden rests on the prosecution to prove the guilt of the accused and, thus, even if the jury disbelieve the evidence of the accused or the evidence called on his or her behalf, they can only convict if they are satisfied beyond a reasonable doubt of his or her guilt.[212]

2–100 Depending on the circumstances of a case, it may also be appropriate for the trial judge to instruct the jury that an accused is not under an obligation to call any witness and he or she should generally refrain from inviting the jury to draw any inference from the failure to call a witness.[213]

2–101 Although an accused does not bear any onus to prove his or her innocence, the jury should be instructed to consider all of the evidence in the case, including that adduced by the defence. It will be a misdirection for the trial judge to instruct the jury or give them the impression that they are required or entitled to consider whether the prosecution have proven the guilt of the accused beyond a reasonable doubt in advance of, or without having regard to, the evidence of the accused or adduced on his or her behalf.[214]

---

[207] *People (DPP) v Pauliukonis* [2009] IECCA 130. *Cf. People (DPP) v Davis* [1993] 2 IR 1 at 13, where Henchy J stated that: "It is open to a judge in an appropriate case to express an opinion that a particular verdict of guilty is the only one which would be reasonable or proper on the evidence, but that must of necessity fall short of the right to direct a verdict of guilty."

[208] *People (DPP) v Morrissey*, unreported, Court of Criminal Appeal, 10 July 1998 at 18.

[209] *People (AG) v Oglesby* [1966] IR 162 at 164. *A fortiori*, it is a misdirection to instruct the jury that, if they disbelieve the explanation of the accused, it would be their duty to convict (*People (AG) v Berber* [1944] IR 405).

[210] *People (AG) v Oglesby* [1966] IR 162 at 164.

[211] *People (AG) v Berber* [1944] IR 405 at 411. *Cf. AG v KJM* (1949) 83 ILTSJ 154 (charge of the trial judge in trial for unlawful carnal knowledge that the issue for the jury to decide in the case was one of which of the witnesses, the complainant or the accused, they believed was incorrect because it might lead the jury to forget that the onus of proof lay upon the prosecution).

[212] *Convening Authority v Byrne*, unreported, Courts-Martial Appeal Court, *ex tempore*, 2 November 1998. *Cf. People (DPP) v Morrisey*, unreported, Court of Criminal Appeal, 10 July 1998 at 19; and *People (DPP) v Rawley* [1997] 2 IR 265.

[213] *People (DPP) v Curran* [2011] IECCA 95 at [39], [2011] 3 IR 785 at 806–807. See also *R. v Wright* [2000] Crim LR 510; *R. v Khan (Shakeel)* [2001] Crim LR 673.

[214] *People (DPP) v Kelly*, unreported, Court of Criminal Appeal, 13 December 1999.

(b) Guidance as to the standard of proof

2–102   In *People (DPP) v DO'T.*,[215] it was held that a trial judge is required to give the jury some guidance as to the application of the standard of proof beyond reasonable doubt. However, the precise nature and extent of the duty of a trial judge in that regard is unclear. Three discrete issues arise: (i) the duty of a trial judge to contrast the criminal and civil standards of proof; (ii) the duty of a trial judge to explain to the jury that the accused is entitled to the benefit of any reasonable doubt; (iii) the duty of a trial judge to explain what is meant by a reasonable doubt.

(i) Contrast of the criminal and civil standards of proof

2–103   One method commonly employed by trial judges to give juries some guidance as to the concept of proof beyond a reasonable doubt is to contrast the criminal and civil standards of proof. This practice has been described as "helpful"[216] and "desirable"[217] and "important as an illustration of the meaning of the phrase 'proof beyond reasonable doubt'".[218] Charges have been criticised where this contrast was not drawn.[219] However, it was held in *People (DPP) v Shortt*[220] that there is no obligation to use this particular way of explaining the standard of proof and, in *People (DPP) v MK*,[221] it was stated that this is not an essential requirement.[222] Accordingly, the failure of the trial judge to contrast the standards of proof will not, of itself, constitute a misdirection provided that he or she adequately explains the concept of proof beyond a reasonable doubt.

(ii) Instruction as to the benefit of the doubt

2–104   In *People (AG) v Byrne*,[223] Kenny J, delivering the judgment of the Court of Criminal Appeal, stated:

> "It is … essential … that the jury should be told that the accused is entitled to the benefit of the doubt and that when two views on any part of the case are possible on the evidence, they should adopt that which is favourable to the accused unless the State has established the other beyond reasonable doubt."[224]

2–105   This passage was classified as *obiter* in *People (DPP) v Kiely*,[225] and it was held that, although an explanation as to the benefit of the doubt was very common and its inclusion in the charge of a trial judge is desirable, its omission in that case was not

---

[215] [2003] 4 IR 286 at 291.

[216] *People (AG) v Byrne* [1974] IR 1 at 9 (*per* Kenny J).

[217] *People (DPP) v MK* [2005] IEHC 93 at [19], [2005] 3 IR 423 at 432.

[218] *People (DPP) v D.O'T.* [2003] 4 IR 286 at 291 (*per* Hardiman J).

[219] See, *e.g. People (DPP) v LG* [2003] 2 IR 517 at 532; *People (DPP) v DO'T* [2003] 4 IR 286 at 291.

[220] Unreported, Court of Criminal Appeal, 23 July 1996.

[221] [2005] IECCA 93 at [19], [2005] 3 IR 423 at 432.

[222] To similar effect, in the Canadian decision of *R v Zebedee* (2006) 81 OR (3d) 583, 211 CCC (3d) 199, it was held that it is not mandatory for a trial judge to instruct a jury that proof beyond a reasonable doubt is much closer to absolute certainty than to a balance of probabilities.

[223] [1975] IR 1.

[224] [1975] IR 1 at 9. See also *Attorney General v O'Connor* [1935] Ir Jur Rep 1 at 2.

[225] Unreported, Court of Criminal Appeal, 21 March 2001. *Cf. People (DPP) v DO'S* [2004] IECCA 23, where the trial judge had given what was regarded as a relatively brief explanation as to the benefit of the doubt but the Court was satisfied that, having regard to the terms of his charge as a whole, he had adequately instructed the jury as to this principle.

fatal.[226] It is not clear, however, that this holding is compatible with the subsequent decision in *People (DPP) v D.O'T.*[227] In that case, Hardiman J described the principle that an accused is entitled to the benefit of any reasonable doubt as a corollary of the presumption of innocence and appears to have regarded it as an integral part of the charge required with regard to the burden and standard of proof.[228] Subsequently, in *People (DPP) v Reid,*[229] the learned judge stated that this principle was "of very great practical importance".

2–106 It is a misdirection for a trial judge to instruct the jury that the accused should be given the benefit of the doubt where two conclusions are equally open on the facts because this may give the jury the mistaken impression that it is only where the probabilities are equal that the accused should be afforded the benefit of the doubt.[230] In *People (DPP) v Cronin,*[231] Hardiman J, delivering the judgment of the Court of Criminal Appeal, stated:

> "There is no doubt … that it is an inadequate statement of the law to say that the inference most favourable to the accused is to be drawn *only* where there are two or more conclusions which, with *equal* plausibility, can be drawn from a particular set of facts. The accused is entitled to have the inference most favourable to him drawn unless it is excluded by the prosecution beyond reasonable doubt. This is unaffected by the fact that the jury may consider the more favourable inference much the less likely of those available. It is, of course, true that where there are two conclusions of equal plausibility, the accused is entitled to have the one most favourable to him drawn, but that is not the whole story: he continues to have this entitlement, even if the favourable inference is relatively unlikely, unless it has been excluded beyond reasonable doubt."[232]

2–107 There is, however, no obligation on a trial judge to instruct the jury to accept the version of events which is more favourable to the accused as this would usurp its function.[233] Similarly, a trial judge is not required to instruct a jury "that it was open to them to consider other ways in which unchallenged facts could be explained and that they should search for some explanation which would be consistent with the innocence of the accused."[234] Furthermore, once this direction is given in such a way that the jury clearly understands its purpose and application, the trial judge is not required to identify each piece of evidence individually and remind the jury to apply the principle to it.[235]

---

[226] See also *People (DPP) v DO'S* [2004] IECCA 23 at [9]–[10].

[227] [2003] 4 IR 286.

[228] [2003] 4 IR 286 at 291–293. The same view was expressed by the learned judge in *People (DPP) v Cronin* [2003] 3 IR 377 at 389.

[229] [2004] IECCA 3 at [10].

[230] *People (DPP) v Wallace*, unreported, Court of Criminal Appeal, 30 April 2001; *People (DPP) v Cronin* [2003] 3 IR 377; *People (DPP) v Reid* [2004] IECCA 3; *People (DPP) v Cagney* [2007] IESC 46, [2008] 2 IR 111.

[231] [2003] 3 IR 377.

[232] [2003] 3 IR 377 at 389–390. *Cf. People (DPP) v Cahill*, unreported, Court of Criminal Appeal, 31 July 2001, where the Court accepted that the charge of the trial judge to the effect that, where there were two interpretations in relation to any particular matter and they were evenly balanced, the benefit of the doubt should be given to the accused, could have been "more happily phrased" but declined to quash the conviction of the applicant on the basis that the trial judge had made it emphatically clear to the jury that they were to determine the issues before them in accordance with the appropriate criminal standard of proof.

[233] *People (DPP) v C* [2001] 3 IR 345 at 356.

[234] *People (AG) v Wickham* [1949] IR 180 at 185.

[235] *People (DPP) v MJ* [2014] IECCA 21 at [85].

(iii) Explanation of the concept of a reasonable doubt

2–108   In *People (AG) v Byrne,* the Court of Criminal Appeal took the view that the expression "beyond reasonable doubt" was understood by jurors.[236] It would seem to follow that a trial judge is not required to give the jury any further explanation of this standard of proof other than to contrast it with the civil standard. Indeed, it can be argued that a trial judge would be better to avoid such explanations because of the inherent difficulties in defining what a "reasonable doubt"[237] is coupled with the obvious potential for error leading to appeals.[238] Nonetheless, a trial judge may take the view that guidance is appropriate because the jury have requested it or otherwise.[239]

2–109   It has been held that it is not a misdirection to tell the jury that a doubt must be a substantial one[240] or that what is required is something short of a mathematical or moral certainty.[241] It is also permissible for a trial judge to instruct a jury to use their common sense and experience of the world in deciding whether a doubt is reasonable.[242] However, a direction that "a reasonable doubt is one for which you could give reasons if you were asked" has attracted criticism at appellate level.[243] When examining whether a trial judge had properly instructed a jury in relation to what constitutes a reasonable doubt, an appeal court will look at the judge's charge as a whole and the use of a word or phrase that might be regarded as infelicitous will not prove fatal where the judge's charge as a whole has made it clear that the jury should have regard to reasonable and not to unreasonable doubts.[244]

2–110   One of the most popular explanations of the concept of a reasonable doubt is to draw an analogy with important affairs. A good example can be seen in *People (DPP) v Kiely*[245] where the trial judge, in the course of his charge, explained the difference between the civil and criminal standards of proof and the standard of proof beyond a reasonable doubt, as follows:

---

[236] [1974] IR 1 at 9. This was also the view of Dixon CJ in *Dawson v The Queen* (1961) CLR 1 at 18, and of the Court of Appeal in *R. v Ching* (1976) 63 Cr App R 7.

[237] In "The Degree of 'Doubt': Warning to Jury in a Charge of Indecent Assault Upon a 'Grown Man'" (1944) 8 J Crim L 307 at 308, it was commented that: "in a court of law it is impossible to measure probabilities and … the unavoidable imperfections of language mean that no set terms can give any definite indication of a place in the scale of probability." See also *People (DPP) v Price* [2004] IECCA 26 at [8], where the Court took the view that it might be "unhelpful" for a trial judge to give practical examples to illustrate the meaning of "reasonable doubt".

[238] In *R. v Ching* (1976) 63 Cr App R 7 at 11, the Court of Appeal cautioned that "if judges stopped trying to define that which is almost impossible to define there would be fewer appeals."

[239] In *R v Layton* [2009] 2 SCR 540, it was held that the trial judge had erred in declining to give an explanation of the concept of "reasonable doubt" when requested by the jury to do so. Similarly, in *R v Cavkic* [2005] VSCA 182, 12 VR 136, where the jury inquired how sure they should be in percentage terms before convicting, the Victoria Court of Appeal considered that the trial judge had been wrong not to give further guidance to the jury and to explain to them that they must not approach their task by reference to percentages.

[240] *People (AG) v Ward* (1944) 78 ILTR 64. However, in the Australian case of *Barr v R* [2004] NTCCA 1, 14 NTLR 164, it was held that a charge to a jury that it did not suffice that there was "some bare possibility that some innocent complexion can be placed on the evidence" which was inconsistent with the guilt of the accused constituted a misdirection.

[241] *People (DPP) v Cotter,* unreported, Court of Criminal Appeal, 28 June 1999; *People (DPP) v Curran* [2011] IECCA 95 at [46]–[48], [2011] 3 IR 785 at 810–811.

[242] *People (DPP) v Byrne* [1998] 2 IR 417 at 436.

[243] *R. v Stafford* (1968) 53 Cr App R 1 at 2.

[244] *People (DPP) v Cunningham* [2007] IECCA 49.

[245] Unreported, Court of Criminal Appeal, 21 March 2001.

"You will have a decision to make and an important decision and you will have to weigh it up. I must refer you to that, during your whole life, you are making decision after decision and they are in various categories. There is one category of decision which I will call of a passing or trivial nature. Will I go to the cinema tonight? Will I buy a lottery ticket? Will I look at the Late Late Show? ... All these things are little decisions that we make. They are not life changing decisions. ... There is another kind of decision which is much more fundamental which we all again make. Are we going to get married or if we are already married are we going to leave our marriage partner and go with someone else? Are we going to sell our house in the rising property market?...They are all decisions which we all have to make from time to time, not very often, but we have to make them, but you make those decisions in a much more fundamental and careful way than the kind of decisions that you are going to watch the Late Late Show or you are going to buy a lottery ticket. They are totally different kinds of decisions. Now the civil standard of proof that I spoke about, the traffic case, injury at work, that kind of thing, you can equate that to the trivial kind of decision and the much more serious decision is equated with the criminal case, so, the difference between the trivial decision and the serious decision gives you some idea of the difference between the civil standards of proof which is lower and the criminal standard of proof which is, much higher. I do not think I can explain it much better than that to you. It is very serious and you have to be satisfied beyond reasonable doubt, that is not mathematical doubt, but beyond reasonable doubt."[246]

2–111 McGuinness J, delivering the judgment of the Court of Criminal Appeal, was satisfied that "no possible criticism" could be made of this charge which she regarded as "admirably clear and comprehensive as well as being geared to the understanding of the ordinary man and woman in the street".[247]

(c) Defences

2–112 Where the trial judge is satisfied that the accused has satisfied the evidential burden in relation to a defence raised by him or her[248] and, thus, decides to leave that defence to the jury, then, except in the case of insanity, he or she is required to clearly instruct the jury that the burden rests on the prosecution to disprove that defence beyond a reasonable doubt and that there is no onus on the accused to establish the defence or

---

[246] The charge of the trial judge is set out at pp.18–19 of the judgment of the Court of Criminal Appeal.

[247] Unreported, Court of Criminal Appeal, 21 March 2001 at 20. *Cf. R. v Ching* (1976) 63 Cr App R 7 at 8, (the Court of Appeal approved as clear and accurate the charge of the trial judge that a reasonable doubt was: "a doubt to which you can give a reason as opposed to a mere fanciful sort of speculation such as 'Well, nothing in this world is certain, nothing in this world can be proved'. ... It is sometimes said the sort of matter which might influence you if you were to consider some business matter. A matter, for example, of a mortgage concerning your house, or something of that nature."); *Walters v R.* [1969] 2 AC 26 at 30 (direction of the trial judge that "a reasonable doubt is that quality and kind of doubt which, when you are dealing with matters of importance in your own affairs, you allow to influence you one way or the other" approved by Privy Council); and *R. v Gray* (1973) 58 Cr App R 177 (reference to everyday affairs suggests too low a standard). By way of contrast, the drawing of an analogy with important decisions in the context of juror's personal lives has been disapproved by the Court of Appeal in New Zealand: *R v Wanhalla* [2006] NZCA 229.

[248] In *People (DPP) v Cronin* [2003] 3 IR 377, the Court of Criminal Appeal held that, other than in exceptional cases, as where an unrepresented accused was incapable of defending his or her interests, there is no duty on a trial judge to consider whether any defences other than those advanced by an accused are open to him or her and, if so, to leave them to the jury. The Court, thus, refused to follow a line of English authorities to this effect on the basis that they were inconsistent with the right of an accused to conduct his or her defence, or to have it conducted professionally on his or her instructions.

prove his innocence.[249] In *People (AG) v Quinn*,[250] Walsh J set out the correct position in the context of the defence of self-defence:

> "In a case where there is evidence, whether it be disclosed in the prosecution case or in the defence case, which is sufficient to leave the issue of self-defence to the jury the only question the jury has to consider is whether they are satisfied beyond reasonable doubt that the accused killed the deceased (if it be a case of homicide) and whether the jury is satisfied beyond reasonable doubt that the prosecution has negatived the issue of self-defence. If the jury is not satisfied beyond reasonable doubt on both of these matters the accused must be acquitted."[251]

2–113 A point which should be noted is that, although the judge is entitled to comment upon the evidence adduced in the case, including the defence put forward by the accused, he or she cannot do so in a manner which undermines the defence made. In *People (DPP) v Clarke*,[252] the defence of the accused to a charge of murder was self-defence. In putting this issue to the jury, the trial judge said that acquittal on this ground was only theoretically possible. This direction was heavily criticised by the Court of Criminal Appeal, who pointed out that it amounted in effect to an invitation to the jury not to consider the possibility at all. While accepting that the judge was entitled to comment on the particular facts of the case, the Court emphasised that once the issue of self-defence was raised, a direction in the terms laid down in *Quinn* was required.[253]

2–114 The position is, of course, different if the defence of insanity, or another statutory defence in respect of which the accused is fixed with a legal burden requiring him to establish a defence on the balance of probabilities[254] is left to the jury. In that case, the trial judge is required to instruct the jury that, by way of contrast to the standard of proof that has to be met by the prosecution, it suffices if the accused makes out the defence on a balance of probabilities.

2–115 Particular care in charging the jury is required where a reverse onus provision places an evidential burden on the accused that requires him or her to establish the existence of a reasonable doubt. This is the case with s.29(2)(a) of the Misuse of Drugs

---

[249] *People (AG) v McMahon* [1946] IR 267 at 275; *People (AG) v Quinn* [1955] IR 57 at 60; *People (AG) v Quinn* [1965] IR 366 at 381; *People (AG) v Dwyer* [1972] IR 416 at 420; *People (DPP) v Shannon*, unreported, Court of Criminal Appeal, 13 July 1994; *People (DPP) v Bambrick*, unreported, Court of Criminal Appeal, 8 March 1999, [1999] 2 ILRM 71 at 75; *People (DPP) v Ceka* [2004] IECCA 25; *People (DPP) v Barnes* [2006] IECCA 165 at [84], [2007] 3 IR 130 at 156. *Cf. People (DPP) v McArdle* [2003] 4 IR 186 at 199, where Keane CJ upheld the charge of the trial judge stating that where the defence of self-defence has been raised, "it is for the prosecution to disprove self-defence; it is for the prosecution to prove that the degree of violence used was not reasonable". In *People (DPP) v Barnes* [2006] IECCA 165, [2007] 3 IR 130, where the trial judge had erroneously directed the jury that the onus of establishing self-defence was on the accused on a balance of probabilities, the Court of Criminal Appeal concluded that the verdict was not unsafe or unsatisfactory in circumstances where he told the jury that he had made "a very, very serious error" and then recharged them properly on this point.

[250] [1965] IR 366.

[251] [1965] IR 366 at 383. The learned judge also suggested that the jury should be instructed as to the difference between the evidential burden on the accused to raise the defence of self-defence and the legal burden on the prosecution to disprove it. However, it is submitted that the question of whether the accused has satisfied the evidential burden is a question for the trial judge only, and the requirement to satisfy it before a defence can be left to the jury should not be mentioned to them at all because it is likely to cause confusion.

[252] [1995] 1 ILRM 355.

[253] [1995] 1 ILRM 355 at 366. See also *People (DPP) v Cremin*, unreported, Court of Criminal Appeal, *ex tempore*, 10 May 1999.

[254] See *Convening Authority v Doyle* [1996] 2 ILRM 213.

Act 1977 which provides that, in any proceedings for possession of a controlled drug, it is a defence for an accused to prove that he did not know and had no reasonable grounds for suspecting that what he had in his possession was a controlled drug or that he was in possession of a controlled drug. In *People (DPP) v Smyth*,[255] it was held that it was a misdirection for the trial judge to suggest to the jury that the accused had to prove beyond a reasonable doubt that they did not know and had no reasonable grounds for suspecting that what was in their possession was a controlled drug. The proper direction to be given was for the trial judge was as follows:

> "In directing the jury on this issue, trial judges should in future, in the view of the court, give the ordinary direction as to the burden and standard and proof and the presumption of innocence. In stating the burden and standard of proof, however, a trial judge should point out that the prosecution are obliged to prove the elements of possession of the substance, and that the substance is a controlled drug, beyond reasonable doubt. A trial judge should then tell the jury that the burden of proof shifts to the defence to prove the existence of a reasonable doubt that the accused did not know and had no reasonable ground for suspecting that what he had in his possession was a controlled drug. It should be clearly stated that this burden cast on the accused is discharged if the defence prove a reasonable doubt, and no more than that, on that issue."[256]

2–116   Variations of that direction will be required in respect of other statutory provisions which are considered to have a similar effect in terms of the incidence of the evidential burden.[257]

2–117   Particular difficulties in instructing the jury can arise where an accused gives evidence in support of his or her defence because of the natural tendency of a jury to use their assessment of whether they believe the accused as a proxy for their decision as to whether the prosecution has proven its case beyond a reasonable doubt. Helpful guidance as to the approach to be adopted in such circumstances was given by the Supreme Court of Canada in *R v WD*[258]:

> "First, if you believe the evidence of the accused, obviously you must acquit.
> Second, if you do not believe the testimony of the accused but you are left in reasonable doubt by it, you must acquit.
> Third, even if you are not left in doubt by the evidence of the accused, you must ask yourself whether, on the basis of the evidence which you do accept, you are convinced beyond a reasonable doubt by that evidence of the guilt of the accused."[259]

2–118   This three step analysis underlines that the ultimate question for the jury is not whether it believes the accused's account or not, but whether the prosecution has proven his or her guilt beyond a reasonable doubt.

---

[255] [2010] IECCA 34, [2010] 3 IR 688, [2011] 1 ILRM 81.

[256] [2010] IECCA 34 at [22], [2010] 3 IR 688 at 697, [2011] 1 ILRM 81 at 89. See further *People (DPP) v Malric* [2011] IECCA 86 and *People (DPP) v Akinola* [2011] IECCA 33 where contentions that the trial judge had failed to properly instruct the jury properly in accordance with the decision in *Smyth* were rejected.

[257] *Cf. People (DPP) v Egan* [2010] IECCA 28, [2010] 3 IR 561 dealing with the direction required to be given in respect of an offence pursuant to s.3(1) of the Criminal Law (Sexual Offences) Act 2006 and *People (DPP) v PJ Carey (Contractors) Ltd* [2011] IECCA 63, [2012] 1 IR 234 where the trial judge was held to have misdirected the jury in relation to the effect of s.50 of the Safety, Health and Welfare at Work Act 1989.

[258] [1991] 1 SCR 742.

[259] See also *R v K(S)* (2003) 177 CCC (3d) 90, 173 OAC 31.

C. Civil Cases

1. Allocation of the Legal Burden

2–119   The general principle applied in civil cases is that he who asserts must prove (*Ei incumbit probatio qui dicit, non qui negat*).[260] Thus, whichever party contends for the existence of a particular fact will bear the burden of proving its existence.[261] A party cannot circumvent this requirement by the device of pleading his or her case by way of negative allegations[262] and a party will have to prove a negative where it is an essential part of his or her claim.[263]

2–120   As a rule of thumb, this will generally mean that proof of the facts necessary to establish a cause of action will rest on the party bringing the proceedings, whilst proof of a defence to the action will lie on the party raising the defence. Thus, in a negligence action, the burden of proving the existence of a duty of care, a breach of that duty and that damage was suffered by the plaintiff as a result of that breach will rest on the plaintiff,[264] while the burden of establishing the defence of contributory negligence rests on the defendant.[265] If a defendant raises a counterclaim, then the defendant will bear the burden of proof in respect of that counterclaim.[266]

2–121   The general principle that the legal burden rests on the party who asserts the matter in question is subject to a number of exceptions discussed below.

(a) Legislative Intervention

2–122   The constitutional constraints applicable in criminal proceedings do not apply in civil proceedings and the legislature, therefore, has much greater freedom, by use of presumptions and deeming provisions, to allocate the legal burden so as to place an onus on a defendant to establish or rebut certain matters.[267] An example can be seen in s.3 of the Proceeds of Crime Act 1996, which provides that, where it appears to the Court on evidence tendered by the applicant that a person is in possession of

---

[260] *Wicklow County Council v Fortune* [2012] IEHC 406 at [19]; *South Dublin County Council v Fallowvale Ltd* [2005] IEHC 408 at [70]. This general principle is based on the supposed difficulty of proving a negative (see Gilbert, *The Law of Evidence* (Dublin, 1754) at pp.104–105.

[261] *Clayton v Cashman* [2006] IEHC 360 at [29]–[30]. See also *McCrystal v Minister for Children* [2012] IESC 53 at [32], [2013] 1 ILRM 217 at 235–236.

[262] See *Soward v Leggatt* (1836) 7 C & P 613 at 615.

[263] *Abrath v North Eastern Railway* (1883) 11 QBD 440 at 457.

[264] *Hanrahan v Merck Sharp & Dohme* [1988] ILRM 629 at 634; *Cosgrove v Ryan* [2008] 4 IR 537 at 547, [2003] 1 ILRM 544 at 553 (*per* Murphy J). The plaintiff's burden in this regard may be eased by the invocation of the principle of *res ipsa loquitur* which is discussed in detail in McMahon and Binchy, *Law of Torts* 4th edn, Chap.9.

[265] *Dillon v Lynch (No.1)* (1957) 95 ILTR 185 at 187; *Clancy v Commissioners of Public Works* [1992] 2 IR 449 at 467; *Boyne v Bus Átha Cliath* [2003] 4 IR 47 at 51. It was held in *Clancy* that, because the onus was on the defendants to establish contributory negligence, the trial judge had been wrong in adopting the view of the facts most favourable to the defendants for the purpose of assessing the issue of contributory negligence. Subsequently, in *Boyne*, Finnegan P held, relying on *Clancy*, that where there is no direct evidence, reliance must be placed on inference as a matter of probability as to what occurred.

[266] See *Rhatigan v Gill* [1999] 2 ILRM 427 at 442.

[267] For an example of where the European legislature has done this, see art.85 of Council Regulation (EC) No. 6/2002 providing protection for community designs which is analysed in *Karen Millen Fashions Ltd v Dunnes Stores* [2007] IEHC 449, [2008] 2 ILRM 368 (HC); [2014] IESC 23 (SC).

control of specified property with a value of not less than £10,000 that constitutes the proceeds of crime or was acquired using the proceeds of crime, it is required to make an interlocutory order to freeze the property unless it is shown to the satisfaction of the court on evidence tendered by the respondent or any other person that it is below the specified value or does not constitute the proceeds of crime and was not acquired using the proceeds of crime. In *Gilligan v Criminal Assets Bureau*,[268] McGuinness J, having concluded that proceedings under that Act are civil rather than criminal in nature, held that this section was not constitutionally infirm.[269]

(b) Agreement of the Parties

2–123 The parties themselves may also agree on the incidence of the legal burden, for example where there is a written contract between them. Where they fail to so agree, the matter is one of construction of the contract, but in construing the contract, the courts will apply the general principles outlined above. In *Gorman v The Hand in Hand Insurance Company*,[270] the plaintiffs were suing on foot of an insurance policy which covered loss caused by fire. A clause in the policy excluded recovery if the fire was caused by arson. It was held that, once the plaintiffs had proved that the loss was caused by fire, the burden of proving that the fire was caused by arson was on the defendants.

(c) Peculiar Knowledge Principle

2–124 There is a long established principle, of uncertain ambit, that the onus of proof can be reversed where a matter is not within the means of knowledge of one party and is peculiarly within the knowledge of the opposing party. In *Mahony v Waterford, Limerick and Western Railway Co.*,[271] a question arose as to whether goods, which had been damaged in transit, had been damaged by the wilful misconduct of the defendant's servants. It was held that the onus of proving that they had not been so damaged rested upon the defendant railway company. Palles CB stated that:

> "although it is the general rule of law that it lies upon the plaintiff to prove affirmatively all the facts entitling him to relief, there is a well-known exception to such rule in reference to matters which are peculiarly within the knowledge of one defendant. In such case the *onus* is shifted."[272]

2–125 More recently, in *Wicklow County Council v Fortune*,[273] Hogan J identified

---

[268] [1998] 3 IR 185.
[269] See also *Murphy v GM PB PC Ltd* [1999] IEHC 5, *FJM v TH*, unreported, High Court, 29 June 2001, *MFM v MC* [2001] 2 IR 385 and *FMcK. v GW.D. (Proceeds of crime outside State)* [2004] IESC 31, [2004] 2 IR 470, [2004] 2 ILRM 419.
[270] (1877) IR 9 C.L. 224. *Cf. Artificial Coal Co. & Hannon v Minister for Finance* [1928] IR 238 at 244 and *Eurofoods (Ireland) Ltd v Meath County Council*, unreported, High Court, 31 October 1985. For a general discussion of the burden of proof and insurance claims, see *Cooper v General Accident Assurance Corporation* [1922] 2 IR 38 at 40.
[271] [1900] 2 IR 273. See also *General Accident Fire and Life Assurance v Robertson* [1909] AC 404.
[272] [1900] 2 IR 273 at 280 [emphasis in original]. But see *Powell v M'Glynn* [1902] 2 IR 154 at 169 where Barton J rejected the proposition that whenever a matter was shown to be peculiarly within a defendant's knowledge, the onus of proof was shifted to him. He suggested, instead, that the fact that a defendant had not given evidence in relation to a matter peculiarly within his own knowledge might serve to reduce the quantum of evidence necessary to establish the plaintiff's case.
[273] [2012] IEHC 406.

the peculiar knowledge principle as the basis for a line of authority in relation to the allocation of the burden of proof in respect of certain issues arising in applications pursuant to s.160 of the Planning and Development Act 2000, stating that this principle "represents a practical recognition of life's realities that certain matters lie almost beyond the effective capacity of an outsider to prove where they relate to events which are largely personal and private to the other party".[274] He went on to base his decision, that the onus of proof of establishing that an application pursuant to s.160 was statute barred rested on the respondent, on the twin bases that this was a matter of defence and the peculiar knowledge principle.

2–126 A somewhat more diluted application of the peculiar knowledge principle, whereby the legal burden of proof was found to shift in respect of a matter considered to be peculiarly within the range of the one party's capacity of proof and where the other party had discharged the evidential burden of establishing a *prima facie* case, can be seen in *Brennan v Windle*.[275] The applicant, who was arrested and committed on foot of a warrant of committal, had been convicted in the District Court of driving without insurance even though he had not been served with the summons and was unaware of the hearing. He brought judicial review proceedings to quash his conviction on the ground, *inter alia*, that the respondent District Judge had acted in breach of fair procedures because he had been convicted without notice of the offence and without an opportunity to make submissions. The DPP did not adduce any evidence in relation to the evidence as to service that had been before the District Court and defended the proceedings on the basis that the applicant had failed to discharge the onus of proving that there was not proper proof of service before the District Judge. This submission was emphatically rejected by Hardiman J who held that the applicant, having established a *prima facie* case, had done enough to shift the onus of proof on the question of whether there was sufficient evidence of service of the summons before the District Court. A similar approach was adopted by the same judge in *Whelan v Kirby*,[276] where it was held that the applicants has sufficiently discharged the onus of proving the record of the court in judicial review proceedings by adducing evidence of two conflicting orders, with the burden of proof shifting to the DPP to provide an explanation for the inconsistency.

2–127 The circumstances in which the burden of proof could be reversed in civil proceedings on the basis that a matter was within the knowledge of an opposing party were considered by the Supreme Court in *Hanrahan v Merck, Sharpe & Dohme*.[277] Delivering the judgment of the Court, Henchy J stated:

> "The ordinary rule is that a person who alleges a particular tort must, in order to succeed, prove … all the necessary ingredients of that tort and it is not for the defendant to disprove anything. Such exceptions as have been allowed to that general rule seem to be confined to cases where a particular element of tort lies or is deemed to lie, pre-eminently within the defendant's knowledge, in which case the onus of proof as to that matter passes to the defendant….The rationale behind the shifting of the onus of proof to the defendant in such cases would appear to lie in the fact that it would be palpably unfair to require a plaintiff to prove something which is beyond his reach and which is peculiarly within the range of the defendant's capacity of proof."[278]

---

[274] [2012] IEHC 406 at [22].
[275] [2003] 2 ILRM 520.
[276] [2004] 2 ILRM 1.
[277] [1988] ILRM 629.
[278] [1988] ILRM 629 at 634–635.

2–128   However, he went on to emphasise that the burden of proof would only be shifted where this was required by the interests of justice and that mere difficulty of proof would not suffice:

> "There are of course difficulties facing the plaintiffs in regard to proof … but mere difficulty of proof does not call for a shifting of the onus of proof. Many claims in tort fail because the plaintiff has not access to full information as to the true nature of the defendant's conduct. The onus of disproof rests on the defendant only when the act or default complained of is such that it would be fundamentally unjust to require the plaintiff to prove a positive averment when the particular circumstances show that fairness and justice call for disproof by the defendant."[279]

2–129   The decision in *Hanrahan* was approved and applied in *Rothwell v Motor Insurers Bureau of Ireland,*[280] with Hardiman J regarding it as having authoritatively set out the circumstances in which, and the basis on which, the onus of proof may shift in civil litigation. In that case, it was held that it is not sufficient that a matter is within the exclusive knowledge of the defendant but it is also required that it be "peculiarly within the range of the defendant's capacity for proof".[281]

2–130   The principles established by *Hanrahan* were also applied by McDermott J in *Jordan v Minister for Children and Youth Affairs*[282] where he rejected the contention that the burden of proof should be reversed on a petition challenging a referendum result, so as to place the burden on the respondents to demonstrate that the result had not been affected by what had been found in a previous decision[283] to be unconstitutional conduct on the part of the State. It was contended that the petitioner faced difficulties in establishing that the referendum result had been affected by the unconstitutional conduct that had been found and that, as a matter of fair procedures, the burden of proof should be placed on the respondents, as wrongdoers. However, McDermott J considered that the result of a referendum should not be lightly overturned and held that it was: "appropriate and proportionate, having regard to the rights of voters and the constitutional primacy of the sovereignty of the people that the burden of proof should be placed on the petitioner to demonstrate how the votes of in excess of one million citizens have been "materially affected" and why those votes should be annulled and each vote deprived of its individual power and effect." In a subsequent decision in related proceedings,[284] he expressed the view that the question of whether unconstitutional conduct had "materially affected" the result of the referendum was not a matter which was either within the peculiar knowledge of the defendants or exclusively within their capacity to prove or disprove.[285] He was, further, satisfied that a shifting of the burden of proof was not required by considerations of due process and rejected the proposition that ss.42 and 43 of the Referendum Act 1994 were

---

[279] [1988] ILRM 629 at 635. This passage was referred to by Geoghegan J in *Cosgrove v Ryan* [2008] IESC 2 at [31], [2008] 4 IR 537 at 570, who divined from it the proposition that "the degree of proof required from a plaintiff in a negligence action may, to some extent at least, depend on what fundamental justice should require". In that case, he also held (at [29], 569) that, in a negligence action, "it is not incumbent on a plaintiff to negative every conceivable possibility provided he puts forward reasonable proof".
[280] [2003] 1 IR 268, [2003] 1 ILRM 521. See also *Brennan v Windle* [2003] 3 IR 494, [2003] 2 ILRM 520.
[281] [2003] 1 IR 268 at 275–276, [2003] 1 ILRM 521 at 529.
[282] [2013] IEHC 458 at [63]–[64].
[283] *McCrystal v Minister for Children and Youth Affairs* [2012] IESC 53.
[284] *Jordan v Minister for Children and Youth Affairs* [2014] IEHC 327.
[285] [2014] IEHC 327 at [65].

unconstitutional because they failed to provide for such a shifting of the burden of proof once a constitutional breach was established.

(d) Proof of Causation

2–131   The question of whether the burden of proof should be reversed or at least relaxed in relation to the requirement of causation has been considered in a number of cases. In *Best v Wellcome Foundation Ltd*,[286] the plaintiff had suffered brain damage, allegedly as the result of the administration of a vaccine to him while an infant. It was held by Hamilton P in the High Court that Wellcome had been negligent in releasing a batch of vaccine which exceeded the recommended levels of potency and toxicity but that the plaintiff had failed to prove on the balance of probabilities that his condition was caused by the administration of the vaccine. On appeal to the Supreme Court, it was argued that the finding of negligence on the part of Wellcome was sufficient to place the onus of disproving causation on them. Rejecting this argument, O'Flaherty J discussed two decisions of the House of Lords which were on point. In the first, *McGhee v National Coal Board*,[287] the plaintiff was suffering from dermatitis. The medical condition showed that his working conditions added materially to the risk that he might develop the disease. Thus, a breach of duty was established but the plaintiff was unable to prove causation. It was held by Lord Wilberforce that "where a person has, by breach of duty of care, created a risk, and injury occurs within the area of that risk, the loss should be borne by him unless he shows that it had some other cause."[288] He went on to refer to the evidential difficulty posed by the burden of proof and stated that "as a matter of policy or justice" the creator of the risk should bear the burden on this issue.[289] However, in the later decision of *Wilsher v Essex Area Health Authority*,[290] doubt was cast on the authority of the decision in *McGhee* and it was reasserted that the legal burden was on the plaintiff to prove the causative link between the defendant's negligence and his injury, although that link could legitimately be inferred from the evidence. In *Best*, there were two alternatives open as to the cause of the plaintiff's condition and O'Flaherty J held that, in this situation, the burden of proof in relation to causation remained upon the plaintiff, and the finding of negligence did not affect the discharge of the burden on the question of causation.

2–132   The question as to when the burden of proof in relation to causation might be reversed or relaxed was revisited by the Supreme Court in *Quinn v Mid Western Health Board*.[291] The plaintiff in that case was a minor who had developed severe brain damage while *in utero* and claimed that this would have been avoided if she had been delivered earlier than she had been. The defendants ultimately admitted negligence but claimed that the outcome would not have been any different if the plaintiff had been delivered earlier. Having engaged in a comprehensive review of the relevant UK and Canadian decisions,[292] Kearns J, delivering the judgment of the Court, held that

286   [1993] 3 IR 421.
287   [1972] 3 All ER 1008, [1973] 1 WLR 1.
288   [1972] 3 All ER 1008 at 1012, [1973] 1 WLR 1 at 6.
289   [1972] 3 All ER 1008 at 1012, [1973] 1 WLR 1 at 6.
290   [1988] AC 1074, [1981] 1 All ER 871.
291   [2005] IESC 19, [2005] 4 IR 1.
292   In a decision delivered after the judgment in *Quinn,* the Canadian Supreme Court in *Resurfice Corp v Hanke* [2007] 1 SCR 333 has reaffirmed the primacy of the "but for" test of causation but has recognised that there are special circumstances where a "material contribution" test will be

the ordinary principles whereby the burden of proof was on the plaintiff to establish causation should be applied and there were no special circumstances present which would justify a relaxation of the causation requirements along the lines adopted in *McGhee* and other cases. Indeed, he made it clear that it would only be in quite exceptional cases that it might be appropriate to adopt an approach that would have the effect of reversing the onus of proof, stating that even in those cases, it would require a decision of a full Supreme Court or, perhaps, legislation before a change of that magnitude to the existing law could take place.[293]

2. The Standard of Proof

2–133　In general, the standard of proof applicable in civil cases is proof on a balance of probabilities and a party will discharge the legal burden and succeed on an issue in a civil case if he or she satisfies the tribunal of fact in relation to that issue on a balance of probabilities.[294] This will also be the position if a legislative provision places a burden of proof on a party, whether by use of a presumption or otherwise.[295] However, it is open to the legislature to impose a higher[296] or lower[297] standard of proof and, as confirmed by McKechnie J in *Competition Authority v Licensed Vintners Association*,[298] there is a well recognised exception at common law that the standard of proof applicable to an allegation of contempt of court is the criminal standard of proof beyond a reasonable doubt, which has to be satisfied in respect of all matters of fact and law required to be established in order for the court to find the person to be in contempt.[299]

2–134　The Irish courts have rejected the contention that there are any other categories of civil cases to which a higher standard than that of proof on the balance of probabilities applies. The seminal case is *Banco Ambrosiano SPA v Ansbacher & Co. Ltd*,[300] where

---

applied instead. See further, Collins and McLeod-Kilmurray, "Material Contribution to Justice? Toxic Causation after Resurfice Corp v Hanke" (2010) 48 Osgoode Hall LJ 411.

[293]　[2005] IESC 19 at [50], [2005] 4 IR 1 at 19.

[294]　*Best v Wellcome Foundation Ltd.* [1993] 3 IR 421 at 441; *Clayton v Cashman* [2006] IEHC 360 at [29]–[30]; *The Leopardstown Club Ltd v Templeville Developments Ltd* [2010] IEHC 152 at [7.68].

[295]　See *Shirley v A. O'Gorman & Co. Ltd* [2012] IESC 5 at [83], [2012] 2 IR 170 at 196.

[296]　See *RJ v MR* [1994] 1 IR 271 at 289 (the word "manifestly" used in Art.10(1) of the Luxembourg Convention required a standard of proof that was something more than the probability appropriate for ordinary proof in civil actions but not as high as proof beyond a reasonable doubt, *i.e.* it required a party to establish their case "to a high degree of probability").

[297]　See *Minister for Justice v Rettinger* [2010] IESC 45, [2010] 3 IR 783 (s.37 of the European Arrest Warrant Act 2003 merely requires a respondent resisting his surrender to establish reasonable grounds for believing that a real risk exists that he will be subjected to torture or inhuman or degrading treatment or punishment contrary to Article 3 of the European Convention on Human Rights and proof on the balance of probabilities is not required).

[298]　[2009] IEHC 439, [2010] 1 ILRM 374.

[299]　The decision was followed in *Kelly v National University of Ireland* [2010] IEHC 48 at [8], [2011] 4 IR 478 at [483]. See also *National Irish Bank Ltd v Graham* [1994] 1 IR 215 at 220; *Anglo Irish Bank Corporation Ltd v Quinn Investments Sweden AB* [2012] IEHC 379 at [11]-[12] and *Re Bramblevale Ltd* [1970] Ch 128. In *Competition Authority v Licensed Vintners Association* [2009] IEHC 439 at [26], [2010] 1 ILRM 374 at 386, the imposition of this higher standard was justified by McKechnie J on the basis that civil contempt of court is a misdemeanour and an application seeking a determination that a person was in contempt of court was quasi-criminal in nature with the possibility that substantial penalties including deprivation of liberty could be imposed.

[300]　[1987] ILRM 669. See also *Superwood Holdings Plc v Sun Alliance & London Insurance Plc*,

the Supreme Court rejected the contention that an intermediate standard, between that of the civil and criminal standards, should be applied in relation to allegations of fraud in civil proceedings.[301] Henchy J adverted to the difficulties of expressing such a standard and the risk of confusing juries and took the view that it would introduce an element of uncertainty into the law.[302] In response to the argument that a higher standard should be required because of the moral condemnation and serious consequences which accompanied a finding of fraud, he pointed out that similar condemnation and consequences could follow a finding against a defendant in other civil proceedings which only required proof on a balance of probabilities. He concluded, therefore, that there was no rational reason why fraud in civil cases should require a higher degree of proof than that required for other issues in civil claims.[303] He did, however, accept that the consequences of a finding of fraud should be taken into account in deciding whether it had been established.[304]

2–135 Subsequent decisions have reaffirmed that the standard of proof to be met in all civil cases (except where contempt of court is alleged) is that of proof on the balance of probabilities.[305] However, it is clear that this standard is applied with a degree of flexibility and where serious allegations are made, they will be required to be clearly proved in evidence.[306] In *Georgopoulus v Beaumont Hospital Board*,[307] Hamilton CJ

---

unreported, Supreme Court, 27 June 1995, which approves and applies the decision in *Banco Ambrosiano*.

[301] See McDonnell & John Monroe (eds.), *Kerr on Fraud and Mistake* 7th edn (London, 1986) at p.669 and *Bater v Bater* [1951] P 35 at 37, [1950] 2 All ER 458 at 459, where Denning LJ had stated that a civil court "when considering a charge of fraud will naturally require a higher degree of probability than that which it would require if considering whether negligence were established."

[302] [1987] ILRM 669 at 701.

[303] [1987] ILRM 669 at 701. A similar decision was reached by the English Court of Appeal in *Hornal v Neuberger Products Ltd.* [1956] 3 All ER 970.

[304] [1987] ILRM 669 at 702.

[305] See *UF (Orse) C v JC* [1991] 2 IR 330 at 358; *Masterfoods Ltd v HB Ice Cream Ltd* [1993] ILRM 145 at 183; *PC v CM (Orse C)*, unreported, High Court, 11 January 1996; *SC v PD*, unreported, High Court, 14 March 1996; *Hanafin v Minister for the Environment* [1996] 2 IR 321, [1996] 2 ILRM 61; *B v B* [1997] 1 IR 305 at 321–330; *Mehigan v Duignan* [1997] 1 ILRM 171; *O'Keefe v Ferris* [1993] 1 IR 39; *Chanelle Veterinary Ltd v Pfizer Ltd* [1998] 1 ILRM 161 at 185; *Georgopoulus v Beaumont Hospital Board* [1998] 3 IR 132 at 150; *O'Laoire v Medical Council*, unreported, Supreme Court, 25 July 1997; *Hearns v Collins*, unreported, High Court, 3 February 1998; *Harlequin Property (SVG) Ltd v O'Halloran* [2013] IEHC 362 at [80]. The same conclusion has been reached in the UK (*Re H (Minors)* [1996] AC 563, [1996] 2 WLR 8; *Re B (Children)* [2008] UKHL 35, [2009] AC 11) and Canada (*FH v McDougall* [2008] 3 SCR 41 at [40]).

[306] *Banco Ambrosiano SPA v Ansbacher & Co. Ltd* [1987] ILRM 669 at 701; *Masterfoods Ltd v HB Ice Cream Ltd* [1993] ILRM 145 at 183; *SC v PD*, unreported, High Court, 14 March 1996; *Chanelle Veterinary Ltd v Pfizer Ltd* [1998] 1 ILRM 161 at 185; *Georgopoulus v Beaumont Hospital Board* [1998] 3 IR 132 at 150; *O'Laoire v Medical Council*, unreported, Supreme Court, 25 July 1997; *Hearns v Collins*, unreported, High Court, 3 February 1998; *Fyffes plc v DCC plc* [2005] IEHC 477 at [191], [2009] 2 IR 417 at 504; *O'Brien v Derwin* [2009] IEHC 2 at [4]; *Kelly v University College Dublin* [2009] IEHC 484 at [30], [2009] 4 IR 163 at 174; *The Leopardstown Club Ltd v Templeville Developments Ltd* [2010] IEHC 152 at [7.68]. See also *Lawlor v Tribunal of Inquiry* [2009] IESC 50, [2009] 2 ILRM 400, where the contention that a tribunal of inquiry was required to apply the criminal standard of proof beyond a reasonable doubt when making findings was rejected by the Supreme Court.

[307] [1998] 3 IR 132.

quoted with approval the following passage from the judgment of Lord Scarman in *Redge v Home Secretary, ex parte Khawaja*[308]:

"My Lords, I have come to the conclusion that the choice between the two standards is not one of any great moment. It is largely a matter of words. There is no need to import into this branch of the civil law the formula used for the guidance of juries in criminal cases. The civil standard as interpreted and applied by the civil courts will meet the ends of justice."[309]

2–136 The position is, perhaps, best summarised by O'Flaherty J in *O'Laoire v Medical Council*[310] where, after a survey of the authorities, he stated:

"The common law panorama at this time gives the impression that there is but one standard of proof in civil cases though, of necessity, it is a flexible one. This flexibility will ensure that the graver the allegation the higher will be the degree of probability that is required to bring home the case against the person whose conduct is impugned."[311]

2–137 This passage was approved and applied by McDermott J in relation to a challenge to a referendum result in *Jordan v Minister for Children and Youth Affairs*.[312] He emphasised the significance of setting aside that result and the need for compelling proof of the matters to be proved by the petitioner before the court would do so:

"Thus, the application of the standard of proof in civil proceedings must have regard to the issues in the case and the consequences of a particular finding of fact, with a view to ensuring that an appropriately cogent body of evidence has been established offering clear and convincing proof of the proposition advanced. In this case, the consequence of a finding in favour of the petitioner would be the annulment of what must be regarded, *prima facie*, as the will of the people as expressed in the result set out in the provisional Referendum Certificate. The court is, therefore, obliged to examine the evidence carefully. It must not draw a conclusion adverse to the Referendum result lightly or without cogent and reliable evidence that the result of the Referendum as a whole was materially affected by unconstitutional wrongdoing."

2–138 It is clear from the foregoing that where serious allegations are made in civil proceedings, the courts will apply the standard of proof in a more rigorous and exacting manner and require clear and convincing proof before they find that the allegation has been proved on the balance of probabilities. Thus, bearing in mind that the consequences of a civil case may be as serious as that of a criminal case, the civil standard of proof will, in appropriate cases, be applied with sufficient stringency to ensure that justice is done and that an adverse finding is not made without satisfactory proof. Ultimately, if the standard of proof in civil proceedings is contextualised in this fashion, then it would appear that the proposition that there is a universal standard of proof in civil proceedings is somewhat illusory. However, this approach does have the merit of avoiding the technicalities and anomalies attendant upon the task of expressly delineating categories where an amplified standard of proof is required. Thus, whilst it may be difficult to defend intellectually, it is justifiable in pragmatic terms.

---

[308] [1984] AC 74, [1983] 1 All ER 765.

[309] [1984] AC 74 at 112, [1983] 1 All ER 765 at 783. This passage was also approved by O'Flaherty J in *O'Laoire v Medical Council*, unreported, Supreme Court, 25 July 1997 at 6.

[310] Unreported, Supreme Court, 25 July 1997. It is apparent from this decision and the later decision of Finnegan P in *Law Society of Ireland v Walker* [2006] IEHC 387 at [31], [2007] 3 IR 581 at 601, that professional bodies such as the Medical Council and the Law Society apply the standard of proof beyond a reasonable doubt when determining whether allegations of misconduct have been proven in inquiries held by them but it is very doubtful whether they are required to apply such a standard.

[311] Unreported, Supreme Court, 25 July 1997 at 9.

[312] [2013] IEHC 458.

3. Proof on a Balance of Probabilities

2–139   In *Miller v Minister of Pensions*,[313] Denning J explained, in relation to the standard of proof on a balance of probabilities, that "[i]f the evidence is such that the tribunal can say: 'we think it more probable than not', the burden is discharged, but if the probabilities are equal it is not."[314] Thus, in order to meet the standard of proof and discharge a legal burden upon it in relation to an issue, a party must satisfy the tribunal of fact that its version of events is more probable than that advanced by his or her opponent and if he or she fails to do this, as where the probabilities are equal or the tribunal of fact is not in a position to decide which version of events is more probable, then the party will lose on that issue.[315]

2–140   Difficulties can arise in the application of this standard of proof in circumstances where the court has to choose between different accounts of how particular events occurred which are in themselves improbable. In *Wright v AIB Finance & Leasing*,[316] an issue arose as to whether the engine of a combine harvester had been engaged at the time that an employee of the plaintiffs suffered personal injuries. Evidence was given by those present that the engine had been disengaged but expert engineering evidence was adduced on the part of the third party that the injuries could not have occurred unless the engine was engaged. However, there was medical evidence adduced that the injuries suffered were not consistent with the engine having been engaged at the time. The trial judge found that the engine had been engaged and the Supreme Court refused to interfere with this finding. Although Clarke J acknowledged that there may be circumstances where the evidence concerning how an event occurred or what caused it may be insufficient to allow any legally sustainable conclusion to be reached, so that a case has to be decided on the basis of the burden of proof, he did not consider the case before him to be such a case.[317] Instead, he used as the starting point of his analysis the maxim of Sherlock Holmes that "when you have excluded the impossible, what remains, however improbable, must be the truth."[318] Thus:

> "… an analysis of the relevant circumstances may reveal that there are, as a matter of logic, only a small number of possibilities. An analysis of those possibilities may demonstrate that an explanation which might, in advance, have appeared to be intrinsically improbable has, in fact, become probable or even very probable. It is important in that context to distinguish between how one might have viewed a situation in advance and how one views the same event after the event in the light of the available evidence concerning what might have occurred.
>
> Thus, a proper analysis of the overall situation may lead the Court to conclude that there are, for example, only two possible explanations as to the manner in which an event occurred. Neither of the possibilities might, before the event, have seemed likely to provide an explanation for a possible future event which, itself, might seem unlikely to occur. However, if the event

---

313   [1947] 2 All ER 372.
314   [1947] 2 All ER 372 at 374. This statement was approved in *O'Brien v Derwin* [2009] IEHC 2 at [5].
315   See *Dillon v Lynch (No.1)* (1957) 95 ILTR 185 at 187; *Buckley v Motor Insurers Bureau of Ireland*, unreported, Supreme Court, *ex tempore*, 12 November 1997; *Quinn v Mid Western Health Board*, unreported, High Court, 14 October 2003, [2005] IESC 19, [2005] 4 IR 1; *O'Brien v Derwin* [2009] IEHC 2 at [6]. For a discussion of how a court should evaluate evidence in determining whether the standard of proof on a balance of probabilities has been met, see *Mero-Schmidlin (UK) plc v Michael McNamara and Company* [2011] IEHC 490 at [2].
316   [2013] IESC 55.
317   *Quinn v Mid Western Health Board*, High Court, 14 October 2003, [2005] IESC 19, [2005] 4 IR 1; *"The Popi M" Rhesa Shipping Co SA v Edmunds* [1985] 1 WLR 948.
318   This comment had also featured in the judgment of Lord Brandon in the Court of Appeal in *"The Popi M" Rhesa Shipping Co SA v Edmunds* [1985] 1 WLR 948.

did, in fact, occur then one or other explanation, however unlikely same might have appeared in advance, must be true. In that context one of the possible explanations may appear, on the evidence, to be more probable than the other. Such an approach seems to me to accord with a proper evidence based approach coupled with logic and may lead a court to properly conclude that an event which might, in advance, have seemed unlikely to occur in a particular manner, has, as a matter of probability, actually occurred in that manner."[319]

2–141 In some cases, the courts have adopted the approach that the discharge by a plaintiff of his or her evidential burden by establishing a *prima facie* case in respect of a matter, coupled with the failure of the defendant to give or call evidence in respect of that matter even though it was within the defendant's capacity to do so, will suffice to meet the standard of proof on a balance of probabilities and discharge the plaintiff's legal burden. In *Cosgrove v Ryan*,[320] Geoghegan J acknowledged that a defendant is not required to give evidence but commented that, if a plaintiff has discharged the evidential burden by putting forward a *prima facie* case then, if the defendant fails to answer that case, the plaintiff will usually succeed. This may be because, in accordance with well established principles, the failure to call evidence that the defendant is in a position to and would be expected to call provides circumstantial evidence of the existence of the matters that the defendant has failed to rebut by evidence.[321]

4. Allocation and Discharge of the Evidential Burden

2–142 The general rule in civil cases is that the party that bears the legal burden in respect of an issue will also bear the evidential burden in respect of that issue. The standard which has to be met is to make out a *prima facie* case.[322] A party will have made out a *prima facie* case when, on the evidence given, it would be open to the tribunal of fact, if no other evidence was given, or if it accepted that evidence even though contradicted in its material facts, to enter a verdict for that party.[323] If a plaintiff has failed to discharge the evidential burden upon him or her with regard to the constituent elements of his or her cause of action then, as discussed below, the case will be dismissed.[324] However, a case should only be withdrawn from a jury in circumstances where a jury could not reasonably conclude that it is more likely than not that the plaintiff's version of events is true or correct.[325] It is sometimes suggested that the discharge by a plaintiff of its evidential burden may lead to the evidential burden shifting to the defendant but, as noted by Clarke J in *Koger Inc v O'Donnell*,[326] this simply reflects the common sense proposition that, if a plaintiff has made out a *prima facie* case and the defendant does not adduce any evidence to rebut it, the plaintiff will be found to have discharged its legal burden of proof.

---

[319] [2013] IESC 55 at [7.6]–[7.7].
[320] [2008] IESC 2 at [8], [2008] 4 IR 537 at 557.
[321] See *Walsh v Sligo County Council* [2010] IEHC 437, [2011] 2 IR 260; *Fyffes plc v DCC plc* [2005] IEHC 477 at [199], [2009] 2 IR 417 at 508; *Quinn v Mid Western Health Board* [2005] IESC 19 at [63]–[64], [2005] 4 IR 1 at 24; *Crofter Properties Ltd v Genport Ltd* [2002] 4 IR 73 at 85; *Doran v Cosgrave*, unreported, Supreme Court, 12 November 1999.
[322] *O'Toole v Heavey* [1993] ILRM 343 at 344.
[323] *O'Toole v Heavey* [1993] ILRM 343 at 344–345.
[324] See, *e.g. Ryan v Cullen* [1957] Ir Jur Rep 65.
[325] *Alexander v Anderson* (1932) NI 158 at 171. See also *Flannery v W & L Railway Co.* (1877) IR 11 CL 30 at 36–37; *Dillon v Lynch (No.1)* (1957) 95 ILTR 185 and *Scanlon v Abbey Service Garage* [1965] IR 700 at 707.
[326] [2013] IESC 28 at [6.5].

5. Application to Dismiss the Plaintiff's Case

2–143   If a defendant contends that a plaintiff has failed to discharge the evidential burden on him or her to make out a *prima facie* case, the defendant can apply to dismiss the plaintiff's case after it has concluded. As noted by Clarke J in *Moorview Developments Ltd v First Active plc*,[327] such an application, which is commonly but inaccurately referred to as an application for a non-suit, stems from the inherent jurisdiction of the court to order its procedure for the purposes of preventing injustice so that, if it becomes apparent that the plaintiff cannot succeed, and if there are no countervailing factors which might lead to a different view being taken, then the justice of the case requires that the proceedings be brought to an end. As discussed further below, on such an application, the question for the trial judge is whether, assuming that the trier of fact was prepared to find that all the evidence of the plaintiff was true and taking the plaintiff's case at its highest, the defendant has a case to meet.[328]

2–144   The principles to be applied by a trial judge in dealing with such an application in a contract or tort action were laid down by the Supreme Court in *Hetherington v Ultra Tyre Service Ltd*[329] and *O'Toole v Heavey*.[330] In the latter case, Finlay CJ differentiated between actions that were tried with a jury and those that were tried by a judge sitting alone. In the case of the former, the judge is required to consider whether the plaintiff had made out a *prima facie* case, *i.e.* whether, on the evidence adduced by the plaintiff, it would be open to a jury, if no other evidence was given, or if they accepted that evidence, even though contradicted in its material facts, to enter a verdict for the plaintiff. [331]

2–145   The situation in relation to an action tried without a jury is somewhat more complex. If an action is brought against one defendant and an application to dismiss the proceedings is brought, the trial judge should, first, inquire from the defendant as to whether in the event of a refusal of that application, it intends to go into evidence. If the defendant indicates that it does intend to go into evidence if the application is refused,[332] then the trial judge has to decide whether the plaintiff has made out a *prima facie* case.[333] If, on the other hand, the defendant indicates that it does not intend to go

---

[327] [2010] IEHC 34 at [8]–[11].

[328] *O'Donovan v Southern Health Board* [2001] 3 IR 385 at 387.

[329] [1993] 2 IR 535, [1993] ILRM 353.

[330] [1993] 2 IR 544, [1993] ILRM 343. The principles laid down in these decisions have been applied in a number of cases including *Bank of Ireland v McCabe*, High Court, 25 March 1993; *Hanafin v Minister for the Environment* [1996] 2 IR 321, [1996] 2 ILRM 61; *Chanelle Veterinary Ltd v Pfizer (Ireland) Ltd* [1999] 1 IR 365, [1998] 1 ILRM 161 (HC); *Cranny v Kelly* [1998] 1 IR 54; *Gill v Egan* [1998] IEHC 152; *Sutton v Wise Finance Company Ltd* [2008] IEHC 364; *The Leopardstown Club Ltd v Templeville Developments Ltd* [2010] IEHC 152 at [7.1]–[7.3].

[331] See also *Alexander v Anderson* (1932) NI 158 at 171; *Flannery v W & L Railway Co.* (1877) IR 11 CL 30 at 36–37; *Dillon v Lynch (No.1)* (1957) 95 ILTR 185 and *Scanlon v Abbey Service Garage* [1965] IR 700 at 707.

[332] As noted by Hardiman J in *Bradley v Independent Star Newspapers* [2011] IESC 17 at [33], [2011] 3 IR 96 at 109, [2012] 2 ILRM 26 at 36, a defendant faces what may be a difficult tactical call in deciding whether to go into evidence because, where a plaintiff's case is weak in some respects, there is a risk that the evidence called by the defendant may improve the plaintiff's case. This indeed is what occurred in *O'Neill v Dunnes Stores* [2010] IESC 53, [2011] 1 ILRM 461 (discussed below) where there was very little evidence to sustain a finding a favour of the plaintiff at the close of his case and most of the evidence that was helpful to the plaintiff was elicited during the cross-examination of the defendant's witnesses.

[333] In *Hetherington v Ultra Tyre Service Ltd* [1993] 2 IR 535 at 541, [1993] ILRM 353 at 358,

into evidence on the issue of liability if the application is refused,[334] then the trial judge is required to determine whether, having regard to his or her view of the evidence of the plaintiff, the plaintiff has established as a matter of probability the facts necessary to support a verdict in his or her favour.[335] If the trial judge is not so satisfied, then the judge must dismiss the action. However, if the judge is so satisfied, he or she must give judgment for the plaintiff.

2–146 The Chief Justice went on to consider the situation where more than one defendant is sued. He stated that, where claims or cross-claims for contribution have been made between the defendants on the basis that they are joint tortfeasors, the trial judge should not decide on an application for a non-suit at the conclusion of the plaintiff's evidence unless he is completely satisfied that the eventual outcome of the case could not result in the patently unjust anomaly that a plaintiff having sued more than one defendant and one of the defendants having been dismissed out of the action at the conclusion of the plaintiff's evidence, the other defendant or defendants could also escape liability by affixing the blame through their evidence on the defendant already dismissed.[336] He took the view that the only way in most cases that a trial judge would be in a position to satisfy himself that such a risk did not exist would be by ascertaining what the intention of all of the defendants was in relation to the calling of evidence and the precise nature of the case which each of them would be making in the event of giving such evidence. However, he did enter the caveat that, where a plaintiff did not make out any form of plausible or arguable case against any of the defendants, the trial judge had a discretion to dismiss the action in its entirety.

2–147 In *Cranny v Kelly*,[337] an appeal was allowed by the Supreme Court because of a departure from those principles. The plaintiff's claim arose out of the death of her husband in a road traffic accident involving a car in which he and the first-named defendant were travelling. The plaintiff contended that the accident had been caused by the negligence of the first-named defendant driving the car. However, while she was able to adduce evidence to show that the car had been driven negligently, none of the witnesses could say who was driving it. At the conclusion of the evidence for the plaintiff, the first-named defendant applied for a non-suit on the basis that the evidence had not established the identity of the driver. The trial judge put the first-named defendant to his election as to whether he intended to call evidence and he was informed by counsel that the first-named defendant would not be calling evidence. Notwithstanding this, the trial judge refused the application on the basis that the first-named defendant had a case to answer and invited him to change his mind and give evidence. The first-named defendant then gave evidence to the effect that the

---

Finlay CJ stated that, where a defendant indicated that he would be going into evidence if the application for a non-suit failed, a judge might properly defer his decision as to whether a case had been made out by the plaintiff until he had heard all the evidence. Subsequently, in *Hanafin v Minister for the Environment* [1996] 2 IR 321 at 420, [1996] 2 ILRM 61 at 179, Hamilton CJ clarified that a trial judge has a discretion in this regard and is not required to adopt this course and defer a decision on the application.

[334] Note that, if the defendant indicates that he intends to go into evidence on the issue of damages but not of liability, the same position obtains (see *O'Toole v Heavey* [1993] 2 IR 544 at 547, [1993] ILRM 343 at 345).

[335] For an example of where this test was applied and it was held that the plaintiff was entitled to succeed, see *The Leopardstown Club Ltd v Templeville Developments Ltd* [2010] IEHC 152.

[336] See *Doran v Cosgrave* [1999] IESC 74 where this approach was applied.

[337] [1998] 1 IR 54.

plaintiff's husband had been driving the car. Although the trial judge rejected much of the evidence given by the first-named defendant, he ultimately held that he was not satisfied that the first-named defendant had been driving the car on the day in question.

2–148   Murphy J, delivering the judgment of the Supreme Court, was satisfied that, in ruling on the application for a non-suit, the trial judge had departed from the principles laid down in *Hetherington* and *O'Toole* in that, having been informed that the first-named defendant did not intend to go into evidence, he did not dismiss the action or give judgment for the plaintiff. While he acknowledged that it would be desirable to avoid the expense and delay of a further trial, he concluded that this was unavoidable and the case was remitted to the High Court for a re-trial.

2–149   A departure from the principles laid down in *O'Toole* also led to a successful appeal in *O'Donovan v Southern Health Board*.[338] An application for a non-suit was made at the end of the plaintiff's case whereupon the trial judge made the required inquiry as to whether, in the event that the application was unsuccessful, the defendant would be going into evidence. Counsel for the defendant indicated that he would be and the trial judge ruled that there was a case to meet. However, the trial judge also stated, in the course of dealing with the application, that, if he were dealing with the case on the basis that no evidence would be offered by the defendant, he would find in its favour as he was satisfied, at that stage, on the balance of probabilities, that the plaintiff was not entitled to succeed. The defendant then went into evidence and, having heard all the evidence, the trial judge dismissed the plaintiff's claim. On appeal, the approach taken by the trial judge was criticised by Keane CJ who stated:

> "Where, as was the situation in this case, the trial judge was of the view that there was, to use the convenient though not altogether accurate, shorthand of a case to meet, then that was all that was required to or indeed should have been said. To give an express and indeed, unequivocal indication as he did in this case that he had already come to the conclusion that the plaintiff on the balance of probabilities had not made out a case, could only be an indication to the defendant that if it called any evidence, other than the absolute minimum of evidence, if it did anything further, then that could only mean that the prospects of it winning the case were, if anything diminished. That would mean, that evidence which it might have called, would not be before the court."[339]

2–150   He, thus, concluded that the comments of the trial judge were not conducive to the satisfactory conduct of the trial and the appeal was allowed.[340]

2–151   Some elaborations on the principles to be applied to an application for a non-suit emerge from the judgment of Clarke J in *Moorview Developments Ltd v First Active plc*.[341] In that case, an issue arose as to the extent to which the court was entitled or obliged to scrutinise expert evidence when dealing with the application for a non-suit. Having considered the decision of the Supreme Court in *Hanafin v Minister for the Environment*,[342] Clarke J said that he was satisfied that it was authority:

> "[T]hat a court can, on a non-suit application, subject, in particular expert evidence, to some degree of scrutiny to ascertain whether there is a reasonable basis for the expert opinion

---

[338] [2001] 3 IR 385.

[339] [2001] 3 IR 385 at 388.

[340] See also *Devlin v National Maternity Hospital* [2007] IESC 50, [2008] 2 IR 222, [2008] 1 ILRM 401 where it was held that the trial judge had correctly applied the principles in *O'Donovan* and an appeal against his decision to grant a non-suit was dismissed.

[341] [2009] IEHC 214.

[342] [1996] 2 IR 321, [1996] 2 ILRM 61.

tendered. The court is not bound to accept the expert view if, when subjected to such scrutiny, the expert view does not stand up even on a *prima facie* basis. It seems to me that the reasoning behind such an approach is clear. The overall test derives from the role of a judge in respect of a trial where facts are to be determined by a jury. The case is not permitted to go to the jury (and will be dismissed by direction) where the evidence is not such as would permit a jury properly directed to reasonably find for the plaintiff. Where expert evidence does not stand up, even on a *prima facie* basis, to scrutiny then it follows that it would have been unsafe to allow a case dependent on such expert evidence to go to a jury, and it equally follows that in a case being tried without a jury a non-suit should be allowed."[343]

2–152   Clarke J went on to make it clear that the question was not whether the court accepted the evidence of the expert concerned but rather, whether in the light of the scrutiny to which the expert evidence is subjected, the evidence remains such as could reasonably be relied on by a jury for the proposition which it is sought to support, so that the plaintiff could be said to have discharged the onus of proof on that issue.

2–153   In its submissions on the non-suit application, the first defendant pointed to a number of matters which it contended gave rise to the inference that the evidence of the principal witness for the plaintiffs lacked credibility and submitted that the evidence of the plaintiffs should be treated with a certain degree of scepticism. However, Clarke J rejected this contention, stating that, at the stage of an application for a non-suit, it was not appropriate to form any generalised view as to the credibility of the plaintiffs' evidence. Instead, the proper approach was to accept this evidence, at its highest, save where, for specific reasons, he did not consider the evidence to be adequate or credible. In that regard, he held[344] that:

> "Where, as a result of internal contradiction, inability to offer an explanation as to the inconsistency of evidence with other facts, or the like, a witness' account, although maintained under cross examination, lacks any real credibility, then it is open to a trial judge on a non-suit application to disregard that evidence for the purposes of assessing whether there is sufficient evidence to discharge the onus of proof at a non-suit stage."[345]

2–154   He went on to reject the suggestion that the application for a non-suit should be refused so that the plaintiffs had an opportunity to cross-examine the defendants' witnesses, stating that, if a plaintiff does not meet the standard of a *prima facie* case, it is inappropriate to require the defendant concerned to go into evidence.

2–155   Clarke J next turned to the complications that arose from the fact that the first defendant had reserved its entitlement to go into evidence in the event that the application for a non-suit was unsuccessful whereas the second defendant indicated that he did not intend to go into evidence. He referred to the decision in *Hetherington v Ultra Tyre Service Ltd*[346] where Finlay CJ had held that, if a co-defendant who was not applying for a non-suit indicated that it intended to present a case against the defendant seeking a non-suit, justice required that all the evidence should be heard before a final determination of the case. He took the view that this was but one example, albeit the most common example, of "a more general principle to the effect that the court should exercise some care in considering an application for a non-suit in multi party litigation, to ensure that no risk of injustice or embarrassment might arise by determining facts as

---

[343] [2009] IEHC 214 at [5.13].
[344] Approving the principles laid down by the English Court of Appeal in *Bentley v Jones Harris & Co.* [2001] EWCA Civ 1724.
[345] [2009] IEHC 214 at [5.17].
[346] [1993] 2 IR 535, [1993] ILRM 353.

a result of a non-suit application at the close of the plaintiff's case".[347] Another example, which arose in the case before him, was where each defendant sought a non-suit but where the basis of the respective applications differed. He observed that it would give rise to a risk of injustice or embarrassment, at least in some cases, if a court was required, at the same time, to form a judgment on a question of fact on two different bases. In particular, the court might decide that the plaintiff's evidence established a *prima facie* case and, thus, allow the case to continue against that defendant but decide that, on the balance of probabilities, the relevant facts were not established and thus allow a second defendant who had elected not to go into evidence to obtain a dismiss. Therefore, he cautioned that a court had to exercise care to ensure that it would not be potentially embarrassed by being required to assess the same facts by reference to two different standards. However, that difficulty ultimately did not arise in the case before him.

2–156 The complexities attendant upon non-suit applications in cases with multiple defendants were also evident in the somewhat unusual case of *Schuit v Mylotte*.[348] This was a medical negligence action against a number of medical practitioners and a health board. At the close of the plaintiff's case, an application for a non-suit was made on behalf of the second defendant. A separate application was made on behalf of the third and fourth defendants. Each of the defendants indicated that, if the application was unsuccessful, they intended to go into evidence. In addition, counsel for the first and second defendants indicated that he was resisting the application by the third and fourth defendants on the basis that the experts to be called by him would corroborate that given by the plaintiff's experts. The trial judge refused the application and the first defendant gave evidence. After his evidence had concluded, but before any expert evidence was called on his behalf, the third and fourth defendants renewed their application for a dismissal of the case against them and counsel for the first defendant now indicated that he was no longer making any case against them. The trial judge acceded to the application and dismissed the plaintiff's case against the second, third and fourth defendants. The case continued against the first defendant and the trial judge ultimately delivered a judgment dismissing the case against him. The plaintiff appealed against the dismissal of the claim against the third and fourth defendants.

2–157 In this judgment, O'Donnell J identified some of the tactical considerations that arise in cases with multiple defendants which meant that the application for a non-suit can be a critical point in the development of a case. He expressed support for the view articulated by McCarthy J in *Hetherington v Ultra Tyre Service Ltd*[349] that the appropriate course in a complex case such as that before him when it had been indicated that the defendants intended to go into evidence was to adjourn the application until all the evidence was heard. He also endorsed the practice often adopted on non-suit applications (but not by the trial judge in the instant case) that, if the court is disposed to grant the application, it gives its reasons for doing so but, if it decides to reject the application, it does not do so because it may distort the trial and the prospect of compromise if the court gives its views on the state of the case. In relation to the standard of review to be exercised by the Supreme Court, he rejected the proposition that the principles laid down in *Hay v O'Grady*[350] were applicable on

---

[347] [2009] IEHC 214 at [5.21].
[348] [2010] IESC 56.
[349] [1993] 2 IR 535, [1993] ILRM 353.
[350] [1992] 1 IR 210.

the basis that the question for an appeal court was one of logic: "is there evidence, whatever its relative cogency or strength, upon which a Court *could* conclude that a defendant was liable".[351] Applying that test, he was satisfied that the trial judge had erred in acceding to the application to dismiss as against the third and fourth defendants and he allowed the appeal.

2–158   It should be noted that, where an unsuccessful application for a non-suit is made by a defendant who thereafter goes into evidence, the Supreme Court, when considering an appeal against the refusal of that application is not confined to assessing the evidence as it stood at the end of the plaintiff's case. In *O'Neill v Dunnes Stores*,[352] O'Donnell J took the view that it would be a denial of justice if the court made its assessment on only that part of the evidence as it stood at the close of the plaintiff's case. Fennelly J concurred on this point, stating that "as a matter of justice, the court must look at the entirety of the evidence".[353] He took the view that the alternative of not considering the evidence called on behalf of the defendant would be patently unjust because, if the defendant had been shown to be negligent, it was no injustice that he should have to compensate the defendant merely because he has suffered a procedural disadvantage.

D. Presumptions

1. Introduction

2–159   A satisfactory categorisation of the wide array of presumptions that exist at common law or have been created by statute is difficult[354] but it is suggested that they can be divided into the following categories: (i) mandatory presumptions; (ii) permissive presumptions; and (iii) bare presumptions.[355] Mandatory presumptions are presumptions that require the tribunal of fact, upon proof of one fact, known as the basic fact, to infer the existence of another fact, known as the presumed fact. Permissive presumptions are similar in structure except that they entitle rather than require the tribunal of fact to infer the existence of the presumed fact upon proof of the basic fact. Finally, bare presumptions are simply statements as to the allocation of the burden of proof and require a conclusion to be drawn unless and until the contrary is proved.

2. Mandatory Presumptions

2–160   As stated above, mandatory presumptions require the tribunal of fact, upon proof of the basic fact, to infer the existence of the presumed fact. They are often

---

[351] [2010] IESC 56 at [41].
[352] [2010] IESC 53, [2011] 1 ILRM 461.
[353] [2011] 1 ILRM 461 at 474.
[354] See, generally, Morgan, "Presumptions" (1937) 12 Wash L Rev 255. Traditionally, at common law, presumptions have been classified into four categories: (i) irrebuttable presumptions of law (*praesumptiones iuris et de iure*); (ii) rebuttable presumptions of law (*praesumptiones iuris sed non de iure*); (iii) presumptions of fact (*praesumptiones hominis*); (iv) presumptions without basic facts. Although this classification is deeply embedded in both the case law and literature, it is not utilised here because it has little explanatory power. Further, it is inappropriate in an Irish context because, as noted below, all presumptions are required to be rebuttable.
[355] *Cf.* the explanation of the role and operation of presumptions given by McKechnie J in *Sweeney v Fahy* [2014] IESC 50 at [37]–[50].

used as a mechanism to make it easier for a party to discharge his or her burden of proof. Thus, instead of having to prove a fact which may be difficult to prove, such as the existence of a specific intention, a party can prove another fact, which is easier to prove, and the tribunal of fact is required to infer the existence of the first fact. A good example is provided by s.15 of the Misuse of Drugs Act 1977.[356] Section 15(1) makes it an offence for a person to have in his or her possession a controlled drug for the purpose of selling or otherwise supplying it to another contrary to regulations made under the Act. In circumstances where a person is found to be in possession of a controlled drug, it could be very difficult for the prosecution to prove beyond a reasonable doubt that he or she had the requisite intention of selling or otherwise supplying it to another. Thus, subs.(2) makes it easier for the prosecution to discharge its onus of proof in that regard by providing that:

> "where it is proved that a person was in possession of a controlled drug and the court, having regard to the quantity of the controlled drug which the person possessed or to such other matter as the court considers relevant, is satisfied that it is reasonable to assume that the controlled drug was not intended for the immediate personal use of the person, he shall be presumed, until the court is satisfied to the contrary, to have been in possession of the controlled drug for the purpose of selling or otherwise supplying it to another..."

2–161 Accordingly, it is not necessary for the prosecution to prove that the accused had an intention to sell or supply, it suffices to prove that he or she was in possession of such a quantity of the controlled drug that it is reasonable to assume that it was not intended for immediate personal use, in which case, the accused is presumed to have had the requisite intention.

2–162 All mandatory presumptions are rebuttable[357] and the quantum of evidence required to rebut the presumption gives rise to two discrete sub-categories of mandatory presumptions: (a) mandatory legal presumptions; and (b) mandatory evidential presumptions. It should be noted that, where the party against whom the presumption operates succeeds in rebutting the presumption, this has the effect of cancelling it out such that it is as if the presumption had never applied at all. In those circumstances, the party who relied on the presumption bears the normal onus of proving the existence of the presumed fact.

(a) Mandatory legal presumptions

2–163 In the case of a mandatory legal presumption, once a party proves the basic fact, the tribunal of fact is required to infer the existence of the presumed fact unless the opposing party disproves the existence of the presumed fact, *i.e.* it places a legal burden of proof on the opposing party to disprove the existence of the presumed fact. Where a mandatory legal presumption applies, it can be said that the burden of proof has shifted from one party to another in respect of the presumed fact.

2–164 Examples at common law of such presumptions include: (i) the presumption

---

[356] No.12 of 1977.

[357] An irrebuttable or conclusive presumption is regarded as an impermissible infringement of the exercise of the judicial power contrary to Art.34.1 of the Constitution (*Maher v AG* [1973] IR 140; *State (McEldowney) v Kelleher* [1983] IR 289; *Sweeney v Fahy* [2014] IESC 50 (para.[47] of the judgment of McKechnie J). *Cf. MR v An tArd Chláraitheoir* [2013] IEHC 91, [2013] 1 ILRM 449 where Abbott J held that the irrebutable presumption of *mater semper certa est* was inconsistent with the provisions of s.35 of the Status of Children Act 1987.

of legitimacy whereby, on proof or admission of the basic fact that a child was born or conceived during the subsistence of a valid marriage, that child is presumed to be legitimate in the absence of proof to the contrary[358]; and (ii) the presumption of death whereby, if a person has been missing for a period of seven years, and persons who would be expected to have heard from him or her have not done so and all reasonable inquires have been made, then he or she is presumed to be dead.[359] There is generally little scope for the application of these or other common law mandatory presumptions in criminal cases but, if one was relied on by the prosecution, it is highly likely that it would be regarded as a mandatory evidential presumption, *i.e.* as placing an evidential burden only on the accused.

2–165 There are numerous statutory provisions applicable in criminal proceedings containing presumptions whereby certain facts are presumed until the contrary is "shown", "proved" or "established" by the accused.[360] At first glance, these provisions would appear to create mandatory legal presumptions but it appears, on the basis of the decisions in *O'Leary v AG*[361] and *Hardy v Ireland*,[362] that such provisions will generally be interpreted as placing an evidential burden only on an accused given the potential constitutional difficulties of placing a legal burden on him or her. If such a rule of construction is adopted, then there will be very few instances of mandatory legal presumptions applicable in criminal proceedings.

(b) Mandatory evidential presumptions

2–166 In the case of a mandatory evidential presumption, it suffices to defeat the operation of the presumption if the party against whom the presumption operates adduces evidence as to the non-existence of the presumed fact, *i.e.* it merely places an evidential burden on the opposing party to adduce some evidence that the presumed fact does not exist.[363] As explained by McKechnie J in *Sweeney v Fahy*[364]:

> "[O]nce the basic fact(s) is established, the onus shifts to the opposing party to negative the existence of the presumed fact(s), proposition(s) or state of affairs; one can do so by producing evidence as to their non-existence. If successful to that end, the result, quite obviously, is that the presumption does not apply and in such circumstances, the party in whose favour the presumption existed, must establish the presumed facts in the normal way."

2–167 Examples of such presumptions include the presumption that a public or official act is presumed to have been regularly and properly performed (*omnia preaesumuntur rite esse acta*),[365] and the presumption contained in s.4(2) of the Criminal

---

[358] See *In re Anderson*, unreported, High Court, 6 July 1995; *Smyth v Smyth* [1948] NI 181 at 183–184.

[359] See *Ford v Weir* (1899) 33 ILTR 30; *In the Goods of Freytag* (1909) 43 ILTR 116; *Allman & Co. v McCabe* [1911] 2 IR 398 at 402; *Cassidy v AG* [1940] Ir Jur Rep 8; *In re the Goods of Doherty* [1961] IR 219 at 221. See generally, Trietel, "The Presumption of Death" (1954) 17 MLR 530 and Stone, "The Presumption of Death: A Redundant Concept?" (1981) 44 MLR 516.

[360] See, *e.g.* s.55(2) of Extradition Act 196 and ss.19(4) and 21 of the Road Traffic Act 1994.

[361] [1995] 1 IR 254, [1995] 2 ILRM 259.

[362] [1994] 2 IR 550.

[363] This passage in the first edition was quoted with approval by White J in *DPP v Tully* [2009] IECCA 1.

[364] [2014] IESC 50 at [46].

[365] With regard to its application in civil cases, see *Rolleston v Sinclair* [1924] 2 IR 157 at 162; *British Wagon Credit Co. v Henebry* (1963) 97 ILTR 123 at 125; *Clarke v Early* [1980] IR 223 at 226. See also *People (DPP) v Farrell* [1978] IR 13 at 25–26; *People (DPP) v Byrne* [1987]

Justice Act 1964[366] that a person charged with murder is presumed to have intended the natural and probable consequences of his conduct.[367] Indeed, as outlined above, it seems that most if not all statutory presumptions applicable in criminal proceedings will be construed as mandatory evidential presumptions.

3. Permissive Presumptions

2–168   As noted above, permissive presumptions differ from mandatory presumptions in that they entitle rather than compel the tribunal of fact to infer the existence of the presumed fact upon proof of the basic fact. Thus, it is open to the tribunal of fact to employ the presumption to find the presumed fact to be proved but it is not obliged to. Notwithstanding their non-binding effect, permissive presumptions are important in that they can defeat a submission of no case to answer on the basis that the presumed fact has not been proved.

2–169   Examples of such presumptions include the presumption of continuance of life,[368] the presumption of seaworthiness[369] and *omnia praesumunter contra spoliatorem* ("everything is presumed against a wrongdoer").[370] Many permissive presumptions are really formalised examples of circumstantial evidence whereby, applying logic, experience, and common sense, it is reasonable to infer the existence of the presumed fact from proof of the existence of the basic fact. As such, whether the presumption will be applied and the strength of the inference that will be drawn is dependent on the nature and extent of the proof of the basic fact. As Lush J explained in *R. v Lumley*[371] in relation to the presumption of continuance of life:

> "This is purely a question of fact. The existence of a party at an antecedent date may, or may not, afford a reasonable inference that he is living at the subsequent date. If, for example, it was proved that he was in good health on the day preceding the marriage, the inference

---

IR 363 at 371, [1989] ILRM 613 at 618–619; *Minister for Agriculture v Cleary* [1988] ILRM 294 at 297, which indicate that it has a somewhat limited application in criminal cases.

[366] No.5 of 1964.

[367] See *People (AG) v Dwyer* [1972] IR 416; *People (DPP) v Murray* [1977] IR 360; *People (DPP) v Cotter,* unreported, Court of Criminal Appeal, 28 June 1999; *People (DPP) v McDonagh* [2001] 3 IR 201, [2002] 1 ILRM 225. It was held in *Dwyer* and confirmed in *Murray* that the subsection places an evidential rather than a legal presumption on an accused and that the onus of proving beyond a reasonable doubt that the presumption has not been rebutted rests on the prosecution. In *Cotter,* the Court of Criminal Appeal acknowledged the difficulties in charging a jury as to the effect of the presumption and suggested a model direction for the guidance of trial judges. See generally, O'Higgins and O'Braonáin, "Section 4 of the Criminal Justice Act 1964: a redundant presumption?" (1991) 1 ICLJ 113 and "Section 4 of the Criminal Justice Act: a constitutional presumption?" (1992) 2 ICLJ 179.

[368] This presumption provides that where a person is proved to have been alive on a particular date, an inference may be drawn that he or she was alive at a later date. See *R. v Lumley* (1869) LR 1 CCR 196; *McDarmaid v AG* [1950] P 218, [1950] 1 All ER 497; *Chard v Chard* [1956] P 259, [1955] 3 All ER 721.

[369] This presumption provides that where a ship sinks or becomes unable to continue its voyage shortly after leaving port, an inference may be drawn that the ship was unseaworthy at the time it left port. See *Pickup v Thames & Mersey Marine Insurance Co. Ltd* (1878) 3 QBD 594 at 597; *Ajum Goolam Hossen & Co. v Union Marine Insurance Co.* [1901] AC 362 at 366.

[370] See *O'Mahony v Bon Secours Hospital,* unreported, Supreme Court, 13 July 2001; *Williamson v Rover Cycle Co.* [1901] 2 IR 615; *Armory v Delamirie* (1722) 1 Stra. 504; *Seager v Copydex Ltd* [1969] 2 All ER 718; *Indian Oil Corporation Ltd v Greenstone Shipping SA* [1988] 1 QB 345, [1987] 3 WLR 869.

[371] (1865–67) L.R. 1 C.C.R. 196.

would be strong, almost irresistible, that he was living on the latter day, and the jury would in all probability find that he was so. If, on the other hand, it were proved that he was then in a dying condition, and nothing further was proved, they would probably decline to draw that inference. Thus, the question is entirely for the jury."[372]

4. Bare Presumptions

2–170 Bare presumptions are not regarded as true presumptions because they do not involve the proof of basic or presumed facts but, instead, dictate conclusions that must be reached in the absence of evidence to the contrary. As such, they are really shorthand expressions for rules of substantive law as to the allocation of the burden of proof in relation to particular issues. Examples of this category of presumptions include: (i) the presumption of innocence,[373] (ii) the presumption of constitutionality,[374] (iii) the presumption of sanity;[375] and (iv) the presumption of testamentary capacity.[376]

---

[372] (1865–67) L.R. 1 C.C.R. 196 at 198.
[373] See *O'Leary v AG* [1993] 1 IR 102 at 107, [1991] ILRM 454 at 458–459 (HC), [1995] 1 IR 254 at 259, [1995] 2 ILRM 259 at 267 (SC); *People (DPP) v D.O'T.* [2003] 4 IR 286 at 290.
[374] See *Pigs Marketing Board v Donnelly* [1939] IR 413; *McDonald v Bord na gCon* [1965] IR 217; *East Donegal Co-Operative Ltd v AG* [1970] IR 317; *Maguire v Ardagh* [2002] 1 IR 385.
[375] See *Attorney General v O'Brien* [1936] IR 263; *Attorney General v Boylan* [1937] IR 449.
[376] See *Scally v Rhatigan* [2010] IEHC 475 at [4.3]; *In re Key, deceased* [2010] 1 WLR 2020 at [97].

CHAPTER 3

ORAL EVIDENCE

A. Introduction

3–01 Under our adversarial model of criminal and civil justice, the primary means by which parties prove their cases is by oral evidence given by witnesses in court.[1] This principle of orality is regarded as a fundamental characteristic of that model, with Murphy J in *Phonographic Performance Ltd v Cody*[2] emphasising that "the examination of witnesses *viva voce* and in open court is of central importance in our system of justice and … it is a rule not to be departed from lightly".[3] This chapter examines the rules and principles governing oral evidence and, in particular, details the rules with regard to the competence and compellability of witnesses, the calling and tendering of evidence, the examination-in-chief, cross-examination and re-examination of witnesses and some related principles. Also considered are the circumstances where, in a departure from the principle of orality, witnesses can give evidence otherwise than *viva voce* in open court.

B. Competence and Compellability

1. Introduction

3–02 The rules in relation to the competence and compellability of witnesses dictate when a witness will be permitted to give evidence and when he or she can be compelled to give evidence. A witness is said to be competent if he or she may be called to give evidence and compellable if, being competent, he or she may be compelled by the court to give evidence. It follows that compellability is predicated upon competence and a witness cannot be compelled if he or she is not competent.

---

[1]   See *The Employment Equality Bill 1996* [1997] 2 IR 321 at 379, where Hamilton CJ observed: "Historically trials, whether in summary form or on indictment, have proceeded *viva voce* although documentary evidence and inferences therefrom may be part and parcel of the trial."

[2]   [1998] 4 IR 504 at 521, [1998] 2 ILRM 21 at 26.

[3]   See also *per* Ó Dálaigh CJ in *Re Haughey* [1971] IR 217 at 261 ("In a criminal trial, evidence may be given orally; a statute may authorise otherwise…"); and *per* Hamilton CJ in *The Employment Equality Bill 1996* [1997] 2 IR 321 at 379 ("It is a fundamental principle in our system that, in general, criminal trials are conducted on *viva voce* evidence.").

3–03   At common law, the competence and compellability of witnesses is governed by two rules. The first is that all persons capable of understanding the nature of the oath, and capable of giving intelligible testimony, are competent witnesses.[4] The second is that all competent witnesses are compellable.[5] These rules, and the exceptions thereto, will be examined further below in relation to various categories of witness. However, it is first necessary to examine the concept of an oath and capacity to give intelligible testimony.

2. Evidence on Oath

3–04   The general rule in both civil and criminal proceedings is that oral evidence must be given on oath or affirmation. The importance of this requirement was emphasised in *Mapp v Gilhooley*[6] where Finlay CJ stated:

> "It is a fundamental principle of the common law that for the purpose of trials in either criminal or civil cases *viva voce* evidence must be given on oath or affirmation."[7]

3–05   The learned Chief Justice explained that the "broad purpose of the rule is to ensure as far as possible that such *viva voce* evidence shall be true by the provision of a moral or religious and legal sanction against deliberate untruth".[8] He, thus, rejected the contention that this requirement was inconsistent with the provisions of the Constitution either on the basis of being discriminatory or on the basis of being an impermissible restriction on the right of access to the courts. It followed from the fundamental nature of this requirement that, unless provided for by statutory exception, the consequence of acting upon *viva voce* evidence that is not given on oath or affirmation would be a mistrial.[9]

3–06   Initially, at common law, a witness could only be sworn if he or she believed in God and divine retribution if he or she lied on oath. However, that requirement was subsequently diluted so that belief in a Supreme Being, and of adverse temporal or spiritual consequences if the person lied on oath, sufficed.[10] The giving of evidence on oath or affirmation is now governed by the Oaths Acts 1888 and 1909.[11] A Christian

---

[4]   As it was put by Denham J in *People (DPP) v Gilligan* [2005] IESC 78 at [145], [2006] 1 IR 107 at 161 (paraphrasing Walsh J in *People (DPP) v JT* (1988) 3 Frewen 141 at 160): "The administration of justice requires that the public has a right to every man's evidence except for that evidence which is excluded by law or by the Constitution."

[5]   *Ex parte Fernandez* (1861) 10 CBN S 3; *Hoskyn v Metropolitan Police Commissioner* [1979] AC 474 at 484, [1978] 2 All ER 136 at 138; *Tribune Newspaper Co. v Fort Frances Pulp & Paper Co.* (1932) 40 Man R 401, [1932] 4 DLR 179.

[6]   [1991] 2 IR 253, [1991] ILRM 695.

[7]   [1991] 2 IR 253 at 262, [1991] ILRM 695 at 700.

[8]   [1991] 2 IR 253 at 262, [1991] ILRM 695 at 700.

[9]   He held that an appellant seeking to rely on the admission of unsworn *viva voce* evidence as constituting a mistrial could only be prevented from so doing: (a) by estoppel arising from an express or unambiguously implied representation that he was waiving his right to challenge the admission of such evidence by reason of the absence of an oath or affirmation, on which the opposing party has acted to his detriment in a manner which would make the finding of a mistrial an injustice; or (b) by reason of a finding that for the party concerned to challenge the validity of the trial on appeal on this ground of want of oath or affirmation would constitute a virtual fraud or abuse of the processes of the court.

[10]   See *Omychund v Barker* (1745) 1 Atk 21; *R. v Brasier* (1779) 1 Leach 199; *Attorney General v Bradlaugh* (1885) 14 QBD 667.

[11]   In its *Report on Oaths and Affirmations* (LRC 34–1990) at p.44, the Law Reform Commission recommended that the oath should be abolished for witnesses who should, instead, be required

takes the oath on the New Testament whereas a person of the Jewish faith takes it on the Old Testament.[12] In the case of a person who is neither a Christian nor Jewish, the oath can be administered in any manner that is lawful.[13] In *R. v Kemble*,[14] it was held that the question of whether the administration of an oath is lawful does not depend upon what might be the considerable intricacies of a particular religion adhered to by a witness but on whether the oath is one that appeared to the court to be binding on the conscience of the witness and which was so considered by the witness.[15] It should be noted that the fact that the witness did not have any religious belief at the time of taking the oath does not affect the validity of the oath.[16]

3–07   In practice, a trial judge will not make any inquiry as to the religious beliefs of an adult witness before he or she is sworn. However, if a witness objects to taking the oath, then the judge should inquire whether an alternative form of oath would bind the conscience of the witness. If so, an oath in that form will be administered.[17] If not, then the witness can give evidence on solemn affirmation.[18]

3. Capacity to Give Intelligible Testimony

3–08   A witness can only give evidence if he or she is capable of giving intelligible testimony. This requirement has a statutory foundation in the case of children and persons with a mental disability, but is of more general application. Thus, a witness may be incompetent to give evidence because of intoxication or mental illness. However, it is important to note that the lack of competency will correspond with the period of intoxication or mental illness and, thus, the witness will be competent when sober or during a period of lucidity.

3–09   If a witness has communicative difficulties, as where he or she is deaf or incapable of speaking, then he or she may give evidence with the aid of interpreters. The better view is that communicative difficulties on the part of a witness should

---

to make a solemn statutory affirmation that the evidence they give "shall be the truth, the whole truth and nothing but the truth".

12   The manner of the administration of oaths is prescribed by s.2(1) of the Oaths Act 1909 which stipulates that: "The person taking the oath shall hold the New Testament, or, in the case of a Jew, the Old Testament, in his uplifted hand, and shall say or repeat after the officer administering the oath the words 'I swear by Almighty God that....', followed by the words of the oath prescribed by law."

13   Section 2(2) of the Oaths Act 1909. See *R. v Entrehman* (1842) Car & M 248; *R. v Wooey* (1902) 2 BCR 569.

14   [1990] 3 All ER 116, [1990] 1 WLR 1111.

15   See also *R. v Chapman* [1980] Crim LR 42. In *R v Majid* [2009] EWCA Crim 2563, it was held that it is improper, in the cross-examination of a muslim, to ask questions designed to challenge whether he regards himself as bound to tell the truth by virtue of the fact that he has affirmed and did not swear on the Koran.

16   Section 3 of the Oaths Act 1888 provides: "Where an oath has been duly administered and taken, the fact that the person to whom the same was administered had, at the time of taking such oath, no religious belief, shall not for any purpose affect the validity of such oath."

17   *R. v Kalevar* (1991) 4 CR (4th) 114.

18   Section 1 of the Oaths Act 1888 provides: "Every person upon objecting to being sworn, and stating, as the ground of such objection, either that he has no religious belief or that the taking of an oath is contrary to his religious belief, shall be permitted to make his solemn affirmation instead of taking an oath in all places and for all purposes where an oath is or shall be required by law, which affirmation shall be of the same force and effect as if he had taken the oath ...".

not lead to a finding of incompetence on the part of a witness unless he or she lacks the intellectual ability to comprehend the questions put to him or her or is unable to effectively communicate his or her response to the questions asked.[19]

4. Determination of Competence

3–10   The question as to whether a particular witness is competent to testify is determined by the trial judge.[20] The burden of proving competence is on the party tendering the witness.[21] If an issue is raised as to competence, the witness can be examined by the party calling him or her and cross-examined by the opposing party in order to reach a determination.[22] The party challenging competence may also adduce other evidence in relation to the issue.[23] In a criminal case, the accused is entitled to have the jury present during the examination of competency[24] but may waive that right and have the issue determined in the absence of the jury.[25]

5. Accused Persons in Criminal Proceedings

3–11   At common law, an accused was not competent and, therefore, not compellable as a witness, whether on his or her own behalf or on behalf of the prosecution. The incompetence of an accused to give evidence on his or her own behalf was predicated on the assumption that, as a person who was interested in the outcome of the proceedings, his or her evidence would be self-serving and unreliable. The lack of competency and compellability at the instance of the prosecution reflected the right of an accused, recognised at common law and now constitutionally protected, not to be compelled to give evidence at his or her trial.[26]

3–12   Section 1 of Criminal Justice (Evidence) Act 1924[27] "remedied the glaring injustice of depriving the accused of the right to swear to his own innocence".[28] Section 1 of that Act provides that an accused "shall be a competent witness for the defence at every stage of the proceedings, whether the person so charged is charged solely or jointly with any other person" and goes on to stipulate that an accused "shall not be called as a witness in pursuance of this Act except upon his own application". It can be seen that the effect of the section is to maintain the common law bar on the competence of the accused as a witness for the prosecution and to make an accused a competent witness on his or her own behalf at any stage of the proceedings.[29]

---

[19] *Cf. Udy v Stewart* (1885) 10 OR 591.

[20] *People (AG) v Kehoe* [1951] IR 70 at 71. This question must be determined in the particular case and a trial judge cannot rely on a previous finding of competence by him or her or any other judge in a previous case: *People (AG) v Keating* [1953] IR 200 at 201.

[21] *R. v Yacoob* (1981) 72 Cr App R 313; *R. v Khan* (1986) 84 Cr App R 44.

[22] *People (AG) v Kehoe* [1951] IR 70 at 71; *R. v Hill* (1851) 2 Den 254.

[23] *People (AG) v Kehoe* [1951] IR 70 at 71; *Dewdney v Palmer* (1839) 4 M & W 664.

[24] *People (AG) v Keating* [1953] IR 200 at 201.

[25] *Attorney General v Lanigan* [1958] Ir Jur Rep 59 at 61.

[26] See further Chap.11.

[27] No.37 of 1924.

[28] *People (DPP) v Ferris* [2008] 1 IR 1 at 7.

[29] In *R. v Wheeler* [1917] 1 KB 283 at 286–287, [1916–17] All ER 1111 at 1112, a broad construction of the words "at every stage of the proceedings" in the equivalent English provision, s.1 of the Criminal Evidence Act 1898, was adopted, with Viscount Reading CJ stating: "Whenever the defence can be heard the prisoner can give evidence on his own behalf." Evidence can, thus, be

3–13   Where an accused is charged jointly with another person or persons, he or she is a competent but not compellable witness for his or her co-accused.[30] However, he or she is not a competent or compellable witness for the prosecution against the co-accused[31] for so long as he or she is jointly charged with the co-accused. A person will cease to be jointly charged with a co-accused and, thus, become competent and compellable for the prosecution as an ordinary witness where: (i) he or she pleads guilty[32]; (ii) he or she is acquitted[33]; (iii) a *nolle prosequi* is entered by the DPP discontinuing the prosecution against him or her; or (iv) the indictment is severed so that he or she is not tried with the co-accused.[34]

6. Spouse of an Accused in Criminal Proceedings

3–14   The issue of the competence and compellability of spouses has been the subject of considerable statutory intervention and was addressed comprehensively in Part IV of the Criminal Evidence Act 1992.[35] For the purpose of analysing these provisions, it is helpful to distinguish between the competence and compellability of the spouse of an accused as: (a) a witness for the prosecution; (b) a witness for the accused; and (c) a witness for a co-accused.

(a) Spouse of an accused as witness for the prosecution

3–15   At common law, the general rule was that the spouse of an accused was not competent to give evidence for the prosecution[36] except in the case of a charge of rape or violence against the spouse.[37] The origin of this rule can be traced to the doctrine of the unity of husband and wife taken together with the right of an accused not to be compelled to give evidence.[38] In effect, the spouse of an accused was treated, for the purpose of the rule as to competency, as if he or she were an accused. The rule was also justified on the basis of the preservation of marital harmony and protection of the institution of marriage.[39]

---

given by an accused on a *voir dire* (*R. v Cowell* [1940] 2 KB 49, [1940] 2 All ER 599) and in mitigation of sentence at a sentencing hearing (*R. v Wheeler*).

[30]   In *Attorney General v Joyce* [1929] IR 526 at 542, the Court of Criminal Appeal rejected the contention that the effect of s.1 of the Criminal Justice (Evidence) Act 1924 was merely to make an accused a competent witness *for* a co-accused but that any evidence given by an accused against a co-accused could not be considered by the jury in determining the guilt of the co-accused. See also *R. v Rudd* (1948) 32 Cr App R 138 and *R. v Paul* [1920] 2 KB 183, [1920] All ER 535.

[31]   *Attorney General v Joyce* [1929] IR 526 at 542.

[32]   *R. v Boal* [1965] 1 QB 402, [1964] 3 All ER 269.

[33]   *R. v Conti* (1973) 58 Cr App R 387.

[34]   *R. v Richardson* (1967) 51 Cr App R 381.

[35]   No.12 of 1992.

[36]   *People (DPP) v JT* (1988) 3 Frewen 141 at 152; *Hoskyn v Metropolitan Police Commissioner* [1979] AC 474 at 484, [1978] 2 All ER 136 at 138 (*per* Lord Wilberforce).

[37]   *R. v Wasson* (1796) 1 Cr & Dix CC 197; *R. v Lord Audley* (1631) 3 St Tr 401; *R. v Lapworth* [1931] 1 KB 117, [1930] All ER 340; *Hoskyn v Metropolitan Police Commissioner* [1979] AC 474, [1978] 2 All ER 136. There appears to have also been an exception in respect of treason (see *R. v Lady Ivy* (1684) 10 St Tr 555).

[38]   *People (DPP) v JT* (1988) 3 Frewen 141 at 154; *Hoskyn v Metropolitan Police Commissioner* [1979] AC 474 at 484, [1978] 2 All ER 136 at 138–139.

[39]   *People (DPP) v JT* (1988) 3 Frewen 141 at 155; *R. v Bailey* (1983) 4 CCC (3d) 21. In *Hawkins v United States* (1958) 358 US 74 at 77, Black J stated: "The basic reason the law has refused to pit wife against husband or husband against wife in a trial where liberty or life is at stake was a belief that such a policy was necessary to foster family peace not only for the benefit of

3–16   However, serious doubts as to the compatibility with the Constitution of the common law rule of spousal incompetence, even as diluted by statute,[40] were raised by the decision of the Court of Criminal Appeal in *People (DPP) v JT*.[41] The appellant was convicted of a number of sexual offences against his daughter, who had Down's Syndrome, including counts of buggery, indecent assault and incest. At the trial, the spouse of the accused gave evidence for the prosecution and the contention, advanced on appeal, that she had been incompetent to do so was rejected. Walsh J examined the historical basis of the rule of spousal incompetence at common law and expressed doubts as to its continued vitality:

> "It could be strongly argued that this rule should no longer be sustained because of the fact that, in the modern age with the independence of women, married or otherwise, and the recognition of the equality of men and women, both within and out of marriage, such a distinction could only be regarded as outmoded and unreal."[42]

3–17   In addition, he pointed out that the reasoning underpinning the rule would not be applicable where the spouses were living apart by mutual consent or by reason of the abandonment or desertion of one by the other.[43]

3–18   The learned judge went on to consider the compatibility of the rule of spousal incompetence with the Constitution. It had been argued by counsel for the applicant that to permit or to compel a spouse to give evidence against the accused spouse would be a violation of Art.41 of the Constitution, which protected the rights of the family. However, Walsh J took the view that this provision was intended to be for the protection and benefit of the family and was not intended to be used to permit the concealment of a criminal assault on one of the members of the family by another member of the family. He pointed out that the Constitution placed an obligation on the courts to enforce the protection conferred by it on the family and he considered it difficult to imagine any matter which would be more subversive of family life than sexual offences of the nature alleged particularly when the child had an intellectual disability. He, therefore, concluded that the application of the common law rule in the circumstances of the case would be incompatible with the obligations imposed by the Constitution:

> "In the form of a common law rule the law has recognised a rule to the effect that one spouse may not give evidence against the other in a criminal prosecution. Insofar as that may be based upon the view that it would tend to rupture family relationships it must be set against a public interest in the vindication of the innocent who have been subjected to injustice. As both may be said to fall within the provisions of Article 41 of the Constitution it is the view of the court that the interests of the child must prevail because what is alleged against the applicant is an attack of a particularly unpleasant kind upon his own child and therefore an attack upon the very fabric of the family itself and the bodily integrity of a member of that family."[44]

3–19   Although it was not necessary to decide the point because the wife in that

---

husband, wife and children, but for the benefit of the public as well. Such a belief has never been unreasonable and is not now … there is a widespread belief, grounded on present conditions, that the law should not force or encourage testimony which might alienate husband and wife, or further influence existing domestic difficulties."
[40]   See, in particular, s.4 of the Criminal Justice (Evidence) Act 1924 and *McGonagle v McGonagle* [1951] IR 123.
[41]   (1988) 3 Frewen 141. For a detailed analysis of the decision in *JT*, see Jackson, "Evidence—Competence and Compellability of Spouses as Prosecution Witnesses" (1989) 11 DULJ 149.
[42]   (1988) 3 Frewen 141 at 156. *Cf. R. v Hawkins* [1996] 3 SCR 1043; (1996) 141 DLR (4th) 193 where the Supreme Court of Canada refused to alter the common law rule of spousal incompetence.
[43]   *Cf. R. v Bailey* (1983) 4 CCC (3d) 21 at 23; *R. v Salituro* (1990) 38 OAC 241.
[44]   (1988) 3 Frewen 141 at 161.

case had been a willing witness, Walsh J stated that it followed from the court's analysis of the constitutional provisions that she would have been compellable if unwilling to testify.[45] It was against this background that the issue of the competence and compellability of spouses at the instance of the prosecution was addressed in the Criminal Evidence Act 1992.

3–20   Section 21 of the 1992 Act deals with the competence of spouses and makes a spouse or former spouse of an accused competent to give evidence at the instance of the prosecution in any criminal proceedings.[46] The only exception to this general rule of competence is where the spouse is charged in the same proceedings with the accused.[47]

3–21   An intermediate approach to the question of spousal compellability is adopted in the 1992 Act, with s.22(1)[48] providing that a spouse is compellable to give evidence at the instance of the prosecution only if the offence: (a) involves violence, or the threat of violence, to the spouse, a child of the spouse or of the accused, or a person who was, at the material time, under the age of 18 years; (b) is a sexual offence[49] alleged to have been committed in relation to a child of the spouse or of the accused, or a person who was, at the material time, under the age of 18 years; or (c) consists of attempting or conspiring to commit, or of aiding, abetting, counselling, procuring or inciting the commission of, an offence falling within the foregoing categories.[50] More extensive compellability is provided for in the case of former spouses[51] who are rendered compellable at the instance of the prosecution unless the offence charged falls outside the categories enumerated in respect of the compellability of spouses and is

---

[45]   The Court, thus, refused to follow the decision of the House of Lords to the contrary in *Hoskyn v Metropolitan Police Commissioner* [1979] AC 474, [1978] 2 All ER 136.

[46]   It was held in *R. v Pitt* [1983] QB 25, [1982] 3 All ER 63 that a spouse who is competent but not compellable is entitled to refuse to give evidence up to the point when he or she takes the oath in the witness box but, once he or she knowingly waives his or her right of refusal, he or she is treated as an ordinary witness and can, if appropriate, be treated as a hostile witness. In order to ensure that a spouse knowingly waives his or her right to refuse to give evidence, the Court of Appeal considered it desirable for a trial judge to explain the position to the spouse in the absence of the jury.

[47]   Section 25 of the Criminal Evidence Act 1992. This exception applies unless the person concerned is not, or is no longer, liable to be convicted at the trial as a result of pleading guilty or for any other reason.

[48]   As amended by s.257(3) of the Children Act 2001.

[49]   The concept of a "sexual offence" is defined in s.2 of the 1992 Act (as amended by s.16 of the Criminal Justice (Miscellaneous Provisions) Act 1997, s.7(2) of the Criminal Law (Sexual Offences) Act 2006, s.4(1) of the Criminal Law (Sexual Offences) (Amendment) Act 2007 and s.12(a) of the Criminal Law (Human Trafficking) Act 2008).

[50]   In *R. v L* [2008] EWCA Crim 973, [2009] 1 WLR 626, the Court of Appeal rejected the proposition that police were obliged to tell the wife of a suspect when interviewing her in respect of offences allegedly committed by her husband that she would not be a compellable witness in criminal proceedings against him but indicated that there might be circumstances where the police should make this clear. It was also held that the admission of a voluntary statement made by the wife to police did not violate s.80 of the Police and Criminal Evidence Act 1984 which provides that a spouse or civil partner is only compellable in certain circumstances. See, further, Omerod, "Witnesses: compellability - spouse as witness for the prosecution" (2008) 10 Crim LR 823 and Brabyn "A criminal defendant's spouse as a prosecution witness" (2011) 8 Crim LR 613.

[51]   Section 20 of the Criminal Evidence Act 1992 (as amended by s.49 of the Family Law (Divorce) Act 1996) defines a former spouse as including a person who, in respect of his or her marriage to an accused: (a) has been granted a decree of judicial separation; (b) has entered into a separation agreement; or (c) has been granted a decree of divorce.

alleged to have been committed at a time when the marriage was subsisting.[52] In the case of both spouses and former spouses, they will not be compellable where they are charged in the same proceedings unless the person concerned is not, or is no longer, liable to be convicted at the trial as a result of pleading guilty or some other reason.[53]

3–22 It is evident that the provisions of the Criminal Evidence Act 1992, particularly those relating to the compellability of spouses, were heavily influenced by the decision in *JT*.[54] However, they have been subjected to cogent academic criticism on the basis that the list of enumerated offences in respect of which a spouse is compellable is either too broad or too narrow.[55] Jackson has also argued, convincingly, that a spouse should be generally compellable subject to a judicial discretion to exempt the spouse where the importance of the spousal testimony is outweighed by either damage to the marital relationship or harshness to the spouse.[56]

3–23 The question of whether Art.8 of the European Convention on Human Rights places any limits on the compellability of spouses or partners was examined recently by the European Court of Human Rights in *Van Der Heijden v The Netherlands*.[57] The Applicant was the unmarried life partner of a man accused of shooting and killing a man in a café and was believed to be with him at the time of the shooting. The relevant provision in Netherlands (Art.217(3) of the Code of Criminal Procedure) provided a testimonial privilege for "spouses" and for "registered partners", but not for those in *de facto* relationships. She was, therefore, compelled to testify and contended that Art.8 had been violated because compelling her to testify would undermine her stable family relationship. The Grand Chamber split 10:7 on this issue, with the majority finding that there had been no violation of Art.8 of the Convention. Although it was held that compelling the applicant to give evidence in criminal proceedings against her partner interfered with the applicant's right to respect for family life, such interference was found to be "necessary" under Art.8(2) in circumstances where she had failed to have the partnership registered:

> "The Court recognises that there are, in fact, two competing public interests at issue in this case. The first is the public interest in the prosecution of serious crime. The second is the public interest in the protection of family life from State interference. Both interests are important, having regard to the common good. In balancing those competing interests the respondent Government have considered that the public interest in the protection of family life weighed heavier in the scales than the public interest in criminal prosecution, but they have

---

[52] It is apparent from s.22(2) that a marriage will not be considered to have been subsisting in circumstances where a decree of judicial separation or a separation agreement was in force and, although it is not specified, it would follow that this would also be the case where a decree of divorce had been granted.

[53] Section 25 of the Criminal Evidence Act 1992.

[54] The Criminal Evidence Act 1992 departs from the recommendations of the Law Reform Commission, *Competence and Compellability of Spouses as Witnesses* (1985) at pp.49–50, which predated the decision in *JT*, that a spouse should be competent but not compellable for the prosecution.

[55] See Jackson, "Competence and Compellability of Spouses to give Evidence" (1993) 15 DULJ 202 and Fennell, *Law of Evidence in Ireland* (Dublin: Butterworths, 1992) at p.91. It might be noted that the rule of spousal non-compellability has been abolished in New Zealand by s.71 of the Evidence Act 2006.

[56] Jackson, "Competence and Compellability of Spouses to give Evidence" (1993) 15 DULJ 202 at 209.

[57] Judgment of the Grand Chamber, 3 April, 2012, [2012] ECHR 588, (2013) 57 EHRR 13. See Stuesser, "Testimonial Privilege: *Van Der Heijden v The Netherlands*" (2012) 16 E & P 323.

set limits on the scope of the 'family life' that attracts statutory protection. They have done so by requiring formal recognition of the "protected" family relationship before permitting the 'testimonial privilege' exception to arise. This formal recognition can be obtained either through marriage or by way of registration of the relationship. The public interest in the prosecution of crime involves, of necessity, putting in place effective criminal-law provisions to deter the commission of offences against the person, backed up by law-enforcement machinery for the prevention, suppression and sanctioning of breaches of such provisions."[58]

3–24   Compliance with Art.8 may require an extension of the provisions of s.21, not just to civil partners of an accused,[59] but to equivalent informal but long standing relationships.[60]

(b) Spouse of accused as witness for the accused

3–25   At common law, the spouse of an accused was not competent as a witness for an accused.[61] However, that rule was abrogated by s.1 of the Criminal Justice (Evidence) Act 1924, which made a spouse competent but not compellable as a witness for the accused. The Criminal Evidence Act 1992 now provides that a spouse or former spouse is competent to give evidence at the instance of an accused in any criminal proceedings.[62] A spouse or former spouse is also made compellable[63] except where he or she is charged in the same proceedings unless the person concerned is not, or is no longer, liable to be convicted at the trial as a result of pleading guilty or for some other reason.[64]

(c) Spouse of accused as witness for a co-accused

3–26   Section 21 of the Criminal Evidence Act 1992 renders a spouse or former spouse of an accused competent to give evidence at the instance of any co-accused. However, a spouse is only compellable in those circumstances that he or she would be compellable for the prosecution.[65] In the case of a former spouse,[66] he or she is compellable unless the offence charged falls outside the categories of enumerated offences and is alleged to have been committed at a time when the marriage was subsisting.[67] In the case of

---

[58]   [2012] ECHR 588, (2013) 57 EHRR 13 at [62].

[59]   Section 21 has not been amended to cover civil partners following the introduction of the Civil Partnership and Certain Rights and Obligations of Cohabitants Act 2010 although the equivalent legislation in the UK now refers to "spouses and civil partners" (s.80 of the UK Police and Criminal Evidence Act 1984 (as amended)).

[60]   The possibility that this may be required has been flagged in the UK in *R v A* [2012] EWCA Crim 1529, [2012] 1 WLR 3378, [2012] 2 Cr App R 34 at [21]–[22]. See, further, Firth, "The Rape Trial and Sexual History Evidence — *R. v A* and the (Un)Worthy Complainant" (2006) 57 NILQ 442.

[61]   *People (DPP) v JT* (1988) 3 Frewen 141 at 152.

[62]   Section 21 of the Criminal Evidence Act 1992. This section enacts the recommendation to this effect by the Law Reform Commission, *Competence and Compellability of Spouses as Witnesses* (1985) at p.39.

[63]   Section 23 of the Criminal Evidence Act 1992.

[64]   Section 25 of the Criminal Evidence Act 1992.

[65]   Section 24(1)(a) of the Criminal Evidence Act 1992.

[66]   Section 20 of the Criminal Evidence Act 1992 (as amended by s.49 of the Family Law (Divorce) Act 1996) defines a former spouse as including a person who, in respect of his or her marriage to an accused: (a) has been granted a decree of judicial separation; (b) has entered into a separation agreement; or (c) has been granted a decree of divorce.

[67]   Section 24(1)(b) of the Criminal Evidence Act 1992. It is evident from that subsection that a marriage will not be considered to have been subsisting in circumstances where a decree of judicial

both spouses and former spouses, they will not be compellable where they are charged in the same proceedings unless the person concerned is not, or is no longer, liable to be convicted at the trial as a result of pleading guilty or some other reason.[68]

7. Children and Persons with a Mental Disability

3–27 At common law, there was no age threshold that had to be reached before a child was competent to give evidence[69] and the issue depended on whether the child could give sworn evidence.[70] The test applied in that regard was whether the child possessed "sufficient knowledge of the nature and consequences of an oath"[71] and this was a matter to be determined by the trial judge by an examination of the child on a *voir dire*.[72]

3–28 The traditional view was that a child could only appreciate the nature and consequences of an oath if he or she believed in the existence of God and understood "the danger and impiety of falsehood".[73] However, modern cases have adopted a more secular approach focussing on an appreciation by the child of the obligation to tell the truth.[74] In *R. v Hayes*,[75] a boy of 12 years who had not heard of the existence of God was tendered as a witness. The English Court of Appeal recognised that, in the present state of society, the divine sanction of the oath is probably not generally recognised amongst the adult population and held, therefore, that the determinative consideration is:

> "whether the child has a sufficient appreciation of the solemnity of the occasion and the added responsibility to tell the truth, which is involved in taking an oath, over and above the duty to tell the truth which is an ordinary duty of normal social conduct."[76]

3–29 The significance of the test as to whether a child understands the nature and consequences of an oath in determining whether a child can give sworn evidence has been reduced considerably by the extensive provision now made for young children to give unsworn evidence where they are in a position to provide an intelligible account of events.

3–30 Section 27(1) of the Criminal Evidence Act 1992 provides that:

---

separation or a separation agreement was in force and, although it is not specified, it would follow that this would also be the case where a decree of divorce had been granted.

[68] Section 25 of the Criminal Evidence Act 1992.

[69] *Attorney General v O'Sullivan* [1930] IR 552 at 556; *R. v Brasier* (1779) 1 Leach 199 at 200.

[70] At common law, a child could not give unsworn evidence: *Mapp v Gilhooley* [1991] 1 IR 253 at 262, [1991] ILRM 695 at 703.

[71] *R. v Brasier* (1779) 1 Leach 199 at 200.

[72] *Attorney General v O'Sullivan* [1930] IR 552 at 556. In that case, it was held that an objection to the reception of the child's evidence on oath could be taken during the course of examination of the child and, if successful, this would result in the trial judge withdrawing the evidence of the child from the jury. However, the better view is that an objection as to competence should be raised in advance of a witness giving evidence where possible so that the tribunal of fact is not exposed to inadmissible evidence.

[73] *R. v Brasier* (1779) 1 Leach 199 at 200. This test was endorsed in *Attorney General v O'Sullivan* [1930] IR 552 at 556, where Kennedy CJ stated that it was a "question of the intelligence and actual mental capacity of the child witness".

[74] See *R. v Hayes* [1977] 2 All ER 288, [1977] 1 WLR 234; *R. v Bellamy* (1985) 82 Cr App R 222; *R. v Bannerman* (1966) 55 WWR 257; *R. v Fletcher* (1982) 1 CCC (3d) 370 at 377.

[75] [1977] 2 All ER 288, [1977] 1 WLR 234.

[76] [1977] 2 All ER 288 at 291, [1977] 1 WLR 234 at 237 (*per* Bridge LJ). This test was approved in *R. v Fletcher* (1982) 1 CCC (3d) 370 at 380.

"in any criminal proceedings the evidence of a person under 14 years of age may be received otherwise than on oath or affirmation if the court is satisfied that he is capable of giving an intelligible account of events which are relevant to those proceedings."[77]

3–31   Subsection (3) extends the application of the section to persons aged 14 years or over with a mental handicap.

3–32   Provision in similar terms for the reception of the unsworn evidence of children in civil cases is made by s.28 of the Children Act 1997.[78] Subsection (1) provides that in any civil proceedings, "the evidence of a child who has not attained the age of 14 years may be received otherwise than on oath or affirmation if the court is satisfied that the child is capable of giving an intelligible account of events which are relevant to the proceedings." Subsection (3) extends the application of the section to persons with a mental disability[79] who are aged 14 years or over.

3–33   Given that it is "a fundamental principle of the common law that for the purpose of trials in either criminal or civil cases *viva voce* evidence must be given on oath or affirmation",[80] it would seem to follow that before a child or a person with a mental disability gives unsworn evidence pursuant to either s.27 of the Criminal Evidence Act 1992 or s.28 of the Children Act 1997, the trial judge should be satisfied that the statutory requirements for doing so are met. This was the view of O'Higgins J in *O'Sullivan v Hamill*,[81] who held that, before a person with a mental handicap could give unsworn evidence pursuant to s.27 of the Criminal Evidence Act 1992, the trial judge must hold an inquiry and be satisfied that: (i) the person has a mental handicap, and (ii) that he or she is capable of giving an intelligible account of events which are relevant to the proceedings.[82] It should be noted that resolution of this issue may require expert medical evidence.[83]

8. Miscellaneous

3–34   There are a number of miscellaneous categories of person who are competent but not compellable to give evidence: (a) a judge in respect of matters of which he or she became aware relating to, and as a result of the performance of, his of her judicial

---

[77]   Shannon, *Report of the Special Rapporteur on Child Protection, Report to the Oireachtas* (2007), at [5.3.2] recommended that: "The Law should be reformed so as to operate on the presumption that a child is competent to appear in a judicial matter, and is capable of providing a sufficiently accurate and intelligible account of the events in question."

[78]   No.40 of 1997.

[79]   The section does not define the meaning of "mental disability" but guidance can be obtained from s.20(b) which applies the provisions of Part III of the 1997 Act to proceedings concerning the welfare of a person who is of full age but who "has a mental disability to such an extent that it is not reasonably possible for the person to live independently".

[80]   *Mapp v Gilhooley* [1991] 1 IR 253 at 262, [1991] ILRM 695 at 700 (*per* Finlay CJ).

[81]   [1999] 2 IR 9.

[82]   [1999] 2 IR 9 at 15.

[83]   *R. v Barratt* [1996] Crim LR 222; *R. v Hawke* (1975) 7 OR (2d) 145 at 154–155.

functions[84]; (b) bankers to produce or prove the contents of bankers books[85]; and (c) diplomats.[86]

C. Adducing Oral Evidence

1. Witness Preparation

3–35 It is common practice in both civil and criminal proceedings for the legal representatives of a party to meet with a witness intended to be called in order to ascertain the evidence that the witness can or will give in the proceedings. Indeed, in the case of witnesses to be called by the prosecution in a criminal case being prosecuted on indictment where service of a book of evidence is required or witnesses to be called by a party in a civil case where an exchange of witness statements has been directed, it will be necessary to do this in order to obtain a statement of the evidence of the witness. On the basis that there "is no property in a witness", whether a witness as to fact or an expert witness, it is also permissible for a party (or the legal representatives of a party) to meet with a witness to be called by an opposing party.[87]

3–36 In *GO'R v DPP*,[88] Charleton J accepted that such pre-trial consultations were necessary and appropriate and served to focus the evidence to be given at trial.[89] He also recognised that some witnesses might require particular reassurance about the process of giving evidence and that some experts would benefit from being assisted as to how their evidence might be best focused and presented. However, any such pre-trial consultations were subject to caveat that the interaction with the witness should be neutral and non-directive and he held that it is impermissible to coach a witness as to the evidence to be given by suggesting the desired content of that evidence:[90]

> "For a witness to be directed as to what they should say in order to prove a case fundamentally

---

[84] *Warren v Warren* [1997] QB 488 at 496, [1996] 4 All ER 664 at 671. Lord Woolf MR pointed out that a judge remained competent in relation to the matters in respect of which he or she was not compellable and expressed the view that, if a situation arises where his or her evidence is vital, he or she should be able to be relied on not to allow the fact that he or she cannot be compelled to give evidence to stand in the way of him or her doing so.

[85] Section 6 of the Bankers' Books Evidence Act 1879 (as amended by s.131 of the Central Bank Act 1989) provides: "A banker or official of a bank shall not, in any legal proceedings, be compellable to produce any banker's book the contents of which can be proved under this Act, or to appear as a witness to prove the matters, transactions and accounts recorded therein, unless by order of a judge made for special cause." It was held in *Gavin v Haughton*, unreported, High Court, 27 May 2004, that s.6 only applies where the bank in question is not a party to the proceedings. See, further, Chap.12 where the Bankers' Books Evidence Act 1879 is discussed.

[86] See s.5 of the Diplomatic Relations and Immunities Act 1967 which incorporates the Vienna Convention on Diplomatic Relations into domestic law. Immunities from being compelled to give evidence are conferred on diplomatic agents and other persons by Arts 31 and 37 of the Convention.

[87] *McGrory v ESB* [2003] IESC 45, [2003] 3 IR 407; *Harmony Shipping Co. v Saudi Export* [1979] 1 WLR 1380; *Versloot Dredging BV v Hdi Gerling Industrie Versicherung AG* [2013] EWHC 581.

[88] [2011] IEHC 368, [2012] 1 IR 193. See also *R. v Momodou* [2005] EWCA 117, [2005] 1 WLR 3442 (discussed in Ellison and Wheatcroft, "Could you ask me that in a different way please? Exploring the Impact of Courtroom Questioning and Witness Familiarisation on Adult Witness Accuracy" [2010] Crim LR 823).

[89] [2011] IEHC 368 at [14], [2012] 1 IR 193 at 201.

[90] [2011] IEHC 368 at [13], [2012] 1 IR 193 at 201.

strikes against the proper administration of justice. The nature of the inquiry through examination-in-chief and cross-examination at trial is that thereby the nature of the person giving evidence and the reliability of that person is, it is to be hoped, exposed. Rehearsal, even as to the form of evidence, may have the effect of undermining the natural presentation of testimony which is expected by any court of trial to be given by witnesses of truth."

3–37   Focusing specifically on coaching of witnesses in the context of criminal trials, he said[91]:

"Whether it is the defence or the prosecution lawyers that feel the need to speak with a witness in a criminal trial, the process must be the same for both; that is a neutral form of inquiry. It is clearly apparent to all involved in criminal litigation that suggestion of any kind to a witness as to the appropriate form or content of evidence, or the putting of only selected and apparently attractive or credible parts of the defence case to prosecution witnesses, would completely undermine the search for truth which remains at the heart of any trial process."

3–38   In that case, the complainant had been counselled by a clinical psychologist who, during the course of the counselling sessions, had engaged in role play with the complainant to prepare her for the trial. While Charleton J regarded this as "undesirable", he was satisfied that it was not directive towards any particular result and could not be regarded as distorting the evidence. Accordingly, it did not mean that a subsequent trial would necessarily carry a real risk of unfairness, although it did create an issue that could be explored by the defence.

3–39   Similar sentiments were expressed by Hogan J in *Byrne v Judges of the Circuit Court*,[92] who regarded it as axiomatic that coaching of witnesses was impermissible. Having noted that this practice would be unethical for legal professionals,[93] he regarded it as objectionable because it creates "the real risk that witnesses will tailor their evidence in the manner which they believe is apparently expected of them … assists the dishonest witness to calculate how his or her evidence may come across as consistent and convincing … [and] helps to create an environment where the evidence of all participating witnesses may be contaminated."[94]

2. Calling and Tendering of Witnesses

3–40   Under our adversarial model of justice, decisions as to the calling of witnesses, and the order in which to call them, are primarily for the parties themselves. However, there are some qualifications to this general principle and it is useful to distinguish, in that regard, between civil and criminal proceedings.

(a) Civil proceedings

3–41   In civil proceedings, each party is free to call any witnesses, in whatever order, it wishes.[95] In general, a judge has no right to call witnesses without the consent of

---

[91]   [2011] IEHC 368 at [15], [2012] 1 IR 193 at 202.
[92]   [2013] IEHC 396 at [68].
[93]   Referring in that regard to rule 5.18 of the Code of Conduct for the Bar of Ireland (adopted on 22 July 2013) which stipulates that: "Barristers may not coach a witness in regard to the evidence to be given."
[94]   See also *R v Momodou* [2005] 1 WLR 3442 at 3453–3454.
[95]   *Briscoe v Briscoe* [1968] P 501, [1966] 1 All ER 465; *Barnes v BPC (Business Forms) Ltd* [1976] 1 All ER 237, [1975] 1 WLR 1565.

the parties,[96] although he or she may do so in cases of civil contempt[97] or child care proceedings.[98] A judge also has the power to recall a witness previously called by a party.[99]

(b) Criminal proceedings

3–42 In indictable proceedings, the general principle is that the prosecution is required to have available in court and call or tender all witnesses whose names are included in the book of evidence.[100] However, a witness should not be called if an acquaintance with a juror is established.[101]

3–43 The prosecution has discretion whether to call a witness in the book of evidence but the exercise of this discretion is circumscribed by considerations of fairness and an overriding duty to ensure that an accused obtains a fair trial. In *R. v Oliva*,[102] Lord Parker CJ summarised the position as follows:

> "The prosecution must of course have in court the witnesses whose names are on the back of the indictment, but there is a wide discretion in the prosecution as to whether they should call them either calling and examining them, or calling and tendering them for cross-examination. The prosecution do not, of course, put forward every witness as a witness of truth, but where the witness's evidence is capable of belief then it is their duty, well recognised, that he should be called, even though the evidence that he is going to give is inconsistent with the case sought to be proved. Their discretion must be exercised in a manner which is calculated to further the interest of justice, and at the same time be fair to the defence. If the prosecution appear to be exercising that discretion improperly, it is open to the judge of trial to interfere and in his discretion in turn to invite the prosecution to call a particular witness, and if they refuse there is the ultimate sanction in the judge himself calling that witness."[103]

3–44 The decision in *Oliva* was approved and applied in *People (DPP) v Casey*.[104] In that case, the prosecution decided not to call a witness named in the book of evidence because the view had been formed that he was an unreliable witness. The trial judge refused an application by the first-named accused to require the prosecution to call him or tender him for cross-examination and, instead, indicated that he would render any assistance necessary to facilitate the defence in calling him. He ordered the production of the witness but he refused to speak to the legal representatives of the first-named

---

[96] *Shea v Wilson & Co.* (1916) 50 ILTR 73 at 75; *Re Enoch and Zaretzky, Bock & Co's Arbitration* [1910] 1 KB 327, [1908–10] All ER 625; *Lissack v Manhattan Loft Corporation Ltd* [2013] EWHC 128 at [32]; *Lindsay v Imperial Steel & Wire Co.* (1910) 21 OLR 375; *Fowler v Fortier* [1949] OWN 244. *Cf. Obacelo Pty v Taveraft Pty Ltd* (1986) 66 ALR 371 and *Clark Equipment Credit of Australia Ltd v Como Factors Pty Ltd* (1988) 14 NSWLR 552.

[97] *Yianni v Yianni* [1966] 1 All ER 231n, [1966] 1 WLR 120.

[98] *Eastern Health Board v Mooney*, unreported, High Court, 20 March 1998. This exception is based on the quasi-inquisitorial nature of these proceedings which do not, generally, involve a *lis inter partes* (see *Eastern Health Board v MK* [1999] 2 IR 99, [1999] 2 ILRM 321).

[99] *Fallon v Calvert* [1960] 2 QB 201, [1960] 1 All ER 281; *French v McKendrick* (1930) 66 OLR 306, [1931] 1 DLR 696.

[100] *R. v Woodhead* (1847) 2 C & K 520 at 520–521; *R. v Oliva* [1965] 3 All ER 116 at 122, [1965] 1 WLR 1028 at 1035; *R. v Russell-Jones* [1995] 3 All ER 239 at 244; *R. v Brown* [1997] 1 Cr App R 112 at 114.

[101] *People (DPP) v O'Brien*, unreported, Court of Criminal Appeal, 17 June 2002, [2005] IESC 29 at [22], [2005] 2 IR 206 at 215.

[102] [1965] 1 WLR 1028 at 1035, [1965] 3 All ER 116 at 122.

[103] See also *R. v Russell-Jones* [1995] 3 All ER 239 at 244; *Ziems v Prohtonotary of the Supreme Court of New South Wales* (1957) 97 CLR 279 at 292; *R. v Fuller* [1966] NZLR 865 at 868.

[104] [2004] IECCA 49.

accused and he was not called by the defence. The Court of Criminal Appeal noted that, in the passage from *Oliva* set out above, it had been held that the trial judge could "invite" the prosecution to call a particular witness and it had not been suggested that the judge could require the prosecution to do so. The Court was satisfied that the trial judge in his ruling had not departed from the principles in *Oliva* and that the interests of fairness and justice had been met by the trial judge's determination to render any assistance necessary to the defence to call the witness.

3–45   The passage from *Oliva* set out above was cited with approval as correctly stating the law in this jurisdiction in *People (DPP) v Lacy*[105] with the important gloss that it is necessary to have regard to the constitutional guarantee of justice and fair procedures when considering the exercise of those principles. Also considered significant were the well established principles in relation to the duty of the prosecution and prosecution counsel to act fairly and impartially and not to try and obtain a conviction by all means at their disposal.[106] It was, thus, held that, while the prosecution retains a discretion as to whether to call or tender all of the witnesses in the book of evidence, a trial judge has a discretion to intervene in the exercise of that discretion where the requirements of a fair and just trial require such an intervention. It is also apparent from that decision that, unlike the position in the UK,[107] where the prosecution decide not to call and merely to tender a witness, the witness is still regarded as a prosecution witness and is available for cross-examination by the defence. This is consistent with the decision of the Supreme Court in *O'Regan v DPP*,[108] where Murphy J declared that "the general and well-accepted practice in this country is for the prosecution to call or tender for cross-examination all witnesses whose names are included in the book of evidence".

3–46   The decision in *Lacy* was distinguished in *People (DPP) v Griffin*,[109] where it was contended that the trial judge had erred in not discharging the jury because of the failure of the prosecution to call the mother of the complainant who had been listed as a witness in the book of evidence. She had given evidence at a previous trial of the accused for the same offences and, by reason of the conflict between her testimony and a statement that she had given to Gardaí, she was, on the application of the prosecution, declared a hostile witness and dealt with on that basis. The witness did not appear at the second trial and medical evidence was led that she would not be in a position to attend because of anxiety caused by fear. The Court of Criminal Appeal held that the prosecution is not required in all circumstances to call a witness who has been listed in the book of evidence although it accepted that "this is the norm, save in unusual or exceptional circumstances". The Court was satisfied that, if the witness had been

---

105   [2005] IECCA 70 at [18], [2005] 2 IR 241 at 245.
106   See *People (DPP) v DO* [2006] IESC 12, [2006] 2 ILRM 61 at 64; *R. v Puddick* (1865) 4 F & F 497 at 499; *R. v Banks* [1916] 2 KB 621 at 623; *Randall v R.* [2002] 1 WLR 2237 at 2242; *Boucher v The Queen* (1954) 110 Can CC 263 at 270.
107   See *R. v Russell-Jones* [1995] 3 All ER 239 at 244–245. Although the passage in *R. v Olivia* [1965] 1 WLR 1028 at 1035, [1965] 3 All ER 116 at 122 set out above might seem to indicate that the prosecution is under an obligation to tender a witness that it does not call for cross-examination by the defence, earlier in his judgment, Lord Parker CJ referred with approval to the decision in *R. v Woodhead* (1847) 2 Car & Kir 520 where it was made clear that, if the defence elected to call a witness who was tendered and not called by the prosecution, that witness would be a defence witness and subject to cross-examination by the prosecution. [1965] 1 WLR 1028 at 1035, [1965] 3 All ER 116 at 122.
108   [2000] 1 ILRM 68 at 73.
109   [2009] IECCA 75.

called at the second trial, she would again have been treated as hostile and, in those circumstances, her evidence could not be considered to be material to the prosecution and there would be no value in calling her as a witness on its behalf. The Court also considered that the trial judge had correctly exercised his discretion not to discharge the jury because it had not been established that her evidence would be centrally supportive of the accused's case.

3–47 The extent to which the prosecution is under a duty to call witnesses who are not named in the book of evidence but who may be in a position to offer relevant evidence is unclear. The position at common law was that the prosecution has a discretion to determine which witnesses were sufficiently relevant to be named on the back of the indictment.[110] However, while that would seem to remain the general position,[111] there may well be situations where, in order to ensure a fair trial, the prosecution may be required to a tender a witness not named in the book of evidence.[112]

3–48 It was held in *O'Regan v DPP*[113] that comparable obligations to those in trials on indictment do not apply in summary proceedings and, subject to "the overriding consideration that the prosecution must not mislead the court or suppress any material evidence which might be of assistance to the defence",[114] it is a matter for the discretion of the prosecution as to what witnesses to call in support of the charges.

3–49 In the case of an accused in criminal proceedings, he or she is afforded great latitude and is entitled to call any witnesses that he or she wishes[115] unless it is patent that the witness does not have any relevant evidence to give or is being called for frivolous or vexatious reasons.[116] It should be noted that, although the accused has a discretion in relation to the order in which he or she calls witnesses, s.2 of the Criminal Justice (Evidence) Act 1924 stipulates that "[w]here the only witness as to the facts of the case called by the defence is the person charged, he shall be called as a witness immediately after the close of the evidence for the prosecution."[117]

3–50 With regard to the calling of witnesses by the judge, in *State (O'Connor) v Larkin*,[118] Ó Dálaigh CJ explained that it necessarily follows from the adversarial character of criminal proceedings "that it is for the prosecution and the defence

---

[110] *Seneviratne v R.* [1936] 3 All ER 36 at 48.

[111] See *People (DPP) v Price* [2004] IECCA 26 and *People (DPP) v Lacy* [2005] IECCA 70, [2005] 2 IR 241.

[112] Although it would seem from the decision in *People (DPP) v Ryan*, unreported, Court of Criminal Appeal, 30 November 1992, that there is no obligation to forewarn the defence of the line of cross-examination that will be taken in respect of a witness who has given a statement to gardaí but is not called.

[113] [2000] 1 ILRM 68.

[114] [2000] 1 ILRM 68 at 74. See also *Geaney v DPP* [2000] 1 IR 412.

[115] *O'Regan v DPP* [2000] 2 ILRM 68 at 75; *Herron v Haughton*, unreported, Supreme Court, 19 May 2000.

[116] See *Herron v Haughton*, unreported, Supreme Court, 19 May 2000, where it was held that the trial judge had been correct to refuse to permit the accused to call as a witness the prosecuting solicitor who she wished to cross-examine on the basis that he was a party to a conspiracy to pervert the course of justice.

[117] See *R. v Wheeler* [1917] 1 KB 283 at 287, where it was held that an accused is not restricted to giving evidence except at that particular point in all cases. See also *R. v Morrison* (1911) 6 Cr App R 159 at 165 and *R. v Smith* (1968) 52 Cr App R 224.

[118] [1968] IR 255.

respectively, and not for the court, to determine what witnesses shall be called to give evidence".[119] However, the trial judge has the power to call a witness not called by either the prosecution or defence if, in his or her opinion, it is in the interests of justice to do so.[120] It has been emphasised that this power should be sparingly used as otherwise the trial judge may give the appearance of acting in a partisan manner.[121] If the trial judge decides to call a witness, neither the prosecution nor the defence are entitled to examine or cross-examine the witness without the leave of the judge,[122] although such leave should be granted if the witness gives evidence that is adverse to either party.[123]

3–51   It appears that a trial judge may require the prosecution to call witnesses in a particular order.[124] However, it is doubtful if the trial judge can interfere with the order of the defence witnesses and, having regard to the presumption of innocence, he or she cannot require the accused to call a witness before the end of the prosecution case.[125]

3. Adverse Inferences From Failure to Call a Witness

3–52   It is well established that a court is entitled to draw an adverse inference from the failure of a party to call a witness who is available to give evidence in relation to a fact in issue. This principle can be traced back to the decision in *M'Queen v Great Western Railway Co.*,[126] where Cockburn CJ stated:

> "If a *prima facie* case is made out, capable of being displaced, and if the party against whom it is established might by calling particular witnesses and producing particular evidence displace that *prima facie* case, and he omits to adduce that evidence, then the inference fairly arises, as a matter of inference for the jury and not as a matter of legal presumption, that the absence of that evidence is to be accounted for by the fact that even if it were adduced it would not disprove the *prima facie* case. But that always presupposes that a *prima facie* case has been established; and unless we can see our way clearly to the conclusion that a *prima facie* case has been established, the omission to call witnesses who might have been called on the part of the defendants amounts to nothing. I cannot say that a *prima facie* case was made out calling upon the company for an answer, and if not, then they would be entitled to take their stand on the evidence as it existed."

3–53   In a passage that has been quoted with approval by the Irish courts,[127] in *R. v IRC, ex p. TC Coombs & Co.*[128] Lord Lowry explained that:

> "In our legal system generally, the silence of one party in face of the other party's evidence may convert that evidence into proof in relation to matters which are, or are likely to be, within the knowledge of the silent party and about which that party could be expected to give

---

[119] [1968] IR 255 at 258.

[120] *State (O'Connor) v Larkin* [1968] IR 255 at 259; *R. v Chapman* (1838) 8 C & P 558; *R. v Holden* (1838) 8 C & P 606.

[121] *Magee v O'Dea* [1994] 1 IR 500 at 507, [1994] 1 ILRM 540 at 545. *Cf. R. v Grafton* (1993) 96 Cr App R 156; *R. v Apostolides* (1983) 11 A Crim R 381, (1984) 154 CLR 563; *R. v Griffis* (1996) 67 SASR 170; *R. v Bishop* [1996] 3 NZLR 399.

[122] *State (O'Connor) v Larkin* [1968] IR 255 at 259; *Coulson v Disborough* [1894] 2 QB 316 at 318; *R. v Cliburn* (1898) 62 JP 232. See *contra Obacelo Pty Ltd v Taveraft Pty Ltd* (1986) 66 ALR 371.

[123] *State (O'Connor) v Larkin* [1968] IR 255 at 259; *Coulson v Disborough* [1894] 2 QB 316 at 318.

[124] See *People (DPP) v McKeown* (1984) 2 Frewen 2.

[125] *State (O'Connor) v Larkin* [1968] IR 255 at 258.

[126] (1875) LR 10 QB 569 at 574.

[127] See *Doran v Cosgrave* [1999] IESC 74; *Crofter Properties Ltd v Genport Ltd* [2002] 4 IR 73 at 85; *Fyffes plc v DCC plc* [2005] IEHC 477, [2009] 2 IR 417.

[128] [1991] 2 AC 283 at 300, [1991] 3 All ER 623 at 636.

evidence. Thus, depending on the circumstances, a *prima facie* case may become a strong or even an overwhelming case. But, if the silent party's failure to give evidence (or to give the necessary evidence) can be credibly explained, even if not entirely justified, the effect of his silence in favour of the other party, may be either reduced or nullified."

3–54 A useful distillation of the relevant principles is to be found in the decision of the Court of Appeal in *Wisniewski v Central Manchester H.A.*,[129] where Brooks LJ summarised the position as follows:

> "(1) In certain circumstances the court may be entitled to draw adverse inferences from the absence or silence of a witness who might be expected to have material evidence to give on an issue in an action.
> (2) If a court is willing to draw such inferences they may go to strengthen the evidence adduced on that issue by the other party or to weaken the evidence, if any, adduced by the party who might reasonably have been expected to call the witness.
> (3) There must, however, have been some evidence, however weak, adduced by the former on the matter in question before the court is entitled to draw the desired inference: in other words, there must be a case to answer on that issue.
> (4) If the reason for the witness's absence or silence satisfies the court, then no such adverse inference may be drawn. If, on the other hand, there is some credible explanation given, even if it is not wholly satisfactory, the potentially detrimental effect of his/her absence or silence may be reduced or nullified."

3–55 The leading Irish authority is *Fyffes plc v DCC plc*[130] where Laffoy J accepted that the principles outlined in *Wisniewski* provided helpful guidelines for the court.[131] In that case, the plaintiff alleged that the defendant had engaged in insider dealing in its shares and contended that the court should draw certain inferences from the failure of the defendants to call a number of witnesses, including a stockbroker who was claimed to be a critical witness in relation to the question of whether the defendant had dealt in the plaintiff's shares. However, Laffoy J declined to draw any inferences from the failure to call these witnesses. With regard to the stockbroker, she had regard to a number of factors in reaching that conclusion including that the onus of proof in respect of the dealing issue was on the plaintiff and the plaintiff was aware that the stockbroker was in a position to give material evidence. Thus, the attendance of the witness could have been procured by the plaintiff, if necessary by service of a *subpoena*, but the plaintiff had decided not to call him. She regarded this as a legitimate tactical decision as she did the decision of the defendant not to call him. She was also not satisfied that it was appropriate to draw the inferences that the plaintiff contended should be drawn from the failure to call him. With regard to the other witnesses, she pointed out that a number of other witnesses had been called to give evidence in relation to the matters in respect of which those witnesses could have been called and cautioned against an overbroad application of the principles laid down in *Wisniewski*, stating[132]:

> "As a general proposition, the fact that every witness who may have material evidence on a particular issue is not called, cannot, in my view, give rise to an adverse inference against the party who might have been expected to call all of the witnesses."[133]

---

[129] [1998] Lloyd's Rep Med 223.

[130] [2005] IEHC 477, [2009] 2 IR 417.

[131] [2005] IEHC 477 at [199], [2009] 2 IR 417 at 508. Those principles were also endorsed by Dunne J in *Nolan v Carrick* [2013] IEHC 523 at [44].

[132] [2005] IEHC 477 at [201], [2009] 2 IR 417 at 510.

[133] Similarly, in *Walsh v Sligo County Council* [2010] IEHC 437 at [306], [2011] 2 IR 260 at 378, McMahon J refused to draw adverse inferences from the failure to call certain witnesses to give evidence in relation to a particular issue where the defendant had called a number of witnesses in relation to that issue and the missing witnesses would have had little to add.

3–56   The decision of Laffoy J on this point in *Fyffes* was approved by the Supreme Court in *Whelan v AIB*,[134] where the decision of Peart J not to draw any adverse inferences from the failure of the first defendant to call a particular witness in circumstances where it had made a tactical decision not to go into evidence at all was upheld. O'Donnell J emphasised the need for a party contending that an inference should be drawn to identify that inference with precision:

> "At the outset I should say that I deprecate the fashion of referring to the "drawing of an inference" in the abstract as if it was an end in itself, akin to the deduction or addition of points which might or might not alter the result of a game. The drawing of an inference in this context, as indeed in any other, is an exercise in logic: when one party asserts a given set of affairs, which the identified witnesses available to the other party could be expected to rebut if untrue, then, if the second party does not call those witnesses to give evidence, the court *may* draw the inference in support of the case made by the first party, that those witnesses were not called to give such evidence because they would not in fact rebut the case made by the first party. Each case therefore, involves a consideration of the *specific* inference which the court is invited to draw."[135]

3–57   Having analysed the case made by the plaintiffs, he was satisfied that there was no *prima facie* evidence of the misconduct alleged by them against the first defendant and the only inference that could be drawn from the failure to call evidence was that the legal advisors for the first defendant (correctly) considered this to be the position.

3–58   A review of the authorities indicates that, while the failure by a party to call a relevant witness is often the matter of critical comment by an opposing party, and sometimes by the court,[136] there are relatively few instances where a court will be satisfied that a party has, without any credible explanation,[137] failed to call a witness to give relevant evidence in respect of a particular issue[138] such that the court is justified in drawing an adverse inference as to the evidence the witness would have given on that issue if called. One of the few examples of where this test was met can be seen in *Smart Mobile Ltd v Commission for Communications Regulation*[139] where the plaintiff had delivered witness statements from two expert witnesses dealing with certain issues who, without any explanation, were not called to give evidence even though the plaintiff was aware that the defendant would be adducing expert evidence covering those issues. Kelly J regarded the principles laid down in *Wisniewski* as having a particular relevance in those circumstances and proceeded to have regard to the failure to call the experts in deciding the issues in the proceedings.[140] Again, in *Dunne v Coombe Women and*

---

[134] [2011] IEHC 544, [2014] IESC 3.

[135] [2014] IESC 3 at [91].

[136] See, *e.g.*, *Walsh v Sligo County Council* [2010] IEHC 437, [2011] 2 IR 260.

[137] See *Whelan v AIB* [2011] IEHC 544 where Peart J refused to draw any adverse inferences from the failure of the plaintiff to call a particular witness who had relevant evidence to give in relation to facts in dispute because he was satisfied that there were several reasons why the plaintiff might have decided not to call the witness including that there had been a "falling out" between the witness and one of the plaintiffs.

[138] If the evidence that the witness might have given is not relevant to an issue in the proceedings, then an adverse inference cannot be drawn: *Walsh v Sligo County Council* [2010] IEHC 437 at [306], [2011] 2 IR 260 at 378. Similarly, an inference will not be drawn if the court would not have been assisted to a material extent by evidence from the witness: *Dunne v Coombe Women and Infants University Hospital* [2013] IEHC 58 at [155].

[139] [2006] IEHC 338.

[140] But see *Doyle v Banville* [2012] IESC 25 at [3.15] where Clarke J expressed doubts as to whether it would be appropriate to draw an adverse inference from the failure to call expert evidence.

Infants University Hospital,[141] where the defendant had not called a nurse who could have given evidence in relation to a key factual controversy in a medical negligence case, Irvine J considered it likely that the defendant had made a tactical decision not to call that witness and the only logical inference to be drawn was that her evidence would not have sat comfortably with the case that the defendant was advancing.

4. Anonymity of Witnesses

3–59   When a witness has been sworn or affirmed, the witness will be identified by name prior to commencing to give evidence. At common law, it had been held that the court had the power to direct that the name or address of a witness not be revealed where the interests of justice so require[142] and such orders had been made in respect of the identity of victims of blackmail called to give evidence for the prosecution in criminal proceedings.[143] However, it was held by the House of Lords in *R v Davis*[144] that a conviction based solely or to a decisive extent on the statements or testimony of an anonymous witness was unfair and inconsistent with Art.6(3)(d) of the European Convention on Human Rights. In this jurisdiction, the position under the Convention is copperfastened by the requirement in Art.34.1 that, "save in such special and limited cases as may be prescribed by law, justice must be administered in public".[145] In a series of decisions, it has been held that proceedings cannot be brought by a party on an anonymous basis[146] and it would seem that it is only in quite exceptional circumstances (if at all) that the identity of a witness could be concealed.

3–60   Statutory provision is, however, made whereby reporting restrictions can be imposed in respect of a witness suffering from a medical condition preventing the disclosure of his or her identity. Section 181 of the Criminal Justice Act 2006 provides that, where a witness has a medical condition, an order may be made prohibiting the publication of any matter relating to the proceedings that would identify the person as having the condition.[147] The order can only be made if the judge is satisfied that: (a) the witness has a medical condition, (b) his or her identification as a person with that condition would be likely to cause him or her undue stress, and (c) the order would not be prejudicial to the interests of justice.[148] An application for such an order may be made at any stage of the proceedings, and should be made on notice to the judge concerned in chambers.[149]

3–61   An analogous jurisdiction to make an order in civil proceedings prohibiting the identification of a person with a medical condition was introduced by s.27 of the Civil

---

[141] [2013] IEHC 58 at [197].
[142] *R. v Gordon* (1913) 8 Cr App R 33.
[143] See *R. v Socialist Worker, ex parte Attorney General* [1975] QB 637, [1974] 3 WLR 801.
[144] [2008] UKHL 36, [2008] 1 AC 1128, [2008] 2 WLR 125. See, further, Omerod, "Coroners and Justice Act 2009: the "Witness Anonymity" and "Investigation Anonymity" Provisions [2010] Crim LR 368
[145] See further *Re R Ltd* [1989] IR 126, [1989] ILRM 757 and *Irish Times Ltd v Murphy* [1998] 1 IR 359.
[146] See *Claimant v Board of St. James's Hospital,* unreported, High Court, 10 May 1989; *Roe v Blood Transfusion Service Board* [1996] 3 IR 67; *Re Ansbacher (Cayman) Ltd* [2002] 2 IR 57, [2002] 2 ILRM 491; *Doe v Revenue Commissioners* [2008] IEHC 5, [2008] 3 IR 328.
[147] Section 181(1).
[148] Section 181(3).
[149] Section 181(7).

Law (Miscellaneous Provisions) Act 2008 which provides that a court can grant such an order where it is satisfied that: (a) the relevant person has a medical condition, (b) his or her identification as a person with that condition would be likely to cause him or her undue stress, and (c) the order would not be prejudicial to the interests of justice.[150] However, it should be noted that the section is considerably wider in scope than s.181 of the Criminal Justice Act 2006 in that its application is not confined to a person whom it is proposed to call to give evidence but extends to any "relevant person".[151]

5. Evidence Taken on Commission

3–62   By way of an exception to the general principle that evidence must be given *viva voce* in open court, evidence may be taken on commission in civil cases pursuant to Ord.39, r.4 of the Rules of the Superior Courts.[152] Evidence taken on commission does not, however, constitute evidence in a case until such time as it is admitted into evidence by the court. This point was made forcefully by Morris J in *Irish Times Ltd v Flood*[153] who stated:

> "When a court, or a tribunal, directs that evidence be taken on commission it is, in my view, clear that the commission … does no more than gather the evidence for the purpose of tendering it to the court or tribunal for its consideration. It is clear from Order 39 of the Rules of the Superior Courts, which set out in detail the procedures and duties of the Commissioner, that he possesses no powers in relation to the evidence other than are necessary for the purpose of harvesting this evidence. The function of receiving or rejecting the evidence is vested not in the commissioner but in the court or tribunal."

3–63   Order 39, rule 4 provides that the court may allow the deposition of a witness, whose evidence has been taken on commission, to be adduced on such terms, if any, as the court may direct. However, the breadth of that discretion appears to be cut down by r.17 which stipulates that, except as otherwise provided by the Order or directed by the court, a deposition cannot be given in evidence at the trial of proceedings without the consent of the party against whom it is offered unless the court is satisfied that the deponent is dead, or beyond the jurisdiction of the court, or unable from sickness or other infirmity to attend the trial. In such cases, the certified deposition of the witness is admissible in evidence though without prejudice to any objections as to the admissibility of the whole or part of the evidence as, for example, on the basis that it is hearsay.[154]

---

[150]   These conditions were found to be satisfied by Hogan J in *PS v Minister for Justice, Equality and Law Reform* [2011] IEHC 92, where the first applicant had an intellectual disability and suffered from a number of medical conditions.

[151]   In *Children's University Hospital v CD* [2011] IEHC 1, [2011] 1 IR 665, where the plaintiff applied for an order sanctioning a blood transfusion for an infant, AB, whose parents had objected to this on religious grounds, Hogan J made an order pursuant to s.27 prohibiting the identification of the infant on the basis that he had a medical condition and notwithstanding that the child was too young to suffer stress from the revelation of his identity. A liberal interpretation of this section was also adopted by Hogan J in *XY v The Clinical Director of St. Patrick's University Hospital* [2012] IEHC 224 at [17]–[19], [2012] 2 IR 355 at 361–362.

[152]   Order 39, r.4 provides that: "The Court may, in any cause or matter where it shall appear necessary, make any order for the examination upon oath before the Court, or any officer of the Court, or any other person, and at any place, of any witness, and may allow the deposition of such witness to be adduced in evidence on such terms (if any) as the Court may direct." The evolution of the practice of taking evidence on commission was traced by Clarke J in *Moorview Developments Ltd v First Active plc* [2008] IEHC 274, [2009] 2 IR 788, 809-810, [2009] 2 ILRM 262, 282–283.

[153]   [1999] IEHC 253 at [5]–[6].

[154]   Order 39, r.17.

3–64 Provision for the taking of evidence on commission in criminal cases is made in s.11 of the Criminal Law (Jurisdiction) Act 1976 which provides that, for the purposes of the trial by the Special Criminal Court of an offence under the Act, the court can by order provide for the taking of evidence from a witness in Northern Ireland by a judge. Section 11(3)(a) provides that:

> "A statement of evidence of a witness taken in compliance with a letter of request under this section, and certified by the judge of the High Court of Justice in Northern Ireland who took it to be a true and accurate statement of the evidence so taken, shall, if all the members of the court were present throughout the taking of the evidence, be admissible at the trial or appeal concerned as evidence of any fact stated therein of which evidence would be admissible at the trial or appeal."[155]

3–65 In *People (DPP) v Mackin*,[156] the issue arose as to whether evidence taken on commission in Northern Ireland in accordance with this section formed part of the evidence at the trial or had to be proved and admitted in evidence. The substantive evidence against the accused had been taken on commission with the members of the Special Criminal Court in attendance. The prosecution contended that the evidence thereby obtained formed part of the evidence without more in circumstances where the judges of the Special Criminal Court, seised of the matter had been present when the evidence was taken. However, the Court of Criminal Appeal, relying on the decision of the Supreme Court in *The Criminal Law (Jurisdiction) Bill, 1975*,[157] disagreed, holding that such a contention was inconsistent with the unitary nature of a criminal trial and the proper construction of the provisions of s.11. As Hardiman J explained, the evidence taken on commission did not form part of the trial, it was evidence taken for production at the trial, and "what is presented to a judge outside the public court is not evidence".[158] Therefore, in line with the position in civil cases, the evidence taken on commission pursuant to s.11 does not constitute evidence until it is proved and admitted in the proceedings.

6. Recording Evidence

3–66 A digital audio recording system ("DAR") exists in both criminal and civil courts which records the evidence given and submissions made by parties. An order for the production of the DAR recording of proceedings can be made if an issue arises as to what evidence was given or otherwise as what transpired in court.[159] In addition, it is open to a party to have a stenographer present to record the evidence and produce a transcript which can then be used for the purpose of cross-examination and closing

---

[155] Section 11(3)(b) further provides that: "A document purporting to be a certificate of a judge of the High Court of Justice in Northern Ireland and to be signed by him shall be deemed, for the purposes of this section, to be such a certificate and to be so signed unless the contrary is shown."

[156] [2010] IECCA 81, [2011] 4 IR 506.

[157] [1977] IR 129.

[158] [2010] IECCA 81 at [23], [2011] 4 IR 506 at 514.

[159] Applications for production of the DAR recording in the Superior Courts are governed by Ord.123 of the Rules of the Superior Courts (as inserted by the Rules of the Superior Courts (Recording of Proceedings) 2008 (SI No. 325 of 2008) and amended by the Rules of the Superior Courts (Order 123) 2013 (SI No. 101 of 2013). In *Hudson v Halpin* [2013] IEHC 4, where an application was made for production of the DAR recording in the context of an application by way of judicial review to quash a conviction in the District Court on the basis of unfair interventions by the District Judge in cross-examination, Hogan J directed the production of the recording because it was essential to know what had happened in the District Court but indicated that such a direction had to be regarded as an exceptional measure.

submissions.[160] However, an accused in criminal proceedings is not entitled to have a stenographer (and transcript) provided as the expense of the State.[161]

7. The Time at Which Evidence Should be Adduced

3–67   In both civil and criminal proceedings, the general principle is that a party should adduce all the evidence on which he or she intends to rely before the close of his or her case.[162] To this general rule, there are two well established exceptions: (a) rebuttal evidence can be called in respect of matters arising *ex improviso*; and (b) evidence of a formal or uncontentious nature can be adduced where it was not called due to inadvertence or oversight. In addition, a trial judge has a broad discretion to admit such evidence whenever the interests of justice or fair procedures so require.

(a) Matters arising ex improviso

3–68   A party will be permitted to adduce rebuttal evidence where the trial judge is satisfied that the party has been taken by surprise by evidence that could not reasonably have been foreseen.[163] It has been emphasised that the question as to whether this test has been satisfied is a matter for the discretion of the trial judge[164] and it appears that it will be difficult to successfully challenge a determination in that regard on appeal.

3–69   An example of a case where the test was satisfied is *People (DPP) v Leahy*.[165] The applicant had been charged with a number of offences involving dishonesty and, in the course of the prosecution case, evidence had been given that the fingerprint of the applicant had been found on a particular bank draft. While giving evidence, the applicant sought to explain the presence of his fingerprint on the bank draft on the basis that a garda officer, when questioning him about another matter, had produced a number of bank drafts to him, and it was in this way that his fingerprint had come to be upon the bank draft. The trial judge then permitted the prosecution to recall the relevant garda witness to give evidence that the bank drafts which he had produced to the applicant on the previous occasion did not contain the draft on which the fingerprint had been found and, thus, the fingerprint could not be explained away in that fashion. The Court of Criminal Appeal stated that a trial judge should be vigilant before

---

[160] In *Tracey v Malone* [2009] IEHC 14 at [16], Cooke J held that, subject to the general entitlement and duty of a judge to ensure the orderly, fair and efficient conduct of proceedings, a party is entitled as of right to have a stenographer present in court to record the proceedings and the consent of the court to the presence of the stenographer is not required. His decision on this point was approved by Irvine J in *Burke v Fulham* [2010] IEHC 448 at [29] and *Burke v Anderson* [2010] IEHC 452 at [28]. However, it should be noted that, in the case of the Superior Courts, Ord.123 of the Rules of the Superior Courts (as inserted by the Rules of the Superior Courts (Recording of Proceedings) 2008 (SI No. 325 of 2008) and amended by the Rules of the Superior Courts (Order 123) 2013 (SI No. 101 of 2013) stipulates that a person (other than the Courts Service) cannot made a record of the proceedings (than by written or shorthand notes) without the permission of the Court.

[161] *Burke v Fulham* [2010] IEHC 448 at [27]–[32]; *Burke v Anderson* [2010] IEHC 452 at [28].

[162] *R. v Frost* (1839) 4 St Tr NS 85; *R. v Rice* (1963) 47 Cr App R 79; *R. v Milliken* (1969) 53 Cr App R 330; *R. v Lee* [1976] 2 NZLR 171.

[163] *People (DPP) v Reid* [1993] 2 IR 186 at 199; *Riordan v O'Shea* (1926) 60 ILTR 61 at 63; *R. v Milliken* (1969) 53 Cr App R 330; *R. v Scott* (1984) 79 Cr App R 49; *R. v Natasien* [1972] 2 NSWLR 227; *R. v Chin* (1985) 59 ALR 1.

[164] *People (DPP) v Reid* [1993] 2 IR 186 at 199; *Riordan v O'Shea* (1926) 60 ILTR 61 at 63.

[165] Unreported, Court of Criminal Appeal, *ex tempore*, 14 February 2000.

allowing the prosecution to adduce evidence after it has closed its case.[166] However, it held that the trial judge had correctly exercised his discretion to allow the evidence to be given because the prosecution could hardly have anticipated the evidence and, even if it had, it was not evidence which a trial judge would normally have permitted the prosecution to use as part of their case because it would have disclosed to the jury that the applicant had been investigated in relation to another matter by the gardaí.[167]

3–70 It appears from the decision in *DPP v Nash*[168] that, where an accused discharges the evidential burden of adducing evidence that is sufficient to rebut a presumption relied on by the prosecution, a trial judge ought to exercise his or her discretion to allow the prosecution to call rebuttal evidence at least where a technical issue requiring expert evidence is thereby raised. In that case, the respondent had been charged with driving while intoxicated and the prosecution relied on print outs from an intoxilyser machine as providing a certificate pursuant to s.17 of the Road Traffic Act 1994 as to the concentration of alcohol in his breath. Section 21 of the Road Traffic Act 1994 provides that a duly completed statement supplied pursuant to s.17 is, until the contrary is shown, sufficient evidence of the facts stated therein and of compliance with the requirements of the Act. On cross-examination of one of the gardaí called by the prosecution, evidence was elicited that the humidity of the room where the machine was used was below the optimal level and the prosecution was dismissed on this basis by the District Judge. On an appeal by way of case stated, Kearns P held that the District Judge had been incorrect to find that there was evidence that the presumption that the certificate was accurate had been rebutted but went on to hold that, even if it had, the trial judge should have permitted the prosecution to call expert rebuttal evidence and to grant an adjournment to enable this to be done. He took the view that not to allow the prosecution this opportunity would be to require it to anticipate every conceivable issue that might be raised by an accused and to have an expert on hand in case a technical issue was raised.

(b) Evidence of a formal nature

3–71 Under this exception, a party can recall a witness (or, as noted below, a judge can direct that a witness be recalled) after it has closed its case to adduce evidence that was not adduced due to inadvertence or oversight. However, the ambit of this exception is circumscribed in criminal cases and can only be invoked by the prosecution to adduce evidence of a formal or uncontentious nature[169] and not evidence relating to a matter

---

[166] This vigilance is required to ensure that the evidence in respect of which it is sought to call rebuttal evidence could not have reasonably been foreseen and that the prosecution is not using it as a means to mend its hand (see *R. v Day* (1940) 27 Cr App R 168).

[167] See also *People (DPP) v Nevin* [2003] 3 IR 321, where it was held that the trial judge had properly allowed rebuttal evidence to be called by the prosecution following the giving of surprise evidence by the accused that her husband had been a member of the IRA. Although this evidence was hearsay and inadmissible, the Court of Criminal Appeal concluded that it could have had an influence on the jury and, therefore, the rebuttal evidence had been properly admitted.

[168] [2011] IEHC 418.

[169] *Attorney General v McTiernan* (1951) 87 ILTR 162; *Attorney General (Corbett) v Halford* [1976] IR 318; *O'Keeffe v Mangan* [2012] IEHC 195 at [9]; *R. v Waller* [1910] 1 KB 364; *R. v Nash* [1958] NZLR 314. *Cf. Carey v Hussey* [2000] 2 ILRM 401 (District Judge had been entitled to adjourn hearing to allow prosecution to procure original or certified copy of safety order).

of substance.[170] This exception was found to have been properly invoked in *O'Keeffe v Mangan*[171] where the applicant had been convicted of driving under the influence of an intoxicant. The garda who had stopped the applicant and taken a sample of urine from him gave evidence that the requirements of s.18 of the Road Traffic Act 1994 in relation to the taking of samples had been complied with but, after the prosecution case had closed, an application for a direction was made on the basis that the garda had failed to provide the applicant with a slip of paper as required by the section to inform him of his right to retain one part of the sample. The District Judge then proceeded to recall the garda and asked her whether she had given the slip to the applicant and she confirmed that she had. Kearns P accepted that, where a statute provides for compliance with specified procedures, there is limited opportunity for the exercise of discretion by a judge in this regard. However, in this case, there was evidence of compliance with the statutory procedures and the only omission on the part of the prosecuting garda was to confirm that the slip of paper had been furnished as required by s.18. In those circumstances, he regarded this as a formal matter and could not see what prejudice or compromise of the applicant's rights had occurred by admitting that evidence.

(c) General discretion

3–72   In addition to the previous two categories of case, a trial judge has a general discretion to permit a witness to be recalled by the prosecution or defence if he or she considers that it is in the interests of justice to do so, even after the summing up.[172] A trial judge may also recall a witness of his or her motion[173] although it has been emphasised that this power should be sparingly exercised in criminal cases as it may interfere with the allocation of the burden of proof to the prosecution and give the appearance that the trial judge is acting in a partisan manner.[174] A narrow view of this jurisdiction was taken in *Bates v Brady*.[175] Having concluded that the evidence given by a garda when recalled by the respondent District Judge after the close of the prosecution case had to be given in order to establish that the applicant had committed an offence and, thus, was not merely formal evidence, Ó Caoimh J proceeded to grant an order of *certiorari* quashing the conviction of the applicant.

---

[170] *Attorney General (Corbett) v Halford* [1976] IR 318 at 324; *Bates v Brady* [2003] 4 IR 111 at 119; *Price v Humphries* [1958] 2 QB 353, [1958] 2 All ER 725.

[171] [2012] IEHC 195.

[172] *People (AG) v O'Brien* [1963] IR 65 at 68; *Dawson v Hamill* [1990] ILRM 257 at 263; *People (DPP) v Hickey* [2007] IECCA 98 at [5]. Alternatively, if the additional evidence may not be contentious, then it is open to the judge in a civil case to give an opportunity to a party to put that additional evidence before the court on affidavit with the facility for cross-examination on the affidavit if this should be required (see *Moorview Developments v First Active plc* [2010] IEHC 275 at [5.13]). See also *Whelan v AIB* [2011] IEHC 544, [2014] IESC 3, where Peart J ruled that evidence proving the sum owed by the plaintiffs to the first defendant bank could be given on affidavit in order to prove its counterclaim, even though it had not gone into evidence, and this ruling was upheld on appeal.

[173] *People (AG) v O'Brien* [1963] IR 65; *O'Keeffe v Mangan* [2012] IEHC 195; *R. v Remnant* (1806) 1 Russ & Ry 136; *R. v Sullivan* [1923] 1 KB 47 at 58; *R. v Bowles* [1992] Crim LR 726. This power is exercisable at any point up until the jury reaches a verdict: *People (AG) v O'Brien* [1963] IR 65; *Attorney General v McDermott* [1933] IR 512.

[174] *Magee v O'Dea* [1994] 1 IR 500 at 507, [1994] 1 ILRM 540 at 545; *Bates v Brady* [2003] 4 IR 111 at 119; *Duff v Dunne* [2004] IEHC 151.

[175] [2003] 4 IR 111. See also *Duff v Dunne* [2004] IEHC 151 where his decision was followed.

D. Examination-in-Chief

3–73   The examination-in-chief of a witness is carried out by or on behalf of the party calling the witness and its object is to elicit evidence that supports the version of the facts in issue advanced by that party. Apart from the requirement that any questions asked must be directed towards obtaining an answer that is relevant and admissible, the principal constraints on a party engaged in examination-in-chief are that he or she may not use leading questions and he or she cannot cross-examine the witness unless the witness has been classified as hostile.

1. Leading Questions

3–74   The general rule is that, on examination-in-chief, a witness may not be asked leading questions.[176] The most common form of leading question is one which suggests the answer desired. An example would be if a plaintiff was asked in a personal injury action, "Did X run you down with his car?" Another objectionable form of question that is classified as leading is one which assumes the existence of a fact or state of facts in dispute. An example would be asking one party in an action for assault what he did after the other party assaulted him when the fact of the assault has yet to be proved. It is, however, important to point out that the dividing line between leading and non-leading questions is not always clear and there is no ready test available to distinguish the two.[177] It is, perhaps, for this reason that evidence elicited by leading questions is not regarded as inadmissible although the weight to be attached to it may be reduced.[178]

3–75   The reason for the prohibition against asking leading questions is to ensure that the witness gives his or her evidence in his or her own words and counterbalances any tendency for the witness to assent to the suggestions put to him or her.[179] It, thus, ensures that the witness gives truthful and balanced evidence rather than evidence which is tailored to the exigencies of the proceedings. However, strict adherence to the rule would make examination-in-chief slower and more cumbersome and there are a number of recognised exceptions to the rule. Thus, a witness may be asked leading questions: (i) in respect of introductory matters; (ii) in respect of facts which are not in dispute[180]; (iii) to help him or her identify people or objects[181]; (iv) if required to

---

[176]   See the criticisms of O'Donnell J in *People (DPP) v Curran* [2011] IECCA 95 at [24], [2011] 3 IR 785 at 800 to the eliciting of crucial evidence by "a plainly inappropriate and leading question". See also *Maves v Grand Trunk Pacific Railway Co.* (1913) 6 Alta LR 396, 14 DLR 70, *R. v Coffin* [1956] SCR 191. See generally, Keane and Fortson, "Leading Questions: A Critical Analysis" [2011] Crim LR 280.

[177]   The test advanced by Lord Ellenborough in *Nicholls v Dowding* (1815) 1 Stark 81 to the effect that a question is leading if the answer of "yes" or "no" is overbroad and of little assistance.

[178]   *Moor v Moor* [1954] 2 All ER 458 at 459, [1954] 1 WLR 927 at 928. There is New Zealand authority that a trial judge should instruct the jury to attach less weight to an answer given to a leading question (*Gabrielsen v Farmer* [1960] NZLR 832 at 835).

[179]   See *Maves v Grand Trunk Pacific Railway Co.* (1913) 6 Alta LR 396, 14 DLR 70; *Connor v Brant (Township)* (1914) 31 OLR 274 at 285.

[180]   *Maves v Grand Trunk Pacific Railway Co.* (1913) 6 Alta LR 396, 14 DLR 70.

[181]   See *Acerro v Petroni* (1815) 1 Stark 100 where counsel for the party that called a witness to prove a partnership was permitted to ask him whether or not specified persons had participated in the partnership. See also *R. v Watson* (1817) 2 Stark 116 at 128; *Maves v Grand Trunk Pacific Railway Co.* (1913) 6 Alta LR 396, 14 DLR 70; *GPI Leisure Corp Ltd v Herdsman Investments Pty Ltd (No.3)* (1990) 20 N.S.WLR 15 at 25.

aid his or her recollection[182]; and (v) if the witness has been classified as hostile. In addition, the rule is often ignored or diluted in practice with the rigour of its application depending on the forbearance of the opposing party and the trial judge.

2. Hostile Witnesses

3–76   At common law, a party is prohibited from cross-examining or attacking the credibility of a witness called by him or her.[183] It has been suggested that:

> "[i]t would be repugnant to principle, and likely to lead to abuse, to enable a party, having called a witness on the basis that he is at least in general going to tell the truth, to question him or call other evidence designed to show that he is a liar."[184]

3–77   Thus, if a witness called by a party turns out to be unfavourable in that he or she fails to give the evidence expected or gives evidence that assists the opposing party, the only avenue open to the party is to call another witness to give evidence of the matters in respect of which the unfavourable witness has failed to come up to proof.[185]

3–78   There is, however, an established exception at common law whereby a party will be permitted to cross-examine a witness called by him or her if the witness is not merely unfavourable but is hostile,[186] *i.e.* a witness who "is not desirous of telling the truth to the court at the instance of the party calling him".[187] That common law jurisdiction has been supplemented by s.3 of the Criminal Procedure Act 1865.[188] This section, which is applicable in both criminal and civil proceedings, provides:

> "A party producing a witness shall not be allowed to impeach his credit by general evidence of bad character, but he may, in case the witness shall, in the opinion of the judge, prove adverse, contradict him by other evidence, or, by leave of the judge, prove that he has made at other times a statement inconsistent with his present testimony; but before such last mentioned proof can be given the circumstances of the supposed statement, sufficient to designate the particular occasion, must be mentioned to the witness, and he must be asked whether or not he has made such statement."[189]

---

[182] *Maves v Grand Trunk Pacific Railway Co.* (1913) 6 Alta LR 396. See also *R v Turner* [2012] EWCA Crim 1786, [2013] 1 Cr App R 25 where undisputed parts of a witness statement were read to the witness who was too embarrassed to read them in open court.

[183] *Ewer v Ambrose* (1825) 3 B & C 746.

[184] Criminal Law Revision Committee, *Eleventh Report* (1972) (Cmnd. 4991), para.162.

[185] *Ewer v Ambrose* (1825) 3 B & C 746; *Bradley v Ricardo* (1831) 8 Bing 57. See also *Greenough v Eccles* (1859) 5 CBN.S. 786 where it was held that the common law rule that a party may contradict a witness by other witnesses called by him or her was unaffected by s.3 of the Criminal Procedure Act 1865.

[186] *O'Flynn v Smithwick* [1993] 3 IR 589 at 595–596, [1993] ILRM 627 at 631–632; *People (DPP) v Cunningham* [2007] IECCA 49; *Price v Manning* (1889) 42 Ch D 372 at 374. *Cf. McMullen v Clancy (No.2)* [2005] 2 IR 445 at 455 where the contention that witnesses were hostile witnesses because they gave evidence that was unfavourable to the plaintiff who called them was rejected.

[187] Stephen, *Digest of Evidence* 12th edn, art.147. See generally Newark, "The Hostile Witness and the Adversary System" [1986] Crim LR 441; Munday, "Calling a Hostile Witness" [1989] Crim LR 866; Pattenden, "The Hostile Witness" (1992) 56 J Crim L 414.

[188] See *O'Flynn v Smithwick* [1993] 3 IR 589, [1993] ILRM 627 and *R. v Thompson* (1977) 64 Cr App R 96 which make it clear that the statutory jurisdiction under s.3 did not displace the common law jurisdiction enjoyed by a trial judge to allow a witness to be treated as hostile.

[189] The drafting used in this section has been the subject of considerable criticism. See *per* Cockburn CJ in *Greenough v Eccles* (1859) 5 CBN S 786 at 806 and Criminal Law Revision Committee, *Eleventh Report* (1972) (Cmnd. 4991), para.161.

3–79 The use of the term "adverse" to mean "hostile"[190] is confusing but the section did clarify the position as to whether a hostile witness could be cross-examined on a previous inconsistent statement which was previously unclear at common law.

3–80 The decision as to whether to treat a witness as hostile is made by the trial judge upon application by the party that called the witness.[191] In the case of a trial by jury, that decision should be made by the trial judge on a *voir dire* in the absence of the jury[192] to ensure that they are not exposed to any prejudicial evidence if the trial judge decides not to grant the application.[193] Among the matters that may be taken into account by the trial judge in deciding whether to classify a witness as hostile are the witness's refusal to answer questions,[194] the existence of an obvious disregard on the part of the witness of his or her duty to the proper administration of justice,[195] and the extent to which any prior statement made by him or her is inconsistent with his or her testimony.[196] A trial judge has a wide discretion as to what matters are relevant in making this decision and an appeal court will be very reluctant to interfere with the exercise of this discretion and substitute its view, especially where the decision is predicated on the judge's view of a witness's demeanour in the witness box.[197] It, thus, appears that an appeal against a decision of a trial judge as to whether to classify a witness as hostile will only succeed in exceptional circumstances.[198]

3–81 If leave is granted to treat a witness as hostile, the party calling the witness may ask leading questions[199] and cross-examine him or her[200] and that cross-examination is not confined to matters contained in any previous inconsistent statement made by the witness.[201] However, it should be noted that the witness may not be asked questions in relation to his or her bad character, previous misconduct or convictions.[202] It has been held that a hostile witness cannot refuse to answer questions about the inconsistencies

---

[190] See *Greenough v Eccles* (1859) 5 CBN S 786 (construing identical language used in s.22 of the Common Law Procedure (Amendment) Bill 1856 which was superseded by s.3).

[191] Although such an application is generally made during examination-in-chief, it can also be made during re-examination: *R. v Powell* [1985] Crim LR 592.

[192] *People (AG) v Taylor* [1974] IR 97 at 99.

[193] *Cf. People (AG) v Hannigan* [1941] IR 252 at 254.

[194] *O'Flynn v Smithwick* [1993] 3 IR 589 at 596, [1993] ILRM 627 at 632. A genuinely forgetful witness will not be treated as hostile: *McLellan v Bowyer* (1961) 106 CLR 95 at 104.

[195] *O'Flynn v Smithwick* [1993] 3 IR 589 at 596, [1993] ILRM 627 at 632.

[196] See *People (AG) v Hannigan* [1941] IR 252; *People (AG) v Taylor* [1974] IR 97; *O'Flynn v Smithwick* [1993] 3 IR 589, [1993] ILRM 627; *R. v Fraser* (1956) 40 Cr App R 160; *R. v Caracella* [1958] VR 382. *Cf. AG v K* (1948) 82 ILTR 67 (leave to cross-examine witness on the basis of a prior inconsistent statement refused where the trial judge was not satisfied that the prior statement was reliable).

[197] *O'Flynn v Smithwick* [1993] 3 IR 589 at 632, [1993] ILRM 627 at 632; *People (DPP) v Cunningham* [2007] IECCA 49.

[198] See *People (AG) v Hannigan* [1941] IR 252 at 254, where it was conceded by counsel for the applicant and apparently accepted by the Court of Criminal Appeal that the decision of the trial judge on this issue will only be overturned in "exceptional circumstances". See also *Rice v Howard* (1886) 16 QBD 681; *Price v Manning* (1889) 42 Ch D 372; *R. v Henry* (1968) 53 Cr App R 150; *McLellan v Bowyer* (1961) 106 CLR 95; *R. v Lawless* [1974] VR 398.

[199] *R. v Thompson* (1977) 64 Cr App R 96 at 99; *R. v Honeyghon* [1999] Crim LR 221 at 222.

[200] *People (AG) v Taylor* [1974] IR 97 at 99; *Bastin v Carew* (1824) Ry & M 127; *R. v Honeyghon* [1999] Crim LR 221 at 222; *R. v Schriek* [1997] 2 NZLR 139.

[201] *O'Flynn v Smithwick* [1993] 3 IR 589 at 596; [1993] ILRM 627 at 632.

[202] But *cf. R. v Hunter* [1956] VLR 31 and *Price v Bevan* (1974) 8 SASR 81.

with a previous statement by invoking the privilege against self-incrimination on the basis that, to do so, would expose the witness to a risk of prosecution for perjury.[203]

3–82   The procedure to be adopted where a witness, who has been classified as hostile in accordance with s.3 of the Criminal Procedure Act 1865, is cross-examined on a previous inconsistent statement was laid down by the Court of Criminal Appeal in *People (AG) v Taylor*[204] as follows:

> "This particular witness had been allowed to be treated as hostile and, when the jury were recalled to court, the proper procedure for the prosecution was to have put to the witness that she had on another occasion made a statement which differed materially from or contradicted the one she was making in the witness-box. If she were to deny that, then the proper procedure would have been to have her stand down from the box, and to prove in fact that she did in fact make a statement by putting into the box the person who took the statement, proving it in the ordinary way without revealing the contents of the statement at that stage. The earlier witness should then have been put back into the box and the statement put to her for identification, and then her attention should have been directed to the passage in which the alleged contradiction or material variation appears. If she had agreed that there was such a contradiction or material variation, that should have been the end of the matter in so far as the question of impugning her credibility was concerned because there would then have been before the jury an admission from the witness to the effect that she had made contrary statements on the same matter. The statement might then be put in evidence, though that would not be strictly necessary at that stage when the admission had been made. If she had persisted in denying the contradiction, then the statement, having already been proved, would have gone in as evidence of the fact that the witness had made a contrary statement."[205]

3–83   A gloss was placed on the decision in *Taylor* by the Court of Criminal Appeal in *People (DPP) v Hanley*.[206] In that case, the accused was charged with assault causing harm and threatening to kill or cause serious injury. The chief prosecution witness was the person who had been assaulted and injured. She failed to turn up for the trial and had to be arrested. When called as a witness, she said that she wanted to retract a written statement made by her to gardaí in which she had given details of an assault on her by the accused. She also said that she was not sure when she had been injured, that she had been fighting with a girl, that she did not know if the accused had any identifying marks even though she had given a detailed description of a tattoo in her garda statement and that the person that she had named as her assailant was not in court. The prosecution applied successfully to have her treated as hostile and counsel for the prosecution then proceeded to cross-examine her by reference to her previous statement and on the oral evidence previously given by her, suggesting that the evidence given by her in court was untrue to the extent that it differed from her garda statement. On appeal, complaint was made that this cross-examination had gone beyond what was permitted by the decision in *Taylor* but this contention was rejected by the Court of Criminal Appeal.

3–84   With regard to the statement by Walsh J in *Taylor* that, if the witness agreed that there was "a contradiction or material variation", that was "the end of the matter in so far as the question of impugning her credibility was concerned", the Court noted that Walsh J had not suggested that the prosecution is inhibited in all cases from cross-examination with the object of persuading the witness to stand by his or her original

---

203 *Singh v R* [2010] NZSC 161 at [39].
204 [1974] IR 97.
205 [1974] IR 97 at 99–100 (*per* Walsh J).
206 [2010] IECCA 101, [2011] 1 IR 247.

statement and the Court did not consider that the prosecution was so circumscribed. In the Court's view, the first and obvious objective of the prosecution where a witness has declined to give evidence in accordance with an earlier garda statement would be to persuade the witness to do this. It was further noted that, since the prior statement is generally not evidence of its contents, there is often little purpose in discrediting the witness, at least where the success of the prosecution depends on the evidence of the witness. Accordingly, it is far more useful to succeed in getting the witness to verify the truthfulness of his or her original statement.[207] In the instant case, the prime objective of the cross-examination (which had been achieved to a significant extent) had been to secure the agreement of the witness with her original statement and to demonstrate inconsistencies between her statement and the evidence that she had given in court. The Court was satisfied that this was a legitimate use of the hostile witness exception.

3–85 Unless a previous inconsistent statement is admitted pursuant to s.16 of the Criminal Justice Act 2006,[208] it is not evidence of the facts stated in it but is only evidence going to the credibility of the witness and this should be made clear to the jury.[209] However, if a hostile witness on being cross-examined on a previous inconsistent statement adopts and confirms its contents, then the contents of the statement become part of his or her evidence and can be acted on by the tribunal of fact.[210] The weight to be attached to this evidence will be affected by the inconsistency in the evidence of the witness, and the trial judge may, and in some instances is under a duty to, direct the jury that little weight should be given to it.[211] It has been held that it is open to the party calling a witness who is treated as hostile to rely on those parts of the witnesses' evidence as supports that party's case.[212]

E. Cross-Examination

1. Introduction

3–86 Cross-examination is considered to be of pivotal importance in the trial process. Wigmore has described cross-examination as "the greatest legal engine ever invented for the discovery of truth".[213] That view was echoed by Hardiman J in *Maguire v Ardagh*,[214] who extolled the value of cross-examination as a truth eliciting process:

"Where a person is accused on the basis of false statements of fact, or denied his civil or constitutional rights on the same basis, cross-examination of the perpetrators of these falsehoods

---

[207] Reference was made to *R. v Thompson* (1977) 64 Cr App R 96 as an example of a case where this objective was achieved.
[208] See Chap.5.
[209] *People (AG) v Taylor* [1974] IR 97 at 100; *People (DPP) v McArdle* [2003] 4 IR 186 at 195; *People (DPP) v Murphy* [2013] IECCA 1 at [20]; *R. v Golder* [1960] 3 All ER 457 at 459, [1960] 1 WLR 1169 at 1172–1173.
[210] *R. v Maw* [1994] Crim LR 841 at 841–842; *R. v Honeyghon* [1999] Crim LR 221 at 222.
[211] *People (DPP) v Kelly* [1987] IR 596 at 598.
[212] See the decision of the Supreme Court of India in *Himanshu @ Chintu v State of NCT of Delhi*, 2011 STPL (Web) 6 SC, 4 January 2011 (noted by Pattenden at (2011) 15 E & P 170).
[213] Wigmore, *Evidence* 3rd edn (Boston: Little Brown and Company, 1940), Vol. V, §1367, p.29. Reservations have, however, been expressed about the forensic value of cross-examination as a technique for discovering the truth about past events (see the Law Reform Commission's *Consultation Paper on Hearsay in Civil and Criminal Cases* (LRC CP 60 – 2010) at [2.88]–[2.91]).
[214] [2002] 1 IR 385 at 704.

is the great weapon available to him for his own vindication. Falsehoods may arise through deliberate calculated perjury (as in the case of Parnell[215]), through misapprehension, through incomplete knowledge, through bias or prejudice, through failure of memory or delusion. In some cases a witness may not be aware that his evidence is false. A witness may be telling the literal truth but refrain, or be compelled to refrain, from giving a context which puts it in a completely different light. And a witness called to prove a fact favourable to one side may have a great deal of information which he is not invited to give in evidence, favourable to the other party."[216]

3–87   Given that effective cross-examination depends on the availability of material to challenge a witness's account and credibility,[217] the right to cross-examine underpins procedural protections such as disclosure of materials that can be used for the purpose of cross-examination[218] and access by an expert to a plaintiff or complainant to conduct an assessment.[219] Concerns about attenuation of the right to cross-examine also subtend the hearsay rule.[220]

2. Constitutional Basis of Right to Cross-Examine

3–88   Given the importance of cross-examination to the trial process, it is unsurprising that the right to cross-examine is considered to be a fundamental procedural right in this jurisdiction, constitutionally guaranteed in both civil and criminal cases. In *State (Healy) v Donoghue*,[221] Gannon J stated that, among the procedural rights enjoyed by an accused by virtue of Art. 38.1, was a right "to hear and test by examination the evidence offered by or on behalf of his accuser".[222] Subsequently, in *Donnelly v*

---

[215] In his judgment, Hardiman J gave details of the cross-examination by Sir Charles Russell QC of the accuser of Charles Stewart Parnell who, he said, was demonstrated to be a perjurer by cross-examination of remarkable skill leading to the vindication of Parnell by the special commission set up to investigate the allegations against him (see [2002] 1 IR 385 at 706).

[216] See also the comments of the same judge in *Murphy v Flood* [2010] IESC 21 at [204], [2010] 3 IR 136 at 196. Part of the efficacy of cross-examination is that a witness is required to answer questions without assistance from his legal advisers or any other person and there is a long standing convention, which is memorialised in the case of solicitors in the Law Society of Ireland, *A Guide to Good Professional Conduct for Solicitors* 3rd edn (2013) at 40, that, when a witness is in the course of being cross-examined, a solicitor should not, without leave of the court or without the consent of counsel or the solicitor for the other side, discuss the case with the witness, whether or not that witness is a client. A similar prohibition applies in the case of counsel with para.5.20 of the Code of Conduct for the Bar of Ireland (adopted on 22 July 2013), stipulating that: "Barristers shall not confer with a witness that they called while such witness is under cross-examination without prior leave of the other parties or the Court."

[217] *Maguire v Ardagh* [2002] 1 IR 385 at 705; *O'Callaghan v Mahon* [2005] IESC 9 at [71], [2006] 2 IR 32 at 65–66.

[218] See *People (DPP) v GK*, unreported, Court of Criminal Appeal, 6 June 2002; *O'Callaghan v Mahon* [2005] IESC 9, [2006] 2 IR 32; *O'Callaghan v Mahon* [2007] IESC 17, [2008] 2 IR 514; *Murphy v Flood* [2010] IESC 21 at [206], [2010] 3 IR 136 at 196. In the first *O'Callaghan* case, Hardiman J said (at [68], 65) that, to deprive the applicant of access to previous statements by a witness, "would be to hamper and possibly to subvert his ability to cross-examine".

[219] *JF v DPP* [2005] IESC 24 at [25], [2005] 2 IR 174 at 183.

[220] *Borges v Medical Council* [2004] IESC 9 at [33], [2004] 1 IR 103 at 105, [2004] 2 ILRM 81 at 92.

[221] [1976] IR 325 at 335.

[222] See also *per* O'Higgins CJ in the Supreme Court who stated ([1976] IR 325 at 349) that: "the words 'due course of law' in Article 38 make it mandatory that every criminal trial shall be conducted in accordance with the concept of justice, that the procedures applied shall be fair, and that the person accused will be afforded every opportunity to defend himself."

Ireland,[223] Hamilton CJ described the right to cross-examine as an "essential ingredient in the concept of fair procedures".[224] In *The Criminal Law (Jurisdiction) Bill, 1975,*[225] O'Higgins CJ summarised the position by saying that:

> "An opportunity to cross-examine on behalf of the accused any witness called against him is fundamental to a trial in due course of law and the taking of evidence for production at such trial without such an opportunity would be contrary to the Constitution."

3–89   The right to cross-examine also enjoys constitutional protection in civil cases by virtue of the guarantee of the personal rights of the citizen contained in Art.40.3. Delivering the judgment of the Supreme Court in *In re Haughey,*[226] Ó Dálaigh CJ stated that Art.40.3 "is a guarantee to the citizen of basic fairness of procedures" which required, *inter alia*, that the defendant in that case "be allowed to cross-examine, by counsel, his accuser or accusers".[227] Again, in *Donnelly v Ireland,*[228] Hamilton CJ stated that:

> "the central concern of the requirements of due process and fair procedures is the same, that is to ensure the fairness of the trial of an accused person. This undoubtedly involves the rigorous testing by cross-examination of the evidence against him or her."[229]

3–90   The constitutional position is reinforced by the position under the European Convention on Human Rights, Art.6(3)(d) of which stipulates that an accused has "the right to examine or have examined witnesses against him". In *Kostowski v The Netherlands,*[230] it was held by the European Court of Human Rights that an accused must be afforded an adequate and proper opportunity to question and challenge a witness giving evidence against him.

3–91   It follows that a party to civil proceedings is entitled to cross-examine any witness called by an adverse party unless there is a statutory curtailment of the right to cross-examine.[231]

---

[223] [1998] 1 IR 321 at 350, [1998] 1 ILRM 401 at 413.

[224] See also *Melton Enterprises Ltd v Censorship of Publications Board* [2004] 1 ILRM 260 at 274.

[225] [1977] IR 129 at 154.

[226] [1971] IR 217 at 264.

[227] See also *Borges v Medical Council* [2004] IESC 9, [2004] 1 IR 103, [2004] 2 ILRM 81 at 90. *Cf. Kiely v Minister for Social Welfare (No.2)* [1977] IR 267 at 281, where Henchy J stated that it was a breach of natural and constitutional justice "if one party is allowed to send in his evidence in writing, free from the truth-eliciting processes of a confrontation which are inherent in an oral hearing, while his opponent is compelled to run the gauntlet of oral examination and cross-examination".

[228] [1998] 1 IR 321, [1998] 1 ILRM 401.

[229] [1998] 1 IR 321 at 356, [1998] 1 ILRM 401 at 418–419. See also *Murray v Commission to Inquire into Child Abuse* [2004] 2 IR 222 at 304–305.

[230] (1990) 12 EHRR 434.

[231] See *DS v Minister for Health and Children* [2005] IEHC 58 where O'Neill J held that the respondent was entitled to cross-examine the applicant on an appeal from a decision of the Hepatitis C Compensation Tribunal even though cross-examination at a hearing before the Tribunal was prohibited by statute. Given that cross-examination was a constitutionally protected right, he was unable to hold that it had been excluded in circumstances where the relevant statutory provisions were silent as to whether cross-examination was available on an appeal. See also *W (A Child) (Cross-examination)* [2010] EWCA Civ 1449, [2011] 1 FLR 1979 where it was held that a failure to provide the opportunity for cross-examination will ordinarily cause any subsequent court order to be quashed.

3. Objectives of Cross-Examination

3–92 Cross-examination of a witness called by a party is carried out by the other parties in the proceedings and has two main objectives: (i) to elicit evidence from the witness in relation to the facts in issue which is favourable to the cross-examining party; and (ii) to cast doubt upon the veracity, accuracy, or reliability of the evidence given by the witness.[232]

3–93 With regard to the first objective, a cross-examining party is entitled to question a witness on any fact in issue or matter relevant to a fact in issue and is not restricted to the evidence given by the witness during examination-in-chief. As for the second objective, there are a number of methods by which a cross-examining party may seek to undermine the credibility of a witness and/or the veracity, accuracy or reliability of the evidence given by him or her. The cross-examining party can question the witness on any errors, contradictions or inconsistencies in the evidence given by the witness and any previous inconsistent statements made by him or her. The party may also question the witness as to his or her powers of perception, memory and recall and any relevant physical or mental disabilities that could affect these. Finally, the cross-examining party may attack the credit of the witness by questioning him or her in relation to previous convictions, bias, partiality or improper motive on his or her part, his or her bad character or general reputation for untruthfulness.[233] When doing so, the cross-examining party may put matters to the witness which are not directly relevant to the facts in issue.[234]

4. Liability to Cross-Examination

3–94 In general, any witness who gives evidence, even if very limited in nature, is liable to cross-examination. However, there is authority to the effect that a witness is not liable to cross-examination if he or she is not sworn and does not give evidence but is simply called to produce a document which does not require proof or is to be proven by other means,[235] or if he or she is called by mistake and the mistake is discovered after the witness has been sworn but before examination-in-chief has commenced.[236]

5. Cross-Examination by Multiple Parties

3–95 The general rule in both civil and criminal proceedings is that a witness may be examined by all other parties to the proceedings even if the witness has not given any evidence adverse to the interests of the party that wishes to cross-examine him or her.[237] Thus, in criminal proceedings, an accused, or a witness called by him or her, may be cross-examined by counsel for a co-accused even if he or she has not given any

---

[232] See *Director of Corporate Enforcement v Seymour* [2006] IEHC 369 at [7] where the second of these two objectives was identified by O'Donovan J.

[233] Most of these matters are dealt with below but the topic of impeaching the character of a witness is examined in Chap.9.

[234] *People (DPP) v Cull* (1980) 2 Frewen 36 at 40; *People (DPP) v Campbell*, unreported, Court of Criminal Appeal, 19 December 2003 at 25.

[235] *Summers v Moseley* (1834) 2 Cr & M 477; *Lyone v Long* (1917) 10 Sask LR 343, 36 DLR 76.

[236] *Wood v Mackinson* (1840) 2 Mood & R 273; *Lyone v Long* (1917) 10 Sask LR 343, 36 DLR 76.

[237] *Allen v Allen* [1894] P 248 at 253; *Dryden v Surrey County Council* [1936] 2 All ER 535 at 537–538.

evidence adverse to that accused.[238] In civil proceedings, a defendant will usually be permitted to cross-examine a co-defendant or a witness called by him or her, subject to a discretion on the part of the judge to refuse to allow such cross-examination where the co-defendants have similar interests.[239]

3–96 Where a witness is subject to cross-examination by multiple parties, as where there are a number of plaintiffs or defendants in civil proceedings, the general rule of practice is that the witness will be cross-examined in accordance with the order in which the parties are named in the proceedings although a trial judge has a discretion to permit cross-examination in a different sequence.[240] Where there are multiple defendants, and one of them calls a witness, the usual practice is that the plaintiff cross-examines that witness and then the other defendants cross-examine the witness in turn. The sequence in which cross-examination occurs may be of some importance because the cross-examining party may not be permitted to cover the same ground, or at least to cover it to the same extent. Thus, the first party to cross-examine may engage in a wide ranging cross-examination but subsequent cross-examining parties may be confined to matters not already covered or of special importance to them.[241]

6. Limits on Cross-Examination

3–97 The central feature of cross-examination, which distinguishes it from examination-in-chief, is that the cross-examining party is permitted to ask leading questions.[242] This enables the cross-examining party to engage in more intensive questioning of the witness and that cross-examination can be "hard, detailed, challenging and bruising".[243] A cross-examiner is also permitted to put questions based on information that is inadmissible or that he or she is unable to prove except through cross-examination and to "pursue any hypothesis that is honestly advanced on the strength of reasonable inference, experience or intuition".[244] However, it is important to note that there are limits to the form, content and length of questioning that is permissible on cross-examination. In particular, cross-examination by counsel is expected to be conducted with restraint and appropriate courtesy and consideration for the witness[245] and he or she cannot put questions based on a factual premise that he or she knows to be false or is reckless as to whether it is false.[246] A cross-examiner

---

[238] *R. v Hilton* [1972] 1 QB 421, [1971] 3 All ER 541; *Murdoch v Taylor* [1965] AC 574 at 584, [1965] 1 All ER 406 at 410; *R. v McLaughlin* (1974) 2 OR (2d) 514, 15 CCC (2d) 562.

[239] See *Millar v B.C. Rapid Transit Co.* (1926) 36 BCR 345, [1926] 1 DLR 1171; *Loslet v Clement* (1970) 3 NBR (2d) 317, 18 DLR (3d) 185.

[240] *Stewart v Walker* (1903) 6 OLR 495 at 506.

[241] *Graydon v Graydon* (1921) 51 OLR 301 at 302–303. Similar guidelines apply if more than one counsel represents a party and they are permitted to cross-examine (see *Omnia Pelts v C.P. Airlines Ltd* (1986) 57 OR (2d) 568; *Phillips v Phillips* [1966] 1 NSWLR 49; *Eva Pty Ltd v Charles Davis Ltd* [1982] VR 515).

[242] *Parkin v Moon* (1836) 7 C & P 408; *McLure v Mitchell* (1974) 6 ALR 471. *Cf. Mooney v James* [1949] VLR 22 (no absolute right to put leading questions in cross-examination).

[243] *People (DPP) v DO* [2006] IESC 12, [2006] 2 ILRM 61 at 73 (*per* Hardiman J).

[244] *R v Lyttle* (2004) 180 CCC (3d) 476 at [46]–[48].

[245] *Mechanical & General Inventions Co. Ltd v Austin* [1935] AC 346 at 360 (*per* Sankey LC).

[246] *R v Lyttle* (2004) 180 CCC (3d) 476 at [46]–[48].

should also avoid comment in the course of cross-examination[247] and refrain from unnecessary and personalised attacks on expert witnesses.[248]

3–98   A trial judge exercises a general supervisory jurisdiction in relation to the cross-examination of witnesses and may disallow questions which he or she considers to be improper. So, for example, in *People (DPP) v R.*,[249] it was held that counsel for the prosecution should not have put a question to the accused, who was on trial for sexual offences, as to whether the complainant was perjuring herself. Barrington J, delivering the judgment of the Court of Criminal Appeal, stated that:

> "a question put in that particular form implying that either the complainant is a perjuress or the applicant is guilty of rape is one which is inherently unfair to the applicant in that the jury might take the view that if they acquitted the applicant they would be implying that the complainant was a perjurer".[250]

3–99   Similarly, a trial judge may disallow questions which he or she regards as vexatious or irrelevant to any matter at issue.[251] A trial judge may also curtail cross-examination which is repetitive or excessive in length[252] if the judge is satisfied that the cross-examiner has been given an adequate opportunity to ask relevant questions of the witness.[253] Particular vigilance may be required by a judge where a vulnerable witness, such as a child or a person with an intellectual disability, is being cross-examined.[254]

3–100   However, given the importance and constitutional basis of the right to cross-examine, the discretion of trial judges to disallow questions or otherwise curtail cross-examination is somewhat circumscribed and a trial judge should not rule out a line of questioning unless it is clearly irrelevant or otherwise objectionable. Thus, in *O'Broin v Ruane*[255] it was held that the respondent District Judge had erred in law in refusing to permit the applicant's solicitor to inquire in a general way as to what procedures had been followed in relation to a specimen taken in connection with a drunk-driving charge. Even though the cross-examination of a garda witness was in essence a "fishing expedition" because the applicant's solicitor had no knowledge of

---

247 See *R. v Farooqi* [2013] EWCA Crim 1649, [2003] All ER (D) 16 at [113].

248 *People (DPP) v Abdi* [2005] 1 ILRM 382 at 393.

249 [1998] 2 IR 106.

250 [1998] 2 IR 106 at 110. See also *R. v Baldwin* [1925] All ER 402, (1925) 18 Cr App R 175 (questions should not be framed in such a way as to invite argument rather than elicit evidence on the facts in issue).

251 *Kenny v Coughlan* [2008] IEHC 28. See in the civil context, Ord.36, r.37 of the Rules of the Superior Courts which provides: "The Judge may in all cases disallow any questions put in cross-examination of any party or other witness which may appear to him to be vexatious, and not relevant to any matter proper to be inquired into in the cause or matter."

252 *O'Broin v Ruane* [1989] IR 214 at 216; *R. v Kalia* [1975] Crim LR 181.

253 *Burke v Fulham* [2010] IEHC 448 at [36]; *Burke v Anderson* [2010] IEHC 452 at [30]–[31]. *Cf.* the position in New Zealand where s.85 of the Evidence Act 2006 which provides that a judge may disallow or direct that a witness is not obliged to answer any unacceptable question, *viz.* "any question that the Judge considers improper, unfair, misleading, needlessly repetitive, or expressed in language that is too complicated for the witness to understand" having regard to a number of factors including the age of the witness and the nature of the proceeding.

254 See the discussion of the difficulties arising in relation to the cross-examination of vulnerable witnesses and judicial control of same in *R v Wills* [2011] EWCA Crim 1938, [2012] 1 Cr App R 2 at [36]–[39]. See, further, Keane, "Cross-examination of vulnerable witnesses – towards a blueprint for re-professionalisation" (2012) 16 E & P 175 and Keane, "Towards a principled approach to the cross-examination of vulnerable witnesses" [2012] Crim LR 407.

255 [1989] IR 214.

any non-compliance with the relevant statutory requirements, it was held by Lynch J that he was entitled to so cross-examine the garda. Otherwise, there was a serious danger that a person might be wrongfully convicted.

3–101 In *People (DPP) v Piotrowski*,[256] a distinction was drawn between cross-examination in relation to the facts in issue and cross-examination as to credibility, and it was held that a trial judge would have greater latitude to intervene and control cross-examination in the case of the latter:

> "The defence is, of course, entitled to some latitude in pursuing issues concerning the credibility of important prosecution evidence. However, it is also true that the trial judge has an important role in ensuring that the case is confined to questions which are at least of sufficient relevance to the issues which the jury has to decide to make their pursuit material. If the issues being pursued by cross-examination are directly relevant to the facts of the case in the sense of the facts which are alleged to constitute the offence charged or the guilt of the accused in respect of that offence, then wide latitude must be allowed. Where the issues raised simply go to general credibility not directly connected with the offence but connected with matters which may have some indirect bearing on the credibility of witnesses in relation to the offence, then it seems to this Court that the trial judge is entitled to exercise a greater degree of control over the extent to which such issues can be pursued."

3–102 It is open to a trial judge to intervene during the cross-examination of a witness to ensure that a witness is given an adequate opportunity to give an answer to a question[257] or to ask questions.[258] However, if the interventions of a trial judge are so frequent, prolonged, or of such a nature as to be unfairly disruptive or to give the impression of partiality in favour of one side of the case, this may result in a verdict being set aside.[259] Further, in a criminal trial before a jury, if the intervention(s) of the trial judge involve adverse comment on the evidence of a witness for the defence which are such as to invite the jury to disbelieve that witness, this may lead to the quashing of a conviction.[260]

3–103 A trial was found to be unsatisfactory and an appeal against a conviction for rape allowed because of excessive interventions by the trial judge in cross-examination in *People (DPP) v McGuinness*.[261] The Court of Criminal Appeal quoted with approval the following passage from the judgment of Denning LJ in *Jones v National Coal Board*[262]:

> "Now it cannot, of course, be doubted that a judge is not only entitled but is, indeed, bound to intervene at any stage of a witness's evidence if he feels that, by reason of the technical nature of the evidence or otherwise, it is only by putting questions of his own that he can properly follow and appreciate what the witness is saying. Nevertheless, it is obvious for more

---

[256] [2014] IECCA 17 at [8.3].

[257] *People (DPP) v Hayes* [2011] IECCA 65.

[258] *R. v Campbell* [1970] VR 120.

[259] *People (DPP) v Scanlon* (1985) 3 Frewen 15; *Browne v Tribune Newspapers plc* [2001] 1 IR 521 at 537–538; *Power v Doyle* [2007] IEHC 375 at [67], [2008] 2 IR 69 at 84; *R. v Hulusi* (1974) 58 Cr App R 378; *Magel v Krempler* (1970) 14 DLR (3d) 593; *R. v Mawson* [1967] VR 205; *EH Cochrane Ltd v Ministry for Transport* [1987] 1 NZLR 146.

[260] See *People (DPP) v Willoughby* [2005] IECCA 4. *Cf. People (DPP) v Kavanagh* [2008] IECCA 100.

[261] [1978] IR 189. See also *McCann v Halpin* [2014] IEHC 276 at [22] where the interventions by the District Judge, though numerous, were not found to be sufficient excessive so as to warrant the grant of relief by way of judicial review but formed part of the circumstances leading to a finding of objective bias on the part of the District Judge.

[262] [1957] 2 QB 55 at 65.

than one reason that such interventions should be as infrequent as possible when the witness is under cross-examination. It is only by cross-examination that a witness's evidence can be properly tested, and it loses much of its effectiveness in counsel's hands if the witness is given time to think out the answer to awkward questions; the very gist of cross-examination lies in the unbroken sequence of question and answer. Further than this, cross-examining counsel is at a grave disadvantage if he is prevented from following a preconceived line of inquiry which is, in his view, most likely to elicit admissions from the witness or qualifications of the evidence which he has given in chief. Excessive judicial interruption inevitably weakens the effectiveness of cross-examination in relation to both the aspects which we have mentioned, for at one and the same time it gives a witness valuable time for thought before answering a difficult question, and diverts cross-examining counsel from the course which he had intended to pursue, and to which it is by no means easy sometimes to return."[263]

3–104   The Court expressed the view that a judge should intervene only when cross-examining counsel mis-states evidence already given or asks a question that the witness may not have understood. The interventions in that case went much further than this and were so numerous that the Court concluded that it had been impossible for counsel for the accused to conduct a cross-examination on the lines he considered most effective and could have had the effect of causing the jury to believe that the judge had formed a definitive opinion on the credibility of the complainant.

3–105   A particularly egregious example of improper intervention in cross-examination by a judge can be seen in *Dineen v Delap*,[264] where the respondent District Judge told a garda witness not to bother responding to counsel for the accused because he was only trying to trip him up. Morris J, unsurprisingly, considered this to be "an unwarranted interference with counsel in the performance of his duty and responsibility of making his defence".[265] The respondent, in rejecting a submission made by counsel for the accused, had also declared that "[t]he days of the garda making a slip in the witness box are long gone and if he does make a slip I will recall him." This suggestion was also characterised by Morris J as improper on the basis that it "would cause an impartial observer to recognise that the judge hearing the case was prepared to support the prosecution to the extent of filling gaps which their evidence might leave".[266]

7. Cross-Examination of an Accused

3–106   If an accused elects to give evidence, then he or she can be cross-examined by the prosecution and by any co-accused with a view to eliciting evidence in relation to the facts in issue or in relation to matters which are not directly relevant to those facts for the purpose of challenging the credibility of the evidence of the accused.[267] That cross-examination can be carried out "with the fullest vigour or robustness appropriate to the context of the trial".[268] However, it was emphasised by the Court of Criminal Appeal in *People (DPP) v Cull*[269] that the cross-examiner should not ask questions or elicit evidence that would undermine the fairness of the trial and "the Court should be

---

[263] This passage was also quoted with approval by Birmingham J in *Power v Doyle* [2007] IEHC 375, [2008] 2 IR 69.

[264] [1994] 2 IR 228.

[265] [1994] 2 IR 228 at 234.

[266] [1994] 2 IR 228 at 234.

[267] See *People (DPP) v Cull* (1980) 2 Frewen 36 at 39–40; *People (DPP) v Campbell*, unreported, Court of Criminal Appeal, 19 December 2003 at 25.

[268] *People (DPP) v DO'S* [2006] IESC 12 at [5], [2006] 3 IR 57 at 59, [2006] 2 ILRM 61 at 65.

[269] (1980) 2 Frewen 36.

alert to prevent the course of cross-examination being used in a manner inconsistent with the presumption of innocence or being abused by the introduction of prejudicial matter neither relevant not pertinent to the issue for trial".[270] In the case of counsel for the prosecution, this obligation is reinforced by the well established principle that his or her duty is not to obtain a conviction at all costs and he or she should present all relevant evidence to the jury fairly and objectively.[271]

3–107   An example of where cross-examination was found to have been unfair can be seen in *People (DPP) v Campbell*,[272] where the accused had been cross-examined in relation to matters that had not been disclosed in the book of evidence or raised as part of the prosecution case and which were prejudicial. The Court of Criminal Appeal took the view that this cross-examination was impermissible and, in circumstances where the evidence thereby elicited had been relied on by the Special Criminal Court to convict the accused, his conviction was quashed.[273]

3–108   Unfairness of a different variety was found to have occurred in *People (DPP) v DO*.[274] The accused was a teacher who had been convicted of a number of sexual offences involving a boy. At trial, he had been cross-examined at length about his sexuality and his involvement in a scouting organisation with a view to showing that he had a disposition towards sexual activity with boys. The Supreme Court held that significant elements of the cross-examination had been "intimidating, disparaging and, if not personally vilifying, demeaning"[275] and "was replete with impermissible innuendos as to the accused's profile or disposition" so that, if "it was not by those means calculated to prejudice the jury, it can only have had that effect".[276] The contention that this cross-examination was justified on the basis of evidence given by the accused of his involvement in scouting activities, the fact that he was unmarried and that he was of a heterosexual orientation were rejected. The Court took the view that the cross-examination, given its nature and extent, could only have distracted and prejudiced the jury in its ability to reach a fair verdict based on the real and admissible evidence placed before them. The conviction was, therefore, quashed because there were such departures from the standards of proper practice to be observed by counsel for the prosecution as to deny the accused the substance of a fair trial.

8. The Admissibility of Evidence Elicited by Cross-Examination

3–109   The rules in relation to the admissibility of evidence apply equally to cross-examination and, therefore, a cross-examining party cannot put questions to a witness

---

[270] (1980) 2 Frewen 36 at 40.

[271] *People (DPP) v DO'S* [2006] IESC 12 at [3], [2006] 3 IR 57 at 59, [2006] 2 ILRM 61 at 64; *R. v Puddick* (1865) 4 F & F 497 at 499; *R. v Banks* [1916] 2 KB 621 at 623; *Randall v R.* [2002] 1 WLR 2237 at 2242; *Boucher v The Queen* (1954) 110 Can CC 263 at 270. See also para.10.19 of the Code of Conduct for the Bar of Ireland (adopted on 22 July 2013) which stipulates that: "It is not the duty of prosecuting barristers to obtain a conviction by all means at their command but rather they shall lay before the jury fairly and impartially the whole of the facts which comprise the case for the prosecution and shall assist the Court with adequate submissions of law to enable the law to be properly applied to the facts."

[272] Unreported, Court of Criminal Appeal, 19 December 2003.

[273] *Cf. People (DPP) v DO'S* [2004] IECCA 23 where this decision was distinguished.

[274] [2006] IECCA 12, [2006] 2 ILRM 61.

[275] [2006] 2 ILRM 61 at 65.

[276] [2006] 2 ILRM 61 at 66.

in relation to inadmissible evidence[277] or which would have the effect of eliciting inadmissible evidence.[278] It is also important to note that it is the answers given by the witness under cross-examination which constitutes evidence in the case, not the questions put by the cross-examiner.[279] Accordingly, if a witness does not accept a factual premise put to him or her in cross-examination, there will be no evidence before the tribunal of fact of that factual premise unless other evidence is called to establish its existence.[280]

9. Previous Inconsistent Statements

3–110   Cross-examination of a witness by reference to previous inconsistent statements made by him or her is one of the most effective methods of both eliciting helpful evidence and impugning the credibility of the witness. As Hardiman J observed in *O'Callaghan v Mahon*[281]: "The cross-examination of a witness on the basis of comparing what he has said on oath with an account given on another occasion is one of the longest established of the conventional methods of contradiction."[282] He went on to state[283]:

> "In my view, it is a matter of common justice and indeed common sense, that a witness who makes a grave allegation against another may be contradicted out of his own mouth where that is possible. If a right to do this were not assured, cross-examination would be gravely hampered and even subverted. It is a statement of the obvious to say that the credibility of a particular statement made by a particular person is reduced or destroyed if he has made a contradictory statement on a previous occasion, unless that can be explained in some way. Conversely, consistency enhances the credibility of a statement."

3–111   The learned judge elaborated in a subsequent instalment of that litigation that[284]:

> "Although a certain amount of technicality has grown up around the circumstances in which a prior statement can be put to a witness, the basic principle is not a technical one at all, but one grounded in ordinary fairness, common sense and every day experience. If a person is shown to have freely given, on two different occasions, contradictory accounts of the same matter within his own knowledge, it follows that he was either lying or mistaken on at least one occasion. If the same person is shown to have given such contradictory accounts on more than one occasion, clear questions arise as to his or her credibility or reliability. Any advocate with experience of litigation with seriously contested factual allegations will have seen cases won and lost on this basis."

---

[277]   *The Leopardstown Club Ltd v Templeville Developments Ltd* [2010] IEHC 152 at [5.28].
[278]   *R. v Thomson* [1912] 3 KB 19; *R. v Treacy* [1944] 2 All ER 229; *R. v Gillespie* (1967) 51 Cr App R 172; *Re P* [1989] Crim LR 897; *R. v Gray* [1998] Crim LR 570.
[279]   *People (DPP) v Connolly* [2003] 2 IR 1 at 5; *People (DPP) v Murphy* [2005] IECCA 1 at [70], [2005] 2 IR 125 at 149.
[280]   *People (DPP) v Connolly* [2003] 2 IR 1 at 5.
[281]   [2005] IESC 9 at [42], [2006] 2 IR 32 at 55.
[282]   To similar effect, the same judge stated in *O'Callaghan v Mahon* [2007] IESC 17 at [356], [2008] 2 IR 514 at 614, that: "a prior statement by a witness which is inconsistent with his subsequent testimony is one of the most effective and best and longest recognised techniques for attacking that witness's credibility. This is so regardless of whether the inconsistency is a positive factual inconsistency or takes the form of an omission to state something relevant in the prior statement". In that case (at [364], 617–618), he gave an example of a case from 1829 where Daniel O'Connell had destroyed the credibility of the chief prosecution witness, thereby saving the lives of all but one of the accused, by cross-examining him on a previous inconsistent statement.
[283]   [2005] IESC 9 at [46], [2006] 2 IR 32 at 58.
[284]   *O'Callaghan v Mahon* [2007] IESC 17 at [357], [2008] 2 IR 514 at 615.

3–112 The procedure for cross-examination on previous inconsistent statements in both civil and criminal proceedings is regulated by the provisions of ss. 4 and 5 of the Criminal Procedure Act 1865.[285] If a witness, on cross-examination, admits that he or she has made a previous oral or written statement that is inconsistent with his or her testimony, then, the credibility of the witness having been impeached, no further proof of that statement is permitted.[286] However, if the witness denies or does not admit making the statement, it may be proved against him or her in accordance with the provisions of ss.4 and 5 if it is relevant to the proceedings.[287]

3–113 Section 4 of the Criminal Procedure Act 1865 applies to both oral and written statements and provides as follows:

> "If a witness, upon cross-examination as to a former statement made by him relative to the subject-matter of the indictment or proceeding, and inconsistent with his present testimony, does not distinctly admit that he has made such a statement, proof may be given that he did in fact make it; but before such proof can be given, the circumstances of the supposed statement, sufficient to designate the particular occasion, must be mentioned to the witness, and he must be asked whether or not he has made such statement."

3–114 As appears, this section applies where a witness "does not distinctly admit" that he made the previous statement and, thus, can be invoked not only where a witness clearly denies that he or she made the statement but also where a witness asserts that he or she cannot remember or refuses to answer.[288]

3–115 Section 5 of the Criminal Procedure Act 1865, which only applies to written statements, provides that:

> "A witness may be cross-examined as to previous statements made by him in writing or reduced into writing relative to the subject-matter of the indictment or proceeding, without such writing being shown to him; but if it is intended to contradict such witness by the writing, his attention must, before such contradictory proof can be given, be called to those parts of the writing which are to be used for the purpose of so contradicting him; provided always, that it shall be competent for the judge, at any time during the trial, to require the production of the writing for his inspection, and he may thereupon make such use of it for the purposes of the trial as he may think fit."

3–116 Although s.5 expressly provides that a witness may be cross-examined on

---

[285] In *O'Callaghan v Mahon* [2005] IESC 9 at [46]–[47], [2006] 2 IR 32 at 57–58, Hardiman J pointed out that neither the Criminal Procedure Act 1865 nor its predecessor, the Common Law Procedure Act 1854, conferred the entitlement to cross-examine on previous inconsistent statements, which existed at common law, but merely regulated its exercise. The Law Reform Commission has recommended the replacement of ss.3–5 of the Criminal Procedure Act 1865 by updated provisions in its *Consultation Paper on Hearsay in Civil and Criminal Cases* (LRC CP 60 – 2010) at [5.40].

[286] *People (AG) v Cradden* [1955] IR 130 at 138; *R. v P (GR)* [1998] Crim LR 663.

[287] The question as to whether a statement is relevant to the proceedings is a matter for the discretion of the trial judge: *R. v Bashir* [1969] 3 All ER 692 at 694, [1969] 1 WLR 1303 at 1306. For an example of where that test was satisfied, see *Attorney General v Murray* [1926] IR 266.

[288] In *People (AG) v Cradden* [1955] IR 130, the appellant succeeded in his appeal on the ground, *inter alia*, that when asked by counsel for the applicant whether she had made a previous inconsistent statement in a pre-trial deposition, she had answered initially that she could not remember saying it and then said that she may have said it. The Court of Criminal Appeal took the view that counsel should have been allowed to question her further in order to get her to adopt a firmer attitude one way or the other. However, in view of the wording of s.5, it does not appear that this was necessary because the answers of the witness did not amount to an explicit admission and thus, her previous inconsistent statement could have been proved on that basis.

a previous inconsistent statement made by him or her without it being shown to the witness, it appears that the cross-examining party must have a copy of the document in court even if he or she does not intend to contradict the witness with it.[289] In *People (DPP) v Diver*,[290] it was held that the procedure for the cross-examination of a witness on a previous inconsistent statement laid down in *People (AG) v Taylor*[291] in the context of hostile witnesses applies equally to the cross-examination of a non-hostile witness and is of general application. Therefore, if the cross-examining party wishes to contradict the witness using the document, the document should first be given to the witness with an invitation to read the document (or the relevant portion of it) and the witness should then be asked whether he or she wishes to change his or her evidence in the light of the contents of the statement.[292] If the witness declines to change his or her evidence, then the cross-examining party can accept that answer and is under no obligation to prove the document. However, if the cross-examining party wishes to contradict the witness using the document, the document must be proved in evidence[293] and, if it is not proved, it cannot be used for any purpose including impeaching credibility.[294] Once proven,[295] the cross-examining party will then read the document (or the relevant portions) aloud to the witness and put it to him or her that the earlier statement in the document is truthful rather than the testimony of the witness.[296] The document will thereby be put into evidence as part of the cross-examiner's case.[297] The document may then be inspected by the tribunal of fact although the trial judge, in the exercise of his or her discretion under s.5, may decide not to leave the entirety of the document to the jury but only those portions that were the subject of cross-examination.[298]

3–117   In general, where a previous inconsistent statement is proved in evidence, it merely goes to the consistency and credibility of the witness and is not evidence of the facts stated therein[299] and the trial judge should expressly instruct the jury to this effect.[300] However, by way of an exception to the hearsay rule, express provision is made in s.16 of the Criminal Justice Act 2006 for the admission of previous inconsistent statements as evidence of the truth of their contents in specified circumstances.[301]

---

[289]   *R. v Yousry* (1914) 11 Cr App R 13; *R. v Anderson* (1929) 21 Cr App R 178; *R. v Derby Magistrates Court, ex parte B* [1996] AC 487, [1995] 4 All ER 526; *R. v Thompson* [1995] 3 NZLR 423.

[290]   [2005] IESC 57 at [47]–[48], [2005] 3 IR 270 at 286.

[291]   [1974] IR 97.

[292]   *O'Callaghan v Mahon* [2005] IESC 9 at [47], [2006] 2 IR 32 at 58; *People (DPP) v Diver* [2005] IESC 57 at [48], [2005] 3 IR 270 at 286; *The Leopardstown Club Ltd v Templeville Developments Ltd* [2010] IEHC 152 at [5.25].

[293]   *O'Callaghan v Mahon* [2005] IESC 9 at [47], [2006] 2 IR 32 at 58; *R. v Riley* (1866) 4 F & F 964; *R. v Wright* (1866) 4 F & F 967.

[294]   *People (DPP) v Diver* [2005] IESC 57 at [49], [2005] 3 IR 270 at 286.

[295]   Although it was held in *People (AG) v Taylor* [1974] IR 97 at 99 that the statement had been proven before the witness was cross-examined on it, the decision in *People (DPP) v Diver* [2005] IESC 57 at [50], [2005] 3 IR 270 at 287, contemplates that the statement could be proven after the witness has given evidence.

[296]   *Cf. Attorney General v Murray* [1926] IR 266 at 282.

[297]   *The Leopardstown Club Ltd v Templeville Developments Ltd* [2010] IEHC 152 at [5.25].

[298]   *R. v Beattie* (1989) 89 Cr App R 302.

[299]   *People (AG) v Cradden* [1955] IR 130 at 138; *People (AG) v Flynn* [1963] IR 255 at 260; *People (DPP) v McArdle* [2003] 4 IR 186 at 195; *R. v White* (1922) 17 Cr App R 60; *R. v Harris* (1927) 20 Cr App R 144; *R. v Askew* [1981] Crim LR 398; *Tepaki v Police* [1967] NZLR 337 at 339.

[300]   *People (AG) v Flynn* [1963] IR 255 at 260; *People (DPP) v McCarthy* [2007] IECCA 64 at [97], [2008] 3 IR 1 at 36; *R. v Carrington* [1969] NZLR 790. *Cf. People (AG) v Taylor* [1974] IR 97 at 100.

[301]   The application of this section is considered in Chap.5.

10. Cross-Examination on Documents

3–118   In addition to the rules addressed in the previous section in relation to cross-examination in relation to the previous inconsistent statements of a witness, there are a number of rules, more honoured in the breach than in the observance, at least in civil cases, that apply in respect of the cross-examination of a witness on the basis of a document that has not been authored by the witness.

3–119   These rules were the subject of a detailed and erudite analysis by Edwards J in *The Leopardstown Club Ltd v Templeville Developments Ltd.*[302] The learned judge commenced by explaining that, depending on the circumstances, a document could be relied on as an item of real evidence, as original evidence or as testimonial evidence which was admitted pursuant to an exception to the hearsay rule, and different rules in terms of what was required to be proven in order to establish the receivability in evidence and admissibility of the document applied depending on which category the document fell into. He drew a clear distinction in that regard between the requirements that have to be satisfied in relation to primary evidence of the contents of the document and proof of due execution in order for a document to be receivable in evidence, either as original evidence or testimonial evidence,[303] and the general rules of admissibility such as the hearsay rule and the rule against opinion evidence that apply if a document is to be relied on testimonially.[304]

3–120   The first matter to be addressed is whether the requirements for receivability of the document have been satisfied. If so, then subject to any issues that arise in relation to the admissibility of the document, a cross-examiner can proceed to question a witness about the document. However, if a document that a cross-examiner wishes to use for the purpose of cross-examination had not already been proven, then he or she either has to prove the document at that juncture (if necessary, by standing the witness down temporarily with the leave of the court to enable this to be done) or, alternatively, continue subject to an express (or more usually an implied) undertaking to do so later.[305] Although not referred to by Edwards J, the position in this regard had been confirmed by the Supreme Court in *People (DPP) v Diver,*[306] where Hardiman J regarded it as well established that it is not proper for counsel to cross-examine out of a document by way of suggesting that the contents of that document and not the evidence of the witness being cross-examined represent the true position unless he or she is in a position to prove the document and its contents.[307]

3–121   Edwards J went on to note that, if the cross-examiner subsequently fails to prove the document, then he or she will not be able to rely on it and, in the case of a trial by jury, the judge will have to give a warning to the jury in strong terms that

---

[302] [2010] IEHC 152 at [5.1]–[5.55].

[303] The rules in relation to the receivability in evidence of documents are examined further in Chap.12.

[304] [2010] IEHC 152 at [5.9] and [5.45].

[305] [2010] IEHC 152 at [5.27]. He thereby affirmed the continued application of the rule in relation to cross-examination on documents laid down by the House of Lords in *The Queen's Case* (1820) 2 Brod & B 284, 129 ER 976 except to the extent that it had been abrogated by the provisions of the Criminal Procedure Act 1865 in relation to prior inconsistent statements.

[306] [2005] IESC 57 at [51], [2005] 3 IR 270 at 287.

[307] See also *Cooper-Flynn v Radio Telifís Éireann* [2004] IESC 27 at [210], [2004] 2 IR 72 at 152; *R v Yousry* (1914) 11 Cr App R 13; *R v Gillespie* (1967) 51 Cr App R 172 at 176–177 and *R v Cross* (1990) 91 Cr App R 115 at 122.

they must not have regard to the document as it does not constitute evidence or it may even be necessary to discharge the jury if the risk of prejudice cannot be ameliorated by such a warning.[308] He also held that, if a cross-examiner is unable or unwilling to prove a document, then only very limited use can be made of it using what has become known as the "Phipson formula":

"[A] document may be placed in the hands of a witness without any indication being given as to its nature or contents and the witness may be asked questions based on its contents but not referring to its contents. So the witness may be asked to look at the document and to say whether he accepts that what the document purports to record is true. If the witness indicates his acceptance then, at that point (subject to any issue as to admissibility, *e.g.* hearsay), the document and its contents become evidence in the case and may be referred to without restriction. They are then available to be considered in conjunction with the witness's oral testimony that the contents of the document are true. However, if the defendant indicates that he does not accept that what the document purports to record is true then the contents of the document cannot be adduced in evidence unless and until the document is proven (or an undertaking is given to do so later), or the requirement has been waived."[309]

3–122   He noted that, where a cross-examiner seeks to put a question to a witness in respect of a document that had not been proven, the party calling the witness can object to the question on that basis or, alternatively, rather than objecting, can call upon the cross-examiner to produce the document and place it before the witness. The cross-examiner then has a choice. He or she had to either desist from pursuing the matter further, or elect to proceed and cross-examine on the document, in which case the document is thereby put into evidence and can be relied on both parties.[310]

3–123   The use that can be made in cross-examination of a document that has been proven depends on whether it is admissible or not. If the document is admissible, then no difficulty arises and the contents of the document may be put to the witness and the witness cross-examined in relation to same. However, if the document is inadmissible, as where it constitutes inadmissible hearsay, then only very limited use may be made of it. As Edwards J explained[311]:

"Unless a receivable document is also admissible only very limited use may be made of it. Inadmissible evidence cannot be made admissible simply by its use in cross-examination. Again, the most that can be done with an inadmissible document is to ask the witness to look at the document and, without describing the nature or contents of the document to the court, to invite the witness to consider whether he or she wishes to give any further or different evidence. (This formula, when employed in jury trials, is sometimes known as the *Phipson formula*, in respect of which there is more below.) If a witness, on being shown a document, asserts or admits that its contents are true, then those contents which he or she so adopts become part of his evidence. But the contents of an inadmissible document cannot be made evidence unless they are so adopted. In this instance the evidence admitted and received by the court is the witness's testimony, not the document which remains inadmissible as evidence in its own right. In particular, where the witness is referred to part only of a document and adopts or admits to the truth of that part, such adoption or admission extends only to that part. No evidence may

---

[308] [2010] IEHC 152 at [5.51]. He also warned that a court might mark its displeasure at the failure to prove the documents by an award of costs against the offending party or against counsel personally.

[309] [2010] IEHC 152 at [5.52]. This appellation derives from the suggested form of questioning in relation to an inadmissible document to be found in the leading text of *Phipson on Evidence* 17th edn, para.12-33.

[310] [2010] IEHC 152 at [5.52].

[311] [2010] IEHC 152 at [5.28].

be led from the witness as to the contents of the remainder of the document and no regard whatever may be had to the actual document itself which is not admissible in evidence."[312]

3–124 The learned judge also pointed out that, if, while the document is before the witness, the cross-examiner makes reference of any sort to either the nature of the document or to the contents of the document, he or she may by his or her conduct be regarded as tendering the document in evidence with the consequent obligation to prove it. Accordingly, it was improper for counsel to do this, unless invited to do so by his opponent, if he was unwilling or unable to prove the document or if the contents of the document were inadmissible. Furthermore, he indicated that a cross-examiner should not refer to the contents of a document that has not been proven or is not admissible without giving his or her opponent advance notice and an adequate opportunity to object.[313]

3–125 In *Leopardstown*, Edwards J also referred to a separate common law rule[314] (which is of little modern relevance) that, if a cross-examiner calls for and inspects in court a document in the possession of his opponent or his opponent's witness, he or she is bound to put that document in evidence as part of the cross-examiner's case.[315]

11. The Finality of Answers to Collateral Questions

3–126 As a general rule, the answers given by a witness under cross-examination to questions concerning collateral matters must be treated as final.[316] Thus, even if a party on cross-examination fails to elicit the desired answer, he or she is generally confined to the terms of that answer and may not call further evidence in rebuttal if the matter is collateral. This "rule of convenience"[317] is based on "the desirability of avoiding a multiplicity of issues".[318] As Rolfe B observed in *Attorney General v Hitchcock*[319]:

> "The laws of evidence as to what ought and what ought not to be received, must be considered as founded on a sort of comparative consideration of the time to be occupied in examinations of this nature, and the time which it is practicable to bestow upon them. If we lived for a thousand years instead of about sixty or seventy, and every case were of sufficient importance, it might be possible, and perhaps proper, to throw a light on matters in which every possible question might be suggested, for the purpose of seeing by such means whether the whole was unfounded, or what portion of it was not, and to raise every possible inquiry as to the truth of the statements made. But I do not see how that could be; in fact, mankind find it to be impossible."[320]

---

[312] See also *Snowden v Branson* [1999] EWCA Civ 1777.
[313] [2010] IEHC 152 at [5.53].
[314] See *Stroud v Stroud (No.1)* [1963] 1 WLR 1080.
[315] [2010] IEHC 152 at [5.29].
[316] *R. v Burke* (1858) 8 Cox CC 44; *People (DPP) v Barr*, unreported, Court of Criminal Appeal, *ex tempore*, 2 March 1992 at 8; *Irish Bank Resolution Corporation Ltd v Quinn Investments Sweden AB* [2012] IESC 51 (p.32 of judgment of Hardiman J); *Harris v Tippett* (1811) 2 Camp. 637; *Attorney General v Hitchcock* (1847) 1 Exch. 91; *R. v Funderbunk* [1990] 2 All ER 482, [1990] 1 WLR 587; *R. v Edwards* [1991] 2 All ER 266, [1991] 1 ALR 207; *R. v Nagrecha* [1997] 2 Cr App R 401; *Piddington v Bennett and Wood Pty Ltd* (1940) 63 CLR 533.
[317] *R. v Burke* (1858) 8 Cox CC 44 at 53 (*per* Christian J); *People (DPP) v McKevitt* [2005] IECCA 139.
[318] *Per* O'Flaherty J in *People (DPP) v Barr*, unreported, Court of Criminal Appeal, *ex tempore*, 2 March 1992 at 8.
[319] (1847) 1 Exch 91.
[320] (1847) 1 Exch 91 at 105.

3–127   The rationale for this rule was considered by Hardiman J in *Nevin v DPP*,[321] who quoted the foregoing passage and observed that:

> "This justification turns on the practical need to limit the length of litigation and the issues, remote from the issues in question at a trial, which may be gone into. If a witness is contradicting a party as to something sufficiently relevant that that party could call evidence on it himself then it is deemed to be of direct relevance and a witness's answers can be contradicted. But if a party seeks to contradict a witness on a matter itself irrelevant to the trial except insofar as reflects on the witness's credibility, he is bound by the answer of the witness and can take the issue no further. I may say that it appears to me that the rule can also be justified on the basis that a witness coming to court, perhaps because he is summoned by the public prosecutor, is entitled to the protection of the Court to ensure that he is not exposed to damaging contradiction or publicity about a matter which happened (if at all) very many years previously and is irrelevant to the trial, in the sense that the opposing party could not call evidence of it during that trial."

3–128   In a similar vein, Kearns J explained in *People (DPP) v McKevitt*[322] that: "The collateral issue rule reflects concern that the longer a trial is allowed to deviate from the facts at issue, the more likely it is that the jury will become sidetracked and the less likely it is that the court will reach an effective decision. The rule is inherently pragmatic, and encourages the court to avoid a 'multiplicity of issues' arising in the trial."[323]

3–129   The question of when a matter can be said to be collateral is a matter of some nicety. The test formulated by Pollock CB in *Attorney General v Hitchcock*,[324] and approved by the Irish Court of Criminal Appeal in *R. v Burke*,[325] is that, if the matter is one in respect of which the cross-examining party would be allowed to introduce evidence-in-chief because of its connection with the issues in the case, it is not collateral and the witness's answers with regard to it may be rebutted. Thus, in general terms, a matter will be considered to be collateral if it goes merely to the credit of a witness, but will not be collateral if it bears upon the facts in issue or a fact relevant to an issue in the proceedings. However, the distinction between matters going merely to the credit of a witness and matters relevant to the facts in issue is not easy to draw, particularly in proceedings relating to sexual offences.[326] It should also be borne in mind that, having regard to the policy behind the rule, the question as to whether a matter is collateral or not may turn on whether the matter is difficult or easy to prove.[327]

3–130   A good example of a collateral matter is furnished by the facts of *R. v Burke*.[328] In that case, a witness was called to give evidence on behalf of the defendant. He pleaded a lack of competence in English, and no objection being taken by the prosecution, he was sworn and gave evidence in Irish. On cross-examination he was asked whether he had, on a recent occasion, spoken in English to two persons who were present in

---

[321] [2010] IECCA 106, [2011] 1 ILRM 479 at 499.

[322] [2005] IECCA 139.

[323] He went on to hold that this rule means that a court of trial is not required to deliver multiple "mini-judgments" on the credibility of a witness or to establish definitively the facts of any such collateral issue. The Court of Criminal Appeal's holding on this issue was referred to with apparent approval by the Supreme Court: [2008] IESC 51, [2009] 1 ILRM 401.

[324] (1847) 1 Exch 91.

[325] (1858) 8 Cox CC 44.

[326] See *R. v Funderburk* [1990] 2 All ER 482; [1990] 1 WLR 587 and *R. v Nagrecha* [1997] 2 Cr App R 401.

[327] *R. v S* [1992] Crim LR 307.

[328] (1858) 8 Cox CC 44.

court and were shown to the witness. He denied this, and the two persons were called to contradict him. On appeal, it was held by a majority of the Court of Criminal Appeal that the evidence had been improperly admitted. Christian J was of the view that the question of whether the witness could speak English was "wholly beside and collateral to the issue which the jury had to try, which was the guilt or innocence of the prisoner."[329] Similarly, in *Attorney General v Hitchcock*,[330] it was held that the question of whether a witness had been offered a bribe to give false evidence which bribe had not been accepted was a collateral matter, being totally irrelevant to the matter in issue.

3–131   The question of whether a matter was collateral also arose in *Nevin v DPP*[331] in the context of an application by the applicant pursuant to s.2 of the Criminal Procedure Act 1993 to have her conviction for the murder of her husband and the solicitation of his murder quashed on the basis that new evidence had become available in relation to the persons solicited including material suggesting that one of them might have had an involvement in the Dublin bombings in 1974. The Court of Criminal Appeal was satisfied that the matters relied on as constituting new or newly discovered evidence were all collateral matters, as they did not go directly to the question of who had killed the deceased or had him killed and were only relevant to the credibility of the witnesses. That being so, then the answer to any question on these matters would have been binding on the questioner and could not have been taken further.

3–132   It appears that the dividing line between matters relevant to an issue and matters relevant only to credit will be differently drawn in the case of sexual offences where the issue of consent arises. In *R. v Nagrecha*[332] it was held that, where consent is an issue, the credibility of the complainant is of such importance that rebuttal evidence going to credibility may be admitted. However, as can be seen from the decision of the Court of Criminal Appeal in *People (DPP) v Onumwere*,[333] that will not be the position where consent is not in issue. The accused was convicted of a sexual assault which was alleged to have taken place in a flat to which the complainant had gone after meeting a number of men in a night club. Under cross-examination, the complainant denied that she had kissed some of the men in the nightclub where she met them. The defence sought to call a witness to rebut this denial but the trial judge refused to allow this evidence to be adduced and the Court of Criminal Appeal held that he had been correct to do so in circumstances where consent was not in issue and this evidence went to credit only and not to a fact in issue.

3–133   There are three established exceptions to the general rule against the finality of answers to collateral questions as follows: (i) previous inconsistent statements; (ii) previous convictions; and (iii) evidence of bias. Proof of inconsistent statements has already been considered and, therefore, only the latter two exceptions will be considered here.

---

[329] (1858) 8 Cox CC 44 at 54.
[330] (1847) 1 Exch 91.
[331] [2010] IECCA 106, [2011] 1 ILRM 479.
[332] [1997] 2 Cr App R 401.
[333] [2007] IECCA 48.

(a) Previous convictions

3–134   The proof of previous convictions in both civil and criminal proceedings is governed by s.6 of the Criminal Procedure Act 1865, which provides as follows:

> "A witness may be questioned as to whether he has been convicted of any felony or misdemeanour, and upon being so questioned, if he either denies or does not admit the fact, or refuses to answer, it shall be lawful for the cross-examining party to prove such conviction."

3–135   Section 6 is broadly drafted and permits a witness to be cross-examined about a conviction for any offence whether or not such an offence is relevant to the issues in the case or the credibility of the witness.[334] However, it would seem that any cross-examination in relation to previous convictions would be subject to the general supervisory discretion of a trial judge discussed above to disallow questions which are irrelevant, vexatious or oppressive.

3–136   It should be noted that the provisions of s.1(f) of the Criminal Justice Act 1924, which is examined in Chapter 9, operate as a powerful disincentive to the use of s.6 by counsel for the accused when cross-examining witnesses in criminal cases.

(b) Bias

3–137   A cross-examining party will not be bound by the answers received if the cross-examination goes further than merely attacking the credibility of the witness and seeks to establish bias, partiality or improper motive on the part of a witness.[335] As formulated in *R. v Burke*,[336] this exception applies "in cases in which the antecedent statements, or acts, of a witness are calculated to show that he was under a bias as regards either party, or ... that he stood in such a position of such dominant influence of either party over him, that a bias must necessarily follow".[337] Thus, "the matter which is to be inquired into, must be of a kind to bring the witness into a special connection with the subject matter of the particular issue, or with one of the parties to that issue."[338] It can be seen, therefore, that the allegation of bias may relate to either the parties to an action or the issues raised therein and, as such, encompasses any matter which might provide an incentive for a party to give testimony that is not wholly truthful.

3–138   In *People (DPP) v McGinley*,[339] the appellant was charged with larceny of cattle. At his trial, the principal evidence against him was that of an alleged accomplice. Counsel for the appellant cross-examined the accomplice as to matters pertaining to his trial in the Circuit Court with the object of showing that he had received a suspended sentence by reason of an undertaking on his part to co-operate in the prosecution of the appellant. The trial judge ruled that the questions went merely to the credit of the witness and, thus, the appellant was bound by his answers and could not adduce affirmative evidence to contradict the answers of the accomplice witness. However, on appeal, it was held that the trial judge had erred because the line of questioning

---

[334]   *Cf. Clifford v Clifford* [1961] 3 All ER 231 at 232, [1961] 1 WLR 1274 at 1276.

[335]   *R. v Burke* (1858) 8 Cox CC 44; *People (DPP) v McGinley* [1987] IR 340; *Attorney General v Hitchcock* (1847) 1 Exch 91; *R. v Shaw* (1888) 16 Cox CC 503; *R. v Mendy* (1976) 64 Cr App R 4.

[336]   (1858) 8 Cox CC 44.

[337]   (1858) 8 Cox CC 44 at 53 (*per* Christian J).

[338]   (1858) 8 Cox CC 44 at 53 (*per* Christian J).

[339]   [1987] IR 340.

fell "within the general category of questioning seeking to lead to the establishing of partiality, bias or improper motive on the part of the witness, as distinct from a general assertion of lack of credit."[340]

12. Requirement to Put Matters to Witness on Cross-Examination

3–139   As a general rule, a party who intends to call evidence to contradict the testimony given by a witness on examination-in-chief is required to put that evidence to him during cross-examination so that he or she has an opportunity of providing an explanation in relation to that evidence.[341] In *Browne v Dunn*,[342] Lord Herschell explained the rationale for this rule as follows:

> "Now, my Lords, I cannot help saying that it seems to me to be absolutely essential to the proper conduct of a cause, where it is intended to suggest that a witness is not speaking the truth on a particular point, to direct his attention to the fact by some questions put in cross-examination showing that that imputation is intended to be made, and not to take his evidence and pass it by as a matter altogether unchallenged, and then, when it is impossible for him to explain, as perhaps he might have been able to do so if such questions had been put to him, the circumstances which it is suggested indicate that the story he tells ought not to be believed, to argue that he is a witness unworthy of credit. My Lords, I have always understood that if you intend to impeach a witness you are bound, whilst he is in the box, to give an opportunity to making any explanation which is open to him; and, it seems to me, that is not only a rule of professional practice in the conduct of a case, but is essential to fair play and fair dealing with witnesses."[343]

3–140   If a party fails to do this, then the trial judge has a discretion as to whether to admit the contradictory evidence but, in general, it will not be admitted unless the witness is recalled and the evidence put to him or her and an opportunity given of commenting on it.[344]

3–141   This requirement to put matters to a witness applies not only to contradictory evidence but also where a party intends to impeach the credibility of a witness in closing

---

[340] [1987] IR 340 at 345. See also *Thomas v David* (1836) 7 C & P 350 (defendant could call evidence to contradict denial of female servant called as witness for the claimant that she was his kept mistress); *R. v Shaw* (1888) 16 Cox CC 503 (accused could call evidence to contradict denial of prosecution witness that he had threatened revenge on the accused); *R. v Phillips* (1936) 26 Cr App R 17 (accused should have been permitted to call witness to prove admissions allegedly made by complainants that that the charges against him were false which they denied on cross-examination).

[341] *Browne v Dunn* (1893) 6 R. 67; *R. v Hart* (1932) 23 Cr App R 202; *R. v Fenlon* (1980) 71 Cr App R 307; *Rahme v Smith & Williamson Trust Corporation Ltd* [2009] EWHC 911 (Ch) at [90]; *Tullow Uganda Ltd v Heritage Oil and Gas Ltd* [2013] EWHC 1656 (Comm) at [61]–[62]; *R. v Hawke* (1974) 3 OR (2d) 210 at 225; *Young v Dawe* (1998) 156 DLR (4th) 626 at 638; *Reid v Kerr* (1974) 9 SASR 367; *R. v Byczko (No.2)* (1977) 17 SASR 460; *Bell Group Ltd v Westpac (No.9)* [2008] WASC 239 at [1023]–[2041]. However, there is authority to suggest that this rule does not apply in the District Court (*O'Connell v Adams* [1973] Crim LR 313). For a discussion of the rule, see Kennedy, "Putting the case against the rule in *Browne v Dunn*" (2006) 11(2) BR 39 who suggests that it is applied too strictly by the Irish courts.

[342] (1893) 6 R. 67.

[343] (1893) 6 R. 67 at 70–71. See also *Gutierrez v R.* [1997] 1 NZLR 192.

[344] See *R. v Cannan* [1998] Crim LR 284.

argument and suggest that a witness is not to be believed in relation to a particular matter.[345] In *Browne v Dunn*,[346] Lord Halsbury stated:

> "To my mind nothing would be more absolutely unjust than not to cross-examine witnesses upon evidence which they have given, so as to give them notice, and to give them an opportunity of explanation, and an opportunity often to defend their own character, and, not having given them such an opportunity, to ask the jury afterwards to disbelieve what they have said, although not one question has been directed either to their credit or to the accuracy of the facts they have deposed to."[347]

3–142 This requirement was reaffirmed in *R. v Fenlon*,[348] where it was held that it applied equally where an accused intended to put forward a version of events that differed from that given by another accused. It was emphasised that:

> "[i]t is the duty of counsel who intends to suggest that a witness is not telling the truth to make it clear to the witness in cross-examination that he challenges his veracity and to give the witness an opportunity to reply. It need not to done in minute detail, but it is the duty of counsel to make it plain to the witness, albeit he may be a co-defendant, that his evidence is not accepted and in which respects it is not accepted."[349]

3–143 In *People (DPP) v Brett*,[350] the applicant and his co-accused had been convicted of the murder of a deceased who had died from stab wounds following a joint trial. On appeal, complaint was made that there had been a failure by counsel for the other co-accused to put to the applicant on cross-examination the evidence of a witness who was subsequently called and testified that the applicant had a knife in his possession a few hours before the deceased had been killed. The trial judge indicated that the applicant could be recalled or could present or call any other witness to address this evidence but the applicant did not do so. In the circumstances, the Court of Criminal Appeal was satisfied that there had not been any prejudice to the fairness of the trial of the applicant.

3–144 It is not necessary for the cross-examining party to expressly suggest that a particular witness is lying if it is evident from the course of cross-examination that it is proceeding on the basis that the witness is inherently incapable of being believed.[351]

13. Unavailability of Witness for Cross-Examination

3–145 There is authority to support the proposition that the evidence of a witness given on examination-in-chief may be taken into consideration by the tribunal of fact even if the witness is unavailable for cross-examination, or cross-examination of the witness is interrupted, by reason of the death or illness of the witness provided that, in the case of a trial before a jury, they are adequately warned in relation to the weight to be attached to the evidence of the witness.[352] However, it is doubtful whether

---

[345] *Browne v Dunne* (1893) 6 R. 67 at 76–77; *R. v Hart* (1932) 23 Cr App R 202; *R. v Fenlon* (1980) 71 Cr App R 307; *Dayman v Simpson* [1935] SASR 320; *Transport Ministry v Garry* [1973] 1 NZLR 120.

[346] (1893) 6 R. 67.

[347] (1893) 6 R. 67 at 76–77.

[348] (1980) 71 Cr App R 307.

[349] (1980) 71 Cr App R 307 at 313.

[350] [2011] IECCA 12.

[351] *R. v Lovelock* [1997] Crim LR 821. *Cf. Palmer v R.* [1980] 1 SCR 759; (1980) 106 DLR (3d) 212.

[352] See *R. v Doolin* (1882) 1 Jebb CC 123 (evidence-in-chief of witness who died before cross-

such a warning can adequately address the prejudice caused by the deprivation of an opportunity to cross-examine, particularly in a criminal case where an accused has not been afforded an opportunity to fully test the evidence of an important prosecution witness.[353] It is submitted that, having regard to the importance of the right to cross-examine, the evidence of a witness who is unavailable for cross-examination should only be left to the jury in exceptional cases as, for example, where the evidence of the witness is of relatively minor importance in the context of proceedings or, possibly, where the witness was fully cross-examined by another party to the proceedings with similar interests.

F. Re-Examination

3–146   A witness who has been cross-examined may be re-examined by the party who called him or her[354] with a view to eliciting further evidence that is favourable to that party and to rehabilitate the credibility of the witness and the veracity, reliability and accuracy of the evidence given by him or her if this has been impugned on cross-examination. The principal rule governing re-examination is that it must be confined to matters that were dealt with on cross-examination and a witness may only be questioned in relation to new matters with the leave to the trial judge.[355]

3–147   It should be noted that evidence which was not admissible on examination-in-chief may become admissible as a result of the nature of the cross-examination. For example, a witness may be re-examined in relation to a previous consistent statement if an allegation of recent fabrication is made upon cross-examination.[356]

G. Refreshing Memory

1. Introduction

3–148   Although, as noted above, the primary means by which parties generally seek to prove their case is oral evidence, human memory is very fallible and exact recollection of events quickly fades. It is therefore permissible, subject to certain conditions, for witnesses to refresh their memory using statements which they made much nearer to the events in question. For the purpose of analysis, it is helpful to distinguish between the use by witnesses of documents to refresh memory in court and out of court.

---

examination admissible though it might be afforded little weight); *R. v Stretton* (1986) 86 Cr App R 7 (trial judge had a discretion to allow a trial for sexual offences to continue and to leave the evidence of the complainant to the jury in circumstances where the complainant, having been cross-examined for some time, became ill and incapable of continuing to give evidence).

[353] *Cf. R. v Lawless* (1993) 98 Cr App R 342.

[354] This is the case even if the witness has been treated as hostile: *R. v Wong* [1986] Crim LR 683.

[355] *Prince v Samo* (1838) 7 Ad & El 627; *Wojcic v Incorporated Nominal Defendant* [1969] VR 323.

[356] See section H below in relation to the admission of previous consistent statements to rebut allegations of recent fabrication.

2. Refreshing Memory in Court

3–149   The general principle is that a witness, while giving evidence,[357] is entitled[358] to refer to a document for the purpose of refreshing his or her memory provided that the document (or the original thereof) was either made or verified by the witness contemporaneously with the events to which it refers.[359] However, it is important to note that this facility cannot be used as a means to circumvent the fundamental requirement of orality and, thus, a witness cannot read from a prepared statement on the stand.[360] A number of rules relating to the use of documents to refresh memory are examined below.

(a) Requirement that document have been made or verified contemporaneously

3–150   The requirement of contemporaneity between the document and the events recorded in it is crucial because it is only where the document was created at a time when the events in question were fresh in the memory of the person who created or verified the document that the rationale of permitting a witness to use the document to refresh memory will apply. A document can, therefore, only be used by a witness to refresh memory if it was made "at the time of the transaction to which it refers, or shortly afterwards when the facts were fresh in his recollection".[361] In *The Leopardstown Club Ltd v Templeville Developments Ltd*,[362] Edwards J identified the requirement as being that the document "was made or verified by the witness, contemporaneously or near contemporaneously with the events to which it relates". However, it should be noted that there is no prescribed lapse of time that will exclude a document from being used to refresh memory because the requirement of contemporaneity is considered to be a matter of fact and degree.[363] In *R. v Richardson*[364] the English Court of Appeal advocated a flexible approach, stating that the requirement of contemporaneity provides "a measure of elasticity and should not be taken to confine witnesses to an over-short period".[365]

3–151   In *R. v Rongonui*,[366] Tipping J identified a number of factors which will be taken into consideration in the assessment of whether a memory was fresh at the time that the document was made or adopted: (a) the relative significance to the witness

---

[357] A witness may refresh his or her memory at any stage while giving evidence including during cross-examination or re-examination: *R. v Sutton* (1992) 94 Cr App R 70.

[358] In *DPP v Clifford*, unreported, High Court, 22 July 2002, it was held by Ó Caoimh J that a witness is entitled, as a matter of law, to refresh his or her memory once the relevant requirements are satisfied and the witness does not require the permission of the trial judge to do so although he or she should indicate his or her intention to do so. It appears that it is open to a trial judge, where the interests of justice so requires, to suggest to a witness that he or she refresh his or her memory (*R. v Tyagi*, The Times, 21 July 1986).

[359] *Lord Talbot de Malahide v Cusack* (1864) 17 ICLR 213; *Northern Banking Co. v Carpenter* [1931] IR 268; *DPP v Clifford*, unreported, High Court, 22 July 2002.

[360] *Dineen v Delap* [1994] 2 IR 228 at 234.

[361] *Lord Talbot de Malahide v Cusack* (1864) 17 ICLR 213 at 217 (*per* O'Brien J). See also *Northern Banking Co. v Carpenter* [1931] IR 268; *DPP v Clifford*, unreported, High Court, 22 July 2002; *AG's Reference (No.3 of 1979)* (1979) 69 Cr App R 411.

[362] [2010] IEHC 152 at [5.21].

[363] *R. v Simmonds* (1967) 51 Cr App R 316 at 330.

[364] [1971] 2 QB 484, [1971] 2 All ER 773.

[365] [1971] 2 QB 484 at 490, [1971] 2 All ER 773 at 777.

[366] [2010] NZSC 279, [2011] 1 NZLR 23 at [52]–[53].

of the events described in the document; (b) the lapse of time between the events in question and the making or adoption of the document; (c) any evidence the witness gives concerning the freshness of their memory; and (d) how detailed and lucid the recollection recorded in the document is.

(b) Past recollection recorded

3–152 Although the principle allowing a witness to use a document to refresh his or her memory proceeds on the basis that sight of the document will "jog" the memory of the witness, in many cases the witness will, in fact, have no recollection of the transaction and the document will not revive his or her memory.[367] As Hayes J stated in *Lord Talbot de Malahide v Cusack*[368]:

> "... in nine cases out of ten the witness's memory is not at all refreshed: he looks at [the document] again and again, and he recollects nothing of the transaction; but, seeing that it is in his own handwriting, he gives credit to the truth and accuracy of his habits; and, though his memory is a perfect blank, he nevertheless undertakes to swear to the accuracy of his entry."[369]

3–153 Such cases were categorised by Wigmore[370] as instances of "past recollection recorded" to be distinguished from instances of "present recollection revived" where the document did, in fact, refresh the memory of the witness.

3–154 It is evident, therefore, that there is no requirement that the witness have a recollection of the transaction or event independently of the document and if "the witness can say that, from seeing his own writing, he is sure of the fact stated therein, such statement by him is admissible in evidence of the fact".[371] This category of "past recollection recorded" effectively constitutes an exception to the hearsay rule.[372] The witness, by swearing to the accuracy of the written document which he or she uses to refresh his or her memory, invests the out-of-court statement with sufficient reliability to justify its reception in evidence. Although it is the oral testimony rather than the written document which constitutes evidence in the case,[373] this is a matter of form only. Where a witness is permitted to refresh his or her memory in this manner, the normal course is for the witness to read the document into the record under the guise of the witness giving evidence from a refreshed memory but without the document becoming evidence itself.[374]

---

[367] A good example of a case where a witness candidly admitted that he had no recollection whatsoever of the events recorded in the written record is furnished by *Northern Banking Co. v Carpenter* [1931] IR 268. See also *People (DPP) v McGinley* [2013] IECCA 7 at [48] (members of staff of the Forensic Science Laboratory cannot be expected to remember the facts of individual cases) and *Maugham v Hubbard* (1828) 8 B & C 14.

[368] (1864) 17 ICLR 213.

[369] (1864) 17 ICLR 213 at 220.

[370] Wigmore, *Evidence* 3rd edn (Boston: Little Brown and Company, 1940), vol. 3, § 735.

[371] *Per* Kennedy CJ in *Northern Banking Co. v Carpenter* [1931] IR 268 at 276. See also *The Leopardstown Club Ltd v Templeville Developments Ltd* [2010] IEHC 152 at [2.36].

[372] *Cf.* Rule 803(5) of the Federal Rules of Evidence provides for an exception to the rule against hearsay in the case of "[a] memorandum or record concerning a matter about which a witness once had knowledge but now has insufficient recollection to enable him to testify fully and accurately, shown to have been made or adopted by the witness when the matter was fresh in his memory and to reflect that knowledge correctly."

[373] *People (DPP) v McGinley* [2013] IECCA 7 at [48]. *R v B (KG)* (1998) 125 CCC (3d) 61. *Cf. People (DPP) v Byrne*, unreported, Court of Criminal Appeal, 7 June 2000.

[374] *The Leopardstown Club Ltd v Templeville Developments Ltd* [2010] IEHC 152 at [2.36].

(c) Use of copies of documents to refresh memory

3–155   In the case of "present recollection revived", where a witness's memory is actually refreshed, a witness is not confined to using the original document created to record the events in issue and can use a copy provided the court is satisfied that the copy is accurate and substantially reproduces the contents of the original.[375] For example, in *R. v Chisnell*,[376] a police officer was permitted to use a statement that had been compiled nine months after an interview because the court was satisfied that a contemporaneous note of the interview, which had been lost, had been accurately transcribed into the statement.

3–156   The requirements in relation to the use of copies are, unsurprisingly, more exacting in the case of "past recollection recorded" because of the need to ensure the accuracy and reliability of the document used to refresh memory in circumstances where the witness does not have any recollection of the events recorded independently of the document. Thus, as a general rule, the witness can only use the original document[377] but, if the original is lost or has been destroyed, and its non-production accounted for, the witness will be allowed to use a true or exact copy of the original.[378]

(d) Cross-examination on the document

3–157   A document used to refresh memory, or at least those portions that refer to the subject-matter of the proceedings, must be produced for inspection by the opposing party.[379] The opposing party is entitled to cross-examine the witness on the contents of the document and, in general, such cross-examination will not make the document admissible in evidence.[380] However, the document may become admissible as evidence going to the credibility of the witness (but not as evidence of the truth of its contents[381]) where: (a) the cross-examination goes beyond the parts of the document used by the witness to refresh his or her memory and raises new matters[382]; (b) the nature of the cross-examination involves a suggestion that the witness has fabricated his or her evidence, in which case the document is admissible to rebut the express or implied suggestion that the document is concocted and for the purpose of allowing the jury to assess where the document is genuine[383]; (c) the document is inconsistent with the witness's evidence in which case it can be admitted as evidence of that inconsistency[384];

---

[375]   *Burton v Plummer* (1834) 2 Ad & El 341; *Topham v McGregor* (1844) 1 Car & Kir 320; *R. v Mills* [1962] 1 WLR 1152; *R. v Chisnell* [1992] Crim LR 507; *R. v Cheng* (1976) 63 Cr App R 20.

[376]   [1992] Crim LR 507.

[377]   *Doe d Church v Perkins* (1790) 3 Term Rep. 749; *Collaton v Correll* [1926] SASR 87; *R. v Bryant (No.2)* [1956] SR Qd 570.

[378]   *Lord Talbot de Malahide v Cusack* (1864) 17 ICLR 213 at 217.

[379]   *The Leopardstown Club Ltd v Templeville Developments Ltd* [2010] IEHC 152 at [5.24]; *Howard v Canfield* (1836) 5 Dowl 417; *Beech v Jones* (1848) 5 CB 696; *R. v Fenlon* (1980) 71 Cr App R 307 at 310; *Owen v Edwards* (1983) Cr App R 191; *R. v Sekhon* (1987) 85 Cr App R 19 at 22.

[380]   *The Leopardstown Club Ltd v Templeville Developments Ltd* [2010] IEHC 152 at [5.24].

[381]   *R. v Virgo* (1978) 67 Cr App R 323; *R. v Britton* (1986) 85 Cr App R 14; *R. v Mills* [1984] 2 NZLR 92.

[382]   *The Leopardstown Club Ltd v Templeville Developments Ltd* [2010] IEHC 152 at [5.24]; *Gregory v Tavernor* (1833) 6 C & P 280; *Senat v Senat* [1965] P 172 at 177, [1965] 2 All ER 505 at 512; *R. v Britton* (1986) 85 Cr App R 14.

[383]   *R. v Sekhon* (1987) 85 Cr App R 19 at 22.

[384]   *R. v Sekhon* (1987) 85 Cr App R 19 at 22.

and (d) the document tends to contradict the evidence and undermine the credibility of the witness.[385]

(e) Inspection of document by the jury

3–158   Even if the document is not admitted in evidence, the jury may be allowed to inspect the document or be furnished with copies where it would be difficult for the jury to follow the cross-examination of the witness who has refreshed his or her memory without having copies of the document before them.[386] The document may also be given to the jury for use as an *aide memoire* where a witness's evidence is long and involved, although the English Court of Appeal in *R. v Sekhon*[387] advised caution in using the document for this purpose because of the danger that the jury might wrongly regard the document as proof of its contents.

(f) Evidential status of document used to refresh memory

3–159   It is important to note that, where a witness is permitted to refresh his or her memory, it is the oral testimony of the witness and not the document from which he or she refreshes his or her memory that constitutes evidence in the case.[388] The document is hearsay and inadmissible as evidence of the truth of its contents.[389] This point is well illustrated by *Northern Banking Co. v Carpenter*.[390] In that case a memorandum which was used to refresh the memory of a witness contained two express statements of fact. When giving evidence, the witness only testified as to the second statement of fact and it was held that, because of the failure of the witness to use the memorandum to enable him to depose to the first statement of fact, neither the memorandum nor his testimony provided any evidence upon that issue. However, as noted above, a document used to refresh memory may, in certain circumstances, be admitted to establish consistency on the part of and, thus, to bolster the credibility of a witness.

(g) Warning to jury in relation to use of document

3–160   In circumstances where a document used to refresh memory is admitted in evidence or inspected by the jury, there is a danger that they may regard it as evidence of its contents and they should be given a warning by the trial judge that the document is not evidence of the truth of its contents and as to the limited purpose for which the document has been admitted or made available to them.[391]

3. Refreshing Memory Out of Court

3–161   It is common practice, in both criminal and civil proceedings, for witnesses to look at and refresh their memories from previous statements made by them or other

---

[385] *R. v Bass* [1953] 1 QB 680 at 687, [1953] 1 All ER 1064 at 1068.

[386] *R. v Sekhon* (1987) 85 Cr App R 19 at 23. See also *R. v Virgo* (1978) 67 Cr App R 323.

[387] (1987) 85 Cr App R 19 at 23.

[388] *Northern Banking Co. v Carpenter* [1931] IR 268; *R. v Virgo* (1978) 67 Cr App R 323; *Young v Denton* [1927] 1 DLR 426.

[389] *R. v Virgo* (1978) 67 Cr App R 323 at 329.

[390] [1931] IR 268.

[391] *R. v Virgo* (1978) 67 Cr App R 323 at 328; *R. v Sekhon* (1987) 85 Cr App R 19 at 23.

documents before going into the witness box. This is considered unobjectionable[392] even if the documents do not satisfy the requirement of contemporaneity applicable to documents used to refresh memory in court.[393] In *Lau Pak Ngam v R.*,[394] the Supreme Court of Hong Kong dismissed the contention that it was improper for witnesses to refresh their memory from their witness statements prior to trial taking the view that:

> "testimony in the witness box becomes not less, but more, a test of memory rather than of truthfulness if witnesses are deprived of the opportunity, normally utilised by prudent men, of checking their recollection beforehand by reference to statements or notes made at a time closer to the events in question."[395]

3–162   The Court also expressed the opinion that "refusal of access to statements would tend to create real difficulties for honest witnesses but is likely to do little to hamper the dishonest witness".[396] That approach was endorsed by the English Court of Appeal in *R. v Richardson*[397] where the view was taken that a general rule to the effect that witnesses could not refresh their memory before giving evidence would be unenforceable and, further, "would militate very greatly against the interests of justice".[398]

3–163   However, it is important that the facility of allowing a witness to refresh his or her memory before trial is not used as an opportunity to coach a witness.[399] Furthermore, if there are a number of witnesses, it is important to ensure that they are not afforded an opportunity to collude or synchronise their evidence. The statement of one witness should not, therefore, be read to another[400] or an opportunity given to witnesses to compare statements.[401]

3–164   It is also undesirable that a witness attempt to memorise his or her statement because, as observed by the Court of Criminal Appeal in *People (DPP) v Donnelly*[402]:

> "There is clearly a danger that if a witness seeks to learn the contents of his or her statement by heart then when such witness gives evidence in court it may not be about what occurred but about what such witness had said in the statement had occurred. This would clearly be wrong."[403]

---

[392] *People (DPP) v Donnelly*, unreported, Court of Criminal Appeal, 22 February 1999 at 7–8; *R. v Richardson* [1971] 2 QB 484, [1971] 2 All ER 773; *R. v Westwell* [1976] 2 All ER 812; *Worley v Bentley* [1976] 2 All ER 449; *R. v Pachonick* [1973] 2 NSWLR 86; *Lau Pak-Ngam v R.* [1966] HKLR 246; [1966] Crim LR 443.

[393] *R. v Richardson* [1971] 2 QB 484 at 489–490, [1971] 2 All ER 773 at 777.

[394] [1966] HKLR 246, [1966] Crim LR 443.

[395] [1966] HKLR 246 at 251, [1966] Crim LR 443 at 444 (*per* Hogan CJ).

[396] [1966] HKLR 246 at 251, [1966] Crim LR 443 at 444 (*per* Hogan CJ).

[397] [1971] 2 QB 484, [1971] 2 All ER 773.

[398] [1971] 2 QB 484 at 490, [1971] 2 All ER 773 at 777. There is also authority to the effect that a judge may, in the exercise of his or her discretion, permit a witness who has begun to give evidence to withdraw from the stand and refresh his or her memory from an earlier statement that does not satisfy the requirement of contemporaneity, provided certain conditions are satisfied (see *R. v Da Silva* [1990] 1 All ER 29, [1990] 1 WLR 31; *R. v South Ribble Magistrates' Court, ex parte Cochrane* [1996] 2 Cr App R 29; *Equiticorp Industries Group Ltd (in Statutory Management) v R.* [1995] 3 NZLR 243).

[399] *R. v Skinner* (1993) 99 Cr App R 212 at 216; *Lau Pak-Ngam v R.* [1966] HKLR 246 at 249, [1966] Crim LR 443 at 444. See also *GO'R v DPP* [2011] IEHC 368, [2012] 1 IR 193 discussed above.

[400] *R. v Skinner* (1993) 99 Cr App R 212 at 216.

[401] *R. v Richardson* [1971] 2 QB 484 at 490, [1971] 2 All ER 773 at 777.

[402] Unreported, Court of Criminal Appeal, 22 February 1999.

[403] Unreported, Court of Criminal Appeal, 22 February 1999 at 7. However, it is evident from

3–165 In *R. v Westwell*,[404] it was held by the English Court of Appeal that the fact that a witness has refreshed his or her memory from a previous statement may go to the weight to be attached to his or her evidence and, thus, in a criminal case, injustice may be caused to the accused if the jury are not informed that this has occurred. This is also important because the accused is entitled to obtain a copy of and cross-examine on the previous statement.[405] It is, therefore, desirable that, if the prosecution is aware that witnesses have seen their statements, they should inform the defence of this fact. However, a failure to do so will not, of itself, be a ground for acquittal or setting aside a conviction.[406]

H. Prior Consistent Statements

3–166 As a general rule, sometimes referred to as the rule against narrative or the rule against self-corroboration,[407] statements made by a witness prior to giving evidence which are consistent with his or her testimony are not admissible.[408] Thus, a witness may not be asked about such statements on examination-in-chief nor may the person to whom the statement was made be called to give evidence as to the making of the statement. This rule is separate and distinct from the rule against hearsay which renders such statements inadmissible if tendered as proof of the truth of their contents. It has the effect of excluding such statements if tendered to establish consistency on the part of a witness or to otherwise bolster his or her credibility.[409]

3–167 One of the principal justifications for excluding these self-serving statements is the ease with which a witness who intended to give false evidence could bolster his or her credibility by repeating his or her version of events to a number of people and then calling them to the stand to show the consistency of his or her story.[410] The danger is that a jury would thereby be misled into giving greater weight to the evidence of the witness than it deserved. Furthermore, such evidence is considered to be irrelevant or superfluous in that it merely duplicates the evidence given by the witness in court.[411]

Donnelly that this is a matter that goes to the weight to be attached to the evidence of the witness rather than its admissibility.

[404] [1976] 2 All ER 812.
[405] *Owen v Edwards* (1983) 77 Cr App R 191.
[406] *R. v Westwell* [1976] 2 All ER 812; *Worley v Bentley* [1976] 2 All ER 449.
[407] For a detailed analysis of this area, see Gooderson, "Previous Consistent Statements" [1968] CLJ 64. See also MacCrimmon, "Consistent Statements of a Witness" (1979) 17 Osgoode Hall LJ 285.
[408] *R. v Coll* (1889) 24 LR Ir 522 at 541; *Cooper-Flynn v Radio Telefís Éireann* [2004] IESC 27 at [217], [2004] 2 IR 72 at 154; *The Leopardstown Club Ltd v Templeville Developments Ltd* [2010] IEHC 152 at [5.21] –[5.22]; *R. v Oyesiku* (1972) 56 Cr App R 240 at 245; *R. v Beattie* (1989) 89 Cr App R 302 at 306. For an example of the application of the rule, see *Fox v General Medical Council* [1960] 3 All ER 225; [1960] 1 WLR 1017.
[409] *R. v Coll* (1889) 24 LR Ir 522 at 529–530; *Flanagan v Fahy* [1918] 2 IR 361 at 366; *Corke v Corke* [1958] P 93 at 111; [1958] 1 All ER 224 at 235; *Fox v General Medical Council* [1960] 3 All ER 225 at 230; [1960] 1 WLR 1017 at 1024; *R. v Nagy* [1990] Crim LR 187.
[410] *R. v Hardy* (1794) 24 St Tr 199 at 1093; *Corke v Corke* [1958] P 93 at 111; [1958] 1 All ER 224 at 235; *R. v Jones* (1988) 44 CCC (3d) 248 at 255.
[411] *R. v Roberts* [1942] 1 All ER 187 at 191; *Fox v General Medical Council* [1960] 3 All ER 225 at 230; [1960] 1 WLR 1017 at 1024; *R. v Beland* (1987) 36 CCC (3d) 481 at 499, [1987] 2 SCR 398; *R. v C.(G.)* (1997) 8 CR (5th) 61 at 70–71.

There is also a policy basis for the rule in that the admission of such evidence would serve to lengthen trials and could give rise to a multiplicity of collateral issues.

3–168   There are, however, a limited number of instances, examined below, where such statements are admissible: (1) complaints in sexual cases; (2) to rebut an allegation of recent fabrication; (3) statements of previous identification; (4) statements admissible as part of the *res gestae*; (5) statements made on accusation; and (6) statements in documents used to refresh memory. Where a previous consistent statement is admitted pursuant to one of these exceptions, it will be a relevant factor, and sometimes a critical factor, in assessing the credibility of the witness.[412] It is important to remember, however, that a statement admitted under one of these exceptions can only be used to demonstrate consistency and bolster the credibility of a witness and cannot, by virtue of the hearsay rule, be used as evidence of any facts stated therein.[413] Given the risk that the jury might so regard it, a trial judge should, in any case where a previous consistent statement is admitted, instruct the jury as to the limited use that can be made of it.[414]

1. Complaints in Sexual Cases

3–169   In a prosecution for a sexual offence, a voluntary complaint made at the first reasonable opportunity after the commission of the offence is admissible to show consistency on the part of the complainant.[415] The origin and rationale of this exception was outlined by Murray J in *People (DPP) v MA*[416]:

> "Centuries ago, evidence that a woman who was the victim of rape or serious sexual assault had raised 'hue and cry' following the commission of the offence was admissible as evidence of conduct consistent with her testimony. Moreover it became effectively a precondition in those times to the initiation of a prosecution for such offences. Of course the making a such a complaint has not been a precondition to a prosecution for a very long time but the fact of making a complaint to a third party soon after the offence was always admissible evidence in the prosecution of such offences. It is evidence which can be introduced to support the credibility of a complainant based on the view that it was the natural expression of the victim's feelings that reasonably soon after the offence she would complain to some person with whom she had a personal or confidential relationship."[417]

3–170   It can be seen, therefore, that this exception to the general prohibition against reception of previous consistent statements is primarily explicable by reference to historical circumstance and it has been criticised on the basis that it lacks a principled foundation.[418] However, the continued admission of complaints in sexual cases can,

---

[412] *O'Callaghan v Mahon* [2005] IESC 9 at [50], [2006] 2 IR 32 at 59.

[413] *People (DPP) v McArdle* [2003] 4 IR 186 at 195.

[414] *R. v A(J)* (1996) 112 CCC (3d) 528 at 536; *R. v Wait* (1994) 69 OAC 63 at 65. *Cf. People (DPP) v MA* [2002] 2 IR 601 at 610 dealing with complaints in sexual cases.

[415] The complaint must be proved by the person to whom it was made and if that person does not give evidence, the complainant will not be permitted to give evidence of complaints allegedly made by her (see *White v R.* [1999] 1 Cr App R 153).

[416] [2002] 2 IR 601.

[417] [2002] 2 IR 601 at 608. *Cf.* the account of the development of this exception given in Tapper (ed), *Cross on Evidence* 7th edn (London: Butterworths, 1990), p.282, which was quoted with approval in *People (DPP) v Brophy* [1992] ILRM 709 at 714–715 and *People (DPP) v Murphy*, unreported, Court of Criminal Appeal, 13 November 2003, where Geoghegan J said that the basis for admission of a complaint was "to show consistency and to negative any inference that it was a malicious complaint". See also the explanation of the rationale for admitting complaints given by Fauteaux J in *Kribs v R.* [1960] SCR 400 at 405.

[418] See the *Report of the Federal/Provincial Task Force on Uniform Rules of Evidence* (Toronto:

perhaps, be justified by reference to the difficulties of proof in cases of sexual offences and the probative value of such complaints in showing consistency.

(a) Conditions of admissibility

3–171   An examination of the authorities in relation to the admission of complaints[419] indicates that there are four conditions of admissibility that have to be satisfied: (i) the prosecution is for a sexual offence; (ii) the complaint was made at the first reasonable opportunity after the commission of the offence; (iii) the complaint was voluntary; and (iv) the complaint is consistent with the evidence of the complainant. Each of these conditions will be considered in turn.

(i) Sexual offence

3–172   It is now settled that a complaint is only admissible in criminal prosecutions for a sexual offence.[420] The precise ambit of the concept of a "sexual offence" is unclear but it has been held to be immaterial whether the offences alleged are against males or females[421] or whether consent is an ingredient of the offence.[422]

(ii) At the first reasonable opportunity

3–173   A complaint is only admissible if it was made at the first reasonable opportunity after the commission of the offence.[423] It is evident from the case law that, although the lapse of time between the alleged commission of the offence and the making of the complaint is very important, this test is not merely a temporal one but is based on

---

Carswell, 1982), p.301, where the admission of complaints in sexual cases was described as "an anomalous and arbitrary exception to the rule against narrative" and Heydon, *Cross on Evidence* 9th Australian edn (Lexis Nexis, 2013) at [17285]. This exception to the rule against narrative was abolished in New Zealand by the Evidence Act 2006. It has also been abrogated in Canada by s.275 of the Canadian Criminal Code. See, further, Craig, "The Relevance of Delayed Disclosure to Complainant Credibility in Cases of Sexual Offence" (2010-2011) 36 Queens LJ 551.

[419]   In *R. v Timm* [1981] 2 SCR 315 at 322–323, Lamer J advocated a broad definition of what could be considered as a complaint for the purpose of this exception: "In my view, any statement made by the alleged victim, which is of some probative value in negating the adverse conclusions the jury might be invited to make and could draw as regards her credibility had she remained silent, is to be considered a complaint. It will have the effect of negating that adverse conclusion if it is in some way supportive of the victim's credibility by showing consistency between the victim's conduct after the alleged ravishment and the victim's narration of same as a witness." This decision was followed by the New Zealand Court of Appeal in *R. v Joseph,* unreported, New Zealand Court of Appeal, 4 June 1998. *Cf. R. v N* [1994] 3 NZLR 641 (no requirement for statement be made with any particular emotion, a narrative statement about the events in issue suffices).

[420]   *People (DPP) v Brophy* [1992] ILRM 709 at 716; *R. v Lillyman* [1896] 2 QB 167; *R. v Osborne* [1905] 1 KB 551; *R. v Jarvis* [1991] Crim LR 374; *R. v Saunders* [1965] Qd. R. 409.

[421]   *R. v Camelleri* [1922] 2 KB 122; *R. v Wannell* (1922) 17 Cr App R 53; *R. v Lebrun* [1951] OR 387, (1951) 100 CCC 16; *R. v McNamara* [1917] NZLR 382.

[422]   *R. v Osborne* [1905] 1 KB 551 at 557–558.

[423]   *Attorney General v McLoughlin* (1937) 71 ILTR 247 at 248; *People (DPP) v Brophy* [1992] ILRM 709 at 716; *People (DPP) v DR* [1998] 2 IR 106 at 109; *R. v Lillyman* [1896] 2 QB 167 at 171; *R. v Timm* [1981] 2 SCR 315 at 337; *R. v Kulak* (1979) 46 CCC (2d) 30; *Suresh v R.* (1998) 153 ALR 145; *R. v N* [1994] 3 NZLR 641. The requirement that the complaint be made as soon as could reasonably be expected was removed in the UK by s.112 of the Coroners and Justice Act 2009 with the timeliness of the complaint now going to weight: *R v Ashraf A* [2011] EWCA Crim 1517.

a consideration of the reasonableness of the conduct of the complainant having regard to all the circumstances.[424]

3–174 In assessing the reasonableness of the conduct of the complainant, an important factor will be the prior opportunities that the complainant had to make a complaint. Thus, a complaint may be ruled inadmissible if the complainant had an earlier opportunity to make a complaint to a family member or friend that was not availed of. An example of where a complaint was excluded on this basis can be seen in *People (DPP) v Kiernan*.[425] The complainant alleged that the accused had brought her to his house on a Friday night and, after plying her with drink, had intercourse with her without her consent. After the alleged incident, the complainant came downstairs where she met the accused's girlfriend and complained that she had been raped. The girlfriend dismissed the complaint suggesting that the complainant had imagined the whole thing because of the alcohol that she had consumed. The complainant then returned to her parents' house but did not make a complaint to any member of her family, for the reason, which was accepted by both the trial judge and the Court of Criminal Appeal, that she was too frightened to tell them. The Court accepted that she was justified in waiting to make a complaint until such time as she had an opportunity to make one to her boyfriend because he had a brother who was a Social Welfare Officer and who the complainant thought would provide good advice. However, the complainant did not make a complaint when she met her boyfriend on Saturday, the day following the incident, but waited until Sunday. In the circumstances, the Court held that the complaint should not have been admitted. If it had been made on Saturday, then the Court would have been satisfied that it was made as soon as reasonably possible but the complaint, having been delayed until this following day, did not satisfy this requirement.[426]

3–175 However, a complaint will not necessarily be excluded because of the existence of a prior opportunity to make a complaint. As Roch LJ emphasised in *R. v Valentine*[427] the relevant question is whether the complaint was made at the first *reasonable* opportunity:

> "The authorities establish that a complaint can be recent and admissible, although it may not have been made at the first opportunity that presented itself. What is the first reasonable opportunity will depend on the circumstances including the character of the complainant and the relationship between the complainant and the person to whom she complained and the

---

[424] *R. v Nazif* [1987] 2 NZLR 122 at 125. *Cf. Attorney General v McLoughlin* (1937) 71 ILTR 247 (complaint of sexual offence committed the previous day admissible but complaint of sexual offence committed four days previously not admissible because it was divorced from the offence by the lapse of time) and the exceptional case of *People (DPP) v JT* (1988) 3 Frewen 141 (complaints made by a girl with an intellectual disability to her mother in respect of sexual abuse by her father were held to be admissible even though they had been made somewhere between three months and eight years after the commission of the alleged offences).

[425] Unreported, Court of Criminal Appeal, 11 March 1994.

[426] See also *People (DPP) v Brophy* [1992] ILRM 709 (prosecution conceded that complaint had not been made as speedily as could reasonably have been expected in circumstances where the complainant did not avail of an opportunity shortly after the alleged offence to complain to her mother but waited until later that day to complain to friends and her father); *R. v Cummings* [1948] 1 All ER 551 (trial judge had not erred in admitting complaint in circumstances where the complainant had not complained to camp warden who she hardly knew or to the girls that she was sharing a hut with but waited until the following day to make a complaint to a friend living near the camp); *R. v Valentine* [1996] 2 Cr App R 213 (trial judge had correctly admitted a complaint made by the complainant the day after the alleged sexual assault to a friend).

[427] [1996] 2 Cr App R 213.

persons to whom she might have complained but did not do so. It is enough if it is the first reasonable opportunity."[428]

3–176 In recent times, greater judicial awareness of the factors such as shame and guilt[429] that may inhibit a complainant from making a complaint even to a trusted friend or close relative has led to an acceptance that a complainant may have made a complaint at the first reasonable opportunity even if there has been a significant lapse of time and the complainant has not availed of an opportunity to complain to a family member or friend. As Roch LJ explained in *R. v Valentine*[430]:

"We now have greater understanding that those who are the victims of sexual offences, be they male or female, often need time before they can bring themselves to tell what has been done to them; that some victims will find it impossible to complain to anyone other than a parent or member of their family whereas others may feel it quite impossible to tell their parents or members of their family."[431]

3–177 This approach is evident in *People (DPP) v DR*[432] where the complainant alleged that she had been raped and sexually assaulted by the accused while staying overnight at the home of her sister-in-law. She did not make any complaint that night to either her husband or her sister-in-law or the next morning while driving home with her husband and it was not until later that day that she told her husband what had happened. Her explanation for the delay was that the assault had had a profound psychological effect upon her which made it difficult for her to talk about it. She found it hard to make a complaint to her sister-in-law who was the partner of the person who had perpetrated the assault on her and was also reluctant to complain to her husband in circumstances where, had she complained to him in the house, there might have been a violent confrontation between him and the accused. This explanation was accepted by the trial judge who took the view that the complainant was in such a psychological state that it was not reasonably possible for her to make the complaint until she did. The Court of Criminal Appeal declined to interfere with the decision of the trial judge which it considered to be supported by the evidence.[433]

(iii) Voluntariness

3–178 A complaint is only admissible if is voluntary in the sense that it is not the result of an inducement or exhortation.[434] However, there is no requirement that the

---

[428] [1996] 2 Cr App R 213 at 223–234. This passage was quoted with approval in *People (DPP) v Murphy*, unreported, Court of Criminal Appeal, 13 November 2003.

[429] *R v D* [2009] Crim LR 591 at [11]. See, further, Úna Ní Raifeartaigh, "The Doctrine of Fresh Complaint in Sexual Cases" (1994) 12 ILT 160 at 162, who refers to the complex cocktail of emotions and feelings including shock, fear, distress, remorse, shame, embarrassment and denial which may result from a sexual assault and inhibit a complainant from making a complaint. See also Foley, "The Doctrine of Recent Complaint Revisited" (2001) 11 ICLJ 20 and Foley, "Hearsay and Recent Complaint" (2001) 19 ILT 234.

[430] [1996] 2 Cr App R 213.

[431] [1996] 2 Cr App R 213 at 224. See further, *People (DPP) v Moloney*, unreported, Court of Criminal Appeal, *ex tempore*, 8 November 1999, where the court refused to interfere with the ruling of the trial judge that a complaint had been made at the first reasonable opportunity because the mother of the complainant, who she had a prior opportunity to complain to, was not, in the circumstances of the case, a person to whom the complainant could be expected to make a complaint.

[432] [1998] 2 IR 106.

[433] See also *People (DPP) v Murphy*, unreported, Court of Criminal Appeal, 13 November 2003 and *People (DPP) v TO'R* [2008] IECCA 38.

[434] *Attorney General v McLoughlin* (1937) 71 ILTR 247 at 248; *People (DPP) v Brophy* [1992]

complaint be spontaneous. Hence, the fact that it was made in answer to questions does not affect its admissibility provided that the questions merely served to elicit a complaint that the complainant would otherwise have made. The relevant principles were outlined by Ridley J in *R. v Osborne*[435]:

> "... the mere fact that the statement is made in answer to a question ... is not of itself sufficient to make it inadmissible as a complaint. Questions of a suggestive or leading character will, indeed, have that effect.... If the circumstances indicate that but for the questioning there probably would have been no voluntary complaint, the answer is inadmissible. If the question merely anticipates a statement which the complainant was about to make, it is not rendered inadmissible by the fact that the questioner happens to speak first. ... "[436]

3–179 In *People (DPP) v DR*,[437] the contention that the complaint made by the complainant should be excluded as involuntary because it had been made in response to a question posed by her husband was rejected. The question had been put by her husband in response to her comment that the accused was "no gentleman" and, in the circumstances, the Court was satisfied that this was not a case of the husband interrogating her and that he merely assisted her in saying something which she herself wished to say.[438]

(iv) Consistency

3–180 The purpose of the admission of complaints in sexual cases is to show consistency on the part of the complainant, *i.e.* that he or she gave the same account in the immediate aftermath of the alleged offence as he or she has given at trial.[439] Therefore, if the complainant does not give evidence, a complaint made by him or her cannot be admitted because there is no testimony with which the complaint can be consistent.[440] Furthermore, even if the complainant gives evidence, a complaint will not be admissible if its terms are not actually consistent with the testimony of the complainant.[441] There is no precise test with regard to the degree of consistency that is required but it would appear that, if the complaint correlates in its main particulars with the testimony of the complainant as to the commission of the offence, it will not be excluded because of minor discrepancies.[442] However, if there are significant differences between the terms of the complaint and the testimony of the complainant, the complaint will be rendered inadmissible.[443] Given that consistency is a condition of admissibility, it follows that the complainant should give evidence prior to evidence

---

ILRM 709 at 716; *People (DPP) v DR* [1998] 2 IR 106 at 109; *R. v Osborne* [1905] 1 KB 551 at 556; *R. v Timm* [1981] 2 SCR 315 at 337; *R. v Kulak* (1979) 46 CCC (2d) 30 at 38.

[435] [1905] 1 KB 551.

[436] [1905] 1 KB 551 at 556. But see *R. v Freeman* [1980] VR 1 where this test was rejected and compare the approach in the Australasian cases of *R. v Adams* [1965] Qd R 255; *R. v Gallagher* (1986) 41 SASR 73; *R. v Walesby* [1919] NZLR 289 at 299; *R. v Duncan* [1992] 1 NZLR 528.

[437] [1998] 2 IR 106.

[438] See also *People (DPP) v Moloney*, unreported, Court of Criminal Appeal, *ex tempore*, 8 November 1999 (Court refused to interfere with the ruling of the trial judge that complaint was voluntary).

[439] *People (DPP) v Gavin* [2000] 4 IR 557 at 563; *People (DPP) v MA* [2002] 2 IR 601 at 606–607; *R. v O'Dowd* [1985] 1 NZLR 388n; *R. v Aramoana* [1985] 1 NZLR 390.

[440] *R. v Wallwork* (1958) 42 Cr App R 153; *Sparks v R.* [1964] AC 964 at 979, [1964] 1 All ER 727 at 734; *Ugle v R.* (1989) 167 CLR 647 at 650–651.

[441] *People (DPP) v Jethi*, unreported, Court of Criminal Appeal, *ex tempore*, 7 February 2000; *People (DPP) v Gavin* [2000] 4 IR 557; *R. v Wright* (1987) 90 Cr App R 91.

[442] See *People (DPP) v Jethi*, unreported, Court of Criminal Appeal, *ex tempore*, 7 February 2000; *People (DPP) v MA* [2002] 2 IR 601 at 607.

[443] See, *e.g. People (DPP) v Gavin* [2000] 4 IR 557. It was held in *R. v Stockman* (1994) 12 CRNZ

of the complaint being adduced as otherwise it will not be possible to assess the consistency of the complaint with the testimony of the complainant.[444]

3–181 If the complaint is admitted notwithstanding the existence of some inconsistencies with the testimony of the complainant, then the defence is entitled to cross-examine the complainant in relation to those inconsistencies[445] and it would appear that, in an appropriate case, the trial judge should draw those inconsistencies to the attention of the jury.[446]

(b) Admissibility of multiple complaints

3–182 The making of a complaint does not render a subsequent complaint inadmissible provided the later complaint satisfies the conditions of admissibility.[447] In *People (DPP) v McDonagh,*[448] a complaint had initially been made to a taxi driver, who afterwards could not be traced, and then to gardaí at a Garda station to which he had brought the two complainants. It was argued on behalf of the two accused that the making of a complaint precluded evidence being given of any subsequent complaint but this submission was rejected by the Court of Criminal Appeal. The Court took the view that it was implicit in the decision in *People (DPP) v Brophy*[449] that evidence of more than one complaint could be given provided that the conditions of admissibility were complied with. However, the Court did acknowledge that a trial judge had a discretion to limit the number of references to complaints in order to ensure fairness in a trial. Although not expressed by the Court of Criminal Appeal in such terms, this can be seen to be an instance where a trial judge might apply his or her general discretion to exclude evidence the prejudicial effect of which exceeds its probative value. It is evident that, once the fact and particulars of a complaint are admitted, repetition of the complaint, especially if it is very similar in its terms, does not add much probative value to the complaint however, it gives rise to a risk of prejudice because of sheer weight of numbers. If a number of witnesses give evidence repeating the particulars of the same complaint, there is a substantial risk that the jury will not treat such evidence as going merely to the credibility of the complainant.[450]

---

312 at 315, that if the complaint mentions matters which the complainant has forgotten or has not given evidence of, the complaint should not be admitted.

[444] *R. v Lillyman* [1896] 2 QB 167 at 170.

[445] *People (DPP) v MA* [2002] 2 IR 601 at 607.

[446] *Cf. People (DPP) v Jethi*, unreported, Court of Criminal Appeal, *ex tempore*, 7 February 2000.

[447] *Attorney General v McLoughlin* (1937) 71 ILTR 247; *People (DPP) v McDonagh*, unreported, Court of Criminal Appeal, 24 July 1990; *R. v Lee* (1912) 7 Cr App R 31; *R. v Wilbourne* (1917) 12 Cr App R 280; *R. v Valentine* [1996] 2 Cr App R 213 at 223–224.

[448] Unreported, Court of Criminal Appeal, 24 July 1990.

[449] [1992] ILRM 709.

[450] See *R. v Valentine* [1996] 2 Cr App R 213 at 224 (*per* Roch LJ): "That is not to say that it is permissible to allow the Crown to lead evidence that the same complaint has been made by the complainant in substantially the same terms on several occasions soon after the alleged offence, where that would be prejudicial in that it might incline the jury to regard the contents of individual complaints as evidence of the truth of what they assert." See also *R. v O* [2006] 2 Cr App r 405, [2006] EWCA Crim 556 at [23] where it was held that, while more than one complaint may be admitted, fairness may demand that evidence of complaint upon complaint which could be merely self-serving should be restricted.

(c) Admission of particulars of complaint

3–183 It is settled that, if evidence of the making of a complaint is admissible, then particulars of the complaint may also be proved.[451] In *R. v Lillyman*,[452] it was held that the particulars of the complaint ought to be admitted so that the jury could make a determination as to whether it was consistent with the testimony of the complainant:

> "The evidence is admissible only upon the ground that it was a complaint of that which is charged against the prisoner, and can be legitimately used only for the purpose of enabling the jury to judge for themselves whether the conduct of the woman was consistent with her testimony on oath given in the witness-box negativing her consent, and affirming that the acts complained of were against her will, and in accordance with the conduct that they would expect in a truthful woman under the circumstances detailed by her. The jury, and they only, are the persons to be satisfied whether the woman's conduct was so consistent or not. Without proof of her condition, demeanour and verbal expressions, all of which are of vital importance in the consideration of that question, how is it possible for them satisfactorily to determine it?"[453]

3–184 In *People (DPP) v Brophy*,[454] the prosecution conceded that the complaint had not been made as soon as could reasonably have been expected and that, therefore, the terms of the complaint were inadmissible, but argued that evidence could be adduced of the fact that it had been made. However, this contention was rejected by the Court of Criminal Appeal which took an "all or nothing" approach that "either evidence of a complaint having been made is admissible or it is not".[455]

(d) Use of complaint by the tribunal of fact

3–185 If a complaint is admitted, it can only be used by the tribunal of fact as evidence of consistency of conduct on the part of the complainant and, in this way, to enhance his or her credibility.[456] The complaint cannot be used as evidence of the facts complained of because it is hearsay if tendered for this purpose.[457] Neither can it provide corroboration of the testimony of the complainant because it fails to satisfy one of the basic criteria for corroboration, *i.e.* that it is evidence independent of the witness to be corroborated.[458]

3–186 There is authority to the effect that, where admitted, a complaint can be used as evidence which is inconsistent with the consent of the complainant where this is in issue.[459] However, the better view would seem to be that a complaint is not admissible,

---

451 *People (DPP) v Brophy* [1992] ILRM 709 at 716; *People (DPP) v Gavin* [2000] 4 IR 557 at 563; *People (DPP) v MA* [2002] 2 IR 601 at 607; *R. v Lillyman* [1896] 2 QB 167 at 171.
452 [1896] 2 QB 167.
453 [1896] 2 QB 167 at 177 (*per* Hawkins J).
454 [1992] ILRM 709.
455 [1992] ILRM 709 at 715. Ni Raifeartagh, "Child sexual abuse cases: the need for cultural change within the criminal justice system" (2009) 5 BR 103 is critical of this approach and suggests that the fact only of the complaint should be admitted unless the defence want the content adduced in evidence in order to highlight inconsistencies in the account given.
456 *People (DPP) v Brophy* [1992] ILRM 709 at 716; *People (DPP) v MA* [2002] 2 IR 601 at 609; *R. v Lillyman* [1896] 2 QB 167 at 170; *Sparks v R.* [1964] AC 964 at 979, [1964] 1 All ER 727 at 734.
457 *People (DPP) v Brophy* [1992] ILRM 709 at 716; *People (DPP) v Gavin* [2000] 4 IR 557 at 563–564; *People (DPP) v MA* [2002] 2 IR 601 at 609; *R. v Lillyman* [1896] 2 QB 167 at 173; *R. v Sparks* [1964] AC 964 at 979; [1964] 1 All ER 727 at 734.
458 *People (AG) v Cradden* [1955] IR 130 at 141; *People (DPP) v Brophy* [1992] ILRM 709 at 716; *People (DPP) v Gavin* [2000] 4 IR 557 at 564; *People (DPP) v MA* [2002] 2 IR 601 at 611.
459 *R. v Lillyman* [1896] 2 QB 167 at 170; *R. v Osborne* [1905] 1 KB 551 at 561.

in derogation from the rule against hearsay, to actually negative consent but rather as evidence that supports the credibility of the complainant's testimony denying consent.[460]

(e) Obligation of trial judge to instruct jury as to use of complaint

3–187 Where a complaint is admitted in a case that is being tried before a jury, there is an obvious danger that the jury might regard the complaint as evidence of the truth of the contents and it is, therefore, necessary for the trial judge to warn the jury as to the limited use that can be made of the complaint.[461]

3–188 The importance of this direction as a safeguard to avert a risk of prejudice to an accused was emphasised in *People (DPP) v MA*.[462] The Court of Criminal Appeal rejected the contention advanced by the DPP that the giving of such a direction to the jury was a desirable practice rather than a mandatory rule and that it was only required to be given where, in the circumstances of the case, it was necessary to avoid injustice. Murray J (as he then was) explained the necessity for the warning as follows:

> "Where evidence of complaint to third parties is tendered by the prosecution, as part of its case against an accused, it is admissible only by virtue of the fact that it may demonstrate consistency of conduct by the complainant with her evidence. If such evidence is incapable of demonstrating such consistency or is not tendered for the purpose of demonstrating consistency, there would appear to be no legitimate basis for the prosecution to call such evidence in a criminal trial. It is the very nature and purpose of the evidence itself which gives rise to a need that the jury are properly instructed and not other facts or circumstances. Accordingly, the direction should be given in all cases were such evidence is tendered by the prosecution. A failure to give such a direction would upset the balance which has long been considered necessary to ensure the fairness of the trial."[463]

3–189 Therefore, in every case in which a complaint is admitted, the trial judge is required to give the jury an instruction as to the use that can be made of it in the following terms:

> "Where evidence of a complaint made by a complainant to third parties in the absence of the accused is admitted in a trial of a sexual offence to establish the consistency of the complaint with the evidence of the complainant the purpose of the evidence should be explained to the jury and it should be made clear to it that such evidence is not evidence of the facts on which the complaint is based but may be considered by them as showing that the victim's conduct in so complaining was consistent with her testimony. It should also be explained to the jury that such evidence does not constitute corroboration, in the legal sense of that term, of the evidence of the complainant."[464]

3–190 In that case, the trial judge had not given the required direction and, accordingly, the court set aside the conviction of the accused.

---

[460] This was the view taken by the High Court of Australia in *Kilby v R*. (1973) 129 CLR 460. *Cf. People (DPP) v MA* [2002] 2 IR 601 at 611.
[461] *People (DPP) v Brophy* [1992] ILRM 709 at 716; *People (DPP) v Gavin* [2000] 4 IR 557 at 563; *People (DPP) v MA* [2002] 2 IR 601; *R. v Lillyman* [1896] 2 QB 167 at 178; *R. v Osborne* [1905] 1 KB 551 at 561; *R. v Islam* [1999] 1 Cr App R 22; *Jones v R*. (1997) 143 ALR 52; *R. v T* [1998] 2 NZLR 257.
[462] [2002] 2 IR 601 at 610.
[463] [2002] 2 IR 601 at 611.
[464] [2002] 2 IR 601 at 611.

(f) Appeals From Decision to Admit a Complaint

3–191   In *People (DPP) v Murphy*,[465] it was held by the Court of Criminal Appeal that the admission of a complaint is a matter for the discretion of the trial judge and it would be very slow to interfere with that discretion although it would do so if the trial judge exercised it wrongly.

2. Recent Fabrication

3–192   The mere fact that the testimony of a witness is impeached in cross-examination, even if the cross-examination relates to previous inconsistent statements, does not render admissible previous consistent statements made by the witness for the purpose of rehabilitating the credibility of the witness.[466] However, if a witness's testimony is challenged in cross-examination as being a recent fabrication, statements made by him or her to the same effect prior to the date of the alleged fabrication may be adduced in order to show his or her consistency.[467] It is important to note that, when admitted, a previous consistent statement is not evidence of the facts stated, but merely goes to rebutting the imputation made,[468] and the jury should be so instructed.[469]

3–193   The parameters of this exception were outlined by Dixon CJ in *Nominal Defendant v Clements*[470] as follows:

> "If the credit of a witness is impugned as to some material fact to which he deposes upon the ground that his account is a late invention or has been lately devised or reconstructed, even though not with conscious dishonesty, that makes admissible a statement to the same effect as the account he gave as a witness if it was made by the witness contemporaneously with the event or at a time sufficiently early to be inconsistent with the suggestion that his account is a later invention or reconstruction."[471]

3–194   Dixon CJ went on to say that, because this rule was an exception to the general principle excluding self-serving statements, great care is required in applying it. A trial judge must be satisfied not only that the testimony of a witness is attacked on the ground of recent fabrication or that the foundation for such an attack has been laid but also that the contents of the statement are consistent with his or her testimony and that, having regard to the time and circumstances in which it was made, it rationally tends to answer the attack.[472] The application of this exception is, thus, primarily a

---

[465] Unreported, Court of Criminal Appeal, *ex tempore,* 13 November 2003.
[466] *R. v Coll* (1889) 24 LR Ir 522 at 541 (*per* Holmes J); *R. v Oyesiku* (1972) 56 Cr App R 240 at 246.
[467] *R. v Coll* (1889) 24 LR Ir 522 at 541; *Fox v General Medical Council* [1960] 3 All ER 225 at 230, [1960] 1 WLR 1017 at 1024; *R. v F (JE)* (1993) 26 CR (4th) 220 at 235; *Nominal Defendant v Clements* (1960) 104 CLR 476 at 479.
[468] *R. v Coll* (1889) 24 LR Ir 522 at 530 (*per* Gibson J); *Transport and General Insurance Co. Ltd v Edmondson* (1961) 106 CLR 23; *R. v Accused* [1993] 2 NZLR 286. It might be noted that, pursuant to rule 801 of the Federal Rules of Evidence, prior consistent statements are not classified as hearsay if tendered to rebut an express or implied charge of recent fabrication and are, thus, admissible as evidence of the truth of their contents.
[469] *R. v Martin* (1996) 65 SASR 590.
[470] (1960) 104 CLR 476.
[471] (1960) 104 CLR 476 at 479. The judgment of Dixon CJ was endorsed as correctly stating the law by the Court of Appeal in *R. v Oyesiku* (1971) 56 Cr App R 240 at 245–246.
[472] (1960) 104 CLR 476 at 479–480.

matter for the discretion of the trial judge, and his or her opinion will be accorded great weight by an appellate court.[473]

3–195   The principal Irish authority on the ambit of this exception is *R. v Coll*.[474] The accused was charged with the murder of a R.I.C. officer who had been killed by a mob. A police officer gave evidence that the accused had been present at the scene of the attack and that he had seen him hit the deceased officer. On cross-examination relating to an earlier information sworn by him, he stated that he believed that he had stated in it the names of all the persons present at the attack whom he knew. This information did not contain the name of the accused but this omission, the officer said, was a mistake. The trial judge permitted the Crown to adduce in evidence a prior deposition in which the officer had mentioned the accused as being present at and taking part in the offence. His decision on this point was upheld by the Court for Crown Cases Reserved which held that the previous statement made by the officer identifying the accused as one of the participants in the offence was admissible in order to rebut the implication of recent fabrication. This was so even though no direct suggestion to this effect had been made on cross-examination. Gibson J took the view that for the purposes of applying the exception, there could be "no difference in principle, whether the imputation is made by one straight question or by skilful circuitry of interrogation, if the same meaning is conveyed."[475] The obvious and natural meaning of the cross-examination was that the officer's testimony identifying the accused "was an invention of late date".[476] Therefore, evidence of the previous deposition made by the officer was admissible to rebut this allegation.

3–196   The decision in *Coll* was followed in *Flanagan v Fahy*[477] which concerned a suit to establish a will. One of the witnesses for the defendants stated that the will had been written after the death of the deceased, that he had been invited to sign as a witness and that he was given a bribe to keep silent. The cross-examination of this witness was directed towards showing that he had fabricated the story because of hostility between him and the plaintiff's family. It was held by the Court of Appeal that the trial judge had properly allowed the witness's employer to be called in order to prove that the witness had told him the same story before the cause of the hostility had arisen.

3–197   An expansive approach to the ambit of this exception was adopted in *Tennants Building Products Ltd v O'Connell*[478] where Hogan J held that a previous consistent statement was admissible not just to rebut an allegation of fabrication but any attack on the credibility of a witness. At issue in that case was whether the defendant had executed

---

[473] *Nominal Defendant v Clements* (1960) 104 CLR 476 at 479. *Cf. Fox v General Medical Council* [1960] 3 All ER 225 at 230, [1960] 1 WLR 1017 at 1024 (application of exception depends on the nature of the challenge made and the relative cogency of the evidence tendered to repel it and must, within limits, be a matter of discretion).

[474] (1889) 24 LR Ir 522.

[475] (1889) 24 LR Ir 522 at 530. Holmes J pointed out that "skillful counsel do not always deal in direct imputation" and that they can produce the same effect as a direct question "in even a more striking way by delicate suggestion" (at 542). See also *R. v Felise* [1985] 1 NZLR 186. *Cf. R. v Campbell* (1977) 38 CCC (2d) 6 at 19 where it was held that the imputation need not be express but may be implied from the circumstances of the case or the conduct of the trial.

[476] (1889) 24 LR Ir 522 at 530.

[477] [1918] 2 IR 361.

[478] [2013] IEHC 197.

a personal guarantee on foot of a representation made by an agent of the plaintiff that it would never be relied on. There was a dispute of fact as to whether that representation had been made at a particular meeting and it was sought to introduce an email which a witness had sent prior to the meeting for the purpose of supporting his denial that the alleged representation had been made at that meeting. An objection to the admission of that email was overruled by Hogan J on the basis that "where the credibility of a witness is impugned, he may by way of exception to the rule against narrative reinforce his own testimony by reference to documents created *before* the actual happening of the event which might be otherwise thought to taint his objectivity qua witness".[479] He considered that the case provided a textbook example of both the reason for the rule and the reason for the exception to it. If the witness had been aware that a dispute might arise as to the circumstances in which the guarantee had been executed, then there could have been a considerable temptation to create a self-serving record whereas this record had been created prior to any controversy arising. He considered that the email was inherently probative and that it would be wholly artificial to confine its admission in evidence to circumstances where the credibility of the witness's account had been first challenged in cross-examination when it was obvious that the credibility of the witness on this issue would be challenged. Given that this evidence was probative of the facts in issue and was introduced during examination-in-chief rather than by way of rebuttal following cross-examination, this is perhaps better viewed as an example of the admission of circumstantial evidence rather than the application of an exception to the rule against self-corroboration.

3. Previous Identification of the Accused

3–198   Where a witness gives evidence identifying the accused as the person who committed the offence charged, evidence of a previous identification of the accused by that witness at the time of the commission of the offence[480] or during the course of a subsequent identification procedure[481] may be given either by the witness himself or by another person. In *R. v Christie*,[482] Lord Haldane explained that evidence of the previous identification was admissible as evidence of the witness's consistency to show that the witness had previously identified the accused and "to exclude the idea that the identification of the prisoner in the dock was an afterthought or mistake".[483]

4. Statements Admissible as part of the *Res Gestae*

3–199   A statement admitted under the inclusionary doctrine of *res gestae, i.e.* a statement which is so closely associated in time, place and circumstance with some act that is in issue that it can be said to form part of the act,[484] can be used as evidence of consistency to support the testimony of a witness to the same effect.[485] The classic

---

479 [2013] IEHC 197 at [9].

480 See *People (DPP) v Fee* [2006] IECCA 102.

481 *R. v Christie* [1914] AC 545; *R. v Fannon* (1922) 2 SR (NSW) 427 at 430.

482 [1914] AC 545.

483 [1914] AC 545 at 551.

484 *Cf. Teper v R.* [1952] AC 480 at 486; *People (AG) v Crosbie* [1966] IR 490 at 497. For a discussion of the *res gestae* doctrine, see Chap.5.

485 *R. v Fowkes,* The Times, 8 March 1856; *Milne v Leisler* (1862) 7 H & N 786; *Meates v Attorney General* [1983] NZLR 308.

example is furnished by *R. v Fowkes*,[486] where the accused, who was charged with murder, was nicknamed "the Butcher". The deceased's son had been sitting in a room with his father and a police officer and had seen a face appear at a window through which the fatal shot was then fired. At the trial the boy gave evidence identifying the face as being that of "the Butcher". Both the boy and the police officer were permitted to give evidence that, at the material time, the boy had shouted "There's Butcher".

5. Statements Made on Accusation

3–200   Statements made by an accused that are wholly exculpatory are not admissible as evidence of their contents under the exception to the hearsay rule in respect of admissions because such self-serving statements do not have the stamp of reliability that a statement against interest has.[487] However, it has been held that the explanation given by an accused when an accusation is first made to him or her[488] or when found in possession of stolen goods[489] is admissible as evidence of consistency if he or she gives the same explanation when testifying. The ambit of this exception has been broadened over time with the English Court of Appeal in *R. v Pearce*[490] holding that statements made by an accused subsequent to the first encounter with his accusers are also admissible although "the longer the time that has elapsed after the first encounter the less the weight which will be attached to the denial".[491] However, a subsequent statement will not be admissible where it adds nothing to the evidence of reaction already before the court.[492] The courts will also be alert to the danger of an accused seeking to take unfair advantage of the rule. Thus, "when an accused produces a carefully prepared written statement to the police, with a view to it being made a part of the prosecution evidence" it will generally be excluded as inadmissible.[493]

6. Statements in Documents Used to Refresh Memory

3–201   By analogy with the exception in respect of recent fabrication, a document used by a witness to refresh his or her memory will become admissible where "the nature of the cross-examination involves a suggestion that the witness has subsequently made up his evidence, which will usually involve, if not expressly at least by implication, the allegation that the record is concocted".[494] In these circumstances, the document is admissible "to rebut this suggestion and, if the document assists as to this, to show whether or not it is genuine, that is to say whether it has the appearance of being a contemporaneous record which has not subsequently been altered".[495]

---

[486] The Times, 8 March 1856.

[487] Cf. *Attorney General v McCabe* [1927] IR 129 at 133–134; *Attorney General v O'Leary* [1926] IR 445 at 452, and *People (AG) v Murphy* [1947] IR 236 at 239; *McCormack v DPP* [2007] IEHC 123 at [4]–[8], [2008] 1 ILRM 49 at 52–54.

[488] *R. v Storey* (1968) 52 Cr App R 334 at 337; *Lucas v R.* [1963] 1 CCC 1 at 10–11; *R. v Coats* [1932] NZLR 401 at 407.

[489] *R. v Abraham* (1848) 3 Cox CC 430; *R. v Exall* (1866) 4 F & F 922; *R. v Graham* (1972) 7 CCC (2d) 93. Cf. *R. v Graham* [1974] SCR 206, (1974) 26 DLR (3d) 579; *R. v Risby* [1978] 2 SCR 139.

[490] (1979) 69 Cr App R 365.

[491] (1979) 69 Cr App R 365 at 369.

[492] *R. v Tooke* (1989) 90 Cr App R 417.

[493] *R. v Pearce* (1979) 69 Cr App R 365 at 370. See also *R. v Newsome* (1980) 71 Cr App R 325.

[494] *R. v Sekhon* (1987) 85 Cr App R 19 at 22.

[495] *R. v Sekhon* (1987) 85 Cr App R 19 at 22.

I. Evidence by Live Television Link

3–202   As noted above, a fundamental element of the adversarial system of justice is the principle of orality whereby witnesses are examined *viva voce* in open court.[496] There has, however, been a legislative trend in recent years towards facilitating the giving of evidence by witnesses by means of live television link. The reasons for introducing these measures vary and are examined below.

1. Sexual or Violent Offences

3–203   It is now recognised that the victims of sexual or violent offences may suffer considerable psychological trauma if required to give evidence in open court in the presence of the persons who have committed those offences.[497] In order to reduce that trauma, Part III of the Criminal Evidence Act 1992[498] permits evidence to be given via live television link at the trial of specified sexual and violent offences.[499] As will be seen below, the provisions of Part III have provided the template for subsequent statutory developments in this area.

(a) Live television link

3–204   Section 13 of the 1992 Act[500] makes provision for the giving of evidence by live television link,[501] with subs.(1) specifying that:

> "In any proceedings (including proceedings under section 4E or 4F of the Criminal Procedure Act 1967) for an offence to which this Part applies a person other than the accused may give evidence, whether from within or outside the State, through a live television link—
>> (a) if the person is under 18 years of age, unless the court sees good reason to the contrary,
>> (b) in any other case, with the leave of the court."[502]

3–205   As a further measure to reduce the stress of giving evidence, s.13(3) stipulates that, while evidence is being given via live television link, neither the judge nor the

---

[496] *Phonographic Performance Ltd v Cody* [1998] 4 IR 504 at 521, [1998] 2 ILRM 21 at 26 (*per* Murphy J); *Mapp v Gilhooley* [1991] 2 IR 253 at 262 (*per* Finlay CJ).

[497] See Law Reform Commission, *Consultation Paper on Child Sexual Abuse* (1989), pp.120–121. See also *Donnelly v Ireland* [1998] 1 IR 321 at 356, [1998] 1 ILRM 401 at 419 (*per* Hamilton CJ).

[498] No.12 of 1992.

[499] The offences to which Part III apply are defined in s.12 (as substituted by s.10 of the Criminal Law (Human Trafficking Act 2008) as being: (a) a sexual offence; (b) an offence involving violence or the threat of violence to a person; (c) an offence under s.3, 4, 5 or 6 of the Child Trafficking and Pornography Act 1998; (d) an offence under s.2, 4 or 7 of the Criminal Law (Human Trafficking) Act 2008; or (e) an offence consisting of attempting or conspiring to commit, or of aiding or abetting, counselling, procuring or inciting the commission of, an offence mentioned in paragraph (a), (b), (c) or (d). The concept of a "sexual offence" is further defined in s.2 of the 1992 Act (as amended by s.16 of the Criminal Justice (Miscellaneous Provisions) Act 1997, s.7(2) of the Criminal Law (Sexual Offences) Act 2006, s.4(1) of the Criminal Law (Sexual Offences) (Amendment) Act 2007 and s.12(a) of the Criminal Law (Human Trafficking) Act 2008).

[500] As amended by s.18(3) of the Criminal Justice Act 1999 and s.257(3) of the Children Act 2001.

[501] For a comprehensive account of how the live television system operates and the safeguards to ensure that a witness is not coached or prompted while giving evidence, see the judgment of Kinlen J in *White v Ireland* [1995] 1 IR 268 at 272–275.

[502] Section 13(2) provides that evidence given by live television link must be videorecorded.

barrister or solicitor concerned in the examination of the witness can wear a wig or gown.

2014 Bill

3–206   Two preliminary points about s.13(1) should be noted. First, the section is not confined in its application to the victims of sexual offences and, secondly, that it applies equally to witnesses proposed to be called by the accused as well as the prosecution. Thus, even though the section would seem to be primarily directed towards the victims of sexual and violent offences, it is not so limited and potentially has a very wide application in prosecutions for such offences.

3–207   It can be seen that, pursuant to s.13(1)(a), persons under the age of 18 years (and persons with a mental handicap who have reached that age[503]) benefit from what is effectively a presumption in favour of being permitted to give evidence via live television link because they are entitled to do so "unless the court sees good reason to the contrary". This appears to reflect a legislative judgment that those persons are likely to suffer trauma if required to testify. However, given the broad application of this category to all persons under the age of 18 (and persons with a mental handicap who have reached that age) and not just the victim of offences, it can be seen that it is potentially applicable to persons who would not run any real risk of trauma if called upon to testify in court. This presumably is the basis for that caveat that the court can require a person under 18 years (and persons with a mental handicap who have reached that age) to give evidence in court rather than via live television link where it "sees good reason" to do so. No guidance is given as to exercise of this discretion although Hamilton CJ in *Donnelly v Ireland*[504] indicated that a trial judge will be obliged to have regard to an accused's right to a fair trial.

3–208   The application of s.13(1)(a) was considered in *O'Sullivan v Hamill*.[505] The applicant was charged with having sexual intercourse with a person who was mentally impaired, contrary to s.5(1) of the Criminal Law (Sexual Offences) Act 1993. An order was made by the respondent District Judge that the victim of the alleged offence could give a deposition via live television link and this order was challenged on the basis that he had acted in excess of jurisdiction in that he heard no evidence that the alleged victim was a person with a mental handicap. However, O'Higgins J rejected the contention that it was necessary for the District Judge to be satisfied that the witness had a mental handicap before she could be permitted to give evidence via live television link. He drew a distinction between the question as to whether a person with a mental handicap could give unsworn evidence and whether such a person could give evidence via television link. He accepted that an inquiry to establish the fact of mental handicap had to be held before unsworn evidence could be given but rejected the contention that such an inquiry was necessary before evidence could be given via television link. He was of the view that Part III conferred jurisdiction on the court to hear evidence by television link in all cases to which it applied and since it applied to the instant case,

---

[503]   Section 19 (as amended by s.4(c) of the Criminal Law (Human Trafficking) (Amendment) Act 2013) extends the application of s.13(1)(a) to a person with a mental handicap who has reached the age of 18 years. No further guidance is given in relation to the concept of "mental handicap" but it should be noted that, under s.20 thereof, the equivalent provisions in Part III of the Children Act 1997 are extended to "a person who is of full age but who has a mental disability to such an extent that it is not reasonably possible for the person to live independently".

[504]   [1998] 1 IR 321 at 357, [1998] 1 ILRM 401 at 420.

[505]   [1999] 2 IR 9.

it followed that the court had jurisdiction to allow a television link to be used. It is submitted, however, that the distinction sought to be drawn by the learned judge cannot be made. As noted above, it has been emphasised that "the examination of witnesses *viva voce* and in open court is of central importance in our system of justice and that it is a rule not to be departed from lightly".[506] Any departure from this cardinal principle requires justification and, where provided for by statute, any conditions precedent must be satisfied. Only a person under 18 years or a person with a mental handicap who has reached that age can give evidence via live television link under s.13(1)(a) and it follows that a judge must be satisfied that one or both of these conditions precedent is satisfied before a witness can be permitted to give evidence in this manner.

3–209 It is clear that persons aged 18 and over (other than persons with a mental handicap) do not have the benefit of any presumption of psychological trauma and they will be required to give evidence *viva voce* in open court unless the court grants leave, following an application made in that behalf by the party calling the witness, for the witness to give evidence via live television link. Again, no guidance is given as how the court should exercise its discretion and as to what circumstances would justify the grant of leave. It is interesting to contrast the wording of s.13(1)(b) with that of s.14(1) dealing with the giving of evidence through an intermediary where the age and mental condition of the witness are identified as the relevant criteria for the exercise of the court's discretion to permit questions to be put through an intermediary. The absence of any such criteria in s.13(1)(b) would seem to indicate that the court has quite a broad discretion although Hamilton CJ in *Donnelly v Ireland*[507] indicated that a trial judge will be obliged to have regard to an accused's right to a fair trial. In practice, an application for leave is most likely to be made and succeed where either the prosecution or the defence can put forward an evidential basis for asserting that a particular witness is likely to suffer trauma if required to give evidence in open court. However, the ambit of the subsection does not appear to be limited to that circumstance.

3–210 In *People (DPP) v McManus*,[508] one the grounds of appeal was that the trial judge had erred in permitting one of the chief prosecution witnesses who was over 18 years of age to give evidence by way of video link. It was contended that fair procedures required that evidence be given *viva voce* in open court so that the jury would have the greatest possible opportunity to assess the demeanour of the witness under examination and cross-examination unless there was "strong evidence" justifying a departure from the standard procedure. It was further contended that such evidence was not present in that case which went no further than establishing that the witness was concerned that she might freeze and be unable to answer questions, she did not want to confront the accused (who was her father) face to face and she did not wish to give evidence in front of a crowd. In addition, there was evidence from a doctor to the effect that the witness had a "strong and direct" personality although he had also said that the witness had great difficulty talking about feelings or things that had happened in the past. In deciding that the decision of the trial judge to permit the witness to give evidence by way of video link could not be criticised, the Court of Criminal Appeal attributed significance to the fact that she had only just reached her

---

[506] *Phonographic Performance Ltd v Cody* [1998] 4 IR 504 at 521, [1998] 2 ILRM 21 at 26 (*per* Murphy J).
[507] [1998] 1 IR 321 at 357, [1998] 1 ILRM 401 at 420.
[508] [2011] IECCA 32.

eighteenth birthday at the time of the trial, that she was giving evidence in a murder trial against her father concerning events that had occurred when she was 15 years of age and that there was evidence that she was a vulnerable person. The Court was also satisfied that the accused had not been unnecessarily or unduly restricted in his defence given that the witness had been cross-examined at length. Accordingly, it concluded that there was no basis for contending that there was a real or serious risk of an unfair trial by reason of the exercise by the trial judge of his discretion to permit the witness to give evidence by video link.

3–211   A restrictive approach to the circumstances in which evidence by way of video link pursuant to s.13 could be permitted was adopted in the particular circumstances that presented in *DO'D v DPP*.[509] The applicant had been charged with five counts of having sexual intercourse with a mentally impaired person. Part of his defence to those charges involved contending that the complainants were not mentally impaired and he sought to quash an order made in the Circuit Criminal Court pursuant to s.13(1)(b) that the complaints could give evidence by live television link on the basis that it would create an inference that the complainants were vulnerable persons who suffered from a mental impairment and pre-determine this issue in contravention of his right to a fair trial. O'Neill J accepted that a problem of perception would arise if the complainants gave evidence by live television link and that it would be difficult for the trial judge to cure this by an appropriate explanation or direction to the jury. In approaching the question of whether the discretion conferred by s.13(1)(b) had been correctly exercised, the learned judge identified the task of the court as being "to achieve a correct balance between the accused's right to a fair trial and the prosecution's right in an appropriate case to have evidence given by video link".[510] He went on to lay down the test to be applied in determining where that balance lay as follows[511]:

> "Where the Court reaches the conclusion that the giving of evidence in this way carries with it a serious risk of unfairness to the accused which could not be corrected by an appropriate statement from the prosecution or direction from the trial judge, it should only permit the giving of evidence by video link where it was satisfied by evidence that a serious injustice would be done, in the sense of a significant impairment to the prosecution's case if evidence had to be given in the normal way, *viva voce,* thus necessitating evidence by video link in order to vindicate the right of the public to prosecute offences of this kind. The fact that the giving of evidence *viva voce* would be very unpleasant for the witness or coming to court to give evidence very inconvenient, would not be relevant factors. In all cases of this nature the giving of evidence by the alleged victim will be very unpleasant and having to come to Court is invariably difficult and inconvenient for most persons. Most witnesses have vital commitments which have to be adjusted to allow them to come to Court. The real question is whether the circumstances of the witness are such that the requirement to give evidence *viva voce* is an insuperable obstacle to giving evidence in a manner that does justice to the prosecution case. The evidence must establish to the satisfaction of the Court hearing the application under s.13 of the Act of 1992 that the probability is that the witness in question will be deterred from giving evidence at all or will, in all probability, be unable to do justice to their evidence if required to give it *viva voce* in the ordinary way, This is necessarily a high threshold, but I am satisfied that in order to strike a fair balance between the right of the accused person to a fair trial and the right of the public to prosecute offences of this kind, it must be so."

3–212   The decision to permit the complainants to give evidence by video link had been made on the basis of the relationship between the applicant and the complainants,

---

[509] [2009] IEHC 559, [2010] 2 IR 605.
[510] [2009] IEHC 559 at [21], [2010] 2 IR 605 at 613.
[511] [2009] IEHC 559 at [22], [2010] 2 IR 605 at 613.

domestic and vocational awkwardness and inconvenience, the unpleasantness of the experience of giving evidence and other matters. The expert evidence in the case was merely that it would be "advantageous" to the complainants to give evidence by video link and there was no evidence that the complainants would be unable to give evidence *viva voce*. Accordingly, O'Neill J was satisfied that the Circuit Court judge had not applied the correct test and he granted the relief sought.

(b) Evidence through an intermediary

3–213   Section 14(1) of the 1992 Act[512] provides that, where a person under 18 years of age (or a person with a mental handicap who has reached that age) is giving, or is to give, evidence through a live television link, the court may, on the application of the prosecution or the accused, if satisfied that, having regard to the age and mental condition of the witness, the interests of justice require that any questions to be put to the witness be put through an intermediary,[513] direct that any such questions be so put. Subsection (2) goes on to stipulate that questions put to a witness through an intermediary must be either in the words used by the questioner or so as to convey to the witness the meaning of the questions being asked in a way which is appropriate to his age and mental condition.

(c) Identification evidence

3–214   Under s.18 of the 1992 Act, the requirements with regard to the identification of the accused in court are relaxed where a witness gives evidence via live television link. If the witness gives evidence that the accused was known to the witness before the date on which the offence was committed, the witness is not required to identify the accused at trial unless the court, in the interests of justice, directs otherwise.[514] In any other case, evidence by a person other than the witness that the witness identified the accused at an identification parade as being the offender is admissible as evidence that the accused was so identified.[515]

(d) Constitutionality of live television links

3–215   The constitutionality of Part III and, in particular, the provision for evidence to be given via live television link was unsuccessfully challenged in *White v Ireland*[516] and *Donnelly v Ireland*.[517]

3–216   In *White*, the contention that an accused person had a right to confront his accuser in open court was rejected by Kinlen J. The learned judge pointed out that, unlike the Sixth Amendment to the United States Constitution, there was no express right to confrontation enshrined in the Constitution and he did not believe that such a right existed as part of due process. Furthermore, even if he was wrong in the conclusion

---

[512] As amended by s.257(3) of the Children Act 1997.

[513] Section 14(3) provides that an intermediary is to be appointed by the court and must be a person who, in its opinion, is competent to act as such.

[514] Section 18(b)(i).

[515] Section 18(b)(ii).

[516] [1995] 2 IR 268. See further Duffy, "Televised testimony and constitutional justice" (1994) 4 ICLJ 178.

[517] [1998] 1 IR 321, [1998] 1 ILRM 401.

that a right to confrontation was not protected as part of the guarantee of due process, he took the view that the purpose of that right was to allow the accused to effectively carry out his cross-examination of witnesses. Therefore, while it was an indispensable part of this right that the tribunal of fact be able to observe the demeanour and credibility of a witness, it was not essential, having regard to the policy considerations involved that the accuser be actually able to see the accused. The learned judge was satisfied that modern technology suitably used is a form of confrontation and pointed out that a trial judge would act in accordance with constitutional and natural justice to ensure that an accused is afforded fair procedures. He also emphasised that the child accuser had rights and took the view that, in the circumstances, the diminution of the accused's right to confrontation was small and had to yield to concern for the wellbeing of the child.

3–217 In *Donnelly*, Costello J in the High Court focused on the question of whether s.13(1)(a) of the 1992 Act, was a breach of the constitutional guarantee of fair procedures contained in Art.38.1 and considered that it was not. His decision was upheld by the Supreme Court. Delivering the judgment of the Court, Hamilton CJ took the view that, although the Constitution did not include a confrontation clause,

> "... the central concern of the requirements of due process and fair procedures is the same, that is to ensure the fairness of the trial of an accused person. This undoubtedly includes the rigorous testing by cross-examination of the evidence against him or her."[518]

3–218 He was satisfied, however, that the provisions of s.13 did not restrict in any way the rights of an accused as protected by Art.38.1 and that the giving of evidence by live television link was not unfair to an accused. In reaching that conclusion, he emphasised the procedural protections that were applicable when a witness was permitted to give evidence via live television link:

> "The Court is satisfied ... that the assessment of such credibility does not require that the witness should be required to give evidence in the physical presence of the accused person and that the requirements of fair procedures are adequately fulfilled by requiring that the witness give evidence on oath and be subjected to cross-examination and that the judge and jury have ample opportunity to observe the demeanour of the witness while giving evidence and being subjected to cross-examination. In this way, an accused person's right to a fair trial is adequately protected and vindicated. Such right does not include the right in all circumstances to require that the evidence be given in his physical presence and consequently there is no such constitutional right."[519]

3–219 The learned Chief Justice went on to reject the contention that the procedures adopted in s.13(1)(a) were unfair and unconstitutional because they did not require a case-by-case determination of the necessity for the child witness to give evidence via live television link and that it placed an unfair burden on an accused to establish the witness's ability to undertake a face-to-face confrontation with the accused. He opined that, once it was established that there was no unfairness involved in allowing evidence to be given in the absence of physical confrontation, then the circumstances in which evidence is given other than in his or her presence is a matter for the Oireachtas. Indeed, he regarded the provision for the trial judge to direct that a witness give evidence in court where "there is good reason to the contrary" to be an additional safeguard for an accused and his or her right to a fair trial.

---

[518] [1998] 1 IR 321 at 356, [1998] 1 ILRM 401 at 418–419.
[519] [1998] 1 IR 321 at 357, [1998] 1 ILRM 401 at 419–420.

2. Criminal Proceedings where Witnesses are in Fear or Subject to Intimidation

3–220   Section 39 of the Criminal Justice Act 1999 provides that, in any proceedings on indictment (including proceedings under Part IA of the Criminal Procedure Act 1967), a person other than the accused may, with the leave of the court, give evidence through a live television link where the court is satisfied that the person is likely to be in fear or subject to intimidation in giving evidence.[520] The requirements with regard to identification in court are relaxed where a witness gives evidence via this medium. If the witness gives evidence that the accused was known to the witness before the date on which the offence in question is alleged to have been committed, the witness is not required to identify the accused, unless the court in the interests of justice directs otherwise.[521] In any other case, evidence by a person other than the witness that the witness identified the accused as being the offender at an identification parade or by other means is admissible as evidence that the accused was so identified.[522]

3. Criminal Proceedings where Witnesses are Outside the State

3–221   Section 29(1) of the Criminal Evidence Act 1992[523] provides that, in any criminal proceedings, or proceedings under the Extradition Acts 1965 to 2001, a person other than the accused or the person whose extradition is being sought, as the case may be, may, with the leave of the court, give evidence through a live television link.[524]

3–222   This subsection, as originally enacted, applied only to witnesses who were outside the State and was predicated on the difficulty and inconvenience of requiring persons outside the State to attend to give evidence at a trial. It does not appear that, in substituting a new subsection so as to extend the entitlement to give evidence via live television link to extradition proceedings, the Oireachtas intended to create a broad new exception that could be availed of by persons in the State. However, the new subsection as substituted by s.24 of the Extradition (European Union Conventions) Act 2001[525] is not confined in its application to persons outside the State and it remains to be seen whether it will be availed of in respect of persons within the State.

4. Civil Proceedings Concerning the Welfare of Children

3–223   Part III of the Children Act 1997 introduces measures similar to those contained in Part III of the Criminal Evidence Act 1992 in civil proceedings concerning the welfare of a child or a person who is of full age but who has a mental disability to such an extent that it is not reasonably possible for the person to live independently.[526]

3–224   Section 21(1) provides that, in any proceedings to which Part III of the 1997

---

[520] Section 39(3) stipulates that evidence given by live television link must be video-recorded.

[521] Section 39(5)(a).

[522] Section 39(5)(b).

[523] As substituted by s.24 of the Extradition (European Union Conventions) Act 2001.

[524] Section 29(2) stipulates that evidence given under subs.(1) must be video-recorded.

[525] No.49 of 2001.

[526] Section 19(1) defines a child as "a person who is not of full age" and subs.(3) provides that where the age of a person at any time is material for the purpose of any proceedings to which Part III applies, "his or her age at that time shall, for the purposes of such proceedings, be deemed, unless the contrary is proved, to be or to have been that which appears to the court to be his or her age at that time".

Act applies, a child may with the leave of the court, give evidence (whether from within or outside the State) through a live television link.[527] It is noteworthy that the leave of the court is required and that a child does not benefit from the presumption of trauma which a child giving evidence in criminal proceedings enjoys. The position is thus analogous to that under s.13(1)(b) of the 1992 Act and, in the absence of any guidelines as to when such leave should be granted, it seems as if a trial judge will enjoy a broad discretion in this regard.

3–225   Section 22(1) provides that, where the evidence of a child is being given or is to be given through a live television link:

> "the court may, of its own motion or on the application of a party to the proceedings, if satisfied that, having regard to the age or mental condition of the child, any questions to be put to the child should be put through an intermediary, direct that any such question be so put".[528]

3–226   This subsection is drafted in similar terms to s.14 of the 1992 Act but one point of departure is that, under s.22(1), the court may direct questions to be put through an intermediary of its own motion. This reflects the more inquisitorial nature of many child care proceedings.[529] Subsection (2) stipulates that questions put to a witness through an intermediary must be either in the words used by the questioner or so as to convey to the witness the meaning of the questions being asked in a way which is appropriate to his age and mental condition.

3–227   Although it is likely to be of less significance in civil proceedings, s.21(3) dispenses with the requirement for identification in court providing that, where evidence is given by a child via live television link that any person was known to him or her before the date of the commencement of the proceedings, the child is not required to identify the person during the course of those proceedings unless the court directs otherwise.

5. Proceedings in the Commercial List

3–228   Under Ord.63A, r.23(1) of the Rules of the Superior Courts[530] a judge hearing proceedings entered in the Commercial List may allow a witness to give evidence, whether from within or outside the State, through a live video link or by other means. This rule does not prescribe any criteria that have to be satisfied in order for this to be permitted and it is clear, therefore, that a judge has a wide discretion in this regard.[531] Such an order is particularly likely to be made in respect of witnesses who are outside of the jurisdiction and whose evidence is not central to the issues in the proceedings. There is no requirement for an application to have evidence taken by video link to be brought by way of motion or made at any particular time but, given the logistics attendant upon the giving of evidence in this manner, such an application should be

---

[527] Section 19(2) stipulates that evidence given through live television link must be video-recorded. The term "video-recorded" is defined in s.19(1) to mean "recorded on any medium (including a film) from which a moving image may by any means be produced, and includes the accompanying soundtrack, if any".

[528] Section 22(3) provides that an intermediary is to be appointed by the court and must be a person who, in its opinion, is competent to act as such.

[529] See *Eastern Health Board v MK* [1999] 2 IR 99, [1999] 2 ILRM 321 for a discussion of the inquisitorial nature of wardship proceedings.

[530] Inserted by the Rules of the Superior Courts (Commercial Proceedings) 2004 (SI No. 2 of 2004).

[531] *Moorview Developments Ltd v First Active plc* [2008] IEHC 274, [2009] 2 IR 788 at 803, [2009] 2 ILRM 262 at 277.

made on the hearing of a motion for directions or by way of a specific motion, if necessary, well in advance of the hearing. Where evidence is given in this manner, r.23(2) specifies that it shall be recorded by video or otherwise as the judge may direct.

3–229 The principles to be applied when considering an application to have evidence taken by video link were considered by Clarke J in unusual circumstances in *Moorview Developments Ltd v First Active plc*.[532] In that case, over three months into the hearing of an action, the plaintiffs applied to have the evidence of a witness, a Mr Michael Lynn, taken by video link. Mr Lynn had acted as solicitor to the plaintiff companies during most of the period that was relevant to the proceedings. A witness statement from Mr Lynn had been filed but he had fled the jurisdiction in circumstances where an order for his attachment for contempt had been made by the President of the High Court arising from his failure to appear before him and it appeared that there were investigations by the gardaí into his affairs. Mr Lynn was unwilling to return to the jurisdiction to give evidence and it was in those circumstances that an application was made to have his evidence taken by video link.

3–230 Clarke J was satisfied that Ord.63A, r.23 conferred a "broad discretion" on the court. He said that, in most cases, the only real issue will be as to the relative convenience of taking evidence by video link or requiring the witness to attend in court. He accepted that there was some disadvantage to the taking of evidence by video link, particularly in cases where the evidence of the witness concerned is likely to be significantly controversial and where the witness's credibility is likely to be attacked. Logistical difficulties could also arise where witnesses were required to deal with a large volume of documents and, although not insurmountable, needed to be weighed in the balance against the potential inconvenience of requiring the witness to come to court. He summarised the position as follows:

> "All in all, in a straightforward case, it seems to me to be likely that the court would be required to balance the undoubted saving of costs that would ensue from permitting foreign witnesses to give evidence by video link with any inconvenience for the run of the case, with that latter fact, in turn, being likely to be significantly dependent on the importance and complexity of the evidence of the witness concerned. That balance also needs to be exercised against the background of the fact that the giving of evidence in person in court remains the default position in the absence of there being some sufficient reason for departing from that course of action."[533]

3–231 Turning to the question of whether evidence by video link should be permitted where a witness is unwilling to travel to Ireland, he commented:

> "If it is the case that it would be convenient, in any event, for the witness concerned to give evidence by video-link, then it may well not be overly important, at least in most cases, to distinguish between a situation where the witness would be prepared to come to Ireland or one where the witness would not be so prepared. However, in cases where the balance would lie against permitting evidence by video-link, the question of the weight to be attached to the reason for the party not being prepared to travel to Ireland is an important factor. There will, of course, be many cases where there are perfectly valid reasons, whether of health or otherwise, which would make it impossible or difficult for a witness to travel to Ireland. Video-link would seem to me to be an entirely appropriate way for dealing with such evidence."[534]

3–232 The position was different, however, where the witness in question was

---

[532] [2008] IEHC 274, [2009] 2 IR 788, [2009] 2 ILRM 262.
[533] [2009] 2 IR 788 at 804, [2009] 2 ILRM 262 at 278.
[534] [2009] 2 IR 788 at 805, [2009] 2 ILRM 262 at 278–279.

unwilling to attend because he was in contempt of court. He took the view that, if this were an ordinary case, the balance of convenience would require that Mr Lynn come to Ireland to give evidence. It was on that basis that he went on to consider what the appropriate approach was where the reason put forward for non-attendance in this jurisdiction was fear of being attached for contempt of court. He summarised his views on this issue as follows:

> "It seems to me that the general consideration of the reason why the witness concerned is unwilling to give evidence in court in the ordinary way remains an important factor to be taken into account. The weight to be attached to such factor is likely to be significantly greater where the person concerned is a plaintiff who has chosen to bring proceedings in this jurisdiction. Less weight may attach in the case of a defendant who has not, after all, chosen the venue for the proceedings. Less weight still must be applied in the case of a mere witness. I would prefer to approach this matter at the level of principle, not on the basis of suggesting that there is any necessary barrier to a fugitive from justice, even as a plaintiff, from obtaining an entitlement, in an appropriate case, to give evidence by video-link. Rather it seems to me to be the case that where, as here, the witness ought ordinarily be expected to give evidence in person in court, the court is entitled to assess the merits of the reason given for the refusal or stated inability of the witness to attend. Where there is no good reason (and it seems to me that in reality a situation where there is no good reason is much the same a situation where a bad reason is put forward), then the court is entitled to take that factor into significant account, most especially where the person unwilling to come to the jurisdiction and give evidence in person is a party (and particularly the moving party). Viewed in that way, there is no breach of the equality of arms identified by the ECHR. The person refused video-link in those circumstances is not being treated any differently to any other potential witness who has not shown a good reason for being unwilling or unable to attend."[535]

3–233   He went on to distinguish the decision of the House of Lords in *Polanski v Condé Nast Publications Ltd*,[536] where the plaintiff who feared extradition to the United States if he gave evidence in the United Kingdom was permitted to give evidence by video link, on the basis that it concerned a situation where it was a plaintiff who was unwilling to give evidence rather than a mere witness. In his view, significant weight had to be attached to the fact that Mr Lynn was not, directly or indirectly, a party to the proceedings. In addition, he could not take the view that his evidence might not be sufficiently material to a reasonable extent and it remained possible that a failure to have his evidence available could lead to an injustice to the plaintiffs. In the circumstances, he concluded that it would be appropriate to allow Mr Lynn's evidence to be given on video link.

6. Civil Proceedings Generally

3–234   Specific provision for the taking of evidence by video link is made in respect of proceedings in the Commercial List only. However, there would seem to be little doubt but that an order permitting this to be done could be made by a court in the exercise of its inherent jurisdiction in any civil proceedings.[537] In recognition of this, a

---

[535] [2009] 2 IR 788 at 810–811, [2009] 2 ILRM 262 at 283–284.
[536] [2005] 1 WLR 637, [2005] 1 All ER 945. This issue was considered by the European Court of Human Rights in *Condé Nast Publications v United Kingdom* [2008] ECHR 107.
[537] As Kelly J explained in *PJ Carroll & Company Ltd v Minister for Health and Children* [2005] IEHC 276, [2005] 3 IR 457 at 466, there "is a jurisdiction inherent in the Court which enables it to exercise control over its process by regulating its proceedings" and this is "a residual source of power which the Court may draw upon as necessary whenever it is just or equitable to do so".

practice direction[538] has been issued specifying when such applications may be made[539] and specifying the steps that must be taken by the solicitor if such an order is made.[540]

J. Certificate Evidence

1. Introduction

3–235   A number of statutory provisions, some of which are examined below, dispense with the requirement for certain matters to be proved by oral evidence in criminal trials by creating an exception to the hearsay rule[541] and permitting those matters to be proved by means of certificate evidence.[542] These provisions, which are based on the inconvenience and expense of requiring witnesses to attend court to give evidence in relation to what are generally technical and/or uncontroversial matters, have the inevitable effect of eroding the orality of the criminal trial. They also sit somewhat uneasily with the constitutional protection of the presumption of innocence and the concomitant rule in criminal cases that the prosecution bears the legal burden of proving every fact essential to its case[543] especially when they are framed so as to give the certificate evidence admitted a particular status in derogation from the normal rules of evidence. However, it appears that such certificate provisions will pass constitutional muster provided that they limited to procedural and/or technical issues.

2. Section 6 of the Criminal Justice (Miscellaneous) Provisions Act 1997

3–236   Section 6 of the Criminal Justice (Miscellaneous) Provisions Act 1997 allows certificate evidence to be given in criminal proceedings of a number of routine and administrative matters thereby dispensing with the requirement for oral evidence to be given by gardaí.[544] This section was introduced in response to the perception that

---

[538] Practice Direction on the Use of Video-Conferencing Link for Taking Evidence in Civil Cases (3 May 2007).

[539] An application must be made not less than three working days prior to the date on which it is intended to hear such evidence.

[540] The solicitor for the party calling the witness is required to do the following: (1) undertake to the court to participate fully in all required test-calls to the remote location; (2) to provide the registrar with the necessary technical information in relation to the remote location and the case in which the application is being made (in the form set out at Appendix I to the Practice Direction); (3) ensure that the appropriate sacred text for taking the oath prior to giving evidence is available to the witness in the remote location; and (4) to ensure that the witness in the remote location is provided with any documents (including pleadings) to which he/she may be referred while giving evidence.

[541] *Power v Hunt* [2013] IEHC 174 at [25].

[542] These provisions include s.23(2) of the Road Traffic (Amendment) Act 1978, s.21 of the Road Traffic Act 1994 (which was considered in *DPP (O'Reilly) v Barnes* [2005] IEHC 245, [2005] 4 IR 176; *DPP v McDonagh* [2008] IESC 57, [2009] 1 IR 767), ss.6 and 11(2) of the Criminal Justice (Miscellaneous Provisions) Act 1997, s.25 of the Non-Fatal Offences Against the Person Act 1997 and s.30 of the Criminal Justice Act 1999. For a comprehensive discussion of these certificate provisions, see Walsh, *Criminal Procedure* (Dublin: Thomson Round Hall, 2002), pp.877–882.

[543] See *O'Leary v AG* [1991] ILRM 454, [1995] 2 ILRM 259 and, generally, Chap.2.

[544] Regulations specifying the form of the certificate have been made and are to be found in the Criminal Justice (Miscellaneous Provisions) Act, 1997 (Section 6) Regulations 1997 (SI No.345 of 1997).

members of the gardaí were tied up for long periods of time by court appearances. As noted by Quirke J in *O'Donnell v Coughlan*[545]:

"The purpose and effect of that statutory provision is to reduce inconvenience and delay in prosecuting certain offences by eliminating the need for the attendance of witnesses to prove routine procedural matters by way of oral evidence.

In many (perhaps most) cases the fact that necessary statutory and other procedural steps have been taken by the prosecuting authorities will not be in issue.

Accordingly, the section has been enacted for the purposes enabling evidence of certain formal, procedural and largely uncontroversial matters to be adduced more conveniently, more efficiently and less expensively than had formally been the case."

3–237 Subsection (1) deals with the evidence required to be given when a person arrested otherwise than under warrant makes his or her first appearance in the District Court and provides that a signed certificate stating that a garda arrested, charged or cautioned a person with regard to a specified offence shall be admissible as evidence of the matters stated in the certificate.[546] Subsection (2) is of more general application and permits evidence to be given by means of certificate in any criminal proceedings, *inter alia*, that a garda commenced duty, or replaced a specified member on duty, at a specified time at a place: (i) where the offence to which such proceedings relate is alleged to have been committed, (ii) adjacent to such a place, or (iii) containing evidence of the offence to which the proceedings relate. In *O'Donnell v Coughlan*,[547] Quirke J emphasised that certificate evidence admitted pursuant to the section is required to be adduced in open court:

"However the section did not abolish the requirement that the requisite evidence should be adduced and admitted in open court as evidence of the commission of the offence with which an accused person has been charged. That is necessary so that an accused person will be openly faced with the evidence upon which the prosecuting authorities rely and will have the opportunity, where appropriate, to challenge that evidence."

3–238 The conviction in that case was quashed in circumstances where the certificate evidence had been placed on the court file after the conviction of the applicant and he, therefore, been deprived of an opportunity to challenge it.

3–239 If a conflict of evidence as to any of the matters the subject of the certificate arises, then s.6(4) can be invoked. This provides that the court may, if it considers that the interests of justice so require, direct that oral evidence of the matters stated in a certificate should be given and, for that purpose, the court can adjourn the proceedings to a later date.

3. Section 30 of the Criminal Justice Act 1999

3–240 Section 30 of the Criminal Justice Act 1999, which is closely modelled on s.6 of the Criminal Justice (Miscellaneous Provisions) Act 1997, allows certificate evidence to be given in relation to the custody of exhibits. Subsection (1) provides that a certificate purporting to be signed by a garda and stating that the garda had custody of an exhibit at a specified place or for a specified period or purpose is admissible as

---

[545] [2006] IEHC 96 at [5].
[546] See *DPP (Ivers) v Murphy* [1999] 1 IR 98, [1999] 1 ILRM 46, where it was held that it was not necessary to prove by oral evidence that the accused had been arrested otherwise than under warrant and a District Judge was entitled to assume that the certificate had been issued in accordance with law.
[547] [2006] IEHC 96 at [5].

evidence of the maters stated in the certificate. However, pursuant to subs.(2), if the court considers that the interests of justice so require, it may direct that oral evidence be given of the matters stated in the certificate and it may, for that purpose, adjourn the proceedings.

4. Criminal Justice Act 2006

3–241   Provision is made in the Criminal Justice Act 2006 for a number of routine matters to be proved by certificate evidence. Thus, provision is made in s.75 for a certificate signed by an officer of the Department of Foreign Affairs to constitute evidence that a person was an Irish citizen on the date on which an offence of conspiracy under s.71 of the 2006 Act was committed; in s.96 for a certificate to be issued as evidence of a convicted person being subject to the requirements of Part 9 of the Act dealing with the obligation of drug trafficking offenders to notify certain information; and in s.97 for the proof of foreign convictions by duly executed documents or certificates in certain cases.

5. The Constitutionality of Certificate Provisions

3–242   The constitutionality of provisions permitting evidence to be given by means of a certificate was considered by the Supreme Court in *The Employment Equality Bill 1996*.[548] At issue in that case was s.63(3) of the Bill which provided that in any proceedings for an offence under the section a document purporting to be certified by the Director of Equality Investigations or to be sealed with the seal of the Labour Court and relating to the circumstances in which the offence was alleged to have occurred was receivable as *prima facie* evidence of the facts stated therein.

3–243   Hamilton CJ, delivering the decision of the Supreme Court, was of the opinion that the subsection encroached upon the essence of a criminal trial:

> "It is a fundamental principle of our system that, in general, criminal trials are conducted on *viva voce* evidence. … Whereas *viva voce* evidence is the normal in the majority of cases, proof by written statement is allowed in certain circumstances but with the consent of the accused, and, in other cases, certificates may provide *prima facie* evidence of specific issues of a scientific or technical nature. Such limitation of *viva voce* evidence is reasonable in circumstances where the nature of the evidence is, for example, technical and by its form appropriate in a certificate, as such form means that, for example, many technicians and officials are not required to be called to court in each case. A reasonable balance is obtained."[549]

3–244   Later in his judgment, he summarised the circumstances where certificate evidence was permissible by saying:[550]

> "Proof by way of certification is an interference with the norm of a trial *viva voce*. A certificate is an appropriate form of proof when it is proportionate to the ends to be achieved. It is a justifiable method of proof when the process is, for example, of a technical nature and there are other issues before the court."

3–245   However, the question of whether an offence had been committed under s.63

---

[548] [1997] 2 IR 321.

[549] [1997] 2 IR 321 at 379. This passage was referred to with approval by Finnegan J in *Criminal Assets Bureau v PS* [2004] IEHC 351 at [49], [2009] 3 IR 9 at 35 and by the Supreme Court in *McGonnell v Attorney General* [2006] IESC 64 at [31], [2007] 1 ILRM 321 at 336, [2007] 1 IR 400 at 418.

[550] [1997] 2 IR 321 at 382–383.

fell into a different category. It was likely to give rise to a sharp conflict of evidence and was not amenable to proof by certification:

> "The idea that a criminal trial could proceed from beginning to end concluding with a verdict of guilty on the production of a document is inconsistent with the concept of trial in due course of law. The use of a certificate as proposed in s.63(3) is to do more than prove evidence of certain technical matters by certificate. It is a document which may be certified by a person with no personal knowledge of or involvement in the events in issue. It purports to relate to all the facts of the offence. No other evidence may be anticipated."[551]

3–246 The learned Chief Justice then considered whether the provision amounted to a proportionate interference with the right to trial in due course of law[552] and concluded that it did not because the subsection failed the first test of proportionality in that the process of certification was not rationally connected to the objective of the Bill. The objective of equality in employment did not require that the offence in s.63 be tried in the manner set out in s.63(3). Thus, there was no rational reason why the process of certification was necessary in this type of case.[553]

3–247 The decision in *The Employment Equality Bill 1996* was subsequently distinguished in *DPP (Ivers) v Murphy*[554] which considered the constitutionality of s.6 of the Criminal Justice (Miscellaneous) Provisions Act 1997. Denham J laid considerable emphasis on the fact that s.6 dealt with the preliminary procedure in the District Court and not the trial itself. In her view, there was no question of the proceedings against the accused being tried by way of certificate and, thus, there was no infringement of the rights of an accused. In addition, she pointed out that the District Judge had a duty to ensure due process at all times and he or she could require oral evidence of the matters stated in the certificate to be given.

3–248 The constitutionality of proof by way of certification in prosecutions for offences contrary to s.49(4) of the Road Traffic Act 1961 was upheld in *McGonnell v Attorney General*.[555] At issue in that case were s.13 of that Act which provided for the taking of samples including a breath specimen, s.17 which provided for two specimens of breath to be taken with a printout from the apparatus used to take the specimens specifying the concentration of alcohol, and s.21 which stipulated that such a printout would be sufficient evidence, until the contrary was shown, in any proceedings under the Road Traffic Acts of the facts stated therein. The Supreme Court rejected the contention that these sections provided for "conviction by printout" and noted that a statement under s.17 specifying the concentration of alcohol was but one of the elements of an offence contrary to s.49(4) of that Act and there were a number of other matters that had to be proved and in respect of which *viva voce* evidence was required in order to obtain a conviction. Also important was that the presumption contained in s.21 was rebuttable and it was open to an accused to apply to conduct an inspection of the apparatus so as to investigate its reliability, to adduce evidence regarding the manner of operation of the apparatus at the relevant time and to adduce evidence of

---

[551] [1997] 2 IR 321 at 382.

[552] Applying the test of proportionality laid down in *R. v Oakes* [1986] 1 SCR 103, (1986) 26 DLR (4th) 200 and *R. v Chaulk* [1990] 3 SCR 1303.

[553] In passing, it might be noted the equivalent section in the Equal Status Bill 1997, s.40(3), was found to be unconstitutional for the same reasons in *Re Article 26 and the Equal Status Bill 1997* [1997] 2 IR 388.

[554] [1999] 1 IR 98, [1999] 1 ILRM 46.

[555] [2006] IESC 64, [2007] 1 ILRM 321, [2007] 1 IR 400.

the amount of alcohol consumed with the object of showing that the apparatus was defective. Accordingly, the Court was satisfied that a reasonable balance had been maintained between the requirement that the State be able to prosecute drunk driving cases effectively whilst preserving the right of an accused to maintain a defence and concluded that the test of proportionality was satisfied.

3–249 In *Criminal Assets Bureau v PS*,[556] Finnegan P held that the effect of a statutory provision providing for prescribed matters to be proved on a *prima facie* basis by certificate was to dispense with the requirement for the party relying on the certificate to adduce oral evidence in respect of the certified matter and thereby shift the evidential burden in respect of those matters to the defendant who could controvert those matters by probative evidence. Once this was done, the certificate ceased to be *prima facie* evidence so that the certified fact has to be proved by admissible evidence. Accordingly, he was satisfied that the provision for proving certain matters in s.966 of the Taxes Consolidation Act 1997 was not unconstitutional.

6. Compliance with Statutory Requirements in relation to Certificate Evidence

3–250 As penal legislation, statutory provisions providing for the admission of certificate evidence will be given a literal interpretation and will be strictly construed.[557] Furthermore, the courts will be astute to ensure that the processes used to create certificate evidence respect the constitutional rights of an accused and are fair.[558]

3–251 It was held in *DPP v Kemmy*[559] that strict compliance with statutory provisions which permit certificate evidence to be adduced and give it a particular evidential status is required, with O'Higgins CJ stating[560]:

> "Where a statute provides for a particular form of proof or evidence in compliance with certain provisions, in my view it is essential that the precise statutory provisions be complied with. The courts cannot accept something other than that which is laid down by the statute, or overlook the absence of what the statute requires. To do so would be to trespass into the legislative field. This applies to all statutory requirements; but it applies with greater general understanding to penal statutes which create particular offences and then provide a particular method for their proof."[561]

3–252 More recently, Clarke J in *DPP v Cullen*[562] stated that "compliance with the statutory regime is in the nature of a condition precedent to the admissibility of the evidence in the first place, for in the absence of such compliance, the certificate simply would not be evidence in the ordinary way."[563]

3–253 However, O'Flaherty J cautioned against adopting an overly strict approach

---

[556] [2004] IEHC 351 at [49]–[50], [2009] 3 IR 9 at 36.
[557] *DPP v Moorehouse* [2006] IESC 52, [2006] 1 IR 421; *DPP v McDonagh* [2008] IESC 57, [2009] 1 IR 767. However, the literal rule will not applied so as to create an absurd result and defeat the clear intention of the legislature: *DPP (Ivers) v Murphy* [1999] 1 IR 98, [1999] 1 ILRM 46; *DPP v McDonagh* [2008] IESC 57 at [65], [2009] 1 IR 767 at 790.
[558] *DPP v McDonagh* [2008] IESC 57 at [31]–[32], [2009] 1 IR 767 at 779.
[559] [1980] IR 160.
[560] [1980] IR 160 at 164.
[561] This passage was approved by the Supreme Court in *DPP v Ennis* [2011] IESC 46 at [10].
[562] [2014] IESC 7 at [2.2].
[563] See also *Sweeney v Fahy* [2014] IESC 50 (judgment of Clarke J at [6.6]).

in *DPP v Somers*[564] so that mistakes in a certificate which did not prejudice the person against whom the certificate evidence was adduced could be overlooked:

> "It is true that in general the law expects strict compliance with the wording of statutes, especially in a penal context. But this is so that the purposes and objects of the legislation are observed. It is impossible to seek perfection at all stages of life and when there is a tiny flaw in the filing out of a document such as this, which flaw is of no significance and cannot possibly work any injustice to an accused and is not in discord with the purposes and objects of the legislation, then the courts are required to say that such a slip, as we have here, cannot be allowed bring about what would be a manifest injustice as far as the prosecution of this offence is concerned."

3–254 These *dicta* were considered by O'Neill J in *DPP (O'Reilly) v Barnes*[565] in circumstances where a certificate as to alcohol detected by an intoximeter in a breath sample, which was admissible as the evidence of the facts contained therein pursuant to s.21(1) of the Road Traffic Act 1994, contained an obvious error. He summarised the position as follows[566]:

> "A court … must approach the matter on the basis of being satisfied that there has been a strict compliance with the relevant statutory provision before admitting the statement into evidence against an accused.
>
> On the other hand where objection has been taken to the statement on the basis of an error in it, if the error is of such an obvious or trivial or inconsequential nature so that it could not be said that it gave rise to any confusion or misleading of the accused or imposed any prejudice on him or in any way exposed him to any injustice, then the court should conclude that the error in question did not detract from the due completion of the statement in question and it should be admitted and permitted the force and effect provided for by, as in this case s.21(1) of the Road Traffic Act 1994."[567]

3–255 In that case, he was satisfied that the error in question was clear and did not mislead, confuse or cause prejudice or injustice to the accused so as to detract from the due completion of the statement which, accordingly, was admissible.

3–256 It has also been held that a certificate can only be used and only has a particular evidential status when used for the statutorily prescribed purpose and will not be admissible for any other purpose.[568]

---

[564] [1999] 1 IR 115 at 119.
[565] [2005] IEHC 245, [2005] 4 IR 176.
[566] [2005] IEHC 245 at [14]–[15], [2005] 4 IR 176 at 181–182.
[567] He went to say, *obiter*, that it was not open to a court to amend a certificate because, by doing so, the court would be altering evidence ([2005] IEHC 245 at [19], [2005] 4 IR 176 at 182).
[568] *Power v Hunt* [2013] IEHC 174 at [26].

CHAPTER 4

UNRELIABLE EVIDENCE

A. Introduction

4–01 There are certain categories of evidence which judicial experience has shown present acute problems of reliability either because of the nature of the offence or some characteristic of the witness giving evidence such that there is an increased risk that a witness may give untruthful evidence or a witness who is endeavouring to give truthful evidence may give evidence that is incorrect or inaccurate.[1] This chapter examines the various safeguards which have been devised to minimise the risk of a wrongful conviction or incorrect verdict consequent upon the admission of such evidence.

4–02 Initial solutions to the problems posed by potentially unreliable evidence focused on the concept of corroboration,[2] *i.e.* independent evidence which implicated the accused in the commission of the offence.[3] Mandatory corroboration requirements were imposed in respect of a number of criminal offences whereby an accused could not be convicted on the uncorroborated evidence of one witness. The availability of such corroboration provided an important reassurance that a conclusion of guilt founded on the potentially unreliable evidence was factually correct.[4] However, the drawback with this solution, which militated against widespread adoption, was that it had the potential to lead to unmeritorious acquittals in circumstances where the evidence of a potentially unreliable witness was considered to be reliable in the particular case by the tribunal of fact but no corroborative evidence was available. Thus, as an alternative to actually requiring corroboration, the practice emerged of judges giving the jury

---

[1] See the distinction between the truthfulness and accuracy of evidence drawn by Hardiman J in *Byrne v O'Leary* [2011] IESC 38 at [31], [2011] 3 IR 667 at 675–676.

[2] The term "corroboration" is derived from the Latin "robur" and the English word "robust" and means "strengthen" *DPP v Hester* [1973] AC 296 at 321, [1972] 3 All ER 1056 at 1070 (*per* Lord Pearson).

[3] See *R. v Sheehan* (1826) Jebb CC 54 and *R. v Baskerville* [1916] 2 KB 658 discussed in detail below.

[4] As Lord Morris explained in *DPP v Hester* [1973] AC 296 at 315, [1972] 3 All ER 1056 at 1065: "Any risk of conviction of an innocent person is lessened if conviction is based on the testimony of more than one acceptable witness. Corroborative evidence in the sense of some other material evidence in support implicating the accused furnishes a safeguard which makes a conclusion more sure than it would be without such evidence."

a warning of the dangers of convicting on the evidence of a suspect witness[5] in the absence of corroboration, *i.e.* a corroboration warning.

4–03 Over time, three categories of suspect witness were identified whose evidence was thought to pose such special and hidden[6] dangers that a corroboration warning was required: (i) accomplices giving evidence on behalf of the prosecution; (ii) complainants in sexual cases; and (iii) children. However, the use of corroboration warnings in respect of these categories of witness created a multitude of difficulties arising from the complexity and technicality of the warning.[7] Accordingly, although it has been held that the categories of suspect witness whose evidence should be the subject of a corroboration warning are not closed,[8] the courts have declined to extend the requirement to give a corroboration warning to other categories of suspect witness with the exception of the evidence of witnesses who have been incentivised to give evidence and/or are participants in the witness protection programme, most of whom are likely to be accomplices in any event.[9] Indeed, the requirement for a mandatory corroboration warning has been abrogated by statute in the case of sexual complainants[10] and children.[11]

4–04 Instead, the modern approach of the courts to the problems posed where evidence may be unreliable has been to develop tailored cautionary instructions which are designed to alert the jury to the potential unreliability of the evidence in the particular circumstances of the case, the reasons for this unreliability, and the need to exercise caution before convicting on the basis of such evidence.[12] The most developed example of such a cautionary instruction, which is discussed in detail below, is that given in respect of identification evidence,[13] but embryonic instructions in relation to other categories of evidence can be identified and are examined.

B. Corroboration Requirements

4–05 In general, the common law eschews any quantitative requirements with regard to testimony, concentrating instead on the qualitative aspect of such evidence.[14] The

---

[5] The term "suspect witness", as a shorthand term for the various categories of witness in respect of which a warning was required, was coined by Lord Diplock in *DPP v Hester* [1973] AC 296 at 324, [1972] 3 All ER 1056 at 1072.

[6] The hidden nature of the dangers posed by these three categories of witness was emphasised by Lord Ackner in *R. v Spencer* [1987] AC 128 at 141, [1986] 2 All ER 928 at 937.

[7] These difficulties are examined below in the context of the accomplice corroboration warning.

[8] *DPP v Kilbourne* [1973] AC 728 at 740, [1973] 1 All ER 440 at 447.

[9] See *People (DPP) v Gilligan* [2005] IESC 78, [2006] 1 IR 107 discussed below.

[10] Criminal Law (Rape) (Amendment) Act 1990, s.7.

[11] Criminal Evidence Act 1992, s.28.

[12] See *People (DPP) v Meehan* [2006] IECCA 104 at [52], [2006] 3 IR 468 at 490, where Kearns J considered that "it makes little sense to relate unreliability to classes of person—be they accomplices, children or complainants in sexual cases, rather than to the circumstances of cases".

[13] See *People (AG) v Casey (No.2)* [1963] IR 33 and subsequent case law.

[14] *Per* Black J in *Weiler v United States* (1945) 323 US 606 at 608: "Our system of justice rests on the general assumption that the truth is not to be determined merely by the number of witnesses on each side of a controversy. In gauging the truth of conflicting evidence, a jury has no simple formulation of weights and measures upon which to rely. The touchstone is always credibility; the ultimate measure of testimonial worth is quality and not quantity. Triers of fact in our fact-finding tribunals are, with rare exceptions, free in the exercise of their honest judgment, to prefer the

general rule is that the evidence of one competent witness is sufficient to support a verdict whether in criminal or civil proceedings.[15] However, as adverted to above, there are a discrete number of criminal offences in respect of which corroboration is required as a matter of law, *i.e.* is mandatory. Thus, in the absence of corroborative evidence, the judge must direct an acquittal, no matter how convincing the testimony against the accused. In addition, there are two miscellaneous categories of civil cases in respect of which corroboration is sought as a matter of practice.

1. Criminal Offences

(a) Evidence of speed

4–06   Section 81(5) of the Road Traffic Act 2010 provides that, where proof of the commission of specified road traffic offences involves proof of the speed at which a person (whether the accused or another person) was driving, the uncorroborated evidence of one witness stating his opinion as to that speed shall not be accepted as proof of that speed.[16]

4–07   This provision is thought necessary because opinion evidence of speed, though admissible, is acknowledged to be unreliable and, in addition, the usual means for identifying error, namely cross-examination, is not very effective in relation to such evidence.[17] The subsection is merely "intended to prevent the conviction of a defendant on evidence given by a single witness of his unsupported visual impression of a defendant's speed".[18] Therefore, where a garda gives evidence of speed based on

---

testimony of a single witness to that of many." There is a general requirement for corroboration in Scottish law, the abolition of which has been recommended in Carloway, *The Carloway Review: Report and Recommendations* (17 November 2011). See further, Duff, "The requirement for corroboration in Scottish criminal cases: one argument against retention" [2012] Crim LR 513; Davidson and Ferguson, "The Corroboration Requirement in Scottish Criminal Trials: should it be retained for some forms of problematic evidence?" (2014) 18(1) E & P 1; Nicolson and Blackie, "Corroboration in Scots law: "archaic rule" or "invaluable safeguard'?" (2013) 17(2) Edinburgh LR 152.

[15] *Burke v Fulham* [2010] IEHC 448 at [65]; *DPP v Kilbourne* [1973] AC 729 at 739, [1973] 1 All ER 440 at 446; *DPP v Hester* [1973] AC 296 at 324, [1972] 3 All ER 1056, 1072; *Vetrovec v R.* [1982] 1 SCR 811, (1982) 136 DLR (3d) 89 at 96; *Radford v MacDonald* (1891) 18 OAR 167 at 171; *Warszower v United States* (1941) 312 US 342 at 348. It appears that a tribunal of fact is not obliged to act on the evidence of one witness, even if uncontradicted (*People (DPP) v Quilligan* [1993] 2 IR 305 at 330). However, there is a strong body of authority to the contrary (*Morrow v Morrow* [1914] 2 IR 183 at 189; *Richards v Jager* [1909] VLR 140 at 147; *Hardy v Gillette* [1976] VR 392 at 396).

[16] This subsection re-enacts s.21(4) of the Road Traffic Act 2002 which had re-enacted a similar requirement in s.105(1) of the Road Traffic Act 1961.

[17] It is arguable that a cautionary instruction rather than an actual corroboration requirement would suffice but, given the ready availability of corroboration from speed measuring apparatus in most cases, a corroboration requirement protects against wrongful convictions without significantly hindering the prosecution of offences. Indeed, it is noteworthy that none of the reports which have examined this requirement in England have recommended its abolition (see CLRC, *Eleventh Report*, para.193; *Road Traffic Law Review Report* (North Report) (London: HMSO, 1988), para.3.18). See also Dennis, "Corroboration Requirements Reconsidered" [1984] Crim LR 316 at 334.

[18] *Per* Bingham LJ in *Crossland v DPP* [1988] 3 All ER 712 at 715 (speaking with regard to then English equivalent, s.89 of the Road Traffic Regulation Act 1984). Where it is sought to found a conviction on the opinion evidence of two witnesses, both must have observed the vehicle at the same time and place (*Brighty v Pearson* [1938] 4 All ER 127).

a reading given by an apparatus for recording speed such as a radar gun, then he or she is not giving opinion evidence of speed and corroboration is not required.[19] The section does not apply in circumstances where evidence is given that a person was driving quickly rather than giving evidence that the person was driving at or above an enumerated speed.[20]

(b) Procuration

4–08 Under s.2 of the Criminal Law Amendment Act 1885,[21] a person cannot be convicted of the offence of procuring a woman or girl to become a prostitute upon the evidence of one witness, unless such witness is corroborated in some material particular by evidence implicating the accused. A similar proviso is contained in s.3[22] in respect of the offences of procuring unlawful sexual connection with a woman by threats, fraud or the administering of drugs or alcohol.[23]

4–09 The standard justification for the requirement of corroboration in relation to procuration is that it is a charge which is easy to make and difficult to defend and, furthermore, the witness to be corroborated is usually the woman procured who may be a person of questionable character and reliability. For these reasons, it is argued that a requirement of corroboration is justified on the grounds of public policy. However, it does not appear that this reasoning can be accepted any longer. The notion that a charge of this nature is easy to make and difficult to defend also underpinned the mandatory corroboration warning in respect of complainants in sexual cases and with the abolition of that warning,[24] the retention of a mandatory corroboration requirement for this category of offences appears anomalous.[25]

(c) Treason

4–10 At common law, the testimony of one witness was sufficient to found a conviction for treason[26] but, in 1821, a requirement that a conviction be based upon the testimony of two witnesses was introduced.[27] That plurality requirement has since

---

[19] *Kenny v Coughlan* [2008] IEHC 28, [2014] IESC 15 at [17].
[20] *People (DPP) v Connaughton*, unreported, Court of Criminal Appeal, 5 April 2001.
[21] 48 & 49 Vic, c.69 (as amended by s.7 of the Criminal Law Amendment Act 1935).
[22] As amended by s.8 of the Criminal Law Amendment Act 1935.
[23] The wording of these sections suggests that the required corroborative evidence must have both an implicatory and a confirmatory quality, *i.e.* it must confirm some material particular of the witness's testimony in addition to implicating the accused (see *R. v Goldstein* (1914) 11 Cr App R 27). Should the matter arise for decision, however, it is likely that the sections would be construed in accordance with the common law definition of corroboration which does not require corroborative evidence to be confirmatory (*People (DPP) v Hogan* [1994] 2 ILRM 74 at 79; *R. v Beck* [1982] 1 All ER 807, [1982] 1 WLR 461; *R. v Galluzzo* (1986) 23 A Crim R 211 at 215).
[24] By s.7(1) of the Criminal Law (Rape) (Amendment) Act 1990.
[25] The equivalent sections in England of the Sexual Offences Act 1956 were repealed by s.33 of the Criminal Justice and Public Order Act 1994 as part of a major overhaul of the law of corroboration which saw the abolition of mandatory warnings in the case of accomplices and sexual complainants.
[26] *R. v Jackson* (1795) 25 St Tr 783 at 871–872 (*per* Lord Clonmell). Coke had earlier advanced the proposition that two witnesses were required for a conviction (3 Inst 26 (1629)) but this contention was not supported by authority (see Wigmore, *Evidence* 3rd edn (Boston: Little Brown and Company, 1940), VII, § 2036).
[27] By St 1 & 2 Geo IV, c.24 which extended the application of the Treason Act 1695, s.2 (St 7 W

been diluted so that the corroborated testimony of one witness suffices to ground a conviction. The relevant provision is s.1(4) of the Treason Act 1939 which provides that no person shall be convicted of treason on the uncorroborated evidence of one witness.[28] Section 2(2) further specifies that no person shall be convicted of the offence of encouraging, harbouring or comforting persons guilty of treason on the uncorroborated evidence of one witness.

4–11   The corroboration requirement is justified on the grounds of the seriousness of the offence,[29] the undefined nature of treason and the fact that false accusations of treason have been used, throughout history, as a means of political oppression.[30]

(d) Perjury

4–12   In a prosecution for perjury,[31] or subornation of perjury,[32] the uncorroborated evidence of one witness is not sufficient to prove the falsity of the statement alleged to be false.[33] This is the one exception at common law to the general rule that a court is entitled to act on the testimony of a single witness if believed.[34]

4–13   The origin of this exception can be traced back to the fact that perjury was originally punished in the Court of Star Chamber.[35] The proceedings of the Star Chamber

---

III, c.3) to Ireland. The latter section provided that "no person could be indicted or tried for high treason except "by and upon the oaths and testimony of two lawful witnesses, either both of them to the same overt act, or one of them to the one and the other of them to another overt act of the same treason". It was repealed by the Statute Law Revision Act 1983 (No.11 of 1983), s.1, Sch., Part 3. For a discussion of the historical origins of the plurality requirement in treason cases, see Wigmore, *Evidence* 3rd edn (Boston: Little Brown and Company, 1940), VII, § 2036.

[28]   A corroboration requirement for treason is also to be found in New Zealand in s.121 of the Evidence Act 2006.

[29]   Section 1(1) of the Treason Act 1939 as originally enacted provided that treason was punishable by death but the death penalty was abolished by s.1 of the Criminal Justice Act 1990.

[30]   See Wigmore, *Evidence* 3rd edn (Boston: Little Brown and Company, 1940), VII, § 2037: "The object of the rule requiring two witnesses in treason is plain enough. It is, as Sir William Blackstone said, to 'secure the subject from being sacrificed to fictitious conspiracies, which have been the engines of profligate and crafty politicians in all ages.' "

[31]   But not the kindred offences of attempting, inciting or conspiring to commit either perjury or subornation of perjury: *R. v Barker* [1986] 1 NZLR 252; *R. v Kyling* (1970) 14 CRNS 257.

[32]   *Hammer v United States* (1926) 271 US 620; *Petite v United States* (1959) 262 F 2d 788 at 794; *R. v Kyling* (1970) 14 CRNS 257 at 261; *R. v Doz* (1984) 52 AR 321, 12 CCC 200; *Lefebvre v R.* (1946) 88 CCC 383 at 386–387. It should be noted, however, that where the perjurer gives evidence for the prosecution on a charge of subornation, he is regarded as an accomplice of the person who suborned him or her and therefore a corroboration warning will be required on that basis.

[33]   *R. v Parker* (1842) Car & M 639 at 645; *R. v Linehan* [1921] VLR 582 at 588; *R. v Sumner* [1935] VLR 197 at 198; *Hammer v United States* (1926) 271 US 620 at 626; *United States v Diggs* (1977) 560 F 2d 266 at 269; *Weiler v United States* (1945) 323 US 606 at 610. In the case of subornation of perjury, it is only the falsity of the statement and not the knowledge of the suborner of the falsity of the statement which requires to be corroborated (*R. v Doz* (1984) 52 AR 321, 12 CCC 200).

[34]   *DPP v Kilbourne* [1973] AC 729 at 739, [1973] 1 All ER 440 at 446 (*per* Lord Hailsham). This common law exception has been placed on a statutory footing in many common law jurisdictions including England (s.13 of the Perjury Act 1911) and Canada (Criminal Code, RSC 1985, c. C–46, s.133).

[35]   This account of the historical origins of the corroboration rule in perjury is based on that of Wigmore, *Evidence* 3rd edn (Boston: Little Brown and Company, 1940), VII, § 2040.

were conducted according to ecclesiastical law and thus required a second witness. When the Star Chamber was abolished[36] and its jurisdiction transferred to the King's Bench, the requirement of a plurality of witnesses, later diluted to a corroboration requirement,[37] was carried over into the common law.[38] A rationale for its adoption was found in the quantitative notion of an oath which was then current. In all other criminal cases, the accused could not testify and thus, one oath for the prosecution was something as against nothing. However, on a charge of perjury the accused's oath was always in issue and thus, if there was only one prosecution witness, then there was "only oath against oath".[39]

4–14 This reasoning has fallen into disfavour[40] and the continuance of the corroboration requirement is justified on the basis of public policy. In *R. v Hook*,[41] Byles J adverted to the danger that "in all judicial proceedings all witnesses, even the most honest, would be constantly exposed to the peril, annoyance and oppression of indictments for perjury if the single oath of another man, without any confirmatory evidence, might, in point of law, suffice to convict."[42] Thus, even though the corroboration requirement makes it more difficult to obtain a conviction for perjury, a concern arises that, to make a prosecution for perjury less difficult, might discourage witnesses from testifying.[43] However, acceptance of this justification as a basis for a mandatory corroboration requirement is not universal.[44]

4–15 Corroboration is only required to prove the falsity of the fact alleged to be

---

[36] In 1640 by St 16 Carl, c.10.

[37] The proposition that the testimony of one witness suffices, if corroborated, has prevailed since at least the middle of the nineteenth century (see, *R. v Mayhew* (1834) 6 C & P 315; *Jordan v Money* (1854) 5 H L Cas 185 at 232; *R. v Braithwaite* (1859) 1 F & F 638 at 640). By 1860, Lefory CJ could declare in *R. v Towey* (1860) 8 Cox CC 328 at 331, that "[t]he rule is now settled and beyond all doubt that corroborative evidence is sufficient to supply the place of a second witness".

[38] A corroboration requirement in respect of perjury and cognate offences has been retained in New Zealand in s.121 of the Evidence Act 2006.

[39] *Per* Parker CJ in *R. v Muscot* (1713) 10 Mod Rep 192 at 194.

[40] The rationale of "oath against oath" was rejected by the English Criminal Law Revision Committee (*Evidence (General): Eleventh Report* (London: HMSO, 1972) (Cmnd 4991), para.178.

[41] (1858) Dears & B 606 at 616.

[42] See also, *Weiler v United States* (1945) 323 US 606 at 609; Best, *The Principles of the Law of Evidence* 12th edn, Phipson (ed.), (London: Sweet & Maxwell, 1922), p.521 at para.607.

[43] Criminal Law Revision Committee, *Eleventh Report* (1972) (Cmnd 4991), para.190; Law Commission, *Offences Relating to Interference with the Administration of Justice* (Law Com No 96), para.2.62; *Weiler v United States* (1945) 323 US 606 at 609. The Law Commission took the view that the requirement of corroboration acted as a safeguard where a principal prosecution witness had a strong interest in securing the accused's conviction. The Criminal Law Revision Committee adverted to the danger that the successful party to litigation might seek to have his opponent or his opponent's witnesses prosecuted for perjury as a result of his evidence having been preferred over theirs but noted that this problem could be cured by the simple expedient of requiring the consent of the DPP before a prosecution for perjury could be brought (at para.221).

[44] *Cf.* The Law Reform Commission of Tasmania, *Report and Recommendations on the Law and Practice relating to Corroboration, with particular reference to the evidence of Treason, Bigamy, Perjury, Forgery, Child Witnesses, Victims in Sex Cases, and Accomplices* (Report No.21) (1978), p.7. It might be noted that, in the US, the contention that the abolition of the corroboration requirement for the offence of perjury is unconstitutional has been rejected in a number of cases (*United States v Isaacs* (1972) 364 F Supp 895 at 903; *United States v McGinnis* (1972) 344 F Supp 89 at 92; *United States v Clizer* (1972) 464 F 2d 121 at 123.

false.[45] Therefore, where the falsity of the statement is not in issue, as where the accused admits the falsity of the statement, either in a formal admission or while giving evidence, corroboration is not required.[46] Where corroboration is required, it may take any form including documentary evidence,[47] a contradictory statement by the accused,[48] or an admission.[49]

2. Civil Cases

(a) Claims against the estates of deceased persons

4–16   Corroboration is sought with respect to this category of case because the creditor making a claim against the estate of a deceased person has a vested interest in the evidence which he is giving and the person "who could best have qualified, explained or contradicted" the claim is no longer alive.[50] Thus, it was feared that, in the absence of a corroboration requirement, the assets of a deceased person "would be exposed to wholesale plunder".[51] The early Irish cases required corroboration as a matter of law.[52] However, consistent with the approach adopted by courts in other jurisdictions,[53] there has been a relaxation of this requirement in modern cases such that, although there is continued recognition that claims of this type must be carefully scrutinised and that corroboration is desirable, it is not essential.[54] In *Murray v Commission to Inquire into Child Abuse*,[55] Abbott J reviewed the authorities and legal commentaries in this area and summarised the position by saying that "in the absence of other convincing evidence, the courts would be very reluctant, as a matter of prudence, to allow a claim against a deceased person unless it was corroborated in relevant material respects".

---

[45]   *R. v Linehan* [1921] VLR 582 at 588; *R. v Allsop* (1899) 24 VLR 812. *Cf.* s.13 of the English Perjury Act 1911 (see *R. v O'Connor* [1980] Crim LR 43 and *R. v Rider* (1986) 83 Cr App R 207).

[46]   *R. v Willmot* [1987] 1 Qd R 53. *Cf. R. v Rider* (1986) 83 Cr App R 207 and *R. v Stokes* [1988] Crim LR 110.

[47]   *R. v Parker* (1842) Car & M 639 at 645; *R. v Mayhew* (1834) 6 C & P 315 (bill of costs for taxation held to be sufficient corroboration and Denman CJ stated that a letter, written by the defendant, contradicting his statement on oath, would suffice). *Cf. R. v Threlfall* (1914) 10 Cr App R 112 (letter held sufficient under s.13 of the Perjury Act 1911).

[48]   The previous statement may be sworn (*R. v Wheatland* (1838) 8 C & P 238) or unsworn (*R. v Hook* (1858) Dears & B 606).

[49]   *R. v Parker* (1842) Car & M 639 at 646; *R. v Towey* (1860) 8 Cox CC 328. *Cf.* the decisions under s.13 of the English Perjury Act 1911: *R. v Peach* [1990] 1 WLR 976 (admission by the accused as to the falsity of his statement which is deposed to by two witnesses suffices to ground a conviction); *R. v Stokes* [1988] Crim LR 110 (admission as to falsity made on two separate occasions suffices).

[50]   *Crone v Hegarty* (1879) 3 LR Ir 50 at 60 (*per* FitzGibbon LJ for the Master of the Rolls).

[51]   *Boak v Moore* (1881) 7 LR Ir 322 at 327 (*per* May CJ). See also *In re Harnett* (1886) 17 LR Ir 543 at 547–548.

[52]   *Hartford v Power* (1869) Ir 3 Eq 602; *Crone v Hegarty* (1879) 3 LR Ir 50; *Boak v Moore* (1879) 3 LR Ir 222 (aff'd (1881) 7 LR Ir 322); *In re Harnett* (1886) 17 LR Ir 543; *Clegg v Clegg* 22 TLR 22; *Mahalm v M'Cullagh* (1891) 27 LR Ir 431 (aff'd (1891) 29 LR Ir 496). For a later case where corroboration was required as a matter of law, see *Robinson v Karmel* (1951) 86 ILTR 1.

[53]   See *Re Hodgson* (1885) 31 Ch. D. 177; *Re Cummins* [1972] Ch. 62; *Morrissy v Clements* (1885) 11 VLR 13; *Tone v Brolly* (1891) 17 VLR 467; *Re B* [1958] NZLR 362.

[54]   *Somers v Erskine (No.2)* [1944] IR 368; *Murray v Commission to Inquire into Child Abuse* [2004] 2 IR 222; *Butler v Regan* [2004] IEHC 326.

[55]   [2004] IEHC 225 at [155], [2004] 2 IR 222 at 295.

(b) Matrimonial cases

4–17 Corroboration is desirable in matrimonial cases because "experience has shown the risk of a miscarriage of justice in acting on the uncorroborated testimony of a spouse in this class of case."[56] Formerly, corroboration was sought in nullity suits as a matter of practice[57] but modern cases do not require corroboration as such. However, given that the courts have emphasised the heavy onus of proof in nullity petitions,[58] the presence or absence of corroborative evidence may be crucial to the petitioner's chance of success.

C. Accomplice Evidence

1. Introduction

4–18 The evidence of an accomplice is admissible and sufficient to ground a conviction, even if uncorroborated.[59] However, such evidence has long been approached with circumspection, and around the end of the eighteenth century a practice of warning juries of the dangers of convicting on such evidence, if uncorroborated, began to emerge.[60] An early example of such a warning can be seen in *R. v Green*,[61] where Jebb J instructed the jury that:

> "although the testimony of an accomplice alone is legal evidence on which a jury may convict, an instance is rarely found, in which a jury will be satisfied to convict upon it because he stands in so degraded a state, from the crimes of which he confesses himself guilty, that but little credit is due to him, and the temptation to save his own life is so strong, that he can seldom be trusted, unless corroborated in some material circumstances."

4–19 The status of this warning was debated by the Irish Court for Crown Cases Reserved in *R. v Sheehan*.[62] The Court was unanimously of the opinion that there was no rule of law requiring a warning to be given but split six to five on what the general

---

56 *Per* Simon P in *Ali v Ali* [1965] 3 All ER 480 at 484 (cited by McCarthy J in *People (DPP) v Quilligan (No.3)* [1993] 2 IR 305 at 342).

57 See *B v B* (1891) 27 LR Ir 587, where Warren J held that a decree of nullity would not, as a rule, be made on the uncorroborated testimony of the petitioner.

58 See *Griffith v Griffith* [1944] IR 35 at 39 (*per* Haugh J, "the onus that lies on the petitioner to satisfy the Court that he is entitled to the relief he seeks is severe and heavy.") and *MF McD v W O'R*, unreported, High Court, 24 January 1984, p.6, (*per* Hamilton J, the onus is on the petitioner to establish the matters alleged "to a high degree of probability").

59 This proposition was first established in a number of English decisions (*R v Rudd* (1775) 1 Cowp 331; *R v Atwood* (1788) 1 Leach 464; *R. v Jones* (1809) 2 Camp 131) and then adopted by the Irish courts (*R. v Green* (1825) 1 Craw & Dix 158; *R. v Sheehan* (1826) Jebb CC 54; *R. v Curtis* (1838) Craw & Dix Ab Not Cas 274 at 275; *R. v Dunne* (1852) 5 Cox CC 507; *M'Clory v Wright* (1860) 10 ICLR 514; *Magee v Mark* (1861) 11 ICLR 449). It was reaffirmed by the Court of Criminal Appeal in *People (AG) v Mazure* [1946] IR 448. However, it appears that the evidence of an accomplice may be inadmissible as illegally obtained evidence if it has been procured in return for payment of money: *People (DPP) v Gilligan*, unreported, Court of Criminal Appeal, 8 August 2003.

60 See, e.g. *R. v Smith* (1784) 1 Leach 479n; *R. v Atwood* (1788) 1 Leach 464; *R. v Hart* (1796) 26 St Tr 387 at 418 (*per* Baron George). For an account of the historical background to the emergence of the corroboration warning with respect to accomplices, see the Law Commission, *Corroboration of Evidence in Criminal Trials* (Working Paper No.15) (London: HMSO, 1990), Appendix A, Part I.

61 (1825) 1 Craw & DixCC 158 at 159.

62 (1826) Jebb CC 54.

practice should be. A minority of the Court took the view that there should not be any special rule of practice applicable to accomplice testimony and that the question of whether a cautionary direction should be given, and in what terms, should depend on the facts of the individual case. However, the majority held that:

> "an accomplice was in *degree* to be treated differently from other witnesses of impeached character; and that a jury, besides being cautioned to regard him with jealousy, ought to be told, that it was the practice to disregard his testimony, unless there were some corroboration".[63]

4–20   Over the course of the next century, this rule of practice began to take on the character of a rule of law[64] and it seems to have crystallised into a peremptory requirement in the decade following the establishment of the Court of Criminal Appeal in 1924.[65] Perhaps the clearest exposition of the modern incarnation of the rule is that of Butler J in *Dental Board v O'Callaghan*[66]:

> "There is no rule of law to the effect that the uncorroborated evidence of an accomplice must be rejected. The rule is that the tribunal of fact, be it District Justice or jury, must clearly bear in mind and be warned that it is dangerous to convict upon the evidence of an accomplice unless it is corroborated; but that having borne that in mind and having given due weight to the warning, if the evidence is nonetheless so clearly acceptable that the tribunal is satisfied beyond doubt of the guilt of the accused to the extent that the danger which is generally inherent in acting on the evidence of an accomplice is not present in the case, then the tribunal may act upon the evidence and convict."[67]

4–21   As Butler J makes clear in this passage, it is a corroboration warning, not corroboration, which is mandatory[68] and such a warning is required whether the tribunal of fact consists of a jury or a judge or judges.[69] Thus, the evidence of an accomplice is sufficient to ground a conviction even if uncorroborated.[70] Further, where the testimony

---

[63]   (1826) Jebb CC 54 at 56–57 (emphasis in the original).

[64]   In *R. v Curtis* (1838) Craw & Dix Ab Not Cas 274 at 275, Doherty CJ stated that although the testimony of an accomplice was admissible, "no judge will permit such testimony to go up [to the jury] without observing strongly upon the questionable nature of evidence derived from a source so polluted". Later, in *M'Clory v Wright* (1860) 10 ICLR 514, Keogh and Christian JJ endorsed the opinion of Lord Abinger CB in *R. v Farler* (1837) 8 Car & P 106 at 107, that the giving of a warning was a "practice which deserves all the reverence of the law".

[65]   In *AG v Corcoran* (1929) 63 ILTR 145 at 146, the rule was described by Kennedy CJ as one of practice. A year later, in *AG v Duffy* [1931] IR 144 at 149, the Chief Justice stated that it was "a very strong, indeed imperative, rule of practice" and by 1932, the rule had hardened sufficiently for O'Byrne J to state in *AG v Levison*, [1932] IR 158 at 166, that the warning had "become such an invariable practice as now to amount to a rule of law". The development of the rule in Ireland thus reflected that in England (see the decision of the House of Lords in *Davies v DPP* [1954] AC 378 at 395–99, [1954] 1 All ER 507 at 510–513, where the development of the rule in England was traced and its peremptory nature in that jurisdiction confirmed).

[66]   [1969] IR 181 at 183.

[67]   This passage was quoted with approval by the Supreme Court in *People (DPP) v Gilligan* [2005] IESC 78 at [71], [2006] 1 IR 107 at 138.

[68]   See also, *M'Clory v Wright* (1860) 10 ICLR 514; *AG v Corcoran* (1929) 63 ILTR 145; *AG v Durnan (No.2)* [1934] IR 540 at 546; *People (DPP) v Gilligan* [2005] IESC 78 at [71]–[72], [2006] 1 IR 107 at 138; *People (DPP) v Meehan* [2006] IECCA 104 at [38], [2006] 3 IR 468 at 483; *Cosgrave v DPP* [2012] IESC 24 at [130], [2012] 3 IR 666 at 730.

[69]   The Special Criminal Court is required to give itself a corroboration warning (see *People (DPP) v Ward*, unreported, Special Criminal Court, 27 November 1998), of its own motion if necessary (*People (DPP) v Dundon* [2013] IESPC 1). However, it has been held that it is not fatal if the Special Criminal Court does not expressly give itself a corroboration warning where it is clear from its decision that it was aware of the dangers of relying on the uncorroborated evidence of an accomplice: *People (DPP) v Gilligan* [2005] IESC 78 at [136], [2006] 1 IR 107 at 158.

[70]   *People (DPP) v Meehan* [2006] IECCA 104 at [38], [2006] 3 IR 468 at 483.

of an accomplice is uncorroborated, the trial judge has no power to withdraw the case from the jury[71] unless the evidence implicating the accused is so tenuous as not to merit consideration by the jury.[72] If, after an adequate and proper warning, the jury convicts, it is within its province to do so[73] because it is for the jurors to decide what weight to attach to the evidence of the accomplice.[74] Indeed, because the assessment of accomplice testimony is a matter peculiarly within the province of the jury, a conviction obtained in the absence of corroboration will be overturned only in exceptional circumstances, where the Court of Criminal Appeal is of opinion that the verdict of the jury is perverse and cannot be supported by the evidence.[75] However, the Court may be more willing to interfere with the verdict of a judge or judges sitting alone.[76]

2. Rationale for the Warning

4–22   The requirement for a corroboration warning in respect of accomplices is predicated on the danger that an accomplice might fabricate evidence and/or falsely implicate an accused. There are a number of reasons why an accomplice might attempt to do so.[77] The first, and perhaps most obvious danger, is that an accomplice may attempt to transfer blame.[78] There is a natural tendency for an accomplice faced with punishment for a criminal offence to minimise his or her own role in the crime[79] and this, consequently, may lead him or her to exaggerate that of the accused.[80]

4–23   Secondly, an accomplice may hope to obtain more favourable treatment by co-

---

71 *People (AG) v Mazure* [1946] IR 448 at 449; *AG v Levison* [1932] IR 158 at 166; *AG of Hong Kong v Wong* [1987] AC 501 at 507, [1987] 2 All ER 488 at 490; *In re Meunier* [1894] 2 QB 415 at 418.

72 *People (DPP) v Egan* [1990] ILRM 780 at 790 (*per* O'Flaherty J).

73 *AG v Durnan (No.2)* [1934] IR 540 at 546; *AG v Levison* [1932] IR 158 at 166. *Cf. People (DPP) v Egan* [1990] ILRM 780 at 789; *People (DPP) v McKevitt* [2008] IESC 51 at [39], [2009] 1 IR 525 at 540–541, [2009] 1 ILRM 401 at 415.

74 *Per* Meredith J in *People (AG) v Williams* [1940] IR 195 at 205, "the weight of evidence, and, therefore, the denomination of each weight and measure that is put into the scales is by law a matter solely for the jury".

75 *AG v Lennon,* unreported, Court of Criminal Appeal, 5 May 1925 (noted in Sandes, *Criminal Practice, Procedure and Evidence in Éire* 2nd edn, (London: Sweet & Maxwell, 1939), p.138; *AG v Lloyd* (1936) 1 Frewen 32; *R. v Baskerville* [1916] 2 KB 658 at 663–664, [1916–17] All ER 38 at 41. *Cf. People (DPP) v O'Brien* (1989) 3 Frewen 195 (notwithstanding the weakness of the evidence, the jury had the advantage of seeing the complainants give evidence and it would be an unwarranted interference with and usurpation of the function of the jury to overturn its verdict).

76 See *People (DPP) v Ward,* unreported, Court of Criminal Appeal, 22 March 2002, where the Court referred to the decision in *People (DPP) v Egan* [1990] ILRM 780, and stated that its function was to consider whether "the evidence accepted by the Special Criminal Court, on its assessment of the credibility of the witnesses, fairly and properly supports the findings of that court, and whether the inferences drawn as disclosed on the transcript were fairly and properly drawn, having regard to the onus of proof which lies on the prosecution" but subject to the caveat that "a decision based on an error of law or logic, or a demonstrable misapprehension of known fact, must be susceptible of correction."

77 The following list of reasons is based on those identified by Heydon, "The Corroboration of Accomplices" [1973] Crim LR 264 at 265–266. See also *Cosgrave v DPP* [2012] IESC 24 at [132]–[140], [2012] 3 IR 666 at 730–732 where the rationale for the rule is summarised by Hardiman J.

78 *People (DPP) v Morgan* [2011] IECCA 36 at 23.

79 *Dental Board v O'Callaghan* [1969] IR 181 at 184; *People (DPP) v Morgan* [2011] IECCA 36 at 23.

80 *People (DPP) v Quilligan (No.3)* [1993] 2 IR 305 at 342 (*per* McCarthy J).

operating with the prosecution and helping them to convict his or her confederates.[81] To this end, "he may be tempted to curry favour with the prosecution by painting their guilt more blackly than it deserves".[82] In some cases, the accomplice may have been granted or promised full or partial immunity in return for his testimony. Such evidence is not to be trusted because, as Lord Abinger CB commented in *R. v Farler*,[83] "when a man is fixed, and knows that his own guilt is detected, he purchases impunity by falsely accusing others".[84] The grant of immunity creates a powerful inducement for an accomplice to adhere to his or her original statement to the police implicating the accused even though this may, in fact, have been false.[85] In other cases, an accomplice may have received or may hope to receive a lighter sentence by virtue of his or her co-operation with the prosecution. This danger is particularly acute when the accomplice remains unsentenced at the time he or she gives evidence.[86]

4–24   In addition, there is the possibility that an accomplice may be actuated by malice or a desire for revenge towards the person implicated by him[87] or that he or she may implicate an innocent party in order to shield the real culprits.[88]

4–25   There is also the objection that the accomplice is by definition a criminal and thus is an inherently unreliable witness because of his moral culpability.[89] In *Cosgrave v DPP*,[90] Hardiman J took the view that an accomplice is necessarily a person of compromised character and his confession of involvement in the crime was sufficient to establish that "but little credit is due to him".

4–26   These dangers may not be obvious to the jury[91] and are accentuated by the fact that "the accomplice knows all the details of the crime and will be able to relate them accurately and in order to involve another person has only to introduce him into the story

---

[81]   *Dental Board v O'Callaghan* [1969] IR 181 at 184; *People (DPP) v Morgan* [2011] IECCA 36 at 23; *R v Gibney* [1986] 4 NIJB 1 at 5; *Vetrovec v R.* [1982] 1 SCR 811, (1982) 136 DLR (3d) 89 at 97; *R. v Sneesby* [1951] St R Qd 26 at 28.

[82]   Heydon, "The Corroboration of Accomplices" [1973] Crim LR 264 at 265.

[83]   (1837) 8 C & P 106 at 108.

[84]   See, to the same effect, the comment of Christian J in *M'Clory v Wright* (1860) 10 ICLR 514 at 523, that accomplices, "[g]uilty themselves, come to purchase impunity by tendering their evidence against their confederates."

[85]   *R. v Chai* (1992) 27 NSWLR 153 at 178; *R. v Dellapatrona* (1993) 31 NSWLR 123 at 148; *R. v Radford*, unreported, Victorian Court of Criminal Appeal, 28 February1992, pp. 9–10.

[86]   The practice of permitting unsentenced accomplices to give evidence has been criticised by the Court of Criminal Appeal in *People (AG) v Shribman* [1946] IR 431 at 445, and *People (AG) v Mazure* [1946] IR 448 at 449, and by the courts in other jurisdictions (see, *e.g. R. v Harris*, unreported, South Australian Full Court, 17 September 1992, paras 21–23).

[87]   *R. v Gibney* [1986] 4 NIJB 1 at 5. For this reason, Pollock CB stated in *R. v Robinson* (1864) 4 F & F 43 at 44, that it was "perilous...to convict a person as receiver on the sole evidence of the thief. This would put in the power of a thief from malice or revenge to lay a crime on any one against whom he had a grudge."

[88]   In *R. v Mullins* (1848) 3 Cox CC 526 at 531, Maule J adverted to the danger that "it often happens that an accomplice is a friend of those who committed the crime with him, and he would much rather get them out of a scrape and fix an innocent man than his real associates."

[89]   See the passage from *R. v Green* (1825) 1 Craw & Dix CC 158 at 159, set out above; *Cosgrave v DPP* [2012] IESC 24 at [135], [2012] 3 IR 666 at 731.

[90]   [2012] IESC 24 at [138], [2012] 3 IR 666 at 731 (quoting from *R. v Green* (1825) 1 Craw & Dix CC 158 at 159).

[91]   *R. v Spencer* [1987] AC 128 at 135 at 141, [1986] 2 All ER 928 at 932 at 937 (*per* Lords Hailsham and Ackner); *R. v Button* [1992] 1 Qd R 552 at 559.

which in its main essentials, is true."[92] Hence, it is easy for an accomplice to weave a detailed and convincing narrative which is difficult to unravel on cross-examination.

3. Definition of "Accomplice"

4–27 The term "accomplice" is derived from substantive criminal law and in that context denotes a person who is chargeable either as a principal or accessory with the principal offender.[93] Thus, for the purposes of the corroboration warning, the "natural and primary meaning" of the term, according to Lord Simonds in *Davies v DPP*,[94] is a person who is *participes criminis* in respect of the offence charged, whether as a principal or accessory before or after the fact (in a felony) or a person committing, procuring or aiding and abetting (in a misdemeanour).[95]

4–28 However, this approach of focusing on the liability of the witness to prosecute for the offence charged against the accused[96] has been criticised because it seeks to apply a concept which evolved to deal with the question of culpability to the very different problem of witness mendacity.[97] The inevitable result is to divorce the definition of accomplice from the rationale of the warning and this leads to anomalies.[98]

4–29 For this reason, a number of decisions have advocated a broader, more purposive approach focusing on the degree of participation of the witness in the events grounding the offence charged and his or her motives to lie rather than on the technical character of that participation. Perhaps, the best known of these is the judgment of Sholl J in *McNee v Kay*.[99] He pointed out that "the temptation to exaggerate or make false accusations would appear to be much more related to the nature and possible punishment of the offence than to its technical identity with that alleged against the accused."[100] Therefore,

---

[92] *Per* Maguire CJ in *People (AG) v Phelan* (1950) 1 Frewen 98 at 100. See also, *R. v Stubbs* (1855) Dears CC 555; *R. v Farler* (1837) 8 Car & P 106; *R. v Graham* [1984] 18 NIJB 1; *R. v John* 1943 TPD 295 at 300; *R. v Ncanana* 1948 (4) SA 399.

[93] *Cosgrave v DPP* [2012] IESC 24 at [123], [2012] 3 IR 666 at 728.

[94] [1954] AC 378 at 400, [1954] 1 All ER 507 at 513.

[95] It should be noted that the distinction between felonies and misdemeanours has been abolished by s.3 of the Criminal Law Act 1997 which also provides that the law and practice in relation to misdemeanours shall apply to all offences. Under s.7(1) of the Act, any person who aids, abets, counsels or procures the commission of an indictable offence shall be liable to be indicted, tried and punished as a principal offender.

[96] Because the definition is predicated on liability to prosecution, it is immaterial whether the witness has previously been convicted or acquitted of the offence in question (*R. v Meston* (1975) 28 CCC (2d) 497 at 509; *Ripley v State* (1950) 227 SW 2d 26, Tenn). The rationale for giving the warning where the witness has previously been convicted or acquitted is that the evidence at the second trial is likely to be a mere repetition of that given at the first (*Attorney General v Linehan* [1929] IR 19 at 23) because the accomplice may fear a prosecution for perjury, reprisals from the police or further prosecution in respect of the events out of which the first trial arose (Heydon, "The Corroboration of Accomplices" [1973] Crim LR 264 at 268).

[97] Zuckerman, *The Principles of Criminal Evidence* (Oxford: Clarendon, 1989), p.158.

[98] See, *e.g. Davies v DPP* [1954] AC 378, [1954] 1 All ER 507 (witness was not an accomplice of the accused on a charge of murder but would have been if he had been charged with the lesser offence of assault).

[99] [1953] VLR 520. See also, *Khan v R.* [1971] WAR 44; *R. v Sneesby* [1951] St R Qd 26; *Horsburgh v R.* (1967) 63 DLR (2d) 699; *R. v Meston* (1975) 28 CCC (2d) 497.

[100] [1953] VLR 520 at 530.

if he had not been constrained by authority, his preferred definition of accomplice would have been[101]:

> "[A person] who is chargeable, in relation to the same events as those founding the charge against the accused, with an offence (whether the same offence or not) of such a character, and who would be if convicted thereof liable to such punishment, as might possibly tempt that person to exaggerate or fabricate evidence as to the guilt of the accused."[102]

4–30   The Irish decisions to date have taken quite an expansive approach. In *People (AG) v Carney*,[103] O'Byrne J, delivering the leading judgment in the Supreme Court, endorsed the following passage from the judgment of the Court of Criminal Appeal in *AG v Linehan*[104]:

> "We do not think that in the case of a rule of caution concerned with the credit of accomplice witnesses and the weight of their uncorroborated evidence, a narrow or precise definition of 'accomplice' should be, or indeed can be, laid down. We think, however, that a person implicated either as principal or as accessory in the crime under investigation is an 'accomplice' within the rule, though the degree and gravity of such complicity may vary, and inasmuch as the extent of the effect of such complicity upon the credit of the witness or the weight of his uncorroborated testimony will vary accordingly, so should the degree and gravity of the warning be measured."

4–31   He went on to state that "a very slight degree of complicity, either as principal or accessory, in the crime charged is sufficient to render a person an accomplice for the purpose of the rule".[105]

4–32   In *People (DPP) v Diemling*,[106] the definition of accomplice was extended to include accessories after the fact, the Court of Criminal Appeal taking the view that even a slight degree of complicity as an accessory after the fact is sufficient to render a witness an accomplice.[107] There is also a series of decisions holding persons to be accomplices although they could not be convicted as a principal or accessory for the same offence as the accused. Thus, it has been held that the perjurer on a charge of

---

[101] [1953] VLR 520 at 530.
[102] This passage was approved by Bray CJ in *R v Rigney* (1975) 12 SASR 30 at 37, and was approved and applied by Crawford J in *R. v Ling* (1981) 6 A Crim R 429 at 451, in relation to the main prosecution witness whom the accused alleged was the actual perpetrator of the offences charged.
[103] [1955] IR 324 at 345.
[104] [1929] IR 19 at 23 (*per* Kennedy CJ).
[105] [1955] IR 324 at 345. See also *People (DPP) v Fee* [2006] IECCA 102 where, applying the approach laid down in *Carney*, it was held a prosecution witness was not an accomplice.
[106] Unreported, Court of Criminal Appeal, 4 May 1992.
[107] See also *People (DPP) v McGrath* [2013] IECCA 12; *Mahadeo v R* [1936] 2 All ER 813 at 817; *Davies v DPP* [1954] AC 378 at 400, [1954] 1 All ER 507 at 513; *Sellars v R* [1980] 1 SCR 527; *Paradis v R* [1978] 1 SCR 264; *Littles v State* (1929) 14 SW 2d 853; *R. v Nhelko* 1960 (4) SA 712. The inclusion of accessories after the fact within the definition has been criticised on the basis that their interest lies in establishing that the crime did not occur (*R. v Ready* [1942] VLR 85 at 93; *R. v Ling* (1981) 6 A Crim R 429 at 452; *R. v Gratton* (1971) 4 NBR (2d) 14 at 17). However, in *McNee v Kay* [1953] VLR 520 at 530, Sholl J adverted to the potential problem of a witness "seeking to minimise his own part in a crime, from which he cannot in the circumstances hope entirely to disassociate himself, by reducing it from that of principal or of accessory before the fact to that of accessory after the fact, by falsifying or exaggerating in evidence the part played by his associates, or by reversing his part and theirs."

subornation of perjury,[108] a woman upon whom an abortion is performed,[109] and willing participants in sexual offences[110] are all accomplices. In addition, it seems likely that the Irish courts will follow the decisions of other courts in applying the warning to receivers at the trial of thieves from whom they receive stolen goods,[111] and thieves at the trial of a receiver to whom they give stolen goods.[112] However, in *People (DPP) v Morgan*,[113] where the applicant had been convicted of managing a brothel and organising prostitution, the Court of Criminal Appeal rejected the proposition that a witness who answered calls and gave directions to the brothel was an accessory and, thus, an accomplice to the offences charged against the accused. The Court held that, however liberal a definition was given to the concept of accomplice, the witness fell outside that definition given her limited involvement. This conclusion seems to have been influenced by the Court's view that she had no motive to lie or falsely implicate the accused whom she spoke highly of.

4–33　A broad rationale-based definition of an accomplice along the lines advocated by Sholl J in *McNee* was endorsed by Hardiman J in *Cosgrave v DPP*.[114] Having referred to various authorities in relation to the rationale for the rule, he stated:

---

[108] *People (DPP) v Murtagh* [1990] 1 IR 339. See also *R. v Atkinson* (1934) 24 Cr App R 123; *Mundy v Commonwealth* (1933) 161 Va 1049 at 1069, 171 SE 691 at 698; *People v Gondelman* (1938) 253 AD 924; 2 NYS 2d 405; *People v Dodge* (1960) 208 NYS 2d 817 at 820. See, *contra, R. v Applegate* (1893) 28 L Jo 759; *United States v Thompson* (1887) 31 F 331; *Boren v United States* (1906) 144 F 801; *Strader v Commonwealth* (1931) 240 Ky 559, 42 SW 2d 736.

[109] *Attorney General v Levison* [1932] IR 158; *People (AG) v Coleman (No.2)* (1945) 1 Frewen 64; *R. v Stephenson* [1947] NI 110; *R. v Price* [1969] 1 QB 541, [1968] 2 All ER 282; *R. v Beebe* (1925) 19 Cr App R 32.

[110] *Attorney General v Duffy* [1931] IR 144; *Attorney General v Troy* (1950) 84 ILTR 193; *People (AG) v Downes* [1944] Ir Jur Rep 40. See also, *R. v Jellyman* (1838) 8 Car & P 604; *R. v Tate* [1908] 2 KB 680; *R. v Stone* (1910) 6 Cr App R 89; *R. v Dimes* (1911) 7 Cr App R 43; *R. v King* [1967] 2 QB 338, [1967] 1 All ER 379; *R. v Sneesby* [1951] St R Qd 26; *R. v Williams* (1914) 19 DLR 676; *McClintock v R.* (1946) 47 WALR 95. See *contra, R. v Pitts* (1912) 8 Cr App R 126. It is immaterial that the witness could not be charged with the same offence as the accused (*Horsburgh v R.* (1967) 63 DLR (2d) 699).

[111] *R. v Jennings* (1912) 7 Cr App R 242; *R. v Dixon* (1925) 19 Cr App R 36; *R. v Jenkins* (1980) 72 Cr App R 354; *R. v Mudgett* (1946) 87 CCC 77; *R. v Kay* [1950] OR 235; *R. v O'Keefe* [1959] QWN 9; *R. v McDonald* [1955] NZLR 699; *Bass v State* (1933) 124 Tex Crim 310, 62 SW 2d 127. In *Davies v DPP* [1954] AC 378 at 400, [1954] 1 All ER 507 at 513, Lord Simonds justified the extension on the ground that not only was the receiver committing a crime intimately allied in character with that of theft, he could not commit the crime of receiving at all without the crime of theft having preceded it—the two crimes are in a relationship of "one-sided dependence". See, *contra, R. v MacDonald* (1946) 87 CCC 257; *R. v Zoccano* [1944] 3 DLR 641; *People v Lima* (1944) 154 P 2d698 at 700.

[112] *R. v Hodgett* [1957] NI 1; *R. v Reynolds* (1927) 20 Cr App R 125; *R. v Lewis* [1937] 4 All ER 360; *R. v Robinson* (1864) 4 F & F 43; *R. v Reeves* (1978) 68 Cr App R 331 at 332; *R. v Meston* (1975) 28 CCC (2d) 497 at 509; *R. v Joseph* [1939] 3 DLR 22; *Medcraft v R.* [1982] WAR 33 at 37; *R. v Lawlor* [1931] QWN 14; *R. v Sneesby* [1951] St R Qd 26; *R. v Ndabeni* 1959 (2) SA 630; *Levit* (1959) 14 PD 1057 at 1062. See *contra, People v Lima* (1944) 154 P 2d 698 at 700, Cal; *State v Wirtanen* (1965) 406 P 2d 376; *State v Mercer* (1943) 114 Mont 142: 133 P 2d 358. In *R. v Vernon* [1962] Crim LR 36, it was held that whether a thief is an accomplice depends on his state of knowledge as to the receiver's *mens rea* but this test has been criticised by Heydon, "The Corroboration of Accomplices" [1973] Crim LR 264 at 279, on the ground that it can make no difference to the reliability of the thief's evidence that he knows or does not know that the receiver thinks the goods are stolen. He advocated, as a better test, that of whether the thief actually hands over the goods to the person charged with receiving.

[113] [2011] IECCA 36.

[114] [2012] IESC 24 at [140], [2012] IESC 666 at [731].

"It appears to me that the rationale for the rule requiring a corroboration warning relates, at least in part, to the character of a person who is an accomplice and not to his precise degree of participation in any particular crime which he alleges. If the character of the witness is an indication for caution in regard to his evidence, that character is a permanent attribute of the witness and does not vary from one part of his statement to another. Accordingly, it appears to me that, once a person has been identified as an accomplice in any crime (or at least any crime arising out of the same sequence of facts of which he gives evidence) he is a witness whose evidence requires a corroboration warning…"

4–34   The application of such an approach can be seen in *People (DPP) v Dundon*.[115] In that case, the accused was charged with the murder of a noted rugby player in Limerick who had been shot in a case of mistaken identity. The prosecution case depended largely on the evidence of three fact witnesses, each of whom had criminal histories of varying degrees of seriousness and one of whom had been in a long term relationship with the accused's brother and another of whom had been in a long term relationship with a first cousin of the accused. Although there was no evidence that any of the witnesses had been involved in the murder of the deceased, there was evidence that they had participated in the theft of a car that had been used in connection with the murder and one of the witnesses had been involved in providing an alibi to one of the participants. Given the lengthy delay in the witnesses coming forward, their involvement in events, and that credibility was central to the evaluation of their testimony, the Special Criminal Court decided that it was appropriate to treat them as accomplices and to give itself a corroboration warning on that basis. Although it may be the case that at least one of the witnesses could properly have been regarded as an accessory after the fact and, thus, categorised as an accomplice in accordance with the authorities discussed above, it is noteworthy that the Special Criminal Court did not engage in any such analysis but instead focused on the reasons why the evidence of the prosecution witnesses might be unreliable in deciding whether to regard them as accomplices, triggering a corroboration warning.

(a) Persons with close relationship to an accomplice

4–35   It is well established that the wife of an accomplice is not, by reason of her marital status, considered to be an accomplice.[116] Therefore, if she gives evidence on behalf of the prosecution, her evidence can be used as corroboration and left to the jury without any warning. However, where she gives evidence supporting that of her accomplice spouse, she has an obvious interest in his welfare and it is necessary to give the jury practically the same warning as that which would have been given in the case of an accomplice.[117] An example can be seen in *People (DPP) v Meehan*[118] where

---

[115] [2013] IESPC 1.

[116] The proposition that she should be treated as an accomplice because a husband and wife are one at law, which seemed to have been accepted in *R. v Neal* (1835) 7 C & P 168, was rejected by the English Court of Criminal Appeal in *R. v Allen* [1965] 2 QB 295, [1964] 3 All ER 401 and by the High Court of Australia in *Tripodi v R.* (1961) 104 CLR 1. In *Allen*, the Court also rejected the argument that the wife should be treated as an accomplice because, in the circumstances of the case, she had the same motives and interests as her accomplice husband.

[117] *Attorney General v Durnan* [1934] IR 308; *People (DPP) v McKeown* (1984) 3 Frewen 2; *R. v Munevich* (1942) 3 DLR 482 (where *Durnan* was cited with approval); *R. v Allen* [1965] 2 QB 295, [1964] 3 All ER 401; *R. v Willis* [1916] 1 KB 933; *R. v Payne* (1913) 8 Cr App R 171. However, it appears that the evidence of the accomplice's wife can still be used as corroboration of his evidence: *R. v Allen* [1965] 2 QB 295, [1964] 3 All ER 401; *Tripodi v R.* (1961) 104 CLR 1 at 9.

[118] Unreported, Special Criminal Court, 29 July 1999.

the Court of Criminal Appeal acceded to the submission of the prosecution that the wife of an accomplice was so closely identified with members of the criminal gang of which he and the accused had allegedly been members that her evidence should be treated as that of an accomplice.

4–36 The same principles may, depending on the circumstances, apply *mutatis mutandis* to other members of an accomplice's family. For example, in *R. v Green*[119] Jebb J instructed the jury to examine the evidence of the accomplice's father with great care where he gave evidence confirming that of his son.

(b) Accomplices outside the ambit of the rule

4–37 Applying the maxim *cessante ratione legis, cessat ipsa lex*, there are two situations where a warning is not required even though a witness comes within the definition of an accomplice. The first is where evidence is given by a police spy or *agent provocateur*.[120] In *Dental Board v O'Callaghan*,[121] Butler J took the view that "the reasons which have led to the requirement as to corroboration in the case of a true accomplice do not apply in the case of a person acting in the course of his duty for the purpose of obtaining evidence of an illegal transaction".[122] He rejected the submission that the ambit of this exception should be restricted to police officers and applied it to an officer of the Dental Board. He pointed out that the Dental Board was a body established by statute to regulate and control the dentistry profession and had been conferred with prosecutorial powers. Therefore, because it had a duty of prevention and detection, its agents were to be treated like police officers for the purpose of the application of the rule.[123]

4–38 The second exception is where the accomplice fails to give any evidence adverse to the accused.[124] If this occurs, then the danger of false implication does not arise. More difficult is the case of an accomplice who gives evidence that is partly

---

[119] (1825) 1 Craw & Dix CC 158 at 160.
[120] *Dental Board v O'Callaghan* [1969] IR 181 at 185; *R. v Mullins* (1848) 3 Cox CC 526; *R. v Bickley* (1909) 2 Cr App R 53; *R. v Heuser* (1910) 6 Cr App R 76; *Sneedon v Stevenson* [1967] 2 All ER 1277, [1967] 1 WLR 1051; *R. v Nation* [1954] SASR 189; *R. v Forgione* [1969] SASR 248; *Moss v Baines* [1974] WAR 7; *R. v Turnbull* (1985) 17 A Crim R 370; *R. v Tyler* [1994] 1 Qd R 675; *R. v Dellapatrona* (1993) 31 NSWLR 123 at 147; *R. v Phillips* [1963] NZLR 855. A person who agrees to co-operate with and spy for the police may, however, be an accomplice with respect to the period before he commenced to act on behalf of the police (*R. v Martin* (1990) 48 A Crim R 208).
[121] [1969] IR 181.
[122] [1969] IR 181 at 185.
[123] [1969] IR 181 at 185–186. He went on to specify that the exception should not be extended to persons acting for merely private as opposed to the public interest. However, some element of private interest will probably not prove fatal so long as the public interest is also implicated. The Dental Board was acting not just on behalf of the general public but also on behalf of its members, in whose interest it was to prevent unlicensed dentists from operating. Perhaps the most important factor is the existence of a legal basis for the body's power to investigate offences. Where that is lacking, the analogy with law enforcement agencies may well break down.
[124] *R. v Peach* [1974] Crim LR 245; *R. v Royce-Bentley* [1974] 2 All ER 347, [1974] 1 WLR 535; *R. v Anthony* [1962] VR 440 at 446 (warning not required even though the jury might reject the exculpatory portion and use the balance to implicate the accused). *Cf. R. v Jacquier* (1979) 20 SASR 543 at 552–553 (court would have applied proviso, if necessary, where no corroboration warning was given with respect to a witness who was favourably disposed to the defence and only reluctantly implicated the accused after being treated as hostile by the prosecution).

favourable to the prosecution and partly favourable to the defence. If his or her testimony is mainly favourable to the accused, the defence may well wish to have it left to the jury unadorned by a corroboration warning which would have the effect of undermining his or her credibility.[125] The best course of action is for the trial judge to consult counsel in the absence of the jury in order to decide whether or not to give a warning.[126] If, having done so, he or she concludes that more harm would be done by giving the warning, then it is not a misdirection to omit it.[127]

(c) Function of judge and jury

4–39   The question of whether a witness is an accomplice is a bifurcated one. It is for the judge to instruct the jury whether, in law, a person is capable of being considered as an accomplice and for the jury to decide whether, in fact, that person is an accomplice.[128]

4–40   In considering the function of the trial judge, it is necessary to distinguish three categories of case.[129] First, if there is no evidence upon which a reasonable jury could find a witness to be an accomplice, then there is no need to give a warning.[130] Secondly, if there is some evidence upon which a reasonable jury could find a witness to be an accomplice, then the issue should be left to them in the form of a conditional warning, *i.e.* if they find the witness to be an accomplice, it is dangerous to convict on his or her uncorroborated evidence.[131] Thirdly, if undisputed evidence establishes that a witness is an accomplice, the jury should be instructed to this effect.[132] This might arise, for example, where the witness confesses to participation in the offence, or pleads guilty, or is convicted of it.[133]

4–41   Some contrariety of opinion exists as to whether an absolute warning should also be given where the issue is disputed but there is very strong evidence pointing towards the categorisation of the witness as an accomplice. In *People (AG) v Carney*,[134] the Court of Criminal Appeal, following its earlier decision in *AG v O'Connor (No.2)*,[135]

---

[125] *Cf. R. v Hoilett* (1991) 3 OR (3d) 449 (conviction quashed where cautionary instruction had been given in relation to evidence of the accused and the main defence witnesses).

[126] *R. v Royce-Bentley* [1974] 2 All ER 347 at 350, [1974] 1 WLR 535 at 539.

[127] In *R. v Wilson, The Times*, 14 April 1988, the English Court of Appeal suggested that where a trial judge takes this course, he or she should state the reason for doing so in open court after the jury has retired to consider its verdict so that a shorthand note may be taken.

[128] *People (DPP) v Diemling*, unreported, Court of Criminal Appeal, 4 May 1992 at 36–37; *People (DPP) v McCarthy* [2007] IECCA 64 at [175], [2008] 3 IR 1 at 58; *Davies v DPP* [1954] AC 378 at 402, [1954] 1 All ER 507 at 514.

[129] See, Coutts, "Accomplices: Functions of Judge and Jury" (1958) 22 J Crim L 61 at 67.

[130] *People (DPP) v McCarthy* [2007] IECCA 64 at [175]–[178], [2008] 3 IR 1 at 58; *Davies v DPP* [1954] AC 378 at 402, [1954] 1 All ER 507 at 514.

[131] *Attorney General v O'Connor (No.2)* [1936] Ir Jur Rep 37; *People (DPP) v Diemling*, unreported, Court of Criminal Appeal, 4 May 1992 at 36–37; *Davies v DPP* [1954] AC 378 at 402, [1954] 1 All ER 507 at 514; *R. v Riley* (1979) 70 Cr App R 1 at 3–4; *R. v Kay* [1950] OR 235 at 242; *R. v MacDonald* [1945] 3 DLR 764 at 776; *R. v O'Neill* (1988) 48 SASR 51 at 61; *R. v Rigney* (1975) 12 SASR 30 at 40. It should be noted that because a very slight degree of complicity is sufficient to make a person an accomplice (*People (AG) v Carney* [1955] IR 324 at 345), very little evidence of complicity is required for the issue to be left to the jury.

[132] *People v Santo* (1954) 273 P 2d 249 at 253; *Ripley v State* (1950) 227 SW 2d 26; *Weaver v State* (1936) 53 P 2d 696 at 699; *Bass v State* (1933) 124 Tex Crim 310, 62 SW 2d127.

[133] *Davies v DPP* [1954] AC 378 at 402, [1954] 1 All ER 507 at 514.

[134] [1955] IR 324.

[135] [1936] Ir Jur Rep 37.

held that, even if the judge is satisfied that the person is an accomplice, he or she must leave the issue to the jury. However, on appeal, a majority of the Supreme Court disagreed. O'Byrne J took the view that where it was clear on the evidence that a person is an accomplice, then the question should not be left to the jury but rather the warning given should be absolute and not conditional.[136] Dixon J delivered a strong dissent on this point. He thought it well settled that the question of whether a witness was an accomplice was a jury question. Therefore, even where the evidence was strongly in favour of a finding that the witness was an accomplice, if it was open, on the evidence, for the jury to take the view that the witness was not in fact an accomplice, then the matter should be left to them.

4–42 The majority view in *Carney* does have the merit of simplicity and would render the corroboration warning more intelligible in many cases. However, the view of Dixon J would seem to be more in accordance with constitutional principles. A line of cases has established the general principle that, consonant with Art. 38.5 of the Constitution, disputed material issues of fact in criminal cases are matters for the jury to decide.[137] Therefore, in the absence of any countervailing policy considerations or practical difficulties,[138] the issue should be left to the jury unless it would be perverse of them to take the view that the witness was not an accomplice.

4. Nature of Corroboration Required

4–43 The question of what kind of evidence could corroborate the evidence of an accomplice was addressed by the Irish Court for Crown Cases Reserved in *R. v Sheehan*.[139] There were, at that time, two lines of authority on this question. In some cases, the view had been taken that it sufficed if the credibility of the accomplice was strengthened by the confirmation of some of the particulars of his story.[140] In others, it had been held that the corroboration had to implicate the accused as well as confirming the commission of the offence.[141]

4–44 In *Sheehan*, the Court split six to five on this issue. A minority of the judges were of the opinion that "generally speaking, a corroboration in the circumstances of the crime charged, though entirely unaccompanied by any circumstance applicable to the prisoner on trial, or to any other person charged by the accomplice, was a substantial corroboration, fit to be examined and weighed".[142] However, a majority of the Court took the view that "the accomplice being supported in his narrative of the transaction only, without corroboration as to any person charged, was so slight a confirmation, as to be entitled to very little, if any, attention, and that a jury should generally be so

---

[136] [1955] IR 324 at 346.
[137] *People (DPP) v Lynch* [1982] IR 64; *People (DPP) v Conroy* [1986] IR 460; *People (DPP) v Curtis* [1985] IR 458, [1986] ILRM 428.
[138] See, *People (DPP) v Conroy* [1986] IR 460, where an exception to the general principle was carved out for facts pertaining to the admissibility of evidence because of the practical difficulties and undesirable consequences of having this issue of fact decided by the jury.
[139] (1826) Jebb CC 54.
[140] *R. v Despard* (1803) 28 St Tr 346 at 487; *R. v Birkett* (1813) Rus & Ry 251; *R. v Tidd* (1820) 33 St Tr 1338 at 1483.
[141] *R. v Green* (1825) 1 Craw & Dix CC 158 at 160; *R. v Carberry* (1826) 1 Craw& Dix CC 160n.
[142] (1826) Jebb CC 54 at 57 (*per* Lord Norbury CJC, M'Clelland and Pennefather BB and Burton and Torrens JJ).

told".[143] The majority opted for the stricter approach because the accomplice was *ex concesso* involved in the crime and knew all the facts. Therefore, confirmation that he was telling the truth with regard to the facts of the commission of the offence did not lead to the inference that he was telling the truth with regard to the persons taking part in it.[144]

4–45   The view that corroboration must implicate the accused in the offence charged was endorsed by the English Court of Criminal Appeal in *R. v Baskerville*[145] where Lord Reading enunciated his canonical definition of corroboration:

> "We hold that evidence in corroboration must be independent testimony which affects the accused by connecting or tending to connect him with the crime. In other words, it must be evidence which implicates him, that is, which confirms in some material particular not only the evidence that the crime has been committed but also that the prisoner committed it."[146]

4–46   This definition of corroboration has been approved and applied by the Irish courts on many occasions[147] and, in *People (AG) v Williams*,[148] Sullivan CJ, though not citing the decision in *Baskerville*, defined corroboration in very similar terms, as "independent evidence of material circumstances tending to implicate the accused in the commission of the crime with which he is charged".[149] More recently, after quoting the passage from *Baskerville* above with approval, Denham J, delivering the judgment of the Supreme Court in *People (DPP) v Gilligan*[150] reiterated that corroborative evidence is independent evidence that tends to implicate the accused in the commission of the offence by establishing "a link which tends to prove that the accused person committed the offence".

4–47   Although it has been asserted that corroboration is a common sense rather than technical concept[151] and that there is nothing complicated in the concept of

---

[143]   (1826) Jebb CC 54 at 57 (*per* Bushe CJ, Smith B and Moore, Johnson, Vandeleur and Jebb JJ).

[144]   See, to the same effect, *per* Lord Abinger CB in *R. v Farler* (1837) 8 C & P 106 at 107–108: "A man who has been guilty of a crime himself will always be able to relate the facts of the case, and if the confirmation be only on the truth of that history, without identifying the persons, that is really no corroboration at all…It would not at all tend to shew that the party accused participated in it." To similar effect, Lord Lowry LCJ observed in *R. v Graham* [1984] 18 NIJB 1 at 10, that "[a]n accurate description of the crime merely strengthens the inference that the witness who gives the description took part".

[145]   [1916] 2 KB 658.

[146]   [1916] 2 KB 658 at 667.

[147]   See, by way of example, *People (AG) v Phelan* (1950) 1 Frewen 98 at 99, *People (DPP) v Murphy* [2005] IECCA 1 at [63], [2005] 2 IR 125 at 148, *People (DPP) v Gilligan* [2005] IESC 78 at [75], [2006] 1 IR 107 at 139 and *People (DPP) v Murphy* [2013] IECCA 1 at [68].

[148]   [1940] IR 195 at 200.

[149]   This definition, which was based on that enunciated by O'Byrne J in *Attorney General v Levison* [1932] IR 158 at 165, was quoted with approval by the Court of Criminal Appeal in *People (DPP) v Murphy* [2005] IECCA 1 at [64], [2005] 2 IR 125 at 148 and adopted and applied by the Supreme Court in *People (DPP) v Gilligan* [2005] IESC 78 at [83], [2006] 1 IR 107 at 142. See also *People (AG) v Travers* [1956] IR 110 at 114; *People (DPP) v D*, unreported, Court of Criminal Appeal, *ex tempore*, 27 July 1993; *People (DPP) v Cornally*, Court of Criminal Appeal, *ex tempore*, 7 November 1994; *People (DPP) v P.C.* [2002] 2 IR 285 at 300.

[150]   [2005] IESC 78 at [77]–[78], [2006] 1 IR 107 at 140.

[151]   In *DPP v Kilbourne* [1973] AC 729 at 750, [1973] 1 All ER 440 at 456, Lord Reid stated that: "There is nothing technical in the idea of corroboration. When in ordinary affairs of life one is doubtful whether or not to believe a particular statement one naturally looks to see whether it fits in with other statements or circumstances relating to the particular matter; the better it fits in,

corroboration,[152] as will be seen below, considerable complexity has developed around the concept. In addition, the *Baskerville* definition of corroboration has been criticised as being too narrow and restrictive. In *Vetrovec v R.*,[153] Dickson J in the Supreme Court of Canada identified three difficulties with that definition. First, it was divorced from and tended to obscure the rationale for the accomplice evidence warning and required a court to focus on whether evidence satisfied that definition, rather than whether it strengthened the credibility of the accomplice. Second, corroboration became a legal term of art with the result that the concept became increasingly complex and technical. Third, the definition was unsound in principle because the reason why corroboration is sought is that the accomplice is a potentially untrustworthy witness and, therefore, any evidence which tends to show that the accomplice is telling the truth should be capable of rehabilitating his or her credibility.[154] Those criticims were echoed by the Court of Criminal Appeal in *People (DPP) v Meehan*[155] which favoured the broader pre-*Baskerville* approach to corroboration and considered a re-evaluation of the *Baskerville* approach to be overdue.[156] It proceeded to review the Irish cases as to what could constitute corroborative evidence which, it believed, indicated that a common sense and nuanced approach had been adopted. Therefore, even without abandoning the *Baskerville* definition of corroboration (which would not have been open to the Court given that it had been expressly approved only months earlier by the Supreme Court in *Gilligan*), the Court was satisfied that "the more nuanced approach adopted in the cases already cited in this jurisdiction already goes some distance to qualify *Rex v Baskerville* towards a more common sense interpretation of what the requirements of corroboration should be".[157] The Court went on to state that[158]:

> "The review of cases demonstrates that the application of *Rex v Baskerville* in Ireland has over the years been of a flexible and nuanced nature. The court believes in any event that the formula of words adopted in *Rex v Baskerville* to define corroboration, including as it does the words "tending to connect him with the crime", leaves a considerable margin of discretion with any court dealing with the issues of corroboration to decide what may or may not constitute corroboration."

4–48 The extent to which this decision has effected a relaxation of the ingredients of corroboration examined below remains to be seen but it certainly indicates that an expansive approach will be taken to the requirement of implication.

(a) Requisite ingredients of corroboration

4–49 In addition to satisfying the threshold criteria that the evidence be relevant and admissible,[159] the requisite ingredients of corroborative evidence are that it must (i)

---

the more one is inclined to believe it." This passage was quoted with approval by the Supreme Court in *People (DPP) v Gilligan* [2005] IESC 78 at [78], [2006] 1 IR 107 at 140.

[152] *People (DPP) v Kenny* [2006] IECCA 137 at 10.

[153] [1982] 1 SCR 811, (1982) 136 DLR (3d) 89 at 101.

[154] See also Wigmore, *Evidence* 3rd edn (Boston: Little Brown and Company, 1940), VII, § 2059 at 327 (drawing on Joy, *On the Evidence of Accomplices* (Dublin: Milliken & Son, 1836), p.8.

[155] [2006] IECCA 104, [2006] 3 IR 468.

[156] [2006] IECCA 104 at [66], [2006] 3 IR 468 at 495.

[157] [2006] IECCA 104 at [65], [2006] 3 IR 468 at 495.

[158] [2006] IECCA 104 at [66], [2006] 3 IR 468 at 495–496.

[159] *R. v Ansell* (1934) 24 Cr App R 177 at 188; *Re a Solicitor, The Times*, 24 March 1978 (hearsay or other inadmissible evidence is not corroboration); *R. v Scarrott* [1978] QB 1016 at 1021, [1978] 1 All ER 672 at 676 (corroborative quality of evidence is a consequence of its admissibility and not vice versa). In order to be corroborative, the evidence must be admissible on the particular

implicate the accused in the offence charged, (ii) be independent of the witness to be corroborated, and (iii) be credible.[160]

(i) Implication of the accused

4–50   Although evidence must implicate the accused in a material particular of the offence in order to be corroborative,[161] it is important to note that, as pointed out by Denham J in *People (DPP) v Gilligan*,[162] evidence will constitute corroboration if "it *tends* to implicate the accused in the commission of the offence."[163] It is, thus, sufficient if the evidence "establishes a link which tends to prove that the accused person committed the offence".[164] It is not necessary that the corroborative evidence establishes any fact beyond a reasonable doubt[165] and evidence will be sufficiently implicatory if it makes it more probable that the accused committed the offence.[166] It follows that evidence which is equally consistent with either the guilt or innocence of the accused cannot constitute corroboration.[167] In *People (DPP) v Slavotic*,[168] it was held that the jury should not be directed that it is open to them to treat such evidence as potentially corroborative but a different approach has been taken in other jurisdictions on the basis that it is ultimately a matter for the jury to decide whether such evidence constitutes corroboration.[169]

4–51   In order to be corroborative, the evidence must implicate the accused in the particular offence charged. Thus, evidence which implicates the accused in a different

---

count (*R. v Hickmet* (1988) 33 A Crim R 75), and against the particular accused (*R. v Graham* [1984] 18 NIJB 1).

[160] *People (DPP) v Gilligan* [2005] IESC 78 at [77], [2006] 1 IR 107 at 140.

[161] *People (DPP) v Murphy* [2005] IECCA 1 at [103], [2005] 2 IR 125 at 159.

[162] [2005] IESC 78 at [77], [2006] 1 IR 107 at 140 (emphasis in the original).

[163] This was also emphasised by the Court of Criminal Appeal in *People (DPP) v Meehan* [2006] IECCA 104 at [61], [2006] 3 IR 468 at 493. See also, *R. v Berrill* [1982] Qd R 508 at 508–509.

[164] *People (DPP) v Gilligan* [2005] IESC 78 at [78], [2006] 1 IR 107 at 140.

[165] *Doney v R.* (1990) 171 CLR 207 at 211.

[166] *People (DPP) v Gilligan* [2005] IESC 78 at [78], [2006] 1 IR 107 at 140; *DPP v Kilbourne* [1973] AC 728 at 758, [1973] 1 All ER 440 at 463 (*per* Lord Simon); *R. v Ralph* (1988) 37 A Crim R 202 at 204; *R. v Nanette* [1982] VR 81 at 86, 3 A Crim R 268 at 279; *R. v Collings* [1976] 2 NZLR 104 at 117. *Cf.* the affiliation cases of *Morrissey v Boyle* [1942] IR 514; *Kiely v Mulvihill* (1948) 82 ILTR 1 and *Cahill v Reilly* [1957] Ir Jur Rep 77 at 79.

[167] *People (DPP) v Slavotic*, unreported, Court of Criminal Appeal, 18 November 2002; *R. v Hodgett* [1957] NI 1 at 8; *R. v Gibney* [1986] 4 NIJB 1 at 29; *Chiu Nang Hong v Public Prosecutor* [1964] 1 WLR 1279 at 1284; *R. v Holland* [1983] Crim LR 545; *Senat v Senat* [1965] P 172. 175, [1965] 2 All ER 505 at 507; *R. v Watson* (1913) 8 Cr App R 249 at 253; *R. v Rogers* (1914) 10 Cr App R 276 at 278; *R. v McNamara (No.1)* (1981) 56 CCC (2d) 193 at 278; *R. v Nanette* [1982] VR 81 at 86; *R. v Stephenson* (1978) 18 SASR 381 at 385; *R. v Lindsay* (1977) 18 SASR 103 at 107; *R. v Ralph* (1988) 37 A Crim R 202 at 204; *R. v Ling* (1981) 6 A Crim R 429 at 442.

[168] Unreported, Court of Criminal Appeal, 18 November 2002.

[169] See *R. v Hodgett* [1957] NI 1 at 6; *R. v Threlfall* (1914) 10 Cr App R 112 at 116; *R. v McK.* [1986] 1 Qd R 476; *R. v Berrill* [1982] Qd R 508; *R. v Kerim* [1988] 1 Qd R 426 at 433; *R. v Kalajzich* (1989) 39 A Crim R 415 at 430–433. In *R. v Collings* [1976] 2 NZLR 104 at 117, it was held that the jury should be instructed, especially where the evidence is not strongly corroborative, that they should not accept it as such unless they find it more consistent with the guilt than the innocence of the defendant.

offence[170] or in a similar offence on another occasion[171] will not suffice. In addition, it should be remembered that evidence which implicates one accused will not necessarily implicate another accused.[172]

4-52 Even where evidence relates to the particular offence charged against an accused, it may not be corroborative because, as O'Byrne J emphasised in *AG v Levison*,[173] the question of corroboration is very contextual, depending on the facts of the case and on the defence set up by the accused.[174] Corroboration can only be provided by evidence relating to matters which are put in issue by the accused, not matters which are admitted by the accused or which are common ground between the prosecution and the defence.[175] Thus, as noted by Denham J in *People (DPP) v Gilligan*,[176] the "nature of the defence may be critical in determining what is corroborative evidence".

4-53 This is apparent from the decision in *People (AG) v Coleman (No.2)*.[177] The accused was charged with two counts of unlawful use of an instrument with intent to procure a miscarriage. Both the woman on whom the instrument had been used and her husband gave evidence on behalf of the prosecution. The woman testified that, on the two material occasions, the accused switched on a large lamp and that, when the operations were being performed, she saw the instrument and the hands of the accused reflected in the lamp. It was held that her evidence was corroborated by the finding in the accused's premises of a chair and lamp upon which experiments had been performed to show that it was possible to see the reflection as described. This evidence implicated the accused because he denied that she had been in his premises on the material occasions or that he had performed any procedure upon her. Therefore, in the absence of an explanation as to how she could otherwise have known that it was possible to see such a reflection, her evidence implicated the accused by tending to rebut his defence. However, if his defence had been that he did see and examine her but did nothing further, then the evidence in respect of the reflection would not have constituted corroboration because she could have acquired it during the course of an "innocent" examination.[178]

---

[170] *R. v Goldstein* (1914) 11 Cr App R 27; *People (DPP) v Kiernan*, unreported, Court of Criminal Appeal, 11 March 1994; *People (DPP) v Cornally*, unreported, Court of Criminal Appeal, *ex tempore*, 7 November 1994.

[171] *AG (Kelly) v Kearns* (1946) 80 ILTR 45; *R. v McCormick* [1984] NI 50.

[172] *Cf. R. v Franklin* [1989] Crim LR 499.

[173] [1932] IR 158 at 165.

[174] This point was also made in *People (DPP) v Gilligan* [2005] IESC 78 at [78], [2006] 1 IR 107 at 140; *People (DPP) v Meehan* [2006] IECCA 104 at [55], [2006] 3 IR 468 at 491 and *People (DPP) v Foley* [2013] IECCA 90 at [39].

[175] *R. v Yates* [1970] SASR 302 at 206; *R. v Lindsay* (1977) 18 SASR 103 at 108 (*per* Bray CJ). But see, *contra*, *R. v Hodgett* [1957] NI 1 at 8 (*per* Curran LJ); *R. v Lindsay* (1977) 18 SASR 103 at 122 (*per* Zelling and Wells JJ); *Murphy v R.* (1976) 70 DLR (3d) 42 at 54; *R. v McKeon* (1987) 31 A Crim R 357 at 361; *R. v K* (1992) 34 FCR 227, (1992) 59 A Crim R 113; *R. v McK.* [1986] 1 Qd R 476.

[176] [2005] IESC 78 at [79], [2006] 1 IR 107 at 141.

[177] (1945) 1 Frewen 64.

[178] See also *R. v Williamson* [1939] GLR 554 (on charge of unlawful use of instrument upon a woman with intent to procure her miscarriage, the fact that the woman was able to accurately describe the interior of the accused's office could be used as corroboration where there was no suggestion by the accused that she had ever been in his office for any purpose). *Cf. Forgive Police* [1969] NZLR 101 (accused's acquaintance with the layout of the complainant's flat did not constitute corroboration where he admitted being present in the flat at the material time).

4–54   The defence run by the accused was also decisive in *People (DPP) v Meehan*[179] on the issue of whether circumstantial evidence was corroborative. The accused had been convicted of the murder of journalist Veronica Guerin together with drugs and firearms offences. The primary prosecution witness, Russell Warren, was an accomplice and gave evidence that he was a member of the same criminal gang as the accused which was headed up by John Gilligan. As corroboration of the involvement of the accused in the murder, the prosecution sought to rely on mobile phone records which established that a number of phone calls had been made between Mr. Warren and the accused and between him and John Gilligan which was consistent with his evidence of calls that he had made on the morning of the killing while tracking Veronica Guerin's movements prior to her murder. The Court of Criminal Appeal was satisfied that the Special Criminal Court had been entitled to treat this evidence as corroborative of the evidence of Mr. Warren when taken together with other circumstantial evidence in the case. Crucial in this regard in terms of the corroborative effect of this evidence was that the defence case was that there had been no contact between the accused and the witness on the day of the killing and this evidence therefore undermined this defence and tended to connect the accused with the killing.

4–55   It is important to note that it is not essential that corroboration confirm any part of the accomplice's testimony in addition to implicating the accused in the offence charged.[180] This is because its value as an additional safeguard derives from its implicatory, rather than its confirmatory quality. *A fortiori*, confirmation of the entirety of an accomplice's testimony is not required as otherwise such testimony would be superfluous.[181]

(ii) Independent evidence

4–56   It has been stated that a person cannot "be his own corroborator"[182] and therefore in order to afford corroboration, an item of evidence must be independent of the witness to be corroborated.[183] The independence requirement excludes from the definition of corroboration much evidence that goes to the credibility of a witness. Thus, corroboration cannot be found in documents admitted to refresh the memory of a witness while giving evidence,[184] or the previous statements of a witness, whether consistent,[185] or inconsistent.[186] Of course, the temptation for a jury to view such

---

[179] [2006] IECCA 104, [2006] 3 IR 468.

[180] *People (DPP) v Hogan* [1994] 2 ILRM 74 at 79; *R. v Beck* [1982] 1 All ER 807 at 815, [1982] 1 WLR 461 at 470–471; *R. v Galluzzo* (1986) 23 A Crim R 211 at 215.

[181] *People (DPP) v Murphy* [2005] IECCA 1 at [103], [2005] 2 IR 125 at 159; *People (DPP) v Murphy* [2013] IECCA 1 at [70]; *R. v Mullins* (1848) 3 Cox CC 526 at 531; *R. v Baskerville* [1916] 2 KB 658 at 664, [1916–17] All ER 38 at 42; *R. v Hodgett* [1957] NI 1 at 4; *R. v K* (1992) 34 FCR 227, (1992) 59 A Crim R 113. *Cf. People (DPP) v C* [2001] 3 IR 345 (dealing with the evidence of sexual complainants).

[182] *DPP v Christie* [1914] AC 545 at 557 (*per* Lord Atkinson).

[183] *People (AG) v Cradden* [1955] IR 130 at 141; *People (DPP) v Gilligan* [2005] IESC 78 at [78], [2006] 1 IR 107 at 140; *People (DPP) v Murphy* [2005] IECCA 1 at [103], [2005] 2 IR 125 at 159; *People (DPP) v Murphy* [2013] IECCA 1 at [69].

[184] *R. v Virgo* (1978) 67 Cr App R 323; *Senat v Senat* [1965] P 172 at 178, [1965] 2 All ER 505 at 509–510; *R. v Boulter* (1852) Cox CC 543 at 546.

[185] *DPP v Christie* [1914] AC 557 at 556; *People (DPP) v Brophy* [1992] ILRM 709 at 716; *People (DPP) v T* (1988) 3 Frewen 141 at 151; *Attorney General v O'Sullivan* [1930] IR 552; *R. v Coyle* [1926] NI 208 at 216–217; *R. v Whitehead* [1929] 1 KB 99, [1928] All ER 186.

[186] *R. v Askew* [1981] Crim LR 398.

evidence as corroborative may be very strong, and therefore a clear direction as to the limited use which may be made of it will be necessary.[187] Whether a jury will in fact heed such a warning is a matter of some conjecture.

4-57 The independence criterion is directed towards the danger of fabrication. By requiring corroborating evidence to come from a source other than the witness to be corroborated, it limits the possibility that such evidence may be fabricated, thereby advancing the objective of providing a guarantee of the truthfulness of the suspect witness. Thus, where evidence is clearly probative of the charge and the risk of fabrication is slight or eliminated, the courts have been prepared to essentially ignore the independence requirement and use such evidence as corroboration. For example, the evidence of the reflection in *People (AG) v Coleman*[188] was considered to be corroborative despite the fact that the evidence did not connect the accused with the commission of the offence except via the testimony of the witness to be corroborated.[189] More recently, in *People (DPP) v Foley*,[190] evidence of the physical reaction and accompanying words of a complainant when found by gardaí in a semi-conscious state were held to be capable of constituting corroboration because they were regarded as spontaneous and independent of her conscious will. Thus, the requirement that corroborative evidence be independent is best viewed as a proxy for reliability and where the court is satisfied that the evidence is reliable, then it will not be a barrier to its use as corroboration.[191] Conversely, if the putative corroboration is potentially unreliable because of a risk of collusion, it can be excluded on the basis of a lack of independence.[192]

(iii) Credibility

4-58 As a matter of common sense, corroborative evidence must be credible in order to be accepted by the tribunal of fact and to have the desired effect of making it safe to convict upon suspect testimony.[193] This was recognised in *R. v Dunne* by Torrens J,[194] who said that corroboration had to be provided by a "faith-worthy witness".[195] In addition, some minimum level of credibility must be expected of the testimony to be corroborated because it is impossible to corroborate that which is incapable of belief. These points were noted by Lord Morris in *DPP v Hester* who stated that:

> "The purpose of corroboration is not to give validity or credence to evidence which is deficient or suspect or incredible but only to confirm and support that which as evidence is sufficient

---

[187] *People (DPP) v Brophy* [1992] ILRM 709 at 716; *R. v Askew* [1981] Crim LR 398; *R. v Virgo* (1978) 67 Cr App R 323.

[188] (1945) 1 Frewen 64.

[189] *Cf. People (DPP) v P.C.* [2002] 2 IR 285 (the description by a witness of features of a room where offences are alleged to have occurred which are unique or unusual or even a combination of everyday features may, in certain circumstances, if verified by evidence independent of the witness's account, be capable of constituting corroboration).

[190] [2013] IECCA 90 at [38].

[191] *Cf. R. v McInnes* (1990) 90 Cr App R 99.

[192] *People (DPP) v Morrissey*, unreported, Court of Criminal Appeal, 10 July 1998.

[193] *People (DPP) v Gilligan* [2005] IESC 78 at [80]–[81], [2006] 1 IR 107 at 141. See also *People (DPP) v Murphy* [2013] IECCA 1 at [69]; *People (DPP) v Foley* [2013] IECCA 90 at [43].

[194] (1852) 5 Cox CC 507.

[195] (1852) 5 Cox CC 507 at 508. See, *e.g. R. v Thomas* (1985) 81 Cr App R 331.

and satisfactory and credible; and corroborative evidence will only fill its role if it itself is completely credible".[196]

4–59   These comments were echoed by Lord Hailsham in *DPP v Kilbourne*,[197] where he said that:

> "[c]orroboration is only required or afforded if the witness requiring corroboration or giving it is otherwise credible…If a witness's testimony falls of its own inanition, the question of his needing, or being capable of giving, corroboration does not arise".

4–60   However, it was held in *People (DPP) v Gilligan*[198] that the requirement of credibility did not involve a two stage test of inquiring, firstly, whether the evidence to be corroborated was credible and, only upon a determination that it was, proceeding to address the question of corroboration. Denham J endorsed the decision of the Privy Council in *Attorney General of Hong Kong v Muk-ping Wong*[199] that such an approach was inappropriate and held that the evidence of a witness, which is the subject of a corroboration warning, should be considered to see how it fits in with all the evidence in the case but should not be considered separately and categorised prior to an analysis of corroboration.[200]

4–61   It should be noted that because credibility is assessed on the basis of all the evidence in a case, both evidence which is corroborative and that which is not can be used by the jury to assess the credibility of an accomplice.[201] Therefore, where there is supporting evidence in a case which fails the criteria for corroboration, such evidence may still be important in convincing a jury that it is safe to convict on the uncorroborated testimony of an accomplice.[202]

(b) Cumulative corroboration

4–62   Corroboration may be found in circumstantial evidence.[203] However, because of the nature of circumstantial evidence, it may be difficult to find one piece of circumstantial evidence which, of itself, sufficiently implicates the accused. It has been held, therefore, that corroboration may be provided by the cumulative effect "of

---

[196] [1973] AC 296 at 315, [1972] 3 All ER 1056 at 1065. This passage was quoted with approval by the Supreme Court in *People (DPP) v Gilligan* [2005] IESC 78 at [80], [2006] 1 IR 107 at 141.

[197] [1973] AC 729 at 746, [1973] 1 All ER 440 at 452.

[198] [2005] IESC 78 at [81], [2006] 1 IR 107 at 141.

[199] [1987] 1 AC 501. See also *R. v Turner* (1975) 61 Cr App R 67 at 84; *R. v McCormick* [1984] NI 50 at 61; *R. v Morris* [1983] 2 SCR 190, (1983) 7 CCC (3d) 97; *R. v Panagiotidis* (1991) 55 SASR 172 at 178–181. See further, Jackson, "Credibility, Morality and the Corroboration Warning" (1988) CLJ 428.

[200] [2005] IESC 78 at [82], [2006] 1 IR 107 at 141. Her decision on this point was applied in *People (DPP) v Cronin* [2008] IECCA 94 at 4–5 and *People (DPP) v Cooke* [2009] IECCA 55 at [17]–[18].

[201] *R. v Turner* (1975) 61 Cr App R 67 at 84.

[202] In *R. v Gibney* [1986] 4 NIJB 1, Gibson LJ observed that: "[i]nsofar as evidence which is supportive falls short of corroboration it seems to recognise that while the acknowledged danger of convicting without corroboration may disappear when corroboration exists, if instead of corroboration there is merely supportive evidence the danger is reduced."

[203] *Attorney General v O'Sullivan* [1930] IR 552; *People (DPP) v Gilligan* [2005] IESC 78 at [84], [2006] 1 IR 107 at 142; *People (DPP) v Meehan* [2006] IECCA 104 at [57], [2006] 3 IR 468 at 491; *R. v Baskerville* [1916] 2 KB 658, [1916–17] All ER 38 at 43; *Thomas v Jones* [1921] 1 KB 22, [1920] All ER 462; *Doney v R.* (1990) 171 CLR 207 at 211; *R. v Lindsay* (1977) 18 SASR 103 at 117; *R. v Colless* [1964–65] NSWR 1243 at 1245.

pieces of circumstantial evidence, each innocuous on its own, which together tend to show that the defendant committed the crime".[204] It is thus immaterial that each item does not of itself implicate the accused in the crime, provided that the cumulative effect of the circumstantial evidence does so. Indeed, it was held in *People (DPP) v Meehan*[205] that circumstantial evidence can provide corroboration even where the corroborative value of the individual items of evidence is low. It is important to note, however, that although each item does not have to implicate the accused, each item does have to be independent.

4–63　Where circumstantial evidence is left to the jury on the basis that it is capable of affording corroboration when viewed cumulatively, the judge should direct the jury as to which items of evidence can be considered as part of this cumulative package.[206]

(c) Rule against mutual corroboration

4–64　There is a considerable body of authority in other jurisdictions to the effect that, while there is no general rule against mutual corroboration between accomplices,[207] corroboration of accomplice testimony may not be found in that of another accomplice where both are *participes criminis*,[208] and the jury must be instructed to this effect.[209] Although there is relatively little Irish authority on the point, it would appear that a broader blanket prohibition on mutual corroboration by persons categorised as accomplices is applied.[210] In addition, mutual corroboration between witnesses where there is a substantial risk of collusion between them to fabricate evidence is also excluded.[211]

---

[204] *Per* Lord Lane LCJ in *R. v Hills* (1988) 86 Cr App R 26 at 30–31. See also, *People (DPP) v Gilligan* [2005] IESC 78 at [84], [2006] 1 IR 107 at 142; *R. v McNamara (No.1)* (1981) 56 CCC (2d) 193 at 278–279; *R. v Galluzo* (1986) 23 A Crim R 211 at 216; *R. v Freeman* [1980] VR 1 at 12; *R. v Lindsay* (1977) 18 SASR 103 at 119–120, (*per* Zelling and Wells JJ); *R. v Duke* (1979) 22 SASR 46 at 52; *R. v Farrelly* [1954] NZLR 1 at 3. *Cf. Attorney General v O'Sullivan* [1930] IR 552.

[205] [2006] IECCA 104 at [62], [2006] 3 IR 468 at 493.

[206] *R. v McNamara (No.1)* (1981) 56 CCC (2d) 193 at 279.

[207] *R. v Cheema* [1994] 1 All ER 639 at 649, [1994] 1 WLR 147 at 158. *Cf. People (DPP) v Murphy* [2013] IECCA 1 at [77] where it was held that the statements of witnesses, in respect of whose evidence a corroboration warning was given even though they were not accomplices, could provide mutual corroboration.

[208] *R. v Noakes* (1832) 5 C & P 326 at 328; *R. v Gay* (1909) 2 Cr App R 327; *R. v Baskerville* [1916] 2 KB 658, [1916–17] All ER 38; *R. v Prater* [1960] 2 QB 464, [1960] 1 All ER 298; *DPP v Hester* [1973] AC 296, [1972] 3 All ER 1056; *R. v Parker* (1983) 8 A Crim R 324 at 336; *J v R.* [1989] Tas R 116 at 139; *R. v Rigney* (1975) 12 SASR 30 at 36; *Khan v R.* [1971] WAR 44; *R. v Webbe* [1926] SASR 108 at 117. See *contra, State v Avon Bottle Store Pty Ltd* 1963 (2) SA 389 at 393.

[209] *R. v Spencer* [1987] AC 128 at 140, [1986] 2 All ER 928 at 936 (*per* Lord Ackner); *Medcraft v R.* [1982] WAR 33; *Khan v R.* [1971] WAR 44; *R. v Lamb* [1975] Qd R 296 at 299. But see *R. v Rance* (1975) 62 Cr App R 118 at 122 (no positive rule which requires such a direction to be given).

[210] *People (DPP) v Dundon* [2013] IESPC 1. See also the direction of the trial judge in *Attorney General v Doyle* (1942) 1 Frewen 33 (the relevant portion of which is set out at p.36 of the judgment of the Court of Criminal Appeal), *People (AG) v Coleman* [1945] IR 237 at 248–249 and the old Irish case of *R. v Aylmer* (1839) 1 Craw & Dix 116 where Bushe CJ took the view that the issue turned on the opportunity which the accomplices had to concoct a story.

[211] *People (DPP) v Morrissey*, unreported, Court of Criminal Appeal, 10 July 1998. See further *People (DPP) v Cooke* [2009] IECCA 55 where the decision in *Morrissey* was distinguished and it was held that a mere allegation of collusion between witnesses was not sufficient to exclude

4–65   This rule is predicated on the proposition that the reasons which may prompt an accomplice to lie apply equally to any other accomplice to the same crime and they may collude together in order to tell the same false story.[212] However, the basic premise of the rule does not hold up to scrutiny. Collusion will not be present in every case and to rule out a valuable source of corroboration[213] because of the possibility that it may exist in a minority of cases is to fasten an *a priori* solution upon a question of fact.[214]

(d) Corroboration by the accused

4–66   It is well established that corroboration can be provided by the actions and statements of the accused. Such evidence will, of course, be independent of the accomplice and, therefore, the main issue is whether it implicates the accused in the commission of the offence.

(i) Misconduct evidence

4–67   Where evidence of the misconduct of the accused on other occasions (commonly known as similar fact evidence) is admitted,[215] it is capable of corroborating the evidence adduced against the accused on the offence charged.[216] Indeed, one of the main purposes of admitting such evidence is often to provide corroboration. Similarly, where there are multiple counts against the accused and the evidence on the counts is cross-admissible, it may be used as corroboration.[217] It should also be noted that, where misconduct evidence is admitted, evidence corroborating the occurrence of the previous incidents can be used as corroboration on the counts charged against the accused.[218]

---

mutual corroboration and the evidence of the witnesses can be left to the jury on the basis that it is capable of providing corroboration if the jury are satisfied that there was no collusion.

[212] *DPP v Hester* [1973] AC 296 at 326, [1972] 3 All ER 1056 at 1074 (*per* Lord Diplock); *DPP v Kilbourne* [1973] AC 728 at 751, [1973] 1 All ER 440 at 456 (*per* Lord Reid); *R. v Rigney* (1975) 12 SASR 30 at 51 (*per* Hogarth J). See also, *R. v King* [1967] 2 QB 338, [1967] 1 All ER 379. In *DPP v Kilbourne* [1973] AC 728 at 747, [1973] 1 All ER 440 at 453, Lord Hailsham opined that the dangers of accomplice evidence might even be greater where more than one accomplice was involved.

[213] With respect to some offences such as conspiracy, the only corroboration which is likely to be available will be that of a fellow accomplice.

[214] See Criminal Law Revision Committee, *Evidence (General): Eleventh Report* (London: HMSO, 1972) (Cmnd 4991), para.194 where the abolition of the rule against mutual corroboration was recommended and this recommendation was endorsed by the English Law Commission, *Corroboration of Evidence in Criminal Trials* (Working Paper No.15) (London: HMSO, 1990), pp.48–49. See also *R. v Parker* (1983) 8 A Crim R 324 at 336, where Gobbo J indicated a willingness to reconsider the binding nature of the rule on the basis that its strict application in the case before him was inappropriate where there were "six separate accounts by persons who fall within the accomplice definition, but who are in no conventional sense joint participators with one another in the crime charged". But *Cf. R. v Rigney* (1975) 12 SASR 30 at 36, where Bray CJ defended the breadth of the rule on the basis that a bright line rule was better because if the question as to whether accomplices had to corroborate each other had to be decided on a case-by-case basis, this would lead to a proliferation of appeals in cases where the accused was convicted and the warning was not given.

[215] See Chap.9.

[216] *DPP v Boardman* [1975] AC 421, [1974] 3 All ER 887; *DPP v Kilbourne* [1973] AC 728, [1973] 1 All ER 440; *R. v Sakail* [1993] 1 Qd R 312 at 317.

[217] *R. v Johannsen* (1977) 65 Cr App R 101.

[218] *R. v Hartley* [1941] 1 KB 5.

(ii) Admissions by the accused

4–68   An admission by the accused as to a fact in issue made out of court,[219] or while testifying,[220] will provide "the strongest possible corroboration".[221]

4–69   The issue of what can constitute an admission is examined in detail in Chap.5 but it should be noted that, apart from express[222] or implied oral admissions by an accused, corroboration may also be provided by an admission by conduct. For example, the silence of an accused in the face of an accusation of wrongdoing may provide corroboration that the accused is guilty of the wrongdoing alleged in circumstances where the accused would reasonably be expected to deny the accusation.[223] Thus, in *R. v Cramp*[224] the accused's silence when confronted by the witness's father who said "I have here those things which you gave my daughter to produce abortion" was held to be capable of corroborating her testimony on a charge of attempting to cause a miscarriage. However, it should be noted that, except where express statutory provision has been made in that regard, the silence of an accused when questioned by gardaí in relation to an offence,[225] or the failure of an accused to testify,[226] cannot provide corroboration.

4–70   Corroboration may also be provided by any attempt by an accused to hinder the investigation or prosecution of an offence, such as flight,[227] the destruction of evidence,[228] or attempts to bribe witnesses[229] or police officers.[230] However, by far the most common example of such conduct is the telling of a lie by the accused[231] in respect

---

[219]   *Cf. People (DPP) v Cornally*, unreported, Court of Criminal Appeal, *ex tempore*, 7 November 1994, and *Morrissey v Boyle* [1942] IR 514.

[220]   *Attorney General v Levison* [1932] IR 158; *R. v Stephenson* [1947] NI 110 at 119–120; *R. v Dossi* (1918) 13 Cr App R 158 at 162; *Scott v Killian* (1985) 40 SASR 38 at 39–40 (*per* King CJ).

[221]   *Per* Deale J in *O'Neill v Kelly* [1957] Ir Jur Rep 81 at 82. See also *DPP v Kilbourne* [1973] AC 728 at 736; [1973] 1 All ER 440 at 443 (*per* Lord Hailsham).

[222]   See, for example, *People (DPP) v MJ* [2014] IECCA 21 at [52]–[53].

[223]   *Cf. R. v Mitchell* (1892) 17 Cox CC 503 at 508. Whether an expectation exists that the accused would reasonably be expected to deny the charge depends on the circumstances (see *Cleeland v M'Cune* (1908) 42 ILTR 202 at 203; *Wiedemann v Walpole* [1891] 2 QB 534; *Thomas v Jones* [1921] 1 KB 22, [1929] All ER 462).

[224]   (1880) 14 Cox CC 390.

[225]   *People (AG) v Quinn* [1955] IR 57; *Attorney General v Fleming* [1934] IR 166 at 186. *Cf. People (DPP) v Finnerty* [2000] 1 ILRM 191; *Heaney v Ireland* [1994] 3 IR 593, [1994] 2 ILRM 420, [1996] 1 IR 580, [1997] 1 ILRM 117.

[226]   *R. v Jackson* [1953] 1 All ER 872; *Tumahole Bereng v R* [1949] AC 253 at 270; *Kolnberger v R.* [1969] SCR 213. However, a failure to testify may have the effect of strengthening the case against an accused and may add weight to any corroborative evidence which exists, or if no corroboration exists may be taken into account by the tribunal of fact in deciding whether it is safe to convict: *R. v Jackson* [1953] 1 All ER 872; *Cracknell v Smith* [1960] 3 All ER 569 at 571; *Jensen v Ilka* [1960] Qd R 274.

[227]   *R. v Melrose* [1989] 1 Qd R 572; *R. v M* [1995] 1 Qd R 213 at 214–15; *R. v Dickson* [1983] 1 VR 227; *R. v McKenna* (1956) 73 WN (NSW) 354; *Coulston v Taylor* (1909) 28 NZLR 807 at 809; *People v White* (1941) 48 Cal App 2d 90 at 95, P 2d 383 at 386; *People v Hoyt* (1942) 20 Cal 2d 306 at 313, P 2d 29 at 33; *Davis v State* (1904) 120 Ga 433 at 437, 48 SE 180 at 183; Wigmore, *Evidence* 3rd edn (Boston: Little Brown and Company, 1940), Vol. 1, § 276.

[228]   *R. v Hodgett* [1957] NI 1 (on a charge of receiving stolen goods, corroboration was provided by the fact that the accused had destroyed certain records which, according to the evidence of the thief, recorded the transactions between them).

[229]   *R. v Mazza* (1975) 24 CCC (2d) 508 at 515. *Cf. People (AG) v Travers* [1956] IR 110.

[230]   *R. v Fox* (1982) 7 A Crim R 28.

[231]   See *R. v Bain* [2004] EWCA Crim 525. For an analysis of the use of lies as corroboration, see JD Heydon, "Can Lies Corroborate?" (1978) 89 LQR 552.

of the offence the subject of the prosecution.[232] Such a lie, whether told in court or out of court,[233] may be used as corroboration[234] where it satisfies the criteria identified by Lord Lane CJ in *R. v Lucas*[235]: (i) it is a deliberate falsehood[236]; (ii) it relates to a material issue[237]; (iii) it is attributable to a consciousness of and an attempt to conceal guilt[238]; and (iv) the statement at issue is clearly shown to be a lie by evidence independent of the accomplice to be corroborated.[239]

---

[232] A lie can only constitute corroboration on a charge if it is an attempt to avoid conviction of that charge and, where there are multiple charges, the jury must be instructed to that effect (*R. v West* (1983) 79 Cr App R 45). However, a lie which relates to a different offence may be held to be corroborative where it also indicates the guilt of the accused on the particular charge in question (see *R. v Court* [1995] Crim LR 310).

[233] In *R. v Lucas* [1981] QB 720 at 725, [1981] 2 All ER 1008 at 1011, the Court of Appeal rejected the suggestion that *R. v Chapman* [1973] QB 774, [1973] 2 All ER 624, was authority for the proposition that lies told by a defendant in court could never provide corroboration. The same conclusion has been reached in other jurisdictions (see *R. v Dehar* [1969] NZLR 763; *R. v Collings* [1976] 2 NZLR 104 at 117; *Edwards v R.* (1993) 178 CLR 193; *Pitman v Byrne* [1926] SASR 207; *R. v Tripodi* [1961] VR 186; *R. v Perera* [1982] VR 901). For criticism of the proposition that lies in court cannot be used as corroboration, see Heydon, "Can Lies Corroborate?" (1973) 89 LQR 552. However, in practice, it may be easier to find corroboration in extra-curial lies: *Pitman v Byrne* [1926] SASR 207 at 212.

[234] *People (DPP) v Murphy* [2005] IECCA 1 at [103], [2005] 2 IR 125 at 159; *People (DPP) v JS* [2013] IECCA 41 at [3].

[235] [1981] QB 720 at 724, [1981] 2 All ER 1008 at 1011.

[236] The mere fact that a statement made by the accused subsequently turns out to be false is not sufficient; it must be shown that the accused was aware of the falsity of the statement at the time he or she made it: *R. v McCormick* [1984] NI 50 at 55. Where a statement of the accused is ambiguous in that it is capable of two interpretations, one of which would be a lie, it can be left to the jury for a determination as to whether it is a lie or not: *R. v Vallance* [1955] NZLR 811.

[237] See, for example, *People (AG) v Lawless* (1968) 1 Frewen 338. A lie will only provide corroboration if it relates to the incriminating features of the offence: *R. v Tripodi* [1961] VR 186 at 193; *Edwards v R.* (1993) 178 CLR 193 at 201; *Ready v R.* [1942] ALR 138. However, it should be noted that a lie about a matter may invest it with more significance than straightforward proof of that matter would have had. This is because "matters which otherwise might be ambiguous or colourless are rendered suspicious and corroborative by reason of the defendant's false denial— the inference open to the tribunal of fact being that, to him, the matter denied suggests guilt, so that, therefore, he is prepared falsely to deny it" (*per* Sholl J in *Popovic v Derks* [1961] VR 413 at 422).

[238] *R. v Collings* [1976] 2 NZLR 104 at 116; *Corfield v Hodgson* [1966] 2 All ER 205, [1966] 1 WLR 590. This test will be satisfied where the inference can be made that the lie was told because the accused knew that the truth of the matter about which he lied would implicate him in the offence: *Edwards v R.* (1993) 178 CLR 193 at 211 (*per* Deane, Dawson and Guadron JJ); *R. v Tripodi* [1961] VR 186 at 193. The standard of proof to be met was addressed in *People (DPP) v Kelly* [2012] IECCA 71 where, following the decision in *R. v Lucas* [1981] QB 720 at 723, [1981] 2 All ER 1008 at 1010, it was held that a court is entitled to draw inferences from lies if it is satsfied beyond reasonable doubt that there was no innocent explanation for the lie.

[239] *R. v Lucas* [1981] QB 720 at 723, [1981] 2 All ER 1008 at 1010; *R. v King* [1967] 2 QB 338 at 349–350; [1967] 1 All ER 379 at 384; *Edwards v R.* (1993) 178 CLR 193 at 211; *Popovic v Derks* [1961] VR 413 at 430. It should be noted that it is not open to the jury to disbelieve the evidence of the accused and then use that disbelief as corroboration of the testimony of the accomplice. To hold otherwise would mean that, if the jury believed the evidence of the accomplice in preference to that of the accused, they could use their disbelief of the accused to corroborate the evidence of the accomplice, thus dispensing with the need for corroboration: *R. v Lucas* [1981] QB 720 at 723, [1981] 2 All ER 1008 at 1010; *R. v King* [1967] 2 QB 338 at 349–350, [1967] 1 All ER 379 at 384; *Edwards v R* (1993) 178 CLR 193 at 211; *R. v Chapman* [1973] 1 QB 774, [1973] 2 All ER 624; *Credland v Knowler* (1951) 35 Cr App R 48 at 55; *Tumahole Bereng v R.* [1949] AC 253 at 270; *R. v Davison* (1974) 6 OR (2d) 103, 20 CCC (2d) 424; *R. v Reid* [1969] 1 OR 158 at 167; *Pitman v Byrne* [1926] SASR 207 at 211; *Tripodi v R.* (1961) 104 CLR 1 at 10.

4–71 A particularly careful direction is required where it is sought to rely on a lie of the accused as corroboration.[240] A direction as to which particular lie or lies are capable of being treated as corroboration and some explanation of the reason will usually be essential.[241] The jury should be instructed that, before using a lie as corroboration, they have to be satisfied that there is no alternative explanation for the lie consistent with the innocence of the defendant[242] and, in an appropriate case, the jury should be reminded that there are a number of reasons why an accused might tell a falsehood other than a consciousness of guilt,[243] including panic,[244] the desire to bolster a just cause,[245] indignation at an officious inquiry,[246] fear of facing an unjust accusation of guilt if suspicious circumstances are admitted,[247] and attempts to conceal discreditable conduct from family and friends,[248] other criminal offences from the police,[249] or the wrongdoing of others from the authorities.[250]

(iii) Statutory provisions

4–72 As explained in Chap.11, a number of statutory provisions have been introduced which provide that certain acts of non-cooperation with investigating gardaí can provide corroboration of the charges against the accused. Thus, corroboration may be provided by: the failure or refusal of an accused when requested to account for objects, substances or marks pursuant to s.18 of the Criminal Justice Act 1984 (as substituted by s.28 of the Criminal Justice Act 2007); the failure or refusal of an accused to provide an account when requested to account for his or her presence at a particular place at or about the time that an offence is alleged to have been committed pursuant to s.19 of the Criminal Justice Act 1984 (as substituted by s.29 of the Criminal Justice Act 2007); the failure of an accused to mention when questioned or charged or informed that he or she might be prosecuted for an offence a fact relied on in his or her defence of the proceedings which clearly called for an explanation pursuant to s.19A of the Criminal Justice Act 1984 (as inserted by s.30 of the Criminal Justice Act 2007); the failure of an accused when questioned about certain offences to answer a question material to the investigation of those offences pursuant to s.2(1) of the Offences Against the State (Amendment) Act 1998 (as amended by s.31 of the Criminal Justice Act 2007) and s.72A of the Criminal Justice Act 2006 (as inserted by s.9 of the Criminal Justice (Amendment) Act 2009); and a refusal without good cause to give consent for

---

[240] *R. v Spencer* [1987] AC 140, [1986] 2 All ER 928 at 936; *R. v Collings* [1976] 2 NZLR 104 at 116.

[241] *R. v Collings* [1976] 2 NZLR 104 at 117.

[242] *Edwards v R.* (1993) 178 CLR 193 at 199; *Eade v R.* (1924) 34 CLR 154; *R. v Toia* [1982] 1 NZLR 555 at 559; *R. v Collings* [1976] 2 NZLR 104 at 117; *R. v Dehar* [1969] NZLR 763 at 765.

[243] In *R. v Collings* [1976] 2 NZLR 104 at 116, McCarthy P observed that "most false statements or denials may…be explicable upon some hypothesis other than the accused's implication in the crime." See also *Lonergan v R.* [1963] Tas SR 158 at 160.

[244] *R. v Clynes* (1960) 44 Cr App R 158 at 163.

[245] *R. v Lucas* [1981] QB 720 at 724, [1981] 2 All ER 1008 at 1011 (*per* Lord Lane CJ); *Moriarty v London, Chatham and Dover Rly.Co.* (1870) LR 5 QB 314 at 319 (*per* Cockburn CJ).

[246] *Popovic v Derks* [1961] VR 413 at 426.

[247] *R. v Collings* [1976] 2 NZLR 104 at 116.

[248] *R. v Sutton* [1967] Crim LR 43; *R. v Dowley* [1983] Crim LR 168; *Harding v Porta* [1934] VLR 79 at 84.

[249] *R. v Wattam* (1952) 36 Cr App R 72.

[250] *Edwards v R.* (1993) 178 CLR 193.

the taking of certain bodily samples pursuant to s.3 of the Criminal Justice (Forensic Evidence) Act 1990.

4–73   In *People (DPP) v Devlin*,[251] the Court of Criminal Appeal held that a failure or refusal to account, as the case may be, must be such as is "capable of amounting to… corroboration of any evidence in relation to which the failure or refusal is material." Thus, in accordance with the decision in *People (DPP) v Gilligan*,[252] the evidence had to be such as tended to implicate the accused in the commission of the offence. However, in *People (DPP) v Donnelly*,[253] the Court of Criminal Appeal, in a judgment delivered by O'Donnell J, differed from *Devlin* in relation to the question of corroboration, stating:

> "Finally, it is perhaps appropriate to observe that a question may arise as to the meaning of "corroboration" in statutory provisions such as s.2 of the Offences Against the State Act 1998 and s. 18 of the Criminal Justice Act 1984. It does not appear to this Court that the reference to such evidence being "capable of amounting to corroboration" amounts to a requirement that such evidence be capable of satisfying the test for corroborative evidence before it can be accepted. On the contrary, such evidence is deemed by statute to be capable of amounting to corroboration, so that in such cases where corroboration is required as a matter of law or practice, it is capable of being supplied by inferences being drawn pursuant to the relevant statutory provisions."[254]

4–74   The Court further held that the Special Criminal Court had been entitled in that case to treat the failure to answer questions as capable of amounting to corroboration of the belief evidence of a garda superintendent that had been admitted pursuant to s.3(2) of the Offences Against the State (Amendment) Act 1972:

> "Under the section it is specifically provided that the failure to answer questions may, on the basis of the inferences to be drawn, be treated as corroboration. However, this is not a case in which there was evidence which required corroboration in the strict sense in which that term is used in the law of evidence. It appears the section uses the term in the more general sense of other evidence of guilt, which by virtue of the section may amount to corroboration, where that is required by law. Furthermore, it is perhaps important to point out that it is not the failure to answer questions which itself amounts to corroboration or indeed is itself evidence. Rather, the failure to answer questions material to the offence permits the court (but does not require it) to draw inferences from such failure as appear proper. It is those inferences which provide the basis on which the failure may amount to the type of corroboration contemplated by the section. Accordingly, any fact finder faced with s.2 must first consider whether there has been a *failure* to answer questions material to the investigation of the offence, and thereafter what *inferences* may be drawn from such failure as a matter of logic. An inference of guilt is not an inevitable consequence of a failure to answer. In some cases one inference may be that the accused did not understand either the import of the question or the consequences of a failure. In another situation, a refusal to answer questions may be indicative of a desire to avoid disclosing matters shameful and reprehensible, though perhaps not illegal. In still other cases, one inference might be that it is a desire to avoid disclosing a matter which is illegal, albeit not the illegality with which the person is being taxed. A further possible inference is that a suspect has already given a comprehensive account and does not see any merit in repetition."[255]

4–75   In that case, the Court of Criminal Appeal was satisfied that the Special Criminal Court had been entitled to conclude that the only possible inference from the sequence of events and the manner in which the accused had responded (or, more accurately, failed to respond) to questions in a number of interviews, which refusal was complete

---

[251]   [2012] IECCA 70.
[252]   [2005] IESC 78, [2006] 1 IR 107.
[253]   [2012] IECCA 78.
[254]   [2012] IECCA 78 at [38].
[255]   [2012] IECCA 78 at [40].

and comprehensive, was that they were members of an unlawful organisation, thus corroborating the belief evidence of the Chief Superintendent.

(e) Function of the judge and jury

4–76   The function of the judge is to decide whether evidence is capable, in law, of amounting to corroboration, and the function of the jury is to decide whether it does, in fact, constitute corroboration.[256] For this reason, a corroboration warning must be given even if there is evidence which indisputably amounts to corroboration.[257] However, as noted above, a trial judge should not direct a jury that it may treat as potentially corroborative, evidence which is reasonably capable of bearing two interpretations, one consistent with the guilt of the accused and the other with his or her innocence.[258]

4–77   Although an assessment of the weight and reliability of corroborative evidence is primarily a matter for the jury, the trial judge has discretion to withdraw potentially corroborative evidence from the jury in exceptional cases where the evidence is so unsatisfactory that it would be highly dangerous to leave it to the jury.[259] Further, as with other evidence, a judge is entitled to comment upon the weight and cogency of corroborative evidence,[260] so long as he or she makes it clear that ultimately, the question of the weight to be attached to the corroboration is a matter for the jury.[261] If a trial judge determines that evidence is capable of amounting to corroboration and so instructs the jury, he or she is generally not obliged to instruct the jury that the evidence is not very strong, if that is his or her view.[262] However, if the judge leaves corroborative evidence to the jury which has little weight or the weight of which may be overestimated by the jury, he or she is obliged to bring the inherent defects and weakness to the notice of the jury.[263]

5. The Corroboration Warning

4–78   The warning which must be given in respect of accomplice testimony has developed into a very complex direction requiring a trial judge to address a number of matters. First, there is the warning itself. This actually consists of two parts, a

---

[256] *People (DPP) v Lynch* [1982] IR 64 at 86 (*per* Walsh J); *R. vHodgett* [1957] NI 1 at 3; *R. v Willoughby* (1989) 88 Cr App R 91 at 93; *R. v Tragen* [1956] Crim LR 332; *R. v McNamara (No.1)* (1981) 56 CCC (2d) 193 at 278; *Manos v R.* [1953] 1 SCR 91; *Eade v R.* (1924) 34 CLR 154 at 159; *Standfield v Byrne* [1929] SASR 352 at 356; *Popovic v Derks* [1961] VR 413 at 420; *R. v Collings* [1976] 2 NZLR 104 at 115. Directions as to the evidence which may be used as corroboration should be given without adverting to the preceding ruling that such evidence was capable of amounting to corroboration, because this is unhelpful to juries who may not understand the distinction (*R. v Small* (1994) 33 NSWLR 575 at 593; *R. v Zorad* (1990) 19 NSWLR 91 at 103).
[257] *R. v Trigg* [1963] 1 All ER 490; *R. v O'Reilly* [1967] 2 QB 722 at 727, [1967] 2 All ER 766 at 768. But *cf.* the Australian approach in *Kelleher v R.* (1974) 131 CLR 534 (where the corroboration is substantial and there is therefore no likelihood that the jury will reject it and have to approach the case on the basis that there is no corroboration, the reason for the warning disappears and it does not have to be given).
[258] *People (DPP) v Slavotic*, unreported, Court of Criminal Appeal, 18 November 2002.
[259] *R. v Thompson* (1992) 57 SASR 397.
[260] *R. v Stephenson* [1947] NI 110 at 119.
[261] *R. v Harris*, unreported, South Australian Full Court, 17 September 1992.
[262] *People (DPP) v Kenny* [2006] IECCA 137 at 12.
[263] *R. v Thompson* (1992) 57 SASR 397.

prohibitive part and a permissive part. The prohibitive part entails warning the jury that it is dangerous to convict on the uncorroborated evidence of an accomplice.[264] The permissive part then informs the jury that, despite the warning, they are entitled to convict on the uncorroborated testimony of the accomplice if they are convinced beyond a reasonable doubt that he or she is a truthful witness.[265]

4–79   No particular formula is required for the warning[266] which should be tailored to the particular circumstances of the case.[267] Indeed, because the strength of the warning will vary in accordance with the degree and gravity of the accomplice's complicity,[268] and the degree and gravity of the risk of accepting his or her evidence,[269] no set wording can be prescribed.[270] Hence, it is not essential to use words such as "danger" or "dangerous"[271] but any alternative formula must adequately convey the frailties of accomplice testimony[272] and the risk of a wrongful conviction attendant upon it.[273] As McKechnie J explained in *People (DPP) v Murphy*[274]: "At its most fundamental, the warning should communicate in clear and unambiguous terms to the jury the risks, howsoever valued or appraised, of convicting an accused on uncorroborated evidence."

4–80   If, in addition to the general dangers, there are particular factors affecting the credibility and reliability of the accomplice, these should be pointed out to the jury. The

---

[264] Frequently, this warning is prefaced by an introduction grounding it in curial experience or some such generalisation. However, where this is done, the trial judge must be careful to relate the generality of the warning to the case before the jury and he or she must not undercut the import of the warning by conveying the impression that, while it is generally dangerous, it may not be dangerous in the particular case before the jury (*R. v Beebe* (1925) 19 Cr App R 22).

[265] The second part of the warning is purely permissive in its terms. Therefore, it is a misdirection to tell the jury that, if they find the accomplice to be a truthful witness, they ought to convict (*R. v Beebe* (1925) 19 Cr App R 22) or would be compelled to convict (*People (AG) v Phelan* (1950) 1 Frewen 98).

[266] *Attorney General v Doyle* (1942) 1 Frewen 33 at 36–37; *People (DPP) v Murphy* [2013] IECCA 1 at [71]; *DPP v Hester* [1973] AC 296 at 309, [1972] 3 All ER 1056 at 1060 (*per* Lord Morris); *R. v Spencer* [1987] AC 128 at 135 at 141, [1986] 2 All ER 928 at 932 at 937 (*per* Lords Hailsham and Ackner); *R. v Price* [1969] 1 QB 541 at 546, [1968] 2 All ER 282 at 285; *R. v Russell* (1968) 52 Cr App R 147 at 150.

[267] *DPP v Hester* [1973] AC 296 at 328, [1972] 3 All ER 1056 at 1076 (*per* Lord Diplock); *DPP v Kilbourne* [1973] AC 728, [1973] 1 All ER 440 (*per* Lord Hailsham); *R. v Spencer* [1987] AC 128 at 135 at 141, [1986] 2 All ER 928 at 932 at 937, (*per* Lords Hailsham and Ackner); *R. v Button* [1992] 1 Qd R 552 at 558.

[268] *Attorney General v Linehan* [1929] IR 19 at 23.

[269] *People (DPP) v Murphy* [2013] IECCA 1 at [72].

[270] *People (AG) v Coleman* (1945) 1 Frewen 64 at 72.

[271] *R. v Spencer* [1987] AC 128 at 141, [1986] 2 All ER 928 at 938 (*per* Lord Ackner); *R. v Taylor* (1985) 80 Cr App R 327 at 333; *R. v Stewart* (1986) 83 Cr App R 327 at 335.

[272] It is essential that the trial judge convey to the jury in clear terms that the evidence of an accomplice is in a special and suspect category. It is, therefore, inappropriate for the judge to use language in his charge which suggests that the credibility of an accomplice is to be judged by the tests which apply to an ordinary witness because this may lessen the force of the warning (*People (AG) v Phelan* (1950) 1 Frewen 98 at 100–101).

[273] *R. v Holland* [1983] Crim LR 545. Exhortations to use "very great care" (*Holland*), "particular care" (*R. v Price* [1967] 1 QB 541, [1968] 2 All ER 282), and "considerable care" (*R. v Stewart* (1986) 83 Cr App R 327 at 335), have all been held to fall short of the required standard because they failed to bring home to the jury the danger of a wrongful conviction. *Cf. R. v Ensor* [1989] 2 All ER 586, where the twice-repeated warning that it was "not safe" to convict on the uncorroborated evidence of the complainant was held to be sufficient.

[274] [2013] IECCA 1 at [71].

jury should, therefore, be cautioned to exercise special care if the accomplice has been granted immunity from prosecution[275] (especially if accompanied by financial or other benefits),[276] is a participant in a witness protection programme,[277] is unsentenced at the time he or she gives evidence[278] or has been pressurised into testifying.[279] A particularly strong warning is required if the witness has previously committed perjury,[280] has previously made false accusations against the accused,[281] has a propensity to lie[282] or has agreed to give evidence against a number of former criminal associates whether or not he or she can be classified as a "supergrass".[283]

4–81 If, in a given case, the trial judge forms the opinion that the accomplice evidence is very unreliable, that opinion can be conveyed to the jury in forceful terms.[284] He or she may even go so far as to advise the jury not to convict on such evidence[285] but, as noted above, the case cannot be withdrawn from the jury.[286] There are also decisions to

---

[275] *People (DPP) v Ward*, unreported, Special Criminal Court, 27 November 1998; unreported, Court of Criminal Appeal, 22 March 2002; *R. v Checconi* (1988) 34 A Crim R 160 at 171; *R. v Falzon*, unreported, Queensland Court of Criminal Appeal, 6 June 1990; *R. v Weightman* [1978] 1 NZLR 79 at 82. In *R. v Dellapatrona* (1993) 31 NSWLR 123 at 148, it was stated that, in addition to pointing out that an accomplice has been granted immunity, the judge should explain how this could lead to the accomplice's evidence being unreliable, viz. the accomplice may have told a false story in order to obtain immunity and then become locked into that story in order to maintain the immunity. See *contra, R. v McNamara (No.1)* (1981) 56 CCC (2d) 193 at 280 (no necessity for a special warning in addition to the usual accomplice warning with respect to witnesses who had been granted immunity—sufficient that trial judge instructed the jury that this was a factor to be taken into account in assessing their credibility).

[276] See *People (DPP) v Ward*, unreported, Special Criminal Court, 27 November 1998; unreported, Court of Criminal Appeal, 22 March 2002 discussed below.

[277] See *People (DPP) v Gilligan* [2005] IESC 78, [2006] 1 IR 107 discussed below.

[278] *R. v Smith* (1924) 18 Cr App R 19 at 20. *Cf. R. v Harris*, unreported, South Australian Full Court, 17 September 1992 (fact that accomplice had not been sentenced was a reason for scrutinising his evidence with particular care). *Cf. Attorney General v Kiely* [1934] LJ Ir 120 (jury adequately instructed as to the weight to be attached to the evidence of an unsentenced accomplice where the trial judge instructed them that it might have been given in hope of mitigation).

[279] *People (DPP) v McKeown* (1984) 3 Frewen 2. In that case, the Court of Criminal Appeal approached the evidence of an accomplice and his wife with even greater care than usual in circumstances where the accomplice had made a statement, on which his evidence at the trial was based, because he was told by a member of the Gardaí that, if he did not, he could be asked to serve the suspended sentence imposed on him. His wife had also been informed by members of the Gardaí that, having made a deposition, she could be charged with perjury if she gave different evidence at the trial.

[280] *R. v Atkinson* (1934) 24 Cr App R 123 at 127; *R. v McNamara (No.1)* (1981) 56 CCC (2d) 193 at 280. See also the direction of the trial judge set out in *Chidiac v R.* (1991) 171 CLR 432 at 438.

[281] *People (DPP) v Berber* [1944] IR 405.

[282] *Cf. People (DPP) v Ward*, unreported, Special Criminal Court, 27 November 1998.

[283] *People (DPP) v Ward*, unreported, Special Criminal Court, 27 November 1998; Court of Criminal Appeal, 22 March 2002 and *People (DPP) v Gilligan*, unreported, Court of Criminal Appeal, 8 August 2003 which are considered below.

[284] See *Attorney General of Hong Kong v Wong Muk-ping* [1987] AC 501 at 506–507, [1987] 2 All ER 488 at 490–491. *Cf. People (DPP) v Ward*, unreported, Court of Criminal Appeal, 22 March 2002, where the Court expressed its scepticism as to whether "one could be confident of eliminating all factors which would motivate and encourage liars, such as Mr Bowden, so as to justify a belief beyond all reasonable doubt in any evidence given by him" and it would appear that, if the case had been tried before a jury, a warning to that effect would have been appropriate.

[285] *R. v Baskerville* [1916] 2 KB 658 at 663; *R. v Beebe* (1925) 19 Cr App R 22 at 25; *R. v Boyes* (1861) 1 B & S 311 at 322.

[286] *People (AG) v Mazure* [1946] IR 448 at 449. This is in contrast with the position in Australia, where the courts have held that where the risks of unreliability are extremely high, as where an

the effect that, if the dangers which underlie the warning are absent or not as prominent, this can be pointed out to the jury.[287] However, the trial judge must be very careful not to negative the warning.[288]

4–82   The warning, to be sufficient, must explain why it is dangerous to act on the evidence of the accomplice on the facts of the particular case, as otherwise it will lack significance.[289] However, because the purpose of doing this is to bring to the jury's attention dangers which would not otherwise be apparent to them, it will not be necessary to do this if it is patent from the nature of the case or the defence of the accused what those dangers are. Thus, in *People (DPP) v Hogan*,[290] the Court of Criminal Appeal rejected the submission that the trial judge had erred in failing to articulate in his charge the reasons why accomplice evidence has to be treated with caution. It was clear from the transcript that counsel for the applicant had placed considerable emphasis on the fact that the accomplice had received a reduction of his sentence on the basis that he had co-operated with the gardaí. Therefore, since it was abundantly clear to the jury why the warning was required, the fact that the judge did not expand further on this point did not render his charge defective.[291]

4–83   If no corroboration exists, the judge should simply make that fact clear to the jury[292] and should refrain from any discussion of the concept.[293] However, where corroborative evidence does exist, the trial judge must go on to explain the nature of

---

accomplice has turned Queen's evidence, the courts have a discretion to exclude this testimony altogether. See *R. v Turner* (1975) Cr App R 67 at 77–79; *R. v Braum* (1983) 21 NTR 6; *R. v McLeon & Funke, ex p. AG* [1991] 1 Qd R 231. However, this discretion should only be exercised in the rare situation where a properly directed jury would be incapable of fairly assessing the probative significance of the evidence: *Rozenes v Beljajev* [1995] 1 VR 533.

[287] See *R. v Riley* (1979) 70 Cr App R 1 at 4 (if trial judge thought that the risk of relying on the accomplices' evidence was not very great in the particular circumstances of the case, then, having given the proper warning, he could have indicated this). *Cf. R. v Price* [1968] 2 All ER 282 (open to the trial judge to indicate to the jury that the degree of risk can vary according to the circumstances of the case).

[288] See *R. v Timmins* [1981] Crim LR 774, where the conviction of the appellant was quashed where the trial judge only paid "lip service" to the warning by reminding the jury that the thief had already been sentenced for his offence and therefore had nothing to gain from lying.

[289] *People (DPP) v Murphy* [2013] IECCA 1 at [72]; *R. v Spencer* [1987] AC 128 at 140, [1986] 2 All ER 928 at 936 (*per* Lord Ackner). See also, *R. v Checconi* (1988) 34 A Crim R 160 at 170–171; *R. v Button* [1992] 1 Qd R 552 at 553. See, *contra, R. v Ling* (1981) 6 A Crim R 429 at 454.

[290] [1994] 2 ILRM 74.

[291] [1994] 2 ILRM 74 at 80. *Cf. Attorney General v Doyle* (1942) 1 Frewen 33 at 35 (dangers of acting on the evidence of accomplices brought home to the jury by the cross-examination and closing speech of counsel for the accused).

[292] *People (DPP) v Murphy* [2013] IECCA 1 at [75]. See also *People (AG) v Williams* [1940] IR 195 at 204; *Attorney General v Troy* (1950) 84 ILTR 193 at 193; *People (AG) v Moore* [1950] Ir Jur Rep 45 at 47; *R. v Nagy* [1990] Crim LR 187; *R. v McKay* [1963] NZLR 407 at 408 which deal with the corroboration warning with regard to sexual complainants.

[293] In *R. v Spencer* [1986] AC 128 at 135, [1986] 2 All ER 928 at 932, Lord Hailsham said that "where no corroboration exists, a disquisition on what can or could amount to such if corroboration were needed is emphatically not required and greatly to be discouraged". See also *DPP v Hester* [1973] AC 296 at 328, [1972] 3 All ER 1056 at 1076 (*per* Lord Diplock); *R. v Jansen* [1970] SASR 531. Such a direction should not be given where there is no corroboration because the very fact that it is given leads the jury to infer that there is evidence capable of amounting to corroboration (*R. v Goddard* [1962] 3 All ER 582 at 586, [1962] 1 WLR 1282 at 1286.

the concept.[294] No particular form of words is required so long as the requirements of implication and independence are brought home to the jury.[295] Indeed, because "corroboration" is not a common term, it is not necessary to use it[296] and it may, in fact, be better not to do so.[297]

4–84 In recent times, it has come to be recognised that the complexity of the concept of corroboration is such that it is insufficient for the trial judge to merely explain the nature of corroboration without going on to provide guidance as to what evidence the jury may use as corroboration.[298] Otherwise, the value of the corroboration warning is undermined and there is a danger of a wrongful conviction arising from juries treating as corroboration that which they should not.[299] The extent of this duty varies according to the amount of corroborative evidence and the complexity of the case. In straightforward cases, where there is little corroborative evidence, the trial judge should point out the specific items of evidence which are capable of constituting corroboration.[300] In more complex cases, there is no obligation to refer to every piece of potentially corroborative evidence: it will suffice for the trial judge to "give a broad indication of the sort of evidence which the jury, if they accept it, may treat as corroboration".[301] To hold otherwise would place an unreasonable burden on the trial judge, confuse juries and enhance the risk of an erroneous direction.[302]

---

[294] *People (DPP) v Kenny* [2006] IECCA 137 at 11; *R. v Clynes* (1960) 44 Cr App R 158 at 161; *R. v Khan* [1971] WAR 44 at 53; *R. v Button* [1992] 1 Qd R 552 at 558.

[295] *R. v Fallon* [1993] Crim LR 591; *R. v Clynes* (1960) 44 Cr App R 158 at 161; *Khan v R.* [1971] WAR 44 at 51; *Chidiac v R.* (1991) 171 CLR 432 at 441. *Cf. People (DPP) v Hogan* [1994] 2 ILRM 74 (use of the word "confirm" in charge not fatal where the charge dealt with all the necessary matters); *R. v Brown* [1992] Crim LR 178 (failure to direct the jury that the putative corroborative evidence must implicate the accused not fatal if it does in fact do so).

[296] *DPP v Hester* [1973] AC 296 at 329, [1972] 3 All ER 1056 at 1076, (*per* Lord Diplock); *R. v O'Reilly* [1967] 2 QB 722, [1967] 2 All ER 766 (summing up described as impeccable even though the deputy chairman did not use the term). But *Cf. R. v Apostolides* (1983) 11 A Crim R 381 at 401–402, (1984) 154 CLR 563, where Kaye J warned against using the word "support" as a substitute for "corroboration" because, contrary to the view of Lord Pearson in *DPP v Hester* [1973] AC 296 at 321, the words are not synonymous.

[297] *DPP v Kilbourne* [1973] AC 728 at 741, [1973] 1 All ER 440 at 447 (*per* Lord Hailsham).

[298] *R. v Charles* (1976) 68 Cr App R 334n at 340; *R. v Reeves* (1978) 68 Cr App R 331 at 332–333; *R. v Timmins* [1981] Crim LR 774; *R. v Cullinane* [1984] Crim LR 420; *R. v Spencer* [1987] AC 128 at 140, [1986] 2 All ER 928 at 936 (*per* Lord Ackner); *R. v McNamara (No.1)* (1981) 56 CCC (2d) 193 at 279; *Khan v R.* [1971] WAR 44 at 51 at 53; *Medcraft v R.* [1982] WAR 33 at 38 at 40; *R. v Baynon* [1960] NZLR 1012 at 1016; *R. v Honey* [1973] 1 NZLR 725 at 730; *R. v Collings* [1976] 2 NZLR 104 at 115. It is particularly important that this should be done where the corroboration is cumulative (*R. v Gold* [1991] Crim LR 447).

[299] *R. v Kelso* (1953) 105 CCC 305 at 308, (*per* Laidlaw JA).*Cf. R. v Honey* [1973] 1 NZLR 725 at 730. There is also the practical difficulty, in the absence of such guidance, of proving that the jury relied on, as corroboration, evidence which did qualify as such.

[300] *People (DPP) v Scanlon* (1985) 3 Frewen 15 at 16; *People (DPP) v Murphy* [2013] IECCA 1 at [74]; *R. v Sherrin (No.2)* (1979) 21 SASR 250 at 255–256; *R. v Small* (1994) 33 NSWLR 575 at 593.

[301] *Per* Parker LJ in *R. v Goddard* [1962] 3 All ER 582 at 586. This statement was approved and applied by the Court of Criminal Appeal in *People (AG) v Lawless* (1968) 1 Frewen 338 at 341, and by the Victorian Full Court in *R. v Matthews* [1972] VR 3 at 20 and 22. Some New Zealand decisions have held that the judge must go further and make it clear to the jury that they cannot rely on anything else as corroboration (*R. v Honey* [1973] 1 NZLR 725 at 730; *R. v Collings* [1976] 2 NZLR 104 at 115 and 120). However, this will generally be implicit in the judge's discussion of corroboration (*R. v Poa* [1979] 2 NZLR 378 at 380), and the point does not have to be expressly made unless there is evidence which the jury might mistakenly regard as corroboration (*Matthews*).

[302] *R. v Matthews* [1972] VR 3 at 22.

4–85   Where there is evidence in a case that supports the testimony or credibility of an accomplice but is incapable of amounting in law to corroboration, there is a risk that a jury may mistakenly so regard it. To neutralise this danger, the jury should be warned not to regard as corroboration of the accomplice's testimony any items of evidence which agree with it or tend to confirm it but do not corroborate it in the strict legal sense.[303] However, it does not follow that such evidence is to be ignored by the tribunal of fact and it can provide supporting evidence of the credibility of the accomplice even though it falls short of corroboration.[304]

4–86   Finally, the judge must clearly instruct the jury that it is for them to decide whether the evidence, which is capable in law of constituting corroboration, does in fact do so.[305]

(a) Multiple defendants or counts

4–87   A particularly careful direction is required where there is more than one accused and/or multiple counts in the indictment. Evidence which corroborates the testimony of an accomplice against one accused will not do so as against another.[306] Therefore, where there is more than one accused, it is important to instruct the jury to treat each accused separately and look for corroboration relating to *each* of the accused.[307]

4–88   Similarly, where there is a multiplicity of counts, the jury must be clearly instructed to treat each count separately and to look for corroboration in respect of each count.[308] Where corroboration exists on some counts but not on others, the duty of the judge is to point out any counts in respect of which there is no corroboration.[309] In addition, it may be necessary to point out which items of evidence are capable

---

[303] *People (AG) v Phelan* (1950) 1 Frewen 98 at 100; *People (AG) v Lawless* (1968) 1 Frewen 338 at 341; *R. v Spencer* [1987] AC 128 at 140, [1986] 2 All ER 928 at 936; *R. v McInnes* (1990) 90 Cr App R 99 at 101; *R. v Goddard* [1962] 3 All ER 582 at 586, [1962] 1 WLR 1282 at 1286.

[304] See *People (DPP) v Meehan* [2006] IECCA 104 at [71], [2006] 3 IR 468 at 498; *People (DPP) v Timmons* [2011] IECCA 13 at 28–29.

[305] *People (DPP) v Lynch* [1982] IR 64 at 86 (*per* Walsh J); *People (DPP) v Murphy* [2013] IECCA 1 at [74]; *R. v McInnes* (1990) 90 Cr App R 99 at 101–102; *R. v Spencer* [1987] AC 128 at 140, [1986] 2 All ER 928 at 936 (*per* Lord Ackner); *R. v Tragen* [1956] Crim LR 332; *R. v Vallance* [1955] NZLR 811. Note that directions as to the evidence which may be used as corroboration should be given without adverting to the preceding ruling that such evidence is capable of amounting to corroboration because this is unhelpful to juries who may not understand the distinction (*R. v Small* (1994) 33 NSWLR 575 at 593; *R. v Zorad* (1990) 19 NSWLR 91 at 103).

[306] *R. v Graham* [1984] 18 NIJB 1 at 17; *R. v Donnelly* [1986] 4 NIJB 32 at 58; *R. v Jenkins* (1845) 1 Cox CC 177; *R. v Stubbs* (1855) Dears CC 555 at 557; *R. v Baskerville* [1916] 2 KB 658 at 670; *R. v Donat* (1985) 82 Cr App R 173 at 178; *R. v Checconi* (1988) 34 A Crim R160 at 169. For an example of a proper charge on this point, see *People (AG) v Lawless* (1968) 1 Frewen 338 at 340–341.

[307] *R. v Webber* [1987] Crim LR 413; *R. v Checconi* (1988) 34 A Crim R160 at 168; *R. v Collings* [1976] 2 NZLR 104 at 115. In *R. v Holland* [1983] Crim LR 545, it was held that, if there is evidence capable of constituting corroboration against one defendant but not another, the jury should be so informed.

[308] The complexity and length of the charge required where there are a multiplicity of counts may necessitate that the warning be given more than once so that the jury adequately appreciate that it applies to each of the counts (*People (AG) v Berber* [1944] IR 405 at 413).

[309] *People (AG) v Shaw* [1960] IR 168 at 172; *R. v Franklin* [1989] Crim LR 499. In *Shaw* it was held that it is insufficient for the trial judge to indicate that corroboration may be lacking on some counts.

of providing corroboration with respect to each count.[310] Problems may arise where there are multiple counts against an accused which relate to very similar offences. In some cases, evidence on one count may be admissible misconduct evidence on another count.[311] However, even where such evidence is not cross-admissible, there is an understandable tendency on the part of a jury to regard the evidence given on one count as corroborative of the evidence given on another count, necessitating a very strong warning that this is not the case.[312]

(b) Failure to give proper warning

4–89   As noted above, the requirement to give the corroboration warning is a rule of law. Therefore, failure to give the warning will lead to the quashing of a conviction, even if there is ample corroboration, unless the Court of Criminal Appeal, applying the proviso contained in s.3(1)(a) of the Criminal Procedure Act 1993, is satisfied that no miscarriage of justice has occurred.[313] This proviso is only applied where the court is satisfied that the jury would inevitably have come to the same conclusion if properly warned.[314] Similarly, failure to give the warning properly by dealing adequately with any of the matters set out above will also result in the conviction being quashed unless the proviso can be applied.[315]

4–90   In order to minimise the risk of an appeal in relation to a defect in the warning, it is considered desirable, except in straightforward cases, for the judge to discuss the terms of the warning with counsel in the absence of the jury.[316] Such a procedure was adopted by the trial judge in *People (DPP) v Cornally*[317] and the Court of Criminal Appeal gave short shrift to a challenge to the charge on the basis that a "measure of agreement" had been reached on what the trial judge would say to the jury.[318]

6. Reform of the Warning

4–91   The accomplice corroboration warning has attracted considerable and justifiable

---

[310] *R. v Watson* [1992] Crim LR 434.
[311] See, *e.g.*, *DPP v Boardman* [1975] AC 421, [1974] 3 All ER 887 and *DPP v Kilbourne* [1973] AC 728, [1973] 1 All ER 440.
[312] *Attorney General v Duffy* [1931] IR 144 at 149. In *Duffy*, it was held that, in some cases, such a warning will not suffice and it will be necessary for the trial judge to exercise his or her discretion to require the prosecution to proceed only with sample counts.
[313] *Davies v DPP* [1954] AC 378 at 399, [1954] 1 All ER 507 at 513; *Khan v R.* [1971] WAR 44 at 50; *R. v Forgione* [1969] SASR 248 at 253.
[314] *R. v McInnes* (1990) 90 Cr App R 99 at 103; *R. v O'Reilly* [1967] 2 QB 722, [1967] 2 All ER 766; *R. v Lewis* [1937] 4 All ER 360 at 363.
[315] *R. v McInnes* (1990) 90 Cr App R 99 at 103; *R. v O'Reilly* [1967] 2 QB 722, [1967] 2 All ER 766; *R. v Lewis* [1937] 4 All ER 360 at 363.
[316] *R. v Beck* [1982] 1 All ER 807 at 815, [1982] 1 WLR 461 at 490 (*per* Ackner LJ); *R. v Ensor* [1989] 2 All ER 586 at 593, [1989] 1 WLR 497 at 505–506, (*per* Lord Lane CJ); *R. v Nagy* [1990] Crim LR 187; *R. v Franklin* [1989] Crim LR 499; *R. v Gold* [1991] Crim LR 447. *Cf. People (DPP) v C* [2001] 3 IR 345, where Murphy J indicated, in the context of sexual complainants, that, in principle, a trial judge should allow counsel to argue in full any question arising concerning the warning to be given to the jury in the absence of the jury before final speeches.
[317] Unreported, Court of Criminal Appeal, 7 November 1994.
[318] Unreported, Court of Criminal Appeal, 7 November 1994 at 8.

criticism from academic commentators,[319] law reform bodies[320] and members of the bench.[321] It is beset by problems which have prompted its demise in other jurisdictions[322] and which, it is submitted, should also happen here.

4–92   First, there is the sheer complexity of the warning and its associated rules. Each new accretion to these rules has added another layer of complexity and technicality to a warning already overburdened with both.[323] The inevitable result has been erroneous directions and successful appeals.[324] Such is the fertility of the warning as a source of appeals that Wigmore commented that it placed "in the hands of counsel a set of juggling formulas with which to practice upon the chance of obtaining a new trial."[325]

4–93   The complexity and technicality of the warning also makes it difficult for the jury to comprehend and apply it. The result is that the warning is "a frequent source of bewilderment".[326] The problem is accentuated by judges attempting to fireproof

---

[319] See, *e.g.* O'Connor, "Corroboration and the Testimony of Accomplices in the Irish Law of Evidence" (1982) 4 DULJ 12; Bronitt, "The Definition of Corroboration Reconsidered" [1991] Crim LR 30; Dennis, "Corroboration Requirements Reconsidered" [1984] Crim LR 316; Williams, "Corroboration: Accomplices" [1962] Crim LR 588. For a discussion of the inadequacies of the rationales underlying the rule and a discussion of its demise in England see Roberts and Zuckerman, *Criminal Evidence* (Oxford University Press, 2004), pp. 477–487.

[320] See, *e.g.* Criminal Law Revision Committee, *Evidence (General): Eleventh Report* (London: HMSO, 1972) (Cmnd 4991) (hereinafter referred to as the "*Eleventh Report*"); Law Commission, *Corroboration of Evidence in Criminal Trials* (Working Paper No.15) (London: HMSO, 1990) (hereinafter referred to as the "*Working Paper on Corroboration*"); Law Commission, *Criminal Law: Corroboration of Evidence in Criminal Trials* (Law Com No. 202) (London: HMSO, 1991) (Cmnd 1620) (hereinafter referred to as the "*Report on Corroboration*"); Law Reform Commission of Canada, *Evidence: 11 Corroboration* (Study Paper) (Ottawa: Law Reform Commission of Canada, 1975) (hereinafter referred to as the "*Study Paper on Corroboration*"); Law Reform Commission of Canada, *Report on Evidence* (Ottawa: Information Canada, 1977) (hereinafter referred to as the "*Report on Evidence*"); Australian Law Reform Commission, *Evidence* (Report No.26 (Interim)) (Canberra: Australian Government Publishing Service, 1985), Vol. I.

[321] The most notable example is of course the decision of the Supreme Court of Canada in *Vetrovec v R.* [1982] 1 SCR 811, (1982) 136 DLR (3d) 89. The criticisms advanced in that case were referred to by the Court of Criminal Appeal in *People (DPP) v Meehan* [2006] IECCA 104, [2006] 3 IR 468.

[322] The mandatory warning has been abrogated in England (Criminal Justice and Public Order Act 1994, s.32), Canada (*Vetrovec v R.* (1982) 136 DLR (3d) 89; *R. v GB (No.1)* [1990] 2 SCR 3; *R. v Winmill* (1999) 131 CCC (3d) 380; *R. v Brooks* [2000] 1 SCR 237; *R. v Kehler* [2004] 1 SCR 328; *R. v Khela* [2009] SCC 4, [2009] 1 SCR 104), Australia (Evidence Act 1995, s.164), and New Zealand (Evidence Amendment Act (No.2) 1986, s.2; see now s.122 of the Evidence Act 2006).

[323] As the Law Reform Commission of Canada observed with regard to the corroboration rules generally, "an enormous superstructure…has been erected on the original basic proposition that the evidence of some witnesses should be approached with caution" (*Study Paper on Corroboration*, p.7, quoted with approval by Dickson J in *Vetrovec v R* [1982] 1 SCR 811, (1982) 136 DLR (3d) 89 at 95). See also, the Law Commission, *Working Paper on Corroboration*, para.4.7, which stated that the corroboration rules and "the structure of law and practice that they now incorporate, impose on the courts an excessively complicated and over-elaborate duty".

[324] CLRC, *Eleventh Report*, para.180; Law Commission, *Report on Corroboration*, para.2.9.

[325] Wigmore, *Evidence* 3rd edn (Boston: Little Brown and Company, 1940), VII, § 2057. This assessment is borne out by the statistics. In a survey of the decisions of the Court of Appeal delivered in a 12-month period, the Law Commission found that corroboration was an issue in 15 per cent of the appeals (*Working Paper on Corroboration*, para.4.16, n.25).

[326] *Per* Lord Diplock in *DPP v Hester* [1973] AC 296 at 327, [1972] 3 All ER 1056 at 1075. See also *R. v Cheema* [1994] 1 All ER 639 at 650, [1994] 1 WLR 147 at 158, where the Court of Appeal, *per* Lord Taylor CJ, voiced its support for a review of the rules which had "become

their summings-up from appellate review by giving complex and elaborate directions which, although they are correct in law, only serve to confuse the jury.[327] A related difficulty is judges repeatedly stressing the dangers of accomplice testimony with the result that the jury may acquit when it would be safe to convict.[328]

4–94 The irony is that the warning stems from judicial distrust of the ability of juries to use common sense and experience in assessing the credibility of witnesses with motives to lie. However, the jury is then expected to understand and apply a complex warning revolving around the highly technical concept of corroboration.[329]

4–95 The warning and the ancillary search for corroboration which it entails also has a tendency to lead to mechanistic decision making. By focusing the jury's attention on the question of whether or not there is corroboration, there is an understandable tendency on the part of the jury to convict where they find corroboration without fully considering whether the guilt of the accused has been established beyond a reasonable doubt.[330] Conversely, the tribunal of fact may be inclined to acquit where there is no corroboration without fully considering whether the accomplice's evidence is, of itself, sufficient to support a verdict of guilty.[331] Thus, the warning may well distract the attention of both the judge and the jury from the central issue of the guilt or innocence of the accused.[332] Reference can be made to the case of *People (DPP) v Ward*, where notwithstanding that the Special Criminal Court expressed itself to be "deeply mindful of the fundamental principle of criminal law that it is unsafe to act upon the evidence of an accomplice which is not corroborated in some material particular implicating the accused",[333] it was held by the Court of Criminal Appeal to have erred in concluding that the evidence supported the charge of murder against him.[334]

---

arcane, technical and difficult to convey to juries", and *R. v Makanjuola* [1995] 3 All ER 730 at 732, [1995] 1 WLR 1348, where Lord Taylor CJ described the full corroboration warning as a "tortuous exercise, which juries must have found more bewildering than illuminating".

[327] In *DPP v Hester* [1973] AC 296 at 327, [1972] 3 All ER 1056 at 1075, Lord Diplock stated that, while the incorporation in the summing up of "a general disquisition on the law of corroboration in the sort of language used by lawyers, may make the summing-up immune to appeal on a point of law...it is calculated to confuse a jury of laymen".

[328] Heydon, *Evidence Cases and Materials* 3rd edn (London: Butterworths, 1991), pp.91–92. See also the concern expressed by the CLRC (*Eleventh Report*, para.180) that the jury may "get the impression that the judge intends to convey to them that they should not convict unless the evidence achieves moral certainty as distinct from proof beyond reasonable doubt".

[329] Dennis, "Corroboration Requirements Reconsidered" [1984] Crim LR 316 at 324.

[330] Roe J, the trial judge in *People (DPP) v Mulvey* [1987] IR 502, was very alive to this danger, stating: "whilst the law is that if there is no corroboration it is dangerous to convict, it doesn't follow that because there is corroboration a jury must convict. That is an error into which a jury may easily fall...Even though there is corroboration in a case the jury must still ask themselves whether, with the corroboration, the guilt of the defendant has been proved beyond all reasonable doubt." (the relevant part of his direction is set out at p.508 of the judgment of the Court of Criminal Appeal). See also, *S v Hlapezula* 1965 (4) SA 439 at 440 (*per* Holmes JA: "Satisfaction of the cautionary rule does not necessarily warrant a conviction, for the ultimate requirement is proof beyond reasonable doubt and this depends upon an appraisal of all the evidence".

[331] A case where an appeal court was satisfied that this had occurred is *McNee v Kay* [1953] VLR 520 at 536.

[332] See *R. v McKay* [1963] NZLR 407 at 409, where Haslam J emphasised that "the direction relating to corroboration must be given in such a manner as not to obscure the fundamental requirement that the verdict of the jury be based upon a consideration of the whole of the evidence."

[333] *People (DPP) v Ward*, unreported, Special Criminal Court, 27 November 1998.

[334] *People (DPP) v Ward*, unreported, Court of Criminal Appeal, 22 March 2002. It is pertinent to

4–96   Another major problem with the warning is that of over-breadth.[335] The hardening of the warning into a rule of practice was criticised on this basis by Joy CB, a judge of the Irish Court of Exchequer, over a century and a half ago[336]:

> "Why the case of an accomplice should require a particular rule for itself; why it should not, like that of every other witness of whose credit there is an impeachment, be left to the unfettered discretion of the judge, to deal with as the circumstances of each particular case may require, seems difficult to explain. Why a fixed, unvarying rule should be applied to a subject which admits of such endless variety as the credit of witnesses, seems hardly reconcilable to the principles of reason. But, that a judge…should come prepared beforehand, to advise the jury to reject without consideration such evidence, even though judge and jury should be perfectly convinced of its truth, seems to be a violation of the principles of common sense, the dictates of morality, and the sanctity of a juror's oath…"

4–97   To similar effect, Dickson J in *Vetrovec v R*.[337] said that "[t]o construct a universal rule singling out accomplices … is to fasten upon this branch of the law of evidence a blind and empty formalism."[338]

4–98   A number of justifications for the rule have already been examined but none of them justifies the scope and blanket nature of the rule. First, it is argued that an accomplice may hope to obtain more favourable treatment by helping the prosecution to convict his or her confederates. However, grants of immunity are a rare occurrence and in the many cases where the accomplice has already been dealt with, he or she will have little to gain from giving false testimony.[339] With regard to the argument that an accomplice may attempt to minimise his or her involvement in the crime, this will not always be the case. The accomplice may well confess the full extent of his or her participation or it may be clear from the evidence that he or she only played a minor role.[340] In addition, the incentive of the witness to lie in order to shift the blame varies with the nature of the offence and the severity of punishment.[341] However, the undiscriminating application of the rule does not take account of such nuances.

4–99   As for the danger that an accomplice may falsely accuse someone out of spite or revenge, this motive will only be present in a very small minority of cases,[342] and the

---

note the comments of the Court of Criminal Appeal that one merit of the non-jury system was that, where an error occurred in the judgment of the court, it could be corrected on appeal whereas a comparable error in a decision reached by a jury might not be detected.

[335] Over-breadth was one of the main criticisms levelled by the CLRC against the warning (*Eleventh Report,* para.183). See also, the Law Commission, *Working Paper on Corroboration*, para.4.7 and *Report on Corroboration*, para.2.7.

[336] Joy, *On the Evidence of Accomplices* (Dublin: Milliken & Son, 1836), p.4.

[337] [1982] 1 SCR 811, (1982) 136 DLR (3d) 89 at 99.

[338] See also, Wigmore, *Evidence* 3rd edn (Boston: Little Brown and Company, 1940), VII, § 2057: "credibility is a matter of elusive variety, and it is impossible and anachronistic to determine in advance that, with or without promise, a given man's story must be distrusted".

[339] Wigmore, *Evidence* 3rd edn (Boston: Little Brown and Company, 1940), VII, § 2057, pointed out that: "The promise of immunity, then, being the essential element of distrust, but not being invariably made, no invariable rule should be fixed as though it had been made. Moreover, if made, its influence must vary infinitely with the nature of the charge and the personality of the accomplice."

[340] *Vetrovec v R* [1982] 1 SCR 811, (1982) 136 DLR (3d) 89 at 98.

[341] Joy, *On the Evidence of Accomplices* (Dublin: Milliken & Son, 1836), p.14, criticised the rule on the basis that it applied "with equal force to the accomplice who may apprehend but a month's imprisonment for the most trifling petit larceny, and to him who may reasonably dread murder for an atrocious murder".

[342] In the opinion of Wigmore, *Evidence* 3rd edn (Boston: Little Brown and Company, 1940), VII,

same can be said of the concern that an accomplice will lie in order to protect his or her friends.[343] Lastly, the notion that an accomplice is morally culpable and therefore his or her evidence must be distrusted does not stand up to scrutiny. The testimony of other criminals is accepted without automatically requiring a warning as to their credit.[344] Also, the moral culpability of an accomplice must vary with the nature of the crime and the degree of his or her involvement in it.[345]

4–100   Despite the fact that these dangers will not be operable in every case and indeed, there will be many cases where none are present, the warning must be given in every case irrespective of the circumstances of the case and the judge's assessment of the credibility of the accomplice. There may be cases where the judge is quite satisfied that none of the accomplice dangers are present and that he or she is an honest and credible witness desirous of telling the truth. However, the judge must still warn the jury that it is dangerous to rely on his or her evidence.

4–101   At a more conceptual level, it can be argued that the over-breadth of the accomplice warning is an impermissible interference with the fact-finding function of the jury. Under Art.38.5, this function is committed exclusively to the jury. They should be free to exercise this function in an untrammelled fashion except where it is necessary to direct them to exercise caution because of a demonstrable danger attaching to a particular category of evidence. However, the category of accomplice evidence does not satisfy this criterion. All that can be said is that some accomplices may be untrustworthy and may fabricate evidence. But the reasons why they may do so will not be present in every case and therefore, any rule predicated on the assumption that they will, is, of necessity, over-broad and an interference with the role of the jury. This is not to suggest that the accomplice warning as currently formulated would be found to be unconstitutional but the constitutional considerations serve to emphasise that the breadth of the warning requires justification.

4–102   Furthermore, the mere existence of motives to fabricate evidence is not a sufficient justification for the warning. Many witnesses have motives to fabricate evidence, yet their evidence is not automatically subject to a corroboration warning. What is required is a demonstration that the normal trial mechanisms for detecting false testimony are less effective with regard to accomplice testimony and that the jury are less capable of discerning false evidence given by accomplices than that given by other witnesses.[346]

4–103   At first glance, it would seem that they should be equal to the task. An accomplice will be subject to cross-examination which will test and challenge the consistency and truthfulness of his or her testimony. If it is thought that any of the motives for falsehood outlined above may be operating, then these can be put to the accomplice. These motives are all cognisable and readily understandable by the jury

---

§ 2057, the "extreme case of the wretch who fabricates merely for the malicious desire to drag others down in his own ruin can be no foundation for a general rule".

[343] Joy, *On the Evidence of Accomplices* (Dublin: Milliken & Son, 1836), p.14, commented that "friendship is not the bond which unites associates in crime; and the accomplice who avows his own guilt, will not feel much disposition to conceal that of his associates".

[344] *Vetrovec v R.* [1982] 1 SCR 811, (1982) 136 DLR (3d) 89 at 99.

[345] Joy, *On the Evidence of Accomplices* (Dublin: Milliken & Son, 1836), p.4.

[346] Dennis, "Corroboration Requirements Reconsidered" [1984] Crim LR 316 at 323.

who will have the opportunity to observe the demeanour of the accomplice and assess his or her credibility. Applying the burden of proof, if there are any doubts as to the credibility of the accomplice, these will be resolved in favour of the accused.[347] Thus, it would seem that the jury is sufficiently equipped to weigh accomplice testimony without being armed with a complex, technical and in many cases, incomprehensible warning.[348]

4–104   However, it is argued that these various filtering mechanisms are nullified by the accomplice's insider knowledge of the offence.[349] This is what sets accomplices apart from other potentially unreliable witnesses and justifies the application of a special warning. Armed with his or her inside knowledge of the crime, the accomplice may be able to weave a detailed and consistent though ultimately false narrative, fooling not only the jury but also the judge, hence the necessity for the mandatory rule which ensures that a warning is given in every case. As Mirfield puts it, the choice is "between a rule which, like all other rules, will be over-inclusive and a discretion which may be inappropriately exercised".[350] Viewed in this way, the mandatory warning is as much a check on trial judges as it is on juries.[351]

4–105   This argument would be persuasive if the warning actually achieved its stated aim. However, it is highly debatable whether the warning as currently structured does confer any additional protection upon innocent defendants.[352] This is because the warning is fundamentally illogical.[353] The prohibitive part of the warning tells the jury that it is dangerous to convict on the uncorroborated evidence of an accomplice but the permissive part then allows them to do precisely that. Thus, the permissive part of the direction significantly undercuts the protection conferred by the prohibitive part and, if the accomplice's false narrative is so convincing that it emerges unscathed from cross-examination, then it is likely that the jury will act upon it and convict despite the warning.

4–106   Indeed, the view has been expressed that the warning may well be counter-

---

[347] See *e.g. People (DPP) v Power*, unreported, Court of Criminal Appeal, 31 July 1975, where the Court upheld a direction of the trial judge in which he had instructed the jury that, if they had "any doubt whatsoever" about the veracity or reliability of the accomplices, they must give the benefit of the doubt to the accused.

[348] The Law Reform Commission of Canada, *Report on Evidence*, p.108, was of the opinion that judges and juries "have the necessary experience and common sense to evaluate the testimony before them, and in doing so to take into account such matters as its source and the fact that it is unsupported by other evidence".

[349] *Cf. R. v Sheehan* (1826) Jebb CC 54 at 57.

[350] Mirfield, "An Alternative Future for Corroboration Warnings" (1991) 107 LQR 450 at 452. He criticises the assumption that the flexibility allowed by a discretion is always to be preferred.

[351] See Carter, "Corroboration Requirements Reconsidered: Two Comments" [1985] Crim LR 143 at 145.

[352] One empirical study indicated that giving a corroboration warning resulted in only a small decrease in convictions (see Hans and Brooks, "Effects of corroboration instructions in a rape case on experimental juries" (1977) 15 Osgoode Hall LJ 701 at 715). An earlier study indicated that an accused was actually more likely to be convicted if a corroboration warning was given but the results were obtained from a very small sample (see LSE Jury Project, "Juries and the Rules of Evidence" [1973] Crim LR 208 at 219–221).

[353] CLRC, *Eleventh Report*, para.181; Law Commission, *Working Paper on Corroboration*, para.4.7, *Report on Corroboration*, para.2.9.

productive. The jury may ignore it because they view it as anomalous,[354] or because it is simply too complex,[355] with the result that the jury do not exercise the requisite caution and the trial judge achieves the contrary effect to that intended. In *Vetrovec v R.*,[356] Dickson J also adverted to the problem of the accused being "in the unhappy position of hearing the judge draw particular attention to the evidence which tends to confirm the testimony the accomplice has given. Cogent prejudicial testimony is thus repeated and highlighted."[357]

4–107 The warning can also have the effect of subverting the presumption of innocence. This is because in many cases, before the jury can employ the warning, they must be satisfied that an offence occurred and that the witness was involved, *i.e.* that the witness comes within the definition of an accomplice. In some cases, especially where some form of joint enterprise is alleged, a conclusion that the witness was involved may very well lead to an almost irresistible inference that the accused was also involved.[358]

4–108 The merit of these arguments has been implicitly recognised by the courts in their refusal to extend the warning requirement to other categories of evidence which pose problems of reliability equal to or perhaps greater than that of accomplices.[359] This lack of faith in the corroboration warning on the part of those who devised it is, perhaps, the most eloquent argument in favour of reform. It is thought that the problems posed by other categories of unreliable evidence can be adequately dealt with by means of a cautionary instruction that is tailored to the facts and deals with the particular deficiencies of the evidence in the case. If this is so, then why is a mandatory sweeping corroboration warning required for accomplices?

4–109 In light of the problems highlighted above, it is submitted that the best course of action would be to abolish the corroboration warning completely and, instead, for

---

[354] See *R. v Chance* [1988] QB 932 at 941–942, [1988] 3 All ER 225 at 231 (*per* Roch J), if the trial judge "is required to apply rigid rules, there will inevitably be occasions when the direction will be inappropriate to the facts. Juries are quick to spot such anomalies, and will understandably view the anomaly, and often (as a result) the rest of the directions, with suspicion, thus undermining the judge's purpose. Directions on corroboration are particularly subject to this danger". See also, the Tasmanian Law Reform Commission, *Report and Recommendations on the Law and Practice relating to Corroboration, with particular reference to the evidence of Treason, Bigamy, Perjury, Forgery, Child Witnesses, Victims in Sex Cases, and Accomplices* (Report No.21) (1978), p.14, which expressed the concern that a corroboration warning "may well result in resentment, and, either intentionally or unintentionally, or even subconsciously, this may operate to the detriment of an accused person".

[355] *Cf. per* Lord Diplock in *DPP v Hester* [1973] AC 296 at 327–328, [1972] 3 All ER 1056 at 1075, "to incorporate in the summing-up a general disquisition on the law of corroboration in the sort of language used by lawyers, may make the summing-up immune to appeal on a point of law, but it is calculated to confuse a jury of laymen and, if it does not pass so far over their heads that when they reach the jury room they simply rely on their native common sense, may...as respects the weight to be attached to evidence requiring corroboration, have the contrary effect to a sensible warning couched in ordinary language directed to the facts of the particular case."

[356] [1982] 1 SCR 811, (1982) 136 DLR (3d) 89 at 95.

[357] See also, *DPP v Hester* [1973] AC 296 at 327–328, [1972] 3 All ER 1056 at 1075, where Lord Diplock expressed the fear that a technical corroboration warning might "have the contrary effect to a sensible warning couched in ordinary language directed to the facts of the particular case".

[358] See *People (AG) v Ryan* (1966) 1 Frewen 304, where an argument along these lines was made but failed on the facts.

[359] See *People (AG) v Casey (No.2)* [1963] IR 33 (identification evidence) and *People (DPP) v Quilligan (No.3)* [1993] 2 IR 305.

a trial judge to adopt an approach similar to that taken in respect of identification evidence (which is outlined in detail below). Thus, whenever the prosecution case is based wholly or substantially on accomplice testimony, it would be necessary for the judge to consider not only whether there was sufficient evidence to prove each of the elements of the charge but also whether it was probative and credible enough to found a conviction. If the testimony of the accomplice was very unreliable and not worthy of credit, then the trial judge could exercise his or her jurisdiction to withdraw such evidence from the jury on the basis that it could not safely ground a verdict. However, because assessment of the credibility of witnesses and the weight to be attached to their evidence is a matter particularly within the province of the jury, this course of action would only be adopted in extreme cases.

4–110   In other cases, the evidence could be left to the jury accompanied by a cautionary instruction, where appropriate. Consistent with the constitutional duty of a trial judge, the risk of a miscarriage of justice, which would depend on the circumstances of the case, would be determinative of both the need for, and the content of, the cautionary instruction.[360] In a given case, the trial judge might point out that the evidence of a given witness was potentially unreliable, explain the reasons why, and then issue an instruction to the jury to examine his or her evidence with great care and exercise caution before acting on it.[361]

4–111   The central point is that these responses to the problems posed by accomplice testimony would be dictated by and moulded by the circumstances of the case. Such an approach would have the advantage of focusing the minds of both the judge and the jury upon the essential question of whether there was sufficient probative and reliable evidence upon which to find the accused guilty. The jury would benefit from a direction grounded in the facts of the case which directed their attention to the potential frailties of the evidence before them. Any caution given could also be interwoven more easily with the other directions given by the judge, especially that on the burden of proof, so that the jury were clear as to their duty and how to discharge it.

4–112   An example of such an approach can be seen in the jurisprudence of the Canadian courts.[362] In *Vetrovec v R*,[363] the mandatory corroboration warning was abolished. It was held that, instead, where there was a concern about the reliability

---

[360]   *Per* Kingsmill Moore J in *People (AG) v Casey (No.2)* [1963] IR 33: "It is the function of a judge in his charge to give to the jury such direction and warnings as may in his opinion be necessary to avoid the danger of an innocent man being convicted, and the nature of such directions and warnings must depend on the facts of the particular case." See also, *Bromley v R.* (1986) 161 CLR 315 at 325 (*per* Brennan J), "[t]he possibility of a miscarriage of justice is both the occasion for the giving of a warning and the determinant of its content".

[361]   *Cf.* the approach to the evidence of accomplices and sexual complainants laid down in *R. v Makanjuola* [1995] 3 All ER 730, [1995] 1 WLR 1348 (and approved in the context of sexual complaints in *People (DPP) v JEM* [2001] 4 IR 385) and the approach to the evidence of accomplices advocated in *Vetrovec v R.* [1982] 1 SCR 811, (1982) 136 DLR (3d) 89 and elaborated and applied in cases including *R. v Babinski* [1992] 3 SCR 467, and *R. v Bevan* [1993] 2 SCR 599.

[362]   See also the approach adopted in the UK post the abolition of the corroboration warnings by s.32 of the Criminal Justice and Public Order Act 1994 where the giving of warnings is now governed by the principles laid down in *R. v Makanjuola* [1995] 3 All ER 730, [1995] 1 WLR 1348. Accordingly, whether a warning is given and, if so, its terms are dictated by the circumstances of the case (see *R. v Causley* [1999] Crim LR 572).

[363]   [1982] 1 SCR 811.

of the evidence of a witness, trial judges should include in their charges "a clear and sharp warning to attract the attention of the juror[s] to the risks of adopting, without more, the evidence of the witness".[364] However, not only was no particular language required in that regard, the trial judge was enjoined from including in the warning any legal definition of "corroboration" when explaining to the jury the type of evidence that is capable of supporting the testimony of the tainted witness.

4-113 Further guidance as to the circumstances in which such a cautionary instruction should be given and its contents were given by the Canadian Supreme Court in *R. v Khela*[365] which took the opportunity to provide a principled framework for instructing juries in relation to the evidence of evidence of witnesses whose evidence was considered to be "unsavoury", "untrustworthy", "unreliable", or "tainted" *viz.* "witnesses who, because of their amoral character, criminal lifestyle, past dishonesty or interest in the outcome of the trial, cannot be trusted to tell the truth-even when they have expressly undertaken by oath or affirmation to do so".[366] The framework has two purposes: first, to alert the jury to the danger of relying on the unsupported evidence of such witnesses and to explain the reasons for special scrutiny of their testimony; and second, in appropriate cases, to give the jury the tools necessary to identify evidence capable of enhancing the trustworthiness of these witnesses.[367] Delivering the majority judgment, Fish J identified four elements of the warning, which were not to be applied in a rigid and formulaic fashion: (1) drawing the attention of the jury to the testimonial evidence requiring special scrutiny; (2) explaining why this evidence is subject to special scrutiny; (3) cautioning the jury that it is dangerous to convict on unconfirmed evidence of this sort, though the jury is entitled to do so if satisfied that the evidence is true; and (4) that the jury, in determining the veracity of the suspect evidence, should look for evidence from another source tending to show that the untrustworthy witness is telling the truth as to the guilt of the accused.[368]

D. Evidence of Witnesses who have Obtained Benefits

1. Introduction

4-114 Considerable controversy has arisen in relation to the use of the evidence of witnesses, usually accomplices, who have received benefits, including participation in the witness protection programme and monetary payments. Such evidence can raise acute problems in terms of its reliability necessitating the taking of particular care before acting on foot of it.

2. Accomplices who have Received Benefits

4-115 The use of testimony from participants in criminal acts who had obtained benefits, such as a grant of immunity from prosecution, as part of an agreement to testify

---

[364] [1982] 1 SCR 811 at 831. This subsequently became known as a *Vetrovec* warning.
[365] [2009] SCC 4, [2009] 1 SCR 104. See the comment by Pattenden at (2009) 13 E & P 243.
[366] [2009] SCC 4, [2009] 1 SCR 104 at [3] (*per* Fish J).
[367] [2009] SCC 4, [2009] 1 SCR 104 at [47].
[368] [2009] SCC 4, [2009] 1 SCR 104 at [37]–[38]. See further, Bryant, Lederman & Fuerst, *Sopinka, Lederman & Bryant: The Law of Evidence in Canada*, 4th edn, (Lexis Nexis, 2014) at §17.1–§17.20.

against others who had allegedly committed criminal offences came to prominence in Northern Ireland in the 1980's where prosecutions were brought and convictions obtained for terrorist offences on the basis of was known as "supergrass" evidence. A "supergrass" in this context was defined as "a terrorist informer who turns Queen's evidence against his alleged former associates, often ... having been granted immunity in respect of his own serious crimes and entertaining a clear expectation of a new life in different surroundings for himself and his family".[369] The reasons why such evidence is particularly unreliable and falls into a special category of untrustworthiness were outlined in *R. v Crumley*[370]:

> "a supergrass is no ordinary criminal and no ordinary accomplice. Therefore, to the extent that what is known about the supergrass's character and situation increases the probability that he will be an unreliable witness, the danger of acting on his uncorroborated evidence is increased.... He is not just a cornered criminal, who is reluctantly disgorging information to save himself from enduring the penalty of perhaps one moderately serious crime, but he has volunteered a veritable mass of damning information against men whom he alleges to have been his confederates, to whom and with whom he is bound by an oath to further a joint cause which he no doubt regarded as patriotic. His motive may be fear, despair or hope of an enormously improved life for the future, or a mixture of the three: Wherever the truth lies, his motive is extremely powerful. It is manifest that the evidence of such a witness must stand up successfully to the sternest criteria before it can be acceptable and become the sole basis for being satisfied beyond reasonable doubt that any accused is guilty of any offence charged against him."[371]

4–116   The approach to be adopted to incentivised accomplice testimony in this jurisdiction arose for consideration in *People (DPP) v Ward*,[372] the first of a number of cases arising from the murder of Veronica Guerin.[373] The accused had been convicted on the uncorroborated evidence of an accomplice, Charles Bowden. At the trial in the Special Criminal Court, Bowden's testimony was attacked on the basis that he was a "supergrass" and, as such, his testimony had to be approached with even greater reserve and suspicion than that of an ordinary accomplice and should be rejected by the Court as utterly unreliable. However, the Court, having examined whether Bowden should be characterised as an "ordinary" accomplice or a supergrass, decided that they were dealing with the former. That conclusion did not, of course, dispose of the concerns about the reliability of Bowden's evidence. As an "ordinary" accomplice, the normal corroboration warning applied and the Court expressed itself to be "deeply mindful of the fundamental principle of criminal law that it is unsafe to act upon the evidence of an accomplice which is not corroborated in some material particular implicating the accused". The Court acknowledged that Bowden was "a self-serving, deeply

---

[369] *Per* Hutton LJ in *R. v Crumley* (1986) 14 NIJB 1.

[370] Unreported, Northern Ireland Court of Appeal, 1984, at 13 (this passage is quoted by Lord Lowry LCJ in *R. v Steenson* (1986) 17 NIJB 36 at 49–50).

[371] The approach to be taken to supergrass evidence following the abrogation of the accomplice corroboration warning in England and Wales (by s.32 of the Criminal Justice and Public Order Act 1994) and in Northern Ireland (by art.45 of the Criminal Justice (NI) Order 1996) was considered in was considered in *R. v Percival (Ricky John)* [2010] EWCA Crim 1326 and *R. v Haddock* [2012] NICC 3 respectively. The use of supergrass evidence in the UK courts and the problems arising therefrom have been examined by Martin, "The recent supergrass controversy: have we learnt from the troubled past?" [2013] Crim LR 273.

[372] Unreported, Special Criminal Court, 27 November 1998; unreported, Court of Criminal Appeal, 22 March 2002.

[373] See also *People (DPP) v Meehan*, unreported, Special Criminal Court, 29 July 1999, [2006] IECCA 104, [2006] 3 IR 468; *People (DPP) v Gilligan*, unreported, Court of Criminal Appeal, 8 August 2003, [2005] IESC 78, [2006] 1 IR 107.

avaricious and potentially vicious criminal" who was, by his own admission, a liar who "would lie without hesitation and regardless of the consequences for others if he perceived it to be in his own interest to do so". It was also conscious of the benefits, including immunity from prosecution for Veronica Guerin's murder, which had accrued to Bowden by reason of his decision to turn State's evidence but took the view that he would appreciate that, in order to achieve these benefits, it would be in his best interest to tell the truth about the murder and the gang's criminal enterprise.

4–117 On the crucial question as to whether Bowden was truthful in describing the accused's part in the murder, the Court was satisfied that his evidence was consistent with the known facts and had "a strong ring of truth about it". Neither was there anything in the evidence which raised a suspicion that Bowden had a motive of self-interest to lie about the accused and wrongly implicate him in the murder. The Court was therefore "satisfied beyond reasonable doubt that Bowden's evidence implicating the accused in the crime [was] correct and ought to be accepted as truthful".[374]

4–118 The approach and the conclusions of the Special Criminal Court in *Ward* were open to criticism on a number of grounds particularly because of the distinction drawn by the Court between "ordinary accomplices" and "supergrasses".[375] That approach proceeded on the implicit basis that there is a neat distinction to be drawn between the two and that the categorisation of Bowden as an "ordinary" accomplice was, in some way, determinative of his credibility. However, no such neat categorisation is possible or indeed desirable because it focuses on a formalistic label to the detriment of a proper assessment of the factors bearing on the credibility of the accomplice. Instead, what is required in each case is an assessment, having regard to the dangers outlined above and all the circumstances of the case, of the creditworthiness and reliability of accomplice testimony. It is arguable that the Court, having satisfied itself that he was not a "supergrass", then fell into error in not having sufficient regard to his acknowledged propensity and the powerful incentives he had to lie in assessing whether his evidence was reliable enough to ground a conviction without corroboration.

4–119 It is not surprising, therefore, that the accused's appeal against conviction was successful. The Court of Criminal Appeal attached little if any importance to the label to be attached to Bowden. Instead, the Court, in a judgment delivered by Murphy J, focused instead on the factors that bore on the reliability of his testimony:

> "It was the unequivocal finding of the Special Criminal Court and it was the frank and unavoidable admission of Mr Bowden himself that he was an inveterate liar. In addition to lies, the cross-examination exposed a variety of errors and inaccuracies in the evidence given against the accused. Some of these were of particular importance. The credibility of Charles Bowden as a witness was further compromised by the fact that he was an accomplice in the particular crime of which Paul Ward was accused. But he was much more than that. He was a witness to whom immunity was granted in respect of the murder of which he had, in effect, confessed and in addition he, his wife and his children were, understandably, afforded the benefit of the witness protection programme under which he was to be given the opportunity of living in a different jurisdiction with a new identity and some unspecified income. The law has always recognised that the evidence of an accomplice—even an accomplice who appears to be a credible witness—must be corroborated from independent sources or alternatively that

---

[374] Unreported, Special Criminal Court, 27 November 1998 at 34.
[375] For an excellent analysis of the decision of the Special Criminal Court in *Ward* and the problems raised by the use of supergrass testimony, see Ingoldsby, "Supergrass Testimony and Reasonable Doubt: An Examination of *D.P.P. v Ward*" (1999) 2 TCLR 29.

the jury should be warned, or a tribunal of fact reminded, of the dangers of acting without such corroboration. Whether or not Charles Bowden fell within the category compromised in the slang expression 'supergrass', clearly his general lack of credibility and his position as a criminal negotiating with the authorities to secure advantages for himself at the expense of his former friends and criminal associates did require that his evidence should be considered with the utmost care."[376]

4–120   The Court went on to express its scepticism as to whether "one could be confident of eliminating all factors which would motivate and encourage liars, such as Mr Bowden, so as to justify a belief beyond all reasonable doubt in any evidence given by him".[377] However, the Court appeared to stop short of laying down a rule that an accused could not be convicted on the uncorroborated evidence of an incentivised accomplice.[378]

3. Witnesses in the Witness Protection Programme

4–121   A somewhat broader issue as to the lawfulness and admissibility of the evidence of accomplices who had obtained benefits in return for their agreement to give evidence through participation in the witness protection programme arose in *People (DPP) v Gilligan*.[379] The applicant had been convicted by the Special Criminal Court of importation of drugs and possession with intention to supply but acquitted of the murder of Veronica Guerin. The case against him depended, to a considerable extent, on the testimony of three accomplices who had been members of a criminal gang of which he was the alleged head and who were participants in the witness protection programme which had been established in order to secure their testimony and which involved them obtaining various incentives. He appealed his conviction on the basis, *inter alia*, that this accomplice evidence had been obtained by offering incentives to the witnesses including participation in the witness protection programme and, therefore, should have been excluded as illegally obtained evidence.

4–122   The Court of Criminal Appeal accepted that it was necessary for the prosecuting authorities to offer protection to certain witnesses which necessarily involves the offering of benefits to such witnesses and held that there was nothing unlawful in doing so. Nonetheless, the Court was satisfied that, if there was an agreement between a witness and the prosecution that he would give certain specific evidence in return for specified payments of money, such evidence would be unlawfully obtained and could be excluded:

"Clearly in seeking to ensure the preservation of public order and the protection of the public, the Gardaí and the prosecuting authorities are entitled to offer protection to witnesses who might be intimidated or fearful that if they gave evidence there would be serious reprisals against them or their family. This in itself necessarily also involves the offering of benefits to such witnesses. They cannot be fully protected unless they are given benefits. That is in the nature of a witness protection programme. If it is not unlawful to offer some benefits,

---

[376]   Unreported, Court of Criminal Appeal, 22 March 2002 at12.
[377]   Unreported, Court of Criminal Appeal, 22 March 2002 at14.
[378]   In the UK, s.73 of the Serious Organised Crime and Police Act 2005 provides a statutory foundation for entering into binding agreements with offenders. The evidence of persons with whom such agreements are reached and who receive benefits on foot thereof will be the subject of a warning of the dangers arising but there is no requirement for a corroboration warning: *R. v Daniels* [2011] 1 Cr App R 18.
[379]   Unreported, Court of Criminal Appeal, 8 August 2003, [2005] IESC 78, [2006] 1 IR 107. See also *People (DPP) v Meehan* [2006] IECCA 104, [2006] 3 IR 468.

then the question arises whether it may become unlawful to offer benefits beyond a certain degree. There is no doubt that if there is an agreement between a witness and the Gardaí or the prosecuting authorities that he will give certain specific evidence and in return will be paid a specific amount of money, that evidence is unlawfully obtained and may be excluded."[380]

4–123   The Court did not, however, believe that this was the situation in the case before it and the contention that the accomplices had been bribed or their testimony "bought" was not borne out by the evidence in the case. The Court went on to highlight a number of "very disturbing factors" in the way in which the authorities had sought to obtain the evidence of the accomplices including a failure on the part of Gardaí to keep notes of meetings with the witnesses and the return of monies that could only have been the proceeds of crime. However, it rejected the contention that their evidence was so suspect as to be rendered inadmissible.[381]

4–124   The judgment of the court of trial was criticised on the basis that it had misdirected itself in relation to the issue of corroboration. However, it was pointed out by the Court of Criminal Appeal that corroboration was not essential and, thus, the court of trial had been entitled to look for and place reliance upon evidence supporting the testimony of the accomplices but which fell short of corroboration in the technical sense. Having reviewed the judgment of the court of trial, the Court was satisfied that it had adequately identified and safeguarded against the dangers of acting on the evidence of the accomplices in the case, and upheld the conviction of the applicant.

4–125   On appeal to the Supreme Court, the accountability and transparency of the witness protection programme that had been operated by the Gardaí was criticised and it was contended that the admission of evidence of the witnesses who were participating in the witness protection programme was incompatible with the guarantee in Art.38.1 of a trial in due course of law. However, in a judgment delivered by Denham J, the Supreme Court rejected the proposition that the evidence of a participant in the witness protection programme was inadmissible. She accepted that witness protection programmes were necessary in order to prosecute certain types of crime and that many cases could not be brought without the evidence of an accomplice or a person in a witness protection programme. She was satisfied that there was no legal reason why such a programme could not be established but said that the conditions of participation should be clearly set out and there should not be any variations which were, or could be perceived to be, related to the giving of evidence.[382] Accordingly, there was no rule excluding such evidence and the ordinary rules of admissibility applied although such evidence should be excluded if the circumtances fell below the fundamental standard of fairness.[383]

4–126   She noted that the witness protection programme at issue in that case was the first such programme in the State and said that there was no doubt but that it was not well organised or executed and had deficiencies. However, she did not consider

---

[380] Unreported, Court of Criminal Appeal, 8 August 2003, at 9–10 (*per* McCracken J).
[381] Reference was made to the Northern Irish cases of *R. v Crumley* [1986] NI 66 and *R. v Steenson*, unreported, Court of Appeal, 23 December 1986, and while the Court believed that these cases were of limited relevance because they dealt with "supergrass" evidence, it was pointed out that, even in the extreme case of "supergrass" witnesses, the courts did not rule out the possibility of a conviction based solely on the evidence of a supergrass.
[382] [2005] IESC 78 at [149], [2006] 1 IR 107 at 162.
[383] [2005] IESC 78 at [150], [2006] 1 IR 107 at 163.

that these deficiencies were fatal to the admissiblity of the evidence.[384] While the shortcomings in how the programme had been administered had compromised the evidence of two of the witnesses, she agreed with the Special Criminal Court that they had not been such as to compromise the criminal justice system so as to render their evidence inadmissible.

4–127 The learned judge noted that a participant in a witness protection programme receives benefits from the State. Consequently, as with accomplice testimony, there were good reasons why such evidence should be approached with caution[385]:

> "The rationale behind the common law rule requiring a warning before acting upon the uncorroborated evidence of an accomplice applies equally to the evidence of a person in, or who is going to join, a witness protection programme. There is a danger that the witness may not tell the truth in the hope of receiving benefits. In relation to the witness protection programme this applies also to expectations the witness may have into the future for him or herself and their family. Thus there is the danger that the witness may seek to obtain additional benefits by his or her evidence. There are dangers especially where there has been a grant of immunity and/or the prosecution has supported the giving of a light sentence. These and other factors may arise in relaiton to a witness in a witness protection programme."

4–128 Accordingly, in order to ensure a fair trial, such evidence should be approached in the same manner as accomplice testimony and was required to be the subject of a corroboration warning and, adapting the exposition of Butler J in *Dental Board v O'Callaghan*,[386] she summarised the position by saying that[387]:

> "[T]here is no rule of law to the effect that the uncorroborated evidence of a person in or going into a witness protection programme must be rejected. The rule should be that the trier of fact must clearly bear in mind and be warned that it is dangerous to convict on the evidence of such a witness unless it is corroborated; but having borne that in mind and having given due weight to the warning, if the evidence is none the less so clearly acceptable that the trier of fact is satisfied beyond reasonable doubt of the guilt of the accused to the extent that the danger which is generally inherent in acting on the evidence of a witness in a witness protection programme is not present in the case, then the trier of fact may act upon the evidence and convict."

4–129 She elaborated later in her judgment that[388]:

> "The testimony of a person in receipt of a benefit from the State, such as a witness protection programme, should be viewed with caution. Such evidence is not inadmissible but the reality of benefit for the witness requires a cautious approach and may reduce the weight which may be attached to such evidence. Such evidence is comparable to the evidence of an accomplice as, both an accomplice and a person receiving benefit from a witness protection programme have a potential motive to perjure himself. It appears to me that the appropriate approach for a court to take to such evidence includes: (a) the testimony from persons receiving a benefit should be viewed with caution; (b) while such evidence is not inadmissible it should be scrutinised carefully; (c) the credibility of such a witness should be analysed in light of all the evidence in the case; (d) all the facts and factors of the case should be analysed to determine the weight, if any, to be given to the evidence; (e) the trial judge should give a warning to a jury of the dangers of relying on such evidence without corroboration; (f) once the warning is given, however, the trier of fact may determine the appropriate weight to be attached to such evidence and may convict in the absence of corroborative evidence; (g) corroborative evidence may include circumstantial evidence."

4–130 She also considered that the Special Criminal Court had applied the analysis

---

[384] [2005] IESC 78 at [91], [2006] 1 IR 107 at 143.
[385] [2005] IESC 78 at [73], [2006] 1 IR 107 at 138–139.
[386] [1969] IR 181 at 184.
[387] [2005] IESC 78 at [74], [2006] 1 IR 107 at 139.
[388] [2005] IESC 78 at [117], [2006] 1 IR 107 at 151.

suggested by her and had adopted a careful and cautious approach to the evidence of the witnesses who were participants in the witness protection programme.

4–131 The dangers of convicting on foot of the evidence of a participant in the witness protection programme are obviously multiplied where, as is generally the case, the witness is also an accomplice. In that case, the presence or absence of corroboration becomes even more important but it remains the position that there is no rule of law requiring corroboration and it is open to the tribunal of fact to convict absent corroboration. Denham J explained that[389]:

> "These multiple factors go to the issues of credibility and to the weight to be attached to the evidence. Thus they should be assessed in light of all the circumstances of the case. However, it is open to the trier of fact to determine that inspite of these multiple factors the credibility of a witness is such that corroboration is not required and that significant weight may be given to his evidence."

4–132 She was satisfied that the dangers of convicting on evidence from persons who were both in a witness protection programme and who were accomplices had been adequately considered by the Special Criminal Court. Accordingly, she dismissed the appeal.

4–133 An appeal against a conviction for murder on foot of the evidence of an accomplice who was in a witness protection programme also failed in *People (DPP) v Kenny*.[390] The Court of Criminal Appeal was satisfied that the trial judge had followed the principles laid down in *Gilligan* and had correctly and adequately warned the jury that it was dangerous to rely on the evidence of the witness on the basis that he was an accomplice and was a participant in the witness protection programme. The Court rejected the contention that the trial judge had erred in that regard by not making a distinction between the nature of the warning that had to be given in respect of accomplice evidence and the nature of the warning that had to be given in respect of evidence under the witness protection programme.

4–134 However, an appeal on the basis that the trial judge had erred in relation to the corroboration warning given in respect of a witness who was a participant in the witness protection programme was successful in *DPP v Ryan*.[391] The trial judge had given a corroboration warning in respect of the witness on the conditional basis that it applied if the jury decided that he was an accomplice but refused to give a corroboration warning on the independent basis that he was in the witness protection programme. The Court of Appeal held that he had erred in that regard and that the decision of the Supreme Court in *Gilligan* was quite clear in requiring a corroboration warning to be given not just in respect of those who were accomplices but in respect of all witnesses in the witness protection programme because such a witness might be influenced directly, or indirectly, by benefits received:

> "The nature of the warning to be given to a jury is ... the same same as the warning to be given in the case of an accomplice although obviously it must be explained to the jury the reasons why, in the particular circumstances of the case, there is a need for such a warning. It is important that they understand that. Thus in the case of an accomplice simpliciter there may be a danger that the witness is seeking credit for his evidence in order to enjoy immunity

---

[389] [2005] IESC 78 at [87], [2006] 1 IR 107 at 143.
[390] [2006] IECCA 137. See (2007) 25(8) ILT 119.
[391] [2011] IECCA 6.

from prosecution or for the purpose of mitigating any punishment that might be imposed on him in the event of a conviction. In the case of a witness on a Witness Protection Programme a jury should be warned as to the desirability of corroboration because the witness might be motivated, in giving evidence, by the benefits to be received from that programme... Accordingly, the evidence of protected witnesses is a category of potentially unreliable evidence in its own right, separate and distinct from the evidence of accomplices. While the evidence of a protected witness, and particularly an innocent protected witness, may well be reliable, both prudence and the interests of justice require that it be received with caution."

4–135 Thus, while the trial judge had given the jury a corroboration warning on the basis that the witness might be an accomplice and had also instructed the jury to exercise caution as regards his evidence on the basis that he was in receipt of benefits from the witness protection programme, he had not, as he was required to do, given a corroboration warning on this basis. In the circumstances, the Court concluded that the verdict of the jury was unsafe.

E. Evidence of Complainants in Sexual Cases

1. Introduction

4–136 The courts have long been suspicious of the evidence of sexual complainants on the premise articulated by Hale that an accusation of a sexual offence is "an accusation easily to be made and hard to be proved and harder to be defended by the party accused, tho' never so innocent".[392] Thus, it was unsurprising that, following the establishment of the warning requirement with respect to accomplices, a rule of practice that juries should be warned of the dangers of acting on the uncorroborated evidence of complainants in sexual cases began to emerge.[393] Initially, the warning requirement was applied in rape cases but it was subsequently extended to all sexual offences,[394] and mirroring the development of the accomplice warning, the rule of practice quickly crystallised into a rule of law.[395]

4–137 Like the warning given with regard to accomplice evidence, the warning was a complex affair. First, the judge had to give the jury a clear and unambiguous warning that it was dangerous to convict on the uncorroborated evidence of a sexual complainant[396] but instruct them that, having taken the warning into account, they were

---

[392] Hale, *Pleas of the Crown* (1678) Vol. I, p.633. For an analysis and criticism of the justifications for the warning requirement, see McGrath, "Two Steps Forward, One Step Back: The Corroboration Warning in Sexual Cases" (1999) 9 ICLJ 16.

[393] The English Law Commission, *Corroboration of Evidence in Criminal Trials* (Working Paper No.15) (1990), Appendix A, Part II, para.13 (hereinafter "*Working Paper on Corroboration*"), attributes the emergence of the rule of practice to a number of statutes in the nineteenth century such as the Criminal Law (Amendment) Act 1885 which required corroboration. The application of these provisions gave rise to the general practice of giving a corroboration warning and this crystallised into a rule of practice in the decade or so following the creation of the English Court of Criminal Appeal in 1909. The Irish courts followed the lead given by their English counterparts and, by the time the Court of Criminal Appeal handed down its decision in *Attorney General v Corcoran* (1929) 63 ITLR 145, the warning was regarded as well established.

[394] See *Attorney General v Corcoran* (1929) 63 ITLR 145 and *People (AG) v Williams* [1940] IR 195.

[395] *People (AG) v Cradden* [1955] IR 130 at 139 (requirement of a corroboration warning was a rule of practice with the force of a rule of law).

[396] *Attorney General v KJM* (1949) 83 ILTSJ 154; *People (AG) v Cradden* [1955] IR 130 at 141. The degree and gravity of the warning varied with the circumstances of the case (*People (AG)*

entitled to convict if they were satisfied that the complainant was a truthful witness.[397] The judge then had to deal with the issue of corroboration. If there was no evidence capable of constituting corroboration, it sufficed to direct the jury that the evidence of the complainant was uncorroborated.[398] However, if potentially corroborative evidence did exist, then he or she had to go on to explain the nature of corroboration,[399] point out any potentially corroborative evidence,[400] and if necessary, warn the jury not to treat as corroboration any evidence which they might, in the absence of such a warning, mistakenly believe to have that quality, *e.g.* complaints admitted under the doctrine of recent complaint.[401]

4–138   However, the warning requirement in respect of sexual complainants was the subject of sustained criticism, not only because of its technicality and complexity but also because it was viewed as misogynistic in conception and application[402] and, acting on the recommendation of the Law Reform Commission,[403] and following the lead of other common law jurisdictions,[404] the warning requirement was abolished by s.7 of the Criminal Law (Rape) (Amendment) Act 1990, which provides as follows:

> "(1) Subject to any enactment relating to the corroboration of evidence in criminal proceedings,[405] where at the trial on indictment of a person charged with an offence of a sexual nature evidence is given by the person in relation to whom the offence is alleged to have been committed and, by reason only of the nature of the charge, there would, but for this section,

---

v Moore [1950] Ir Jur Rep 45 at 48) and the degree and gravity of the risk involved in accepting the uncorroborated evidence of the complainant (*Cradden*). No particular form of words was required (*Attorney General v Connick* (1942) 76 ITLR 173; *R. v Henry* (1968) 53 Cr App R 150 at 153; *R. v O'Reilly* [1967] 2 QB 722 at 727, [1967] 2 All ER 766 at 768; *R. v Turnsek* [1967] VR 610 at 614).

[397] *R. v Henry* (1968) 53 Cr App R 150 at 154.

[398] *Attorney General v KJM* (1949) 83 ILTSJ 154; *People (AG) v Moore* [1950] Ir Jur Rep 45 at 47; *R. v Donald* (1982) 7 A Crim R474 at 477.

[399] *People (AG) v Cradden* [1955] IR 130 at 141; *R. v Lindsay* (1977) 18 SASR 103 at 116.

[400] In straightforward cases, the trial judge had to draw the jury's attention to specific items of evidence which were capable of amounting to corroboration, but in more complex cases it was sufficient for the judge to refer to the broad categories of evidence which could be used as corroboration (see *R. v Sorby* [1986] VR 753 at 780; *R. v Sherrin (No.2)* (1979) 21 SASR 250 at 255–256). It was also important for the trial judge to make it clear to the jury that it was a matter for them to decide whether any item of evidence actually did corroborate the testimony of the complainant (*People (DPP) v Cornally*, Court of Criminal Appeal, *ex tempore*, 7 November 1994).

[401] *R. v Allen* [1965] 2 QB 295 at 302; [1964] 3 All ER 401 at 403; *R. v Lillyman* [1896] 2 QB 167 at 178.

[402] Temkin, "Towards a Modern Law of Rape" (1982) 45 MLR 399 at 418, took the view that the warning was highly insulting to women as it was based on "folkloric assumption that women are by nature peculiarly prone to malice and mendacity and particularly adept at concealing it". See also Fennell, "Criminal Law and the Criminal Legal Justice System: Women as Victim" in Connelly (ed.), *Gender and the Law in Ireland* (Oak Tree Press, Dublin, 1993), pp.153 and 165, and LeGrand, "Rape and Rape Laws: Sexism in Society and Law" (1973) 61 Calif L Rev 919 at 931.

[403] Law Reform Commission, *Report on Rape and Allied Offences* (LRC 24–1988), paras 29–32. See also the earlier *Consultation Paper on Rape* (1987), paras 97–103.

[404] The warning was abolished in New Zealand in 1986, in Canada in 1975, and in England in 1994. While a trial judge still has a discretion to give the warning in England, a corroboration warning is expressly prohibited in Canada (by s.274 of the Criminal Code RSC 1985) and Australia (by s.294AA of the Criminal Procedure Act 1986). See generally, Lewis, 'A Comparative Examination of Corroboration and Caution Warnings in Prosecutions of Sexual Offences' [2006] Crim LR 889.

[405] This clause makes it clear that the section does not affect the corroboration requirements contained in ss.2 and 3 of the Criminal Law (Amendment) Act 1885 which deal with procuration offences.

be a requirement that the jury be given a warning about the danger of convicting the person on the uncorroborated evidence of that other person, it shall be for the judge to decide in his or her discretion, having regard to all the evidence given, whether the jury should be given the warning; and accordingly any rule of law or practice by virtue of which there is such a requirement as aforesaid is hereby abolished.

(2) If a judge decides, in his discretion, to give such a warning as aforesaid, it shall not be necessary to use any particular form of words to do so." [406]

2. The Discretion to Give a Warning

4–139   In the aftermath of the enactment of s.7, the extent of the reform effected thereby was unclear. Given that the requirement to give a warning had been a judicially created rule reflecting the views and prejudices of judges in relation to sexual complainants, it was feared by some commentators that the section would effect merely a change in form but not in substance. [407] This fear appeared to be well founded having regard to the comments of Keane J (as he then was) in *People (DPP) v Reid* [408] soon after s.7 came into force that, that notwithstanding its enactment, "there will still be cases in which trial judges will consider it desirable to warn the jury as to the dangers of convicting on the uncorroborating evidence of the complainant". [409] Subsequently, in *People (DPP) v Molloy* [410] the decision of the trial judge not to give a corroboration warning was trenchantly criticised by the Court of Criminal Appeal which stated that:

"where the charge is essentially supported by the evidence of the Complainant alone without collateral forensic evidence or any other form of corroboration, it is a prudent practice for the trial Judge to warn the jury that unless they are very very satisfied with the testimony of the Complainant that they should be careful not to convict in the absence of corroborative evidence". [411]

4–140   Although these comments were, strictly speaking, *obiter*, because the trial judge had issued a warning following a requisition, they seemed to indicate a firm view on the part of the Court as to the continued desirability of giving a corroboration warning, at least where there is no corroboration.

4–141   The approach taken in *Molloy* stood in stark contrast to that taken in respect of similar reforms enacted in other jurisdictions. In *Longman v R.*, [412] the High Court of Australia had considered the proper construction of a statutory provision which had abrogated the warning requirement. It took the view that the purpose of the section was to remove sexual complainants from the categories of suspect witness and that, by doing so, it overrode the reasons underpinning the warning. Thus, sexual complainants

---

[406] See generally, O'Malley, *Sexual Offences*, 2nd edn (Dublin: Thomson Reuters Round Hall, 2013), Chap.19; Charleton and Byrne, "Sexual Violence: Witnesses and Suspects. A Debating Document" (2010) 1 IJLS 1; Leahy, "Summing up in Rape Trials: The Challenge of Guiding Effectively and Without Prejudice" (2013) 4 ICLJ 102; Leahy, 'The Corroboration Warning in Sexual Offence Trials: Final Vestige of the Historic Suspicion of Sexual Offence Complainants or a Necessary Protection for Defendants?' (2014) 18(1) E&P 41.

[407] See the comments of Caroline Fennell in relation to s.7 in [1990] ICLSA, 32–16: "The chosen route to reform may have just the appearance or form of change, while the requirement reasserts itself in substance in practice as the same factors considered to justify the original rule, might also be deemed to justify a continual exercise of their discretion by the judiciary."

[408] [1993] 2 IR 186.

[409] [1993] 2 IR 186 at 197.

[410] Unreported, Court of Criminal Appeal, 28 July 1995.

[411] Unreported, Court of Criminal Appeal, 28 July 1995 at 6.

[412] (1989) 168 CLR 79.

were no longer to be viewed as a suspect class and it was inappropriate for judges to continue to give juries a general warning grounded in curial experience that allegations of sexual offences are easy to make or more likely to be fabricated than other classes of allegations.[413]

4–142   The decision of the English Court of Appeal in *R. v Makanjuola*[414] contained an even more trenchant rejection of the contention that the reasoning underpinning the corroboration warning in respect of sexual complainants had any continuing validity. At issue in that case was the interpretation and effect of s.32(1) of the Criminal Justice and Public Order Act 1994, which abrogated the mandatory corroboration warnings with respect to both accomplices and sexual complainants. Lord Taylor CJ emphasised that:

> "The circumstances and evidence in criminal cases are infinitely variable and it is impossible to categorise how a judge should deal with them. But it is clear that to carry on giving 'discretionary' warnings generally and in the same terms as were previously obligatory would be contrary to the policy and purpose of the 1994 Act. Whether, as a matter of discretion, a judge should give any warning and if so its strength and terms must depend upon the contents and manner of the witnesses evidence, the circumstances of the case and the issues raised. The judge will often consider that no special warning is required at all. Where, however, the witness has been shown to be unreliable, he or she may consider it necessary to urge caution. In a more extreme case, if the witness is shown to have lied, to have made previous false complaints, or to bear the defendant some grudge, a stronger warning may be thought appropriate and the judge may suggest it would be wise to look for some supporting material before acting on the impugned witness's evidence."[415]

4–143   The learned judge went on to summarise the relevant principles to be applied in a series of numbered propositions as follows:

> "(1) Section 32(1) abrogates the requirement to give a corroboration direction in respect of an alleged accomplice or a complainant of a sexual offence simply because a witness falls into one of those categories.
>
> (2) It is a matter for the judge's discretion what, if any, warning he considers appropriate in respect of such a witness, as indeed in respect of any other witness in whatever type of case. Whether he chooses to give a warning and in what terms will depend on the circumstances of the case, the issues raised and the content and quality of the witness's evidence.
>
> (3) In some cases, it may be appropriate for the judge to warn the jury to exercise caution before acting upon the unsupported evidence of a witness. This will not be so simply because the witness is the complainant of a sexual offence nor will it necessarily be so because a witness is alleged to be an accomplice. There will need to be an evidential basis for suggesting that the evidence of the witness may be unreliable. An evidential basis does not include mere suggestions by cross-examining counsel.
>
> (4) If any question arises as to whether the judge should give a special warning in respect of a witness, it is desirable that the question be resolved by discussion with counsel in the absence of the jury before final speeches.
>
> (5) Where the judge does decide to give some warning in respect of a witness, it will be appropriate to do so as part of the judge's review of the evidence and his comments as to how the jury should evaluate it rather than as a set piece legal direction.
>
> (6) Where some warning is required, it will be for the judge to decide the strength and terms of the warning. It does not have to be invested with the whole florid regime of the old corroboration rules.
>
> (7) … Attempts to re-impose the straight-jacket of the old corroboration rules are strongly to be deprecated.

---

[413] See also *Pahuja v R.* [1988] VR 261; *Question of Law (No.1 of 1993)* (1993) 59 SASR 214; *R. v Gilbert* [2002] 2 AC 531; and *State v K* [2000] 4 LRC 129.

[414] [1995] 3 All ER 730, [1995] 1 WLR 1348.

[415] [1995] 3 All ER 730 at 732, [1995] 1 WLR 1348.

(8) Finally, this court will be disinclined to interfere with a trial judge's exercise of his discretion save in a case where that exercise is unreasonable in the *Wednesbury* sense…"[416]

4–144 These principles were endorsed in this jurisdiction by the Court of Criminal Appeal in *People (DPP) v JEM*.[417] The applicant in *JEM* sought leave to appeal against his conviction of four counts of sexual assault on a 15-year-old girl and one of the main grounds of appeal raised by him was that the trial judge had erred in refusing to give to the jury a corroboration warning in respect of the evidence of the complainant. Denham J, delivering the judgment of the Court, examined the terms of s.7 and emphasised that the warning was no longer mandatory and that the decision whether it should be given is now a matter for the discretion of the trial judge.[418] As to the circumstances where, as a matter of discretion, a judge ought to give a cautionary instruction to the jury and in what terms, she referred with approval to the decision of *Makanjuola* and the principles laid down therein. Although the wording of s.32(1) was not the same as s.7 of the 1990 Act, the learned judge said that the legal principle underpinning both statutes was similar.

4–145 A similar view was taken in *People (DPP) v Wallace*,[419] where Keane CJ referred with approval to the decision in *JEM* and stated that:

> "the express legislative provision for the abolition of the mandatory warning … must not be circumvented by trial judges simply adopting a prudent or cautious approach of giving the warning in every case where there is no corroboration or where the evidence, might not amount, in the view of the trial judge, to corroboration. That would be to circumvent the clear policy of the legislature and that, of course, the courts are not entitled to do".[420]

4–146 Those *dicta* were in turn endorsed in *People (DPP) v Ferris*,[421] where Fennelly J added the gloss that "the legislature is not only entitled to but has the function under the constitution of evaluating changes in social and cultural circumstances, including sexual mores, and, while giving them legislative form where warranted".[422] It has, accordingly, been held that, in order for a corroboration warning to be given, there has to be something in the case which warrants the giving of the corroboration warning such as an indication of unreliability on the part of the complainant.[423]

---

[416] [1995] 3 All ER 730 at 733. See also *R. v Muncaster* [1999] Crim LR 449, where the Court of Appeal reaffirmed *Makanjuola*, and held that these principles apply generally to all cases where a witness may be suspect because he falls into a particular category. In all such cases, whether a warning is given and, if so, the strength of its terms is a matter of judicial discretion. See also *R. v Causley* [1999] Crim LR 572 (regardless of the category of suspect witness in question the decision as to whether a warning is necessary and, if so, its terms is dictated by the particular circumstances of the case).

[417] [2001] 4 IR 385.

[418] See also *People (DPP) v D O'S.* [2004] IECCA 23. In *People (DPP) v Gentleman* [2003] 4 IR 22 at 25, it was held that, although it can be a useful and effective procedure, there is no requirement for a trial judge to indicate to counsel in advance whether he or she intends to give a warning.

[419] Unreported, Court of Criminal Appeal, 30 April 2001.

[420] Unreported, Court of Criminal Appeal, 30 April 2001 at 6–7. The learned judge stated that the decision in *Molloy* should be confined to its own facts and expressly held that the case was not authority for the proposition that trial judges should give a corroboration warning as a matter of prudence. See also *People (DPP) v Slavotic*, unreported, Court of Criminal Appeal, 18 November 2002 at 4; *People (DPP) v Keogh* [2009] IECCA 93 at [3].

[421] [2008] 1 IR 1.

[422] [2008] 1 IR 1 at 12. That the warning is discretionary was also emphasised in *People (DPP) v Mulligan* [2009] IECCA 24 at [2] and *People (DPP) v D* [2014] IECCA 20 at [8].

[423] *People (DPP) v Mulligan* [2009] IECCA 24 at [3].

4–147   However, the traditional corroboration warning has proven very resilient and continues to be deployed by judges.[424] Indeed, the continued use of the corroboration warning has received appellate approval in some cases. In *People (DPP) v Gentleman*,[425] the evidence of the complainant was uncorroborated, the offences were alleged to have happened some 22 years earlier and no complaint had been made at the time. In those circumstances, Keane CJ regarded it to be "a case in which one would not be in the least surprised to find that a trial judge would consider it necessary to give a warning".

4–148   Similarly, in *People (DPP) v PJ*,[426] the comments of Keane J in *People (DPP) v Reid*[427] (set out above) were referred to with approval and McGuinness J stated that, although it is no longer mandatory for a corroboration warning to be given, it "may still … be desirable in particular cases."[428] In that case, the Court was satisfied that the trial judge was justified in his decision to give a warning having regard to a number of factors: (i) the complainant's evidence was not corroborated in any way,[429] contained a number of inconsistencies and was vague in some respects, especially in relation to dates; (ii) the offences were alleged to have taken place in a house with many inhabitants; and (iii) no evidence was given as to physical injuries which might have been suffered by the complainant.[430] Again, in *People (DPP) v MK*,[431] the Court of Criminal Appeal noted that the warning was no longer mandatory but stated that it might be desirable in particular cases and the trial judge could not be criticised for having given such a warning.[432]

4–149   The question of whether a trial judge must give a reasoned ruling for refusing

---

[424] See, by way of example, *People (DPP) v MK* [2005] IECCA 93, [2005] 3 IR 423; *People (DPP) v Boyce* [2008] IESC 62, [2009] 2 IR 124, [2009] 1 ILRM 253; *People (DPP) v Bangu* [2008] IECCA 90; *People (DPP) v O'Brien* [2010] IECCA 103, [2011] 1 IR 273; *People (DPP) v McCurdy* [2012] IECCA 76; *People (DPP) v C.C. (No.2)* [2012] IECCA 86; *People (DPP) v MJ* [2014] IECCA 21.

[425] [2003] 4 IR 22 at 25.

[426] [2003] 3 IR 550, [2004] 1 ILRM 220.

[427] [1993] 2 IR 186 at 197.

[428] [2003] 3 IR 550 at 566, [2004] 1 ILRM 220 at 236.

[429] In *PL v Buttimer* [2004] 2 IR 494 at 516, Geoghegan J expressed the view, *obiter*, that a corroboration warning should always be given as a matter of discretion when a case involved a contest between the evidence of the complainant and that of the accused.

[430] *Cf. People (DPP) v Boyce* [2005] IECCA 143 where the Court of Criminal Appeal noted on appeal that a corroboration warning was discretionary and had been given in that case in ease of the defence without any suggestion that it would have been preferable if a different form of warning had been given and *People (DPP) v C.C. (No.2)* [2012] IECCA 86 at [16] where it was stated that, in deciding to give a corroboration warning, the trial judge had "acted with scrupulous care and fairness towards the accused".

[431] [2005] IECCA 93, [2005] 3 IR 423.

[432] One circumstance where a court might decide to exercise its discretion to give a warning is where the evidence of the complainant as to the commission of the alleged offences relates to a period when he or she was very young. The Research Board of the British Psychological Society, *Guidelines on Memory and the Law* (2010), p.13, indicates that memories relating to events that occurred below 7 years of age should be treated with caution, those relating to events that occurred below 5 years of age should be viewed with considerable caution and those relating to events that occurred at 3 years and below should be viewed with great caution without independent corroborating evidence. However, the English courts have resisted the imposition of any obligation to give a warning with respect to the risk of relying on supported testimony of events that occurred when the witness was very young (*R. v E* [2009] EWCA Crim 1370; *R. v H* [2011] EWCA Crim 2344, [2012] 1 Cr App R 30).

to give a warning arose in somewhat unusual circumstances in *People (DPP) v Dolan*.[433] In that case, the trial judge refused to accede to the application of counsel for the accused to give a warning on the basis that another judge had said that the warning was "demeaning of women" and that, insofar as the Court of Criminal Appeal had indicated in a particular case that the warning should be given, this was to overrule the laws passed by the Oireachtas. The Court of Criminal Appeal was satisfied that the trial judge had failed to give a reasoned basis or any legally valid reason for his decision and, in circumstances where the ruling was one of considerable significance in the trial, it proceeded to quash the conviction. The ambit of that decision was subsequently confined in *People (DPP) v Ryan*[434] where the Court of Criminal Appeal clarified that the decision in *Dolan* had not laid down a universal rule that, if a judge is asked to give a corroboration warning, he or she must always give a reasoned ruling for doing so. In that case, the Court did not consider that a reasoned ruling was necessary because it could not identify any particular feature of the evidence that gave rise to the necessity to give the warning and expressed the view that it had been appropriate for the trial judge to leave the conflicts of evidence in the case to the unfettered judgment of the jury to decide where the truth lay. The position was summarised in *People (DPP) v D*[435] as being that it is unnecessary for a trial judge to deliver an elaborate ruling but the decision must be susceptible to analysis on the basis of whether it is a decision that was judicially made.

3. Review of Decision not to Give a Warning

4–150   If a trial judge exercises his or her discretion not to give a warning, this will not ground a successful appeal unless the trial judge can be shown to have exercised his or her discretion improperly either because the decision was made upon an incorrect legal basis or was clearly wrong in fact.[436] In *People (DPP) v Ryan*,[437] Geoghegan J summarised the position by saying that "an appellate court would not interfere with that discretion but, as in the case of all discretionary orders, an appellate court may interfere if, on the facts of any particular case, a failure to give a warning was manifestly a wrong exercise of the discretion".[438] With regard to the standard of review that will be applied if an appeal is taken on the ground of the failure of a trial judge to give a warning, it should be noted that, in *JEM,* Denham J rejected the use of *Wednesbury*[439] unreasonableness as the standard for review.[440] Although she did not articulate her reason for doing so, she was clearly correct to reject what is an inappropriate standard in the context of the review of the exercise of a discretion by a trial judge. A better test is that used by the Australian courts of whether the failure to give a warning has given rise to the risk of a miscarriage of justice.[441]

---

[433] [2007] IECCA 30.
[434] [2010] IECCA 29.
[435] [2014] IECCA 20 at [18].
[436] See *People (DPP) v Wallace*, unreported, Court of Criminal Appeal, *ex tempore*, 30 April 30 2001; *People (DPP) v P.C.* [2002] 2 IR 285 at 361–362; *People (DPP) v Ferris* [2008] 1 IR 1.
[437] [2010] IECCA 29.
[438] In *People (DPP) v Mulligan* [2009] IECCA 24 at [4], it was stated by Fennelly J in the Court of Criminal Appeal that "the question is not whether this court would have decided to give it but rather whether the trial judge exercised his discretion wrongly".
[439] *Associated Provincial Picture Houses Ltd v Wednesbury Corp.* [1948] 1 KB 223; [1947] 2 All ER 680.
[440] See also *People (DPP) v D* [2014] IECCA 20 at [14].
[441] See *Bromley v R.* (1986) 161 CLR 315.

4. Terms of the Warning

4–151   It is clear from s.7(2) of the 1990 Act and the principles laid down in *Makanjuola* and endorsed in *JEM* and *Wallace* that, where a trial judge exercises his or her discretion to give a warning, no particular form of words is required. It would seem to follow that a trial judge enjoys a considerable margin of discretion in relation to the terms of the warning, provided that he or she gives a warning or cautionary instruction which is sufficient to meet the risk of a miscarriage of justice by alerting the jury to the particular dangers of acting on the evidence of the complainant in the case before them. This was the approach adopted by the Court of Criminal Appeal in *People (DPP) v O'Connor*[442] where a challenge to the terms of the warning given by the trial judge failed. In the warning, the trial judge had instructed the jury as to the "grave and serious danger of convicting on a charge such as rape on the uncorroborated evidence of the complainant" and told them that it was "unsafe and dangerous to convict on the evidence of [the complainant] alone". This direction was impugned by the applicant on the basis that the warning was insufficiently strong and that the trial judge should have used a formula such as "very, very satisfied" but the Court, having adverted to the stipulation in s.7(2) that it is not necessary to use any form of words, was satisfied that "the warning given by the trial judge was sufficiently clear and strong to meet the circumstances of the case".[443]

4–152   An appeal on the basis of the alleged inadequacy of a warning also failed in *People (DPP) v Griffin*.[444] The trial judge declined to give a corroboration warning but, in his charge, he warned the jury there was no evidence independent of the complainant such as forensic evidence or an admission which provided corroboration of the complaint's evidence and that the case involved a swearing match between the complainant and the accused. Having noted that it is a matter for a trial judge to decide whether to give a warning and reiterated that no particular format for the warning is required, the Court of Criminal Appeal concluded that the relatively terse warning given by the trial judge was sufficient when taken in conjunction with other warnings given by him and the rest of the charge including his instructions to the jury in relation to the difficulties for an accused of defending old charges and the burden of proof on the prosecution.

4–153   However, the warning given was found to be inadequate in *People (DPP) v Gentleman*.[445] Although the trial judge had instructed the jury that great care should be taken before convicting the accused on the uncorroborated evidence of the complainant and had highlighted the antiquity of the alleged offences and the failure to make an earlier complaint, that instruction was held to be deficient because of the failure to indicate to the jury why the law considered it dangerous to convict on the uncorroborated evidence of a complainant and of the need to exercise special care in deciding whether it was satisfied beyond a reasonable doubt of the veracity of the complainant's evidence. The decision in *Gentleman* was approved and applied in *People (DPP) v D*[446] where MacMenamin J derived from it the requirement that a warning,

---

[442] Unreported, Court of Criminal Appeal, 29 July 2002.
[443] See also *People (DPP) v O'Brien* [2010] IECCA 103, [2011] 1 IR 273 where a challenge to the strength of the warning given was rejected.
[444] [2009] IECCA 75.
[445] [2003] 4 IR 22.
[446] [2014] IECCA 20.

if given, must be "*clear, unmistakable* and *contextualised*"[447] which standard had not been met in that case.

4-154 Where a judge decides to give a corroboration warning, then notwithstanding the discretion afforded by s.7(2), it appears that it is not open to a judge to give attenuated version of the warning and a full corroboration warning explaining the rationale for the warning is required. In *People (DPP) v C.C. (No.2)*,[448] the Court of Criminal Appeal expressed concern that the trial judge had failed to adequately explain the reason for the warning:

> "[T]he warning on corroboration was not in this court's view sufficient to convey the essence required by the law once it is decided, within the court's discretion, to give such a warning. To say that "the law requires care and caution to be exercised before you arrive at a view of guilt" is likely to be confusing, since a jury might well consider that they were obliged to exercise care and caution before coming to a view of guilt in any case. It is not clear what was added by these words. Furthermore, all warnings given to juries are an attempt to give to a jury approaching a one off task something of the general experience of courts. Thus whatever language is used, it is necessary to convey to a jury that the law considers it dangerous to convict in the absence of corroboration, because by definition these offences occur in private, or at least in circumstances of some furtiveness, and there have been occasions where evidence apparently plausible, has subsequently been shown to be untrue. Accordingly, over and above the degree of care and caution they would normally expect to exercise in coming to a verdict of guilt beyond any reasonable doubt, the jury should recognise that it is the law's experience that it is dangerous to convict on the uncorroborated evidence of a complainant, and should only do so when, having considered the warning, they nevertheless feel a very high degree of assurance that the evidence is true. Unless something of this nature is conveyed to the jury, there seems little benefit in giving a corroboration warning at all."[449]

4-155 A trial judge giving a corroboration warning is also required to give a clear explanation of the concept of corroboration and to correctly identify evidence that is potentially corroborative and any misdirection in this regard may lead to the quashing of a conviction.[450]

4-156 In *People (DPP) v PJ*,[451] the applicant had been convicted of a number of sexual offences relating to the sexual abuse of the complainant over a period from 1973 to 1979. The evidence of the complainant was uncorroborated and the trial judge decided to give a corroboration warning. As noted above, this decision was endorsed by the Court of Criminal Appeal which was, however, critical of the terms of the warning. McGuinness J referred to some of the pre-1990 authorities[452] which had stressed the necessity for a clear and emphatic warning and stated that, although the corroboration warning was no longer mandatory, once a trial judge had elected to give a

---

[447] [2014] IECCA 20 at [14] (emphasis in original).

[448] [2012] IECCA 86.

[449] [2012] IECCA 86 at [35].

[450] *People (DPP) v P.C.* [2002] 2 IR 285; *People (DPP) v PJ* [2003] 3 IR 550, [2004] 1 ILRM 253; *People (DPP) v MK* [2005] IECCA 93, [2005] 3 IR 423. Where a complaint is raised in relation to the adequacy of the instruction given in respect of the definition of corroboration or the identification of items of evidence that are potentially corroborative, a critical factor on appeal in determining whether it is meritorious will be whether a requisition was raised at the time: *People (DPP) v Boyce* [2008] IESC 62 at [94]–[97], [2009] 2 IR 124 at 146 - 148, [2009] 1 ILRM 253 at 272–273. However, a point may succeed in this regard on appeal even if it was not the subject of a requisition: *People (DPP) v C.C. (No.2)* [2012] IECCA 86 at [45].

[451] [2003] 3 IR 550, [2004] 1 ILRM 220. See also *People (DPP) v Gentleman* [2003] 4 IR 22 at 25–26.

[452] *People (AG) v Cradden* [1955] IR 130; *People (AG) v Williams* [1940] IR 195.

warning, "the necessity remains for that warning to be clear and unmistakable".[453] The "perfunctory" warning given in that case was unsatisfactory because it failed to convey any clear message to the jury and the trial judge had failed to emphasise the specific difficulties to which the absence of corroboration gave rise. The trial judge was also criticised for failing to explain the meaning of corroboration to the jury with the Court taking the view that the meaning of corroboration, as defined in *R. v Baskerville*,[454] had to be clearly explained to the jury. A similar approach was taken in *People (DPP) v P.C.*[455] where the Court of Criminal Appeal set aside the conviction of the applicant in circumstances where the trial judge had misdirected the jury as to the evidence that could constitute corroboration of the testimony of the complainant. Murray J. referred with approval to the *Baskerville* definition of corroboration and emphasised that there was "a substantive difference between evidence or an item of evidence which may tend to support or reinforce the testimony of a witness and independent evidence which in law is capable of amounting to corroboration".[456]

4–157 A misdirection in relation to the evidence that could constitute corroboration also led to the quashing of a conviction in *People (DPP) v MK*.[457] The Court of Criminal Appeal summarised the position by stating that:

> "The concept of corroboration and its proper definition in law is quite a difficult one but one which is of considerable importance to a jury in deciding the guilt or innocence of an accused person. It is essential that a clear definition of the principle of corroboration be given but it is also of great importance that it be clearly and unequivocally pointed out to the jury what, if any, of the evidence before them is capable of amounting to corroboration as defined."[458]

4–158 In that case, the trial judge had succinctly and correctly set out the legal principles in relation to corroboration. However, in circumstances where there was no issue but that the complainant had been sexually assaulted, with the issue for determination being whether the accused had assaulted her, the trial judge had failed to clearly distinguish between evidence that confirmed that the complainant had been assaulted and evidence that connected the accused with the commission of the offence. This could have led to confusion in the minds of the jury rendering the trial unsatisfactory.

4–159 Although these decisions confirm the continued application of the narrow *Baskerville* definition of corroboration to sexual offences where a corroboration warning is given, it should be noted that, in other decisions, the Court of Criminal Appeal has expressed a preference for a more expansive and less technical approach to the question of what can constitute corroboration such that it can include evidence

---

[453] [2003] 3 IR 550 at 567, [2004] 1 ILRM 220 at 236–237.
[454] [1916] 2 KB 658 at 667 (*per* Lord Reading CJ).
[455] [2002] 2 IR 285.
[456] [2002] 2 IR 285 at 301. See also *People (DPP) v Cornally*, unreported, Court of Criminal Appeal, *ex tempore*, 7 November 1994 (where a warning is given, the judge ought to point out to a jury the evidence capable of amounting to corroboration) and *People (DPP) v D*, unreported, Court of Criminal Appeal, *ex tempore*, July 27, 1993 (the judge must warn the jury not to treat as corroboration evidence which they might mistakenly believe to have that quality). But *Cf. People (DPP) v Murphy*, unreported, Court of Criminal Appeal, *ex tempore*, 3 November 1997, where it was held that the trial judge had not misdirected the jury by instructing them that dirt on the complainant's clothes and body could provide corroborative evidence which supported her account that she had been sexually assaulted.
[457] [2005] IECCA 93, [2005] 3 IR 423.
[458] [2005] IECCA 93 at [56], [2005] 3 IR 423 at 445.

that is supportive of the evidence of a complainant because it connects the accused with the commission of the offence.[459] Such an approach was evident in *People (DPP) v Foley*[460] where it was held that the trial judge had correctly instructed the jury that the distress of the complainant and the words spoken by her when found by gardaí in a semi-conscious state were capable of providing corroboration. The Court of Criminal Appeal considered that the requirement of independence was satisfied because the complainant's physical reaction and accompanying words were capable of being treated as involuntary and spontaneous by virtue or her emotional and semi-conscious condition and the evidence implicated the applicant in the commission of the offence because it was inconsistent with his defence that the complainant had willingly participated in the sexual acts in question.

4–160   Where there are multiple complainants, the trial judge should instruct the jury as to the extent to which the evidence of one complainant can be used to corroborate that of another.[461] In *People (DPP) v C.C. (No.2)*,[462] the corroboration warning given by the trial judge was criticised on appeal on the basis that it was insufficiently clear and detailed in terms of the evidence that could constitute corroboration and particularly as to the extent to which the evidence of one complainant was admissible in support of and could provide corroboration of the evidence of another complainant.

4–161   Given the complexities and the potential for error that arises in relation to the decision to give a warning and the terms of any warning given, particularly in relation to the evidence that can potentially be treated by the jury as corroborative, the Court of Criminal Appeal recommended in *People (DPP) v MK*[463] that there should be a discussion of this issue between counsel and the trial judge prior to his or her charge to the jury.[464] Arising from this discussion, the trial judge should indicate to counsel prior to their closing speeches whether he or she proposes to give a warning and the reasons for that decision.[465] He or she should also identify the evidence (if any) that he or she considers capable of constituting corroboration.[466]

4–162   The continued vitality of the traditional corroboration warning with the attendant technicalities in respect of corroboration is disappointing because it undermines, to a considerable degree, the reform effected by s.7. By way of contrast, the English Court of Appeal in *Makanjuola* emphatically disagreed with the suggestion

---

[459] See *People (DPP) v Cooke* [2009] IECCA 55 and *People (DPP) v Hardiman* [2011] IECCA 69.
[460] [2013] IECCA 90.
[461] In *People (DPP) v Cooke* [2009] IECCA 55, the Court of Criminal Appeal confirmed that there can be mutual corroboration between complainants where offences are not committed on one complainant in the presence of the other. Further, although *People (DPP) v Morrissey*, unreported, Court of Criminal Appeal, 10 July 1998 is authority for the proposition that there cannot be mutual corroboration between complainants where there is collusion between them, it was held in *Cooke* that mutual corroboration is not precluded merely because collusion is alleged. The Court also rejected the proposition that the evidence of one complainant could only be used as corroboration of that of another if the jury was satisfied that the offence against the first complainant had been proven beyond a reasonable doubt. See also *People (DPP) v McCurdy* [2012] IECCA 76 dealing with mutual corroboration where there is admissible misconduct evidence.
[462] [2012] IECCA 86.
[463] [2005] IECCA 93 at [53], [2005] 3 IR 423 at 445.
[464] See the comments to similar effect in *People (DPP) v Ryan* [2010] IECCA 29 at [7].
[465] *People (DPP) v D* [2014] IECCA 20 at [20].
[466] *People (DPP) v Foley* [2013] IECCA 90 at [17].

made in *Archbold*[467] that, if a judge decided to give a warning, the previous law would continue to apply and thus, the judge would have to explain to the jury what is meant by corroboration and identify the evidence capable of being corroborative, stating that "attempts to re-impose the straitjacket of the old corroboration rules are strongly to be deprecated".[468] Furthermore, a strong argument can be made that the concept of corroboration, which was devised to deal with the problem of insider knowledge with regard to the evidence of accomplices,[469] is too narrow when applied to the very different problems raised by the evidence of sexual complainants. With a sexual complainant, the concern is that he or she may, for a variety of reasons, make a false accusation. Thus, any evidence which bolsters the credibility of the complainant and which tends to show that he or she is telling the truth should be capable of being corroborative and not just independent evidence which implicates the accused in the commission of the offence.[470]

5. Additional Warning Required where there has been Delay

4–163 The dangers inherent in a trial which takes place many years after the sexual offences alleged and the difficulties such a trial creates for an accused, particularly where there is generally little or no non-testimonial evidence available which can be used to test the veracity of the complainant's evidence, have repeatedly been pointed out.[471] As Hardiman J explained in *JB v DPP*[472]:

> "a trial of a very old case has inherently dangerous aspects to it: memories fade, witnesses or potential witnesses die or become unavailable, the allegations in themselves lack specificity and the capacity to contradict a complainant on specific details may have been wholly lost due to these things, either one of them or in combination."

4–164 The test applied to determine whether a trial should be prevented from proceeding because of delay, which is whether there is a real and serious risk of an unfair trial which cannot be avoided by appropriate rulings and directions on the part of the trial judge,[473] underlines the obligation on a trial judge to give such directions. It

---

[467] *Archbold's Criminal Pleading, Evidence and Practice* (Sweet & Maxwell, London, 1995), Vol.1, para.16–36.

[468] [1995] 3 All ER 730 at 733. It might be noted that, in Canada, following the abolition of the mandatory corroboration warning in respect of accomplices in *Vetrovec v R.* [1982] 1 CR SCR 811, (1982) 136 DLR (3d) 89, the courts rejected the technical corroboration rules in favour of a commonsense approach and the adequacy of a cautionary instruction given by a trial judge will no longer be assessed by reference to those rules (see *R. v B(G) (No.1)* [1990] 2 CR SCR 3).

[469] See *R. v Sheehan* (1826) Jebb CC 54 and *People (AG) v Phelan* (1950) 1 Frewen 98 at 100.

[470] *Cf.* the Commonwealth cases holding that corroboration may be found in evidence which is more consistent with the truth of the complainant's evidence than its falsity: *Warkentin v R.* [1977] 2 CR SCR 355, (1976) 70 DLR (3d) 20; *R. v B (G) (No.1)* [1990] 2 CR SCR 3, (1990) 56 CCC (3d) 200; *Kelleher v R.* (1974) 131 CLR 534.

[471] See, by way of example, *JL v DPP* [2000] 3 IR 122; *JO'C v DPP* [2000] 3 IR 478; *H v DPP* [2006] IESC 55, [2006] 3 IR 575, [2007] 1 ILRM 401; *JB v DPP* [2006] IESC 66; *People (DPP) v C.C. (No.2)* [2012] IECCA 86 at [1].

[472] [2006] IESC 66 at [9].

[473] In *Z v DPP* [1994] 2 IR 476 at 507, [1994] 2 ILRM 481 at 499, Finlay CJ held that "where one speaks of the onus to establish a real risk of an unfair trial it necessarily and inevitably means an unfair trial which cannot be avoided by appropriate rulings and directions on the part of the trial judge". This remains the position after the re-setting of the law in this area by the Supreme Court in *H v DPP* [2006] IESC 55, [2006] 3 IR 575, [2007] 1 ILRM 401. In *CK v DPP* [2007] IESC 5 at [17]. Kearns J (as he then was) explained that: "the first question to be addressed is whether or not the applicant has discharged the onus of establishing on the balance of probabilities that he

has been emphasised that a trial judge has a constitutional duty to ensure due process in a trial[474] and, in discharge of this duty, it is necessary for a trial judge to give a warning to the jury of the problems arising from delay and give such directions to the jury as are necessary to mitigate the prejudicial effect of delay.[475]

4–165   The rationale and basis for the warning that is required to be given was elaborated upon by O'Donnell J in *People (DPP) v C.C. (No.2)*[476] who highlighted the difficulties for an accused in defending charges of alleged sexual offences committed on unspecified dates many years previously where there is little evidence beyond that of the complainant and the accused:

> "Such minimal evidence reduces the trial as has regularly been observed, to little more than a charge countered by a denial, contained in this case in the statement of the accused, and necessarily involved the jury in an attempt to determine whether or not they believed each complainant beyond any reasonable doubt. This necessarily places heavy reliance on the perception of the jury in relation to the demeanour of the witness. But as Lord Atkin famously pointed out in *Société d'avances Commerciales (Société Anonyme Egyptienne) v. Merchants' Marine Insurance Co.* [1924] 20 Lloyd's L. Rep. 140 at p.152 "an ounce of intrinsic merit or demerit in the evidence, that is to say, the value of the comparison of evidence with known facts, is worth pounds of demeanour". That is an observation borne of lengthy experience, and with which many judges have agreed. It is significant that those with the greatest experience of judging the credibility of witnesses have the least faith in the capacity of any person to simply observe the witness giving evidence and determine if he or she is telling the truth. However, almost by definition, that is an experience which a jury does not have. That is partly why it has been considered necessary to give the jury an explicit warning as to the dangers of conviction of persons where there has been a significant lapse of time, blurring of memory, and evaporation and loss of evidence. It is an added complicating feature that the stark singling out of an allegation of a criminal offence without the clutter of context and surrounding provable and therefore contestable facts, may make a false allegation appear more convincing to a jury and a true allegation less convincing than such evidence given closer to the time, and in a more fact rich context. The warning which must be given to a jury is designed to provide a jury encountering evidence of any sort for the first time with the accumulated experience of trial courts to the effect that it is normally by the testing of evidence against observable provable facts that credibility is more persuasively established, and that the stark and isolated evidence of the assertion of a criminal offence on a day without specification, definition or description, rather than providing clarity and persuasiveness, is something to be approached with considerable caution."[477]

---

has been prejudiced by the consequences of delay to the extent that there is a real risk of an unfair trial. If that question is answered affirmatively, the applicant must further satisfy the court that it is a degree or type of prejudice which can not be overcome or countered by appropriate directions or warnings to the jury to be given by the trial judge. Only if he succeeds in both respects is he entitled to an order." See also *K v Moran* [2010] IEHC 23 at [9]; *MC v DPP* [2011] IEHC 378 at [6.2].

[474]   *DC v DPP* [2005] IESC 77 at [2], [2005] 4 IR 281 at 283, [2006] 1 ILRM 348 at 351; *People (DPP) v O'C* [2006] IESC 54 at [18], [2006] 3 IR 238 at 246; *JB v DPP* [2006] IESC 66 at [7] (*per* Denham J).

[475]   *B v DPP* [1997] 3 IR 140 at 204, [1997] 2 ILRM 118 at 134; *People (DPP) v PJ* [2003] 3 IR 550 at 568, [2004] 1 ILRM 220 at 238; *People (DPP) v Hegarty* [2013] IECCA 66 at [36]. The English courts have taken a similar approach, and a number of convictions have been quashed on the grounds that no direction was given to the jury on the issue of delay: *R. v Dutton* [1994] Crim LR 910; *R. v Egan* [1996] 1 Cr App R 88, [1996] Crim LR 205; *R v B* [1996] Crim LR 406; and *R. v King* [1997] Crim LR 298. However, there is no absolute rule that a charge must be given in such cases, see Lewis and Mullis, "Delayed Criminal Prosecutions for Childhood Sexual Abuse: Ensuring a Fair Trial" [1999] LQR 265 at 281 and Birch, "Commentary on J." [1997] Crim LR 297 at 298, discussing *R. v J* [1997] Crim LR 297.

[476]   [2012] IECCA 86 at [18].

[477]   See also *JO'C. v DPP* [2000] 3 IR 478 at 504 where Hardiman J stated: "If a defendant who is innocent is exposed to a trial where the only evidence is unsupported assertion and the only

4–166   It is apparent from the decision of the Court of Criminal Appeal in *People (DPP) v EC*,[478] that the point has now been reached whereby the requirement to give a warning where there has been significant delay is a rule of law and the failure to give such a warning will result in a conviction being quashed unless the proviso in s.3 of the Criminal Procedure Act 1993 can be applied. The Court observed that, while the difficulties that arise by reason of delay may be obvious to lawyers and judges, it could not be assumed that they would be understood by a jury in the absence of an appropriate warning. It considered that the authorities established that "in sexual abuse cases where there has been lengthy delay, a warning to the jury of the dangers thereby arising should be given by the trial judge in the course of his summing up".[479] In that case, the Court was satisfied that, even though it had not been requested by either side, some sort of warning was essential. Such a warning not having been given, it proceeded to quash the conviction, holding that the proviso could not be applied because the omission of the warning went to a central and critical aspect of the case.

4–167   Where it is required to be given, the warning in respect of delay is independent from, and should not be conflated with, any corroboration warning that may be given.[480] The topic of delay requires entirely separate treatment in the judge's charge, and the failure of the trial judge to give adequate directions as to the issue of delay in its own right may result in the finding that a conviction is unsafe.

4–168   Guidance as to the content of the warning is provided by *People (DPP) v RB*.[481] The trial judge, Haugh J gave a lengthy charge, the first part of which dealt, in some detail, with the issue of delay. Given that this "lucid and clear charge" was found by the Court of Criminal Appeal in that case to have been adequate[482] and has been referred to in a number of subsequent cases as providing an appropriate template for a warning in respect of delay,[483] it is worth quoting the relevant portion in full:

> "I now want to move from the general, not totally to the particular, but to this kind of case. You have heard in this case, and it is undoubtedly a further difficulty for the case, that this is a case of an old complaint. The events that you have to decide here are alleged to have occurred more than fifteen years ago. It obviously makes the task for a jury and the task for a court in

---

> defence bare denial, his position is indeed perilous. Where these cases have been succesfully defended, it has, in my experience, always been because it has been possible to show that the complainant's account is inconsistent with objectively provable facts relevant to the allegation, or that the complainant has made other allegations against other people which are lacking in credibility."

[478] [2006] IECCA 69, [2007] 1 IR 749.
[479] [2006] IECCA 69 at [18], [2007] 1 IR 749 at 757.
[480] *People (DPP) v JH*, unreported, Court of Criminal Appeal, December 3, 2001; *People (DPP) v PJ* [2003] 3 IR 550 at 565; [2004] 1 ILRM 220 at 235; and *People (DPP) v LG* [2003] 2 IR 517 at 529. This is in marked contrast to the position adopted by the Australian Court in *Longman v R.* (1989) 168 CLR 79, in which it was held that the jury should have been warned of the danger of a conviction on the basis of the uncorroborated testimony of a witness as to events experienced when the witness was a young child, testimony given so long after the event that it was difficult for the accused to effectively test the evidence through cross-examination. See also *R. v K* (1997) 68 SASR 405 and *R. v Young* [1998] 1 VR 402.
[481] Unreported, Court of Criminal Appeal, 12 February 2003.
[482] Unreported, Court of Criminal Appeal, 12 February 2003 at 20.
[483] See *People (DPP) v PJ* [2003] 3 IR 550, [2004] 1 ILRM 220; *People (DPP) v C.C.* [2006] IECCA 1 at [20], [2006] 4 IR 287 at 294–295; *People (DPP) v EC* [2006] IECCA 69 at [19], [2007] 1 IR 749 at 757–758; *People (DPP) v MJ* [2014] IECCA 21 at [73]. In *People (DPP) v D* [2014] IECCA 20 at [25], this charge was described as "exemplary".

trying these cases a lot more difficult. As Mr. McKeon says, they normally degenerate into one man's word against another, a 'you did, I didn't, you did, I didn't kind of a contest and that is because when you are dealing with old complaints, you are dealing with events from a long time ago and for the very reason that they are so old they generally lack precision, they generally lack detail. And it is in precision and in detail that cross-examinations generally take place. Witnesses seldom change their stories and admit that what they had said was a fabrication or a lie. You probe looking for the truth by questioning people in relation to detail. If there are contests, as there is in this case or any case where there is a plea of not guilty, again it is much easier to defend an allegation when there is detail alleged against you. If somebody alleged that any one of you had assaulted me in the middle eighties and left it no more than that, it is very, very hard for you to defend it. I think that would be accepted by all of you and it is, no doubt, so. But if I had complained that one of you had assaulted me last July, if I had complained that one of you had assaulted me on the 17th of July, the chances are that you will be able to work out your whereabouts at that time and who can vouch for you at that time and be able to grapple with issues on the basis of detail. You will be able to look up your diaries maybe, if you keep them, or check with your employers if you have them and you may have been on holidays. But how can a person be expected to attack the allegation, to contest the allegation with any subtlety, with any detail, with any forensic form of attack if all you are told about it is that you did it about fifteen years ago on some date unknown over a period of eighteen months? That, I suggest to you, makes it far harder to defend it than it is to prosecute it. In fact, to prosecute it is easier if you do not nail your colours to the mast because there is less you can be cross-examined on. But the law does not say that stale cases, old cases, cannot be tried. But what I must tell you is that an accused person cannot in your minds or in your consideration be disadvantaged because the case is old, because the complaint is related to events from a long time ago. You have to be all the more careful and it should be much harder to satisfy you in relation to an event that is phrased in a vague and general way, rather than an event which carries details or particulars. You cannot let the fact that Mr. B. is handicapped by reason of the lack of precision in the charge cause you to come easier to a decision adverse to him. The State should not take benefit from old cases. Their life should not be made easier by bringing old cases. Juries must, with their hand on their heart, recognise the huge difficulty that accused persons have of dealing with old cases and be all the more careful and take that into account when arriving at a decision."

4–169 In *People (DPP) v EC*,[484] the Court of Criminal Appeal described this cautionary instruction as a good example of how a trial judge should convey to a jury the dangers that go with lengthy delay. However, it refrained from saying that it was appropriate in every case and emphasised that "the extent and nature of the warning will vary from case to case and turn on the particular facts of the case in question".[485] The same point was made by the Court of Criminal Appeal in *People (DPP) v Walsh*[486] which pointed out "that a charge is not a *formulaic* matter" and stressed that[487]:

"It does not have to follow a specific absolute template in terms of the charge to be enunciated by the judge to a jury, provided at all time that all issues necessary to be raised in the charge are fully, sufficiently and clearly put to the jury, so as to enable the jury to make the decisions it is entitled and obliged to make, and to follow any appropriate warnings that a jury is obliged to take into account."

4–170 In that case, the charge, although less elaborate than that in *RB,* was considered to address all of the essential ingredients and the Court attached some importance to the fact that there had not been any requisitions raised on the charge.

4–171 As explained by MacMenamin J in *People (DPP) v D*,[488] the required charge

---

[484] [2006] IECCA 69, [2007] 1 IR 749.
[485] [2006] IECCA 69 at [18], [2007] 1 IR 749 at 757.
[486] [2011] IECCA 101.
[487] [2011] IECCA 101 at [6].
[488] [2014] IECCA 20 at [26].

in respect of delay contains two parts. First, it consists of general illustrations of the difficulties which generally arise in cases where there has been a long lapse of time. Second, there is a contextualisation of those difficulties by explaining how they arise in the particular circumstances of the case before the jury. Accordingly, in order for a warning to be effective and to adequately address the risk of a miscarriage of justice, it must not only highlight the general difficulties encountered by an accused who faces charges of sexual offences allegedly committed many years earlier but those general difficulties must be related to the particular circumstances of the case.

4–172 In *People (DPP) v PJ*,[489] it was held that, while it might not always be necessary for a trial judge to go into the same level of elaborate detail as to the effects of delay as in *RB*, he or she was required to deal reasonably fully with the various aspects of the problems caused by delay in the making of a complaint of a sexual offence. In that case, the direction given by the trial judge with regard to delay was found not to be adequate because it did not deal with the specific problems caused by delay in that particular case.[490] The direction of the trial judge on the issue of delay was also deemed to be inadequate in *People (DPP) v LG*[491] because it failed to deal with elements of possible prejudice specific to the proceedings. The Court of Criminal Appeal held that the trial judge should have drawn the jury's attention to the failure to provide an explanation for the delay in making a complaint after the relationship of dominion ended. The Court also rejected the submission that a detailed instruction was not required because counsel for the applicant laid stress on the importance of delay in his closing address to the jury. Given the weight that the jury would attach to specific directions from the trial judge, the fact that these matters were the subject of comment from counsel for the applicant did not relieve the trial judge of his or her obligation to give appropriate directions to the jury.[492]

4–173 The compounded difficulties that arise where there has not just been delay but allegations are made by multiple complainants were addressed in *People (DPP) v C.C.*.[493] The applicant had been convicted on 180 counts of indecent assault which offences were alleged to have taken place between 1968 and 1977 when he was a teacher and the complainants were students. The Court of Criminal Appeal accepted that "the nature and detail of the warning to be given to the jury in an old case will turn very much on the facts and circumstances peculiar to the case in question"[494] but held that the trial judge had failed to deal adequately with the problems caused by delay in that case, particularly given that there were multiple complainants[495]:

> "It seems to us that whatever prejudice arises by virtue of delay in the case of a single complainant can only be seen as exponentially magnified where there are multiple complainants and a single accused. His difficulties of recollection, his difficulties of finding witnesses, or of even remembering the identity of individual complainants are all magnified in direct relation to the number of complainants who come forward. So, while the difficulties of delay may

---

[489] [2003] 3 IR 550, [2004] 1 ILRM 220.

[490] The same deficiency in the charge of the trial judge was identified in *People (DPP) v D* [2014] IECCA 20 at [28].

[491] [2003] 2 IR 517.

[492] *Cf. People (DPP) v Mulligan* [2009] IECCA 24 at [4], where criticism of the trial judge's charge on the basis that he had referred to the submissions made by counsel for the applicant in her closing speech rather than expressing his own warning was rejected.

[493] [2006] IECCA 1, [2006] 4 IR 287.

[494] [2006] IECCA 1 at [20], [2006] 4 IR 287 at 294.

[495] [2006] IECCA 1 at [23], [2006] 4 IR 287 at 296.

in such circumstances recede to some degree from the prosecution's point of view, they are multiplied and exaggerated from a defendant's point of view."

4–174 In those circumstances, the Court considered that the trial judge should have dwelt at some length on the particular difficulties that arose for the applicant in that case in defending charges of such antiquity where there were few areas of objectively provable fact that could be addressed by him.[496]

4–175 In *People (DPP) v Cooke*[497] the Court of Criminal Appeal analysed the adequacy of a delay warning in the context of the well established principle that:

> "There is no requirement in law that a charge by a trial judge must follow a particular fixed rigid or established formula of words, a matter clearly recognised in the jurisprudence, the details of which it is not necessary for the court to cite. A charge is always a matter for the trial judge, in which he or she must exercise his/her appropriate judicial function in accordance with the law, and the facts of a particular case."

4–176 The question, therefore, was whether the warning concerning delay was sufficiently detailed by reference to the specific difficulties for the defence in that case. Having reviewed charges from other cases including *RB*, and having considered the particular features of the case and the difficulties that arose for the defence, the Court was satisfied that the charge was adequate in the circumstances.[498]

4–177 It should be noted that, although there seems to be a consensus in the jurisprudence of the Court of Criminal Appeal as to the contents of the warning to be given to a jury in respect of delay, in *JB v DPP*,[499] Hardiman J in the Supreme Court opined that the warning in *RB* fell short of what was required because it failed to tell the jury how it should act on the dangers identified. He referred to the warning in respect of identification evidence that was laid down by the Supreme Court in *People (DPP) v Casey*[500] (discussed below) and said that its force derived from the fact that it was related to the courts' experience of error in other cases. He referred to a number of cases where "very alarming effects even of relatively short periods of delay" had come to the attention of the courts and he stated that consideration would have to be given as to whether, in cases where delay had occurred, a specific warning, perhaps along *Casey* lines, should be given.

6. Recovered Memory

4–178 In some instances, a complainant may not have a recollection of the occurrence of the alleged sexual offences in advance of counselling or some other form of therapeutic intervention, leading to the "recovery" of a memory of the offences taking

---

[496] The applicant was retried and an appeal against the adequacy of the charge given by the trial judge in respect of delay at the retrial failed in circumstances where the Court of Criminal Appeal was satisfied that the trial judge had highlighted the difficulties faced by the applicant in defending the offences and the impact of delay in terms of the loss of available evidence, particularly when taken in conjunction with the address of counsel for the prosecution to the jury which had also contained an extensive warning of the dangers created by charges of such antiquity: *People (DPP) v C.C. (No.2)* [2012] IECCA 86.

[497] [2009] IECCA 55.

[498] A challenge to the adequacy of a warning in relation to the difficulties caused by delay also failed in *People (DPP) v Hegarty* [2013] IECCA 66.

[499] [2006] IESC 66.

[500] [1963] IR 33.

place.[501] Courts in other jurisdictions have held that it is appropriate to give a warning to the jury of the dangers of acting on evidence of "recovered memory"[502] and, in *People (DPP) v McKenna*,[503] the Court of Criminal Appeal appeared to be open to the proposition that a cautionary instruction in respect of such evidence might be appropriate.

F. Evidence of Children

1. Introduction

4–179   A number of dangers have traditionally been associated with the evidence of children. Firstly, there are problems stemming from the intellectual immaturity of children which mean that their comprehension of events and of questions put to them and their powers of expression may be imperfect.[504] Secondly, children are prone to fantasise[505] and may have trouble distinguishing reality from fantasy. Thirdly, children are suggestible and are susceptible to the influence of third persons.[506] Fourthly, a child has a less developed sense of moral responsibility[507] and may give evidence out of spite or a desire to make mischief.[508] Furthermore, the usual means for identifying unreliable and untruthful testimony, namely cross-examination, is less effective with respect to children. Counsel is forced to exercise more restraint when cross-examining children in order to avoid distressing the child because, especially where the child is the victim of an offence, this can only serve to heighten the natural sympathy felt by the jury towards the child to the detriment of the accused.[509]

4–180   For these reasons, children were identified as a category of suspect witness in respect of whose evidence the safeguard of corroboration was required. In the case of unsworn testimony of children, corroboration was mandatory,[510] whilst in respect

---

[501] As to what is meant by "recovered memory", see *People (DPP) v McKenna*, unreported, Court of Criminal Appeal, 19 October 2001 and *People (DPP) v C.C. (No.2)* [2012] IECCA 86. The recovery of memory through or by reason of a therapeutic process is distinct from the spontaneous recovery of memory such as occurred in *Hickey v McGowan* [2014] IEHC 19.

[502] See *R. v G* [1996] 1 NZLR 615 and *R. v McFelin* [1985] 2 NZLR 750.

[503] Court of Criminal Appeal, 19 October 2001.

[504] *DPP v Hester* [1973] AC 296 at 325, [1972] 3 All ER 1056 at 1073 (*per* Lord Diplock); *R. v Spencer* [1987] AC 128 at 141, [1986] 2 All ER 928 at 937 (*per* Lord Ackner); *Kendall v R.* [1962] SCR 469 at 473, (1962) 132 CCC 216 at 220 (*per* Judson J).

[505] *People (DPP) v Quilligan* [1993] 2 IR 305 at 342 (*per* McCarthy J). See also *R. v Dossi* (1918) 13 Cr App R 158 at 161.

[506] *People (AG) v Casey (No.2)* [1963] IR 33 at 37 (*per* Kingsmill Moore J); *People (DPP) v Quilligan* [1993] 2 IR 305 at 342 (*per* McCarthy J).See also *R. v Dossi* (1918) 13 Cr App R 158 at 161.

[507] *Kendall v R.* [1962] SCR 469 at 473, (1962) 132 CCC 216 at 220 (*per* Judson J).

[508] Dennis, "Corroboration Requirements Reconsidered" [1984] Crim LR 316 at 330.

[509] Zuckerman, *Principles of Criminal Evidence* (Oxford: Clarendon, 1989), pp.164–165. Indeed, it may be noted that the effectiveness of cross-examination has been further reduced by the introduction of live television links by Part III of the Criminal Evidence Act 1992 (No.12 of 1992).

[510] Section 30 of the Children Act 1908 (as amended by s.28(2) of the Criminal Justice (Administration) Act 1914) permitted the reception of the unsworn evidence of a child if the child was possessed of sufficient intelligence to justify the reception of the evidence and understood the duty of speaking the truth, but went on to specify that a person could not be convicted of an offence under the section by virtue of such evidence unless it was "corroborated by some other material evidence in support thereof implicating the accused".

of the sworn evidence of children, a warning had to be given of the dangers of acting on such evidence in the absence of corroboration.[511]

4–181   However, research which indicated that many of the assumptions underpinning the corroboration requirements in respect of children were unfounded[512] coupled with mounting concern about the incidence and difficulty of prosecuting child sexual abuse, prompted the Law Reform Commission to recommend the abolition of the corroboration requirements[513] and this was effected by the Criminal Evidence Act 1992. The requirement that the unsworn evidence of a child be corroborated was abolished by s.28(1) of the 1992 Act,[514] and s.28(2)(a) abolished any requirement that a jury be given a warning by the judge about convicting the accused on the uncorroborated evidence of a child by reason only that the evidence is that of a child.[515] It is now for the judge to decide, in his or her discretion, having regard to all the evidence given, whether the jury should be given the warning[516] and where the judge decides to give a warning, it is not necessary to use any particular form of words.[517]

4–182   Section 28(3) further provides that the unsworn evidence given by virtue of s.27 of the Act[518] may corroborate evidence (sworn or unsworn) given by any other person.[519] Of course, in an appropriate case, where there is a danger of collusion, a judge may warn of the dangers of accepting the evidence of one child whether sworn or unsworn as corroboration of the evidence of another, though he cannot, consistent with s.28(3), direct the jury that such evidence is not capable of amounting to corroboration.

2. Discretion to Give a Warning

4–183   The pattern of reform recommended by the Law Reform Commission and implemented in s.28 is similar to that adopted in s.7 of the Criminal Law (Rape)

---

[511] *Attorney General v O'Sullivan* [1930] IR 552; *R. v Campbell* [1956] 2 QB 432, [1956] 2 All ER 272; *R. v Cleal* [1942] 1 All ER 203; *R. v Dossi* (1918) 13 Cr App R 158.

[512] See Hedderman, *Children's Evidence: The Need for Corroboration* (Research and Planning Unit Paper 41) (Home Office, London, 1987) where much of this research is discussed. See also, the *Report of the Committee on Sexual Offences Against Children and Youths* (Minister of Supply and Services, Ottawa, Canada, 1984) at p.381, which concluded that "the requirement of corroboration for a young child's testimony has traditionally been based on both untested and unfounded assumptions about the intrinsic reliability of children's evidence".

[513] *Consultation Paper on Child Sexual Abuse* (1989), at pp.101–102; *Report on Child Sexual Abuse* (LRC 32–1990), at p.60.

[514] The constitutionality of the removal of the corroboration requirement was raised but not resolved in *White v Ireland* [1995] 2 IR 268 at 283.

[515] The words "by reason only" make it clear that if a warning should be necessary for some other reason, *e.g.* because the child is an accomplice, then the warning should be given: *R. v Pryce* [1991] Crim LR 379.

[516] Section 28(2)(a).

[517] Section 28(2)(b).

[518] Section 27(1) provides that the evidence of a person under 14 years of age can be received otherwise than on oath or affirmation if the court is satisfied that he is capable of giving an intelligible account of events which are relevant to those proceedings.

[519] The section thus reverses the decision in *Attorney General (Kelly) v Kearns* (1946) 80 ITLR 45, where it was held, following *R. v Coyle* [1926] NI 208, that the unsworn evidence of a child admitted by virtue of s.30 of the Children Act 1908 could not be corroborated by the unsworn evidence of any number of other children similarly admitted. However, it was the case that unsworn evidence could corroborate and be corroborated by sworn evidence (*DPP v Hester* [1973] AC 296, [1972] 3 All ER 1056; *R. v Campbell* [1956] 2 QB 432, [1956] 2 All ER 272).

(Amendment) Act 1990[520] and the question again arises as to how trial judges will exercise their discretion to give a warning.

4–184 Proceeding by analogy with sexual complainants, it seems clear that, by abrogating the legislative corroboration requirements with regard to the evidence of children, the legislature has disavowed the proposition that the evidence of children is inherently unreliable and should automatically be the subject of a warning or cautionary instruction.[521] Therefore, a warning or cautionary instruction should not be given in relation to the evidence of a child simply because of his or her tender years as this would amount to re-introducing the abrogated rule requiring a corroboration warning in another guise.[522] However, a cautionary instruction should be given in an appropriate case[523] where there is an evidential basis for suggesting that the evidence of a child witness may be unreliable.[524]

4–185 In assessing whether a cautionary instruction should be given, for example on the basis that a child's recollection of events is poor and unspecific, it is important to bear in mind that children's perception and recollection of events is different to that of adults and it would be incorrect to apply adult tests for credibility to the evidence of children.[525]

G. Identification Evidence

1. Introduction

4–186 It has long been recognised that visual identification evidence poses a serious risk of a miscarriage of justice because an honest and responsible witness who is sure

---

[520] In its *Report on Child Sexual Abuse* (LRC 32–1990), p.60, the Law Reform Commission declined to adopt the Australian approach of setting out a statutory framework for giving a warning. The Commission took the view that introducing new and detailed legislative provisions would give rise to the possibility of confusion and litigation.

[521] See also the Canadian approach in *R. v W (R)* [1992] 2 CR SCR 122; (1992) 74 CCC (3d) 134; *R. v B (G)* [1990] 2 CR SCR 3; (1990) 56 CCC (3d) 200. However, the Oireachtas has not gone as far as the New Zealand legislature which, in s.125 of the Evidence Act 2006, prohibited the giving of a corroboration warning in respect of the evidence of children except where expert evidence is adduced that provides a basis for doing so.

[522] *R. v Pryce* [1991] Crim LR 379. But see Spencer, "Child Witnesses, Corroboration and Expert Evidence" [1987] Crim LR 239 at 242, where Spencer takes the view that children's evidence is not as reliable as that of adults and points out that children do, sometimes, make false accusations. Judges do retain a discretion to give a warning following *Makanjuola*, but whether any direction should be given and the terms of same must depend on the circumstances of the particular case: *R. v L* [1999] Crim LR 489.

[523] The Law Reform Commission, *Report on Child Sexual Abuse* (LRC 32–1990), p.58, envisaged that a warning would continue to be given in appropriate cases. See also *R. v W(R)* [1992] 2 CR SCR 122 at 266, where McLachlin J stated that: "The repeal of the provisions creating a legal requirement that children's evidence be corroborated does not prevent the judge or jury from treating a child's evidence with caution where such caution is merited in the circumstances of the case."

[524] Cf. *R. v Makanjuola* [1995] 3 All ER 730 at 733.

[525] *R. v B (G)* [1990] 2 CR SCR 3, (1990) 56 CCC (3d) 200; *R. v W (R)* [1992] 2 CR SCR 122; (1992) 74 CCC (3d) 134; *R. v S (W)* (1994) 29 CR (4th) 143.

that he or she is identifying the correct person may be mistaken.[526] In *People (DPP) v Mekonnen*,[527] McKechnie J explained that:

> "Where the conviction of an accused person is wholly or substantially dependent on evidence derived from visual identification, both human and legal experience has in a marked way alerted us to the risk of mistaken identity. This risk exists even where the opportunity for observation appears adequate. It exists even with a witness who conscientiously strives for truth and accuracy and who is convinced that in his present situation the threshold for both has been surpassed. It also exists even in the case of multiple witnesses, all of whom possess the same determination. Evidently, any slippage in such commitment increases the possibility of resulting injustice: the greater the slippage the greater risk. Hence, time after time courts at all levels have warned of such dangers. That is why a particular duty of enhanced scrutiny and critical appraisal is required in all cases where the issue is in play."

4–187   Indeed, visual identification evidence was singled out by the English Criminal Law Revision Committee as "by far the greatest cause of actual or possible wrong convictions".[528] More recently, in *State v Henderson*,[529] having considered the report of a Special Master appointed by the New Jersey Supreme Court to consider and evaluate scientific and other evidence about eyewitness identification, Rabner CJ summarised that evidence and the dangers of wrongful conviction posed by identification evidence as follows:

> "Study after study revealed a troubling lack of reliability in eyewitness identifications. From social science research to the review of actual police lineups, from laboratory experiments to DNA exonerations, the record proves that the possibility of mistaken identifications is real. Indeed, it is now widely known that eyewitness misidentification is the leading cause of wrongful convictions across the country.
>
> We are convinced from the scientific evidence in the record that memory is malleable, and that an array of variables can affect and dilute memory and lead to misidentifications."

4–188   The danger of mistake and of a consequent miscarriage of justice with this class of evidence is acute because the ostensibly simple act of identification by an eyewitness of a perpetrator is actually the culmination of a complex memory process[530] comprising three main stages: (a) acquisition of information; (2) storage of information; and (3) retrieval of information.[531] In the case of identification evidence, which involves the

---

[526] See generally, Lambert, "Swearing Blind With Pointed Fingers" (2000) 10 ICLJ 11; Tinsley, "Even Better than the Real Thing? The Case for the Reform of Identification Procedures (2001) 5 E & P 99; Roberts, "The problem of mistaken identification: Some observations on process" (2004) 8 E & P 100; Morgan et al, "Accuracy of Eyewitness Memory for Persons Encountered during Exposure to Highly Intense Stress" (2004) 27 International Journal of Psychiatry and the Law 265; Ferguson & Raitt, "If a picture paints a thousand words...": the development of human identification techniques in forensic anthropology and their implications for human rights in the criminal process" (2013) 17(2) E & P 127.

[527] [2011] IECCA 74 at [14], [2012] 1 IR 210 at 216-217, [2012] 2 ILRM 328 at 330.

[528] *Eleventh Report*, Cmnd 4991, para.196.

[529] (2011) NJ LEXIS 927. See the casenote by Pattenden (2012) 16 E & P 106 and "New Jersey Supreme Court uses Psychological Research to update Admissibility Standards for Out-of-Court Identifications" (2011-2012) 125 Harv L Rev 1514. See also, Rabner, "Evaluating Eyewitness Identification Evidence in the Twenty-First Century" (2012) 87 NYU L Rev 1249. For an analysis of the significance of the decision in an Irish context, see Berry, "The Perils of ID Parades" (2014) 19(4) BR 92.

[530] See *Craig v R.* (1933) 49 CLR 429 at 446 (*per* Evatt and McTiernan JJ).

[531] See Loftus, *Eyewitness Testimony* (Harvard University Press, Cambridge, 1979); Brigham, Wasserman and Meissner, "Disputed Eyewitness Identification Evidence; Important Legal and Scientific Issues" (1999) (36) American Judge Association Court Review, Summer, 12; Penrod, Loftus, and Winkler, "The Reliability of Eyewitness Testimony: A Psychological Perspective" in NL Kerr and RM Brady (eds), *The Psychology of the Courtroom* (Academic Press, Orlando,

perception, storage and recall of the identity of a person, a potential for error arises at each of these three stages.

4–189   During the acquisition stage, error may arise in the perception of the person if the conditions under which the observation was made by the witness were sub-optimal as where the witness has poor eyesight or was not wearing corrective lenses, or the witness obtained only a momentary or partial glimpse of the perpetrator's face or because the lighting or weather conditions were bad or because the witness was overcome by fear or shock. These factors can render unreliable, even so-called "recognition evidence" where a witness purports to identify someone with whom he or she is already acquainted. Further, even where the conditions of initial observation were good, an identification may be unreliable where the person observed is of a different race, ethnic background, age and, perhaps, class to the witness, because of the "all outsiders look alike" syndrome.

4–190   Turning to the second stage, the committal to memory of the image of the person perceived and the accuracy with which this is done will depend on whether the witness had any special reason to remember the person observed. Thus, there is a higher risk of error if a witness is asked to identify someone who was observed by him or her in circumstances which were not such as to put the witness on notice that it would be necessary to identify the person at a later date.

4–191   With regard to the third stage, the process of recalling the image of the person is obviously rendered more difficult and the potential for error increases the longer the lapse of time between the initial observation and the subsequent identification. Furthermore, it is rare for a witness to be able to recall the face and build of a perpetrator with exact clarity. Instead, what will generally be recalled by a witness is a relatively hazy impression which crystallises into a positive identification upon confrontation with the person again. It is evident, therefore, that eye witnesses are very vulnerable to suggestion and to having their imperfect recollection overlain or supplemented. Therefore, where improper identification procedures are used by the gardaí, there is a serious danger that a witness's recollection may crystallise into a mistaken identification.

4–192   The foregoing dangers are compounded by the fact that the usual method of detecting testimonial error, namely cross-examination, is not very effective in this context. While it can identify physical deficiencies on the part of the witness such as poor eyesight, and to a lesser extent deficiencies in the conditions of observation, it is not well-suited to uncovering mistaken identifications. This is because an identification is either right or wrong and cannot be parsed by careful cross-examination to reveal error. In addition, witnesses who have made identifications tend to exhibit great certitude in the correctness of their identification[532] and counsel seeking to elicit an admission from a witness that they could be mistaken may find such a line of cross-examination

---

1982); and O'Hagan, "When Seeing is not Believing: The Case for Eyewitness Expert Testimony" (1993) 81 Geo LR 741. This three stage theory is now well established, to the extent that this structure is commonly used by expert witnesses on eyewitness psychology while giving evidence in the US (see *US v Smith* (1984) 736 F. (2d) 1103 at 1107) and Canada (see *R. v Marinelli* (1988) 5 WCB (2d) 437).

[532] *People (DPP) v O'Reilly* [1990] 2 IR 415 at 424; *Scott v R.* [1989] AC 1242 at 1260–1261, [1989] 2 All ER 305 at 314, (1989) 89 Cr App R 153; *R. v Dickson* [1983] 1 VR 227.

to be counter-productive in that it results only in a trenchant reaffirmation by the witness of the opposite.[533]

4–193 Because of these dangers and problems, the courts have developed a number of safeguards to minimise the risk of a wrongful conviction from the admission of identification evidence. Thus, as will be seen below, a trial judge has a discretion to withdraw from the jury identification evidence which is considered to be particularly unreliable and, in any case where the prosecution case depends substantially on the accuracy of identification evidence, a trial judge is required to give the jury a cautionary instruction as to the danger of acting on foot of such evidence.[534] Furthermore, recognising that the reliability of an identification made by a witness in court and the consequent risk of a miscarriage of justice is crucially dependent on the quality of the identification procedures used at the pre-trial stage, the courts have laid down a number of rules and safeguards with regard to those procedures.

2. Pre-Trial Identification Procedures

(a) Introduction

4–194 Identification of the accused by a witness in court for the first time,[535] traditionally referred to as a "dock identification", has, as emphasised by the Supreme Court in *People (DPP) v Cooney*,[536] long been recognised as an undesirable and unsatisfactory procedure giving rise to a high risk of testimonial error.[537] This is because the procedure is extremely suggestive as the witness, operating on the assumption that the right person is being prosecuted, expects the accused to be the perpetrator. As Keane J commented in *Cooney*, "the identification of the accused for the first time when he or she is sitting in the place normally reserved for the accused and usually flanked by prison officers is of limited probative value".[538] Furthermore, a person, having been called as an eye witness may feel under pressure to "come up to proof" and identify the accused as the perpetrator and may, therefore, put aside any doubts that he or she entertains as to the correctness of the identification.[539] For these reasons, an in-court identification is regarded as having very limited probative value which will generally be outweighed by the risk of a miscarriage of justice attendant upon its admission, and

---

[533] *R. v Atfield* (1983) 25 Alta LR (2d) 97 at 98.

[534] In the US, the trial judge has a discretion to admit expert eyewitness testimony to counteract the prejudicial effects of identification evidence and alert the jury to the features of the memory which render it so unreliable. In *US v Dowling* (1988) 855 F 2d 114, the court recognised the established nature of the field of expertise relating to eyewitness identifications. These are psychologists specialising in human memory and perception, and an entire division of the American Psychologists Association (Division 41) is now devoted to the domain of psychology and law.

[535] See *People (DPP) v Lee* [2004] IECCA 18 at [14], [2004] 4 IR 166 at 173, where it was pointed out that, where prior identification of an accused has occurred, either by means of an identification parade or through a more informal method, it is a normal proof for a prosecution witness to identify the accused in court as the person of whom they are speaking. This, however, is not a "dock identification" or "in-court identification".

[536] [1998] 1 ILRM 321 at 328.

[537] See also *R. v Cartwright* (1914) 10 Cr App R 219.

[538] [1998] 1 ILRM 321 at 328.

[539] It is noteworthy that, in a number of cases, witnesses have purported to identify a defendant in court despite having failed to do so at an earlier identification parade. See, *e.g. People v Bond* [1966] IR 215; *R. v Murray* (1913) 9 Cr App R 248; *R. v Tricoglus* (1977) 65 Cr App R 16; and *Davies v R.* (1937) 57 CLR 170.

while a trial judge has a discretion to admit such evidence, it will only be exercised in exceptional circumstances.[540] Such exceptional circumstances were found to exist in *Cooney*. The evidence of identification by a number of witnesses of the accused at properly conducted identification parades had been excluded because the accused was in unlawful custody at the time and the Court was satisfied that the trial judge had correctly permitted dock identifications, and that he was entitled to take the view that "the admittedly prejudicial nature of a "dock identification" did not outweigh its probative value".

4–195   The general rule, therefore, is that a witness will not be permitted to identify the accused in court unless his or her ability to make an identification has been tested by an identification parade or other appropriate form of pre-trial identification procedure.[541] The one exception where in-court identification will routinely be allowed is in the case of "recognition evidence" where the witness purports to identify a person already known to him or her because, in those circumstances, the holding of a pre-trial identification procedure would be redundant.[542]

4–196   Initially, the courts declined to be prescriptive as to the precise form of the pre-trial identification procedure that was required.[543] However, in a number of decisions, the courts have identified a properly conducted identification parade as the preferred option[544] with recourse to another form of identification procedure permissible only where the holding of an identification parade is impracticable. Therefore, although there is no rule of law or practice requiring an identification parade to be held,[545] it has been emphasised that:

> "... the proper, regular and optimum method of holding an identification [procedure] for a witness who believes he or she can visually identify an accused person in a criminal case is

---

[540] *People (DPP) v Cooney* [1998] 1 ILRM 321 at 330. In *Holland v HM Advocate* [2005] HRLR 25, the proposition that the admission of a dock identification infringed the accused's rights under the Article 6 of the European Convention on Human Rights was rejected.

[541] *People (DPP) v Cooney* [1998] 1 ILRM 321 at 328.

[542] *People (DPP) v O'Reilly* [1990] 2 IR 415 at 420, [1991] ILRM 10 at 15; *People (DPP) v Cooney* [1998] 1 ILRM 321 at 328; *People (DPP) v Farrell*, unreported, Court of Criminal Appeal, *ex tempore*, 13 July 1998; *People (DPP) v Meehan*, unreported, Special Criminal Court, 29 July 1999; *People (DPP) v Gilligan* [2005] IESC 78 at [133] – [135], [2006] 1 IR 107 at 157–158; *People (DPP) v Costa* [2008] IECCA 1; *R v Capron* [2006] UKPC 34; *John v Trinidad and Tobago* [2009] UKPC 12. It follows that, if an identification parade is held, the recognition evidence will not be rendered inadmissible by any shortcomings in the manner in which the parade is held: *People (DPP) v McDonagh* [2001] 3 IR 411 at 428.

[543] In *People (AG) v Martin* [1956] IR 22, it was held that there was no rule of law or practice requiring the visual identification of a person to be proved by means of an identification parade and that each case required to be considered on its own facts. Subsequently, in *People (AG) v Fagan* (1974) 1 Frewen 375, the Court of Criminal Appeal acceded to the suggestion that: "... other types of identification may in certain circumstances be fairer and more dependable than a formal identification parade which, because of its surroundings, atmosphere, range of choice and limited opportunity for observation, may be a less than satisfactory means of achieving a reliable identification."

[544] *People (DPP) v O'Reilly* [1990] 2 IR 415 at 421, [1991] ILRM 10 at 15–16; *People (DPP) v Behan,* unreported, Court of Criminal Appeal, *ex tempore*, 1 February 1993 at 4; *People (DPP) v Duff* [1995] 3 IR 296 at 300; *People (DPP) v Lee* [2004] IECCA 18 at [27], [2004] 4 IR 166 at 179; *People (DPP) v Mekonnen* [2011] IECCA 74, [2012] 1 IR 210, [2012] 2 ILRM 325.

[545] *People (AG) v Martin* [1956] IR 22 at 30; *People (DPP) v McDermott* [1991] 1 IR 359 at 361; *People (DPP) v Cahill* [2001] 3 IR 494 at 505. *Cf. People (DPP) v Lee* [2004] IECCA 18 at [27], [2004] 4 IR 166 at 180.

an identification parade. Any other method of visual identification where it is a real issue in the case is necessarily a second-best."[546]

4–197 The desirability of holding identification parades where possible was also stressed in *People (DPP) v Lee*,[547] where Murray J stated:

"… because of certain inherent dangers in relying exclusively or predominantly on evidence of visual identification there is an onus on the investigating gardaí and the prosecution to ensure that evidence of visual identification is obtained in the most reasonably reliable form which, in the absence of reasonable cause, should be in the form of a formal identification."

4–198 The reason for this preference for formal identification parades stems, in part, from a recognition that it is accompanied by a number of procedural safeguards (examined below) which make it fairer to an accused than other informal methods of pre-trial identification.[548] Furthermore, it is considered to generally provide a much superior test of the ability of a witness to make an identification. However, it is very important to enter the caveat that, even in the case of identification parades, there is statistical evidence to support the view that they are overrated as a safeguard against the danger of mistaken identification.[549] Williams points out that:

"It is the experience of the police that at the majority of such parades the witness picks out nobody or the 'wrong' man. … It will be obvious that this fact seriously discounts the probative value of a positive identification. Quite apart from this, and even granting a reasonably good memory on the part of the witness, the danger of the identification parade is that the witness expects to find the guilty person present, and therefore, points out the man who he thinks is most like the one he remembers. Thus all that an identification parade can really be said to establish is that the accused resembled that criminal much more closely than any other members of the public did, which is not saying very much."[550]

4–199 For this reason, a cautionary instruction as to the dangers inherent in identification evidence must be given even where an identification parade has been held.[551]

[546] *Per* Finlay CJ in *People (DPP) v Duff* [1995] 3 IR 296 at 300. See also *People (DPP) v O'Reilly* [1990] 2 IR 415 at 421, [1991] ILRM 10 at 15–16, where O'Flaherty J, delivering the judgment of the Court of Criminal Appeal, "deprecate[d] any suggestion that the holding of formal identification parades have out-lived their usefulness", and *People (DPP) v Behan,* unreported, Court of Criminal Appeal, *ex tempore,* 1 February 1993 at 4, where O'Flaherty J stated "insofar as is practicable a proper identification parade is the ideal thing and should whenever possible be put in place".
[547] [2004] IECCA 18 at [27], [2004] 4 IR 166 at 179.
[548] See *People (DPP) v O'Reilly* [1990] 2 IR 415 at 421, [1991] ILRM 10 at 15, where O'Flaherty J stated: "The Court is also mindful that an important difference between a formal identification parade and an informal identification, such as in the present case, is that in the former the accused (and his legal adviser if one is present) has full knowledge about the composition of the parade and may object if it is perceived to be unfair. Furthermore, the court of trial will have the benefit of a detailed account of the parade and a description of those who participated in it. By contrast, an accused has no input where there is an informal identification and is unlikely even to have knowledge of it happening. Therefore, he may be seriously inhibited in challenging its fairness at the trial."
[549] *Report of the Committee on Evidence of Identification in Criminal Cases* (Devlin Committee), Cmnd 338 (1976), Table 1.
[550] Glanville Williams, *The Proof of Guilt* 3rd edn (London: Steven and Sons, 1963), pp.120–121.
[551] *People (DPP) v O'Reilly* [1990] 2 IR 415 at 421, [1991] ILRM 10 at 15.

(b) Procedure for holding an identification parade X

4–200   The procedure for holding an identification parade is well settled.[552] It involves placing the suspect among[553] eight or nine persons of the same sex and of similar age, height, appearance and dress as the suspect[554] and who come from the same socio-economic background[555] (termed "foils"). The suspect or his or her solicitor can object to the composition of the parade[556] and any reasonable objections should be addressed.[557] Such objections might relate to, for example, the likeness of the other participants to the suspect, the way they are dressed or the presence or lack of facial hair.[558] Although the fairness of the parade and its value as a filtering mechanism obviously depends on the likeness of the foils to the suspect, it should be noted that only rough similarity is required because it has been judicially accepted that it will generally be impossible to get foils who are similar in all respects to the actual suspect.[559] ,

4–201   If a witness indicates that he or she has made an identification, he or she will generally be asked to touch the person identified on the shoulder. However, if a witness is a child or an old person or is frightened it will suffice if he or she makes the identification by pointing at and describing the person in question.

4–202   It was emphasised in *People (DPP) v Mekonnen*[560] that Gardaí have an overriding duty to ensure the fairness of a parade, to adopt whatever safeguards are necessary to achieve this and to be "vigilant and proactive in this regard". One of the principal safeguards is that the identification parade should be conducted by an independent garda who is not connected with the investigation[561] and he or she is responsible for ensuring that the parade is conducted fairly. To that end, he or she should ensure that the witnesses do not have the opportunity to see the suspect in

---

[552] See the summary of the elements of the parade in *People (DPP) v Mekonnen* [2011] IECCA 74 at [17], [2012] 1 IR 210 at 218, [2012] 2 ILRM 325 at 331. Detailed guidelines for the conduct of identification procedures in the UK are to be found in Code D: Code of Practice for the Identification of Persons by Police Officers issued pursuant to the Criminal Evidence Act 1984 and a discussion of the appropriate procedures and safeguards is to be found in *State v Henderson* (2011) NJ LEXIS 927.

[553] See *People (AG) v Martin* [1956] IR 22 at 25, where the suspects stood apart from the foils during the parade, a procedure which was characterised by the Court of Criminal Appeal as "very unsatisfactory".

[554] *People (DPP) v O'Reilly* [1990] 2 IR 415 at 420, [1991] ILRM 10 at 14; *People (DPP) v Mekonnen* [2011] IECCA 74 at [17], [2012] 1 IR 210 at 218, [2012] 2 ILRM 325 at 331.

[555] *People (DPP) v Mekonnen* [2011] IECCA 74 at [17], [2012] 1 IR 210 at 218, [2012] 2 ILRM 325 at 331.

[556] *People (DPP) v O'Reilly* [1990] 2 IR 415 at 421, [1991] ILRM 10 at 15.

[557] If the suspect has a solicitor present at the parade and no objection is taken to the composition of the parade or any objection made has been addressed, it will be very difficult to subsequently challenge the fairness of the conduct of the parade at trial: *People (DPP) v Cawley*, unreported, Court of Criminal Appeal, *ex tempore*, 22 March 1999.

[558] Although the suspect and his or her solicitor are entitled to object to the composition of the parade, it would appear that they cannot insist upon the inclusion of persons of their own choosing: *R. v Thorne* [1981] Crim LR 702.

[559] *People (DPP) v O'Hanlon*, unreported, Court of Criminal Appeal, 12 October 1998.

[560] [2011] IECCA 74 at [17], [2012] 1 IR 210 at 218, [2012] 2 ILRM 325.

[561] *People (DPP) v O'Reilly* [1990] 2 IR 415 at 420, [1991] ILRM 10 at 15; *People (DPP) v Mekonnen* [2011] IECCA 74 at [17], [2012] 1 IR 210 at 218, [2012] 2 ILRM 325 at 331. In *People (DPP) v Brazil*, unreported, Court of Criminal Appeal, 22 March 2002, where the identification parade was organised by a garda who was not the investigating garda, it was held that the fairness of the parade was not vitiated by the fact that the investigating garda was present during the parade.

advance of the holding of the parade.[562] It is important that the garda in charge keeps a meticulous record of the conduct of the parade including full details and descriptions of all the persons taking part in the parade,[563] any objections made by the suspect or his or her solicitor about the composition of the parade, and any identification made by the witness or witnesses.

4–203   A suspect is entitled to have a solicitor present at the parade[564] and evidence of an identification where a suspect has not been afforded an adequate opportunity to have a solicitor present is likely to be excluded.[565]

4–204   If a parade is not conducted properly, as where the procedures specified above are not adhered to or there is any element of suggestiveness in the way that it was held, then this will reduce the probative value of any identification made.[566] At a minimum, the shortcomings in the conduct of the parade will have to be brought to the attention of the jury as part of the cautionary instruction which the trial judge is obliged to give to the jury, and where the conduct of the parade has been unfair to the accused this may lead to the withdrawal of the identification evidence from the jury.

(c) Participation by a suspect in identification parade

4–205   A suspect has a right to refuse to participate in an identification parade[567] and, prior to a parade being held, should be told of his or her right not to participate.[568] However, in *People (DPP) v Marley*[569] it was held that, if an identification parade is conducted notwithstanding the objections of the suspect, evidence of the parade is admissible at the discretion of the trial judge.[570]

---

[562] *People (DPP) v O'Reilly* [1990] 2 IR 415 at 420, [1991] ILRM 10 at 15.

[563] *People (DPP) v O'Reilly* [1990] 2 IR 415 at 420, [1991] ILRM 10 at 14; *People (DPP) v Mekonnen* [2011] IECCA 74, [2012] 1 IR 210, [2012] 2 ILRM 325. But see *People (DPP) v Brazil*, unreported, Court of Criminal Appeal, 22 March 2002, where it was held that the fairness of an identification parade was not affected by the fact that there was no record of the description of the foils who participated in the parade.

[564] *People (DPP) v Mekonnen* [2011] IECCA 74 at [17], [2012] 1 IR 210 at 218, [2012] 2 ILRM 325 at 331.

[565] In *People (DPP) v Marley* [1985] ILRM 17, it was held that evidence of a parade held in the absence of the suspect's solicitor (the solicitor not having arrived in time) was admissible at the discretion of the trial judge. However, that decision predates the decision of the Supreme Court in *People (DPP) v Healy* [1990] 2 IR 73, [1990] ILRM 313, elevating the right of reasonable access to a solicitor to constitutional status and, if a parade is held notwithstanding the request of a suspect for his or her solicitor, it would seem to follow that evidence of any identification should be inadmissible in accordance with the principles laid down in *People (DPP) v Kenny* [1990] 2 IR 110, [1990] ILRM 569 and *People (DPP) v Gormley and White* [2014] IESC 17, [2014] 1 ILRM 377.

[566] *People (AG) v Martin* [1956] IR 22 at 29.

[567] *People (AG) v Martin* [1956] IR 22 at 28; *People (DPP) v Marley* [1985] ILRM 17; *People (DPP) v Maples*, unreported, Court of Criminal Appeal, 26 February 1996; *People (DPP) v O'Toole*, unreported, Court of Criminal Appeal, 26 May 2003 at 11.

[568] *People (DPP) v Mekonnen* [2011] IECCA 74 at [17], [2012] 1 IR 210 at 218, [2012] 2 ILRM 325 at 331.

[569] [1985] ILRM 17 at 22.

[570] *People (DPP) v Marley* [1985] ILRM 17 at 22. The Court went on to hold that, if the trial judge rules the evidence to be admissible, the jury should be told: (a) that the suspect was not obliged to take part in the identification parade, even though he was in lawful custody at the time, and (b) that in assessing the weight to be given to the identifications effected at the parade, the jury

4–206 As will be seen below, if an accused refuses to participate in a parade or frustrates the parade when held, then gardaí may have recourse to an informal identification procedure.[571] The question whether an accused must be informed of these consequences arose for decision in *People (DPP) v Maples*.[572] The conviction of the applicant was challenged on the ground, *inter alia*, that the trial judge had erred in law in admitting informal identification evidence because it was not preceded by a clear and intelligent waiver by him, founded on a warning that his failure to stand on an identification parade might lead to an informal identification taking place. The argument was made that, although there is no obligation on the gardaí to hold an identification parade in all circumstances, when they do hold a parade, it must be conducted in accordance with fair procedures. The corollary of this requirement of fair procedures was that it should have been explained to the accused that, if he did not stand on the identification parade, recourse might be had to informal identification and so he might come to be identified in less favourable circumstances. Thus, it was submitted that there is a constitutional right to an identification parade, and before that right can be waived the consequences of such waiver must be explained to an accused so that he or she can give a full and free consent to the waiver.

4–207 The Court of Criminal Appeal declined to hold that there was any constitutional right to the holding of an identification parade. Instead, it characterised the holding of a parade as a police procedure which, once embarked upon, must be carried out in accordance with fair procedures. O'Flaherty J quoted his previous comments in *People (DPP) v O'Reilly*[573] that, if a suspect refuses to take part in an identification parade or attempts to frustrate the parade, then "he may have to live with the consequences".[574] Thus, there was a limit, which had been reached in that case, as to what was to be expected of investigating officers in the way of explaining a suspect's options to him.

4–208 Due to the terms in which the Court construed the applicant's submission, the ultimate conclusion of the Court is unsurprising. However, there was considerably more merit to the applicant's submission than the judgment of the Court would seem to indicate. A number of Supreme Court decisions[575] have embraced the idea that a suspect in custody is an autonomous individual who is entitled to make free and fully informed decisions as to whether to co-operate with the gardaí or not. To hold that a suspect has a right to be informed of the consequences of refusal to participate in an identification parade is not to create a constitutional right to the holding of an identification parade but to recognise that fair procedures are to be accorded to both the co-operative and the non co-operative alike. If a suspect is to lose the benefit of a procedure conducted in accordance with the requirements of due process, then it is submitted that the consequences of that decision should be drawn to his or her attention.

---

should bear in mind that the probative value of an identification parade is reduced by the refusal of the suspect to consent to its being held. The basis of direction (b) is not clear. Although the lack of consent of the accused to participation in the parade raises questions of fairness, it is difficult to see how the probative force of the evidence of the parade is affected.

[571] It appears from *People (DPP) v O'Toole*, unreported, Court of Criminal Appeal, 26 May 2003, that if an accused is aware of and attempts to frustrate an informal identification procedure, an identification can be made if it is possible and will be admissible in evidence.

[572] Unreported, Court of Criminal Appeal, 26 February 1996.

[573] [1990] 2 IR 415.

[574] [1990] 2 IR 415 at 421.

[575] See, in particular, *People (DPP) v Healy* [1990] 2 IR 73, [1990] ILRM 313, and *People (DPP) v Hoey* [1987] IR 637, [1988] ILRM 666.

4–209   Finally, it should be noted that, as O'Flaherty J pointed out in *People (DPP) v O'Reilly*,[576] an identification parade provides a filter for both the prosecution and the defence. Thus, while identification parades are generally held at the instigation of the gardaí, a suspect may sometimes request one to be held. In the UK, a formal identification procedure is mandatory where the suspect consents to participating[577] but there is no authority in this jurisdiction directly on the question of whether a suspect has an entitlement to insist on a parade being held.[578] Although the decision in *People (DPP) v Maples*[579] would seem to militate against the recognition of such an entitlement, it is submitted that a serious issue as to the admissibility of identification evidence would arise if the gardaí, despite request and without a good objective justification, refused to hold an identification parade.

(d) Recourse to other identification procedures

4–210   The holding of an identification parade may not be practicable or of probative value in certain circumstances as where the suspect is known to the witness,[580] the witness has previously identified the suspect,[581] where the identification is aural rather than visual,[582] the suspect is of a unique or singular appearance,[583] it is not possible to get together sufficient people to make up a fair parade,[584] or the suspect refuses to participate in or frustrates a parade.[585] In those circumstances, gardaí are permitted to

---

576 [1990] 2 IR 415 at 421, [1991] ILRM 10 at 15.
577 Para.3.12 of Code D: Code of Practice for the Identification of Persons by Police Officers issued pursuant to the Criminal Evidence Act 1984.
578 *Cf. People (DPP) v Cox*, unreported, Court of Criminal Appeal, 28 April 1995, where a complaint made by the accused as to the failure of the gardaí to hold an identification parade following a request by him to do so was dismissed in a cursory fashion by the Court, in circumstances where the gardaí had refused to hold the parade because the perpetrators had worn disguises and no useful purpose would have been served by having a parade.
579 Unreported, Court of Criminal Appeal, 26 February 1996.
580 *People (DPP) v O'Reilly* [1990] 2 IR 415 at 420, [1991] ILRM 10 at 15; *People (DPP) v Cooney* [1998] 1 ILRM 321 at 328; *People (DPP) v Mekonnen* [2011] IECCA 74 at [19], [2012] 1 IR 210 at 218, [2012] 2 ILRM 325 at 332. But see *John v Trinidad and Tobago* [2009] UKPC 12 where it was held that an identification parade should have been held even though the identification at trial was made by someone who knew the accused because he was on trial for capital murder and the holding of a parade would have eliminated the risk, however small, of a mistaken dock identification.
581 *People (DPP) v Christo* [2005] IECCA 3 (the suspect was arrested by Gardaí after the witness, who had been assaulted, saw the suspect on the street and identified him as the man who assaulted her); *People (DPP) v Mekonnen* [2011] IECCA 74, [2012] 1 IR 210, [2012] 2 ILRM 325 (witness had previously identified the accused in the course of an informal identification procedure in a public building).
582 *People (DPP) v Kavanagh*, unreported, *ex tempore*, 7 July 1999 (identification parade would have been an "unreal" exercise because witnesses purported to recognise the accused principally on the basis of his voice). See also *R. v Hersey* [1998] Crim LR 281. In relation to voice identification, see generally, Ormerod, "Sounds Familiar? – Voice Identification Evidence" [2001] Crim LR 595 and Warurton and Lewis, "Opinion Evidence: Admissibility of *Ad hoc* Voice Recognition: *R. v Flynn* (2009) 13 E & P 50.
583 *People (DPP) v O'Reilly* [1990] 2 IR 415 at 420, [1991] ILRM 10 at 15; *People (DPP) v Mekonnen* [2011] IECCA 74 at [19], [2012] 1 IR 210 at 218, [2012] 2 ILRM 325 at 332.
584 *People (DPP) v O'Reilly* [1990] 2 IR 415 at 420, [1991] ILRM 10 at 15; *People (DPP) v Mekonnen* [2011] IECCA 74 at [19], [2012] 1 IR 210 at 218, [2012] 2 ILRM 325 at 332.
585 *People (DPP) v O'Reilly* [1990] 2 IR 415 at 420–421, [1991] ILRM 10 at 15; *People (DPP) v Maples*, unreported, Court of Criminal Appeal, 26 February 1996; *People (DPP) v Cooney* [1998] 1 ILRM 321 at 328; *People (DPP) v Rapple* [1999] 1 ILRM 113 at 116; *People (DPP) v*

have recourse to an informal identification procedure. It was emphasised, however in *People (DPP) v Mekonnen*[586] that recourse to other identification procedures is not permissible as a matter of course or routine but will only be permitted in quite exceptional circumstances.

4–211 Where a formal identification has not been held, the courts will require an objectively reasonable justification for the failure to hold such a parade.[587] In *People (DPP) v Mekonnen,*[588] the Court of Criminal Appeal held that:

> "[W]here the conviction of a person is wholly or substantially dependent on visual evidence, such evidence should have resulted from a formal identification parade unless the Director of Public Prosecutions and gardaí can satisfy the court that the explanation for the alternative source of such evidence is objectively justified. In other words, the onus is on the prosecution to show why second best, in the particular circumstances, is the best available. This requirement reflects the oft recited nature of visual identification evidence and the court's duty to ensure that where relied upon, the best possible method has been utilised so as to obtain it. It will only be in the rarest of cases that the court, in the absence of objective justification, will consider secondary evidence: when available for consideration the procedures appropriate to the method used must satisfy the normal rules."

4–212 Accordingly, the explanation given by the prosecution authorities for the failure to hold an identification parade will be carefully scrutinised and the courts have criticised as unacceptable the following reasons for not holding a parade: that the suspect did not reside at home and was not, therefore, always readily available;[589] that the witness was reluctant to personally confront the perpetrators;[590] and that the gardaí considered it "more beneficial" to the accused not to hold a parade.[591] An acceptable justification was found to have existed in *People (DPP) v Mekonnen,*[592] where the gardaí had not formed a reasonable suspicion that the suspect had committed the offence so that he could be arrested and there was a limited timeframe within which to conduct an identification procedure before the accused left Dublin.

Cahill [2001] 3 IR 494 at 505; *People (DPP) v O'Toole,* unreported, Court of Criminal Appeal, 26 May 2003; *People (DPP) v Lee* [2004] IECCA 18 at [27], [2004] 4 IR 166 at 180; *People (DPP) v Mekonnen* [2011] IECCA 74 at [19], [2012] 1 IR 210 at 218, [2012] 2 ILRM 325 at 332. In *O'Reilly,* O'Flaherty J stated that, if a suspect refused to participate in or parade or frustrates the parade when held, then he or she "may have to live with the consequences".

[586] [2011] IECCA 74 at [23], [2012] 1 IR 210 at 220, [2012] 2 ILRM 325 at 333.

[587] *People (DPP) v Mekonnen* [2011] IECCA 74 at [22], [2012] 1 IR 210 at 219, [2012] 2 ILRM 325 at 333. The Australian courts have taken a similar approach, as s.114(2) of the Australian Evidence Act 1995 provides that eyewitness identification is not admissible unless an identification parade was held, or it would not have been reasonable to hold a parade. In England, para.3.12 of Code D: Code of Practice for the Identification of Persons by Police Officers issued pursuant to the Criminal Evidence Act 1984, para.3.12 stipulates that, when a suspect disputes being the person the witness claims to have seen, an identification procedure (which will normally be a video identification rather than a formal identification parade) is required to be held unless it is not practicable or it would serve no useful purpose in proving or disproving whether the suspect was involved in committing the offence. See, further, *R. v Forbes* [2001] 1 AC 473, [2001] 2 WLR 1.

[588] [2011] IECCA 74 at [24], [2012] 1 IR 210 at 220, [2012] 2 ILRM 325.

[589] *People (AG) v Fagan* (1974) 1 Frewen 375.

[590] *People (DPP) v Duff* [1995] 3 IR 296.

[591] *People (DPP) v O'Reilly* [1990] 2 IR 415 at 420, [1991] ILRM 10 at 13. O'Flaherty J observed that: "[w]hile it is right that those in charge of prosecutions should be scrupulous in looking to the rights of the accused, nonetheless, the decision as to what is most beneficial for an accused, in the preparation and conduct of his defence, must be primarily a matter for the decision of the accused and his legal adviser (if he has a legal adviser at the time)."

[592] [2011] IECCA 74 at [40], [2012] 1 IR 210 at 227, [2012] 2 ILRM 325.

4–213   Where recourse to an informal identification procedure is permissible, the precise form of procedure used is a matter for the gardaí subject to the overriding requirement that the procedure adopted must be fair to the accused[593] and this duty of fairness permeates all aspects of any alternative procedure adopted.[594] As emphasised by Lord Hewart CJ in *R. v Dwyer*[595] in the context of photographic identification, "it is the duty of the police to behave with exemplary fairness, remembering always that the [prosecution] has no interest in securing a conviction, but has an interest only in securing the conviction of the right person".[596]

4–214   It is considered desirable that an informal identification procedure should resemble as closely as possible the procedures of a formal identification parade although the extent to which this is possible will depend on considerations of practicality in light of the prevailing circumstances.[597] One important safeguard is that the procedure should be overseen by an independent garda who is not involved with the investigation of the offence.[598]

4–215   The most common and acceptable form of informal identification procedure is an identification in a public place whereby a witness is brought to a location, such as the precincts of a building, where it is anticipated that the accused will be present in order to ascertain whether the witness can make an identification.[599] In *People (DPP) v Mekonnen*,[600] the Court of Criminal Appeal regarded as fairly conducted, an identification of the accused, who was a male of African origin, that took place in Busáras in circumstances where there were about 400 people in total and approximately 11 or 12 black males there at the relevant time. Although it is sometimes done,[601] such an identification procedure should not be conducted in the environs of a court building as this may cause prejudice at trial if the accused seeks to challenge the fairness of the procedure.

4–216   Another method of identification is that of a confrontation, where a witness is

---

[593] *People (DPP) v Rapple* [1999] 1 ILRM 113 at 115–116; *People (DPP) v O'Toole*, unreported, Court of Criminal Appeal, 26 May 2003 at 11.

[594] *People (DPP) v Mekonnen* [2011] IECCA 74 at [30], [2012] 1 IR 210 at 223, [2012] 2 ILRM 325 at 336.

[595] [1925] 2 KB 799.

[596] *R. v Dwyer* [1925] 2 KB 799 at 803; *People (DPP) v Rapple* [1999] 1 ILRM 113 at 118; *People (DPP) v Mekonnen* [2011] IECCA 74 at [30], [2012] 1 IR 210 at 223, [2012] 2 ILRM 325 at 336. In *People (DPP) v O'Toole*, unreported, Court of Criminal Appeal, 26 May 2003, the view appears to have been taken that the question of fairness of informal identification procedures is a matter for the jury to assess. However, given that identification evidence from an informal identification may be ruled inadmissible where the procedures adopted are unfair, it is also a matter for the trial judge to consider in deciding whether the identification evidence is sufficiently reliable to be left to the jury.

[597] *People (DPP) v Dumbrell*, unreported, Court of Criminal Appeal, 10 December 2007; *People (DPP) v Mekonnen* [2011] IECCA 74 at [31], [2012] 1 IR 210 at 224, [2012] 2 ILRM 325 at 336.

[598] *People (DPP) v Mekonnen* [2011] IECCA 74, [2012] 1 IR 210, [2012] 2 ILRM 325.

[599] See, *e.g. People (DPP) v Duff* [1995] 3 IR 296; *People (DPP) v Mekonnen* [2011] IECCA 74, [2012] 1 IR 210, [2012] 2 ILRM 325. Empirical research by Robert et al, "Should we be concerned about street identification?" [2014] Crim LR 633 indicates that an on-street identification may not be any less reliable than the video identification procedures commonly used in the UK. However, whether this is so will depend, very much, on how the on-street identification is conducted.

[600] *People (DPP) v Mekonnen* [2011] IECCA 74, [2012] 1 IR 210, [2012] 2 ILRM 325.

[601] See, *e.g. People (AG) v Fagan* (1974) 1 Frewen 375; *People (DPP) v Behan*, unreported, Court of Criminal Appeal, *ex tempore*, 1 February 1993; and *People (DPP) v Cahill* [2001] 3 IR 494.

brought face to face with the suspect. However, an identification produced under these circumstances is of very limited probative value because of the inherent suggestibility of this procedure and recourse should only be had to it where no other method is possible or practicable.[602]

4–217 It is important to avoid any element of suggestion in the conduct of an informal identification procedure and it has been emphasised that gardaí must not do anything to influence the witness who is attempting to make an identification.[603] A suggestion made by a garda to the identifying witness in *People (AG) v Fagan*[604] that the witness would see the perpetrator drew the ire of the Court of Criminal Appeal with Henchy J stating that any identification made consequent upon such a comment would be "virtually valueless" as the witness might have felt bound to identify somebody

(e) Use of photographs

4–218 Section 12(1) of the Criminal Justice Act 2006 provides that a person arrested by the gardaí may be photographed in the garda station after their arrest[605] "for the purpose of assisting with the identification of him or her for the offence in respect of which he or she is arrested."[606] The use of photographs as part of the criminal investigative process is a common investigative technique but creates a number of difficulties. In the first place, there is a tendency for a witness who has been shown photographs "to substitute a photographic image once seen for a hazy recollection of the person initially observed".[607] Thereafter, "his recollection of the culprit and recollection of the photograph are likely to be so merged that he can no longer separate them, even though in fact his identification was mistaken".[608] This problem is compounded by the "Hobson's choice"[609] faced by an accused who wishes to challenge identification evidence by virtue of the fact that, by disclosing that photographs including one of the accused were shown by gardaí to the witness, he or she risks the jury drawing the inference that the accused has a criminal record.[610]

---

[602] See *R. v Ladlow* [1989] Crim LR 219; *R. v Samms* [1991] Crim LR 197; *R. v Miaponnose* (1996) 110 CCC (3d) 445.

[603] *People (DPP) v O'Toole*, unreported, Court of Criminal Appeal, 26 May 2003 at 11–12; *People (DPP) v Mekonnen* [2011] IECCA 74 at [26], [2012] 1 IR 210 at 221, [2012] 2 ILRM 325 at 334.

[604] (1974) 1 Frewen 375.

[605] Section 12(5) stipulates that a person who refuses to allow themselves to be photographed pursuant to this section is liable for a fine up to €3,000 and/or six months imprisonment.

[606] It should be noted that the power conferred by the section is not exhaustive. Subsection (6) provides that the power conferred by the section is without prejudice to any other power exercisable by a member of the Garda Síochána to photograph a person. See *People (DPP) v Boyce* [2008] IESC 62, [2009] 2 IR 124, [2009] 1 ILRM 253, where it was held that the provisions of the Criminal Justice (Forensic Evidence) Act 1990, which confer powers to take, or cause to be taken, certain bodily samples, did not oust the common law power to take samples for forensic testing on the basis of a free and voluntary consent of a person detained.

[607] *Per* Mason J in *Alexander v R.* (1981) 145 CLR 395 at 426.

[608] G Williams, *The Proof of Guilt* (3rd edn, Steven and Sons, London, 1963), p.122. *Cf.* the comments of Lord Hewart CJ in *R. v Dwyer* [1925] 2 KB 799 at 803, that where a witness picks a person out from photographs, "it is quite evident that afterwards the witness who has so acted in relation to a photograph is not a useful witness for the process of identification, or at any rate the evidence of that witness for the purpose of identification is to be taken subject to this, that he has previously seen a photograph."

[609] *People (DPP) v O'Reilly* [1990] 2 IR 415 at 421, [1991] ILRM 10 at 15–16.

[610] *People (DPP) v O'Reilly* [1990] 2 IR 415 at 421, [1991] ILRM 10 at 15–16; *People (DPP) v Rapple* [1999] 1 ILRM 113. Because of the prejudice that may be caused by the admission of

4–219   In recognition of these difficulties, the Court of Criminal Appeal in *People (DPP) v Rapple*[611] distinguished between two situations in which photographs may be shown to a witness.[612] The first is where the gardaí, having taken a description from a witness, show him or her a series of photographs in an attempt to generate a suspect ("suspect generation"). The second is where the gardaí have a suspect in mind and wish to confirm that he or she is the perpetrator seen by the witness ("suspect confirmation").

4–220   So far as the use of photographs for the purpose of suspect generation is concerned, the Court in *Rapple* accepted that this is a necessary investigative technique which is justified by reference to the exigencies of criminal investigation and is, therefore, permissible subject to the observation of certain safeguards.[613] The first is that the gardaí should behave with "exemplary fairness" when showing photographs to a witness so as to minimise any prejudice to the accused.[614] Thus, any element of suggestiveness should be avoided and, to that end, it is important that a series of photographs and not just one or two is shown to the witness.[615] The second is that a witness who identifies a suspect from photographs should also identify him or her "in the flesh" by means of an identification parade or, where this is not practicable, by some other informal identification procedure.[616] Finally, the trial judge should, in a case where the photographs have been referred to in evidence, draw the attention of the jury to the fact that photographs were shown to a witness and explain to them how his or her identification could have been affected by this.[617]

4–221   With regard to the use of photographs for the purpose of suspect confirmation, this procedure was criticised by the Court in *Rapple* as "clearly prejudicial and unfair".[618] This disapproval of the procedure was reiterated in *People (DPP) v Mekonnen*[619] where it was stated that the evidence resulting therefrom was valueless. Therefore, if photographs are used for this objective in advance of a formal identification parade or informal identification procedure, this is very likely to lead to the exclusion of the identification evidence of that witness.[620] In *People (DPP) v Brazil*,[621] Keane CJ stated that it would be unsafe for a jury to consider the identification evidence of

---

the photographs, they can only be put into evidence by the defence and not by the prosecution: *People (AG) v Mills* [1957] IR 106 at 108–109.

[611] [1999] 1 ILRM 113 at 117–118.
[612] See also *R. v Dwyer* [1925] 2 KB 799 at 803; *R. v Melany* (1923) 18 Cr App R 2 at 3.
[613] [1999] 1 ILRM 113 at 116.
[614] See *People (DPP) v Rapple* [1999] 1 ILRM 113 at 118, where Barron J approved the principle laid down in *R. v Dwyer* [1925] 2 KB 799 at 803, that "it is the duty of the police to behave with exemplary fairness, remembering always that the Crown has no interest in securing a conviction, but has an interest only in securing the conviction of the right person".
[615] *People (AG) v Mills* [1957] IR 106 at 109; *R. v Melany* (1923) 18 Cr App R 2; *R. v Dwyer* [1925] 2 KB 799 at 803.
[616] *People (DPP) v Rapple* [1999] 1 ILRM 113 at 115–116.
[617] *People (AG) v Mills* [1957] IR 106 at 109; *R. v Melany* (1923) 18 Cr App R 2. It should be noted that, in *People (DPP) v Rapple* [1999] 1 ILRM 113 at 116, the Court of Criminal Appeal rejected the submission that, because of the risk of prejudice consequent upon referring to photographs in open court, the accused should be entitled to cross-examine garda witnesses as to the circumstances in which the photographic identification was made in the absence of the jury.
[618] [1999] 1 ILRM 113 at 118.
[619] [2011] IECCA 74 at [28], [2012] 1 IR 210 at 222, [2012] 2 ILRM 325 at 335.
[620] *People (DPP) v O'Reilly* [1990] 2 IR 415 at 421, [1991] ILRM 10 at 15–16; *R. v Goss* (1923) 17 Cr App R 196.
[621] Unreported, Court of Criminal Appeal, 22 March 2002.

a witness who had been shown a photograph of the accused before an identification parade as such evidence would be "tainted and rendered almost valueless".[622] In that case, a photograph was shown to a witness after she had picked out the accused at an identification parade and, although this was criticised as "a not particularly desirable feature of the identification parade",[623] it was held that the identification evidence of the witness had been properly admitted.

4-222 The Irish courts have not yet had to grapple with the difficulties arising where an identification is made by a witness using photographs accessed through Facebook or other social media but these have been addressed in other jurisdictions.[624] In *Strauss v Police*,[625] the Supreme Court of South Australia highlighted the problems that can arise where an identification is made by a witness using Facebook in the first instance. Not only do such identifications lack the safeguards accompanying a properly executed formal identification procedure, there is a very significant risk of contamination from the views of other Facebook users, there is a lack of foils and there is a tendency for the witness to make a positive identification of a person who looks like the perpetrator followed by a displacement effect whereby the image of the person so identified overlays that of the original perpetrator. The admission of such identification evidence was one of the factors that led to the quashing of the conviction in that case. In the decision of the English Court of Appeal in *R. v McCullough*,[626] it was held that identification evidence which had been preceded by a Facebook identification was not inadmissible but the obvious weaknesses of such evidence had to be drawn to the attention of the jury. Subsequently, in *R. v Alexander*,[627] it was held that the prosecution should obtain as much information as possible in relation to the initial Facebook identification including the images that were accessed so that this material can be put before the jury in order that they can properly assess the reliability of the identification.

3. Withdrawal of Identification Evidence From the Jury

4-223 Whenever the prosecution case depends wholly or substantially on identification evidence which is challenged by the defence as unreliable (on an application for a direction or otherwise), the trial judge has to decide whether the identification evidence is sufficiently reliable to be left to the jury with a cautionary instruction of the dangers of acting on foot of it or whether it should be withdrawn from the jury.[628]

(a) The test to be applied

4-224 There has been surprisingly little judicial consideration of the test to be applied by a trial judge when deciding whether identification evidence should be withdrawn

---

[622] Unreported, Court of Criminal Appeal, 22 March 2002 at 5.
[623] Unreported, Court of Criminal Appeal, 22 March 2002 at 4.
[624] See, generally, O'Floinn and Omerod, "Social Networking Material as Criminal Evidence" [2012] Crim LR 486.
[625] [2013] SASC 3.
[626] [2011] EWCA Crim 1413.
[627] [2012] EWCA Crim 2768, [2013] 1 Cr App R 26 at [22].
[628] *People (DPP) v O'Reilly* [1990] 2 IR 415 at 421, [1991] ILRM 10 at 15; *R. v Turnbull* [1977] QB 224, [1976] 3 All ER 549.

from the jury. In *People (DPP) v O'Toole*,[629] the issue was decided by reference to the general principles laid down by the English Court of Appeal in *R. v Galbraith*[630] in relation to applications to withdraw cases from the jury.[631] However, it is submitted that the use of these principles, which are primarily directed towards circumstances where concerns are raised about the credibility of the evidence adduced on behalf of the prosecution, is inappropriate where the reliability of identification evidence is challenged. This is because the risk of a miscarriage of justice which arises in respect of identification evidence relates not to the danger that a witness may be lying but rather to the danger that an honest witness may be mistaken.[632] The test should, instead, be whether the identification evidence is sufficiently reliable that it can safely ground a conviction or whether it is so unreliable that there would be a risk of a miscarriage of justice if it is left to the jury. This accords with the approach taken in *R. v Turnbull*,[633] where it was held by the Court of Appeal that, if a trial judge forms the opinion that the quality of identification evidence is "poor", he or she should withdraw the case from the jury and direct an acquittal unless there is other evidence which serves to support the correctness of the identification. This was the approach adopted by the Court of Criminal Appeal in *People (DPP) v Christo*.[634]

(b) Application of the test

4–225 The decision as to whether identification evidence is sufficiently reliable to be safely left to the jury is ultimately based on an assessment of the possibility of a mistaken identification. A trial judge is, therefore, required to consider all facts and circumstances which bear upon the reliability/correctness of the identification evidence including the conditions of initial observation, the characteristics of the witness, the demeanour of the witness giving evidence and the adequacy of the identification procedures used.[635] Where it is present, the trial judge should also have regard to any other evidence which implicates or connects the accused with the crime, as this may provide a satisfactory basis for a conviction when taken in conjunction with the impugned identification evidence.[636]

---

[629] Unreported, Court of Criminal Appeal, 26 May 2003.

[630] [1981] 2 All ER 1060.

[631] It is important to note that both parties agreed that the *Galbraith* principles were applicable and the Court proceeded on the basis of that consensus.

[632] See *Daley v R.* [1994] 1 AC 117 at 129, [1993] 4 All ER 86 at 94.

[633] [1977] QB 224 at 229–230, [1976] 3 All ER 549 at 553.

[634] [2005] IECCA 3 at [8]–[9]. By way of contrast, in the US, eyewitness identification evidence will not be withdrawn from the jury unless there are shortcomings in the pre-trial identification procedures which create a substantial likelihood of misidentification (see *Simmons v United States* (1968) 390 US 377).

[635] In *State v Henderson* (2011) NJ LEXIS 927, the factors bearing upon the reliability of identification evidence were divided by the Supreme Court of New Jersey into system variables like lineup procedures, which are within the control of the criminal justice system, and estimator variables like lighting conditions or the presence of a weapon, over which the legal system has no control.

[636] *R. v Turnbull* [1977] QB 224 at 230, [1976] 3 All ER 549 at 553. See, *e.g. People (DPP) v Cahill* [2001] 3 IR 494 (held that the identification evidence in respect of one applicant should have been withdrawn at the close of the prosecution case but different conclusion reached in respect of co-accused in circumstances where there was other evidence implicating him in the offence that the jury was entitled to consider).

(i) Conditions of initial observation

4–226 A very important factor to be taken into account in considering the reliability and probative value of an identification will be the conditions under which the witness initially observed the perpetrator. In assessing these, all circumstances which affected the opportunity of the witness to observe the perpetrator have to be considered including the length of time the witness observed the perpetrator,[637] whether the witness saw the whole or merely part of the perpetrator's face,[638] the distance the witness was from the perpetrator,[639] the lighting conditions,[640] the weather conditions, whether the witness had consumed alcohol or drugs[641] and whether the witness was in a state of fear or shock.[642] Even if the conditions of observation were not ideal, the identification evidence will be left to the jury if the trial judge is satisfied that the witness had an adequate opportunity to observe the accused.[643]

(ii) Characteristics of the witness

4–227 The characteristics of the witness may also have an important bearing upon the reliability of an identification. Obviously, physical characteristics of the witness, particularly his or her ocular abilities, will be important but the age of a person may also be relevant.[644] A particular witness may, by training or experience, be better equipped to observe or identify persons. This was recognised in *People (DPP) v O'Callaghan*[645] where the applicant had been convicted of armed robbery on the basis of the evidence of a security officer. The perpetrators wore masks and the officer was face-to-face with one of them for only a couple of seconds. However, it later occurred to him that the man who had confronted him was one of two men who had entered the bank two days earlier and acted suspiciously. Having reviewed the videotapes from both occasions, he identified the applicant as one of the robbers. Endorsing the trial judge's decision to leave the evidence of the officer to the jury, O'Hanlon J observed that the "witness was not a mere casual passer-by, but a security officer who had worked in that capacity in the bank for over a year prior to the robbery. His duties required him to stand near the entrance to the bank and observe carefully people who entered and left the bank."[646] It would seem that the evidence of a garda or customs officer would also be entitled to extra weight because of these considerations.[647]

(iii) The Lapse of Time between the Initial Observation and the Identification

4–228 Given the inevitable fading of memory, the lapse of time that occurs between

---

[637] *Cf. People (DPP) v O'Callaghan,* unreported, Court of Criminal Appeal, 30 July 1990; *People (DPP) v Duff* [1995] 3 IR 296; *R. v Turnbull* [1976] 3 All ER 549 at 552.

[638] See *People (DPP) v Duff* [1995] 3 IR 296; *State v Henderson* (2011) NJ LEXIS 927.

[639] *State v Henderson* (2011) NJ LEXIS 927.

[640] *State v Henderson* (2011) NJ LEXIS 927. *Cf. People (DPP) v Smith* [1999] 2 ILRM 161.

[641] *State v Henderson* (2011) NJ LEXIS 927.

[642] See the emphasis placed on this factor in *People (DPP) v O'Reilly* [1990] 2 IR 415, [1991] ILRM 10. See also *State v Henderson* (2011) NJ LEXIS 927 where stress was identified as a factor as was whether a weapon was visible during the crime.

[643] See, *e.g. People (AG) v Hughes* (1958) 92 ITLR 179.

[644] *State v Henderson* (2011) NJ LEXIS 927.

[645] Unreported, Court of Criminal Appeal, 30 July 1990.

[646] Unreported, Court of Criminal Appeal, 30 July 1990 at 8.

[647] *R. v Ramsden* [1991] Crim LR 295 at 296; *R. v Tyler* (1993) 96 Cr App R 332. But see, *contra, Reid v R.* [1990] 1 AC 363 at 392.

the initial observation by the witness of the perpetrator and the subsequent identification of the accused is relevant,[648] particularly if a significant period of time has elapsed.

(iv) Familiarity of the witness with Persons with the Appearance of the Accused

4–229   As noted above, an identification may be unreliable where the person observed is of a different race, ethnic background, age and, perhaps, class to the witness, because of the "all outsiders look alike" syndrome. Where the case involves a cross-racial identification, this is a factor to which particular regard should be had.[649]

(v) Accuracy of Prior Description

4–230   The court will also have regard to any discrepancies between the description given by the witness to the gardaí of the perpetrator and the actual appearance of the accused, as these may cast doubt on the reliability of the identification made by the witness.[650]

(vi) Confidence of the Witness

4–231   A judge will also have regard to the degree of certitude displayed by the witness as to the correctness of his or her identification in the course of the identification procedure[651] and at trial.[652] While, as explained above, certitude is not, of itself, any guarantee that the identification is correct and does not relieve the trial judge of his or her duty to give a warning,[653] its absence is some indication that an identification may be mistaken.[654]

(vii) Pre-trial identification procedures

4–232   A very important consideration in deciding whether identification evidence is sufficiently reliable to be left to the jury will be the adequacy of the pre-trial procedures. As noted above, the courts now take the view that the optimum method of pre-trial identification is an identification parade.[655] A properly conducted identification parade may provide an *imprimatur* of reliability for identification evidence where the conditions of initial observation were not good.[656] Where the initial conditions of observation were poor, or there are other factors which undermine the reliability of

---

[648] *State v Henderson* (2011) NJ LEXIS 927.

[649] See *People (DPP) v Christo* [2005] IECCA 3 and *State v Henderson* (2011) NJ LEXIS 927.

[650] See *People (DPP) v Cahill* [2001] 3 IR 494 at 506 . Any descriptions given by a witness which differ materially from the appearance of the accused should be disclosed to the defence before trial: *R. v Turnbull* [1977] QB 224 at 228, [1976] 3 All ER 549 at 551–552.

[651] *State v Henderson* (2011) NJ LEXIS 927.

[652] See *R. v McCook* [2012] EWCA Crim 2817.

[653] *People (DPP) v O'Reilly* [1990] 2 IR 415 at 424, [1991] ILRM 10 at 18.

[654] See *People (AG) v Fagan* (1974) 1 Frewen 375 at 378–379.

[655] *People (DPP) v Duff* [1995] 3 IR 296 at 300; *People (DPP) v O'Reilly* [1990] 2 IR 415 at 421, [1991] ILRM 10 at 15; *People (DPP) v Behan,* unreported, Court of Criminal Appeal, *ex tempore,* 1 February 1993 at 4; *People (DPP) v Lee* [2004] IECCA 18 at [27], [2004] 4 IR 166 at 179.

[656] The importance not just of holding an identification parade but of holding one that is properly conducted with appropriate safeguards is apparent from the scientific evidence considered by the Supreme Court of New Jersey in *State v Henderson* (2011) NJ LEXIS 927. See further, Berry, "The Perils of ID Parades" (2014) 19(4) BR 92.

the identification evidence, the failure to hold a properly conducted parade may well prove fatal to its admissibility.

4–233   The importance of holding an identification parade as a factor to be considered by a trial judge in the exercise of his discretion to grant a direction can be seen in the decision of the Court of Criminal Appeal in *People (DPP) v Duff*.[657] The conviction of the applicant depended solely on the testimony of a bank official identifying him as one of the participants in the robbery. The official in question had observed a side profile of the perpetrator for a period of about 30 seconds during the robbery. Subsequent to the robbery, she was brought to the Juvenile Court in Smithfield to see if she could identify the perpetrator. Although, she was initially unsure because she saw the other side of his face, she identified the applicant after seeing the same profile as that presented during the robbery. In the circumstances of the case, the Court was satisfied that, having regard to the very limited time during which the witness had the opportunity of seeing the perpetrator, and having regard to the limited part of his face which she saw coupled with the lack of a formal identification parade, the trial judge should not have refused the application for a direction.[658]

4–234   One point of note about the decision in *Duff* was that Finlay CJ expressed the opinion, *obiter*, that the case might have been left to the jury if the on-street identification had been followed by a formal identification parade. However, it is submitted that, while the holding of an identification parade will generally provide some degree of reassurance as to the reliability of an observation made under unfavourable conditions, it cannot do so where it is preceded by an informal identification procedure. This is because the almost inevitable result of a formal parade will be that the witness will pick out the person previously identified during the course of the informal identification (even if that person is not actually the perpetrator) because the image of the person initially observed will be overlain by the face of the person identified during the informal procedure.[659] Therefore, while a subsequent formal parade is indeed likely to validate the result of the informal identification procedure, it will do so without any increase in the reliability or probative value of the identification. Reference can be made to the decision in *People (DPP) v Cahill*,[660] where evidence of identifications by witnesses made during an informal identification in a courthouse were excluded in circumstances where the witnesses had previously participated in an informal identification procedure in a garda station. Keane CJ stated that the identifications in the courthouse were "irremediably flawed" by the fact that they had previously seen the applicant in the garda station and knew him to be a suspect.[661]

---

[657] [1995] 3 IR 296.

[658] See also *People (DPP) v Lee* [2004] IECCA 18, [2004] 4 IR 166. *Cf.* the approach taken in New Zealand where s.45(2) of the Evidence Act 2006 stipulates that, if a formal procedure is not followed by officers of an enforcement agency in obtaining visual identification evidence of a person alleged to have committed an offence and there was no good reason for not following a formal procedure, that evidence is inadmissible in a criminal proceeding unless the prosecution proves beyond reasonable doubt that the circumstances in which the identification was made have produced a reliable identification.

[659] This was the finding of the empirical research conducted by Robert et al, "Should we be concerned about street identification?" [2014] Crim LR 633.

[660] [2001] 3 IR 494.

[661] [2001] 3 IR 494 at 506. It was undoubtedly an important factor in the decision that, when the informal identification procedure was held in the garda station, two of the witnesses failed to identify anyone and the third picked out the wrong person.

4–235 If photographs have been shown to the witness prior to the holding of an identification parade or informal identification procedure, then this will be taken into account as a factor significantly undermining the value of an identification made thereafter. In *People (DPP) v O'Reilly*,[662] a witness had been shown a number of photographs including one of the applicant prior to identifying him during an "on-street" identification. In these circumstances, O'Flaherty J expressed the view that the "trial judge's ruling should certainly have been sought on the admissibility of the identification evidence obtained in such frail circumstances."[663]

4. Cautionary Instruction

(a) Introduction

4–236 As the dangers posed by identification evidence came to be recognised, the practice was adopted by trial judges of warning the jury of the dangers of acting on such evidence. At first, the decision to give a warning and its terms was considered to be a matter for the discretion of the trial judge[664] but this quickly crystallised into a requirement to give a cautionary instruction in relation to such evidence in all cases. This process began in cases where identification rested solely on the evidence of one witness. In *People (AG) v Hughes*,[665] the conviction of the applicant was quashed by the Court of Criminal Appeal because of the failure to give a warning. Maguire CJ drew attention to the fact that the case against the applicant, who had not been professionally represented, depended upon the identification of him by only one witness and characterised the case as one requiring "the greatest care … in charging the jury, as to the way in which they should approach the case and particularly of the dangers inherent in evidence of visual identification."[666] Subsequently, in *People (AG) v Keffard,*[667] the Court of Criminal Appeal went even further, laying down a rule to the effect that "the jury should be directed on the necessity of exercising care in all cases where the visual identification is that of one witness only".

4–237 It was against this background that the Supreme Court handed down its seminal decision in *People (AG) v Casey (No.2)*.[668] The appellant in that case was convicted upon a re-trial of charges related to the assault and indecent assault of two young boys. There being no physical evidence to link the accused with the assaults, the case against him rested principally on the correctness of the identifications made by one of the victims and by a man who had given chase and had caught a momentary glimpse of the perpetrator in the headlights of his car.

4–238 The Court was of the opinion that juries might not be fully aware of the dangers inherent in visual identification evidence or of the numerous instances of mistaken identification and also that they might be inclined to attribute too much probative effect to identification. For these reasons, it was held that a cautionary instruction should be given in all cases where the prosecution case depended substantially on the

---

[662] [1990] 2 IR 415, [1991] ILRM 10.

[663] [1990] 2 IR 415 at 421, [1991] ILRM 10 at 16.

[664] *People (AG) v Casey* [1961] IR 264 at 280 (CCA) (*per* Teevan J).

[665] (1958) 92 ITLR 179.

[666] (1958) 92 ITLR 179 at 182.

[667] Unreported, Court of Criminal Appeal, 26 February 1962.

[668] [1963] IR 33.

correctness of identification evidence. Kingsmill Moore J, delivering the judgment of the Court, stated:

> "In our opinion it is desirable that in all cases, where the verdict depends substantially on the correctness of an identification, [the jury's] attention should be called in general terms to the fact that in a number of instances such identification has proved erroneous, to the possibilities of mistake in the case before them and to the necessity of caution. Nor do we think that such warning should be confined to cases where the identification is that of only one witness. Experience has shown that mistakes can occur where two or more witnesses have made positive identifications. We consider juries in cases where the correctness of an identification is challenged should be directed on the following lines, namely, that if their verdict as to the guilt of the prisoner is to depend wholly or substantially on the correctness of such identification, they should bear in mind that there have been a number of instances where responsible witnesses, whose honesty was not in question and whose opportunities for observation had been adequate, made positive identifications on a parade or otherwise, which identifications were subsequently proved to be erroneous; and accordingly that they should be specially cautious before accepting such evidence of identification as correct; but that if after careful examination of such evidence in the light of all the circumstances, and with due regard to all the other evidence in the case, they feel satisfied beyond reasonable doubt of the correctness of the identification they are at liberty to act upon it."[669]

4–239 On the facts of the case, the Court pointed out that the conviction of the appellant depended substantially, if not entirely, on the correctness of the identification by two witnesses, neither of whom had any previous acquaintance with him. While the trial judge had directed the jury adequately as to the deficiencies of the identification evidence, he had not given them the general warning as laid down by the Court and for this reason, the conviction was set aside.

(b) Terms of the cautionary instruction

4–240 In *Casey*, Kingsmill Moore J emphasised that the direction mandated therein was "not meant to be a stereotyped formula"[670] and this point was reiterated in *People (DPP) v Kavanagh*[671] by O'Flaherty J:

> "The Court rejects the idea that there should be a mechanical repetition of everything that is set forth in the *Casey* judgment. On the contrary, a judge should be accorded a wide discretion to express the warning in the way that he thinks best—having regard to the underlying rationale of the *Casey* decision."[672]

4–241 Accordingly, no particular form of words is necessary provided that the judge addresses all the relevant matters.[673]

---

[669] [1963] IR 33 at 39–40. *Cf.* the cautionary instruction requirements laid down by the UK courts (*R. v Turnbull* [1977] QB 224; *Scott v R.* [1989] AC 1242, [1989] 2 All ER 305, (1989) 89 Cr App R 153; *R. v Bentley* (1994) 99 Cr App R 342; *Rose v R* [1995] Crim LR 939; *R v Vasco (Pedro)* [2012] EWCA Crim 2004; *France v Queen* [2012] UKPC 28), the Canadian courts (*R. v Artfield* (1983) 42 AR 294; *R. v Collins* (1989) 32 O.AC 296; 48 CCC (3d) 343; *R. v Burke* [1996] 1 CR SCR 474; *R. v Henry* [2010] BCJ No. 2072) and by statute in New Zealand (s.46A of the Evidence Act 2006). A cautionary instruction is also required where evidence of voice identification is relied on by the prosecution (see *R. v Hersey* [1998] Crim LR 281 and *R. v Roberts* [2000] Crim LR 183).
[670] [1963] IR 33 at 40.
[671] Unreported, Court of Criminal Appeal, *ex tempore*, 7 July 1997.
[672] Unreported, Court of Criminal Appeal, *ex tempore*, 7 July 1997 at 9.
[673] See *People (AG) v O'Driscoll* (1972) 1 Frewen 351; *People (DPP) v Kavanagh*, unreported, Court of Criminal Appeal, *ex tempore*, 7 July 1997; *People (DPP) v Farrell*, unreported, Court of Criminal Appeal, *ex tempore*, 13 July 1998; *People (DPP) v McCarthy* [2007] IECCA 64 at

4-242   While it is open to a trial judge as part of the warning to read the relevant passage from the judgment in *Casey* to the jury because it is "so clear and easily grasped",[674] there is no obligation to recite that passage[675] and the mere recitation of that passage as a "stereotyped formula" will not be sufficient because the warning is required to be applied to the facts of the particular case before the jury.[676]

4-243   Also, while it is open to a trial judge to point out to the jury facts or matters that would tend to support the identification evidence,[677] it is important that the trial judge unequivocally convey the dangers of acting on identification evidence. He or she must not undermine the cautionary instruction by giving the jury the impression that those dangers may not be present in the case before them, as where an identification was described as "genuine"[678] or where gardaí giving identification evidence were described, without any evidential foundation, as "trained observers".[679] Furthermore, a trial judge must be careful to draw the jury's attention to any matters which would tend to cast doubt on the correctness of the identification.[680]

4-244   It was stressed by Kingsmill Moore J in *Casey* that the Court was merely articulating the minimum warning which had to be given in every case and that the facts in an individual case might require a stronger warning to be given.[681] Therefore, it

---

[146], [2008] 3 IR 1 at 48; *People (DPP) v Mekonnen* [2011] IECCA 74 at [47], [2012] 1 IR 210 at 229, [2012] 2 ILRM 325 at 341.

[674] *People (DPP) v McCarthy* [2007] IECCA 64 at [145], [2008] 3 IR 1 at 48.

[675] The advantages and disadvantages of using particular formulae when charging a jury in this regard were discussed in *People (DPP) v Mekonnen* [2011] IECCA 74 at [53], [2012] 1 IR 210 at 231, [2012] 2 ILRM 325 at 342–343, where McKechnie J said that: "there cannot be any objection in principle to conveying the import of any formulae to a jury, by words other than those used in the formula. Indeed, depending on how it is phrased and how it is delivered, such informal communication may be far more beneficial to a jury's understanding of the principles involved, than if a verbatim version was delivered. However, a formula should not be rejected simply because it is that and is so described. Unless its essence can be at least equalled, if not urpassed by informal language, there should be no unnecessary hesitancy in adopting its use. Much will depend on the subject matter involved and how the guidance has been framed. If it is couched in highly legalistic terms, informality may be most useful; taking care however, that all of the essential points are covered. On the other hand if what has been stated is described in plain and understandable language, the court sees no reason why it should not be adopted and would not stand over criticism of the trial judge for so doing. It just might be that such formulas cannot be bettered."

[676] *People (DPP) v O'Donovan* [2004] IECCA 48 at [15]–[19], [2005] 1 IR 385 at 391–392. In *France v Queen* [2012] UKPC 28 at [14], it was emphasised by the Privy Council that: "a formulaic recital of possible dangers of relying on identification evidence, if pitched at a hypothetical rather than a practical (in the sense of being directly related to the circumstances of the actual case that the jury has to consider) level may do more to mislead than enlighten. The purpose of what has become known as a Turnbull direction is to bring to the jury's attention possible dangers associated with identification evidence but that purpose is not achieved by rehearsing before the jury, difficulties that might attend the evidence on a purely theoretical basis…"

[677] See *People (DPP) v Kavanagh*, unreported, Court of Criminal Appeal, *ex tempore*, 7 July 1997 (not a misdirection to tell the jury that the case is stronger where more than one person recognised the accused).

[678] *People (DPP) v O'Hanlon*, unreported, Court of Criminal Appeal, 12 October 1998.

[679] *People (DPP) v O'Donovan* [2004] IECCA 48 at [19], [2005] 1 IR 385 at 392.

[680] *People (DPP) v O'Toole*, unreported, Court of Criminal Appeal, 26 May 2003.

[681] [1963] IR 33 at 40. See also *State (AG) v O'Brien* (1969) 103 ILTR 109; *People (DPP) v Lee* [2004] IECCA 18, [2004] 4 IR 166; *People (DPP) v McCarthy* [2007] IECCA 64 at [146], [2008] 3 IR 1 at 48; *People (DPP) v O'Donovan* [2004] IECCA 48 at [16], [2005] 1 IR 385 at 391.

is necessary for the trial judge in every case[682] where the prosecution case rests wholly or substantially on identification evidence to carefully examine the identification evidence with a view to pointing out to the jury any matters which might have affected its reliability.[683] These would include any deficiencies in the conditions under which the initial observation was made such as the fact that the witness only observed the perpetrator for a short period[684] or at a distance,[685] or in poor weather conditions,[686] the fact that the perpetrator was in motion,[687] or that the witness was in a state of fear or shock[688] or was drunk.[689] The judge should also draw the attention of the jury to any discrepancies between the description initially given by the witness and the appearance of the accused,[690] any inconsistencies in the evidence given by the eye witness, and any uncertainty expressed by him or her as to the correctness of the identification.[691]

4-245   It was held in *People (DPP) v Christo*[692] that a special warning of the difficulties that arise in relation to inter-racial identifications will be required where this issue is raised at trial. In that case, the main prosecution witness had identified the accused, who was black, as the man who had assulted her. She rejected the suggestion put to her in cross-examination that she identified the accused on the basis that her assailant was black and the accused was black and said that she did not think that all black people looked the same. The Court of Criminal Appeal held that the trial judge had erred in not pointing out to the jury the added difficulty of inter-racial difficulty and reminding the jury of the necessity to assess and weigh up the evidence of the witness as to her claimed ability to make an inter-racial identification in the light of all the other evidence in the case.[693]

---

[682] But see *People (DPP) v Lavery*, unreported, Court of Criminal Appeal, *ex tempore*, 19 March 2002, where it was held that the instruction of the trial judge was not deficient by reason of his failure to deal with the particular circumstances of the identification and the factors affecting its reliability because the trial had only lasted one day and all the evidence was fresh in the mind of the jury and had been drawn to their attention by counsel for the accused.

[683] See *People (DPP) v McDermott* [1991] 1 IR 359 at 362. See also *People (DPP) v McDonagh* [2010] IECCA 127, [2012] 1 IR 49 where an appeal on the basis that the trial judge had failed to sufficiently relate the warning to the evidence in the case was rejected. The English courts have taken a similar approach, holding that it is not sufficient to simply set out the guidelines and reference must be made to any matters potentially effecting the accuracy of the identification in the particular circumstances: *R. v Graham* [1999] Crim LR 212 and *R. v Doldur* [2000] Crim LR 178. This is also a requirement in Canada: *R v Henry* [2010] BCJ No. 2072.

[684] *People (AG) v Casey (No.2)* [1963] IR 33 at 40.

[685] *People (DPP) v O'Donovan* [2004] IECCA 48 at [19], [2005] 1 IR 385 at 392. *Cf. People (DPP) v Farrell*, unreported, Court of Criminal Appeal, *ex tempore*, 13 July 1998.

[686] *People (DPP) v O'Donovan* [2004] IECCA 48 at [19], [2005] 1 IR 385 at 392.

[687] *People (DPP) v McDermott* [1991] 1 IR 359 at 362.

[688] *People (DPP) v O'Reilly* [1990] 2 IR 415 at 423, [1991] ILRM 10 at 17; *People (DPP) v McDermott* [1991] 1 IR 359 at 362.

[689] *People (DPP) v Mekonnen* [2011] IECCA 74 at [48], [2012] 1 IR 210 at 229, [2012] 2 ILRM 325 at 341.

[690] *Ricketts v R.* [1998] 1 WLR 1016.

[691] *Cf. People (AG) v Fagan* (1974) 1 Frewen 374.

[692] [2005] IECCA 3 at [26]. See Byrne, "Inter-racial recognition and the Casey Warning" (2005) 15(3) ICLJ 29.

[693] As might be expected, this issue has arisen in a number of US cases and convictions have been quashed because of the failure to instruct the jury in relation to the difficulties arising in respect of cross-racial identification (see, for example, *State v Cromedy* (1999) 727 A 2d 457). See further, Aaronson, "Cross-Racial Identification of Defendants in Criminal Cases – A Proposed Model Jury Instruction" (2008-2008) 3 Crim Just 4; Aaronson, "Proposed Maryland Jury Instruction on Cross-racial Identification" (2007-2008) 3 Crim L Brief 2 and Rutledge, "They All Look Alike:

4–246   A very careful direction is required where there have been any shortcomings in relation to the pre-trial identification procedures.[694] In particular, if an informal identification procedure has been utilised rather than an identification parade:

> "there must … be added … to the very special warnings which must be given to a jury, a warning as to the difference in opportunity, control and credibility between an informal identification, even if organised so as to permit the picking out from a great number of people and an ordinary controlled identification parade."[695]

4–247   A particularly strong warning will be required if an identification parade or other informal procedure was preceded by the showing of photographs to the witness,[696] and in the exceptional circumstances where an in-court identification of the accused by a witness who was previously unacquainted with him or her is permitted.[697]

4–248   Where there are a number of counts on the indictment and the identification evidence relates to some but not all of the counts or there is separate identification evidence in respect of the different counts, then the jury must be warned to treat each count separately and that the evidence on one cannot be used in support of the evidence on another.[698]

4–249   If the case against an accused rests wholly or substantially on identification evidence, then a misdirection in relation to identification will lead to the quashing of the conviction and the Court of Appeal will not apply the proviso in s.3(1)(a) of the Criminal Procedure Act 1993.[699]

(c) Recognition evidence

4–250   A series of cases have confirmed the application of the *Casey* warning to recognition evidence,[700] and in *People (DPP) v Stafford*,[701] the Court of Criminal Appeal endorsed the proposition laid down by Lord Widgery CJ in *R. v Turnbull*[702] that, though recognition evidence "may be more reliable than identification of a

---

The Inaccuracy of Cross-Racial Identifications" (2000-2001) 8 Am J Crim L 207. This is also something that is required to be addressed in Canada (see *R v Richards*, [2004] OJ No. 2096 (QL) at para.32, 186 CCC (3d) 333, 70 O.R. (3d) 737) but not necessarily in Australia (see *R. v Dodd* (2002) 135 A Crim R 32 at [31]).

[694] See *People (DPP) v O'Reilly* [1990] 2 IR 415, [1991] ILRM 10.

[695] *People (DPP) v McDermott* [1991] IR 359 at 361. See also, *People (DPP) v Lee*, [2004] IECCA 18, [2004] 4 IR 166 and *People (DPP) v Mekonnen* [2011] IECCA 74, [2012] 1 IR 210, [2012] 2 ILRM 325. *Cf. People (DPP) v Behan*, unreported, Court of Criminal Appeal, *ex tempore*, 1 February 1993.

[696] *People (AG) v Mills* [1957] IR 106. *Cf. People (DPP) v O'Reilly* [1990] 2 IR 415 at 421, [1991] ILRM 10 at 15–16.

[697] *People (DPP) v Cooney* [1998] 1 ILRM 321 at 328–329.

[698] See *People (DPP) v Wallace* (1982) 2 Frewen 125; and *People (DPP) v Goulding* (1964) 1 Frewen 292.

[699] *People (DPP) v O'Donovan* [2004] IECCA 48 at [20], [2005] 1 IR 385 at 392.

[700] *State (AG) v O'Brien* (1969) 103 ITLR 109; *People (AG) v O'Driscoll* (1972) 1 Frewen 351; *People (DPP) v Stafford* [1983] IR 165; (1981) 2 Frewen 119; *People (DPP) v O'Reilly* [1990] 2 IR 415 at 420–421, [1991] ILRM 10 at 14–15; *People (DPP) v Murphy*, unreported, Court of Criminal Appeal, *ex tempore*, 3 November 1997; *People (DPP) v Smith* [1999] 2 ILRM 161 at 165; *People (DPP) v McNamara*, unreported, Court of Criminal Appeal, *ex tempore*, 22 March 1999; *People (DPP) v O'Donovan* [2004] IECCA 48 at [10], [2005] 1 IR 385 at 390.

[701] [1983] IR 165, (1981) 2 Frewen 119.

[702] [1977] QB 224, [1976] 3 All ER 549.

stranger ... the jury should be reminded that mistakes in recognition of close relatives and friends are sometimes made."[703] This position was reaffirmed in *People (DPP) v Smith*[704] where Murphy J, delivering the judgment of the Court of Criminal Appeal, stated that, "whilst there is a distinction in degree between recognition and mere visual identification of a person not previously known to the witness, this distinction would not justify abandoning or neglecting the rules in *Casey's* case."[705] Thus, a cautionary instruction must be given in all cases where recognition evidence is relied upon although "the degree of emphasis with which the rule must be applied will ... depend on the nature of the case and the evidence available".[706] Indeed, in certain circumstances, a strong warning may be required in respect of identification evidence that is classified as recognition evidence.[707]

4–251   Given that the position in this regard is so well established, it is surprising that, in *People (DPP) v Fee*,[708] the Court of Criminal Appeal drew a distinction between identification evidence and recognition evidence and held that there had been no requirement for the Special Criminal Court to give itself a cautionary instruction in relation to the risk of mistake in respect of the recognition evidence of a garda witness. However, there can be circumstances where a cautionary instruction in respect of recognition evidence may be unnecessary, particularly if the correctness of the identification is not actually disputed. In *People (DPP) v Freiberg*,[709] the contention that the trial judge had erred in refusing to give a cautionary instruction was rejected on the basis that the witness in question had been involved in an intimate relationship with the accused, no issue of mistaken identification had been raised during the hearing and she had, instead, been cross-examined on the basis that she was lying.

(d) Corroboration

4–252   In *Casey*, Kingsmill Moore J made it clear that he was not creating another corroboration warning and that the cautionary instruction was not dependent upon the concept of corroboration because "[a]n item of evidence falling within this formula may, according to its nature, have very little or very great probative value".[710] Nevertheless, many trial judges began to import references to corroboration into the warning, a tendency which was the subject of criticism in *People (AG) v O'Driscoll*[711] with Walsh J stating emphatically that:

> "The question of corroboration has nothing to do with the matter...The warning which must be given to the jury in respect of identification following the directions laid down by the Supreme Court in *People v Casey* must be given even in cases where there is ample corroboration because the whole point of the warning is that errors in identification can be

---

[703] [1977] QB 224 at 228, [1976] 3 All ER 549 at 552. See also *R. v Bentley* (1994) 99 Cr App R 342; *Beckford v R* (1993) 97 Cr App R 409; *R. v Capron* [2006] UKPC 34 and *R. v Ali* [2008] EWCA Crim 1522, [2009] Crim LR 40.
[704] [1999] 2 ILRM 161.
[705] [1999] 2 ILRM 161 at 165.
[706] [1999] 2 ILRM 161 at 165.
[707] *People (DPP) v Costa* [2008] IECCA 1 at [19].
[708] [2006] IECCA 102.
[709] [2010] IECCA 33 at [37].
[710] [1963] IR 22 at 40.
[711] (1972) 1 Frewen 351.

made even when the testimony as to the identification is given by several person in the same case to the same effect."[712]

4–253   Thus, a trial judge should not make any reference to the concept of corroboration in giving the cautionary instruction[713] although it appears that he or she may, in an appropriate case, draw the jury's attention to evidence which supports the correctness of the identification evidence.[714]

(e) Where presence at the scene of the crime is admitted

4–254   It appears from the decision in *People (DPP) v McCarthy*[715] that, where the presence of an accused at the scene of a crime is admitted and the only question is whether he engaged in the acts complained of, a *Casey* direction need not be given although the trial judge should ensure that he or she puts the defence case fairly and adequately to the jury and gives the jury such directions as may be necessary to avoid a miscarriage of justice.[716]

4–255   In *McCarthy*, the three applicants had been convicted of having participated with three other men in the gang rape of a young woman. The first applicant admitted being present at the time of the alleged offences but denied that he had had sex with the complainant. In her evidence, the complainant alleged that he was the first to have sex with her and that he had helped one of the others to take off her clothes. The Court of Criminal Appeal took the view that the principles laid down in *Casey* and subsequent cases were of "limited relevance" to a case where the accused admitted being present at the scene of the crime. However, the case against the applicant was wholly dependent on the correctness of the identification by the complainant of him as one of those who took part in the sequence of rapes. Therefore, it was essential that the defence of the applicant which was that the complainant had mistakenly identified him due to poor lighting, the amount of drink she had consumed, and the terrifying nature of her ordeal, was put "in clear and unmistakable terms to the jury".[717]

(f) Where it is alleged that the identification evidence is fabricated

4–256   The Irish courts have not yet addressed the question of whether it is necessary to give a cautionary instruction in respect of identification evidence where the defence case is not that the witness making the identification is mistaken but that he or she is lying. There are a number of English authorities to the effect that a warning is not required in those circumstances because such a direction would be pointless.[718] However, there is Privy Council authority[719] that the warning should always be given

---

[712] (1972) 1 Frewen 351 at 357. See also *People (DPP) v Quilligan (No.3)* [1993] 2 IR 305 at 355 (*per* O'Flaherty J).

[713] But see *People (DPP) v Costa* [2008] IECCA 1 for an example of a case where a trial judge nonetheless gave a corroboration warning in respect of the identification evidence of the main prosecution witness.

[714] *Cf. R. v Turnbull* [1977] QB 224 at 230, [1976] 3 All ER 549 at 553.

[715] Unreported, Court of Criminal Appeal, 31 July 1992.

[716] See *People (AG) v Casey (No.2)* [1963] IR 33 at 37.

[717] Unreported, Court of Criminal Appeal, 31 July 1992 at 8. See also *R. v Ockwell* [1978] 1 WLR 32 and *R. v Thornton* [1995] 1 Cr App R 578.

[718] *R. v Courtnell* [1990] Crim LR 115; *R. v Cape, Jackson and Gardner* [1996] 1 Cr App R 191.

[719] *Shand v R.* [1996] 1 WLR 67; *Capron v R.* [2006] UKPC 34.

on the basis that, even if the witness is honest, there is still a risk of mistake and this would seem to be the preferable approach.[720]

5. Video Evidence

4–257   In *People (DPP) v Maguire*,[721] the Court of Criminal Appeal considered the admission and use of video evidence for the purposes of identification in circumstances where the applicant had been convicted of robbery on the basis of video footage of the robbery and still photographs taken from the film without any other evidence of identification. Barron J, delivering the judgment of the Court, distinguished three situations in which video evidence or stills taken from video footage may be put before a jury.

4–258   Firstly, such evidence could be used to augment the evidence of a witness at the scene of the crime in order to show whether or not the witnesses had a reasonable opportunity to make an identification[722] or to explain why they were unable to make an identification. Where evidence was used for this purpose, the role of the jury was not to decide the issue of identification based on the video evidence but rather to decide whether the identification evidence of the witnesses was credible.

4–259   Secondly, the video tape or stills taken from it could be used by persons who were not at the scene but who knew the accused in order to identify him or her as the perpetrator of the crime.[723] Such an identification will almost certainly follow the recognition by the witness of the accused following a viewing of the video tape or stills before the trial and, in *R. v Smith (Dean Martin)*,[724] the English Court of Appeal emphasised the importance of implementing proper procedures to ensure that a record of the initial reactions of the witness to the tape or stills and the basis on which the recognition occured. Absent such a record, it would not be possible to assess the reliability of the recognition.

4–260   In order to lay the foundation for the admission of such an identification, it is necessary for the witnesses to indicate the capacity in which and how well they know the accused and they should also indicate any feature which, in their view, identifies the accused with the person in the still.[725] Once more, the video evidence is not admitted in this situation to allow the jury to make an identification themselves from it but, rather, to enable them to assess the credibility of the witnesses making the identification. The Court acknowledged that identification evidence of this type may cause difficulties where the witness making the identification from the video is a garda or other person in authority because of the danger of prejudice to the accused arising from the occupation

---

[720] See the qualified warning given in *R. v Giga* [2007] EWCA Crim 345.

[721] [1995] 2 IR 286. See also *People (DPP) v Allen* [2003] 4 IR 295; *People (DPP) v Foley* [2006] IECCA 72, [2007] 2 IR 486 and *People (DPP) v Larkin* [2008] IECCA 138, [2009] 2 IR 381, where the decision in *Maguire* was applied.

[722] See, *e.g. People (DPP) v O'Callaghan*, unreported, Court of Criminal Appeal, 30 July 1990 where the admission of evidence for this purpose was described by the Court as helpful to the jury.

[723] See, *e.g. Kajala v Noble* (1982) 75 Cr App R 149 (witness permitted to identify the accused from the tape of a television news programme) and *R. v Leaney* [1989] 2 SCR 393 (videotape may be used as basis of identification where a witness has sufficient familiarity with accused).

[724] [2008] EWCA 1342, [2009] 1 Cr App R 36 at [68]–[69].

[725] [1995] 2 IR 286 at 289.

of the witness and the consequent inference that might be drawn by the jury that the accused was a previous wrongdoer. Barron J. stated that such evidence is admissible but the accused must be protected from the prejudice which may arise and, thus, the evidence should be excluded if, in all the circumstances of the case, its prejudicial effect would outweigh its probative value.[726]

4–261 It is, however, clear from the decision in *People (DPP) v Foley*[727] that this discretion does not have to be exercised in favour of the exclusion of such evidence of a garda witness. In that case it was held that the probative value of the evidence outweighed its prejudicial effect because, without it, it would probably have been impossible to bring a prosecution against the accused at all and the garda only referred in his evidence to knowing the accused socially. In *People (DPP) v Larkin*[728] it was held that prejudice arising from the admission of such evidence and the consequent risk of an unfair trial can be overcome by means of suitable warnings from the trial judge. In that case, the Court of Criminal Appeal also rejected the proposition that evidence from gardaí identifying an accused from still photographs is inadmissible where there is other identification evidence available. However, the Court reiterated that a trial judge is required to engage in a balancing exercise so that such evidence should not be admitted where it did not have sufficient probative value. Furthermore, garda witnesses who are called should, where possible, be able to point to some non-criminal background context where the garda is in a position to recognise the accused.[729] The Court signalled that, where this is not possible, a very real difficulty may arise.

4–262 Thirdly, although the Court in *Maguire* regarded it is unsatisfactory to do so, video evidence can be left to the jury to form its own view on the question of identity in circumstances where no witnesses who are acquainted with the accused can be found who can or are prepared to come to court to identify him or her.[730] In reaching that conclusion the Court followed *R. v Dodson*,[731] where the English Court of Appeal had rejected the argument that identification by the jury could not be allowed because in carrying out this function, they were acting as experts. The Court took the view that no special training or expertise was required to make an identification and that the jury "were called upon to do no more than the average person in domestic, social and other situations does from time to time, namely to say whether he is sure that a person shown in a photograph is the person he is then looking at or whom he has seen recently."[732]

---

[726] See *People (DPP) v Allen* [2003] 4 IR 295 and *People (DPP) v Foley* [2006] IECCA 72, [2007] 2 IR 486 where evidence of a garda witness that he recognised the accused from a still photograph was excluded on this basis. In *Foley*, one garda witness who was in a position to say that he knew the accused socially was permitted to give evidence but the evidence of another garda witness who was not in a position to do so was excluded. See also *R. v Fowden* [1982] Crim LR 588 and *R v Grimer* [1982] Crim LR 674.

[727] [2006] IECCA 72, [2007] 2 IR 486.

[728] [2008] IECCA 138 at [22], [2009] 2 IR 381 at 390.

[729] [2008] IECCA 138 at [28], [2009] 2 IR 381 at 391.

[730] [1995] 2 IR 286 at 292. See also *Kajala v Noble* (1982) 75 Cr App R 149; and *R. v Nikolovski* [1996] 3 SCR 1197, (1996) 141 DLR (4th) 647 (if the evidence establishes that a videotape showing a crime being committed has not been altered, it may be used by the tribunal of fact to determine whether a crime has been committed and whether the accused is the perpetrator but it must be of sufficient clarity and quality and show the accused for a sufficient period to prove identification beyond a reasonable doubt).

[731] [1984] 1 WLR 971, (1984) 79 Cr App R 220.

[732] [1984] 1 WLR 971 at 979.

4–263 The Court in *Maguire* emphasised that, whenever video evidence is admitted, the *Casey* direction must be given and they should be instructed that, before they can convict, they must be satisfied beyond a reasonable doubt that the accused is the person shown on the film.[733] In that regard, it may be appropriate to warn the jury that the witness was aware that the accused was "in the frame" for the offence when identifying him from the video and that this is a factor to be taken into account.[734] The jury should also be warned of any inadequacies in the procedures leading to the identification from the video tape or stills before the trial.[735] Further, with the exception of those cases where there is no independent evidence of identification, the trial judge should make it clear to the jury that its function is to assess the credibility of the witnesses rather than to form its own view of the identity of the accused.

4–264 Although not addressed by the Court in *Maguire*, it should be noted that there is precedent in other jurisdictions for the admission of evidence from experts in facial mapping in order to give evidence as to the similarity between the face of the accused and that of a perpetrator as recorded on CCTV footage.[736]

H. Other Categories of Unreliable Evidence

4–265 As noted above, the traditional solution to the problems posed by potentially unreliable evidence was the creation of a corroboration warning. However, although it had been stated that the categories of suspect witness are not closed,[737] for reasons explored above in relation to the accomplice evidence warning, it is clear that the courts have lost faith in the utility and effectiveness of corroboration warnings. Accordingly, with the exception of the evidence of witnesses who have been incentivised to give evidence and/or are participants in the witness protection programme, most of whom are likely to be accomplices in any event,[738] the courts have refused to create any further corroboration warnings requirements. Thus, the courts have declined to extend the requirement to give a corroboration warning to identification evidence,[739] confessions,[740] prior inconsistent statements admitted pursuant to s.16 of the Criminal Justice Act

---

[733] [1995] 2 IR 286 at 290.
[734] *People (DPP) v Larkin* [2008] IECCA 138 at [29], [2009] 2 IR 381 at 391.
[735] *R. v Smith (Dean Martin)* [2008] EWCA 1342, [2009] 1 Cr App R 36 at [72].
[736] See *AG's Reference (No 2 of 2002)* [2002] EWCA Crim 2373; *R. v Atkins* [2009] EWCA Crim 1876, [2010] 1 Cr App R 8; *R. v Tang* [2006] NSWCCA 167, [2006] 65 NSWLR 681; *R. v Gardner* [2004] EWCA Crim 1639 and *Shepherd v R.* [2011] NZCA 666, [2012] 2 NZLR 609. See also, Roberts "*R. v Atkins* (D and M): evidence — expert — 'facial mapping'" (2010) 2 Crim LR 141, Edmond et al, "Law's Looking Glass: Expert Identification Evidence Derived from Photographic and Video Images" (2009) 20(3) CICJ 337 and Edmond et al, "Atkins and The Emperor: the 'cautious' use of unreliable 'expert' opinion" (2010) 14 (2) E & P 146. In *R. v Otway* [2011] EWCA Crim 3, an expert in podiatry was permitted to testify as to similarities between the walking gait of a person filmed on CCTV and the accused.
[737] *DPP v Kilbourne* [1973] AC 728 at 740, [1973] 1 All ER 440 at 447.
[738] See *People (DPP) v Gilligan* [2005] IESC 78, [2006] 1 IR 107 discussed above.
[739] *People (AG) v Casey (No.2)* [1963] IR 33.
[740] *People (DPP) v Quilligan (No.3)* [1993] 2 IR 305.

2006,[741] witnesses with a motive to fabricate evidence,[742] dying declarations,[743] the evidence of mentally unsound patients with criminal records,[744] the evidence of unwilling witnesses,[745] and tracker dog evidence.[746] Instead, it appears that the courts will deal with the problems posed by particular categories of unreliable evidence by means of a more tailored cautionary instruction in accordance with the principles laid down by the Supreme Court in *People (AG) v Casey (No.2)*.[747]

4–266   In that case, Kingsmill Moore J, delivering the judgment of the Supreme Court, stated that:

> "It is the function of a judge in his charge to give to the jury such direction and warnings as may in his opinion be necessary to avoid the danger of an innocent man being convicted, and the nature of such directions and warnings must depend on the facts of the particular case. But, apart from the directions and warnings suggested by the facts of an individual case, judicial experience has shown that certain general directions and warnings are necessary in every case and that particular types of warnings are necessary in particular types of case. ... The category of circumstances and special types of case which call for special directions and warnings from the trial judge cannot be considered as closed. Increased judicial experience, and indeed further psychological research, may extend it."[748]

4–267   Furthermore, as emphasised by Brennan J in *Bromley v R.*,[749] the necessity for a warning in an individual case is dictated by the risk of a miscarriage of justice:

> "When a warning is needed to avoid a miscarriage of justice, it must be given; when none is needed to avoid a miscarriage, none need be given. The possibility of a miscarriage of justice is both the occasion for the giving of a warning and the determinant of its content."[750]

4–268   Applying the above principles, it seems that, in general, concerns about the reliability of particular evidence or witnesses can be adequately accommodated within the rubric of the general duty of trial judges to put the defence case fairly and adequately. Thus, if the defence challenge the credibility and/or reliability of a witness and allege that his or her evidence must be treated with caution for some reason, that issue can normally be dealt with as part of the trial judge's charge to the jury. The situations where a more generalised direction or cautionary instruction such as that laid down in the *Casey* decision itself are required because of the risk of a miscarriage of justice will necessarily be limited but a number of categories of evidence in respect of which a more formalised duty may devolve on a trial judge are examined below.

---

[741] In *People (DPP) v Murphy* [2013] IECCA 1, the trial judge gave a corroboration warning in circumstances where the case against the accused was based almost entirely on statements given by a number of witnesses to Gardaí which were later retracted and admitted at the trial pursuant to s.16 of the Criminal Justice Act 2006 but, on appeal, the Court of Criminal Appeal gave guidance in relation to the charge that should be given in these circumstances which was quite different from a corroboration warning.

[742] *R. v Beck* [1982] 1 All ER 807, [1982] 1 WLR 461.

[743] *Nembhard v R.* [1982] 1 All ER 183, [1981] 1 WLR 1515.

[744] *R. v Spencer* [1987] AC 128, [1986] 2 All ER 928.

[745] *R. v Wilkins* [1985] Crim LR 222.

[746] *R. v Montgomery* [1966] NI 120.

[747] [1963] IR 33.

[748] [1963] IR 33 at 37–38. *Cf. Per* Lord Morris in *DPP v Hester* [1973] AC 296 at 309, [1972] 3 All ER 1056 at 1059.

[749] (1986) 161 CLR 315.

[750] (1986) 161 CLR 315 at 325. See also *R. v Miletic* [1997] 1 VR 593 at 605: "the judge should give any direction that is necessary and practical, in the circumstances of the case, to avoid a perceptible risk of miscarriage of justice".

1. Lies of an Accused

4–269 In *R. v Lucas*,[751] Lord Lane CJ identified four conditions governing the use of lies as corroboration as follows:

> "To be capable of amounting to corroboration the lie told out of court must first of all be deliberate. Secondly it must relate to a material issue. Thirdly the motive for the lie must be a realisation of guilt and a fear of the truth. The jury should in appropriate cases be reminded that people sometimes lie, for example, in an attempt to bolster up a just cause, or out of shame or out of a wish to conceal disgraceful behaviour from their family. Fourthly the statement must be clearly shown to be a lie by evidence other than that of the accomplice who is to be corroborated, that is to say by admission or by evidence from an independent witness."

4–270 The holding that the jury should be reminded in appropriate cases of the reasons, other than a realisation of guilt or fear of the truth, why a person might lie was the foundation of what became known in the UK as a "Lucas direction" and in this jurisdiction as a "Lucas warning".

4–271 The authorities in the UK in relation to the Lucas direction were reviewed by the Court of Appeal in *R. v Burge*[752] and four circumstances where such a direction is usually required were identified as follows:

> "1. Where the defence relies on an alibi.
> 2. Where the judge considers it desirable or necessary to suggest that the jury should look for support or corroboration of one piece of evidence from other evidence in the case, and amongst that other evidence draws attention to lies told, or allegedly told, by the defendant.
> 3. Where the prosecution seek to show that something said, either in or out of court, in relation to a separate and distinct issue was a lie, and to rely on that lie as evidence of guilt in relation to the charge which is sought to be proved.
> 4. Where although the prosecution have not adopted the approach to which we have just referred, the judge reasonably envisages that there is a real danger that the jury may do so."

4–272 The starting point in this jurisdiction is the decision of the Court of Criminal Appeal in *People (DPP) v Brady*[753] where the accused, who was charged with a sexual offence, had twice told Gardaí when questioned about the offence that he had been at work at the time of the assault but later admitted that he had been present although he denied assaulting the complainant. The Court considered it obvious that the fact that the accused had given a completely false account was certain to discredit him in the eyes of the jury and that this was an appropriate case for the jury to be warned along the lines recommended in *Lucas*:

> "[I]t seems common sense that when a particular problem arises in the evidence the judge should direct the jury as to how they are to handle it and it was not in the view of the court sufficient in the present case for the judge to rely on the general directions with regard to the burden of proof. This was clearly something that was going to weigh with the jury and they should have been directed in the view of the court that the evidence in question could be used against the applicant, as of course it could, but only on the basis that they were entitled to rely on it and if they were satisfied beyond reasonable doubt, that being the general standard of proof, that there was no innocent, that is to say no non-criminal explanation for the untruthful answers."

4–273 That decision was subsequently analysed by the Court of Criminal Appeal in

---

[751] [1981] QB 720 at 724, [1981] 2 All ER 1008 at 1011.
[752] [1996] 1 Cr App Rep 163.
[753] Unreported, Court of Criminal Appeal, 5 May 2005.

People (DPP) v Doyle[754] where the view was taken that the Court had not established a principle that in each and every case in which lies have been told, there is a positive obligation on the trial judge to give a specific direction in the course of his or her charge in relation to those lies.[755] However, the Court accepted that there would undoubtedly be cases in which a trial judge would be obliged to give such a warning and the failure to do so could constitute a good ground of appeal.

4–274   In *People (DPP) v Curran*[756] the Court of Criminal Appeal did not regard the question as to whether a Lucas warning should be given to a jury as definitively settled but it was in no doubt but that there were cases in which it would be appropriate to do so, particularly where the accused admits or concedes at or before the trial that an earlier account given is false and untruthful.[757] O'Donnell J explained the necessity for such a warning as follows:

> "The admission, or proof, that an accused person has been telling lies can have a very potent impact upon a criminal trial. There is a natural tendency to assume that if it has been established that the accused was lying on a previous occasion, then there is no reason to believe that he or she is telling the truth when in court. In such circumstances it is necessary to remind the jury that they should not necessarily make the leap from an acknowledgement of lying to a determination of guilt. Human experience, and indeed the experience of courts, can show that while it may not be very creditable, persons who have been involved in incidents, and particularly those in which another person has lost their life, may not always be forthcoming about their role in the events, and in particular may seek to exculpate themselves by denying involvement or possibly asserting some other exculpation such as self defence."

4–275   As can be seen from this passage, the main purpose of the warning is to explain to the jury that there may be reasons other than a sense of guilt why an accused has lied. As to how this should be conveyed, in *People (DPP) v Cronin*,[758] the trial judge gave what the Court of Criminal Appeal regarded as a model warning by identifying numerous examples of circumstances which might encourage a person otherwise innocent to tell lies. In the course of delivering the judgment of the Court, Finnegan J referred to the decision in *R. v Richens*[759] where Lord Taylor had approved of the model direction suggested by the UK Judicial Studies Board which was in the following terms:

> "The defendant has admitted that he lied to the police. You must consider why he lied. The mere fact that the defendant tells a lie is not in itself evidence of guilt. A defendant may lie for many reasons, for example: to bolster a true defence, to protect someone else, to conceal disgraceful conduct of his, short of commission of the offence, or out of panic or confusion. If you think that there is, or may be, some innocent explanation for his lies, then you should take no notice of them but if you are sure that he did not lie for some such other reason then his lies can support the prosecution case."

4–276   However, it is clear that a trial judge is not required to use any particular formula of words. In *People (DPP) v JS*,[760] the Court of Criminal Appeal emphasised that it is not its function to lay down precise or definitive terms in which a Lucas

---

[754] [2006] IECCA 163.
[755] This is consistent with the approach adopted in the intervening decision in *People (DPP) v Cleary* [2006] IECCA 25 which had been decided without the judgment in *People (DPP) v Brady*, unreported, Court of Criminal Appeal, 5 May 2005, having been drawn to the attention of the Court.
[756] [2011] IECCA 95, [2011] 3 IR 785.
[757] [2011] IECCA 95 at [41], [2011] 3 IR 785 at 808.
[758] [2008] IECCA 94 at [6].
[759] [1993] 4 All ER 877.
[760] [2013] IECCA 41.

warning, if required to be given, should be given. This was a matter for the trial judge to decide on the facts of each case and the Court made it clear that an accused does not have an entitlement to have the trial judge use words of his or her counsel's choosing. However, while underlining the breadth of the discretion enjoyed by a trial judge, the Court did accept that the warning would have to be contextualised to the degree that this is necessary.[761] It was also held that it is incumbent on a trial judge to instruct the jury that the prosecution must satisfy them beyond reasonable doubt that the particular statements relied on were deliberate falsehoods and not due to mistake or confusion or some erroneous but nonetheless legitimate and genuine belief on the part of the accused.

4–277 It can be seen from the foregoing that it is now well established in this jurisdiction that there is a requirement to give a direction in an appropriate case in relation to lies told by an accused. However, the jurisprudence in this area is somewhat more embryonic than in the UK and there is no certainty that it will develop along precisely the same lines.

2. False Evidence by Garda Witnessses

4–278 The approach to be taken where garda witnesses called by the prosecution are found to have engaged in the fabrication of evidence and to have committed perjury while giving evidence arose for consideration in *People (DPP) v Murphy*.[762] The accused had been convicted by the Special Criminal Court of conspiracy to cause an explosion. The prosecution relied, *inter alia*, on a number of alleged admissions by the accused. Prior to the trial, the defence had engaged an expert to carry out electrostatic detection apparatus (ESDA) analysis on the garda interview notes which established that the notes for one of the interviews had been altered in a significant way in order to conceal an earlier fabrication by two gardaí as to what the accused had said in the course of that interview. The two gardaí gave evidence that they had not altered the interview notes but the Special Criminal Court was satisfied that they had lied and committed perjury. While evidence as to that interview was excluded, the Court had not ruled inadmissible other admissions made by the accused and had also refused an application for a direction. On appeal, the Court of Criminal Appeal followed the decision of the Northern Ireland Court of Appeal in *R. v Lattimer*[763] and held that there was no automatic rule that an accused was entitled to a direction because police officers were found to have lied while giving evidence.[764] However, the alteration of the interview notes raised a question as to the extent to which other garda officers had colluded in this. It was accepted that the Special Criminal Court had been entitled to find that there was evidence which could support the contention that the other garda officers had not colluded to falsify interviews but it was held that, at the very least, the circumstances of the case demanded a warning that, having excised the tainted evidence, the surviving garda evidence would have to evaluated in the most critical and careful manner. It was stated that, in the case of a trial by jury, a very strong warning to this effect would have had to be given. The Court of Criminal Appeal proceeded to quash

---

[761] See further *People (DPP) v Massoud* [2009] IECCA 94 where a complaint that there had been a failure to properly contextualise a Lucas warning was dismissed in circumstances where the lie in question was stark and admitted by the accused and an explanation for it had been offered by him.

[762] [2005] IECCA 1, [2005] 2 IR 125.

[763] [1992] NI 45.

[764] [2005] IECCA 1 at [54], [2005] 2 IR 125 at 143.

the conviction of the accused as unsafe because it was not satisfied that the trial court had evaluated the suriving garda evidence with the degree of extra critical analysis which was required and, in particular, had failed to take into account the impact on the evidence of another garda witness of criticisms made of him by the Special Criminal Court in another case[765] and had engaged in speculation that other gardaí did not have knowledge of the wrongdoing.

3. Witnesses With Motive to Fabricate Evidence

4–279 Apart from accomplices, there are many witnesses who, for a variety of reasons, have a motive to give false or inaccurate evidence and the question arises as to what warning, if any should be given in respect of their evidence.

4–280 The solution initially suggested by Edmund Davies J in *R. v Prater*[766] was to extend the requirement to give a corroboration warning to witnesses with a purpose of their own to serve. However, this development would have had the had the effect of completely outflanking the definition of an accomplice laid down in *Davies v DPP*[767] and of extending the technicality of the corroboration warning to a new and amorphous category of witness. It was not surprising, therefore, that this solution was rejected by the Court of Appeal in *R. v Beck*.[768] However, the Court was at pains to stress that it did not, in any way "wish to detract from the obligation on a judge to advise a jury to proceed with caution where there is material to suggest[769] that a witness's evidence may be tainted by an improper motive, and the strength of that advice must vary according to the facts of the case".[770]

4–281 Thus, in accordance with the principles identified in *Casey*, it would appear that there is a general obligation on a trial judge to give a jury such cautionary instruction as is necessary and appropriate to avoid a miscarriage of justice whenever there is an evidential basis for suggesting that a witness may have a motive for giving false or inaccurate testimony.[771] It is possible to identify a wide variety of such motives as where the witness may be the perpetrator of the offence,[772] the witness may be trying to shield the perpetrator of the offence,[773] the witness has a financial or personal interest

---

[765] *People (DPP) v Gilligan*, Special Criminal Court, 5 March 2001.

[766] [1960] 2 QB 464, [1960] 1 All ER 298.

[767] [1954] AC 378, [1954] 1 All ER 507.

[768] [1982] 1 All ER 807, [1982] 1 WLR 461.

[769] The mere suggestions of counsel for the defence are not sufficient: *R. v Mouqni*, unreported, Court of Appeal, 29 March 1994.

[770] [1982] 1 All ER 807 at 813, [1982] 1 WLR 461 at 469. See also, *R. v Stainton* [1983] Crim LR 171 and *R. v Petkar* [2003] All ER 278, [2004] Crim LR 157. It is clear that the cautionary instruction is to be distinguished from a corroboration warning and there is no requirement to mention the concept of corroboration: *R. v Spencer* [1987] AC 128 at 142, [1986] 2 All ER 928 at 938. In *R. v Muncaster* [1999] Crim LR 409, the English Court of Criminal Appeal extended the principles as set out in *Makanjuola* to this category of witnesses, holding that whether a warning is given, and the strength of that warning where given, are matters of judicial discretion.

[771] In New Zealand, s.122 of the Evidence Act 2006 requires a judge, in proceedings tried with a jury, to consider whether to give a warning of the need for caution whenever evidence is given by a witness who may have a motive to give false evidence that is prejudicial to a defendant. See further, *Taylor v R* [2010] NZCA 69 and *Hudson v R* [2011] NZSC 51, [2011] 3 NZLR 289.

[772] *R. v Whitaker* (1976) 63 Cr App R 193; *R. v Ling* (1981) 6 A Crim R429.

[773] *R. v Ashgar* [1995] 1 Cr App R 223.

in the outcome,[774] or there is evidence to suggest that a witness has something to gain from giving evidence.[775]

4–282   The issue has not been squarely addressed by the Irish courts but, in *People (DPP) v Meehan*,[776] the Special Criminal Court accepted the submission of the prosecution that, although a witness who was a social acquaintance of the accused and other members of the criminal gang of which the accused was alleged to be a member should not be regarded as an accomplice, his evidence should be treated with caution because of his close association with witnesses who were accomplices.

4. Confessions

4–283   In *People (DPP) v Quilligan (No.3)*,[777] the Supreme Court rejected the contention that there should be a rule of practice that a judge should give a warning that it is unsafe to convict on the uncorroborated evidence of a confession made by an accused. However, such a requirement was introduced by s.10 of the Criminal Procedure Act 1993 which stipulates that, in all cases tried on indictment where evidence is given of a confession made by the accused that that evidence is not corroborated, the judge is required to advise the jury to have due regard to the absence of corroboration. The content of this charge and the circumstances in which it is required are discussed further in Chap.8.

5. Prior Inconsistent Statements Admitted Pursuant to s.16 of the Criminal Justice Act 2006

4–284   In *People (DPP) v Murphy*,[778] the Court of Criminal Appeal gave guidance as to the terms of a cautionary instruction that should be given to the jury where the prior inconsistent statement of a witness is admitted pursuant to s.16 of the Criminal Justice Act 2006. The content of this cautionary instruction and the circumstances in which it is required are discussed further in Chap.5.

6. Witnesses With a Mental Disability

4–285   Another category of evidence in respect of which some form of generalised cautionary instruction may be required is where a witness is suffering from a mental

---

[774] *R. v Beck* [1982] 1 All ER 807, [1982] 1 WLR 461. See also *R. v Cheema* [1994] 1 All ER 639, [1994] 1 WLR 147.

[775] In *Chan Wai-keung v R.* [1995] 2 All ER 438, the chief prosecution witness, who had been convicted of a serious offence in separate proceedings, gave evidence against the appellant in the expectation of obtaining a reduction in sentence. In those circumstances, it was held that the potential fallibility of his evidence had to be put squarely before the jury. See also, *R. v Collie* (1991) 55 A Crim R139; *Collett v Bennett* (1986) 21 A Crim R410 at 415 (*per* Zelling J).

[776] Unreported, Special Criminal Court, 29 July 1999.

[777] [1993] 2 IR 305.

[778] [2013] IECCA 1.

disorder or disability.[779] In *Bromley v R.*,[780] a majority of the High Court of Australia took the view that, if, in a criminal trial, it appears that a witness whose evidence is important has some mental disability which may affect his or her capacity to give reliable evidence, the jury should be given a warning of the possible danger of convicting on the testimony of that person unless it is confirmed by other evidence.[781] Again, the issue has not really been considered by the Irish courts although it should be noted that, in *People (DPP) v Molloy*,[782] the Court of Criminal Appeal stated that one of the matters which should have been brought to the attention of the jury in that case was the mental status of the complainant, *i.e.* that she had a childlike mind.[783]

---

[779] It might be noted that in its *Report on Sexual Offences Against the Mentally Handicapped* (LRC 33–1990, p.24) the Law Reform Commission recommended that there should be no corroboration requirement with respect to the testimony of the mentally handicapped. Under English law, s.77 of the Police and Criminal Evidence Act 1984 imposes on a court a duty to given a corroboration warning as regards a confession of an accuse with a mental disability in certain circumstances.

[780] (1986) 161 CLR 315.

[781] See also *R. v Spencer* [1987] AC 128, [1986] 2 All ER 928; and *R. v Adams* [1997] 1 Cr App R 369.

[782] Unreported, Court of Criminal Appeal, 28 July 1995.

[783] Unreported, Court of Criminal Appeal, 28 July 1995 at 6–7. *Cf. People (DPP) v Gillane*, unreported, Court of Criminal Appeal, 14 December 1998 (conviction not unsafe and unsatisfactory because it was based on the evidence of a witness who gave evidence that he had a microchip in his head and he thought that people could read his mind in circumstances where trial judge had given proper charge in relation to these matters to the jury).

CHAPTER 5

THE RULE AGAINST HEARSAY

A. Introduction

5–01 By virtue of the exclusionary rule in respect of hearsay evidence, a statement, whether made orally, in writing or by communicative conduct, other than one made by a person testifying in the proceedings in which it is sought to be admitted, is inadmissible if tendered as evidence of the truth of any fact asserted.[1] Perhaps the most helpful judicial explanation of the rule in this jurisdiction is to be found in *Cullen v Clarke*[2] where Kingsmill Moore J stated:

> "[I]t is necessary to emphasise that there is *no* general rule of evidence to the effect that a witness may not testify as to the words spoken by a person who is not produced as a witness. There is a general rule subject to many exceptions that evidence of the speaking of such words is inadmissible to prove the truth of the facts which they assert. ... This is known as the rule against hearsay."[3]

---

[1] One of the most commonly cited definitions of hearsay is that found in various editions of *Cross on Evidence*, viz. "An assertion other than one made by a person while giving oral evidence in the proceedings is inadmissible as evidence of any fact asserted". This definition, taken from Cross and Tapper, *Cross on Evidence* 8th edn (London: Butterworths, 1999), p.46 was quoted with approval in *People (DPP) v Murphy*, unreported, Court of Criminal Appeal, 8 July 2003 at 12, and the same definition, taken from Cross, *Cross on Evidence* 6th edn, p.38, was endorsed in *People (DPP) v Gartland* [2010] IECCA 100. To similar effect, in *Horncastle v R.* [2009] UKSC 14 at [20], [2010] 2 WLR 47 at 99, Lord Philips defined hearsay as follows: "Hearsay evidence is any statement of fact other than one made, of his own knowledge, by a witness in the course of oral testimony." However, these definitions do not really capture all of the complexities of the concept and a more complete formulation of the concept of hearsay is that proposed by the Law Reform Commission in its *Consultation Paper on Hearsay in Civil and Criminal Cases* (LRC CP60–2010) at [2.13]: "any statement, whether a verbal statement, written document or conduct, which is made, generated or which occurred out of court involving a person who is not produced in court as a witness, and where the statement is presented as testimony to prove the truth of the facts which they assert". See also the definition of "hearsay" contained in rule 801 of the Federal Rules of Evidence: "'Hearsay' is a statement, other than one made by the declarant while testifying at the trial or hearing, offered in evidence to prove the truth of the matter asserted." The concept of "statement" is further defined to mean "(1) an oral or written assertion or (2) nonverbal conduct of a person, if it is intended by him as an assertion".

[2] [1963] IR 368.

[3] This passage was described as the *locus classicus* on the rule against hearsay in this jurisdiction by Keane J in *Eastern Health Board v MK* [1999] 2 IR 99 at 123, [1999] 2 ILRM 321 at 345. See to similar effect, *Ratten v R.* [1972] AC 378 at 387, [1971] 3 All ER 801 at 805; *Subramaniam v Public Prosecutor* [1956] 1 WLR 965 at 970.

5–02   This passage serves to emphasise a cardinal and, at times, misunderstood, aspect of the rule against hearsay which is that it does not exclude all out-of-court statements, just those that are offered for the purpose of proving the truth of their contents. As Fish J noted in *R. v Baldree*,[4] this is one of the defining features of hearsay.

5–03   The hearsay rule is regarded as a fundamental principle of the law of evidence.[5] Unfortunately, it is also one of the most complicated with the result that it is difficult to provide an entirely satisfactory exposition of the rule and its exceptions.[6] These difficulties are compounded in this jurisdiction by the relative paucity of case law in this area in recent decades.

B. Basis of the Rule

5–04   A variety of justifications have been advanced for the hearsay rule[7] and these are discussed below. Each can be seen to have played some part in the development of the rule and, in some cases at least, provide a rationale for its continued vitality. However, it is doubtful if any of the rationales identified below provides an entirely satisfactory justification for the current parameters of the exclusionary rule.[8]

5–05   One general principle that appears to have underpinned the early development of the hearsay rule[9] is the "best evidence rule", *i.e.* the rule that a party should adduce the best evidence available having regard to the nature of the case.[10] Thus, the direct evidence of a witness in court is preferred to hearsay evidence of what that witness is reported to have stated. Although there continues to be isolated references to this principle as a rationale for the exclusion of hearsay evidence,[11] the best evidence rule

---

4   [2013] SCC 35 at [30], [2013] 2 SCR 520 at 531.

5   *People (DPP) v McGinley* [1998] 2 IR 408 at 413; [1998] 2 ILRM 233 at 237; *Teper v R.* [1952] AC 480 at 486, [1952] 2 All ER 447 at 449; *R. v Blastland* [1986] AC 41 at 54, [1985] 2 All ER 1095 at 1099; *R. v Kearley* [1992] 2 AC 228 at 261, [1992] 2 All ER 345 at 368 (*per* Lord Oliver). Wigmore, *Evidence* 3rd edn, 1940, Vol. V, § 1364, p.27 famously described the rule against hearsay as "that most characteristic rule of the Anglo-American Law of Evidence—a rule which may be esteemed, next to jury trial, the greatest contribution of that eminently practical legal system to the world's methods of procedure".

6   See the comments of Lord Reid in *Myers v DPP* [1965] AC 1001 at 1019–1020, [1964] 2 All ER 881 at 884, that it "is difficult to make any general statement about the law of hearsay evidence which is entirely accurate". For an excellent discussion of the rule, as well as its many exceptions, see Ashworth and Pattenden, "Reliability, Hearsay Evidence and the English Criminal Trial" (1986) 102 LQR 292.

7   See, generally, Wigmore, *Evidence* (3rd edn, 1940), Vol. V, § 1362, p.3; Spencer, *Hearsay Evidence in Criminal Proceedings* (Hart Publishing, 2008), pp.9–14; Choo, *Hearsay and Confrontation in Criminal Trials* (OUP, 1996); Morgan, "Hearsay Dangers and the Application of the Hearsay Concept" (1948) 62 Harv L Rev 177; Maguire, "The Hearsay System: Around and Through the Thicket" (1961) 14 Vand L Rev 741 at 743.

8   Spencer, *Hearsay Evidence in Criminal Proceedings* (Hart Publishing, 2008), pp.9–14, engages in a detailed analysis of the rationales for the hearsay rule and concludes that none of them justifies a total ban on its reception.

9   For an account of the historical development of the hearsay rule, see the Law Reform Commission's *Consultation Paper on Hearsay in Civil and Criminal Cases* (LRC CP 60–2010), Chap.1.

10   The best known formulation of this principle is to be found in *Omychund v Barker* (1744) 1 Atk 21 at 48, where Lord Hardwicke stated that "the judges and sages of the law have laid it down that there is but one general rule of evidence, the best that the nature of the case will admit".

11   See *Dascalu v Minister for Justice*, unreported, High Court, 4 November 1999 at 4, where O'Sullivan J stated that he was not entitled to have regard to hearsay evidence because he was

has fallen into desuetude[12] and it is doubtful if it continues to provide a justification for the hearsay rule.[13]

5–06 Underlying the hearsay rule is a concern that, if evidence could be given of the out-of-court statements of persons who were not called to testify, those assertions could be false[14] and it would be easy to fabricate and concoct evidence. This danger is particularly acute in the case of statements attributed to unidentified witnesses but is also present when the witness is identified but not available to attend.[15] Apart from the dangers of deliberate fabrication and distortion, hearsay evidence is also considered to be unreliable because of the risks of mistake, misperception, or inaccuracy.[16] It is obvious that these dangers increase as the levels of hearsay multiply.[17]

5–07 Concerns as to the reliability of hearsay evidence are further heightened by a lack of faith in the ability of jurors to properly weigh and evaluate hearsay evidence. In *R. v Blastland*,[18] Lord Bridge identified as the rationale for the hearsay rule:

> "[A] recognition of the great difficulty, even more acute for a juror than for a trained judicial mind, of assessing what, if any, weight can properly be given to a statement by a person whom the jury have not seen or heard and who has not been subject to any test of reliability by cross-examination. ... The danger against which this fundamental rule provides a safeguard is that untested hearsay evidence will be treated as having a probative force which it does not deserve."[19]

5–08 Of course, this rationale is undermined considerably by the fact that many criminal cases and the great majority of civil cases are tried before a judge alone and, even in those cases where the tribunal of fact is a jury, a judge can give the jury appropriate directions as to how to evaluate, and the weight to be attached to, hearsay evidence.

5–09 It is also feared the reception of hearsay evidence would lead to the prolonging

---

[12] bound by the "best evidence" rule. *Cf. Teper v R.* [1952] AC 480 at 486, [1952] 2 All ER 447 at 449.

[12] *Hussey v Twomey* [2009] IESC 1 at [31], [2009] 3 IR 293 at 306, *sub nom. Hussey v MIBI* [2009] 1 ILRM 321 at 332–333. See also *per* Henchy J in *Martin v Quinn* [1980] IR 244 at 249.

[13] See the comments of the Law Reform Commission in its *Consultation Paper on Hearsay in Civil and Criminal Cases* (LRC CP60–2010) at [2.51]–[2.54].

[14] *R. v Kearley* [1992] 2 AC 228 at 258, [1992] 2 All ER 345 at 366; *Horncastle v R* [2009] UKSC 14 at [21], [2010] 2 All ER 359 at 368; *R. v Baldree* [2013] SCC 35 at [32], [2013] 2 SCR 520 at 531.

[15] *Per* Lord Bridge in *R. v Blastland* [1986] AC 41 at 52–53, [1985] 2 All ER 1095 at 1098: "To admit in criminal trials statements confessing to the crime for which the defendant is being tried made by third parties not called as witnesses would be to create a very significant and, many might think, a dangerous new exception."

[16] *Donohoe v Killeen* [2013] IEHC 22 at [15]; *R. v Baldree* [2013] SCC 35 at [32], [2013] 2 SCR 520 at 531.

[17] Baker, *The Hearsay Rule* (Pitman, London, 1950), p.19, provides an illustration of the problem with statements made other than from personal knowledge: "Everyone is familiar with the ease and rapidity with which a story grows. As it is passed from mouth to mouth some additional fact is added; perhaps, too, a little colour to make it a better tale. With each handing on of the story, the further away from the truth it becomes; detail is added to detail as the story grows and in the end the accumulated mass swamps the core of truth at its centre. Misunderstanding, faulty memory, and misreporting make the story increasingly inaccurate and unreliable."

[18] [1986] AC 41, [1985] 2 All ER 1095.

[19] [1986] AC 41 at 54, [1985] 2 All ER 1095 at 1099; *Horncastle v R.* [2009] UKSC 14 at [21], [2010] 2 All ER 359 at 368. *Cf. Eastern Health Board v MK* [1999] 2 IR 99 at 123, [1999] 2 ILRM 321 at 344 (*per* Keane J); *R. v Lucier* [1982] 1 SCR 28 at 31. See also Coen, "Hearsay, bad character and trust in the jury: Irish and English contrasts" (2013) 17 E & P 250.

of trials and would give rise to a multiplicity of side issues as to the reliability of that evidence.[20] There is the related danger that, in criminal trials, the defence would seek to confuse or distract the jury with hearsay evidence or that the admission of such evidence would lead to unmeritorious acquittals where it is used to raise a reasonable doubt.

5–10 Whilst the foregoing factors are clearly important, in more recent times the primary focus has been on the absence of fundamental procedural protections where hearsay evidence is admitted, namely: (a) the absence of an oath[21]; (b) the absence of an opportunity on the part of the tribunal of fact to observe the demeanour of the declarant when the statement was made[22]; and (c) the absence of an opportunity for cross-examination by the party adversely affected by it.[23]

5–11 With regard to the lack of an oath, this was clearly a factor in the development of the rule[24] and continues to be identified as a rationale.[25] However, it can hardly have been decisive because it was decided, at an early point, that hearsay statements were to be excluded even if sworn.[26] Furthermore, provision is made for the reception of unsworn evidence.[27] Turning to the lack of an opportunity to observe the demeanour of the declarant, this has only been identified as a justification for the rule on a somewhat fitful basis and it has been suggested that the importance of this factor may be overstated.[28] Thus, it is the lack of opportunity to cross-examine which must be

---

[20]   Heydon, *Evidence Cases and Materials* 2nd edn (London: Butterworths, 1984), p.308.

[21]   *Cullen v Clarke* [1963] IR 368 at 378; *Eastern Health Board v MK* [1999] 2 IR 99 at 108, 123, [1999] 2 ILRM 321 at 331, 345 (*per* Denham J and Keane J respectively); *Teper v R.* [1952] AC 480 at 486, [1952] 2 All ER 447 at 449; *R. v Abbey* [1982] 2 SCR 24 at 41, (1982) 138 DLR (3d) 202 at 216.

[22]   *Eastern Health Board v MK* [1999] 2 IR 99 at 108, [1999] 2 ILRM 321 at 331 (*per* Denham J); *Teper v R.* [1952] AC 480 at 486, [1952] 2 All ER 447 at 449; *R v Rowley* [2012] EWCA Crim 1434 at [24], [2013] 1 WLR 895 at 901; *Mattox v United States* (1895) 156 US 237 at 242; *Ohio v Roberts* (1980) 448 US 56. See also Welborn, "Demeanour" (1991) 76 Cornell LR 1075.

[23]   *Cullen v Clarke* [1963] IR 368 at 378; *Eastern Health Board v MK* [1999] 2 IR 99 at 108, 123, [1999] 2 ILRM 321 at 331, 344 (*per* Denham J and Keane J respectively); *Teper v R.* [1952] AC 480 at 486, [1952] 2 All ER 447 at 449; *R. v Y* [2008] EWCA Crim 10 at [56], [2008] 1 WLR 1683 at 1696; *R. v Rowley* [2012] EWCA Crim 1434 at [24], [2013] 1 WLR 895 at 901; *R. v Abbey* [1982] 2 SCR 24 at 41, (1982) 138 DLR (3d) 202 at 216.

[24]   Gilbert CB explained the hearsay rule in *The Law of Evidence* (2nd edn, London, 1760), at p.152, on the basis that: "though a person testify what he hath heard upon oath, yet the person who spoke it was not upon oath; and if a man had been in court and said the same thing and had not sworn it, he had not been believed in a court of justice." See also Hawkins, *Pleas of the Crown* (1716), Book II, c.46, § 44.

[25]   *R. v Rowley* [2012] EWCA Crim 1434 at [24], [2013] 1 WLR 895 at 901.

[26]   *R. v Inhabitants of Eriswell* (1790) 3 Term Rep 707; *R. v Nuneham Courtney Inhabitants* (1801) 1 East 373.

[27]   See s.27(1) of the Criminal Evidence Act 1992 and, generally, Chap.3.

[28]   In *Lek v Mathews* (1926) 25 Lloyd's Rep 525 at 543, Lord Atkin cautioned that: "The lynx-eyed judge who can discern the truth teller from the liar by looking at him is more often found in fiction or in appellate judgments than on the bench." For that reason, the same judge stated in *Société d'Avances Commerciales v Merchants Marine Insurance Co.* (1924) 20 Lloyds Reports 140 at 152 that: "an ounce of intrinsic merit or demerit in the evidence, that is to say, the value of the comparison of the evidence with known facts is worth pounds of demeanour". That statement was quoted by O'Donnell J in *People (DPP) v C.C. (No.2)* [2012] IECCA 86 at [18] who said that it was an observation borne of lengthy experience and regarded it as "significant that those with the greatest experience of judging the credibility of witnesses have the least faith in the capacity of any person to simply observe the witness giving evidence and determine if he or she is telling the truth".

regarded as the principal foundation of the hearsay rule.[29] In *Director of Corporate Enforcement v Bailey*,[30] Hardiman J declared that "the fundamental objection to the admissibility of hearsay evidence in proceedings before a court is that, to the extent that it is admitted, it deprives the applicant of his right to cross-examine".

5–12　Wigmore has described cross-examination as "beyond any doubt the greatest legal engine ever invented for the discovery of truth".[31] Cross-examination is the principal means available to a party of testing the powers of perception, the extent and accuracy of recall, and the truthfulness of testimony given by a witness. As Bayley J stated in *In re Berkeley*[32]:

> "Whoever has attended to the examination, the cross-examination, and the re-examination of witnesses…has observed what a very different shape their story appears to take in each of these stages…"

5–13　However, when hearsay evidence is admitted, the party adversely affected by it is deprived of the opportunity to test its veracity, accuracy and reliability and the credibility of the declarant by means of cross-examination. The difficulties thus created were adverted to by Chancellor Kent in *Coleman v Southwick*:

> "A person who relates a hearsay is not obliged to enter into any particulars, to answer any questions, to solve any difficulties, to reconcile any contradictions, to explain any obscurities, to remove any ambiguities; he entrenches himself in the simple assertion that he was told so, and leaves the burden entirely on his dead or absent author."[33]

5–14　In a similar vein, Hardiman J in *People (DPP) v McLoughlin*[34] commented that the admission of hearsay evidence effectively stymies cross-examination because: "One cannot hope to shake a witness who can repeat that he is only saying what he was told, or even hope to qualify the effect of his evidence." These difficulties are compounded by the lack of opportunity on the part of the tribunal of fact to observe the demeanour of the hearsay declarant under cross-examination.[35]

5–15　The hearsay rule can, thus, be seen to be a requirement of fair procedures and to have a constitutional foundation in this jurisdiction.[36] Article 38.1 guarantees

---

[29]　*Director of Corporate Enforcement v Bailey* [2007] IEHC 365, [2008] 2 ILRM 13 at 30, [2011] IESC 24 at [89], [2011] 3 IR 278 at 307 (*per* Hardiman J); *People (DPP) v McLoughlin* [2009] IESC 65 at [41] and [46], [2010] 1 IR 590 at 601 and 603, [2010] 1 ILRM 1 at 10 and 11–12 (*per* Hardiman J); *Clarke v Governor of Cloverhill Prison* [2011] IEHC 199 at [20]; *Donohoe v Killeen* [2013] IEHC 22 at [12]; *R. v Rowley* [2012] EWCA Crim 1434 at [24], [2013] 1 WLR 895 at 901; *R. v B (KG)* [1993] 1 SCR 740 at 768 (*per* Lamer CJ); *R. v Khelawon* [2006] SCC 57 at [56], [2006] 2 SCR 787 at 819; *R. v Baldree* [2013] SCC 35 at [30], [2013] 2 SCR 520 at 531; *Pointer v Texas* (1965) 380 US 400 at 404; *California v Green* (1970) 399 US 149 at 158.

[30]　[2011] IESC 24 at [89], [2011] 3 IR 278 at 307.

[31]　Wigmore, *Evidence* (3rd edn, 1940), Vol. V, §1367, p.29. Reservations have, however, been expressed about the forensic value of cross-examination as a technique for discovering the truth about past events (see the Law Reform Commission's *Consultation Paper on Hearsay in Civil and Criminal Cases* (LRC CP60–2010) at [2.88]–[2.91].

[32]　(1811) 4 Camp 401 at 405.

[33]　(1812) 9 John 50 (quoted in Wigmore, *Evidence* (3rd edn, 1940), Vol. V, §1362, p.4)).

[34]　[2009] IESC 65 at [41], [2010] 1 IR 590 at 601, [2010] 1 ILRM 1 at 10.

[35]　*People (DPP) v Gartland* [2010] IECCA 100 at 6.

[36]　*Cf.* The position in the US where the Sixth Amendment which guarantees the right of an accused to be confronted by the witnesses against him has been held to render inadmissible testimonial hearsay evidence subject to certain exceptions. See *Crawford v Washington* (2004) 541 US 36, *Davis v Washington* (2006) 547 US 813 and *Michigan v Bryant* (2011) 113 S Ct 1143 and, generally, Broun (ed.), *McCormick on Evidence* (Thomson Reuters, 2013), Vol. II, § 252, Fishman

the right to a trial in due course of law and, in *State (Healy) v Donoghue*,[37] Gannon J stated that among the procedural rights enjoyed by an accused was a right "to hear and test by examination the evidence offered by or on behalf of his accuser".[38] This right was subsequently described by Hamilton CJ in *Donnelly v Ireland*[39] as an "essential ingredient in the concept of fair procedures". The right to cross-examine also enjoys constitutional protection in civil cases by virtue of the guarantee of the personal rights of the citizen contained in Art.40.3. Delivering the judgment of the Supreme Court in *In re Haughey*,[40] Ó Dálaigh CJ stated that Art.40.3 "is a guarantee to the citizen of basic fairness of procedures" which required, *inter alia*, that the defendant in that case "be allowed to cross-examine, by counsel, his accuser or accusers".[41] In a passage that underlines the equivalence of the right to cross-examine enjoyed in criminal and civil proceedings, Hamilton CJ in *Donnelly v Ireland*[42] stated that:

> "[T]he central concern of the requirements of due process and fair procedures is the same, that is to ensure the fairness of the trial of an accused person. This undoubtedly involves the rigorous testing by cross-examination of the evidence against him or her."[43]

5–16   The constitutional protection of the right to cross-examine is reinforced by Art.6 of the European Convention on Human Rights which guarantees a fair hearing and stipulates in Art.6(3)(d) that a person charged with a criminal offence has the right "to examine or to have examined witnesses against him".[44] In *Al-Khawaja v United Kingdom*,[45] the Grand Chamber of the European Court of Human Rights held that the admission of a hearsay statement which is the "sole or decisive evidence" against an accused will not automatically result in a breach of Art.6(1). However, the proceedings in which such a statement was admitted would have to be subjected to "the most searching scrutiny" and, because of the dangers of the admission of such evidence, the question in each case is "whether there are sufficient counterbalancing

---

"*Crawford v Washington*: the Supreme Court opts for new (old?) approach to the Confrontation Clause" (2004) 8 E & P 240; Ho, "Confrontation and hearsay: a critique of *Crawford*" (2004) 8 E & P 147; Friedman, "'Face to face': Rediscovering the right to confront prosecution witnesses" (2004) 8 E & P 1; Bellin, "Incredible Shrinking Confrontation Clause" (2012) 92(6) Boston University Law Review 1865; and O'Brian Jr, "Confrontation and ongoing emergencies: *Michigan v Bryant*" (2011) 15 E & P 357. See also, O'Brian, "The Right of Confrontation: US and European Perspectives" (2005) 121 LQR 481.

[37]   [1976] IR 325 at 335.

[38]   See also *per* O'Higgins CJ in the Supreme Court who stated ([1976] IR 325 at 349) that: "the words 'due course of law' in Art. 38 make it mandatory that every criminal trial shall be conducted in accordance with the concept of justice, that the procedures applied shall be fair, and that the person accused will be afforded every opportunity to defend himself."

[39]   [1998] 1 IR 321 at 350, [1998] 1 ILRM 401 at 413.

[40]   [1971] IR 217 at 264.

[41]   See also *Borges v Medical Council* [2004] IESC 9, [2004] 1 IR 103 at 113, [2004] 2 ILRM 81 at 90. *Cf. Kiely v Minister for Social Welfare (No.2)* [1977] IR 267 at 281, where Henchy J stated that it was a breach of natural and constitutional justice "if one party is allowed to send in his evidence in writing, free from the truth-eliciting processes of a confrontation which are inherent in an oral hearing, while his opponent is compelled to run the gauntlet of oral examination and cross-examination".

[42]   [1998] 1 IR 321, [1998] 1 ILRM 401.

[43]   [1998] 1 IR 321 at 356, [1998] 1 ILRM 401 at 418–419.

[44]   See *Kostovski v Netherlands* (1990) 12 EHRR 434; *Unterpertinger v Austria* (1991) 13 EHRR 175; *Windisch v Austria* (1991) 13 EHRR 281; *Van Mechelen v Netherlands* (1998) 25 EHRR 647; *Luca v Italy* (2003) 36 EHRR 46; *Al-Khawaja v United Kingdom* [2009] 49 EHRR 1, (2012) 54 EHRR 23. See also the decision of the UK Supreme Court in *R. v Horncastle* [2009] UKSC 14, [2010] 2 AC 373, [2010] 2 WLR 47.

[45]   (2012) 54 EHRR 23.

factors in place, including measures that permit a fair and proper assessment of the reliability of that evidence to take place".[46] The jurisprudence of the Court in this regard potentially creates a limit to the extent to which hearsay can be admitted and a conviction grounded on it.[47]

5–17 It can be seen, therefore, that the rule against hearsay is not just a rule of evidence but is a constitutionally mandated ingredient of fair procedures. This was the view taken in *Borges v Medical Council*,[48] where Keane CJ, delivering the judgment of the Court, explained that:

> "[T]he right of a person to have the evidence against him given orally and tested by cross-examination before the tribunal in question may be of such importance in a particular case that to deprive the person concerned of that right would amount to a breach of the basic fairness of procedure to which he is entitled by virtue of Article 40.1 [sic] of the Constitution. It is not simply because the tribunal is in greater danger of arriving at an unfair conclusion, absent the safeguard of material evidence being given orally and tested by cross-examination....It is because, depending on the nature of the evidence, its admission in that form may offend against fundamental concepts of fairness which are not simply rooted in the law of evidence, either in its statutory or common law vesture."[49]

5–18 Of course, as acknowledged by Keane CJ in that case, this does not mean that there cannot be exceptions to the hearsay rule but it does indicate the context in which the application of existing exceptions and the creation of any new exceptions must be approached.

C. Scope and Application of the Hearsay Rule

1. Introduction

5–19 As noted above, in approaching the admissibility of out-of-court statements, it is important to distinguish hearsay evidence from non-hearsay or original evidence.

---

[46] (2012) 54 EHRR 23 at [147]. This decision has resulted in a considerable amount of academic commentary, particularly as the UK Supreme in *R. v Horncastle* [2009] UKSC 14, [2010] 2 WLR 47, had refused to follow an earlier decision of a chamber of the Fourth Section of the European Court of Human Rights ((2009) 49 EHRR 1). See Pattenden, "Hearsay and the right of confrontation—United Kingdom and the European Convention on Human Rights" (2012) E & P 216; O'Brien, "Confrontation: the defiance of the English Courts" (2011) 15(2) E & P 93; Dennis, "The right to confront witnesses: meanings, myths and human rights" [2010] Crim LR 255; Wallace, "The Empire strikes back: hearsay rules in common law legal systems and the jurisprudence of the European Court of Human Rights" (2010) Eur HRL Rev 408; Stockdakle and Piasecki, "The safety-valve: discretion to admit hearsay evidence in criminal proceedings" (2012) 76 (4) J Crim L 314; Du Bois-Pedain, "Hearsay exceptions and fair trial rights in Strasbourg" (2012) 71(2) CLJ 257; Redmayne, "Hearsay and Human Rights—Al Khawaja in the Grand Chamber" (2012) 75(5) MLR 865; de Wilde, "A fundamental review of the ECHR right to examine witnesses in criminal cases". Subsequent decisions considering the effect of the judgment include *R. v Ibrahim* [2012] 2 Cr App R 32, *R. v Riat* [2012] EWCA Crim 1509, [2013] 1 WLR 2592 and *R. v Shabir* [2012] EWCA Crim 2564. See also Stark, "Reconciling the Irreconcilable?" (2012) 71(3) CLJ 475.

[47] For a discussion of this decision and the potential implications on the Irish law in relation to hearsay, see Heffernan, "Hearsay in Criminal Trials: the Strasbourg Perspective" (2013) 49 Ir Jur 113 and Heffernan and Ni Raifeartaigh, *Evidence in Criminal Trials* (Bloomsbury, 2014), pp.351–362.

[48] [2004] IESC 9, [2004] 1 IR 103, [2004] 2 ILRM 81.

[49] [2004] 1 IR 103 at 115, [2004] 2 ILRM 81 at 92. See also *Director of Corporate Enforcement v Bailey* [2011] IESC 24 at [89]–[92], [2011] 3 IR 278 at 307–308.

The mere fact that a statement is made out of court does not render it inadmissible if it is tendered, not to prove the truth of its contents, but the fact that it was made.[50] To repeat what was stated by Kingsmill Moore J in *Cullen v Clarke*[51]:

"[I]t is necessary to emphasise that there is *no* general rule of evidence to the effect that a witness may not testify as to the words spoken by a person who is not produced as a witness. There is a general rule subject to many exceptions that evidence of the speaking of such words is inadmissible to prove the truth of the facts which they assert…This is known as the rule against hearsay."[52]

5–20   This explanation of the nature and scope of the hearsay rule is echoed in a well-known passage from the judgment of Lord Wilberforce in *Ratten v R.*[53] where he drew a distinction between hearsay and original evidence:

"The mere fact that evidence of a witness includes evidence as to words spoken by another person who is not called is no objection to its admissibility. Words spoken are facts just as much as any other action by a human being. If the speaking of the words is a relevant fact, a witness may give evidence that they were spoken. A question of hearsay only arises when the words spoken are relied on 'testimonially', *i.e.* as establishing some fact narrated by the words."[54]

5–21   Thus, the dividing line between out-of-court statements that are hearsay and *prima facie* inadmissible, and those that are admissible as original evidence to prove that they were made, is drawn according to the purpose for which the statement is being tendered.[55] As noted by Kingsmill Moore J in *Cullen v Clarke*,[56] "[t]he actual question put and the object for which it was put in each case has to be considered". The importance of considering the purpose for which it is sought to introduce an out-of-court statement into evidence was highlighted by Macdonald JA in *R. v Baltzer*[57] who explained:

"Essentially it is not the form of the statement that gives it its hearsay or non-hearsay characteristics but the use to which it is put. Whenever a witness testifies that someone said something, immediately one should then ask, 'what is the relevance of the fact that someone said something'. If, therefore, the relevance of the statement lies in the fact that it was made, it is the making of the statement that is evidence—the truth or falsity of the statement is of no consequence: if the relevance of the statement lies in the fact that it contains an assertion which is, itself, a relevant fact, then it is the truth or falsity of the statement that is in issue. The former is not hearsay, the latter is."[58]

5–22   The importance of identifying the purpose for which an out-of-court statement is tendered was also emphasised by Wigmore who stated:

---

[50]   *Cullen v Clarke* [1963] IR 368 at 378; *Subramaniam v Public Prosecutor* [1956] 1 WLR 965 at 970; *Mawaz Khan v R.* [1967] 1 AC 454 at 462, [1967] 1 All ER 80 at 82; *Ratten v R.* [1972] AC 378 at 387, [1971] 3 All ER 801 at 805.

[51]   [1963] IR 368 at 378.

[52]   In *R. v Baldree* [2013] 2 SCR 520 at 531, Fish J identified as one of the defining features of hearsay, "the fact that the statement is adduced to prove the truth of its contents".

[53]   [1972] AC 378, [1971] 3 All ER 801.

[54]   [1972] AC 378 at 387, [1971] 3 All ER 801 at 805. See, to the same effect, *per* LMD de Silva in *Subramaniam v Public Prosecutor* [1956] 1 WLR 965 at 970: "Evidence of a statement made to a witness by a person who is not himself called as a witness may or may not be hearsay. It is hearsay and inadmissible when the object of the evidence is to establish the truth of what is contained in the statement. It is not hearsay and is admissible when it is proposed to establish, not the truth of the statement, by the fact that it was made." That statement was quoted with approval by Lamer CJC in *R. v Smith* [1992] 2 SCR 915 at 924, (1992) 94 DLR (4th) 590 at 597.

[55]   *Wicklow County Council v Jessup* [2011] IEHC 81 at [2.6].

[56]   [1963] IR 368 at 378.

[57]   (1974) 27 CCC (2d) 118.

[58]   (1974) 27 CCC (2d) 118 at 143.

"The prohibition of the Hearsay rule, then, does not apply to all words or utterances merely as such. If this fundamental principle is clearly realized, its application is a comparatively simple matter. The Hearsay rule excludes extrajudicial utterances only when offered for a special purpose, namely, as assertions to evidence the truth of the matter asserted".[59]

5–23 This restriction on the application of the hearsay rule to out-of-court statements that are tendered as proof the truth of their contents is considered to be justified by reference to the underlying rationale of the rule. As noted above, the primary justification for the rule is the lack of opportunity of the party adversely affected to cross-examine the declarant. However, a party is only deprived of an opportunity to cross-examine where an out-of-court statement is tendered to prove the truth of its contents because it is only in those circumstances that an issue as to credibility of the declarant, who is not called as a witness, arises. If a statement is relevant and is tendered simply to prove the fact that it was made, then only the credibility of the witness giving evidence is at issue. The witness may be lying, or mistaken because he or she misheard or misunderstood what was said, or his or her recollection may be poor but these are all matters that can be put to the witness in cross-examination and the party against whom the statement is made has a full opportunity to explore and attack the credibility of the witness as to whether the statement was made and it precise contents. By way of contrast, if it is sought to tender an out-of-court statement as proof of the truth of its contents, then an issue arises not only as to the credibility of the witness who relates the statement in court but also as to the out-of-court declarant who made the statement. That person is not, however, available for cross-examination and the party adversely affected by it is deprived of the opportunity to test the credibility of the declarant as to whether he or she might be lying or mistaken because of poor conditions of observation, misperception, faulty memory, etc.

5–24 It should be noted that the hearsay rule is not applied with the same vigour in civil proceedings as in criminal proceedings. The rule will often be relaxed to the extent of permitting a witness to give evidence of statements made out of court if the person who made the statement or to whom it was made has been or will be called to give evidence. In addition, as discussed below, documents are frequently admitted without any objection on hearsay grounds and it is becoming increasingly common for parties to agree that specified categories of documents can be admitted as *prima facie* evidence of their contents as against the party that created the original of the document subject to the entitlement of an opposing party. The position in criminal cases is quite different and the hearsay rule is generally applied with rigour.

5–25 Although in practice there is a degree of asymmetry as to how rigorously the hearsay rule is applied in criminal cases to evidence that is inculpatory of an accused versus evidence that is exculpatory, it is important to note that the rule is equally applicable to exculpatory evidence. So, in *People (DPP) v Gartland*,[60] the Court of Criminal Appeal refused an application for leave to admit additional evidence on the basis that the evidence, comprising a written statement by the son of the accused that inculpated him and exculpated the accused of the offence of which he had been convicted, was inadmissible hearsay.[61]

---

[59] Wigmore, *Evidence* (3rd edn, 1940), Vol. VI, § 1766, at p.178.
[60] [2010] IECCA 100.
[61] See also *People (DPP) v Piotrowski* [2014] IECCA 17 at [6.3]; *R. v Blastland* [1986] AC 41, [1985] 2 All ER 1095 and *R. v Lawless* [2003] EWCA Crim 271. See also Heffernan and Imwinkelried,

5–26   In the following sections the scope of the hearsay rule will be examined by reference to its application to oral statements, written statements and statements by conduct. Before doing so, however, some circumstances where an out-of-court statement is relevant and admissible for a purpose other than to prove the truth of its contents will be outlined.

2. Non-Hearsay Statements

5–27   There are a diverse range of circumstances where an out-of-court statement may be admissible as original evidence for the purpose of proving that it was made rather than to prove the truth of its contents. As Edwards J explained in *The Leopardstown Club Ltd v Templeville Developments Ltd*[62] in relation to documents:

> "Where a document is produced by a party who proposes to rely upon the statements it contains, not as evidence of their truth by way of an exception to the hearsay rule, but to show for some legitimate purpose that the statements (whether or not they be true) were in fact made, then the document is properly characterised as non-hearsay original evidence (otherwise original evidence)."[63]

5–28   Some of the more important examples where an out-of-court statement can be admitted as original evidence are: (a) where the making of the statement is a fact in issue; (b) to establish the ability of the declarant to communicate; (c) to establish the state of mind of the recipient of the statement; (d) where words having a legal effect are used; (e) to establish the falsity of the statement; and (f) where the statement provides circumstantial evidence.[64]

5–29   However, before examining these categories, two general points can be made. The first is that the making of the non-hearsay statement must be proved by admissible evidence that does not itself infringe the hearsay rule. In simple terms, a witness can, for a non-hearsay purpose, give evidence of what he or she heard the declarant say but cannot give evidence of what he or she was told that the declarant said. This distinction is neatly illustrated by the Canadian case of *Enge v Trerise*.[65] The plaintiff had been injured in a car accident which left her with a large scar on her face. In order to establish that the schizophrenia that she subsequently suffered from was caused by the scar, her doctor gave evidence that she had told him that people were talking about her and it was held that this was hearsay evidence. Sheppard JA explained:

> "The plaintiff's counsel argued that the statement of a patient to a doctor that she was queen of America would be a verbal act and therefore admissible. The fact that a person would make such a statement may be evidence of a certain mental condition: in such a case the making of the statement would be a fact to be proved and would be a verbal act. However that may be, it would be quite a different matter for the doctor to testify that the patient had told him that she at some earlier time had stated that she was queen of America. That she had stated that she was queen of America would be the fact to be proved, but the doctor would be offering

---

"The Accused's Constitutional Right to Introduce Critical, Demonstrably Reliable Exculpatory Evidence" (2005) 40 Ir Jur 111.

[62]   [2010] IEHC 152 at [5.13].

[63]   It should also be noted that a document may also be admitted in some circumstances as real evidence (see further, Chap.12).

[64]   Having referred to the section of the first edition of this text dealing with non-hearsay evidence, a summary of the circumstances in which an out-of-court statement may be admitted as original evidence was given in very similar terms by Edwards J in *The Leopardstown Club Ltd v Templeville Developments Ltd* [2010] IEHC 152 at [5.13].

[65]   (1960) 33 WWR 577, 26 DLR (2d) 529.

hearsay evidence in testifying that she told him that she, at some earlier time, had so stated. That appears to be what happened in this case."[66]

5–30   Secondly, it is important to note that a statement may be relevant both for a hearsay and a non-hearsay purpose. Where that is the case, the danger obviously arises that the tribunal of fact will use the statement not only for the non-hearsay purpose but also as evidence of the truth of its contents. Indeed, a party may try to identify a non-hearsay purpose in order to get an out-of-court statement admitted in the hope that the tribunal of fact will do just that. Therefore, it is important that, in the case of a jury, it is instructed by the trial judge as to the limited purpose for which the statement has been received and can be used. Whether it will actually heed such a warning is open to question and, in circumstances where the truth of the contents of the statement is an issue that is central to a case, a judge might decide that the probative value of the evidence, *i.e.* the relevance of the statement for the non-hearsay purpose, is outweighed by its prejudicial effect, *i.e.* the danger that the jury would impermissibly use it as evidence of the truth of its contents.[67]

(a) Where the making of the statement is a fact in issue

5–31   An out-of-court statement can be admitted where its making is a fact in issue in a case. The obvious example is defamation proceedings where evidence that the impugned words were spoken or written is admissible to prove that fact as an essential ingredient of the action for slander or libel.[68] Conversely, where it is relevant to prove whether a particular statement was made, records wherein such a statement would be expected to be recorded if made may be admitted for the purpose of establishing that the statement was not made.[69]

(b) To establish the ability of the declarant to communicate

5–32   A statement will be admissible if any issue arises as to the ability of the declarant to speak or communicate at the time when the statement was made.[70] So, in *R. v Ferber*,[71] evidence of a telephone call made by the deceased to a witness was admitted in a murder trial in order to establish that the deceased was alive at the time of the call.

(c) To establish the state of mind of the recipient of the statement

5–33   A statement may be relevant, regardless of the truth of its contents, to establish the state of mind of the person to whom it was made, *i.e.* to establish what he or she

---

[66]   26 DLR (2d) 529 at 595–596, 546–547.
[67]   As to the exercise of this discretion generally, see Chap.1.
[68]   As Edwards J noted in *The Leopardstown Club Ltd v Templeville Developments Ltd* [2010] IEHC 152 at [5.13], the plaintiff in a libel action will want to rely on the document to establish what was published but will not be relying on the truth of the contents because his whole case is that they are false and misleading.
[69]   See *DPP v Leigh* [2010] EWHC 345.
[70]   See, *Donohoe v Killeen* [2013] IEHC 22 at [12], where Hogan J gave the example of the admission of evidence of a conversation with a participant in a road traffic accident to show that the participant was sufficiently composed after the accident to engage in such a conversation.
[71]   (1987) 36 CCC (3d) 157.

knew or believed.[72] The classic example is *Subramaniam v Public Prosecutor*,[73] where the defence of the accused to a charge of unlawful possession of ammunition was that he was acting under duress. The trial judge refused to allow the accused to give evidence as to the threats made to him by the terrorists and the Privy Council advised that he had been incorrect to do so:

> "The fact that the statement was made, quite apart from its truth, is frequently relevant in considering the mental state and conduct thereafter of the witness or of some other person in whose presence the statement was made. In the case before their Lordships statements could have been made to the appellant by the terrorists, which, whether true or not, if they had been believed by the appellant, might reasonably have induced in him an apprehension of instant death if he failed to conform to their wishes."[74]

5–34   Similarly, in *R. v Buckley*,[75] the deposition of a deceased police officer wherein he stated that he had seen the accused commit theft and had arrested him with the stolen articles on him was admitted to prove motive at the trial of the accused for his murder.[76]

5–35   Out-of-court statements have also been admitted on this basis to establish the effect of an alleged libel on the reputation of the plaintiff,[77] to prove notice or knowledge of a defect or danger in a negligence action,[78] to establish that a complaint of unlawful activity was made,[79] to show whether someone alleging fraud was misled,[80] to establish the belief of a person as to the contents of a document,[81] to establish the belief of the police as to the existence of grounds for securing a warrant,[82] to establish that an accused was aware that he was harbouring a fugitive,[83] to establish that the accused had been forewarned that he was going to be arrested and of incriminating evidence found by the police,[84] and to explain the conduct of the accused when questioned and charged.[85]

(d) Where words having a legal effect are used

5–36   A statement may be relevant and admissible because it contains words, sometimes referred to as "operative words" that have a particular legal effect simply because they have been uttered. The classic example is a statement establishing contractual relations. If a dispute arises as to whether a contract was concluded between two parties, evidence may be given of any statement relied upon as constituting an offer

---

[72]   See Carter, "Hearsay, Relevance and Admissibility: Declarations as to State of Mind and Declarations Against Penal Interest" [1987] LQR 106. *Cf. People (DPP) v O'Reilly* [2009] IECCA 18 at 34.
[73]   [1956] 1 WLR 965.
[74]   [1956] 1 WLR 965 at 970 (*per* LMD de Silva). *Cf. United States v Williams* (1991) 952 F 2d 1504; *United States v Herrera* (1979) 600 F 2d 502.
[75]   (1873) 13 Cox CC 293 at 295.
[76]   See also *United States v Cline* (1978) 570 F 2d 731; *Emich Motors Corporation v General Motors Corporation* (1950) 181 F 2d 70.
[77]   *Fullam v Associated Newspapers Ltd* [1953–4] Ir Jur Rep 79.
[78]   See *Safeway Stores Inc v Combs* (1960) 273 F 2d 295; *Player v Thompson* (1972) 259 SC 600, 193 SE 2d 531; *Smedra v Stanek*(1951) 187 F 2d 892 at 894; *Johnson v Misericordia Community Hospital* (1980) 97 Wis 2d 521 at 549–551, 294 NW 2d 501 at 515–516.
[79]   *Wicklow County Council v Jessup* [2011] IEHC 81 at [2.6].
[80]   *Gray v New Augarita Porcupine Mines Ltd.* [1952] 3 DLR 1.
[81]   *Doe d Small v Allen* (1799) 8 Term Rep 147.
[82]   *Minnesota v Purdy* (1967) 153 NW 2d 254.
[83]   *United States v Kutas* (1976) 542 F 2d 527.
[84]   *R. v T* [2007] EWCA Crim 1250.
[85]   *R. v Willis* [1960] 1 All ER 331, [1960] 1 WLR 55.

or acceptance for the purpose of showing that a contract came into being.[86] Similarly, an out-of-court statement may be admitted to establish consent,[87] the vesting of ownership of goods,[88] adverse possession,[89] and that a conveyance was in trust.[90]

5–37 A variety of official documents and communications may potentially be admissible on this basis where the existence of a document or communication is relevant. For example, a licence or other statutory consent can be admitted to establish that the holder is authorised to carry out specified activities.[91] Evidence of a direction given by the DPP in relation to a prosecution is also admissible to establish that it was given though not the reasons why it was given.[92] Similarly, a request by a judicial authority pursuant to the provisions of the European arrest warrant scheme will be admitted and regard can be had to any facts stated therein to provide context for the request rather than being admitted as proof thereof.[93]

5–38 Words may also have a legal effect by virtue of their utterance where the declarant is under a legal obligation to utter them. In *DPP v O'Kelly*,[94] the respondent had been arrested for drink driving and an issue arose as to compliance with the provisions of the Custody Regulations which require an accused to be informed of certain rights enjoyed by him or her while in custody.[95] At the trial of the accused, a garda gave evidence that he had heard the member-in-charge of the garda station inform the accused of those rights. This evidence was objected to on the basis that it was hearsay, an objection that was upheld by the District Judge. However, McCracken J held that the District Judge had erred in so ruling because the Custody Regulations simply required that the accused be informed of his rights and it did not matter whether the accused understood those rights. That being the case, the only evidence that was required was that the words were spoken and the required notice handed to the accused and this evidence could be given by any garda who heard the words being spoken and saw the notice being handed over.[96]

5–39 The crucial point in *O'Kelly* was that it was sufficient compliance with the statutory requirements that the statement was made. However, if it is necessary to go further and prove that the statement was made with a particular belief or state of mind, then the hearsay rule applies and it is necessary to call the declarant to give evidence of that state of mind.[97]

---

[86] See *NLRB v H Koch & Sons* (1978) 578 F 2d 1287; *Gyro Brass Manufacturing Corporation v United Auto Aircraft and Agricultural Implement Workers* (1959) 147 Conn 76, 157 A 2d 241.

[87] *People (DPP) v Bishop* [2005] IECCA 2 at 10.

[88] See *Hanson v Johnson* (1924) 161 Minn 229, 201 NW 322.

[89] *Rush v Collins* (1937) 366 Ill 307, 8 NE 2d 659.

[90] *Butler v Butler* (1962) 253 Iowa 1084, 114 NW 2d 595.

[91] *Cf. People (DPP) v O'Reilly* [2009] IECCA 18 at 29.

[92] *Cosgrave v DPP* [2012] IESC 24 at [120], [2012] 3 IR 666 at 727.

[93] *Minister for Justice, Equality and Law Reform v O'Sullivan* [2011] IEHC 230.

[94] Unreported, High Court, 11 February 1998.

[95] See reg.8 of the Criminal Justice Act 1984 (Treatment of Persons in Custody in Garda Síochána Stations) Regulations 1987 (SI No.119 of 1997). See, generally, Chap.8.

[96] *Cf. R. v Chapman* [1969] 2 QB 436, [1969] 2 All ER 321 (evidence by police officer that medical practitioner had not objected to proposal to require breath specimen admissible to establish the fact that he had made no objection).

[97] *Cf. People (DPP) v Byrne* [1987] IR 363, [1989] ILRM 613 and *DPP v Owens* [1999] 2 IR 16, [1999] 2 ILRM 421.

(e) To establish falsity

5–40   An out-of-court statement will not be hearsay if it is tendered to establish its falsity. For example, in *Mawaz Khan v R.*,[98] the appellants were charged with murder and separate statements made by them to the police in which they set up a common alibi were admitted to show that they had fabricated a joint story and had co-operated for that purpose after the alleged murder. It was held that the statements were admissible, not to establish the truth of the assertions contained therein but, rather, for the purpose of inviting the jury to find that the assertions were false and to draw inferences from their falsity.[99]

(f) Circumstantial evidence

5–41   An out-of-court statement may be relevant because the fact that it was made or its contents provide circumstantial evidence of a fact which is in issue or relevant to an issue in proceedings. An example can be seen in *Bradley v Independent Star Newspapers*[100] where an issue of identification arose in a libel action as to whether the plaintiffs were the persons referred to in a newspaper article and it was held that evidence could be given of comments made by persons not called as witnesses stating or implying that they thought that the article referred to the plaintiffs.[101]

5–42   Another example is where an out-of-court statement is relevant to prove the identity of the declarant, as in *R. v Evans*[102] where statements made to the vendors of a car by the purchaser that he worked in chain-link fencing and had a big dog who was going to have pups were admitted as circumstantial evidence to establish that the accused, who had carried on that occupation and had such a dog, had purchased the car, which was subsequently used in an armed robbery. Sopinka J explained that:

> "On the issue of identity, the fact that certain representations are made is probative as it narrows the identity of the declarant to the group of people who are in a position to make similar representations. The more unique or unusual the representations, the more probative they will be on the issue of identity. ... The statement has probative value without assuming the truth of the statement because the mere fact that it was made tells us something relevant about the declarant that connects him to the accused."[103]

5–43   Similarly, a statement may be relevant because it tends to establish a link between the declarant and some other person, object or place. A good example is furnished by *R. v Lydon*,[104] where the appellant, whose defence was one of alibi, had been convicted of the robbery of a post office. About one mile from the post office, on the verge of the road taken by the car used in the robbery, a gun was found. Nearby, two pieces of paper were found on which the words "Sean rules" and "Sean rules 85" were written. Ink of a similar appearance and composition to that on the paper was

---

[98]   [1967] 1 AC 454, [1967] 1 All ER 80.

[99]   *Cf. People (DPP) v Wharrie* [2013] IECCA 20 where, without any hearsay issue being raised, a false passport and evidence that the accused had used it to enter Ireland was admitted as circumstantial evidence to link him to the offences at issue.

[100]   [2011] IESC 17 at [123], [2011] 3 IR 96 at 130, [2012] 2 ILRM 26 at 54.

[101]   See also *Fullam v Independent Newspapers Ltd* [1955-56] Ir Jur Rep 45 (in a defamation action by a professional footballer, evidence of chants and jeers by supporters was admitted in order to prove identity).

[102]   [1993] 3 SCR 653, (1993) 108 DLR (4th) 32.

[103]   (1993) 108 DLR (4th) 32 at 38.

[104]   [1987] Crim LR 407. See also *R. v Owens* [2006] EWCA Crim 2206.

found on the barrel of the gun. The Court of Appeal held that the statements were not hearsay and had been properly admitted as circumstantial evidence. If the jury were satisfied that the gun was used in the robbery and that the pieces of paper were linked to the gun, the references to Sean could be a fact which would fit in with the appellant having committed the offence. This decision is correct because the written statements were not admitted to prove the truth of their contents, *i.e.* that Sean ruled anything but, rather, to prove the fact that they were made which provided circumstantial evidence of a relevant fact in the proceedings.

5–44   In *Lydon*, the connection between the statement and the gun and thus, the value of the statement as circumstantial evidence was established by forensic evidence but, in other instances, the link may be established by virtue of some esoteric knowledge contained therein as, for example, if a person possesses a document containing the address or telephone number of another person.[105]

5–45   This line of authority was followed by the Court of Criminal Appeal in *People (DPP) v Morgan*[106] where, at the trial of the accused for the offence of managing a brothel, the prosecution had adduced evidence of documents including an employment contract, spreadsheets and internet printouts in relation to the availability of prostitution services. Those documents had been found when the premises, allegedly a brothel, was searched. The contention of the accused that these documents constituted inadmissible and prejudicial hearsay was rejected by the Court. It was satisfied that the documents were not relied on testimonially in order to establish some fact narrated by the words such as that "Lisa" was a gorgeous "Carribean" or that "Jessie" was a "curvy Austrian brunette" but rather as circumstantial evidence linking the accused with the operation of a brothel.

3. Oral Statements

5–46   A straightforward example of the application of the hearsay rule to an oral statement can be seen in the old case of *R. v Gibson*.[107] The accused was charged with the unlawful and malicious wounding of a person by throwing a stone at him. At the trial, the victim gave evidence that, immediately after he had been struck by the stone, a passer by had pointed to the door of the accused's house and said: "The person who threw the stone went in there". On appeal, it was conceded that this statement was inadmissible. Similarly, in *Teper v R.*,[108] the Privy Council evinced little difficulty in classifying as hearsay the evidence of a police officer, at the trial of the accused for maliciously setting fire to a shop with intent to defraud, that shortly after the fire had started, he heard an unidentified woman shouting at the driver of a car who resembled the accused: "Your place burning and you going away from the fire."

5–47   The issue of oral hearsay was considered in this jurisdiction in *Cullen v Clarke*.[109] The applicant was a builder's labourer who had suffered an occupational injury and sought an order that, as a result of the injury, he was totally incapacitated.

---

[105] *R. v Romeo* (1982) 30 SASR 243. *Cf. R. v Olisa* [1990] Crim LR 721 and *R. v Chin* (1985) 157 CLR 671.
[106] [2011] IECCA 36.
[107] (1887) 18 QBD 537.
[108] [1952] AC 378.
[109] [1963] IR 368.

At the hearing of the application, he gave evidence that he had made a number of unsuccessful attempts to obtain work but the Circuit Court Judge ruled that he could not quote statements made to him by these potential employers in order to establish why they refused to employ him. That ruling was upheld by the Supreme Court with Kingsmill Moore J stating:

> "I find difficulty in seeing how the proposed evidence would not be hearsay. ... If reliance is placed on the truth of what is stated by a person not called as a witness it is hearsay evidence, admissible only if it falls within one of the exceptions to the rule excluding hearsay."[110]

5–48   A more recent example of oral hearsay can be seen in *Donohoe v Killeen*.[111] In a personal injuries action arising out of a road traffic accident, an issue arose as to whether the plaintiff had run a red light. On cross-examination, counsel for the defendant sought to elicit from the plaintiff evidence of a conversation after the accident with an unidentified foreign national who allegedly had accosted her and asserted that she had broken the light. An objection to this line of questioning was upheld by Hogan J who regarded the evidence sought to be elicited as a textbook example of inadmissible hearsay. He took the view that it would be unfair to admit such evidence, observing that, "were the court to admit this hearsay evidence it would be tantamount to admitting such evidence without having the witness available to run the gauntlet of cross-examination".[112]

5–49   It is important to note that, although it is commonly done, the courts have deprecated attempts to avoid the hearsay rule by avoiding direct questions with regard to the contents of a statement but, instead, asking a series of questions from which the jury can infer what the statement was. In *Glinski v McIver*,[113] Lord Devlin referred with disapproval to such devices:

> "The first consists in not asking what was said in a conversation or written in a document but in asking what the conversation or document was about; it is apparently thought that what would be objectionable if fully exposed is permissible if decently veiled. ... The other device is to ask by means of 'Yes' or 'No' questions what was done. (Just answer 'Yes' or 'No': Did you go to see counsel? Do not tell us what he said but as a result of it did you do something? What did you do?) This device is commonly defended on the ground that counsel is asking only about what was done and not about what was said. But in truth what was done is relevant only because from it there can be inferred something about what was said. Such evidence seems to me to be clearly objectionable. If there is nothing in it, it is irrelevant; if there is something in it, what there is in it is inadmissible."[114]

5–50   Also objectionable is an attempt by a witness to give disguised hearsay whereby the witness does not directly refer to an out-of-court statement but gives evidence that is not based on personal knowledge but on statements made or information supplied by others. In *People (DPP) v Bowes*[115] evidence was given at the trial of the accused for drug offences that the Gardaí, acting on "confidential information" had targeted a particular motor vehicle which was being driven by the accused and was subsequently found to contain drugs. The adducing of this evidence was criticised by the Court of Criminal Appeal on the basis that it was not probative of any element of the case against

---

110 [1963] IR 368 at 381.
111 [2013] IEHC 22.
112 [2013] IEHC 22 at [14].
113 [1962] AC 726, [1962] 1 All ER 696.
114 [1962] 1 All ER 696 at 780–781, 723.
115 [2004] IECCA 44, [2004] 4 IR 223.

the accused and was tantamount to giving hearsay evidence that he was involved in the importation and distribution of drugs.[116]

4. Written Statements

5–51   A statement in a document is hearsay if it is sought to be admitted in order to prove the truth of the statement[117] and it is immaterial in that regard that the author of the document is called to prove it.[118]

5–52   A straightforward application of the hearsay rule to written statements can be seen in *Patel v Comptroller of Customs*.[119] The accused was charged with making a false declaration on a customs entry form on the basis that, in the form, the origin of a consignment of coriander seed was stated to be India but the bags containing the seed bore the legend "Produce of Morocco". However, it was held that these words were clearly hearsay and inadmissible to prove that the seeds had, in fact, originated in Morocco. Similar reasoning applies even if the designation of a country of origin is indelibly stamped on an item—it is still hearsay if relied upon to prove that the item originated in that country.[120] Another example of the exclusion of documentary hearsay can be seen in *People (AG) v O'Brien*[121] where it was held that the trial judge had correctly excluded hospital records that the accused sought to introduce into evidence in order to establish that he suffered from epilepsy.

5–53   The most infamous case on documentary hearsay is *Myers v DPP*,[122] where the accused was charged with a number of offences arising from a car fraud that involved passing off stolen cars as models re-built from wrecked cars. This was accomplished by transferring from the wrecked cars to the stolen cars small plates that contained the engine and chassis numbers to ensure that this would coincide with the details in the log books of the wrecked cars. However, it wasn't possible to substitute the cylinder block number from the wrecked cars as this was indelibly stamped on the engine and the prosecution case rested upon the mismatch between the numbers which could be changed and the cylinder block number. In order to establish the relevant combination of numbers, the prosecution called as a witness the custodian of the relevant manufacturer's records. These had been complied by unidentified workmen, who had not been called as witnesses, and therefore the House of Lords held that the records were hearsay because they were tendered to prove the truth of their contents, *i.e.* that the cylinder block of a particular car when manufactured bore a particular number. This conclusion was reached despite the fact that the records were undoubtedly reliable and no oral testimony would have been credible, even if those who compiled the records could have been identified and found.[123]

---

[116] [2004] IECCA 44 at [14], [2004] 4 IR 223 at 231. *Cf. Wicklow County Council v Jessup* [2011] IEHC 81 at [2.11].

[117] See, by way of example, *Director of Corporate Enforcement v Bailey* [2007] IEHC 365, [2008] 2 ILRM 13.

[118] *Cooper-Flynn v Radio Telefís Éireann* [2004] IESC 27 at [214], [2004] 2 IR 72 at 153.

[119] [1966] AC 356, [1965] 3 All ER 593.

[120] *Comptroller of Customs v Western Electric Co. Ltd* [1962] AC 367, [1965] 3 All ER 599.

[121] (1969) 1 Frewen 343.

[122] [1965] AC 1001, [1964] 2 All ER 881.

[123] The decision in *Myers* was considered but distinguished on the facts in *People (DPP) v Marley* [1985] ILRM 17.

5–54   The decision in *Myers* was distinguished by the Court of Appeal in *People (DPP) v Meehan*[124] where it was held that a document generated by an automated computerised process without human intervention is not hearsay and is admissible as real evidence.[125] However, before such evidence can be admitted, it is necessary to call appropriate evidence to describe the function and operation of the computer.[126] Further, where data has been inputted into the computer system, the printout will be regarded as being equivalent to a statement by the person who inputted the data and will be treated as hearsay which will be inadmissible unless it falls within one of the exceptions to the hearsay rule such as that applicable to business records under Part II of the Criminal Evidence 1992 which is discussed below.[127] It should also be noted that, before the application of the hearsay rule to a document arises for consideration, the document must be properly proven in evidence.[128]

5–55   In practice, the hearsay rule has quite an attenuated application to documentary evidence in civil cases because parties routinely waive any objection on hearsay grounds to the admission of documents.[129] Indeed, in more recent times, the practice has developed of the parties formally agreeing that identified documents can be admitted as *prima facie* evidence of their contents on what has become known as the *Bula/Fyffes* basis.[130] Where this is agreed, the documents the subject of the agreement (usually the discovered documents and/or the documents compiled in core books) are also admitted as *prima facie* evidence of the truth of their contents as against the party who created the original of the document in question. However, documents, the originals of which were created by any other party to the proceedings or a non-party, are not so admitted. Such an agreement, which will result in significant savings in time at a hearing, recognises the reality that, in most cases, the documents created by a party will be admissible by way of an exception to the hearsay rule as an admission.[131]

5. Statements by Conduct

5–56   Conduct will also come within the ambit of the hearsay rule where it is intended

---

[124]   [2006] IECCA 104, [2006] 3 IR 468.

[125]   [2006] IECCA 104 at [31], [2006] 3 IR 468 at 480. See also *People (DPP) v Murphy* [2005] IECCA 1 at [78], [2005] 2 IR 125 at 151; *Sapporo Maru (Owners) v Statute of Liberty (Owners), The Statue of Liberty* [1968] 1 WLR 739; *R. v Wood* (1982) 76 Cr App 23; *Castle v Cross* [1984] 1 WLR 1372; *R. v Spiby* (1990) 91 Cr App R 186. For a more detailed discussion of the admissibility of the outputs of mechanical and computerised systems as real evidence, see Chap.12.

[126]   [2006] IECCA 104 at [33], [2006] 3 IR 468 at 480; *R. v Cochrane* [1993] Crim LR 48.

[127]   *People (DPP) v Meehan* [2006] IECCA 104 at [34]–[35], [2006] 3 IR 468 at 481; *R. v Coventry Justices, Ex parte Bullard* (1992) 95 Cr App R 175.

[128]   As outlined in Chap.12, a party tendering a document is required, firstly, to prove the contents of a document by producing the original of the document or, in certain circumstances, by adducing a copy or other secondary evidence of its contents and, secondly, to prove the authenticity of the document. The distinction between compliance with these requirements and the hearsay rule was drawn in *People (DPP) v Byrne* [1987] IR 363, [1989] ILRM 613 but seems to have been overlooked in *People (DPP) v Byrne*, unreported, Court of Criminal Appeal, 7 June 2000.

[129]   See by way of example, *Hughes v Staunton*, unreported, High Court, 16 February 1990 and *Shelley-Morris v Bus Atha Cliath* [2003] 1 IR 232.

[130]   See *Moorview Developments Ltd v First Active plc* [2008] IEHC 211 at [3.4]–[3.8] and [2009] IEHC 214 at [3.1].

[131]   The admission of documents on the *Bula/Fyffes* and some of the problems that can thereby arise are discussed in Chap.12.

to be communicative.[132] Everyday examples of statements by conduct are where a person nods his or her head to signify "yes" or shakes his or her head to signify "no" and the use of sign language by a person who cannot speak. In *Chandrasekera v R.*,[133] signs made by a woman whose throat had been cut that were interpreted as identifying the accused and the nodding by her of her head when asked if was the accused who had cut her throat were held to be hearsay statements. A less obvious example of conduct that was intended to be communicative can be seen in *Stevenson v Commonwealth of Virginia*.[134] The accused was suspected of homicide and a police officer asked the accused's wife to give him the clothes that the accused had been wearing on the day of the homicide. It was held that the giving by the wife of a shirt, which was later found to have bloodstains on it matching the blood of the deceased, was a non-verbal assertion that the accused had worn that shirt on the day of the homicide and was inadmissible hearsay.

6. Implied Assertions

5–57   One question that has generated considerable controversy is whether, and to what extent, the hearsay rule applies to out-of-court statements which are tendered, not to prove the truth of their contents but for the purpose of inviting the jury to draw an inference from the contents of the statement that is circumstantially relevant.

5–58   Applying a definitional approach to hearsay, it would seem that the hearsay rule is confined to express assertions of fact. As noted above, in *Cullen v Clarke*, Kingsmill Moore J stated that out-of-court statements are "inadmissible to prove the truth of the facts which they *assert*".[135] To assert means to positively declare.[136] Again, in *Ratten v R.*,[137] Lord Wilberforce stated that "[a] question of hearsay only arises when words spoken are relied on "testimonially", *i.e.* as establishing some fact *narrated* by the words".[138] Thus, it would seem to follow that the hearsay rule only applies where a statement is tendered to prove the truth of a fact which is expressly asserted in the statement and not where a fact, the truth of which is relevant to the proceedings, is

---

[132] In *Wright v Doe d Tatham* (1837) 7 Ad & El 313, Parke B suggested that the hearsay rule would apply to conduct which was tendered to prove to prove any fact or belief that could be implied from it giving the following illustrative examples: "the supposed conduct of the family or relations of a testator, taking the same precautions in his absence as if he were a lunatic; his election, in his absence, to some high and responsible office; the conduct of a physician who permitted a will to be executed by a sick testator; the conduct of a deceased captain on a question of seaworthiness, who, after examining every part of the vessel, embarked in it with his family; all these, when deliberately considered, are, with reference to the matter in issue in each case, mere instances of hearsay evidence, mere statements, not on oath, but implied in or vouched by the actual conduct of persons by whose acts the litigant parties are not to be bound." However, the balance of authority in commonwealth jurisdictions appears to be against this proposition (see *R. v McKinnon* (1989) 33 OAC 11) and rule 801 of the Federal Rules of Evidence stipulates that conduct is only a statement for the purposes of the hearsay rule when it is intended by the declarant to be an assertion.

[133] [1937] AC 220.

[134] (1977) 218 Va. 462, 237 SE2d 779.

[135] [1963] IR 368 at 378.

[136] *US v Zenni* (1980) 492 F Supp 464 at 468.

[137] [1972] AC 378, [1971] 3 All ER 801.

[138] [1972] AC 378 at 387, [1971] 3 All ER 801 at 805. See further Weinberg, "Implied Assertions and the Scope of the Hearsay Rule" (1973) 9 Mel ULR 26 and Guest, "The Scope of the Hearsay Rule" (1985) 10 LQR 385.

implicit or can be inferred from the statement. Furthermore, as noted above, the key to the application of the hearsay rule is the identification of the purpose for which the evidence is tendered. Thus, even if a statement has a double relevance for both a hearsay and a non-hearsay purpose, it is admissible provided that it is tendered for the non-hearsay purpose only.

5–59 This was the approach taken in *Ratten v R*.[139] where the defence of the accused to a charge of murdering his wife was that his gun had gone off accidentally while he was cleaning it. In order to rebut this defence, the prosecution called as a witness a telephonist from the local telephone exchange who gave evidence that, shortly before the shooting, she had received a call from the house in which the accused and deceased lived from a hysterical woman who said "Get me the police please". This evidence was objected to on the basis that it was hearsay but the Privy Council was satisfied that this evidence was not hearsay because it was relevant as establishing, if the jury thought it proper to draw the inference that the deceased was, at the time of the call, in a state of emotion of fear. The contents of the statement, that the deceased wanted the police, helped to indicate the nature of emotion, anxiety or fear at an existing or impending emergency. Thus, even though the statement "Get me the police please" would have been inadmissible hearsay if tendered for the purpose of showing that she wanted the police and, thus, by inference that she needed the police because she was being attacked by the accused, the statement was admissible because a relevant non-hearsay purpose, showing the state of mind of the declarant, had been identified. Of course, it would have been necessary to carefully instruct the jury as to the limited purpose for which the statement could be used.

5–60 The decision in *Ratten* was subsequently applied in *Woodhouse v Hall*[140] where an issue arose, in a prosecution of the accused for managing a brothel, as to the admissibility of the evidence of police officers as to offers made to them while on the relevant premises of "immoral services". Donaldson LJ dismissed the contention that the evidence of the offers made should be regarded as hearsay:

> "I suspect that the justices were mislead ... and thought that this was a hearsay case, because they may have thought that they had to be satisfied as to the truth of what the ladies said or were alleged to have said in the sense that they had to satisfy themselves that the words were not a joke but were meant seriously. ... But this is not a matter of truth or falsity. It is a matter of what was really said – the quality of the words, the message being transmitted.... There is no question of the hearsay rule arising at all. The relevant issue was did these ladies make these offers? The offers were oral and the police officers were entitled to give evidence of them."

5–61 This case illustrates the difficulties posed by out-of-court statements with a double relevance. Here, the Court of Appeal was correct in concluding that the fact that a number of offers of "immoral services" had been made on the same premises was relevant to the issue of whether the accused was managing a brothel on the basis of the unlikelihood of coincidence that such offers would be made if the premises was not being used as a brothel. However, the statements would also have been very relevant if tendered to prove the truth of their contents, *i.e.* that the offerors would provide "immoral services" for specified sums of money. Again, a careful instruction as to the limited purpose for the reception of the offers would have been necessary.

5–62 An example of the distinction between hearsay and original evidence that was

---

[139] [1972] AC 378, [1971] 3 All ER 801.
[140] (1981) 72 Cr App R 39.

circumstantially relevant in the context of a written statement arose in *R. v Rice*.[141] The accused were charged with conspiracy and, at the trial, a used airline ticket which bore the names of two of the accused was admitted to prove that they had travelled on a particular flight. The Court of Criminal Appeal stated that the ticket would have been hearsay if tendered for the purposes of speaking its contents, *i.e.* that it was issued to the persons named on the ticket. However, it took the view that it had been properly admitted as evidence from which the jury could infer that persons with those names had travelled on the specified flight. Winn J explained that:

> "The relevance of that ticket in logic and its legal admissibility as a piece of real evidence both stem from the same root, *viz.*, the balance of probability recognised by common sense and common knowledge that an air ticket which has been used on a flight and which has a name upon it has more likely than not been used by a man of that name or by one of two men whose names are upon it. A comparable document would be a passport, which is more likely on the whole to be in the possession of the person to whom it was issue than that of anyone having no right to it."[142]

5–63   The example of the passport referred to is instructive. If it were relevant to prove that a person had been in a particular airport, then evidence that his or her passport had been found in that airport would provide circumstantial evidence of that fact on the basis that it is more likely to have been deposited in the airport by the person to whom the passport has been issued than some other person. If tendered for the limited purpose of proving the connection between the person to whom it was issued and the place where it was found, it is not hearsay even though the probative force of the evidence depends on the underlying proposition that the passport is that of the person, *i.e.* its contents are true.

5–64   However, there is a line of English and commonwealth authority to the effect that it is not possible to "circumvent" the hearsay rule in this manner and which has extended its application to circumstances where the relevance of an out-of-court statement is derived from or depends on the truth of an inference that is implicit in the statement. The seminal authority in this regard is the infamous case of *Wright v Doe d Tatham*.[143] One of the principal issues in that case was the mental competence of a testator and it was sought to introduce into evidence a number of letters written to the testator by some of his acquaintances from which it could be inferred that they considered him to be sane. Having regard to the outline of the hearsay rule above, it would seem to quite clear that these letters should not be regarded as hearsay because they were not being tendered to prove the truth of their contents, *i.e.* the truth of any of the matters stated in the letters. However, it was held that the letters were hearsay and inadmissible for the purpose for which they were tendered. The reasoning behind this conclusion is most clearly set out in the judgment of Parke B:

> "But the question is, whether the contents of those letters are evidence of the fact to be proved upon this issue—that is, the actual existence of the qualities which the testator is, in those letters, by implication, stated to possess: and those letters may be considered in this respect to be on the same footing as if they had contained a direct and positive statement that he was competent. For this purpose they are mere hearsay evidence, statements of the writers, not

---

[141] [1963] 1 QB 857. See Cross, "The Periphery of Hearsay" (1969) 7 Mel. ULR 1 for a discussion of the case.
[142] [1963] 1 QB 857 at 871.
[143] (1837) 7 Ad & El 313.

on oath, of the truth of the matter in question, with this addition, that they have acted upon the statements on the faith of their being true, by their sending the letters to the testator."[144]

5–65   This passage explains the reasoning behind the decision. If one of the letter writers had opened his or her letter with words along the lines of "I am glad to hear that you are in good health and still sane", this statement would have been clearly inadmissible if tendered to prove that this statement was correct and that the testator was sane. However, the only relevance of the letters was to prove that the writers believed that the testator was sane and to allow the tribunal of fact to infer that there was a reasonable basis for that belief. The effect of the ruling in *Wright v Doe'd Tatham* was that an out-of-court statement from which a relevant fact could be inferred was inadmissible as hearsay if an express assertion in similar terms would be inadmissible.

5–66   The application of the reasoning in *Wright* can be seen in *R. v Van Vreden*,[145] a decision that is difficult to square with *Rice*. In that case, it was alleged that the accused had committed various offences using a South African Barclaycard issued to a South African woman and of which they had unauthorised possession. In order to prove that the Barclaycard had issued to a person other than the accused, an application form in the name of that person was tendered in evidence. It was submitted that the connection between the application form and the card used by the accused was established by the fact that the number of the card was to be found in the space for the account number which in the ordinary course of business would have been inserted after the application had been approved. However, the Court of Criminal Appeal held that the application form was hearsay and had been improperly admitted. The Court accepted the argument that the application form was the equivalent of a statement made by a bank clerk in South Africa asserting that he had issued a card to the person named thereon bearing the number which he had entered as the account number. Similarly, in *R. v Romeo*,[146] it was held that a sales docket could not be admitted on a charge of drugs trafficking in order to establish a link between the accused and materials used to wrap and distribute the drugs.[147]

5–67   After, arguably, being ignored in decisions such as *Ratten* and *Rice*, the reasoning in *Wright v Doe d Tatham* was approved and applied by a majority of the House of Lords in *R. v Kearley*.[148] In that case, the police found drugs in the accused's flat, but not in sufficient quantities to raise the inference that he was a dealer. The police remained there for several hours and intercepted 10 telephone calls in which the callers asked to speak to the defendant and asked for drugs. Seven people also called to the flat, asking for the defendant and to be supplied with drugs. At the accused's trial for possession with the intent to supply, the officers gave evidence of these conversations

---

[144] (1837) 7 Ad & El 313 at 385–386.

[145] (1973) 57 Cr App R 818.

[146] (1982) 30 SASR 243.

[147] It is noteworthy that the decision in *R. v Rice* [1963] 1 QB 857, [1963] 1 All ER 832 was expressly disapproved. See also *Re Gardner* (1968) 13 FLR 345.

[148] [1992] 2 AC 228, [1992] 2 All ER 345. See Pattenden, "Conceptual Versus Pragmatic Approaches to Hearsay" (1993) 56 MLR 138; Taylor, "Two English hearsay heresies'" (2005) 9 E & P 110. As confirmed in *R. v Singh* [2006] EWCA Crim 660, [2006] 1 WLR 1564, the effect of the Criminal Justice Act 2003 has been to reverse the decision in *Kearley* and to remove implied assertions from the scope of the hearsay rule. See also *R. v MK* [2007] EWCA Crim 3150, *R. v Leonard* [2009] EWCA Crim 1251, *R. v Twist* [2011] EWCA Crim 1143, [2011] 2 Cr App R 17, *R. v Mateza* [2011] EWCA Crim 2587, *R. v Ahmed* [2012] EWCA Crim 288 and Duff, "The Demise of Kearley—A Hearsay Problem Solved?" (2005) International Commentary on Evidence (2) 1.

in order to prove intention to supply. However, a majority of the House of Lords held that this evidence had been improperly admitted on the grounds that it was irrelevant and, further, than even if it could be regarded as relevant, it was only relevant by means of an implied assertion and was, thus, inadmissible hearsay.

5–68   The majority took the view that the evidence of the requests made by the callers and visitors was irrelevant because it could only be evidence of the state of mind or belief of those making the requests, which was not a relevant issue at the trial, the issue being whether the defendant intended to supply drugs. It made no difference, in that regard, that there were a large number of such requests all made at the same place on the same day. Secondly, in so far as the evidence was relevant to the issue of the defendant's intent to supply, *i.e.* as an implied assertion that the defendant was a supplier, it was inadmissible hearsay as much as an express out of court assertion to the same effect. According to Lord Ackner, the object of tendering the evidence was to establish the truth of what was contained in the statements which was precisely what the hearsay rule prohibited:

> "What is sought to be done is to the use the oral assertion, even though it may be an implied assertion, as evidence of the truth of the proposition asserted. That the proposition is asserted by way of necessary implication rather than expressly cannot, to my mind, make any difference."[149]

5–69   Strong dissenting judgments were delivered by Lord Griffiths and Lord Browne-Wilkinson. They agreed that the calls would be irrelevant if offered merely as evidence of belief on the part of the callers but took the view that the large number of telephone calls and visitors implied that "the appellant had established a market as a drug dealer by supplying or offering to supply drugs and was thus attracting customers".[150] Therefore, "the existence of a substantial body of potential customers provides some evidence which a jury could take into account in deciding whether the accused had an intent to supply".[151] With regard to the contention that the evidence was hearsay, Lord Griffiths justified its admissibility by reference to a classic hearsay analysis of focusing on the purpose for which it had been admitted:

> "The evidence is offered not for the purpose of inviting the jury to draw the inference that the customers believed they could obtain drugs but to prove as a fact that the telephone callers and visitors were acting as customers or potential customers, which was a circumstance from which the jury could if so minded draw the inference that the appellant was trading as a drug dealer.... The request for drugs made by the callers were not hearsay as generally understood, namely an out-of-court narrative description of facts which have to be proved in evidence. The callers were neither describing the appellant as a drug dealer nor stating their opinion that he was a drug dealer. They were calling him up or visiting him as customers, a fact revealed by the words they used in requesting drugs from him."[152]

5–70   It is interesting to contrast the decision in *Kearley* with that reached in *US v Zenni*,[153] where evidence of phone calls intercepted by government agents by unknown callers seeking to place bets on various sporting events was held to be admissible on charges relating to illegal bookmaking activities. It was held by the United States District Court that under Rule 801 of the Federal Rules of Evidence the hearsay rule only applied to "assertions" and the dividing line between hearsay and non-hearsay was

---

[149] [1992] 2 AC 228 at 255, [1992] 2 All ER 345 at 364. See above.
[150] [1992] 2 AC 228 at 238, [1992] 2 All ER 345 at 349 (*per* Lord Griffiths).
[151] [1992] 2 AC 228 at 279, [1992] 2 All ER 345 at 383 (*per* Lord Browne-Wilkinson).
[152] [1992] 2 AC 228 at 238, [1992] 2 All ER 345 at 350 .
[153] (1980) 492 F Supp 262. See also *US v Giraldo* (1987) 822 F 2d 205; *People v Morgan* (2005) 125 Cal App 4th 935, 23 Cal Rptr 3d 224 *US v Rodriguez-Lopez* (2009) 565 F 3d 312.

an intention to assert. Thus, the calls were admitted as non-assertive verbal conduct which were relevant to support an inference that bets could be placed at the premises being telephoned.

5–71   The issue of whether implied assertions fall within the scope of the hearsay rule has recently been considered by the Canadian Supreme Court in *R. v Baldree*,[154] the facts of which bear some similarity to *Kearley*. The accused had been convicted of possession of drugs with an intent to supply. At the trial, evidence was given by a police officer that, after the accused had been arrested, he had answered a call to the accused's mobile phone and the caller had asked for the accused, requested "one ounce of weed" and gave an address for delivery. No effort was made to find and interview the caller or to call him as a witness. The Supreme Court held that this evidence should not have been admitted. Delivering the judgment of the majority, Fish J declined to draw any distinction between express and implied assertions for the purpose of the application of the hearsay rule on the basis that the risks associated with the admission of hearsay evidence applied just as much in the case of implied assertions as express assertions:

> "Accordingly, there is no principled reason, in determining their admissibility, to distinguish between express and implied assertions adduced for the truth of their contents. Both function in precisely the same way. And the benefits of cross-examining the declarant are not appreciably different when dealing with one form of testimony than the other. If an out-of-court statement implicates the traditional hearsay dangers, it constitutes hearsay and must be dealt with accordingly."[155]

5–72   However, while the approach of the majority in *Kearley* on this issue was endorsed, Fish J emphasised that this would not lead to an overbroad application of the hearsay rule because of the recognition by the Canadian courts of a broad inclusionary discretion to admit hearsay evidence where the twin criteria of necessity and reliability were satisfied:

> "Under our law, hearsay evidence that is not admissible under a traditional exception may nonetheless be admitted pursuant to a principled analysis of its necessity and reliability. This "sensible scheme" recognises that "some implied assertions, like some express assertions, will be highly reliable even in the absence of cross-examination": Finman, at p. 693. Pursuant to its terms, implied assertions that are necessary and reliable may be admitted while those that are unreliable or unnecessary will be excluded."[156]

5–73   Surprisingly, there is no Irish authority on the question as to whether implied assertions fall within the scope of the hearsay rule. When the matter does arise, the courts will have the choice between adopting a narrow rule that focuses on the purpose for which the evidence is admitted and the presence of an intention to assert as the dividing line between hearsay and non-hearsay and a hearsay rule that includes implied assertions.[157] A narrower hearsay rule allows more evidence to go to the tribunal of fact and a strong argument can be made that, contrary to the views expressed by some

---

[154] [2013] SCC 35, [2013] 2 SCR 520. See Hunt & Rankin, "Hearsay by implication: *R. v Baldree*" (2014) 18 E & P 181. See Bryant, Lederman and Fuerst, *Sapinko, Lederman & Bryant: The Law of Evidence in Canada* 4th edn (Lexis Nexis, 2014) §6.57–§6.60.

[155] [2013] SCC 35 at 49, [2013] 2 SCR 520 at 536.

[156] [2013] SCC 35 at 66, [2013] 2 SCR 520 at 540.

[157] The Law Commission in England addressed this issue in its Report on "Evidence in Criminal Proceedings: Hearsay and Related Topics" (1997) LCR 245. It concluded that the narrow rule should be adopted as regards implied assertions, such that these only constitute hearsay where there was an intention to assert. This recommendation has been incorporated into s.115 of the Criminal Justice Act 2003, which focuses on the purpose of the person making the statement.

judges, juries are well equipped to weigh and evaluate such evidence provided that they are properly instructed.[158] Furthermore, hearsay dangers such as mendacity and insincerity are lessened considerably where a statement is only relevant by means of some assertion to be implied from it.[159] On the other hand, it has to be conceded that there are some hearsay dangers involved in the admission of such evidence and further, a party against whom such evidence is admitted may not have a full opportunity to cross-examine the declarant on the statement. Nonetheless, it is submitted that these matters should go to weight rather than admissibility and that the Irish courts should take an approach to the hearsay rule along the lines of that adopted in Rule 801 of the Federal Rules of Evidence and confine the hearsay rule to express assertions.[160]

D. Exceptions to the Hearsay Rule

5–74 It is evident from the discussion of the hearsay rule above that it has the potential to exclude a lot of very probative evidence and, as acknowledged by Keane J in *People (DPP) v McGinley*,[161] "is capable of producing injustice in individual cases, particularly if applied in a rigid and unyielding manner". It is, therefore, unsurprising that the exclusionary rule is subject to a large number of exceptions developed at common law or by legislation. Although it is difficult to make any generalisations about these exceptions given the rather *ad hoc* manner in which they have developed, it is apparent that most of them developed on the basis of, and can be justified by, reference to the twin criteria for exceptions identified by Wigmore[162] of necessity and reliability.[163]

1. Statements Forming Part of the Res Gestae

5–75 The phrase "*res gestae*" means "transaction" and, under the inclusionary doctrine of *res gestae*, a statement which is so closely associated in time, place and circumstance with some act that is in issue that it can be said to form part of the act rather than a reported statement, is admissible in evidence to prove the truth of its contents.[164] In *Teper v R.*,[165] Lord Normand explained that the application of the doctrine of *res gestae* to hearsay statements as follows:

---

[158] As may be seen from the successful operation of the narrow rule in Scotland (where such evidence has never been regarded as hearsay), the United States (Rule 801(a) of the Federal Rules of Evidence), and Australia (s.59 of the Evidence Act 1995).

[159] See Falknor, "The 'Hear-Say' Rule as a 'See-Do' Rule: Evidence of Conduct" (1961) Rocky Mt. Law Rev. 133; Marshall, "Admissibility of Implied Assertions: Towards a Reliability Based Exception to the Hearsay Rule" (1997) 23 (1) Mon ULR 201. *Cf.* cl. 77(2)(b) of the Draft Evidence Code 131 prepared by the Canadian Law Reform Commission; the New Zealand Law Commission Preliminary Paper No. 15, "Evidence Law: Hearsay" (1991), pp. 32–33; and the Report of the Law Commission in England (LC245: 2004), para 7.21.

[160] See McCormick, "The Borderland of Hearsay" (1929–30) 39 Yale LJ 489 at 502; Falkner, "Silence as Hearsay" (1940) 89 UPaLRev 192 at 206; McGinlay & Waye, "Implied Assertions and the Hearsay Prohibition" (1993) 67 ALJ 657.

[161] [1998] 2 IR 408 at 413, [1998] 2 ILRM 233 at 237.

[162] Wigmore, *Evidence* (3rd edn, 1940), Vol. 5, § 1420.

[163] See *Eastern Health Board v MK* [1999] 2 IR 99 at 124, [1999] 2 ILRM 321 at 345 (*per* Keane J).

[164] Paraphrasing Lord Normand in *Teper v R.* [1952] AC 480 at 486 in a passage which was quoted with approval in *People (AG) v Crosbie* [1966] IR 490 at 497. See generally, Davidson, "Res Gestae in the Law of Evidence" [2007] 11 Edin LR 379.

[165] [1952] AC 480.

"It appears to rest ultimately on two propositions, that human utterance is both a fact and a means of communication, and that human action may be so interwoven with words that the significance of the action cannot be understood without the correlative words, and the dissociation of the words from the action would impede the discovery of the truth."[166]

5–76   However, he conceded that "the judicial applications of these two propositions, which do not always combine harmoniously, has never been precisely formulated in a general principle"[167] and the *res gestae* doctrine has been subjected to considerable criticism, with Lord Tomlin in *Homes v Newman*[168] dismissing it as "a phrase adopted to provide a respectable legal cloak for a variety of cases to which no formula of precision can be applied".[169] Indeed, that comment seems to be borne out with regard to its application to the hearsay rule because the *res gestae* exception actually encompasses four distinct exceptions to the hearsay rule: (a) spontaneous declarations; (b) declarations explaining the performance of an act; (c) declarations as to contemporaneous state of mind of the declarant; and (d) declarations as to the contemporaneous physical state of the declarant.

(a) Spontaneous declarations

5–77   Statements concerning an event in issue, made in circumstances of such spontaneity or involvement in an event that the possibility of concoction, distortion or error can be disregarded, are admissible as evidence of the truth of their contents. The rationale for the admission of this category of out-of-court statements is evident from the formulation of the exception—they are made in circumstances where the declarant's mind is so dominated by a startling or overwhelming event that the statement is a spontaneous and instinctive reaction, made without any opportunity for the declarant to devise a false statement.[170] This rationale is open to criticism on the basis that the circumstances that ground admissibility actually increase the risks of error and inaccuracy. However, as will be seen below, the absence of the risks of distortion or error form part of the conditions of admissibility.

5–78   The origin of this category of *res gestae* can be traced to the decision in *Thompson v Trevanion*[171] where, in an action for assault, Holt CJ stated that "what the wife said immediate upon the hurt received, and before that she had time to devise or contrive anything for her own advantage, might be given in evidence". However, the emphasis on the requirements of spontaneity and the lack of an opportunity to concoct a false statement was lost in subsequent decisions. The focus shifted, instead, to the question of whether the statement formed part of the same transaction as the act. One of the more indefensible examples of this approach was *R. v Bedingfield*[172] where the statement of a woman made after she had emerged from the room where her throat had

---

[166] [1952] AC 480 at 486. This passage was quoted with approval by the Court of Criminal Appeal in *People (AG) v Crosbie* [1966] IR 490 at 497.

[167] [1952] AC 480 at 486.

[168] [1931] 2 Ch 112 at 120.

[169] See also *People (DPP) v O'Callaghan* [2001] 1 IR 584 at 588, [2001] 2 ILRM 184 at 189, where Hardiman J endorsed judicial and academic criticisms of the doctrine of *res gestae*.

[170] See *Ratten v R.* [1972] AC 378 at 389, [1971] 3 All ER 801 at 807; *R. v Andrews* [1987] AC 281 at 301, [1987] 1 All ER 513 at 520; *R. v Barlien* [2008] NZCA 180 at [38], [2009] 1 NZLR 170.

[171] (1693) Skin 402.

[172] (1879) 14 Cox CC 341. See also *R. v Leland* [1951] OR 12, (1951) 98 CCC 337.

been cut was held to be inadmissible because "it was something stated by her after it was all over, whatever it was, and after the act was completed".[173]

5–79 However, the law in this area was harmonised again with the underlying rationale in *Ratten v R.*[174] where Lord Wilberforce, delivering the judgment of the Privy Council, stated:

> "[T]he test should be not the uncertain one whether the making of the statement was in some sense part of the event or transaction. This may often be difficult to establish: such external matters as the time which elapses between the events and the speaking of the words (or vice versa), and differences in location being relevant factors but not, by themselves, decisive criteria. As regards statements made after the event it must be for the judge, by preliminary ruling, to satisfy himself that the statement was so clearly made in circumstances of spontaneity or involvement in the event that the possibility of concoction can be disregarded. Conversely, if he considers that the statement was made by way of narrative of a detached prior event so that the speaker was so disengaged from it as to be able to construct or adapt his account, he should exclude it. And the same must in principle be true of statements before the event."[175]

5–80 Applying those principles to the facts of the case (which have been outlined above), it was held that the evidence of the telephonist was admissible as part of the *res gestae*. Not only was there a close association in place and time between the statement and the shooting, but also the way in which the statement came to be made, in a call for the police, and the tone of voice used, showed intrinsically that the statement was being forced from the wife by an overwhelming pressure of contemporary events.[176]

5–81 The approach taken in *Ratten* was subsequently endorsed by the House of Lords in *R. v Andrews*[177] with Lord Ackner summarising the principles to be applied:

> "(1) The primary question which the judge must ask himself is: can the possibility of concoction or distortion be disregarded? (2) To answer that question the judge must first consider the circumstances in which the particular statement was made, in order to satisfy himself that the event was so unusual or startling or dramatic as to dominate the thoughts of the victim, so that his utterance was an instinctive reaction to that event, thus giving no real opportunity for reasoned reflection. In such a situation the judge would be entitled to conclude that the involvement or pressure of the event would exclude the possibility of concoction or distortion, providing that the statement was made in conditions of approximate but not exact contemporaneity. (3) In order for the statement to be sufficiently 'spontaneous' it must be so closely associated with the event which has excited the statement that it can fairly be stated that the mind of the declarant was still dominated by the event ... (4) Quite apart from the time factor, there may be special features in the case, which relate to the possibility of concoction or distortion. In the instant appeal the defence relied on evidence to support the contention that the deceased had a motive of his own to fabricate or concoct, namely ... malice ... (5) As to the possibility of error in the facts narrated in the statement, if only ordinary fallibility of human recollection is relied on, this goes to the weight to be attached to and not to the

---

[173] (1951) 98 CCC 337 at 343. In *Ratten v R.* [1972] AC 378 at 390, [1971] 3 All ER 801 at 807, Lord Wilberforce stated that "there could hardly be a case where the words uttered carried more clearly the mark of spontaneity and intense involvement".

[174] [1972] AC 378, [1971] 3 All ER 801.

[175] [1971] 3 All ER 801 at 389, 807.

[176] *Cf. R. v Newport* [1998] Crim LR 581 (evidence of contents of the telephone call made by deceased approximately 20 minutes before she was stabbed was held not to be admissible as part of the *res gestae* because it was a fairly long telephone call whose content was in no sense a spontaneous and unconsidered reaction to an immediately impending emergency and the accused was not even present).

[177] [1987] AC 281, [1987] 1 All ER 513. The decision in *Ratten* had been applied in a number of intervening cases including *R. v Nye* (1977) 66 Cr App R 252 and *R. v Turnbull* (1984) 80 Cr App R 104.

admissibility of the statement and is therefore a matter for the jury. However, here again there may be special features that may give rise to the possibility of error. ... In such circumstances the trial judge must consider whether he can exclude the possibility of error."[178]

5–82   In that case, the deceased had been stabbed during a burglary of his flat by two men. He went to the flat below for assistance and the police arrived within a matter of minutes. One of the constables asked him how he had received his injuries and he identified the accused and another man. There was evidence that the accused had drunk to excess and had a motive to fabricate because of malice he bore the accused. However, applying the principles set out above, their Lordships were satisfied that the statement had been properly admitted.

5–83   The principles in *Andrews* were subsequently applied in *R. v Carnall*[179] where statements made by deceased more than an hour after he had been attacked, badly beaten and stabbed were held to have been properly admitted notwithstanding the lapse of time, evidence that the deceased had acted dishonestly in the past and medical evidence that the loss of blood could have caused confusion, delusion or paranoia.[180]

5–84   The traditional approach of the Irish courts was to focus on the requirement of contemporaneity. In *People (AG) v Crosbie*,[181] a statement made the deceased within one minute of being stabbed identifying the first accused as his assailant was held to be admissible as part of the *res gestae* on the basis that "the words were so clearly associated with the stabbing in time, place and circumstances that they were part of the thing done and so an item or part of real evidence and not merely a reported statement".[182] However, given that the approach laid down in *Ratten/Andrews* has been followed in other common law jurisdictions,[183] it is unsurprising that it has been adopted in this jurisdiction. In *People (DPP) v Longeran*,[184] the applicant had been convicted of the murder of his brother who had died from stab wounds. At the trial, a number of statements made by the deceased identifying his brother as the person who had stabbed him were admitted. On appeal, it was contended that the trial judge had erred in admitting the evidence of a witness to whom such a statement had been made approximately ten minutes after the stabbing had occurred. It was argued that the trial judge had gone further than permitted by *Crosbie* by adopting a composite test premised on the possibility of concoction or fabrication rather than contemporaneity. However, the Court of Criminal Appeal took the view that the modern English approach merely represented an evolution of that adopted in *Crosbie*:

"The composite approach adopted by the trial judge, which gave due weight to both the

---

[178] [1987] AC 281 at 301, [1987] 1 All ER 513 at 520–521.

[179] [1995] Crim LR 944.

[180] See also *R. v Glover* [1991] Crim LR 48.

[181] [1966] IR 490.

[182] [1966] IR 490 at 498. *Cf.* The old Irish case of *R. v Lunny* (1854) 6 Cox CC 477 (statement of the deceased to a girl who had heard his cry and came to his aid was held to be admissible at the trial of the accused for his murder as part of the *res gestae*).

[183] *Walton v R.* (1989) 166 CLR 283 at 295 (*per* Mason CJ), 84 ALR 59; *Pollitt v R.* (1992) 174 CLR 558 at 582–583 (*per* Brennan J), 108 ALR 1; *R. v Clark* (1983) 42 OR (2d) 609, 1 DLR (4th) 46; *Conway v R.* (2000) 172 ALR 185; *R. v Accused* (1997) 14 CRNZ 656; *R. v Pennell* (2003) 1 NZLR 289. *Cf.* the excited utterance exception to the hearsay rule in rule 803 of the Federal Rules of Evidence which renders admissible: "A statement describing or explaining an event or condition made while the declarant was under the stress of excitement caused by the event or condition."

[184] [2009] IECCA 52, [2009] 4 IR 175.

requirement of contemporaneity and the possibility of concoction or fabrication, appear to this court to represent the correct approach to this issue. It would be quite wrong to hold that admissibility should be determined by reference solely to a given time period as to do so would lead to arbitrary and unfair results. Time in this context is an important factor but not a determinant. The true importance of the requirement of contemporaneity is to eliminate the possibility of concoction. Where it is clear that no such opportunity existed on the facts of a given case it would be quite wrong to exclude statements on some arbitrary time basis. It is more a matter of factoring in both components when deciding whether or not to admit such statements as part of the *res gestae*. In every case the trial judge will have to exercise his discretion having regard to the particular circumstances of the case."[185]

5–85　Applying that approach to the facts of the case before it, the Court regarded it as significant that it had not been suggested to any of the witnesses that the statements had not been made by the deceased, that no alternative version of events or other possible perpetrator had been put forward and no motive for concocting or fabricating evidence had been identified. Furthermore, the evidence of other witnesses as to the statements made by the deceased had been admitted without serious challenge. In those circumstances, the Court was satisfied that the challenged statements had been correctly admitted because they formed part of the transaction, were sufficiently contemporaneous and there was no opportunity on the part of the deceased to concoct or fabricate an explanation.

5–86　There are authorities in the UK which appeared to contemplate that a statement admitted as part of the *res gestae* can be adduced even where the witness is available to give evidence.[186] However, having regard to the requirements of fair procedures in this jurisdiction, and particularly, the emphasis placed on the importance of the right to cross-examine, it seems likely that a spontaneous declaration will be excluded if the declarant is available but not called as a witness.

(b) Declarations explaining the performance of an act

5–87　If an act is in issue, or relevant to an issue, a contemporaneous statement made by the person performing the act, explaining his or her intentions in performing the act, is admissible to prove the truth of its contents.[187] The rationale for admitting such a statement appears to be that it is the best and often the only evidence available to explain the motive for the performance of the act.[188] Further, a limited guarantee of reliability is afforded by the requirement of contemporaneity.

5–88　The conditions of admissibility are as follows: (i) the act is in issue or relevant to an issue; (ii) the statement explains the performance of the act; (iii) the statement was made contemporaneously with the act performed; and (iv) the statement was made by the person performing the act.

---

[185] [2009] IECCA 52 at [22], [2009] 4 IR 175 at 183.

[186] See *R. v Andrews* [1987] AC 281 at 302, [1987] 1 All ER 513 at 521; and *Tobi v Nicholas* [1987] Crim LR 774. *Cf. Edwards v DPP* [1992] Crim LR 576.

[187] But see *Cullen v Clarke* [1963] IR 368 at 378–379, where Kingsmill Moore J appeared to identify two distinct sub-categories of statements within this category of *res gestae*, some of which he regarded as falling outside the scope of the hearsay rule altogether and some of which were admissible under this *res gestae* exception.

[188] See *per* Best CJ in *Rawson v Haigh* (1824) 2 Bing 99 at 103: "The going abroad was of itself an equivocal act, and where an act is equivocal, we must get at the motive with which it was committed. In ninety-nine cases out of a hundred, this can only be got at by the declarations of the party himself."

(i) Act in issue or relevant to an issue

5–89   It is a pre-requisite to the admission of a statement explaining the performance of an act that the act must itself be in issue or relevant to an issue without the statement.[189] As Lord Coleridge pointed out in *Wright v Doe d Tatham*,[190] "[i]t is merely arguing in a circle first to pray in aid the declaration to make the action relevant, and then to make the declaration admissible by shewing it to be a part of the act". A good example of an act that was relevant in itself can be seen in *R. v Edwards*[191] where, at the trial of the accused for the murder of his wife, evidence was given by a neighbour that, a week before she was killed, the deceased had visited her house and given her an axe and carving knife to take care of. She was permitted to give evidence that the deceased told her when giving her the items: "Please to put them up, and when I want them I'll fetch them, for my husband always threatens me with these, and when they're out of the way I feel safer."[192] However, this condition was found not to be satisfied in *Gresham Hotel Co Ltd v Manning*[193] where, in an action for obstruction of light, employees of the hotel gave evidence that guests had refused to take certain rooms on the basis that they were dark. The contention that this testimony was properly admitted in order to explain the acts of the guests in refusing the rooms was rejected on the basis that "if (as in the present case) the act without the accompanying declaration would not be admissible in evidence of the fact in controversy, then the union of the two cannot render them legal evidence".[194]

(ii) Explanation of act

5–90   In order to be admissible, a statement must explain or, at a minimum, relate to the performance of the act.[195] For example, in *Chase v Chase*,[196] a grantor executed a deed and handed it to the defendant saying, "There's your deed, Ruth, do what you want with it". These words were admitted as part of the *res gestae* on the basis that the words accompanied and explained the act and gave it legal significance. Similarly, a police officer was permitted to give evidence in *R. v McCay*[197] that another witness, who testified that he had identified the accused in an identification parade but could not remember his number, had picked out the accused saying: "It is number 8."[198]

(iii) Contemporaneity

5–91   The statement must be contemporaneous with the act as otherwise the rationale

---

[189] *Wright v Doe d Tatham* (1828) 4 Bing 496 at 498; *Hyde v Palmer* (1863) 3 B & S 657 at 661.
[190] (1828) 4 Bing 496 at 498.
[191] (1872) 12 Cox CC 230.
[192] See also *Rawson v Haigh* (1824) 4 Bing 99 (person left country leaving debts unpaid and contemporaneous letters written by him were admitted in evidence to show that he left the country with the intention of defrauding his creditors and, thus, to prove an act of bankruptcy).
[193] (1867) IR 1 CL 125.
[194] (1867) IR 1 CL 125 at 128 (*per* O'Brien J).
[195] See *R. v Bliss* (1837) 7 Ad & El 550, [1835–42] All ER Rep 372; *Hyde v Palmer* (1863) 3 B & S 657 at 661 (what was said was not important as an explanation of the act in question, but as a statement in its own right); *Freel v Robinson* (1909) 18 OLR 651 at 654–655; *Chase v Chase* (1963) 48 MPR 12, 36 DLR (2d) 251.
[196] (1962) 48 MPR 12, 36 DLR (2d) 251.
[197] [1990] 1 WLR 645.
[198] See also *R. v Lynch* [2008] 1 Cr App R 338 in relation to the equivalent hearsay exception in s.118(1), rule 4(b) of the Criminal Justice Act 2003.

for admitting it breaks down.[199] However, contemporaneity is a matter of degree and it suffices that the statement was made shortly before or after the act in question.[200] Where the act can be construed as a continuing act, then it is sufficient that the statement is made during its continuance.[201]

(iv) Statement by performer of act

5–92   It follows almost inexorably from the rationale for the exception that, in order to be admissible, the statement must have been made by the person performing the act.[202] However, a statement made by a person who witnessed the act could potentially be admitted if it was adopted by the person performing the act.

(c) Declarations as to contemporaneous state of mind

5–93   If the state of mind of a person is an issue or relevant to an issue, statements made by the person as to his or her contemporaneous state of mind are admissible as evidence of the existence of that state of mind at the time the statement was made.[203] Again, the rationale for the admission of such statements appears to be one of necessity—that the declarant is the person in the best position to state what his or her state of mind is. As Mellish LJ explained in *Sugden v Lord St. Leonards*[204] in relation to statements of intention:

> "Wherever it is material to prove the state of a person's mind, or what was passing in it, and what were his intentions, then you may prove what he said, because that is the only means by which you can find out what his intentions are."[205]

5–94   Statements may be admitted under this heading to prove a variety of matters including knowledge of a matter,[206] political opinion,[207] fear and apprehension,[208]

---

[199] See *Peacock v Harris* (1836) 5 Ad & El 449 at 454, where Lord Denman CJ stated that "a contemporaneous declaration may be admissible as part of a transaction, but an act done cannot be varied or qualified by insulated declarations made at a later time".

[200] *Rawson v Haigh* (1824) 2 Bing 99 at 103; *R. v M (ML)* (1993) 78 CCC (3d) 318 at 323.

[201] *Rawson v Haigh* (1824) 2 Bing 99 at 103.

[202] *Cf. Howe v Malkin* (1878) 40 LT 196.

[203] See *People (DPP) v Murphy*, unreported, Court of Criminal Appeal, 8 July 2003. There is some controversy as to whether declarations as to state of mind are hearsay with Lord Bridge in *R. v Blastland* [1986] AC 41 at 54, [1985] 2 All ER 1095 at 1098–1099, taking the view within they do not fall within the scope of the hearsay rule at all. The judgment of Kingsmill Moore J in *Cullen v Clarke* [1963] IR 368 at 379, is somewhat unclear on this point. He seems to take the view that statements to prove the contemporaneous state of mind of the declarant were not hearsay but that statements made to prove a state of mind at an earlier point were admissible by way of an exception to the hearsay rule. However, the Court of Criminal Appeal in *Murphy* has clarified that declarations as to state of mind are admissible by way of an exception to the hearsay rule and, further, are only admissible if they are declarations as to the contemporaneous state of mind of the declarant.

[204] (1876) 1 PD 154.

[205] (1876) 1 PD 154 at 251.

[206] See *Thomas v Connell* (1838) 4 M & W 267 (statement admitted to prove that bankrupt knew he was insolvent at the time that payment was made) and *R. v Blastland* [1986] AC 41, [1985] 2 All ER 1095 (knowledge of murder at point before the body was discovered).

[207] *R. v Tooke* (1794) 25 State Tr 344.

[208] *R. v Vincent* (1840) 9 C & P 275; *R. v Gandfield* (1846) 2 Cox CC 43; *Neill v North Antrim Magistrates' Court* [1992] 4 All ER 846 at 854; *R. v Gregson* [2003] EWCA Crim 1099; *Re JA's Application for Judicial Review* [2008] NI 74.

feelings of ill-will[209] and the opinions of members of the public by means of opinion polls.[210]

5–95 In *People (DPP) v Murphy*,[211] the Court of Criminal Appeal emphasised that this exception only applies to statements by a person as to his or her contemporaneous state of mind and not statements of their state of mind at an earlier time. The Court quoted with approval from the judgment of Kingsmill Moore J in *Cullen v Clarke*[212] where he stated:

> "The [proposition] that the admission of evidence of words spoken by a person who is not a witness in order to prove the state of his mind is not a transgression of the general hearsay rule must, I think, be confined to cases where such words are the spontaneous and unrehearsed expression of contemporary feelings, words which reveal rather than declare the condition of the mind."

5–96 One category of declarations as to state of mind which merits particular examination is statements of intention. These are admissible as evidence that the particular intention expressed existed at the time the statement was made.[213] A statement of intention may also support the inference that the intention existed at a time prior to or after the declaration. In *Cullen v Clarke*,[214] Kingsmill Moore J stated that the modern tendency is to admit declarations as to state of mind even where they are made prior to or subsequent to an act and unconnected therewith.[215] However, such an inference will not be drawn when a statement is self-serving as "otherwise it would be easy for a man to lay grounds for escaping the consequences of his wrongful acts by making such declarations".[216]

5–97 It is unclear whether a statement of intention is admissible as evidence that it was carried into effect. In *R. v Wainwright*[217] Cockburn CJ excluded evidence of a statement by a murder victim that she was going to the accused's premises because "it was only a statement of intention which might or might not have been carried out".[218] However, in *Mutual Life Insurance Co. v Hillmon*,[219] letters wherein the writer

---

[209] *R. v Hagan* (1873) 12 Cox CC 357.

[210] *Cf. Hanafin v Minister for the Environment* [1996] 2 IR 321, [1996] 2 ILRM 61, where it was held that evidence obtained by a properly conducted research survey was admissible proof of the fact that the opinions obtained had in fact existed and was therefore, not hearsay. However, if (which it is submitted is the correct approach), the opinion polls were regarded as hearsay, they were admissible by way of an exception to the hearsay rule as evidence of the state of mind of the public. See also *Customglass Boats Ltd v Salthouse Brothers Ltd* [1976] 1 NZLR 36, [1976] RPC 589 and *Lego Systems Aktienelskab v Lego M Lemelstrich Ltd* [1983] FSR 155.

[211] Unreported, Court of Criminal Appeal, 8 July 2003.

[212] [1963] IR 368 at 380.

[213] See, *e.g. Moffett v Moffett* [1920] 1 IR 57 (declarations of intention to return to a country admissible in relation to the issue of domicile) and *Murray v Murray* [1939] IR 317 at 327 (statement of donor's intentions admissible to rebut presumption of a resulting trust). See also *Hoare v Allen* (1801) 3 Esp 276; *Sudgen v Lord St. Leonards* (1876) 1 PD 154; *Scappaticci v AG* [1955] 1 All ER 193n, [1955] 2 WLR 409; *Great West Uranium Mines Ltd v Rock Hill Uranium Mines Ltd* (1955) 15 WWR 404, [1995] 4 DLR 307.

[214] [1963] IR 368 at 379.

[215] See *Robson v Kemp* (1802) 4 Esp 233; *Re Fletcher* [1917] 1 Ch 339 at 342; *R. v Moghal* (1977) 65 Cr App R 56 at 62–63; *Shanklin v Smith* (1932) 5 MPR 204.

[216] *Per* Crampton J in *R. v Petcherini* (1855) 7 Cox CC 79 at 83.

[217] (1875) 13 Cox CC 171.

[218] (1875) 13 Cox CC 171 at 172. See also *R. v Thomson* [1912] 3 KB 19; *Cuff v Frazee Storage & Cartage Co.* (1907) 14 OLR 263.

[219] (1892) 145 US 285.

had expressed the intention of leaving a particular place with a man by the name of Hillmon were admitted as evidence that "he had the intention of going, and of going with Hillmon, which made it more probable both that he did go and that he went with Hillmon, than if there had been no proof of such intention".[220] The reasoning in the latter case seems more persuasive. A statement of intention furnishes circumstantial evidence of the carrying into effect of the declaration by the declarant which may, depending on the circumstances, be entitled to very little or a great deal of weight.

5–98   It is important to point out that a statement may only be admitted under this head of *res gestae* to prove a state of mind but not any underlying facts. Thus, in *Thomas v Connell*,[221] evidence of a statement by the bankrupt that he knew he was insolvent was admitted to prove his knowledge of that fact, but not to prove the fact of insolvency.

(d) Declarations as to contemporaneous physical state

5–99   If the physical state of a person is in issue or is relevant to an issue, a statement made by that person as to his or her contemporaneous physical state is admissible to prove the existence of that state at the time the statement was made. Again, the argument in favour of admissibility proceeds on a basis of necessity with Cherry LJ in *Wright v Kerrigan*[222] justifying the admission of this category of statements on the basis that "there are no other means possible of proving bodily or mental feelings than by statements of the person who experiences them".[223] Statements admissible under this head include statements as to the declarant's good health,[224] statements of the declarant's ill-health,[225] complaints of pain,[226] and a complaint of hunger.[227]

5–100   To be admissible, a statement must be about the contemporaneous physical state of the declarant.[228] However, exact contemporaneity is not required and a statement, for example, that the declarant experienced a pain the previous day would be admissible.[229]

5–101   It is important to note that a statement as to physical sensation is admissible to prove the physical state of the declarant only and not the underlying cause.[230] Thus,

---

[220] (1892) 145 US 285 at 295–296. See also *R. v Buckley* (1873) 13 Cox CC 293; *R. v Moghal* (1977) 65 Cr App R 56; *R. v Moore* (1984) 5 OAC 51, 15 CCC (3d) 541; *R. v P(R)* (1990) 58 CCC (3d) 334.

[221] (1838) 4 M & W 267 at 269.

[222] [1911] 2 IR 301 at 310.

[223] *Cf. Per* Lord Ellenborough CJ in *Aveson v Lord Kinnaird* (1805) 6 East 188 at 195: "What were the complaints, what the symptoms, what the conduct of the parties themselves at the time, are always received in evidence upon such inquiries, and must be resorted to from the very nature of the thing." See also *per* Grose J in the same case (at 196–197): "The next question was, why was she in bed? Now who could possibly give so good an account of that as the party herself. It is not only good evidence but the best evidence which the nature of the case afforded."

[224] *R. v Johnson* (1847) 2 Car & Kir 354.

[225] *Aveson v Lord Kinnaird* (1805) 6 East 188.

[226] *Donaghy v Ulster Spinning Co. Ltd* (1912) 46 ILTR 33; *Gilbey v Great Western Railway Co.* (1910) 102 LT 202 at 203.

[227] *R. v Conde* (1867) 10 Cox CC 547.

[228] *R. v Gloster* (1888) 16 Cox CC 471.

[229] See *R. v Black* (1922) 16 Cr App R 118 at 119. *Cf. Youlden v London Guarantee & Accident Co.* (1912) 26 OLR 75, 4 DLR 721 (statement made shortly after act alleged to have caused injury admitted).

[230] *R. v Gloster* (1888) 16 Cox CC 471 at 473.

in a personal injury action, a statement by the injured person as to the pain caused by his injury is admissible but a statement as to the cause of the injury is not.[231]

2. Admissions

5–102   An admission, which is a statement made by a party (or a person in privity with him or her) which is adverse to his or her case,[232] may be proved by the other party in both civil and criminal cases. However, it should be noted that the special rules governing the reception of admissions in criminal cases are dealt with in Chap. 8 and will not be considered here.

5–103   Admissions are admitted on the basis, articulated in the criminal sphere, that "it is fairly presumed that no man would make such a confession against himself if the facts confessed were not true."[233] Furthermore, there is no basis for objecting to the reception in evidence of admissions because of the lack of opportunity to cross-examination or the lack of an oath. As Morgan has stated: "[a] party can hardly object that he had no opportunity to cross-examine himself or that he is unworthy of credence save when speaking under the sanction of an oath."[234] The requirement of necessity is satisfied by the unlikelihood of the party repeating the admission in court and, in criminal cases, the non-compellability of the accused.

5–104   There are a number of species of admissions which, for ease of exposition, are treated separately below: (a) express admissions; (b) admissions by conduct; and (c) vicarious admissions.[235]

(a) Express admissions

5–105   A statement by a party, either orally or in writing, that is adverse to his or her case is admissible as an admission.[236] A straightforward example can be seen in *DPP v Buckley*[237] where the statement by the accused that a brown substance found in his pocket was cannabis was admissible as an admission on a charge of possession of a controlled substance.

---

[231] *Donaghy v Ulster Spinning Co. Ltd.* (1912) 46 ILTR 33 at 34; *Gilbey v Great Western Railway Co.* (1910) 102 L.T. 202 at 203; *Amys v Barton* [1912] 1 KB 40; *Youlden v London Guarantee & Accident Co.* (1912) 26 OLR 75, 4 DLR 721. But see *Wright v Kerrigan* [1911] 2 IR 301 (evidence admitted that deceased had told doctor that he was in pain as a result of an accident admissible in action taken by his widow under Workmen's Compensation Act 1906) and *Somerville v Prudential Insurance Co. of America* [1935] 3 WWR 81 (statements by deceased as to the cause of his pain and distress admitted as evidence of the manner in which the accused received his injury).

[232] *Walsh v Sligo County Council* [2010] IEHC 437 at [152], [2011] 2 IR 260 at 326. *Cf. Per* Ó Dálaigh CJ in *Bord na gCon v Murphy* [1970] IR 301 at 310: "the only exceptions which are admissible in evidence as exceptions to the rule rejecting hearsay are such admissions as are declarations against interest or, as these are sometimes called, disserving statements".

[233] *Per* Grose J in *The King v Lambe* (1791) 2 Leach 552 at 555.

[234] Morgan, *Basic Problems of Evidence* (Joint Committee on Continuing Legal Education of the American Law Institute and the American Bar Association), 1962, at p.266 (quoted in Broun (ed.), *McCormick on Evidence* (Thomson Reuters, 2013), Vol. II, § 254, at p.260).

[235] This categorisation of admissions was adopted by McMahon J in *Walsh v Sligo County Council* [2010] IEHC 437 at [153], [2011] 2 IR 260 at 327.

[236] *Walsh v Sligo County Council* [2010] IEHC 437 at [153], [2011] 2 IR 260 at 327; *Bank of Ireland v O'Donnell* [2012] IEHC 475 at [35].

[237] [2007] IEHC 150 at [15], [2007] 3 IR 745 at 753.

5–106 It is not necessary that evidence of the admission be given by the person to whom it was made. It was held in *R. v Simons*[238] that evidence could be given of what a party was overheard saying to another or even to himself if it was an admission.[239]

5–107 If an issue arises as whether a particular statement constitutes an admission, this is a question of fact to be decided by the tribunal of fact having regard to the words used, the context in which the statement was made and all the surrounding circumstances.[240] An example of the analysis required in this regard can be seen in *People (DPP) v Pringle*,[241] where the first applicant, after being questioned by gardaí for a lengthy period about a bank robbery in which two gardaí had been killed, stated: "I know that you know I was involved, but on the advice of my solicitor I am saying nothing and you will have to prove it all the way." It was contended that this statement did not necessarily mean that the applicant was saying that he was involved in those offences. However, the Court of Criminal Appeal was satisfied that the words, when viewed in the context in which they were spoken, were an admission by the first applicant that he was involved in the offences about which he was being questioned and in respect of which the gardaí had given him detailed evidence which they claimed implicated him in those offences:

> "It is to be noted that the accused did not acknowledge that the Gardaí had a suspicion that he was involved in those crimes—such an acknowledgment would not have implied an admission by him of his guilt in the crimes. Nor was he acknowledging that the Gardaí had a belief in his guilt—again, a statement by him that his interrogators believed in his guilt would not convey any admission on his part that their belief was a correct one. What he in fact said amounted to an admission of his appreciation that those who were accusing him of the crimes of murder and armed robbery knew that he had committed them, and this admission was accompanied by a statement that on the advice of his solicitor he was going to say nothing and an observation that the Gardaí were going to have to prove the case themselves. It is to be noted that the acknowledgment which he made of the knowledge of the Gardaí was not qualified in any way. It can only be regarded as an admission by him of his involvement in the crimes they were investigating."[242]

5–108 It should be noted that, if evidence of an admission made by a party is given, then the whole statement of which the admission forms part or conversation in which it was made may be adduced in evidence including parts favourable to the party who made the admission.[243] In *The Queen's Case*,[244] Abbott CJ explained that:

> "The conversations of a party to the suit relative to the subject matter of the suit are in themselves evidence against him in the suit, and if a counsel chooses to ask a witness as to anything which may have been said by an adverse party, the counsel for that party has a right to lay before the court the whole which was said in the same conversation: not only so much as may explain or qualify the matter introduced by the previous examination but even matter not properly connected with the part introduced upon the previous examination, provided only that it relates to the subject matter of the suit; because it would not be just to take part of

---

[238] (1834) 6 C & P 540.

[239] *Cf. R. v Maqsud Ali* [1966] 1 QB 688, [1965] 2 All ER 464 (tape recording of conversation between two appellants in which admissions were made admitted in evidence)

[240] *Walsh v Sligo County Council* [2010] IEHC 437 at [153], [2011] 2 IR 260 at 327. See further the civil case of *Vandeleur v Glynn* [1905] 1 IR 483 at 506–507 and 530 and the criminal cases of *People (AG) v Sherlock* (1975) 1 Frewen 383; *People (DPP) v Pringle* (1981) 1 Frewen 57; *People (DPP) v Rose*, unreported, Court of Criminal Appeal, 21 February 2002.

[241] (1981) 1 Frewen 57.

[242] (1981) 1 Frewen 57 at 76.

[243] *Walsh v Sligo County Council* [2010] IEHC 437 at [153], [2011] 2 IR 260 at 327.

[244] (1820) 2 Bro & Bing 397.

a conversation as evidence against a party without giving to the party, at the same time, the benefit of the entire residue of what he said on the same occasion."

5–109   This principle is now well established and has been applied in both civil[245] and criminal[246] cases.

(b) Admissions by conduct

5–110   Admissions may be made by conduct, both in the form of actions or omissions.[247] The conduct of a person will be treated as an admission by that person where it indicates a consciousness of guilt in relation to an offence charged in the case of criminal offences or an acceptance of the weakness of a party's case in the context of civil proceedings. The examples of conduct that may give rise to an admission are diverse but include the following: (i) an offer by a party to settle proceedings; (ii) where an accused accepts an accusation by words, conduct, action or demeanour; (iii) the lies of a party; (iv) attempts to interfere with the course of proceedings; (v) the possession of documents; (vi) the use of documents in previous proceedings; and (vii) the failing of certain tests.

(i) Offer to settle

5–111   An offer made by a party to settle proceedings, whether made prior to or after the institution of proceedings may be considered to be an admission of the allegations made in the proceedings.[248] It is for this reason that negotiations to settle proceedings are generally conducted on a without prejudice basis.[249]

(ii) Acceptance of accusations

5–112   A statement made in the presence of a party accusing him or her of wrongdoing may amount to an admission by that party if he or she, by his or her words, conduct, actions or demeanour, can be considered to have accepted or admitted the truth of what was stated.[250] An example of such an admission can be seen in *Morrissey v Boyle*[251] which involved an affiliation suit brought by the applicant against the defendant on the basis that he was the father of her illegitimate child. Evidence was given by the applicant's father that he met the defendant after his daughter had given birth and said to him: "Now, Mr. Manning [a false name used by the defendant], this is my daughter and she'll tell you her tale". He then left them to talk for 10 or 15 minutes after which the defendant made an arrangement to meet him the following night. It was held by

---

[245] See *Walsh v Sligo County Council* [2010] IEHC 437 at [153], [2011] 2 IR 260 at 327; *Smith v Blandy* (1825) Ry & Mood 257; *Capital Trust Co. v Fowler* (1921) 64 DLR 289, 50 OLR 48; *Albert v Tremblay* (1963) 49 MPR 407.

[246] See *People (AG) v Crosby* (1961) 1 Frewen 231 at 246; and *People (DPP) v Clarke* [1995] 1 ILRM 355 at 367.

[247] *Walsh v Sligo County Council* [2010] IEHC 437 at [154], [2011] 2 IR 260 at 327.

[248] See *Tait v Beggs* [1905] 2 IR 525.

[249] See Chap.10 for a discussion of without prejudice privilege.

[250] *People (DPP) v Finnerty* [1999] 4 IR 364 at 376, [2000] 1 ILRM 191 at 203; *People (AG) v Finkel*(1951) 1 Frewen 123 at 128; *R. v Christie* [1914] AC 545 at 554, [1914–15] All ER 63 at 67 (*per* Lord Atkinson).

[251] [1942] IR 514.

a majority of the Supreme Court that the conduct of the defendant was capable of providing corroboration of the evidence of the mother. Sullivan CJ explained:

> "[T]he only reasonable interpretation of the appellant's evidence is that in the interview in question she charged the respondent with the paternity of her child....If such a charge was made, then the fact that the respondent did not repudiate it in the presence of the appellant's father, but made an appointment to meet him on the following night, obviously with the object of discussing the matter, is to my mind a most material circumstance from which the more probable inference is that the charge was well founded."

5–113   Given that the attribution of an admission to a party depends on some indication of acceptance by him or her of the accusation made, it might be thought that mere silence in the face of an accusation could never, in view of its inherent ambiguity, give rise to an admission. However, proceeding on the basis that the natural reaction of a person when falsely accused is to protest his or her innocence and deny the accusation,[252] it has been held that failure to do so may be construed as an indication that the accusation is true.[253] As stated by Cave J in *R. v Mitchell*,[254] the principle is that "when persons are speaking on even terms, and a charge is made, and the person charged says nothing, and expresses no indignation, and does nothing to repel the charge, that is some evidence to show that he admits the charge to be true". For example, in *R. v Cramp*[255] the accused's silence when confronted by the witness's father who said "I have here those things which you gave my daughter to produce abortion" was held to be capable of corroborating her testimony on a charge of attempting to cause a miscarriage.

5–114   Some limitations on the principle that silence can be construed as an admission should be noted. The first is that it is only applicable where the circumstances are such that the party would reasonably be expected to deny the accusation.[256] The second is that the silence of a person when questioned by gardaí cannot be construed as any form of admission of any accusations or facts put to him or her. This limitation was formerly justified by reference to the caution given to criminal suspects on the basis articulated by FitzGibbon J in *Attorney General v Fleming*,[257] that "mere silence, when the accused person is told that he is not bound to say anything but that anything he does say may be used against him, cannot be tortured into an admission of guilt"[258] but is now referable to the constitutional protected right to silence enjoyed by a suspect.[259]

---

[252] This proposition is enshrined in the Latin maxim, *"qui tacet consentire videtur, ubi tractatur de ejus commodo"* i.e. silence is considered as assent, when the interest of the person keeping silent is at stake.

[253] *Walsh v Sligo County Council* [2010] IEHC 437 at [155], [2011] 2 IR 260 at 328; *R. v Mitchell* (1892) 17 Cox CC 503 at 508; *Thomas v Jones* [1920] All ER 462 at 472.

[254] (1892) 17 Cox CC 503 at 508.

[255] (1880) 14 Cox CC 390.

[256] *Cleeland v M'Cune* (1908) 42 ILTR 202 at 203 (*per* Gibson J); *Walsh v Sligo County Council* [2010] IEHC 437 at [156], [2011] 2 IR 260 at 328; *Bessela v Stern* (1877) 2 CPD 265; *R. v Mitchell* (1892) 17 Cox CC 503. There is no expectation, in the ordinary course of events, that a person who receives an accusatory letter will reply and thus, failure to reply to such a letter does not constitute corroboration: *Wiedemann v Walpole* [1891] 2 QB 534; *Thomas v Jones* [1921] 1 KB 22, [1929] All ER 462. But *cf. Ex p. Freeman* (1922) 39 WN (NSW) 73, where the failure of the defendant to reply to a letter from the plaintiff's father alleging paternity and threatening legal proceedings if no reply was received was held to constitute corroboration in an affiliation suit taken by the plaintiff.

[257] [1934] IR 166 at 186.

[258] See also *AG v Durnan (No.2)* [1934] IR 540 and *People (AG) v Quinn* [1955] IR 57.

[259] See *Heaney v Ireland* [1994] 3 IR 593, [1994] 2 ILRM 420; *People (DPP) v Finnerty* [1999] 4 IR 364, [2000] 1 ILRM 191, and generally Chap.11.

5–115   By way of an extension of the proposition that a failure to deny an accusation may be construed as an acceptance of that accusation, it could be argued that a failure to controvert an assertion as to the existence of a particular state of facts is an admission that that state of facts exists. In *Walsh v Sligo County Council*,[260] the failure of the predecessor in title of the plaintiffs to take issue with assertions made in the course of conversations with him to the effect that rights of way existed over his land was considered by McMahon J in the High Court to be an admission on his part that those rights of way existed. However, in circumstances where no express admission had been made, the Supreme Court regarded it as very doubtful that his silence in the face of such statements could give rise to an admission,[261] noting that no authority had been cited in support of the proposition that the mere silence of a person when he could be expected to address a matter in contention constituted an admission.[262]

(iv) Lies

5–116   The circumstances in which a lie told by an accused will be construed as an admission by conduct on his or her part have principally been considered in criminal cases dealing with the question of when the lies of an accused can be used as corroboration.[263] However, irrespective of any issue of corroboration, a lie told by an accused in court or out of court may be admissible as an admission if it can be attributed to a realisation on his or her part that, if he or she told the truth about the matter to which the lie relates, it would implicate him or her in the offence.[264] So, for example, in *People (DPP) v Madden*,[265] it was held that the conduct of the accused in making false denials in relation to the parking of a car connected to the murder of the person "was conduct which was not reasonably consistent with any explanation other than that he was at the time he parked in this car aware of the general nature of the purpose of which it was intended to be used", *i.e.* it was conduct that implicated him in the commission of the offence.

5–117   It is important to remember, however, that there are a number of reasons why an accused might tell a lie other than a consciousness of guilt including panic,[266] the desire to bolster a just cause,[267] indignation at an officious inquiry,[268] fear of facing an unjust accusation of guilt if suspicious circumstances are admitted,[269] attempts to conceal discreditable conduct from family and friends,[270] other criminal offences

---

[260] [2010] IEHC 437 at [164], [2011] 2 IR 260 at 330.
[261] [2013] IESC 48 at [272].
[262] [2013] IESC 48 at [264].
[263] The leading case is *R. v Lucas* [1981] QB 720, [1981] 2 All ER 1008, which is considered in Chap.4.
[264] *Cf. R. v Lucas* [1981] QB 720, [1981] 2 All ER 1008; *Edwards v R.* (1993) 178 CLR 193 at 211; *R. v Tripodi* [1961] V.R. 186 at 193 which emphasise this criterion in the context of the use of lies as corroboration.
[265] [1977] IR 336 at 349.
[266] *R. v Clynes* (1960) 44 Cr App R 158 at 163.
[267] *R. v Lucas* [1981] QB 720 at 724, [1981] 2 All ER 1008 at 1011; *Moriarty v London, Chatham and Dover Rly. Co.* (1870) LR 5 QB 314 at 319. *Cf. Curran v Gallagher*, unreported, Supreme Court, 7 May 1997.
[268] *Popovic v Derks* [1961] VR 413 at 426.
[269] *R. v Collings* [1976] 2 NZLR 104 at 116.
[270] *R. v Sutton* [1967] Crim LR 43; *R. v Dowley* [1983] Crim LR 168; *Harding v Porta* [1934] VLR 79 at 84.

from the police,[271] or the wrongdoing of others from the authorities.[272] Indeed, it has been observed that "most false statements or denials may ... be explicable upon some hypothesis other than the accused's implication in the crime".[273] Thus, it is important that the tribunal of fact eliminate these and any other possible motives for the lie before using it as an admission.

5–118 Whilst the vast majority of the authorities deal with criminal cases, it is clear that a lie told by a party before or while giving evidence in a civil case may also constitute an admission. However, the difficulties of identifying the motive for a lie and using it as an admission are evident from the decision of the Supreme Court in *Curran v Gallagher*.[274] The plaintiff had been injured in an accident when the car in which he was travelling as a passenger collided with a wall and lamp post late at night. One of the major issues in the case was whether the first named defendant had permission to drive the car which belonged to her mother and the plaintiff gave a version of events which was rejected as untrue by the trial judge. A divergence of opinion was evident in the Supreme Court as to the motive for the plaintiff's lies and the inference to be drawn from them. Lynch J, for the majority, pointed out that it is "a regrettable and reprehensible fact that litigants sometimes exaggerate and even grossly exaggerate their cases" and he took the view that, in this case, the plaintiff had fabricated evidence in an effort to strengthen his case. It did not, therefore, establish as a matter of probability that he knew that the first named defendant did not have authority to take the car. Murphy J, dissenting, took a different view, stating that while there were different reasons why the plaintiff might have concocted his account, "the proper inference to draw from the fact that he was prepared to give and did give untruthful evidence was that he was understandably apprehensive that a court of law would draw the same conclusions as he had drawn from the facts as they truly were."

(v) Interference with the course of proceedings

5–119 An attempt by a party to interfere with the course of proceedings may be construed as an admission by conduct. This principle was established in the old Irish case of *Annesley v Earl of Anglesea*,[275] where evidence was admitted in an action for ejectment that the defendant, knowing that the plaintiff claimed title to the lands at issue, employed an attorney to prosecute the plaintiff for the murder of a man who, as the defendant was aware, the plaintiff had shot by accident and declared that he would spend ten thousand pounds to get the plaintiff hanged because he would then be easy in his title and his estates. Mounteney B explained the relevance of this evidence on the basis that "every act done by the defendant, which has a tendency to shew a consciousness in him of title in the lessor of the plaintiff, must, be thought to be admitted beyond all controversy, to be pertinent and legal evidence".[276] That decision was followed in *Moriarty v London, Chatham and Dover Railway Co*.[277] where evidence that the plaintiff had attempted to suborn witnesses to give false evidence was held to

---

[271] *R. v Wattam* (1952) 36 Cr App R 72.
[272] *Edwards v R.* (1993) 178 CLR 193.
[273] *Per* McCarthy P in *R. v Collings* [1976] 2 NZLR 104 at 116.
[274] Unreported, Supreme Court, 7 May 1997.
[275] (1743) 17 How St Tr 1139.
[276] (1743) 17 How St Tr 1139 at 1221.
[277] (1870) LR 5 QB 314.

constitute an admission, by conduct, of the plaintiff that he had a bad case.[278] Other examples of conduct which may give rise to an admission by conduct include flight by an accused,[279] the destruction of evidence,[280] and attempts to bribe police officers.[281]

5–120   It is important to remember that, as in the case of lies by a party, attempts to interfere with the course of proceedings do not inexorably lead to a conclusion that a plaintiff has a fabricated claim or that an accused is guilty. As Cockburn CJ cautioned in *Moriarty v London, Chatham and Dover Railway Co.*,

> "it does not follow, because a man, not sure he shall be able to succeed by righteous means, has recourse to means of a different character, that that which he desires, namely, the gaining of the victory, is not his due, or that he has not good ground for believing that justice entitles him to it".[282]

(vi) Possession of documents

5–121   There is some authority to suggest that possession and control by a party of documents authored by another person may constitute an admission by him or her of the contents of those documents.[283] However, in *Duke of Devonshire v Neill*[284] the Court of Exchequer rejected as having no solid foundation the proposition:

> "... that a person is to be deemed bound, by way of recognition or adoption of their truth, by the statements of fact contained in every document made by any person whomsoever, of his own knowledge or upon hearsay, for any purpose, known or unknown, provided only that such document be after his death found among his muniments."

5–122   Thus, it would appear that it will only be in very limited circumstances that an admission under this heading will be established.

(vii) Use of documents in previous proceedings

5–123   An affidavit or document used by a party in proceedings to prove a particular fact is admissible against him or her in subsequent proceedings to prove the same fact if a party, knowing of the contents of the document, elects to put it forward as true.[285] This latter requirement was emphasised by Crompton J in *Richards v Morgan*[286] who emphasised that: "It must always be remembered that it is not the obtaining the affidavit

---

[278] See also *Pitman v Bryne* [1926] SASR 207 at 212 and *R. v Mazza* (1975) 24 CCC (2d) 508 at 515.

[279] *R. v Ellis* [1910] 2 KB 746 at 749, [1908–10] All ER 488 at 490; *R. v M.* [1995] 1 Qd R 213 at 214–215; *R. v Dickson* [1983] 1 VR 227; *R. v McKenna* (1956) 73 WN (NSW) 354; *Coulston v Taylor* (1909) 28 NZLR 807 at 809; *People v White* (1941) 48 Cal App 2d 90 at 95; 119 P 2d 383 at 386.

[280] *R. v Hodgett* [1957] NI 1 (on a charge of receiving stolen goods, corroboration was provided by the fact that the accused had destroyed certain records which, according to the evidence of the thief, recorded the transactions between them).

[281] *R. v Fox* (1982) 7 A Crim R 28.

[282] (1870) LR 5 QB 314 at 319.

[283] See *Alderson v Clay* (1816) 1 Stark 405.

[284] (1877) 2 LR Ir 132 at 160.

[285] *White v Dowling* (1845) 8 Ir LR 128 at 131; *Brickell v Hulse* (1837) 7 Ad & E 454; *Gardner v Moult* (1839) 10 Ad & E 464. *Cf. Evans v Merthyr Tydfil UDC* [1899] 1 Ch 241 at 251–252, where the proposition that an affidavit or document used by a predecessor in title could be admissible against a party where it had been put forward as a true statement of the contents was accepted.

[286] (1863) 4 B & S 641 at 657.

or deposition, but the making use of it as true with knowledge of the contents, which is the ground on which such evidence is supposed to be receivable."

(viii) Failure of tests or examinations

5–124   Where a party undergoes a test or examination, such as a DNA test, and the results are adverse to a party, the result will (apart from any other basis for its reception) be admissible against the party as an admission. An example in the criminal context can be seen in *Sullivan v Robinson*[287] where it was held by Davitt P that the failure of an accused of a test of sobriety constituted an admission of drunkenness by him.[288]

(c) Vicarious admissions

5–125   In general, a party will not be bound by an admission made by another person.[289] However, a statement made by another may, in certain circumstances, be construed as an admission against a party because of some privity of interest between them. The categories of person considered to have the requisite privity are: (i) agents; (ii) predecessors in title; and (iii) partners.[290] In addition, there are a number of miscellaneous relationships that are considered below. However, the necessity privity of interest does not arise between a parent and a child,[291] joint tenants,[292] co-parties to proceedings,[293] or a party and a witness called by him or her.[294]

(i) Admissions by agents

5–126   An admission by an agent is admissible against his or her principal if it was made: (1) at a time when the agency existed; (2) in the course of a communication which the agent was expressly or impliedly authorised by the principal to make; and (3) the communication was with a third party and not the principal himself or herself.[295]

5–127   The question of whether the agency existed at the time that an admission was made by an agent is a question of fact and depends on the nature of the agency. A person may be an agent for a particular purpose but not more generally.[296] If a person has been appointed as an agent for a specific purpose, for example to negotiate a

---

[287] [1954] IR 161 at 168.
[288] *Cf. People (DPP) v Murray*, unreported, Court of Criminal Appeal, 12 April 1999, concerning the examination of a mark on the lip of the accused.
[289] See *Foster v McMahon* (1847) 11 Ir Eq R 287 at 299; *Walsh v Sligo County Council* [2010] IEHC 437 at [157], [2011] 2 IR 260 at 328; *Tucker v Oldbury UDC* [1912] 2 KB 317.
[290] *Walsh v Sligo County Council* [2010] IEHC 437 at [157], [2011] 2 IR 260 at 328.
[291] *G(A) v G(T)* [1970] 2 QB 643, [1970] 3 All ER 546.
[292] *Turner v AG* (1847) IR 10 Eq 386.
[293] *Morton v Morton* [1937] P 151 at 154, [1937] 2 All ER 470.
[294] *Gardner v Moult* (1839) 10 Ad & E 464; *Boileau v Rutlin* (1848) 2 Ex 675; *British Thomson-Houston Co. Ltd v British Insulated and Helsby Cables Ltd* [1924] 2 Ch 160.
[295] This summary was approved as correctly stating the law in *Fyffes plc v DCC plc* [2005] IEHC 477 at [204], [2009] 2 IR 417 at 511.
[296] See *Director of Corporate Enforcement v Bailey* [2007] IEHC 365, [2008] 2 ILRM 13 at 43–44, where Irvine J held that a statement made by an auditor of a company that proper books of account had not been kept by a company was admissible as an admission, in reliance on the view expressed in Keane, *Company Law* 4th edn, at [30.142], that an auditor appointed under s.160 of the Companies Act 1963 may be regarded as an agent when carrying out his duties under the Companies Acts but not as an agent for other purposes.

particular contract, then the agency and the authority of the agent to bind the principal will expire when the transaction is completed.[297]

5–128   The second condition requires the admission to have been authorised by the principal. In *Swan v Miller, Son and Torrance Ltd*,[298] O'Connor LJ summarised the position as follows:

> "The question whether a statement of an agent is to be treated as the statement of (and therefore binding) the principal is to be determined by the ordinary rule by which the responsibility of a principal for the acts of his agent is determined. That rule is, that the principal is responsible for the acts of his agent done within the scope of his authority. ... To test whether the statement binds the principal one has to consider the nature of the statement and the circumstances in which it is made, including for example, the person to whom, and the time at which, the statement is made."[299]

5–129   A straightforward example of where the requirement of authorisation was not met can be seen in *Dwyer v Larkin*[300] where statements made by two barmen at an inquest following the death of a customer were held to be inadmissible as an admission against the publican at subsequent criminal proceedings because they did not have any authority to make any statement in relation to the incident in question.[301] This was also the conclusion reached by Laffoy J in *Fyffes plc v DCC plc*[302] who was quite satisfied that the agent in question was neither expressly nor impliedly authorised to discuss the matter in issue. Again, in *Bord na gCon v Murphy*[303] it was held by the Supreme Court that evidence could not be given of a statement made by the defendant's solicitor in a letter, ostensibly written on the defendant's instructions, because no evidence had been offered to establish that the letter had been written with the defendant's authority. It will be difficult for a party to prove such authority given the holding in that case that evidence of the existence of the authority must be found outside the terms of the admission itself because this is not receivable in evidence until authority has first been proved. It should, however, be noted that there is no requirement to show that the admission was expressly authorised by the principal; it will be sufficient if it was made in the ordinary course of business of the agent.

5–130   In order to be received as an admission against a principal, it is settled that the statement in question must have been made in a communication to a third party, not to the principal. In *Swan v Miller, Son and Torrance Ltd*,[304] O'Connor LJ rejected the contrary proposition in robust terms stating: "The notion that a principal should be bound by what his agent says to him seems to me to have no warrant whatever, either in law or sense."[305]

(ii) Predecessors in title

5–131   A statement against proprietary interest made by a predecessor in title of a party is admissible against him or her provided that it was made at a time when

---

[297] *Swan v Miller, Son and Torrance Ltd* [1919] 1 IR 151 at 183.
[298] [1919] 1 IR 151.
[299] [1919] 1 IR 151 at 182–183. See also *Bord na gCon v Murphy* [1970] IR 301 at 313–314.
[300] (1905) 39 ILTR 40.
[301] See also *Burr v Ware RDC* [1939] 2 All ER 688.
[302] [2005] IEHC 477 at [204], [2009] 2 IR 417 at 511.
[303] [1970] IR 301.
[304] [1919] 1 IR 151 at 183.
[305] See also *In re Devala Provident Gold Mining Company* (1883) LR 22 Ch D 593 at 596.

the declarant had an interest in the property.[306] In *Walsh v Sligo County Council*[307] McMahon J explained that:

> "[W]here a predecessor in title makes statements which, if that predecessor was a party to the action, could be considered to be admissions, these will bind those with subsequent title in the property and may be admitted as evidence in an action against him or her."

5–132   In that case, admissions made by the predecessor in title of the plaintiffs as to the existence of rights of way were held to be admissible on this basis. Similarly, in *M'Kenna v Earl of Howth*[308] maps made by a predecessor of a landlord were held to be admissible against a person claiming under a lease subsequently executed by him. An extension of this principle to declarations concerning planning permission was made in *South Dublin County v Balfe*[309] where a special condition in a contract for the sale of lands to the defendant by his predecessor in title, which stated that a number of buildings had been erected without planning permission, was held to be admissible against the defendant as evidence of unauthorised development.

(iii) Partners

5–133   At common law, an admission made by a partner about the business of a partnership could be admitted against the other partners[310] and this exception is now given statutory form in s.15 of the Partnership Act 1890 which provides: "An admission or representation made by any partner concerning the partnership affairs, and in the ordinary course of its business, is evidence against the firm."

(iv) Miscellaneous relationships

5–134   The authorities indicate that, apart from the foregoing three categories, there are a number of other miscellaneous relationships which will create the necessary privity of interest such that the admission of one person may bind another: (1) if a party refers a person upon particular business to a third person, a statement made by the third person concerning the business will be admissible against the party[311]; (2) entries relevant to the performance by a person of obligations undertaken by him are admissible in proceedings against a surety on foot of a bond guaranteeing the performance of those obligations[312]; (3) corporation books are evidence by way of admissions between members of the corporation[313]; and (4) admissions made by a

---

[306] *Walsh v Sligo County Council* [2010] IEHC 437 at [158], [2011] 2 IR 260 at 329; *South Dublin County Council v Balfe*, unreported, High Court, 3 November 1995. See also *Woolway v Rowe* (1834) 1 Ad & El 114, (1835) 1 Cr M & R 919; *Evans v Merthyr Tydfil UDC* [1899] 1 Ch 241 at 251–252; *Falcon v Famous Players Film Co. Ltd.* [1926] 2 KB 474 at 488. *Cf. Foster v McMahon* (1847) 11 Ir Eq R 287.

[307] [2010] IEHC 437 at [158], [2011] 2 IR 260 at 329. It should be noted that, although this passage was not disapproved on appeal, his finding that there had been admissions by the predecessor in title was seriously doubted by the Supreme Court ([2013] IESC 48 at [272]).

[308] (1893) 27 ILTR 48.

[309] Unreported, High Court, 3 November 1995.

[310] See *Jaggers v Binnings* (1815) 1 Stark 64; *Wood v Braddick* (1808) 1 Taunt 104 (even after the partnership has ceased in respect of transactions entered into while they were partners).

[311] *Williams v Innes* (1808) 1 Camp 364 at 365.

[312] *Guardians of the Poor of the Abbeyleix Union v Sutcliffe* (1890) 26 LR Ir 32.

[313] *Waterford Corporation v Price* (1846) 9 Ir LR 310 at 314.

deceased are admissible against dependants of the deceased who bring wrongful death proceedings arising from his or her death.[314]

3. Declarations Against Interest

5–135   A declaration by a deceased person as to a fact which, to his or her knowledge, was against his or her pecuniary or proprietary interest at the time he or she made it, is admissible as evidence of that fact. The rationale for the admission of such statements is similar to that in respect of admissions, *i.e.* the unlikelihood that a person will make a declaration against their own interests which is false.[315] The requirement of necessity is obviously satisfied by the fact that the declarant is dead.

5–136   It should be noted that, when a declaration against interest is admitted, the entire statement of which it forms part is admissible to explain the context in which it was made and the meaning of the statement even if other parts of the declaration are in the interest of the declarant.[316] In that way, it appears that a declaration against interest may be used to prove facts that are collateral to the declaration.[317]

5–137   The conditions of admissibility of a declaration against interest are that: (a) the declarant is deceased; (b) the statement is against the proprietary or pecuniary interest of the declarant; (c) the statement was against the interest of the declarant at the time it was made; (d) the declarant knew that it was against his or her interest; and (e) the declarant had personal knowledge of the facts stated.

(a) Declarant is deceased

5–138   It is well settled that this exception only applies if the declarant is dead[318] and

---

[314] *Power v Dublin United Tramway Co. Ltd* [1926] IR 302. That decision related to proceedings brought under the Fatal Accidents Act 1846, but see now Part IV of the Civil Liability Act 1961 dealing with fatal injuries. See, *contra*, *Tucker v Oldbury UDC* [1912] 2 KB 317 at 321.

[315] See *per* Fletcher Moulton LJ in *Tucker v Oldbury UDC* [1912] 2 KB 317 at 321 ("Such declarations are admitted as evidence in our jurisprudence on the ground that declarations made by persons against their own interests are extremely unlikely to be false."); *per* Stuart-Smith LJ in *R. v Rogers* [1995] 1 Cr App R 374 at 380 ("The rationale of the exception is that a man will not say something which is against his pecuniary interest unless it is true.") and *per* Powell J in *Chambers v Mississippi* (1973) 410 US 284 at 299 (the exception is "founded on the assumption that a person is unlikely to fabricate a statement made against his own interest at the time it is made"). However, this rationale was criticised by Hamilton LJ in *Ward v HS Pitt & Co.* [1913] 2 KB 130 at 138 as "sordid and unconvincing" on the basis that: "Men lie for so many reasons and some for no reason at all and some tell the truth without thinking or even in spite of thinking about their pockets."

[316] *Whaley v Carlisle* (1866) 17 ICLR 792 at 817; *Conner v Fitzgerald* (1883) 11 LR Ir 106 at 111; *Higham v Ridgway* (1808) 10 East 109; *Ward v HS Pitt & Co.* [1913] 2 KB 130 at 136.

[317] *Higham v Ridgway* (1808) 10 East 109; *Churchwardens, Overseers and Guardians of the Parish of Birmingham* (1861) 1 B & S 763 at 768; *Taylor v Whitham* (1876) 3 Ch D 605; *Ward v HS Pitt & Co.* [1913] 2 KB 130 at 136. In *Lalor v Lalor* (1879) 4 LR Ir 678 at 681, FitzGibbon LJ referred to the decision in *Highway v Ridgway* as "a questionable extension of a dangerous principle" and the Court of Appeal sought to confine it in *R. v Rogers* [1995] 1 Cr App R 374 at 380–381, holding that "it is only in so far as collateral matters are necessary to explain the nature of the transaction in question that they are admissible".

[318] *La Touche v Hutton* (1875) LR 9 Eq 166 at 170; *Guardians of the Poor of the Abbeyleix Union v Sutcliffe* (1890) 26 LR Ir 32; *Ranbaxy Laboratories Ltd v Warner-Lambert Company* [2005] IEHC 178 at 28.

it is not sufficient that the declarant is otherwise unavailable to testify.[319] However, it should be noted that Rule 804 of the United States Federal Rules of Evidence makes provision for the reception of statements against interest in a range of circumstances where the declarant is unavailable and the Canadian courts have also held in a series of cases that this exception can apply where the witness is not deceased but is unavailable.[320]

(b) Contrary to interest of declarant

5–139   There is a difference in the authorities as to whether the declaration against interest must be one that "never could be available for the person himself"[321] or whether it suffices that the declaration is one which is *prima facie* against his interest, "that is, to say, the natural meaning of the entry standing alone must be against the interest of the main who made it".[322] The former view appears to be more consistent with the rationale for the exception but the latter seems a more a common sense approach to take.[323]

(i) Contrary to pecuniary interest

5–140   The question of whether a statement is contrary to pecuniary interest is one of fact and depends on all of the circumstances including the other evidence adduced in the case. Nonetheless, two categories of statement that will generally be considered to be contrary to the pecuniary interest of the declarant are: statements acknowledging a debt due to another[324]; and statements acknowledging receipt of monies owed by another.[325] However, it appears that a statement evidencing the existence of a contract is not a statement against interest because it is presumed to have been made on fair and equitable terms that benefit both parties to it.[326]

(ii) Contrary to proprietary interest

5–141   A statement will be contrary to proprietary interest if it cuts down or fetters the interest of a person in land. Thus, in *Conner v Fitzgerald*,[327] where the plaintiff brought proceedings for specific performance of an agreement to let certain lands, an entry in a rent book by his deceased father, who had previously owned the lands, to the effect that he had agreed to let land for a certain term at a certain rent was held

---

[319] *Stephen v Gwenap* (1831) 1 Mood & R 120 (declarant had left the jurisdiction).

[320] See *R. v Lucier* [1982] 1 SCR 28, (1982) 132 DLR (3d) 244; *R. v Demeter* [1978] 1 SCR 538, (1978) 75 DLR (3d) 251; *R. v Pelletier* (1978) 38 CCC (2d) 515.

[321] *Per* Blackburn J in *Smith v Blakey* (1867) LR 2 QB 326 at 332. This approach was applied in *Massey v Allen* (1879) 13 Ch D 558 at 562–563.

[322] *Per* Jessel MR in *Taylor v Witham* (1876) 3 Ch D 605 at 607.

[323] See, *contra*, *Ward v HS Pitt & Co.* [1913] 2 KB 130 at 137, where Hamilton LJ, who questioned the justification for the exception, preferred the narrower view expressed by Blackburn J in *Smith v Blakey*.

[324] See *R. v Rogers* [1995] 1 Cr App R 374 at 379. In that case, the Court of Appeal rejected the contention that there was any requirement that there be a legal or moral obligation to pay the sum acknowledged to be due.

[325] See *Richards v Gogarty* (1870) 4 ICLR 300; *Higham v Ridgway* (1808) 10 East 109; *Marks v Lahee* (1837) 3 Bing NC 408; *Taylor v Whitam* (1876) 3 Ch D 605.

[326] *R. v Inhabitants of Worth* (1843) 4 QB 132 at 138. *Cf. Ward v HS Pitt & Co.* [1913] 2 KB 130 at 140.

[327] (1883) 4 LR Ir 106.

to be admissible. Chatterton VC held that this entry had been correctly admitted as a declaration against proprietary interest on the basis that the deceased had been, at the time, in possession of the estate, and was presumed to be seised in fee and he considered that any statement "tending to cut down his interest or to charge or fetter it, is a declaration against proprietary interest within this rule".[328]

(iii) Contrary to penal interest

5–142   The conventional view is that this exception does not extend to declarations against penal interest.[329] For example, in *R. v Gray*[330] a death-bed confession by a third party that he had committed the murder with which the accused was charged was held to be inadmissible. Torrens J expressed the view that "it would tend to establish a dangerous precedent if [he] were to admit the evidence".[331] In the *Sussex Peerage Case*,[332] Lord Brougham staunchly defended the exclusion of declarations contrary to penal interest:

> "[T]o say, if a man should confess a felony for which he would be liable to prosecution, that therefore, the instant the grave closes over him, all that was said by him is to be taken as evidence in every action and prosecution against another person, is one of the most monstrous and untenable propositions that can be advanced."[333]

5–143   However, the exclusion of statements against penal interest from the ambit of this exception has been subjected to sustained and cogent criticism[334] with Wigmore describing it as a:

> "… barbarous doctrine, which would refuse to let an innocent accused vindicate himself even by producing to the tribunal a perfectly authenticated written confession, made on the very gallows, by the true culprit now beyond the reach of justice."[335]

5–144   It is unsurprising, therefore, that this limitation has been abandoned in other jurisdictions. In *R. v O'Brien*,[336] Dickson J, delivering the decision of the Supreme Court of Canada, rejected the distinction drawn between statements against pecuniary

---

[328] (1883) 4 LR Ir 106 at 111. A similar approach was adopted in *Garland v Cope* (1848) 11 Ir LR 514 at 534, and *La Touche v Hutton* (1875) LR 9 Eq 166 at 171. See also *Flood v Russell* (1891) 29 LR Ir 91 at 96; *Domvile v Calwell* [1907] 2 IR 617; *Crease v Barrett* (1835) 1 Cr M & R 919 at 931; *Homes v Newman* [1931] 2 Ch 112, [1931] All ER 85.

[329] *R. v Gray* (1841) 2 Cr & Dix 129, (1841) Ir Cir Rep 76; *Sussex Peerage Case* (1844) 11 Cl & Fin 85 at 105; *Tucker v Oldbury UDC* [1912] 2 KB 317 at 321; *Ward v HS Pitt & Co.* [1913] 2 KB 130 at 138; *R. v Rogers* [1995] 1 Cr App R 374 at 379; *Donnelly v US* (1913) 288 US 243; *Re Van Beelen* (1974) 9 SASR 163; *Baker v R.* (2012) 289 ALR 614. See also *R. v Thomson* [1912] 3 KB 19 and *R. v Blastland* [1986] 1 AC 41, [1985] 2 All ER 1095. *Cf.* Carter, "Hearsay, Relevance and Admissibility: Declarations as to State of Mind and Declarations Against Penal Interest" [1987] LQR 107.

[330] (1841) 2 Cr & Dix 129, (1841) Ir Cir Rep 76.

[331] (1841) 2 Cr & Dix 129 at 130, (1841) Ir Cir Rep 76.

[332] (1844) 11 Cl & Fin 85 at 111–112.

[333] See also *per* Lord Bridge in *R. v Blastland* [1986] AC 41 at 52–53 [1985] 2 All ER 1095 at 1098: "To admit in criminal trials statements confessing to the crime for which the defendant is being tried made by third parties not called as witnesses would be to create a very significant and, many might think, a dangerous new exception."

[334] See, *e.g.* Jefferson, "Declarations Against Interest: An exception to the Hearsay Rule" (1944) 58 Harv L Rev 1; Morgan, "Declarations Against Interest" (1952) 5 Vand L Rev 451; Baker, *The Hearsay Rule* (Pitman, London, 1950), p.64; New South Wales Law Reform Commission, *Report on the Rule Against Hearsay* (1978), pp.44–47.

[335] Wigmore, *Evidence* (3rd edn), Vol. V, § 1477.

[336] [1978] 1 SCR 591, (1978) 76 DLR (3d) 513.

and proprietary interest and those against penal interest as "arbitrary and tenuous" and held that:

> "There is little or no reason why declarations against penal interest and those against pecuniary or proprietary interest should not stand on the same footing. A person is as likely to speak the truth in a matter affecting his liberty as in a matter affecting his pocketbook. For these reasons and the ever-present possibility that a rule of absolute prohibition could lead to grave injustice, I would hold that, in a proper case, a declaration against penal interest is admissible according to the law of Canada. ..."[337]

5-145 However, in that and other cases, the Court has also identified a number of principles and safeguards regarding the admission of such statements in an effort to provide some guarantee of their trustworthiness.[338]

5-146 The entitlement of an accused to adduce evidence of incriminating statements made by third parties was given a constitutional anchor in *Chambers v State of Mississippi*.[339] In that case, a third party had confessed to a murder in respect of which the accused was being prosecuted, and at his trial the accused sought to adduce the testimony of three witnesses as to oral confessions made to them by the third party. The trial court excluded this evidence as inadmissible hearsay but the US Supreme Court held that the exclusion of this evidence violated the accused's due process right to a fair trial. Powell J, delivering the judgment of a majority of the Court, stated that "where constitutional rights directly affecting the ascertainment of guilt are implicated, the hearsay rule may not be applied mechanistically to defeat the ends of justice".[340] In the instant case, it was held that the accused's due process right to call witnesses on his own behalf was violated because there were persuasive assurances of trustworthiness in relation to the testimony excluded which was critical to the accused's defence.

(c) Statement was contrary to interest at the time it was made

5-147 In order for a declaration against interest to be admissible, it must be shown to have been contrary to the interest of the declarant at the time that it was made.[341] In *Lalor v Lalor*,[342] FitzGibbon LJ emphasised the importance of this requirement by reference to the rationale for the exception:

> "[T]he interest against which the statement appears to be made must, in order to supply that sanction which, after the death of the party, is accepted as a substitute for an oath, be an interest existing at the time of making the statement."[343]

5-148 Thus, in *Re Tollemache, ex p. Edwards*[344] it was held that the statement of a

---

[337] [1978] 1 SCR 591 at 599, (1978) 76 DLR (3d) 513 at 518–519.

[338] See also *Demeter v R.* [1978] 1 SCR 538, (1978) 75 DLR (3d) 251 and *Lucier v R.* [1982] 1 SCR 28, (1982) 132 DLR (3d) 244. However, the High Court of Australia has declined to create an exception to the hearsay rule in respect of third party confessions that are exculpatory of an accused: *Baker v R* [2012] HCA 27.

[339] (1973) 410 US 284.

[340] (1973) 410 US 284 at 302.

[341] *La Touche v Hutton* (1875) LR 9 Eq 166 at 169–170; *Lalor v Lalor* (1879) 4 LR Ir 678; *Power v Dublin United Tramway Co. Ltd* [1926] IR 302 at 316; *Doe d Sweetland v Webber* (1834) 1 Ad & El 733; *Re Tollemache, Ex p. Edwards* (1884) 14 QBD 415; *Ward v HS Pitt & Co.* [1913] 2 KB 130 at 137; *R. v Rogers* [1995] 1 Cr App R 374 at 379.

[342] (1879) 4 LR Ir 678.

[343] (1879) 4 LR Ir 678 at 681.

[344] (1884) 14 QBD 415 at 416 (*per* Brett MR); "The rule is that an admission which is against the interest of the person who makes it, at the time when he makes it, is admissible; not that an

bankrupt acknowledging a debt could not be admitted as a declaration against interest merely because he might, at some future date, possess assets sufficient to settle the debt.

(d) Declarant knew that statement was against interest

5–149   The logical extension of the previous condition is that, not only must the statement have been against interest at the time it was made but, in addition, the declarant must have known that the statement was against his or her interest.[345] In *Tucker v Oldbury UDC*,[346] Fletcher-Moulton LJ linked this requirement to the rationale underpinning the exception, explaining that:

> "Such declarations are admitted on the ground that declarations made by persons against their own interest are extremely unlikely to be false. It follows therefore that to support the admissibility it must be shewn that the statement was to the knowledge of the deceased contrary to his interest."[347]

5–150   In that case, the dependants of a blacksmith brought a claim for workman's compensation following his death. It was held that a statement by him concerning the nature and cause of the injury which caused his death was inadmissible because it had not been proved that he knew it to be contrary to his pecuniary interest.

(e) Personal knowledge of declarant of the facts stated

5–151   The balance of authority is in favour of a requirement that the declarant must have personal knowledge of the facts stated as a condition of admissibility.[348]

4. Public Documents

5–152   At common law, there is a wide ranging exception to the hearsay rule that permits the admission of public documents[349] as *prima facie* evidence of facts stated therein. This exception is justified on the basis that public officials can be expected to perform their duties honestly and conscientiously particularly where the documents are open to inspection by members of the public. As Parke B stated in *The Irish Society v The Bishop of Derry*[350] in relation to certain returns made by the Bishops:

> "The writs related to a public matter, the revenue of the Crown, and the Bishops, in making the return, discharged a public duty, and faith is given that they would perform their duty correctly.

---

admission which may or may not turn out at some subsequent time to have been against his interest is admissible".

[345]   *Ward v HS Pitt & Co.* [1913] 2 KB 130 at 137–138; *R. v Rogers* [1995] 1 Cr App R 374 at 379.
[346]   [1912] 2 KB 317.
[347]   [1912] 2 KB 317 .at 321.
[348]   See *Roe d Lord Trimlestown v Kemmis* (1843) 9 Cl & Fin 749 at 780 and 785, *Sussex Peerage Case* (1844) 11 Cl & Fin 85 at 105; *Sturla v Freccia* (1880) 5 App Cas 623 at 632–633; *Ward v HS Pitt & Co.* [1913] 2 KB 130 at 137; *R. v Rogers* [1995] 1 Cr App R 374 at 379. See, *contra*, *Crease v Barrett* (1835) 1 Cr M & R 919 at 925.
[349]   The Law Reform Commission in its *Consultation Paper on Documentary and Electronic Evidence* (LRC CP 57–2009), at [1.41] has provisionally recommended that a "public document" should be defined as "a document retained in a depository or register relating to a matter of public interest whether of concern to sectional interests or to the community as a whole, compiled under a public duty and which is amenable to public inspection". It also provisionally recommended (at [3.82]) that such a public document should be presumed to be admissible as proof of its contents subject to any contrary evidence as to its authenticity.
[350]   (1846) 12 Cl & Finn 641.

... In public documents, made for the information of the Crown, or all the King's subjects who may require the information they contain, the entry by a public officer is presumed to be true when it is made, and is for that reason receivable in all cases. ..."[351]

5–153 Therefore, public documents are considered to be sufficiently reliable to be admitted as proof of their contents. The requirement of necessity is satisfied by the possible unavailability through death or illness of the public official who brought the document into being and, more generally, by the administrative inconvenience of requiring public officials to attend court to give evidence of the matters recorded in the document. There is also the added consideration that, in most instances, a public official is likely to have little if any recollection of the matters the subject of the public document independent of the document itself. The public document is, therefore, the best evidence of the matters recorded therein.

5–154 This common law exception has been supplemented by a miscellany of statutory provisions that allow for the admissibility of certain classes of public documents.

(a) Public documents admissible at common law

5–155 A wide variety of public documents have been held to be admissible as *prima facie* evidence of their contents under this exception including: the Poor Law valuation,[352] rate books of Poor Law Unions,[353] Down survey,[354] the Book of Distributions consisting of extracts from the Down survey,[355] a finding of lunacy by inquisition,[356] the census,[357] the Dublin Gazette,[358] a map of the Curragh prepared and deposited for the purposes of the Curragh of Kildare Act 1961.[359]

5–156 Unsurprisingly, given the diversity of documents that have been held to be admissible in a line of authorities stretching back four centuries, it is difficult to identify common criteria for their admission. However, in general terms, to be admissible under this exception, a document must: (i) contain matters of a public nature; (ii) have been compiled by a public official in the exercise of a duty to inquire into and record those matters; and (iii) have been intended to be retained for and be available for public inspection.[360]

---

[351] (1846) 12 Cl & Finn 641. at 668–669. See also *per* O'Brien LCJ in *Dublin Corporation v Bray Township Commissioners* [1900] 2 IR 88 at 93 ("the census is a public paper made out by public officers under a sanction and responsibility which impel them to make it out accurately") and *Lilley v Pettit* [1946] 1 KB 401 at 405, [1946] 1 All ER 593 at 595.

[352] *Welland v Middleton* (1847) 11 Ir Eq R 603 at 604.

[353] *Cf. Castlebar Guardians v Lord Lucan* (1849) 13 Ir LR 44.

[354] *Archbishop of Dublin v Coote* (1849) 12 Ir Eq R 251 at 266; *Poole v Griffith* (1864) 15 ICLR 277 at 280.

[355] *Poole v Griffith* (1864) 15 ICLR 277 at 280. See, *contra*, *Archbishop of Dublin v Coote* (1849) 12 Ir Eq R 251 at 267.

[356] *Hassard v Smith* (1872) IR 6 Eq 429 at 431–432.

[357] [1900] 2 IR 88 at 92–93.

[358] *R. (Lanktree) v McCarthy* [1903] 2 IR 146 (a copy of the *Dublin Gazette* published under the authority of His Majesty's Stationery Office admissible to prove that a particular district was included in a proclamation made under the Criminal Law and Procedure (Ireland) Act 1887).

[359] *Minister for Defence v Buckley* [1978] IR 314 at 321.

[360] The requirement that the document be available for public inspection as a condition of admissibility has been doubted in Canada: *R. v P(A)* (1996) 109 CCC (3d) 385.

5–157 It should be noted that there is no requirement that the record be made contemporaneously with or promptly after the events that it records—this is a matter that goes to weight and not admissibility.[361] A factor which also goes to weight rather than admissibility is that the entry was made by an interested party.[362]

(i) Matters of a public nature

5–158 In *Sturla v Freccia*,[363] Lord Blackburn explained that a matter could be considered to be of a public nature even if it is of concern to only a section of the public and not the public at large.[364] However, he emphasised the requirement that, in order to be admissible under this exception, the document had to be public, meaning "a document that is made for the purpose of the public making use of it, and being able to refer to it".[365] This condition was not satisfied in *Heyne v Fischel and Co.*,[366] where it was held that documents kept by the Post Office showing the times of the receipt and delivery of telegrams were not public documents because they were not the result of public inquiry and did not deal with general public rights but were merely kept for the purpose of regulating the employment of Post Office employees.

(ii) Duty of public official to inquire into and record facts

5–159 The document is required to have been compiled by a public official[367] in pursuance of a common law or statutory duty.[368] This condition was found not to be satisfied in *Mulhearn v Clery*,[369] in the case of parish registers of births, deaths, baptisms, and marriages which could not, therefore, be regarded as public documents.[370]*A fortiori*, a certificate of marriage by a clergyman has been held to be inadmissible to prove the fact of marriage.[371] It should be noted that the document is only admissible as evidence of facts that the public official was under a duty to record and not of other facts stated therein.[372]

5–160 The traditional approach was that a document could only be admitted under this exception where the public official compiling the document had personal knowledge

---

[361] *R. v Halpin* [1975] QB 907 at 913, [1975] 2 All ER 1124 at 1126.

[362] *Irish Society v Bishop of Derry* (1846) 12 Cl & Fin 641 at 668–669.

[363] (1880) 5 App Cas 623.

[364] *Sturla v Freccia* (1880) 5 App Cas 623 at 643. He gave the examples of the books of the manor which would be public in the sense that they concerned all the people interested in the manor (these were held to be public documents in *Heath v Deane* [1905] 2 Ch 86) and books of a corporation (*cf. Hill v Manchester & Salford Waterworks Co.* (1833) 5 B & Ad 866).

[365] (1833) 5 B & Ad 866 at 643.

[366] (1913) 30 TLR 190.

[367] A record made by or at the direction of a private individual does not qualify: *Doe d France v Andrews* (1850) 15 QB 756 at 759; *Daniel v Wilkin* (1852) 7 Exch 429 at 437.

[368] *Mulhearn v Clery* [1930] IR 649 at 684. It does not appear to be essential to identify a precise statutory duty: *Poole v Griffith* (1864) 15 ICLR 277 at 280.

[369] [1930] IR 649 at 683–686 (*per* FitzGibbon J).

[370] See also *Miller v Wheatley* (1890) 28 LR Ir 144 (entry of marriage in parochial register of a Protestant parish held not to be admissible as evidence of marriage). *Cf. Re Woodward* [1913] 1 Ch 392 (parochial registers of births, marriages, deaths and burials kept by Quakers not admissible under this exception).

[371] *Farrell v Maguire* (1841) 3 Ir LR 187.

[372] *Cf. R. v Clapham* (1829) 4 C & P 29 where it was held that a parish register of baptisms was admissible to prove the baptism of a person but not their date of birth.

of the facts recorded or was under a duty to inquire into and ascertain the accuracy of facts before recording them.[373] However, in *R. v Halpin*,[374] the view was taken that "the common law should move with the times and recognise that the official charged with recording matters of public import can no longer in this highly complicated world, as like as not, have personal knowledge of their accuracy". That case concerned the admissibility of annual returns filed with the Registrar of Companies Office and it was held that those returns were *prima facie* proof of the truth of their contents in circumstances where there was a statutory duty on a company to make accurate returns and on the Registrar to make that document available for public inspection. It can be seen that, in *Halpin*, the statutory duty on the persons filing the annual return to ensure their accuracy (under pain of penalty) afforded some reassurance of the reliability of the records and it is doubtful if the requirement that the public official have personal knowledge of, or have inquired into the accuracy of the facts recorded, will be relaxed in circumstances where there is no such duty on the person furnishing information to the public official.

5–161   In *Director of Corporate Enforcement v Bailey*,[375] the proposition that a report of a tribunal of inquiry could be considered to be a public document[376] was rejected by Irvine J who referred with approval to a passage from the judgment of Gibson J in *Savings and Investment Bank v Gasco Investments (Netherlands) BV*[377] in which he commented:

> "To my mind it is obvious that a report by inspectors, containing as it does a selection of evidence put before the inspectors and their comments and conclusions thereon, is not a record in any ordinary sense of the word. It falls short of simply compiling the information supplied to them in the sense that some information will not be included in the report, and it goes beyond such a compilation in that it expresses opinions thereon."

(iii) Availability for public inspection

5–162   A document can only be considered to be a public document if it is was brought into existence with the intention of being made retained indefinitely[378] for inspection by members of the public.[379] Thus, in *R. v Sealby*,[380] it was held that registers of motor vehicles kept by county councils which could be inspected by persons with an adequate interest were public documents but a car registration book could not be considered to

---

[373] *Doe d France v Andrews* (1850) 15 QB 756 at 759; *Sturla v Freccia* (1880) 5 App Cas 623 at 643–644; *AG v Antrobus* [1905] 2 Ch 188 at 194; *ThrasyvoulosIoannou v Papa Christoforos Demetriou* [1952] AC 84 at 95, [1952] 1 All ER 179 at 186; *R. v Sealby* [1965] 1 All ER 701 at 703; *White v Taylor* [1967] 3 All ER 349 at 351.

[374] [1975] QB 907 at 915, [1975] 2 All ER 1124 at 1128.

[375] [2007] IEHC 365, [2008] 2 ILRM 13 at 33. Her decision on this point was followed by Kearns P in *Lowry v Smyth* [2012] IEHC 22 at [40], [2012] 1 IR 400 at 412.

[376] This proposition had been put forward by the Law Reform Commission in its *Consultation Paper on Public Inquiries including Tribunals of Inquiry* (LRC CP 22/2003) at [11.14].

[377] [1984] 1 All ER 296 at 307.

[378] A document intended to be of temporary effect such as a draft (*White v Taylor* [1969] 1 Ch 150) or designed to serve only temporary purposes (*Mercer v Denne* [1905] 2 Ch 538) will not be considered to be a public document.

[379] *Sturla v Freccia* (1880) 5 App Cas 623 at 644; *Heyne v Fishchel and Co.* (1913) 30 T LR 190; *Lilley v Pettit* [1946] KB 401 at 406–407, [1946] 1 All ER 593 at 596; *ThrasyvoulosIoannou v Papa Christoforos Demetriou* [1952] AC 84 at 93, [1952] 1 All ER 179 at 186.

[380] [1965] 1 All ER 701.

be such a document because it was a private document issued to a car owner who could only be obliged to produce it to a police officer or a local taxation officer.

(b) Public documents admissible by statute

5–163 A miscellany of statutory provisions render various classes of public documents admissible as proof of their contents including: s.4 of the County Boundaries (Ireland) Act 1872 which provides that every copy of any ordnance map made under that Act or the Survey (Ireland) Acts 1854–1859 and purported to be duly certified as a true copy shall be conclusive evidence of the original map for all purposes and is admissible in evidence to prove the boundary of a county[381]; s.27 of the Pharmacy Act (Ireland) 1875 which provides that copies of the register of pharmacists or certified copies of extracts therefrom are admissible as evidence of the matters specified in the section[382]; s.5(5) of the Criminal Evidence Act 1992 which provides that, where a document purports to be a birth certificate issued in pursuance of the Births and Deaths Registration Acts 1863 to 1987, and a person is named therein as father or mother of the person to whom the certificate relates, the document is admissible in any criminal proceedings as evidence of the relationship indicated therein[383]; and s.11 of the Criminal Evidence Act 1992 which provides that, in any criminal proceedings, evidence of the passing of a resolution of either House of the Oireachtas, whether before or after the commencement of the section, may be given by the production of a copy of the Journal of the proceedings of that House relating to the resolution and purporting to have been published by the Stationery Office.

5–164 Of particular importance are the provisions of the Civil Registration Act 2004. Section 13(4) provides that evidence of an entry in the register of births, the register of stillbirths, the register of adoptions, the register of deaths, the register of marriages, the register of decrees of divorce and the register of decrees of nullity, and of the facts stated therein, may be given by the production of a document purporting to be a legible copy of the entry and to be certified to be a true copy by an tArd-Chláraitheoir, a person authorised in that behalf by an tArd-Chláraitheoir, a Superintendent Registrar, an authorised officer or a registrar. However, under s.68(1), an entry in the register of births, the register of stillbirths or the register of deaths is not evidence of the birth, stillbirth or death unless: (a) the entry purports to be signed by the person who gave the required particulars in relation to the birth, stillbirth or death to the registrar concerned, (b) that person was a person who, at the time of the making of the entry, was required by the Act or a statutory provision repealed by the Act, to give particulars in relation to the event concerned to a registrar, and (c) the entry was made in accordance with the relevant provisions of the Act or a statutory provision repealed by the Act.[384] Section 68(3) further provides that, where a birth, stillbirth or death is registered more than 12 months from the date of its occurrence, the relevant entry in the register of births, the register of stillbirths or the register of deaths, is not evidence of the occurrence unless it purports to have been made with the authority of an tArd-Chláraitheoir or an authorised officer of the relevant authority.

---

[381] See *Brown v Donegal County Council* [1980] IR 132 where these provisions are considered.

[382] See *Barrett v Henry* [1904] 2 IR 693.

[383] See now the provisions of the Civil Registration Act 2004.

[384] Subs.(2) provides that paras (a) and (b) of subs.(1) do not apply to: (i) an entry in the register of births made pursuant to s.3 of the Births, Deaths and Marriages Registration Act 1972, or (ii) an entry in the register of deaths made pursuant to that section or s.41 of the 2004 Act.

5–165 It should also be noted that provision for the admissibility of domestic legislation is made by the Documentary Evidence Act 1925[385] and of European legislation and decisions of the European Courts by the European Communities (Judicial Notice and Documentary Evidence) Regulations 1972.[386]

5. Declarations in the Course of Duty

5–166 A statement made by a person, since deceased, in pursuance of a duty owed to another to record the performance of an act, is admissible as evidence of the truth of its contents provided that the statement was made contemporaneously with the performance of the act and the declarant had no motive to misrepresent the facts.

5–167 This exception, the genesis of which is generally traced back to the decision in *Price v Earl of Torrington*,[387] appears to have developed on the basis of reasoning similar to that underpinning the exception applicable in respect of public documents that contemporaneous records of the performance of an act, compiled pursuant to a duty owed to another, and subject to potential sanction if inaccurate, are likely to be reliable. The routine nature of the entries together with the lack of a motive to misrepresent the facts furnish additional safeguards.[388] The criterion of necessity is, of course, met by the stipulation that the declarant must be dead.

5–168 In order for a statement to be admissible under this exception, it must be established that: (a) the declarant is deceased; (b) the declarant made a statement recording his or her performance of an act; (c) the declarant owed a duty to another to record the performance of the act; (d) the declaration was made contemporaneously with the act; (e) the declarant had personal knowledge of the facts recorded; and (f) the declarant had no motive to misrepresent the facts.

(a) Declarant is deceased

5–169 It is well settled that this exception only applies if the declarant is dead.[389] This is an essential pre-condition that has to be proved by a party seeking to admit a statement under this exception though it appears that, if there is a sufficient lapse of time since the statement was made, the court may be willing to presume the death of the declarant.[390] However, the requirement that the declarant be deceased has been

---

[385] See s.2 (Acts of the Oireachtas), s.3 (Proclamations and certain Orders) and s.4 (Rules, Regulations and Bye laws).

[386] SI No. 341 of 1972.

[387] (1703) 1 Salk 285. In that case, entries that a deceased drayman, employed by a brewer, made in a book every night accounting for the beer that he had delivered were admitted to prove certain deliveries of beer. One of the earliest cases applying the exception established in *Price v Earl of Torrington* in this jurisdiction is *Malone v L'Estrange* (1839) 2 Ir Eq R 16 in which it was held that the books of Roman Catholic Chapels were admissible as evidence of marriages and baptisms recorded therein because they contained "the entries of deceased person, made in the exercise of their vocation, contemporaneously with the events themselves, and without any interest or intention to mislead".

[388] See *Poole v Dicas* (1835) 1 Bing NC 649 at 652.

[389] *Malone v L'Estrange* (1839) 2 Ir Eq R 16; *Dillon v Tobin* (1879) 12 ILTR 32 at 33; *Guardians of the Poor of the Abbeyleix Union v Sutcliffe* (1890) 26 LR Ir 32; *Poole v Dicas* (1835) 1 Bing NC 649; *Esch v Nelson* (1885) 1 TLR 610.

[390] See *Miller v Wheatley* (1890) 28 LR Ir 144 at 166.

abandoned in Canada[391] and, should the issue arise in this jurisdiction, there would seem to be a strong argument in favour of the application of a broader test of unavailability.

(b) Statement recording performance of act

5–170   The statement which it is sought to admit must be one wherein the declarant recorded his or her performance of an act.[392] Thus, the exception will not apply to records of acts performed by other persons,[393] or records of acts that the declarant intends to perform.[394] It was also held in *R. v McGuire*[395] that only statements of fact fall within the scope of the rule and a declaration cannot be admitted as evidence of expressions of opinion contained therein.

5–171   It should be noted that, in the case of a written declaration, there is authority that indicates that it is necessary to prove the handwriting of the declarant.[396] This reduces the practical utility of this exception because of the difficulty of doing so in respect of persons long deceased. As O'Brien J stated in *Miller v Wheatley*,[397] insistence on proof of handwriting "makes it a question between insisting upon a condition of proof impossible in nature, and depriving the party of evidence which time makes more authentic as it destroys all living account of it". This difficulty is compounded by the dictum of FitzGibbon J in *Mulhern v Clery*[398] that "there is no presumption ... that the handwriting is that of the person by whom the entry ought to have been made". It is submitted that, if the issue arises again, this line of authority should be revisited.

(c) Duty to record performance of act

5–172   The declaration must be established to have been made in pursuance of a duty owed by the declarant to another to record the performance of the act.[399] It is evident from the decision in *Price v Torrington*[400] and confirmed in *Dillon v Tobin*[401] that the duty does not have to be one imposed by law. Thus, in the latter case, which concerned the admission of an entry recording a baptism in the Baptism Book of a Roman Catholic parish church, it sufficed that the clergyman who made the entry was obliged pursuant to Church rules to make the entry and neglect of such duty would render him liable to ecclesiastical penalties.[402]

5–173   In England, it has been held that "[t]he duty must be to do the very thing

---

[391]   See *Ares v Venner* [1970] SCR 608.
[392]   *Polini v Gray* (1879) 12 Ch D 411 at 426; *Sturla v Freccia* (1880) 5 App Cas 623 at 640; *Mercer v Dunne* [1905] 2 Ch 538 at 558.
[393]   *Ryan v Ring* (1889) 25 LR Ir 184 at 185; *The Henry Coxon* (1878) 3 PD 156.
[394]   *Rowlands v De Vecchi* (1882) Cab & El 10 (ledger recording letters to be posted rejected as evidence that a particular letter had actually been posted).
[395]   (1985) 81 Cr App R 323.
[396]   *Malone v L'Estrange* (1839) 2 Ir Eq R 16; *Miller v Wheatley* (1890) 28 LR Ir 144 at 166; *Mulhearn v Clery* [1930] IR 649 at 688.
[397]   (1891) 28 LR Ir 144 at 159.
[398]   [1930] IR 649 at 688.
[399]   *Miller v Wheatley* (1890) 28 LR Ir 144 at 166; *Mulhearn v Clery* [1930] IR 649 at 686. *Cf. Doe v Turford* (1832) 3 B & Ad 890.
[400]   (1703) 1 Salk 285
[401]   (1879) 12 ILTR 32.
[402]   *Cf. Miller v Wheatley* (1890) 28 LR Ir 144 at 166.

to which the entry relates and then to make a report or record of it".[403] However, a broader approach has been taken by the Irish courts. In *Harris v Lambert*[404] a deceased solicitor had made notes in his diary of what had transpired at meetings with regard to negotiations for a deed of family settlement. The admission of these entries was objected to on the grounds of their not having been made in the performance of his duty to his client but rather for the purposes of recording and later claiming costs. However, Meredith J rejected the narrow view that a statement, to be admissible, must be made in pursuance of a specific duty to do a specific thing:

> "[T]he question of whether the duty was to do this specific thing or whether the notes were merely kept in discharge of what was generally advisable, is really a question which, from the point of view of science, logic and common sense, can only be one of the weight and value of the evidence, not a question of whether or not the notes are evidence at all. Only a peculiarity of the law of evidence would make the distinction vital."[405]

5–174 He took the view that, although the notes would be used for the purpose of assessing costs, they were also made for the purpose of having a record to be used in further negotiations. It was advisable for the solicitor to keep such a record in order to properly discharge his ultimate duty to the client of approving the settlement and, therefore, the notes were admissible.[406]

5–175 It is important to note, however, that a statement can only be admitted as evidence of facts that the declarant was under a duty to report or record and not of any other facts that the declarant chose to record.[407] This limitation on the scope of the exception was neatly summarised in *Chambers v Bernasconi*[408] by Lord Denman CJ, who stated that "whatever effect may be due to an entry made in the course of any office reporting facts necessary to the performance of a duty, the statement of other circumstances, however naturally they may be thought to find a place in the narrative, is no proof of those circumstances". Thus, in *Mulhearn v Clery*,[409] statements relating to the legitimacy of an infant in a baptismal register were held to be inadmissible because it had not been established that the declarant was under a duty to record that matter.

(d) Record must be contemporaneous

5–176 Although it is well established that, to be admissible, a declaration must be contemporaneous with the performance of the act to which it relates,[410] the precise

---

[403] *Per* Blackburn J in *Smith v Blakey* (1867) LR 2 QB 326 at 332. See also *Massey v Allen* (1879) 13 Ch D 558; *Mercer v Dunne* [1905] 2 Ch 538 at 556; *Dawson v Dawson* (1906) 22 TLR 52.

[404] [1932] IR 504.

[405] [1932] IR 504 at 506. It is clear that the decision of the learned judge was influenced by his view that, to reject the notes in circumstances where the other solicitor who had participated in the settlement discussions was using his notes to refresh his memory, "would lead to manifest injustice" (at 509).

[406] See also *Somers v Erskine (No.2)* [1944] IR 368 at 385 (held by the Supreme Court that the trial judge had been incorrect to exclude notes made by a deceased solicitor which were admissible "as being a record of instructions given by the client to his solicitor, which it was the latter's duty to record, and which it was necessary to record for the purpose of having such instructions carried into effect") and *Esch v Nelson* (1885) 1 TLR 610. See, *contra*, *Mercer v Mercer* [1924] 2 IR 50 (Northern Ireland Court of Appeal held that memorandum made by deceased solicitor of consultation with client had been improperly admitted).

[407] *Mulhearn v Clery* [1930] IR 649 at 686–687; *Chambers v Bernasconi* (1834) 1 CM & R 347.

[408] (1834) 1 CM & R 347 at 368.

[409] [1930] IR 649 at 686.

[410] *Malone v L'Estrange* (1839) 2 Ir Eq R 16; *Dillon v Tobin* (1879) 12 ILTR 32 at 33; *Champneys*

degree of contemporaneity required is not clear. In *Ryan v Ring*,[411] Warren J merely stated that the record must have been made "at or near the time when the matter stated occurred". This requirement was found to be satisfied when the record was made on the same day as the act[412] but not where it was made one month later[413] but where the dividing line between the two will be drawn is not clear. In *The Henry Coxon*[414] entries made two days after the events in question were excluded but there were a number of reasons for the rejection of the entries in that case and it is not clear that they would have been excluded on the basis of lack of contemporaneity alone. It is submitted that a strict requirement of contemporaneity should not be applied. Rather, the degree of contemporaneity should be a factor going to the weight, and not the admissibility of the records.

(e) Personal knowledge

5–177 It has been emphasised in a number of cases that the declarant must have had personal knowledge of the facts recorded.[415] Thus, in *Ryan v Ring*,[416] an entry in a baptismal register was inadmissible to prove that the parents of the child were married because there was no evidence that the priest had officiated at the marriage or had personal knowledge of it. Again, in *Mulhearn v Clery*,[417] one of the reasons advanced by FitzGibbon J for excluding statements relating to the legitimacy of an infant in a baptismal register was that the declarant priest had no "peculiar knowledge" of the parentage of a child presented to him for baptism.

(f) Lack of motive to misrepresent the facts

5–178 There is a long established requirement that, in order for a declaration to be admissible, the declarant must not have any motive to misrepresent the facts.[418] One of the grounds for the rejection of log entries recording the details of a collision between two ships in *The Henry Coxon*[419] was that the first mate who made the entries had an interest to misrepresent the role of his ship in the collision.

6. Business Records

5–179 At common law, the principal hearsay exception applicable to business records was that in respect of declarations in the course of duty. However, as can be seen from the previous section, the conditions of admissibility of such declarations were quite strict with the result that many records that were produced in the ordinary

---

v Beck (1816) 1 Stark 404; *Poole v Dicas* (1835) 1 Bing NC 649; *Mercer v Dunne* [1905] 2 Ch 538 at 558; *Re Djiambi (Sumatra) Rubber Estates Ltd* (1913) 107 LT 631 at 633; *R. v McGuire* (1985) 81 Cr App R 323 at 330.

[411] (1889) 25 LR Ir 184 at 185.
[412] *Price v Earl of Torrington* (1703) 1 Salk 285.
[413] *Re Djiambi (Sumatra) Rubber Estates Ltd* (1913) 107 LT 631 at 633.
[414] (1878) 3 PD 156.
[415] *Ryan v Ring* (1889) 25 LR Ir 184 at 185; *Mulhearn v Clery* [1930] IR 649 at 687; *Sturla v Freccia* (1880) 5 App Cas 623 at 633.
[416] (1889) 25 LR Ir 184. See also *Mulhearn v Clery* [1930] IR 649 at 687.
[417] [1930] IR 649 at 687.
[418] *Malone v L'Estrange* (1839) 2 Ir Eq R 16; *Marks v Laheè* (1837) 3 Bing NC 408; *The Henry Coxon* (1878) 3 PD 156 at 158.
[419] (1878) 3 PD 156.

course of business and could be considered to be quite reliable did not fall within the scope of the exception and were excluded as inadmissible hearsay. This lacuna was highlighted in *Myers v DPP*[420] where it was held that manufacturer's records compiled in the ordinary course of business were inadmissible.[421]

5–180 Legislative reform in this area has, therefore, been necessary. An early instance of legislative intervention came in the Bankers' Books Evidence Acts but the most important reform came in the Criminal Evidence Act 1992 which makes provision for the admission, by way of exception to the hearsay rule, of a wide variety of records that have been compiled in the ordinary course of business. It should be noted that there has been no equivalent reform to the Criminal Evidence Act 1992 in civil cases with the result that records compiled in the ordinary course of business that are relied on as proof of the truth of their contents will be excluded as hearsay unless admissible under the Bankers' Books Evidence Acts or some other exception to the hearsay rule.[422] In the absence of a judicially recognised exception in respect of such business records, further statutory intervention to address this disparity seems likely.[423]

(a) Bankers' Books

5–181 The Bankers' Books Evidence Acts 1879 and 1959[424] (as amended by s.131 of the Central Bank Act 1989[425] and s.126 of the Building Societies Act 1989[426]) provide for the admissibility of copies of entries from the books and records of a bank[427] against

---

[420] [1965] AC 1001.

[421] *Cf. People (DPP) v Byrne*, unreported, Court of Criminal Appeal, 7 June 2000, where the decision in *Myers* was distinguished, though it is not clear on what basis.

[422] See *Ulster Bank Ireland Ltd v Dermody* [2014] IEHC 140 at [46]. In that decision, O'Malley J declined to follow the judgments of Clarke J in *Moorview Developments Ltd v First Active plc* [2010] IEHC 275, Finlay Geoghegan J in *Bank of Scotland plc v Fergus* [2012] IEHC 131 and Ryan J in *Bank of Ireland v Keehan* [2013] IEHC 631 who had taken the view that bank records were admissible as *prima facie* evidence of their contents if proven by a bank official who could swear to their accuracy. A similar view was also taken by McGovern J in *Permanent TSB v Beades* [2014] IEHC 81 at [15] which was not referred to in *Dermody*. In *Ulster Bank Ireland Ltd v Kavanagh* [2014] IEHC 299, Baker J refused to give the decision in *Dermody* retrospective effect so as to set aside a judgment obtained before that decision was handed down.

[423] The Law Reform Commission in its *Consultation Paper on Documentary and Electronic Evidence* (LRC CP 57–2009), at [4.09] has provisionally recommended that "business records" should be presumed to be admissible in evidence and (at [4.15]) that business documents be accepted as admissible evidence if the document was created or received in the course of a business and where: (a) the information in the statement is derived from a person who had, or may reasonably to supposed to have had, direct personal knowledge of that information; (b) the documentary statement has been produced for the purposes of a business; and (c) the information is contained in a document kept by a business.

[424] See, generally, Dunne and Davies, "The Bankers' Books Evidence Acts 1879 and 1959" (1997) 2 (7) BR 297. The Law Reform Commission in its *Consultation Paper on Documentary and Electronic Evidence* (LRC CP 57–2009), at [4.162] provisionally recommended the retention of the Bankers' Book Evidence Act 1879 (as amended) with their application extended to all credit institutions.

[425] No.16 of 1989.

[426] No.17 of 1989.

[427] The concept of "bank" and "banker" are defined in s.9 of the 1879 Act (as amended by s.2 of the Bankers' Books Evidence (Amendment) Act 1959 (No.21 of 1959) and s.126 of the Building Societies Act 1989 (No.17 of 1989)).

any person[428] as *prima facie* evidence of their contents in any proceedings.[429] If a book or record can be proven utilising the provisions of the Act, then an officer of the bank is not compellable to produce that book or record or to appear as a witness to prove the matters therein recorded except by order of a judge made for special cause.[430]

5–182   At a time when banks recorded transactions by way of handwritten entries in books, the purpose of allowing proof of such entries by secondary evidence was to avoid the inconvenience that resulted from requiring a bank official to bring the original books of the bank to court which were not then available to the bank to make entries therein.[431] Given that bank records are no longer maintained by way of handwritten entries in books, the modern day purpose of these provisions is to provide a convenient means of proving information contained in bank records and avoid the necessity of requiring a bank official to attend, most likely on foot of a subpoena *duces tecum*, to give such evidence.[432] Although the provisions can be availed of by a bank in order to prove bank records in any proceedings,[433] this is not the primary purpose of the legislation.[434]

5–183   The application of the these Acts turns on the concept of "bankers' books" which are defined in s.9 of the 1879 Act (as amended[435]) to include any records used in the ordinary business of a bank, or used in the transfer department of a bank acting as registrar of securities, whether comprised in bound volume, loose-leaf binders or other loose-leaf ledger sheets, pages, folios, or cards, or kept on microfilm, magnetic tape or in any non-legible form (by the use of electronics or otherwise[436]) which is capable of being reproduced in a permanent legible form together with documents in manuscript, documents which are typed, printed, stencilled or created by any other mechanical or partly mechanical process in use from time to time and documents which are produced by any photographic or photostatic process.[437] It was held by Murphy J in *Volkering v Haughton*[438] that this definition of bankers' books is wide enough to include correspondence from a customer to a bank relating to an account with has been retained and forms part of the records of the bank.[439]

---

[428] *Harding v Williams* (1880) 14 Ch D 197 at 199.
[429] Section 3 of the Bankers' Books Evidence Act 1879.
[430] Section 6. As noted by O'Malley J in *Ulster Bank Ireland Ltd v Dermody* [2014] IEHC 140 at [19], until amended by s.131 of the Central Bank Act 1989, s.6 only applied to legal proceedings to which the bank was not itself a party.
[431] *Bank of Scotland plc v Stapleton* [2012] IEHC 549 at [9]; *JB O'C v PCD* [1985] IR 265 at 274; *Larkins v National Union of Mineworkers* [1985] IR 671 at 695.
[432] *Moorview Developments Ltd v First Active plc* [2010] IEHC 275 at [4.8]; *Walsh v National Irish Bank Ltd* [2013] IESC 2 at [7.5]. See also *JB O'C v PCD* [1985] IR 265 at 274.
[433] *Ulster Bank Ireland Ltd v Dermody* [2014] IEHC 140 at [48].
[434] *Moorview Developments Ltd v First Active plc* [2010] IEHC 275 at [4.8]; *Bank of Ireland v Keehan* [2013] IEHC 631.
[435] By s.2 of the Bankers' Books Evidence (Amendment) Act 1959 and s.131 of the Central Bank Act 1989.
[436] Where computer printouts are relied upon, it is necessary to prove that the computer accurately records the relevant data and was operating correctly: *R. v Chow* (1991) 68 CCC 190.
[437] *Cf. Williams v Williams* [1988] 1 QB 161 (addition of cheque or credit slip to the bundles of such documents retained by a bank could not be regarded as making an entry in the records of the bank) and *Barker v Wilson* [1980] 1 WLR 884, [1980] 2 All ER 81 (entry in bankers' books included any form of permanent record kept by the bank by means made available by modern technology including records on microfilm).
[438] [2005] IEHC 240, [2010] 1 IR 417.
[439] He did not follow the narrower view of Murphy J in *JB O'C v PCD* [1985] IR 265, a decision

5–184   In order for an entry in a bankers' book to be admitted in evidence, it must be proved by the person seeking to admit the copy that, at the time of the making of the entry, the book was one of the ordinary books of the bank,[440] the entry was made in the usual and ordinary course of business, and the book is in the custody or control of the bank.[441] In accordance with s.4 of Bankers' Books Evidence Act 1879, such evidence must be given by a partner or officer[442] of the bank (orally or by affidavit) and it was held in *Bank of Scotland plc v Stapleton*[443] that delegation in this regard is not permissible so that such evidence cannot be given by a person who is not a partner or officer of the bank even if authorised by the bank to do so and even if that person has direct access to the records of the bank.[444] *A fortiori*, the Acts cannot be invoked if the person giving evidence is not an employee and therefore not an officer of the bank in question.[445]

5–185   It must also be proved by evidence given orally or on affidavit by a person who has examined the original entry and the copy that the copy of the entry in the bankers' book is an accurate copy.[446] However, such evidence does not have to given by a partner or official in the bank.[447]

---

which predated the amendment to s.9 effected by s.131 of the Central Bank Act 1989, that the concept of bankers' books did not extend to items of correspondence because the removal of those documents would not inconvenience the business of a bank. He also distinguished English cases including *R. v Dadson* (1983) 77 Cr App R 91 on the basis that the definition of bankers' books in s.9 (as amended) is wider than the amended definition in the UK.

[440] See *Permanent TSB v Beades* [2014] IEHC 81 at [21] where McGovern J was satisfied that the description of documents in an affidavit as "books, documents and records of the Plaintiff bank" was sufficient to establish that they were "bankers' books" for the purpose of the 1897 Act.

[441] Section 4 of the Bankers' Books Evidence Act 1879. Such proof may be given by a partner or officer of the bank orally or by affidavit.

[442] An employee of the bank will be considered to an officer for the purposes of the Acts: *Ulster Bank Ireland Ltd v Dermody* [2014] IEHC 140 at [50].

[443] [2012] IEHC 549 at [15].

[444] In *Permanent TSB v Beades* [2014] IEHC 81, McGovern J rejected a contention that the plaintiff bank had failed to establish that the deponents of affidavits, who described their functions within the bank but did not expressly state they were officers of the bank, were in fact officers of the bank.

[445] *Ulster Bank Ireland Ltd v Dermody* [2014] IEHC 140 at [52].

[446] Section 5 of the Bankers' Books Evidence Act 1879 as originally enacted required proof that the copy had been examined with the original entry and was correct. Section 5 (as substituted by s.131 of the Central Bank Act 1989) now provides that a copy of an entry in a bankers' book cannot be received in evidence unless it is proved that: (a) in the case where the copy sought to be received in evidence has been reproduced in a legible form directly by either or both mechanical and electronic means from a bankers' book maintained in non-legible form, it has been so reproduced; (b) in the case where the copy sought to be received in evidence has been made (either directly or indirectly) from a copy to which paragraph (a) of the section would apply, the copy sought to be so received has been examined with a copy so reproduced and is a correct copy and the copy so reproduced is a copy to which paragraph (a) would apply if it were sought to have it received in evidence; and (c) in any other case, the copy has been examined with the original entry and is correct. Under s.5(2), proof that the foregoing requirements have been met can be only be given by the categories of persons specified therein and may be given either orally or on affidavit.

[447] *Bank of Scotland plc v Stapleton* [2012] IEHC 549 at [12]; *R. v Albutt* (1911) 6 Cr App R 55.

(b) Records admissible under the Criminal Evidence Act 1992

5–186   Part II of the Criminal Evidence Act 1992 Act (the "1992 Act")[448] creates an exception to the hearsay rule in respect of documents compiled in the ordinary course of business.[449] The rationale for this exception was explained by Thomas LJ in *R v Horncastle*[450] as follows:

> "Business records are admissible … because in the ordinary way, they are compiled by persons who are disinterested and, in the ordinary course of events, such statements are likely to be accurate; they are therefore admissible as evidence because *prima facie* they are reliable."

5–187   It is important to emphasise that this exception applies to criminal proceedings only and, thus, the admission of business records in civil cases is still governed by common law, principally by the exception in respect of declarations made in the course of duty. Part II also contains provisions regulating the admission of such evidence, the weight to be attached to them and requirements for advance notice which are examined below.[451] These provisions provide safeguards to ensure that the admissibility of such documentary evidence does not contravene the constitutional guarantee of fair procedures.[452]

(i) Admissibility of records

5–188   Section 5(1) of the 1992 Act provides that information[453] contained in a document[454] is admissible in any criminal proceedings[455] as evidence of any fact therein of which direct oral evidence would be admissible[456] provided that the information: (a) was compiled in the ordinary course of a business,[457] (b) was supplied by a person

---

[448] Part II implements recommendations for reform contained in the Law Reform Commission, *Report on Receiving Stolen Property* (LRC 23–1987) at 144.

[449] It should be noted that s.2(2) of the 1992 Act stipulates that nothing in Part II shall prejudice the admissibility in evidence in any criminal proceedings of information contained in a document that is otherwise so admissible. In *People (DPP) v McCann*, Special Criminal Court, 31 July 1996, *People (DPP) v Murphy* [2005] IECCA 1 at [80], [2005] 2 IR 125 at 152 and *People (DPP) v Meehan* [2006] IECCA 104 at [30], [2006] 3 IR 468 at 480, the proposition that Part II of the 1992 Act had abrogated or abolished the existing common law rules for the admissibility of documents was rejected.

[450] [2009] EWCA Crim 964 at [15].

[451] The comparable English provision is s.24 of the Criminal Justice Act 1988 while in the US it is set out in rule 803 of the Federal Rules of Evidence.

[452] *People (DPP) v Murphy* [2005] IECCA 1 at [90], [2005] 2 IR 125 at 155.

[453] The concept of "information" is defined in s.2 of the 1992 Act to include "any representation of fact, whether in words or otherwise". It would, thus, seem that s.5 creates an exception to the hearsay rule only and not to the exclusionary rule in respect of opinion evidence.

[454] A "document" is defined in s.2 of the 1992 Act to include of: (i) a map, plan, graph, drawing or photograph, or (ii) a reproduction in permanent legible form, by a computer or other means (including enlarging), of information in non-legible form. *Cf. Campofina Bank v ANZ Banking Group* [1982] 1 NSWLR 409 and *H v Schering Chemicals Ltd* [1983] 1 All ER 849 for a discussion of what constitutes a "business record".

[455] Criminal proceedings are defined in s.2 of the 1992 Act to include proceedings before a court-martial and proceedings on appeal.

[456] Any inadmissible evidence may have to be excised from the document: *Re Marra Developments* [1979] 2 NSWLR 193.

[457] The concept of "business" is broadly defined in s.4 of the 1992 Act to include "any trade, profession or other occupation carried on, for reward or otherwise, either within or without the State and includes also the performance of functions by or on behalf of: (a) any person or body remunerated or financed wholly or partly out of moneys provided by the Oireachtas; (b) any institution of the European Communities; (c) any national or local authority in a jurisdiction outside the State;

(whether or not he so compiled it and is identifiable) who had, or may reasonably be supposed to have had, personal knowledge[458] of the matters dealt with, and (c) in the case of information in non-legible form[459] that has been reproduced in permanent legible form, was reproduced in the course of the normal operation of the reproduction system concerned.[460] Subsection (2) goes on to provide that the information is admissible whether it was "supplied directly or indirectly but, if it was supplied indirectly, only if each person (whether or not he is identifiable) through whom it was supplied received it in the ordinary course of a business".

5–189   In *People (DPP) v Murphy*,[461] it was held that telephone records produced mechanically and without human intervention by a telecoms service provider fell within s.5(1). However, it is difficult to see how such evidence satisfies the requirement in subs.(1)(b) that the information in the document was supplied by a person (whether or not he so compiled it and is identifiable) who had, or may reasonably be supposed to have had, personal knowledge of the matters dealt with. In circumstances where the information is compiled automatically by a computer system and having regard to the contents of those records, it can hardly be said that it has been supplied by a person who has personal knowledge of the matters dealt with.

5–190   Where information is admissible under s.5 but is expressed in terms that are not intelligible to the average person without explanation, an explanation of the information is also admissible if either (a) it is given orally by a person who is competent to do so, or (b) it is contained in a document and the document purports to be signed by such a person.[462]

5–191   There are a number of important limitations on the applicability of the hearsay exception established by s.5(1). It does not apply to information that is privileged from disclosure in criminal proceedings,[463] or where the information is supplied by a person who would not be compellable to give evidence at the instance of the party wishing to give the information by virtue of s.5.[464] Furthermore, it does not apply in respect of information compiled for the purposes of or in contemplation of any (i) criminal investigation, (ii) investigation or inquiry carried out pursuant to or under any enactment, (iii) civil or criminal proceedings, or (iv) proceedings of a disciplinary

---

or (d) any international organisation. The meaning of the phrase "in the course of business" has given rise to some controversy in the US and Canada. *Cf. Palmer v Hoffman* (1943) 318 US 109; *Otney v US* (1965) 340 F 2d 696; *R. v Zundel* (1987) 18 OAC 161, 35 DLR (4th) 338.

[458] It is not necessary that the individual who created the record be identified so that their personal knowledge can be assessed (*R. v Ewing* [1983] QB 1039, [1983] 2 All ER 645) because such personal knowledge may be inferred (*R. v Foxley* [1995] 2 Cr App R 523 at 536). See, further, Williams, "The New Proposals in Relation to Double Hearsay and Record" [1973] Crim LR 139.

[459] The concept of "information in non-legible form" is defined in s.2 of the 1992 Act to include "information on microfilm, microfiche, magnetic tape or disk".

[460] *Cf. O'Brien v Shantz* [1998] OJ No. 4072 for a discussion of a similar requirement contained in Canadian legislation.

[461] [2005] IECCA 1, [2005] 2 IR 125 (see the commentary by Murphy, "The Use of Business Records in Prosecution" (2004) 14(1) ICLJ 19). See also *People (DPP) v Hickey* [2007] IECCA 98.

[462] Section 5(6).

[463] Section 5(3)(a). See Chaps 10 and 11 for a discussion of the privileges applicable in criminal proceedings.

[464] Section 5(3)(b). See Chap.3 dealing with the competence and compellability of witnesses.

nature except in limited circumstances except in certain specified circumstances.[465] The first is where the information contained in the document was compiled in the presence of a District Judge and supplied on oath by a person in respect of whom an offence was alleged to have been committed and who is ordinarily resident outside the State, where it was not possible or practicable to obtain a deposition pursuant to s.4F of the Criminal Procedure Act 1967,[466] and the person in respect of whom the offence was alleged to have been committed has either died or is outside the State and it is not reasonably practicable to secure his or her attendance at the criminal proceedings concerned.[467] The second is where the document containing the information is: (a) a map, plan, drawing or photograph (including any explanatory material in or accompanying the document concerned); (b) a record of a direction given by a member of the Garda Síochána pursuant to any enactment; (c) a record of the receipt, handling, transmission or storage of anything by the Forensic Science Laboratory of the Department of Justice, Equality and Law Reform in connection with the performance of its functions to examine and analyse things or samples of things for the purposes of criminal investigations or proceedings or both, (d) a record of the receipt, handling, transmission, examination or analysis of any thing by any person acting on behalf of any party to the proceedings; or (e) a record by a registered medical practitioner of an examination of a living or dead person.

5–192 In accordance with general principles with regard to the admission of evidence,[468] where a party proposes to adduce information in a document pursuant to the provisions of Part II, that party bears the onus of establishing that the requirements of s.5 have been satisfied and, if the party fails to do so, he or she will be unable to avail of the exception under s.5.[469] However, s.6 of the 1992 Act eases the burden on parties by making provision for proof of compliance with the conditions of admissibility by means of a certificate rather than oral evidence.[470] Oral evidence may, nevertheless, be

---

[465] Section 5(3)(c) and (4) (as amended by s.188 of the Criminal Justice Act 2006). *Cf. R. v Heilman* (1983) Man R (2d) 173.

[466] Section 4F of the Criminal Procedure Act 1967 (as amended by the Criminal Justice Act 1999) provides that where, on the application of the prosecutor or an accused person, a District Judge is of the opinion that a prospective witness may be unable to attend or be prevented from attending to give evidence at the trial of the accused and that it is necessary in the interests of justice to take his evidence by way of sworn deposition, he may order accordingly.

[467] Subsection (4)(a).

[468] *Cf. People (DPP) v Dillon* [2003] 1 ILRM 531.

[469] *Cf. Convening Authority v Company Sergeant Berigan*, unreported, Courts-Martial Appeal Court, 1 November 2001.

[470] Subsection (1) provides that a certificate: (a) stating that the information was compiled in the ordinary course of a specified business; (b) stating that the information is not of the kind mentioned in para.(a) or (b) of s.5(3); stating either that the information was not compiled for the purposes or in contemplation of any investigation, inquiry or proceedings referred to in s.5(3)(c) or, as the case may be, specifying which of the provisions of s.5(4) applies in relation to the document containing the information; (d) stating that the information was supplied, either directly or, as the case may be, indirectly through an intermediary or intermediaries (who, or each of whom, received it in the ordinary course of a specified business), by a person who had, or may reasonably be supposed to have had, personal knowledge of the matters dealt with in the information and, where the intermediary, intermediaries or person can be identified, specifying them; (e) where the information is information in non-legible form that has been reproduced in permanent legible form, stating that the reproduction was effected in the course of the normal operation of a specified system; (f) where appropriate, stating that the person who supplied the information cannot reasonably be expected to have any, or any adequate, recollection of the matters dealt with in the information, having regard to the time that has elapsed since he supplied it or to any other

required in some cases. Where notice has been served objecting to the admissibility in evidence of the whole or any specified part of the information concerned, the court must, notwithstanding that a certificate may have been given, require oral evidence to be given of any matter stated or specified in the certificate.[471] In addition, the court has a general discretion to require such oral evidence in any other case.[472]

5–193 Even where a document satisfies the conditions of admissibility specified in s.5, it may not be admitted because s.8(1) confers on a court a broad discretion to exclude information or any part thereof where "the court is of opinion that in the interests of justice the information or that part ought not to be admitted". Guidance as to how that discretion should be exercised is provided in subs.(2) which provides as follows:[473]

> "In considering whether in the interests of justice all or any part of such information ought not to be admitted in evidence the court shall have regard to all the circumstances including—
> (a) whether or not, having regard to the contents and source of the information and the circumstances in which it was compiled, it is a reasonable inference that the information is reliable,[474]
> (b) whether or not, having regard to the nature and source of the document containing the information and to any other circumstances that appear to the court to be relevant, it is a reasonable inference that the document is authentic, and
> (c) any risk, having regard in particular to whether it is likely to be possible to controvert the information where the person who supplied it does not attend to give oral evidence in the proceedings, that its admission or exclusion will result in unfairness to the accused or, if there is more than one, to any of them."

(ii) Notice requirement

5–194 Section 7 contains an important procedural protection for persons against whom it is intended to adduce documentary hearsay pursuant to Part II by laying down a notice requirement.[475] Subsection (1) provides that information in a document shall not, without the leave of the court, be admissible in evidence by virtue of s.5 unless a copy of the document and, where appropriate, of a certificate as to admissibility, has

---

specified circumstances; (g) unless the date on which the information was compiled is already shown on the document, specifying the date (or, if that date is not known, the approximate date) on which it was compiled; (h) stating any other matter that is relevant to the admissibility in evidence of the information and is required by rules of court to be certified for the purposes of the subsection; and purporting to be signed by a person who occupied a position in relation to the management of the business in the course of which the information was compiled or who is otherwise in a position to give the certificate shall be evidence of any matter stated or specified therein. Subsection (2) further provides that, for the purposes of subs. (1), it is sufficient for a matter to be stated or specified to the best of the knowledge and belief of the person stating or specifying it.

[471] Section 6(3).
[472] Section 6(3).
[473] This section is modelled on s.23 of the English Criminal Justice Act 1988 which has since been replaced by s.117 of the Criminal Justice Act 2003. See Malek (ed.), *Phipson on Evidence* (18th edn), paras 30–35 to 30–40.
[474] For example, such evidence may be inadmissible if the maker of the statement had a motive to misrepresent, or the statement is a self serving statement. See *Northern Wood Preserves Ltd v Hall Corp (Shipping) 1969 Ltd.* [1972] 3 OR 751, (1972) 29 DLR (3d) 413. *Cf. Setak Computer Services Corp. v Burroughs Business Machines Ltd* (1977) 15 OR (2d) 750 at 758, 76 DLR (3d) 641.
[475] Under s.52(6)(b) of the Criminal Justice (Theft and Fraud Offences) Act 2001, the provisions of s.7 are extended to documents that it is sought to admit pursuant to that section.

been served on the accused as part of the Book of Evidence[476] or, not later than 21 days before the commencement of the trial, a notice of intention so to give the information in evidence, together with a copy of the document and, where appropriate, of the certificate, is served by or on behalf of the party proposing to give it in evidence on each of the other parties to the proceedings. Subsection (2) goes on to provide that a party to the proceedings on whom a notice has been served pursuant to subs. (1) cannot, without the leave of the court, object to the admissibility in evidence of the whole or any specified part of the information concerned unless, not later than 7 days before the commencement of the trial, a notice objecting to its admissibility is served by or on behalf of that party on each of the other parties to the proceedings.

(iii) Weight to be attached to information

5–195   Section 8(3) provides that, in estimating the weight, if any, to be attached to information which is adduced in evidence under Part II of the 1992 Act, regard must be had to all the circumstances from which any inference can reasonably be drawn as to its accuracy or otherwise.[477]

5–196   Important in the assessment of weight will be the credibility of the declarant and s.9 makes provision for the reception in evidence of a number of categories of evidence relevant to assessing the credibility of the declarant:

> "(a) any evidence which, if the person who originally supplied the information had been called as a witness, would have been admissible as relevant to his credibility as a witness shall be admissible for that purpose,
>
> (b) evidence may, with the leave of the court, be given of any matter which, if that person had been called as a witness, could have been put to him in cross-examination as relevant to his credibility as a witness but of which evidence could not have been adduced by the cross-examining party, and
>
> (c) evidence tending to prove that that person, whether before or after supplying the information, made (whether orally or not) a statement which is inconsistent with it shall, if not already admissible by virtue of section 5, be admissible for the purpose of showing that he has contradicted himself."

5–197   The purpose of the section is to place the declarant whose hearsay statement is admitted in the same position, for the purpose of impeaching credibility, as if he or she had been called as a witness.

7. Proceedings Concerning the Welfare of Children

5–198   The question of whether and the extent to which hearsay evidence of sexual abuse should be admitted in proceedings concerning the welfare of children is a difficult one. In some cases, reported allegations of sexual abuse may be the only evidence available and if they are excluded, the court will not be in a position to properly assess the risks to the welfare of a child. However, the admission of such evidence is fraught with risks and potentially may work an injustice to the other parties involved in such

---

[476] See ss.4B and 4C of the Criminal Procedure Act 1967 (as amended by the Criminal Justice Act 1999).

[477] The Canadian courts have interpreted a similar provision so as to assess the reliability of the document by reference to the promptness with which the transaction was recorded. A contemporaneous document is viewed as more reliable (*Matheson v Barnes* [1981] 2 WWR 435, 438). *Cf. Setak Computer services Corp. v Burroughs Business Machines Ltd* (1977) 76 DLR (3d) 641.

proceedings. The matter is now governed by Part III of the Children Act 1997[478] but, before examining those provisions, it is instructive to outline the position at common law because some of the principles laid down will still be of relevance under the statutory regime.

(a) The common law position

5–199   In a number of cases in the late 1990s, the issue of the admission of hearsay in wardship and analogous proceedings arose for consideration, and the leading decision is that of the Supreme Court in *Eastern Health Board v MK*.[479] The Eastern Health Board instituted proceedings seeking an order taking three children, MK, SK and WK into wardship. At the hearing of the summons, Costello P admitted certain contested hearsay evidence on a *de bene esse* basis: (i) the evidence of Mrs H, a speech therapist, who stated that SK had confided to her that he had, with the knowledge of his mother, been subjected to sexual abuse by his father on a regular basis for a number of years; and (ii) the evidence of Mr McG, a senior social worker with considerable experience of child abuse allegations, as to what SK said and did at an interview which he had with him in the Children's Hospital, Temple Street. A videotape of this interview had been made. The President was satisfied that if the hearsay evidence was excluded, the rest of the evidence would not justify the making of an order of wardship and he addressed the admissibility of this evidence as a preliminary issue. He ultimately decided to admit it and, on the basis of that evidence, he made a finding that SK had been grossly sexually abused by his father and that his mother knew of the abuse but was powerless to stop it. On appeal, the respondents submitted that the hearsay evidence should not have been admitted or, alternatively, that it had not been scrutinised sufficiently.

5–200   The five members of the Supreme Court were unanimous that the reported statements of SK had been improperly admitted but adopted different approaches in allowing the appeal. Two members of the Court, Denham and Keane JJ, supported the existence of an exception allowing the admission of hearsay evidence in wardship cases provided that certain threshold tests were met. Barrington J took the view that hearsay evidence could be admitted in relation to administrative matters but not contested issues. Lynch J's very short concurring judgment seems to support that approach. Finally, Barron J took the view that the reported statements could be received but only as the basis for an expert opinion on their veracity.

5–201   The most detailed analysis of the issue before the Court is to be found in the judgment of Keane J. He laid emphasis on the special nature of the wardship jurisdiction which flowed from the fact that it is not concerned with a *lis inter partes* and, accordingly, its exercise is generally administrative rather than judicial in nature. It followed that a judge exercising that jurisdiction is not necessarily bound by the rules which apply where a court is engaged in the administration of justice and cases could arise where the paramount object of the wardship procedure, namely the welfare of the persons under protection, might require a departure from those rules. Therefore,

---

[478]   No.40 of 1997
[479]   [1999] 2 IR 99 (reported *sub nom In the Matter of MK, SK and WK* [1999] 2 ILRM 321). See also *Re M., S. and W. Infants* [1996] 1 ILRM 370, *Southern Health Board v CH.* [1996] 1 IR 219 and *Eastern Health Board v Mooney*, unreported, High Court, 20 March 1998. *Cf. McGlinchey v Ryan* [2012] IEHC 536 (where the admissibility of hearsay evidence was considered in the context of a non statutory inquiry into allegations of sexual abuse).

at least where the judge exercising that jurisdiction is acting as an administrator, "the strict application of the rule against hearsay would be impracticable, undesirable and unnecessary".[480]

5–202   Different considerations arose where something in the nature of a *lis inter partes* arose, as where it was sought to admit hearsay evidence of allegations of child sexual abuse. However, after surveying a number of English decisions, he found authority in the decision of the Court of Appeal in *Re W (Minors)*[481] for the proposition that hearsay evidence of allegations of sexual abuse by children, whether in the form of videotaped interviews or in other forms, is admissible in wardship proceedings. He also examined the decision of *R. v Khan*[482] which dealt with the admission of hearsay evidence of children in the criminal context. In that case, McLachlin J advocated a flexible approach to the reception of the hearsay evidence of children and held that such evidence was admissible where the twin criteria of necessity and reliability were met:

> "The first question should be whether reception of the hearsay statement is necessary. Necessity for these purposes must be interpreted as 'reasonably necessary'. The inadmissibility of the child's evidence might be one basis for a finding of necessity. But sound evidence based on psychological assessments that testimony in court might be traumatic for the child or harm the child might also serve...The next question should be whether the evidence is reliable. Many considerations such as timing, demeanour, the personality of the child, the intelligence and understanding of the child, and the absence of any reason to expect fabrication in the statement may be relevant on the issue of reliability."[483]

5–203   She stressed, however, the need to proceed with caution and stated that the admission of such evidence should be subject to such safeguards as the judge considers necessary and any considerations affecting its weight.

5–204   Keane J declined to express a concluded opinion as to whether the law as stated in *Khan* should be adopted in this jurisdiction. Instead, he decided the case on the ground that the President had failed to establish whether the circumstances in which the statement was allegedly made by SK were such as to justify the reception of hearsay evidence of that statement. On the basis of *Khan*, the correct procedure would be that the trial judge should consider, first, whether the child is competent to give evidence. If that condition is satisfied, then it would be necessary to consider whether the trauma that the child would suffer would make it undesirable that he or she should give evidence. In this case, the trial judge had merely addressed the issue of trauma and had not made an inquiry into the preliminary condition of whether SK was competent to give evidence. In addition, the trial judge had failed to consider the reliability of the statements prior to admission in accordance with the criteria set out in *Khan*.

5–205   Denham J adopted quite a similar approach. She acknowledged that the hearsay rule had been developed "to protect fair trial process"[484] but took the view that it continued to evolve and that there was no reason why such evolution could not take place in the wardship jurisdiction. She opined that the creation of an exception to the hearsay rule in wardship proceedings was justified by the unique nature of wardship proceedings which are centred on the welfare of the child and place the court in an

---

[480] [1999] 2 IR 99 at 125.
[481] [1990] 1 FLR 203.
[482] [1990] 2 SCR 531.
[483] [1990] 2 SCR 531 at 546–567.
[484] [1999] 2 IR 99 at 108.

inquisitorial role in determining what, in all the circumstances, is in the best interests of the child. Thus, it was "entirely consistent that a judge exercising the wardship jurisdiction has a discretion as to the use of hearsay evidence and may admit hearsay evidence in certain circumstances".[485] However, she went on to emphasise that the wardship jurisdiction had to be exercised in a manner consistent with the constitutional rights of all the parties involved:

> "Wardship proceedings must be fair and in accordance with constitutional justice. The constitutional rights of all parties, the children and the parents, must be protected. Where rights are in conflict they must be balanced appropriately. Due process must be observed by the court while exercising this unique jurisdiction. Consequently, if a legal right or a constitutional right is to be limited or taken away by a court this must be done with fair procedures."[486]

5–206   She pointed out that there are special concerns which must be addressed in relation to children's evidence and, in cases of alleged child sexual abuse, especially where the allegations are against a person in close relationship to the child, there are often added difficulties. In the circumstances of the particular case, she was not satisfied that the admission of hearsay evidence had been in accordance with the requirements of fair procedures because of the failure of the trial judge to conduct an adequate preliminary inquiry as to whether SK could have given evidence.

(b) The Children Act 1997

5–207   As stated above, the reception of the hearsay evidence of children in any civil proceedings concerning the welfare of a child is now governed by the provisions of Part III of the Children Act 1997.[487] Section 23 now provides that:

> "(1) Subject to subsection (2), a statement made by a child shall be admissible as evidence of any fact therein of which direct oral evidence would be admissible in any proceeding to which this Part applies, notwithstanding any rule of law relating to hearsay, where the court considers that—
>   (a) the child is unable to give evidence by reason of age, or
>   (b) the giving of oral evidence by the child, either in person or under section 21, would not be in the interest of the welfare of the child.
>   (2) (a) Any statement referred to in subsection (1) or any part thereof shall not be admitted in evidence if the court is of the opinion that, in the interests of justice, the statement or that part of the statement ought not to be so admitted.
>   (b) In considering whether the statement or any part of the statement ought to be admitted, the court shall have regard to all the circumstances, including any risk that the admission will result in unfairness to any of the parties to the proceedings."

5–208   It can be seen that the hearsay evidence is admissible in two situations. The first is where the child is not competent as a witness by reason of age. However, since a child can now give unsworn evidence in civil proceedings if he or she is capable of giving an intelligible account of events,[488] it would seem that it is only in exceptional circumstances that a hearsay statement should be admitted under this head because it will necessarily be the statement of a child who is incapable of giving an intelligible account of events. In those circumstances, there is considerable force in the question

---

[485] [1999] 2 IR 99 at 110.
[486] [1999] 2 IR 99 at 111.
[487] See McMahon, "Can Anybody Hear Me? The Duty to Promote the Voice, Wishes and Interests of Children" (2014) IJFL 4.
[488] Section 28 of the Children Act 1997.

posed by Dodd J in *R. v Burke*:[489] "How can the secondhand version of her evidence
be good if her own testimony be deemed unfit for credence?"[490] The second scenario
provided for in the section is where the giving of oral evidence by a child, either in
person or by means of a television link, would not be in the best interests of the child.
Again, it would seem that the admission of hearsay evidence under this exception
should be rare because it is only applicable where a child will suffer trauma even if
the option of giving evidence via live television link is utilised.

5–209   In order to prevent surprise, s.23(3) introduces a notice obligation. A party
proposing to introduce hearsay evidence under the section is obliged to give such notice
and particulars as is reasonable and practicable in the circumstances for the purpose
of enabling the other parties to deal with any matter arising from its being hearsay. It
is noteworthy that the notice obligation is drafted in broad terms couched in terms of
reasonableness. It thus eschews the strict and complicated notice requirements for the
admission of business records in s.7 of the Criminal Evidence Act 1992. This means
that, even though it is a mandatory requirement, the flexibility of the obligation is such
that, in practice, a trial judge will enjoy considerable discretion to decide whether
adequate notice has been given. In some circumstances, he or she might decide that it
was not reasonable or practicable to give any notice, *e.g.* if such evidence is introduced
at an *ex parte* or interlocutory hearing. It should also be noted that the parties can, by
agreement, decide to disregard the notice requirement.[491]

5–210   With concession of the principle of the admissibility of hearsay statements,
the main question becomes one of the weight to be attributed to such statements. This
is a difficult question and guidance is provided by s.24:[492]

> "(1) In estimating the weight, if any, to be attached to any statement admitted in evidence
>   pursuant to section 23, regard shall be had to all the circumstances from which any
>   inference can reasonably be drawn as to its accuracy or otherwise.
> (2) Regard may be had, in particular, as to whether[493]—
>   (a) the original statement was made contemporaneously with the occurrence or
>   existence of the matters stated,[494]
>   (b) the evidence involves multiple hearsay,

---

[489] (1912) 47 ILTR 111 at 112.

[490] It is worth noting that the Law Reform Commission, *Report on the Rule Against Hearsay in Civil
Cases* (LRC 25–1990), p.22, recommended that an out-of-court statement of a child who is not
competent to give evidence should not be admissible.

[491] Section 23(4).

[492] The drafting of this section owes a fairly obvious debt to s.4 of the English Civil Evidence
Act 1995 and, for a discussion of this provision, see Keane & McKoewn, *The Modern Law of
Evidence* 10th edn (OUP, 2014), pp.352–353, and Salako, "The Civil Evidence Rule and The Civil
Evidence Act 1995: Where Are We Now" (2000) CJQ 371 at 375–376. It might be noted that the
importance of s.4 was emphasised in *R. (McCann) v Crown Court at Manchester* [2003] 1 AC
787 at 835, where it formed the basis of Lord Hutton's decision that the 1995 Act is compatible
with the European Convention on Human Rights. He held that there was no unfairness in the
admission of hearsay under the Act due to the safeguards provided for in s.4.

[493] In interpreting s.4 of the Civil Evidence Act 1995, the English courts have held that the onus is
on the party tendering the evidence to provide evidence from which an inference may be drawn
that the evidence is reliable: *Mulloy v Chief Constable of Humberside Police* [2002] EWCA Civ
1851.

[494] The English courts have emphasised the importance of this requirement, as well as its capacity
to overcome other problems with reliability (see *Rowland v Boyle* [2003] STC 855).

(c) any person involved has any motive to conceal or misrepresent matters,[495]
(d) the original statement was an edited account or was made in collaboration with another for a particular purpose, and
(e) the circumstances in which the evidence is adduced as hearsay are such as to suggest an attempt to prevent proper evaluation of its weight."

5–211   As to the factors specified in subs.(2), factors (a) and (b) have an obvious bearing on the reliability of any hearsay statement. With regard to factor (c), the phrase "any person involved" is broad enough to encompass not just the child declarant but the person hearing/reading/seeing the statement and where multiple hearsay is involved, the person giving evidence of the statement and any intermediaries. This factor is likely to prove particularly important in situations where there is some form of custody dispute involving the child and it is contended that allegations of child sexual abuse are being fabricated at the instigation of one of the parties seeking custody. Indeed, the phrase is wide enough such that it would seem to cover any person who may have prompted the child to make the statement. In addition, the purpose for which a statement was made will, as acknowledged by factor (e), have an important bearing on its reliability. Where a statement was made at a point before the proceedings in which it was sought to admit it had commenced or were contemplated, then this reduces the risk that it is being made at the suggestion of a third person for a motive connected with the proceedings.

5–212   Apart from the specific factors identified in subs.(2), it can be seen that subs.(1) contains a catch-all provision that the court should have regard to "all the circumstances from which any inference can reasonably be drawn as to its accuracy or otherwise". In that regard, it should be noted that in *Eastern Health Board v MK*, Denham J lists a number of factors which will go to this question, including the child's age, intelligence, comprehension of the circumstances of the case, skill in communication, and coherence.[496] She also stressed that the circumstances in which the hearsay evidence is obtained will be relevant as will its content and its consistency, both internally and with the other relevant evidence in the case.

5–213   Finally, it should be noted that s.25 (which is drafted in virtually identical terms to s.9 of the 1992 Act) makes provision for the admission of evidence as to the credibility of the hearsay declarant. The purpose of the section is to place the child whose hearsay statement is admitted in the same position, for the purpose of impeaching credibility, as if he or she had been called as a witness.

Hague Convention Cases

5–214   Article 13 of the Hague Convention on the Civil Aspects of International Child Abduction, which is implemented in this jurisdiction by the Child Abduction and Enforcement of Custody Orders Act 1991, requires the judicial and administrative authorities dealing with abduction and custody matters to take into account the information relating to the social background of the child provided by the Central Authority or other competent authority of the state of the child's habitual residence. This article was relied on by White J in *RP v SD*[497] to overrule a hearsay objection and admit in evidence a report compiled by social services in England as to the ability of the

---

[495] For example, if the witness in question has "an axe to grind" as regards the accused: *Brownville Holdings Ltd v Adamjee Insurance Co. Ltd.* [2000] 2 Lloyd's Rep 458.
[496] [1999] 2 IR 99 at 114, [1999] 2 ILRM 321 at 336.
[497] [2012] IEHC 579 at 6.

respondent to care for the child in question as he regarded the report to be information provided by the English Central Authority.

8. Dying Declarations

5–215   A statement of a deceased person in relation to the cause of his or her death is admissible as evidence of the truth of its contents at a trial for the homicide of the deceased provided that he or she was under a settled hopeless expectation of death at the time he or she made it.

5–216   The rationale underpinning this exception was outlined by Eyre CB in *R. v Woodcock*[498] who explained that:

> "The principle on which this species of evidence is admitted is, that they are declarations made in extremity, when the party is at the point of death, and when every hope of this world is gone; when every motive to falsehood is silenced, and the mind is induced by the most powerful considerations to speak the truth; a situation so solemn and so awful is considered by law as creating an obligation equal to that which is imposed by a positive oath administered in a court of justice."[499]

5–217   In *Nembhard v R.*[500] it was stated that there was a further consideration which was "that it is important in the interests of justice that a person implicated in a killing should be obliged to meet in court the dying accusation of the victim". Implicit in this statement is a justification of necessity, which is that dying declarations are often the best available evidence and, if they were not admitted, offenders would escape punishment.

5–218   The exception has, however, been subjected to criticism.[501] Although the expectation of death might be equated to the sanction of an oath, it is not a guarantee of truthfulness and there are a variety of reasons why a person, even on his or her deathbed, might wish to level a false accusation. Furthermore, there is no opportunity to cross-examine the declarant and the circumstances under which such declarations are made when the declarant is mortally ill with weakened faculties serve to increase a number of the other hearsay dangers including ambiguity, misperception and mistake. In *R. v Stephenson*,[502] the Northern Ireland Court of Criminal Appeal highlighted some of the dangers attendant upon the admission of dying declarations:

> "Like evidence given in the witness box, they may be lacking in veracity or they may be lacking in accuracy. Indeed in most cases they deserve even closer scrutiny, inasmuch as the jury have no opportunity of seeing and hearing the declarant and forming their own judgment as to the declarant's reliability and, moreover, as it can seldom happen, in the nature of things, that the accused will have been present or have had any opportunity for cross-examination. Again

---

[498] (1789) 1 Leach 500.

[499] (1789) 1 Leach 500 at 502. See also, *per* Lush LJ in *R. v Osman* (1881) 15 Cox CC 1 at 3 (no one "who is immediately going into the presence of his Maker, will do so with a lie on his lip"); *per* MacDermott LJ in *R. v Stephenson* [1947] NI 110 at 121 ("Made in the settled hopeless expectation of impending death, the solemnity of the occasion is regarded at law as imposing a sanction equivalent to that of an oath.") and *per* Sir Owen Woodhouse in *Nembhard v R.* [1982] 1 All ER 183 at 185 ("any sanction of the oath in the case of a living witness is thought to be balanced at least by the final conscience of the dying man. Nobody, it is has been said, would wish to die with a lie on his lips. So it is considered quite unlikely that a deliberate untruth would be told, let alone a false accusation of homicide, by a man who believed that he was face to face with his own impending death.").

[500] [1982] 1 All ER 183 at 185.

[501] See Munday, "Musings on the Dying Declaration" (1993) 22 Anglo-Am L Rev 42.

[502] [1947] NI 110.

speaking generally, it is this lack of opportunity to test and amplify the declaration which, more than anything else, makes it desirable to weigh and ponder the evidence contained in such a declaration with special care and attention. For one of the dangers in admitting such declarations is the danger that omissions, failure to tell the whole story, or misrepresentations, even quite unintentional, or mere turns of phrase, may have the effect of giving a colour which could have been corrected by cross-examination."[503]

5–219   This passage indicates the need for caution where dying declarations are admitted. Although there is no requirement that a dying declaration be corroborated or that the jury be given a corroboration warning in respect of it,[504] a trial judge, in discharge of the general duty to give such directions as may be necessary to avoid the danger of miscarriage of justice,[505] should give the jury a cautionary instruction, tailored to the facts of the particular case, pointing out the dangers of unreliability associated with a dying declaration and the lack of an opportunity to cross-examine the declarant.[506]

5–220   In order to be admitted, the party tendering a dying declaration in evidence must satisfy the following conditions of admissibility: (a) the trial must be for the homicide of the declarant; (b) the statement must relate to the cause of death of the declarant; and (c) the declarant must have been under a settled hopeless expectation of death at the time that he or she made the statement. In the South Australian decision of *R. v Buzzacott*,[507] it was held that, as an exception to the hearsay rule, strict proof of the preconditions of admissibility is required. However, in *Mills v R.*,[508] Lord Steyn, delivering the judgment of the Privy Council, indicated a willingness to re-examine the conditions governing the admissibility of dying declarations so as to concentrate on the probative value of such declarations in a manner analogous to that of the reformulation which has occurred with respect to the branch of res gestae*res gestae* dealing with spontaneous statements.

5–221   Before examining the conditions of admissibility in detail, some preliminary points should be noted. Firstly, although dying declarations are most commonly tendered in evidence by the prosecution, they may also be adduced by the accused.[509] Secondly, a dying declaration is not rendered inadmissible because it was made in response to questions—this is a matter which goes to the weight to be attached to it.[510] Finally, although there is some authority suggesting that the statement of a declarant

---

[503] [1947] NI 110 at 122 (*per* MacDermott J). See also, *per* Byles LJ in *R. v Jenkins* (1869) 11 Cox CC 250 at 257: "We should guard with jealousy the admissibility of such declarations, the admissibility of which is an exception to the ordinary rules of evidence; for they may be made without the sanction of an oath, and when the party is in no fear or danger of the penalties of perjury, and when the persons making them are very liable to the influences of misrepresentation or error."

[504] *Nembhard v R.* [1982] 1 All ER 183. However, it appears that a corroboration warning may be required where the deceased declarant is an accomplice for the purpose of the accomplice corroboration warning (*cf.R. v Stephenson* [1947] NI 110 at 118–120).

[505] See *People (AG) v Casey (No.2)* [1963] IR 33 at 37–38 and, generally, Chap.4, section G.

[506] *Cf. R. v Stephenson* [1947] NI 110 at 122–123 and *Nembard v R.* [1982] 1 All ER 183 at 185–186.

[507] [2012] SASC 234 at [6].

[508] [1995] 3 All ER 865 at 875–876, [1995] 1 WLR 511 at 521–522.

[509] See, *e.g.* *R. v Scaife* (1836) 2 Lew CC 150 where the following statement of the declaration of the deceased was admitted in favour of the accused: "He would not have struck me but that I provoked him to it".

[510] *R. v Fitzpatrick* (1910) 46 ILTR 173 at 174–175; *R. v Stephenson* [1947] NI 110 at 116; *R. v Smith* (1865) Le & CA 606; *R. v Bottomley* (1903) 115 LT Jo 88. See, *contra, R. v Mitchell* (1892) 17 Cox CC 503. It would appear that one of the principal factors to be taken into account in assessing

should not be admitted if he or she does not have belief in,[511] or sufficient appreciation of,[512] the spiritual consequences of dying with a lie on one's lips, this, again, appears to be a matter that should go to weight only.

(a) Trial for the homicide of the declarant

5–222   It is well settled that a dying declaration is only admissible at a trial of a person for the homicide of the deceased declarant.[513] Thus, it is inadmissible in proceedings for a charge of using an instrument with intent to procure a miscarriage,[514] perjury,[515] robbery,[516] rape,[517] and, *a fortiori*, a quasi-criminal matter.[518] This limitation on the use of dying declarations makes little sense having regard to the rationale underpinning the exception which would seem to apply to any statement made by a declarant who believes that he or she is going to die[519] and it is noteworthy that the exception has been broadened in the United States to encompass civil actions.[520]

(b) Cause of death

5–223   In *R. v Mead*,[521] Abbott CJ said that a dying declaration "is only admissible where the death of the deceased is the subject of the charge, and the circumstances of the death are the subject of the dying declaration.[522]

(c) Settled hopeless expectation of death

5–224   The requirement that the declarant be conscious that he or she was dying at the time he or she made the statement sought to be admitted[523] is closely linked to the rationale for the exception because truthfulness can only be assured in circumstances

---

the weight to be attached to a dying declaration obtained in response to questioning is whether the questions were leading in nature.

[511] See *R. v Madobi-Madogai* [1963] P&NGLR 252 at 253 (dying declaration excluded because the local people believed that after death they moved to live on a neighbouring island).

[512] See *R. v Pike* (1829) 3 Car & P 598, where it was held that the dying declaration of a four-year-old child could not be admitted because, *per* Parke B, "a child of such tender years could not have had that idea of a future state which is necessary to make such a declaration admissible".

[513] *Smith v Cavan County Council* (1924) 58 ILTR 107 at 108; *R. v Mead* (1824) 2 B & C 605 at 608; *R. v Hind* (1860) 8 Cox CC 300 at 301. In Canada, it has been held to be applicable on a charge of criminal negligence causing death: *R. v Jurtyn* [1958] OWN 355, (1958) 121 CCC 403.

[514] *R. v Hind* (1860) 8 Cox CC 300.

[515] *R. v Mead* (1824) 2 B & C 605.

[516] *R. v Lloyd* (1830) 4 C & P 233.

[517] *R. v Newton* (1859) 1 F & F 641.

[518] *Smith v Cavan County Council* (1924) 58 ILTR 107 at 108.

[519] The Law Reform Commission was critical of this limitation in its *Consultation Paper on Hearsay in Civil and Criminal Cases* (LRC CP 60–2010) at [3.05]. See also Broun (ed.), *McCormick on Evidence* 7th edn (Thomson Reuters, 2013), Vol. II, § 311, p.515.

[520] Rule 804(b) of the Federal Rules of Evidence makes dying declarations concerning the cause or circumstances of the declarant's impending death admissible in a civil action or proceeding as well as in a prosecution for homicide.

[521] (1824) 2 B & C 605.

[522] (1824) 2 B & C 605 at 608. This passage was approved in *R. v Hind* (1860) 8 Cox CC 300 at 301–302.

[523] *Cf. R. v Smith* (1865) 10 Cox CC 82 (declaration made by deceased and taken down in writing while she was ill and then read over to her at a point when she knew that she was dying was held to be admissible).

where "the deceased herself apprehended that she was in such a state of mortality as would inevitably oblige her soon to answer before her Maker for the truth or falsehood of her assertions".[524] There is Irish authority to the effect that the declarant must have been under a settled expectation of *immediate* death[525] but the English Court of Criminal Appeal has rejected this suggestion[526] and it appears to be an unduly restrictive approach to take.

5–225 The formula "settled hopeless expectation of death" appears to have been first used by Willes J in *R. v Peel*[527] and has now passed into common currency.[528] It serves to emphasise that, in order for a declaration to be admissible, the deceased must be aware that he or she is dying and must not entertain any hope of recovery.[529] In deciding whether the deceased was under a "settled hopeless expectation of death", a trial judge will have regard, in particular, to the contents of any statements made by the declarant as to his or her condition and expectations of recovery.[530] For example, in *R. v Jenkins*,[531] the deceased had amended a deposition taken from her which included the words "with no hope of my recovery" so as to read "with no hope at present of my recovery". Kelly CB stated that "the declaration of a dying person in order to be admissible in evidence must be made under a belief, and a belief without hope, that the declarant is about to die".[532] In the instant case, the suggestion that the deceased entertained some small hope of recovery rendered the statement inadmissible.[533]

5–226 It is not sufficient that the declarant was dying at the time that the declaration was made or even, it would appear, that he or she was told that that he or she was dying—what is required to be established is that the declarant accepted and believed that he or she was dying. As Pigot CB stated in *R. v Mooney*,[534] "[i]t must be proved, to the satisfaction of the court, that [the declarant] was dying, and that she was aware of the fact". In that case, the accused had been charged with the manslaughter of his wife and the prosecution sought to admit certain declarations made by her before her death. She had been told by her doctor that she was dangerously ill and by a clergyman to prepare for death and had been heard recommending her soul to God. However, she had not told anyone that she knew she was dying and, in the circumstances, the declarations were held to be inadmissible.[535]

---

[524] *Per* Eyre CB in *R. v Woodcock* (1789) 1 Leach 500 at 503.

[525] *R. v Cunnane* (1903) 4 NIJR 49. See also *R. v Osman* (1881) 15 Cox CC 1.

[526] *R. v Perry* [1909] 2 KB 697 at 702; *R. v Austin* (1912) 8 Cr App R 27 at 28–29.

[527] (1860) 2 F & F 21 at 22.

[528] It was approved by the Court of Criminal Appeal in *R. v Perry* [1909] 2 KB 697 at 702–703.

[529] See *R. v Gloster* (1888) 16 Cox CC 471 at 476 (*per* Charles J) ("there must be an unqualified belief in the nearness of death; there must be a belief without hope in the declarant that he is about to die"); *R. v Perry* [1902] 2 KB 697 at 703 (held that test was "whether all hope of life has been abandoned so that the person making the statement thinks that death must follow"); *R. v Austin* (1912) 8 Cr App R 27 at 28–29 (Court of Criminal Appeal approved as perfectly accurate the following statement by Avory J of the law: "The principle is this, to make such a statement admissible it must appear that it was made under the influence of a settled—that means one not wavering—hopeless—which means where hope is abandoned—expectation of death.")

[530] In *State v Harper* (2009) 770 NW 2d 316, the statement by the dying declarant who had suffered severe burns, "I think I am going to die", was sufficient to indicate a settled expectation of death.

[531] (1869) 11 Cox CC 250.

[532] (1869) 11 Cox CC 250 at 256.

[533] See also *R. v Gloster* (1888) 16 Cox CC 471 (declaration held not to be admissible because it appeared from various statements made by her that the declarant had not entirely given up hope).

[534] (1851) 5 Cox CC 318.

[535] See also *R. v Mitchell* (1892) 17 Cox CC 503 (there was not sufficient proof that deceased had

5–227   However, such an exacting approach does not seem to have been taken in other cases. For example, in *R. v Woodcock*,[536] a statement was admitted in circumstances where the deceased had not expressed any view as to whether she thought she was dying or recovering, Eyre CB taking the view that "she must have felt the hand of death, and must have considered herself to be a dying woman".[537] Again, in *R. v Spilsbury*,[538] it was held that, apart from any statements made by the declarant as to his expectations of recovery, the court should consider whether the conduct of the deceased was consistent with that of a person who thought he was dying. In that case, the court concluded that the accused must have had some hope of recovery, as he did not settle his affairs, give directions as to his funeral, or take leave of his friends and family.[539]

5–228   The requirement of a settled hopeless expectation of death falls to be assessed at the time the statement was made. Thus, it is immaterial that the deceased entertained hopes of recovery after the statement was made, provided that he or she had the requisite state of mind at the point when the statement was made.[540]

9. Testimony in Earlier Proceedings

(a) Admissibility at Common Law

5–229   At common law, a statement made by a person while giving evidence, whether orally or on affidavit, is admissible in subsequent proceedings between the same parties or their privies concerning the same subject matter if the witness is unavailable to give evidence. The application of this exception in civil cases is long established[541] and its application in criminal cases was confirmed in *R. v Hall*.[542]

5–230   This exception to the hearsay rule[543] is justified on the basis that the requirement of necessity is met by the unavailability of the witness and the circumstances in which the statement was made address the concerns underlying the hearsay rule. In particular, the statement is made under oath and the party against whom the statement is admitted has had an opportunity to cross-examine the witness. Although such reported evidence

---

settled hopeless expectation of death in circumstances where doctor had told her that there was little or no chance of her recovery) and *R. v Buzzacott* [2012] SASC 234 (the deceased made a number of statements implicating the accused shortly before he died but without indicating that he was aware of his impending death).

[536]   (1789) 1 Leach 500.
[537]   (1789) 1 Leach 500 at 504.
[538]   (1835) 7 Car & P 187 at 190.
[539]   *Cf. R. v Morgan* (1875) 14 Cox CC 337 (doubt expressed as to whether a dying declaration could be admitted solely on the basis of an inference drawn from the seriousness of the wound that the deceased must have known that he was dying) and *R. v Bedingfield* (1879) 14 Cox CC 341 at 343 (statement by woman whose throat had been cut and who died a few moments later not admissible because it did not appear that she was aware that she was dying).
[540]   *R. v Hubbard* (1881) 14 Cox CC 565 at 566; *R. v Austin* (1912) 8 Cr App R 27 at 29.
[541]   *Mayor of Doncaster v Day* (1810) 3 Taunt 262; *Wright v Tatham* (1834) 1 Ad & E 3 at 18–19; *Morgan v Nicholl* (1866–67) LR 2 CP 117; *Llanover v Homfray* (1881) 19 Ch D 224; *Walkertown (Town) v Erdman* [1894] 23 SCR 352.
[542]   [1973] 1 QB 496, [1973] 1 All ER 1. See also *R. v Radbourne* (1787) 1 Leach 457; *R. v Smith* (1817) Russ & Ry 339; *R. v Beeston* (1854) Dears CC 405; *R. v Lee* (1864) 4 F & F 63 and *R. v Edmunds* (1909) 2 Cr App R 257.
[543]   But see Wigmore, *Evidence*, Vol. V, §1370, p.50, who took the view that testimony in former proceedings was not subject to the hearsay rule at all because the hearsay rule was designed to exclude statements that were not made under oath or subject to cross-examination.

is not as satisfactory as if given in the proceedings because the tribunal of fact will not be in a position to observe the demeanour of the witness while giving evidence and, particularly, under cross-examination, the testimony in the former proceedings is reliable enough to warrant admission.

5–231 There are a number of conditions that must be met before testimony in former proceedings will be admitted: (i) the witness is unavailable; (ii) the previous proceedings were between the same parties or their privies; (iii) the issues are substantially the same in both proceedings; and (iv) the party against whom it is sought to admit the testimony had an adequate opportunity to cross-examine the witness in the earlier proceedings.

(i) Unavailability of witness

5–232 The requirement of unavailability will undoubtedly be satisfied where the witness is dead[544] but also, it would appear, where he or she is too ill to attend court,[545] has been prevented from attending by the party against whom the evidence is to be admitted,[546] is out of the jurisdiction[547] or cannot be located following extensive inquiries.[548]Although this exception was not expressly considered by the Supreme Court in *Borges v Medical Council*,[549] it appears from that decision that the requirement of unavailability will not be satisfied where a witness is simply unwilling to testify.

(ii) Same parties

5–233 In order to ensure that a party is not unfairly bound by cross-examination conducted by an unrelated party, testimony by a witness in earlier proceedings is only admissible if the subsequent proceedings are between the same parties or their privies.[550] Thus, in *Morgan v Nicholl*,[551] evidence given in earlier proceedings was excluded even though the party in the second proceedings was the father of a party in previous proceedings about the same premises because there was no privity of estate between them.

(iii) Same subject-matter

5–234 In order for the exception to apply, the issues raised in both sets of proceedings must have been substantially the same.[552] An example of a case where this requirement was met is *Walkertown (Town) v Erdman*[553] where proceedings had been brought by the widow claiming damages arising from the death of her husband allegedly caused

---

[544] *Mayor of Doncaster v Day* (1810) 3 Taunt 262; *Wright v Tatham* 1834) 1 Ad & E 3 at 18; *Morgan v Nicholl* (1866–67) LR 2 CP 117; *Llanover v Homfray* (1881) 19 Ch D 224; *R. v Hall* [1973] 1 QB 496, [1973] 1 All ER 1.

[545] *R. v Thompson* [1982] 1 QB 647, [1982] 1 All ER 907.

[546] *R. v Scaife* (1851) 2 Den 281.

[547] *Sutor v McLean* (1859) 18 UCQB 490.

[548] *Fleming v Canadian Pacific Railway Co.* (1905) 5 OWR 589.

[549] [2004] IESC 9, [2004] 1 IR 103, [2004] 2 ILRM 81.

[550] *Morgan v Nicholl* (1866–67) LR 2 CP 117; *Llanover v Homfray* (1881) 19 Ch D 224; *Insco Sarnia Ltd v Polysar Ltd* (1990) 45 CPC (2d) 53.

[551] (1866–67) LR 2 CP 117.

[552] *Wright v Tatham* (1834) 1 Ad & E 3 at 18; *Llanover v Homfray* (1881) 19 Ch D 224 at 229; *Walkertown (Town) v Erdman* (1894) 23 SCR 352.

[553] (1894) 23 SCR 352.

by the negligence of the defendant town. Prior to his death, her husband had instituted proceedings in his own name against the town claiming damages for negligence. It was held that evidence given by him in the course of those proceedings was admissible in the proceedings taken by his wife because the material issues were substantially the same in both sets of proceedings.

(iv) Opportunity to cross-examine

5–235 As noted above, the hearsay rule in this jurisdiction is based primarily on considerations of fair procedures and, in particular, the constitutionally protected right of cross-examination. Thus, testimony can only be tendered under this exception where the party against whom it is sought to adduce it had an adequate opportunity to cross-examine the witness in the previous proceedings.[554] This condition was also found to be fulfilled in *Walkertown (Town) v Erdman*[555] because the defendant had been afforded and availed of the right to cross-examine in the earlier proceedings.

(b) Statutory Provision

5–236 The common law exception in respect of the admission of testimony in earlier proceedings has been extended by s.4G of the Criminal Procedure Act 1967[556] to provide for the admission of depositions and videorecordings made during the pre-trial stage of proceedings. Subsection (2) provides that a deposition taken in accordance with the provisions of s.4F of the 1967 Act may be admitted in evidence at the trial of the accused if the following conditions are satisfied: (a) the witness is dead, is unable to attend to give evidence at the trial, is prevented from so attending, or does not give evidence at the trial through fear or intimidation; (b) the accused was present at the taking of the evidence; and (c) an opportunity was given to cross-examine and re-examine the witness; unless the court is of opinion that it would not be in the interests of justice to admit the deposition. In the case of a videorecording of evidence given through live television link, this is admissible at the trial of the offence with which the accused is charged as evidence of any fact stated therein of which direct oral evidence by the witness would be admissible provided that the accused was present at the taking of the evidence and an opportunity was given to cross-examine and re-examine the witness unless the court is of the opinion that in the interests of justice the videorecording ought not to be admitted.[557]

10. Prior Statements of Witness

5–237 At common law, it is well established that, where admitted, the previous statements of a witness, whether consistent or inconsistent, go to credibility only and are inadmissible as evidence of the truth of their contents.[558] Indeed, the trial judge is

---

[554] *Llanover v Homfray* (1881) 19 Ch D 224 at 229–230; *R. v Hall* [1973] 1 QB 496 at 504, [1973] 1 All ER 1 at 7; *Walkertown (Town) v Erdman* (1894) 23 SCR 352; *Insco Sarnia Ltd v Polysar Ltd* (1990) 45 CPC (2d) 53.

[555] (1894) 23 SCR 352.

[556] As inserted by s.9 of the Criminal Justice Act 1999.

[557] Section 4G(3). The provisions of this subsection are stated to be subject to those of s.16 of the Criminal Evidence Act 1992 dealing with the admissibility at trial of a videorecording of evidence given by a witness under 17.

[558] *People (AG) v Taylor* [1974] IR 97; *People (AG) v Cradden* [1955] IR 130; *People (AG) v Flynn*

under an obligation to instruct the jury of the limited purpose for which the statement has been admitted.[559]

5–238 This traditional rule can be seen to be an application of the hearsay rule.[560] However, the classification and the exclusion of the previous statements of a witness as hearsay has been criticised on the basis that problems of unreliability flowing from the absence of the safeguards of an oath, an opportunity on the part of the tribunal of fact to observe the demeanour of the declarant when the statement was made, and an opportunity for cross-examination by the party adversely affected by it, are much lessened in the case of previous statements.

5–239 With regard to the absence of an oath, it has been argued that this can no longer be regarded as a safeguard of the trustworthiness of testimony[561] and the witness is, in any event, under oath when the prior statement is put to him or her at trial. Further, as McCormick has pointed out, that there are numerous exceptions to the hearsay rule where evidence is admitted despite not being sworn.[562] Turning to the lack of an opportunity for the tribunal of fact to observe the demeanour of the declarant at the time the statement was made, this justification was dismissed by Learned Hand J in *Di Carlo v United States*[563] on the basis that:

> "The possibility that the jury may accept as the truth the earlier statements in preference to those made upon the stand is indeed real, but we find no difficulty in it. If, from all that the jury see of the witness, they conclude that what he says now is not the truth, but what he said before, they are none the less deciding from what they see and hear of that person and in court."

5–240 Furthermore, in some cases at least, the prior statement which it is sought to admit will have been videorecorded so that this difficulty does not arise.[564] Finally, with regard to the lack of an opportunity to cross-examine the declarant, the witness is available to be cross-examined and, thus, the principal rationale for the hearsay rule does not exist.[565] As argued by McCormick,[566] in relation to prior inconsistent statements:

> "The witness who has told one story earlier and another at trial has invited a searching examination of credibility through cross-examination and re-examination. The reasons for the change, whether forgetfulness, carelessness, pity, terror, or greed, may be explored by the adversaries in the presence of the trier of fact, under oath, casting light on which is the true story and which the false."

5–241 It has been argued that cross-examination after the fact is not sufficient and

---

[1963] IR 255.

[559] *People (AG) v Taylor* [1974] IR 97 at 100; *People (DPP) v McArdle* [2003] 4 IR 186 at 198.

[560] See Broun (ed.), *McCormick on Evidence* 7th edn (Thomson Reuters, 2013), Vol. II, § 251, at p.211; Delisle, *Evidence: Principles and Problems* (2nd edn, 1989), p.247; Schiff, "The Previous Inconsistent Statements of Opponent's Witness" (1986) 36 UTLJ 440 at 451; Stuesser, "Admitting Prior Inconsistent Statements for Their Truth" (1992) 71 Can Bar Rev 48 at 53.

[561] Morgan, "Hearsay Dangers and the Application of the Hearsay Concept" (1948) 62 Harv L Rev 177; Stuesser, "Admitting Prior Inconsistent Statements for Their Truth" (1992) 71 Can Bar Rev 48 at 53–54.

[562] Broun (ed.), *McCormick on Evidence* 7th edn (Thomson Reuters, 2013), Vol. II, § 251, at p.211.

[563] (1925) 6 F 2d 364.

[564] *R. v B(KG)* [1993] 1 SCR 740 at 766.

[565] See Wigmore, *Evidence* (Chadbourn rev. 1970), Vol. 3A, §1018, p.996: "But the theory of the hearsay rule is that an extrajudicial statement is rejected because it was made out of court by an absent person not subject to cross-examination…Here, however, by hypothesis the witness is present and subject to cross-examination. There is ample opportunity to test him as to the basis for his former statement. The whole purpose of the hearsay rule has been already satisfied."

[566] Broun (ed.), *McCormick on Evidence* 7th edn (Thomson Reuters, 2013), Vol. II, § 251, p.214.

what is required is contemporaneous cross-examination.[567] However, as pointed out by White J in *California v Green*:

> "It may be true that a jury would be in a better position to evaluate the truth of the prior statement if it could somehow be whisked magically back in time to witness a gruelling cross-examination of the declarant as he first gives his statement. But the question as we see it must be not whether one can somehow imagine the jury in 'a better position', but whether subsequent cross-examination at the defendant's trial will still afford the trier of fact a satisfactory basis for evaluating the truth of the prior statement."[568]

5–242 As a result of these criticisms, there has been a general trend in common law jurisdictions to move away from the traditional rule excluding prior inconsistent statements (and to a lesser extent prior consistent statements) as evidence of their contents.[569] The abrogation of the rule has been taken furthest in the United States under Rule 801(d)(1) of the Federal Rules of Evidence[570] and while other jurisdictions have not gone so far, an exception in respect of prior inconsistent statements has been created in Australia[571] and Canada[572] and, having been canvassed judicially, has been created by statute in this jurisdiction. It is proposed to examine these judicial developments first and then to outline legislative intervention in this area.

(a) Admission of prior inconsistent statements at common law

5–243 In the leading Canadian decision of *R. v B(KG)*,[573] the accused and three of his friends had been involved in a fight with two men in the course of which one of the men was stabbed and killed. The accused's friends were subsequently interviewed and made statements to the effect that the accused had told them he thought that he had been responsible for the death of the deceased by using a knife. These statements were videotaped. The accused was charged with second degree murder but, at the trial, his friends recanted their statements and stated that they had lied to the police to exculpate themselves from possible involvement. Although the trial judge had no doubt but that the recantations were false, he held that their prior inconsistent statements could only

---

[567] See *State v Saporen* (1939) 205 Minn 358 at 362, 285 NW 898 at 901, where Stone J, delivering the opinion of a majority of the Supreme Court of Minnesota, stated: "The chief merit of cross-examination is not that at some future time it gives the party opponent the right to dissect adverse testimony. Its principal virtue is the immediate application of the testing process. Its strokes fall while the iron is hot. False testimony is apt to harden and become unyielding to the blows of truth in proportion as the witness has opportunity for reconsideration and influence by the suggestions of others..."

[568] (1970) 399 US 149 at 160–161.

[569] See Foley, "Hearsay and Recent Complaint" (2001) 15 ILT 234, for a discussion of this trend in the context of evidence of recent complaint by sexual complainants and, further, Gorman, "Hearsay in Sexual Offence Prosecutions" [1997] 39 CLQ 493.

[570] Rule 801(d)(1) provides that a prior statement of a witness is not hearsay if: "The declarant testifies at the trial or hearing and is subject to cross-examination concerning the statement, and the statement (A) is inconsistent with the declarant's testimony and was given under penalty of perjury at a trial, hearing, or other proceeding, or in a deposition, (B) is consistent with the declarant's testimony and is offered to rebut an express or implied charge that the declarant recently fabricated it or acted from a recent improper influence or motive in so testifying, or (C) identifies a person as someone the declarant perceived earlier."

[571] *Driscoll v R.* (1977) 137 CLR 517.

[572] *R. v B(KG)* [1993] 1 SCR 740.

[573] [1993] 1 SCR 740. See Bryant, Lederman and Fuerst, *Sopinke, Lederman & Bryant: The Law of Evidence in Canada* 4th edn (Lexis Nexis, 2014), §6.119. See also *R. v Khelawon* (2006) 2 SCR 787, (2006) SCJ No.57.

be used to impeach the credibility of these witnesses and not as evidence of these admissions. In the absence of any other sufficient evidence, he acquitted the accused.

5–244 On appeal, the Supreme Court decided that the time had come for the orthodox rule limiting the use of prior inconsistent statements to impeaching the credibility of witnesses to be replaced by a new rule recognising the changed means and methods of proof in modern society. However, it was emphasised that a reformed rule had to carefully balance the accused's interests in a criminal trial with the interests of society in seeing justice done. Since the orthodox rule was an incarnation of the hearsay rule, the reformed rule had to deal with the "hearsay dangers" of admitting prior inconsistent statements as evidence of the truth of their contents, namely, the absence of an oath or solemn affirmation when the statement was made, the inability of the trier of fact to assess the demeanour and, therefore, the credibility of the declarant when the statement was made, and the lack of contemporaneous cross-examination by the opponent. It was, therefore, necessary to adapt the criteria of necessity and reliability identified in *R. v Khan*[574] and *R. v Smith*[575] to the admission of prior inconsistent statements.

5–245 With regard to necessity, which was the primary criterion, the Court took the view that there would be a sufficient circumstantial guarantee of reliability to allow a jury to make substantive use of a statement: (1) if the statement was made under oath, solemn affirmation or solemn declaration following an explicit warning to the witness as to the existence of severe criminal sanctions for the making of a false statement; (2) if the statement is videotaped in its entirety; and (3) if the opposing party, whether the Crown or the defence, has a full opportunity to cross-examine the witness at trial respecting the statement. These criteria were not, however, regarded as exhaustive and it was held that such statements could be admissible in other instances provided that the judge was satisfied that the circumstances were such as to provide adequate assurances of reliability in place of those which the hearsay rule traditionally requires. Turning to necessity, a flexible approach was advocated and it was held that unavailability was not an indispensable condition of necessity.

5–246 The Court also laid down a threshold requirement that a prior inconsistent statement would only be admissible if a statement in the same terms would have been admissible if given by the witness in court, *i.e.* a prior inconsistent statement could not be used as a means to admit otherwise inadmissible evidence by the back door. Furthermore, the Court specified that, before a prior inconsistent statement could be used as evidence of the truth of its contents, its admissibility for this purpose would have to be decided by a trial judge following a *voir dire*.

5–247 In *People (DPP) v McArdle*,[576] an attempt to convince the Court of Criminal Appeal to follow the decision in *R. v B (KG)* and abandon the rule that prior inconsistent statements go to credibility only was unsuccessful. The accused had been convicted of manslaughter arising out of a fight that had taken place late at night. In the course of the trial, a number of witnesses were cross-examined on prior inconsistent statements made by them and it was contended that the trial judge should have directed the jury that, in the case of witnesses who had made prior inconsistent statements, they were entitled to treat those statements as evidence of the truth of their contents and not simply

---

[574] [1990] 2 SCR 531.
[575] [1992] 2 SCR 915, (1992) 94 DLR (4th) 590.
[576] [2003] 4 IR 186.

as going to the credibility of those witnesses in court. The relevance of these prior inconsistent statements was that they were more helpful to the accused in making out a defence of self-defence. It was accepted by counsel for the accused that the traditional rule was that stated in *Phipson on Evidence* as follows:

> "Any inconsistency between a witness's evidence and an earlier statement goes to credibility and the earlier statement cannot be treated as evidence of the truth of its contents."[577]

5–248 However, it was argued that this rule should be departed from given the widespread criticism of it and the decisions in other common law jurisdictions to the effect that a prior inconsistent statement could establish the truth of its contents.

5–249 Keane CJ, delivering the judgment of the Court of Criminal Appeal, considered the decision in *R. v B (KG)* and pointed out that one of the essential indicia of reliability identified by the Supreme Court of Canada in that case, namely that the statements had been videotaped, was not satisfied in the instant case. However, there was an even more fundamental difficulty in that there had been no application by the accused to have the prior inconsistent statements treated as evidence of their contents and no *voir dire* had been held to determine if the statements were sufficiently reliable to be used for this purpose. Indeed, he ventured the opinion that it was difficult to see how the reformed rule proposed in *R. v B (KG)* could work in this jurisdiction. Furthermore, the Court was satisfied that the failure to instruct the jury in the terms advocated did not make any material difference in the circumstances of the case. Having regard to the contents of the prior inconsistent statements, even if the jury had been instructed to treat them as evidence, they would still have been entitled to conclude beyond a reasonable doubt, on the entire evidence in the case that a defence of self-defence was not available to the accused.

5–250 As will be seen below, possible developments at common law in this area have been been overtaken by statutory intervention whereby provision is now made for the admission of prior statements in a wide range of circumstances.

(b) Section 16 of the Criminal Evidence Act 1992

5–251 Section 16 of the Criminal Evidence Act 1992[578] makes provision for the admission by way of an exception to the hearsay rule of videorecordings made in specified circumstances during pre-trial procedures.[579] Under subs.(1)(a), a video-recording of any evidence given by a person under 17 through a live television link in proceedings under Part IA of the Criminal Procedure Act 1967[580] in relation to certain offences of a sexual or violent nature,[581] is admissible at the trial of the offence as

---

[577] 15th edn (London: Sweet & Maxwell, 2000), para.11.31.

[578] As amended by s.20 of the Criminal Justice Act 1999 and s.4(b) of the Criminal Law (Human Trafficking) (Amendment) Act 2013.

[579] It should be noted that these provisions only apply in criminal proceedings, and do not impact on the admissibility of such evidence in civil proceedings: *Southern Health Board v C.H.* [1996] 1 IR 219 at 228. *Cf.* O'Doherty, "Recent Cases on Hearsay Evidence in Civil Child Sexual Abuse Proceedings" (1996) ILT 284.

[580] As inserted by s.9 of the Criminal Justice Act 1999.

[581] The offences to which Part III apply are defined in s.12 (as substituted by s.10 of the Criminal Law (Human Trafficking Act 2008) as being: (a) a sexual offence; (b) an offence involving violence or the threat of violence to a person; (c) an offence under s.3, 4, 5 or 6 of the Child Trafficking and Pornography Act 1998, (d) an offence under s.2, 4 or 7 of the Criminal Law (Human Trafficking) Act 2008, or (e) an offence consisting of attempting or conspiring to commit, or of aiding or

evidence of any fact stated therein of which direct oral evidence by the person would be admissible.[582] A similar exception is applicable in respect of a videorecording of any statement made during an interview with a member of An Garda Síochána or any other person who is competent for the purpose (i) by a person under 14 years of age (being a person in respect of whom such an offence is alleged to have been committed), or (ii) by a person under 18 years of age (being a person other than the accused) in relation to a specified offence.[583] during an interview with a member of the gardaí or any other person who is competent for the purpose but subject to the proviso that such person is available for cross-examination.[584]

5–252 Under s.16(2), the court is given a discretion to exclude a videorecording or any part thereof if it is of the opinion that, in the interests of justice, the videorecording concerned or that part should not be admitted. In considering whether the interests of justice require the videorecording or part thereof to be excluded, the court is mandated to have regard to all the circumstances including any risk that its admission will result in unfairness to the accused.[585] Subsection (3) goes on to provide that, in estimating the weight, if any, to be attached to any statement[586] contained in such a videorecording, a court is required to have regard to all the circumstances from which any inference can reasonably be drawn as to is accuracy or otherwise.

(c) Part 3 of the Criminal Justice Act 2006

5–253 A significant extension of the circumstances in which the prior statements of a witness may be admitted in evidence as evidence of the truth of their contents is provided for in Part 3 of the Criminal Justice Act 2006[587] which makes provision in s.16 for the admission in specified circumstances of a statement[588] made by a

---

abetting, counselling, procuring or inciting the commission of, an offence mentioned in paragraph (a), (b), (c) or (d). The concept of a "sexual offence" is further defined in s.2 of the 1992 Act (as amended by s.16 of the Criminal Justice (Miscellaneous Provisions) Act 1997 (No.4 of 1997), s.7(2) of the Criminal Law (Sexual Offences) Act 2006, s.4(1) of the Criminal Law (Sexual Offences) (Amendment) Act 2007 and s.12(a) of the Criminal Law (Human Trafficking) Act 2008).

[582] In *O'Sullivan v Hamill* [1999] 2 IR 9 at 15, O'Higgins J pointed out that direct oral evidence is only admissible if a person is competent to give evidence. As such, the requirement that a witness be capable of giving an intelligible account of event persists under the Act.

[583] The offences specified are those under s.3(1), (2) or (3) of the Child Trafficking and Pornography Act 1998 or s.2, 4 or 7 of the Criminal Law (Human Trafficking) Act 2008.

[584] Section 16(1)(b) (as substituted by s.4(b) of the Criminal Law (Human Trafficking) (Amendment) Act 2013). See Delahunt, "Video Evidence and s.16(1)(b) of the Criminal Evidence Act 1992" (2011) BR 2.

[585] Section 16(2)(b).

[586] The term "statement" is defined in subs.(4) to mean "any representation of fact, whether in words or otherwise".

[587] See Coonan, "Admitting "Statements" in Evidence Pursuant to Section 16 of the Criminal Justice Act 2006" (2007) 2 BR 53; Fitzgerald, "Reluctant Witnesses and Section 16 of the Criminal Justice Act 2006" (2008) 13(6) BR 126; Walsh, "The Criminal Justice Act 2006: A Crushing Defeat for Due Process Values?" (2007) 7 JSIJ 45.

[588] A statement is defined in s.15 of the 2006 Act as meaning a statement the making of which is duly proved and includes: (a) any representation of fact, whether in words or otherwise, (b) a statement which has been videorecorded or audiorecorded, and (c) part of a statement. In *People (DPP) v O'Brien* [2010] IECCA 103 at [55], [2011] 1 IR 273 at 293, it was noted that the definition of statement is not exhaustive and considered that a videorecording in which the complainant demonstrated certain matters fell within the definition.

witness[589] in any criminal proceedings[590] relating to an arrestable offence.[591] In *People (DPP) v Murphy*,[592] McKechnie J, delivering the judgment of the Court of Criminal Appeal, described this section as "a fundamental departure from traditional common law principles which for good reason, have always placed such high regard on sworn evidence given directly, immediately, and spontaneously before the fact adjudicator." He went on to say that "both the section's interpretation and application must be viewed not only in light of the public interest which it is said to enhance but also within the bedrock of criminal justice overall".[593] However, a somewhat different note was struck in the decision of the Court of Criminal Appeal a month later in *People (DPP) v Rattigan*[594] where O'Donnell J stated:

> "This provision permits the introduction of the out-of-court statement of a witness which would otherwise be excluded as hearsay, and is therefore one further statutory exception to the hearsay rule. Section 16 is consonant with developments in the common law world. In some jurisdictions an exception to the hearsay rule was effected by case law and in others, as here, by statute. The objective however, is the same. The most obvious circumstance in which a witness who has given a detailed witness statement might nevertheless refuse to give evidence at the trial is when there has been interference with the witness, whether by way of inducement or intimidation or otherwise, or where the witness has developed a reluctance to giving evidence without any direct threat or inducement. The capacity of any legal system to compel the production of relevant testimony and real evidence is central to its ability to perform the function of the administration of justice. Interference with witnesses is not just an ugly and insidious crime which is by definition difficult to detect and punish, it is also fundamentally subversive of the administration of justice and its capacity to provide a fair trial of a charge. A provision such as section 16 therefore provides a partial remedy for a real problem and in doing so removes, or at least reduces, the incentive for anyone to seek to encourage a witness not to testify. While counsel for the applicant argued that the Court should approach the section on the basis that it was a very powerful provision since a statement so admitted could not be cross examined, this is a necessary consequence of the admission of any out-of-court statement under an exception to the hearsay rule. Indeed, under section 16 the opposing party is in a somewhat better position since the witness must be available for cross examination, and the opposing party can seek to exploit the witness's uncertainty, or professed lack of memory, if he or she thinks it desirable. That possibility is not available in other exceptions to the hearsay rule. The fact that evidence admitted under the rule may be effective and even powerful in some cases, is not itself a reason to approach the section with any skepticism."

5–254   Although the enactment of Part 3 would seem to have been precipitated by particular problems with witnesses recanting from statements made by them to Gardaí in relation to gangland type offences, in *People (DPP) v O'Brien*,[595] the Court of Criminal Appeal held that it was not restricted expressly or by implication to such crimes or any

---

[589] It is clear from the provisions of s.16, especially when interpreted in the light of the provisions of s.17 dealing with the making of witness statements, that the application of the section is confined to the statements of witnesses only and not accused persons.

[590] It is evident from the definition of "proceedings" in s.15 and the provisions of s.16, that the admissibility of a witness statement is not confined to the trial of person on an arrestable offence but extends to an application under s.4E of the Criminal Procedure Act 1967 (as amended) and any other proceeding after the accused has been sent forward for trial.

[591] An "arrestable offence" is defined by s.2 of the Criminal Law Act 1997 (as amended by s.8 of the 2006 Act) as meaning "an offence for which a person of full capacity and not previously convicted may, under or by virtue of any enactment or the common law, be punished by imprisonment for a term of five years or by a more severe penalty and includes an attempt to commit any such offence".

[592] [2013] IECCA 1 at [21].

[593] [2013] IECCA 1 at [22].

[594] [2013] IECCA 13 at [9].

[595] [2010] IECCA 103 at [69], [2011] 1 IR 273 at 297.

particular category of offences but, on the contrary, was of general application.[596] In that case, it was held that it had been correctly invoked by the trial judge so as to admit at the trial of the accused for sexually abusing his two daughters, prior statements of one of the daughters describing the abuse and identifying the accused as the perpetrator in circumstances where she failed to give that evidence when called to testify.

5–255 It should also be noted that, in *People (DPP) v Rattigan*,[597] the Court of Criminal Appeal held that the changes effected by s.16 were procedural or evidential in nature and applied only to events occurred at trials after the enactment of the section. The Court, thus, rejected the proposition that s.16 could not be applied in respect of the trial of offences allegedly committed and statements made prior to the enactment of the section as this would be to give an impermissible retrospective effect to the section.

(i) The Admission of a Witness Statement

5–256 Section 16(1) of the 2006 Act provides that a relevant prior statement of a witness may, with leave of the court, be admitted as evidence of any fact mentioned in it if the witness, although available for cross-examination: (a) refuses to give evidence, (b) denies making the statement, or (c) gives evidence which is materially inconsistent with it. The circumstances in which such a statement may be admitted are further prescribed by subss.(2) to (4).

5–257 Taking all of these subsections together, it can be seen that a statement will only be admitted if a court is satisfied of each of the following matters: (i) the statement is relevant to the proceedings; (ii) the contents of the statement are admissible in evidence; (iii) the statement was made by the witness; (iv) the witness understood the requirement to tell the truth; (v) the statement was made voluntarily; (vi) it is necessary to admit the statement; (vii) the statement is reliable; (viii) the witness is available for cross-examination; and (ix) the admission of the statement would not be contrary to the interests of justice. Each of these requirements will be examined in turn but, at the outset, it should be noted that it was held in *People (DPP) v Murphy*[598] that the use of the word "may" rather than "shall" in subs.(1) "clearly implies a residual discretion in the court of trial, to the effect that the reception of such a statement does not automatically follow, even if the statutory requirements have been met". While the Court went on to link this discretion to the stipulation that the trial court must be satisfied that the admission of the statement would not be contrary to the interests of justice, it failed to elaborate on the circumstances where a court might decide to exercise its discretion to exclude a statement where all of the requirements identified had been satisfied and the circumstances in which this would be appropriate are not readily apparent.

Relevance

5–258 As noted in Chap.1, it is a fundamental prerequisite to the admission of any evidence that it is relevant to the matters in issue in proceedings. Accordingly,

---

[596] A similar conclusion was reached in *People (DPP) v Murphy* [2013] IECCA 1 at [22] where the Court of Criminal Appeal acknowledged that Part 3 was largely intended to deal with gangland or organised criminality but stated that its provisions were not so limited and noted, in the case before it, the entire absence of any of the features which had underlain its enactment.

[597] [2013] IECCA 13.

[598] [2013] IECCA 1 at [24].

although the insertion of an express requirement of relevance in s.16 might seem to be unnecessary, it serves to emphasise that a prior statement will only be admitted where it is sufficiently relevant to the issues that arise in the proceedings that invocation of this exception to the hearsay rule is justified. It will be a matter for the trial judge to determine whether the test of relevance is satisfied.[599]

Admissibility of Contents of Statement

5–259 Under s.16(2), a statement can only be admitted if the court is satisfied that direct oral evidence of the fact concerned would be admissible in the proceedings. Thus, a statement can only be admitted as evidence of facts stated therein of which the witness had personal knowledge and not in order to prove a hearsay statement or statement of opinion contained therein. So, for example, if an issue arose in criminal proceedings as to whether certain goods were stolen, the prior statement of a witness that he or she believed the goods to be stolen would not be admissible as evidence that the goods were actually stolen.[600]

Proof of Making of Statement

5–260 Proof of the making of the statement is not required if the witness confirms that he or she made it but, if such confirmation is not forthcoming, it will be necessary to prove the making of the statement. If the statement was recorded by audio or video, it will be a straightforward matter for the person(s) who took the statement to prove that it was made by the accused. If the statement was recorded in writing, then the court will have to be satisfied, by the evidence of the person(s) who were present when the statement was made, that it was made and that it is accurately recorded in the written statement. Finally, if the statement was not recorded in writing, proof will be required from the person(s) who were present when the statement was made that it was made and as to the contents of the statement.

5–261 Given the conflicts of evidence that might arise as to whether a statement was made, particularly, if the witness denies making the statement, it would, arguably, have been better to restrict the availability of the exception under s.16 to witness statements that had been videorecorded or, at a minimum, been recorded contemporaneously in writing. In this way, an important incentive would have been provided to ensure that statements from witnesses were properly recorded.

Understanding of the Requirement to Tell the Truth

5–262 Section 16(2)(c) stipulates that, to be admissible, the statement must have been given on oath or affirmation,[601] or contain a statutory declaration by the witness to the

---

[599] *Cf. R. v Bashir* [1969] 1 WLR 1303 at 1306, [1969] 3 All ER 692 at 694, dealing with s.4 of the Criminal Procedure Act 1865.

[600] *Cf. People (DPP) v McHugh* [2002] 1 IR 352 and *AG's Reference (No.4 of 1979)* [1981] 1 WLR 667, [1981] 1 All ER 1193 dealing with the use of admissions made by accused persons as proof of facts stated therein.

[601] Section 17(3) of the Act contains provision for the making of a taking of a statement on oath or affirmation and for a member of the Garda Síochána to administer the oath or affirmation to a witness.

effect that the statement is true to the best or his or knowledge or belief,[602] or the court is otherwise satisfied that, when the statement was made, the witness understood the requirement to tell the truth. In *People (DPP) v O'Brien*[603] the Court of Criminal Appeal expressed the view that the requirement that a witness understood the requirement to tell the truth "is readily or most securely, met by evidence that the statement was prefaced by a warning, or even a reminder, to the witness to tell the truth, or by a statement of the consequences that might flow from a failure to do so".[604] However, the Court noted that admissibility was not confined to those circumstances and that it was a matter for the trial judge to satisfy himself, in the particular circumstances of each case, that the witness understood the requirement to be truthful. At issue in that case was the admission of the videotaped interviews of a child complainant by a psychologist. Although the interviews were not prefaced by the administration of any warning of the necessity to tell the truth or as to what would happen if the truth was not told, the trial judge, having viewed the interviews, was nonetheless satisfied that this requirement was met on the basis that the child was aware that the matters under discussion in the interview were very important and that it was important to tell the truth. The Court of Criminal Appeal refused to interfere with this conclusion which it considered to have been open on the evidence.

Voluntariness of Statement

5-263   Section 16(2)(b)(ii) imposes a requirement that a witness statement should be made voluntarily but does not provide any further guidance in that regard. In *People (DPP) v O'Brien*[605] the question of voluntariness was approached as a question of fact by the trial judge who, having viewed the videotapes of the interviews with the child in question, was satisfied that the statements were voluntary.[606] The Court of Criminal Appeal declined to reverse that decision but without engaging in any discussion of the relevant principles to be applied. The test that should be applied was, however, addressed in its subsequent decision in *People (DPP) v Murphy*[607] where it was held that the voluntariness test laid down in the context of the admissibility of confessions should be applied.[608] Having considered a number of the authorities in that regard, the Court summarised the position by saying that the task of the trial court when considering the admissibility of a statement pursuant to s.16:

> "is to determine whether any relevant statement was made under the influence of an inducement from a person in authority which was calculated to induce that result. The motive or intention of such person is irrelevant. The test has both objective and subjective elements. Even if such inducement is found to have been made, but it did not in fact influence the mind of the person

---

[602] Section 17(1) of the Act contains provision for the making by a witness, who makes a statement to a member of the Garda Síochána, of a statutory declaration that a statement is true to the best of the person's knowledge and belief. Similar provision is contained in section 18 for a statutory declaration to be made where a witness makes a statement to a person employed by a public authority in the course of the performance of that person's official duties.

[603] [2010] IECCA 103, [2011] 1 IR 273.

[604] [2010] IECCA 103 at [64], [2011] 1 IR 273 at 295.

[605] [2010] IECCA 103, [2011] 1 IR 273.

[606] In *People (DPP) v Murphy* [2013] IECCA 1 at [55]–[57], the Court of Criminal Appeal rejected the proposition that, where available, videotapes must be viewed in order to determine whether the requirements of voluntariness and reliability have been satisfied but held that, where there is a conflict of evidence, it would be better to view the videotapes.

[607] [2013] IECCA 1.

[608] The voluntariness test is considered in detail in Chap.8.

in making the statement, the same shall be regarded as having been made voluntarily and therefore is inadmissible in evidence. Finally, the burden of proof lies on the prosecution, where it invokes the section, to show beyond reasonable doubt that the statement was made voluntarily."[609]

5–264   It went on to say that the test of voluntariness was linked to the test of reliability in subs.(2)(b)(iii) but without exploring further the relationship and potential overlap between these two concepts.

5–265   In that case, the relevant witnesses alleged that the statements made by them prior to the trial and which had been admitted pursuant to s.16 had been made as a result of threats made by Gardaí to them, allegations which were denied by the Gardaí witnesses resulting in a direct conflict of fact as to the circumstances in which the statements had been made.

5–266   While it is unsurprising that the Court in *Murphy* should import the well developed principles in relation to voluntariness from the law relating to confessions, a note of caution should be sounded. The concept of voluntariness developed in relation to the admissibility of confessions is based on and owes its contours to concerns not just about the reliability of confessions[610] but also the protection of the right to silence.[611] However, when dealing with the voluntariness of witness statements, concerns about protecting the right to silence of the witness do not arise and the focus of the voluntariness test will be on the reliability of any statement obtained. Furthermore, there are important differences in the factual matrix in which questions as to voluntariness of witness statements will arise in that a witness will not be under arrest or detained in a garda station and is unlikely to be subjected to prolonged questioning. However, it is possible to conceive of circumstances where a witness statement might be regarded as involuntary where the gardaí have gone further than merely asking the witness questions and have applied pressure, whether by reason of a threat or otherwise, or have made a promise of a benefit, in order to obtain a statement.

Necessity to Admit the Statement

5–267   As noted above, one of the core criteria that has to be satisfied for any exception to the hearsay rule is that of necessity.[612] In general, the necessity for an exception to the hearsay rule arises because of the death or unavailability of the person who made the statement in question. However, the exception to the hearsay rule provided for in s.16 is predicated on the availability of the witness and, thus, the necessity for the admission of the witness statement arises because: (a) the witness refuses to give evidence, (b) denies making the statement, or (c) gives evidence which is materially inconsistent with it. It would seem that these three scenarios should be sufficient to cover any circumstances where a witness fails to come up to proof. Although the situation where a witness testifies but fails to give evidence of facts set out in previous statement is not expressly provided for, it has been held that this falls within the category of a witness who gives evidence that is materially inconsistent with a prior statement.[613] Similarly,

---

[609]   [2013] IECCA 1 at [37].

[610]   See *R. v Warickshall* (1783) 1 Leach 263.

[611]   See *People (AG) v O'Brien* [1965] IR 142.

[612]   See Wigmore, *Evidence* (3rd edn, 1940), Vol. V, § 1420; *Khan v R.* [1990] 2 SCR 531; *Eastern Health Board v MK* [1999] 2 IR 99 at 124, [1999] 2 ILRM 321 at 345.

[613]   *People (DPP) v O'Brien* [2010] IECCA 103 at [57], [2011] 1 IR 273 at 293.

a material inconsistency will arise where a witness professes a lack of memory in respect of a matter dealt with in a prior statement.[614]

5–268   The requirement of necessity is buttressed by s.16(4)(b) which stipulates that a witness statement cannot be admitted in evidence if the court is of opinion that its admission is unnecessary having regard to the other evidence in the proceedings. Thus, even if a witness fails to come up to proof, the previous statement of that witness will not be admitted if the party who called the witness is in a position to prove by other admissible evidence the matters in respect of which the witness has failed to give evidence.[615] Commenting on this requirement in *People (DPP) v Murphy*,[616] the Court of Criminal Appeal stated:

> "The key therefore is "necessity"; evidence which is merely supportive, useful, helpful or even desirable is not sufficient. It must be essential in a material and substantive respect. This obviously means that every statement, certainly from different witnesses, must, at this time of assessment, be critically judged against the existing evidence. Anything less will not be in compliance with the "necessity" test."

5–269   In that case, it was held that this test had not been satisfied and the trial judge had erred in considering and ruling on applications to admit the statements of three witnesses together rather than considering and ruling on them separately.[617]

Reliability of the Statement

5–270   Apart from necessity, the other critical criterion that has to be satisfied by any exception to the hearsay rule is reliability[618] and s.16 makes it clear that a witness statement can only be admitted if the court is satisfied that it is reliable. In deciding whether the statement is sufficiently reliable to be admitted, the court is required to have regard to whether it was given on oath or affirmation or was videorecorded[619] or whether, by reason of the circumstances in which it was made, there is other sufficient evidence in support of its reliability.[620] In determining the reliability of a statement, the court is also required to have regard to any explanation by the witness for refusing to give evidence or for giving evidence which is inconsistent with the statement or, where the witness denies making the statement, any evidence given in relation to the denial.[621]

5–271   When considering the criterion of "reliability", the question for a trial judge is whether the witness statement which it is sought to admit appears to be sufficiently reliable, whether by reason of its contents, the person who made it and/ or the circumstances in which it was made, that it can be admitted and left to the jury. Some guidance as to test of reliability that must be met can be obtained from case law

---

[614] *People (DPP) v Rattigan* [2013] IECCA 13 at [10].

[615] That was not the case in *People (DPP) v O'Brien* [2010] IECCA 103, [2011] 1 IR 273 where the prior statement of the witness constituted the only direct evidence of that complainant in relation to the alleged sexual abuse.

[616] [2013] IECCA 1.

[617] [2013] IECCA 1 at [61].

[618] See Wigmore, *Evidence* (3rd edn, 1940), Vol. V, § 1420; *Khan v R.* [1990] 2 SCR 531; *Eastern Health Board v MK* [1999] 2 IR 99 at 124, [1999] 2 ILRM 321 at 345.

[619] Section 19 makes provision for the Minister to make regulations in relation to the manner in which videorecordings or audiorecordings of statements made by witnesses to members of the Garda Síochána are to be made and preserved and the period for which they are to be retained.

[620] Section 16(3).

[621] Section 16(3).

in other jurisdictions. In the Canadian case of *R. v Smith*,[622] Lamer CJC stated that, if a hearsay statement "is made under circumstances which substantially negate the possibility that the declarant was untruthful or mistaken, the hearsay evidence may be said to be 'reliable,' *i.e.* a circumstantial guarantee of trustworthiness is established". To similar effect, Tipping J in the New Zealand case of *R. v Manase*[623] stated that "hearsay evidence must have sufficient apparent reliability either inherent or circumstantial, or both, to justify its admission in spite of the dangers against which the hearsay rule is designed to guard".

5–272   The test of reliability in this context was considered by the Court of Criminal Appeal in *People (DPP) v O'Brien*[624] which stated:

> "It seems relatively clear that the Act, in requiring that the statement be found to be "reliable", appears to mandate the court to examine the circumstances and factors surrounding the making of the statement, to ensure this is a reliable statement in the sense that it is one which can be relied upon, rather than requiring the court to be satisfied that the actual content of the statement is reliable in the sense that it is true…A consideration of later subsections of the Act of 2006 also suggests that the emphasis is on the circumstances of the making and taking of the statement itself, rather than the reliability of the content of the statement…"[625]

5–273   However, it is difficult to confine the concept of reliability to the circumstances in which the statement is made and to exclude consideration of the truthfulness and accuracy of the contents of the statement and later in its judgment, the court stated:

> "If the concept of reliability is to be correctly or, in part, measured also by reference to the reliability of the content of the statement, or its substance, there were factors present in this trial which indicate clearly that the content of the statement was reliable. In substance, it was supported by the very significant medical findings and also, to a certain degree, by the account given by the witness's sister, which was admissible having regard to the "similar facts" doctrine."[626]

5–274   Accordingly, the court was satisfied that there was evidence on the basis of which the trial judge could conclude that the statement was reliable.

Availability of Witness for Cross-Examination

5–275   It is clear from the provisions of s.16, that the exception to the hearsay rule provided for therein can only be invoked if the witness, whose statement it is sought to admit, is available for cross-examination. It is this availability of the witness for cross-examination which ultimately ensures that no injustice will take place where his or her prior statement of is admitted.

5–276   However, issues are likely to arise as to what is meant by the concept of "availability" and whether it means available in a physical sense or available to answer questions. In the United States, under Rule 804(a) of the Federal Rules of Evidence, a witness will be regarded as unavailable if he persists in refusing to testify despite an order of the court to do so or testifies to a lack of memory in relation to the subject matter of the statement. Given that s.16 is expressly stated to apply in circumstances where a witness refuses to give evidence, it appears that the requirement of availability

---

[622] [1992] 2 SCR 915 at 933, (1992) 94 DLR (4th) 590 at 604.
[623] [2001] 2 NZLR 197.
[624] [2010] IECCA 103, [2011] 1 IR 273.
[625] [2010] IECCA 103 at [62], [2011] 1 IR 273 at 294.
[626] [2010] IECCA 103 at [64], [2011] 1 IR 273 at 296.

for cross-examination is directed merely towards physical availability. However, it is questionable whether a witness who refuses or fails to answer any questions under cross-examination could, in any meaningful sense, be said to be "available for cross-examination". As pointed out in the Canadian decision of *R. v Conway*,[627] where a witness said that he could not remember making a statement, cross-examination in such circumstances "becomes, to a large extent, an exercise in futility and does not serve as a substitute for contemporaneous cross-examination on the prior statement". Accordingly, even if a court were to conclude that a witness was "available" for cross-examination in such circumstances, it would be necessary to assess whether the admission of the previous statement was in the interests of justice.

5–277 Although the witness must be available for cross-examination, it does not appear that the witness must be actually present in court. Accordingly, the provisions of s.16 could be utilised to admit a statement if a witness was giving evidence through a live television link pursuant to s.39 of the Criminal Justice Act 1999 on the basis that the witness was likely to be in fear or subject to intimidation in giving evidence.

5–278 It might be noted that the proposition that the admission of the previous statement of a witness pursuant to s.16 violated the guarantee in art. 38.1 of a trial in due course of law or breached art. 6 of the European Convention on Human Rights because it deprived the accused of an opportunity to cross-examine the witness at the time that the statement admitted was made was rejected in *People (DPP) v O'Brien*.[628] In that case, the accused had twice been afforded the opportunity to cross-examine the witness, firstly, during the *voir dire* and, secondly, when she gave evidence before the jury but did not avail of those opportunities. In those circumstances, the Court dismissed summarily the contention that there has been any breach of the guarantee of a trial in due course of law because the right to cross-examine had been fully vindicated. Turning to the contention that there was a breach of art.6, the Court noted that it guaranteed the right of cross-examination to persons charged with a criminal offence and held that the key element of the case law of the European Court of Human Rights on this Article was that it attached importance to the right to cross-examine in the course of trial. The Court characterised as extraordinary the proposition that this right applied at the stage at which police were investigating an offence leading to the possibility of a charge.

Interests of Justice

5–279 Section 16(4) stipulates that a statement cannot be admitted in evidence if the court is of opinion, having had regard to all the circumstances, including any risk that its admission would be unfair to one or more of the accused, that in the interests of justice it ought not to be admitted.[629]

5–280 Apart from the reference to the risk of unfairness to an accused, no guidance is given as how a court is to decide when the admission of a previous statement by

---

[627] (1997) 36 OR (3d) 579, 121 CCC (3d) 397.
[628] [2010] IECCA 103 at [69], [2011] 1 IR 273 at 297.
[629] In *People (DPP) v Rattigan* [2013] IECCA 13, the contention that the invocation of s.16 and the admission of a statement pursuant thereto was unfair because of the delay in the prosecution of the appellant was rejected with the Court taking the view that the appellant had not suffered the type of prejudice which would render the trial or the admission of the statements unfair.

a witness will be contrary to the interests of justice. However, it is submitted that one important component of this test will be the degree to which a party adversely affected by the admission of the witness statement would be in a position to test it and expose any potential unreliability by cross-examination. In the Canadian case of *R. v U(FJ)*,[630] Lamer CJC emphasised the importance of cross-examination at trial in addressing the lack of contemporaneous cross-examination of the witness at the time the statement was made and in justifying the admission of hearsay evidence of this nature. As pointed out in *R. v Conway*[631] what is required in this regard is effective cross-examination and, in that case, where the witness stated that he did not remember making the statement, "the cross-examination was rendered virtually ineffectual". Accordingly, where an application is made to admit a previous statement made by a witness, a trial judge, in deciding whether it is in the interests of justice to admit it, will have to pay particular attention to the circumstances in which the witness has recanted from the earlier statement and whether the party adversely affected by the admission of the statement has a meaningful opportunity to test the potential unreliability of the statement by cross-examination.[632] If, for example, a witness in a statement made before trial purported to identify an accused as the perpetrator of an offence, the admission of the statement could be unfair to an accused and contrary to the interests of justice if the witness, although available for cross-examination, refused to answer any questions in relation to the previous statement thereby depriving counsel for the accused of the opportunity of cross-examining the witness as to the conditions of initial observation and other factors that could affect the accuracy and reliability of the identification made.

5–281   Although the focus of this subsection would seem to be on potential unfairness to an accused, somewhat surprisingly, in *People (DPP) v O'Brien*,[633] it was held that, in deciding that it was not unfair to admit the statements at issue, the court had been entitled to be influenced by the fact that there was powerful evidence to support the view that the witness was sexually abused in the manner she described, and that her account that the abuse had been perpetrated by the accused, was supported by her sister's similar complaints.

(ii) Weight

5–282   The weight to be given to a statement admitted pursuant to s.16 is a matter for the tribunal of fact. Guidance in that regard is given by s.16(5) which provides that:

> "In estimating the weight, if any, to be attached to the statement regard shall be had to all the circumstances from which any inference can reasonably be drawn as to its accuracy or otherwise."

5–283   The terms of this subsection are quite broad and enable the tribunal of fact to look at a broad range of factors including the circumstances in which the statement was taken, its content, the contents of the testimony (if any) of the witness, his or her demeanour and the reasons given (if any) for refusing to give evidence or for the inconsistencies with the previous statement. In *People (DPP) v Murphy*,[634] it was held

---

630   [1995] 3 SCR 764, 128 DLR (4th) 121.
631   (1997) 36 OR (3d) 579, 121 CCC (3d) 397.
632   See, by way of example, the analysis conducted in *R. v M(A)* (2004) ONCJ 185.
633   [2010] IECCA 103 at [68], [2011] 1 IR 273 at 297.
634   [2013] IECCA 1 at [27].

that "as weight is a sole matter for the trier of fact, it is of primary importance that the jury should be properly instructed in this regard".

(iii) Instruction to the Jury

5–284   Although no requirement for any form of instruction to a jury is contained in s.16, unsurprisingly, in *People (DPP) v Murphy*,[635] it was held that a trial judge is required to give a jury an instruction as to the weight to be attached to a statement that is admitted pursuant to the section and the factors that can be considered in that regard.[636] The Court of Criminal Appeal pointed out that the weight to be attached to a statement admitted pursuant to s.16 may differ greatly depending on circumstances from treating a statement as having no value to considering it to be entirely reliable. This assessment was of fundamental importance and, thus, the jury had to be given guidance in relation to it:

> "It is scarcely open to argument but that appropriate directions must be given to the jury, so that they are properly equipped to conduct the exercise demanded. This means that all matters directly and indirectly relevant to accuracy and reliability must be brought to their attention. In the instant case these would include the circumstances by reference to which the statements were admitted, and on the Gardaí side, the fact that each was supported by statutory declarations and on the lay witnesses' side, the individual explanations offered by them for making the statements and for later recanting them. There are but examples of specific matters and do not take from the more general instruction which is required. Unless the jury is so fully informed, their critical role in this context will almost certainly be impaired and could easily be fatally jeopardised."[637]

5–285   The Court went on to elaborate in relation to the required instruction to the jury:

> "The approach suggested could conveniently have a general and specific level to it. General as in all cases where s.16 is invoked and specific as to particular circumstances, relating to the individual case and that or those aspects of the section which are involved. In addition it will be necessary to isolate the evidence at issue and to treat it quite distinctly from the more general observations which trial judges usually make on the body of the evidence available.
>
> On the general side, it seems to this Court that reference should be made: to the historical role of the hearsay rule and the reasons that lay behind it; to the court's longstanding preference to have guilt or "innocence" determined by direct sworn evidence, tested by the safeguards which exist; to the differences between oral evidence and witness statements made pre-trial without judicial control; to the existence of such statements and to sworn evidence which may deny their existence, or their content or be materially inconsistent with them; to the difficulties of reliability presented by such conflict involving the same witness and to the potential dangers of relying on anything which that person may have said, either then or on oath before them, and if they should so rely, what on and to what extent. Finally however, they should also be told that, having regard to the direction given, it remains a matter exclusively for them to determine what weight or value, if any, they place on the witness's overall evidence, whether given outside trial or before them.
> On the specific side they should be instructed, having regard to s.16(5) of the Act in such a manner as to reflect the circumstances peculiar to the case at trial…"[638]

5–286   In that case, the direction given by the trial judge fell well short of addressing all of these matters and, insofar as he summarised the comments of defence counsel

---

[635] [2013] IECCA 1 at [27].
[636] Such a requirement had also been laid down by the Canadian Supreme Court in *R. v B(KG)* [1993] 1 SCR 740 at 804.
[637] [1993] 1 SCR 740 at [82].
[638] [1993] 1 SCR 740 at [84]–[86].

in relation to the potential unreliability of the statements, it was held that this was no substitute for observations coming directly from the judge.

5–287   If the experience in relation to other cautionary instructions such as that in relation to identification evidence provides any guide, this direction could potentially involve quite a complex instruction and provide fertile ground for appeals having regard to the range of factors to be considered in assessing the weight to be attached to a statement and the need to tailor the instruction to the particular circumstances of the case.

11. Common Enterprise

5–288   Although not yet recognised in this jurisdiction, there is a long standing exception to the hearsay rule whereby, where two or more persons are engaged in a common and unlawful enterprise, the statements of any of them in pursuance of that common enterprise, including statements made in the absence and even without the knowledge of the others, are admissible.[639] The rationales advanced for this exception include the principle of agency and an extension of the *res gestae* principle.[640]

12. Evidence of Pre-Trial Identification

5–289   The out-of-court statement of a witness identifying an accused at a pre-trial identification procedure is admissible on principles analogous to *res gestae* as part of the act of identification.[641] Evidence of the statement of identification may be given by the witness himself or herself and, it would appear, by another person present, where the witness gives evidence and identifies the accused in court.[642]

5–290   More controversial is the question whether another person who was present when the identification was made can give evidence of it in circumstances where the witness does not give evidence or is unable to identify the accused in court. The old Irish case of *R. v Burke*[643] and more modern English authorities[644] indicate that such evidence may be given. However, in *People (AG) v Casey (No.1)*,[645] the Court of Criminal Appeal, while not going so far as to hold that such evidence was inadmissible, stated that it was "extremely dangerous" to admit it and stated that the trial judge should

---

[639] See *R. v Hardy* (1794) 24 How St Tr 451; *R. v Devonport* [1996] 1 Cr App R 211; *R. v Jones* [1997] 2 Cr App R 119; *Ahern v R.* (1988) 80 ALR 161; *R. v Humphries* [1982] 1 NZLR 353; *R. v Buckton* [1985] 2 NZLR 257 *R. v Qiu* [2008] 1 NZLR 1; *R. v Mapara* [2005] 1 SCR 358; *US v Doerr* (1989) 886 F 2d 944. See generally, Malek (ed.), *Phipson on Evidence* 18th edn, para. 31—44. This exception has been put on a statutory basis in England and Wales in s.118(1) of the Criminal Justice Act 2003 (see *R. v Kiernen* [2008] EWCA Crim 972; *R. v Sofroniou* [2009] EWCA 1360; *R. v King* [2012] EWCA Crim 805).

[640] See Spencer, "The common enterprise exception to the hearsay rule" (2007) 11 E & P 106; *Levie, "Hearsay and Conspiracy: A Re-examination of the Co-Conspirator's Exception to the Hearsay Rule"* (1954) 52 Mich LR 1159.

[641] *R. v Christie* [1914] AC 545.

[642] *R. v Christie* [1914] AC 545.

[643] (1847) 2 Cox CC 295 (victim had identified one of the accused as his assailant before the trial but was unable to make a definitive identification in court and the prosecution was permitted to call other witnesses to establish that the accused had been identified by the victim before trial).

[644] *R. v Osborne* [1973] 1 QB 678 at 690, [1973] 1 All ER 649; *R. v McCay* [1991] 1 All ER 232. See, *contra, per* Lord Morris in *Sparks v R.* [1964] 1 AC 964 at 981, [1964] 1 All ER 727 at 735.

[645] [1961] IR 264.

have considered whether the evidence should have been excluded on the basis that its prejudicial effect outweighed its probative value. It should be noted that provision for the admission of such evidence is made in s.18(6) of the Criminal Evidence Act 1992. This subsection provides that, where a witness is giving evidence via live television link in accordance with the provisions of Part III of that Act, evidence by a person other than the witness that the witness identified the accused at an identification parade as the offender is admissible as evidence that the accused was so identified.

13. Bail Applications

5–291   In general, the hearsay rule applies with full vigour to bail applications, even though they are interlocutory in character, although the rule may be relaxed so as to admit hearsay where there is a good reason why the declarant is not available to give evidence.[646]

5–292   The leading authority is *People (DPP) v McGinley*[647] where the accused, who had been charged with unlawful carnal knowledge of a girl, applied for bail. This was opposed by the prosecution, and a garda gave evidence of attempts by members of the accused's family to intimidate the complaint's family and of offers of inducements to them to withdraw the complaint. Notwithstanding the hearsay nature of this evidence, the trial judge decided to admit it and refused bail on the basis that there was a grave likelihood that the applicant would interfere with witnesses. On appeal, it was held that the trial judge had erred in admitting and relying on the hearsay evidence. Keane J (as he then was), delivering the judgment of the Supreme Court, held that, in general, an applicant for bail was entitled to have the evidence on which the court was being asked to rely given *viva voce* on oath and tested by cross-examination. While he accepted that a bail application could properly be described as interlocutory in character, he rejected any analogy with civil interlocutory proceedings on the basis that "if bail is refused, the accused person is deprived of his liberty in circumstances where he must be presumed to be innocent" and, if subsequently acquitted at trial, "the fact that he has spent a period of custody, however lengthy, awaiting his trial affords him no remedy".[648] However, he went on to state:

> "The constitutional right of the applicant for bail to liberty must, in every case where there is an objection to the granting of bail, be balanced against the public interest in ensuring that the integrity of the trial process is protected. Where there is evidence which indicates as a matter of probability that the applicant, if granted bail, will not stand his trial or will interfere with witnesses, the right to liberty must yield to the public interest in the administration of justice. It is in that context that hearsay evidence may become admissible, where the court hearing the application is satisfied that there are sufficient grounds for not requiring the witness to give *viva voce* evidence. In such a case, it would be for the court to consider what weight should be given to the evidence, having regard to the fact that the author of the statement had not been produced and to any other relevant circumstances which arose in the particular case."[649]

5–293   Although it was common for a prosecuting garda to collate information from a number of sources and unusual for objection to be taken to hearsay evidence of that

---

[646] See O'Higgins, "Hearsay Evidence in Bail Applications" (1998) BR 129, for a discussion of the application of the hearsay rule in this context and the policy considerations at play.
[647] [1998] 2 IR 408, [1998] 2 ILRM 233. *Cf. People (DPP) v McKeon*, unreported, Supreme Court, 12 October 1995 and *People (DPP) v McNamara*, unreported, Supreme Court, 21 June 2002.
[648] [1998] 2 IR 408 at 414, [1998] 2 ILRM 233 at 238.
[649] [1998] 2 IR 408 at 414, [1998] 2 ILRM 233 at 238.

nature, where, as in the instant case, the hearsay evidence contradicted the evidence of the applicant in relation to a crucial issue, the objection to its admission had to be upheld.

5–294   The decision in *McGinley* was approved by the Supreme Court in *People (DPP) v McLoughlin*[650] where Hardiman J reiterated the general principle that hearsay evidence is not admissible on bail applications:

> "there is a *prima facie* right in an applicant for bail to have the evidence deployed against his application given orally, by its author and not simply by a person who heard it said. The reason for this has already been alluded to, but cannot be too often repeated. To allow hearsay evidence, or written evidence, or certificate evidence, in an important matter (and a grant of refusal to bail is certainly such) is to deny to an applicant the essential and vital tool of cross-examination of the persons giving evidence against him, without which, in the great majority of cases, he cannot hope to be successful in his application. It wholly stymies the applicant and confers a huge and normally insuperable advantage on his opponent."[651]

5–295   However, he acknowledged that "the exigencies of the practice of criminal law, particularly in interlocutory applications, make it absolutely necessary that hearsay be admissible *in some such interlocutory applications*, but on a very restricted basis".[652] There was, therefore, no question of there being a general exception to the hearsay rule in bail applications and the evidence relied on to ground the admission of hearsay evidence had to establish more than that it would be convenient if evidence in this form was admitted and that all reasonable steps had been taken to procure *viva voce* evidence. He emphasised that hearsay would only be admitted in rare and exceptional cases:

> "The result of this is that hearsay evidence may be admissible in a bail application, but quite exceptionally, and when a specific, recognised, ground for its admission has been properly established by ordinary evidence."[653]

5–296   He went on to say that it is for the courts to keep the use of hearsay within proper bounds and, where it is proposed to adduce hearsay evidence, there must be a full and proper hearing of the objection and of the evidence relied on in support of the admission of hearsay and a proper ruling on its admissibility. In that case, it was held that it has been reasonable for the trial judge to admit hearsay evidence where witnesses were unwilling to come to court to give evidence as to intimidation.[654]

5–297   One situation where hearsay evidence may be admitted on a bail application is where an objection to bail is based on information provided on a confidential basis by a garda informant. In *People (DPP) v McKeon*,[655] a garda gave evidence that she was in receipt of confidential information indicating that the applicant had received a false

---

[650]   [2009] IESC 65, [2010] 1 IR 590, [2010] 1 ILRM 1.

[651]   [2009] IESC 65 at [46], [2010] 1 IR 590 at 603, [2010] 1 ILRM 1 at 11–12.

[652]   [2009] IESC 65 at [49], [2010] 1 IR 590 at 603, [2010] 1 ILRM 1 at 12 (emphasis in the original).

[653]   [2009] IESC 65 at [51], [2010] 1 IR 590 at 603, [2010] 1 ILRM 1 at 12. This test was applied in *McCann v Governor of Castlerea Prison* [2011] IEHC 244 where the applicant's bail had been revoked on the basis of hearsay evidence given by a garda as to the involvement of the applicant in criminal activity and Hogan J held that the admission of hearsay evidence without a sufficient legal basis amounted to a fundamental legal error on the part of the District Judge which vitiated the legality of the applicant's detention.

[654]   See also *Galvin v Governor of Cloverhill Prison* [2012] IEHC 497 where Peart J accepted that hearsay evidence as to intimidation could be given in exceptional cases but held that there had to be some evidence provided as to why the person alleging intimidation was not able to give *viva voce* evidence on which he could be cross-examined.

[655]   Unreported, Supreme Court, 12 October 1995.

passport and money from an unlawful organisation in order to assist him in leaving the country. Costello P held that the hearsay evidence of the garda was admissible in order to preserve the anonymity of a garda informer and that decision was upheld on appeal.[656]

5–298 Sufficient grounds for admitting hearsay evidence were also found to exist in *Vickers v DPP*.[657] The applicant had been charged with the murder of his wife and his application for bail was opposed, *inter alia*, on the basis that there was a risk that, if granted bail, the applicant would harm his children and himself. This contention was based on the evidence of the best friend of the deceased that the deceased had told her some months prior to her death that the applicant had threatened to kill her, their children and himself. The applicant objected to the admission of this evidence as hearsay but, given that the person who could have given *viva voce* evidence of this threat was deceased, Kearns J, delivering the judgment of the Supreme Court, was satisfied that it had been open to the trial judge to receive and act on that evidence. He noted in that regard that the trial judge had ruled that he would receive such evidence only from the person with the most direct contact with the deceased and would not extend the admissibility of hearsay evidence beyond what was strictly necessary. Kearns J emphasised that, where hearsay evidence is admitted, there is an obligation on a trial judge to weigh it carefully with the other evidence in the case including the sworn evidence of the applicant. In circumstances where the applicant had failed to demonstrate any improper motive on the part of the witness, he was satisfied that the trial judge had been entitled to attribute weight to the hearsay evidence of that witness in deciding to refuse bail.

14. Sentencing Hearings

5–299 There is a long established practice that the rules of evidence including the hearsay rule are not applied to sentencing hearings.[658] The existence of this exception to the hearsay rule was confirmed and its parameters considered by the Court of Criminal Appeal in *People (DPP) v McDonnell*.[659] The appellant and his co-accused had pleaded guilty to possession of a controlled drug with intent to supply. At his sentencing hearing, the trial judge intervened in the cross-examination of a garda witness to inquire how long the accused had been involved "in the trade" which elicited evidence that the appellant had been known to Gardaí for a number of years and that he was the target of the operation which led to his arrest. The appellant contended that this evidence was inadmissible hearsay but the Court of Criminal Appeal took the view that an accused person would be singularly disadvantaged if the rules of evidence on sentencing hearings were applied in precisely the same manner as at trial:

> "This is a valuable relaxation of the strict rules of evidence which operates for the benefit of convicted persons and has enabled the sentencing judge to construct a sentence which places the offence in context and which reflects the rule of law that the sentence is not for the offence, but rather for the offence committed by the particular offender. Were hearsay evidence to be regarded as inadmissible in sentencing as at trial, as contended for by counsel for the accused, one might argue that its exclusion would have to operate even handedly so as to also rule out, or at least render objectionable, the leading of hearsay evidence which is

---

[656] See also *Clarke v Governor of Cloverhill Prison* [2011] IEHC 199.
[657] [2009] IESC 58, [2010] 1 IR 548.
[658] See Law Reform Commission, *Consultation Paper on Sentencing* (1993) at para.1.22.
[659] [2009] IECCA 16, [2009] 4 IR 105.

favourable to the accused as well as evidence which is unfavourable. The importance attached by the European Court of Human Rights to the principle of *égalité des armes* would seem, if one were to apply it in this context, to suggest no less. Moreover, a sentencing judge would be severely disadvantaged if obliged to approach sentencing in such a blinkered manner. A sentencing judge should not be obliged to structure the sentence in a case in a kind of factual vacuum devoid of all relevant contextual and background information."[660]

5–300   Having reviewed the Irish authorities on point and surveyed authorities from other common law jurisdictions, the Court concluded that:

"Hearsay evidence of character, antecedents, and as to the background to the particular offence being dealt with, including the extent of the role played therein by an accused may, at the discretion of the sentencing judge, be received, subject to the requirement that if a particular fact assumes specific significance or is disputed the court's findings should require strict proof. It is a matter for the sentencing judge to decide what weight should be attached to such hearsay evidence as is received, noting any objection taken thereto and any arguments or evidence offered in rebuttal."[661]

5–301   However, this exception to the hearsay rule was subject to an important limitation that the admission at a sentencing hearing of hearsay evidence to suggest the commission of prior criminal offences on the part of a convicted person for which he had not been tried and found guilty or, if charged, he did not require to be taken into account, would infringe Arts 38 and 40.1 of the Constitution.[662]

5–302   Applying those principles, the Court was satisfied that the question asked by the trial judge had crossed the line into the realms of inadmissibility because, not only was it irrelevant, there was implicit in it a suggestion of other uncharged criminality. However, in circumstances where the trial judge was entitled on the other evidence before him to impose the sentence under appeal, the Court declined to interfere with it.

5–303   The principles laid down in *McDonnell* were approved and applied by the Court of Criminal Appeal in *People (DPP) v O'Neill*[663] where it was emphasised that: "While the sentencing judge is entitled to receive hearsay evidence and opinion evidence, he or she must be astute to ensure that extraneous matters whose evidential value is inherently more prejudicial than probative so far as the accused is concerned are thereby excluded."[664]

15. Extradition Applications

5–304   Extradition applications have traditionally been regarded as *sui generis*, being neither civil nor criminal in nature and with an inquisitorial as well as an adversarial character.[665] For this reason, the rule against hearsay is not applied with the same rigour as in criminal or civil proceedings and documents issued by or information provided by a requesting State / judicial authority can be admitted in evidence as proof of the facts stated therein without the need for an official of the requesting State / judicial

---

[660] [2009] IECCA 16 at [26], [2009] 4 IR 105 [2009] 4 IR 105 at 114.

[661] [2009] IECCA 16 at [49], [2009] 4 IR 105 at 120.[2009] 4 IR 105

[662] See also *People (DPP) v Delaney,* Court of Criminal Appeal, 28 February 2000 and *People (DPP) v Gilligan (No.2)* [2004] 3 IR 87.

[663] [2012] IECCA 37.

[664] [2012] IECCA 37 at [22].

[665] *AG v Parke* [2004] IESC 100; *Minister for Justice, Equality and Law Reform v Sliczynski* [2008] IESC 73; *AG v O'Gara* [2012] IEHC 179 at [7.3]; *AG v Pocevicius* [2013] IEHC 229 at 26.

authority to give direct evidence of those matters.[666] Specific provision in that regard is made in ss.7B(1) and 37 of the Extradition Act 1965 (as amended by the Extradition (European Union Conventions) Act 2001).

5–305 A similar approach applies in respect of applications pursuant to the provisions of the European Arrest Warrant Act 2003 which are also regarded as *sui generis* and having an inquisitorial dimension.[667] Section 12(8) of that Act makes provision for the reception into evidence without further proof of a European arrest warrant and other specified documents and, in *Minister for Justice, Equality and Law Reform v Sliczynski,*[668] the question arose as to whether other information provided by a requesting judicial authority could be admitted without direct evidence from the judicial authority. In that case, the surrender of the respondent was sought pursuant to the provisions of the 2003 Act on foot of a European arrest warrant issued by a Polish judicial authority. Section 20 of the Act provided that additional information could be obtained from the issuing State/judicial authority but did not provide for the admission of such information by way of an exception to the hearsay rule. However, the Supreme Court held that s.20 had to be interpreted in light of the objectives of the Framework Decision which underlay the European arrest warrant system and was satisfied that the Oireachtas intended that the High Court would be able to have regard to such information in addition to the information contained in the European arrest warrant for the purpose of deciding whether a person should be surrendered on foot of that warrant. Murray CJ took the view that, to interpret the provisions of the Act otherwise and require direct evidence to be given would be to render them meaningless. Furthermore, it was noted that the a high level of confidence and mutual trust was an integral part of the European arrest warrant scheme so that it could be assumed that information provided by the judicial authority of a requesting State would be true and accurate and should be accorded the appropriate mutual respect. Accordingly, it was held that the information provided by the requesting judicial authority was to be taken as *prima facie* evidence of the facts set out therein and it was to be assumed that such facts were correct until there was some reason to believe to the contrary.[669]

5–306 Outside of the statutory exceptions referred to above, the rule against hearsay applies to an application for extradition or for surrender on foot of a European arrest warrant so that the evidence adduced by a respondent can be excluded if it is hearsay.[670]

16. Interlocutory Applications in Civil Cases

5–307 The hearsay rule is generally applied with considerably less vigour in interlocutory applications in civil cases and Ord.40 r.4 of the Rules of the Superior

---

[666] *AG v O'Gara* [2012] IEHC 179 at [7.3].
[667] *Minister for Justice, Equality and Law Reform v Sliczynski* [2008] IESC 73 at 14.
[668] [2008] IESC 73.
[669] This decision was followed and applied in *Minister for Justice, Equality and Law Reform v Sawczuk* [2011] IEHC 41 and *Minister for Justice, Equality and Law Reform v O'Sullivan* [2011] IEHC 230.
[670] *AG v Pocevicius* [2013] IEHC 229.

Courts[671] allows for the inclusion of hearsay in affidavits on interlocutory applications.[672] The rationale for this exception is that, when dealing with interlocutory matters, the court does not decide the rights of the parties but merely makes a decision for the purpose of preserving the status quo until those rights are decided or for the purpose of progressing the proceedings so that those rights can be decided.[673] It has been held that this rule permits a deponent to give "second hand hearsay evidence" whereby he or she avers that he or she has been told something by a person who in turn has been told it by another person.[674] However, the inclusion of hearsay in an affidavit should be avoided where possible and a court may refuse relief where an affidavit grounding an interlocutory application is sworn by a deponent who does not have first hand knowledge of the facts.[675]

5–308 Furthermore, the courts have traditionally been wary of attributing too much probative value to hearsay evidence adduced on interlocutory applications. The reason for such circumspection is evident from *Smithkline Beecham v Antigen Pharmaceuticals Ltd*.[676] The plaintiff sought an interlocutory injunction in a passing off action. In support of its argument that there was a likelihood of confusion, the plaintiff relied on the affidavit of a sales representative wherein he gave hearsay evidence of three occasions on which he had been told by pharmacists that they were confused between the plaintiff's and the defendant's product. However, the defendant produced affidavits from two of the three named persons and both said that they were not confused. This led McCracken J to comment that while hearsay evidence is admissible in interlocutory applications, the case showed the dangers of relying on it.[677]

17. Miscellaneous Common Law Exceptions

5–309 Apart from those exceptions to the hearsay rule already dealt with above, the courts have created a number of miscellaneous exceptions to the hearsay rule. The list below is not meant to be exhaustive but outlines the main exceptions that have not already been discussed.

(a) Declarations as to public and general rights

5–310 The statement of a deceased person concerning the reputed existence or non-existence of a public or general right is admissible as evidence of the existence of such a right provided that the declaration was made before the dispute in which it is tendered had arisen.

5–311 A public right is one affecting the entire population such as a claim of a public

---

[671] Ord.40 r.4 of the Rules of the Superior Courts stipulates that: "Affidavits shall be confined to such facts as the witness is able of his own knowledge to prove, and shall state his means of knowledge thereof, except on interlocutory motions, on which statements as to his belief, with the grounds thereof, may be admitted."

[672] See *O'D v Minister for Education and Science* [2009] IEHC 227 at 14.

[673] *Director of Corporate Enforcement v Bailey* [2007] IEHC 365, [2008] 2 ILRM 13 at 24; *Rossage v Rossage* [1960] 1 WLR 249; *Gilbert v Endean* [1878] 9 Ch Div 259 at 268.

[674] *Bula Ltd v Tara Mines Ltd*, unreported, High Court, 17 September 1990; *Savings and Investment Bank Ltd v Gasco Investments (Netherlands) BV* [1984] 1 WLR 271.

[675] See, *e.g. Darcy v Roscommon County Council*, unreported, Supreme Court, 11 January 1991.

[676] [1999] 2 ILRM 190.

[677] [1999] 2 ILRM 190 at 196.

right of way,[678] the existence of a fishery in tidal waters,[679] a right of ferry,[680] and the right to use part of a river bank as a public landing place.[681] It was held in *Crease v Barrett*[682] that, in the case of a public right, no connection with the locus or personal knowledge on the part of the declarant is required because in "a matter in which all are concerned, reputation from anyone appears to be receivable".[683] However, it was conceded that, if the declarant did not have means of knowledge of the facts, any declaration made by him in relation to the right "would be almost worthless".[684]

5–312   A general right is one that affects a particular class of person and includes rights of commonage,[685] the rights of corporations[686] and a custom of mining in a particular district.[687] In the case of a general right, it is not necessary for the person to be living in the area in question[688] but it must be shown that the declarant has some connection to the area and, thus, particular knowledge of the right in question.[689] In the absence of such proof, a declaration as to the reputed existence of the right is inadmissible.[690]

5–313   In general, a private right cannot be proved by evidence of reputation.[691] However, evidence of reputation is admissible when private and public rights are co-extant as, for example, when the boundary between two estates is the same as that between two hamlets.[692]

5–314   In England, there is a line of authority to the effect that a declaration is only admissible to prove reputation and not as evidence of particular facts contained in it from which the existence of the right may be inferred.[693] However, a less rigid approach has been taken in Ireland and in the *Giant's Causeway Co. Ltd v Attorney General*[694] the Court of Appeal held that an original Ordnance Survey map was admissible as reputation to prove the existence of a public right of way.

5–315   As noted, the declaration[695] must have been made *ante litem motam, i.e.* before

---

[678] *Crease v Barrett* (1835) 1 Cr M & R 919 at 929; *R. v Bliss* (1837) 7 Ad & El 550, [1835–42] All ER Rep 372.

[679] *Duke of Devonshire v Neill and Fenton* (1877) 2 LR Ir 132.

[680] *Pim v Curell* (1840) 6 M & W 234 at 266.

[681] *Drinkwater v Porter* (1835) 7 C & P 181.

[682] (1835) 1 Cr M & R 919.

[683] (1835) 1 Cr M & R 919 at 929 (*per* Parke B). See also *Duke of Devonshire v Neill and Fenton* (1877) 2 LR Ir 132 at 159, where *Crease v Barrett* was cited with approval on this point.

[684] (1835) 1 Cr M & R 919 at 929.

[685] *Evans v Merthyr Tydfil UDC* [1899] 1 Ch 241.

[686] *Davies v Morgan* (1831) 1 Cr & J 587.

[687] *Crease v Barrett* (1835) 1 Cr M & R 919.

[688] *Duke of Newcastle v Hundred of Broxtowe* (1832) 4 B & Ad 273; *Crease v Barrett* (1835) 1 Cr M & R 919 at 929.

[689] *Rogers v Wood* (1831) 2 B & Ad 245; *Crease v Barrett* (1835) 1 Cr M & R 919 at 928.

[690] *Crease v Barrett* (1835) 1 Cr M & R 919 at 929.

[691] *Talbot v Lewis* (1834) 1 Cr M & R 495 at 497; *Earl of Dunraven v Llewellyn* (1850) 15 QB 791 at 809–810; *White v Taylor* [1969] 1 Ch 150 at 154, [1967] 3 All ER 349 at 351.

[692] *Thomas v Jenkins* (1837) 6 Ad & El 525.

[693] *Crease v Barrett* (1835) 1 Cr M & R 919 at 930; *Pim v Currell* (1840) 6 M & W 234 at 266; *R. v Inhabitants of Lordsmere* (1866) 16 Cox CC 65; *R. v Berger* [1894] 1 QB 823; *Mercer v Denne* [1905] 2 Ch 538.

[694] (1905) 5 NIJR 381.

[695] In the case of a written declaration, it must be proved to have been made or adopted by the putative declarant in order to be admissible. In *Duke of Devonshire v Neill* (1877) 2 LR Ir 132 at 160, Palles CB refused to admit an unsigned document stating that it had never been decided that

the dispute in which it is tendered had arisen.[696] However, provided this condition is satisfied, the fact that the declaration was in the interests of the person making it does not affect its admissibility and is merely a matter going to weight.[697]

(b) Declarations as to pedigree

5–316   The declaration of a deceased person as to pedigree, *i.e.* an issue of birth, death, marriage, legitimacy or the relationship by blood or marriage between persons, is generally admissible. Declarations as to pedigree may take many forms including direct assertions of fact,[698] conduct,[699] family tradition,[700] an entry in a family Bible,[701] an inscription on a tombstone[702] or a pedigree hung up in the family mansion.[703]

5–317   The conditions of admissibility are: (i) that the proceedings involve a question of pedigree[704]; (ii) the declaration was made by a blood relation or the spouse of a blood relation of the person whose pedigree is in issue[705]; and (iii) the declaration was made *ante litem motam*, *i.e.* before the dispute in which it is tendered had arisen.[706] However, there is no requirement for personal knowledge on the part of the declarant.[707]

(c) Testamentary declarations

5–318   In the case of *In the Goods of Ball*,[708] Warren J approved and applied the principle laid down by the House of Lords in *Sugden v St. Leonards*[709] that "declarations made by a testator, both before and after the execution of his will, are, in the event of its loss, admissible as secondary evidence of its contents".[710] There does not appear

---

"an unsigned and unrecognised document is evidence as reputation because it is kept amongst muniments".

[696] *Berkeley Peerage Case* (1811) 4 Camp 401.

[697] *Moseley v Davies* (1822) 11 Price 162 at 174.

[698] *Goodright v Moss* (1777) 2 Cowp 591 at 594.

[699] *Cf. Goodright d Stevens v Moss* (1777) 2 Cowp 591 at 594 (if child had always been treated as illegitimate and another child had been considered to be the heir of the family).

[700] *Per* Lord Eldon in *Whitelocke v Baker* (1807) 13 Ves 510 at 514, the tradition must prevail among persons having such a connection with the person to whom it relates that it is natural and likely, from their domestic habits and connections, that they are speaking the truth and could not be mistaken. However, this is a matter which goes to weight, rather than to admissibility.

[701] *Cf. Goodright v Moss* (1777) 2 Cowp 591 at 594.

[702] *Cf. Goodright v Moss* (1777) 2 Cowp 591 at 594.

[703] See, generally, *Duke of Devonshire v Neill* (1877) 2 LR Ir 132 at 160; *Goodright v Moss* (1777) 2 Cowp 591 at 594. See also *Whitelocke v Baker* (1807) 13 Ves 510 at 514 (family tradition); *Monkton v AG* (1831) 2 Russ & Myl 161.

[704] In Ireland, it suffices that an issue of pedigree arises in the course of proceedings (*Palmer v Palmer* (1885) 18 LR Ir 192; *Smith v Smith* (1878–79) 1 LR Ir 206) whereas a more restrictive approach is taken in England that the question of pedigree must be directly in issue (*Haines v Guthrie* (1884) 13 QBD 818).

[705] *Johnson v Lawson* (1824) 2 Bing 86; *Crease v Barrett* (1835) 1 Cr M & R 919 at 928; *Shrewsbury Peerage Case* (1858) 7 HL Cas 1. However, the statement may be proved by a person who is not a member of the family: *Re Holmes* [1934] IR 693.

[706] *Berkeley Peerage Case* (1811) 4 Camp 401; *Butler v Mountgarret* (1859) 7 HL Cas 633. Provided that this condition is satisfied, the fact that the declaration is in the interest of the declarant is a matter going to weight rather than admissibility: *Doe d Jenkins v Davies* (1847) 10 QB 314.

[707] *Davies v Lowndes* (1843) 6 Man & G 471.

[708] (1890) 25 LR Ir 556.

[709] (1876) 1 PD 154.

[710] *Cf. Woodward v Goulstone* (1886) 11 App Cas 469 (where the proposition that post-testamentary

to be any modern authorities in this jurisdiction that consider this exception and it is of limited importance.

(d) Ancient documents affecting an interest in land

5–319   Ancient documents such as leases and licences demonstrating acts of possession or ownership and coming from proper custody[711] may be admitted as evidence of a proprietary interest in land.[712] In *Malcomson v O'Dea*,[713] Willes J justified the admission of such evidence on the basis of the difficulties of proving ancient possession: "Time has removed the witnesses who could speak to acts of ownership of their own personal knowledge, and resort must necessarily be had to written evidence".[714]

5–320   Many commentators treat this category of documentation as an example of original evidence falling outside of the scope of the hearsay rule that is admitted on the basis that it allows circumstantial inferences of possession to be drawn from the documents.[715] However, the better view seems to be that such documentation is admitted by way of an exception to the hearsay rule in recognition that a court is unlikely to restrict the use of these documents to drawing inferences of possession but will use them as evidence of the facts contained therein.[716]

5–321   It should be noted that this common law exception has been supplemented by statute. Under s.2 of the Vendor and Purchaser Act 1874, recitals, statements and descriptions of facts, matters and parties in deeds, instruments, Acts of Parliament or statutory declarations 20 years old at the date of a contract for the sale of land are to be taken as sufficient evidence of the truth of such facts, matters and descriptions, unless and except so far as they are proved to be inaccurate.

(e) Published works of reference

5–322   Authoritative published works of reference are admissible to prove facts of a public nature stated therein or, as appropriate, to provide a foundation for a judge to

---

declarations are admissible to prove the contents of a will was doubted) and *In the Goods of Gilliland* [1940] NI 125 at 131, where Andrews LCJ expressed a willingness, *obiter*, to follow *Sugden* notwithstanding the doubts expressed in *Woodward*.

[711]   The concept of proper custody was explored in *Blandy-Jenkins v Earl of Dunraven* [1899] 2 Ch 121, where Lindley MR held that a document had been found in proper custody in circumstances where it is was found where one would expect such a document to be kept, *i.e.* in the papers of a successor in title of the person named in the document.

[712]   *Malcomson v O'Dea* (1863) 10 HL Cas 593; *Blandy-Jenkins v Earl of Dunraven* [1899] 2 Ch 121. See generally Winokur, "Notes: The Effect of the Ancient Document Rule on the Hearsay Rule" (1935) 83 U Pa L Rev 247.

[713]   (1863) 10 HL Cas 593.

[714]   (1863) 10 HL Cas 593 at 614.

[715]   See Tapper (ed.), *Cross and Tapper on Evidence* 9th edn (London: Butterworths, 1999) p.47; Baker, *The Hearsay Rule* (London: Pitman, 1950) pp.162–163.

[716]   See Bryant, Lederman and Fuerst, *Sopinka, Lederman & Bryant: The Law of Evidence in Canada* 4th edn (Lexis Nexis, 2014), § 6.287; Broun (ed.), *McCormick on Evidence* 7th edn (Thomson Reuters, 2013), § 323.

take judicial notice of those facts. Examples include dictionaries,[717] historical works in order to ascertain ancient facts of a public nature,[718] and certain published maps.[719]

(f) Note of evidence on application for judicial review

5–323 It has been held that it would be inappropriate and contrary to the public interest for a judge whose decision is the subject of an application for judicial review to swear an affidavit because this would leave him or her open to cross-examination in relation to the judicial process.[720] On the basis that it would be "quite wrong that the only person who could not be heard was the judge himself", Kearns J in *McQuaid v McBride*[721] decided to admit a note of the evidence taken by the respondent District Judge which was exhibited in an affidavit sworn by the District Court clerk defending an application for judicial review. While he accepted that this was hearsay evidence, he agreed with the submission made by counsel for the DPP that "there need be no exclusionary rule for such evidence in judicial review where it is relevant and where there are public policy considerations which preclude the respondent from swearing an affidavit". He signalled that he was conscious of the fact that the note of evidence was not in affidavit form. However, he failed to specify if this would affect the weight to be attached to it.

18. Miscellaneous Statutory Exceptions

5–324 The common law exceptions to the hearsay rule have been supplemented by a growing number of statutory exceptions, a number of which have already been examined above, and further miscellaneous examples of which are set out below. Given the existence of numerous express statutory exceptions, the courts have been reluctant to infer the existence of implied statutory exceptions.[722]

(a) Section 21 of the Criminal Justice Act 1984

5–325 Section 21 of the Criminal Justice Act 1984 provides a mechanism to avoid calling witnesses to give routine and non-controversial evidence in criminal proceedings by providing that a written statement by a person is admissible to the like extent as oral evidence as to the like effect by that person would be admissible provided that: (a) the

---

[717] See, e.g. *O'Sullivan v Aquaculture Licences Appeal Board* [2001] 1 IR 646 at 650 (meaning of "strands" in Oxford English Dictionary); *Grant v Roche Products (Ireland) Ltd*, unreported, Master of the High Court, 25 June 2003 (meaning of "hippocampus" in Oxford English Dictionary).

[718] *Read v Bishop of Lincoln* [1892] AC 644 at 653, [1891–4] All ER 227 at 229. *Cf. Foyle & Bann Fisheries Ltd v AG* (1949) 83 ILTR 29 at 37–38. It appears that historical works are only admissible in relation to matters of general history and are not admissible to prove facts of local history (*Stainer v Burgesses of Droitwich* (1695) 1 Salk 281; *Evans v Getting* (1834) 6 C & P 586) or particular facts (*Fowke v Berington* [1914] 2 Ch 308).

[719] See *Re Application of McNeill*, unreported, High Court, 14 December 2001, where Barr J was satisfied, on the basis of a street map dated 1726, having an acceptable provenance and which was likely to be reasonably accurate, that a particular lane in Cork City was a public right of way. As to the position in relation to ordnance survey maps, see the County Boundaries (Ireland) Act 1872 and the Survey (Ireland) Acts 1854–1859 which are considered in *Brown v Donegal County Council* [1980] IR 132.

[720] *O'Connor v Carroll* [1992] IR 160 at 166.

[721] Unreported, High Court, 21 February 2001.

[722] See *Director of Corporate Enforcement v Bailey* [2007] IEHC 365, [2008] 2 ILRM 13, [2011] IESC 24, [2011] 3 IR 278.

statement purports to be signed by the person who made it; (b) the statement contains a declaration by the person to the effect that it is true to the best of his knowledge and belief and that he made the statement knowing that, if it were tendered in evidence, he would be liable to prosecution if he stated in it anything which he knew to be false or did not believe to be true; (c) a copy of the statement is served on each of the other parties to the proceedings; and (d) none of the other parties objects within 21 days to the statement being tendered.[723] Even if there is no objection, the party who served the statement retains a discretion to call the person to give evidence and the court may also, of its own motion, or on the application of any party to the proceedings, require the person to attend and give evidence.[724] If a statement is admitted pursuant to this section, then it will be read aloud at the hearing unless the court otherwise directs.[725]

(b) Applications under the Proceeds of Crime Act 1996

5–326 Section 8 of the Proceeds of Crime Act 1996[726] renders admissible the evidence of the belief of a garda or authorised officer as to certain matters in applications for interim and interlocutory orders freezing the proceedings of crime under that the Act.[727] Such evidence is likely to based on and contain a significant hearsay element. The contention that s.8 was unconstitutional on this basis was rejected by the Supreme Court in *Murphy v GM*[728] which noted that a court was required to act in accordance with the principles of constitutional justice and held that it was a matter for the trial judge to determine what weight, if any, should be given to such hearsay evidence. However, concern about the admission of hearsay evidence pursuant to this section has been expressed in a number of decisions which indicate that the courts will approach such evidence with considerable caution and will be reluctant to make orders on foot of it without other evidence.[729] In *FMcK v TH (Proceeds of crime)*,[730] Hardiman J observed:

> "Any court will, of course, be conscious of the very great potential unfairness of permitting hearsay evidence and belief evidence to be given in legal proceedings. They are capable of gross abuse, and capable of undermining the ability of a person against whom they are deployed to defend himself by cross-examination. It is, accordingly, essential to ensure that the conditions under which this court held their use constitutionally justifiable in this unique statutory context are in fact met."

5–327 In *PB v AF*,[731] Feeney J emphasised that, while s.8 permits the introduction of hearsay evidence, such evidence is not conclusive and is open to challenge by a respondent. Accordingly, the court has to have regard to the ability of the person against whom such evidence is deployed to defend himself or herself by way of cross-examination of the persons giving such evidence and the extent of the respondent's

---

[723] See subss.(1) and (2).

[724] Subsection (5).

[725] Subsection (7).

[726] No.30 of 1996.

[727] The admission of opinion evidence pursuant to this section and the weight to be attached to it is considered in Chap.6.

[728] [2001] 4 IR 113 at 155.

[729] See *M v D*, unreported, High Court, 10 December 1996 and *Gilligan v Criminal Assets Bureau* [1998] 3 IR 185 at 243; *P.B. v A.F.* [2012] IEHC 428 at [3.6]. *Cf. Criminal Assets Bureau v Craft* [2001] 1 IR 121 where a submission was made but not dealt with by O'Sullivan J that s.8 was unconstitutional because it deprived the defendant of the opportunity to cross-examine the garda as to his sources.

[730] [2006] IESC 63 at [22], [2007] 4 IR 186 at 194, [2007] 1 ILRM 338 at 345–346.

[731] [2012] IEHC 428 at [3.6].

ability, if any, to give contradictory evidence. This was a significant factor in the determination by a court as to whether it should rely on such evidence.

5–328   Apart from the provisions of s.8, it appears that hearsay evidence is admissible on interlocutory applications under the Proceeds of Crime Act 1996 on the same basis as in other civil proceedings although the weight to be attached to it is a matter for the court.[732]

5–329   A separate exception to the hearsay rule of somewhat indeterminate scope that is also relevant to applications under the Proceeds of Crime Act 1996 is created by the provisions of s.8, subss.(5)[733] and (7)[734] of the Criminal Assets Bureau Act 1996.[735] The effect of these subsections is that an officer of the Criminal Assets Bureau may disclose information obtained for the purposes of the Act to specified other persons and those persons, including other officers of the bureau, may exercise or perform their duties on foot of any such information including forming a belief that is admissible by virtue of s.8 of the Proceeds of Crime Act 1996.[736] If this occurs, then any information, documents or other material obtained is admissible in evidence in any subsequent proceedings.

5–330   The extent of the abrogation of the hearsay rule by these provisions was considered by the Supreme Court in *Criminal Assets Bureau v Hunt*.[737] In the course of inquires into the affairs of the defendant, an officer of the plaintiff had obtained orders for the production of accounts in the names of the defendants in certain financial institutions and, on foot of those orders, was furnished with relevant documents including bank statements. The defendants argued that the plaintiff was not entitled to rely on these bank statements in proceedings brought by it for the recovery of the taxes due unless they were properly proved in evidence as otherwise they were hearsay. In response, the plaintiff claimed that it was entitled to rely on those documents by virtue of the provisions of s.8(5) and (7). Delivering the judgment of the Supreme Court, Keane CJ acknowledged that the "precise scope of the abridgement of the rule of hearsay effected by those provisions is difficult to identify"[738] but it appeared that:

> "[W]here it is a necessary proof in proceedings, whether under the Act of 1996 or other legislation, that a bureau officer takes certain actions as a result of information, documents or other material received by him from another bureau officer, the court may act on the sworn evidence of the bureau officer that he received the information, documents or other material

---

[732] See *Murphy v GM PB PC Ltd* [1999] IEHC 5, where O'Higgins J rejected the contention that it was constitutionally unfair to admit hearsay evidence on interlocutory applications under the Proceeds of Crime Act because there was no requirement for an undertaking as to damages and the substantive hearing could not take place for seven years.

[733] Subs. (5) provides that: "A bureau officer may exercise of perform his or her powers or duties on foot of any information received by him or her from another bureau officer or on foot of any action taken by that other bureau officer in the exercise or performance of that other bureau officer's powers or duties for the purposes of this Act, and any information, documents or other material obtained by bureau officers under this subsection shall be admitted in evidence in any subsequent proceedings."

[734] Subs. (7) provides that: "Any information or material obtained by a bureau officer for the purposes of this Act may only be disclosed by the bureau officer to [certain specified persons]...and information, documents or other material obtained by a bureau officer or any other person under the provisions of this subsection shall be admitted in evidence in any subsequent proceedings."

[735] No.31 of 1996.

[736] *FMcK v TH (Proceeds of crime)* [2006] IESC 63 at [26]–[27], [2007] 4 IR 186 at 195, [2007] 1 ILRM 338 at 347.

[737] [2003] 2 IR 168, [2003] 2 ILRM 481.

[738] [2003] 2 IR 168 at 189, [2003] 2 ILRM 481 at 501.

from the other bureau officer. To that extent, the rule against hearsay is relaxed and the court is entitled to accept as truthful an unsworn statement made out of court by a bureau officer to the bureau officer who gives evidence that he acted on foot of the information in question."

5–331 However, the Chief Justice cautioned against adopting an over broad interpretation of the subsections:

"However, it certainly does not follow from the fact that the unsworn out-of-court statement of the first bureau officer to the bureau officer giving evidence is admissible that any evidence which he obtained and of which he informs the bureau officer giving evidence, is also admissible. That would have the absurd consequence that a bureau officer would be precluded by the operation of the rule against hearsay from giving evidence as to what he was told by another person not before the court, but that the same plainly admissible evidence could be rendered admissible if he informed another bureau officer of the contents of the conversation."

5–332 This was a construction that he was only prepared to give to the provisions if they were incapable of any other construction and he was satisfied that this was not the case. Thus, the plaintiff was required to properly prove the bank statements in evidence and, as it had failed to do so, they should not have been admitted in evidence.

(c) Material under the Criminal Justice (Theft and Fraud Offences) Act 2001

5–333 Under s.52(2) of the Criminal Justice (Theft and Fraud Offences) Act 2001, a District Judge, if satisfied as to certain matters,[739] can make an order that a person produce material to a garda for the member to take away, or give the garda access to it. Pursuant to s.52(6)(a), information contained in a document which was produced to a garda, or to which a garda was given access, in accordance with an order under the section is admissible in any criminal proceedings as evidence of any fact therein of which direct oral evidence would be admissible unless the information: (a) is privileged from disclosure in such proceedings; (b) was supplied by a person who would not be compellable to give evidence at the instance of the prosecution, (c) was compiled for the purposes or in contemplation of any: (i) criminal investigation, (ii) investigation or inquiry carried out pursuant to or under any enactment, (iii) civil or criminal proceedings, or (iv) proceedings of a disciplinary nature. Subsection (6)(b) applies the provisions of ss.7, 8 and 9 of the Criminal Evidence Act 1992 to such a document and it is stipulated in subs.(6)(a) that a document will not be admissible unless those provisions are complied with.

(d) Section 50 of the Criminal Justice Act 2007

5–334 Section 50(4C)(a) of the Criminal Justice Act 2007[740] provides that a member of an Garda Síochána applying for an extension of time of the period of detention for the investigation of a specified offence may give evidence in relation to any matter within the knowledge of another member of the Garda Síochána that is relevant to the application notwithstanding that it is not within the personal knowledge of the member. However, the Court hearing such an application may, if it considers it to be in the interests of justice to do so, direct that another member of the Garda Síochána

---

[739] The District Judge, on hearing evidence on oath given by a garda, must be satisfied that: (a) the Gardaí are investigating an offence to which the section applies; (b) a person has possession or control of particular material or material of a particular description; and (c) there are reasonable grounds for suspecting that the material constitutes evidence of or relating to the commission of the offence.

[740] As inserted by s.23 of the Criminal Justice (Amendment) Act 2009.

give oral evidence and the Court may adjourn the hearing of the application for the purpose of receiving such evidence.[741]

(e) The Report of an Inspector appointed pursuant to the Companies Act 1990

5–335   Section 22 of the Companies Act 1990 provides that a document purporting to be a copy of a report of an inspector appointed under the provisions of that Act is admissible in civil proceedings as evidence: "(a) of the facts set out therein without further proof unless the contrary is shown, and (b) of the opinion of the inspector in relation to any matter contained in the report." This section therefore creates not just a wide ranging exception to the hearsay rule but also accords a particular evidential status to such a report. The construction and application of this section was considered by Laffoy J in *Countyglen plc v Carway*[742] who held that:

> "...the word "facts" means primary or basic facts and not secondary or inferred facts. The words "without further proof", in my view, indicate that what the legislature intended was that facts which would be provable by witnesses in the ordinary way, and not deductions from facts found or admitted, should acquire the status of proven facts under section 22."[743]

5–336   She went on to observe that the section does not prescribe that facts thereby given the status of proven facts have any special probative value or that any particular weight should be attached thereto so that the ordinary rules apply to the assessment of such evidence and the weight to be applied to it.

E. Development of the Hearsay Rule

5–337   The rule against hearsay has been criticised judicially as "absurdly technical"[744] and "a branch of the law which has little to do with commonsense".[745] It is evident that it can operate to exclude the only or the best evidence that can be obtained in relation to a particular issue[746] and there is little doubt that, as stated by Keane J in *People (DPP) v McGinley*,[747] the rule "is capable of producing injustice in individual cases, particularly if applied in a rigid and unyielding manner". This is particularly true in criminal cases where, applying a principle of mutuality, the courts have refused to relax the hearsay rule in respect of probative evidence that is crucial to the defence

---

[741] Section 50(4C)(b).

[742] [1998] 2 IR 540.

[743] [1998] 2 IR 540 at 550–551. Her decision on this point was followed by McGovern J in *Director of Corporate Enforcement v Stakelum* [2007] IEHC 486 at [16].

[744] *Per* Lord Reid in *Myers v DPP* [1965] AC 1001 at 1019, [1964] 2 All ER 881 at 884.

[745] *Per* Diplock LJ in *Jones v Metcalfe* [1967] 3 All ER 205 at 208.

[746] See the comments of Cherry LJ in *Donaghy v Ulster Spinning Company Ltd* (1912) 46 ILTR 33 at 34.

[747] [1998] 2 IR 408 at 413, [1998] 2 ILRM 233 at 237. This comment was endorsed by Hardiman J in *People (DPP) v McLoughlin* [2009] IESC 65 at [40], [2010] 1 IR 590 at 601, [2010] 1 ILRM 1 at 10.

of an accused.[748] In *People (AG) v O'Brien*,[749] the Court of Criminal Appeal rejected the contention that the hearsay rule should be relaxed in favour of the accused with Kenny J stating that:

> "In a criminal trial, the administration of justice according to law means justice for the People and for the accused and the admission in evidence of matters which either side wishes to produce must be decided by the same principles of law."[750]

5–338 Furthermore, as will be evident from the review of the exceptions to the hearsay rule above, these have developed piecemeal and on an *ad hoc* basis with the result that there is, in relation to many of the exceptions, a dissonance between the parameters of the exception and the underlying rationale. In *Myers v DPP*,[751] Lord Reid reviewed the development of the exceptions to the hearsay rule and commented:

> "[I]n most cases we do not know how or when the exception came to be recognised. It does seem, however, that in many cases there was no justification either in principle or logic for carrying the exception just so far and no farther. One might hazard a surmise that when the rule proved highly inconvenient in a particular kind of case it was relaxed just sufficiently far to meet that case, and without regard to any question of principle."[752]

5–339 Furthermore, as Keane J pointed out in *Eastern Health Board v MK*,[753] the result of the development of a number of intricate exceptions by both the courts and the legislature designed "to avoid the injustice and inconvenience which would flow from an unyielding adherence to the rule" has been "a body of law which is confusing, complex and not entirely logical".

5–340 In such circumstances, it would seem natural that the courts should continue to develop the contours of the hearsay rule and its exceptions. However, such a jurisdiction was disavowed by a majority of the House of Lords in the landmark case of *Myers v DPP*[754] with Lord Reid stating that any further development of the rule or its exceptions would have to be by way of legislation following a wide survey of the field.[755] A different view was taken by Lords Pearce and Donovan in their dissenting judgments with Lord Donovan advocating the position that:

> "The common law is moulded by the judges, and it is still their province to adapt it from time

---

[748] See *R. v Gray* (1841) 2 Cr & Dix 129 (evidence of death bed confession to crime with which accused was charged excluded); *R. v Thomson* [1912] 3 KB 19 (on a charge of procuring a miscarriage, statements made by the deceased woman before her miscarriage that she had intended to operate upon herself and, shortly after her miscarriage that she had operated upon herself, were excluded). However, the Law Reform Commission, *The Rule Against Hearsay* (Working Paper No. 9–1980), pp. 11–12, stated that the courts freely allow hearsay evidence which is of probative value to be given on behalf of the defence in criminal cases and concluded that "there are very few reported cases in the last fifty years, apart from those dealing with confessions, where evidence of any probative value has been shut out by the operation of the rule against hearsay".

[749] (1969) 1 Frewen 343.

[750] (1969) 1 Frewen 343 at 345. See, to the same effect, *per* Lord Alverstone in *R. v Thomson* [1912] 3 KB 19 at 21: "If put in the popular way, the argument for the appellant, that what the woman had said she had done to herself ought to be admissible evidence for the defence, might be attractive; but upon consideration it is seen to be a dangerous argument, and, in the opinion of the Court, the rejection of evidence of that kind is much more in favour of the accused than of the prosecution. If such evidence is admissible for one side it must also be admissible for the other."

[751] [1965] AC 1001, [1964] 2 All ER 881.

[752] [1965] AC 1001 at 1020, [1964] 2 All ER 881 at 884.

[753] [1999] 2 IR 99 at 124, [1999] 2 ILRM 321 at 345.

[754] [1965] AC 1001, [1964] 2 All ER 881.

[755] [1965] AC 1001 at 1021, [1964] 2 All ER 881 at 886.

to time so as to make it serve the interests of those it binds. Particularly is this so in the field of procedural law. Here the question is posed—'Shall the courts admit as evidence of a particular fact authentic and reliable records by which alone the fact may be satisfactorily proved?' I think that the courts themselves are able to give an affirmative answer to that question."[756]

5–341   That approach of the majority in *Myers* has, not, however, found favour in other jurisdictions. In *Ares v Venner*[757] the Canadian Supreme Court preferred the approach of the minority in *Myers*, that the courts could develop the hearsay rule and in that case created a new exception for hospital records that satisfied certain conditions.[758] Subsequently, in *R. v Khan*,[759] McLachlin J, delivering the judgment of the Supreme Court, criticised the rigidity of the hearsay rule and advocated a more flexible approach:

> "The hearsay rule has traditionally been regarded as an absolute rule, subject to various categories of exceptions…While this approach has provided a degree of certainty to the law on hearsay, it has frequently proved unduly inflexible in dealing with new situations and new needs in the law. This has resulted in courts in recent years on occasion adopting a more flexible approach, rooted in the principle and the policy underlying the hearsay rule rather than the strictures of the traditional exceptions."[760]

5–342   She identified the twin considerations that should govern the creation of new exceptions as being (i) the necessity of the evidence to prove a fact in issue, and (ii) the reliability of the evidence. Applying those criteria in that case, it was held that a statement made by the complainant to her mother was admissible in evidence on a charge of sexual assault against the accused on the basis that she was incompetent to testify and the circumstances in which it was made were such that it was reliable.

5–343   As interpreted in subsequent decisions, the effect of the decision in *Khan* was to create a general inclusionary exception to the hearsay rule based on the criteria of necessity and reliability.[761] In *R. v Smith*,[762] Lamer CJC stated that the decision in *Khan* "should be understood as the triumph of a principled analysis over a set of ossified judicially created categories" and emphasised the sweeping nature of the change effected by that decision:

> "*Khan* should not be understood as turning on its particular facts, but, instead, must be seen as a particular expression of the fundamental principles that underlie the hearsay rule and the exceptions to it. What is important, in my view, is the departure signalled by *Khan* from a view of hearsay characterised by a general prohibition on the reception of such evidence, subject to a limited number of defined categorical exceptions, and a movement towards a flexible approach governed by principles which underlie the rule and its exceptions alike…. The court's decision in *Khan*, therefore, signalled an end to the old categorical approach to the admission of hearsay evidence. Hearsay evidence is now admissible on a principled basis, the governing principles being the reliability of the evidence, and its necessity."[763]

---

[756] [1965] AC 1001 at 1047, [1964] 2 All ER 881 at 902.
[757] (1970) 14 DLR (3d) 4.
[758] *Cf. Hughes v Staunton,* unreported, High Court, 16 February 1990, where Lynch J indicated a willingness to admit nursing records notwithstanding the rule against hearsay, stating that such notes are "quite reliable and probably every bit as good as if a nurse were called to verify them provided that there is no ambiguity or uncertainty in them and even though they are technically speaking pure hearsay".
[759] [1990] 2 SCR 531, (1990) 79 CR (3d) 1 at 9.
[760] [1990] 2 SCR 531 at 540.
[761] See *R. v Smith* [1992] 2 SCR 915, (1992) 94 DLR (4th) 590; *R. v B. (K.G.)* [1993] 1 SCR 740; *R. v Finta* [1994] 1 SCR 701, (1994) 112 DLR (4th) 513.
[762] [1992] 2 SCR 915, (1992) 94 DLR (4th) 590.
[763] [1992] 2 SCR 915 at 932–933, (1992) 94 DLR (4th) 590 at 603–604.

5–344 He went on to explain further what was meant by the concepts of necessity and reliability. He said that the criterion of necessity must be given a flexible definition but gave as examples of where it would be satisfied, where the declarant was dead, insane, out of the jurisdiction or otherwise unavailable to testify. As regards reliability, if a hearsay statement "is made under circumstances which substantially negate the possibility that the declarant was untruthful or mistaken, the hearsay evidence may be said to be 'reliable,' *i.e.* a circumstantial guarantee of trustworthiness is established."[764]

5–345 However, the approach taken in those decisions did not met with universal acclaim[765] and, following a number of attempts to refine the principles applicable in deciding whether hearsay statements were sufficiently reliable to be admissible,[766] the Supreme Court of Canada revisited this question in *R. v Khelawon*.[767] At issue in that appeal was the admissibility of the videotaped unsworn statement of a resident of a nursing home who alleged that the accused had assaulted him but who had died by the time of the trial. In a unanimous judgment delivered by Charron J, the Supreme Court held that the statement should not have been admitted because it was not sufficiently reliable and the unavailability of the complainant for cross-examination significantly impaired the accused's ability to test the evidence and the trier of fact's ability to assess it. Charron J comprehensively reviewed the previous jurisprudence and emphasised that hearsay is presumptively inadmissible and, even where the twin criteria of necessity and reliability are satisfied, the trial judge retained a discretion to exclude the evidence:

> "In determining the question of threshold reliability, the trial judge must be mindful that hearsay evidence is presumptively *inadmissible*. The trial judge's function is to guard against the admission of hearsay evidence which is unnecessary in the context of the issue to be decided, or the reliability of which is neither readily apparent from the trustworthiness of its contents, nor capable of being meaningfully tested by the ultimate trier of fact. In the context of a criminal case, the accused's inability to test the evidence may impact on the fairness of the trial, thereby giving the rule a constitutional dimension. Concerns over trial fairness not only permeate the decision on admissibility, but also inform the residual discretion of the trial judge to exclude the evidence even if necessity and reliability can be shown. As in all cases, the trial judge has the discretion to exclude admissible evidence where its prejudicial effect is out of proportion to its probative value."[768]

5–346 With regard to the criteria of necessity and reliability, she stressed the duty of the trial judge to ensure the integrity of the trial process which meant that hearsay evidence could not be admitted where it would compromise the fairness of the trial:

> "The broader spectrum of interests encompassed in trial fairness is reflected in the twin

---

[764] [1992] 2 SCR 915 at 933, (1992) 94 DLR (4th) 590 at 604.

[765] See Carter, "Hearsay: Whether and Whither?" (1993) 109 LQR 573 at 582 where it is argued that *R. v Smith* should be strictly construed so as to place a limitation on the invocation of the residual exception, in order to avoid the sacrifice of certainty and predictability and the complication of the judicial task. Schiff, *Evidence in the Litigation Process*, Master ed., Vol 1 4th edn (Toronto: Carswell, 1993), p.661, questions whether this approach is consistent with the adversarial nature of the trial, in light of the reduced opportunity to cross-examine. He also suggests that such a step should have been left to the legislature (at p.682), and that it may lengthen the trial process (pp.660–661). See also Rosenberg, "B(KG) – Necessity and Reliability: the New Pigeonholes" (1993) 19 CR (4th) 69 at 71.

[766] See *R. v U(FJ)* [1995] 3 SCR 764, 128 DLR (4th) 121; *R. v Rockey* [1996] 3 SCR 829; *R. v Hawkins* [1996] 3 SCR 1043; *R. v Starr* [2000] SCR 40; *R. v Parrott* [2001] 1 SCR 178; *R. v Mapara* [2005] 1 SCR 358.

[767] [2006] 2 SCR 787. See Ives, *"R. v Khelawon* – continuing reform of the law of hearsay in Canada"* (2007) 11 E & P 213.

[768] [2006] 2 SCR 787 at [3].

principles of necessity and reliability. The criterion of necessity is founded on society's interest in getting at the truth. Because it is not always possible to meet the optimal test of contemporaneous cross-examination, rather than simply losing the value of the evidence, it becomes necessary in the interests of justice to consider whether it should nonetheless be admitted in its hearsay form. The criterion of reliability is about ensuring the integrity of the trial process. The evidence, although needed, is not admissible unless it is sufficiently reliable to overcome the dangers arising from the difficulty of testing it. As we shall see, the reliability requirement will generally be met on the basis of two different grounds, neither of which excludes consideration of the other. In some cases, because of the circumstances in which it came about, the contents of the hearsay statement may be so reliable that contemporaneous cross-examination of the declarant would add little if anything to the process. In other cases, the evidence may not be so cogent but the circumstances will allow for sufficient testing of evidence by means other than contemporaneous cross-examination. In these circumstances, the admission of the evidence will rarely undermine trial fairness. However, because trial fairness may encompass factors beyond the strict inquiry into necessity and reliability, even if the two criteria are met, the trial judge has the discretion to exclude hearsay evidence where its probative value is outweighed by its prejudicial effect."[769]

5–347   A conservative approach to the admission of hearsay evidence was also advocated by the New Zealand Court of Appeal in *R. v Manase*.[770] In that case, the accused was charged with sexual offences against a child who was three and a half years old at the time of the offences. The victim was not called to give evidence because she could not remember any of the incidents or statements that she had made and the prosecution sought to adduce in evidence statements made by the child to her mother and another person. The trial judge admitted the evidence but the Court of Appeal held that he had been incorrect to do so.

5–348   The Court, in a judgment delivered by Tipping J, began by reviewing and criticising the approach taken in the Canadian cases:

"Our review of these cases leads us to the view that the concept of reasonable necessity as a criterion for admitting hearsay is imprecise and problematic. It has led the Canadian Courts to allow hearsay to be introduced in circumstances which depend on little more than the trial Judge's subjective opinion that it would be desirable to let it in.

The Canadian concept of necessity now reaches well beyond the idea of the primary witness being unavailable. It encompasses cases in which the primary witness is available, in any ordinary sense of the term, but the Judge considers it would be unduly onerous to require that person to give evidence. There is force in [the] submission that in Canada the grounds for admission of hearsay have been diluted to little more than relevance coupled with a sufficient degree of reliability. We consider that this is going too far, at least as a general touchstone of admissibility. The common law of New Zealand should not be developed in this way, nor should we adopt terminology which is apt to encourage gradual slippage to this effect."[771]

5–349   While he confirmed that existence of a general residual exception to the hearsay rule, he stressed the importance of applying it within well defined parameters:

"We do not consider the Court should confine itself to specific categories. The flexibility provided by a residual category is appropriate, provided the residual category has sufficient signposts to enable this part of the law of evidence to be administered in a way which is not only reasonably predictable, but also consistent and fair to the competing interests. Too great an element of subjectivity is not likely to achieve those objectives."[772]

5–350   He then went on to identify the requirements that had to be satisfied before a hearsay statement could be admitted under the residual exception:

---

[769] [2006] 2 SCR 787 at [49].
[770] [2001] 2 NZLR 197. See also *R. v S&H* [2007] NZCA 37.
[771] [2001] 2 NZLR 197 at 202.
[772] [2001] 2 NZLR 197 at 203.

"(a) **Relevance.** This is not strictly a requirement directed to this exception to the hearsay rule. Rather it is an affirmation and a reminder of the overriding criterion for the admissibility of all and any evidence. It is a self-contained issue. The evidence in question either has sufficient relevance or it does not. The same test applies as would have applied to the primary (*i.e.* non-hearsay) evidence.

(b) **Inability.** This requirement will be satisfied when the primary witness is unable for some reason to be called to give primary evidence. If the primary witness is personally able to give that evidence, it will seldom, if ever, be appropriate to admit hearsay evidence simply because the witness would prefer not to face the ordeal of giving evidence or would find it difficult to do so. To adopt that approach would be to tilt the balance too far against the accused or opposite party who is thereby deprived of the ability to cross-examine.

(c) **Reliability.** The hearsay evidence must have sufficient apparent reliability, either inherent or circumstantial, or both, to justify its admission in spite of the dangers against which the hearsay rule is designed to guard. We use the expression 'apparent unreliability' to signify that the Judge is the gatekeeper and decides whether to admit the evidence or not. If the evidence is admitted, the jury or the Judge, as the trier of fact, must decide how reliable the evidence is and therefore what weight should be placed on it. If a sufficient threshold level of apparent reliability is not reached, the hearsay evidence should not be admitted. The inability of a primary witness to give evidence is not good reason to admit unreliable hearsay evidence.

As a final check, as with all evidence admitted before a jury, the Court must consider whether the hearsay evidence which otherwise might qualify for admission should nevertheless be excluded because its probative value is outweighed by its illegitimate prejudicial effect."[773]

5–351 The extent of the willingness on the part of the Irish courts to further develop the hearsay rule and, in particular, to develop a general inclusionary exception along the lines of either the Canadian or New Zealand model is not clear. After some initial indications that any major extension of the exceptions would have to be by way of legislation,[774] it now appears that the courts accept that they do have the jurisdiction to develop the hearsay rule and its exceptions.

5–352 In *Eastern Health Board v MK*,[775] it was argued strongly by counsel for the second respondent that the exceptions to the hearsay rule could not be extended by the courts and, if a new exception to the hearsay rule was to be created, this should be done by the Oireachtas. However, this proposition was rejected by Denham J who said that the fact that the legislature had extended the exceptions to the hearsay rule did not exclude the jurisdiction of the courts to do so. She was strongly of the view that the hearsay rule and its exceptions "are not set in stone" and the courts retained the jurisdiction to develop modern jurisprudence on the use of hearsay evidence. Keane J also referred to the existence of exceptions designed "to avoid the injustice and inconvenience which would flow from an unyielding adherence to the rule". Although he was more sympathetic to the argument that any major new exception to the hearsay rule would be best effected by the legislature, he did not rule out the possibility of new judicially-created exceptions grounded on the twin criteria of necessity and reliability which he identified as the common underlying features of exceptions to the hearsay rule. Indeed, the decision provides support for, at least, a limited exception to the hearsay rule for videotape evidence of interviews with children, with both Keane and Barrington JJ expressing doubts as to whether evidence adduced by means of a video recording could properly be described as hearsay evidence because the court could see and hear an exact electronic recording of the statement as it was actually made.

---

[773] [2001] 2 NZLR 197 at 206 (emphasis in the original).
[774] *Cf. People (DPP) v Prunty* [1986] ILRM 716 at 718.
[775] [1999] 2 IR 99 (also reported *sub nom. In the Matter of MK, SK, and WK* [1999] 2 ILRM 321).

5–353   In *Borges v Medical Council*,[776] Keane CJ once more left open the question as to whether the approach in the Canadian cases of developing exceptions to the hearsay rule based on the criteria of necessity and reliability would be followed in this jurisdiction taking the view that it was, in the particular circumstances of that case, sufficient to hold that the applicant could not "be deprived of his right to fair procedures, which necessitate the giving of evidence by his accusers and their being cross-examined, by the extension of the exceptions to the rule against hearsay to a case in which they are unwilling to testify in person."[777]

5–354   Taken together the decisions of the Supreme Court in *Eastern Health Board* and *Borges* indicate a consistent view on the part of the Court that the hearsay rule is not merely a rule of evidence but has a constitutional foundation as a requirement of fair procedures and an ingredient of a fair trial. That being the case, it seems unlikely that the Court will favour a relaxation of the hearsay rule to the extent that is evident in the Canadian jurisprudence. Instead, any new exceptions to the hearsay rule, whether specific or of a general residual nature, are likely to have carefully and narrowly drawn parameters with a focus on the two crucial criteria of necessity and reliability.

5–355   Given the academic and judicial criticisms of the hearsay rule and the reluctance of the courts to develop broad new exceptions to it, pressure has built for legislative reform in this area. As far back as 1980, the Law Reform Commission expressed the view that it was undesirable to retain the rule against hearsay rule as a rigid exclusionary rule of evidence although it limited its detailed recommendations for reform to civil cases.[778] Some of those recommendations provided the basis for legislative intervention in this area such as the provisions in the Children Act 1997 discussed above. The Law Reform Commission has recently revisited the hearsay rule in both civil and criminal cases[779] and re-evaluated the approach that should be adopted in light of the jurisprudence discussed above which has identified a constitutional basis for the hearsay rule. In relation to civil cases, the Commission has reiterated its previous recommendation that there should be a general inclusionary rule in civil cases subject to safeguards,[780] a proposal which it believes would pass constitutional muster.[781] However, it has advocated a more cautious approach in criminal cases,[782] rejecting a broad inclusionary discretion,[783] and recommending that the hearsay rule

---

[776] [2004] IESC 9, [2004] 1 IR 103, [2004] 2 ILRM 81.

[777] [2004] IESC 9, [2004] 1 IR 103 at 119, [2004] 2 ILRM 81 at 96.

[778] See the Law Reform Commission's *Working Paper on the Rule Against Hearsay* (LRC WP 9–1980) at 201. These recommendations were repeated in the Law Reform Commission's *Report on the Rule Against Hearsay in Civil Cases* (LRC 25–1988). A template in that regard may be provided by the Civil Evidence Act 1995 in England and Wales which implemented the recommendations of the Law Commission, *The Hearsay Rule in Civil Proceedings* (Law Com. No. 216, Cm23a21 (1993)) and abolished the hearsay rule in civil cases and introduced certain safeguards relating to the reception of hearsay evidence. See generally, Malek (ed.), *Phipson on Evidence* 18th edn, Chap.29. The hearsay rule has also been abolished in civil cases in Scotland by s.2(1) of the Civil Evidence (Scotland) Act 1988 (see Ross and Chalmers, *Walker and Walker The Law of Evidence in Scotland* (Tottel, 2009), Chap.8).

[779] See Law Reform Commission, *Consultation Paper on Hearsay in Civil and Criminal Cases* (LRC CP 60–2010).

[780] LRC CP 60–2010 at [4.106]–[4.117].

[781] LRC CP 60–2010 at [2.121].

[782] LRC CP 60–2010 at [2.122].

[783] Such an approach is adopted in South Africa where the Law of Evidence Amendment Act 1988 confers a wide discretion to admit hearsay evidence in accordance with specified criteria in both

should continue to operate on an exclusionary basis subject to the existing common law and statutory inclusionary exceptions.[784] It can be anticipated that the recommendations of the Commission will drive legislative (and perhaps curial) reform in this area in the coming years.

---

civil and criminal cases (see *State v Ramavhale* [1996] ZASCA 14; *State v Ndhlovu* [2002] ZASCA 70; *State v Mamushe* [2007] ZASCA 58; *State v Libazi* [2010] ZASCA 91; *State v Mpungose* [2011] ZASCA 60 and Mujuzi, "Hearsay evidence in South Africa—should courts add the "sole and decisive rule" to their arsenal?" (2013) 17 E & P 347 where the authorities are reviewed). An inclusionary approach has also been adopted in New Zealand where s.18 of the Evidence Act 2006 provides that hearsay is admissible if the circumstances relating to the statement provide reasonable assurance that the statement is reliable and the maker of the statement is unavailable or the Judge considers that undue expense or delay would be caused if the maker of the statement were required to be a witness.

[784] LRC CP 60–2010 at [5.46]. That recommendation chimes with the view expressed in the Report of the Balance in the Criminal Law Review Group (2007) at p.231 that, while it would be useful to codify and clarify the law, the hearsay rule "should not generally be relaxed". It could also pave the way for a regime along the lines currently adopted in England and Wales in the Criminal Justice Act 2003 which maintains an exclusionary approach to hearsay but has replaced and broadened a number of the common law exceptions and introduced new statutory exceptions together with an inclusionary discretion. See generally, *Phipson on Evidence* 18th edn, Chap.30, Birch, "Criminal Justice Act 2003 (4) Hearsay: Same Old Story, Same Old Song?" [2004] Crim LR 556 and Worthen, "The Hearsay Provisions of the Criminal Justice Act 2003: so far, not so good? [2008] Crim LR 431.

CHAPTER 6

OPINION EVIDENCE

A. Introduction

6–01   The exclusionary rule relating to opinion evidence was summarised as follows by Kingsmill Moore J in *AG (Ruddy) v Kenny*[1]:

> "It is a long standing rule of our law of evidence that, with certain exceptions, a witness may not express an opinion as to a fact in issue. Ideally, in the theory of our law, a witness may testify only to the existence of facts which he has observed with one or more of his own five senses. It is for the tribunal of fact – judge or jury as the case may be – to draw inferences of fact, form opinions and come to conclusions."[2]

6–02   Thus, witnesses are generally confined to giving evidence of facts that they perceived and it is the function of the tribunal of fact to make inferences or draw conclusions from those facts.[3] However, the line between fact and inference is often difficult to draw and it has been observed, with some justification, that "[e]xcept for the sake of convenience there is little, if any, virtue in any distinction resting on the tenuous and frequently false antithesis between fact and opinion".[4]

6–03   The primary rationale for the exclusionary rule is that it prevents witnesses from usurping the role of the tribunal of fact whose function it is to make inferences from, and reach conclusions on the basis of, the facts deposed to by witnesses.[5] In addition, there are risks attendant upon the admission of such evidence because factors such as "prejudice, faulty reasoning and inadequate knowledge" may undermine the reliability of the opinion expressed but may not be evident to the tribunal of fact.[6] These dangers are thought to be particularly acute in the case of jury trials where it is feared that a jury might give undue weight to statements of opinion of a witness. Thus, in the context of a jury trial in a criminal case, the rule arguably has a constitutional anchor in Art.38.1 which guarantees a right to trial by jury for non-minor offences.

---

[1]   (1960) 94 ILTR 185.

[2]   (1960) 94 ILTR 185 at 190. For an account of the origins and development of the use of expert evidence, see the Law Reform Commission's *Consultation Paper on Expert Evidence* (LRC CP 52–2008), Chap.1.

[3]   *AG (Ruddy) v Kenny* (1960) 94 ILTR 185 at 186 (*per* Davitt P); *Director of Corporate Enforcement v Bailey* [2007] IEHC 365, [2008] 1 ILRM 13 at 30; *Sherrard v Jacob* [1965] NI 151 at 156.

[4]   *Per* Dickson J in *R. v Graat* [1982] 2 SCR 819 at 835.

[5]   This rationale has been strongly criticised in Wigmore, *Evidence* (Chadbourn rev., 1978) Vol. VII, para.1917 on the basis that: "There is no such reason for the rule, because the witness, in expressing his opinion, is not attempting to 'usurp' the jury's function; nor could if he desired."

[6]   *AG (Ruddy) v Kenny* (1960) 94 ILTR 185 at 190 (*per* Kingsmill Moore J).

6–04   There are two well established exceptions to the general exclusionary rule. The first is that expert witnesses may give opinion evidence as to matters within the sphere of their expertise on the basis that they possess expertise that permits them to analyse the facts and make inferences which the tribunal of fact is not qualified or capable of making.[7] The second is that non-experts are allowed to give opinion evidence where it is necessary to do so either because of the indivisibility of fact and inference in their testimony, where the tribunal of fact is not in as good a position as the witness to make the inference, or where it is simply expedient to admit such evidence.[8] These exceptions are examined below together with a number of statutory provisions which allow for the admission of opinion evidence in specified circumstances.

B. Expert Evidence

1. Introduction

6–05   Expert evidence[9] is admitted in relation to matters calling for specialised knowledge and expertise on the basis, articulated by Kingsmill Moore J in *AG (Ruddy) v Kenny*,[10] that:

> "The nature of the issue may be such that even if the tribunal of fact had been able to make the observations in person he or they would not have been possessed of the experience or the specialised knowledge necessary to observe the significant facts, or to evaluate the matters observed and to draw the correct inferences of fact."[11]

6–06   Thus, as stated by Lord Cooper in *Davie v Edinburgh Magistrates*,[12] the function of expert witnesses:

> "… is to furnish the judge or jury with the necessary scientific criteria for testing the accuracy of their conclusions, so as to enable the judge or jury to form their own independent judgment by the application of these criteria to the facts proved in evidence."[13]

6–07   In *Wright v AIB Finance & Leasing*[14] Clarke J noted that expert evidence may

---

7   *AG (Ruddy) v Kenny* (1960) 94 ILTR 185 at 186 (*per* Davitt P).
8   *AG (Ruddy) v Kenny* (1960) 94 ILTR 185 at 186 (*per* Davitt P).
9   See generally, Hodgkinson and James, *Expert Evidence: Law and Practice* 3rd edn (London: Sweet & Maxwell, 2010); Dwyer, *The Judicial Assessment of Expert Evidence* (Cambridge: Cambridge University Press, 2008); Dockrell, *A Guide to Expert Witness Evidence* (Bloomsbury Publishing, 2010); Bond et al, *The Expert Witness*, (Sweet & Maxwell, 2007); L Blom Cooper (ed.), *Experts in the Civil Courts'* (Oxford University Press, 2006); Heffernan, *Scientific Evidence: Fingerprints and DNA* (Dublin: Firstlaw, 2006).
10   (1960) 94 ILTR 185.
11   (1960) 94 ILTR 185 at 190. See, to similar effect, *per* Pigot CB in *McFadden v Murdock* (1867) 1 ICLR 211 at 218: "without such evidence, a jury will in some cases find it difficult, and in some almost, if not wholly, impossible to arrive at a just conclusion; because the subject matter may be, to a great extent, or altogether, without the range of their own observation and experience, and not belonging to the ordinary occurrences or transactions among men."
12   1953 SC 34.
13   1953 SC 34 at 40. This passage has been approved in a number of decisions including *L v DPP*, unreported, High Court, 16 April 2002; *People (DPP) v O'Reilly* [2009] IECCA 30 at [27]; *Re Glaxo Group Ltd* [2009] IEHC 277 at [24]; *James Elliott Construction Ltd v Irish Asphalt Ltd* [2011] IEHC 269 at [10]. To similar effect, in *Condron v ACC Bank plc* [2012] IEHC 395 at [19], [2013] 1 ILRM 113 at 123, Charleton J said that: "The purpose of an expert witness is to enable the court to be instructed on arcane disciplines which are outside the experience of a judge or jury."
14   [2013] IESC 55 at [5.1]–[5.4].

be relevant for two different purposes in cases such as personal injury actions. The first is to assist the court in deciding what actually happened on a relevant occasion by providing forensic findings which can be used by the court to assess the credibility and reliability of testimony from fact witnesses in relation to the events in question. The second is to assist the court in deciding whether wrongdoing occurred. He considered the distinction between the two purposes to be important because expert evidence in relation to the first purpose falls to be evaluated in conjunction with the factual evidence whereas evidence directed towards the second purpose will be predicated on but evaluated separately from the factual evidence.

6–08 Although statutory provision is made for the appointment by the Court of experts in a number of specified instances,[15] this is not commonly done outside of the family law arena,[16] and the calling of experts is left to the parties as part of the adversarial process.

6–09 As pointed out by Hardiman J in *JF v DPP*,[17] the admission of expert evidence has the potential to cause unfairness and to give rise to a breach of the principle of *égalité des armes* if an opposing party is not given an adequate opportunity to challenge that evidence and adduce its own expert evidence. In a number of decisions of the European Court of Human Rights, violations of Art. 6 have been found on this basis.[18]

2. Matters in Respect of Which Experts May Give Evidence

6–10 Expert evidence is admissible in respect of matters that call for expertise, *i.e.* matters which fall outside of the ordinary knowledge or expertise of a tribunal of fact.[19] Indeed, in respect of a matter calling for expertise, only expert evidence will be admitted.[20] Such matters traditionally included issues relating to engineering,[21]

---

[15] See, for example, s.20 of the Civil Liability and Courts Act 2004 which provides that, in a personal injuries action, the court may appoint such approved persons as it considers appropriate to carry out investigations into, and give expert evidence in relation to, such matters as the court directs. See further, Holland, "Civil Liability and Courts Act 2004: Some Thoughts on Practicalities" (2006) 6(1) JSIJ 43.

[16] See s.47 of the Family Law Act 1995, discussed below.

[17] [2005] IESC 24, [2005] 2 IR 174.

[18] See *Bonisch v Austria* (1985) 9 EHRR 191; *Brandstetter v Austria* [1991] ECHR 39, (1993) 15 EHRR 378; *Stoimenov v Macedonia* [2007] ECHR 257; *Mirilashvili v Russia* [2008] ECHR 1669; *Masar v Slovakia* [2012] ECHR 806; *CB v Austria* [2013] ECHR 268; *Khodorkovskiy v Russia* [2013] ECHR 747, (2014) 59 EHRR 7; *Matytsina v Russia* [2014] ECHR 334; *Ivanovski v The Former Yugoslav Republic of Macedonia* [2014] ECHR 440. See generally Cummings, *Expert Evidence Deficiencies in the Judgments of the Court of European Union and the European Court of Human Rights* (Kluwer Law International, 2014).

[19] *Condron v ACC Bank plc* [2012] IEHC 395 at [19], [2013] 1 ILRM 113 at 123; *Flynn v Bus Átha Cliath* [2012] IEHC 398 at [9]; *Folkes v Chadd* (1782) 3 Doug KB 157 at 159; *R. v Turner* [1975] QB 834 at 841, [1975] 1 All ER 70 at 74; *R. v Abbey* [1982] 2 SCR 24 at 42; *R. v Mohan* [1994] 2 SCR 9. For a discussion of the approach of the Australian courts, see Gillies, "Opinion Evidence" (1986) 60 ALR 597 and Arnold, "Expert and Lay Opinion Evidence" (1990) Aust BR 219.

[20] See *R. v Wilbain* (1863) 9 Cox CC 448 (evidence as to comparison of handwriting could only be given by expert); *AG v Shearne* [1955–56] Ir Jur Rep 55 at 56 (expert evidence required to establish that particular matter was a material fact which would have influenced an insurer in deciding whether to accept or refuse a proposal); *Confetti Records v Warner Music* [2003] EWHC 1274 (expert evidence required as to meaning of slang used by drug dealers contained in song lyrics).

[21] See *Folkes v Chadd* (1782) 3 Doug KB 157.

science,[22] medicine,[23] accountancy,[24] economics,[25] insurance,[26] actuary,[27] statistics,[28] customs in particular trades,[29] and the practice and standards of competence of professions.[30] However, the categories calling for specialist knowledge are not closed and expert evidence is admissible "wherever peculiar skill and judgment, applied to a particular subject, are required to explain results, or trace them to their causes."[31] With advances in science and technology and ever greater specialisation of knowledge, expert evidence in relation to an increasingly wide range of specialist areas has been admitted including analysis of CCTV footage,[32] accident reconstruction and seatbelt effectiveness,[33] and establishing the time of death on the basis of insect activity.[34]

6–11   Given the rationale for the admission of expert evidence, it necessarily follows that the evidence of an expert must be confined to his or her area of expertise[35] and he or she will not be permitted to give opinion evidence in relation to matters that fall outside that expertise.[36]

6–12   When a matter is within the knowledge and experience of the tribunal of fact,

---

[22]   See *People (DPP) v Allen* [2003] 4 IR 295 (DNA evidence); *In the Goods of Benn* [1938] IR 313 (comparison of handwriting).

[23]   See, *e.g. O'Donovan v Cork County Council* [1967] IR 409; *Best v Wellcome Foundation Ltd* [1993] 3 IR 421 and *Bolton v Blackrock Clinic Ltd*, unreported, Supreme Court, 23 January 1997.

[24]   See, *e.g. Murnaghan Bros. v O'Maoldhomhnaigh* [1991] 1 IR 455; *Carroll Industries plc v Ó Culacháin* [1988] IR 705. See the comments as to expert accountancy evidence by O'Donnell J in *Emerald Meats Ltd v Minister for Agriculture* [2012] IESC 48 at [28].

[25]   See *Yun v MIBI* [2009] IEHC 318.

[26]   See, *e.g. Chariot Inns v Assicurazioni Generali* [1981] IR 199 at 225 and *AG v Sheane* [1955-56] Ir Jur Rep 55 at 56.

[27]   *O'Sullivan v Córas Iompair Éireann* [1978] IR 409.

[28]   See, generally, Malek (ed.), *Phipson on Evidence* (18th edn), Chap.34; Aitken & Taroni "Fundamentals of Statistical Evidence—A Primer for Legal Professionals" (2008) 12 E & P 181.

[29]   See, *e.g. O'Connail v The Gaelic Echo (1954) Ltd* (1958) 92 ILTR 194.

[30]   See, *e.g. O'Donovan v Cork Co Council* [1967] IR 173 (practice of medical practitioners); *Roche v Peilow* [1986] ILRM 189 (practice of solicitors).

[31]   *Per* Pigot CB in *McFadden v Murdock* (1867) 1 ICLR 211 at 218.

[32]   See *People (DPP) v O'Reilly* [2009] IECCA 18. See also *R v Atkins* [2009] EWCA Crim 1876, [2010] 1 Cr App R 8 where evidence from an expert in facial mapping comparing the face of the accused with the face of the offender as recorded on CCTV footage was admitted. Similar evidence was also admitted in *R. v Tang* [2006] NSWCCA 167, [2006] 65 NSWLR 681 as to points of resemblance between photographs of one the accused and surveillance images of one of the offenders. For an analysis of the issues arising in relation to the admissibility of such evidence, see *R. v Gardner* [2004] EWCA Crim 1639, *Shepherd v R* [2011] NZCA 666, [2012] 2 NZLR 609. See also, Roberts "*R. v Atkins* (D and M): evidence — expert — 'facial mapping'" (2010) 2 Crim LR 141; Edmond et al "Law's Looking Glass: Expert Identification Evidence Derived from Photographic and Video Images" (2009) 20(3) CICJ 337; Edmond et al "Atkins and The Emperor: the 'cautious' use of unreliable 'expert' opinion" (2010) 14(2) E & P 146.

[33]   See *McNeilis v Armstrong* [2006] IEHC 269.

[34]   See *People (DPP) v Kavanagh* [2009] IECCA 29.

[35]   *Director of Corporate Enforcement v Bailey* [2007] IEHC 365, [2008] 2 ILRM 13 at 30.

[36]   See *R. v Barnes* [2005] EWCA 1158 and *R. v Bjordal* [2006] Crim LR 183; *Hawkes v London Borough of Southwark* [1998] EWCA Civ 310; *Clark v Ryan* (1960) 103 CLR 486. The dangers of an expert giving evidence outside his area of expertise are illustrated by *R. v Clark (Sally)* [2003] EWCA Crim 1020, [2004] 2 FCR 447 where a renowned paediatrician gave evidence as to the incidence of cot deaths at the trial of the accused for the murder of her sons. He had no experience in relation to statistical analysis and gave what turned out to be seriously flawed statistics about the probabilities of two cot deaths in one family. The conviction was subsequently quashed as unsafe. See Wilson, "Expert testimony in the dock" (2009) 64(4) J Crim L 330.

expert evidence is inadmissible.[37] Such evidence is superfluous because, having regard to the rationale for the admission of expert evidence set out above, it is only required and its admission justified in relation to matters calling for expertise not possessed by the tribunal of fact. In addition, if such evidence is admitted, there is a danger that the tribunal of fact will give such evidence more weight than it deserves.[38] As Sopinka J cautioned in *R. v Mohan*:

> "Dressed up in scientific language which the jury does not easily understand and submitted through a witness of impressive antecedents, this evidence is apt to be accepted by the jury as being virtually infallible and as having more weight than it deserves."[39]

6–13 A good example of the dividing line between matters within and matters without the knowledge and experience of the tribunal of fact can be seen in *McMullen v Farrell*[40] where Barron J was prepared to admit expert evidence relating to the everyday practice of solicitors but indicated that the position would be different in relation to matters concerning the conduct of litigation because the court would itself have knowledge as to how litigation is conducted.

6–14 However, this dividing line is not always respected in practice. In *O'Neill v Dunnes Stores*[41] one of the criticisms made on appeal of a finding of negligence against the defendant arising out of an incident in which the plaintiff had sustained injuries while assisting a security guard employed by the defendant who was trying to apprehend a shoplifter was that no expert evidence had been adduced to support the plaintiff's case. O'Donnell J in the Supreme Court acknowledged that it is not always necessary "to have so called expert evidence, sometimes fanciful and nearly always expensive, on matters that are little more than common sense" and observed that there was no academic discipline of management of shopping centres. Nonetheless, while expert evidence was not essential, he regarded as a convenient way of giving evidence of general practice.[42]

6–15 The issue of the admissibility of expert medical evidence in relation to the mental state of accused persons has generated some difficulties. The general approach of the courts is that such evidence is admissible where it relates to matters that are clearly outside the ordinary knowledge and experience of judges and jurors such as

---

37   *Flynn v Bus Átha Cliath* [2012] IEHC 398 at [9]; *R. v Turner* [1975] QB 834 at 841, [1975] 1 All ER 70 at 74; *R. v Robb* (1991) 93 Cr App R 161 at 164; *R. v Ugoh* [2001] EWCA Crim 1381; *Transport Publishing Co Pty Ltd v Literature Board of Review* (1955) 99 CLR 111 at 119. The question of whether the rule excluding expert evidence in respect of matters that fall within the common knowledge of the tribunal of fact should be abolished or retained has been considered by the Law Reform Commission in its *Consultation Paper on Expert Evidence* (LRC CP 52–2008) which provisionally recommended its retention (at [2.192]).

38   *R. v Turner* [1975] QB 834 at 841, [1975] 1 All ER 70 at 74. *Cf. People (DPP) v Kehoe* [1992] ILRM 481 at 485.

39   [1994] 2 SCR 9 at 21.

40   [1993] 1 IR 123 at 148, [1992] ILRM 776 at 791.

41   [2010] IESC 53, [2011] 1 IR 325, [2011] 1 ILRM 461.

42   [2010] IESC 53 at [33], [2011] 1 IR 325 at 338, [2011] 1 ILRM 461 at 468. In a similar vein, the same judge commented in *Karen Millen Fashions Ltd v Dunnes Stores* [2014] IESC 23 at [17], that: " It is often the case that expert evidence is useful in identifying key issues and presenting them clearly to the court."

insanity,[43] mental illness,[44] mental defect,[45] diminished responsibility,[46] automatism,[47] hypoglycaemia[48] or "battered wife syndrome".[49] However, the courts have refused to admit such evidence in relation to behaviour and matters that are viewed as falling within the experience of the tribunal of fact because it is then regarded as being in a position to evaluate such evidence without any expert assistance.[50]

6–16 A good example can be seen in *R. v Turner*[51] where the appellant had killed his girlfriend by bludgeoning her to death. At his trial for her murder, he put forward a defence of provocation on the basis that he had been in love with her and thought she was carrying his child so that, when she told him that she had been having affairs with other men and the child was not his, he had lost control and hit her with a hammer but without realising what he was doing and without intending to harm her. On appeal, the appellant challenged the refusal of the trial judge to permit him to call a psychiatrist to give evidence, *inter alia*, that he had a deep emotional relationship with his deceased girlfriend which was likely to have caused an explosive release of blind rage when she confessed her infidelity to him. However, the Court of Appeal upheld the ruling of the trial judge with Lawton LJ explaining:

> "We all know that both men and women who are deeply in love can, and sometimes do, have outbursts of blind rage when discovering unexpected wantonness on the part of their loved ones.... Jurors do not need psychiatrists to tell them how ordinary folk who are not suffering from any mental illness are likely to react to the stresses and strains of life. It follows that the proposed evidence was not admissible to establish that the appellant was likely to have been provoked. The same reasoning applies to its suggested admissibility on the issue of credibility. The jury had to decide what reliance they could put on the appellant's evidence.... The jury in this case did not need, and should not have been offered the evidence of a psychiatrist to help them decide whether the appellant's evidence was truthful."[52]

6–17 The decision in *Turner* was approved in this jurisdiction by the Court of Criminal Appeal in *People (DPP) v Kehoe*.[53] The defence of the accused to a charge of murder was provocation. The background to the killing was that the accused had a relationship a woman called Sheila and they had a child together. However, she then became involved with the deceased (his best friend). On the night of the murder, the accused and Sheila had been out drinking and he went back to her apartment with her. While there, he went into one of the bedrooms to see his son but instead discovered

---

[43] See *People (AG) v Fennell (No.1)* [1940] IR 445; *People (AG) v Kelly* (1962) 1 Frewen 267.

[44] See *R. v Riley* [1967] Crim LR 656 (psychoneurosis).

[45] *R. v Masih* [1986] Crim LR 395 (expert evidence may be adduced where person has an IQ of 69 or below and is, therefore, classified as mentally defective but not where he or she has an IQ above 69).

[46] *R. v Dix* (1981) 74 Cr App R 306. The defence of diminished responsibility was introduced in this jurisdiction by s.6(1) of the Criminal Law (Insanity) Act 2006.

[47] *R. v Smith* (1994) 99 Cr App R 326, [1979] 3 All ER 605; *Hill v Baxter* [1958] 1 QB 277, [1958] 1 All ER 193.

[48] *R. v Toner* (1991) 93 Cr App R 382

[49] *Cf. R. v Thornton (No.2)* [1996] 2 All ER 1023, [1996] 1 WLR 1174; *R. v Lavallee* [1990] 1 SCR 852; *R. v Kontinnen* (1991) SASR 114; *R. v Guthrie* (1997) 15 CRNZ 67.

[50] For a general discussion of this area, see Paciocco, "Evaluating Expert Opinion Evidence for the Purpose of Determining Admissibility: Lessons from the Law of Evidence" (1994) 27 CR (4th) 302.

[51] [1975] QB 834, [1975] 1 All ER 70.

[52] [1975] QB 834 at 841–842, [1975] 1 All ER 70 at 74. See also *R. v Weightman* (1991) 92 Cr App R 291. *Cf.* Mackay and Coleman, "Excluding Expert Evidence: A Tale of Ordinary Folk and Common Experience" [1991] Crim LR 800.

[53] [1992] ILRM 481.

the deceased. He gave evidence that this had shocked, upset and annoyed him and he went to the kitchen where he obtained a knife that he used to stab the deceased. In order to bolster his defence of provocation, the accused had called a psychiatrist to give evidence. However, the Court of Criminal Appeal held that such evidence should not have been admitted. The psychiatrist could not give relevant, admissible evidence in relation to the state of mind or temperament of the accused which he could not do himself. Thus, despite the opinion of the expert that he was in a strong position to give a clinical pronouncement on the reality of the accused's defence, the Court took the view that he was merely seeking to articulate in a fuller way the defence of the accused which was properly to be considered by the jury without such elaboration:

"The court is of the opinion that the accused's defence was properly to be considered by the jury without such elaboration and that, further, in the course of his evidence it is clear that Dr Behan overstepped the mark in saying that he believed the accused did not have an intention to kill and that the accused was telling the truth. These are clearly matters four-square within the jury's function and a witness no more than the trial judge or anyone else is not entitled to trespass on what is the jury's function."[54]

6–18 An Australian example of this approach can be seen in *R. v LM*[55] where the Queensland Court of Appeal held that evidence of a psychiatrist about Munchausen's Syndrome by proxy at the trial of a mother for torturing and harming her children was inadmissible. Munro P observed:

"A close examination of Dr Reddan's evidence as to the medical term, factitious disorder (Munchausen's Syndrome) by proxy, used to describe people exhibiting behaviour like that alleged by the prosecution to have been exhibited by the appellant here, demonstrates that it does not relate to matters outside the sound judgment of a reasonable juror without any particular special knowledge or experience. Ordinary people are capable of understanding that some mothers may harm their children through deceitfully manipulating unnecessary medical treatment. As the term factitious disorder (Munchausen's Syndrome) by proxy is merely descriptive of a behaviour, not a psychiatrically identifiable illness or condition, it does not relate to an organised or recognised reliable body of knowledge or experience."[56]

6–19 The reasoning subtending these decisions is that psychiatric evidence is not necessary and is inadmissible where it seeks to deal with matters that judges and juries, applying their common sense and life experience, are adequately equipped to deal with.[57] Indeed, such evidence "if it is given dressed up in scientific jargon"[58] may make

---

54 [1992] ILRM 481 at 485. The decision in *Kehoe* was applied in *People (DPP) v Kavanagh* [2008] IECCA 100 where the Court of Criminal Appeal held that the trial judge had correctly ruled out as inadmissible evidence proposed to be given by a consultant psychiatrist about the personality of the applicant to suggest that she would have found it difficult to refuse to obey and instructions of her co-accuseds.

55 [2004] QCA 192. See also *US v Welch* (2004) 368 F 3d 970 where evidence of a psychologist as to frailties of human memory and the risk of a mistaken identification was held to be in admissible because the risks were understood by jurors.

56 [2004] QCA 192 at [67].

57 *Cf. DW v DPP*, unreported, Supreme Court, 21 October 2003, where, in the context of an application to prevent a trial of sexual offences on the ground of delay, McGuinness J distinguished between cases where the court would be in a position to understand, from its own common sense and general experience of life as to why there was a delay in reporting sexual abuse and cases where the reasons for the delay were less clear and ascertainable. In relation to the first category of cases, any expert evidence would be limited to a general exposition of the reasons for delay in reporting sexual abuse and it would then be for the court to form its own opinion of the influence of these factors. However, in the second category of cases, expert evidence in greater depth might be required.

58 *R. v Turner* [1975] QB 834 at 841, [1975] 1 All ER 70 at 74 (*per* Lawton LJ).

it more difficult for the tribunal of fact to reach a decision. This danger is heightened where, as in *Kehoe*, the evidence goes directly to the issues that the jury have to decide such as whether the accused had an intention to kill.[59] However, it should be noted that, in the decision of the Court of Criminal Appeal in *People (DPP) v Abdi*[60] (which is discussed below), Hardiman J referred with apparent approval to decisions of the English Court of Appeal in *R. v O'Brien*[61] and the High Court of Australia in *Murphy v R.*[62] which indicated that a broader approach to the admission of psychiatric evidence might be taken than that adopted in *Turner*.

6–20 The decisions in *Turner* and *Kehoe* were distinguished in *People (DPP) v Abdi*[63] where the applicant had been convicted of the murder of his infant son. The applicant alleged that he was legally insane at the time and had been acting on the instructions of voices addressing him in his native Somali language. Evidence was given by a consultant psychiatrist on behalf of the prosecution who expressed the opinion that the applicant was not legally insane and that his actions were motivated by his inability to accept that he would be unable to rear his child in his own religious faith, coupled with the threat of losing custody of the child. The applicant appealed his conviction on the basis that the trial judge had erred in admitting that evidence which, it was contended, related to the questions of intention and motive which were matters peculiarly for the jury.

6–21 Delivering the judgment of the Court of Criminal Appeal, Hardiman J noted that insanity had not been alleged in either of *Turner* or *Kehoe* and was of the view that the case before the Court was quite different because insanity had been positively alleged and the prosecution was entitled to call expert evidence to counter that allegation. He further noted that the consultant psychiatrists who gave evidence on behalf of the applicant to the effect that he was legally insane relied on the very violent manner in which the infant had been killed to express the view that a normal person would not have committed the act without a very considerable degree of malice or personality disturbance or psychopathic tendency. That opinion having been expressed, the prosecution was entitled to counter it and, accordingly, the evidence of the consultant psychiatrist for the prosecution was, in principle, admissible. The Court also rejected the contention that there was no factual basis for that opinion. Hardiman J took the opportunity to reaffirm the central role of the jury on the issue of insanity and the permissible limits of expert evidence on this issue[64]:

> "The role of the expert witness is not to supplant the tribunal of fact, be it judge or jury, but to inform that tribunal so that it may come to its own decision. Where there is a conflict of expert evidence it is to be resolved by the jury or by the judge, if sitting without a jury, having regard to the onus of proof and the standard of proof applicable in the particular circumstances. Expert opinion should not be expressed in a form which suggests that the expert is trying to subvert the role of the finder of fact."

---

[59] In Canada, the judiciary has expressed particular concern about psychiatric evidence as regards personality traits: see *R. v Mohan* [1994] 2 SCR 9, (1994) 114 DLR (4th) 419, and *R. v McMillan* [1977] 2 SCR 824, (1977) 73 DLR (3d) 759.
[60] [2005] 1 ILRM 382 at 392.
[61] Unreported, Court of Appeal, 25 January 2000.
[62] (1989) 167 CLR 94.
[63] [2005] 1 ILRM 382. See Kennedy, "Limits of Psychiatric Evidence in Criminal Courts: Morals and Madness" (2005) 1 Medico-Legal Journal of Ireland 13.
[64] [2005] 1 ILRM 382 at 393.

3. Reliability Test

6–22   A matter of controversy is the extent to which a court is required to evaluate the reliability of expert evidence, particularly that which involves novel scientific techniques which have not achieved widespread acceptance, in order to determine its admissibility.

6–23   An exacting reliability test is applied by the US courts. In *Daubert v Merrell Dow Pharmaceuticals, Inc. Daubert v Merrell Dow Pharmaceuticals, Inc*,[65] the US Supreme Court held that rule 702 of the Federal Rules of Evidence[66] imposes an obligation to ensure that scientific testimony is not only relevant but also reliable. A number of criteria were identified by Blackmun J to assist a court in establishing whether a particular theory or technique is reliable or not: (a) whether the theory can be and has been tested; (b) whether it has been subjected to peer review and publication; (c) whether it has a known or potential error rate and there are standards that exist and can be maintained to control its usage; and (d) whether it has attracted general acceptance.[67] Subsequently, in *Kumho Tire Co Ltd v Carmichael*,[68] the application of these criteria was extended beyond scientific evidence to all types of expert evidence and it was emphasised that they were to be applied flexibly.

6–24   The Canadian courts have adopted a similar approach.[69] In *R. v Mohan*,[70] Sopinka J reviewed the authorities and summarised the position as follows:

> "In summary, therefore, it appears from the foregoing that expert evidence which advances a novel scientific theory or technique is subjected to special scrutiny to determine whether it meets a basic threshold of reliability and whether it is essential in the sense that the trier of fact will be unable to come to a satisfactory conclusion without the assistance of the expert."[71]

6–25   In *R. v J-LJ*,[72] Binnie J, delivering the judgment of a unanimous Canadian Supreme Court, referred with approval to the *Daubert* criteria. He emphasised that a trial judge had a function as "gatekeeper" and that: "The admissibility of the expert evidence should be scrutinized at the time it is proffered, and not allowed too easy an entry on the basis that all of the frailties could go at the end of the day to weight

---

[65]   (1993) 509 US 579. For an analysis of this decision and its possible adoption into Irish law, see Imwinkelried, "'Junk Science' in the Courtroom: Will the Changes in the American Law of Expert Testimony Influence the Irish Courts?" (2004) 26 DULJ 83.

[66]   Rule 702 provides: "If scientific, technical, or other specialized knowledge will assist the trier of fact to understand the evidence or to determine a fact in issue, a witness qualified as an expert by knowledge, skill, experience, training, or education, may testify thereto in the form of an opinion or otherwise."

[67]   This last factor had been formulated as the main test in *Frye v US* (1923) 54 App DC 46, 293 F 2013, which decision was held to have been overruled by Rule 702 of the Federal Rules of Evidence.

[68]   (1999) 526 US 137.

[69]   See generally, Bryant, Lederman and Fuerst, *Sopinka, Lederman & Bryant: The Law of Evidence in Canada* 4th edn (Canada: Lexis Nexis, 2014), §12.69ff. See also Cunliffe "Without fear or favour? Trends and possibilities in the Canadian approach to expert human behaviour evidence" (2006) 10 E & P 280; Arvisais, "Daubert comes to Canada: Closing the Gates on Unreliable Scientific Evidence" (2008) 66 Advocate (Vancouver) 539; Dufraimont, "New Challenges for the Gatekeeper: The Evolving Law on Expert Evidence in Criminal Cases" (2011-2012) 58 Crim LQ 531.

[70]   [1994] 2 SCR 9.

[71]   [1994] 2 SCR 9 at 25.

[72]   [2000] 2 SCR 600.

rather than admissibility."[73] This approach and the *Daubert* criteria were subsequently applied by the Supreme Court in *R. v Trochym*[74] to hold that post-hypnosis testimony was not sufficiently reliable and was, therefore, not admissible. Deschamps J observed that: "Reliability is an essential component of admissibility. Whereas the degree of reliability required by courts may vary depending on the circumstances, evidence that is not sufficiently reliable is likely to undermine the fundamental fairness of the criminal process."

6–26 However, a more liberal approach to the admission of expert evidence has been adopted in the United Kingdom.[75] In *R. v Luttrell*,[76] where an issue arose as to the admissibility of lip-reading evidence, the Court of Appeal rejected the contention that expert evidence could not be admitted unless the scientific methods involved were so well established and understood that they could be tested on cross-examination. It also held that an assessment of the reliability of expert evidence was primarily a matter of weight rather than admissibility:

> "In some cases, the reliability of the evidence might be relevant to whether the conditions of admissibility are satisfied. Thus in *R. v Gilfoyle* [2001] 2 Cr App R 57 at para.25, it was observed that English law will not consider expert evidence properly admissible if it is "based on a developing new brand of science or medicine ... until it is accepted by the scientific community as being able to provide accurate and reliable opinion"...Similarly, evidence might be so lacking in "*prima facie* reliability" that it has no probative force or its probative force is too slight to influence a decision: *R. v Clarke* [1995] 2 Cr App R 425, 432.
>
> However, while reliability of evidence can be relevant to whether the conditions of admissibility are met, in itself reliability goes to its weight... Although at one time a more conservative approach had been adopted, the policy of the English courts has been to be flexible in admitting expert evidence and to enjoy "the advantages to be gained from new techniques and new advances in science": Clarke , at p.430...The preferred view, and in our judgment the proper view, is "that so long as a field is sufficiently well-established to pass the ordinary tests of relevance and reliability, then no enhanced test of admissibility should be applied, but the weight of the evidence should be established by the same adversarial forensic techniques applicable elsewhere": Cross and Tapper (loc cit)."[77]

6–27 The position as confirmed by the Court of Appeal in *R. v Reed*[78] is that, although "expert evidence of a scientific nature is not admissible where the scientific basis on which it is advanced is insufficiently reliable for it to be put before the jury", there is "no enhanced test of admissibility for such evidence".[79] Accordingly:

> "If the reliability of the scientific basis for the evidence is challenged, the court will consider whether there is a sufficiently reliable scientific basis for that evidence to be admitted, but,

---

73 [2000] 2 SCR 600 at [28].
74 [2007] 1 SCR 239 at [27].
75 A comparable approach is adopted in Australia. See *R. v Bonython* (1984) 38 SASR 45; *R. v Tang* [2006] NSWCCA 167, [2006] 65 NSWLR 681 and, generally, Edmond, "Specialised Knowledge, the Exclusionary Discretions and Reliability: Re-Assessing Incriminating Opinion Evidence" (2008) 31 UNSWLJ 1; Edmond and Roberts, "Procedural Fairness, the Criminal Trial and Forensic Science and Medicine" (2011) 33 Sydney LR 359. For the approach in South Africa, see *R. v Parenzee* [2007] SASC 143.
76 [2004] EWCA Crim 1344, [2004] 2 Cr App R 31. See comment by Pattenden at (2004) 8 E & P 248.
77 [2004] EWCA Crim 1344 at [34]–[37], [2004] 2 Cr App R 31 at 538–539.
78 [2009] EWCA Crim 2698, [2010] 1 Cr App R 23 at [111]. See Jamieson, "LCN DNA analysis and opinion on transfer: *R. v Reed & Reed*" (2011) 15 E & P 161; Naughton & Tan, "The need for caution in the use of DNA evidence to avoid convicting the innocent" (2011) 15 E & P 245.
79 [2010] 1 Cr App R 23 at [111].

if satisfied that there is a sufficiently reliable scientific basis for the evidence to be admitted, then it will leave the opposing views to be tested in the trial."[80]

6–28   Thus, provided that this threshold of reliability is met, the fact that the scientific method or technique used by an expert has not gained widespread acceptance or is not readily capable of testing does not affect the admissibility of his or her evidence but goes merely to weight. So, for example, in *R. v Atkins*,[81] evidence from an expert in facial mapping as to the similarities between the face of the accused and the face of an offender recorded on CCTV footage was admitted even though there was no statistical database to support his findings or by reference to which those findings could be tested.[82]

6–29   There has been little judicial consideration of this issue in this jurisdiction. Although there have been some instances where doubt has been expressed as to whether a particular scientific technique has achieved the requisite degree of expert peer approval,[83] and evidence has been rejected on the basis that it is not scientifically robust,[84] thus far, the Irish courts have not propounded a test of admissibility which requires expert evidence or the science underpinning it to achieve a specified threshold of reliability before it can be admitted.[85] However, the Law Reform Commission has recently examined this issue and has provisionally recommended the introduction of a reliability test as an additional requirement for admissibility of all expert testimony with the introduction of a judicial guidance note outlining a non-exhaustive and non-binding list of factors, based on empirical validation, which can be used to help the court to assess the reliability of tendered expert evidence.[86]

---

[80]   [2010] 1 Cr App R 23 at [111]. See also *R. v Dallagher* [2003] 1 Cr App R 195 (ear print analysis); *R. v O'Doherty* [2003] 1 Cr App R 77 (voice identification); *R. v G* [2004] 2 Cr App R 38 (financial instrument fraud); *R. v Broughton* [2010] EWCA Crim 549 (DNA evidence); *R. v Henderson* [2010] EWCA Crim 1269, [2010] 2 Cr App R 24 (baby shaking); *R. v T* [2010] EWCA Crim 2439, [2011] 1 Cr App Rep 9 (footwear impressions); *R. v Ahmed* [2011] EWCA Crim 184, [2011] Crim LR 734 (international terrorism). See generally, Roberts, "Drawing on Expertise: Legal Decision-making and the Reception of Expert Evidence" [2008] Crim LR 443.

[81]   [2009] EWCA Crim 1876, [2010] 1 Cr App R 8.

[82]   See also *R. v Dlugosz* [2013] EWCA Crim 2, [2013] 1 Cr App R 425 where the evaluative opinion of experts in relation to low-template DNA match probability was admitted even though there was no statistical basis to provide a random match probability.

[83]   See *People (DPP) v Kelly* [2008] IECCA 7, [2008] 3 IR 697, [2008] 2 ILRM 217 where the Court of Criminal Appeal was not satisfied that CUSUM analysis, which was used to determine whether documents had been authored by one person or more than one person, was a technique that had a properly established scientific provenance and concluded that it had not achieved the requisite degree of expert peer approval.

[84]   See *People (DPP) v Fox*, Special Criminal Court, 23 January 2002, where handwriting evidence from an expert was rejected on the basis that it was not supported by scientific criteria that would have enabled the tribunal of fact to test the accuracy of the conclusions reached by the expert.

[85]   In *Wright v AIB Finance & Leasing* [2013] IESC 55, it was suggested that such a test should be introduced but it was not necessary for the Supreme Court to deal with this submission on the particular facts of that case.

[86]   Law Reform Commission, *Consultation Paper on Expert Evidence* (LRC CP 52–2008) at [2.295]–[2.407]. The introduction of a *Daubert* style test for admissibility of expert evidence in England and Wales has also been recommended by the Law Commission: Law Commission, *Admissibility of Expert Evidence in Criminal Proceedings in England and Wales* (Consultation Paper No. 190) (2009) and *Expert evidence in Criminal Proceedings in England and Wales (*Law Com No. 325) (2011). See further, Roberts, "Rejecting General Acceptance, Confounding the Gate-Keeper: the Law Commission and Expert Evidence" [2009] Crim LR 551; Heffernan & Coen, "The Reliability of Expert Evidence: reflections on the Law Commission's Proposals for Reform (2009) 73 J Crim L 488; Edmond, "Is reliability sufficient? The Law Commission and Expert Evidence" (2012) 16 E & P 30.

4. Evidence as to the Ultimate Issues

6–30   Historically, expert witnesses were not permitted to give opinion evidence as to the ultimate issues in the case.[87] This prohibition, known as the ultimate issue rule, was designed to prevent expert witnesses from usurping the tribunal of fact whose function it was to decide those issues.[88] However, in the case of expert evidence, this rule was illogical because, as noted above, the rationale underlying the admission of such evidence is that the tribunal of fact does not have the necessary expertise and requires assistance in making inferences from the proven facts.[89] Further, the rule was ignored in some cases and was circumvented by careful questioning in others so that it became "a matter of form rather than substance".[90] Thus, although the rule is still invoked sporadically,[91] it is generally recognised to be obsolete at least in civil cases.[92] This was the view of Barron J in *McMullen v Farrell*,[93] who stated that there are cases where professional witnesses are entitled to express their opinion on the question which the court has to decide.[94] This was also the view of Charleton J in *Condron v ACC Bank Plc*[95] who commented on the privileged position occupied by expert witnesses in that they were entitled to express a view, at least in some cases, on the ultimate issue before the court.[96] In *Karen Millen Fashions Ltd v Dunnes Stores*[97] the pragmatic reasons for abandoning the ultimate issue rule were identified by O'Donnell J:

> "For my own part, I can see how it is at least convenient to permit experts to give evidence in general as to their conclusions, so long as it is very clearly understood that what is important are the reasons leading the expert to that conclusion rather than the fact of the conclusion itself. Anything else is somewhat artificial. It is a matter of near certainty that the only expert

---

[87]   See *R. v Wright* (1821) Russ & Ry 456 at 458; *British Drug Houses Ltd v Battle Pharmaceuticals* [1944] 4 DLR 577 at 580 (*per* Thorson J).

[88]   See *Hayes v Doman* [1899] 2 Ch 13 at 24 (*per* Lindley MR) (evidence from persons in the trade giving their views as to the reasonableness of a restraint of trade clause was inadmissible because this was a question for the court alone to determine).

[89]   See *McFadden v Murdock* (1867) 1 ICLR 211 at 218; *AG (Ruddy) v Kenny* (1960) 94 ILTR 185 at 190.

[90]   *R. v Stockwell* (1993) 97 Cr App R 260 at 265; *DPP v A and BC Chewing Gum Ltd* [1968] 1 QB 159 at 164, [1967] 2 All ER 504 at 506.

[91]   See *People (DPP) v Kehoe* [1992] ILRM 481 at 485, where the evidence given by a psychiatrist on behalf of the accused was criticised on the basis that he had: "overstepped the mark in saying that he believed the accused did not have an intention to kill and that the accused was telling the truth. These are clearly matters four-square within the jury's function and a witness no more than the trial judge or anyone else is not entitled to trespass on what is the jury's function." The Law Reform Commission in its *Consultation Paper on Expert Evidence* (LRC CP 52–2008) considered whether the ultimate issue rule should be abolished and provisionally recommended that it should not and should have continued application as it does not impose any excessive difficulties in practice (at [2.242]). The Commission also provisionally recommended that courts should continue to be entitled to allow expert evidence to inform and educate the judge and/or the jury about the background to the ultimate issue where necessary whilst emphasising that the ultimate decision on such issues is for the court and not the expert (at [2.243]).

[92]   *McMullen v Farrell* [1993] 1 IR 123; *DPP v A & BC Chewing Gum Ltd* [1968] 1 QB 159 at 164; *R. v Stockwell* (1993) 97 Cr App R 260 at 265; *R. v Howe* [1982] NZLR 618 at 628; *Cooper v R.* [1980] 1 SCR 1149 at 1158; *R. v Lupien* [1970] SCR 263, (1970) 9 DLR (3d) 1. Rule 704 of the US Federal Rules of Evidence makes express provision for the admissibility of expert evidence as to the ultimate issue.

[93]   [1993] 1 IR 123.

[94]   See, *e.g. Bolton v Blackrock Clinic Ltd*, unreported, Supreme Court, 23 January 1997.

[95]   [2012] IEHC 395 at [19], [2013] 1 ILRM 113 at 123.

[96]   See also *James Elliott Construction Ltd v Irish Asphalt Ltd* [2011] IEHC 269 at [10]; *Flynn v Bus Átha Cliath* [2012] IEHC 398 at [9].

[97]   [2014] IESC 23 at [23].

witnesses called by either side will have formed an opinion favourable to that side and their evidence can often be best understood when both the reasons and conclusions are stated so long as it is understood and appreciated that the reasons leading an expert to a particular conclusion are the important matters for the court to consider."[98]

6–31   Thus, while it is open to an expert to express an opinion on the ultimate issue that the court has to decide, and there is little point in trying to exclude it, it carries little weight and what really matters are the reasons that underpin that opinion. It followed that the trial judge could not be said to have erred in that case by adhering to the traditional rule and excluding evidence as to the ultimate issue.

6–32   However, the prohibition against experts opining on the ultimate issue still has some vitality in jury trials, particularly criminal trials before a jury. As noted above, in *People (DPP) v Abdi*[99] Hardiman J emphasised that[100]:

> "The role of the expert witness is not to supplant the tribunal of fact, be it judge or jury, but to inform that tribunal so that it may come to its own decision. Where there is a conflict of expert evidence it is to be resolved by the jury or by the judge, if sitting without a jury, having regard to the onus of proof and the standard of proof applicable in the particular circumstances. Expert opinion should not be expressed in a form which suggests that the expert is trying to subvert the role of the finder of fact."

6–33   It is, thus, impermissible for an expert in a criminal trial to express a view on the guilt or innocence of an accused or to say that he or she is satisfied of a matter the subject of his or her expert opinion "beyond a reasonable doubt" because this will be regarded as subverting the role of the jury.[101] However, subject to that caveat, an expert is entitled to express confidence,[102] or even certitude in relation to the correctness of his or her opinion. In *People (DPP) v White,*[103] the Court of Criminal Appeal referred to the passage in *Abdi* set out above and the injunction against subverting the role of finder of fact and said:

> "As to whether that occurs in each and every circumstance where an expert expresses a strong, or very strong, confidence in his opinion, even "no doubt" in his opinion, depends on the circumstances of the case, the type of evidence being tendered, the manner in which the evidence has been tendered, even perhaps the tenor in which the evidence is tendered, the charge to the jury, and all other relevant factors enabling a court to determine whether or not there has been, in reality, an attempt by an expert to usurp the role of the finder of fact

---

[98]   See, to similar effect, *per* Jacob LJ in *Routestone v Minories France* [1977] BCC 180 at 188, who observed that, just because an opinion as to the ultimate issue is admissible: "it by no means follows that the court must follow it. On its own (unless uncontested) it would be "a mere bit of empty rhetoric" Wigmore, *Evidence* (Chadbourn rev) para. 1920. What really matters in most cases is the reasons given for the opinion. As a practical matter a well-constructed expert's report containing opinion evidence sets out the opinion and the reasons for it. If the reasons stand up the opinion does, if not, not. A rule of evidence which excludes this opinion evidence serves no practical purpose. What happens if the evidence is regarded as inadmissible is that experts' reports simply try to creep up to the opinion without openly giving it. They insinuate rather than explicate". See also *Rockwater Ltd v Technip France* [2002] EWCA Civ 381 at [14]–[15].

[99]   [2005] 1 ILRM 382. See Kennedy, "Limits of Psychiatric Evidence in Criminal Courts: Morals and Madness" (2005) 1 Medico-Legal Journal of Ireland 13.

[100]   [2005] 1 ILRM 382 at 393.

[101]   *People (DPP) v Gormley and White* [2014] IESC 17 at [12.6] and [12.7], [2014] 1 ILRM 377 at 417 and 418.

[102]   *People (DPP) v Rattigan* [2013] IECCA 13 at [35].

[103]   [2011] IECCA 78 at 10 (appeal *sub nom. People (DPP) v Gormley and White* [2014] IESC 17, [2014] 1 ILRM 377).

(whether judge or jury), or whether his/her evidence might reasonably be interpreted as being such an attempt, or as having that effect."[104]

6–34 The Court went on to reject the contention that an expert had impermissibly usurped the role of the jury by stating that he had "no doubt" as to the correctness of his opinion in relation to certain fingerprint evidence. An appeal to the Supreme Court against that decision failed. Clarke J considered that the phrase "no doubt" was one that was frequently used in everyday discourse and was merely a way of indicating that the expert held the opinion with a high degree of confidence:

> "As was pointed out by the trial judge, it is in the nature of any expert opinion that it may be held with a greater or lesser degree of confidence. There is no necessarily correct way in which an expert ought to express the degree of confidence with which the expert holds the opinion of which evidence is given. If there is a basis, whether because of the generally accepted principles of the area in question or because of a contrary view expressed by another expert witness, for suggesting that the expert has been exaggerated in the degree of confidence expressed, then that is a matter which can be the subject of a challenge to the expert's opinion."[105]

6–35 He went on to say that it was exclusively a matter for the jury to decide what weight, if any, to attach to the evidence and to decide on the guilt or innocence of the accused.

5. Persons who are Qualified to give Expert Evidence

6–36 A witness who gives evidence as an expert must have sufficient expertise in relation to the matter upon which he or she is to give evidence to be considered an expert[106] and the burden of establishing this rests on the party calling the witness. Such expertise may be acquired by reason of experience, training or knowledge.[107] In *Galvin v Murray*,[108] Murray J stated that, in general terms, "an expert may be defined as a person whose qualifications or expertise give an added authority to opinions or statements given or made by him within the area of his expertise".[109] No formal qualifications are necessary if the judge is satisfied that the witness has the requisite expertise.[110] Thus, in *McFadden v Murdock*,[111] a shopkeeper was allowed to testify as to the amount of wastage that it was reasonable to expect in the course of a grocery business.[112] Provided that an expert is appropriately qualified, the admissibility of his

---

[104] [2011] IECCA 78 at 10.
[105] [2014] IESC 17 at [12.5], [2014] 1 ILRM 377 at 417.
[106] *People (DPP) v Boyce* [2005] IECCA 143.
[107] *AG (Ruddy) v Kenny* (1960) 94 ILTR 185 at 190 (*per* Kingsmill Moore J). Cf. the definition of "expert witness" in s.34(9) of the Criminal Procedure Act 2010 as meaning "a person who appears to the court to possess the appropriate qualifications or experience about the matter to which the witness's evidence relates".
[108] [2001] 2 ILRM 234 at 239.
[109] See also *People (DPP) v Fox*, Special Criminal Court, 23 January 2002, where the following definition of an expert was propounded: "a person who is well qualified to express a credible opinion or belief on the subject so much so that the Court is entitled to regard such opinion and belief as admissible evidence for the purpose of supplying the Court with information which is outside of the range and knowledge of the Court."
[110] *McFadden v Murdock* (1967) 1 ICLR 211 at 217–218; *R. v Silverlock* [1894] 2 QB 766 at 771; *R. v Marquard* [1993] 4 SCR 233, (1993) 108 DLR (4th) 47.
[111] (1867) 1 ICLR 211.
[112] See also *R. v Silverlock* [1894] 2 QB 766 (evidence of solicitor who had studied handwriting as amateur could give evidence as to comparison of handwriting).

or her evidence does not depend on the court's view as to how expert the person is, that is a matter that goes to weight.[113]

6–37   The special knowledge and experience of the expert must be demonstrated to the court as a threshold requirement before he or she gives evidence.[114] However, the oral testimony of an expert attesting to his expertise, qualifications and experience is accepted as *prima facie* evidence of those facts and it is not necessary for him or her to adduce primary evidence of his or her qualifications in the absence of evidence rebutting that oral testimony.[115]

6–38   The appropriate time to challenge the expertise of a person called to give evidence as an expert witness, whether generally or in relation to a particular portion of evidence, is at the time that he or she gives evidence and, if this is not done, his or her evidence will be admissible as expert evidence and can be considered by the tribunal of fact on that basis.[116]

6. Independence of an Expert

6–39   Having regard to the function and role of an expert, it is obviously desirable that an expert is independent of the parties.[117] A party cannot give expert evidence[118] but a pre-existing relationship between an expert and a party will not disqualify the expert from giving evidence although it may affect the weight to be given to his or her evidence.[119] In *Galvin v Murray*[120] it was held that engineers employed by a County Council were experts for the purposes of disclosure obligations in a personal injuries action. Murphy J held that:

> "The fact that an engineer is employed by one or other of the parties may affect his independence with a consequent reduction in the weight to be attached to his evidence but could not deprive him of his status as an expert."[121]

6–40   In *Toth v Jarman*,[122] it was held that the existence of a conflict of interest on the part of an expert does not automatically disqualify an expert but is likely to lead the court to decline to act on his evidence.[123]

---

[113] *R. (Doughty) v Ely Magistrates' Court* [2008] EWHC 522; *Tong v R.* [2011] NZCA 211.

[114] *R. v Marquard* [1993] 4 SCR 233, (1993) 108 DLR (4th) 47.

[115] *Martin v Quinn* [1980] IR 244; *Minister for Agriculture v Concannon*, unreported, High Court, 14 April 1980; *DPP v O'Donoghue* [1991] 1 IR 448.

[116] *People (DPP) v Connolly* [2011] IESC 6 at [24].

[117] *R. (Factortame) v Secretary of State for Transport* [2002] EWCA Civ 932 at [70].

[118] *Sheeran v Meehan*, unreported, High Court, 6 February 2003.

[119] *AG v Shearne* [1955–56] Ir Jur Rep 55; *Galvin v Murray* [2001] 2 ILRM 234; *R. (Factortame) v Secretary of State for Transport* [2002] EWCA Civ 932; *Armchair Passenger Transport Ltd v Helical Bar plc* [2003] EWHC 367; *ANZ National Bank Ltd v Commissioner of Inland Revenue* (2005) 18 PRNZ 114 at 121.

[120] [2001] 2 ILRM 234.

[121] [2001] 2 ILRM 234 at 239. *Cf. Field v Leeds City Council* (2000) 17 EGLR 54 at 55, where Lord Woolf MR in the Court of Appeal stressed that, if the defendant city council wished to use an employee as an expert, it was important that they show that he had full knowledge of the requirements for an expert to give evidence before the court and that he was fully familiar with the need for objectivity.

[122] [2006] EWCA Civ 1028, [2006] 4 All ER 1276.

[123] In relation to conflicts of interest that may arise in respect of expert evidence and how to reduce the prevalence of bias in expert testimony, see Law Reform Commission, *Consultation Paper on Expert Evidence* (LRC CP 52–2008), Chap.4.

6–41 Any fact that bears upon the independence of the expert such as a prior relationship with the party calling him or her should be disclosed.[124] In *ANZ National Bank Ltd v Commissioner of Inland Revenue*,[125] MacKenzie J emphasised that an expert should "make clear the nature of the involvement with the affairs of the party calling the witness, and should not assert an independence which does not exist".

6–42 In order to ensure that the evidence of an expert is independent and uninfluenced by the exigencies of the litigation, it has been held that it is inappropriate for an expert to be remunerated on the basis of a contingency fee. In *R. (Factortame Ltd) v Secretary of State for Transport (No.8)*,[126] Lord Phillips MR stated:

> "To give evidence on a contingency fee basis gives an expert, who would otherwise be independent, a significant financial interest in the outcome of the case. As a general proposition, such an interest is highly undesirable. In many cases the expert will be giving an authoritative opinion on issues that are critical to the outcome of the case. In such a situation the threat to his objectivity posed by a contingency fee arrangement may carry greater dangers to the administration of justice then would the interest of an advocate or solicitor acting under a similar agreement. Accordingly, we consider that it will be in a very rare case indeed that the Court will be prepared to consent to an expert being instructed under a contingency fee arrangement."

6–43 It should be noted that, as was confirmed in *Harmony Shipping Co SA v Saudi Europe Line Ltd*,[127] there "is no property in an expert witness as to the facts he has observed and his own independent opinion on them". Therefore, an expert who has been consulted by one party can be called to give evidence on behalf of an opposing party subject to the constraints imposed by legal professional privilege not to disclose any privileged communications with the first party.

7. Facts on Which Expert Opinion may be Based

6–44 The primary facts upon which the opinion of an expert is based must be proved by admissible evidence.[128] These facts may be proved either by the expert himself or by other witnesses.[129] If the expert does not have first hand knowledge of the facts upon which his opinion is based, he or she can state a hypothesis upon assumed facts.[130] However, if the primary facts which provide the foundation for that opinion are not proved by admissible evidence,[131] the opinion of the expert will be entitled to little,

---

[124] *Proton Energy Group SA v Lietuva* [2013] EWHC 2872. See further, Hutchinson, "Expert Witnesses and the Duty to Disclose" (2013) 20(11) CL Pract 246.

[125] (2005) 18 PRNZ 114 at 121.

[126] [2002] EWCA Civ 932 at [73].

[127] [1979] 1 WLR 1380 at 1386 (*per* Denning MR).

[128] *R.T v VP* [1990] 1 IR 545 at 551; *People (DPP) v Boyce* [2005] IECCA 143. See also *R. v Lanigan* [1987] NI 367; *English Exporters (London) Ltd v Eldonwall Ltd* [1973] Ch 415 at 421, [1973] 1 All ER 726 at 731; *R. v Turner* [1975] QB 834 at 840, [1975] 1 All ER 70 at 73.

[129] *R.T v VP* [1990] 1 IR 545 at 551; *AG (Ruddy) v Kenny* (1960) 94 ILTR 185 at 190.

[130] *R.T v VP* [1990] 1 IR 545 at 551.

[131] So, in general, the primary facts relied on by an expert cannot be proved by hearsay evidence but such evidence is admissible on interlocutory applications in civil cases in accordance with Order 40, rule 4 of the Rules of the Superior Courts: *O'D v Minister for Education and Science* [2009] IEHC 227 at [12]–[14].

if any, weight.[132] Indeed, in *Dasreef Pty v Hawchar*,[133] Heydon J in the High Court of Australia considered that a failure to prove the primary facts on which an expert opinion is based would render it inadmissible.

6–45 Greater latitude is afforded to an expert when it comes to the material that he or she relies on in order to draw inferences from those primary facts. An expert will generally have acquired a certain amount of expertise from his or her first hand experience and can give evidence of any relevant facts of which he or she has personal knowledge.[134] In addition, given that the nature of expertise is such that it will usually be based, at least in part, on material of which the expert does not have personal knowledge or experience, an expert may rely, in reaching a conclusion, on the work of others in his or her field of expertise including material such as reference works, published studies and even unpublished material of which he or she is aware.[135] In *People (DPP) v Boyce*[136] an opinion had been expressed by an expert as to the probability of a DNA match in reliance on DNA databases that had not been proven in evidence. However, it was held by the Court of Criminal Appeal that these did not have to be proven by direct evidence because:

> "in a long established exception to the hearsay rule, an expert can ground or fortify his or her opinion by referring to works of authority, learned articles, recognised reference norms and other similar material as comprising part of the general body of knowledge falling within the field of expertise of the expert in question."[137]

6–46 That conclusion was upheld by the Supreme Court with Fennelly J endorsing the holding of the Court of Criminal Appeal that the expert had been "entitled to explain his reliance on the databases in question by reference to accepted scientific standards, scientific studies in published scientific data and norms accepted by the science in question".[138] Thus, it is not an objection to the admissibility of the opinion evidence of an expert that it is based, in part, on inadmissible evidence.[139] However, the evidence of an expert should not be used as a vehicle to try and get inadmissible evidence before the tribunal of fact.

6–47 The foregoing principles have been considered in a number of cases dealing with expert evidence in nullity cases. In the first of these, *RT v VP (Orse VT)*,[140] a

---

[132] *R. v Abbey* [1982] SCR 24 at 42, 44–6; *Ramsay v Watson* (1961) 108 CLR 642 at 649. *Cf. Conley v Strain* [1988] IR 628. In New Zealand, the courts require a warning to be given where an opinion is not based on direct evidence that it may affect the weight to be attached to it: *R. v Rongonui* [2000] NZLR 385.

[133] (2011) 277 ALR 611 at [66].

[134] See *McFadden v Murdock* (1867) 1 ICLR 211 where a shopkeeper called to give expert evidence as to the amount of wastage that it would be reasonable to expect in the course of a grocery business was permitted to give evidence as to the wastage incurred in running his own business. See also *English Exporters Pty Ltd v Eldonwall Ltd* [1973] 1 Ch 415.

[135] *Foyle & Bann Fisheries Ltd v AG* (1949) 83 ILTR 29 at 37–38; *English Exporters (London) Ltd v Eldonwall Ltd* [1973] Ch 415, [1973] 1 All ER 726 at 730–731; *R. v Abadom* [1983] 1 All ER 364 at 368; *City of Saint John v Irving Oil Co Ltd* (1966) 58 DLR 404; *Wilband v The Queen* [1967] SCR 14; *Commissioner of Taxation v Hammersley Iron Pty Ltd* (1980) 11 ATR 303 at 321. See further Pattenden, "Expert Opinion Evidence Based on Hearsay" [1982] Crim LR 85.

[136] [2005] IECCA 143; [2008] IESC 62, [2009] 2 IR 124, [2009] 1 ILRM 253.

[137] [2005] IECCA 143.

[138] [2008] IESC 62 at [154]–[155], [2009] 2 IR 124 at 161, [2009] 1 ILRM 253 at 285.

[139] *Foyle & Bann Fisheries Ltd v AG* (1949) 83 ILTR 29 at 37–38; *Wicklow County Council v Jessup* [2011] IEHC 81 at [2.14]; *Wilband v R.* [1967] SCR 14 at 21.

[140] [1990] 1 IR 545.

psychiatrist called on behalf of the petitioner sought to give opinion evidence about the respondent on the basis of what he had been told by the petitioner about her and from reading a report prepared by a court-appointed expert psychiatrist who had examined her. Lardner J upheld the objection of the respondent to the admission of this evidence on the basis that it was based on hearsay. However, it seems incorrect to classify such evidence as hearsay because both the petitioner and the court-appointed expert were called to give evidence. The real objection to the evidence in the case was that the opinion of the psychiatrist had little probative value in circumstances where it was based on second hand information because he had not met or examined the respondent.[141] However, this is a matter that, in the case of expert evidence, goes go to the weight to be attached to such evidence and not to its admissibility.

6–48 This, indeed, was the approach taken by O'Higgins J in two nullity cases, *DK v TH (Orse TK)*[142] and *JWH (Orse W) v GW*.[143] In both cases, evidence was given at the hearing of the petition by an eminent psychologist who formed the opinion, based on an interview with the petitioner, that the respondent did not have the capacity to enter into a marital relationship. The learned judge cautioned that an expert opinion based on information supplied by the petitioner only and without an examination of the respondent was of limited value only. In *JWH (Orse W) v GW*, where there was no psychiatric or psychological evidence before the court by anyone who had examined the respondent, he was unable to attach sufficient weight to the opinion of the psychiatrist who had given evidence to satisfy him that the respondent had been unable to enter a marital relationship.

6–49 In *R. v Turner*,[144] it was held that a party calling an expert should ask him or her to state the facts on which his or her opinion is based.[145] Lawton LJ pointed out that:

> "Before a court can assess the value of an opinion it must know the facts on which it is based. If the expert has been misinformed about the facts or has taken irrelevant facts into consideration or has omitted to consider relevant ones, the opinion is likely to be valueless."[146]

6–50 In doing so, it is permissible for the expert to refer to hearsay evidence if that formed part of the material underlying his or her opinion in order to explain the basis of the opinion.[147] However, it is important to point out that it is the opinion of the expert and not the underlying materials used by him or her which constitutes the evidence in the case.[148]

6–51 Similar principles were laid down in this jurisdiction in the context of

---

[141] See the distinction drawn between the hearsay rule and the rule requiring first-hand knowledge in Broun (ed.), *McCormick on Evidence,* 7th edn, (Minnesota: Thomson Reuters) Vol. II, § 247, p.186.

[142] Unreported, High Court, 25 February 1998.

[143] Unreported, High Court, 25 February 1998. *Cf. Wilband v R.* [1967] SCR 14 at 21 and *R. v Lupien* [1970] SCR 263 at 273, where expert evidence based on reports and materials compiled by another party were held to be admissible.

[144] [1975] QB 834, [1975] 1 All ER 70.

[145] *Cf. Trade Practices Commission v Arnotts Ltd (No.5)* (1990) 24 FCR 313.

[146] [1975] QB 834 at 840, [1975] 1 All ER 70 at 73.

[147] *R. v Bradshaw* (1985) 82 Cr App R 79 at 83.

[148] *Foyle v Bann Fisheries Ltd v AG* (1949) 83 ILTR 29 at 38; *R. v Bradshaw* (1985) 82 Cr App R 79 at 83; *Phillion v The Queen* [1978] 1 SCR 18 at 24; *R. v Abbey* [1982] SCR 24 at 45; *R. v Lavallee* [1990] 55 CCC 97 at 127–128.

proceedings concerning the welfare of children in *State (D and D) v Groarke*.[149] The respondents had obtained a "fit person" order removing a child from the custody of her parents on the basis that she was being sexually abused by her father and that order was challenged by the parents on the basis that it had not been obtained in accordance with fair procedures. The allegation of sexual abuse rested primarily on the opinion of a doctor who had interviewed the child and questioned her with the aid of anatomical dolls. This interview was recorded on video and Finlay CJ, delivering the judgment of the Supreme Court, was satisfied that:

> "[I]n order to determine with safety, having regard to the nature of this interview, such a vital matter as to whether the conclusion reached by the doctor carrying it out is a sound conclusion which would warrant such a drastic step as the possibly long-term removal of the care of the child out of the custody of its parents, it would be necessary for the tribunal before which such evidence of conclusion was given to have, in addition, the basic evidence from which that conclusion was reached, namely, the video recording (where it existed) of the interview between the doctor and the child and a demonstration, in addition, of the precise use and the expert witness's belief in the meaning of the use by the child, of the anatomical dolls.[150]

6–52 The decision in *Groarke* was followed in *Southern Health Board v CH*[151] which also concerned an application for a fit person order. Again, the application was grounded on allegations of sexual abuse made against the father of the child. The evidence relating to these allegations consisted of the opinion evidence of a social worker who had interviewed the child together with videotapes of those interviews. Objection was taken to the admissibility of the videotapes on the basis that they constituted hearsay evidence. However, O'Flaherty J, delivering the judgment of the Supreme Court, emphasised that the key evidence was that of the expert and the tapes were simply material that would back up his testimony. It was for the District Judge to accept or reject that evidence, and the defence would have the right to adduce such expert or other evidence, in rebuttal or otherwise as it thought fit.

6–53 These decisions appear to push back the traditional boundaries as to the evidence that is admissible in support of expert opinion. It is one thing to say that an expert may base his or her opinion on hearsay evidence and may refer to such hearsay evidence in order to illustrate the basis for that opinion. It is a quite a different matter to admit, on this basis, videotape evidence in which allegations of sexual abuse are made untested by cross-examination. In such circumstances, notwithstanding any admonition that it is the testimony of the expert and not the underlying material that constitutes the evidence in the case, the rules regarding expert evidence are being used as a backdoor means of admitting hearsay evidence.[152] The use of expert evidence as a vehicle for adducing inadmissible hearsay evidence is something which was deprecated in *Director of Corporate Enforcement v Bailey*.[153]

8. Provision of Information to Experts

6–54 As noted below, the weight to be attributed to an expert's opinion will depend,

---

149 [1990] 1 IR 305.
150 [1990] 1 IR 305 at 310.
151 [1996] 1 IR 219, [1996] 2 ILRM 142.
152 Concerns in that regard can be seen to underpin the decision of Budd J in *PMcG v AF* [2000] IEHC 11 not to permit a medical inspector appointed by the court pursuant to Ord.70, r.32 to interview third party informants.
153 [2007] IEHC 365, [2008] 1 ILRM 13.

inter alia, on the extent of the expert's first hand knowledge of the facts upon which he or she has based his or her expert opinion and the nature and extent of the investigations carried out by the expert. It follows that a party may be required to provide access by an expert engaged by an opposing party to the information required for him or her to form an opinion. For this reason, it has long been a requirement in personal injury actions that a plaintiff make himself available for an examination by the medical experts retained by the defendant.[154] In addition, an order for inspection of property or any item in issue will be made if this is necessary for an expert to form an opinion and give expert evidence.[155]

6–55 Where an issue arises as to the psychological or psychiatric condition of a party or witness, then access by an opposing expert so that he or she can form an opinion on the basis of having examined and assessed the person himself or herself is crucial. In *JF v DPP*,[156] Hardiman J pointed out that: "where there are conflicting views of a psychological or psychiatric nature as to why a particular person behaved in a particular way, an expert who has seen and assessed the person in question is at an enormous advantage over an expert who has not done so". He, therefore, considered that fair procedures[157] and the principle of *égalité des armes*[158] required that access for the purpose of carrying out such an assessment be afforded to the expert retained by an opposing party.

9. Regulation of Expert Evidence in Civil Cases

6–56 With increasing specialisation of knowledge in recent decades, there has been a marked multiplication in the number and variety of expert witnesses giving evidence with a consequent increase in the complexity of proceedings and costs associated with such evidence. This has given rise to understandable judicial concern and a desire to try and ensure that proceedings are not unnecessarily lengthened and costs increased by such evidence. There is also a serious risk of unfairness because of surprise.

6–57 One response to these concerns has been to impose disclosure obligations in relation to expert evidence. The traditional common law position was that litigation privilege could be claimed in respect of all communications between a client or his or her lawyer and experts made for the purposes of litigation and the work product of that expert.[159] Thus, there was no requirement for a party to disclose the identity of any

---

[154] See *McGrory v ESB* [2003] 3 IR 407.
[155] See *Wymes v Crowley* [1987] IEHC 68 and *Bula Ltd v Tara Mines Ltd (No.1)* [1987] IR 85.
[156] [2005] IESC 24, [2005] 2 IR 174.
[157] See *Re Haughey* [1971] IR 217 at 263.
[158] See *Steel and Morris v United Kingdom*, unreported, European Court of Human Rights, 15 February 2005 at [59].
[159] See *Ahern v Mahon* [2008] IEHC 119 at [65], [2008] 4 IR 704 at 720, [2009] 1 ILRM 458 at 471, where Kelly J, delivering the judgment of a Divisional High Court, approved the summary in this regard to be found in Passmore, *Privilege* 2nd edn (2006), para.3.109: "Traditionally, whenever a professional third party has been engaged as an expert witness by or on behalf of a party to actual, pending or contemplated proceedings, litigation privilege has protected (i) confidential communications between any of the client, his solicitors or counsel and the expert, and (ii) the work of the expert prior to its disclosure or use in the litigation, so long as those communications or the expert's work are referable to the litigation concerned and satisfy the dominant purpose test. This is so, whether the expert has been instructed with a view to assisting his client to understand, for example, the technical aspects of the claim, to assist in the preparation of a claim or its defence, or to provide expert evidence at the trial of the action."

experts that he or she intended to call, still less to serve an expert report in advance of trial. However, in personal injuries cases, detailed disclosure requirements have been introduced which require the disclosure in advance of trial of all reports from expert witnesses intended to be called.[160] This will often act as a precursor to meetings between the experts. Similarly, in proceedings in the Commercial List, directions are almost invariably made in plenary actions requiring a sequential exchange of expert reports followed by a meeting of the experts who are required to produce a memorandum setting out the areas of agreement and disagreement between them.[161] Outside of these categories of cases, equivalent directions are increasingly made on an *ad hoc* basis and Clarke J in *Wright v AIB Finance & Leasing*[162] highlighted the undesirability of a situation where expert reports are not exchanged or exchanged so late that the parties' respective experts do not have a sufficient opportunity to consider the views of opposing experts and the facts on which they are based. In *Emerald Meats Ltd v Minister for Agriculture*[163] O'Donnell J highlighted the advantages of experts meeting before trial to identify the real areas in dispute. Indeed, it has been stated that experts are under a duty to try and limit the matters in contention between them.[164]

6–58 In recent times, disquiet has also been voiced about situations where two or more experts are called to give evidence in relation to the same area of expertise leading to duplication and an increase in the complexity, length and cost of trials. In *Weavering Macro Fixed Income Fund Ltd v PNC Global Investment Servicing (Europe) Ltd*[165] Charleton J highlighted the escalating complexity, length and cost of trials and the costs involved in retaining experts and queried whether some regulation of the number of experts who could be called at trial was required in order to redress an imbalance in resources that may exist in some cases. He also expressed some dissatisfaction with the traditional trial process so far as it related to expert evidence and suggested that consideration should be given to the Australian approach of swearing opposing experts at the same time to debate the issues under the control of the trial judge.[166] The learned judge returned to this theme in *Condron v ACC Bank Plc*,[167] where he commented:

> "It is clear that expert evidence, in contrast to evidence as to fact, may be controlled either by rules of court or by the entitlement of a court to hear cases in a focused manner. For the benefit of the constitutional right of access, the courts may exclude repetition and take such steps as are necessary to render hearings a fair contest. Such control serves to establish a balance between those who may be rich enough to engage several experts and those who have limited funds. Hearings are very expensive. Long hearings made repetitive by multiple experts addressing the same issue for the same party are prohibitively expensive. The courts are entitled to control their own procedures in the interests of fairness. That is what the Constitution predicates by establishing an entitlement to fair trials."

---

[160] See the Rules of the Superior Courts (No.6) (Disclosure of Reports and Statements) 1998. For an analysis of these Rules and the disclosure obligations imposed thereby, see Delany and McGrath, *Civil Procedure in the Superior Courts* 3rd edn (Dublin: Round Hall) Chap.28, section F.

[161] See RSC Ord.63A r.6(1)(ix).

[162] [2013] IESC 55 at [6.5]–[6.6].

[163] [2012] IESC 48 at [28].

[164] *Graigola Merthyr Co Ltd v Swansea Corporation* [1928] 1 Ch 31; *Stanton v Callaghan* [1998] EWCA Civ 1176.

[165] [2012] IEHC 25.

[166] This was a suggestion which had earlier been made by O'Sullivan J, writing extra judicially ("A Hot Tub for Expert Witnesses" (2004) 4 JSIJ 1).

[167] [2012] IEHC 395 at [19], [2013] 1 ILRM 113 at 123.

6–59   Again in *Flynn v Bus Átha Cliath*,[168] Charleton J was critical of the tendency to call experts to give evidence in relation to matters, such as driving, which he regarded as being within common experience and for a multiplicity of experts such as medical experts to be called, commenting that: "The proliferation of experts renders trials immensely expensive and draws out the court time required for even simple cases."[169] In that case, he signalled that costs sanctions might be imposed in respect of unnecessary expert evidence.

6–60   In its *Consultation Paper on Expert Evidence*,[170] the Law Reform Commission has identified a number of shortcomings in the present system for the giving of expert evidence and has recommended a range of procedural reforms which it believes would have a beneficial impact in terms of improving access to the courts, limiting delay and expense and avoiding possible abuse.

10. Leave to Adduce Expert Evidence in Criminal Cases

6–61   Traditionally, a very asymmetrical approach has been adopted to disclosure of information in advance of criminal trials so that, while the prosecution has extensive disclosure obligations (at least in relation to offences tried on indictment), those placed on an accused are very limited.[171] As the use of expert evidence on behalf of accused persons has increased and, with the increasing specialisation of knowledge, this has created difficulties for the prosecution in trying to anticipate and deal with expert evidence that may be adduced on behalf of an accused. These difficulties were noted in the Final Report of the Balance in the Criminal Law Review Group which recommended the creation of a disclosure obligation in respect of experts whom an accused intended to call.[172] That recommendation was implemented in s.34 of the Criminal Procedure Act 2010 which introduced a notice obligation and a requirement for an accused to obtain leave to adduce expert evidence.[173]

6–62   The constitutionality of s.34 was unsuccessfully challenged in *Markey v Minister for Justice and Law Reform*.[174] The contentions that this section breached the principle of equality of arms or limited an accused's right to cross-examination were summarily rejected by Kearns P. Having noted that there were general disclosure obligations placed on the prosecution but equivalent obligations were not placed on an accused, he regarded the proposition that the imposition on an accused of a notice obligation and requirement to seek leave in respect of expert evidence altered the balance between the prosecution and defence as "astonishing and unreal".[175] He identified the purpose of s.34 as being to limit trial by ambush and referred to jurisprudence from other jurisdictions

---

[168] [2012] IEHC 398 at [7]–[9].

[169] Similar criticisms were voiced by Stuart-Smith LJ in *Liddell v Middleton* [1996] PIQR 36 who commented: "We do not have trial by expert in this country: we have trial by Judge. In my judgment, the expert witnesses contributed nothing to the trial in this case except expense."

[170] LRC CP 52–2008, Chap.5.

[171] The most important disclosure obligation in practice is that imposed by s.20 of the Criminal Justice Act 1984 in relation to alibi evidence.

[172] See the *Final Report of the Balance in the Criminal Law Group* (2007) at 167–174.

[173] As noted by Kearns P in *Markey v Minister for Justice* [2011] IEHC 39 at [20], [2012] 1 IR 62 at 72, s.34 goes further than the recommendation of the Balance in the Criminal Law Review Group by imposing a requirement to obtain leave in addition to a notice obligation.

[174] [2011] IEHC 39, [2012] 1 IR 62.

[175] [2011] IEHC 39 at [27], [2012] 1 IR 62 at 74.

which recognised that "trial by ambush is inherently unfair and damaging to the justice system".[176] He also noted that there is no rule of law or constitutional requirement that the procedures available to an accused must be identical to those available to the prosecution.[177] He was also unpersuaded by arguments that the section interfered with the right of an accused not to testify or infringed legal professional privilege. He concluded that any interference by s.34 with any constitutionally protected right of the applicant under Art.38 or 40 of the Constitution was limited and proportionate having regard to the nature, scope and effect of the section when placed in balance with the public interest in an effective and balanced prosecution system.[178] He was also satisfied that the section was not incompatible with the State's obligations under art.6 of the European Convention on Human Rights.[179]

6–63   Section 34(2) imposes a notice requirement, stipulating that, where the defence intends to call an expert witness[180] or adduce expert evidence,[181] whether or not in response to such evidence presented by the prosecution, notice of the intention shall be given to the prosecution at least 10 days prior to the scheduled date of the start of the trial. That notice is required to be in writing and to include the name and address of the expert witness and any report prepared by the expert witness concerning a matter relevant to the case including details of any analysis carried out by or on behalf or, or relied upon by, the expert witness, or a summary of the findings of the expert witness.[182] It is clear from the section that the obligation only applies in respect of an expert witness that the accused intends to call and does not extend to other experts consulted by an accused.[183] However, the section is less clear as to whether there is an obligation to disclose all reports from the expert including earlier drafts of his or her report[184] and whether there is any obligation to include in the expert report information that is unfavourable to the accused.[185] Having regard to the purpose of the section as identified by the Kearns P in *Markey v Minister for Justice and Law Reform*,[186] it is likely that it will be construed as regarding disclosure of the evidence that the expert proposes to give only although the duties owed by an expert witness may dictate that views unfavourable to the accused are expressed.[187]

---

[176] [2011] IEHC 39 at [27], [2012] 1 IR 62 at 74.

[177] See *Fitzgerald v DPP* [2003] 3 IR 247.

[178] [2011] IEHC 39 at [39], [2012] 1 IR 62 at 78.

[179] [2011] IEHC 39 at [43]–[44], [2012] 1 IR 62 at 79–80.

[180] An "expert witness" is defined in subs.(9) to mean "a person who appears to the court to possess the appropriate qualifications or experience about the matter to which the witness's evidence relates".

[181] Subs.(9) defines "expert evidence" to mean "evidence of fact or opinion given by an expert witness".

[182] Subsection (3).

[183] *Cf. Kincaid v Aer Lingus Teoranta* [2003] 2 IR 314 dealing with the disclosure obligations imposed by s.45(1)(a) and RSC Ord.39, r.46 in personal injuries actions.

[184] *Cf. Payne v Shovlin* [2004] IEHC 430, [2006] IESC 5, [2007] 1 IR 114, [2006] 2 ILRM 1, where it was held, dealing with the disclosure obligations imposed by s.45(1)(a) and RSC Ord.39, r.46 in personal injuries actions, that all reports from the particular expert must be disclosed.

[185] *Cf.* the differing views expressed in this regard in relation to the disclosure obligations imposed by s.45(1)(a) and RSC Ord.39, r.46 in personal injuries actions which are discussed in Delany and McGrath, *Civil Procedure in the Superior Courts* (3rd edn) at [28-67]–[28-72].

[186] [2011] IEHC 39, [2012] 1 IR 62.

[187] In *Markey* (at [37], 77), Kearns P said that it had to be assumed that such expert evidence would be exculpatory rather than inculpatory and, thus, an expert report disclosed in accordance with s.34 would not be admissible as an admission against interest by the accused or his agent. However, that assumption would not necessarily hold true in all cases.

6–64 The notice obligation is reinforced by the requirement to obtain leave to adduce expert evidence. Subsection (1) provides that an accused cannot call an expert witness or adduce expert evidence unless leave to do so has been granted by the court. The application for leave is made by the defence[188] and the prosecution is entitled to be heard on it.[189] The court is required to grant leave where it is satisfied, firstly, that the expert evidence to be adduced satisfies the requirements of any enactment or rule of law relating to evidence and, secondly, that the notice obligation has been complied with or non-compliance has been satisfactorily excused. In *Markey v Minister for Justice and Law Reform*,[190] Kearns P commented that the discretion exercised by a trial judge on an application for leave is a limited one and that "his primary duty and obligation is to grant leave except in those limited circumstances provided for by the section".

6–65 With regard to the first test for the grant of leave, it is apparent that the court must be satisfied that the evidence proposed to be adduced constitutes "expert evidence" and is otherwise admissible. Thus, a court could refuse to grant leave if it is not satisfied that the proposed witness has the appropriate qualifications or experience about the matter to which the witness's evidence relates so that he or she fails to satisfy the definition of "expert witness" in sub.(9). A court might also refuse leave if it formed the view that the expert evidence sought to be adduced was not relevant to the issues in the case or if it is inadmissible because it relates to a matter that is within the knowledge and experience of the tribunal of fact as was the case with regard to the psychiatric evidence in *People (DPP) v Kehoe*.[191]

6–66 Although a court generally has to be satisfied that the notice obligation imposed by subs.(2) has been complied with, leave can still be granted if: (a) notice was given of the name and address of the expert witness but no report or summary of the findings of that expert was provided if the court is satisfied that the accused took all reasonable steps to secure the report or summary before giving the notice;[192] (b) in all the circumstances of the case, it was not reasonably possible for the defence to give notice at least 10 days prior to the scheduled date of the start of the trial[193]; or (c) where the prosecution has adduced expert evidence and a matter arose from that expert's testimony that was not reasonably possible for the defence to have anticipated so that it would be in the interests of justice for that matter to be further examined in order to establish its relevance to the case.[194] If there has been delay in bringing an application for leave which has prejudiced the prosecution, then leave may be refused as in *Writtle v DPP*[195] where an expert report raising a new issue was not served and leave sought until after the prosecution had closed its case. In addition, leave will be refused if the court is satisfied that the application has been made late as a deliberate tactical ploy to ambush the prosecution.[196]

6–67 Where the court grants leave for the adducing of expert evidence, the

---

[188] Subsection (5).
[189] Subsection (6).
[190] [2011] IEHC 39 at [35], [2012] 1 IR 62 at 76.
[191] [1992] ILRM 481.
[192] Subsection (4).
[193] Subsection (5)(b).
[194] Subsection (5)(c).
[195] [2009] RTR 28.
[196] *R. v Ensor* [2009] EWCA Crim 1269, [2010]1 Cr App R 18.

prosecution must be given a reasonable opportunity to consider the report or summary before the expert witness gives the evidence or the evidence is otherwise adduced.[197]

6–68   In *Markey v Minister for Justice and Law Reform*,[198] Kearns P held that expert reports disclosed pursuant to s.34 can only be used by the prosecution subject to the control of the trial judge and it had to be assumed that the trial judge will exercise his or her powers "in such a manner as to ensure a fair trial and to avoid unfairness to the accused". Thus, by analogy with the position in relation to alibi evidence, the prosecution will not be permitted to adduce evidence in respect of expert evidence which has been notified by an accused in accordance with s.34 but which the accused subsequently decides not to adduce.[199]

11. Duties of Expert Witnesses

6–69   As noted above, the function of expert witnesses as identified by Lord Cooper in *Davie v Edinburgh Magistrates*[200] is to furnish the tribunal of fact "with the necessary scientific criteria for testing the accuracy of their conclusions" so as to enable it to form an "independent judgment by the application of these criteria to the facts proved in evidence". It follows that the expert owes an overriding duty to the court when giving evidence to give objective and unbiased evidence on the matters falling within the scope of his or her expertise.[201] However, the required degree of independence and objectivity is not generally achieved in practice[202] leading in some cases to the rejection of expert evidence on this basis.[203] As Taylor commented, "it is often quite surprising to see with what facility and to what extent, their [experts'] views can be made to correspond with the wishes or the interests of the parties who call them."[204]

6–70   The failure by experts to discharge their obligation to form an independent view uninfluenced by the exigencies of litigation inevitably leads to a conflict, and sometimes a stark conflict, of evidence between them and the inability of opposing experts to agree matters has been the subject of adverse comment in a number of decisions.[205] In *Emerald Meats Ltd v Minister for Agriculture*,[206] O'Donnell J highlighted the very divergent approaches taken by the expert accountants in that case and emphasised

---

[197] Subsection (8).
[198] [2011] IEHC 39 at [36], [2012] 1 IR 62 at 76.
[199] See *People (DPP) v Cahill* [2001] 3 IR 494.
[200] 1953 SC 34 at 40.
[201] *R. v O'Connell* (1844) 7 ILR 261; *Polivitte Ltd v Commercial Union Assurance Co plc* [1987] 1 Lloyd's Rep 379 at 386.
[202] See, *per* Mr Justice Robert Barr, "Expert Evidence—A Few Personal Observations and the Implications of Recent Statutory Developments" (1999) 4 (4) BR 185 at 185, where he notes that, while experts are rarely dishonest or deliberately fair, "they seem to lack a true understanding of their function, i.e. to assist the court in arriving at the truth by providing a skilled expert assessment, which is objective and fair, of matters requiring a specialised appreciation of the particular problem at issue".
[203] See *News Datacom Ltd v Lyons* [1994] 1 ILRM 450 at 456, where Flood J, in refusing to grant an interlocutory injunction, was quite dismissive of what he termed "the opinion of a partisan expert".
[204] *Treatise on the Law of Evidence* 12th edn (London: Sweet & Maxwell, 1931), p.59.
[205] See the comments of Charleton J in *People (DPP) v O'Reilly* [2009] IECCA 30 at [26] and *James Elliott Construction Ltd v Irish Asphalt Ltd* [2011] IEHC 269 at [10].
[206] [2012] IESC 48 at [28].

the requirement for independence on the part of experts and the duty owed by them to the court:

> "In theory, expert witnesses owe a duty to the court to provide their own independent assessment. It is only because of their expertise and assumed independence that they are entitled to offer opinion evidence on matters central to the court's determination. If this process functions properly, there should not be wide and unbridgeable gaps between the views of experts. Where there are differences, those should be capable of identification along with the relevant considerations so that the particular issue or issues which require judicial determination should be capable of ready exposition…It is important that experts, and particularly accountancy witnesses, do not simply accept their client's instructions as to certain matters and then construct calculations on the basis of those instructions. If that is all that is done, then the expert report is no more than the provision of a very expensive calculator. The court is entitled to expect that such experts will apply their critical faculties and their expertise to the case being made by their clients. Furthermore, experts who are willing to provide such realistic advice to their clients are entitled to expect that the courts will, where appropriate, identify and be critical of exaggeration and lack of realism when that is detected."

6–71 In a number of decisions, the courts have felt the need to emphasise the requirement of objectivity on the part of experts and to lay down some guidelines with regard to their evidence. A very useful list of the duties and responsibilities of expert witnesses was given by Creswell J in *National Justice Compania Naviera S.A v Prudential Assurance Co Ltd (The Ikarian Reefer)*[207] the first five of which are as follows:

> "1. Expert evidence presented to the Court should be, and should be seen to be, the independent product of the expert uninfluenced as to form or content by the exigencies of litigation…
> 2. An expert witness should provide independent assistance to the Court by way of objective unbiased opinion in relation to matters within his expertise. … An expert witness should never assume the role of advocate.[208]
> 3. An expert witness should state the facts or assumptions upon which his opinion is based.[209] He should not omit to consider material facts which could detract from his concluded opinion. …[210]
> 4. An expert witness should make it clear when a particular question or issue falls outside his expertise.
> 5. If an expert's opinion is not properly researched because he considers that insufficient data is available, then this must be stated with an indication that the opinion is no more than a provisional one. …"

6–72 These principles were subsequently reformulated by Toulmin J in *Anglo Group*

---

[207] [1993] 2 Lloyd's Rep 68 at 81–82. See also *R. v Harris* [2006] 1 Cr App R 55 where these guidelines were approved and refined. A number of guidance documents relating to expert testimony drawn up in other jurisdictions are considered in the Law Reform Commission's *Consultation Paper on Expert Evidence* (LRC CP 52–2008).

[208] This point was also made in *Flynn v Bus Átha Cliath* [2012] IEHC 398 at [9] and *R. v Tihi* [1990] 1 NZLR 540 at 548. *Cf.* Mahon, "Expert Evidence" [1979] NZLJ 123.

[209] See also *per* Heydon J in *Dasreef Pty Ltd v Hawciar* [2011] HCA 21 at [65] who went so far as to say that expert evidence is inadmissible unless the facts on which the opinion is based are stated by the expert.

[210] See *Re J (Child Abuse: Expert Evidence)* [1991] FCR 193 at 206 where an expert report was criticised by Cazalet J on the basis that it was "misleading in a number of material respects and in my view was a failure to comply with the duty of an expert witness to provide an objective opinion and not to mislead either by omission or otherwise as to the nature and basis of his written opinion". See also, *R. v Clark (Sally)* [2003] EWCA Crim 1020, [2004] 2 FCA 447 where the accused had been convicted of the murder of her two sons and the Court of Appeal was very critical of an expert witness for the prosecution who had failed to disclose test results tending to show that one of the children had died from natural causes.

Plc v Winther Brown & Co Ltd[211] to take account of the reforms in relation to expert evidence introduced in England and Wales by rule 35 of the Civil Procedure Rules as follows:

> "1.   An expert witness should at all stages in the procedure, on the basis of the evidence as he understands it, provide independent assistance to the court and the parties by way of objective unbiased opinion in relation to matters within his expertise. This applies as much to the initial meetings of experts as to evidence at trial. An expert witness should never assume the role of an advocate.
>
> 2.   The expert's evidence should normally be confined to technical matters on which the court will be assisted by receiving an explanation, or to evidence of common professional practice. The expert witness should not give evidence or opinions as to what the expert himself would have done in similar circumstances or otherwise seek to usurp the role of the judge.
>
> 3.   He should co-operate with the expert of the other party or parties in attempting to narrow the technical issues in dispute at the earliest possible stage of the procedure and to eliminate or place in context any peripheral issues. He should co-operate with the other expert(s) in attending without prejudice meetings as necessary and in seeking to find areas of agreement and to define precisely arrears of disagreement to be set out in the joint statement of experts ordered by the court.
>
> 4.   The expert evidence presented to the court should be, and be seen to be, the independent product of the expert uninfluenced as to form or content by the exigencies of the litigation.
>
> 5.   An expert witness should state the facts or assumptions upon which his opinion is based. He should not omit to consider material facts which could detract from his concluded opinion.
>
> 6.   An expert witness should make it clear when a particular question or issue falls outside his expertise.
>
> 7.   Where an expert is of the opinion that his conclusions are based on inadequate factual information he should say so explicitly.
>
> 8.   An expert should be ready to reconsider his opinion, and if appropriate, to change his mind when he has received new information or has considered the opinion of the other expert. He should do so at the earliest opportunity."

6–73   These principles have not yet been approved in this jurisdiction but the Law Reform Commission[212] has provisionally recommended that a formal guidance code for expert witnesses based on the principles laid down in *The Ikarian Reefer* should be developed which would outline the duties owed by expert witnesses and which would be made available to all persons seeking to act as expert witnesses.

6–74   In the absence of such a code, the duties owed by expert witnesses have been addressed in a somewhat *ad hoc* way. In a series of cases dealing with allegations of delay in the prosecution of sexual offences, the courts have had occasion to emphasise the general duty of experts to make an objective judgment when called upon to give a professional opinion and the concomitant duty on them to investigate fully the factual foundation for their opinion.[213] An example can be seen in *Fitzpatrick v DPP*[214] where the applicant brought judicial review proceedings seeking an order of prohibition preventing his trial for the sexual abuse of two complainants on the ground of delay. One of the affidavits filed by the respondent was sworn by a senior clinical psychologist who

---

[211]   [2000] EWHC 127, 72 Con LR 118, [2000] All ER (D) 294 at [109].

[212]   Law Reform Commission, *Consultation Paper on Expert Evidence* (LRC CP 52–2008) at [3.246].

[213]   See *Fitzpatrick v DPP*, unreported, High Court, 5 December 1997; *AW v DPP*, unreported, High Court, 23 November 2001; *BJ v DPP*, unreported, High Court, 12 February 2002; *L v DPP*, unreported, High Court, 16 April 2002 and *JS v DPP* [2004] IEHC 100, unreported, High Court, 2 April 2004.

[214]   Unreported, High Court, 5 December 1997.

sought to explain why such a long period had elapsed between the alleged offences and the ultimate complaints. However, in the affidavit, the psychologist failed to mention sexual abuse of the complainants by members of their family and the psychological effect which this might have had on them. Under cross-examination, he sought to explain this omission on the basis that he did not know of the allegations against the members of the family and he did not think that the fact that the complainants had been abused by someone else should form part of his report. Commenting on this failure, which he characterised as "astonishing", McCracken J said that:

> "It is my strongly held view that where a witness purports to give evidence in a professional capacity as an expert witness, he owes a duty to ascertain all the surrounding facts and to give that evidence in the context of those facts, whether they support the proposition which he is being asked to put forward or not."

6–75 These comments were approved by Hardiman J in *JL v DPP*[215] who stressed "the need for caution and for a very full and impartial presentation of psychiatric or psychological evidence".

6–76 If these principles are to be complied with, then it is obvious that an expert cannot be directed by a party as to what to say although it is permissible for an expert, particularly one who is unfamiliar with giving evidence, to be provided with some guidance as to how best to focus and present his or her evidence.[216]

6–77 The necessity for an expert to place all relevant facts before the tribunal of fact and the potential consequences if this is not done is evident from the decision in *People (DPP) v Allen*.[217] The accused had been convicted of armed robbery and possession of a firearm and one of the primary items of evidence against him consisted of DNA evidence obtained from a piece of cloth found near the scene of the robbery that had been matched to him. At the trial, expert evidence was given by a forensic scientist who estimated that the chance of an unrelated person having the same profile was less than one in a thousand million. She also indicated that a matching profile was more likely between the siblings but did not give any probability figure. On appeal, the Court of Criminal Appeal accepted the submission that the conviction should be quashed because of the failure of the forensic scientist to give a probability figure for the possibility of siblings of the accused having a matching DNA profile. Having reviewed the evidence given by the forensic scientist during examination-in-chief and cross-examination, the Court was satisfied that the jury would have been left with the "very clear impression" that the chances of the DNA belonging to anybody other than the accused were so remote as to lead them to the view that they would not have a reasonable doubt that the DNA was that of the accused. Thus, the failure to disclose any probability figures in relation to siblings to the jury "had the potential to confuse or mislead the jury into believing that, even among brothers, an increased probability starting from a base of one in one thousand million would still be so improbable that they could disregard it."[218] The Court explained that it had no way of knowing what attitude a jury would have taken if the probability figures in relation to brothers had been disclosed to it and, so, it quashed the conviction and ordered a re-trial.

6–78 The importance of expert witnesses disclosing the facts on which their opinions

---

[215] [2000] 3 IR 122 at 149.
[216] *GO'R v DPP* [2011] IEHC 368 at [13]–[14], [2012] 1 IR 193 at 201–202.
[217] [2003] 4 IR 295.
[218] [2003] 4 IR 295 at 301.

are based and the basis on which that opinion has been formed was also emphasised by Charleton J in *Condron v ACC Bank Plc*[219] who commented:

> "Experts have a particular privilege before the courts. They are entitled to express an opinion. In doing so, their entitlement is predicated upon also informing the court of the factors which make up their opinion and supplying to the court the elements of knowledge which long study and experience has equipped them so that, armed with that analysis and the elements of arriving there, the court may be enabled to take a different view to their opinion."[220]

6–79   An expert who gives evidence can be questioned in relation to the instructions which were given to him or her and as to the factual material that he or she used in order to form his or her expert opinion and litigation privilege will be waived to that extent.[221]

12. Weight to be Attached to Expert Evidence

6–80   The weight to be attached to the evidence of a particular expert witness will depend on a number of factors including the qualifications and experience of the expert,[222] his or her degree of expertise,[223] the extent to which the particular area of expertise is recognised by the courts,[224] whether the views or methodology of the expert accord with those generally accepted in that field of expertise,[225] the extent to which the facts upon which the opinion of the expert have been proved in evidence,[226] the extent of the expert's first hand knowledge of the facts upon which he or she has based his or her expert opinion,[227] the nature and extent of the investigations carried out by the expert,[228] the extent to which the expert has relied on information provided by the party who has engaged him or her or has sought to verify that information from

---

[219] [2012] IEHC 395 at [19], [2013] 1 ILRM 113 at 123.

[220] He made very similar comments in *Flynn v Bus Átha Cliath* [2012] IEHC 398 at [9].

[221] *Ahern v Mahon* [2008] IEHC 119 at [117], [2008] 4 IR 704 at 729–730, [2009] 1 ILRM 458 at 480.

[222] See *R. v Silverlock* [1894] 2 QB 766 at 771, where it was held that the lack of formal qualifications of an expert witness would go to the weight to be attached to his or her testimony.

[223] *Re Glaxo Group Ltd* [2009] IEHC 277 at [74]; *ACC v Deacon* [2013] IEHC 427 at 16.

[224] Contrast the approach of Murphy J in *KWT v DAT* [1992] 2 IR 11 (evidence of psychiatrist in nullity suit) with the approach of the same judge in *Murnaghan Bros v O'Maoldomhnaigh* [1991] 1 IR 455 (evidence of accountant in tax case).

[225] See *R. v Robb* (1991) 93 Cr App R 161 at 165, 166. See also *People (DPP) v Kelly* [2008] IECCA 7, [2008] 3 IR 697 where the Court of Criminal Appeal was not satisfied that CUSUM analysis, which was used to determine whether documents had been authored by one person or more than one person, was a technique that had a properly established scientific provenance and had not achieved the requisite degree of expert peer approval.

[226] See *Conley v Strain* [1988] IR 628 and *O'K v O'K* [2005] IEHC 384. *Cf. R. v Lavelle* [1990] 55 CCC 97, *per* Wilson J at 127–128, where it was held that, unless the facts on which an expert's opinion is based have been found to exist, no weight may be given to that opinion. The courts in New Zealand took a similar approach in *R. v Makaore* [2001] 1 NZLR 318, where it was held that there must be admissible evidence of the underlying facts.

[227] See *DK v TH (Orse TK)*, unreported, High Court, 25 February 1998 and *JWH (Orse W) v GW*, unreported, High Court, 25 February 1998. In each case, O'Higgins J attached little weight to the evidence of a psychiatrist concerning the respondent's capacity to enter into a marital relationship in circumstances where he had not actually examined the respondent but relied on information supplied by the petitioner. See also *Conley v Strain* [1988] IR 62, where Lynch J preferred the evidence of medical witnesses who had the plaintiff under their care over that of medical witnesses whose opinions were based solely on medical records.

[228] See *Fitzpatrick v DPP*, unreported, High Court, 5 December 1997; *AW v DPP*, unreported, High Court, 23 November 2001; *BJ v DPP*, unreported, High Court, 12 February 2002; *L v DPP*, unreported, High Court, 16 April 2002. In each of these cases, the evidence of a clinical psychologist as to the reasons for the delay in complainants making complaints of sexual offences

other sources,[229] and the extent to which the expert has applied his or her expertise in a critical manner to the information provided by the engaging party.[230] In *James Elliott Construction Ltd v Irish Asphalt Ltd*[231] Charleton J quoted with approval a passage from the judgment of Stewart-Smyth LJ in *Loveday v Renton*[232] where he outlined his approach to the evaluation of expert evidence as follows:

> "The mere expression of opinion or belief by a witness, however eminent... does not suffice. The Court has to evaluate on the soundness of his opinion. Most importantly this involves an examination of the reasons given for his opinions and the extent to which they are supported by the evidence. The judge also has to decide what weight to attach to a witnesses' opinion by examining the internal consistency and logic of his evidence; the care with which he has considered the subject and presented his evidence; his precision and accuracy of thought as demonstrated by his answers; how he responds to searching and informed cross-examination and in particular the extent to which a witness faces up to and accepts the logic of a proposition put in cross examination or is prepared to concede points that are seen to be correct; the extent to which a witness has conceived an opinion and is reluctant to re-examine it in the light of later evidence, or demonstrates a flexibility of mind which may involve changing or modifying opinions previously held; whether or not a witness is biased or lacks independence... there is one further aspect of a witness's evidence that is often important; that is his demeanour in the witness box. As in most cases where the court is evaluating expert evidence, I have placed less weight on this factor in reaching my assessment. But is not wholly unimportant; and in particularly in those instances where criticisms have been made of a witness, on the grounds of bias or lack of independence, which in my view are not justified, the witnesses' demeanour has been a factor which I have taken into account"[233]

6–81 Although the tribunal of fact is entitled to give particular weight to,[234] and will generally accept uncontradicted expert evidence,[235] it is not obliged to do so.[236] In *Davie v Edinburgh Magistrates*[237] Lord Cooper cautioned that:

> "Expert witnesses, however skilled and eminent, can give no more than evidence. They cannot usurp the functions of the jury or judge sitting as a jury...The scientific opinion evidence, if intelligible, convincing and tested, becomes a factor (and often an important factor) for consideration along with the whole other evidence in the case, but the decision is for the judge or jury."[238]

6–82 Thus, the courts are quite conscious of the dangers of uncritical acceptance of the evidence of experts and it has been emphasised in a number of cases that a judge cannot abdicate his or her function to an expert, no matter how distinguished. For example,

---

was given little weight because of serious deficiencies in the methodology employed by him and the failure to carry out any validation process. See also *ACC v Deacon* [2013] IEHC 427 at [33].

[229] See *Carey v Minister for Finance* [2010] IEHC 166 at [4.33]–[4.44], where Irvine J held that medical practitioners should, wherever possible, try to avoid relying solely on the account of the claimant and should have regard to any other primary sources of information available to them when coming to their conclusions.

[230] *Emerald Meats Ltd v Minister for Agriculture* [2012] IESC 48 at [28].

[231] [2011] IEHC 269 at [12].

[232] [1989] 1 Med LR 117.

[233] See further, Bell, "Judicial Assessment of Expert Evidence" [2010] 2 JSIJ 55.

[234] *Quinn v Mid Western Health Board* [2013] IESC 19 at [63], [2005] 4 IR 1 at 24.

[235] *JW v VW* [1990] 2 IR 437 at 459; *Murnaghan Bros v O'Maoldomhnaigh* [1991] 1 IR 461; *R. v Saunders* (1991) 93 Cr App R 245 at 249.

[236] *Molamphy v Nenagh Co-Operative Creamery Ltd* (1952) 89 ILTR 159 at 162; *Hanrahan v Merck, Sharp & Dohme* [1988] ILRM 629 at 645; *Ryan v Walsh*, unreported, Supreme Court, *ex tempore*, 18 July 1996; *GC v DPP* [2006] IEHC 44 at [4.3]; *Sparrow v Minister for Agriculture, Fisheries and Food* [2010] IESC 6 at [18]; *Nerney v Thomas Crosbie Holdings Ltd* [2013] IEHC 127 at [39].

[237] 1953 SC 34 at 40.

[238] This passage was approved by Charleton J in *Re Glaxo Group Ltd* [2009] IEHC 277 at [24].

in *F (Orse C) v C*,[239] Keane J said that, while the evidence of psychiatrists could assist the court, "it is the responsibility of the Courts alone and not of psychiatrists, however eminent, to determine whether a decree of nullity should be granted."[240] However, that case dealt with psychiatric evidence which has traditionally been treated with some degree of caution,[241] not least because eminent psychiatrists may quite properly differ on a psychiatric question to which their expertise relates.[242] Greater deference will be shown to the opinions of experts in respect of more traditional categories of expert evidence. This is evident from *Murnaghan Bros v O'Maoldomhnaigh*,[243] where Murphy J accepted that the trial judge had been correct in saying that the court must not abdicate to experts the role of the court in determining matters of law and fact but went on to say that the value of expert evidence in relation to accounting matters is well recognised. Therefore, because the accountant had not been shown to have erred as a matter of law in his approach and his evidence had not be challenged on the grounds that it did not represent the practice of the accountancy profession, the learned judge was of the view that there had not been sufficient grounds for the rejection of his evidence.

13. Directions as to the Weight to be attached to Expert Evidence in Criminal Cases

6–83   With certain types of expert evidence, there is a danger that a jury might attach too much weight to it. In *People (DPP) v Allen*,[244] the Court of Criminal Appeal adverted to this possibility in the context of DNA evidence:

> "Expert evidence comparing D.N.A. profiles is a comparatively recent scientific technique and indeed it would appear that it is still being perfected. As in many scientific advances, the jury have to rely entirely on expert evidence. One of the primary dangers involved in such circumstances is that, the matter being so technical, a jury could jump to the conclusion that the evidence is infallible. That, of course, is not so in the case of D.N.A. evidence, at least in the present state of knowledge."[245]

6–84   In such circumstances, there is an obligation on the trial judge to give directions to the jury as to how it should approach the expert evidence and to caution the jury against attaching too much weight to it.[246]

---

239   [1991] 2 IR 330.

240   [1991] 2 IR 330 at 344. See, to similar effect, *per* Murphy J in *KWT v DAT* [1992] 2 IR 11 at 21–22, that, while the evidence of psychiatrists, psychologists and social workers was of "paramount importance" in nullity cases, "at the end of the day it seems to me that I cannot abdicate my function to the experts, however distinguished".

241   For a discussion of psychiatric evidence and the problems with its reliability, see Mackay and Coleman, "Equivocal Rulings on Expert Psychological and Psychiatric Evidence; Turning a Muddle into a Nonsense" [1996] Crim LR 88; Beaumont, "Psychiatric Evidence: Over-Rationalising the Abnormal" [1988] Crim LR 290; Sheldon and MacLeod, "From Normative Data: Expert Psychological Evidence Re-Examined" [1991] Crim LR 811.

242   As noted by Hardiman J in *O'Callaghan v DPP* [2011] IESC 30 at [12].

243   [1991] 1 IR 455.

244   [2003] 4 IR 295.

245   [2003] 4 IR 295 at 299. But see *People (DPP) v Boyce* [2008] IECCA 62 at [155], [2009] 2 IR 124 at 161, [2009] 1 ILRM 253 at 285, where the Supreme Court seemed to have less concerns about the potential unreliability of DNA evidence with Fennelly J stating that "DNA constitutes one of the astonishing scientific advances of the age".

246   In *People (DPP) v Murphy* [2005] IECCA 52, [2005] 4 IR 504, the Court of Criminal Appeal was satisfied that the trial judge had given an adequate direction in this regard in relation to DNA evidence.

14. Conflict Between the Evidence of Experts and Non-Experts

6–85   Although the tribunal of fact may, in circumstances of a given case, prefer expert evidence to that of lay witnesses,[247] it is clear that expert evidence is not to be afforded additional weight simply because it has been given by an expert and, where a conflict arises between the evidence of experts and that of non-experts, it is open to the tribunal of fact to prefer that of the non-experts. Reference can be made to the case of *People (AG) v Fennell (No.1)*[248] where the defence of the defendant to a charge of murder was insanity. Two medical experts testified on his behalf that he was insane at the time of the killing. However, there was a body of lay evidence showing that the accused had been acting normally around the time of the fatal attack. The jury found the accused to be sane and guilty of murder, a verdict which was upheld on appeal. The Court of Criminal Appeal expressed the view "that the testimony of the medical experts, either considered by itself and fully tested by cross-examination, or when weighed against the lay testimony of sanity, was not so convincing or coercive as to compel a jury of reasonable men to accept it."[249] The same conclusion was reached when the issue arose again in *People (AG) v Kelly*[250] where the Court of Criminal Appeal rejected the proposition that the jury was bound to accept the medical evidence of insanity tendered, stating that the jury, "while they were bound to give the greatest attention to the medical evidence … were entitled, and indeed bound, to give equal attention to the conduct of the accused".[251]

15. Resolving a Conflict between Experts

6–86   When resolving a conflict of evidence between experts, the tribunal of fact will have regard to the factors identified above in relation to the weight to be attached to expert evidence. In particular, a court will consider their relative expertise,[252] the extent to which their respective opinions are supported by the facts,[253] the nature and extent of the investigations in respect of matters relevant to the opinions expressed by them,[254] the authority and persuasiveness of their evidence,[255] the extent to which their

---

[247] See, e.g. *Furey v Suckau*, unreported, High Court, 14 July 2000 and *Conlan v O'Malley*, unreported, High Court, 18 November 2002. In both cases, expert evidence was preferred to direct oral evidence in determining the cause of a road traffic accident.

[248] [1940] IR 445.

[249] [1940] IR 445 at 452.

[250] (1962) 1 Frewen 267.

[251] (1962) 1 Frewen 267 at 271. See also *R. v Khan* [2009] EWCA Crim 1569, [2010] 1 Cr App R 4 where the Court of Appeal refused to overturn a conviction for murder despite the fact that there was uncontradicted expert evidence that that the appellant was suffering from an abnormality of mind induced by disease. In the view of the Court of Appeal there was ample evidence on which the jury could reject the defence of diminished responsibility and conclude that it was not satisfied, on a balance of probabilities, that the abnormality of the mind of the appellant substantially impaired the mental responsibility of the appellant in committing the acts in question. *Cf. Poynton v Poynton* (1903) 37 ILTR 54 and *Glynn v Glynn* [1990] 2 IR 326 where the evidence of lay witnesses was preferred to medical evidence in cases dealing with testamentary capacity.

[252] See *Quinn v Midwestern Health Board*, High Court, 14 October 2003; [2005] IESC 19 at [60]–[62], [2005] 4 IR 1 at 22–23; *Re Glaxo Group Ltd* [2009] IEHC 277 at [74].

[253] See, by way of example, *Griffin v Patton* [2004] IESC 46; *Dunne v Coombe Women and Infants University Hospital* [2013] IEHC 58 and *People (DPP) v Moore* [2005] IECCA 141.

[254] See *People (DPP) v Moore* [2005] IECCA 141.

[255] While it is natural that a court would have regard to this factor, the Law Reform Commission in its *Consultation Paper on Expert Evidence* (LRC CP 52–2008) at [2.278], observed that it effectively means "that in the 'battle of the experts,' the opinion given by the witness with the

evidence has been presented objectively and in discharge of the duties owed to the court,[256] and the extent to which their opinion was undermined by cross-examination.[257] In *James Elliott Construction Ltd v Irish Asphalt Ltd,*[258] Charleton J, having endorsed the criteria for the evaluation of expert evidence identified by Stewart-Smyth LJ in *Loveday v Renton,*[259] explained that:

> "the most important reasons whereby I have chosen one expert over another have been the manner in which an opinion has been reasoned through and the extent to which opposing views have been genuinely and objectively considered on the basis of their merit. A judge must bear in mind that, notwithstanding that an expert may firmly declare a duty to the court, it is a natural aspect of human nature that even a professional person retained on behalf of a plaintiff or defendant may feel themselves to be part of that side's team. Of particular importance in this case, therefore, has been the extent to which an expert has been able to step back and to consider and to think through an opposing point of view. As with demeanour, this is not readily demonstrated on a transcript of evidence. Rather, to a trial judge, it can be possible to see the degree to which a witness is thinking through the potential for an opposing theory before giving a reasoned answer. Experience in other cases demonstrates that there is a danger that experts may erect a barrier of apparent learning in order to disguise what would be an answer awkward to their side were it to be expressed plainly. Apart from the attractions of logic and reasoning, therefore, assessing an answer based on what is seen and heard in the courtroom remains important."

6–87 A tribunal of fact may also draw on its own common sense and experience in deciding which evidence to prefer. In *Cassidy v Wellman International Ltd,*[260] conflicting evidence had been given by expert witnesses as to whether an accumulation of water on the floor of a premises had caused the plaintiff to slip and fall. Tests had been carried out by an expert engineer called on behalf of the defendant which showed that the floor met required standards and had sufficient skid resistance. However, the trial judge preferred the evidence of the engineer called on behalf of the plaintiff that, even if this was the case, the floor could still be dangerous where water accumulated on it because this tallied with his own experience. Although the finding of the trial judge on this point was criticised on the basis that he had preferred to rely on his own experience instead of expert engineering evidence, Keane CJ took the view that the trial judge could not be faulted "for preferring the evidence of one expert engineer to another where he finds the evidence of one engineer most closely according with the facts of human experience as he saw it".[261]

6–88 As noted by Finlay CJ in *Best v Wellcome Foundation Ltd,*[262] where competing scientific theories are put forward by opposing expert witnesses, it is not the function of the court to resolve scientific controversies but simply to decide which evidence is to be preferred:

> "I am satisfied that it is not possible for either a judge of trial or for an appellate court to

---

greater oratorical skills may be the one that sways the opinion of the judge or jury, particularly where complex issues are in question, regardless of whether the opinion is the more reliable in the circumstances."

[256]   *James Elliott Construction Ltd v Irish Asphalt Ltd* [2011] IEHC 269 at [13].
[257]   See, by way of example, *Re Glaxo Group Ltd* [2009] IEHC 277 at [79].
[258]   [2011] IEHC 269 at [13].
[259]   [1989] 1 Med LR 117.
[260]   Unreported, Supreme Court, 31 October 2001.
[261]   It should be noted that there is no obligation on a trial judge to give any reasons why he or she has accepted the evidence of one expert witness rather than another: *O'Sullivan v Sherry*, unreported, Supreme Court, *ex tempore,* 2 February 1996.
[262]   [1993] 3 IR 421.

take upon itself the role of a determining scientific authority resolving disputes between distinguished scientists in any particular line of scientific expertise. The function which the court can and must perform is to apply common sense and a careful understanding of the logic and likelihood of events to conflicting opinions and conflicting theories concerning a matter of this kind."[263]

6–89 This was the approach adopted by Peart J in *McNeilis v Armstrong*[264] who had to choose between conflicting evidence of engineering and medical experts as to whether the injuries suffered by a number of children who were rear passengers involved in a road traffic accident would have been less severe if they had been wearing seatbelts at the time and decided this issue as a matter of probability taking in account all of the evidence adduced.[265]

6–90 However, the difficulties in asking a tribunal of fact to decide between conflicting expert evidence when the rationale for admitting that evidence is that the tribunal of fact does not have the necessary specialised knowledge or skill are obvious.[266] As can be seen from *Quinn v Mid Western Health Board*,[267] in some instances, a court may be unable to choose between competing theories propounded by experts so that it has to decide the relevant issue on the basis that the party bearing the burden of proof has failed to discharge it. But this will not be necessary where there is evidence from fact witnesses which enables the court to decide between the competing theories and reach a conclusion as to what occurred.[268]

6–91 Turning to a trial before a jury, it was suggested in *R. v Cannings*[269] that a case may have to be withdrawn from jury where the outcome of the trial depends exclusively or almost exclusively on scientific evidence which was the subject of a serious disagreement between distinguished and reputable experts. However, in *R. v Kai-Whitewind*,[270] it was noted that such disagreements are not uncommon and it was held that: "Evidence of this kind must be dealt with in accordance with the usual principle that it is for the jury to decide between the experts, by reference to all the available evidence, and that it is open to the jury to accept or reject the evidence of the experts on either side."

---

[263] [1993] 3 IR 421 at 462. This approach was approved and applied in *Quinn v Midwestern Health Board*, High Court, 14 October 2003, [2005] IESC 19 at [55]–[56], [2005] 4 IR 1 at 21.

[264] [2006] IEHC 269.

[265] See also *Ward v South Western Health Board* [2008] IEHC 81.

[266] As Learned Hand queried in "Historical and Practical Considerations Regarding Expert Testimony" (1901) 15 Harvard LR 40 at 54–55: "But how can the jury judge between two statements each founded upon an experience confessedly foreign in kind to their own? It is just because they are incompetent for such a task that the expert is necessary at all.... If you would get at the truth in such cases, it must be through someone competent to decide."

[267] High Court, 14 October 2003, [2005] IESC 19 at [57]–[59] [2005] 4 IR 1 at 21. See also *Rhesa Shipping Co SA v Edmunds* [1985] 1 WLR 948 at 955. The trial judge in *Quinn* was O'Sullivan J who subsequently commented ("A Hot Tub for Expert Witnesses" (2004) 4 JSIJ 1) that the task of trying to resolve the stark conflict between the medical expert evidence in the case left him "feeling like an intellectual pygmy looking up at two giants: from that vantage point one simply cannot tell which of them is taller".

[268] *Fyffes plc v DCC plc* [2005] IEHC 477 at [193], [2009] 2 IR 417 at 505. This was the position in *Wright v AIB Leasing & Finance* [2013] IESC 55.

[269] [2004] 2 Cr App R 7 at [178].

[270] [2005] EWCA Crim 1092, [2005] 2 Cr App R 31 at [89].

16. Proof of Foreign Law

6–92   It is well established that expert evidence is not admissible in respect of any matter of domestic law.[271] However, it is not only admissible but is mandatory in respect of matters of foreign law[272] and the evidence of a non-expert as to a foreign law is inadmissible.[273]

6–93   In general, the dividing line between domestic law and foreign law[274] is straightforward but it should be noted that, where the construction or application of legislation that is common to both Ireland and the England arises in the context of a question of English law, this will be considered to be an issue of foreign law.[275] Similarly, where the interpretation and application in another jurisdiction of a convention that has been incorporated into domestic law such as the European Convention on Human Rights arises, this again is considered to be a question of foreign law.[276]

6–94   The leading Irish case on the proof of foreign law is *O'Callaghan v O'Sullivan*[277] where it was held that, where an issue of foreign law arises, it:

> "…must be proved as a fact in the particular case, and … it must be so proved by the testimony and opinion of competent expert witnesses shown to possess the skill and knowledge, scientific or empirical, required for stating, expounding, and interpreting that law."[278]

6–95   Thus, foreign law can only be proven by the evidence of a suitably qualified lawyer and, in the absence of such evidence, cannot be established by referring to statutory provisions or case law from the relevant jurisdiction.[279]

6–96   It is ultimately a question of fact as to whether a person has sufficient expertise in a foreign law but it is likely that a person will have the requisite expertise if he or

---

[271]   *SPUC v Grogan (No. 3)* [1992] 2 IR 471 at 475 (interpretation of solemn declaration regarding the seventeenth protocol to the Maastricht Treaty); *F v Ireland* [1995] 1 IR 345 (evidence as to essential features of a Christian marriage in the context of the issue of constitutional interpretation); *Glancré Teoranta v Cafferkey* [2004] IEHC 123 at [10]–[11], [2004] 3 IR 401 at 407 (evidence of planning consultant as to whether An Bord Pleanála had correctly applied relevant statutory provisions); *O'Carroll v Diamond* [2005] IESC 21 at [31], [2005] 4 IR 41 at 56 (evidence as what a solicitor should have done in a particular situation). Cf. *Byrne v Conroy* [1998] 3 IR 1 at 10 (affidavits of lawyers and economists, whilst of some help in relation to the question of whether a particular offence was a revenue offence within the meaning of s.50 of the Extradition Act 1965 were not determinative of the question because it was a matter of Irish law).

[272]   *O'Callaghan v O'Sullivan* [1925] 1 IR 90 at 112; *MacNamara v Owners of the Steamship "Hatteras"* [1933] IR 675 at 698–700; *Kutchera v Buckingham International Holdings Ltd* [1988] IR 61 at 68; *McMahon v McDonald*, unreported, High Court, 3 May 1988 at 29; *Attorney General v Pocevicius* [2013] IEHC 229 at 21.

[273]   *Attorney General v O'Gara* [2012] IEHC 179 at [7.2].

[274]   Canon law is considered to be a foreign law and must be proven by expert evidence: *McNally v Ireland* [2009] IEHC 753 at [62], [2011] 4 IR 431 at 448, [2011] 1 ILRM 40 at 54.

[275]   *McMahon v McDonald*, unreported, High Court, 3 May 1988 at 29.

[276]   *McMahon v McDonald*, unreported, High Court, 3 May 1988 at 30.

[277]   [1925] 1 IR 90.

[278]   [1925] 1 IR 90 at 112 (*per* Kennedy CJ).

[279]   *Walsh v National Irish Bank Ltd* [2013] IESC 2 at [6.3].

she is a practitioner,[280] a former practitioner,[281] or a person qualified to practice[282] in the particular foreign jurisdiction, or is person who, though unqualified, has acquired sufficient expertise by academic study[283] or, in matters of commerce, by practical experience.[284] However, regardless of how the witness has acquired his expertise, he or she should be an independent expert.[285]

6–97 Where an expert witness gives evidence upon a matter of foreign law, the general rule is that it is the testimony of the witness which constitutes evidence on that issue and not the textbooks or other legal materials referred to by him.[286] This is because the court "has not organs to know and to deal with the text of that law, and therefore requires the assistance of a lawyer who knows how to interpret it."[287] Thus, a judge is generally not permitted to consult the sources used by the expert[288] but he may do so when the evidence given is unclear[289] or where there is a conflict between the experts.[290] In no circumstances, however, may the judge go beyond the sources used by the expert and conduct his or her own researches into foreign law.[291] Furthermore, where admissible expert evidence of foreign law is tendered, the court is required to accept it "unless obviously false or discredited in some way"[292] and the court cannot reject the evidence of the expert because it would itself have come to a different conclusion on perusal of the text of the foreign law or on consideration of the terms of the document that falls to be interpreted or whose validity is to be decided in accordance with that law.[293] However, where the expert evidence establishes that a discretion is enjoyed by

---

[280] *In re Anderson*, unreported, High Court, 6 July 1995; *Baron de Bode's Case* (1845) 8 QB 208; *Attorney General v Dyer* [2004] IESC 1 at [13], [2004] 1 IR 40 at 44. It is apparent from the decision in *Dyer* that it is sufficient if the person is a practitioner and he or she does not have to furnish evidence of any particular or special expertise.

[281] *Glentanar v Wellington* [1947] Ch 506, [1947] 2 All ER 854.

[282] *Barford v Barford* [1918] P 140 (witness had been called to the Bar in a number of countries and was entitled, as a matter of course, to be admitted to practise in the relevant jurisdiction).

[283] *O'Callaghan v O'Sullivan* [1925] 1 IR 90 (one of the experts in Canon Law had acquired his expertise through study in Maynooth and Rome).

[284] See *Ajami v Comptroller of Customs* [1954] 1 WLR 1405 (bank manager permitted to give evidence as to whether certain bank notes were legal tender); *De Beéche v South American Stores* [1935] AC 148, [1934] All ER 284 (evidence of banker admitted in relation to proper construction of contractual term); *Vander Donckt v Thellusson* (1849) 8 CB 812 (merchant who had carried on business in Belgium permitted to give evidence to prove the law in relation to the presentment of a promissory note).

[285] *Per* Fennelly J in *ICDL v The European Computer Driving Licence Foundation Ltd* [2012] IESC 55 at [107], [2012] 3 IR 327 at 362.

[286] *O'Callaghan v O'Sullivan* [1925] 1 IR 90 at 119; *Sussex Peerage Case* (1844) 11 Cl & F 85 at 115; *Baron de Bode's Case* (1845) 8 QB 208 at 250.

[287] *Per* Lord Brougham in the *Sussex Peerage Case* (1844) 11 Cl & F 85 at 115.

[288] *Earl Nelson v Lord Bridport* (1845) 8 Beav 527.

[289] *O'Callaghan v O'Sullivan* [1925] 1 IR 90 at 121; *Earl Nelson v Lord Bridport* (1845) 8 Beav 527.

[290] *McC v McC* [1994] 1 IR 293; *McNamara v Owners of S.S. Hatteras (No.2)* [1933] IR 675 at 699–700; *O'Callaghan v O'Sullivan* [1925] 1 IR 90 at 121.

[291] *Bumper Development Corp. Ltd v Commissioner of Police* [1991] 4 All ER 638; *Duchess Di Sora v Phillips* (1863) 10 HL Cas 624.

[292] [1925] 1 IR 90 at 119. See also *MacNamara v Owners of the SS "Hatteras"* [1933] IR 675 at 699 and *Waterford Harbour Commissioners v British Railways Board* [1979] ILRM 296 at 306.

[293] *MacNamara v Owners of the SS "Hatteras"* [1933] IR 675 at 699.

a court under the foreign law, an Irish judge will not necessarily be bound by the view of an expert as to how that discretion should be exercised.[294]

6–98   If there is a conflict between the experts as to either the content of the foreign law, its interpretation, or how the question at issue would be decided by a court in foreign jurisdiction, then, in accordance with the approach laid down by Fitzgibbon J in *MacNamara v Owners of the SS "Hatteras"*,[295] "the court must make up its own mind as best it can, using the material at its disposal, and deciding between the experts as it would have to do if they were giving their opinion upon any scientific question".[296]

6–99   It is important to note that an issue of foreign law is regarded as a matter of fact.[297] Therefore, the finding of the court on the issue has no precedential value and if the point arises again, it must be decided anew by reference to fresh expert evidence.[298] It also follows that the determination of the trial judge on the issue of foreign law is regarded as a finding of primary fact for the purposes of any appeal from that determination.[299]

C. Non-Expert Opinion Evidence

6–100   There are a number of circumstances where, in derogation from the general exclusionary rule, the opinion evidence of non-experts is admissible. These defy precise categorisation but, for ease of analysis, can be placed into four non-exclusive and non-exhaustive[300] categories.

6–101   The first category is where a matter is one which "is not capable of exact observation and where the most that could be expected is an appreciation or an extenuation."[301] Examples falling within this category include the speed of vehicles,[302] the size of a crowd, the apparent age of a person,[303] and any question of measurement. In respect of these matters, a witness is permitted to give evidence which is a mixture of observed facts and opinion based on that observation.[304]

6–102   The second category "includes instances in which the primary facts and the inferences to be drawn therefrom are so adherent or closely associated that it may be

---

[294] See *Kelly v Groupama* [2012] IEHC 177 (which the assessment of damages in accordance with French law for personal injuries was considered).

[295] *Kelly v Groupama* [2012] IEHC 177 at 699–700.

[296] See *M McC v J McC* [1994] 1 IR 293 and *HI v MG* [1999] 2 ILRM 1 where this approach was applied.

[297] *O'Callaghan v O'Sullivan* [1925] 1 IR 90 at 112; *MacNamara v Owners of the SS "Hatteras"* [1933] IR 675 at 698; *Walsh v National Irish Bank Ltd* [2013] IESC 2 at [6.2]; *McCaughey v Irish Bank Resolution Corporation* [2013] IESC 17 at 45; *Earl Nelson v Lord Bridport* (1845) 8 Beav 527 at 536.

[298] *McCormick v Garnett* (1854) 23 LJ Ch 777.

[299] *McCaughey v Irish Bank Resolution Corporation* [2013] IESC 17 at [45].

[300] *Sherrard v Jacob* [1965] NI 151 at 156 (*per* Lord MacDermott LCJ); *R. v Graat* [1982] 2 SCR 819 at 837.

[301] *Per* Kingsmill Moore J in *AG (Ruddy) v Kenny* (1960) 94 ILTR 185 at 190.

[302] *Cf.* s.81(5) of the Road Traffic Act 2010 which lays down a requirement for corroboration in respect of opinion evidence of speed.

[303] *R. v Cox* [1898] 1 QB 179.

[304] *AG (Ruddy) v Kenny* (1960) 94 ILTR 185 at 190 (*per* Kingsmill Moore J); *Lithgow City Council v Jackson* [2011] HCA 36 at [45].

hard, if not impossible, to separate them".[305] Evidence of identification is, perhaps, the best example of this category. A witness who identifies a person as one whom he or she has seen before "does not consciously arrive at his conclusion by an observation of separate features."[306] Even though a witness could give a description of the person he saw and then leave it to the jury to decide whether that description matches that of the defendant, the jury who did not actually observe the defendant are not in as good a position as the witness to make that identification. Other examples include evidence as to the condition of objects. Thus, a non-expert may describe the condition of objects, using adjectives such as "good", "new", "worn", and "old".

6–103   The third category enables evidence as to "matters of common experience within the ken of ordinary men ... to be conveniently summarised or distilled in opinion form which in practice could not reasonably be called for in all its multitudinous detail".[307] A good example is an expression of opinion as to the sanity of a person.[308] Instead of requiring a witness to give detailed evidence of the facts underlying that inference, the witness is permitted to express the opinion as "a compendious mode of ascertaining the result of the actual observation of the witness."[309] Other examples are expressions of opinion as to the emotional or physical state of a person, such as that a person was distressed, angry, sick or depressed.[310] One physical condition that has generated a degree of controversy is drunkenness, but it is now settled that opinion evidence can be given in relation to it.[311]

6–104   Finally, there is a residual category accommodating a miscellany of circumstances where non-experts are allowed to express opinions where it is convenient and they do not go to the issues in a case.[312] In *AG (Ruddy) v Kenny*,[313] Lavery J took quite a broad view of the admission of non-expert opinion evidence saying that there were "innumerable incidents of everyday life upon which an ordinary person can express a useful opinion and one which ought to be admitted."[314] Such an approach was also advocated by Dickson J, delivering the judgment of the Supreme Court of Canada in *R. v Graat*:

> "I can see no reason in principle or in common sense why a lay witness should not be permitted

---

[305] *Sherrard v Jacob* [1965] NI 151 at 156 (*per* Lord MacDermott LCJ). *Cf. R. v Barker* (1988) 34 ACR 141.

[306] *Per* Kingsmill Moore J in *AG (Ruddy) v Kenny* (1960) 94 ILTR 185 at 190.

[307] *Per* Lord MacDermott LCJ in *Sherrard v Jacob* [1965] NI 151 at 156.

[308] *Wright v Doe d Tatham* (1838) 4 Bing NC 489; *Glynn v Glynn* [1990] 2 IR 326; *Cooper v R.* [1980] 1 SCR 1149 at 1165. *Cf. Royal Trust Ltd v McClure* [1945] 4 DLR 373, [1946] 2 SCR 622.

[309] *Per* Parke B in *Wright v Doe d. Tatham* (1838) 4 Bing NC 489 at 543–544.

[310] See *People (DPP) v Keogh* [2009] IECCA 93 where a garda gave evidence that the upset of a sexual complainant was "genuine" and the Court of Criminal Appeal rejected the contention that this evidence was inadmissible, stating that it "was in reality merely giving a description of the appearance and demeanour and visible upset of the complainant".

[311] In *AG (Ruddy) v Kenny* (1960) 94 ILTR 185, it was held that a garda could give opinion evidence that an accused was drunk and that he was thereby unfit to drive a vehicle. That was also the conclusion reached in *R. v Graat* [1982] 2 SCR 819 at 838. *Cf. R. v Davies* [1962] 1 WLR 1111 and *Sherrard v Jacob* [1965] NI 151 at 156 where it was held that opinion evidence of drunkenness could be given but not of capacity to drive.

[312] *Cf. AG (Ruddy) v Kenny* (1960) 94 ILTR 185 at 191 (*per* Kingsmill Moore J).

[313] (1960) 94 ILTR 185.

[314] (1960) 94 ILTR 185 at 189.

to testify in the form of an opinion if, by doing so, he is able more accurately to express the facts he perceived."[315]

6–105   It is also worth noting the approach taken in Rule 701 of the US Federal Rules of Evidence whereby lay witnesses are permitted to express opinions or inferences which are (a) rationally based on the perception of the witness, and (b) helpful to a clear understanding of the witnesses' testimony or the determination of a fact in issue.[316]

6–106   While, as noted above, the ultimate issue rule no longer appears to be extant, a non-expert witness will not be permitted to give an opinion as to a legal issue such as, for example, whether or not a person is negligent.[317]

D. Statutory Provisions

6–107   A number of miscellaneous statutory provisions have made provision for the admission of evidence of the belief and opinion of specified persons in particular contexts. These provisions, which differ in their purpose and effect, are considered in outline below.

1. Offences Against the State (Amendment) Act 1972

6–108   Section 3(2) of the Offences Against the State (Amendment) Act 1972[318] provides that, where a garda officer, not below the rank of Chief Superintendent, in giving evidence in proceedings related to an offence of membership of an unlawful organisation under s.21 of the Offences Against the State Act 1939,[319] states that he believes that the accused was at a material time a member of an unlawful organisation, the statement shall be evidence that he was then such a member. It should be noted that the subsection renders admissible the belief evidence of the garda officer only[320] and not the material upon which the belief is based and, thus, does not provide for the admission of the hearsay evidence of the statements of informants and other persons.[321] A practice has also developed that the garda officer giving belief evidence will make it clear that the belief has not been formed on the basis of any matters in respect of which direct evidence has or will be given in court so that there is no element of duplication.[322]

---

[315] [1982] 2 SCR 819 at 837.

[316] See Broun (ed.), *McCormick on Evidence* (7th edn), Vol. II, p.896.

[317] *Sherrard v Jacob* [1965] NI 151 at 156; *R. v Graat* [1982] 2 SCR 819 at 839.

[318] No.26 of 1972. See Heffernan, "Evidence and National Security: Belief Evidence in the Irish Special Criminal Court" (2009) 15 Pub Law 65.

[319] No.13 of 1939.

[320] In *People (DPP) v Doran* [2009] IECCA 113 an appeal was allowed on the basis, *inter alia*, that the Special Criminal Court had in its judgment erroneously ascribed to the Chief Superintendent who gave belief evidence, evidence given by another garda officer that had no particular statutory standing.

[321] *People (DPP) v Donnelly* [2012] IECCA 78 at [27].

[322] See, by way of example, *People (DPP) v Birney* [2006] IECCA 58 at [88], [2007] 1 IR 337 at 364. In *People (DPP) v Kelly* [2006] IESC 20 at [29], [2006] 3 IR 115 at 126, [2006] 2 ILRM 321 at 331, Fennelly J suggested that belief evidence could not be based on matters in respect of which direct evidence was before the court but O'Donnell J in *People (DPP) v Donnelly* [2012] IECCA 78 at [28] was of the view that this was not necessarily required.

6–109 In *People (DPP) v Kelly*[323] Geoghegan J noted that s.3(2) had been enacted in the context of preserving the security of the State and the legitimate concern that it will not in practice be possible in many, if not most cases, to adduce direct evidence from lay witnesses establishing that somebody is a member of a prescribed organisation because of the fear of reprisal.[324] In *People (DPP) v Mulligan*,[325] Keane CJ acknowledged that, by enacting the subsection, "the legislature has significantly altered the normal law of evidence and altered it unambiguously and unequivocally in favour of the prosecution and against the defence in a case of this nature". The extent to which the admission of such evidence constitutes a departure from the normal rules of evidence was also emphasised by Fennelly J in *People (DPP) v Kelly*[326] who pointed out that:

> "This is evidence of a quite exceptional kind. Whether or not an accused person is a member of an unlawful organisation is a question of fact. The Chief Superintendent gives evidence not of fact but of belief. His belief does not have to be based on direct knowledge of the involvement of the accused in the unlawful organisation in question. It is patently based on statements of others, whether inside or outside the force. It is probably frequently based on intelligence available to An Garda Síochána. That is precisely what is permitted by the section. Such evidence, if given openly, would infringe the hearsay rule, an objection which is circumvented by the section. The Chief Superintendent simply says what his belief is."

6–110 It has repeatedly been affirmed that belief evidence admitted pursuant to s.3(2) does have any special status and has to be evaluated and weighed in light of all other admissible evidence.[327] It has also been held that, where a claim of privilege is made in respect of the sources on which the belief is based so that these cannot be tested by way of cross-examination, this will reduce the weight to be attached to the evidence of belief and it will be necessary to weigh such evidence and any corroborating evidence against a denial on oath of membership of the unlawful organisation (if any).[328]

6–111 It has been held that a court of trial is entitled to assume that an officer of the rank of Chief Superintendent will give evidence of his or her belief that an accused person is a member of an unlawful organisation only where he or she has satisfied himself or herself of this fact beyond a reasonable doubt.[329] Accordingly, it is open to a court to convict solely on the basis of belief evidence admitted pursuant to s.3(2),[330] particularly if that evidence is unchallenged, and there are a number of cases where prosecutions have been brought and convictions obtained on the basis of such evidence

---

[323] [2006] IESC 20 at [10], [2006] 3 IR 115 at 120–121, [2006] 2 ILRM 321 at 326.

[324] See also the comments of Hardiman J in *People (DPP) v Birney* [2006] IECCA 58 at [81], [2007] 1 IR 337 at 361.

[325] Unreported, Court of Criminal Appeal, 17 May 2004.

[326] [2006] IESC 20 at [42], [2006] 3 IR 115 at 130, [2006] 2 ILRM 321 at 335.

[327] *O'Leary v AG* [1993] 1 IR 102, [1991] ILRM 454; *People (DPP) v Gannon*, unreported, Court of Criminal Appeal, 21 March 2003; *People (DPP) v Kelly* [2006] IESC 20 at [16], [2006] 3 IR 115 at 122, [2006] 2 ILRM 321 at 327; *People (DPP) v Binead* [2006] IECCA 374 at [39], [2007] 1 IR 374 at 396; *People (DPP) v Donnelly* [2012] IECCA 78 at [27]. See also *Donohoe v Ireland*, Application No. 19156/08, Judgment of the Fifth Chamber, 12 December 2013 at [91], where it was noted that the belief evidence admitted is not conclusive and "has no special status it being one piece of admissible evidence to be considered by the trial court having regard to all the other admissible evidence."

[328] *People (DPP) v Kelly* [2007] IECCA 110; *People (DPP) v Maguire* [2008] IECCA 67.

[329] *People (DPP) v Kelly* [2006] IESC 20 at [52], [2006] 3 IR 115 at 135, [2006] 2 ILRM 321 at 339 (*per* Fennelly J). See to similar effect, *per* Gannon J in *People (DPP) v Cull* (1980) 2 Frewen 36 at 41.

[330] *People (DPP) v Kelly* [2006] IESC 20 at [52], [2006] 3 IR 115 at 134–135, [2006] 2 ILRM 321 at 339; *People (DPP) v Donnelly* [2012] IECCA 78 at [24].

alone.[331] Indeed, in *People (DPP) v Kelly*,[332] Fennelly J expressed the view that, where the Chief Superintendent is not cross-examined in relation to his or her belief or the basis for it and no other basis is laid for questioning the truth or cogency of his or her evidence, it was difficult to envisage a court deciding to acquit. However, in recent times, the practice has been adopted by the DPP of not bringing a prosecution, and by the Special Criminal Court of not convicting, on such evidence alone.[333]

6–112 In *O'Leary v AG*,[334] Costello J rejected the contention that s.3(2) infringes the presumption of innocence, holding the effect of the subsection is simply to render admissible the non-expert opinion evidence of the Garda which would otherwise be inadmissible.[335] Such evidence, if admitted, had to be weighed and considered and did not place a legal burden on the accused because the court could still hold that the prosecution had not proved its case beyond a reasonable doubt.

6–113 The contention that a fair trial cannot be obtained where belief evidence is admitted pursuant to s.3(2) and informer privilege is asserted was rejected in *People (DPP) v Kelly*.[336] The appellant contended that he had not received a fair trial because of the restriction placed on the right to cross-examination in circumstances where the Chief Superintendent who gave belief evidence claimed informer privilege. However, Geoghegan J considered that this limitation on cross-examination was inherent in the subsection itself which enjoyed the presumption of constitutionality. Thus, while the learned judge accepted that the basis for the belief expressed by the garda officer could be explored on cross-examination, he held that the garda officer is entitled to claim informer privilege and this did not, of itself, render the trial of the accused unfair. In his view, it was a matter for the trial court to balance the conflicting rights and interests of the accused and the necessity to protect confidential garda sources. The contention that the maintenance of a claim of privilege in respect of the sources grounding belief evidence constituted a violation of art.6 of the European Convention on Human Rights was considered and rejected by Fennelly J in his concurring judgment. A broader challenge to the constitutionality of s.3(2) and its compatibility with the European Convention on Human Rights on the basis that it deprived an accused of the rights to be informed of the substance of the allegations against him or her, to test the evidence against him or her and cross-examine his accusers, to give effective rebutting evidence and to a fair trial also failed in *Redmond v Ireland*.[337]

---

[331] See, by of example, *People (DPP) v Ferguson*, unreported, Court of Criminal Appeal, 27 October 1975; *People (DPP) v Gannon*, unreported, Court of Criminal Appeal, 2 April 2003.

[332] [2006] IESC 20 at [52], [2006] 3 IR 115 at 134, [2006] 2 ILRM 321 at 339.

[333] As noted by Geoghegan J in *People (DPP) v Kelly* [2006] IESC 20 at [14], [2006] 3 IR 115 at 122, [2006] 2 ILRM 321 at 327 and Hardiman J in *People (DPP) v Birney* [2006] IECCA 58 at [83] and [93], [2007] 1 IR 337 at 362 and 366.

[334] [1993] 1 IR 102, [1991] ILRM 454.

[335] See, *e.g. People (DPP) v McManus*, unreported, Court of Criminal Appeal, 21 March 2003 (statement by garda during sentencing hearing of his belief that accused was operating on behalf of criminal gang held to be clearly inadmissible).

[336] [2006] IESC 20, [2006] 3 IR 115, [2006] 2 ILRM 321. See also *People (DPP) v Matthews* [2006] IECCA 103, [2007] 2 IR 169; *People (DPP) v Binead* [2006] IECCA 374, [2007] 1 IR 374; *People (DPP) v Birney* [2006] IECCA 58, [2007] 1 IR 337; *People (DPP) v Donohue* [2007] IECCA 97, [2008] 2 IR 193; *People (DPP) v Kelly* [2007] IECCA 110; *People (DPP) v Maguire* [2008] IECCA 67; *People (DPP) v Bullman* [2009] IECCA 84; *People (DPP) v Donnelly* [2012] IECCA 78.

[337] [2009] IEHC 201, [2009] 2 ILRM 419.

6–114   The contention that the admission of belief evidence pursuant to s.3(2) rendered a trial unfair in breach of art.6 of the Convention was also rejected by the Fifth Chamber of the European Court of Human Rights in *Donohoe v Ireland*.[338] The applicant had been convicted of membership of the IRA by the Special Criminal Court. At the trial, belief evidence had been given by a Chief Superintendent who said that he had formed the belief based on confidential information but refused to identify his sources, asserting informer privilege.[339] The Fifth Chamber began its assessment of whether there had been a breach of art.6 by reiterating that its primary concern under art.6(1) is to evaluate the overall fairness of the criminal proceedings and, in doing so, it will look at the proceedings as a whole having regard to the rights of the defence but also to the interests of the public and the victims that crime is properly prosecuted and, where necessary, to the rights of witnesses.[340] It also reaffirmed that the admissibility of evidence is primarily a matter for regulation by national law, it is not within the province of the Court to substitute its assessment of the facts for that of the domestic courts and its task under the Convention is to ascertain whether the proceedings as a whole, including the way in which evidence was taken, were fair.

6–115   The Court referred to the decision of the Grand Chamber in *Rowe and Davis v the United Kingdom*[341] which dealt with the disclosure of evidence by the prosecution and held that:

> "60. It is a fundamental aspect of the right to a fair trial that criminal proceedings, including the elements of such proceedings which relate to procedure, should be adversarial and that there should be equality of arms between the prosecution and defence. The right to an adversarial trial means, in a criminal case, that both prosecution and defence must be given the opportunity to have knowledge of and comment on the observations filed and the evidence adduced by the other party ... In addition Article 6 § 1 requires ... that the prosecution authorities disclose to the defence all material evidence in their possession for or against the accused...
> 61. However, ... the entitlement to disclosure of relevant evidence is not an absolute right. In any criminal proceedings there may be competing interests, such as national security or the need to protect witnesses at risk of reprisals or keep secret police methods of investigation of crime, which must be weighed against the rights of the accused ... In some cases it may be necessary to withhold certain evidence from the defence so as to preserve the fundamental rights of another individual or to safeguard an important public interest. However, only such measures restricting the rights of the defence which are strictly necessary are permissible under Article 6 § 1 ... Moreover, in order to ensure that the accused receives a fair trial, any difficulties caused to the defence by a limitation on its rights must be sufficiently counterbalanced by the procedures followed by the judicial authorities ..."[342]

6–116   Reference was also made to the decision in *Al-Khawaja and Tahery v the United Kingdom*[343] where the Grand Chamber had accepted that the admission into evidence of statements of absent witnesses which were the "sole or decisive" evidence against the accused would not automatically result in a breach of art.6(1) but the most "searching scrutiny" was required to be applied to the consideration of two key points. The first was whether it was necessary to admit the witness statements. The second was whether the untested evidence was the sole or decisive basis for the conviction

---

[338] Application No. 19156/08, Judgment of the Fifth Chamber, 12 December 2013.
[339] An appeal (*sub nom. People (DPP) v Binead* [2006] IECCA 374, [2007] 1 IR 374) was unsuccessful with the Court of Criminal Appeal applying the principles established in *People (DPP) v Kelly* [2006] IESC 20, [2006] 3 IR 115, [2006] 2 ILRM 321.
[340] Application No. 19156/08, Judgment of the Fifth Chamber, 12 December 2013 at [73].
[341] (2000) 30 EHRR 1.
[342] (2000) 30 EHRR 1 at [60]–[61].
[343] (2012) 54 EHRR 23.

and, if it was, whether there were sufficient counterbalancing factors, including strong procedural safeguards, in place to ensure that the trial, judged as a whole, was fair within the meaning of art.6 of the Convention.

6–117   Applying the principles established in those cases, the Court noted that the case before it did not involve the evidence of an absent or an anonymous witness. The prosecution relied on the testimony of the Chief Superintendent and the non-disclosed evidence as to the sources relied on by him did not form part of the prosecution's case. However, the Court identified a potential unfairness in the upholding of the claim of privilege and it proceeded to address three questions: (i) whether it was necessary to uphold the claim of privilege asserted by the Chief Superintendent as regards the source of his belief; (ii) if so, whether the Chief Superintendent's evidence was the sole or decisive basis for the applicant's conviction; and, (iii) if it was, whether there were sufficient counterbalancing factors, including the existence of strong procedural safeguards, in place to ensure that the proceedings, when judged in their entirety, were fair within the meaning of art.6 of the Convention.

6–118   The Court was satisfied that the first question should be answered affirmatively, stating that the public and victims have a strong interest in ensuring that organised and subversive crime is prosecuted and allowing police informers to provide information anonymously is a vital tool in prosecuting such crimes. With regard to the second question, the Special Criminal Court had expressly stated that it would not convict the applicant on the basis of the belief evidence alone and it had identified other corroborative evidence against him. Accordingly, the Court was satisfied that the belief evidence had not been the sole or decisive evidence grounding the applicant's conviction. Nonetheless, given that this evidence had clearly carried some weight in the establishment of the applicant's guilt, the Court went on to examine whether there were adequate counterbalancing factors and safeguards in place in order to ensure that the disadvantage caused to the applicant by upholding the claim of informer privilege did not restrict the applicant's defence rights to an extent incompatible with the requirements of art.6 and concluded that there were. In particular, the Court was of the view, that while the upholding of the claim of privilege restricted the scope of cross-examination, the possibility of cross-examination was not entirely eliminated and the Chief Superintendent's evidence could still be tested with regard to a variety of matters. The Court, therefore, concluded that the applicant's trial had not been rendered unfair.

6–119   It is noteworthy that the focus of the Court's analysis was on the potential for unfairness arising from the upholding by the Special Criminal Court of the Chief Superintendent's claim of informer privilege. This would seem to indicate that no significant issue in terms of the fairness of a trial or compliance with art.6 arises from the admission of belief evidence *per se*.

2. Proceeds of Crime Act 1996

6–120   The Proceeds of Crime Act 1996[344] permits the seizure and disposal of the proceeds of crime. In order to make it easier to obtain interim and interlocutory orders freezing assets, s.8 of the Act provides that where a member of An Garda Síochána[345]

---

[344] No.30 of 1996.
[345] Section 1(1) defines "member" as meaning a member of the Garda Síochána not below the rank

or an authorised officer states in proceedings for an interim order under s.2 or an interlocutory order under s.3 that he or she believes (i) that the respondent is in possession or control of specified property and that the property constitutes, directly or indirectly, proceeds of crime, and/or (ii) that the respondent is in possession of or control of specified property and that the property was acquired, in whole or in part, with or in connection with property that, directly or indirectly, constitutes proceeds of crime, and that the value of the property is not less than £10,000 (€12,697.38), then, if the Court is satisfied that there are reasonable grounds for the belief, the statement shall be evidence of the matter referred to and the value of the property.[346]

6–121 A challenge to the constitutionality of this section was unsuccessful in *Murphy v GM PB PC Ltd*[347] O'Higgins J rejected the proposition that opinion evidence of the type admissible under s.8 was unconstitutional because of the inequality to which its admission gave rise and its decisive effect. He held that s.8 does not, of itself, alter the onus of proof but merely renders the opinion of an authorised officer admissible as part of the evidence if the court is satisfied that there are reasonable grounds for such a belief.[348] Thus, the onus does not shift to the respondent to rebut that evidence unless it appears to the court that a number of matters have been established and, even then, the court cannot make the order if it is satisfied that there would be a serious risk of injustice. There was, therefore, adequate protection for respondents to prevent the admission of belief evidence from being unfair. He also rejected as unsustainable the proposition that evidence of belief could not be received if it was that of the applicant himself. He pointed out that the applicant had no personal interest in the outcome of the case and was simply the applicant because he was entitled under the legislation to bring the proceedings. There was no breach of the maxim of *nemo iudex in causa sua* because the entitlement of the applicant to give opinion evidence did not make him a judge in his own cause but merely a witness. Finally, the learned judge rejected the contention that, because a statement of belief admissible under s.8 was based on hearsay, the court should not be satisfied that there are reasonable grounds for it. However, he did indicate that there would be circumstances where a court might refuse to act on such a statement of belief depending on the basis of same.

6–122 It can be seen from s.8 that there are two conditions of admissibility of the belief evidence referred to therein.[349] The first is that the garda or authorised officer must hold and express that belief. The second is that the court must be satisfied that there are reasonable grounds for the belief. In *FMcK v TH (Proceeds of Crime)*,[350] Hardiman J highlighted the risk of "very great potential unfairness" and the possibility

---

of Chief Superintendent and in *DPP v Hollman*, unreported, High Court, 29 July 1999, O'Higgins J adopted a strict approach to the interpretation of s.8 and held that the reference to an officer not below the rank of Chief Superintendent had to be construed as a reference to a person who is a Chief Superintendent at the time of the giving of oral evidence. He, therefore, held to be inadmissible in that case the evidence of a Chief Superintendent who had retired by the time he gave evidence.

[346] That statement of belief may be given on affidavit in interim proceedings unless the court directs that it be given by oral evidence and by oral evidence in interlocutory proceedings.

[347] [2001] 4 IR 113 (his judgment rejecting a wide ranging challenge to the constitutionality of various provisions of the 1996 Act was upheld by the Supreme Court ([2001] 4 IR 113)).

[348] *Cf. O'Leary v AG* [1993] 1 IR 102, [1991] ILRM 454.

[349] *FMcK v TH (Proceeds of Crime)* [2006] IESC 63 at [25], [2007] 4 IR 186 at 195, [2007] 1 ILRM 338 at 356.

[350] [2006] IESC 63 at [25], [2007] 4 IR 186 at 195, [2007] 1 ILRM 338 at 356.

of "gross abuse" arising from the admission of belief evidence pursuant to s.8 which could undermine the ability of persons against whom it is deployed to defend themselves by cross-examination. Accordingly, he held that it is essential that the conditions for the admissibility of such evidence is actually met.

6–123   In order to establish that there are reasonable grounds for the belief expressed by the garda or authorised officer, the practice has developed of specifying in his or her affidavit the particular matters that are relied on to ground the belief which matters can then be assessed by the court to decide whether they provide reasonable grounds for the belief. Insofar as reliance is placed on particular factual matters, admissible evidence of these matters has to be adduced either by the garda or authorised officer himself or herself or by other witnesses and it is not open to him or her to ground his or her belief on hearsay.[351]

6–124   If a trial judge is satisfied that there are reasonable grounds for the belief expressed by the garda or authorised officer such that it is admissible in evidence, he or she then has to proceed to evaluate the weight to be attached to that belief. In *FMcK v GWD (Proceeds of crime outside State)*[352] Fennelly J explained that s.8 envisages a two stage process. Firstly, the authorised officer has to give evidence which becomes evidence only if the court was satisfied that there were reasonable grounds for the belief. Secondly, the court has to evaluate the weight to be attached to that evidence of belief.

6–125   In *FMcK v TH (Proceeds of Crime)*,[353] Hardiman J explained that, where evidence is admitted pursuant to s.8, it is not conclusive but it will be sufficient to discharge the evidential burden on the applicant and to make out a *prima facie* case that the respondent is in possession or control of specified property that constitutes, directly or indirectly, proceeds of crime or which was acquired, in whole or in part, with or in connection with property that, directly or indirectly, constitutes proceeds of crime, above the requisite value.[354] That evidence may be contradicted or undermined by evidence called by or on behalf of the respondent[355] or by cross-examination of the person expressing the belief.[356]

6–126   The approach to be adopted by a trial judge to the evaluation of belief evidence admitted pursuant to s.8 is complicated by the inclusion of a reverse onus provision in s.3 of the Proceeds of Crime Act 1996. In *FMcK v GWD (Proceeds of crime outside State)*[357] Fennelly J held that the trial judge had erred in holding that the admission of such evidence was sufficient, of itself, to transfer the burden of proof to the defendant in accordance with s.3. In his concurring judgment, McCracken J

---

[351] *FMcK v SMcD* [2005] IEHC 205 at 11–12.
[352] [2004] IESC 31, [2004] 2 IR 470, [2004] 2 ILRM 419.
[353] [2006] IESC 63 at [25], [2007] 4 IR 186 at 195, [2007] 1 ILRM 338 at 356.
[354] See to similar effect, *per* Fennelly J in *FMcK v GWD (Proceeds of crime outside State)* [2004] IESC 31 at [48], [2004] 2 IR 470 at 486, [2004] 2 ILRM 419 at 433, who emphasised that the section does not abrogate the fact-finding function of the court. See also *FMcK v SMcD* [2005] IEHC 205 at [15] where Finnegan P expressed the view that the effect of s.8(1) was that, once evidence of belief is given together with evidence as to the grounds of that belief, the evidential burden shifts to the defendant.
[355] *FMcK v TH (Proceeds of Crime)* [2006] IESC 63 at [25], [2007] 4 IR 186 at 195, [2007] 1 ILRM 338 at 356.
[356] *FMcK v SMcD* [2005] IEHC 205 at 15.
[357] [2004] IESC 31, [2004] 2 IR 470, [2004] 2 ILRM 419.

examined the interaction between ss.3 and 8 and held that correct procedure for a trial judge to adopt was as follows:[358]

(1) "he should firstly consider the position under s.8. He should consider the evidence given by the member or authorised officer, such as that of the two police officers in the present case, which might point to reasonable grounds for that belief;

(2) if he is satisfied that there are reasonable grounds for the belief, he should then make a specific finding that the belief of the member or authorised officer is evidence;

(3) only then should he go on to consider the position under s.3. He should consider the evidence tendered by the plaintiff, which in the present case would be both the evidence of the member or authorised officer under s.8 and indeed the evidence of the other police officers;

(4) he should make a finding whether this evidence constitutes a *prima facie* case under s.3 and, if he does so find, the onus shifts to the defendant or other specified person;

(5) he should then consider the evidence furnished by the defendant or other specified person and determine whether he is satisfied that the onus undertaken by the defendant or other specified person has been fulfilled;

(6) if he is satisfied that the defendant or other specified person has satisfied his onus of proof then the proceedings should be dismissed;

(7) if he is not so satisfied he should then consider whether there would be a serious risk of injustice…"

6–127 This suggested procedure is one that has been followed in subsequent cases[359] and, in *PB v AF*,[360] Feeney J identified a number of factors which would bear upon the evaluation of evidence adduced on applications pursuant to s.3 including belief evidence admitted pursuant to s.8.

3. Misuse of Drugs Act 1977

6–128 Section 15A of the Misuse of Drugs Act 1977 (as inserted by s.4 of the Criminal Justice Act 1999) creates an offence of possession of a controlled drug with a market value of €12,697 or greater for the purpose of sale of supply. Subsection (3) provides that, if the court is satisfied that a member of the Garda Síochána or an officer of customs and excise has knowledge of the unlawful sale or supply of controlled drugs, that member or officer, as the case may be, is entitled in any proceedings for an offence under that section to give evidence as to the market value of the controlled drug in question. The subsection thereby renders admissible such evidence which might otherwise be open to objection on the basis that it constituted opinion evidence.[361] However, it should be noted that the subsection does not provide the only means by which evidence of the market value of controlled drugs may be given and expert evidence may be given by any person who has sufficient expertise to give such evidence such as, for example, a retired garda.[362]

4. Section 71B of the Criminal Justice Act 2006

6–129 Section 71B of the Criminal Justice Act 2006[363] makes provision for the

[358] [2004] IESC 31 at 70, [2004] 2 IR 470 at 492, [2004] 2 ILRM 419 at 438–439.
[359] See *Criminal Assets Bureau v O'Brien* [2010] IEHC 12 at [7]; *Criminal Assets Bureau v AW* [2010] IEHC 166 at [7]; *PB v AF* [2012] IEHC 428 at [3.7].
[360] [2012] IEHC 428 at [3.9].
[361] See *People (DPP) v Heaphy* [2010] IECCA 86.
[362] See *People (DPP) v Hanley* [2010] IECCA 99.
[363] As substituted by s.7 of the Criminal Justice (Amendment) Act 2009.

admission of opinion evidence in prosecutions relating to organised crime. Subsection (1) provides that the opinion of any member or former member of the Garda Síochána who appears to the Court to possess the appropriate expertise[364] is admissible in evidence in relation to the issue of the existence of a particular criminal organisation. Subsection (3) goes on to provide that such an expert is entitled, in the formation of an opinion in that regard, to take into account *inter alia* any previous convictions for arrestable offences of persons believed by that expert to be part of the organisation to which the opinion relates.[365]

5. Domestic Violence Act 1996

6–130   Section 3(4) of the Domestic Violence Act 1996[366] attempts to avert potential constitutional difficulties with regard to the grant of barring orders by providing that a court shall not make a barring order in respect of the place where the applicant resides where the respondent has a legal or beneficial interest in that place but the applicant has no such interest or the applicant's interest is, in the opinion of the court, less than that of the respondent. However, in order to assist potential applicants to surmount this potentially significant hurdle, s.3(4)(b) goes on to provide that where, in proceedings for a barring order, the applicant states the belief, in respect of the place to which para. (a) relates, that he or she has a legal or beneficial interest in that place which is not less than that of the respondent, then such belief shall be admissible in evidence. The purpose and expediency of this provision is evident but it must be questioned whether, given the complexities that can arise in relation to the legal and beneficial ownership of the family home, an applicant, who will usually be a person with little or no legal knowledge, should be allowed to express such a belief. Of course, such belief is only evidence and a judge is not obliged to act on foot of it. However, it is likely that he or she will do so in many cases especially at the interim stage. Thus, any protection which the section affords to the property rights of a respondent will, in many cases, be more apparent than real.

6. Family Law Act 1995

6–131   Section 47 of the Family Law Act 1995[367] applies to a range of family law proceedings and provides that a court may, of its own motion or on application to it in that behalf by a party to the proceedings, by order give such directions as it thinks proper for the purpose of procuring a report in writing on any question affecting the welfare of a party to the proceedings or any other person to whom they relate from a probation and welfare officer, a person nominated by the Health Service Executive or any other person specified in the order. The person who provides a section 47 report is considered to be an expert and the rules governing expert reports generally apply to expert reports commissioned pursuant to s.47.[368] However, in *AB v CD*,[369] a number

---

[364] Subsection (2) provides that "expertise" means "experience, specialised knowledge or qualifications".

[365] Subsection (4) also provides for the admission of certain documents and records as evidence that a particular group constitutes a criminal organisation.

[366] No.1 of 1996.

[367] As amended by s.75 of the Health Act 2004. See Hogan & Kelly, "Section 47 Reports in Family Law Proceedings: Purpose, Evidential Weight and Proposals for Reform" (2011) 2 IJFL 27.

[368] *JMcD v PL* [2008] IEHC 96, [2009] IESC 81, [2010] 2 IR 199, [2010] 1 ILRM 461.

[369] [2011] IEHC 543 at [111].

of fundamental differences between a section 47 expert witness and the general run of expert witnesses were noted arising from the nature of the proceedings in which such a report is submitted and the manner in which that person obtains information for the purpose of that report.

6–132   Although a section 47 report is ordered by the court, the author of that report is not considered to be the court's expert witness and may be called by either or both of the parties.[370] That report may also be challenged by further expert witnesses although the permission of the court should be sought in that regard and such report may be ordered as a section 47 report.[371]

6–133   It was held in *JMcD v PL*[372] that the rules governing expert reports generally apply to expert reports commissioned pursuant to s.47. However, it should not be given undue weight and a court is not obliged to accept the views expressed in the section 47 report or to specify the reasons for non-acceptance of the views expressed in that report. It was also emphasised that the court is the decision maker and it is for the court and the court alone to determine, in accordance with the law, what was in the best interests of the child.

7. Competition (Amendment) Act 1996

6–134   Section 4 of the Competition (Amendment) Act 1996[373] provides that in proceedings for an offence under s.2 of the Act, the opinion of any witness who appears to the court to possess the appropriate qualifications or experience in respect of the matter to which his or her evidence relates shall be admissible in evidence as regards any matter calling for expertise or special knowledge that is relevant to the proceedings and, in particular, the following matters, namely: (a) the effects that types of agreements, decisions or concerted practices may have, or that specific agreements, decisions or concerted practices have had, on competition in trade; (b) an explanation to the court of any relevant economic principles or the application of such principles in practice, where such an explanation would be of assistance to the judge or, as the case may be, the jury. The purpose of this section is clearly to copper-fasten the admissibility of the expert evidence of economists in prosecutions under s.2 of the Act. However, the terms in which it is drafted, which mirror closely the common law requirements with regard to the admission of expert evidence, raise the question as to whether the section is in fact, superfluous. The evidence of economists is routinely admitted in civil cases regarding competition matters[374] and it would seem as if such evidence would have been admissible in criminal prosecutions under s.2 even without s.4(1).

6–135   Section 4(2) goes on to provide that a court may, where in its opinion the interests of justice require it, direct that evidence of a general or specific kind referred to subs.(1) shall not be admissible in proceedings for an offence under s.2 or shall be admissible in such proceedings for specified purposes only. This subsection obviously gives a court a very wide discretion to exclude expert evidence but no guidance is

---

[370] *AB v CD* [2011] IEHC 543 at [111].
[371] *AB v CD* [2011] IEHC 543 at [111].
[372] [2009] IESC 81 at [134]–[135], [2010] 2 IR 199 at 268, [2010] 1 ILRM 461 at 486–487.
[373] No.19 of 1996.
[374] See, *e.g. Masterfoods Ltd v HB Ice Cream Ltd* [1993] ILRM 145.

given as to the circumstances where it will be appropriate to exercise it and this will have to be worked out on a case-by-case basis.

CHAPTER 7

IMPROPERLY OBTAINED EVIDENCE

A. Introduction

7–01 The term "improperly obtained evidence" is used as an umbrella term to cover three distinct though related categories of evidence which are examined in this chapter: unconstitutionally obtained evidence; illegally obtained evidence; and unfairly obtained evidence.[1] As will be seen below, different principles apply in each scenario. In the case of evidence obtained as a result of a breach of the constitutional rights of the accused, the evidence will be excluded unless there are extraordinary excusing circumstances. In the case of illegally obtained evidence, the court has a discretion to admit or exclude such evidence which will be exercised on the basis of a number of factors including the seriousness of the breach and the conduct of the wrongdoer. With regard to unfairly obtained evidence, the jurisdiction of the courts to exclude such evidence is undeveloped but it is contended that a court has a discretion to exclude evidence that has been obtained in a manner that is fundamentally unfair.

B. Unconstitutionally Obtained Evidence

1. Rationales for an Exclusionary Rule

7–02 At common law, the traditional approach of the courts was that evidence which was relevant to the matters at issue would not be excluded because it had been obtained illegally[2] unless it had been procured by torture.[3] This inclusionary approach was predicated on the proposition that the purpose of a criminal trial is to adjudicate upon the guilt or innocence of the accused and that it is no part of the function of a judge to engage in a collateral inquiry as to the means used to obtain evidence which is

---

[1] See generally, Jackson, "Human Rights, Constitutional Law and Exclusionary Safeguards in Ireland" in Roberts & Hunter (eds), Criminal Evidence and Human Rights: Reimagining Common Law Procedural Traditions (Oxford: Hart Publishing, 2012), pp.119–43.

[2] *People (AG) v McGrath* (1965) 99 ILTR 59 at 74; *Kuruma v R.* [1955] AC 197; *R. v Wray* (1970) 11 DLR (3d) 673. The attitude of the common law courts was, perhaps, most memorably encapsulated in the assertion of Crompton J in *R. v Leatham* (1861) 8 Cox CC 498 at 501, that "[i]t matters not how you get it; if you steal it even, it would be admissible".

[3] In *A v Secretary of State for the Home Department (No.2)* [2006] 2 AC 221, [2005] 3 WLR 1249, it was held that evidence obtained by torture is absolutely inadmissible in any judicial proceedings, civil or criminal. See Rasiah, "*A v Secretary of State for the Home Department (No 2)*: Occupying the Moral High Ground" (2006) 69 MLR 995.

relevant to the issues at trial[4] or to attempt to discipline the police for any misconduct in obtaining evidence.[5] It was argued that, if the law was broken by police officers in order to obtain evidence, recourse should be had to police disciplinary procedures, tortious remedies or the criminal law as appropriate rather than affording an accused an evidential windfall with the result that both the police officer and the accused would escape conviction.[6] The view was taken that, by refusing to exclude evidence on the basis that it had been illegally obtained, the court does not "excuse, condone or encourage the illegality; it merely ignores it".[7] There are, however, three main principles which have been invoked to justify the application of exclusionary rules to evidence obtained in breach of constitutional provisions.[8]

7–03   The first principle, which has been articulated in a number of US decisions,[9] has been referenced in some cases in this jurisdiction,[10] and is the foundation of the exclusionary rule in Canada,[11] is concern for the reputation and integrity of the criminal justice system. This rationale, which is rooted in the principle of the rule of law, proceeds on the basis that the legitimacy of the criminal justice system is undermined and criminal behaviour encouraged if the State can break the law in an effort to bring wrongdoers to justice.[12] In *Youman v Commonwealth*,[13] Carroll J expressed the view that it was "much better that a guilty individual should escape punishment then that a court of justice should put aside a vital fundamental principle of the law in order to

---

4   Wigmore, *Evidence* 3rd edn (Boston: Little Brown and Company, 1940), § 2183, pp.4–5. The argument that the courts should not engage in such a collateral inquiry was rejected in *People (AG) v O'Brien* [1965] IR 142 at 161–162, where Kingsmill Moore J pointed out that a similar collateral inquiry was involved when the admissibility of a confession and other categories of evidence was considered.

5   *People (AG) v O'Brien* [1965] IR 142 at 167–169 (*per* Walsh J).

6   Wigmore, *Evidence* 3rd edn (Boston: Little Brown and Company, 1940), § 2184, pp.35–40.

7   *People (AG) v McGrath* (1965) 99 ILTR 59 at 74 (*per* Davitt P).

8   For a discussion of these rationales, see Choo, "Improperly Obtained Evidence: A Reconsideration" (1989) 9 LS 261; Martin, "The Rationale of the Exclusionary Rule of Evidence" (1992) ICLJ 1.

9   See, for example, *Olmstead v United States* (1928) 277 US 438; *Terry v Ohio* (1968) 392 US 1 at 12; *Calandra v United States* (1974) 414 US 338 at 357 (*per* Powell J); *People v Cahan* (1955) 282 P 2d 912; and *Youman v Commonwealth* (1920) 189 Ky 152, 224 SW 860.

10   In *People (DPP) v Lynch* [1982] IR 64 at 76, [1981] ILRM 389 at 393, the rationale of concern for the integrity of the criminal justice system, as expounded by Warren CJ in *Terry v Ohio* (1968) 392 US 1, was endorsed by O'Higgins CJ.

11   Section 24(2) of the Canadian Charter of Rights and Freedoms provides that where "a court concludes that evidence was obtained in a manner that infringed or denied any rights or freedoms guaranteed by this Charter, the evidence shall be excluded if it is established that, having regard to all the circumstances, the admission of it in the proceedings would bring the administration of justice into disrepute." See *R. v Collins* [1987] 1 SCR 265; *R. v Hebert* [1990] 2 SCR 151; *R. v Stillman* [1997] 1 SCR 607, (1997) 144 DLR (4th) 193; *R. v Cook* [1998] 2 SCR 597, (1998) 164 DLR (4th) 1; *R. v Grant* [2009] 2 SCR 353. See also, Penney, "Unreal Distinctions: The Exclusion of Unfairly Obtained Evidence Under s.24(2) of the Charter" (1994) 34 (4) Alberta Law Rev 782, and Fenton, "Recent Developments in section 24(2) Jurisprudence" (1997) 39 Crim LQ 279.

12   *Per* Brandeis J in *Olmstead v US* (1928) 277 US 438 at 485: "In a government of laws, existence of the government will be imperilled if it fails to observe the law scrupulously. Our Government is the potent, the omnipresent teacher. For good or for ill, it teaches the whole people by its example. Crime is contagious. If the Government becomes a lawbreaker, it breeds contempt for law."

13   (1920) 189 Ky 152 at 166, 224 SW 860 at 866. See, to similar effect, the statement of Holmes J in *Olmstead v United States* (1928) 277 US 438 at 470, that "it is a less evil that some criminals should escape than that the government should play an ignoble part".

secure his conviction". Furthermore, it is suggested that the courts cannot simply ignore unconstitutionality, as to do so is to condone it and, in effect, to make the court a party to the breaChap. As Warren CJ explained in *Terry v Ohio*,[14] a ruling admitting evidence in a criminal trial "has the necessary effect of legitimizing the conduct which produced the evidence, while an application of the exclusionary rule withholds the constitutional imprimatur".[15] This rationale necessarily incorporates an element of balancing because of the recognition that the exclusion of evidence may also bring the administration of justice into disrepute.[16] Thus, a court is required to make an assessment of whether greater damage would be caused to the administration of justice by the admission or the exclusion of the evidence.

7–04   The second principle, which provides the current rationale for the exclusionary rule in the United States,[17] and a subsidiary rationale in this jurisdiction,[18] is the deterrence principle.[19] According to the proponents of this principle, the primary purpose of the exclusionary rule is "to deter future unlawful police conduct and thereby effectuate the guarantee of the Fourth Amendment against unreasonable searches and seizures".[20] This is achieved by removing the incentive to disregard that guarantee, i.e. by excluding the evidence obtained.[21] An exclusionary rule predicated on the deterrence principle is primarily prospective in its application and the exclusion of evidence in an individual case is merely a by-product of the deterrent effect of the rule. It follows that, where the exclusion of evidence cannot be shown to have a deterrent effect, as in circumstances where the police officer exercised his or her powers in good faith and did not realise that he or she was breaching the rights of the accused, the evidence will not be excluded.[22]

---

[14]   (1968) 392 US 1 at 13.

[15]   See also *Elkins v United States* (1960) 364 US 206 at 223. *j*

[16]   See *Stone v Powell* (1976) 428 US 465 at 491 (*per* Burger CJ). *Cf. People (AG) v O'Brien* [1965] IR 142 at 148, where Lavery J stated: "If a judge were to hold inadmissible the evidence in question in this case, or in any comparable case, his ruling would, in my opinion, be wrong to the point of absurdity and would bring the administration of the law into well-deserved contempt."

[17]   See *United States v Calandra* (1974) 414 US 338 at 348; *Stone v Powell* (1976) 428 US 465 at 486; *United States v Leon* (1983) 468 US 897 at 906. For a discussion of *Calandra* and the shift in the rationale of the exclusionary rule, see Billy and Rehnberg, "The Fourth Amendment Exclusionary Rule: Past, Present, No Future" (1975) 12 Am Crim Law Rev 507.

[18]   In *People (DPP) v Kenny* [1990] 2 IR 110 at 133, [1990] ILRM 569 at 578, Finlay CJ stated that the absolute protection principle enunciated by him would provide a positive encouragement to those involved in the investigation and prosecution of offences in addition to a negative deterrent against a garda acting in a manner which he or she knew to be unconstitutional or from acting in a manner reckless as to whether his or her conduct was unconstitutional. Subsequently, in *Kennedy v Law Society of Ireland (No.3)* [2002] 2 IR 458 at 489, Fennelly J expressed the view that the Supreme Court in *People (DPP) v Kenny* [1990] 2 IR 110, [1990] ILRM 569, "was motivated by the need, in the course of the criminal process, to adopt a rule which would act as a sufficiently powerful deterrent against the abuse by the police arm of the state of the exceptional powers which they may exercise, while engaged in the investigation of crime." In *People (DPP) v AD* [2012] IESC 33 at [41], [2012] 2 IR 332 at 345, 346, Clarke J declined to apply the exclusionary rule so as to exclude statements made by an accused during a period of lawful detention because his or her detention later become unconstitutional as this would "be to impose an unnecessarily excessive exclusionary rule not warranted by the need to discourage improper activity by those investigating crime".

[19]   See Friedman, "Controlling the Administrators of Criminal Justice" (1989) 11 DULJ 10.

[20]   *United States v Calandra* (1974) 414 US 338 at 348 (*per* Powell J).

[21]   *Per Elkins v United States* (1960) 364 US 206 at 217.

[22]   *United States v Leon* (1983) 468 US 897 at 906. See Fleissner, "Glide Path to an Inclusionary

7–05 The third principle, which underpins the exclusionary rule in this jurisdiction, is the vindication principle.[23] According to this principle, the courts are required to uphold the provisions of the Constitution[24] and to protect the constitutional rights of an accused from violation.[25] Therefore, if the constitutional rights of an accused have been violated in the course of a criminal investigation, the courts are required to vindicate those rights by providing the accused with an effective remedy, i.e. the exclusion of the evidence obtained as a result of that violation.[26] An exclusionary rule based on this principle is, thus, designed to have a compensatory effect in that it attempts to place the accused in the same position in which he or she would have been if his or her rights had not been breached by excluding the evidence obtained as a result of the breach.

2. Development of the Exclusionary Rule

7–06 The seminal case in relation to the exclusionary rule in respect of unconstitutionally obtained evidence is the decision of the Supreme Court in *People (AG) v O'Brien*.[27] At issue in the case was the admissibility of evidence that had been obtained on foot of an invalid search warrant. The warrant incorrectly described the premises concerned as "118 Cashel Road, Crumlin", the correct address being "118 Captain's Road, Crumlin". It was not clear whether the mistake had been adverted to before the execution of the warrant but the appeal was dealt with on the assumption that it had not.

7–07 In the Supreme Court, two different approaches were adopted in the judgments delivered by Kingsmill Moore and Walsh JJ.[28] In his judgment, Kingsmill Moore J did

---

Rule: How Expansion of the Good Faith Exception Threatens to Fundamentally Change the Exclusionary Rule" (1997) 48 Mercer LR 1023.

[23] See *People (DPP) v Kenny* [1990] 2 IR 110, [1990] ILRM 569, which is examined in detail below. It is also part of the underlying rationale of the exclusionary rule in New Zealand (see *R. v Goodwin* [1993] 2 NZLR 153; *R. v Shaheed* [2002] 2 NZLR 377) and was formerly the basis for the exclusionary rule in the United States (see *Weeks v United States* (1914) 232 US 383).

[24] In *People (DPP) v Lynch* [1982] IR 64 at 76, [1981] ILRM 389 at 393, it was pointed out by O'Higgins CJ that, in countries with a written constitution, judges are generally required by their oath and office to uphold the constitution.

[25] *People (AG) v O'Brien* [1965] IR 142 at 170 (*per* Walsh J); *People (DPP) v Lynch* [1982] IR 64 at 76, [1981] ILRM 389 at 393 (*per* O'Higgins CJ).

[26] It should be noted in that regard that it was held by Clarke J in *Osbourne v Minister for Justice* [2006] IEHC 117 at [27], [2009] 3 IR 89 at 96–97, that a claim in damages (whether for breach of constitutional rights or in tort) cannot be brought in respect of actions taken on foot of a warrant which, although it appeared valid was technically infirm, unless there was a deliberate and conscious breach of the rights concerned, meaning that the person who applied for or executed the warrant was aware of the defect.

[27] [1965] IR 142.

[28] There has been a degree of controversy as to whether the judgment of Walsh J or that of Kingsmill Moore J should be regarded as the majority judgment in relation to the principles to be applied regarding the admission of unconstitutionally obtained evidence. Although Ó Dálaigh CJ was the only member of the court to expressly concur in the judgment of Walsh J, Kingsmill Moore J did signify some level of agreement with the central holding of Walsh J regarding the test to be applied in the case of unconstitutionally obtained evidence, and in *People (DPP) v Shaw* [1982] IR 1 at 32, Walsh J stated that this proposition had been agreed to by all the members of the court. However, in *Shaw*, Griffin J stated that the majority judgment had been given by Kingsmill Moore J. This was also the view of O'Higgins CJ in *People (DPP) v Lynch* [1982] IR 64 at 76, [1981] ILRM 389 at 393, who stated that the judgment of Kingsmill Moore J had the approval, in one or two respects of a majority of the Court, and, in the other, of the entire of the Court. See also *People (DPP) v Morgan* (1979) 114 ILTR 60 at 62; *per* Finlay CJ in *DPP v McMahon* [1986]

not draw any particular distinction between illegally and unconstitutionally obtained evidence and regarded the fact that a breach of a constitutional right was involved in obtaining the impugned evidence simply as a factor to be weighed in the balance in the exercise by a trial judge of his or her discretion to exclude it. However, for Walsh J, the distinction between illegally and unconstitutionally obtained evidence was crucial. In the case of the latter, he took the view that:

> "The vindication and the protection of constitutional rights is a fundamental matter for all Courts established under the Constitution. That duty cannot yield place to any competing interest.... The defence and vindication of the constitutional rights of the citizen is a duty superior to that of trying such citizen for a criminal offence. The Courts in exercising the judicial powers of government of the State must recognise the paramount position of constitutional rights and must uphold the objection of an accused person to the admissibility at his trial of evidence obtained or procured by the State or its servants or agents as a result of a deliberate and conscious violation of the constitutional rights of the accused person where no extraordinary excusing circumstances exist, such as the imminent destruction of vital evidence or the need to rescue a victim in peril.... In my view evidence obtained in deliberate conscious breach of the constitutional rights of an accused person should, save in the excusable circumstances outlined above, be absolutely inadmissible".[29]

7–08 Applying those principles to the facts of the case, in circumstances where the gardaí had been unaware of the error, the learned judge was of the view that there had been no deliberate or conscious violation of the appellant's constitutional right to inviolability of the dwelling under Art.40.5.

7–09 As can be seen from the passage above, the application of the exclusionary rule enunciated by Walsh J in *O'Brien* was predicated on the existence of a "deliberate and conscious breach of the constitutional rights of the accused person". The most natural reading of this formula is that it incorporates an element of *mens rea* or premeditation. Thus, in order to trigger the operation of the exclusionary rule, the person responsible for the breach of the constitutional rights of the accused has to be aware that his or her actions constituted such a breach. This reading of the judgment was reinforced by the decision of the Court in *O'Brien* to admit the evidence because the error invalidating the search warrant was inadvertent and the gardaí were unaware of the error. However, it is also evident from the passage set out above, that the exclusionary rule advocated by Walsh J in *O'Brien* was based on a vindication principle, *i.e.* it was, in his view, required to vindicate the constitutional rights of an accused whose constitutional rights have been breached by the actions of the executive. As noted above, an exclusionary rule based on the vindication principle is designed to have a compensatory effect, *i.e.* it places the accused person in the position he or she would have been if the breach had not occurred by excluding evidence obtained as a result of the breach, rather than any sort of deterrent or punitive effect. It follows that its operation is triggered by the fact that a breach of the accused's constitutional rights has occurred and is not dependent on the state of mind of the person who breached those rights. Thus, the intention of the person who breached those rights is irrelevant.

7–10 This fundamental contradiction between the rationale and formulation of the

---

IR 393, [1987] ILRM 87; and *per* McCarthy J in *DPP v Gaffney* [1987] IR 173 at 184, [1988] ILRM 39 at 46. See also the analysis of the ratio of *O'Brien* by O'Connor, "The admissibility of unconstitutionally obtained evidence in Irish law" (1982) 17 Ir Jur 257 at 275–276. The issue is one of academic interest only now as the judgment of Walsh J. has, whether correctly or not, come to be regarded as containing the ratio of the decision of the Supreme Court on this issue.
29 [1965] IR 142 at 170.

exclusionary rule in *O'Brien* subsequently led to considerable judicial disagreement as to the precise meaning of the phrase "deliberate and conscious" and particularly as to whether it referred to the commission of the act complained of or the knowledge of the actor.[30] The divergence of views on this issue crystallised in the decision of the Supreme Court in *People (DPP) v Shaw*.[31] Walsh J, dissenting on this point, took the view that:

> "When the act complained of was undertaken or carried out consciously and deliberately, it is immaterial whether the person carrying out the act may or may not have been conscious that what he was doing was illegal or, even if he knew it was illegal, that it amounted to a breach of the constitutional rights of the accused. It is the doing of the act which is the essential matter, not the actor's appreciation of the legal consequences or incidents of it ... there is nothing whatever in *O'Briens Case* to suggest that the admissibility of the evidence depends upon the state or degree of the violator's knowledge of constitutional law or, indeed, of the ordinary law. To attempt to import any such interpretation of the decision would be to put a premium on ignorance of the law."[32]

7-11 However, Griffin J, with whom a majority of the Supreme Court concurred, disagreed:

> "I [do not] find myself able to support the opinion that the person's statement is to be ruled out as evidence obtained in deliberate and conscious violation of his constitutional rights, even though the taker of the statement may not have known that what he was doing was either illegal or unconstitutional. ... In my opinion, it is the violation of the person's constitutional rights, and not the particular act complained of, that has to be deliberate and conscious."[33]

7-12 The Supreme Court also split in relation to this issue in *People (DPP) v Healy*.[34] Griffin J defended the decision of the majority of the Court on this point in *Shaw* but Finlay CJ and McCarthy J rejected his interpretation of the "deliberate and conscious" formula. McCarthy J stated:

> "[I]f 'conscious and deliberate' is a term of art appropriate to be used in the context of constitutional rights and their violation, the only test is whether or not the act or omission that constituted such violation was itself a conscious and deliberate act; the fact that the violator did not realise he was in breach of a constitutional right is irrelevant."[35]

7-13 This controversy as to the ambit and effect of the exclusionary rule established in *O'Brien* was finally resolved definitively by a five judge Supreme Court in *People (DPP) v Kenny*.[36] In *Kenny,* the appellant's flat had been searched by Gardaí pursuant to a search warrant issued under s.26 of the Misuse of Drugs Act 1977 and the only evidence against him had been gathered during the course of that search. It was held

---

[30] In a number of cases including *People (DPP) v Madden* [1977] IR 336; *People (DPP) v O'Loughlin* [1979] IR 85; and *People (DPP) v Shaw* [1982] IR 1, and the judgment of Henchy J in *People (DPP) v Quilligan* [1986] IR 495 at 513, [1987] ILRM 606 at 628, the necessity for some form of *mens rea* on the part of the person breaching the constitutional rights of the accused was emphasised. However, Walsh J in *People (DPP) v Walsh* [1980] IR 294 at 313 and *People (DPP) v Shaw* [1982] IR 1 at 31–34, stated that, once the act complained of was deliberate and conscious, it was immaterial that the person was unaware that he or she was breaching the constitutional rights of the accused. For a comprehensive and insightful analysis of *O'Brien* and its interpretation in subsequent cases, see O'Connor, "The Admissibility of Unconstitutionally Obtained Evidence in Irish Law" (1982) 17 Ir Jur 257.

[31] [1982] IR 1.

[32] [1982] IR 1 at 32–33.

[33] [1982] IR 1 at 55–56.

[34] [1990] 2 IR 73, [1990] ILRM 313.

[35] [1990] 2 IR 73 at 88–89, [1990] ILRM 313 at 328.

[36] [1990] 2 IR 110, [1990] ILRM 569.

by the Court of Criminal Appeal that the warrant was invalid and the question therefore arose as to whether the evidence obtained on foot it should be excluded because of the breach of the appellant's right to inviolability of the dwelling. There was no question that the gardaí had intentionally violated this constitutional right as the procedure adopted to obtain the warrant had been in use for many years without any suggestion that it was constitutionally suspect.

7–14 The majority judgment of the Supreme Court was delivered by Finlay CJ who took the view that *O'Brien* had left open the choice between the deterrent principle and, what he termed, the "absolute protection principle". He pointed out that the courts had a duty, pursuant to Art.40.3.1, in as far as practicable, to defend and vindicate personal rights. Therefore:

> "As between two alternative rules or principles governing the exclusion of evidence obtained as a result of the invasion of the personal rights of a citizen, the court has ... an obligation to choose the principle which is likely to provide a stronger and more effective defence and vindication of the right concerned.
> To exclude only evidence obtained by a person who knows or ought reasonably to know that he is invading a constitutional right is to impose a negative deterrent. It is clearly effective to dissuade a policeman from acting in a manner which he knows is unconstitutional or from acting in a manner reckless as to whether his conduct is or is not unconstitutional.
> To apply, on the other hand, the absolute protection rule of exclusion whilst providing also that negative deterrent, incorporates as well a positive encouragement to those in authority over the crime prevention and detection services of the State to consider in detail the personal rights of the citizens as set out in the Constitution, and the effect of their powers of arrest, detention, search and questioning in relation to such rights.
> It seems to me to be an inescapable conclusion that a principle of exclusion which contains both negative and positive force is likely to protect constitutional rights in more instances than is a principle with negative consequences only."[37]

7–15 He acknowledged the anomalies that would be caused by this principle of absolute exclusion which would limit the truth-finding capacity of the courts. However, in his view, the objectives of crime control could not outweigh the constitutional mandate to defend and vindicate, as far as practicable, the personal rights of the citizen. He, therefore, concluded that:

> "the correct principle is that evidence obtained by invasion of the constitutional personal rights of a citizen must be excluded unless a court is satisfied that either the act constituting the breach of constitutional rights was committed unintentionally or accidentally, or is satisfied that there are extraordinary excusing circumstances which justify the admission of the evidence in its (the court's) discretion."[38]

7–16 On the facts of the case, neither of the gardaí involved had any knowledge that they were invading the constitutional rights of the accused. However, their acts in forcibly entering the dwelling were neither unintentional nor accidental and, thus, the evidence obtained from the search should have been excluded.

7–17 Dissenting judgments were delivered by Lynch and Griffin JJ. Griffin J reiterated the view which he had expressed in *People (DPP) v Shaw*.[39] He pointed out that the gardaí in the case had, for the purpose of obtaining the search warrant, adopted a procedure that had been in almost universal use throughout the country for

---

[37] [1990] 2 IR 110 at 133, [1990] ILRM 569 at 578. See O'Gorman, "The Rationale of the Exclusionary Rule" (1991) ILT 142 for a discussion of the rationale adopted in *Kenny*.
[38] [1990] 2 IR 110 at 134, [1990] ILRM 569 at 579.
[39] [1982] IR 1.

many years.[40] Therefore, he was satisfied that there had not been any deliberate and conscious breach of the rights of the appellant. Lynch J was also of the opinion that evidence should only be excluded if there was a deliberate disregard by the gardaí of constitutional rights and there were no adequate excusing circumstances. In his view, for evidence to be rejected, there had to be some element of blame or culpability or unfairness in order to bring the exclusionary rule into operation. Such was not present in that case which he thought was on all fours with *O'Brien*.[41]

3. Scope of the Exclusionary Rule

7–18 The exclusionary rule formulated in *Kenny* applies to evidence sought to be adduced at the trial of an accused and the courts have resisted attempts to extend its application any further than this. In *People (DPP) v Cooney*,[42] evidence of identifications made by witnesses of the appellant at pre-trial identification procedures was excluded because the appellant had been in unlawful detention at the time but the witnesses were permitted to make an in-court identification of him. It was contended by the appellant that the "dock identifications" were irremediably tainted because of their association with the earlier identifications and, thus, constituted the fruits of an unconstitutional procedure. However, it was held by the Supreme Court that the constitutional rights of the accused had been vindicated in full by the exclusion of the evidence of the pre-trial identifications and "it was not in any sense a necessary consequence of their vindication that the further identification by the witnesses of the appellant in court ... should be excluded".[43]

7–19 A similar approach was taken in *Curtin v Dáil Éireann*.[44] The applicant was a Circuit Court judge who had been acquitted of charges of possession of child pornography after material seized during a search of his home including a computer had been excluded by the application of the exclusionary rule. Following the proposal of a motion to remove the applicant from office pursuant to Art.35.4.1, a direction was made by an Oireachtas committee that he produce to it all documents and materials including the computer that had been seized at his home by Gardaí. The applicant sought to quash that direction on a number of bases including that, by virtue of the exclusionary rule, the Committee could not lawfully take possession of the computer as it had been seized in breach of his constitutional rights. This contention was given short shrift by the Supreme Court which held that the computer could have been returned to the applicant's possession and it could not be said that the exclusionary

---

[40] This echoes comments made by O'Hanlon J in *Farrell v Farrelly* [1988] IR 201 who stated, *obiter*, that even if there had been an unconstitutional invalidity in the procedure whereby the applicants were arrested, there had not been any deliberate and conscious violation of their constitutional rights because the application to the peace commissioner for warrants had been made pursuant to statutory procedures which had been followed without challenge within living memory.

[41] But see *People (DPP) v Balfe* [1998] 4 IR 50 at 59–62, where the Court of Criminal Appeal, somewhat unconvincingly it is suggested, sought to reconcile the decisions in *O'Brien* and *Kenny* on the basis that, in *O'Brien*, the defect was patent and there was "sufficient validity in the warrant or order to justify the admission in evidence of the goods which were in fact seized pursuant to the warrant despite its defects" whereas, in *Kenny*, the warrant had an inherent or fundamental flaw "which deprived it of legal effect". See, further, *People (DPP) v Mallon* [2011] IECCA 29, [2011] 2 IR 544.

[42] [1998] 1 ILRM 321.

[43] [1998] 1 ILRM 321 at 331–332.

[44] [2006] IESC 14, [2006] 2 IR 556.

rule meant that it was forever immune, in all circumstances, from a lawful seizure or order for production.[45]

7–20 An even more ambitious submission failed in *DPP (Walsh) v Cash*[46] where gardaí were unable to state whether fingerprints stored in a database which had been used to identify an accused as the perpetrator of a burglary leading to his arrest, but which it is was not proposed to adduce in evidence, had been lawfully retained. The accused contended that there was an obligation on the State to establish that any administrative step in the criminal process, including arrest, was taken on foot of evidence which was proved to have been lawfully obtained. However, Charleton J rejected this contention and the proposition that the exclusionary rule could have any application, stating:

> "This argument seeks to import into the rules of evidence into police procedures. It has no place there. If the prosecution was obliged to prove legality in respect of every step leading to an arrest or charge, this would have the result that the prosecution, in presenting a case, would be required not only to show, against objection by the defence, that the evidence which they proposed to lead was lawfully obtained, but to open to the court every facet of the investigation to ensure that no illegality ever tainted any aspect of police conduct."[47]

7–21 That conclusion was upheld by the Supreme Court. Fennelly J summarised the question before the Court as being whether the exclusionary rule laid down in *Kenny* should be extended to cover facts, not being offered as part of the evidence of a criminal trial, but giving rise to the suspicion which led to the arrest. He was quite satisfied that this question should be answered in the negative. He pointed out that the decision in *Kenny* was not concerned with the lawful provenance of evidence used to ground suspicion and the judgment of Finlay CJ did not advert to the possibility that the exclusionary rule could be applied to such an issue. He held that the lawfulness of an arrest and the admissibility of evidence at trial are different matters which will normally be considered in distinct contexts and agreed with the holding of Charleton J that a reasonable suspicion was not required to be grounded on evidence that would be admissible at a criminal trial. Therefore, there was no onus on the prosecution to establish the lawful provenance of material relied on to ground such a reasonable suspicion and the exclusionary rule could not have any application.[48]

4. Application of the Exclusionary Rule

7–22 The exclusionary rule will apply so as to exclude evidence where: (i) there has been a breach of the constitutional rights of an accused; (ii) there is a causative link between that breach and the evidence; and (iii) there are no extraordinary excusing circumstances.[49]

---

[45] [2006] IESC 14 at [166], [2006] 2 IR 556 at 637.
[46] [2007] IEHC 108, [2008] 1 ILRM 443; [2010] IESC 1, [2010] 1 IR 609, [2010] 1 ILRM 389.
[47] [2007] IEHC 108 at [13], [2008] 1 ILRM 443 at 451.
[48] The decision in *Cash* was applied in *DPP (McDonnell) v McDonnell* [2014] IEHC 35 at [37] in relation to the formation of opinion by a garda that a person had driven a vehicle after consuming an intoxicant prior to making a demand for a specimen of blood or urine. O'Malley J held that the opinion has to be genuinely and reasonably held but there was no requirement that it based upon matters that would themselves be admissible.
[49] In keeping with the general principle that the prosecution bears the onus of establishing the admissibility of evidence and any facts required to be proved in order to establish the admissibility of evidence (*People (DPP) v Dillon* [2003] 1 ILRM 531), where the admission of evidence is challenged on the basis that it has been obtained in breach of the constitutional rights of the accused,

(a) Breach of constitutional rights of the accused

7–23   A consideration of the circumstances where a breach of the constitutional rights of an accused will be found is beyond the scope of this chapter but the following points should be noted. First, the exclusionary rule will apply only where there has been a breach of the constitutional rights of the accused, not where there has been a breach of the constitutional rights of a third party. So, in *People (DPP) v Lawless*,[50] where an unlawful search of a dwelling which was not occupied by the applicant had been carried out, it was held by the Court of Criminal Appeal that no constitutional rights of the applicant had been breached and the court proceeded to deal with the admissibility of the evidence on the basis that it had been illegally rather than unconstitutionally obtained. However, subsequent decisions have broadened the scope of protection of Art.40.5 to any person who resides in a property[51] even if he or she has little or no proprietary interest in the property or is a trespasser.[52] In addition, it had been held that the exclusionary rule may be invoked where there is an unlawful search of a commercial premises in which the accused has or previously had an interest.[53] Accordingly, where evidence is obtained on foot of an unlawful search, there is relatively little scope for avoiding the exclusionary rule on the basis that the constitutional rights of a third party only have been breached.[54]

7–24   Secondly, as can be seen from the decision in *People (DPP) v Mallon*,[55] there is an obvious temptation for the courts to shape the contours of the law relating to arrest and searches so that a finding of illegality and a consequent breach of constitutional rights is not made and the application of the exclusionary rule is avoided. In that case, there had been a misdescription in the address in a search warrant which described the premises searched as "4 Marrowbone Close, Dublin 8" rather than "4 Marrowbone Lane Close, Dublin 8". Following a very detailed review of the relevant authorities, O'Donnell J held that "a mere error will not invalidate a warrant, especially one which is not calculated to mislead, or perhaps just as importantly, does not mislead".[56] He justified this approach on the basis that, "particularly in so long as Irish law maintains

---

the prosecution bears the onus of proving that there has not been a breach of the constitutional rights of the accused (*People (DPP) v Madden* [1977] IR 336 at 345), that there is no causative link between the breach the evidence sought to be excluded (*R. v Bartle* (1995) 118 DLR (4th) 83, 110; *Noort v Ministry for Transport* [1992] 3 NZLR 260 at 283) or that there are extraordinary excusing circumstances (*People (DPP) v Walsh* [1980] IR 294 at 317; *People (DPP) v Shaw* [1982] IR 1 at 31, 32).

[50]   (1985) 3 Frewen 30.
[51]   *People (DPP) v Bowes*, unreported, Court of Criminal Appeal, 25 February 2002.
[52]   *People (DPP) v Lynch* [2009] IECCA 31, [2010] 1 IR 543.
[53]   See *People (DPP) v Joyce* [2008] IECCA 53 at [27], [2009] 4 IR 656 at 668. *Cf.* the civil case of *The Competition Authority v The Irish Dental Association* [2005] IEHC 361, [2006] 1 ILRM 383 discussed below.
[54]   It is possible that a premises will not be regarded as the dwelling of a person for the purposes of Art.40.5 if he or she is a transient visitor and only stays overnight there occasionally. In the United States, the test of whether a person found on premises has standing to raise a challenge to the search of the premises as unconstitutional and invoke the exclusionary rule is whether the person has a legitimate expectation of privacy in the premises. Thus, a casual visitor to an apartment does not have standing (*United States v Burnett* (1989) 890 F2d 1233) but an overnight guest has (*Minnesota v Olson* (1988) 487 US 533). However, even if the premises was not regarded as a dwelling, a court might still find that an unlawful search breached the accused's right of privacy and exclude the evidence obtained on that basis.
[55]   [2011] IECCA 31, [2011] 2 IR 544.
[56]   [2011] IECCA 31 at [44], [2011] 2 IR 544 at 567.

an almost absolute exclusionary rule for evidence obtained as a result of an illegal and therefore unconstitutional search of a dwelling house, courts should be slow to invalidate warrants on the grounds of typographical, grammatical or transcription errors, which are neither calculated to mislead, nor in truth do mislead, any reasonable reader of the words".[57]

7–25 Thirdly, it is important to note that there are circumstances where an apparent breach of the constitutional rights of an accused may be justified by the necessity to protect or vindicate a competing and "superior" constitutional right such that no breach of the constitutional right of the accused actually occurs and the application of the exclusionary rule does not arise.[58] This is evident from the decision in *People (DPP) v Shaw*.[59] In that case, the accused and another man had been arrested by gardaí without a warrant for being in possession of a stolen car. However, the gardaí failed to bring the two men before the District Court at the first reasonable opportunity, as required at common law, because the gardaí suspected that they were involved in the disappearance of two young women. Instead, the gardaí kept them in custody for the purpose of questioning them in relation to the disappearance of the women, one of whom had disappeared four days earlier and whom gardaí hoped might still be alive.

7–26 Although the failure to bring the accused before the District Court at the first reasonable opportunity *prima facie* rendered his detention unlawful, a majority of the Supreme Court held that the accused had not been unlawfully detained as the interference with his constitutional right to liberty was justified by the necessity to vindicate the superior constitutional right to life of the woman who gardaí believed might still be alive.[60] Griffin J rejected the proposition that the right to liberty protected by Art.40.4.1 was absolute and stated that it could be limited by reference to the obligation placed on the State by Art.40.3 to protect and vindicate the personal rights of every citizen. In the circumstances of the case, there had been a conflict between the right to liberty of the accused and the right to life of the woman and Griffin J was in no doubt that it was the duty of the State to protect the more important constitutional right:

> "[T]he State must weigh each right for the purpose of evaluating the merits of each and strike a balance between them and, having done so, take such steps as are necessary to protect the more important right. Although the right to personal liberty is one of the fundamental rights, if a balance is to be struck between one person's right to personal liberty for some hours or even

---

[57] [2011] IECCA 31 at [58], [2011] 2 IR 544 at 573.

[58] *Cf. People (DPP) v Shaw* [1982] IR 1 at 33, where Walsh J stressed that "nothing in the admissibility rule renders lawful what was and is unlawful. By definition the question of admissibility arises only because there was an illegality."

[59] [1982] IR 1. For an analysis of this aspect of the decision in *Shaw*, see P O'Connor, "The Admissibility of Unconstitutionally Obtained Evidence in Irish Law" (1982) 17 Ir Jur 257 at 268–273.

[60] Walsh J, who dissented, took the view ([1982] IR 1 at 40–41) that: "[t]here is nothing in the Constitution which authorises the commission of an unlawful act. If an act is unlawful and the law or the laws which render it unlawful is or are not inconsistent with, or invalid having regard to the provisions of the Constitution, it is quite clear that the Constitution cannot and does not purport to render lawful an act which is unlawful and that no court is competent or permitted to do so. To suggest that an effort in vindicating the life of another person, *e.g.* to enable that person to gain the benefit of the constitutional provision for the protection or vindication of his life, is sufficient in itself to render lawful any act however unlawful, provided it is motivated by an honest desire to save or vindicate a life, is simply to state that the end may justify the means, unlawful though they may be."

days and another person's right to protection against danger to his life, then in any civilised society, in my view, the latter right must prevail…"[61]

7–27   A similar approach was taken in *DPP v Delaney*[62] where it was held that there had not been any breach of the constitutional right to inviolability of the dwelling in circumstances where gardaí had entered a dwelling in the *bona fide* belief that it was necessary to do so to safeguard the constitutional right to life and bodily integrity of persons present therein. O'Flaherty J stated:

> "The sergeant was entitled to enter the premises to safeguard the life and limbs of the woman who was there as well as the children. The fact that he may have thought that he was relying on some common law power is neither here nor there. He was entitled to make the choice that he did and such choice, far from being in breach of the Constitution, was in fulfilment of the obligation that devolves on all citizens to observe and implement the requirements of the Constitution because the safeguarding of life and limb must be more important than the inviolability of the dwelling of the citizen, especially when it is under attack in any event."[63]

7–28   Therefore, provided that the garda sergeant had been acting *bona fide* in belief that he should enter the premises to safeguard life and limb, no breach of the constitutional right to inviolability of the dwelling had occurred.

7–29   Finally, it is necessary that the breach of a constitutional right is "deliberate and conscious" and the exclusionary rule will not apply where the act that violates the constitutional right was accidental or unintentional. While the *Kenny* case made it quite clear that the motive or intention of the actor is irrelevant,[64] there are still cases where the distinction between the intention of the actor and the act is not observed.[65] In *People (DPP) v Creed*,[66] manifestly inadequate efforts had been made to contact a solicitor nominated by the accused while in custody with the garda. Although it was a Saturday night, all the garda did was to ring the office number of the solicitor and no attempt was made to obtain a mobile or other number and, further, contrary to the Custody Regulations, he did not inform the accused that he had failed to make contact. As Geoghegan J commented in the Court of Criminal Appeal, this "behaviour by the garda seemed to show a lack of common sense and proper care in efforts to procure the named solicitor and in failing to seek alternative instructions (if any) from the prisoner".[67] Nonetheless, the trial judge ruled that the failures had not been conscious and there had not been a deliberate and conscious failure to vindicate the accused's constitutional rights, a finding that the Court of Criminal Appeal refused to interfere with. Geoghegan J expressed the view that it was not contrary to the holding

---

[61] [1982] IR 1 at 55. In his concurring judgment, Kenny J explained (at 63) that there is "a hierarchy of constitutional rights and, when a conflict arises between them, that which ranks higher must prevail".

[62] [1997] 3 IR 453, [1998] 1 ILRM 507 (overturning the decision of Morris J on this point who had opined ([1996] 3 IR 556 at 561–562, [1996] 1 ILRM 536 at 541) that *O'Brien* was not: "authority for the general proposition that a member of An Garda Síochána may violate a constitutional right provided that there are extraordinary excusing circumstances. It is authority for no more than the proposition that where such a violation occurs and evidence is harvested as a result, it is for the court of trial to decide all the issues as to the admissibility of this evidence including a consideration of any extraordinary excusing circumstances alleged.")

[63] [1997] 3 IR 453 at 460, [1998] 1 ILRM 507 at 512–513.

[64] See *People (DPP) v Laide* [2005] IECCA 24 at 49–50 and *DPP v McCrea* [2009] IEHC 39, where this distinction was clearly drawn.

[65] See, by way of example, *People (DPP) v McGartland*, unreported, Court of Criminal Appeal, 20 January 2003; *People (DPP) v Creed* [2009] IECCA 95.

[66] [2009] IECCA 95.

[67] [2009] IECCA 95 at [6].

in *Kenny* "that subjective factors like motive or personal knowledge are not relevant when considering whether infringement of a constitutional right is conscious and deliberate".[68] However, it is difficult to see how this is so because each of the acts and omissions of the garda was deliberate and, therefore, fell squarely within the "deliberate and conscious" requirement.

(b) Causative link

7–30 Given that the exclusionary rule is a compensatory remedy designed to place the accused in the position in which he or she would have been if his or her rights had not been breached, it logically follows that it is only applicable where evidence has been obtained *as the result of* a breach of the constitutional rights of the accused. Thus, in order for the exclusionary rule to apply, there must be a causative link between the evidence sought to be excluded and the breach of constitutional rights in question.

7–31 Although implicit in the judgment of Walsh J in *O'Brien*,[69] the requirement for a causative link was not highlighted until the decision in *People (DPP) v Healy*,[70] where Finlay CJ, in the context of an issue as to the admissibility of a confession allegedly obtained in breach of what was recognised in that case to be a constitutionally protected right of access to a solicitor, stated:

> "The vital issue which arises, therefore, if a breach of the right of access to a solicitor has occurred as a result of a conscious and deliberate act of a member of the Garda Síochána, is as to whether there is a causative link between that breach and the obtaining of an admission."[71]

7–32 In *People (DPP) v AD*,[72] Clarke J in the Supreme Court regarded the causative link test as well established and expressed the view that it "meets the legitimate requirements of discouraging a constitutionally impermissible investigation while at the same time permitting lawfully obtained evidence to be placed before the court as part of the criminal process."

7–33 The potency of the requirement of a causative link as a potential means for circumscribing the ambit of the exclusionary rule is illustrated by *People (DPP) v O'Donnell*.[73] The appellant in that case had been stopped by gardaí while driving a car and searched. A walkie-talkie was found in one pocket of the jacket he was wearing and a quantity of explosives in the other. On appeal, the legality of the search was challenged. The Court of Criminal Appeal held that the search had been lawful and that no breach of the constitutional rights of the appellant had occurred. However, the Court went on to say that, even if it were conceded that the removal of the walkie-talkie from the pocket of the appellant had in some way infringed his constitutional rights, no causative link had been shown to exist between this act and the later production of the explosives from the other pocket because the garda was intent on carrying out

---

[68] [2009] IECCA 95 at [6].

[69] In *O'Brien*, Walsh J stated ([1965] IR 142 at 170) that: "The Courts in exercising the judicial powers of government of the State must recognise the paramount position of constitutional rights and must uphold the objection of an accused person to the admissibility at his trial of evidence obtained or procured by the State or its servants *as a result of* a deliberate and conscious violation of the constitutional rights of the accused. ..."

[70] [1990] 2 IR 73, [1990] ILRM 313.

[71] [1990] 2 IR 73 at 81, [1990] ILRM 313 at 320.

[72] [2012] IESC 33 at [42], [2012] 2 IR 332.

[73] [1995] 3 IR 551.

a search of the applicant and had invoked the appropriate powers before proceeding to assert his right to search the other pocket.[74] The court, thus, indicated that it was prepared to use the requirement of a causative link to atomise the sequence of events leading up to the arrest of the appellant so as to uphold the constitutionality of one part of the search even if an earlier part of the search was tainted by unconstitutionality. However, it would seem to be impossible to identify *ex post facto* the extent to which the discovery of the walkie-talkie in one pocket of the appellant's jacket influenced the decision of the garda to insist on seeing, and to invoke his legal powers in order to see the contents of the other pocket. Thus, having regard to the onus of proof on the prosecution to establish that the evidence was not unconstitutionally obtained,[75] it would seem that any doubt in relation to the issue of causation should be resolved in favour of the accused.

(i) Breach of Right of Access to a Lawyer

7–34   Particular difficulties can arise in applying the requirement of a causative link to evidence obtained after a breach of an accused's right of access to a lawyer. As discussed in more detail in the next chapter, in a series of cases,[76] culminating in the decision of the Supreme Court in *People (DPP) v Buck*,[77] it was held that the effect of a breach of the right of reasonable access to a solicitor was to render the detention of the person detained unlawful. It logically followed that, if this right was breached, the person was thereafter in unlawful detention and any inculpatory statement made thereafter was inadmissible.[78] However, as held in *People (DPP) v O'Brien*,[79] once the access to a solicitor was afforded and the constitutional right ceased, the detention ceased to be unlawful and any statement made subsequently would be admissible, subject to the caveat that:

> "If the inculpatory statement or admission ultimately made by the accused was elicited from him by the use of information disclosed by him while he was in unlawful detention, there would clearly have been a causative link between the breach of his constitutional rights and the making of the statements of admissions. In those circumstances, material which had been wrongfully obtained in breach of the accused's constitutional rights would have been used to obtain an inculpatory statement or admission."[80]

---

[74] [1995] 3 IR 551 at 558. See also *Freeman v DPP* [1996] 3 IR 565, where a similar approach was adopted.

[75] *People (DPP) v Madden* [1977] IR 336 at 345.

[76] See *The Emergency Powers Bill 1976* [1977] IR 159 at 173; *People (DPP) v Madden* [1977] IR 336 at 355; *People (DPP) v Shaw* [1982] IR 1 at 35 (*per* Walsh J); *People (DPP) v Quilligan (No.3)* [1993] 2 IR 305 at 321; *Barry v Waldron*, unreported, High Court, 23 May 1996 at 5; *People (DPP) v Finnegan*, unreported, Court of Criminal Appeal, 15 July 1997 at 42; *Lavery v Member in Charge, Carrickmacross Garda Station* [1999] 2 IR 390 at 395; *People (DPP) v Buck* [2002] 2 IR 268, [2002] 2 ILRM 454; *People (DPP) v O'Brien*, unreported, Court of Criminal Appeal, 17 June 2002, [2005] IESC 29, [2005] 2 IR 206; *DPP v McCrea* [2009] IEHC 39.

[77] [2002] 2 IR 268.

[78] *People (DPP) v Madden* [1977] IR 336; *People (DPP) v Farrell* [1978] IR 13; *People (DPP) v O'Loughlin* [1979] IR 85; *People (DPP) v Higgins*, unreported, Supreme Court, 22 November 1985; *People (DPP) v Byrne* [1989] ILRM 613: *People (DPP) v Quilligan* [1986] IR 495 at 503, [1987] ILRM 606 at 618; *Larkin v O'Dea* [1994] 2 ILRM 448, [1995] 2 ILRM 1.

[79] Unreported, Court of Criminal Appeal, 17 June 2002; [2005] IESC 29, [2005] 2 IR 206.

[80] [2005] IESC 29 at [13], [2005] 2 IR 206 at 211–212. See, further, *DPP v Ryan* [2011] IECCA 6 for an example of a case where this causation inquiry was undertaken in relation to statements made after a remedied breach of the right of access to a lawyer.

7–35 In *People (DPP) v AD*,[81] it was held by Clarke J in the Supreme Court that a breach of the right of reasonable access to a solicitor will not affect the admissibility of any statements made prior to the occurrence of the breach on the basis that there is no causal link between a breach of that right resulting in detention becoming unconstitutionally unlawful and a statement made earlier while the suspect was in lawful custody. He went on to hold that a court could sever those portions of a statement made by an accused during a period of constitutionally unlawful custody from those which were made during a period of lawful custody which were, in principle, admissible. He added that, unless there was some sufficient nexus between the two parts of the statement or interview process so as to taint the otherwise lawful portion, then there was no reason to exclude that part of the interview or statement which was made while the accused was in lawful custody. However, where there was a real risk of unfairness by admitting only part of the statement, a trial judge might have to exclude the entirety of the statement concerned.

7–36 Somewhat different issues arise where forensic samples are obtained from a suspect after a breach of his or her right of access to a lawyer has been occurred. In *Walsh v O'Buachalla*,[82] the applicant had been convicted of driving while intoxicated contrary to s.49(2) of the Road Traffic Act 1961. While in custody, he had been given an information leaflet that stated that an arrested person could communicate privately with a solicitor, either by telephone or at the garda station but he made no attempt to do so until a doctor arrived to take a sample. That request was refused by the arresting garda because he believed that the request was not genuine and was made merely for the purpose of delay. Even assuming that the applicant's right to a solicitor had been infringed, which he doubted, Blayney J went on to hold that that there must be shown that there was a causal connection between the infringement and the obtaining of the evidence. On the facts of the case, he was satisfied that the evidence had been obtained after the violation but not as a result of it. The applicant was obliged by statute to give a specimen of his blood or urine and no advice from a solicitor could have altered that. Therefore, refusing access to a solicitor did not in any way lead to a specimen of blood being obtained. If a solicitor had been present to give advice, all he could have done would have been to confirm that the applicant was required by law to provide a specimen of blood or urine.[83]

---

[81] [2008] IECCA 101; [2012] IESC 33, [2012] 2 IR 332.

[82] [1991] 1 IR 56.

[83] See also *Director of Public Prosecutions v Spratt* [1995] 2 ILRM 117, and *People (DPP) v Cullen*, unreported, Court of Criminal Appeal, 30 March 1995, which also dealt with alleged breaches of the constitutional right of reasonable access to a solicitor, where a similar approach was adopted. These three decisions have been criticised by Butler and Ong, "Breach of the Constitutional Right of Access to a Lawyer and the Exclusion of Evidence—The Causative Link" (1995) 5 ICLJ 156 on the basis that they applied the causative link requirement too strictly and thereby failed to vindicate the constitutional right of access to a lawyer and, further, that even applying a strict test of causation, a causative link was present in these cases. In *Noort v Ministry of Transport* [1992] 3 NZLR 260 at 274, it was held that absence of causation in circumstances similar to those in *Walsh* could not be safely assumed and that "legal advice, even of an elementary kind, might have helped the persons detained to decide whether to elect to undergo the tests or face the consequences of prosecutions for refusing". A strict causation requirement was also rejected in similar circumstances by the Canadian Supreme Court in *R. v Bartle* (1995) 118 DLR (4th) 83 where it was held that all evidence obtained as part of the "chain of events" involving the Charter breach will fall within the scope of s.24(2). Lamer CJC expressed the view that courts should take a generous approach and that a strict causal link between the infringement and the discovery of the evidence was not required.

7–37   In *DPP v McCrea*,[84] Edwards J accepted that the effect of the decisions in *Buck* and *O'Brien* and the holding that a breach of the right of access to a lawyer rendered the detention of a suspect unconstitutional was that *Walsh v O'Buachalla* no longer represented the law and that there was no longer a requirement to establish a causative link between a sample taken during a period of unconstitutional detention and the breach of that right. However, it would appear that the decision of the Supreme Court in *People (DPP) v Gormley and White*[85] has effectively reversed that holding. In that case, it was held that a suspect has a right of access to a lawyer after arrest and prior to questioning and that the conviction of an accused wholly or in significant reliance incriminating statements obtained where that right had been breached would be an unfair trial. However, a different approach was adopted in relation to forensic samples and the conclusion was reached that there is no constitutional impediment to "the taking of objective forensic samples from a suspect while that suspect is in custody, after the relevant suspect has requested legal advice and before the relevant legal advice becomes available".[86] It was accepted that the position might be different where the suspect had a genuine legal choice available in respect of the taking of samples and where it would be reasonably necessary for the suspect concerned to have access to legal advice before making such choices. However, it was emphasised that the fact that a suspect might be able, by committing a separate criminal offence of refusing to cooperate with the giving of samples, to frustrate the process, could not amount to the making of a choice by the suspect.[87]

(ii) Derivative evidence

7–38   The Irish courts have not yet had occasion to expressly address the issue of derivative evidence, *i.e.* evidence that is derived from evidence obtained as a result of a breach of constitutional rights. In the United States, evidence obtained as an indirect result of unconstitutionality is rendered inadmissible by the application of "fruit of the poisonous tree doctrine"[88] unless it is obtained from a source independent of the unconstitutionality[89] or the taint of unconstitutionality has dissipated.[90] However, the European Court of Human Rights declined to establish a general rule excluding derivative evidence in *Gäfgen v Germany*.[91] In that case, the Court of Human Rights noted that, outside of circumstances where statements were obtained as a result of torture or inhuman or degrading treatment involving a breach of Art.3, there was no clear consensus among the Contracting States, the courts of other states and human rights monitoring institutions about the exact scope of the exclusionary rule that should apply to the fruits of inadmissible evidence. Accordingly, it held that a case by case analysis of the impact of the admission of such evidence on the fairness of the trial was

---

[84]   [2009] IEHC 39 at 27.

[85]   [2014] IESC 17, [2014] 1 ILRM 377. This decision is discussed further in Chaps 8 and 11.

[86]   [2014] IESC 17 at [10.4], [2014] 1 ILRM 377 at 407. A similar conclusion had been reached by the Court of Criminal Appeal in one of the cases under appeal (*People (DPP) v White* [2011] IECCA 78).

[87]   [2014] IESC 17 at [10.6], [2014] 1 ILRM 377 at 408.

[88]   See *Silverthorne Lumber Co. v United States* (1920) 251 US 385 at 392; *Wong Sun v United States* (1963) 371 US 471 at 484–88.

[89]   See *Silverthorne Lumber Co. v United States* (1920) 251 US 385 at 392; *United States v Crews* (1980) 445 US 463; *Murray v United States* (1988) 487 US 533.

[90]   *Nardone v United States* (1939) 308 US 338; *Wong Sun v United States* (1963) 371 US 471; *United States v Ceccolini* (1978) 435 US 268.

[91]   [2010] ECHR 759, (2011) 52 EHRR 1 (see case comment at (2009) 13 E & P 58).

required and "factors such as whether the impugned evidence would, in any event, have been found at a later stage, independently of the prohibited method of investigation, may have an influence on the admissibility of such evidence".[92]

7–39 In this jurisdiction, the question would seem to be simply one of causation; evidence will be excluded where it would not have been obtained "but for" the breach of the accused's constitutional rights. This approach can be illustrated by the decision of the Canadian Supreme Court in *R. v Burlingham*.[93] The accused, who had been arrested in connection with a murder, made a number of incriminating statements to the police, took them to the murder scene and pointed out where he had disposed of the gun. He subsequently made an incriminating statement to his girlfriend. The confession was ruled inadmissible on the basis of a breach of the accused's right to counsel under s.10(b) of the Canadian Charter of Rights and Fundamental Freedoms and the evidence of the gun and of his girlfriend were also excluded on the basis that they were derivative evidence which would not have been obtained but for the incriminating statements made in violation of the accused's right to counsel.[94]

(iii) Inevitable discovery

7–40 The case law in relation to the requirement for a causative link also raises the question as to whether the Irish courts would apply the doctrine of inevitable discovery whereby evidence, which has been obtained in breach of an accused's constitutional rights, will be admitted if the prosecution can establish that it would have been obtained in any event by lawful means.[95] Having regard to the remedial nature of the exclusionary rule in this jurisdiction, a strong argument can be made that, if it can be demonstrated that the evidence sought to be excluded would have been discovered in any event, no prejudice to the defendant accrues by admitting such evidence and the necessity to vindicate his or her rights does not arise. The difficulty with this principle is, of course, its lack of clarity and the uncertainty which it would introduce into the application of the exclusionary rule. It remains to be seen whether the Irish courts would be attracted to this doctrine as a means of curtailing the ambit of the exclusionary rule.

(iv) Intentional breach of constitutional rights

7–41 It appears that, where a breach of constitutional rights has been deliberate or *mala fide,* the courts will eschew the strict causation requirement and exclude not just evidence obtained as a result of the breach but also evidence obtained after the breach occurs in order to deprive the gardaí of the "fruits" of their unconstitutional actions. The leading authority in this regard is *Trimbole v Governor of Mountjoy Prison*,[96] where the prosecutor had been arrested and detained under s.30 of the Offences Against the State Act 1939 without any reasonable suspicion to ground the arrest, in order to ensure that he would be available for extradition. Finlay CJ, having reviewed

---

[92] [2010] ECHR 759, (2010) 52 EHRR 1 at [274]. A similar conclusion was reached by the UK Supreme Court in *Her Majesty's Advocate v P* [2012] UKSC 108, [2011] 1 WLR 2497.
[93] [1995] 2 SCR 206, (1995) 124 DLR (4th) 7. See Wiseman, "The Derivative Imperative: An Analysis of Derivative Evidence in Canada" (1997) 39 Crim LQ 435.
[94] See also *R. v Stillman* [1997] 1 SCR 607, (1997) 144 DLR (4th) 193.
[95] See *Nix v Williams* (1984) 467 US 431; *R. v Black* [1989] 2 SCR 138; *R. v Stillman* [1997] 1 SCR 607, (1995) 144 DLR (4th) 193; *Gäfgen v Germany* [2010] ECHR 759, (2011) 52 EHRR 1.
[96] [1985] IR 550, [1985] ILRM 465.

a number of authorities including *O'Brien*, laid down three principles which he said were of general application:

> "The courts have not only an inherent jurisdiction but a positive duty:
> (i)   to protect persons against the invasion of their constitutional rights;
> (ii) if invasion has occurred, to restore as far as possible the person so damaged to the position in which he would be if his rights had not been invaded; and
> (iii) to ensure as far as possible that persons acting on behalf of the Executive who consciously and deliberately violate the constitutional rights of citizens do not for themselves or their superiors obtain the planned results of that invasion."[97]

7–42   It can be seen from the third of these principles that the courts can use the exclusionary rule as a means, not only to vindicate the constitutional rights of an accused, but also to deter unconstitutional actions on the part of the gardaí. It is noteworthy that, in rejecting the application of the *Trimbole* principles on the facts in *People (DPP) v Cooney*,[98] Keane J laid emphasis on the fact that "[t]he infringement by the garda officers of the appellant's constitutional rights was not *mala fide*: his unlawful detention was the result of their misunderstanding of the true legal position".[99] The implication appears to be that, if the gardaí had acted *mala fides*, the Court might have applied the exclusionary rule in a more expansive fashion so as to preclude the impugned in-court identification evidence from being given.

(c) Extraordinary excusing circumstances

7–43   Evidence obtained as a result of a breach of the constitutional rights of an accused may be admitted at the discretion of the trial judge where he or she is satisfied that there are extraordinary excusing circumstances which excuse the violation of the rights of the accused. In *People (AG) v O'Brien*,[100] Walsh J gave three examples of such "extraordinary excusing circumstances": (i) the need to prevent the imminent destruction of vital evidence; (ii) the need to rescue a victim in peril; and (iii) evidence obtained by a search incidental to and contemporaneous with a lawful arrest although made without a valid search warrant.[101] However, only the first of these can properly be regarded as an extraordinary excusing circumstance because a breach of constitutional rights is not actually involved in the case of the need to rescue a victim in peril[102] or in the case of evidence obtained by a search incidental to and contemporaneous with a lawful arrest although made without a valid search warrant.[103]

7–44   The leading authority with regard to the exception in respect of the imminent

---

[97]   [1985] IR 550 at 573, [1985] ILRM 465 at 484.
[98]   [1998] 1 ILRM 321.
[99]   [1998] 1 ILRM 321 at 331.
[100] [1965] IR 142 at 170.
[101] Kingsmill Moore J, in his judgment (at 162), agreed that there might be certain "extraordinary excusing circumstances" which could warrant the admission of unconstitutionally obtained evidence but preferred not to enumerate such circumstances by anticipation going so far as to say that the "facts of individual cases vary so widely that any hard and fast rules of a general nature seem to me dangerous".
[102] See *People (DPP) v Shaw* [1982] IR 1, and *DPP v Delaney* [1997] 3 IR 453, [1998] 1 ILRM 536, discussed above.
[103] At common law, the power of a police officer who had effected a lawful arrest to conduct a search of the arrested person and retain objects found in the course of the search without a search warrant was, at the time of the decision in *O'Brien*, well established and was subsequently confirmed in *Jennings v Quinn* [1968] IR 305 at 309, and *People (DPP) v McFadden* [2003] 2 ILRM 1.

destruction of vital evidence is the decision of Carney J in *Freeman v DPP*.[104] In that case, two gardaí had gone to the appellant's house in Cabra where he had been seen, with two other men, unloading goods from a van and carrying them into the house. When the gardaí approached the house, they were spotted by the men who ran into the house and slammed the door behind them. After banging on the door and identifying themselves, the gardaí entered the house where they found cigarettes, spirits and other items. On an appeal by way of case stated, Carney J held that the gardaí had violated the guarantee of inviolability of the dwelling in Art.40.5 and went on to consider whether the evidence obtained could be admitted because of the need to prevent the imminent destruction of vital evidence. He was conscious of the fact that to give too wide a scope to this exception might "undermine the rationale of a rule which by its nature is invoked in circumstances where well meaning haste on the part of the gardaí may lead to unconstitutional acts".[105] Thus, he emphasised that the exception is directed towards the "imminent destruction" of vital evidence rather than the gathering of such evidence. However, he was of opinion that the facts of the case fell squarely within the exception. The gardaí had caught the appellant and his associates *in flagrante delicto* and there had not been enough time for the gardaí to obtain the necessary search warrant.

7–45   It is, however, difficult to square the actual decision on the facts in *Freeman* with the ostensible determination of Carney J not to adopt an expansive interpretation of the "imminent destruction of evidence" exception. Although the gardaí had come upon the appellant and his associates acting suspiciously and they fled into the house upon their arrival, it would seem as if the gardaí had no *specific* reason to believe that the appellant and his associates were about to destroy vital evidence other than a general belief to that effect. Indeed, the nature of the contraband involved was such that, unlike drugs, for example, it would be difficult to destroy or conceal the evidence.[106] It would seem, therefore, as if it was the element of haste and the view of the gardaí that there was not enough time to get a warrant which was determinative. This would not appear to be consistent with the requirement that there be a risk of *imminent destruction* of vital evidence.

7–46   Although it is clear that the examples of extraordinary excusing circumstances given by Walsh J in *O'Brien* were non-exhaustive,[107] there has, to date, been relatively little consideration of what other categories of circumstances might qualify. However, it appears that the courts, mindful of the risk of undercutting the protection afforded by the exclusionary rule, will adopt a restrictive approach in this regard. Most notably, in *People (DPP) v O'Loughlin*,[108] it was held by the Court of Criminal Appeal that the trial judge had been wrong to take the view that the illegal detention of the applicant could be excused by the requirements of the public interest in the investigation of criminal offences.[109]

---

[104] [1996] 3 IR 565.

[105] [1996] 3 IR 565 at 576.

[106] *Cf. People (DPP) v Lawless* (1985) 3 Frewen 30 (forced entry into premises on foot of a search warrant granted under the Misuse of Drugs Act 1977 in circumstances where the noise of a flushing toilet was heard).

[107] In *People (DPP) v Shaw* [1982] IR 1 at 33, Walsh J stated that the examples given in *O'Brien* were simply illustrative and were not meant to be exhaustive.

[108] [1979] IR 85.

[109] See also *People (DPP) v Dillon* [2003] 1 ILRM 531, where Hardiman J stated, *obiter*, that if the gardaí had acted entirely outside the terms of the Postal and Telecommunications Services

4. Civil Cases

7–47 Having regard to the doctrinal basis of the exclusionary rule, which as seen above is grounded in the provisions of Art.40.3, there does not appear to be any reason, as a matter of principle, why it should not also be applied in civil cases. Indeed, given the seriousness of the findings that may be made in some civil cases,[110] it is clear that the availability of the compensatory remedy of the exclusionary rule may be just as important in the civil context. It is not surprising, therefore, that it has been held that the exclusionary rule may apply in civil cases[111] and even in administrative proceedings.[112]

7–48 The leading authority is *The Competition Authority v The Irish Dental Association*.[113] In that case, a search warrant executed by the plaintiff contained an error which rendered it invalid. McKechnie J was satisfied that the defendant's constitutional rights of freedom of association, freedom of expression and privacy had been breached by the illegal search and that the exclusionary rule applied. He accepted that the error in the warrant had not been adverted to before it had been executed and that the plaintiff had acted *bona fide*. However, applying the decision in *People (DPP) v Kenny*,[114] he held that the breach of constitutional rights was "deliberate and conscious" because the plaintiff had knowingly, deliberately and intentionally entered and searched the defendant's premises and taken away material. Accordingly, the court had no discretion and the material obtained on foot of the invalid search warrant had to be excluded.

5. Reform of the Exclusionary Rule

7–49 The strictness of the absolute exclusionary rule adopted by the Supreme Court in *People (DPP) v Kenny*[115] stands in marked contrast to the approaches adopted in other jurisdictions which all seek to strike a balance between the competing public interests.[116]

7–50 A century ago, in *Weeks v United States*,[117] the US Supreme Court declared that, if documents that were unlawfully seized could be used in evidence against an accused, "the protection of the Fourth Amendment declaring his right to be secure against such searches and seizures is of no value, and, so far as those thus placed are concerned,

---

Act 1983 in intercepting a telephone call, it would be very difficult for the State to establish "extraordinary excusing circumstances".

[110] See the decision in *Banco Ambrosiano Spa v Ansbacher & Co. Ltd* [1987] ILRM 669 and the subsequent case law on the standard of proof in civil cases which is discussed in Chap.2.

[111] *OC v TC*, unreported, High Court, 9 December 1981 at 5–6; *Universal City Studios Ltd v Mulligan* [1999] 3 IR 392 at 404. There was a suggestion in *P v Q* [2012] IEHC 593 at [36], [2012] 3 IR 805 at 812, [2014] 1 ILRM 144 at 151 that the exclusionary rule may have a more attenuated application in proceedings concerned with the welfare of a minor because of the requirement to balance rights.

[112] *Kennedy v Law Society of Ireland (No.3)* [2002] 2 IR 458 at 490. However, Fennelly J pointed out in that case that the application of the exclusionary rule in the sphere of administrative proceedings would necessarily be limited.

[113] [2005] IEHC 361, [2006] 1 ILRM 383.

[114] [1990] 2 IR 110, [1990] ILRM 569.

[115] [1990] 2 IR 110, [1990] ILRM 569.

[116] For a review of the approaches in Canada, Australia and New Zealand, see Choo & Nash, "Improperly obtained evidence in the Commonwealth: lessons for England and Wales?" (2007) 11 E & P 75.

[117] (1914) 232 US 383 at 393.

might as well be stricken from the Constitution". In *Mapp v Ohio*,[118] the exclusionary rule was held to be an essential part of both the Fourth and Fourteenth Amendment with the result that it was also binding on the States. However, with a change in the doctrinal basis of the exclusionary rule from a concern about the legitimacy of the criminal justice system[119] to a deterrence rationale[120] came curtailment of the scope of application of the rule. In particular, the introduction in *United States v Leon*[121] of a "good faith" exception so that the exclusionary rule did not apply where a police officer did not realise that he or she was breaching the rights of the accused had a significant attenuating effect. That process of retrenchment has continued[122] with a majority of the Supreme Court holding in *Herring v United States*[123] that an accused's Fourth Amendment rights are not violated and the exclusionary rule does not apply when police mistakes that lead to unlawful searches are the result of isolated instances of negligence. Delivering the Opinion of the Court, Roberts CJ said:

> "To trigger the exclusionary rule, police conduct must be sufficiently deliberate that exclusion can meaningfully deter it, and sufficient culpable that such deterrence is worth the price paid by the justice system. As laid out in our cases, the exclusionary rule serves to deter deliberate, reckless, or grossly negligent conduct or in some circumstances recurring or systemic negligence."[124]

7–51 Although the majority accepted that the application of the rule in circumstances of negligence created an incentive to act with greater care and would have some deterrent effect, they considered that exclusion in those circumstances was not worth the cost.[125]

7–52 Across the border in Canada, the exclusionary rule is constitutionally mandated with s.24(2) of the Canadian Charter of Rights and Freedoms stipulating that where, "a court concludes that evidence was obtained in a manner that infringed or denied any right of freedoms guaranteed by this Charter, the evidence shall be excluded if it is established that, having regard to all the circumstances, the admission of it in the proceedings would bring the administration of justice into disrepute". The leading authority on the application of this exclusionary rule is *R. v Grant*[126] where the Canadian Supreme Court established a three part test to be applied in deciding whether to exclude evidence because of a Charter violation:

> "A review of the authorities suggests that whether the admission of evidence obtained in

---

[118] (1961) 367 US 643.

[119] See *Olmstead v United States* (1928) 277 US 438; *Terry v Ohio* (1968) 392 US 112.

[120] See *United States v Calandra* (1974) 414 US 338; *Stone v Powell* (1976) 428 US 465; *United States v Leon* (1983) 468 US 987.

[121] (1983) 468 US 987 at 906.

[122] See *Hudson v United States* (2006) 547 US 586; *Herring v United States* (2009) 555 US 135; *Davis v United States* (2011) 131 St Ct 2419.

[123] (2009) 555 US 135.

[124] (2009) 555 US 135 at 144.

[125] For commentary on recent developments in relation to the exclusionary rule in the US, see Alschuler, "Herring v. United States: A Minnow or a Shark?" (2009) 7 Ohio State J Crim Law 463; Tomkovicz, "The Exclusion Revolution Continues" (2011) 9 Ohio State J Crim Law 381; Bradley, "Is the Exclusionary Rule Dead?" (2012) 102 J Crim Law & Criminology 1; Maclin & Rader "No More Chipping Away: The Roberts Court Uses an Axe to Take Out the Fourth Amendment Exclusionary Rule." (2012) 81 Miss LJ 1183; Re, "The Due Process Exclusionary Rule" (2014) 127 Harv Law Rev 1885.

[126] [2009] 2 SCR 353. See Jocelson & Kramar "Situating exclusion of evidence analysis in its socio-legal place: a tale of judicial populism" (2014) 61 CL & SC 541.

breach of the *Charter* would bring the administration of justice into disrepute engages three avenues of inquiry, each rooted in the public interests engaged by s. 24(2), viewed in a long-term, forward-looking and societal perspective. When faced with an application for exclusion under s. 24(2), a court must assess and balance the effect of admitting the evidence on society's confidence in the justice system having regard to: (1) the seriousness of the *Charter*-infringing state conduct (admission may send the message the justice system condones serious state misconduct), (2) the impact of the breach on the *Charter*-protected interests of the accused (admission may send the message that individual rights count for little), and (3) society's interest in the adjudication of the case on its merits. The court's role on a s. 24(2) application is to balance the assessments under each of these lines of inquiry to determine whether, considering all the circumstances, admission of the evidence would bring the administration of justice into disrepute."[127]

7–53   Turning to the southern hemisphere, in *HKSAR v Muhammad Riaz Khan*,[128] the Court of Final Appeal in Hong Kong summarised the test to be applied in determining whether or not to admit evidence that has been obtained in a manner that violates an accused's constitutional rights as follows:

"Evidence obtained in breach of a defendant's constitutional rights can nevertheless be received if, upon a careful examination of the circumstances, its reception (i) is conducive to a fair trial, (ii) is reconcilable with the respect due to the right or rights concerned, (iii) appears unlikely to encourage any future breaches of that, those or other rights. The risk-assessment called for under the third element will always be made by the courts, vigilantly of course, in the light of their up-to-date experience. Thus is achieved, consistently with the constitution, a proper balance between the interests of individual defendants and those of society as a whole. It cannot have been the framers' intention – and is not the constitution's effect – to stand in the way of such of [sic] balance being struck. Just as rationality and proportionality can justify an impact on a non-absolute constitutional right, so can they justify a discretion to receive evidence obtained in breach of a constitutional right. Under the test stated above, the discretion concerned is rational and proportionate. The factors to be taken into account in applying this test and the weight to be accorded to each such factor will depend on the circumstances of each case."[129]

7–54   A balancing test has also been adopted in New Zealand. In a series of cases, including *R. v Goodwin*,[130] in which the decision in *Kenny* was referred to with approval, the New Zealand Court of Appeal had adopted the vindication principle and laid down a *prima facie* rule of exclusion in respect of evidence obtained in breach of the New Zealand Bill of Rights Act 1990. However, in *R. v Shaheed*,[131] the Court of Appeal, while maintaining the vindication principle as the doctrinal basis for the exclusionary jurisdiction, abandoned the *prima facie* rule of exclusion in favour of a balancing exercise:

"To be sure, there are some good arguments favouring a rule expressed in *prima facie* terms: it recognises the importance of a guaranteed right; exclusion may be the only effective means of vindicating a breach; it diminishes the appearance that the Courts are deciding cases on

---

[127]   [2009] 2 SCR 353 at [71]. For a detailed review of the Canadian authorities, see Lederman, Bryant and Fuerst, *Sopinka, Lederman & Bryant: The Law of Evidence in Canada* 4th edn (Lexis Nexis, 2014), Chap.9. See also Jocelson & Kramar "Situating exclusion of evidence analysis in its socio-legal place: a tale of judicial populism" (2014) 61 CL & SC 541.

[128]   [2012] HKCFA 38, [2012] 4 HKC 66. See Mujuzi, "The admissibility of evidence obtained as a result of violating the accused's rights: analysing the test set by the Hong Kong Court of Final Appeal in *HKSAR v Muhammad Riaz Khan*" (2012) 16 E & P 425.

[129]   [2010] NKCFA 38, [2012] 4 HKC 66 at [20].

[130]   [1993] 2 NZLR 153.

[131]   [2002] 2 NZLR 377. See Optican, "The new exclusionary rule: interpretation and application of *R. v Shaheed*" [2004] NZ Law Rev 451.

the basis of ends rather than means; and it makes it clear to the police that there is no utility in obtaining evidence via a breach of rights.

There is much force in these arguments, although the last of them is of greater relevance to a deterrence-centred regime. But a balancing test in which, as a starting point, appropriate and significant weight is given to the fact that there has been a breach of a quasi-constitutional right, can accommodate and meet them. Importantly, a *prima facie* rule does not have the appearance of adequately addressing the interest of the community that those who are guilty of serious crimes should not go unpunished. That societal interest, in which any victim's interest is subsumed, rather than being treated as a separate interest, will not normally outweigh an egregious breach of rights—particularly one which is deliberate or reckless on the part of law enforcement officers. But where the disputed evidence is strongly probative of guilt of a serious crime, that factor too must be given due weight. A system of justice will not command the respect of the community if each and every substantial breach of an accused's rights leads almost inevitably to the exclusion of crucial evidence which is reliable and probative of a serious crime. The vindication will properly be seen as unbalanced and disproportionate to the circumstances of the breach. ...

A careful consideration of the experience in this country and the other broadly comparable jurisdictions is persuasive that the proper approach is to conduct a balancing exercise in which the fact that there has been a breach of the accused's guaranteed right is a very important but not necessarily determinative factor. The breach of a right would be given considerable weight...But it might, in the end, be held to be outweighed by the accumulation of other factors. In such a case, the conscientious carrying out of the balancing exercise will at least demonstrate that the right has been taken seriously."[132]

7–55 The exclusion of evidence by reason of a breach of the Bill of Rights Act is now governed by s.30 of the Evidence Act 2006, subs.(2) of which requires the trial judge, where evidence has been improperly obtained, to "determine whether or not the exclusion of the evidence is proportionate to the impropriety by means of a balancing process that gives appropriate weight to the impropriety but also takes proper account of the need for an effective and credible system of justice." Section 30(3) enumerates a non-exhaustive list of matters to which regard may be had: (a) the importance of any right breached by the impropriety and the seriousness of the intrusion on it; (b) the nature of the impropriety, in particular, whether it was deliberate, reckless, or done in bad faith; (c) the nature and quality of the improperly obtained evidence; (d) the seriousness of the offence with which the defendant is charged; (e) whether there were any other investigatory techniques not involving any breach of the rights that were known to be available but were not used; (f) whether there are alternative remedies to exclusion of the evidence which can adequately provide redress to the defendant; (g) whether the impropriety was necessary to avoid apprehended physical danger to the police or others; and (h) whether there was any urgency in obtaining the improperly obtained evidence.

7–56 The leading authority in New Zealand on the exercise of the discretion conferred by s.30 is *Hamed v R*.[133] Tipping J emphasised that the concept of "an effective and credible system of justice" was not solely a counterpoint to the impropriety involved in

---

[132] [2002] 2 NZLR 377 at 418–419 (*per* Richardson P, Blanchard and Tipping JJ.). The Court went on (at 419–421) to identify the factors which are likely to be relevant to the balancing exercise as follows: the value which the right protects and the seriousness of the intrusion on it; whether the breach has been committed deliberately or with reckless disregard of the suspect's rights or has arisen through gross carelessness on the part of the police; whether other investigatory techniques, not involving any breach of rights, were known to be available and not used; the nature and quality of the disputed evidence; the centrality of the evidence to the prosecution's case; and, in some cases, the availability of an alternative remedy or remedies.

[133] [2011] NZSC 10. See Gallavin & Wall, "Search and surveillance, and the exclusion of evidence in New Zealand: clarity or confusion?" (2012) 16 E & P 199.

obtaining the evidence and involved not only a focus on the immediate case before the court but also a longer term and wider focus on the administration of justice generally:

> "The admission of improperly obtained evidence must always, to a greater or lesser extent, tend to undermine the rule of law. By enacting s.30 Parliament has indicated that in appropriate cases improperly obtained evidence should be admitted, but the longer-term effect of doing so on an effective and credible system of justice must always be considered, as well as what may be seen as the desirability of having the immediate trial take place on the basis of all relevant and reliable evidence, despite its provenance. As the Supreme Court of Canada recently put it in *R. v Grant*,[134] the short-term public clamour for a conviction in a particular case must not deafen the judge to the longer-term repute of the administration of justice. Moreover, while the public has a heightened interest in seeing a determination on the merits where the offence charged is serious, it also has a vital interest in having a justice system that is above reproach, particularly when the penal stakes for the accused are high. The seriousness of the offence charged is apt to cut both ways."[135]

7–57 He went on to analyse the individual factors listed in s.30(3) and said that "the ultimate assessment involves striking a balance between the weight of the factors which favour exclusion and the weight of those which favour admission".[136]

7–58 What emerges from this very condensed overview of other jurisdictions is that Ireland is something of an outlier with the strictest exclusionary rule of any major common law jurisdiction. While that does not, of itself, indicate that the decision in *People (DPP) v Kenny*[137] is wrong, it does give pause for thought as why Ireland is so out of step with other jurisdictions with similar legal systems which share similar constitutional values. The review also indicates the dynamic nature of the jurisprudence in this area with significant changes in the formulation and application of the exclusionary rule occurring in jurisdictions as the assessment of where the balance should be struck between the rights of a criminal defendant and societal interests change over time.

7–59 It is also of some significance that, apart from evidence obtained by torture or inhuman or degrading treatment in breach of art.3 of the European Convention on Human Rights,[138] the European Court of Human Rights has eschewed a *Kenny* style exclusionary rule. In *Schenk v Switzerland*[139] the Court emphasised that the rules of admissibility of evidence were primarily a matter for national courts unless the admission of evidence imperilled the fairness of a trial guaranteed by art.6:

> "While art.6 of the Convention guarantees the right to a fair trial, it does not lay down any rules on the admissibility of evidence as such, which is therefore primarily a matter for regulation under national law.
> The Court therefore cannot exclude as a matter of principle and in the abstract that unlawfully obtained evidence of the present kind may be admissible. It has only to ascertain whether Mr. Schenk's trial as a whole was fair."[140]

7–60 That approach was endorsed in *Khan v UK*.[141] In that case, the applicant had been convicted of drugs offences solely on the basis of evidence obtained by the use of

---

[134] [2009] 2 SCR 353 at [84].
[135] [2011] NZSC 10 at [230].
[136] [2011] NZSC 10 at [231].
[137] [1990] 2 IR 110, [1990] ILRM 569.
[138] *Jalloh v Germany* [2006] ECHR 721, (2007) 44 EHRR 32; *Gäfgen v Germany* [2010] ECHR 759, (2011) 52 EHRR 1; *Levinta v Moldova* (2011) 52 EHRR 40.
[139] (1991) 13 EHRR 242.
[140] (1991) 13 EHRR 242 at 265–266.
[141] [1997] AC 558, [1996] 3 All ER 289 (HL), (2000) 31 EHRR 1016 (ECHR).

an aural surveillance device in circumstances which were found to constitute a breach of art.8 of the Convention. At his trial, he failed to have the evidence excluded under the provisions of s.78 of the Police and Criminal Evidence Act 1984 which confers on a trial judge a general exclusionary discretion that may be exercised where, having regard to all the circumstances, including the circumstances in which the evidence was obtained, the admission of the evidence would have such an adverse effect on the fairness of the proceedings that the court ought not to admit it. His appeal against conviction was dismissed with the House of Lords holding that, having regard to the circumstances, including the facts that the trespass was slight and the criminal conduct being investigated was very serious, the breach of art.8 was outweighed by the public interest in the detection of crime and could not be regarded as having such an adverse effect on the fairness of the proceedings that the judge ought to have exercised his discretion to exclude it under s.78.[142] A majority of the European Court of Human Rights held that the admission of the evidence did not involve a breach of art.6(1) of the Convention:

> "While article 6 guarantees the right to a fair hearing, it does not lay down any rules on the admissibility of evidence as such, which is therefore primarily a matter for regulation under national law. It is not the role of the court to determine, as a matter of principle, whether particular types of evidence—for example, unlawfully obtained evidence—may be admissible or, indeed, whether the applicant was guilty or not. The question which must be answered is whether the proceedings as a whole, including the way in which the evidence was obtained, were fair. This involves an examination of the 'unlawfulness' in question and, where violation of another Convention right is concerned, the nature of the violation found."[143]

7–61 The Court, thus, rejected the mandatory exclusionary rule for breaches of the Convention propounded by Judge Loucaides in his dissenting opinion.[144]

7–62 The Court identified the central issue as being whether the proceedings as a whole were fair and, in reaching the conclusion that they were, the Court emphasised the fact that the applicant had ample opportunity to challenge the admissibility of the evidence at his trial. Further, at each level of jurisdiction, the domestic courts had assessed the effect of the admission of the evidence on the fairness of the trial by reference to s.78 of the Police and Criminal Evidence Act 1984. The Court emphasised that "had the domestic courts been of the view that the admission of the evidence would have given rise to substantive unfairness, they would have had a discretion to exclude it under section 78 of PACE."[145]

---

[142] For a general discussion of this area, see Grievling, "Fairness and the Exclusion of Evidence under s.78(1) of the Police and Criminal Evidence Act" (1997) 113 LQR 667, and Fitzpatrick and Taylor, "Human Rights and the Discretionary Exclusion of Evidence" (2001) 65 JCL 349.

[143] (2000) 31 EHRR 1016 at 1025–1026. The wide margin of appreciation afforded by the European Court of Human Rights in this regard has been the subject of academic criticism: see Friedman, "From Due Deference to Due Process" [2002] EHRLR 216.

[144] Judge Loucaides stated (at 1031): "I cannot accept that a trial can be 'fair', as required by Art.6, if a person's guilt for any offence is established through evidence obtained in breach of the human rights guaranteed by the Convention. It is my opinion that the term 'fairness', when examined in the context of the European Convention on Human Rights, implies observance of the rule of law and for that matter it presupposes respect of the human rights set out in the Convention."

[145] This approach was reaffirmed by both the English courts and the European Court of Human Rights in *PG v UK*, Application No.44787/98, 25 September 2001, [2002] Crim LR 308 and *Allan v UK* (2003) 36 EHRR 143. For a discussion of these cases and the current position in the UK, see Ashworth, "Article 6 and the Fairness of Trials" [1999] Crim LR 261; Ormerod, "ECHR and the Exclusion of Evidence: Trial Remedies for Article 8 Breaches?" [2003] Crim LR 61; Ashworth,

7–63   Against the backdrop of that comparative survey, some observations can be made about the decision in *People (DPP) v Kenny*[146] and the absolute exclusionary rule established thereby. It is submitted that the Supreme Court was correct to endorse the vindication principle. This principle provides the most satisfactory doctrinal base for the exclusionary rule in this jurisdiction because it is consistent with the general jurisprudence of the courts relating to the protection of constitutional rights. Article 40.3.1 imposes a duty on the organs of State, including the courts, to defend and vindicate the personal rights of the citizen.[147] It follows that if those rights are violated, an effective remedy must be provided. As O'Dálaigh CJ emphasised in *State (Quinn) v Ryan*[148]:

> "It is not the intention of the Constitution in guaranteeing the fundamental rights of the citizen that these rights should be set at nought or circumvented. The intention was that rights of substance were being assured to the individual and that the courts were the custodians of these rights. As a necessary corollary it follows that no one can with impunity set these rights at nought or circumvent them and that the courts' powers in this regard are as ample as the defence of the Constitution requires."[149]

7–64   Thus, as stated by Finlay CJ in *Trimbole v Governor of Mountjoy Prison*,[150] if an invasion of constitutional rights occurs, the courts "have not only an inherent jurisdiction but a positive duty … to restore as far as possible the person so damaged to the position in which he would be if his rights had not been invaded". Although other remedies exist, such as police disciplinary procedures, tortious remedies and criminal law, and these have been promoted as alternatives to the exclusion of unconstitutionally obtained evidence, they are not as effective as an exclusionary rule[151] and, in particular, do not have an equivalent compensatory effect.

7–65   It is, therefore, submitted that the judicially created remedy of the exclusionary rule can properly be regarded as constitutionally mandated in fulfilment of the State's obligation to protect and vindicate the constitutional rights of the citizen.[152] However, a number of criticisms can be made of the decision of the majority in *Kenny*. The first, and most obvious, is that the judgment of Finlay CJ is based on the false premise that the

---

"Commenting on *PG v UK*" [2002] Crim LR 308; Nash, "Case Note: Balancing Convention Rights: *PG & JH v UK*" (2002) 6 IJEP 125.

[146]   [1990] 2 IR 110, [1990] ILRM 569.

[147]   *People (DPP) v Shaw* [1982] IR 1 at 62 (*per* Kenny J); *People (DPP) v Kenny* [1990] 2 IR 110 at 133, [1990] ILRM 569 at 578 (*per* Finlay CJ). In *Shaw*, Kenny J drew attention to the use of the words "the State" in Art.40.3 and stated that the "obligation to implement this guarantee is imposed not on the Oireachtas only but on each branch of the State which exercises the powers of legislating, executing and giving judgment on those laws: Art. 6". In the context of the courts, this obligation is reinforced by the oath which judges are required to take pursuant to Art.34.5 to uphold the provisions of the Constitution.

[148]   [1965] IR 70 at 122.

[149]   See also *Byrne v Ireland* [1972] IR 241 at 281 where Walsh J stated: "Where the People by the Constitution create rights against the State or impose duties upon the State, a remedy to enforce these must be deemed to be also available."

[150]   [1985] IR 550 at 573, [1985] ILRM 465 at 484.

[151]   See *Wolf v Colorado* (1949) 338 US 25 at 42–43, where Murphy J discusses and discounts, as alternatives to the exclusionary rule, the prosecution of or civil actions against police officers who violate the constitutional rights of accused persons.

[152]   *DPP v McCrea* [2009] IEHC 39 at 33. O'Connor, "Admissibility of Unconstitutionally Obtained Evidence" (1982) 17 Ir Jur 257 at 290–293, has argued that the exclusionary rule is not just a judicially created remedy and that an accused has, by virtue of Art.40, a correlative right to have unconstitutionally obtained evidence excluded from his trial.

Court was required to make a choice between *two* possible alternatives, the "deterrent principle" and the "principle of absolute protection". Central to the judgment of Finlay CJ was the unstated proposition that, once the theory of vindication is accepted as the rationale for the exclusionary rule, it necessarily follows that all unconstitutionally obtained evidence must be excluded, i.e. an "absolute rule of exclusion" must be adopted. However, this is not the case.

7–66 In the first place, it is important to emphasise that the exclusionary rule is a judicially created remedy. It is open to the courts to fashion the parameters of the rule and to hold that the compensatory effect of the rule should only be available where the person who breached the constitutional rights of the accused had a particular intention or state of knowledge.

7–67 Secondly, insofar as the vindication principle is grounded on the provisions of the Constitution and, in particular, of Art. 40.3, it is evident that the obligations imposed on the State by Art. 40.3 are qualified by considerations of practicality in that the State guarantees to defend and vindicate the personal rights of the citizen "as far as practicable" and to protect those personal rights "as best it may" from unjust attack. These limitations were adverted to in *Moynihan v Greensmith*,[153] where O'Higgins CJ stated:

> "…the guarantee of protection given by Article 40, s.3, subs.2, is qualified by the words 'as best it may'. This implies circumstances in which the State may have the balance its protection of the rights as against other obligations arising from regard for the common good."[154]

7–68 Arguably, the impairment of the truth-finding function of the courts entrusted, under the Constitution, with the task of administering justice places a limit on the practicality of vindicating the constitutional rights of the citizen. The courts could, therefore, consistent with the text and underlying policy of Art. 40.3, decide that the judicially created remedy of the exclusionary rule should be tempered in its application by having regard to the constitutional rights of others such as the rights of life, bodily integrity and property of the victims of crime or, more generally, the interest of the community in the prosecution of offenders.[155]

7–69 Thirdly, the exclusionary rule espoused by Finlay CJ in *Kenny* does not, in fact, provide an "absolute rule of exclusion" because he endorsed the holding in *O'Brien* that the exclusionary rule would not apply if there are extraordinary excusing circumstances. These exceptions which, as enumerated by Walsh J in *O'Brien*, include the imminent destruction of vital evidence and the need to rescue a victim in peril, are clearly predicated on the proposition that there are circumstances where the vindication of the constitutional rights of the accused is not required because of competing constitutional

---

[153] [1977] IR 55.

[154] [1977] IR 55 at 71.

[155] It must be acknowledged that this argument was expressly rejected in *People (DPP) v Healy* [1990] 2 IR 73 at 87–88, [1990] ILRM 313 at 327. McCarthy J, responding to the argument of the DPP that there had to be a balancing of the constitutional rights of the accused and those of the public, said that it overlooked the fact that "[q]uite apart from the interest of the public in the investigation of, punishment for and suppression of crime, the public has a deep interest in ensuring that the individual citizen is not denied any personal right." This is correct but does not explain why, in a conflict between the two interests, the rights of an accused must necessarily win out.

rights or the public interest in the prosecution of offenders. Thus, balancing is required in a limited number of instances.

7–70   Another criticism of the decision in *Kenny* is that the Court, having effectively re-cast the *O'Brien* exclusionary rule, failed to dispense with the requirement that a breach of constitutional rights be "deliberate and conscious".[156] Although the etymology of this formulation is evident, its retention is confusing and, furthermore, its re-interpretation as meaning that the act constituting the breach must be intentional is illogical. If the Court, as Finlay CJ states, is adopting an "absolute rule of exclusion", then it would seem to be irrelevant whether the act that breached the constitutional right of the accused was "deliberate and conscious" because the application of the exclusionary rule would be triggered by the mere fact that the constitutional right had been breached. Thus, the retention of the requirement that the breach be "deliberate and conscious" does not make any sense and the only value in its retention would be its function as a quasi *de minimis* qualification. Yet, it performs this function only inadequately, and it would be much better to actually articulate a *de minimis* threshold.

7–71   In recent times, there have been expressions of judicial discontent in this jurisdiction about the harshness of what Geoghegan J has referred to as the "somewhat controversial principle" established in *Kenny*[157] and, in particular, the failure to give any sufficient weight to the public interest in the prosecution of offenders and the interests of the victims of crime. The most detailed and pointed critique to date has been delivered by Charleton J in *DPP (Walsh) v Cash*.[158] He identified three practical (and undesirable) consequences of the exclusionary rule as formulated in *Kenny*. The first is that every error on the part of agents of the State which takes their action outside the strict letter of the law causes the exclusion at trial of any evidence which directly results therefrom. The second is that every breach of an accused's rights is pleaded at trial as an infringement of the Constitution and the courts invariably accept that any breach of a legal right leads to an infringement of a constitutional right. The third is that it has become practically impossible to say when a constitutional right begins and ends.

7–72   He went on to express trenchant criticism of the exclusionary rule on the basis that it fails to weigh the public interest in the prosecution of offences and the rights of victims of crime in the balance, stating that, since *Kenny*, "the entire focus is on the accused and his rights; the rights of the community to live safely has receded out of view".[159] He noted that, in other areas where a conflict between constitutional rights has arisen, it was sought to strike a balance.[160] Further, the requirement to strike a

---

[156] It appears that this requirement remains an ingredient in the formulation of the exclusionary rule. In *Kennedy v Law Society of Ireland (No.3)* [2002] 2 IR 458 at 489, where Fennelly J referred to the decisions in *O'Brien, Shaw* and *Kenny* and stated: "That line of cases depends for the basic proposition it lays down on a finding by the court that there has been a knowing and deliberate breach of the constitutional rights of the person against whom the impugned evidence is to be tendered."

[157] *People (DPP) v Creed* [2009] IECCA 95 at [6]. In that case, a somewhat strained approach to the concept of "deliberate and conscious" was taken in order to categorise a failure to make reasonable efforts to contact a solicitor nominated by the accused as amounting to an illegality only rather than an unconstitutionality in order to avoid the application of the exclusionary rule.

[158] [2007] IEHC 108, [2008] 1 ILRM 443.

[159] [2007] IEHC 108 at [31], [2008] 1 ILRM 443 at 463.

[160] Charleton J instanced the decision in *Re Article 26 of the Constitution and the Regulation of Information (Services Outside the State for the Termination of Pregnancy) Bill 1995* [1995] 1 IR 1 in this regard.

balance between the competing rights of the accused to have the law observed and that of the community to prosecute criminal offences has been expressly recognised in other cases.[161] He expressed "difficulty in accepting that the separation of powers doctrine allows the courts to invent rules whereby juries, or judges as triers of fact in criminal cases, are deprived, on a non-discretionary basis, of considering evidence which is inherently reliable" and suggested that a "rule which remorselessly excludes evidence obtained through an illegality occurring by a mistake does not commend itself to the proper ordering of society which is the purpose of the criminal law".[162] He noted that the exclusionary rule as formulated in other jurisdictions such as New Zealand allowing a balancing of the competing interests and, having referred to the decision of the European Court of Human Rights in *X and Y v Netherlands*,[163] went so far as to suggest that "a rule providing for the automatic exclusion of evidence obtained in consequence of any mistake that infringes any constitutional right of an accused, may be incompatible with Ireland's obligations [under the Convention] to provide, for both the accused and the community, a fair disposal of criminal charges".[164] Accordingly, he was of the view that it should be possible:

> "in considering whether to exclude evidence which has been unlawfully obtained, to take into account factors other than the isolated interests of the accused, divorced from any other consideration. Criminal trials are about the rights and obligations of the entire community; of which the accused and the victim are members. It is not the function of the criminal courts to discipline police officers by causing the exclusion of evidence. Sometimes, however, the balancing of competing interests requires that exclusion in the overall interests of the administration of justice. The cases of *JT* and *B* and *X and Y* make it clear that the victim, being the subject of a crime, can have interests which should be weighed in the balance as well as those of the accused. But I would hold that the primary interest in the prosecution of crime is the maintenance of social order under the Constitution as provided for in the preamble."[165]

7–73 It was not necessary for the Supreme Court in that case to engage with those criticisms or to reconsider the decision in *Kenny*.[166] However, there has been some judicial endorsement of the views of Charleton J in subsequent decisions[167] including, perhaps most significantly, by O'Donnell J sitting in the Court of Criminal Appeal in *People (DPP) v Mallon*[168] who noted that the "remorseless logic" of *Kenny*, which led to "the automatic exclusion of evidence, sometimes as a result of quite trivial errors", had been the subject of criticism. The decision in *Kenny* was also the subject of adverse comment by a majority of the Balance in the Criminal Law Review Group[169] who considered it to be "too strictly calibrated" and were in favour of its relaxation

---

[161] Referring to the decision of the Supreme Court in *B v DPP* [1997] 3 IR 140 and of the Court of Criminal Appeal in *People (DPP) v JT* (1988) 3 Frewen 141.

[162] [2007] IEHC 108 at [65], [2008] 1 ILRM 443 at 478.

[163] (1986) 8 EHRR 235.

[164] [2007] IEHC 108 at [45], [2008] 1 ILRM 443 at 469.

[165] [2007] IEHC 108 at [50], [2008] 1 ILRM 443 at 472.

[166] Although Hardiman J did note that the portion of the judgment of Charleton J dealing with the exclusionary rule was *obiter* ([2010] IESC 1 at [31], [2010] 1 IR 609 at 621, [2010] 1 ILRM 389 at 410).

[167] In *DPP v McCrea* [2009] IEHC 39 at 30, Edwards J agreed that "the automatic exclusion of evidence due to a mistake made in good faith arguably represents an unjustifiable anomaly in the law and something which is inimical to the public's interest in the prosecution of crime" and supported Charleton J's call for a re-examination of the exclusionary rule.

[168] [2011] IECCA 31 at [5], [2011] 2 IR 544 at 550.

[169] Balance in the Criminal Law Review Group, *Final Report* (2007), p.161.

such that the "the court would have a discretion to admit the evidence or not, having regard to the totality of the circumstances and in particular the rights of the victim".[170]

7–74   At the time of writing, judgment is awaited from a seven judge Supreme Court in the case of *People (DPP) v C* where the Court has been invited by the DPP to overrule the decision in *Kenny* and replace the absolute protection rule of exclusion with a balancing test which would permit the public interest to be taken into account. The scene is, therefore, set for a re-evaluation and, quite possibly, a significant reformulation of the exclusionary rule.

C. Illegally Obtained Evidence

1. General Principles to be Applied

7–75   In *People (AG) v O'Brien*,[171] the Supreme Court split in relation to the principles to be applied in respect of illegally obtained evidence. In his judgment, Walsh J took the view that the primary function of the rules of evidence was to ensure the fair trial of an accused and that it was not the function of the courts either to deter police illegality or discipline the police. He therefore concluded that there was no discretion to exclude evidence on the ground that it had been illegally obtained. However, Kingsmill Moore J, with whom a majority of the Court concurred on this point,[172] rejected an absolute inclusionary rule as well as an absolute exclusionary rule.

7–76   He opted instead for an intermediate approach which sought to reconcile the competing policy interests in this area:

> "It is desirable in the public interest that crime should be detected and punished. It is desirable that individuals should not be subjected to illegal or inquisitorial methods of investigation and that the State should not attempt to advance its ends by utilising the fruits of such methods. It appears to me that in every case a determination has to be made by the trial judge as to whether the public interest is best served by the admission or by the exclusion of evidence of facts ascertained as a result of, and by means of, illegal actions, and that the answer to the question depends on a consideration of all the circumstances."[173]

---

[170]   The Chairman of the Group, Gerard Hogan SC (as he then was) delivered a dissenting note on the exclusionary rule (at pp.287–295) in which he argued for its retention on the basis that it was constitutionally required and that any relaxation woud significantly undermine the effectiveness of the rule. See Buggy, "A comparative analysis of the exclusionary rule: the laws of the United States and New Zealand" (2014) 24(1) ICLJ 2, which suggests that the New Zealand balancing test approach offers a preferable middle course between the US deterrence approach and the current Irish protectionist approach. See also Twomey "Poisonous fruit from a poisonous tree: reforming the exclusionary rule for Ireland—Part 1" (2012) 30(18) ILT 270 and "Poisonous fruit from a poisonous tree: reforming the exclusionary for Ireland—Part 2" (2012) 30(19) ILT 288 for a review of the position in other jurisdictions and suggestions for reform. The arguments in favour of relaxation and retention of the exclusionary rule are cogently marshalled by Mícheál P O'Higgins, "High Time to Reconsider the Exclusionary Rule?" (delivered at the Thomson Reuters Round Hall Criminal Law Conference 2013).

[171]   [1965] IR 142.

[172]   See *DPP v McMahon* [1986] IR 393 at 398–399, where the question of whether the judgment of Kingsmill Moore J should be considered a majority judgment in relation to the issue of illegally obtained evidence is discussed by Finlay CJ who took the view that it should properly be so regarded.

[173]   [1965] IR 142 at 160.

7–77   Thus, the matter was one to be decided by the exercise of judicial discretion. He went on to outline the criteria to be taken into account in the exercise of this discretion:

> "On the one hand, the nature and extent of the illegality have to be taken into account. Was the illegal action intentional or unintentional, and if intentional, was it the result of an *ad hoc* decision or does it represent a settled or deliberate policy? Was the illegality one of a trivial and technical nature or was it a serious invasion of important rights the recurrence of which would involve a real danger to necessary freedoms? Were there circumstances of urgency or emergency which provide some excuse for the action? ... The nature of the crime being investigated may also have to be taken into account."[174]

7–78   These principles have subsequently been approved and applied in a number of cases including *DPP v McMahon*.[175] In that case, the defendants had been convicted of a number of offences in respect of gaming machines on licensed premises and one of the issues raised on a case stated to the Supreme Court was in relation to the admissibility of evidence obtained unlawfully by gardaí while present on the licensed premises without a search warrant. Delivering the judgment of the Supreme Court, Finlay CJ approved the principles laid down by Kingsmill Moore J in *O'Brien,* although he expressed the opinion that the criteria enunciated by him were not to be considered as being exclusive or complete.[176] Applying these criteria to the case before him,[177] he attached particular importance to the fact that the gardaí had entered the licensed premises as trespassers only and were not involved in any criminal or opprobrious conduct. Also important, in his view, was that the offence of permitting gaming on licensed premises could be considered as having grave social consequences. He therefore, answered the case stated by saying that the evidence was admissible in evidence unless the trial judge, in the exercise of his discretion, refused to admit it.[178] McCarthy J, concurring, expressed the view, *obiter*, that if the District Judge found that there was a policy to conduct searches without a warrant, his or her discretion could only be properly exercised so as to exclude the evidence.

7–79   It is interesting to note the form of Finlay CJ's answer to the case stated. In *O'Brien*, Kingsmill Moore J was careful not to set up a presumption of admissibility or inadmissibility, the matter being one to be decided on the balance of public interest in each case. However, in *McMahon*, Finlay CJ comes close to doing so by saying that the evidence was admissible unless the trial judge chose, in his discretion, to exclude it. It is understandable that the discretionary test should be weighted towards admission because one of the main factors to be considered in the exercise by a trial judge of

---

[174] [1965] IR 142 at 160. *Cf.* the list of factors identified in *Bunning v Cross* (1978) 141 CLR 54 at 74.

[175] [1986] IR 393. See also *People (AG) v Hogan* (1972) 1 Frewen 360; *People (DPP) v Morgan* (1979) 114 ILTR 60; *People (DPP) v Lawless* (1985) 3 Frewen 30; and *McKenna v Deery* [1998] 1 IR 62. But *cf. DPP v Lennon,* unreported, High Court, 26 June 1998, where Morris J expressed the view that evidence obtained in breach of a statutory right would be inadmissible *per se*.

[176] [1986] IR 393 at 400. See also *Kennedy v Law Society of Ireland (No.3)* [2002] 2 IR 458 at 490, where Fennelly J stated that Kingsmill Moore J in *O'Brien* had "stressed the need to have regard to all the circumstances".

[177] He said that these criteria should be applied in the light of the evidence already given by the prosecution, any evidence relevant to the issue that might be adduced on behalf of the defendants and the submissions of the parties (at 400). The necessity for the trial judge to hear the evidence sought to be excluded before ruling on its admissibility was stressed in *DPP v McCutcheon* [1986] ILRM 433. See also *DPP v Clifford*, unreported, High Court, Ó Caoimh J, 22 July 2002.

[178] McCarthy J concurred with the judgment of the Chief Justice but added the rider that the trial judge might conclude, in light of the multiplicity of searches and the rank of the searching officers, that there was a policy to conduct searches without a warrant.

his or her discretion is the seriousness of the illegality.[179] Most serious illegalities are likely to also result in the breach of a constitutional right of the accused and will, thus, fall for consideration under the heading of unconstitutionally obtained evidence. Therefore, it is likely that the illegalities which fall for consideration under this heading will generally be of a relatively minor nature and, at least where the offence charged is serious, evidence obtained as a result thereof will, in most cases, be admitted.

7–80 The nature and extent of the discretion enjoyed to exclude illegally obtained evidence was also considered in *People (DPP) v Jagutis*.[180] Delivering the judgment of the Court of Criminal Appeal, Clarke J commented:

> "It is appropriate to pause to emphasise that the use of the term 'discretion' in this context does not imply that the Court can do as it pleases… In truth what the law requires is that in deciding whether to admit or exclude evidence obtained on foot of the execution of a defective warrant the court is required to take into account a broad range of circumstances before determining whether, on balance, the evidence should be admitted or excluded. The role of the court is, therefore, non-automatic. It does not automatically follow from a determination that a warrant is defective that evidence obtained on foot of the execution of the warrant is either to be admitted or to be excluded."

7–81 He went on to say that what is mandated is "a broad ranging inquiry into all relevant circumstances before determining whether illegally obtained evidence is to be admitted".[181]

2. The Custody Regulations

7–82 The Criminal Justice Act 1984 (Treatment of Persons in Custody in Garda Síochána Stations) Regulations 1987 (as amended)[182] (the "Custody Regulations") were enacted pursuant to the Criminal Justice Act 1984 (the "1984 Act")[183] and lay down various rules regulating the custody of arrested/detained persons with the object of ensuring that they are fairly treated.[184] The provisions of the Custody Regulations and the principles that are applied to the admissibility of confessions obtained where there has been a breach thereof are examined in detail in Chap.8. However, given that a breach of the Custody Regulations may also lead to the exclusion of non-testimonial evidence, the relevant principles are also dealt with in outline here.

7–83 The effect of a breach of the Custody Regulations is governed by s.7(3) of the Criminal Justice Act 1984, which provides as follows:

> "A failure on the part of any member of the Garda Síochána to observe any provision of the regulations shall not of itself render that person liable to any civil or criminal proceedings or itself affect the lawfulness of the custody of the detained person or the admissibility in evidence of any statement made by him."

---

[179] *Cf. Kennedy v Law Society of Ireland (No.3)* [2002] 2 IR 458 at 490, where Fennelly J stated that the questions posed by Kingsmill Moore J in *O'Brien* suggested that "a comparatively serious case of intentional illegality has to be established".

[180] [2013] IECCA 4.

[181] [2013] IECCA 4 at [4.10].

[182] SI No. 119 of 1987 (as amended by the Criminal Justice Act 1984 (Treatment of Persons in Custody in Garda Síochána Stations) (Amendment) Regulations 2006).

[183] Although the scope of application is not specified in the Custody Regulations, unlike the Criminal Justice Act 1984 (Electronic Recording of Interviews) Regulations 1997 (SI No.74 of 1997), it would appear that they apply whenever a person is arrested and/or detained under any legislation: *cf. DPP v Spratt* [1995] 1 IR 585, [1995] 2 ILRM 117.

[184] *Cf. People (DPP) v Smith*, unreported, Court of Criminal Appeal, 22 November 1999 at 6.

7–84 The construction of this subsection was considered in *DPP v Spratt*[185] where O'Hanlon J. stated:

> "The phrase 'of itself' is obviously an important one in the construction of the statutory provisions, and I interpret the subsection as meaning that non-observance of the regulations is not to bring about automatically the exclusion from evidence of all that was done and said while the accused person was in custody. It appears to be left to the court of trial to adjudicate in every case as to the impact the non-compliance with the regulations should have on the case for the prosecution."[186]

7–85 In *DPP (Lenihan) v McGuire*,[187] Kelly J endorsed the approach taken in *Spratt* and stated that:

> "[T]here must be a causal link between failure to comply with the relevant regulations and whatever prejudice is alleged to have been suffered by the accused as a result thereof. The appropriate question to ask it is: if a breach of the regulations has taken place, was the accused prejudiced thereby?"[188]

7–86 These principles have since been applied in a number of cases and it was been emphasised that, where a breach of the Regulations is found, it is necessary for the trial judge to adjudicate on the impact that non-compliance with the Regulations has had on the case for the prosecution and whether the accused has been prejudiced by the breach.[189]

7–87 A somewhat different approach was taken by the Court of Criminal Appeal in *People (DPP) v McFadden*[190] where greater emphasis was laid on the importance of the provision that has been breached. Keane CJ stated:

> "It is understandable that the legislature provided that a failure to observe any provision of the regulations would not of itself affect the lawfulness of the custody of the detained person or the admissibility in evidence of any statements made by him. As one would expect, the regulations contain detailed requirements as to the treatment of persons in custody, including such matters as the accurate recording of a number of aspects of his detention in documentary form. A failure to observe the requirements of the regulations could clearly in some instances be of so trivial or inconsequential a nature as not to afford a sufficient ground for treating the detention of the person as unlawful or statements made by him inadmissible."[191]

7–88 In that case, the failure of a garda to give any explanation to the applicant as to why his wallet was being searched as required by art.17(1) of the Regulations, was not regarded as being a trivial or inconsequential departure from the Regulations. It was held, therefore, that the evidence obtained as a result of the search should have been excluded. It, thus, appears that where common law or constitutional requirements are given statutory form in a provision of the Regulations, the test of admissibility may be weighted in favour of exclusion.

7–89 These authorities were considered and an alternative test, focused on the impact

---

[185] [1995] 1 IR 585, [1995] 2 ILRM 117.

[186] [1995] 1 IR 585 at 591, [1995] 2 ILRM 117 at 122.

[187] [1996] 3 IR 586.

[188] [1996] 3 IR 586 at 596. In that case, Kelly J took the view that it was extremely difficult to see how the failure complained of in that case, namely the failure of a garda to sign his name in the Station diary, could cause prejudice to the respondent.

[189] *DPP v Devlin*, unreported, High Court, 2 September 1998; *DPP v Cullen*, unreported, High Court, 7 February 2001; *DPP v Clark*, unreported, High Court, 31 May 2001; *DPP v Gillespie* [2011] IEHC 236.

[190] [2003] 2 ILRM 201.

[191] [2003] 2 ILRM 201 at 208.

of the breach of the Custody Regulations on the fairness of the trial, was put forward by Hardiman J when delivering the judgment of the Supreme Court in *People (DPP) v Diver*.[192] In that case, there had been numerous breaches of the Custody Regulations including a failure to record in any of the interviews exculpatory statements by the appellant while recording any statements consistent with guilt and it was held that:

> "Where there has been a breach of the regulations due to a failure to record 'so far as practicable' an interview with an accused, the task of the trial judge is to determine, whether in all the circumstances, the effect of the failure to observe the regulation has prejudiced the fairness of the trial of the accused other than by the fact of a breach of the regulations in themselves. The issue is not so much whether or not the breach of the regulations was of a 'trivial and inconsequential nature', although that is a factor to be taken into account, but whether the fairness of the trial of the accused would be prejudiced by the admission of statements made by him or her in respect of which the regulations were not followed."[193]

7–90 It can be seen, therefore, that where there is a serious breach of the Custody Regulations which will impact on the fairness of the trial, this will lead to the exclusion of the statements so obtained. This is consistent with applying the protective principle. However, given that the Regulations are intended to require adherence by the gardaí to certain standards of conduct in the treatment of arrested persons, it is possible that the courts, applying a deterrence/disciplinary rationale, might also exclude evidence obtained as a result of a deliberate breach of the Regulations in an appropriate case even if prejudice to an accused or an impact on the fairness of his or her trial could not be established.[194]

3. Civil Cases

7–91 The discretion to exclude illegally obtained evidence also applies in civil cases[195] including administrative proceedings.[196] However, the need for caution in applying the rule in the context of administrative tribunals was stressed in *Kennedy v Law Society of Ireland (No.3)*,[197] where Fennelly J stated:

> "The courts should be slow to adopt any mechanical exclusionary rule which makes it easy to prevent disciplinary tribunals from receiving and hearing relevant and probative material. The balance should be struck between the rights of individuals and those professional bodies assigned the task of supervising their behaviour so as to give careful weight to competing considerations: firstly, the test adopted should not unduly impede the latter types of bodies from performing their duty of protecting the public from professional misbehaviour; secondly, members of professional body should be protected from such clear abuse of power as would render it unfair that the evidence gathered as a result be received."[198]

---

[192] [2005] IESC 57, [2005] 3 IR 270.

[193] [2005] IESC 57 at [29], [2005] 3 IR 270 at 280.

[194] *Cf. DPP v Devlin*, unreported, High Court, 2 September 1998, where Budd J appeared to attach some significance to the fact that there was no finding by the District Judge that there had been a conscious and deliberate violation of the Custody Regulations or that there had been reprehensible or oppressive behaviour on the part of the gardaí.

[195] *Universal City Studios Ltd v Mulligan* [1999] 3 IR 392. That discretion has also been extended to civil cases in Scotland (*MacColl v MacColl* (1946) SLT 312) and Australia (*Pearce v Button* (1985) 60 ALR 537).

[196] *Kennedy v Law Society of Ireland (No.3)* [2002] 2 IR 458.

[197] [2002] 2 IR 458.

[198] [2002] 2 IR 458 at 490.

7–92 It was, thus, held that "an element of deliberate and knowing misbehaviour must be shown, before evidence is excluded".[199]

7–93 The decision in *Kennedy* was distinguished by McKechnie J in *The Competition Authority v The Irish Dental Association*[200] on the basis, *inter alia*, that the case before him did not involve administrative or disciplinary matters or the exercise by a professional body of a supervisory function. Accordingly, if he had concluded that the evidence at issue had been illegally obtained rather than unconstitutionally obtained by reason of the defective warrant, he would have exercised his discretion to exclude it even though he was satisfied that the error in the warrant had not been adverted to before it had been executed and that the plaintiff had acted *bona fide*. He accepted that there was a major public interest in the enforcement of competition law. However, the rights of persons thereby affected had to be protected. He noted that the Competition Act 2002 conferred considerable powers on the plaintiff which could be used for the purposes of both criminal and civil proceedings. He also observed that there had not been any pressing need for the plaintiff to move with haste and that there had been ample opportunity and time for it to make sure that the warrant relied on by it was correct. He considered that there as a major public interest underpinning public confidence in the business community with regard to the operation of the Competition Act 2002 and it was "absolutely crucial that the most core and basic document which founds the searching of premises, namely the search warrant, is correct".[201] He, therefore, concluded that the competing public interests required him to exercise his discretion so as to exclude the material in question.

D. Unfairly Obtained Evidence

7–94 In *R. v Sang*,[202] it was held that a trial judge does not have a discretion to exclude relevant evidence, other than confessions or other incriminating evidence obtained from an accused after commission of the offence, on the basis that it has been obtained by improper or unfair means. However, in New Zealand, it was accepted in a series of cases that a trial judge had a broad discretion to exclude unfairly obtained evidence where its admission would be calculated to bring the administration of justice into disrepute.[203] Examples of improper or unfair conduct which potentially attracted the exercise of that discretion included misrepresentations by police officers,[204] and the use of tricks to obtain evidence.[205] The existence of that discretion has been confirmed and the factors governing its exercise codified in s.30 of the Evidence Act 2006 by including unfairly obtained evidence within the concept of improperly obtained evidence.

---

[199] [1996] 3 IR 565 at 490.

[200] [2005] IEHC 361, [2006] 1 ILRM 383.

[201] [2005] IEHC 361 at [38], [2006] 1 ILRM 383 at 398.

[202] [1980] AC 402, 437, [1979] 2 All ER 46 at 62. *Cf.* the Canadian decision of *R. v Wray* [1971] SCR 272, (1970) 11 DLR (3d) 673.

[203] *R. v Capner* [1975] 1 NZLR 411; *Police v Lavelle* [1979] 1 NZLR 45; *R. v Loughlin* [1982] 1 NZLR 236; *R. v Smith (Malcolm)* [2000] 2 NZLR 656 at 663; *R. v Shaheed* [2002] 2 NZLR 377 at 396.

[204] *Howden v Ministry of Transport* [1987] 2 NZLR 747.

[205] *R. v Hapeta* (1988) 3 CRNZ 570.

7–95 It is submitted that such a discretion should be recognised in this jurisdiction on the basis articulated by Knight Bruce VC in *Pearse v Pearse*[206] that:

> "The discovery and vindication and establishment of truth are main purposes certainly of the existence of the courts of justice; still, for the obtaining of these objects, which however valuable and important, cannot be usefully pursued without moderation, cannot be either usefully or creditably pursued unfairly or gained by unfair means, not even channel is or ought to be open to them. ... Truth, like all other good things, may be loved unwisely—may be pursued too keenly—may cost too much."[207]

7–96 It is also consistent with the test of fundamental fairness formulated by Griffin J in the context of confession evidence in *People (DPP) v Shaw*[208]:

> "Because our system of law is accusatorial and not inquisitorial, and because ... our constitution postulates the observance of basic or fundamental fairness of procedures, the Judge presiding at a criminal trial should be astute to see that, although a statement may be technically voluntary, it should nevertheless be excluded if, by reason of the manner or of the circumstances in which it was obtained, it falls below the required standard of fairness. The reason for exclusion here is not so much the risk of an erroneous conviction as the recognition that the minimum standards must be observed in the administration of justice."

7–97 Although the test of fundamental fairness was not expressly invoked, considerations of fairness were considered in the context of the admission of non-testimonial evidence in *People (DPP) v Creed*.[209] The Court of Criminal Appeal upheld the ruling of the trial judge that, although manifestly inadequate efforts had been made to contact the solicitor nominated by the accused, there had not been a deliberate and conscious breach of his right of reasonable access to a solicitor while in custody so that the exclusionary rule in respect of unconstitutionally obtained evidence did not apply. However, it went on to hold that the trial judge had a discretion whether to admit a hair sample taken from him while in custody, saying that it did not follow that, because there had not been a deliberate and conscious breach of the right, it would be a fair procedure to admit the evidence that had been obtained in the absence of a solicitor, reasonable efforts not having been made to obtain one. Ultimately, the Court was satisfied that the trial judge had been entitled to exercise his discretion in the particular circumstances of the case to rule that the hair sample was admissible having regard to a number of factors including that the hair sample could have been obtained under the Criminal Justice (Forensic Evidence) Act 1990 without consent and that the request for a solicitor had been clearly related to the questioning which the accused was about to undergo.

---

[206] (1846) 1 De G & Sm 12.
[207] (1846) 1 De G & Sm 12 at 28–29.
[208] [1982] IR 1 at 61.
[209] [2009] IECCA 95.

CHAPTER 8

CONFESSIONS

A. Introduction

8–01 As outlined in Chapter 5, confessions (and inculpatory statements which fall short of full confessions) are admissible, by way of an exception to the hearsay rule, to prove the truth of their contents on the basis that "it is fairly presumed that no man would make such a confession against himself if the facts confessed were not true."[1] Indeed, it has been stated that a "free and voluntary confession is deserving of the highest credit, because it is presumed to flow from the strongest sense of guilt".[2]

8–02 However, the courts have long been wary of the reliability of confessions and suspicious of the methods by which they have been obtained. This judicial scepticism has, perhaps, been most memorably expressed in *R. v Thompson*,[3] where Cave J stated:

> "I always suspect these confessions, which are supposed to be the offspring of penitence and remorse, and which nevertheless are repudiated by the prisoner at the trial. It is remarkable that it is of very rare occurrence for evidence of a confession to be given when the proof of the prisoner's guilt is otherwise clear and satisfactory; but, when it is not clear and satisfactory, the prisoner is not unfrequently alleged to have been seized with the desire born of penitence and remorse to supplement it with a confession; a desire which vanishes as soon as he appears in a court of justice."[4]

8–03 The validity of those concerns has been demonstrated by a number of high profile instances of miscarriages of justice involving the admission of untrue confessions such as the Birmingham Six and the Guildford Four cases in England and the Sallins train robbery case in this jurisdiction.[5]

---

[1] *Per* Grose J in *The King v Lambe* (1791) 2 Leach 552 at 555.

[2] *R. v Warickshall* (1873) 1 Leach 263 at 263 (*per* Nares J and Eyre B.). See also, *per* Sir William Scott in *Mortimer v Mortimer* (1820) 2 Hag Con 310 at 315, "confession generally ranks high, or I should say, highest in the scale of evidence" and, *per* Erle J in *R. v Baldry* (1852) 2 Den 430 at 444, "when a confession is well proved it is the best evidence that can be produced".

[3] [1893] 2 QB 12.

[4] See also, *per* Sir William Scott in *Williams v Williams* (1798) 2 Hag Con 310 at 315, "confession is a species of evidence which, although not inadmissible, is regarded with great distrust".

[5] See further, Langwallner, "Miscarriages of Justice in Ireland; a survey of the jurisprudence with suggestions for the future" (2011) 2(1) IJLS 22; Langwallner, "Miscarriages of Justice in Ireland"

8–04   To meet concerns about the reliability of confessions and in order to protect the rights of suspects including, in particular, their right not to be compelled to incriminate themselves, a number of tests have to be met and safeguards adhered to before a confession, or an admission falling short of a full confession,[6] can be admitted in evidence. Thus, a confession will not be admitted if it was obtained in breach of an accused's constitutional rights. It will also be inadmissible if it cannot be proven by the prosecution to be a voluntary statement. In addition, a confession may be excluded, at the discretion of the trial judge, if it was obtained in breach of the Judges' Rules, the Custody Regulations,[7] the Electronic Recording Regulations[8] or in breach of the standards of fundamental fairness. Each of these different tests of admissibility is examined in detail below together with safeguards and rules that apply after a confession has been admitted into evidence.

B. Breach of Constitutional Rights

8–05   As we have seen in Chap.7, evidence obtained as a result of a breach of the constitutional rights of an accused will be inadmissible unless there are extraordinary excusing circumstances.[9] In *People (DPP) v Shaw*,[10] Griffin J, with whom a majority of the Supreme Court agreed, took the view that the exclusionary rule established in *People (AG) v O'Brien*[11] was confined in its application to real evidence and did not extend to confession evidence. The admissibility of confession evidence where there had been a breach of the constitutional rights of the accused fell, instead, to be determined by the trial judge in the exercise of his or her discretion in accordance with the standard of fundamental fairness.[12] However, this approach was subsequently repudiated in *People (DPP) v Lynch*,[13] with O'Higgins CJ stating emphatically that: "Once the Constitution has been violated for the purpose of securing a confession, the fruits of that violation must be excluded from evidence on that ground alone."[14]

(2011) BR 50; Conway & Schweppe, "What is a Miscarriage of Justice? The Irish Answer to an International Problem" (2012) DULJ 1.

[6]   In *Commissioners of Customs and Excise v Harz* [1967] 1 AC 760 at 818, [1967] 1 All ER 177 at 182, it was held that there is no difference, in the application of the rules of admissibility, between a full confession and an admission falling short of a confession.

[7]   The Criminal Justice Act 1984 (Treatment of Persons in Custody in Garda Síochána Stations) Regulations 1987 (SI No. 119 of 1987).

[8]   Criminal Justice Act 1984 (Electronic Recording of Interviews) Regulations 1997 (SI No. 74 of 1997).

[9]   *People (AG) v O'Brien* [1965] IR 142; *People (DPP) v Kenny* [1990] 2 IR 110, [1990] ILRM 569.

[10] [1982] IR 1.

[11] [1965] IR 142.

[12] Walsh J, dissenting, took the view that the principles laid down in *O'Brien* were equally applicable to confession evidence (at 31).

[13] [1982] IR 64.

[14] [1982] IR 64 at 79. He, thus, rejected the contention that the admissibility of confessions could be decided by reference to whether it had been obtained voluntarily and fairly, quoting from the judgment of Warren CJ in *Terry v Ohio* (1968) 392 US 1 at 13, to the effect that if a confession was admissible on this basis, the courts would "be made party to lawless invasions of the constitutional rights of citizens by permitting unhindered governmental use of the fruits of such invasions". See also *per* Walsh J (at 84–85): "No valid distinction can be drawn between a statement or an admission obtained by reason of the unconstitutional deprivation of an accused's liberty and any other type of evidence so obtained. As has been so often pointed out, it is the protection and

8–06   In the context of confessions, there are a number of constitutional rights which might be violated in the course of obtaining an inculpatory statement, including the right to bodily integrity[15] if any form of torture or physical violence is used,[16] the right to inviolability of the dwelling[17] if an admission was made in the course of an unlawful search of an accused's dwelling,[18] and the right to privacy[19] if there is an unlawful interception of communications by the accused.[20] However, the rights which are most commonly breached are the right to liberty and the right of access to a lawyer and these are considered in more detail below.

1. The Right to Liberty

8–07   Article 40.4.1 stipulates that "[n]o citizen shall be deprived of his personal liberty save in accordance with law" and any inculpatory statement made by the accused while unlawfully detained will be inadmissible[21] unless there are extraordinary excusing circumstances.[22] While an analysis of the circumstances in which a person can be lawfully detained is beyond the scope of this chapter,[23] the following points should be noted.

8–08   First, the prosecution bears the onus of proving beyond a reasonable doubt that an accused was lawfully detained[24] and the general approach of the courts to statutory

---

upholding of the Constitution which is the dominant consideration and not the preferment of one type of evidence over another. "

[15] See *Ryan v AG* [1965] IR 294; *In re a Ward of Court (No.2)* [1996] 2 IR 79.

[16] Although there is, perhaps, unsurprisingly no decision directly on point as any confession obtained by violence would automatically be excluded, it might be noted that, in *People (AG) v O'Brien* [1965] IR 142 at 150, it was conceded by the State that evidence obtained as a result of gross personal violence or methods which offended against the essential dignity of the human person could not be received in evidence and Kingsmill Moore J stated that: "To countenance the use of evidence extracted or discovered by gross personal violence would, in my opinion, involve the State in moral defilement." In *Murray v Ireland* [1985] IR 532 at 539, Costello J opined that the right not to be tortured is one of the personal rights protected but not expressly enumerated in Art.40.3.1.

[17] See Art.40.5 which guarantees that "[t]he dwelling of every citizen is inviolable and shall be not be forcibly entered save in accordance with law".

[18] See, *e.g. People (DPP) v Kenny* (1989) 3 Frewen 169, [1990] 2 IR 110, [1990] ILRM 569 (inculpatory statements made by the accused during the course of unlawful search of his dwelling were excluded as unconstitutionally obtained).

[19] See *Kennedy v Ireland* [1987] IR 587, [1988] ILRM 472; *X v Flynn,* unreported, High Court, 19 May 1994; *O'T v B* [1998] 2 IR 321; *Hanahoe v Hussey* [1998] 3 IR 69.

[20] See, *e.g. People (DPP) v Dillon* [2003] 1 ILRM 531 (unlawful interception of telephone conversation with accused contrary to s.98 of the Postal and Telecommunications Services Act 1983. *Cf. Kennedy v Ireland* [1987] IR 587.

[21] *People (DPP) v Madden* [1977] IR 336; *People (DPP) v Farrell* [1978] IR 13; *People (DPP) v O'Loughlin* [1979] IR 85; *People (DPP) v Higgins*, unreported, Supreme Court, 22 November 1985; *People (DPP) v Byrne* [1989] ILRM 613: *People (DPP) v Quilligan* [1986] IR 495 at 503, [1987] ILRM 606 at 618; *Larkin v O'Dea* [1994] 2 ILRM 448, [1995] 2 ILRM 1.

[22] See *People (DPP) v Shaw* [1982] IR 1.

[23] For a comprehensive analysis of the powers of arrest and detention, see O'Malley, *The Criminal Process*, (Dublin: Round Hall Thomson Reuters, 2009) at Chap.10; Conway, *Irish Criminal Justice: Theory, Process and Procedure* (Dublin: Clarus Press, 2010), Chap.2; Orange, *Police Powers in Ireland* (Bloomsbury Professional, 2014), Chap. 6; and Coen, *Garda Powers: Law and Practice* (Dublin: Clarus Press, 2014), Chap.5.

[24] *DPP v Finn* [2003] 1 IR 372 at 378.

provisions permitting detention is that they will be strictly construed and compliance with the statutory provisions must be strictly proved.[25]

8–09   Secondly, at common law, a person may only be arrested for the purpose of being charged and brought before a court as soon as reasonably possible and it is not permissible to arrest or detain a person for the purpose of questioning him or her in relation to the commission of an offence.[26] However, this is lawful where the person is arrested and detained pursuant to the statutory powers granted to the gardaí in that behalf, *e.g.* pursuant to (i) s.30 of the Offences Against the State Act 1939,[27] (ii) s.4 of the Criminal Justice Act 1984,[28] (iii) s.2 of the Criminal Justice (Drug Trafficking) Act 1996,[29] or s.50 of the Criminal Justice Act 2007.[30] Indeed, not only is questioning in such instances permissible,[31] it has become one of the primary investigative tools

---

[25] *People (DPP) v Farrell* [1978] IR 13 at 25; *People (DPP) v Shaw* [1982] IR 1 at 30; *DPP v McGarrigle*, unreported, Supreme Court, 22 June 1987; *DPP v Finn* [2003] 1 IR 372 at 384.

[26] *Dunne v Clinton* [1930] IR 366 at 372; *People (DPP) v O'Loughlin* [1979] IR 85 at 91; *People (DPP) v Walsh* [1980] IR 294 at 299–300, 313; *People (DPP) v Shaw* [1982] IR 1 at 28–29 (*per* Walsh J); *People (DPP) v Higgins*, unreported, Supreme Court, 22 November 1985.

[27] Under s.30 (as amended by s.10 of the Offences Against the State (Amendment) Act 1998 and s.21 of the Criminal Justice (Amendment) Act 2009), a person may be detained for an initial period not exceeding 24 hours which can be extended for a further period not exceeding 24 hours if a garda officer not below the rank of Chief Superintendent so directs, and for an additional period not exceeding 24 hours on foot of a warrant granted by a District Judge on the application of a garda officer not below the rank of Chief Superintendent in circumstances where the judge is satisfied that such further detention is necessary for the proper investigation of the offence concerned and that the investigation is being conducted diligently and expeditiously.

[28] Under s.4 (as amended by s.2 of the Criminal Justice (Miscellaneous) Provisions Act 1997, s.9 of the Criminal Justice Act 2006 and s.7 of the Criminal Justice Act 2011), a person may be arrested and detained for a period not exceeding six hours if there are reasonable grounds for believing that his or her detention is necessary for the proper investigation of an offence to which the section applies. The period of detention may be extended for a period not exceeding 12 hours, and then for a further period not exceeding 12 hours, where a garda officer not below the rank of Chief Superintendent has reasonable grounds for believing that such further detention is necessary for the proper investigation of the offence. Thus, it is possible for a person arrested pursuant to s.4 to be detained for a maximum of 24 hours excluding a rest period from midnight to 8am.

[29] Under s.2 (as amended by s.10 of the Criminal Justice Act 2006 and s.22 of the Criminal Justice (Amendment) Act 2009), a person may be detained for an initial period not exceeding six hours if the member in charge of the station to which the arrested person is brought has reasonable grounds for believing that his or her detention is necessary for the proper investigation of a drug trafficking offence. That period may be extended for a further period, not exceeding 18 hours, if a garda officer, not below the rank of superintendent, has reasonable grounds for believing that such further detention is necessary for the proper investigation of the offence, and, subsequently, for a further period, not exceeding 24 hours, if that view is formed by a garda officer, not below the rank of Chief Superintendent. The period of detention may be extended further for a period not exceeding 72 hours and, subsequently for a period not exceeding 48 hours, pursuant to a warrant granted by a District Judge on the application of a garda officer not below the rank of Chief Superintendent, if the judge is satisfied that such further detention is necessary for the proper investigation of the offence concerned and that the investigation is being conduct diligently and expeditiously. Thus, it is possible for a person arrested pursuant to s.2 to be detained for a maximum of seven days.

[30] Under s.50 of the Criminal Justice Act 2007, enacted to deal with organised crime, a person can be detained in respect of a number of specified serious offences for periods identical to those set out in s.2 of the Criminal Justice (Drug Trafficking) Act 1996 (as amended).

[31] See *Lavery v Member in Charge, Carrickmacross Garda Station* [1999] 2 IR 390 and *TH v DPP* [2004] IEHC 76 at [47]–[51]. See *contra* the views expressed by Walsh J in *People (DPP) v Quilligan* [1986] IR 495 at 509, [1987] ILRM 606 at 624.

employed by the gardaí.[32] Moreover, even where there is evidence that implicates a suspect in an offence, the gardaí are not required to immediately charge him or her upon arrest but can arrest him or her for the purpose of questioning where this is necessary for the proper investigation of the offence.[33] Inculpatory statements made by a suspect who has been detained but before he or she has been arrested may be excluded.[34]

8–10 Thirdly, even where a person has been lawfully arrested and detained for questioning pursuant to one of these sections, their detention may be rendered unlawful if the constitutional rights of the person are violated while he or she is in custody, as for example where the person is not afforded access to a solicitor.[35]

8–11 Fourthly, if a person attends voluntarily at a garda station for the purpose of assisting the gardaí with their enquiries, he or she should be made aware that all times he or she is free to leave[36] until the point is reached when that is not the case and, from that point on, the person will be considered to be unlawfully detained unless arrested or detained pursuant to statute.[37]

8–12 Finally, it appears from the decision in *People (DPP) v Madden*[38] that, if the detention of an accused becomes unlawful in the course of making a confession, the whole of the confession, and not just the portion made during the period of unlawful detention, will be excluded. However, as will be seen below, inculpatory statements made prior to the detention becoming unlawful can be admitted.[39]

2. Right of Access to a Lawyer

8–13 The common law right of a person in detention to reasonable access to a solicitor,[40] which had received a measure of statutory protection in the provisions of the Criminal Justice Act 1984 (Treatment of Persons in Custody in Garda Síochána

---

[32] See the comments of Hardiman J in *People (DPP) v Gormley and White* [2014] IESC 17, [2014] 1 ILRM 377 at 418–419.

[33] *People (DPP) v Murphy* [2005] IECCA 52 at [44], [2005] 4 IR 504 at 517–518.

[34] In *People (DPP) v Breen* [2008] IECCA 136, [2009] 2 IR 262, the accused was alleged to have made verbal admissions, which were not contemporaneously noted, at a time after he was under physical restraint by gardaí and had been searched but before he was arrested. Without ruling explicitly on the lawfulness of his detention, the Court of Criminal Appeal held that those admissions should not have been admitted.

[35] *People (DPP) v Buck* [2002] 2 IR 268 at 281, [2002] 2 ILRM 454 at 466; *People (DPP) v Finnegan*, unreported, Court of Criminal Appeal, 15 July 1997; *Barry v Waldron*, High Court, 23 May 1996; *People (DPP) v Shaw* [1982] IR 1 at 35 (*per* Walsh J.); *People (DPP) v Madden* [1977] IR 326 at 355. *Cf. The Emergency Powers Bill, 1976* [1977] IR 159 at 173, where it was indicated that denial of an accused's rights in respect of matters such as the right to communication, the right to have legal and medical assistance and the right of access to the courts could render a detention illegal and unconstitutional. See also *People (DPP) v Quilligan* [1986] IR 495 at 508, where Walsh J stated that, if a person was detained under s.30 of the Offences Against the State Act 1939 in breach of those rights, the High Court might grant an order for release pursuant to the provisions of Art.40.

[36] *People (DPP) v Lynch* [1982] IR 64 at 86 (*per* Walsh J). See also *People (DPP) v Coffey* [1987] ILRM 727.

[37] *People (DPP) v O'Loughlin* [1979] IR 85 at 91.

[38] [1977] IR 336.

[39] *People (DPP) v AD* [2008] IECCA 101; [2012] IESC 33, [2012] 2 IR 332.

[40] See *People (DPP) v Madden* [1977] IR 336 at 355.

Stations) Regulations 1987,[41] was elevated to the constitutional plane in *People (DPP) v Healy*.[42] Finlay CJ identified the purpose of the right as follows:

"The undoubted right of reasonable access to a solicitor enjoyed by a person who is in detention must be interpreted as being directed towards the vital function of ensuring that such person is aware of his rights and has the independent advice which would be appropriate in order to permit him to reach a truly free decision as to his attitude to interrogation or to the making of any statement, be it exculpatory or inculpatory. The availability of advice from a lawyer must, in my view, be seen as a contribution, at least, towards some measure of equality in the position of a detained person and his interrogators."[43]

8–14   He was satisfied that:

"such an important and fundamental standard of fairness in the administration of justice as the right of access to a lawyer must be deemed to be constitutional in its origin, and that to classify it as merely legal would be to undermine its importance".[44]

8–15   The importance of this right was also emphasised by Clarke J in *People (DPP) v Gormley and White*[45] who commented that it was "an important constitutional entitlement of high legal value" and recast it as a right of access to a lawyer.[46]

8–16   As will be seen below, the right of access to a lawyer is also protected under Art.6(1) of the European Convention on Human Rights. In addition, it is protected under EU law. Article 47 of the Charter of Fundamental Rights of the European Union provides that: "Everyone shall have the possibility of being advised, defended and represented". Furthermore, Directive 2013/48/EU on the right of access to a lawyer in criminal proceedings and in European arrest warrant proceedings, on the right to have a third party informed upon deprivation of liberty and to communicate with third persons and with consular authorities while deprived of liberty ("Directive 2013/48/ EU") imposes an obligation on Member States to "ensure that suspects and accused persons have the right of access to a lawyer in such time and in such a manner so as to allow the persons concerned to exercise their rights of defence practically and

---

41   SI No. 119 of 1987. These are considered in detail below.
42   [1990] 2 IR 73, [1990] ILRM 313. Earlier authorities were divided on whether the right was legal or constitutional in status. In *People (DPP) v Farrell* [1978] IR 13, the Court of Criminal Appeal rejected the contention that there was a constitutional right to have the services of a solicitor and doctor before being questioned. However, in *People (DPP) v Conroy* [1986] IR 460 at 478, Walsh J took the view that a person in custody had a constitutional right of reasonable access to a legal adviser. *Cf.* Fenwick, "Access to Legal Advice in Police Custody: A Fundamental Right?" (1989) 52 MLR 104.
43   [1990] 2 IR 73 at 81, [1990] ILRM 313 at 320. Given this stated purpose of the right, it follows that the solicitor must be independent of the State: *People (DPP) v Birney* [2006] IECCA 58 at [98], [2007] 1 IR 337 at 367.
44   [1990] 2 IR 73 at 81, [1990] ILRM 313 at 320.
45   [2014] IESC 17 at [9.14], [2014] 1 ILRM 377 at 405. *Cf. per* T.C. Smyth J in *Mart v Minister for Justice*, unreported, High Court, 19 April 2002: "The right to access to a solicitor by a person in custody is one of the most important of constitutional rights".
46   See generally, Daly, "Does the Buck stop here? An examination of the pre-trial right to legal advice in light of *O'Brien v DPP*" (2006) DULJ 345; Wycherley, "Custodial Legal Advice in Ireland—Lessons Learned from England and Wales (Part 1)" (2010) 28 ILT 170; Wycherley, "Custodial Legal Advice in Ireland—Lessons Learned from England and Wales (Part 2)" (2010) 28 ILT 190; Storan, "Right of Access to a Solicitor in Garda Custody" (2011) BR 27; Heffernan, "The Right to Legal Advice, Reasonable Access and the Remedy of Excluding Evidence" (2011) 1 Crim L & Proc Rev 111; Ni Raifeartaigh, "Interviewing Suspects in Detention: The Changing Landscape" (2012) 2 Crim L & Proc Rev 22.

effectively."[47] Although Ireland is not required to transpose this Directive, having opted out of Lisbon Treaty measures on police and judicial cooperation in criminal matters,[48] it underlines the strong European consensus as to the importance of the right of access to a lawyer and is likely to provide some guidance as to the substantive content of the right.

8–17   Given that the right of access to a solicitor is protected on both a statutory, constitutional and European level, and that its importance has been repeatedly emphasised, it is somewhat surprising how frequently inculpatory statements are ruled inadmissible because of a breach of that right, a phenomenon which has attracted judicial censure.[49]

(a) The Basis and Scope of the Right

8–18   Somewhat surprisingly, in *Healy*, Finlay CJ failed to identify the precise constitutional locus of the right of reasonable access to a solicitor. In the course of his judgment, he referred to the statement of Walsh J in *People (DPP) v Conroy*[50] that the right:

> "is based upon the constitutional obligation imposed upon the Garda Síochána to abide by the provisions of Art. 40.3 of the Constitution, which postulates the observance of basic or fair procedures during interrogations by members of the Garda Síochána".[51]

8–19   He also placed considerable emphasis, when explaining the purpose of the right, on the importance of ensuring that a person in detention "is aware of his rights and has the independent advice which would be appropriate in order to permit him to reach a truly free decision as to his attitude to interrogation or to the making of any statement, be it exculpatory or inculpatory".[52] Similar comments were made by Griffin J who expressed the opinion that the:

> "main, if not the sole, purpose of the right of access to a legal adviser is to enable the detained person to obtain advice as to his rights, and in particular advice as to whether, in the circumstances, it would be in his best interest to make a statement or to refuse to make one."[53]

8–20   He acknowledged that, in most cases, "the prudent legal adviser would be likely to advise his client that it would not be in his interest to make a statement" but was of the opinion that the detained person was "entitled to obtain that advice, and it is then for him alone to decide whether to make a statement or not, and he cannot make an informed decision until he has received that advice".[54] These *dicta* suggested that the right was primarily directed towards protecting the right of a detainee not to be compelled to incriminate himself or herself and enjoyed protection under Art.40.3 either as an adjunct of that right or as an independent right directed towards that

---

[47]   Article 3(1).
[48]   Protocol 21 to the Treaty of Lisbon on the position of the United Kingdom and Ireland in respect of the area of freedom, security and justice (OJ C 306/01, 17 December 2007). Ireland has the option of opting into the Directive and the measures that would be required to be taken in order to do so were the subject of review in the *Final Report of the Working Group to Advise on a System Providing for the Presence of a Legal Representative during Garda Interviews* (July 2013).
[49]   See *DPP v Ryan* [2011] IECCA 6 at 14.
[50]   [1986] IR 460.
[51]   [1986] IR 460 at 478.
[52]   [1990] 2 IR 73 at 81, [1990] ILRM 313 at 320.
[53]   [1990] 2 IR 73 at 84, [1990] ILRM 313 at 323.
[54]   [1990] 2 IR 73 at 84, [1990] ILRM 313 at 324.

purpose.[55] This view that the right was adjectival in nature is, perhaps, the reason why, notwithstanding its newly conferred constitutional status, the Supreme Court in *Healy* continued to describe it as one of reasonable access to a solicitor rather than access simpliciter.

8–21 A different constitutional anchor for the right was identified by the Supreme Court in *People (DPP) v Buck*[56] where the view was taken that it was a concomitant right to the right to liberty protected by Art.40.4.1 which provides that "[n]o citizen shall be deprived of his personal liberty save in accordance with law". Keane CJ referred to the decision in *The Emergency Powers Bill 1976*[57] as authority for the proposition that a person detained under the provisions of the Criminal Justice Act 1984, or any other statutory provision, is entitled to the benefit of specific constitutional protections including the right to legal assistance. Delivering the judgment of the Court in that case, O'Higgins CJ stated:

> "While it is not necessary to embark upon an exploration of all the incidents or characteristics which may not accompany the arrest and custody of a person under [the impugned section], it is nevertheless desirable, in view of the submissions made to the court, to state that the section is not to be read as an abnegation of the arrested person's rights (constitutional or otherwise) in respect of matters such as the right of communication, the right to have legal and medical assistance, and the right of access to the courts. ... It is not necessary for the court to attempt to give an exhaustive list of the matters which would render a detention under the section illegal or unconstitutional."[58]

8–22 Keane CJ regarded it as a logical corollary of this statement of the law that the detention of a person against his or her will pursuant to a statutory power is permissible only where his constitutional right of reasonable access to a solicitor is observed. Thus, it would seem that the purpose of the right was not confined to affording a detainee advice in relation to his or her right not to be compelled to incriminate himself or herself but served a broader purpose of ensuring that a person who has been deprived of his or her personal liberty has access to legal advice in relation to all of his or her legal and constitutional rights.

8–23 The effect of the holding in *Buck* that the right of reasonable access to a solicitor was one of a penumbra of rights which had to be complied with in order for a person to be detained in accordance with law was that, if that right was breached, then the detention of the person became unconstitutional. However, this approach created some conceptual as well as practical problems. First, a breach of the right resulted in a situation where a person was considered to be in lawful custody, having been lawfully detained pursuant to a statutory power, but yet was simultaneously regarded as being in unconstitutional custody. In *People (DPP) v O'Brien*,[59] McCracken J held that, from the moment that the breach of the accused's constitutional right of reasonable access to a solicitor had occurred, his detention had become unlawful and remained unlawful so long as the breach continued but entered the caveat that, having been lawfully detained pursuant to s.4 of the Criminal Justice Act 1984, the accused had remained

---

[55] *Cf.* the approach in Canada where the right to counsel, right to silence, and the common law confession rules are viewed as interrelated, as they operate together to provide a standard of reliability with respect to evidence obtained from detained persons and to ensure fairness in the investigative process: *R. v Whittle* [1994] 2 SCR 914.

[56] [2002] 2 IR 268, [2002] 2 ILRM 454.

[57] [1977] IR 159.

[58] [1977] IR 159 at 173.

[59] Unreported, Court of Criminal Appeal, 17 June 2002, [2005] IESC 29, [2005] 2 IR 206.

in lawful custody.[60] Subsequently, in *People (DPP) v AD*,[61] Clarke J used the phrase "unconstitutionally unlawful custody" to describe the legal character of the custody of a suspect where there had been a breach of the right of reasonable access to a solicitor. Secondly, given that the unconstitutionality could be cured whenever reasonable access to a solicitor was belatedly afforded,[62] the result was to create a detention of ambulatory legality which caused difficulties in determining the admissibility of testimonial and real evidence obtained during the period of detention. The difficulties in that regard were compounded by the formulation of the right as one of *reasonable* access so that the extent of the right and the question of whether it had been breached so that a lapse into unconstitutionality had occurred, involved a very fact-specific inquiry.

8–24 Some of these difficulties have been resolved by the quite different approach adopted by the Supreme of Court in the landmark decision in *People (DPP) v Gormley and White*.[63] At issue in those joined appeals was the question of whether the gardaí were obliged to postpone questioning when a detainee requested access to a solicitor and, whether, inculpatory statements made and real evidence obtained after such a request was made but before the solicitor arrived were admissible. Having reviewed the authorities, Clarke J (with whom the other members of the Court concurred) summarised the law as it stood as follows:

> "It is clear that the current state of the jurisprudence in Ireland recognises that the right to have access to a lawyer while in custody is a constitutionally recognised right. A failure to provide reasonable access after a request from a suspect in custody can, on that basis, render the custody unconstitutional and thus lead to any evidence obtained on foot of such unconstitutional custody becoming inadmissible."[64]

8–25 The starting point of his analysis was a review of the relevant jurisprudence of the European Court of Human Rights, starting with the decision in *Salduz v Turkey*[65] where the Grand Chamber, having reiterated that the guarantee of a fair trial in Art.6 could also apply during the pre-trial period because the fairness of a trial could be compromised by what occurred during the pre-trial period, emphasised that "although not absolute, the right of everyone charged with a criminal offence to be effectively defended by a lawyer, assigned officially if need be, is one of the fundamental features of a fair trial".[66] The Court explained that access to a lawyer served to protect an accused against abusive coercion, contributed to the prevention of miscarriages of justice and also promoted an equality of arms between the investigating or prosecuting authorities and the accused. It also identified access to a lawyer as a key protection for the right of an accused not to incriminate himself or herself, saying:

> "Early access to a lawyer is part of the procedural safeguards to which the Court will have particular regard when examining whether a procedure has extinguished the very essence of the privilege against self-incrimination…"[67]

---

[60] [2005] IESC 29 at [17]–[18], [2005] 2 IR 206 at 213–214.
[61] [2008] IECCA 101; [2012] IESC 33 at [41], [2012] 2 IR 332 at 345.
[62] *People (DPP) v O'Brien*, unreported, Court of Criminal Appeal, 17 June 2002; [2005] IESC 29, [2005] 2 IR 206.
[63] [2014] IESC 17, [2014] 1 ILRM 377.
[64] [2014] IESC 17 at [5.7], [2014] 1 ILRM 377 at 389–390.
[65] (2009) 49 EHRR 19. See also *Panovits v Cyprus* [2008] ECHR 1688; *Amutgan v Turkey* [2009] ECHR 184; *Plonka v Poland* [2009] ECHR 2277; *Dayanan v Turkey* [2009] ECHR 2278
[66] (2009) 49 EHRR 19 at [51].
[67] (2009) 49 EHRR 19 at [54].

8–26   Accordingly, the Grand Chamber went on to hold that a suspect was entitled to access to a lawyer from the commencement of his detention:

"[T]he Court finds that in order for the right to a fair trial to remain sufficiently "practical and effective" (see para. 51 above) Art. 6 § 1 requires that, as a rule, access to a lawyer should be provided as from the first interrogation of a suspect by the police, unless it is demonstrated in the light of the particular circumstances of each case that there are compelling reasons to restrict this right. Even where compelling reasons may exceptionally justify denial of access to a lawyer, such restriction – whatever its justification – must not unduly prejudice the rights of the accused under Art. 6 …. The rights of the defence will in principle be irretrievably prejudiced when incriminating statements made during police interrogation without access to a lawyer are used for a conviction."[68]

8–27   That conclusion was affirmed by the Court in *Dayanan v Turkey*[69] where it was held that:

"an accused person is entitled, as soon as he or she is taken into custody, to be assisted by a lawyer, and not only while being questioned (for the relevant international legal materials see Salduz, cited above, §§ 37–44). Indeed, the fairness of proceedings requires that an accused be able to obtain the whole range of services specifically associated with legal assistance. In this regard, counsel has to be able to secure without restriction the fundamental aspects of that person's defence: discussion of the case, organisation of the defence, collection of evidence favourable to the accused, preparation for questioning, support of an accused in distress and checking of the conditions of detention."

8–28   On the basis of these and other authorities, Clarke J considered it clear that:

"the protection against self-incrimination which is guaranteed by the European Convention on Human Rights ("ECHR") is breached where a person makes an incriminating statement which forms a substantial part of the evidence leading to their conviction in circumstances where the relevant person does not have the benefit of legal advice at the time in question and where they have not waived any entitlement to legal advice."[70]

8–29   That being the position, the question arose as to whether the interpretative obligations imposed on the Irish courts under s.2 of the European Convention on Human Rights Act 2003 required Irish law to be interpreted so as prevent the use of statements made or evidence of samples taken during a period between a request for a solicitor being made and the attendance of the solicitor concerned. However, in circumstances where this question would be moot if Irish law achieved that result by virtue of interpreting the right of trial in due course of law as recognised in Art.38.1 as encompassing a right to legal advice prior to either or both of the conduct of an interrogation of a suspect or the taking of forensic samples from such a suspect, he turned to deal with the Irish constitutional position first.

8–30   Clarke J then engaged in a review of the international jurisprudence,[71] starting with the US and the decision of the US Supreme Court in *Miranda v Arizona*[72] where

---

68   (2009) 49 EHRR 19 at [55].

69   [2009] ECHR 2278 at [32].

70   [2014] IESC 17 at [2.11], [2014] 1 ILRM 377 at 384–385.

71   Somewhat surprisingly, he did not advert to the position in England where questioning must generally be suspended once an accused has requested legal advice until he or she has consulted with a solicitor: Code C, para. 6.6. of Code C of the Revised Code of Practice for the Detention, Treatment and Questioning of Persons by Police Officers (May 2014).

72   (1966) 384 US 436. For an analysis of this decision and its progeny, see Broun (ed.), *McCormick on Evidence* 7th edn (West Academic Publishing, 2014), Vol. I, § 150. See also MacGuckian, "Judge or Politician? The Political Role of the Judiciary in Society" (2005) 27 DULJ 302; Allen, "Miranda's Hollow Core" (2006) 100 Nw UL Rev 71; Duke, "Does Miranda Protect the Innocent

it had been held not only that there was a right to consult a lawyer prior to questioning but also to have a lawyer present during questioning. Moving to Canada, he noted that, in *R. v Sinclair*,[73] the Canadian Supreme Court had held that s.10(b) of the Canadian Charter of Rights and Freedoms required a detainee to be advised of his right to counsel and that the detainee had to be given a right to exercise that right which imposed a duty on police to hold off questioning until the detainee had a reasonable opportunity to consult counsel. Next, he recorded the current practice in Australia which is that police are required to inform suspects that they may communicate or attempt to communicate with a lawyer and, normally, if a lawyer is contacted and indicates that he or she will attend the police station, the police will not commence an interview until the lawyer has arrived. He rounded off his tour with New Zealand where s.23(1)(b) of the Bill of Rights Act 1990 confers a right on an arrested or detained person to consult a lawyer without delay and a police officer has a duty to refrain from taking any positive or deliberate step to elicit evidence from the detainee until he or she has had a reasonable opportunity to consult with a lawyer.[74] On the basis of this review of the international landscape, it was apparent that "there is, at a minimum, an obligation in most circumstances (possibly subject to some exceptions) on investigating police to refrain from interrogating a suspect at a time after the suspect has requested a lawyer and before that lawyer has arrived to advise the suspect concerned".[75]

8–31   Turning to the issues before the Court, the first question to be addressed was whether the guarantee in Art. 38.1 of a trial in due course of law extended to any part of the pre-trial investigative stage. Having noted that the European Court of Human Rights had interpreted the protection conferred by art. 6 of the European Convention on Human Rights as extending to the pre-trial stage, Clarke J, concluded that Art.38.1 and the guarantee of due process was engaged from the time of arrest of a suspect:

> "I am persuaded that the point at which the coercive power of the State, in the form of an arrest, is exercised against a suspect represents an important juncture in any potential criminal process. Thereafter the suspect is no longer someone who is simply being investigated by the gathering of whatever evidence might be available. Thereafter the suspect has been deprived of his or her liberty and, in many cases, can be subjected to mandatory questioning for various periods and, indeed, in certain circumstances, may be exposed to a requirement, under penal sanction, to provide forensic samples. It seems to me that once the power of the State has been exercised against a suspect in that way, it is proper to regard the process thereafter as being

---

or the Guilty?" (2007) 10 Chapman L Rev 551; Weisselberg, "Mourning Miranda" (2008) 96 Cal L Rev 1519; Kamisar, "The Rise, Decline, and Fall (?) of Miranda" (2012) 87 Washington Law Review 965.

[73] [2010] 2 SCR 310. See also *R. v Singh* [2007] 3 SCR 3. For an analysis of *Sinclair*, see Stuart, "Sinclair Regrettably Completes the *Oickle* and *Singh* Manual for Coercive and Lawless Interrogation" (2010) 77 CR (6th) 303; Boyle, "*R. v. Sinclair*: A Comparatively Disappointing Decision on the Right to Counsel" (2010) 77 CR (6th) 310; Ives & Sherrin, "R. v. Singh—A Meaningless Right to Silence with Dangerous Consequences" (2007) 51 CR (6th) 250; Dufraimont, "The Interrogation Trilogy and the Protections for Interrogated Suspects in Canadian Law" (2011) 54 SCLR 2d 309; Bershadaski, "A Trio of Cases, A Trio of Opinions: The Right of Access to Counsel in Canada's Police Stations" [2011] Journal of Commonwealth Criminal Law 170; Boyle and Cunliffe, "Right to Counsel during Custodial Interrogation in Canada: Not Keeping Up with the Common Law Joneses" in Roberts and Hunter (eds), *Criminal Evidence and Human Rights: Reimagining Common Law Procedural Traditions* (Oxford: Hart Publishing, 2012), pp.79–102.

[74] This has been established in a series of cases including *Ministry of Transport v Noort; Police v Curran* [1992] 3 NZLR 260, 280; *R. v Gordon* [1990–92] 3 NZBORR 191 at 200 and *R. v Taylor* [1993] 1 NZLR 647. See Butler, "Exercising the Right to Counsel and the Due Diligence Requirement—The Need for a Graduated Approach" [1995] NZLJ 406.

[75] [2014] IESC 17 at [7.11], [2014] 1 ILRM 377 at 398.

intimately connected with a potential criminal trial rather than being one at a pure investigative stage. It seems to me to follow that the requirement that persons only be tried in due course of law, therefore, requires that the basic fairness of process identified as an essential ingredient of that concept by this Court in *State (Healy) v. Donoghue* applies from the time of arrest of a suspect. The precise consequences of such a requirement do, of course, require careful and detailed analysis. It does not, necessarily, follow that all of the rights which someone may have at trial (in the sense of the conduct of a full hearing of the criminal charge before a judge with or without a jury) apply at each stage of the process leading up to such a trial. However, it seems to me that the fundamental requirement of basic fairness does apply from the time of arrest such that any breach of that requirement can lead to an absence of a trial in due course of law. In that regard it seems to me that the Irish position is the same as that acknowledged by the ECtHR and by the Supreme Court of the United States."[76]

8–32   Having so extended the ambit of the protection conferred by Art.38.1, he had little difficulty in concluding that the guarantee of a trial in due course of law carried with it an entitlement not to be interrogated after a request for a lawyer had been made and before that lawyer had become available to give advice:

"There may be many reasons why an arrested suspect may wish to have access to a lawyer. There may also be many reasons why such access may be required at an early stage. Some of those reasons may not be very closely connected with either questioning or the taking of forensic samples. It might, for example, be necessary to put in place early enquiries which might assist in the building of a defence. The suspect might require advice on the lawfulness of the arrest and of his or her custody. However, there can be little doubt but that advice on the immediate events which often occur on the arrest of a suspect (such as questioning) is one of the most important aspects of the advice which any suspect is likely to require as a matter of urgency. There would be little point in giving constitutional recognition to a right of access to a lawyer while in custody if one of the principal purposes of that custody in many cases, being the questioning of the relevant suspect, could continue prior to legal advice being obtained. At a minimum any such right would be significantly diluted if questioning could continue prior to the arrival of the relevant lawyer. In those circumstances, it seems to me that the need for basic fairness, which is inherent in the requirement of trial in due course of law under Art.38.1 of the Constitution, carries with it, at least in general terms and potentially subject to exceptions, an entitlement not to be interrogated after a request for a lawyer has been made and before that lawyer has become available to tender the requested advice."[77]

8–33   He emphasised that "the right is one designed to provide support for the right against self-incrimination amongst other rights including the right to a fair trial".[78]

8–34   He then went on to draw a distinction between the two cases before the court and circumstances where incriminating statements were made after the request for a solicitor had been made and circumstances where real evidence had been obtained. In the case of the former, he regarded it as clear that such evidence was inadmissible:

"The right to a trial in due course of law encompasses a right to early access to a lawyer after

---

[76]   [2014] IESC 17 at [8.8], [2014] 1 ILRM 377 at 400–401.

[77]   [2014] IESC 17 at [9.2], [2014] 1 ILRM 377 at 402. Interestingly, this conclusion was reached without any discussion of the previous authorities on this point. Although Walsh J had expressed the view in *People (DPP) v Conroy* [1986] IR 460 at 479 that interrogation by the gardaí after a solicitor had been requested but before his arrival was "a constitutionally forbidden procedure", scepticism about this proposition had been expressed in *People (DPP) v Cullen*, unreported, Court of Criminal Appeal, 30 March 1993 and it had been held in *People (DPP) v Buck* [2002] 2 IR 268, [2002] 2 ILRM 454, that the constitutional right of reasonable access to a solicitor would not necessarily be denied in such circumstances. In that case, Finlay CJ took the view that the issue was best dealt with by the exercise of a discretion by the trial judge based on considerations of fairness to the accused and public policy rather than by the application of a rigid exclusionary rule.

[78]   [2014] IESC 17 at [9.15], [2014] 1 ILRM 377 at 405.

arrest and the right not to be interrogated without having had an opportunity to obtain such advice. The conviction of a person wholly or significantly on the basis of evidence obtained contrary to those constitutional entitlements represents a conviction following an unfair trial process."[79]

8–35   However, the position was quite different where real evidence only had been obtained. It was clear from the decisions of the European Court of Human Rights in *Saunders v United Kingdom*[80] and *Jalloh v Germany*[81] that the forcible taking of samples was not regarded as a breach of the privilege against self-incrimination unless the procedures used were sufficiently invasive and unnatural so as to bring the case outside the norm. Furthermore, the results of forensic testing are objective and the results do not depend on the will of a suspect or comments made by him or her in circumstances where the right to self-incrimination could have been invoked. Accordingly:

"On that basis, at the level of principle, I am not satisfied that the mere fact that otherwise lawful forensic sampling is properly taken prior to the attendance of a legal adviser renders any subsequent trial, at which reliance is placed on the results of tests arising out of that forensic material, unfair. It remains, of course, the case that the suspect is entitled to reasonable access to a lawyer. The authorities in whose custody the suspect is held are required to take reasonable steps to facilitate such access. What consequences may flow, in respect of the admissibility of forensic evidence taken from a suspect where such reasonable steps are not taken, is a matter to be decided in a case where those circumstances arise. However, I am not satisfied that there is any fair trial constitutional prohibition on the taking, without prior legal advice, of a sample in a minimally intrusive way which is justified in law."[82]

8–36   However, Clarke J acknowledged that the position might be different where the suspect had a genuine legal choice available in respect of the taking of samples and where it would be reasonably necessary for the suspect concerned to have access to legal advice before making such choices.

8–37   The decision in *Gormley and White* is very important because it not only significantly extends the scope of the right of access to a lawyer[83] beyond its previously established parameters but also because it recasts the rationale and scope of the right. The rationale for the right is firmly rooted in the right of a suspect not to be compelled to incriminate himself or herself. As explained in Chap.11, the right to silence enjoyed by a suspect during the pre-trial investigative period developed on the basis that, without it, the right of an accused not to give evidence at trial would be "illusory".[84] The right of access to a lawyer during the pre-trial investigative phase is a concomitant right which protects the right to silence by ensuring that suspects are properly advised as to the existence of that right, their entitlement to assert it where appropriate and, in an appropriate case, the circumstances in which inferences may be drawn from its exercise. As explained in *Salduz*, access to a lawyer also has a range of other benefits in terms of ensuring that there is no ill-treatment of the suspect, that any other legal protections applicable to his or her detention are adhered to, preventing miscarriages of justice and in evening the scales between the investigating authorities and the suspect.[85]

---

79   [2014] IESC 17 at [9.13], [2014] 1 ILRM 377 at 405.
80   (1996) 23 EHRR 313.
81   [2006] ECHR 721, (2007) 44 EHRR 32.
82   [2014] IESC 17 at [10.3], [2014] 1 ILRM 377 at 407.
83   Clarke J acknowledges (at [8.4.], 399) that the decision amounted to a significant development of the jurisprudence in the area.
84   *R. v Hebert* [1990] 2 SCR 151 at 174 (*per* McLachlin J). *Cf.* Zuckerman. "Trial by Unfair Means—The Report of the Working Group on the Right of Silence" [1989] Crim LR 855.
85   In his concurring judgment in *Gormley and White* [2014] IESC 17, [2014] 1 ILRM 377 at 420,

Thus, a breach of this right impacts directly on the fairness of the trial process which is what a court is primarily concerned with when ruling on the admissibility of evidence obtained during the period of detention. Hence, Art.38.1 is the most natural locus for the protection of the right.

8–38   A second significant aspect of the decision is that, although the right at issue is variously referred to in the judgment of Clarke J as "a right to legal advice" and "a right to have access to a lawyer", what is notably lacking is any qualification of the right as one of *reasonable* access.[86] The removal of this adjective from the formulation of the right is important because it underlines the increased status accorded to the right. It also underpins the conclusion that, once the right of access is exercised, questioning cannot begin or is required to stop as the case may be, until that access is afforded. As to whether the right is more correctly described as right to legal advice or a right of access to a lawyer, it is submitted that the second formulation is more correct because, as will be seen below, the obligation on gardaí is to afford access to a lawyer not to ensure that the lawyer actually provides adequate or even any legal advice to the suspect.

8–39   Another striking feature of the decision is the importance accorded to the right and the repeated emphasis on the obligation to ensure that the right is respected and vindicated. In the course of his judgment, Clarke J said that "it must be clearly understood that there is an obligation on the arresting authorities to genuinely respect that right".[87] As discussed below, the decision clearly signals an openness to the proposition that a suspect is entitled to have his or her solicitor present during questioning and may also lead to a recognition of an entitlement to the provision of a lawyer by the State for impecunious detainees. Not surprisingly, therefore, it has led to very significant changes in garda practice with solicitors now permitted to be present during questioning. It has, thus, pre-empted the changes envisaged by s.5A of the Criminal Justice Act 1984[88] and the regulations to be made thereunder.[89]

(b) When the Right Applies

8–40   In *People (DPP) v Gormley and White*,[90] Clarke J identified the arrest of a suspect as the point at which the guarantee of due process contained in Art.38.1 was engaged and the right of access to a solicitor arose on the basis that "once the power of the State has been exercised against a suspect in that way, it is proper to regard the process thereafter as being intimately connected with a potential criminal trial rather than being one at a pure investigative stage". This is consistent with the approach

---

Hardiman J described in graphic terms the unsatisfactory conditions that might have to be endured by a suspect when brought to a garda station.

[86]   The pre *Gormley and White* authorities consistently described the right as one of reasonable access only: *People (DPP) v Healy* [1990] 2 IR 73, [1990] ILRM 313; *Lavery v Member in Charge, Carrickmacross Garda Station* [1999] 2 IR 390 at 395; *Ward v Minister for Justice* [2007] IEHC 39 at [12], [2007] 2 IR 726 at 732.

[87]   [2014] IESC 17 at [9.15], [2014] 1 ILRM 377 at 405–406.

[88]   As inserted by s.9(a) of the Criminal Justice Act 2011. This section has not been commenced as of the time of going to print.

[89]   The comments made by the Court of Criminal Appeal in *DPP v Ryan* [2011] IECCA 6 about the need for additional training of gardaí in relation to interview practices and the principles relating to same should also be noted.

[90]   [2014] IESC 17 at [8.8], [2014] 1 ILRM 377 at 400–401.

adopted by the UK Supreme Court in *Ambrose v Harris*[91] where it was held that the trigger point for the application of Art.6(1) rights including the right of access to a lawyer was when a person was no longer a potential witness but had become a suspect and that this would be the case where a person was in custody or his freedom to act had otherwise been significantly impaired. It follows that the right does not apply in circumstances where a person is questioned by the gardaí in advance of being taken into custody.[92]

(c) Exceptions to the Right

8–41   In the course of his judgment in *Gormley and White*, Clarke J accepted that the right of access to a lawyer could be abridged[93] but only in truly exceptional circumstances:

> "It should also be emphasised that the right to legal advice before interrogation is an important constitutional entitlement of high legal value. If any exceptions to that right are to be recognised, then it would be necessary that there be wholly exceptional circumstances involving a pressing and compelling need to protect other major constitutional rights such as the right to life. This judgment is not the place to attempt to define any possible exceptions with precision. The basis of any exception would need to meet the criteria just noted and also be clearly established in fact supported by contemporaneous records."[94]

8–42   While Clarke J did not attempt to enumerate the "wholly exceptional circumstances" where the right of access to a lawyer could be curtailed, it is evident from the requirement for a "pressing and compelling need" and the reference to the right to life that he had in mind something quite restrictive, perhaps along the lines of art.3(6) of Directive 2013/48/EU which provides that Member States may temporarily derogate from the right of access to a lawyer in exceptional circumstances and only at the pre-trial stage to the extent justified in the light of the particular circumstances of the case, on the basis of one of two compelling reasons: (a) where there is an urgent need to avert serious adverse consequences for the life, liberty or physical integrity of a person; and (b) where immediate action by the investigating authorities is imperative to prevent substantial jeopardy to criminal proceedings. A serious doubt must arise as to whether s.5A(4) of the Criminal Justice Act 1984,[95] if commenced, which prescribes a much wider range of circumstances where questioning may commence without the detainee having had an opportunity to consult with a solicitor would pass constitutional muster.[96]

---

[91]   [2011] UKSC 43, [2011] 1 WLR 2435.

[92]   It is noteworthy that the right may be activated at an earlier juncture pursuant to the provisions of Art.3(2) of Directive 2013/48/EU which stipulates that suspects and accused persons have to be given access to a lawyer without undue delay and, in any event, from whichever is the earliest of: (a) before they are questioned by the police or by another law enforcement or judicial authority; (b) upon the carrying out by investigating or other competent authorities of an investigative or other evidence-gathering act; (c) without undue delay after deprivation of liberty; (d) where they have been summoned to appear before a court having jurisdiction in criminal matters in due time before they appear before that court.

[93]   He noted that the US courts had developed a "public safety" exception to the right of access to a lawyer in *New York v Quarles* (1984) 467 US 649.

[94]   [2014] IESC 17 at [9.14], [2014] 1 ILRM 377 at 405.

[95]   As inserted by s.9 of the Criminal Justice Act 2011 but not commenced as of the date of going to print.

[96]   Subsection (5) provides that: "A member of the Garda Síochána in charge of a Garda Síochána station may authorise the questioning of a person who is being detained pursuant to section 4 and who has not yet consulted with a solicitor where the member concerned has reasonable grounds

8–43   Furthermore, even if circumstances exist which justify gardaí in restricting access to a lawyer, it does not follow that any inculpatory statements made during the period when this right was denied will be admissible. In *Salduz v Turkey*[97] it was held that:

> "Article 6 § 1 requires that, as a rule, access to a lawyer should be provided as from the first interrogation of a suspect by the police, unless it is demonstrated in the light of the particular circumstances of each case that there are compelling reasons to restrict this right. Even where compelling reasons may exceptionally justify denial of access to a lawyer, such restriction – whatever its justification – must not unduly prejudice the rights of the accused under Art. 6 …. The rights of the defence will in principle be irretrievably prejudiced when incriminating statements made during police interrogation without access to a lawyer are used for a conviction."

8–44   It remains to be seen whether the Irish courts will adopt the same approach but, given that the effect of the decision in *Gormley and White* has been to align Irish constitutional law in this area with the position under the Convention, it would not be surprising if they did so.

(d) Informing a Detainee of the Right

8–45   After being left open in a number of cases,[98] the question of whether a detainee has the right or entitlement to be informed of his or her right of access to a lawyer was answered affirmatively in *People (DPP) v Gormley*.[99] Although no justification for this was provided, it is readily found in the pithy reasoning of O'Higgins CJ in *State (Healy) v O'Donoghue*[100] as to why an accused should be informed of his right to legal aid: "If the person charged does not know of his right, he cannot exercise it; if he cannot exercise it, his right is violated."[101] This issue did not directly arise on the appeal to the Supreme Court in *Gormley and White* although the judgment of Clarke J clearly proceeds on the assumption that the right of access to a lawyer carries with it an entitlement on the part of a suspect to be informed of that right at the outset of a period of detention and before any questioning of the suspect takes place or any other step is taken in respect of which the suspect may require legal advice.

8–46   While the decision in *Gormley and White* does not identify any particular language that has to be used when explaining the right,[102] it is apparent that a clear explanation of the right of access to a lawyer must be given and the gardaí must be careful not to, in any way, discourage the suspect from exercising that right. Clarke J emphasised that: "Suspects should have explained to them their entitlements in a fair

---

for believing that to delay the questioning would involve a risk of (a) interference with, or injury to, other persons, (b) serious loss of, or damage to, property, (c) the destruction of, or interference with, evidence, (d) accomplices being alerted or the securing of their apprehension being made more difficult, or (e) hindering the recovery of property obtained as a result of an offence or the recovery of the value of any proceeds of an offence.

[97]   (2009) 49 EHRR 19 at [55].
[98]   See *People (DPP) v Conroy* [1986] IR 460 at 478; *People (DPP) v Healy* [1990] 2 IR 73 at 78, [1990] ILRM 313 at 317; *DPP v Spratt* [1995] 1 IR 585 at 592, [1995] 2 ILRM 117 at 123.
[99]   [2010] IECCA 22 at [7], [2010] 2 IR 409 at 414.
[100]   [1976] IR 325.
[101]   [1976] IR 325 at 352.
[102]   The question of what must be said to a suspect about their entitlement to have the assistance of a lawyer was expressly left over by the Supreme Court ([2014] IESC 17 at [9.3], [2014] 1 ILRM 377 at 402).

and appropriate way which could not, objectively speaking, be considered to in any way encourage waiver or non-invocation."[103]

8–47 As noted below, a statutory obligation has been imposed on the gardaí to inform a detainee of his or her right of access to a solicitor.[104] However, this simply requires the detainee to be informed that he or she is entitled to consult a solicitor without telling him or her that, if a request for access to a solicitor is made, questioning will not take place until the solicitor arrives and that right can be exercised at any time.

8–48 Given the importance attributed to the right of access to a lawyer in *Gormley and White*, it would seem that gardaí are required to go further than merely informing a detainee about the existence of the right but also to furnish information to the detainee to ensure that he or she has a realistic opportunity to exercise that right. One of the authorities that Clarke J referred to was the decision of the European Court of Human Rights in *Panovits v Cyprus*[105] where it has held that Art.6 had been violated because of the failure to provide sufficient information in relation to the applicant's right to consult a lawyer before his questioning began.[106] So, for example, if a detainee does not know the names of any solicitors, gardaí will be expected to provide information about practitioners specialising in the area of criminal law. This could be done by maintaining a list in the garda stations of locally based solicitors who are available to act.[107]

(e) Waiver of Right

8–49 In *Gormley and White*, it was accepted that a detainee could waive his or her right of access to a lawyer but only if this waiver was fully informed and freely given. Clarke J stated:

> "[I]t must be clearly understood that there is an obligation on arresting authorities to genuinely respect that right. Whatever parameters may exist in relation to the question of whether a person might be said either to have waived the right, or to have failed to invoke the right, the circumstances surrounding the actions of the relevant suspect will require to be carefully scrutinised to ensure that any decision made or, indeed, any inaction on the part of the suspect concerned, was not inappropriately influenced by any contrived conditions brought about or

---

[103] [2014] IESC 17 at [9.16], [2014] 1 ILRM 377 at 406.
[104] See s.5 of the Criminal Justice Act 1984 and reg.8 of the Custody Regulations, which are discussed below.
[105] [2008] ECHR 1688.
[106] Clarke J also referred to the decision of the US Supreme Court in *Miranda v Arizona* (1966) 384 US 436 which established this as one of the *Miranda* rights enjoyed by a criminal suspect, the decision of the Canadian Supreme Court in *R. v Sinclair* [2010] 2 SCR 310 where a requirement that a detainee be informed of his right to retain and instruct counsel was identified, and s.23(1)(b) of the New Zealand Bill of Rights Act 1990 which expressly creates a right to be informed of the right to consult a lawyer. For a discussion of the approach to this issue in Canada and New Zealand, see Butler, "An Objective or Subjective Approach to the Right to be Informed of the Right to Counsel? A New Zealand Perspective" (1994) 36 Crim LQ 317. It is also worth noting that Art.3(4) of Directive 2013/48/EU imposes an obligation on Member States to make general information available to facilitate the obtaining of a lawyer by suspects and accused persons.
[107] It might be noted that a suggestion to this effect was made nearly 35 years ago in *People (DPP) v Shaw* [1982] IR 1 at 35, where Walsh J said: "it is not too much to expect that every garda station should have a list of all local solicitors to supply to prisoners when a request for a solicitor is made, so as to enable the prisoner to make a choice—particularly if he is a stranger in the area or has not already the name of the solicitor whom he wishes to contact".

contributed to by arresting authorities designed or which would be likely to encourage any such waiver or non-invocation."[108]

8–50   This is consistent with the position under the Convention with the European Court of Human Rights having confirmed in *Trymbach v Ukraine*[109] that a waiver of the right to a lawyer is permissible but such a waiver "must not run counter to any important public interest, must be established in an unequivocal manner, and must be attended by minimum safeguards commensurate to the waiver's importance".[110]

8–51   It also appears from the concurring judgment of Hardiman J that there may be a requirement that any waiver is adequately recorded:

> "In my opinion, it is important that every formal stage of detention in the Garda Station, from the original decision to detain onwards, and in particular the explanation of the rights to consult a solicitor, should be both audio and video-recorded. In my opinion, a failure to do this requires explanation: the suggestion that there was an earlier, or different, conversation on this subject before the recording started, or after it finished, or while the recording machines were turned off, should trigger scepticism on the part of any court asked to consider it."[111]

8–52   A useful template of the requirements for an effective waiver can be found in art.9(1) of Directive 2013/48/EU which stipulates that Member States must ensure that: (a) the suspect or accused person has been provided orally or in writing, with clear and sufficient information in simple and understandable language about the content of the right concerned and the possible consequences of waiving it; and (b) the waiver is given voluntarily and unequivocally. There is also a requirement that the waiver, whether made in writing or orally, and the circumstances under which the waiver was given, are recorded and that suspects or accused persons are informed that the waiver may be revoked subsequently which revocation will take place immediately if it occurs.

8–53   It should be noted that s.5A(4) of the Criminal Justice Act 1984[112] makes provision for the waiver of the right to consult a solicitor and that section also envisages that regulations will be made providing for how that waiver is to be recorded.

(f) Exercise of the Right

8–54   While the decision in *Gormley and White* makes it clear that, once access to a lawyer is requested, questioning cannot commence or must cease as the case may be, it does not address the question of whether such questioning is entirely prohibited thereafter or whether it can commence if a solicitor fails to arrive within a reasonable timeframe. In both of those cases, the solicitors in question had attended with promptitude and the Court preferred to leave that question over to a case where it

---

[108] [2014] IESC 17 at [9.14], [2014] 1 ILRM 377 at 405–406. *Cf.* the comments of Murray CJ in *DPP v Ryan* [2011] IECCA 6 at [14] that the adoption and giving effect to a protocol which ensured that the right of an arrested person's access to a solicitor was routinely respected would in turn ensure that evidence properly and fairly obtained during interviews with suspects would be admissible at trial which he said would be "in the interests of justice from every perspective".

[109] [2012] ECHR 36 at [61].

[110] See also *Bodaerenko v Ukraine*, unreported, European Court of Human Rights, 14 May 2013, *Tarasov v Ukraine* [2013] ECHR 1070 and *Sebalj v Croatia* [2011] ECHR 1048 at [256]. In *Panovits v Cyprus* [2008] ECHR 1688 at [73], it was held that a waiver must be made in "an explicit and unequivocal manner".

[111] [2014] IESC 17, [2014] 1 ILRM 377 at 423.

[112] As inserted by s.9(a) of the Criminal Justice Act 2011. This section has not been commenced as of the time of going to print.

actually arose. In New Zealand, it has been held that a suspect must exercise his or her right to consult a lawyer without delay and the police are not obliged to wait indefinitely for a lawyer to arrive.[113] However, given the reference by Clarke J to "extreme situations where the lawyer just does not arrive within any reasonable timeframe",[114] it would seem that the circumstances where this will be permissable are quite confused. Such circumstances might include where the right was not being *bona fide* exercised or there were exceptional circumstances whereby, despite the best efforts of gardaí, the attendance of one or more solicitors nominated by the accused could not be procured.

8–55   There are a number of authorities which deal with the nature and extent of the efforts which gardaí were required to make to secure the attendance of a nominated solicitor when the right was formulated as one of reasonable access. These established that gardaí were obliged to act without delay[115] and *bona fide*,[116] and were required to make reasonable efforts to contact the nominated solicitor,[117] but were not obliged to actually procure the attendance of the nominated or any other solicitor.[118]

8–56   Those authorities, which examined the efforts required by gardaí in circumstances where gardaí were permitted to question the detainee in the interval before the arrival of that solicitor, might seem to have little continuing relevance given the holding in *Gormley and White* that, when a detainee decides to exercise his or her right of access to a lawyer, no questioning, or no further questioning, can take place until that access is afforded. It is noteworthy in that regard that, in *People (DPP) v Gormley*,[119] the Court of Criminal Appeal lauded what it regarded as the exemplary efforts made by gardaí to secure legal advice for the accused and expressed the view

---

[113] *R. v Etheridge* (1992) 9 CRNZ 268. It has also been held in Canada that a detainee is required to exercise reasonable diligence and act without delay in exercising the right to retain counsel: *R. v Sinclair* [2010] 2 SCR 310.

[114] [2014] IESC 17 at [9.10], [2014] 1 ILRM 377 at 404.

[115] *People (DPP) v Healy* [1990] 2 IR 73 at 83, [1990] ILRM 313 at 322. A delay in acting on foot of the request constituted a violation of the right of access to a solicitor even if the garda considered that there was a good reason to delay compliance with the request: *DPP v McCrea* [2009] IEHC 39, [2010] IESC 60.

[116] See *People (DPP) v O'Brien*, unreported, Court of Criminal Appeal, 17 June 2002, [2005] IESC 29, [2005] 2 IR 206, where the trial judge excluded certain inculpatory statements on the basis that there had been a breach of the right of access to a solicitor in circumstances where the gardaí chose to get in contact with a solicitor who was a sole and busy practitioner and whose offices were some distance from the station. The trial judge was satisfied that, in selecting the particular solicitor, the gardaí must have known that a significant and unnecessary delay would ensue. In *People (DPP) v Gormley* [2010] IECCA 22 at [9], [2010] 2 IR 409 at 415, *O'Brien* was cited as an example of the adoption by gardaí of a "colourable manoeuvre" designed to thwart the right of reasonable access to a solicitor. See also *People (DPP) v Connell* [1995] 1 IR 244, where it was held that there had been a breach of the accused's constitutional right of reasonable access to a solicitor in circumstances where a garda had abandoned efforts to contact a solicitor because he was told, incorrectly, that the applicant's solicitor had been in contact.

[117] *People (DPP) v Healy* [1990] 2 IR 73 at 83, [1990] ILRM 313 at 322. What was regarded as "reasonable steps" to carry out a request to contact a solicitor was a question of fact to be decided having regard to the circumstances of each individual case including, in particular, the time at which access is requested and the availability of the solicitor sought: *People (DPP) v Madden* [1977] IR 336 at 355. See, for example, the analysis in *People (DPP) v Darcy*, unreported, Court of Criminal Appeal, 29 July 1997; *People (DPP) v Buck* [2002] 2 IR 268, [2002] 2 ILRM 454 and *People (DPP) v O'Brien*, unreported, Court of Criminal Appeal, 17 June 2002, [2005] IESC 29, [2005] 2 IR 206.

[118] *People (DPP) v Darcy*, unreported, Court of Criminal Appeal, 29 July 1997 at 25.

[119] [2010] IECCA 22, [2010] 2 IR 409.

that they took every possible step to vindicate the rights of the accused. However, these authorities may have some continuing vitality given that the effect of the exercise of the right may be to extend the period of detention of the suspect. This is provided for in s.5A of the Criminal Justice Act 1984[120] which provides:

> "Subject to subsections (4) and (5), no questioning of a person detained pursuant to section 4 shall take place until such time as the person has had an opportunity to consult with a solicitor and, the period of time commencing from the time the detained person makes the request to consult a solicitor and ending upon the commencement of such a consultation, shall be excluded in reckoning a period of detention permitted by section 4."

8–57   In his concurring judgment in *Gormley and White*, Hardiman J was critical of what he termed dawn arrests and the problems that they posed for securing expeditious access to a solicitor. He gave a graphic description of the unsatisfactory conditions that might have to be endured by detainees and voiced disquiet at the prospect that they could be detained for a significant additional period if they decided to exercise their right of access to a lawyer. Clarke J also stressed that:

> "Situations should not arise which would place a suspect in a position where the price which they would have to pay for invoking their right to legal advice prior to interrogation would be an unreasonably lengthened period of incarceration or the acceptance of other adverse conditions. The conditions of custody must reflect the fact that the suspect at that stage has not even been charged. Such conditions must be such as could not objectively be considered in any way oppressive or otherwise such as might lead a suspect to reasonably consider waiving any rights which they may have."[121]

8–58   The obvious way of ensuring that this does not occur would be for gardaí, where possible, to arrest persons during normal business hours coupled with the establishment of a duty panel of solicitors to provide legal advice where persons are arrested out of hours. Hardiman J commented adversely on the failure of the State to put such a system in place and an expectation that this would be done was underlined by the strong endorsement by both Clarke and Hardiman JJ[122] of the holding in *Cadder v Her Majesty's Advocate*[123] that: "contracting states are under a duty to organise their systems in such a way as to ensure that, unless in the particular circumstances of the case there are compelling reasons for restricting the right, a person who is detained has access to advice from a lawyer before he is subjected to police questioning."[124]

8–59   A question that was expressly left open in *Gormley and White* is whether there is any obligation on the State to provide legal aid for impecunious detainees.[125]

---

[120] As inserted by s.9(a) of the Criminal Justice Act 2011. This section has not been commenced as of the time of going to print.

[121] [2014] IESC 17 at [9.16], [2014] 1 ILRM 377 at 406.

[122] [2014] IESC 17 at [9.7], [2014] 1 ILRM 377 at 404 (Clarke J) and 420–421 (Hardiman J).

[123] [2011] UKSC 13 at [48], [2010] 1 WLR 2601 at 2623. See Ferguson, "Repercussions of the Cadder Case: the ECHR's Fair Trial Provisions and Scottish Criminal Procedure" [2011] Crim LR 743; J. McCluskey, "Supreme Error" (2011) Edin LR 276; F. Leverick, "The Supreme Court Strikes Back" (2011) Edin LR 287; F. Stark, "The Consequences of Cadder" (2011) Edin LR 293; White and Ferguson, "Sins of the Father? The 'Sons of Cadder'" [2012] Crim LR 357.

[124] It is worth noting in this regard that, in *People (DPP) v Cullen,* unreported, Court of Criminal Appeal, 30 March 1993, opposition was expressed to the proposition that gardaí were obliged to suspend questioning until a solicitor arrived on the basis that it carried with it the necessary consequential assertion that there existed an obligation on the State to provide, in relation to all Garda stations in which persons might be obtained, a panel of solicitors who would always be available at the request of an arrested person to attend and give advice.

[125] [2014] IESC 17 at [9.3], [2014] 1 ILRM 377 at 402.

However, given the holding that the guarantee of a trial in due course of law in Art.38.1 applies after a suspect has been arrested, and the reliance placed on the decision in *State (Healy) v Donoghue*[126] which established a right to legal aid, this would be an unsurprising extension of that decision. This question is, perhaps, somewhat moot because the Garda Station Legal Aid Scheme[127] which provided for legal aid in respect of consultations with detainees has been replaced by the Garda Station Legal Aid Revised Scheme which makes provision for legal aid in respect of attendance by solicitors during questioning or time otherwise spent at garda stations for the purpose of advising detainees.[128]

(g) Affording Access to a Lawyer

8–60   If a detainee has requested access to a solicitor, then he or she must be afforded immediate access to that solicitor upon his or arrival at the garda station. That was the position when the right was couched as one of reasonable access and is, *a fortiori*, the position now. In *People (DPP) v Healy*,[129] it was held that the right of reasonable access meant "in the event of the arrival of a solicitor at the garda station in which a person is detained, an immediate right of that person to be told of the arrival and, if he requests it, immediate access".[130] It was further stated that the only thing which could justify the postponement of informing the detained person of the arrival of the solicitor, or of immediately complying with a request made by the detained person when so informed for access to him, would be reasons which objectively viewed from the point of view of the interest or welfare of the detained person, would be viewed by a court as being valid.[131] Such an objective justification did not lie, as contended by the DPP in that case, in the fact that a detained person was in the course of making a statement at the time of the arrival of the solicitor. Although the Supreme Court in that case seemed to accept that there could be reasons which would justify delaying access to a lawyer after he or she had arrived, it must be seriously doubted if, in practice, such reasons exist.

8–61   The right of access to a lawyer also means that, even if the detainee has not requested access (and, perhaps, even if he or she has expressly waived that right), he or she must be told if a solicitor retained on his or her behalf attends at the garda station. That was the position in *People (DPP) v Healy*[132] where a solicitor who had been retained by the family of the accused called to the garda station and sought to see the accused. Finlay CJ was satisfied that there was no distinction to be drawn between the right of a detained person to have reasonable access during his detention to a solicitor whose presence he or she has requested and that of reasonable access to

[126] [1976] IR 325.
[127] Details of the operation of this scheme were given in the *Final Report of the Working Group to Advise on a System Providing for the Presence of a Legal Representative during Garda Interviews* (July 2013).
[128] Details of the revised scheme are set out in a letter from the Department of Justice and Equality to the Director General of the Law Society dated 22 July 2014.
[129] [1990] 2 IR 73, [1990] ILRM 313.
[130] [1990] 2 IR 73 at 81, [1990] ILRM 313 at 320 (*per* Finlay CJ). A similar opinion was expressed by Griffin J who emphasised that delay in informing a detainee of the arrival of a solicitor could amount to a denial of the right of access (at 83; 322). *Cf. State v Reed* (1993) 133 NJ 237, where it was held that a failure to inform an accused of his attorney's attempts to contact him rendered a waiver of the privilege against self-incrimination invalid.
[131] [1990] 2 IR 73 at 81, [1990] ILRM 313 at 320.
[132] [1990] 2 IR 73, [1990] ILRM 313.

a solicitor whose attendance had been requested by other persons acting *bona fide* on his or her behalf.[133]

8–62   It should be noted that, although access to a solicitor will generally take the form of a face to face consultation between the suspect and the solicitor, it can be facilitated through a telephone call.[134] As discussed below, one facet of the right of access is the right to consult a solicitor by phone in private.[135]

8–63   Given that one of the purposes of the right of access to a solicitor is to redress the imbalance between a detained person and his interrogators,[136] it has been held that the solicitor must be independent of the State.[137] It follows that the State or gardaí cannot be held responsible for the content of the advice given or any shortcomings in it.[138] Thus, provided that access to a solicitor has been afforded, it would seem that gardaí have no obligation to satisfy themselves that the legal advice obtained was adequate or that it was actually obtained. In *DPP v Ryan*,[139] after initially being denied access to a solicitor, the accused had been given an opportunity to speak to his solicitor by telephone which he did in a call that lasted approx. 90 seconds. The call was not curtailed by gardaí and, when asked afterwards whether he was happy with the call, he confirmed that was. In those circumstances, the Court of Criminal Appeal was satisfied that the trial judge had been correct to conclude that the earlier breach of his right of reasonable access to a solicitor had been cured by that call, notwithstanding its brevity, and that his decision to admit that portion of an interview which took place after that call was correct. A similar approach was adopted in *People (DPP) v Cronin*.[140] After the accused had been arrested, an enquiry was made as to whether he wished to consult his solicitor to which he gave an affirmative response. He was given access to a telephone and made a two minute telephone call prior to the commencement of the first interview. When asked whether he had consulted a solicitor, he indicated that he had but, in fact, he had merely gotten through to a secretary. Unsurprisingly, the Court

---

[133] [1990] 2 IR 73 at 78, [1990] ILRM 313 at 317–318. As regards persons acting *bona fide* on behalf of a detained person, Finlay CJ did not enumerate the persons who would fall within this category but Griffin J stated that they would include members of his family, his employer or a close friend (at 83, 322).

[134] *People (DPP) v Gormley* [2010] IECCA 22 at [13], [2010] 2 IR 409 at 416.

[135] As held in *People (DPP) v Finnegan*, Court of Criminal Appeal, 15 July 1997.

[136] *People (DPP) v Healy* [1990] 2 IR 73 at 81, [1990] ILRM 313 at 320; *Salduz v Turkey* (2009) 49 EHRR 19 at [53].

[137] In *People (DPP) v Birney* [2006] IECCA 58 at [98], [2007] 1 IR 337 at 367, Hardiman J stated: "In the first place, it is of course important that a person held in custody for the purpose of an investigation have access, if he wishes, to a legal adviser. Such an adviser, normally a solicitor practising in the locality, must of course be entirely independent of the State and of the gardaí. Sometimes a person held in custody will have his own solicitor, though there may be logistical difficulties in contacting a specific practitioner for various reasons, notably the time of the day or night when advice is required and the practitioner's other commitments. In some circumstances a person may be given a list of solicitors or told of certain solicitors available in the locality. But whichever course is adopted it is essential that the advice be quite independent of the State and the gardaí." See also *People (DPP) v Gormley* [2010] IECCA 22 at [7], [2010] 2 IR 409 at 414 where Finnegan J referred to the right "to independent legal advice".

[138] *People (DPP) v Birney* [2006] IECCA 58 at [99], [2007] 1 IR 337 at 368. See also *People (DPP) v O'Callaghan* [2005] IECCA 72 where it was held that the fact that answers which a suspect gives to the gardaí are ones which he or she has been advised by a solicitor to give and which are untrue or misleading does not, of itself, render such answers inadmissible.

[139] [2011] IECCA 6.

[140] [2008] IECCA 165.

of Criminal Appeal rejected the contention that there had been a breach of his right of reasonable access to a solicitor on the basis that the gardaí should have been more proactive in satisfying themselves that an actual consultation with the solicitor had taken place. The court did not think that the brevity of the call was such as to arouse suspicions on the part of the gardaí that there had not been any effective access in the absence of being told that a consultation had not taken place.

8–64 An issue that has yet to be decided is the extent of the access that must be afforded. In *DPP v Ryan*,[141] the Court of Criminal Appeal accepted the proposition that the right of reasonable access to a solicitor (as it then stood) "embraces being afforded a meaningful opportunity to obtain legal advice". However, there is no authority as to the length of the consultation that a detainee is entitled to have. Also yet to be decided is the extent to which a detainee, having had a consultation with his or her solicitor prior to the commencement of questioning, is entitled thereafter to have further consultations. Although the Supreme Court of Canada in *R. v Sinclair*[142] held that a detainee was not entitled to additional consultations with a lawyer unless there were developments in the course of the interview which made this necessary to serve the purpose underlying the right to a lawyer guaranteed by s.10(b) of the Charter, such an approach seems very unlikely to be followed here, particularly as, for the reasons discussed below, it seems that a suspect has a right to have a lawyer present during questioning.

(h) Right of private access to a solicitor

8–65 In *People (DPP) v Finnegan*,[143] it was confirmed that the constitutional right to obtain legal advice carries with it the ancillary right to obtain such legal advice in private.[144] The appellant was arrested on suspicion of larceny and, while in custody, he asked to speak to his solicitor. He was permitted to telephone him but a number of gardaí stayed in the room while he made the call and the conversation took place in the hearing of at least one garda. The Court of Criminal Appeal held that the right to of access to a solicitor:

> "… necessarily implies, except in the most exceptional circumstances, a right to consult with the solicitor in private, in the sense of out of the hearing of police officers or prison warders. Indeed the right to consult a Solicitor would usually be of little value unless it carried with it, as a necessary concomitant, the right to consult him in private."[145]

8–66 Furthermore, when the appellant asked to speak with his solicitor by telephone, that request carried with it the necessary implication that he wished to speak to his solicitor in private. The gardaí were not entitled to assume that he did not require privacy simply because he did not mention it.

---

[141] [2011] IECCA 6 at [12].
[142] [2010] 2 SCR 310.
[143] Unreported, Court of Criminal Appeal, 15 July 1997.
[144] The ECHR made a similar finding in *Brennan v UK* (2002) 34 EHRR 18 at [58], where it was held that "an accused's right to communicate with his advocate out of hearing of a third person is part of the basic requirements of a fair trial and follows from Article 6(3)(c)".
[145] Unreported, Court of Criminal Appeal, 15 July 1997, at 33. As can be seen from the decision in *Ward v Minister for Justice* [2007] IEHC 39, [2007] 2 IR 726, the right of a detained person to consult with his legal advisers in private out of the hearing of members of the Gardaí or prison staff is more attenuated where the consultation takes place outside of the confines of a garda station or prison and it is not a breach of the broader right of reasonable access to a solicitor for an applicant to remain handcuffed to a prison officer when consulting with his legal advisors in the environs of the courts.

8–67   The decision in *Finnegan* is clearly correct.[146] The conclusion that the right of access to a lawyer entails a right to consult that solicitor in private necessarily follows from the purpose of the right. It has long been recognised in the sphere of legal professional privilege that confidential communication is essential so that a client may make a "clean breast" of it to his or her legal adviser.[147] Similarly, if, as envisaged in *Healy*, a suspect in custody is to make a free and full informed decision as to whether to make a statement, then it is essential that he or she should be able to consult and put all the facts before his or her solicitor in private so that the appropriate legal advice can be received.

3. Whether Solicitor is Entitled to be Present during Questioning

8–68   Although the contention that a suspect was entitled to have a lawyer present during questioning was rejected by the Supreme Court of Canada in *R. v Sinclair*,[148] a strong argument can be made that the presence of a lawyer during questioning is an important safeguard and serves, in particular, to protect the constitutional right of a suspect not to be compelled to incriminate himself or herself.[149] It was for this reason that the US Supreme Court held in *Miranda v Arizona*[150] that an accused was entitled to have his attorney present during questioning:

> "The circumstances surrounding in-custody interrogation can operate very quickly to overbear the will of one merely made aware of his privilege by his interrogators. ... Even preliminary advice given to the accused by his own attorney can be swiftly overcome by the secret interrogation process. ... Thus, the need for counsel to protect the Fifth Amendment privilege comprehends not merely a right to consult with counsel prior to questioning, but also to have counsel present during any questioning if the defendant so desires."[151]

8–69   In the UK, legal advice is available from a duty solicitor who is allowed to be present while the accused is being interviewed.[152] It is also noteworthy that art.3(3)(b) of Directive 2013/48/EU stipulates that:

> "Member States shall ensure that suspects or accused persons have the right for their lawyer to be present and participate effectively when questioned. Such participation shall be in accordance with procedures under national law, provided that such procedures do not prejudice the effective exercise and essence of the right concerned. Where a lawyer participates during questioning, the fact that such participation has taken place shall be noted using the recording procedure in accordance with the law of the Member State concerned;"

---

[146] It should be noted that art.3(3)(a) of Directive 2013/48/EU imposes an obligation on Member States to ensure that suspects or accused persons have the right to meet in private and communicate with the lawyer representing them, including prior to questioning.

[147] *Anderson v Bank of British Columbia* (1876) 2 Ch D 644 at 649 (*per* Jessel MR).

[148] [2010] 2 SCR 310.

[149] See White, "The Confessional State—Police Interrogation in the Irish Republic: Part 1" (2000) 10(1) ICLJ 17; White, "The Confessional State—Police Interrogation in the Irish Republic: Part 2" (2000) 10(2) ICLJ 2, and Costelloe, "Detention for Questioning and Oppressive Interrogation" (2001) 11(1) ICLJ 12.

[150] (1966) 384 US 436. For a general discussion of the US approach to confessions, see Link, "Fifth Amendment—The Constitutionality of Custodial Confessions" (1992) 82 (4) JCL & Crim 878.

[151] Indeed, it seems to have been precisely because the presence of a solicitor during questioning would have served to neutralise the psychological pressure that the gardaí were able to bring to bear that Carney J refused to recognise a right to have the solicitor present during questioning in *Barry v Waldron*, unreported, High Court, *ex tempore*, 23 May 1996.

[152] Code C of the Revised Code of Practice for the Detention, Treatment and Questioning of Persons by Police Officers (May 2014) at [6.8].

8–70 While the jurisprudence of the European Court of Human Rights has not yet reached the point where a universal right to have a lawyer present during questioning has been recognised,[153] there are some indications that such a right may be recognised in the future.[154]

8–71 In this jurisdiction, the position taken thus far has been that a detainee does not have an entitlement to have a solicitor present during questioning.[155] The contention that the gardaí were required to provide notes of interviews to a solicitor while the questioning of his or her client was ongoing was rejected in *Lavery v Member in Charge, Carrickmacross Garda Station*.[156] O'Flaherty J summarised the position as follows:

> "[T]he gardaí must be allowed to exercise their powers of interrogation as they think right, provided they act reasonably. Counsel for the State submitted to the High Court Judge that in effect what [the solicitor for the applicant] was seeking was that the gardaí should give him regular updates and running accounts of the progress of their investigations and that this was going too far. I agree. The solicitor is not entitled to be present at the interviews. Neither was it open to the applicant, or his solicitor, to prescribe the manner by which the interviews might be conducted, or where."[157]

8–72 Thus, although the applicant and his solicitor would have been entitled to all relevant documentation if a prosecution took place, the applicant's solicitor was not entitled to be present during interviews with him or furnished with secondary evidence of them on a contemporaneous basis.[158]

8–73 This issue was revisited in *JM (A Minor) v Member in Charge of Coolock Garda Station*[159] where it was contended, in the context of an inquiry pursuant to Art.40.4.2, that the refusal by gardaí to allow the applicant's solicitor to be present during questioning in circumstances where the applicant was a minor with mental health problems was a breach of the right of reasonable access to a solicitor and rendered his detention unlawful. Sheehan J rejected the argument that the passage from *Lavery* set out above was *obiter* and held that it represented the law as to the entitlement to have a solicitor present during questioning in garda custody. The applicant had been arrested on suspicion of having committed a serious offence under the Misuse of

---

[153] In *Brennan v UK* (2002) 34 EHRR 18 at [53], it was held that the attendance of lawyer during interview of suspect is not an indispensable precondition of fairness within the meaning of art.6(1) of the Convention.

[154] See *Mader v Croatia* [2011] ECHR 973 at [157] and *Sebalj v Croatia* [2011] ECHR 1048 at [256].

[155] *People (DPP) v Cornally,* unreported, Court of Criminal Appeal, *ex tempore*, 7 November 1994 at 12; *Barry v Waldron,* unreported, High Court, 23 May 1996; *Lavery v Member in Charge, Carrickmacross Garda Station* [1999] 2 IR 390 at 396; *People (DPP) v Yu Jie* [2005] IECCA 95 at [6].

[156] [1999] 2 IR 390.

[157] [1999] 2 IR 390 at 395–396.

[158] It should be noted that in *Lavery* the applicant's solicitor sought the interview notes specifically so that he could advise him in relation to the application of ss.2 and 5 of the Offences Against the State (Amendment) Act 1998 (No.39 of 1998) which permit inferences to be drawn from the failure to answer questions. The Supreme Court did not attach any particular significance to this factor but Breen and McEntee, "The Right to Silence" (1999) 5 BR 6, have made a strong argument that the complex provisions of ss.2 and 5 of the Offences Against the State (Amendment) Act 1998 place a premium on the availability of legal advice and, therefore, require the presence of a solicitor in interviews. See also *Murray v UK* (1996) 22 EHRR 29 at [66] and *Averill v UK* (2001) 31 EHRR 36 at [58], where the importance of access to legal advice in circumstances where adverse inferences can be drawn has been emphasised.

[159] [2013] IEHC 251.

Drugs Act 1977 and it was contended on his behalf that issues could arise if the gardaí invoked ss.18 or 19 of the Criminal Justice Act 1984 and as to whether a mandatory sentence might be imposed after conviction pursuant to s.15A of the Misuse of Drugs Act 1977 (as amended) which would require careful advice so that the presence of a parent or suitable adult (as required by s.61(1) of the Children Act 2001) would not be sufficient. However, Sheehan J was satisfied that the applicant had failed to establish the likelihood of unfairness arising in the course of the interviews as a result of the absence of a solicitor during those interviews. He also concluded that the decisions of the European Court of Human Rights relied on by the Applicant[160] did not support the contention advanced because they only established a right of access to legal advice prior to questioning and none of them went so far as to hold that a suspect has a right to have a solicitors present during police questioning.

8–74 However, these decisions must be considered to be of very doubtful authority following the decision in *Gormley and White*. Although Clarke J acknowledged that the question of whether a suspect is entitled to have a lawyer present during questioning did not arise, he nonetheless commented:

> "However, it does need to be noted that the jurisprudence of both the ECtHR and the United States Supreme Court clearly recognises that the entitlements of a suspect extend to having the relevant lawyer present."[161]

8–75 Hardiman J was even more forthright in signalling the Court's likely view on this question, stating:

> "For many years now judicial and legal authorities have pointed to the likelihood that our system's option for the very widespread questioning of suspects who are held in custody for that purpose, was very likely to attract a right on the part of such suspects, not merely to be advised by lawyers before interrogation, but to have lawyers present at the interrogation, and enabled to intervene where appropriate. This has now come to pass in countries with similar judicial systems: see in the developments surveyed by Mr. Justice Clarke, and also under the ECHR, to which Ireland is a signatory and which it has incorporated to a limited extent in Irish law by an Act of 2003.
>
> It is notable, however, that Mr. Gormley has not asserted that right to its full extent but has asserted only a right to have a lawyer to advise him, in custody, before the questioning starts. Manifestly, however, it will not be long before some person or other asserts a right to legal advice in custody on a broader basis. I say this in explicit terms in order that this may be considered by those whose duty it is to take account of potential developments."[162]

8–76 Taking those comments together with the evolving jurisprudence of the European Court of Human Rights and the position adopted in Directive 2013/48/EU, it seems inevitable that, when this issue is reconsidered by the Supreme Court, it will be held that the constitutional right of access to a lawyer extends to an entitlement to have the lawyer present during questioning.

8–77 The reality of this situation has been recognised and new procedures have been put in place to facilitate the presence of lawyers during questioning.

---

[160] The Applicant relied in particular on the decisions in *Salduz v Turkey* (2009) 49 EHRR 421 and *Panovits v Cyprus* [2008] ECHR 1688 and the decision of the UK Supreme Court in *Cadder v Her Majesty's Advocate (Scotland)* [2010] UKSC 43, [2010] 1 WLR 2601 which had considered the relevant jurisprudence of the European Court of Human Rights.

[161] [2014] IESC 17 at [9.10], [2014] 1 ILRM 377 at 404–405.

[162] [2014] IESC 17 at [9.10], [2014] 1 ILRM 377 at 419.

(a) Effect of a breach of the right

8–78   In *People (DPP) v Healy*,[163] Finlay CJ stated that, if a breach of the right of reasonable access to a solicitor occurred, the "vital issue" was "whether there is a causative link between that breach and the obtaining of an admission". Thus, if a breach of the right occurred, this did not automatically lead to the exclusion of an inculpatory statement made thereafter but only if there was a causative link between the breach and the obtaining of the statement.[164] However, in a series of cases,[165] culminating in the decision of the Supreme Court in *People (DPP) v Buck*,[166] it was held that the effect of a breach of the right of reasonable access to a solicitor was to render the detention of the person detained unlawful. In *People (DPP) v Buck*,[167] Keane CJ referred to the decision in *The Emergency Powers Bill 1976*[168] where it was held that the detention of a person against his or her will is permissible only where his or her constitutional right of reasonable access to a solicitor is observed. In his view, it followed "inexorably" that his or her detention became unlawful as soon as that right is denied.[169] Therefore, if the right of a detained person of reasonable access to a solicitor was breached, the person was thereafter in unlawful detention[170] and any inculpatory statement made during that period of unlawful detention was inadmissible[171] unless there are extraordinary excusing circumstances.[172]

8–79   As discussed above, the unlawfulness of a period of detention has been held to subsist only for so long as the person detained is deprived of reasonable access to a solicitor and will cease to be unlawful once that is afforded. In *People (DPP) v O'Brien*,[173] the trial judge had found that there had been a deliberate and conscious breach by Gardaí of the accused's constitutional right of reasonable access to a solicitor because, when the accused requested a solicitor, Gardaí recommended and made contact with a busy sole practitioner whose office was distant from the station and whose attendance would inevitably be delayed. He, accordingly, ruled inadmissible the statements made by the accused prior to the arrival of the solicitor but admitted statements made by him after the accused had consulted with the solicitor. In the Court

---

[163] [1990] 2 IR 73 at 78, [1990] ILRM 313 at 317.

[164] See also *People (DPP) v Connell* [1995] 1 IR 244 at 252, where the Court of Criminal Appeal appeared to apply a test of causation stressing that the "inexcusable" breach of the accused's right of access to a solicitor was "a matter of great importance as the applicant might well have avoided making the inculpatory statement had he received advice that morning from his solicitor".

[165] See *The Emergency Powers Bill 1976* [1977] IR 159 at 173; *People (DPP) v Madden* [1977] IR 336 at 355; *People (DPP) v Shaw* [1982] IR 1 at 35 (*per* Walsh J); *People (DPP) v Quilligan (No.3)* [1993] 2 IR 305 at 321; *Barry v Waldron*, unreported, High Court, 23 May 1996 at 5; *People (DPP) v Finnegan*, unreported, Court of Criminal Appeal, 15 July 1997 at 42; *Lavery v Member in Charge, Carrickmacross Garda Station* [1999] 2 IR 390 at 395; *People (DPP) v Buck* [2002] 2 IR 268, [2002] 2 ILRM 454; *People (DPP) v O'Brien*, unreported, Court of Criminal Appeal, 17 June 2002, [2005] IESC 29, [2005] 2 IR 206; *DPP v McCrea* [2009] IEHC 39.

[166] [2002] 2 IR 268.

[167] [2002] 2 IR 268, [2002] 2 ILRM 454.

[168] [1977] IR 159.

[169] [2002] 2 IR 268 at 281, [2002] 2 ILRM 454 at 466.

[170] See also *DPP v McCrea* [2009] IEHC 39 at [27].

[171] *People (DPP) v Madden* [1977] IR 336; *People (DPP) v Farrell* [1978] IR 13; *People (DPP) v O'Loughlin* [1979] IR 85; *People (DPP) v Higgins*, unreported, Supreme Court, 22 November 1985; *People (DPP) v Byrne* [1989] ILRM 613: *People (DPP) v Quilligan* [1986] IR 495 at 503, [1987] ILRM 606 at 618; *Larkin v O'Dea* [1994] 2 ILRM 448, [1995] 2 ILRM 1.

[172] See *People (DPP) v Shaw* [1982] IR 1.

[173] Unreported, Court of Criminal Appeal, 17 June 2002; [2005] IESC 29, [2005] 2 IR 206.

of Criminal Appeal, Keane CJ stated that it was clear that a conscious and deliberate violation by the gardaí of an applicant's constitutional right of access to a solicitor would render a detention, that was otherwise lawful, unlawful. However, it did not follow that statements made after a solicitor had arrived and an applicant had been advised as to his rights were also inadmissible. The applicant had been in otherwise lawful detention and, accordingly, once the violation of the applicant's right to consult a solicitor had been remedied, there was no reason in law why his detention should, thereafter, be regarded as unlawful.

8–80   The same conclusion was reached by a unanimous Supreme Court. McCracken J held that, from the moment that the breach of the accused's constitutional right of reasonable access to a solicitor occurred, his detention became unlawful[174] and remained unlawful so long as the breach continued. It followed logically that, once the solicitor attended and consulted with the accused so that the breach of this constitutional right ceased, the detention ceased to be unlawful. Accordingly, the accused had been in lawful detention when he made the statements at issue and these had been correctly admitted in evidence. However, having considered the decisions in *Healy* and *Buck* which had referred to the requirement for a causative link, he entered the significant caveat that:

> "If the inculpatory statement or admission ultimately made by the accused was elicited from him by the use of information disclosed by him while he was in unlawful detention, there would clearly have been a causative link between the breach of his constitutional rights and the making of the statements of admissions. In those circumstances, material which had been wrongfully obtained in breach of the accused's constitutional rights would have been used to obtain an inculpatory statement or admission."

8–81   Thus, while inculpatory statements made by an accused after reasonable access to a solicitor has been afforded and the lawfulness of the detention has been restored will generally be admissible, if a causative link is established between those statements and an earlier breach of the accused's constitutional right to such access, those statements will be inadmissible.

8–82   This aspect of the decision in *O'Brien* was applied and elaborated upon in *DPP v Ryan*,[175] a case which underlines the very fact-specific inquiry which is required to identify whether there is a causative link between an inculpatory statement made during a period of lawful detention after a breach of the right of reasonable access to a solicitor has been remedied and statements made and/or information obtained during an earlier period of unlawful detention. During a twenty four hour period of detention, the accused had been interviewed six times. The accused had a telephone consultation with a solicitor prior to the first interview and again after the first interview. No admissions were made by him in the first and second interviews. In the course of the third interview, the accused requested further access to his solicitor which request was not conveyed to the member-in-charge or otherwise acted on. He subsequently made a

---

[174] In the course of his judgment (at [17]–[18], 213–214), McCracken J explained that he used the phrase "unlawful detention" because it had been used in earlier decisions but expressed doubts as to whether this was the correct description of the accused's position during the period while the breach of the accused's constitutional rights subsisted. He pointed out that the accused had been detained pursuant to s.4 of the Criminal Justice Act 1984 and explained that what was unlawful was not his detention in the garda station but the delay in providing him with access to a solicitor. He was, therefore, of the view that an application for his release pursuant to Art. 40 of the Constitution could not have been made because the accused was in lawful custody pursuant to s.4.

[175] [2011] IECCA 6.

number of admissions in that interview and again in the fourth interview. The accused did not get an opportunity to speak to his solicitor until the following morning when the solicitor rang the station while the accused was in the course of the fifth interview and the applicant spoke briefly to him. In the course of the sixth interview, the accused again made admissions but after requesting to see his solicitor. The trial judge found that there had been a flagrant breach of the accused's right of reasonable access to a solicitor and excluded all of the statements made by the accused except for those made in the portion of the fifth interview after he had an opportunity to speak to his solicitor to the extent that these did not relate to matters divulged in earlier interviews of which the gardaí were not otherwise aware. The Court of Criminal Appeal held that the trial judge had applied the correct approach, stating:

> "The '*O'Brien* test', as the applicant characterises it, speaks of '*the use of information*' gained. The word 'use' as deployed in the particular context connotes the positive or active sense of that word, namely the conscious employment of relevant unconstitutionally obtained information towards the achievement of a specific end, namely the obtaining of an inculpatory statement or admission (whether that be a new statement/admission or a reiterated statement/admission). This Court considers that for an inculpatory statement to be excluded on those grounds there must be clear evidence that the sole source of the material used to elicit that statement was the accused. The inculpatory statement must have been 'obtained' exclusively by the use of the unlawfully sourced material. If material used to obtain an inculpatory statement is also available to the police from another, lawful, source then the police may legitimately use that material in questioning an accused notwithstanding that he may have spoken about it previously in the course of an unconstitutional interview."

8–83 The Court, thus, rejected the proposition advanced by the accused that a causative link between what had been stated in the fifth interview and the contents of the earlier interviews should be inferred on the basis of "human psychology". A causative link might exist in some cases but not in others, and what was required and what the Court engaged in, was a careful review of the contents of the interviews and the evidence generally to ascertain whether the admissions obtained in the admissible portion of the fifth interview had been elicited using information obtained during the earlier interviews that was not otherwise known to gardaí.

8–84 It has also been held that, while a breach of the right of reasonable access to a solicitor will render inadmissible any inculpatory statement made thereafter, it will not affect the admissibility of any statements made prior to the occurrence of the breach. In *People (DPP) v AD*,[176] the accused was in the course of making an exculpatory statement when his solicitor arrived. He was asked if he wanted to consult with his solicitor and replied that he did but, before his solicitor was afforded access, the accused was asked a further question and the statement was read over, amended and signed by the accused. The trial judge excluded that portion of the statement which had been made after the accused had confirmed that he wished to see his solicitor and the written statement that had been signed by him but allowed evidence to be given of a note of the interview and a videorecording of the interview up to that point. The accused contended that the entirety of the statement ought to have been excluded because of the conscious and deliberate breach of his constitutional right.

8–85 Delivering the judgment of the Supreme Court, Clarke J held that the decisions in *Healy, Buck* and *Finnegan* all supported the proposition that a causal connection with a breach of constitutional rights had to be established in order for a statement to

---

[176] [2008] IECCA 101; [2012] IESC 33, [2012] 2 IR 332.

be excluded. Having noted that there was a clear causative link where the statement under challenge was made during a period of unlawful detention because, if the accused had been released, the statement would not have been made, he continued[177]:

> "Where, however, a statement is made in circumstances where there was no illegality, let alone unconstitutionality, attaching to the accused's custody or to the taking of the statement concerned up to a certain point in time, is there any reason in principle why the statement up to that point in time should not be admissible? There is, at least in the ordinary way, no obvious causal link between a subsequent lapse into constitutionally unlawful custody[178] and previous statements made by an accused during entirely lawful custody. To impose an exclusionary rule, at the level of principle, to statements made by an accused during lawful custody simply because the accused's custody later, albeit while the statement taking process was continuing, became unconstitutional would, in my view, be to impose an unnecessarily excessive exclusionary rule not warranted by the need to discourage improper activity by those investigating crime.
>
> The causative link test is well established in the jurisprudence to which reference has been made. It seems to me that that test meets the legitimate requirements of discouraging a constitutionally impermissible investigation while at the same time permitting lawfully obtained evidence to be placed before the court as part of the criminal process. I am not, therefore, satisfied that there is any legitimate basis for departing from the causative link test identified by Finlay CJ in *The People (Director of Public Prosecutions) v Healy* [1990] 2 IR 73."

8–86   He went on to express the view that a court could sever those portions of a statement made by an accused during a period of constitutionally unlawful custody from those which were made during a period of lawful custody and these were, in principle, admissible. He approved of the approach laid down in *O'Brien* of analysing whether the breach of the right of reasonable access to a solicitor had caused or contributed to the making of the statement and that held that it could equally be applied to two portions of a statement taken during an interview process where one portion is made during lawful custody and another portion is made during constitutionally unlawful custody. He added that, unless there was some sufficient nexus between the two parts of the statement or interview process so as to taint the otherwise lawful portion, then there was no reason to exclude that part of the interview or statement which was made while the accused was in lawful custody. That might be necessary if it proved impossible, with any degree of confidence, to disentangle those aspects of the statement which had been made within and without periods of lawful custody.[179] The entirety of a statement might also be excluded where the interview ranged forward and backwards over the events under investigation so that it was not possible to sever the portion of the statement made in constitutionally unlawful custody without giving the jury a misleading account of what had been said by the accused thereby creating a real risk of unfairness. He summarised the position as follows[180]:

> "I am, therefore, satisfied that the causal link test is one which needs to be applied in

---

[177] [2012] IESC 33 at [41]–[42], [2012] 2 IR 332 at 345–346.

[178] The use by Clarke J of the phrase "unconstitutionally unlawful custody" chimes with the views expressed by McCracken J in *People (DPP) v O'Brien*, unreported, Court of Criminal Appeal, 17 June 2002, [2005] IESC 29, [2005] 2 IR 206 noted above in relation to the continued lawfulness at a statutory level of the detention when there has been a breach of the constitutionally guaranteed right of reasonable access to a solicitor.

[179] He noted (at [47], 347) that this was the position in *People (DPP) v Healy* [1990] 2 IR 73 where the trial judge had been unable to determine whether the admissions had been made prior to or after the breach of the accused's constitutional rights leading him to exclude the entirety of the statement. However, he noted that it was much less likely that such difficulties would arise in modern conditions with videotaping of interviews.

[180] At [53], 349.

circumstances where an accused comes to be detained in conscious and deliberate violation of constitutional rights. It follows that a part of a statement made or interview given during a period when the accused is in constitutionally unlawful custody must be excluded but that, *prima facie*, any part of the statement made or interview given during a period of lawful custody can be admitted. However, that latter statement is subject to the caveat that, if it can be shown that there is a real risk of unfairness by admitting only part of a statement, then it may well be that the trial judge will have to exclude the entirety of the statement concerned."

8–87 On the facts of that case, he was satisfied that none of the matters which occurred after the accused was denied access to his solicitor and his detention became constitutionally unlawful were such as to create a nexus between what occurred during his constitutionally unlawful custody and what had gone before while he was in lawful custody or any real risk of unfairness.

8–88 It is unclear whether these decisions and the approach adopted therein will be followed post *Gormley and White*. As noted above, this decision has identified a different doctrinal basis for the right of access to a lawyer, rooting it firmly in the guarantee of due process in Art.38.1, and highlighting its role in protecting the right to silence of a detainee. This approach is very similar to that adopted by the European Court of Human Rights in *Salduz v Turkey*[181] so it would be expected that the question in each case is whether the breach of the right has deprived the accused of a fair hearing, a question that will almost certainly be answered in the affirmative if an inculpatory statement is made by an accused after a breach of the right of access to a lawyer has occurred. However, Clarke J referred, without any disapproval, to the existing jurisprudence including the decision in *Buck* where this question was analysed by reference to whether the detention of the accused was lawful or unlawful by reason of a breach of the right at the time that an inculpatory statement was made.

8–89 The significance of the difference in the two approaches potentially lies in a situation where the gardaí take forensic samples or obtain other items of real evidence after a breach of the right of access to a lawyer has occurred and can be illustrated by reference to the decision in *People (DPP) v Creed*.[182] The accused had been arrested pursuant to s.4 of the Criminal Justice Act 1984 on a Saturday night. He requested the services of a named local solicitor. The member in charge made a number of attempts to contact that solicitor but they were confined to ringing the landline at her office, which predictably did not result in contact being made. The member in charge did not make any effort to obtain a mobile or other number for the solicitor and did not inform the accused that he had failed to make contact. While the manifest inadequacy of these efforts led the trial judge to exercise his discretion to exclude any statements made by the accused while in custody, he nonetheless ruled that there has not been a deliberate and conscious failure to vindicate the accused's constitutional rights and admitted a hair sample that had been obtained. On appeal, it was argued that the breach of the right to a solicitor had been deliberate and conscious with the result that the detention of the accused thereafter become unlawful and all evidence obtained during that period of unlawful detention including the sample was inadmissible.

8–90 Geoghegan J accepted that the "behaviour by the garda seemed to show a lack of common sense and proper care in efforts to procure the named solicitor and

---

[181] (2009) 49 EHRR 19.
[182] [2009] IECCA 95.

in failing to seek alternative instructions (if any) from the prisoner".[183] However, he did not think that it was in any way contrary to the exclusionary rule established by *Kenny* (which he described as a "somewhat controversial principle") "that subjective factors like motive or personal knowledge are not relevant when considering whether infringement of a constitutional right is conscious and deliberate".[184] He observed:

> "A deliberate and conscious violation of rights may indeed render a detention wholly unlawful and render any evidence taken as a consequence of it, in admissible. Where, however, there has been no deliberate and conscious violation of the constitutional right to access to a solicitor but where reasonable efforts have not been made to obtain a solicitor and the accused has not acquiesced in that situation, it must then be a matter of discretion for the trial judge to rule as to whether any particular evidence obtained in that context should be admitted or not."[185]

8–91   He went on to hold that the trial judge had been entitled to exercise his discretion in the particular circumstances of the case to rule that the hair sample was admissible. He noted a number of factors in that regard including that the hair sample could be obtained under the Criminal Justice (Forensic Evidence) Act 1990 without consent and that the request for a solicitor had been clearly related to the questioning which the accused was about to undergo.

8–92   The decision in *Creed* indicates some level of judicial discomfort with the combined effect of the decisions in *Buck* and *Kenny*. Given that *Buck* held that the effect of a breach of the right of reasonable access to a solicitor is to render the detention of the person detained unlawful and that detention will remain unlawful until such time as the breach of the right of reasonable access is remedied, it would seem to follow that all evidence obtained thereafter, whether in the form of an incriminating statement or real evidence, will be inadmissible[186] in accordance with the exclusionary rule laid down in *Kenny* unless it can be said that the act constituting the breach of that right was committed unintentionally or accidentally or there were extraordinary excusing circumstances. In order to avoid this result, the Court of Criminal Appeal in *Creed* adopted a strained interpretation of the formula "deliberate and conscious" which is difficult to reconcile with *Kenny*. However, such an approach would not be necessary under the approach adopted in *Gormley and White* where Clarke J said that he was "not satisfied that the mere fact that otherwise lawful forensic sampling is properly taken prior to the attendance of a legal adviser renders any subsequent trial, at which reliance is placed on the results of the tests arising out of that forensic material, unfair".[187]

8–93   Another issue that has yet to be determined is the admissibility of evidence that has been obtained as a result of an inculpatory statement made by an accused in circumstances where there was a breach of his or her right to a lawyer. In *Gäfgen v Germany*[188] the European Court of Human Rights reviewed its previous case law which established that "both the use in criminal proceedings of statements obtained as a result of a person's treatment in breach of art.3—irrespective of the classification of that treatment as torture, inhuman or degrading treatment—and the use of real evidence obtained as a direct result of acts of torture made the proceedings as a whole

---

[183]   [2009] IECCA 95 at [6].
[184]   [2009] IECCA 95 at [6].
[185]   [2009] IECCA 95 at [6]–[7].
[186]   This was the conclusion reached by Edwards J in *DPP v McCrea* [2009] IEHC 39.
[187]   [2014] IESC 17 at [10.3], [2014] 1 ILRM 377 at 407.
[188]   [2010] ECHR 759, (2011) 52 EHRR 1 (case comment at (2009) 13 E & P 58).

automatically unfair, in breach of art. 6…"[189] However, outside of circumstances where a breach of art.3 was involved, it noted that there was no clear consensus among the Contracting States, the courts of other states and human rights monitoring institutions about the exact scope of the exclusionary rule that should apply to the fruits of inadmissible evidence in other cases. It went on to say that "factors such as whether the impugned evidence would, in any event, have been found at a later stage, independently of the prohibited method of investigation, may have an influence on the admissibility of such evidence".[190]

8–94 It is apparent, therefore, that the European Court of Human Rights has not laid down any hard and fast rule that the admission of real or other evidence derived from an inadmissible inculpatory statement will necessarily render a trial unfair irrespective of the other circumstances of the case. On the contrary, it would seem that a case by case analysis is required in that regard. This was the conclusion reached by the UK Supreme Court in *Her Majesty's Advocate v P*.[191]

C. The Voluntariness Rule

1. Introduction

8–95 A confession[192] is inadmissible unless it is proved by the prosecution beyond reasonable doubt to have been voluntarily made.[193] If the prosecution fails to discharge this burden of proof, then the trial judge must exclude the confession and has no discretion to admit it in evidence.[194] This common law voluntariness rule has now been given a constitutional foundation by the decision of the Supreme Court in *Re National Irish Bank*[195] that the guarantee in Art.38.1 of a trial in due course of law requires the exclusion of involuntary confessions. Delivering the judgment of the Court, Barrington J stated:

> "It appears to me that the better opinion is that a trial in due course of law requires that any confession admitted against an accused person in a criminal trial should be a voluntary confession and that any trial at which an alleged confession other than a voluntary confession were admitted in evidence against the accused person would not be a trial in due course of law within the meaning of Art.38 of the Constitution and that it is immaterial whether the compulsion or inducement used to extract the confession came from the Executive or from

---

[189] [2010] ECHR 759, [2010] 52 EHRR 1 at [173].

[190] [2010] ECHR 759, [2010] 52 EHRR 1 at [174]. The US courts have developed a doctrine of inevitable discovery whereby evidence, which has been obtained in breach of an accused's constitutional rights, will be admitted if the prosecution can establish that it would have been obtained in any event by lawful means (*Nix v Williams* (1984) 467 US 431). A similar approach is adopted by the Canadian courts (*R. v Black* [1989] 2 SCR 138; *R. v Stillman* [1997] 1 SCR 607, (1995) 144 DLR (4th) 193).

[191] [2012] UKSC 108, [2011] 1 WLR 2497.

[192] Or an admission falling short of a full confession: *Commissioners of Customs and Excise v Harz* [1967] 1 AC 760 at 818, [1967] 1 All ER 177 at 182.

[193] *State v Treanor* [1924] 2 IR 193; *DPP v Patterson* (1979) 113 ILTR 6 at 8; *People (DPP) v Hoey* [1987] IR 637, [1988] ILRM 666; *People (DPP) v Buck* [2002] 2 IR 268 at 277, [2002] 2 ILRM 454 at 462. In *People (DPP) v Boylan* [1991] 1 IR 477, it was stated that this incidence of the burden does not require the prosecution to go through a litany to disprove involuntariness; voluntariness is a matter to be looked at in the light of any particular case.

[194] *McCarrick v Leavy* [1964] IR 225; *People (AG) v Cummins* [1972] IR 312; *People (DPP) v Shaw* [1982] IR 1 at 48.

[195] [1999] 3 IR 145, [1999] 1 ILRM 321.

the Legislature … it can be stated, as a general principle, that a confession, to be admissible at a criminal trial must be voluntary. Whether, however, a confession is voluntary or not must in every case in which the matter is disputed be a question to be decided, in the first instance, by the trial Judge."[196]

8–96   As will be seen below, the voluntariness test seeks to protect the free will of a person who is questioned in relation to an offence.[197] A person is free to make an inculpatory statement if he or she wishes but cannot be forced to do so and if improper or undue pressure is applied or means are used which vitiate the free will of the person, any confession made by him or her will be rejected as involuntary. As originally developed, the voluntariness test excluded confessions that had been obtained as the result of threats or promises (referred to collectively as inducements) made by persons in authority. However, over time, it has come to be recognised that a person's free will may be overborne by factors other than threats and promises and what is referred to below as the traditional voluntariness test has been supplemented by the concept of oppression and a broader test of voluntariness.[198]

8–97   At the outset, it should be noted that the cases in this area are not all easily reconcilable[199] due to the fact that the voluntariness test is very contextual and its application is dependant on all of the circumstances of an individual case. In addition, as will be seen below, the test is underlain by a number of different and sometimes competing policy considerations.[200] This is an area of the law of evidence where the interaction between the State and the individual in the context of the criminal justice system is at its most fraught and it is evident from a review of the cases that judges in particular cases have been influenced by their perception of where the balance between the two should be struck.

2. Development and Rationale of the Voluntariness Rule

8–98   The origins of the voluntariness rule can be traced back to the eighteenth century when it developed because of concerns about the reliability of confessions that were, at the time, being increasingly relied upon to sustain criminal charges against accused persons. The contours of the rule seem to have been reasonably well settled by the time of the decision in *R. v Warickshall*[201] where Nares J and Eyre B stated:

"A free and voluntary confession is deserving of the highest credit, because it is presumed to flow from the strongest sense of guilt, and therefore it is admitted as proof of the crime to which it refers; but a confession forced from the mind by the flattery of hope, or by the torture of fear, comes in so questionable a shape when it is to be considered as evidence of guilt, that no credit ought to be give to it; and therefore it is rejected."[202]

8–99   That formulation of the voluntariness rule was approved as an authoritative statement of the law by the Irish Court for Crown Cases Reserved in *R. v Gillis*[203] and

---

[196] [1999] 3 IR 145 at 186–187, [1999] 1 ILRM 321 at 359. See McGuckian, "Confessions and the Constitution" (2004) 26 DULJ 272.
[197] See *per* Henchy J in *People (DPP) v Hoey* [1987] IR 637 at 651–652, [1988] ILRM 666 at 673.
[198] See *People (DPP) v Shaw* [1982] IR 1 at 60–61.
[199] As was acknowledged by Kenny J in *People (AG) v Galvin* [1964] IR 325 at 330; and Henchy J in *People (DPP) v Hoey* [1987] IR 637 at 652, [1988] ILRM 666 at 673.
[200] See O'Connor, "Observations on the Voluntariness Test in Irish Law" (1980) 11 *Gazette* 198.
[201] (1783) 1 Leach 263.
[202] (1783) 1 Leach 263 at 263–264.
[203] (1866) 17 ICLR 512 at 531.

forms the basis of the traditional voluntariness test as formulated in the seminal Irish authority of *State v Treanor*.[204]

8–100   In *R. v Warickshall*,[205] Nares J and Eyre B. were quite emphatic that the voluntariness rule was not based on any notion of "public faith" or the right of an accused person not to be compelled to incriminate himself or herself:

> "It is a mistaken notion, that the evidence of confessions and facts which have been obtained from prisoners by promises or threats, is to be rejected from a regard to public faith: no such rule ever prevailed. The idea is novel in theory, and would be as dangerous in practice as it is repugnant to the general principles of criminal law. Confessions are received in evidence, or rejected as inadmissible, under a consideration whether they are or are not intitled to credit."[206]

8–101   Thus, the voluntariness rule was concerned only with the reliability of confessions and the focus in the rule on threats and promises reflected the view of the courts that hope or fear engendered by such inducements could cause an accused to confess to an offence that he did not commit.[207] It followed logically from this rationale for the rule, and was confirmed in subsequent cases, that only inducements which were calculated to induce an untrue confession fell foul of the rule.[208]

8–102   In the late eighteenth and the first half of the nineteenth century, the trend was towards a very expansive interpretation of what could constitute an inducement and, hence, render an inculpatory statement inadmissible by the application of the voluntariness requirement. The reasons for such a lenient approach were identified by Lord Hailsham in *DPP v Ping Lin*[209] as follows:

> "At that time almost every serious crime was punished by death or transportation. The law enforcement officers formed no disciplined police force and were not subject to effective control by the Central Government Watch Committee or an inspectorate. There was no legal aid. There was no system of appeal. To crown it all the accused was unable to give evidence on his own behalf and was therefore largely at the mercy of any evidence, either perjured or oppressively obtained, that might be brought against him. The judiciary was therefore compelled to devise artificial rules designed to protect him against dangers now avoided by other and more rational means."[210]

8–103   An attempt was made by the Court for Crown Cases reserved in *R. v Baldry*[211] to reverse this trend, with Parke B stating:

> "By the law of England, in order to render a confession admissible in evidence, it must be perfectly voluntary; and there is no doubt that any inducement in the nature of a promise or of a threat held out by a person in authority vitiates a confession...but I think there has been too much tenderness towards prisoners in this matter. I confess that I cannot look at the decisions

---

[204] [1924] 2 IR 193 at 208.
[205] (1783) 1 Leach 263.
[206] (1783) 1 Leach 263 at 263. See also, *per* Blain J in *R. v Ovenell* [1968] 1 All ER 933 at 937: "The basic reason for the rejection of involuntary statements in our system is the greater risk that an induced or involuntary statement may be untrue".
[207] But *cf. R. v Baldry* (1852) 2 Den 430 and *Ibrahim v R.* [1914] AC 599 at 610–611, [1914-15] All ER 874 at 878. In *Ibrahim*, Lord Sumner described the voluntariness rule as one of policy and stated: "It is not that the law presumes such statements to be untrue, but from the danger of receiving such evidence judges have thought it better to reject it for the due administration of justice".
[208] See *R. v Court* (1836) 7 Car & P 486 at 487, and *R. v Thomas* (1836) 7 Car & P 345 at 346.
[209] [1976] AC 574, [1975] 3 All ER 175.
[210] [1976] AC 574 at 600, [1975] 3 All ER 175 at 182. These reasons are elaborated upon by Heydon, *Cases and Materials* 2nd edn (London: Butterworths, 1984), pp.178–179.
[211] (1852) 2 Den 430.

without some shame when I consider what objections have prevailed too far, and justice and common sense have, too frequently, been sacrificed at the shrine of mercy."[212]

8–104 However, the courts continued to adopt an indulgent approach to the question of what could constitute an inducement and in *R. v Smith*[213] Lord Parker CJ observed that:

"In deciding whether an admission is voluntary the court has been at pains to hold that even the most gentle, if I may put it that way, threats or slight inducements will taint a confession."[214]

8–105 Although that lenient approach has been the subject of some judicial criticism,[215] it was defended by Lord Reid in *Commissioners of Customs and Excise v Harz*[216] who explained:

"It is true that many of the so-called inducements have been so vague that no reasonable man would have been influenced by them, but one must remember that not all accused are reasonable men or women: they may be very ignorant and terrified by the predicament in which they find themselves. So if may have been right to err on the safe side."[217]

8–106 In the twentieth century, it came to be recognised that one of the animating principles of the voluntariness test was the maxim *nemo tenetur se ipsum accusare*. As McLachlin J stated in *R. v Hebert*,[218] "one of the themes running through the jurisprudence on confessions is the idea that a person in the power of the state's criminal process has the right to freely choose whether or not to make a statement to the police".[219] The linkage between the principle that no one should be compelled to incriminate himself or herself and the voluntariness test appears to have been first made in this jurisdiction in *State (McCarthy) v Lennon*.[220] This change in doctrinal basis was acknowledged by Walsh J in *People (AG) v O'Brien*[221] who explained that:

"While the rule of law relating to the non-admissibility of … confession[s] was a judge-made rule and based, originally at least, upon the question of the credit to be attached to

---

[212] (1852) 2 Den 430 at 444.

[213] [1959] 2 QB 35, [1959] 2 All ER 193.

[214] See also *per* Parke B. in *R. v Moore* (1852) 2 Den 522 (if an inducement was held out the confession must be excluded "however slight the threat or inducement"), *per* Finnemore J in *R. v Cleary* (1963) 48 Cr App R 116 at 119: ("What is plain is this, that any kind of inducement made by a person in authority will make the statement inadmissible") and *per* Winn LJ in *R. v Richards* [1967] 1 All ER 829 at 830 ("Whatever be the nature of the inducement so made and however trivial it may seem to the average man to have been, such an inducement will be at least capable of rendering the statement then made inadmissible.").

[215] See, *e.g. R. v Northam* (1967) 52 Cr App R 97 at 102 (*per* Winn LJ).

[216] [1967] 1 AC 760, [1979] 1 All ER 177.

[217] [1967] 1 AC 760 at 820, [1979] 1 All ER 177 at 184. See, to similar effect, *per* Winn LJ in *R. v Northam* (1967) 52 Cr App R 97 at 104: "It is not the magnitude, it is not the cogency to the reasonable man or to persons with such knowledge as is possessed by lawyers and others which is the proper criterion. It is what the average, normal, probably quite unreasonable person in the position of the appellant at the time might have thought was likely to result to his advantage from the suggestion agreed to by the police officer."

[218] [1990] 2 SCR 151 at 173, (1990) 57 CCC (3d) 1 at 32.

[219] See also *R. v Hodgson* [1998] 2 SCR 449 at 463–466; *R. v Oickle* [2000] 2 SCR 3; *R. v Singh* [2007] 3 SCR 405; *R. v Spencer* [2007] SCC 11, 44 CR (6th) 199. For an analysis of the voluntariness test in Canada, see Dufraimont, "The Common Law Confessions Rule in the Charter Era: Current Law and Future Directions" (2008) 40 SCLR 2d 249; Akhtar, "Whatever Happened to the Right to Silence?" (2009) 62 CR (6th) 73; Stewart, "The Confessions Rule and the Charter" (2009) 54 McGill LJ 517; Dufraimont, "The Interrogation Trilogy and the Protections for Interrogated Suspects in Canadian Law" (2011) 54 SCLR 2d 309.

[220] [1936] IR 485.

[221] [1965] IR 142.

such a statement, the rule has also come to be based partly upon the idea that in fairness to an accused person he should not by way of trick or otherwise improperly be compelled to incriminate himself."²²²

8–107   This change led to the decision of the Court of Criminal Appeal in *AG v Cleary*²²³ that it was irrelevant to the application of the voluntariness rule whether an inducement was of a type that would "affect the person in the direction of telling or not telling the truth", *i.e.* the rule was directed towards the inducement of statements irrespective of their truth or falsity.²²⁴ The recognition of the right of a person not to be compelled to incriminate himself or herself as a basis for the rule can also be seen to underlie its constitutionalisation as a requirement of a trial in due course of law protected by Art.38.1 in *Re National Irish Bank*.²²⁵

8–108   The change in the rationale for the voluntariness rule, coupled with the increasing reliance by the gardaí on interrogation of suspects as a means of obtaining incriminating statements and the use of more sophisticated interrogation techniques, also led to a recognition by the courts that there were a broader range of factors than just threats and promises which could result in an involuntary confession. An initial response was the development of the concept of oppression as a distinct category of involuntariness but this is just one example of a factor other than a threat or a promise that may vitiate the free will of a suspect and render a confession involuntary. The best exposition of the broad scope of the modern voluntariness rule is, perhaps, to be found in the judgment of Griffin J in *People (DPP) v Shaw*²²⁶:

> "The primary requirement is to show that the statement was voluntary, in the sense in which that adjective has been judicially construed in the decided cases. Thus, if the tendered statement was coerced or otherwise induced or extracted without the true and free will of its maker, it will not be held to have been voluntarily made. The circumstances which will make a statement inadmissible for lack of voluntariness are so varied that it would be impossible to enumerate or categorize them fully. It is sufficient to say that the decided cases show that a statement will be excluded as being involuntary if it was wrung from its maker by physical or psychological pressures, by threats or promises made by persons in authority, by the use of drugs, hypnosis, intoxicating drink, by prolonged interrogation or excessive questioning, or by any one of a diversity of methods which have in common that result or the risk that what is tendered as a voluntary statement is not the natural emanation of a rational intellect and a free will."²²⁷

8–109   A final strand in the policy basis of the voluntariness rule which should be

---

²²² [1965] IR 142 at 166. The privilege against self incrimination has also been recognised as one of the principal rationales of the voluntariness rule in England (see *Commissioners of Customs and Excise v Harz* [1967] 1 AC 760 at 820, [1967] 1 All ER 177 at 184 and *Lam Chi-ming v R.* [1991] 2 AC 212 at 220, [1991] 3 All ER 173 at 178) and Canada (see *R. v Hebert* [1990] 2 SCR 151, (1990) 57 CCC (3d) 1; *R. v Oickle* [2000] 2 SCR 3).
²²³ (1934) 1 Frewen 14 at 17–18.
²²⁴ See also *People (DPP) v Hoey* [1987] IR 637 at 649, [1988] ILRM 666 at 670 (*per* Walsh J); *Sparks v R.* [1964] AC 964, [1964] 1 All ER 727 at 739; *R. v Hodgson* [1998] 2 SCR 449 at 463–465.
²²⁵ [1999] 3 IR 145 at 186–187, [1999] 1 ILRM 321 at 359. *Cf. R. v Hebert* [1990] 2 SCR 151 at 164, (1990) 57 CCC (3d) 1 at 26, where it was held that the right to silence protected by s.7 of the Canadian Charter of Rights and Freedoms was rooted in the voluntariness rule and the privilege against self-incrimination which were united by the common theme "that a person in the power of the state in the course of the criminal process has the right to choose whether to speak to the police or remain silent".
²²⁶ [1982] IR 1.
²²⁷ [1982] IR 1 at 60–61.

noted is a concern for the reputation and integrity of the criminal justice system.[228] As Lord Hailsham commented in *Wong Kam-ming v R.*[229]:

"[A]ny civilised system of criminal jurisprudence must accord to the judiciary some means of excluding confessions or admissions obtained by improper methods. This is not only because of the potential unreliability of such statements, but also, and perhaps mainly, because in a civilised society it is vital that persons in custody or charged with offences should not be subjected to ill treatment or improper pressure in order to extract confessions."[230]

8–110 In a number of older decisions, judicial disapproval of the practice of interrogating suspects with a view to obtaining incriminating statements was expressed[231] and this disapproval can be seen to have influenced the application of the voluntariness rule in some cases. A good example can be seen in *People (AG) v Flynn*,[232] where the Court of Criminal Appeal held that an incriminating statement made by the accused should have been excluded because it could not be satisfied that it was voluntary having regard to:

"the undoubted facts that the purpose of arresting the applicant and bringing him to the station was to get a statement from him…that he was kept nearly seven hours in custody, and that he was released only when he had made a statement admitting nearly all [the complainant's] allegations".[233]

8–111 There is now a much greater acceptance of the practice of interrogating suspects, with O'Flaherty J in *People (DPP) v McCann*[234] observing that "the very word "interrogation" means more than some form of gentle questioning and, provided that there are no threats or inducements or oppressive circumstances, then the gardaí are always entitled to persist with their questioning of a suspect".[235] However, judicial distaste for some of the interrogation practices used by the gardaí is still evident[236] and the voluntariness rule is susceptible to use as a means of deterring/disciplining improper conduct on the part of the gardaí.

3. The Traditional Voluntariness Test

8–112 The *locus classicus* of the traditional test of voluntariness in Irish law is to found in the judgment of Fitzgibbon J in *State v Treanor*[237]:

---

[228] This was explicitly recognised by McLachlin J in *R. v Hebert* [1990] 2 SCR 151 at 173, (1990) 57 CCC (3d) 1 at 32, adopting the views of Lamer J (dissenting) in *R. v Rothman* [1981] 1 SCR 640 at 696.

[229] [1980] AC 247, [1979] 1 All ER 939.

[230] [1980] AC 247 at 261, [1979] 1 All ER 939 at 946. See also *King v R.* [1969] 1 AC 304, [1968] 2 All ER 610 and *Lam Chi-ming v R.* [1991] 2 AC 212 at 220, [1991] 3 All ER 173 at 178.

[231] See *R. v Hughes* (1839) 1 Cr & Dix CC 13; *R. v Johnston* (1864) 15 ICLR 60 (*per* Pigot C.B.); *People (AG) v C.* [1943] Ir Jur Rep 74; *People (AG) v Murphy* [1947] IR 236; *People (AG) v Galvin* [1964] IR 325.

[232] [1963] IR 255.

[233] [1963] IR 255 at 261–262. See also *People (AG) v C* [1943] Ir Jur Rep 74, where Gavan Duffy J excluded certain statements because he regarded the practice of interrogating suspects as being contrary to the principles of criminal justice.

[234] [1998] 4 IR 397 at 410.

[235] See also *Barry v Waldron*, unreported, High Court, 23 May 1996 and *Lavery v Member in Charge, Carrickmacross Garda Station* [1999] 2 IR 390 at 395. For a discussion of the effectiveness of police interrogation techniques, see Brooke, "Police Interrogation: For Justice Not Punishment-Part 1" (2010) 28 ILT 28 and Brooke, "Police Interrogation: For Justice Not Punishment—Part 2" (2010) 28 ILT 48.

[236] *Cf. People (DPP) v Ward*, unreported, Special Criminal Court, 27 November 1998

[237] [1924] 2 IR 193.

"A confession made to any person under the influence of a promise or threat held out by a person in authority, calculated to induce a confession, is inadmissible, unless it be clearly proved to the satisfaction of the Judge, whose duty it is to decide the question, that the promise or threat did not operate upon the mind of the accused, and that the confession was voluntary notwithstanding, and that the accused was not influenced to make it by the previous promise or threat."[238]

8–113 Thus, a confession by an accused will be excluded as involuntary where it has been preceded by a threat or promise made by a person in authority to him or her[239] unless the prosecution establish that the threat or promise did not actually induce the accused to make the confession.

(a) Person in authority

8–114 It is well settled that, in order for the traditional voluntariness test to apply, the impugned inducement must have been held out by a person in authority.[240] In *People (DPP) v McCann*,[241] a "person in authority" was defined to mean "someone engaged in the arrest, detention, examination or prosecution of the accused or someone acting on behalf of the prosecution".[242] Obviously, this category of persons would include, in appropriate cases, the gardaí,[243] customs and excise officers,[244] and military officers.[245]

8–115 Decisions in other jurisdictions have extended the definition of a person in authority to include, in certain circumstances, the captain of a ship vis-à-vis a sailor,[246] a school headmistress vis-à-vis a pupil,[247] employers vis-à-vis employees,[248] the victim of an offence,[249] and a social worker.[250] Although it is not immediately evident

---

[238] [1924] 2 IR 193 at 208. This statement of the law was approved and applied by the Court of Criminal Appeal in *People (AG) v O'Shea* (1943) 1 Frewen 50. *Cf.* the formulation of the rule by Lord Sumner in *Ibrahim v R.* [1914] AC 599 at 609, [1914–15] All ER 874 at 877: "It has long been established as a positive principle of English criminal law, that no statement by an accused is admissible in evidence against him unless it is shown by the prosecution to have been a voluntary statement, in the sense that it has not been obtained from him either by fear of prejudice or hope of advantage exercised or held out by a person in authority." This formulation of the rule has been cited with approval in many Irish cases including *AG v McCabe* [1927] IR 129; *People (AG) v Murphy* [1947] IR 236; and *People (DPP) v Hoey* [1987] IR 637, [1988] ILRM 666.

[239] An inducement must be made to the accused and it is not sufficient that he overhears an inducement offered to another suspect (*R. v Jacobs* (1849) 4 Cox CC 54) or entertains unsolicited hopes that he will be better off confessing (*R. v Godinho* (1911) 7 Cr App R 12; *R. v Rennie* (1981) 74 Cr App R 207 at 212).

[240] See *R. v Doherty* (1874) 13 Cox CC 23; *R. v Row* (1809) Russ & Ry 153; *R. v Gibbons* (1823) 1 C & P 97; *R. v Tyler* (1823) 1 C & P 129; and *R. v Moore* (1852) 2 Den 522.

[241] [1998] 4 IR 397 at 412.

[242] *Cf. R. v Hodgson* [1998] 2 SCR 449 at 471, where Cory J stated that a "'person in authority' typically refers to those persons formally engaged in the arrest, detention, examination or prosecution of the accused".

[243] *AG v Cleary* (1938) 72 ILTR 84, (1934) 1 Frewen 14; *People (DPP) v Hoey* [1987] IR 637, [1988] ILRM 666.

[244] *R. v Ovenell* [1969] 1 QB 17, [1968] 1 All ER 933; *R. v Grewal* [1975] Crim LR 159.

[245] *R. v Smith* [1959] 2 QB 35, [1959] 2 All ER 193.

[246] *R. v Parratt* (1831) 4 Car & P 570.

[247] *R. v McLintock* [1962] Crim LR 549.

[248] *R. v Richards* (1832) 5 Car & P 318; *R. v Hewett* (1842) Car & M 534; *R. v Stanton* (1911) 6 Cr App R 198. *Cf. R. v Thompson* [1893] 2 QB 12, [1891–94] All ER 376 (chairman of a company was held to be person in authority in relation to an employee of the company).

[249] *R. v Downey* (1976) 32 CCC (2d) 511.

[250] *R. v Sweryda* (1987) 34 CCC (3d) 325.

that these categories of persons can be said to be engaged in the arrest, detention or prosecution of those over whom they were held to exercise authority, it has been held that a subjective approach should be used, *i.e.* the question is whether the accused believed, on reasonable grounds, that the person holding out the inducement was in a position to influence his or her arrest, detention, examination or prosecution in relation to the offence.[251] In *R. v Hodgson*,[252] it was emphasised by the Supreme Court of Canada that, apart from police officers and prison guards, there is no catalogue of people who will automatically be considered to be "persons in authority". A case by case consideration of the accused's belief as to the ability of the person to influence the investigation or prosecution of the offence is required.

8–116   The person in authority requirement will also be satisfied where an inducement is held out by a person not in authority in the presence of a person in authority and the latter does not dissent from it.[253] In *People (AG) v Murphy*[254] an inducement was held out by a civilian who was acting in concert with and under the instructions of a garda. Having regard to that fact, and also to the fact that the inducement was uttered in the presence of the garda and without any demur by him, the court was of opinion that the civilian was to be treated for the purposes of the rule as a person in authority. It also appears from the definition advanced in *McCann* that a lay person who is considered, on the facts of a particular case, to have been acting as an agent for or on behalf of the prosecution will be considered to be a person in authority.[255]

8–117   In *Deokinian v R.*[256] the Privy Council rejected the argument that the decision in *Commissioner of Customs and Excise v Harz*[257] had impliedly abolished the person in authority requirement. Viscount Dilhorne acknowledged that untrue confessions could be induced by inducements held out by persons who were not in authority but regarded the requirement as well-settled and advanced the view that the "fact that an inducement is made by a person in authority may make it more likely to operate on the accused's mind and lead him to confess".[258] Whether the requirement should be retained in this jurisdiction depends to a certain extent on the view taken as to the proper doctrinal basis for the voluntariness rule. Applying the reliability principle, it is evident, and was conceded in *Deokinian*, that untrue confessions could be induced by threats and promises held out by persons who are not in authority and, thus, it would seem to follow that this requirement should be dispensed with. However, if the voluntariness rule is considered to be primarily predicated on protecting the constitutionally protected right

---

[251] *R. v Hodgson* [1998] 2 SCR 449 at 472–473; *R. v Dally* [1990] 2 NZLR 184.

[252] [1998] 2 SCR 449 at 474–475.

[253] *People (AG) v Murphy* [1947] IR 236; *R. v Cleary* (1963) 48 Cr App R 116 at 119; *R. v Laugher* (1846) 2 Car & K 225. The mere fact that an inducement has been held out by the person not in authority prior to the making of a confession to a person in authority is not sufficient, it must be held out in the presence of the person in authority: *R. v Gibbons* (1823) 1 C & P 97; *R. v Tyler* (1823) 1 C & P 129; *R. v Richards* (1832) 5 Car & P 318.

[254] [1947] IR 236.

[255] In *Deokinian v R.* [1961] 1 AC 20, [1968] 2 All ER 346, a person who had been placed by police in a cell with the accused in the hope that he would obtain information from him was not considered to be a person in authority because the accused did not regard him as such. However, a different conclusion might be reached if the issue were to arise in this jurisdiction.

[256] [1961] 1 AC 20, [1968] 2 All ER 346.

[257] [1967] 1 AC 760, [1967] 1 All ER 177.

[258] [1969] 1 AC 20 at 33, [1968] 2 All ER 346 at 350. See also *R. v Hodgson* [1998] 2 SCR 449 at 469–470, where the Supreme Court of Canada also decided to retain the person in authority requirement.

of a person not to be compelled to incriminate himself or herself, then some degree of State action would seem to be required, *i.e.* the person holding out the inducement must be an agent of the State.[259]

(b) Inducements

8–118   At the core of the traditional voluntariness test is the concept of an inducement, which is used as an umbrella term to cover both threats and promises. There are a large number of decisions on the question of what can constitute an inducement but, before examining these, some general principles should be noted. The first point, which was clarified in *People (DPP) v Hoey*,[260] is that, in determining whether a particular statement constitutes an inducement, the intention or motive on the part of the person making the statement is irrelevant. Walsh J stated that the test is "what effect [the inducement] was calculated to produce upon the person to whom it was made and not the subjective test of what was intended or even hoped for by the person who made it".[261]

8–119   The second point, which emerges from the decision in *People (DPP) v McCann*[262] is the test of whether a statement which constitutes an inducement has both an objective and a subjective element. In that case, the Court of Criminal Appeal approved the following test laid down in *Phipson on Evidence*:[263]

> "As regards what constitutes an inducement, the test would appear to be (a) were the words used by the person or persons in authority, objectively viewed, capable of amounting to a threat or promise? (b) Did the accused subjectively understand them as such? (c) Was his confession in fact the result of the threat or promise?"[264]

8–120   It can thus be seen that the test is primarily subjective in nature, involving an inquiry as to whether an accused regarded the statement as an inducement coupled with an inquiry as to whether it actually caused the accused to confess. Indeed, such a subjective approach to the question of what can constitute an inducement would seem to be mandated by the underlying rationale of protecting the right of a criminal suspect not to be compelled to incriminate himself or herself. It helps to ensure that protection is afforded by the voluntariness test to the weak-willed individual. However, it is evident that a purely subjective test would be open to abuse by criminal suspects who could allege that they were induced to confess by very mild inducements. Thus, the objective element of the test performs an important filtering function by excluding innocuous statements from the ambit of inducements.

(i) Statements capable of amounting to an inducement

8–121   As noted above, there are a large number of decisions as to whether particular statements are capable of constituting inducements which provide some guidance in that regard. However, it is important to enter the caveat that the value of some of the

---

[259] For a discussion of the policy issues surrounding the person in authority requirement, see *R. v Hodgson* [1998] 2 SCR 449 at 467–470.

[260] [1987] IR 637, [1988] ILRM 666.

[261] [1987] IR 637 at 649, [1988] ILRM 666 at 670–671. See also *DPP v Ping Lin* [1976] AC 574 at 607, [1975] 3 All ER 175 at 188 (*per* Lord Salmon).

[262] [1998] 4 IR 397. See also *People (DPP) v Murphy* [2013] IECCA 1 at [34].

[263] Buzzard, May and Howard (eds.), *Phipson on Evidence* 13th edn (London: Sweet and Maxwell, 1982), para.2–20.

[264] [1998] 4 IR 397 at 411.

decisions, especially the older decisions, as precedents is limited because they were decided in the context of quite a different criminal justice system[265] and, as pointed out above, adopted interpretations of alleged inducements that were deliberately favourable to accused persons. Moreover, regard should be had to the cautionary words of Lord Morris in *DPP v Ping Lin*[266] who pointed out that these decisions "merely record what the ruling of another judge has been in another case and in the particular circumstances of that case and on the basis of its own particular facts" and that "considerations of space may often make it difficult to record in a report all the relevant circumstances and facts".

8–122   (a) Threats   It is evident that any threat of violence or ill-treatment of the accused or members of his family would be considered to be an inducement[267] as would any such threat directed towards friends of the accused or even a person with little or no connection to the accused.[268] A threat to charge or interrogate members of an accused's family or, possibly, friends of the accused, will also suffice.[269] Other threats that have been held to be capable of amounting to inducements include threats to commit the accused to prison,[270] to prosecute the accused if he or she fails to answer questions,[271] to prosecute the accused for additional offences,[272] to keep troops on parade until someone confesses,[273] and to have an accused suspected of having murdered her baby brought to a doctor who she was told would be able to determine if her baby had been born

---

[265] See the description by Lord Hailsham in *DPP v Ping Lin* [1976] AC 574 at 600, [1975] 3 All ER 175 at 182, of the conditions obtaining in the late eighteenth and early nineteenth century when many of the early decisions were made. In *R. v Northam* (1967) 52 Cr App R 97 at 102, Winn LJ suggested that, given the change in conditions since then, the approach adopted in some of the older authorities was out of date. Indeed, in *R. v Priestly* (1966) 50 Cr App R 183 at 188, Melford Stevenson J went so far as to suggest that the authorities that pre-dated the Criminal Evidence Act 1898, which made accused persons competent to testify, no longer had any relevance in practice.

[266] [1976] AC 574 at 594, [1975] 3 All ER 175 at 177.

[267] *People (DPP) v Boylan* [1991] 1 IR 477 at 480.

[268] In *People (DPP) v Hoey* [1987] IR 637 at 649, [1988] ILRM 666 at 671, Walsh J, drew a distinction, in the context of a threat of interrogation, between members of an accused's family and persons for whom an accused "would not normally have such a natural concern". However, in *R. v Middleton* [1975] QB 191 at 197, [1974] 2 All ER 1190 at 1194, it was held that a confession could be rendered inadmissible by a threat of violence towards a person who was a complete stranger to the accused.

[269] See *People (DPP) v Hoey* [1987] IR 637, [1988] ILRM 666 where the threat was to interrogate members of the accused's family, and *R. v Jackson* (1977) 34 CCC (2d) 35 where the threat was to charge a friend of the accused. *Cf. R. v Oickle* [2000] 2 SCR 3 at 50–51 (threat to question fiancé of accused or ask her to take polygraph was not strong enough inducement to raise a reasonable doubt as to the voluntariness of confession). In *R. v Middleton* [1975] QB 191 at 197, [1974] 2 All ER 1190 at 1194, Edmund Davies LJ observed that: "As a matter of common sense, of course, the more remote the person involved in the threat is from the person or close circle of the accused man the more difficult it may be to establish that the confession was improperly obtained; but that is a consideration which goes to the weight of the evidence that a threat was made and not to the admissibility of a confession if the threat was, in fact, established."

[270] *R. v Parratt* (1831) Car & P 570.

[271] *Commissioners v Customs and Excise v Harz* [1967] 1 AC 760 at 815, [1967] 1 All ER 177 at 180.

[272] *Sparks v R.* [1964] AC 964, [1964] 1 All ER 727.

[273] *R. v Smith* [1959] 2 QB 35, [1959] 2 All ER 193.

alive.[274] It is not, however, a threat to indicate to an accused a desire or need to take a statement[275] or to express frustration at the failure of a suspect to make a statement.[276]

8–123   (b) Promises   In the case of promises, the question is whether the accused has been offered some benefit or advantage of a type that might induce him or her to confess. Examples of such promises that have been held to constitute inducements include: an offer of bail if the accused makes a statement[277]; promises to the effect that, if a confession is made and/or stolen goods returned, a complaint will not be made to the authorities or the accused will not be prosecuted[278]; promises that the accused will receive a lighter sentence or more favourable treatment from the prosecuting authorities or the court if he confesses[279]; the avoidance of publicity in relation to the prosecution of the offence[280]; and, it would appear, statements couched in terms that suggest that it would be "better" for an accused to make a statement.[281] It appears that the benefit or advantage does not have to accrue to the accused personally provided that it is of a type that could cause him to confess.[282]

8–124   An inducement may be found to have been held out even where the suggestion of the benefit or advantage originates with the accused himself or herself. In *R. v*

---

[274] *AG v Cleary* (1938) 72 ILTR 84, (1934) 1 Frewen 14.

[275] *R. v Joyce* [1957] 3 All ER 623, [1958] 1 WLR 140.

[276] *People (AG) v Galvin* [1964] IR 325 (remark of a garda to the accused: "You should not be keeping us here all night—tell the truth and be finished with it" held not to constitute an inducement).

[277] *R. v Zavecka* [1970] All ER 413; *R. v Northam* (1967) 52 Cr App R 97 at 100.

[278] See *R. v Gillis* (1866) 17 ICLR 512 (promise not to prosecute); *R. v Thompson* (1783) 1 Leach 291 ("Tell me where the things are and I will be favourable to you"); *R. v Jones* (1809) Russ & Ry 152 (accused had produced money in response to statement by victim that "he only wanted his money, and if the prisoner gave him that, he might go to the devil if he pleased"); *R. v Stanton* (1911) 6 Cr App R 198 ("If you will give me back my rings, I will forgive you").

[279] See *R. v Cooper* (1833) 5 Car & P 535 (where the accused was told by the committing magistrate that, if he confessed, he would do all that he could for him); *R. v Nugent* (1988) 84 NSR (2d) 191 (confession excluded where accused had been told that, if he confessed, the charge could be reduced from murder to manslaughter). But *cf. DPP v Ping Ling* [1976] AC 574, [1975] 3 All ER 175 (statement of police officer to the accused, "If you can show the judge that you have helped the police to trace bigger drug people, I am sure he will bear it in mind when he sentences you", was held not to constitute an inducement on the particular facts of the case). In *R. v Oickle* [2000] 2 SCR 3 at 32, Iacobucci J stated that the classic "hope of advantage" is the prospect of leniency from the courts and that it is improper for a person in authority to suggest to a suspect that he or she will take steps to procure a reduced charge or sentence if the suspect confesses.

[280] *Sparks v R.* [1964] AC 964, [1964] 1 All ER 727. *Cf. People (AG) v Kelly* (1962) 1 Frewen 267 (request by accused that his children would not learn of what he done to which the garda responded that: "In so far as possible we will avoid bringing your children into it").

[281] See *R. v Doherty* (1874) 13 Cox CC 23 ("It is better for you to tell the truth, and not put people to the extremities you are doing"); *R. v Cheverton* (1862) 2 F & F 833 ("You had better tell all about it; it will save trouble"); *R. v Thompson* [1893] 2 QB 12, [1891–4] All ER 376 ("It will be the right thing…to make a clean breast of it"); *R. v Cleary* (1963) 48 Cr App R 116 ("Put your cards on the table and tell them the lot … If you did not hit him, they can't hang you."); *R. v Richards* [1967] 1 All ER 829 ("I think it would be better if you made a statement and told me exactly what happened"). *Cf. People (AG) v Murphy* [1947] IR 236 at 245, where the Court of Criminal Appeal upheld the ruling of the trial judge that the statement "You are all right" meaning "You will be alright" was an inducement. But see, *contra, R. v Oickle* [2000] 2 SCR 3 at 48–49, where it was held that suggestions by police that the accused would feel better if he confessed did not contain any implied threat or promise and did not render his confession involuntary.

[282] See *People (DPP) v Pringle* (1981) 1 Frewen 57 at 84–85 (promise that person with whom accused had close relationship would not be charged with any offence or have to give evidence); *Sparks v R.* [1964] AC 964, [1964] 1 All ER 727 (freedom for accused's wife to leave the jurisdiction).

Zaveka,[283] the appellant asked a police officer if he would get bail at once if he made a statement. The police officer said "yes" and the appellant then made an inculpatory statement. It was held that the question asked by the appellant together with the police officer's answer amounted to an inducement and it made no difference that it was the appellant who had inquired about bail being available first rather than an offer having been made.[284]

8–125   (c) Spiritual inducements   A number of old authorities indicate that, to come within the scope of the voluntariness rule, the threat or promise must involve temporal as opposed to spiritual or moral consequences.[285] For example, the exhortation, "Don't run your soul into more sin, but tell the truth", was held not to render a confession inadmissible in *R. v Sleeman*.[286] The reasons advanced for this limitation are that a spiritual or moral threat is unlikely to produce a false confession[287] and the person in authority has no control over the suggested threat or benefit.[288] However, with the recognition that the voluntariness rule is also predicated on the right of a person not to be compelled to incriminate himself or herself, it makes little sense to exclude spiritual or moral inducements from the ambit of the rule because these undoubtedly could cause an accused to confess when he or she would otherwise have remained silent.[289]

8–126   (d) Whether inducement has to relate to the prosecution   In *People (AG) v Kelly*,[290] the Court of Criminal Appeal applied the orthodox view[291] that a statement to an accused "could be an inducement only if it might cause him to believe that his own position in relation to the charge would be altered by his making or not making a statement".[292] However, this requirement was rejected by the House of Lords in *Commissioners of Customs and Excise v Harz*[293] as illogical and unreasonable and one that had not been applied in practice. It is submitted that the criticisms of the requirement in *Harz* are well made and that the decision in *Kelly* should not be regarded as good law.

---

[283] [1970] All ER 413.

[284] See also *R. v Northam* (1967) 52 Cr App R 97 (reply of police officer that the police would have no objection to the suggestion of the accused that an offence in respect of which he was being questioned could be taken into consideration at his forthcoming trial for a different offence held to constitute an inducement).

[285] *R. v Johnston* (1864) 15 ICLR 60 at 71 (*per* Deasy B.); *R. v Gilham* (1828) 1 Mood CC 186; *R. v Wild* (1835) 1 Mood CC 452; *R. v Sleeman* (1853) Dears 249.

[286] (1853) Dears 249.

[287] Joy, *Confessions* (J.S. Littell, Philadelphia, 1848), p.51, explained: "It seems difficult to imagine a man under spiritual convictions and the influence of religious impressions would therefore confess himself guilty of a crime of which he was *not* guilty. ... Such spiritual convictions or exhortations seem, from the nature of religion, the most likely of all motives to produce truth. ... If temporal hopes exist, they may lead to falsehood. Spiritual hopes can lead to nothing but truth."

[288] *R. v Oickle* [2000] 2 SCR 3 at 37.

[289] *Cf. People (AG) v Cummins* [1972] IR 312 at 328, where Walsh J referred to the fact that the accused was not labouring under "any degree of moral compulsion" as a factor indicating voluntariness.

[290] (1962) 1 Frewen 267.

[291] *R. v Lloyd* (1834) 6 Car & P 393; *R. v Joyce* [1957] 3 All ER 623. See also Joy, *On the Admissibility of Confessions and Challenge of Jurors in Criminal Cases in England and Ireland* (J.S. Littell, Philadelphia, 1843), p.12 ("But the threat or inducement held out must have reference to the prisoner's escape from the charge and be such as would lead him to suppose it will be better for him to admit himself to be guilty of an offence which he never committed.").

[292] (1964) 1 Frewen 267 at 271.

[293] [1967] 1 AC 760 at 821, [1967] 1 All ER 177 at 184.

8–127   (e) Statements that do not Constitute Inducements   Despite some early authorities to the contrary,[294] it now seems clear that an exhortation to an accused to tell the truth, unaccompanied by any promised benefit for doing so, cannot amount to an inducement.[295] Neither will it be an inducement for a garda to express sympathy or understanding to the accused in respect of the offence that he is alleged to have committed[296] or to downplay the moral culpability of that offence.[297]

(ii) Whether the Accused Considered the Statement to be an Inducement

8–128   As noted above, it is clear from the decision in *People (DPP) v McCann*[298] that the question of whether a particular statement is objectively capable of amounting to an inducement within the meaning of the traditional test is only the first part of the application of the test. The trial judge must then go on to consider whether the accused regarded the statement as an inducement. In practice, there are likely to be very few instances in which a statement, which is objectively capable of amounting to an inducement, will not be regarded by an accused subjectively as such. However, it is possible to envisage circumstances where a particular threat or promise is made by a garda to an experienced criminal who is aware that it cannot be fulfilled and, thus, does regard it subjectively as a threat or promise.

(iii) Whether inducement caused the accused to confess

8–129   The final step of the test is to consider whether the accused's confession is, in fact, the result of the threat or promise. A confession will not be excluded if the prosecution succeed in establishing that the accused was not actually induced to make the confession by the inducement.[299] An example can be seen in *R. v Richards*[300] where a servant girl was told by her mistress that if she did not admit to a suspected offence that night, a police constable would be sent for in the morning to take her before the magistrates. She made a statement that night and made a further statement the next morning to a police constable while on the way to the magistrates. It was held that the statement was admissible because the accused must have known when she made the statement that she was being taken to the magistrates and, thus, her statement could not have been caused by the promise not to take her. A similar approach was adopted in *DPP v Ryan*[301] where a misrepresentation was made by gardaí in the course of an interview that, if the accused did not take the opportunity to admit to an involvement in an offence at a level less than murder, he would not be permitted to put forward a defence to that effect at trial. The Court of Criminal Appeal upheld the finding of the trial judge that this did not constitute an inducement in circumstances where the

---

[294] In *R. v Jarvis* (1867) LR 1 CCR 96, it was held that the words "you had better tell the truth" had acquired a technical meaning as an inducement.

[295] *People (DPP) v McCann* [1998] 4 IR 397 at 409; *People (AG) v Galvin* [1964] IR 325; *R. v Court* (1836) 7 Car & P 216; *R. v Reeve* (1872) LR 1 CCR 362; *R. v Stanton* (1911) 6 Cr App R 198; *R. v Cleary* (1963) 48 Cr App R 116 at 119.

[296] *R. v Ovenell* [1969] 1 QB 17 at 23–24, [1968] 1 All ER 933 at 937.

[297] *R. v Oickle* [2000] 2 SCR 3 at 45–46.

[298] [1998] 4 IR 397.

[299] *State v Treanor* [1924] 2 IR 193 at 208; *People (DPP) v Murphy* [2013] IECCA 1 at [36]; *Sparks v R.* [1964] AC 964 at 975, [1964] 1 All ER 727 at 740; *R. v Priestley* (1966) 50 Cr App R 183 at 187.

[300] (1832) 5 Car & P 318.

[301] [2011] IECCA 6.

accused gave evidence at a *voir dire* into the admissibility of the statements made by him and did not, at any stage, refer to this misrepresentation, much less contend that it caused him to harbour any hope of advantage or influenced his decision to answer questions. However, it would have been more correct to hold that an inducement had been held out but that it did not have any causative effect.

8–130   The nature of the analysis required to determine whether an inducement caused an accused to confess is evident from the decision in *People (DPP) v Hoey*.[302] The appellant in that case had surrendered himself at a garda station and was questioned in connection with a search of his house at 78 Rossmore Avenue, Ballyfermot, during which a quantity of firearms and ammunition had been discovered. On the advice of his solicitor, he refused to answer any questions and maintained this attitude until a Detective Inspector asked him: "Will I have to get some member to go up to your family and find out from them if anybody at 78 Rossmore is going to take responsibility for the property in the house." The appellant replied that he would make a statement but that he was not involving any other person and proceeded to make the inculpatory statement which formed the basis of his conviction in the Special Criminal Court. On appeal to the Supreme Court, it was held that this statement had been wrongly admitted. Walsh J stated that the test applicable was "whether the inducement was of a nature calculated under the particular circumstances of the case to induce the confession irrespective of its truth or falsity"[303] and he was satisfied, in the circumstances of the case, that it was:

> "On the facts of this case it certainly produced an immediate result. It produced an acceptance of responsibility and in effect a confession in respect of the offences charged from a person who hitherto had adamantly refused to answer any question or to accept any responsibility or to make damaging admissions....In the present case it is clear beyond all doubt that the appellant was unwilling to make any form of admission or confession whatsoever until the question put to him, or the suggestion made to him, by Detective Inspector Anders. It is also clear beyond doubt that the effect of that statement was to cause him to make the confession".[304]

8–131   Reference can also be made to the decision in *DPP v Ping Lin*[305] where the very fact-specific nature of the causation inquiry required was emphasised. Lord Morris explained the proper approach to be adopted as follows:

> "In considering whether the statement of the accused was brought about by hope or fear the judge will have to ascertain all the facts concerning the alleged and so-called 'inducement'. If it is said to have consisted in something said by a person conducting an interview then the facts must be ascertained as to what was said and as to what were the circumstances. Then what was said must be considered in a common sense way in the light of all the circumstances; and what was said must be given in a common sense meaning which it would rationally be understood to have by the person to whom it was said[306] ... The test is simply whether the Crown have proved that a statement made by an accused was voluntary in the sense that it was not obtained from him either because some person in authority 'exercised' fear or prejudice or 'held out' hope of advantage. Stated otherwise, was it as a result of something said or done by a person in authority that an accused was caused or led to make a statement? Did he make it because he was caused to fear that he would be prejudiced if he did not or because he was

---

[302]   [1987] IR 637, [1988] ILRM 666.
[303]   [1987] IR 637 at 649, [1988] ILRM 666 at 670.
[304]   [1987] IR 637 at 649, [1988] ILRM 666 at 671.
[305]   [1976] AC 574, [1975] 3 All ER 175.
[306]   *Cf. R. v Bodsworth* [1968] 2 NSWR 132 at 139, where it was stated that it was desirable "to avoid putting ingenious constructions on colourless words so as to detect a hint of improper inducement, as was at one time the case, but rather to construe the words only according to their natural, obvious and commonsense meaning". See further, O'Donnell, "The Admissibility of Confession Evidence in New South Wales" (1996) 14 Aust BR 61.

caused to hope that he would have advantage if he did? The prosecution must show that the statement did not owe its origin to such a cause".

8–132   That approach was echoed in *Hoey* with Henchy J stressing that the test "is essentially situational rather than self-operating" and "depends on the circumstances of the case".[307]

(c) Dissipation of the effect of an inducement

8–133   In some cases, the prosecution may succeed in establishing the admissibility of a confession on the basis that the causative link between the inducement and the confession has been broken because the effect of the inducement had dissipated by the time the inculpatory statement was made.[308] For example, in *People (AG) v Galvin*,[309] it was held that, even if a remark made to the accused at 12.10am constituted an inducement, the effect of it had been spent by the time the accused made an inculpatory statement in an interview with his parents at 2.40am. This was because of the fact that the accused had been cautioned twice in the intervening period, the status of his detention had changed in that he had been told that he was being detained in connection with the murder being investigated, and the questioning of him by the gardaí had ceased some hours before. Therefore, the Court concluded that the earlier remark could not have had any effect on the mind of the accused when he made the later admission.[310] Again, in *People (DPP) v Pringle*,[311] the Court of Criminal Appeal upheld the ruling of the court of trial that the effect of an inducement held out by gardaí had dissipated by the time that the accused made an inculpatory statement the following morning and had not induced him to make the statement.

8–134   In deciding whether the effect of an inducement has been dissipated, relevant factors include the nature of the inducement, the lapse of time between the making of the inducement and the statement,[312] any intervening visits from the accused's solicitor, whether the accused was cautioned before making the statement[313] and the contents of the statement.[314] Ultimately, however, the question is one of fact and it is clear from the authorities that it will be difficult for the prosecution to satisfy a court that the effect of an inducement has dissipated because, as emphasised in *People (AG) v Murphy*,[315] "the Judge must be judicially satisfied that that inducement had ceased to operate on the mind of the accused, and that the statement was not made under the influence of that inducement."[316] For example, in *R. v Doherty*[317] the court rejected the submission that an inducement held out at 10am had been dissipated by the time

---

[307] [1987] IR 637 at 652, [1988] ILRM 666 at 673–674.
[308] The prosecution bears the burden of proving that the inducement had ceased to affect the mind of the accused: *R. v Caputo* (1997) 114 CCC (3d) 1 at 13.
[309] [1964] IR 325.
[310] See also *R. v Clewes* (1830) 4 C & P 221 at 224.
[311] (1981) 1 Frewen 57 at 85–86.
[312] *People (AG) v Galvin* [1964] IR 325; *People (DPP) v Pringle* (1981) 1 Frewen 57.
[313] *People (AG) v Galvin* [1964] IR 325; *R. v Bate* (1871) 11 Cox CC 686 (caution administered by person of superior rank to the person in authority who held out the inducement negatived the inducement). *Cf. Sparks v R.* [1964] AC 964, [1964] 1 All ER 727 (caution did not negative the inducement).
[314] *People (DPP) v Pringle* (1981) 1 Frewen 57 at 87.
[315] [1947] IR 236.
[316] *People (AG) v Murphy* [1947] IR 236 at 244.
[317] (1874) 13 Cox CC 23.

the accused made an admission at 6pm by reason of the time interval and the fact that the accused has been cautioned before making the admission. Whiteside CJ said that it was necessary to show that the subsequent caution had the effect of removing the effect of the inducement from the accused's mind and he was not satisfied on the facts that it had done so.[318]

(i) Multiple confessions

8–135   Similar principles apply in circumstances where an accused has made more than one inculpatory statement and it is sought to admit a second or subsequent statement on the basis that it was not caused by the inducement held out before the first involuntary statement.[319] The test to be applied was outlined by Lord Parker CJ in *R. v Smith*[320] as follows:

> "The court thinks that the principle to be deduced from the cases is really this: that if the threat or promise under which the first statement was made still persists when the second statement is made, then it is inadmissible. Only if the time-limit between the two statements, the circumstances existing at the time and the caution are such that it can be said that the original threat or inducement has been dissipated can the second statement be admitted as a voluntary statement."[321]

8–136   A review of the authorities indicates that, in general, it will be very difficult for the prosecution to establish that a subsequent inculpatory statement was made free of the inducement that preceded the first.[322] Such a strict approach is justifiable on the basis articulated by Jackson J in *U.S. v Bayer*,[323] that:

> "… after an accused has once let the cat out of the bag by confessing, no matter what the inducement, he is never thereafter free of the psychological and practical disadvantages of having confessed. He can never get the cat back in the bag."[324]

8–137   However, the prosecution has, in some cases, succeeded in establishing the voluntariness of a subsequent statement. For example, in *R. v Smith*,[325] after making a confession that was ruled to be inadmissible, the accused had confessed again nine hours later. The Court held that the second statement was admissible having regard to a number of factors; the accused had been cautioned twice, nine hours had elapsed and the circumstances had changed considerably from when the first inculpatory statement had been made. Having regard to the foregoing, the Court was satisfied that the effect of the inducement was spent by the time the second statement had been made.[326]

4. Oppression

8–138   It is well settled that Gardaí are entitled to interrogate suspects provided

---

[318] See also *R. v Meynell* (1834) 2 Lew CC 122; *R. v Cooper* (1833) 5 Car & P 535, and *R. v Hewett* (1842) Car & M 534 at 536, where statements were ruled inadmissible where the court was not satisfied that the inducements had ceased to affect the mind of the accused.

[319] See Mirfield, "Successive Confessions and the Poisonous Tree" [1996] Crim LR 554.

[320] [1959] 2 QB 35, [1959] 2 All ER 193.

[321] [1959] 2 QB 35 at 41, [1959] 2 All ER 193 at 196.

[322] See *R. v Cooper* (1833) 5 Car & P 535; *R. v Meynell* (1834) 3 Lew CC 122; *R. v Sherrington* (1838) 2 Lew CC 123; *R. v Hewett* (1842) Car & M 623; *R. v Rue* (1876) 13 Cox CC 209.

[323] (1947) 331 US 532.

[324] (1947) 331 US 532 at 540.

[325] [1959] 2 QB 35, [1959] 2 All ER 193.

[326] See also *R. v Lintock* [1962] Crim LR 549 where the principles laid down in *Smith* were applied.

that they act reasonably and in a manner that does not breach the suspect's legal or constitutional rights. [327] It should be noted in that regard that it does not constitute a breach of the suspect's right of silence for Gardaí to continue an interrogation even if the suspect has indicated that he or she does not wish to answer any questions.[328] However, the courts have developed a test of oppression as a discrete sub-set of the general voluntariness rule in response to the use by the gardaí of lengthy interrogations as a means of obtaining confessions from suspects.[329]

8-139   After some initial expressions of unease at the increased used of interrogation and its effect on the voluntariness of confessions,[330] the Court of Criminal Appeal held in *People (AG) v Galvin*[331] that, independent of the traditional voluntariness test, a trial judge could, in his discretion, refuse to admit a statement when he was of the opinion "that the statement was obtained under circumstances of such pressure that it ceased to be one freely made."[332] The oppression test then developed in a series of cases in the late 1970s and early 1980s which shared the common features of disputed confessions/admissions having been made after long periods of intensive questioning and with allegations of physical ill-treatment having been rejected by the trial judges in each case.

8-140   In the first of these cases, *People (DPP) v Madden*,[333] it was contended that an inculpatory statement made by one of the accused was inadmissible on the basis that he had been in custody for a period of approximately 36 hours prior to making it. He had been interviewed for lengthy periods by 12 to 14 members of the Garda Síochána during that period and it was argued that this made it impossible for a Court to find that he was not thereby subjected to oppression which vitiated his will and left

---

[327] *Lavery v Member in Charge, Carrickmacross Garda Station* [1999] 2 IR 390 at 395; *Ward v Minister for Justice* [2007] IEHC 39 at [13], [2007] 2 IR 726 at 733.

[328] *People (DPP) v Yu Jie* [2005] IECCA 95 at [3]–[4], [2005] IECCA 137 at [2]–[3]. A similar conclusion was reached by the Canadian Supreme Court in *R. v Singh* [2007] 3 SCR 405, where the proposition that police must cease questioning when a detainee asserts his or her right to silence was rejected.

[329] *Cf.* O'Mahony, "The Ethics of Police Interrogation and the Garda Síochána" (1996) 6 ICLJ 46.

[330] See, in particular, *People (AG) v Murphy* [1947] IR 236 at 242 where O'Byrne J, delivering the judgment of the Court of Criminal Appeal, stated: "it is within our judicial knowledge that, in recent years, a practice has grown up whereby police officers obtain, by questions, statements of great, and sometimes inordinate, length from accused persons and, subsequently, these statements are tendered in evidence on the trial of such persons. We are not to be taken as approving of this practice, and if the practice is continued, it may become necessary for trial Judges to consider with great care whether, and to what extent, statements made in such circumstances can be considered to be free and voluntary statements and, as such, admissible in evidence." See also *AG v McCabe* [1927] IR 129.

[331] [1964] IR 325.

[332] [1964] IR 325 at 330. *Cf. Callis v Gunn* [1964] 1 QB 495 at 501, [1963] 3 All ER 677 at 680. Lord Parker CJ stated that it was "a fundamental principle of law that no answer to a question and no statement is admissible unless it is shown by the prosecution not to have been obtained in an oppressive manner and to have been voluntary in the sense that it has not been obtained by threats or inducements" and principle (e), stated to be overriding and applicable in all cases, included in the revised Judges' Rules issued by Practice Note in 1964 ([1964] 1 WLR 152, [1964] 1 All ER 327): "That it is a fundamental condition of the admissibility in evidence against any person, equally of any oral answer given by that person to a question put by a police officer and of any statement made by that person, that it shall have been voluntary in the sense that it has not been obtained from him by fear of prejudice or hope of advantage, exercised or held out by a person in authority, or by oppression."

[333] [1977] IR 336.

his statement involuntary. On the facts, the Court of Criminal Appeal was satisfied that the evidence did not support such a finding but O'Higgins CJ acknowledged that:

"Obviously it would be possible for a protracted period of detention, coupled with persistent interviewing or interrogation, to constitute oppression even without physical violence or threats of violence. It would be possible also for such treatment or circumstances so to reduce the will of a suspect that the statement made by him during the course of it or at its conclusion would not be a voluntary statement."[334]

8–141   In the next case, *People (DPP) v Lynch*,[335] the argument of oppression made on behalf of the appellant succeeded. The appellant made a number of inculpatory statements admitting that he had committed a murder after being subjected to intensive questioning over a 22-hour period by successive teams of gardaí during which he was not afforded any opportunity of sleeping or resting and his family were not permitted to see or make contact with him. On appeal to the Supreme Court, it was held that the statements should not have been admitted. While accepting that it was not open to the Court to disturb the findings of fact made by the trial judge that the allegations made by the appellant that he had been intimidated and threatened and had not been permitted to leave the garda station were untrue, O'Higgins CJ said that the trial judge had been wrong to ignore the length of the interrogation and that it would be unfair and unjust to allow the statements to be given in evidence:

"… so obtrusive and dominating a feature of this interrogation was its length, that such should not have been ignored or overlooked. The fact that the appellant was subjected for almost 22 hours to sustained questioning, never had the opportunity of communicating with his family or friends and never being permitted to rest or sleep until he made an admission of guilt, all amount to such circumstances of harassment and oppression as to make it unjust and unfair to admit in evidence anything he said. The trial judge exercised his discretion to admit these statements on the basis that the allegations made by the appellant were untrue. In so doing, he ignored that the features of oppression, harassment and fatigue which I have mentioned and which should have caused the statement, even if *prima facie* voluntary, to be excluded."[336]

8–142   In his concurring judgment, Walsh J emphasised that:

"All the circumstances surrounding the taking of any…statement or circumstances which go to create the atmosphere in which a written or non-written admission is made must be examined with a view to ascertaining whether or not any such statement may be regarded as the free and voluntary act or admission of the person purporting to make it."[337]

8–143   Having regard to the fact that "the accused spent a long time without sleep in a strange and unaccustomed environment and in a position of isolation from all he was accustomed to and under constant surveillance of which he was conscious"[338] plus the proven untruth of essential part of the admissions, he was also satisfied that the statement had not been voluntarily obtained.

8–144   The principles to be applied in determining when a confession would be found to have been obtained by oppression were elaborated upon by the Court of Criminal Appeal in *People (DPP) v McNally*.[339] The applicants had been convicted, along with Nicky Kelly, in the Special Criminal Court of the Sallins train robbery. The only evidence connecting either of the applicants with the offence was inculpatory

---

[334] [1977] IR 336 at 354.

[335] [1982] IR 64, [1981] ILRM 389.

[336] [1982] IR 64 at 74, [1981] ILRM 389 at 391–392.

[337] [1982] IR 64 at 87, [1981] ILRM 389 at 401.

[338] [1982] IR 64 at 87, [1981] ILRM 389 at 401.

[339] (1981) 2 Frewen 43.

statements allegedly made by them. Both applicants gave evidence at trial that they had been physically assaulted by gardaí during questioning but their evidence in that regard had been rejected with the trial court finding that injuries suffered by them were "self-inflicted" and/or "mutually inflicted". These findings of fact were not disturbed by the Court but, in the case of the second applicant, the Court concluded that, having regard to the circumstances in which it had been taken, his inculpatory statement should have been excluded as having been obtained by oppression.

8–145   The Court approved the description of oppressive questioning that had been given by Lord MacDermott[340] and adopted by the Court of Appeal in *R. v Prager*[341]:

> "... questioning which by its nature, duration or other attendant circumstances (including the fact of custody) excites hopes (such as the hope of release) or fears, or so affects the mind of the suspect that his will crumbles and he speaks when otherwise he would have stayed silent".

8–146   It also cited with the approval the definition advanced by Sachs J in *R. v Priestley*[342] that the word "oppression" "imports something which tends to sap, and has sapped, that free will which must exist before a confession is voluntary".[343]

8–147   Applying those principles to the inculpatory statement made by the second applicant, the Court regarded the following factors as significant: (a) the unexplained change of attitude on the part of the applicant to questioning concerning the offence, the applicant having previously refused to answer questions during a period of 40 hours in custody; (b) the fact that the questioning which immediately preceded the making of the statement did not take place in a normal interview room but in what had to be considered as the menacing environment of an underground passage; (c) the fact that the alleged statement was made in the early hours of the morning after the applicant had been woken up; and (d) the fact that, notwithstanding the request of the applicant to consult a solicitor, and his consistent refusal on a previous occasion that he had been arrested in relation to the offence to be questioned without consulting a solicitor, no solicitor had been obtained for him before the making of the alleged statements. Having regard to the foregoing, the Court was not satisfied beyond reasonable doubt that the statements of the second applicant had been voluntarily made or that they had been obtained in a manner that satisfied the requirements of basic fairness.[344]

8–148   In *People (DPP) v Pringle*,[345] it was emphasised that, in applying the test of oppression, regard must be had to the physical, mental and emotional characteristics of the person whose will is alleged to have been overborne by oppressive questioning. The first applicant had been arrested and questioned in relation to a bank robbery in which two gardaí had been killed. At a point when he had been interviewed for a total of 43 hours over a three-day period, he made the statement: "I know that you know that I was involved, but on the advice of my solicitor I am saying nothing and you will have to prove it all the way."[346] On appeal, it was contended that the statement should

---

[340] Lord MacDermott, "The Interrogation of Suspects in Custody" (1968) 21 CLP 1 at 10.
[341] [1972] 1 All ER 1114 at 1119, [1972] 1 WLR 260 at 266.
[342] (1967) 51 Cr App R 1.
[343] (1967) 51 Cr App R 1 at 1. *Cf. R. v Alexis* (1994) 35 CR (4th) 117 at 155.
[344] See *People (DPP) v Shaw* [1982] IR 1.
[345] (1981) 2 Frewen 57.
[346] This statement was an example of what Hardiman J classified as an indirect admission in *Rattigan v DPP* [2008] IESC 34 at [17]–[18], [2008] 4 IR 639, 647–648, a species of admission which

have been excluded as involuntary. However, the Court of Criminal Appeal upheld the ruling of the trial court that it had not been obtained by oppression:

> "The length of the duration of the interviewing of the accused combined with the shortness of the duration of the sleep he obtained do not in themselves establish the validity of the submission now being considered. It is obvious, as the Court of trial pointed out, that 'what may be oppressive as regards a child, an invalid, or an old man or somebody inexperienced in the ways of the world may turn out not to be oppressive when one finds that the accused person is of tough character and an experienced man of the world' (see judgment of Sachs J in *R. v Priestley* (1967) 51 Cr App Rep 1). And so when a Court is considering an allegation such as has been made in this case, the physical, mental and emotional characteristics of the person whose will it is said was undermined must be considered."[347]

8–149   In that case, the first applicant was 42 years of age, in good health, and for some years prior to his arrest, had been a fisherman in the Galway area. He was, thus, "an experienced man of the world not unused to conditions of physical hardship" and the Court was satisfied that it was open to the trial court to conclude that "the will of such a man would not have been so undermined by the interviews he had experienced and the lack of sleep that he spoke the inculpatory words when otherwise he would have remained silent".[348] In reaching that conclusion, one factor of particular significance was that the first applicant had had the benefit of five visits from his solicitor during the period of custody leading up to the inculpatory statement.[349] He had been advised by his solicitor that he was entitled to remain silent and that he was not required to answer questions and the Court considered that those visits and the advice that he obtained would "have strengthened his resolve and assisted in counteracting any weakness of will which the conditions of his custody and the questioning by the Gardaí may have produced".[350] Furthermore, this was not a case where the first applicant had made a full confession for no apparent reason after a long period of silence. Instead, his admission was "a laconic one", accompanied by a statement that he was going to say nothing and that the gardaí would have to prove their case against him. Indeed, although not characterised by the Court as such, the statement could be regarded as defiant in tone.

8–150   It is clear from this review of the authorities that the test of oppression involves a detailed factual inquiry into all of the circumstances surrounding the questioning of and the making of an inculpatory statement by an accused.[351] A statement will not be found to be involuntary merely because it is obtained after "intensive and persistent interrogation"[352] or vigorous questioning[353] although there is a point at which interrogation, "by reason of its nature, the manner in which it is conducted,

---

he regarded as insidious because, if invented, it might be considered by the tribunal of fact to be more convincing than a direct admission.

[347] (1981) 2 Frewen 57 at 82. See *DPP v Patterson* (1979) 113 ILTR 6 where Finlay P. excluded a statement of a 16-year-old boy, who had no parent or guardian with him, in circumstances where he was questioned for a number of hours by two gardaí, even though he acknowledged that if the defendant had been an adult or "a tough young man" he would have held it to be admissible.

[348] (1981) 2 Frewen 57 at 82.

[349] Emphasis was also laid on this factor in rejected a contention that interrogation had been oppressive in *People (DPP) v McGing* (1985) 3 Frewen 18 at 29.

[350] (1981) 2 Frewen 57 at 83.

[351] *Cf. R. v Oickle* [2000] 2 SCR 3 at 39 where Iacobucci J stated that the list of factors that can create an atmosphere of oppression included "depriving the suspect of food, clothing, water, sleep, or medical attention; denying access to counsel; and excessively aggressive, intimidating questioning for a prolonged period of time".

[352] *People (AG) v Conmey* (1973) 1 Frewen 371 at 373 (*per* Gannon J).

[353] *People (DPP) v Kavanagh* [2009] IECCA 29 at [17].

its duration or the time of day, or of its persistence into the point of harassment" will become oppressive.[354] It is clear that oppression is not and cannot be a precise concept marking as it does the point along the continuum of interrogation which separates "permissible" questioning from "impermissible questioning".[355] Such a determination depends on an assessment of the level of psychological pressure brought to bear on a suspect and, as emphasised in *People (DPP) v Pringle*,[356] the "physical, mental and emotional characteristics" of the particular accused.

8–151   The above cases pre-dated the introduction of the Custody Regulations which regulate the treatment of persons in custody including the conduct of interviews. As appears from the overview of the provisions of the Custody Regulations below, a number of the requirements laid down therein are directed towards the indicia of oppressive questioning identified in the cases above. It follows, therefore, that if the Custody Regulations are complied with, there is little scope for the application of the oppression test.[357] This is illustrated by the decision of the Court of Criminal Appeal in *DPP v Ryan*.[358] The accused was detained for 24 hours and was interviewed on six occasions. By reasons of breaches of the accused's right of reasonable access to a solicitor, all of statements made by him in the course of those interviews were excluded except for those made during a portion of the fifth interview after he had been afforded an opportunity to speak to his solicitor. On appeal from his conviction for murder, it was contended that the trial judge had erred in failing to exclude those statements also on the basis that they have been obtained by oppression. A number of matters were relied on in that regard including: that his requests for access to his solicitor were not acted upon; the accused was told by garda interrogators that, unless he admitted participation at some level, he would be convicted of murder and imprisoned for 30 years and, that if he received a lengthy sentence, his partner would take up with another man and his daughter would be raised by another man; it was suggested to him that he could have been involved without necessarily having an intent to kill thereby seeking to downplay the seriousness of his involvement; and it was suggested to him that, if he did not take the opportunity during garda interviews to admit involvement at a level less than that of murder, he would not be permitted to put forward a defence to that effect at trial. The trial judge reviewed the videotapes of the interviews which disclosed that the interrogation alternated between vigorous and robust and being sympathetic and cajoling. However, there were no threats of physical violence or any improper inducements held out. Further, the fifth interview had taken place after the accused had had the benefit of resting overnight and it was apparent from the videotape of this interview that the accused was relaxed, in jocular form and more than capable of deciding which questions he would answer. Therefore, notwithstanding what he considered to be a flagrant breach of the right of reasonable access to a solicitor and the wholly improper suggestion that the accused would not

---

[354] *People (DPP) v Quilligan* [1987] ILRM 606 at 624 (*per* Walsh J). *Cf. People (AG) v Conmey* (1973) 1 Frewen 371 at 374, where the decision of the trial judge as to the voluntariness of an inculpatory statement was upheld even though the Court of Criminal Appeal characterised the treatment of the applicant as "harsh and oppressive".

[355] See further Leo, "Inside the Interrogation Room" (1996) 86(2) JCL Crim 266, and Skolnick and Leo, "The Ethics of Deceptive Interrogation" (1992) 11(1) Crim Justice Ethics 3, for a discussion of the impact of interrogation techniques on suspects and the conduct of interviews.

[356] (1981) 1 Frewen 57 at 82. See also *People (DPP) v Kavanagh* [2009] IECCA 29 at [17].

[357] *Cf. People (DPP) v McCann* [1998] 4 IR 397 at 409–410, *People (DPP) v O'Neill*, unreported, Court of Criminal Appeal, 28 January 2002 and *People (DPP) v PA* [2008] IECCA 21.

[358] [2011] IECCA 6.

be permitted to put forward a defence that he did articulate to the gardaí, he concluded that the accused had not been oppressed, that his questioning was not unfair and that his answers were freely and voluntarily given. That conclusion was supported by his negative assessment of the credibility of the accused who gave evidence during the *voir dire* that he was "mentally worried". The Court of Criminal Appeal was quite satisfied that that conclusion was correct and was supported by the evidence.[359]

8–152 A submission that an inculpatory statement should have been excluded on the basis of oppression also failed in *People (DPP) v Bishop*.[360] It was contended that the accused had not been in a fit state to be questioned because he had sustained a gunshot wound but the trial judge had rejected that contention having heard that the doctors treating him had not told gardaí that he should not be questioned and one of them had expressly advised gardaí that he was fit to be questioned. A complaint of oppression was also made on the basis that the accused had been required to remove all his clothes including underwear in front of gardaí and wear a paper suit and was, as a consequence, frozen throughout the questioning failed. However, the trial judge was satisfied that the removal of the accused's clothes was reasonable having regard to the requirements of the investigation and that, although the accused was momentarily naked before gardaí, this could not have humiliated him to such an extent as to render the questioning thereafter unfair or oppressive. He also accepted the evidence of the gardaí that the room was not cold and that the accused had not made any complaints about coldness. The Court of Criminal Appeal refused to interfere with those findings.

5. Other Causes of Involuntariness

8–153 As noted above, the traditional voluntariness test and the oppression test are but two limbs of a broader voluntariness rule which seeks to protect the free will of a person who is questioned in relation to an offence.[361] The best explanation of the scope of this rule is to be found in the judgment of Griffin J in *People (DPP) v Shaw*[362]:

> "The primary requirement is to show that the statement was voluntary, in the sense in which that adjective has been judicially construed in the decided cases. Thus, if the tendered statement was coerced or otherwise induced or extracted without the true and free will of its maker, it will not be held to have been voluntarily made. The circumstances which will make a statement inadmissible for lack of voluntariness are so varied that it would be impossible to enumerate or categorize them fully. It is sufficient to say that the decided cases show that a statement will be excluded as being involuntary if it was wrung from its maker by physical or psychological pressures, by threats or promises made by persons in authority, by the use of drugs, hypnosis, intoxicating drink, by prolonged interrogation or excessive questioning, or by any one of a diversity of methods which have in common that result or the risk that what is tendered as a voluntary statement is not the natural emanation of a rational intellect and a free will."[363]

---

[359] See also *People (DPP) v Yu Jie* [2005] IECCA 95 (will of the accused not overborne because gardaí continued to ask questions after he had indicated that he did not want to answer any more questions).

[360] [2005] IECCA 2. See also *People (DPP) v Gallagher* [2006] IECCA 110, [2007] 2 IR 246, where the contention that statements made by the accused were involuntary and made in oppressive circumstances because he was a drug addict suffering from withdrawal symptoms was rejected on the facts by the trial judge and the Court of Criminal Appeal refused to interfere with that finding.

[361] See *per* Henchy J in *People (DPP) v Hoey* [1987] IR 637 at 651, [1988] ILRM 666 at 673.

[362] [1982] IR 1.

[363] [1982] IR 1 at 60–61. *Cf.* the approach of the Canadian Supreme Court in *R. v Hebert* [1990] 2 SCR 151 at 166 and *R. v Oickle* [2000] 3 SCR 3 at 22–23.

8–154 Thus, in deciding whether a statement is voluntary, it is necessary for a court to have regard to all of the circumstances in which it was made[364] and, in particular, any factors that could have vitiated the free will of the accused in deciding whether it is admissible. This approach was applied in *People (DPP) v Ward*[365] (the facts of which are set out below) so as to exclude inculpatory statements which the Special Criminal Court was satisfied had been induced "by grievous psychological pressure" that had affected the free will of the accused to such an extent as to render those statements involuntary.

(a) Requirement of State action

8–155 It should be noted that, although Griffin J in *Shaw* described a wide range of factors that could render a confession involuntary, it is clear the alleged cause of the involuntariness must emanate from a person in authority rather than from the accused. Thus, in the case of drugs and alcohol, what will render a confession involuntary is not the fact that the accused is under the influence of drugs or alcohol but the use of drugs or alcohol by a person in authority in order to obtain a confession.

8–156 This accords with the approach taken in *People (AG) v Sherlock*.[366] At the time that the first applicant was arrested and brought to the garda station, he was very obviously under the influence of drink and possibly drugs. After arriving at the station, he slept for some time before awaking and making an incriminating statement. After getting ill, he then made further inculpatory statements. It was contended that these statements should have been excluded because, at the time he made them, the first applicant was in a physical and mental state such that he did not know what he was doing. However, the Court of Criminal Appeal upheld the ruling of the trial judge that the statements were voluntary saying that:

> "The fact that his debilitated condition may have either prompted him or not restrained him from making his statements which incriminated himself either because of carelessness for his own safety or perhaps because of feelings of remorse does not make the statements involuntary. There may be elements in the circumstances surrounding the making of such statements which might cause a jury to consider whether having regard to these circumstances the statements could be accepted as being true but that is not the consideration which the learned trial Judge had to rule upon on the question of admissibility."[367]

8–157 The Court noted that later when it came to making a written statement, the accused made one which was entirely exculpatory. This indicated that, faced with the formality of making a written statement, he became more alert and conscious of his own safety but that did not indicate that the earlier oral statements he had made, which were spontaneous and not prompted by questions, were other than voluntary. The matter of what weight to attach to these statements was for the jury to consider having regard to all the circumstances of the case.

8–158 It is submitted that this approach is correct. As set out above, one of the primary

---

[364] See *People (DPP) v Conroy* [1986] IR 460 at 473, where Finlay CJ said that "the entire atmosphere of an investigation or interrogation leading to a confession must be ascertained in order for a decision to be made as to whether the confession is voluntary or fairly obtained or not." *Cf. R. v Oickle* [2000] 2 SCR 3 at 31.

[365] Unreported, Special Criminal Court, 27 November 1998.

[366] (1975) 1 Frewen 383.

[367] (1975) 1 Frewen 383 at 391.

purposes of the voluntariness test is to protect the right of a suspect not to be compelled to incriminate himself or herself. This right is predicated on the personal autonomy and dignity of an accused and seeks to preserve an accused's freedom of choice when he or she is subjected to the overweening power of the state whilst in custody by protecting him or her from any coercion or pressure which would have the effect of overbearing his or her will.[368] It is, thus, a right enjoyed by a criminal suspect vis-à-vis the State and does not, generally, have any paternalistic application to protect a suspect from his or her own misjudgment or inability to make an intelligent decision whether to make a statement. As Rehnquist CJ put it in *Colorado v Connelly*,[369] "[a]bsent police conduct causally related to the confession, there is simply no basis for concluding that any state actor has deprived a criminal defendant of due process of law". The situation might, however, be different if there was some element of unfairness as where gardaí sought, in some way, to take advantage of an accused's debilitated condition.

(b) Confessions obtained by false pretence or trick

8–159   A confession obtained by means of a false pretence or trick is not, on that ground alone, inadmissible in evidence but will be if the effect of the false pretence or trick has been to produce an involuntary confession.[370] The most common example of this is where this may occur is where a suspect is told that gardaí have particular evidence that implicates him or her in the commission of the offence such as a DNA sample or CCTV footage which is not the case.[371]

8–160   Applying the reliability rationale, the traditional test in that regard was whether the false pretence or trick would tend to produce an untrue confession.[372] However, following the recognition in *People (AG) v O'Brien*[373] that the voluntariness rule was also "based partly upon the idea that in fairness to an accused person he should not by way of trick or otherwise improperly be compelled to incriminate himself",[374] it was held in *People (AG) v Cummins*[375] that confessions obtained by false pretence or trick would also be excluded where there was an element of compulsion. Walsh J explained:

> "Naturally very many tricks would have no element of compulsion attached to them, but there may nevertheless be types of tricks or false pretences which produce such an effect upon an accused person as to make him feel constrained to follow a particular course of action even though it is not his wish to do so; and the circumstances may be such that, having regard to the mental abilities of the accused, the general atmosphere, the relationship of the parties to

---

[368] *Cf.* the approach in Canada where, applying an "operating mind test", a high degree of intoxication which has significantly diminished the accused's intellectual ability is required in order to render a statement involuntary (see *R. v Clarkson* [1986] 1 SCR 383 at 399 and *McKenna v R.* [1961] SCR 660).

[369] (1986) 479 US 157 at 164.

[370] *People (AG) v Cummins* [1972] IR 312 at 325. See also *People (DPP) v Kavanagh* [2009] IECCA 29 at [18]–[19], where the contention that an admission had been obtained by a trick failed on the facts.

[371] See, by way of example, *People (DPP) v O'Neill* [2007] IECCA 8 at [19], [2007] 4 IR 564 at 570, where a statement was excluded because a garda had told the accused that there was CCTV footage which implicated him when this was not true.

[372] *People (DPP) v O'Neill* [2007] IECCA 8 at [19], [2007] 4 IR 564 at 570. *Cf. R. v Collins* [1987] 1 SCR 265, where Lamer J held that a confession would not be inadmissible unless the trick was a "dirty trick" in the sense that it would shock the community.

[373] [1965] IR 142.

[374] [1965] IR 142 at 166 (*per* Walsh J)

[375] [1972] IR 312.

each other and other relevant factors, the trial judge may very well come to the conclusion that in such a given situation the accused person was not in truth doing a voluntary act and that, although not offered any improper inducements or promises, he was nonetheless so affected by the situation as no longer to be fully a free agent. In such a cases the trial judge ought to exclude from evidence any confession so obtained as not being a voluntary confession."[376]

8–161   This test of compulsion was subsequently applied in *People (AG) v Sherlock*[377] where a submission that the trial judge had erred in admitting evidence of an inculpatory statement made following an innocent misrepresentation that a fingerprint of the second named applicant had been found at the scene of the crime was rejected. The Court held that the trial judge had properly exercised his discretion as there was nothing in the evidence to show that the effect of the misrepresentation on the second applicant "was so overwhelming as to make him no longer fully a free agent and that he was in effect coerced into making a statement."[378]

8–162   It is submitted that the approach adopted in *Cummins* and *Sherlock* is correct. The core of the right of a person not to be compelled to incriminate himself or herself is that a suspect when questioned should be allowed to make a free and informed decision as to whether or not to make a statement. If he or she has effectively been deprived of that choice by reason of a trick or subterfuge, then any resulting confession should be excluded. As stated by McLachlin J in *R. v Hebert*[379]:

> "To permit the authorities to trick the suspect into making a confession to them after he or she has ... declined to make a statement, is to permit the authorities to do indirectly what the Charter does not permit them to do directly."[380]

8–163   In that case, it was held that the right to silence of the accused was breached and a confession made by him to an undercover police officer placed in a cell with him was inadmissible.[381] A similar conclusion was reached in *Allan v United Kingdom*[382] where the European Court of Human Rights held that:

> "While the right to silence and the privilege against self-incrimination are primarily designed to protect against improper compulsion by the authorities and the obtaining of evidence through methods of coercion or oppression in defiance of the will of the accused, the scope of the right is not confined to cases where duress has been brought to bear on the accused or where the will of the accused has been directly overborne in some way. The right, which the Court has previously observed is at the heart of the notion of a fair procedure, serves in principle to protect the freedom of a suspected person to choose whether to speak or to remain silent when questioned by police. Such freedom of choice is effectively undermined in a case in which, the suspect having elected to remain silent during questioning, the authorities use subterfuge to elicit, from the suspect, confessions or other statements of an incriminatory nature, which

---

[376] [1972] IR 312 at 328.

[377] (1975) 1 Frewen 383.

[378] (1975) 1 Frewen 383 at 387. *Cf. People (DPP) v Burke* (1986) 3 Frewen 92, where an allegation of misrepresentation was dismissed on the basis that it amounted, at most, to the gardaí having obtained evidence by means of a relatively minor trick or subterfuge without any actual illegality, which could not in itself constitute a ground for excluding a statement. However, neither *Cummins* nor *Sherlock* was referred to and the case must be regarded as having limited precedential value. See also *People (DPP) v Yu Jie* [2005] IECCA 95, where the contention that the accused had been tricked by Gardaí into identifying himself in a photograph by the manner in which those photographs had been presented to him during an interview was rejected on the facts.

[379] [1990] 2 SCR 151, (1990) 57 CCC (3d) 1.

[380] [1990] 2 SCR 151 at 180–181, (1990) 57 CCC (3d) 1 at 38.

[381] *Cf. R. v Oickle* [2000] 2 SCR 3 at 58 (confronting a suspect with adverse evidence and even exaggerating its accuracy and reliability will not, of itself, render a confession involuntary).

[382] (2003) 36 EHRR 12.

they were unable to obtain during such questioning and whether the confessions or statements
thereby obtained are adduced in evidence at trial."[383]

8–164   The Court went on to hold that the decision as to whether the right to silence
is undermined to such an extent as to give rise to a violation of Art.6 depends on all
the circumstances of the case.[384]

6. Statutory Compulsion

8–165   At common law, the position was that an inculpatory statement made by an
accused under statutory compulsion was admissible and would not be excluded as
involuntary.[385] However, in *Re National Irish Bank*[386] it was held that the guarantee of a
trial in due course of law in Art.38 requires the exclusion of an involuntary confession
and it was immaterial whether the compulsion or inducement used to obtain the
confession comes from the executive or the legislature.[387] However, the mere fact that
a confession has been obtained in circumstances where the questioner enjoys statutory
powers to compel a person to make a statement does not automatically mean that the
statement is involuntary; the voluntariness of the statement is a matter to be decided
by the trial judge in each case.[388]

8–166   Furthermore, it would appear that information that is required pursuant to
general regulatory requirements in a non-adversarial context will not be regarded as
involuntary. In *EPA v Swalcliffe*,[389] the accused had been charged with a number of
offences under the Waste Management Act 1996.[390] At the hearing before the District
Court, reliance was sought to be placed by the prosecutor on information contained
in records, which the accused had been obliged to keep pursuant to its waste licence,
and a Waste Licence Audit Report compiled on the basis of those records. Under
the 1996 Act, it was a criminal offence not to keep records in accordance with the
conditions of the licence and it was argued by the accused that these records were
involuntary confessions and, as such, inadmissible. However, Kearns J held that no
question of involuntariness or a breach of the right not to incriminate oneself arose in
the circumstances of the case:

> "In my view none of the purposes or concerns which underlie the principle against self-
> incrimination are meaningfully brought into play in the circumstance of this particular case.
> Firstly, it cannot be said that there is any real coercion by the State in obtaining the information
> contained in the records. Secondly, there was no adversarial relationship between the accused
> and the State at the time the material was obtained. I do not see any increased risk of 'unreliable
> confessions' as a result of the statutory compulsion, nor do I perceive any increased risk of
> abuses of power by the State as a result of the statutory compulsion."[391]

8–167   Thus, the Waste Licence Audit Report or waste records could not properly be
characterised as "confessions" for the purposes of the involuntariness test.

---

[383] (2003) 36 EHRR 12 at [50].
[384] It was also held that guidance could be obtained from the decisions of the Canadian Supreme Court
in *R. v Hebert* [1990] 2 SCR 151; *R. v Broyles* [1991] 3 SCR 595; and *R. v Liew* [1999] 2 SCR
914. See also *Bykov v Russia* [2009] ECHR 441 where the decision in *Allan* was distinguished.
[385] See *People (DPP) v McGowan* [1979] IR 45.
[386] [1999] 3 IR 145, [1999] 1 ILRM 321.
[387] [1999] 3 IR 145 at 186–187, [1999] 1 ILRM 321 at 359.
[388] [1999] 3 IR 145 at 188, [1999] 1 ILRM 321 at 360.
[389] [2004] IEHC 190, [2004] 2 IR 549, [2005] 1 ILRM 120.
[390] No.10 of 1996.
[391] [2004] IEHC 190 at [18].

D. The Judges' Rules

1. Introduction

8–168   The Judges' Rules date from 1912,[392] when the first four rules set out below were drawn up by the judges of the King's Bench Division at the request of the Home Secretary for clarification of the circumstances in which police officers[393] could question a person and, in particular, as to when a caution was required.[394] By 1922, further guidance as to the questioning of suspects had been provided and the rules had increased to a total of nine. It is these nine rules which are in force in this jurisdiction[395]:

1.   When a police officer is endeavouring to discover the author of a crime there is no objection to his putting questions in respect thereof to any person or persons, whether suspected or not, from whom he thinks that useful information may be obtained.

2.   Whenever a police officer has made up his mind to charge a person with a crime, he should first caution such person before asking him any questions, or any further questions as the case may be.

3.   Persons in custody should not be questioned without the usual caution being first administered.

4.   If the prisoner wishes to volunteer any statement, the usual caution should be administered. It is desirable that the last two words of such caution should be omitted, and that the caution should end with the words "be given in evidence".

5.   The caution to be administered to a prisoner when he is formally charged should therefore be in the following words: "Do you wish to say anything in answer to the charge? You are not obliged to say anything unless you wish to do so, but whatever you say will be taken down in writing and may be given in evidence." Care should be taken to avoid the suggestion that his answers can only be used in evidence *against* him, as this may prevent an innocent person making a statement which might assist to clear him of the charge.

6.   A statement made by a prisoner before there is time to caution him is not rendered inadmissible in evidence merely because no caution has been given, but in such a case he should be cautioned as soon as possible.

7.   A prisoner making a voluntary statement must not be cross-examined, and no questions should be put to him about it except for the purpose of removing ambiguity in what he has actually said. For instance, if he has mentioned an hour without saying whether it was morning or evening, or has given a day of the week and day of the month which do not agree, or has not made it clear to what individual or what place he intended to refer in some part of his statement, he may be questioned sufficiently to clear up the point.

8.   When two or more person are charged with the same offence and their statements are taken separately, the police should not read these statements to the other persons charged, but each of such persons should be given by the police a copy of such statements and nothing should be said or done by the police to invite a reply. If the person charged desires to make a statement in reply the usual caution should be administered.

9.   Any statement made in accordance with the above rules should, whenever possible,

---

[392] Although their origin can be traced to 1906 (see Practice Note (Judges' Rules) [1964] 1 WLR 15, [1964] 1 All ER 327).

[393] See *R. v Ovenell* [1968] 1 All ER 933 at 938, where it was stated that the Judges' Rules are directed to the police only but that it was understandable that investigating officers of other services might be thought to be comparably placed with police officers.

[394] See *R. v Voisin* [1918] 1 KB 531 at 539; *People (AG) v Cummins* [1972] IR 312 at 323.

[395] *People (AG) v Cummins* [1972] IR 312 at 323 (the Rules are set out at 317–318); *People (AG) v Regan* [1975] IR 367. In *Cummins*, Walsh J noted the distinction between the 1922 Rules and the 1964 Rules then in force in England, but held that it was the 1922 Rules which were applicable in Ireland.

be taken down in writing and signed by the person making it after it has been read to him and he has been invited to make any corrections he may wish.

8–169   In *People (DPP) v Kavanagh*,[396] it was stated that the Rules had been framed to try and ensure that incriminating statements made in police custody are not admitted in evidence when their admission would be either unsafe or unfair. While the Rules continue to serve this purpose, it is surprising that, notwithstanding the very significant changes in investigative practices and procedures and the development of a considerable body of jurisprudence in relation to the rights of suspects under the Constitution and the European Convention on Human Rights, the Rules have not been updated in close to a century. It is difficult to disagree with the view expressed in the *Final Report of the Balance in the Criminal Law Group*[397] that, while "the Rules contain a good deal of practical common sense which is worth preserving, an overhaul and re-examination of these Rules in the light of modern circumstances is overdue".

2. Rules 1 to 6

8–170   In *People (DPP) v Finnerty*,[398] Keane J outlined the genesis of these rules as follows:

> "Our criminal law, deriving ultimately from the Anglo-American system, historically reflected a tension between two competing principles. The first was the right and duty of the police to investigate crime of every sort in the interests of the community as a whole and the corresponding obligation on citizens to assist them in that task. The second was the right of a suspect at a defined stage in the investigation to refuse to answer any questions and the obligation on the police to inform him of that right in the almost universally known formula of the traditional police caution."[399]

8–171   These two principles can be seen to be enshrined in rules 1–6 of the Judges' Rules which permit a garda to question any person from whom he or she thinks that useful information may be obtained but require him or her to give a suspect a caution in two circumstances: (i) where the garda has made up his or her mind to charge the person; or (ii) where the suspect is in custody. A number of issues relating to the application of these Rules are examined below.

(a) Entitlement of garda to question persons

8–172   At common law, a police officer was entitled to ask questions of any person likely to be able to give him or her information, whether he or she suspected that person of complicity in an offence or not.[400] Rule 1 of the Judges' Rules essentially codifies

---

[396]   (1989) 3 Frewen 243 at 247.

[397]   (2007), p.32.

[398]   [1999] 4 IR 364, [2000] 1 ILRM 191.

[399]   *Cf. per* Parker CJ in *Rice v Connolly* [1966] 2 QB 414 at 419, "though every citizen has a moral duty or, if you like, a social duty to assist the police, there is no legal duty to that effect, and indeed the whole basis of the common law is that right of the individual to refuse to answer questions put to him by persons in authority, and to refuse to accompany those in authority to any particular place; short, of course, of arrest."

[400]   *R. v Knight* (1905) 21 TLR 310; *R. v Reason* (1872) 12 Cox CC 228. In *McMahon v Special Criminal Court*, unreported, High Court, 30 July 1998, the contention that there was anything illegal or irregular in gardaí questioning a person without having arrested him or her was rejected. McGuinness J took the view that there is no legal requirement to arrest and detain a suspect in order to interview him or her and stated that "it should never be forgotten that the voluntary interview is in fact the norm under the common law, and that a very large part of the detection

this position and, in *DPP v Byrne*,[401] O'Sullivan J summarily rejected the contention that the questioning referred to in rule 1 was permissible only after the police officer had come to the conclusion that a crime had been committed and was endeavouring to discover the author thereof. If this were the case, then it would effectively mean that all preliminary inquiries and investigations were prohibited.[402]

8–173   It is also clear from rule 1, taken in conjunction with rules 2 and 3, that a garda is entitled to question a person suspected of having committed an offence without first administering a caution provided that he or she has not made up his or mind to charge the person or the person is not in custody. In *Moore v Martin*,[403] the applicant had been convicted of drink driving arising out of a collision involving the applicant's car and a parked vehicle. A garda who arrived on the scene was informed by the owner of the parked vehicle that the applicant had left the scene on foot. When the guard caught up with the applicant, he questioned the applicant who admitted that he had been driving his car at the time of the collision. Finnegan J rejected the contention put forward by the applicant that the respondent District Judge should have excluded his statement to the garda on the basis that he ought to have been cautioned before being questioned. Finnegan J referred to rule 1 of the Judges' Rules and stated that he was satisfied that the garda had been doing no more than trying to discover whether or by whom an offence had been committed and that he had been entitled to ask the applicant as to whether or not he had been driving at the relevant time. Therefore, notwithstanding the absence of a caution, the statement made by the applicant in relation to his driving of the car at the relevant time was admissible. A similar approach was taken in *People (DPP) v O'Reilly*[404] where the contention that there had been a breach of the Judges' Rules by reason of the failure to caution the accused prior to Gardaí taking a detailed statement from him was rejected on the basis that, even though he was a suspect, he was not a person whom the garda officer taking the statement had made up his mind to charge.

8–174   *A fortiori*, there is no requirement to administer a caution if a garda is not even investigating an offence at the time. In *People (DPP) v McDonagh*,[405] the accused had been convicted of firearms offences arising out of a shooting incident. The accused was a suspect and had been arrested in connection with a shooting incident but made no admissions. Subsequently, a decision was taken to provide an armed patrol in the area and a garda called to the house of the accused in connection with concerns about the safety of the accused. The garda gave evidence that the accused was in an agitated state and, without any forewarning, he made an inculpatory remark. In those circumstances, the Court of Criminal Appeal was satisfied that the remark was not

---

work of the Gardaí must and should depend on voluntary interviews and on information gained from statements made during such interviews".

[401] [1999] 1 ILRM 500.

[402] See also *DPP v Cowman* [1993] 1 IR 335, where O'Hanlon J rejected the contention that a garda could not approach a member of the public unless he had already formed an opinion that some grounds existed for suspecting that the person he was approaching was planning to commit some breach of the criminal law, or had already committed some offence. He took the view that there was no restriction imposed by law on the right of a garda to approach members of the public from time to time as he or she saw fit for the purpose of speaking to them and having communications with them on an informal basis.

[403] Unreported, High Court, 29 May 2000.

[404] [2009] IECCA 18.

[405] [2010] IECCA 127, [2012] 1 IR 49.

made in the contextual framework of the Judges' Rules. Further, even if there had been any non-compliance, it was not such as to render the statement inadmissible.

(b) Intention to charge a person

8–175   Rule 2 requires a garda to caution a person before asking any questions or further questions if he or she has made up his or her mind to charge the person with an offence. In *People (DPP) v Darcy*,[406] Keane J said that the purpose of this rule was to ensure fairness to persons who have not been arrested or detained but who are "assisting the police with their enquiries".

8–176   It is clear that the question of whether the garda had the requisite intention falls to be tested subjectively, on the basis of whether the garda had, as a matter of fact, made up his or her mind to charge the person and not objectively according to whether the garda was in a position to charge the accused.[407] The problem with such a subjective test is that it involves an *ex post facto* evaluation at a point when the accused is on trial and a garda has a significant incentive to give evidence that he had not made up his or her mind to charge the accused, a fact which is not otherwise objectively verifiable. The inevitable tendency of the formulation of the rule must be to prompt a garda to push back in time the point at which he or she had made up his or her mind to charge the accused, at least beyond the point at which an incriminating statement was made.[408]

8–177   In *People (DPP) v Breen*,[409] objection was taken to the admissibility of incriminating statements made by the accused in the course of a conversation with a garda. The conversation had taken place against the backdrop of a search of the accused's farm for firearms and explosives and, in the course of same, the accused became very agitated and intimated that he wished to say something but was afraid to do so. The court of trial found that there had been no breach of rule 2 in the failure to administer a caution because the garda had not made up his mind to charge the accused. On appeal, it was argued that the rule had been breached because, even if the garda had not made up his mind to charge the applicant, he intended to do so should the search discover anything of an incriminating nature. This contention was, however, rejected by the Court of Criminal Appeal which stated that the wording of the rule 2 is quite specific and does not apply to a conditional intention of the kind which was alleged to exist.[410] However, it should be noted that the Court decided to exclude the statement on the basis that it had been taken in breach of the requirements of fundamental fairness.

(c) Requirement to administer caution to person in custody

8–178   Rule 3 requires a person in custody to be given a caution before questioning and the purpose of this rule was identified by Finlay CJ in *Re Gunner Buckley*[411] as follows:

---

[406] Unreported, Court of Criminal Appeal, 29 July 1997.

[407] *People (AG) v Cummins* [1972] IR 312 at 326.

[408] Of course, the trial judge may disbelieve the garda when he says that he had not made up his mind to charge the accused: see *McCarrick v Leavy* [1964] IR 225.

[409] Unreported, Court of Criminal Appeal, 13 March 1995.

[410] Unreported, Court of Criminal Appeal, 13 March 1995 at 4.

[411] [1998] 2 IR 454.

"It is clear in the view of the Court that r.3 of the Judges' Rules is a precaution ... the necessity for which arises not from the legal origin of the custody of the person concerned, but from the fact of custody. The essential precaution of giving to a person, before asking questions, a caution that they are not obliged to answer those questions unless they wish to do so, but that if they do, what they say may be taken down and given in evidence, arises from the fact that the person concerned, if he is in custody, cannot leave and avoid being subjected to the questions which are being put before him, whereas, if he were a person who has merely accompanied a policeman to a garda station for the purpose of assisting him with his inquiries and voluntarily subjected himself to the questions, he can at any moment terminate the interview by standing up and leaving."[412]

8–179   In that case, the appellant had been required to attend for, and subject himself to, interview by the military police and would not have been entitled to leave without a breach of military discipline. The Courts-Martial Appeal Court was, thus, satisfied that the position of the appellant had been equivalent to that of a civilian in custody being interviewed by the gardaí in that the essential requirement that he could not leave was satisfied. Indeed, there was an additional factor in that the order with which the appellant had complied was to attend for interview which made it even more important that a caution should be given before the interview commenced. The Court, therefore, proceeded to quash the conviction because of the breach of r.3, taking the view that it would not be a proper exercise of discretion to admit the inculpatory statements made by the appellant.

8–180   It is clear from *Re Gunner Buckley* that it is the fact of custody rather than the legal basis for same which is important and triggers the obligation to caution. It is, thus, immaterial that the custody is not related to the matter in respect of which the accused is being questioned[413] or that the person is in the custody of civilians rather than the gardaí.[414] It also appears that the concept of custody will be interpreted broadly and is not confined to where a person has been arrested and detained in a garda station. It extends to circumstances where a person is in custody in the sense that he or she is under restraint, whether physical or verbal, and is not free to leave.[415]

(d) The caution

8–181   The requirement for the caution is clearly grounded in the pre-trial right to silence enjoyed by a suspect[416] and serves to ensure that a person who may be charged with the commission of an offence understands that he does not have to answer any questions.[417] Its purpose was explained by Murnaghan J in *AG v Durnan (No.2)*[418] in the following terms:

"The proper caution will bring home to the mind of the accused when he has been charged that he need not make any statement; but, on the other hand, that, if he does volunteer a statement,

---

[412] [1998] 2 IR 454 at 462.

[413] *People (AG) v Cummins* [1972] IR 312 at 324; *R. v Buchan* [1964] 1 All ER 502 at 503.

[414] *People (AG) v Kearns* (1938) 72 ILTR 115.

[415] *Cf. R. v Narayan* [1992] 3 NZLR 145 where it was held that a person will be under *de facto* arrest if a police officer deprives him or her of liberty to go where he or she pleases or by actions or words restrains him or her from moving anywhere beyond the arrester's control.

[416] See Chap.12.

[417] See *People (DPP) v Lynch* [1982] ILRM 64 at 86, where Walsh J, referring to the caution, stated: "Generally speaking, nobody is obliged to answer any questions and, if one were to assume that everybody knows that that is the law, there would be no need for the warning: but practical experience has show that there is a need for such a warning."

[418] [1934] IR 540.

it may be used in evidence at his trial. This caution enshrines the result of long experience and it is no idle formula. The first part in substance warns the accused that on an occasion when it might reasonably be expected that some answer should be made the law does not require any answer; while the second part of the caution warns the accused that if he makes any statement it should be no glib or untrue excuse, and further, it being a principle that the prosecution must prove the guilt of the accused, it gives a warning that admissions made at the time may be used to prove the guilt of the accused."[419]

8–182   In *Heaney v Ireland*,[420] the Supreme Court held that the right to silence is constitutionally protected by the guarantee of freedom of expression in Art.40.6.1 and, as discussed in Chap.11, a strong argument can be made that the effect of that decision has been to constitutionalise the requirement to give a caution. If this is the case, it would have significant repercussions because, as matters stand, a failure to give a caution merely gives rise to a discretion to exclude any confession obtained thereafter whereas a breach of the right to silence would, arguably, give rise to the application of the exclusionary rule as formulated in *People (DPP) v Kenny*.[421] This would very likely result in the exclusion of a confession if a caution had not been given.

8–183   It is obviously important that the caution be administered properly so as to convey the substance of same to a suspect and in *AG v Cleary*,[422] Kennedy CJ, adverting to the danger of "parrot-like repetition", stated that:

> "It is not enough that the words shall be glibly or rapidly spoken, but the sense of the caution and of every limb of it must be conveyed to the mind of the person to whom it is addressed, otherwise it ceases to be a caution."[423]

8–184   It is also important that the gardaí do not, by their actions or words, undermine the terms of the caution by, for example, immediately urging the suspect to speak.[424]

8–185   Although it is good practice to do so, it appears that it is not necessary to caution an accused at the start of every session of questioning. In *People (DPP) v Morgan*,[425] the accused had been questioned by gardaí and was cautioned at least once, perhaps twice, in accordance with the Judges' Rules. An identification parade was then held and after the parade, interviewing recommenced. The accused was told by a garda that he was still under caution and, according to the garda, the accused indicated that he understood this. However, he later challenged an admission made by him during the course of this interview on the basis that he had not been cautioned. The Court of Criminal Appeal concluded that there had not been any breach of the Judges' Rules. O'Flaherty J said that it is not necessary for the police officers "to repeat in parrot like fashion" the words of the caution on every occasion. The point of giving the caution is the person should understand what it is about. The accused had been under caution originally and understood it. He had also had the benefit of legal advice while in custody so he knew his rights.

---

[419] [1934] IR 540 at 548.
[420] [1996] 1 IR 580, [1997] 1 ILRM 117.
[421] [1990] 2 IR 110.
[422] (1934) 1 Frewen 14.
[423] (1934) 1 Frewen 14 at 17.
[424] *DPP v WF* (1980) 114 ILTR 110 at 112. *Cf. People (DPP) v Coll*, unreported, Court of Criminal Appeal, 18 May 1998 (inculpatory statement was taken in breach of the Judges' Rules in circumstances where the accused had been cautioned but immediately questioned with the object of obtaining such a statement).
[425] Unreported, Court of Criminal Appeal, *ex tempore*, 28 July 1997.

8–186 If an accused alleges that a caution was not given, the prosecution bear the onus of proving that a caution in accordance with the Judges' Rules was given.[426] However, because the terms of the caution are well known, it is not generally necessary for the prosecution to prove the terms of caution and the court will, in the absence of evidence to the contrary, assume that the caution given was a proper one.[427]

8–187 It should be noted that s.32 of the Criminal Justice Act 2007 confers on the Minister for Justice the power to make regulations providing for the administration of cautions by members of the Garda Síochána to persons in relation to offences. However, to date, no such regulations have been made and the traditional caution continues to apply.

3. Rule 7

8–188 Rule 7 prohibits a suspect from being cross-examined in the course of making a statement and stipulates that questions can only be put to him or her for the purpose of removing ambiguity in what he or she has said. Thus, in *AG v Lanigan*,[428] an incriminating statement was excluded in circumstances where a garda had put questions to the accused while in the course of making a statement in order "to establish the crime".[429] However, r.7 does not prevent a suspect from being questioned in relation to a statement, and any inconsistencies contained therein, after it has been made.[430] Neither, would it appear, does it affect the admissibility of a statement made by the accused which has been preceded by intensive questioning provided that the accused is not questioned (except in relation to ambiguities) in the course of making the statement.

4. Rule 8

8–189 Rule 8 stipulates that, when two or more accused persons are charged with the same offence and their statements are taken separately, the gardaí should not read these statements to the other persons charged. Instead, each accused should simply be given a copy of those statements and nothing should be done by the gardaí to invite a reply. If the accused wishes to make a statement in reply, he or she should first be cautioned in the usual terms.[431]

8–190 The application of r.8 arose for consideration in *People (DPP) v Burke*.[432] In the course of questioning a garda had told the second appellant that the first appellant had made a statement implicating him in the crime. However, the Court of Criminal

---

[426] *McCarrick v Leavy* [1964] IR 225 at 237.
[427] *AG v Durnan (No.2)* [1934] IR 540 at 548. *Cf. AG v McGrath* [1938] Ir Jur Rep 25, a decision of a differently constituted Court of Criminal Appeal which held that the actual terms of the caution used had to be proved. However, it should be noted that in *McGrath*, the accused, who was unrepresented, alleged that no caution had been given.
[428] [1958] Ir Jur Rep 59.
[429] *Cf. People (DPP) v McCann* [1998] 4 IR 397 at 409 (no breach of Judges' Rules where suspect had asked garda to lead with questions and questions were not put for the purpose of cross-examination but for the purpose of maintaining direction and coherence).
[430] *People (DPP) v O'Driscoll*, unreported, Court of Criminal Appeal, *ex tempore*, 19 July 1999 at 3.
[431] In *People (DPP) v Mulligan* (1980) 2 Frewen 16, the Court of Criminal Appeal rejected the argument that a special form of caution is required pursuant to rule 8, pointing out that the rule specified that the "usual" caution should be given.
[432] (1986) 3 Frewen 92.

Appeal rejected the contention that there had been a breach of r.8 because the second appellant had not been charged at the time and the rule only applies when two or more persons "are charged" with the same offence. The Court was also satisfied that there had not been a breach of the spirit of the rule as the second appellant was illiterate and little would have been achieved by giving him a copy of Burke's statement. In *People (DPP) v Palmer*,[433] it was argued that there had been a number of breaches of r.8 in that statements made by other persons questioned by gardaí had been read to the applicant. Applying the decision in *Burke*, the Court held that the literal terms of r.8 had not been breached but was of the view that there had been a breach of the spirit of the rule. However, the Court was satisfied that any admissions made by the applicant thereafter could not be said to have resulted from the breach of the spirit of the rule and, further, even if the spirit of the rule was breached, the trial judge was entitled, in the exercise of his discretion, to admit the applicant's admissions.

8–191   It was held in *AG v Durnan (No.2)*[434] that, where a statement of an accomplice is handed to a suspect, this fact, the contents of the statement and the fact that the accused remained silent are permitted to be placed before the jury. However, this holding must be considered to be of very doubtful authority having regard to the decision in *People (DPP) v Finnerty*.[435]

5. Rule 9

8–192   Rule 9 stipulates that a statement should, whenever possible, be taken down in writing and signed by the person making it after it has been read to him or her and he or she has been invited to make any corrections he or she may wish.[436] In *People (DPP) v Pringle*,[437] O'Higgins CJ identified the purpose of rule 9 as follows:

> "It seems clear that this Rule, which, of course, is not a rule of law but rather an admonition for the carrying out of fair procedures of interrogation, was designed to achieve a situation in which (a) there would be accuracy in the recording of any statement made to be achieved by the early writing down of it so as to obviate errors of recollection and (b) in which an accused person would, at a time when he should have a sufficient memory of what he had said, be given an opportunity of challenging the accuracy of the record made."[438]

8–193   Subsequently, in *People (DPP) v Towson*,[439] he elaborated that the mischief at which rule 9 is aimed is "to prevent a situation in which invented or planted oral statements are adduced in evidence by the stronger side to the detriment and harm and injury of a weak and oppressed defendant".[440]

8–194   Rule 9 merely requires a "statement" made by an accused to be taken down in writing and does not require gardaí to reduce to writing everything said in the

---

[433] Unreported, Court of Criminal Appeal, 22 March 2002.
[434] [1934] IR 540 at 546.
[435] [1999] 4 IR 364, [2000] 1 ILRM 191. This decision is discussed in Chap.11, section E.
[436] It should be noted that it is the statement of the accused, not the record of it, that is the evidence in the case: *People (DPP) v Farrell* [1978] IR 13 at 21.
[437] (1981) 2 Frewen 57.
[438] (1981) 2 Frewen 57 at 98. This statement was accepted and adopted in *People (DPP) v Kelly (No.2)* [1983] IR 1. Consistent with this identification of the purpose of rule 9, it was held in *People (DPP) v Ebbs* [2011] IECCA 5 at [3], [2011] 1 IR 778 at 781, that it principally addresses the making of formal statements rather than verbal exchanges in the course of arrest.
[439] [1978] ILRM 122.
[440] [1978] ILRM 122 at 126.

course of an interview.[441] It was held in *People (DPP) v McKeever*[442] that there had been no breach of the Judges' Rules because of the failure of gardaí to record "general conversations" with the accused.[443] However, the gardaí should record anything of consequence said during the interview.[444]

(a) Contemporaneous recording of statement

8–195 Having regard to the purpose of the rule, it appears that rule 9 envisages the reduction of a statement to writing and its signing within a short time after it has been made but the courts have declined to be prescriptive in relation to the lapse of time that is permissible. In *People (DPP) v Pringle*[445] it was held that "the permissible time-lag between the making of a statement, the recording of it and the reading over of it must, of necessity, vary from case to case and in particular be governed by the circumstances of each case".[446] In that case, the applicant had been questioned over a two-day period and notes had been taken on an ongoing basis. On the evening of the second day, the detective sergeant who had taken the notes read them over to the accused and asked him if they were correct. The applicant agreed that they were correct but declined the invitation to sign them. The applicant had not challenged the accuracy of the notes at the trial and, in the circumstances, the Court was satisfied that the evidence supported the ruling of the court of trial that the object and purpose of rule 9 had been achieved and there had been compliance with it.[447] Furthermore, even if a breach of the rule had occurred, it would have been open to the court of trial to have exercised its discretion to admit the statements.

(b) Failure to reduce statement to writing or read it over to accused

8–196 A number of cases have considered the admissibility of statements where there has been a failure to reduce the statements to writing as required by rule 9 or to read it over and proffer it to the accused for signature. In *People (DPP) v McNally*,[448] verbal admissions of the first applicant had been taken in breach of r.9 and no explanation was given by the garda witnesses, other than a previous course of conduct, for the failure to take a note of the alleged verbal admissions of McNally. Coupled with the

---

[441] *McCormack v DPP* [2007] IEHC 123 at [10], [2008] 1 ILRM 49 at 55. *Cf.* the description of the process of compiling the statement of an accused which is given in the *Report of Committee to Enquire into Certain Aspects of Criminal Procedure* (Report of the Martin Committee) (1990), p.22: "During the course of what is best described as a question and answer session, the police officer involved may from time to time write down some of the answers received. In most instances once the questioning, which may have lasted for hours, comes to an end, the officer converts into narrative form what appears to him to be a fair summary of the answers received, and when this has been put in writing it is read over, alterations or additions are invited and, whether the person in question agrees or declines to sign the document, it is eventually produced in court as the 'statement of the accused'".

[442] [1994] 2 ILRM 186.

[443] O'Flaherty J pointed out (at 196) that the caution required under the Judges' Rules warns an accused that what he says *may be* taken down in writing and may be given in evidence.

[444] *People (DPP) v McKeever* [1994] 2 ILRM 186 at 196.

[445] (1981) 2 Frewen 57.

[446] (1981) 2 Frewen 57 at 98–99.

[447] But see *People (DPP) v Reddan* [1995] 3 IR 560 at 566, where the Court of Criminal Appeal had no doubt that the Judges' Rules had not been complied with in circumstances where the note of an interview was not made until one hour after the interview had concluded.

[448] (1981) 2 Frewen 43.

facts that each of the alleged verbal admissions had been made in the early hours after 44 hours of interrogation, interrupted by only one night's sleep, the Court of Criminal Appeal was not satisfied that there were any circumstances which would have justified the trial court in exercising its discretion to admit the statements. Another case where the Court of Criminal Appeal refused to interfere with the exercise of the trial judge's discretion is *People (DPP) v Kelly (No.2)*.[449] In that case, two oral statements had been taken in contravention of rule 9 but a third written statement had been made by the accused and acknowledged and signed by him. The Court held that the trial judge had exercised his discretion correctly in admitting evidence of the two oral statements, having regard to the fact that the material contained in them was in substance identical to the facts contained in the written statement.[450]

8–197   An example of where statements that had been reduced to writing but not read over or proffered to the accused for signing were held to be admissible can be seen in *People (DPP) v Callan*.[451] The statements had not been read over to the accused or proffered to him for signing because he had lapsed into an apparent state of unconsciousness. However, having regard to the fact that the medical evidence indicated that the applicant had been feigning this state of unconsciousness, the Court of Criminal Appeal was satisfied that there had not been any injustice in the admission of these statements into evidence.

(c) Refusal of accused to sign statement

8–198   Rule 9 does not require that a statement be signed to be admitted in evidence, merely that the suspect be invited to sign it.[452] If an accused refuses to sign a statement when invited to do so, an issue may obviously arise at trial as to whether the statement is accurate or was even made by the accused. It is, therefore, good practice for the gardaí present to sign and date the statement so that the Court has some means of knowing that the statement is contemporaneous and that it was been read out to the accused.[453]

8–199   It should be noted that the procedure for the admission of an inculpatory statement is different if it is not signed. In *People (AG) v Keane*,[454] it was held that the correct procedure is for the witness to whom the statement was made and who reduced it to writing to give oral testimony of what the accused said to him. Only if that oral testimony establishes that the accused acknowledged the document to be a correct

---

[449] [1983] IR 1.
[450] The decision of the Court of Criminal Appeal on this point was upheld on appeal to the Supreme Court. See also *People (DPP) v Towson* [1978] ILRM 122 where it was held that the trial court had correctly exercised its discretion to admit a verbal statement in circumstances where the prosecution had advanced what was considered to be an adequate explanation for the failure to reduce it to writing.
[451] (1986) 3 Frewen 92.
[452] See *People (DPP) v McKeever* [1994] 2 ILRM 186 at 195.
[453] *Cf. People (DPP) v Kavanagh* (1989) 3 Frewen 243 at 246.
[454] (1975) 110 ILTR 1.

record of what he said in his statement can be it put in evidence.[455] Once such oral evidence is given, then the document is treated as if it has been signed by the accused.[456]

6. Discretion to Exclude Evidence Obtained in Breach of the Rules

8–200   Where the admission of a statement is challenged on the basis of a breach of the Judges' Rules, the onus is on the prosecution to establish that the Rules were complied with.[457] In *R. v Voisin*[458] the effect of a breach of the Rules was explained by the English Court of Criminal Appeal as follows:

> "These rules have not the force of law; they are administrative directions the observance of which the police authorities should enforce upon their subordinates as tending to the fair administration of justice. It is important that they should do so, for statements obtained from prisoners, contrary to the spirit of these rules, may be rejected as evidence by the judge presiding at the trial."[459]

8–201   A similar approach was adopted in *McCarrick v Leavy*[460] where Walsh J distinguished between an involuntary statement and a statement obtained in breach of the Judges' Rules on the basis that an involuntary statement was inadmissible *per se* whereas a breach of the Judges' Rules did not, of itself, render a statement inadmissible but gives rise to a discretion on the part of a trial judge to exclude it.[461] Thus, a breach of the Rules does not result in automatic exclusion but confers a discretion on the trial judge to exclude a statement so obtained.

8–202   The decision of the Court of Criminal Appeal in *People (DPP) v Farrell*[462] indicates that the discretion to exclude evidence obtained in breach of the Judges' Rules is weighted in favour of exclusion. O'Higgins CJ stated:

> "The Judges' Rules are not rules of law. They are rules for the guidance of person taking statements. However, they have stood up to the test of time and will be departed from at peril. In very rare cases such as *R. v Mills and Lemon*[463] a statement taken in breach may be admitted in evidence but in very exceptional circumstances. Where ... there is a breach of

---

[455] (1975) 110 ILTR 1 at 6. In *People (AG) v Murphy* [1947] IR 236 at 241, it was held that a document containing answers to questions put to an accused but which was not signed or adopted by him was not admissible in evidence. However, that decision has not been followed and in *People (DPP) v Brazil*, unreported, Court of Criminal Appeal, 22 March 2002, it was held that the trial judge had acted properly in admitting portions of the interview notes even though they were not signed. It should be noted, however, that Keane CJ stated that the statements "retained their status of being purely verbal admissions alleged to have been made by the applicant".

[456] *Per* Maguire CJ in *People (AG) v Wickham* [1949] IR 180 at 182: "There is no discoverable difference between a document containing a record of a statement made by the accused which is read over to him and acknowledged but not signed by him. In both cases the document is acknowledged by him to contain, in precise terms, the confession or statements made by him."

[457] *McCarrick v Leavy* [1964] IR 225 at 237.

[458] [1918] 1 KB 531.

[459] [1918] 1 KB 531 at 539 (*per* A.T. Lawrence J). See also *R. v Bass* [1953] 1 QB 680, [1953] 1 All ER 1064; *R. v Ovenell* [1968] 1 All ER 933 at 939, and *R. v Corr* [1968] NI 193 at 211.

[460] [1964] IR 225.

[461] [1964] IR 225 at 236–238. See also *People (AG) v Cummins* [1972] IR 312 at 322–323; *People (DPP) v Buck* [2002] 2 IR 268 at 277, [2002] 2 ILRM 454 at 462; *People (DPP) v O'Reilly* [2009] IECCA 18. A similar approach has been adopted in New Zealand and Australia, where on a breach of the Rules, the trial judge has a discretion as to whether to admit the evidence or not: *R. v Convery* [1968] NZLR 426 at 433; *R. v Cobcroft* [1967] 2 NSWR 97; *Ryan v Marshall* [1965] Tas SR 1; *Collins v R.* (1980) 31 ALR 257.

[462] [1978] IR 13.

[463] [1947] KB 297.

the Judges' Rules ... each of such breaches calls for an adequate explanation. The breaches and the explanations (if any) together with the entire circumstances of the case are matters to be taken into consideration by the trial Judge before exercising his judicial discretion as to whether or not he will admit such statement in evidence."[464]

8–203 This statement of principle was been approved and applied in a number of cases[465] but it is not clear that the approach laid down in *Farrell*, which effectively sets up a presumption of exclusion in the absence of an adequate and acceptable explanation for a breach, has been universally followed in subsequent cases. Instead, many of the cases concerning breaches of the Judges' Rules appear to have been decided by reference to the test of whether the accused has suffered any prejudice by reason of the breach.

(a) Effect of breach of Judges' Rules on subsequent statement

8–204 As noted above, if a person makes an incriminating statement which is involuntary, this will taint and render inadmissible any subsequent incriminating statement because of the possibility that the inducement or oppression continues to affect the mind of the person when making the subsequent statement. However, in *People (DPP) v Buckley*[466] it was held by the Court of Criminal Appeal that a statement taken in compliance with the Judges' Rules will not be rendered inadmissible because earlier statements were taken in breach of the Rules and have been ruled inadmissible on that basis.[467] The Court did not expand upon the reasons why different considerations apply in the case of breaches of the Judges' Rules and it is doubtful that a general proposition that the admissibility of a statement taken in compliance with the Rules will not be affected by an earlier breach of the Rules can be accepted without qualification. For example, if an accused made an inculpatory statement which was ruled inadmissible because of the failure to administer a caution, it is certainly possible that that breach could affect the admissibility of a statement made in similar terms though preceded by a caution. The rationale employed in the context of involuntary statements, that an accused may well confess a second time when "the cat is out of the bag", might well be applicable.

E. The Custody Regulations

1. Introduction

8–205 The Criminal Justice Act 1984 (Treatment of Persons in Custody in Garda Síochána Stations) Regulations 1987 (as amended)[468] (the "Custody Regulations") were enacted pursuant to the Criminal Justice Act 1984 (the "1984 Act")[469] and expand on

---

[464] [1978] IR 13 at 21.

[465] See *People (DPP) v McNally* (1981) 2 Frewen 43 at 50; *People (DPP) v Towson* [1978] ILRM 122; *People (DPP) v Ebbs* [2011] IECCA 5, [2001] 1 IR 778.

[466] [1990] 1 IR 14.

[467] See also *People (DPP) v Reddan* [1995] 3 IR 560 at 566.

[468] SI No. 119 of 1987 (as amended by the Criminal Justice Act 1984 (Treatment of Persons in Custody in Garda Síochána Stations) (Amendment) Regulations 2006. It might be noted that a series of amendments to the Custody Regulations and additional safeguards were recommended in the *Report of the Committee to Enquire into Certain Aspects of Criminal Procedure* (1990) which have not been implemented.

[469] Although the scope of application is not specified in the Custody Regulations (unlike the Electronic

certain protections contained in that Act.[470] They lay down various rules regulating the custody of arrested/detained persons[471] including questioning and are intended to provide additional safeguards[472] for persons arrested and questioned in the context of the greater powers conferred on gardaí by the 1984 Act.[473] The purpose of the provisions is to ensure that accused persons are fairly treated.[474]

2. Outline of the Custody Regulations

(a) Member in charge

8–206 One of the central features of the Custody Regulations is the creation of the position of "member in charge".[475] This is the garda, generally of a senior rank, who is in charge of a garda station and who is responsible for overseeing the application of the Regulations to persons in custody in that garda station.[476] This role is reinforced by the stipulation that, in as far as practicable, he or she should not be a member who was involved in the arrest of the person for the offence in respect of which he or she is in custody or in the investigation of that offence.[477]

Recording Regulations), it would appear that they apply whenever a person is arrested and/or detained under any legislation: *cf. DPP v Spratt* [1995] 1 IR 585, [1995] 2 ILRM 117.

[470] Section 5 of the Criminal Justice Act 1984 (as extended by s.9 of that Act and s.5 of the Criminal Justice (Drug Trafficking) Act 1996 and amended by s.67 of the Children Act 2001) stipulates in subs.(1) that, where a person not below the age of 18 years is detained in a garda station pursuant to s.4 of that Act, s.30 of the Offences Against the State Act 1939 or s.2 of the Criminal Justice (Drug Trafficking) Act 1996), the member in charge must inform him or her or cause him or her to be informed without delay that he or she is entitled to consult a solicitor and to have notification of his or her detention and of the station where he or she is being detained sent to one other person reasonably named by him or her and the member in charge is required, on request, to cause the solicitor and the named person to be notified accordingly as soon as practicable. The consequences of a failure to comply with s.5 are not specified but it would appear that, if the requirements of the section were not complied with, any statement obtained would constitute illegally obtained evidence and a trial judge would have a discretion to exclude same in accordance with the principles laid down by Kingsmill Moore J in *People (AG) v O'Brien* [1965] IR 142 at 160.

[471] As the title of the Custody Regulations suggests, they only apply where a person is detained in a garda station: *Seeruttun v The Governor of Cloverhill Prison* [2013] IEHC 217 at [23].

[472] In *People (DPP) v Darcy*, unreported, Court of Criminal Appeal, 29 July 1997 at 23, it was held that the Custody Regulations do not, in any way, deprive a person detained in custody of the protection of the Judges' Rules. Indeed, as was pointed out in that case, the Judges' Rules may have a wider application in that they apply not only to arrested persons but also to persons who are "assisting the police with their enquiries".

[473] *Cf. DPP v Devlin*, unreported, High Court, 2 September 1998 at 13.

[474] *Cf. People (DPP) v Smith*, unreported, Court of Criminal Appeal, 22 November 1999 at 6.

[475] The concept of "member in charge" is defined in reg.4(1) of the Regulations to mean "the member who is in charge of a station at a time when the member in charge of a station is required to do anything or cause anything to be done pursuant to [the] Regulations". In *DPP (Lenihan) v McGuire* [1996] 3 IR 586 at 593–594, Kelly J held that the definition of the term "member in charge" relates to a factual position which obtains in a garda station at any relevant time. Thus, the "member in charge" within the meaning of the Regulations is the person who is actually in charge of a station when such person is required to do anything or cause to be done anything pursuant to the Regulations.

[476] Regulation 5(1). This was described by Kelly J in *DPP (Lenihan) v McGuire* [1996] 3 IR 586 at 593, as "an important responsibility placed on the shoulders of such a person". As part of the discharge of that responsibility, the member in charge is required by reg.5(1) to visit persons in custody from time to time and make necessary enquiries.

[477] Regulation 4(3). The circumstances in which the arresting officer can act as the member in charge were considered in *DPP v Devlin*, unreported, High Court, 2 September 1998, where the difficulties

(b) Custody record

8–207   One of the primary duties of the member in charge is the keeping of a custody record in respect of each person in custody.[478] This is designed to act as an important safeguard of the rights of an accused while in custody and also as a source of information for a court of trial if any issue later arises as what transpired during custody. Under the Regulations, the member in charge is required to record in the custody record specified information about every significant event during the period of detention including: the arrest and detention of the person;[479] details of any extension of the period of detention;[480] the times during which an arrested person is interviewed and the members present at each interview;[481] and details of compliance with various other requirements under the Custody Regulations[482] and the Electronic Recording Regulations.[483] There is an obligation to preserve the custody record[484] which may be accessed by a detainee or his or her legal representative after he or she ceases to be in custody.[485]

(c) Right of access to solicitor

8–208   The member in charge has a vital role in ensuring that arrested persons are informed of their right to consult a solicitor.[486] Thus, pursuant to reg.8(1), the member in charge is required to inform an arrested person orally and without delay, or cause him or her to be so informed, that he or she is entitled to consult a solicitor.[487] The member in charge must also go on to explain or cause to be explained that failure to

---

of complying with this requirement in the context of rural garda stations were acknowledged by Budd J.

[478] Regulation 6. Under reg.6(4), the member in charge is responsible for the accuracy and completeness of all entries made in the custody record while he or she is the member in charge.

[479] Regulation 7(1) requires a record to be made in relation to an arrested person of (a) the date, time and place of arrest and the identity of the arresting member (or other person effecting the arrest), (b) the time of arrival at the station, (c) the nature of the offence or other matter in respect of which he or she was arrested, and (d) any relevant particulars relating to his or her physical or mental condition. Regulation 7(2) stipulates that, when a person is detained pursuant to s.4 of the Criminal Justice Act 1984, the member of charge is required to certify that he or she has reasonable grounds for believing that the detention of the person is necessary for the proper investigation of the offence in respect of which he or she has been arrested in accordance with s.4(2) of that Act.

[480] Regulation 7(3) and (4).

[481] Regulation 12(12).

[482] See regs 8(2), 12(8)(b), 12(12), 13(4), 14(5), 15(2), 17(6) and (7), 18(2)–(4), 20(5) and (7), 21(3), (5) and (7), and 23.

[483] See regs 4(4) and 13.

[484] Regulation 24(1) requires custody records to be preserved for at least 12 months or, if any proceedings to which a custody record would be relevant are instituted or any complaint is made in respect of the conduct of a member while a person was in custody, until the final determination of the proceedings or complaint, whichever is the later.

[485] Regulation 24(2) provides that, when a person ceases to be in custody, he or she or his or her legal representative must, on request made within 12 months thereafter, be supplied as soon as practicable with a copy of the custody record relating to him or her, or of such entries in it as he or she may specify.

[486] The importance of this obligation was emphasised by Hardiman J in *DPP v McCrea* [2010] IESC 60 at [14] who noted that, in the absence of access to a solicitor, the Gardaí themselves are the only source of legal advice available to the accused.

[487] The member in charge is not relieved of this obligation on the basis that the arrested person is not in a condition, due to intoxication, to understand his or her rights: *DPP v Devlin*, unreported, High Court, 2 September 1998.

exercise that right immediately will not preclude the person from doing so later.[488] Further, under reg.8(2), the member in charge is also required to, without delay, give the arrested person or cause him or her to be given a written notice informing him or her, *inter alia*, of his or her entitlement to consult a solicitor.[489] However, it does not appear that a lengthy exposition of those rights is required,[490] provided that the arrested person actually receives the required information.[491] In *DPP v O'Kelly*[492] it was held that the obligation on a member in charge is simply to inform an accused of his rights and hand him the required notice, not to ensure that he understands his rights.[493]

8–209   Regulation 9(2)(a) stipulates that, if an arrested person asks for a solicitor to be notified of his or her being in custody, the member in charge is obliged to notify the solicitor, or cause him or her to be notified, as soon as practicable.[494] If the solicitor cannot be contacted within a reasonable time, or if the solicitor is unable or unwilling to attend at the station, the arrested person must be given an opportunity to ask for another solicitor and the member in charge is required to notify the solicitor, or cause him or her to be notified, as soon as practicable.[495] It appears that an arrested person is also entitled to make a telephone call or communicate in writing with his or her solicitor.[496] Under reg.12(6), where an arrested person asks for a solicitor, he or she cannot be asked to make a written statement in relation to an offence until a reasonable time for the attendance of the solicitor has elapsed. However, there does not appear to be any impediment to questioning continuing during that period with a record being made of any incriminating statements made by the arrested person.

8–210   Provision is made in reg.10(1) for information to be given as to the station where an arrested person is in custody in response to enquiries by solicitors.[497] Where an arrested person has not had access to a solicitor and a solicitor whose presence has not been requested presents himself or herself at the station and informs the member

---

[488] Regulation 8(1).

[489] Regulation 8(2).

[490] In *People (DPP) v Reddan* [1995] 3 IR 560, where the member in charge stated that the explanation of the accused's right to a solicitor only took two minutes, the Court of Criminal Appeal was satisfied that such a period was ample to impart the required information.

[491] In *DPP v Gillespie* [2011] IEHC 236, it was contended that reg.8(1) had not been complied with because the accused was on his mobile telephone at the time that the information specified by reg.8(1) was given to him. It was held by Hedigan J (at [5.5]) that it was highly undesirable for the arrested person to be on a phone call when notice of his rights was given to him but it did not follow that there had been a breach of the Custody Regulations and it was a question of fact as to whether the article had been complied with.

[492] Unreported, High Court, 10 February 1998.

[493] It was also held that evidence of compliance with the requirements of reg.8 does not have to be given by the member in charge or the garda responsible but may be given by any garda who heard the required information given orally and saw the written notice being given to the arrested person. McCracken J rejected the submission that such evidence would be hearsay.

[494] Regulation 9(2)(a)(i).

[495] Regulation 9(2)(a)(ii). Regulation 9(2)(b) (as amended) extends the provisions of para.(a) to a request for a solicitor by a parent, guardian or spouse of a person under the age of eighteen or by an adult who is present during the questioning in accordance with the provisions of reg.13(2).

[496] Regulation 11(5).

[497] Regulation 10(1) provides that information as to the station where an arrested person is in custody is required to be given, if the arrested person consents, in response to an enquiry by a solicitor whose presence has not been requested by him.

in charge that he or she wishes to visit the arrested person, he or she must be asked if he or she wishes to consult the solicitor.[498]

8–211   Regulation 11(1) stipulates that an arrested person is to have reasonable access to a solicitor of his or her choice and to be enable to communicate with him or her privately.[499] However, a consultation with a solicitor may take place in the sight but out of the hearing of a garda.[500]

8–212   These regulations will be largely, if not entirely, superseded when s.5A of the Criminal Justice Act 1984[501] is commenced and the regulations that it is envisaged will be made pursuant thereto are made.

(d) Right of access to other persons

8–213   As noted above, one of the features of oppressive questioning is the keeping of a suspect incommunicado without access to family and friends.[502] To ensure that this does not occur, the Regulations contain a number of provisions dealing with the right of an accused person of access to persons other than his or her solicitor.[503] It is noteworthy that most of these provisions relate to persons *reasonably* named by him or her. No guidance is given in the Regulations as to when a person will be considered to have been reasonably named by an arrested person. However, it appears to be a person whose access to the arrested person will not hinder or delay the investigation of crime.

8–214   The provisions governing access to other persons are reasonably similar to those relating to access to a solicitor. Thus, under reg.8, the member in charge is required to inform an arrested person, without delay, orally and in writing, that he or she is entitled to have notification of his of her being in custody sent to another person

---

[498]   Regulation 11(2).
[499]   *Cf. People (DPP) v Finnegan*, unreported, Court of Criminal Appeal, 15 July 1997, where it was held that right of access to a solicitor necessarily implies, except in exceptional circumstances, a right to consult with the solicitor in private.
[500]   Regulation 11(3).
[501]   As inserted by s.9(a) of the Criminal Justice Act 2011.
[502]   See the emphasis placed on this factor in *People (DPP) v Lynch* [1982] IR 64 at 74, [1981] ILRM 389 at 391. In *Miranda v Arizona* (1966) 384 US 436 at 457–478, Warren CJ, delivering the judgment of a majority of the US Supreme Court, stated that the "practice of incommunicado interrogation is at odds with one of our Nation's most cherished principles—that the individual may not be compelled to incriminate himself".
[503]   The decision in *The Emergency Powers Bill 1976* [1977] IR 159 at 173, indicates that a detainee has, at a minimum, a legal right to communicate with other persons. *Cf. People (DPP) v Quilligan (No.3)* [1993] 2 IR 305 at 337, where Hederman J stated that a person in custody has a right not to be detained incommunicado. It might be noted that Art. 5(1) of Directive 2013/48/EU imposes an obligation on Member States to ensure that suspects or accused persons who are deprived of their liberty have the right to have at least one person, such as a relative or employer, nominated by them, informed of their deprivation of liberty without undue delay if they so wish. Pursuant to sub-article (2), this right can only be temporarily derogated from where justified in the light of the particular circumstances of the case on the basis of one of two compelling reasons: (a) where there is an urgent need to avert serious adverse consequences for the life, liberty or physical integrity of a person; or (b) where there is an urgent need to prevent a situation where criminal proceedings could be substantially prejudiced. Article 6(1) further requires Member States to ensure that suspects or accused persons who have been deprived of their liberty have the right to communicate without undue delay with at least one third person, such as a relative, nominated by them. Pursuant to sub-article (2), Member States may limit or defer the exercise of this right in view of imperative requirements or proportionate operational requirements

reasonably named by him or her, and to explain or cause to be explained, that failure to exercise that right immediately will not preclude the person from doing so later.[504] Under reg.9, if an arrested person asks for a named person to be notified of his or her being in custody, the member in charge is obliged to notify the named person, or cause him or her to be notified, as soon as practicable.[505] If the named person cannot be contacted within a reasonable time, the arrested person must be given an opportunity to name another person to be notified of his or her custody and the member in charge is required to notify that named person, or caused them to be notified, as soon as practicable.[506] An arrested person is also entitled to make a telephone call or communicate in writing with a person reasonably named by him or her provided that the member in charge is satisfied that it will not hinder or delay the investigation of crime.[507] Provision is made in reg.10(1) for information to be given as to the station where an arrested person is in custody in response to enquiries by solicitors and other persons.[508]

8–215　An arrested person may receive a visit from a relative, friend or other person with an interest in his or her welfare provided that he or she so wishes and the member in charge is satisfied that the visit can be adequately supervised and that it will not hinder or delay the investigation of crime.[509] However, before an arrested person has a supervised visit or communicates with a person other than his or her solicitor, he or she must be informed that anything he or she says during the visit or in the communication may be given in evidence.[510]

(e) Access to medical practitioners

8–216　A detainee has, at a minimum, a legal right to medical assistance while in custody[511] and provision is made in that regard by reg.21(4) which stipulates that, if a person in custody asks to be examined by a doctor of his or her choice at his or her

---

[504] The member in charge is not relieved of this obligation on the basis that the arrested person is not in a condition, due to intoxication, to understand his or her rights: *DPP v Devlin*, unreported, High Court, 2 September 1998. In *People (DPP) v O'Kelly*, unreported, High Court, 10 February 1998, it was held that the member of charge is simply required to inform a person in custody of his rights, not to ensure that he understands them.

[505] Regulation 9(2)(a)(i).

[506] Regulation 9(2)(a)(ii). Regulation 9(2)(b) extends the provisions of para.(a) to a request for a solicitor by a parent, guardian or spouse of a person under the age of 17 or by an adult who is present during the questioning in accordance with the provisions of reg.13(2).

[507] Regulation 11(5). A garda may listen to and terminate such a telephone call and read and decline to send such a letter if he or she is not satisfied that it will not hinder or delay the investigation of crime.

[508] Regulation 10(1) provides that information as to the station where an arrested person is in custody is required to be given: (a) if the arrested person consents, in response to an enquiry by a solicitor whose presence has not been requested by him; (b) if the arrested person consents and the member in charge is satisfied that giving the information will not hinder or delay the investigation of crime, in response to an enquiry by any other person.

[509] Regulation 11(4). The Regulations do not specify any limit to the number of visits that may be received but it is worth noting that, in *People (DPP) v McCann* [1998] 4 IR 397 at 411, a complaint that there had been excessively liberal access to an accused by his family was dismissed as "quite extraordinary".

[510] Regulation 11(6).

[511] *The Emergency Powers Bill 1976* [1977] IR 159 at 173; *People (DPP) v Quilligan (No.3)* [1993] 2 IR 305 at 322.

own expense, the member in charge must, as soon as practicable, make arrangements accordingly.[512]

8–217   Regulation 21 also makes provision for medical attention to be sought without prior request on the part of the person in custody. Thus, if a person in custody is injured, under the influence of intoxicating liquor or drugs and cannot be roused, fails to respond normally to questions or conversation (otherwise than owing to the influence of intoxicating liquor alone), appears to the member in charge to be suffering from a mental illness, or otherwise appears to the member in charge to need medical attention, the member in charge is required to summon a doctor or cause him or her to be summoned unless the person's condition appears to the member in charge to be such as to necessitate immediate removal to a hospital or other suitable place.[513] The member in charge is also charged with ensuring that any instructions given by a doctor in relation to the medical care of a person in custody are complied with.[514] Where a person in custody makes a complaint of physical ill-treatment, the member in charge must arrange for the person to be medically examined as soon as practicable unless, in circumstances where the complaint relates to another garda, he or she considers the complaint to be frivolous and vexatious.[515]

(f) Conduct of interviews

8–218   The Regulations, and, in particular, reg.12, contain what is effectively a Code of Practice with regard to the conduct of interviews and lay down a number of specific requirements and safeguards that must be complied with.

8–219   Regulation 12(7) provides that, except with the authority of the member in charge, an arrested person shall not be questioned between midnight and 8am in relation to an offence, which authority shall not be given unless: (i) he or she has been taken to the station during that period (but, subject to the caveat, that he or she must be allowed reasonable time for rest),[516] (ii) in the case of a person detained under s.4 of the Criminal Justice Act 1984, he or she has not consented in writing to the suspension of questioning in accordance with s.4(6), or (iii) the member in charge has reasonable grounds for believing that to delay questioning the person would involve a risk of injury to persons, serious loss of or damage to property, destruction or interference with evidence or escape of accomplices.

8–220   That regulation has been superseded by a new s.4(6) as substituted by s.7 of the Criminal Justice Act 2011. That subsection provides that, if a person is being detained pursuant to s.4 in a garda station between midnight and 8am, any questioning of that person for the purpose of the investigation shall be suspended during that period unless the detained person objects to the suspension (and the member in charge is required to inform the detained person or cause him or her to be informed that he or she may

---

[512] This does not preclude his examination by another doctor summoned by the member in charge provided that the person in custody consents to the examination: reg.21(4).
[513] Regulation 21(1). Under reg.21(2), medical advice must also be sought if the person in custody claims to need medication relating to a heart condition, diabetes, epilepsy or other potentially serious condition, or the member in charge considers it necessary because the person has in his or her possession any such medication.
[514] Regulation 21(2).
[515] Regulation 20(7).
[516] Regulations 12(7)(b) and 19(2).

object to the suspension) which objection is required to be recorded in writing or by electronic or other similar means. However, pursuant to subs.(6)(d), the member in charge may authorise the questioning of the detained person between midnight and 8am where the member has reasonable grounds for believing that to suspend the questioning would involve a risk of: (i) interference with, or injury to other persons, (ii) serious loss of, or damage to, property, (iii) the destruction of, or interference with, evidence, (iv) accomplices being alerted or the securing of their apprehension being made more difficult, or (v) hindering the recovery of property obtained as a result of an offence or the recovery of the value of any proceeds of an offence.

8–221 Where an arrested person is deaf or there is doubt about his or her hearing ability, he or she cannot be questioned in relation to an offence in the absence of an interpreter, if one is reasonably available, without his or her written consent or in circumstances where the member in charge has reasonable grounds for believing that to delay questioning the person would involve a risk of injury to persons, serious loss of or damage to property, destruction or interference with evidence or escape of accomplices.

8–222 Special provision is made in relation to the questioning of arrested persons under the influence of alcohol or drugs. Regulation 12(9) provides that an arrested person who is under the influence of intoxicating liquor or drugs to the extent that he or she is unable to appreciate the significance of questions put to him or her, or his or her answers, cannot be questioned in relation to an offence while he or she is in that condition[517] except with the authority of the member in charge. That authority cannot be given except where the member in charge has reasonable grounds for believing that to delay questioning the person would involve a risk of injury to persons, serious loss of or damage to property, destruction or interference with evidence or escape of accomplices.

8–223 As far as practicable, interviews must take place in rooms set aside for that purpose[518] and, before an interview commences, the garda conducting the interview must identify himself or herself and any other person present by name and rank to the arrested person.[519]

8–224 The conduct of interviews is subject to the overriding requirement laid down by reg.12(2) that they must be conducted "in a fair and humane manner". This provision is reinforced by the general duty imposed on gardaí by reg.3(1) that they "act with due respect for the personal rights of persons in custody and their dignity as human persons, and shall have regard for the special needs of any of them who may be under a physical or mental disability". Furthermore, reg.20(1) stipulates that no garda shall subject a

---

[517] *Cf. People (DPP) v Smith*, unreported, Court of Criminal Appeal, 22 November 1999, where the contention that the appellant was not in a fit state to be interviewed in circumstances where he had been drinking heavily the previous day, was suffering from gastritis attributable to alcohol and had vomited in the course of an interview was rejected. In reaching that conclusion, reliance seems to have been placed on the fact that a doctor who saw the appellant did not suggest that his condition required any postponement of the interview that had commenced.

[518] Regulation 12(5). See *People (DPP) v McNally* (1981) 2 Frewen 43 at 54, where one of the factors that led to a finding that the statements made by the second applicant had been obtained by oppression was that the questioning which immediately preceded the making of the statements did not take place in a normal interview room but in the "possibly menacing environment" of an underground passage in the garda station.

[519] Regulation 12(1).

person in custody to ill-treatment of any kind or the threat of ill-treatment (whether against the person himself or herself, his or her family or any other person connected with him or her) or permit any other person to do so.[520] Regulation 20(2) stipulates that force can only be used against a person in custody in very limited circumstances.[521]

8–225 Regulation 12(3) specifies that, not more than two members can question the arrested person at any one time and not more than four members can be present at any one time during the interview. In *People (DPP) v Connolly*,[522] Hardiman J, delivering the judgment of the Court of Criminal Appeal, identified the purpose of reg.12(3) as being to avoid a situation where a detained person might be intimidated by numbers. That being the case, the Court was satisfied that there was no breach of the Regulations and there was no basis for arguing that there was any impropriety in one garda questioning a suspect. This was a matter that, at most, might be urged against the reliability of a statement.[523] In *People (DPP) v Smith*,[524] it was held that only two of the gardaí present at an interview may question the accused.

8–226 Regulation 12(4) provides that, if an interview has lasted for four hours, it shall be either terminated or adjourned for a reasonable time.[525] What constitutes a "reasonable time" is not specified but some guidance can perhaps be gained from reg.19(2) which specifies that a person in custody "shall be allowed such reasonable time for rest as is necessary". It has been held that this is a mandatory requirement which cannot be waived by the person being questioned.[526]

8–227 Regulation 12(11) requires a record to be made of each interview either by the garda conducting it or by another garda who is present.[527] It must include particulars of the time the interview began and ended, any breaks in it, the place of the interview and

---

[520] As noted above, reg.20(7) stipulates that, if a complaint of ill-treatment is made by a person in custody, the member in charge must arrange for the person to be medically examined as soon as practicable except where, in the case of an allegation relating to another member, he considers the complaint to be frivolous or vexatious.

[521] Regulation 20(2) provides that no garda shall use force against a person in custody except such reasonable force as is necessary: (a) in self-defence; (b) to secure compliance with lawful directions; (c) to prevent his escape; or (d) to restrain him from injuring himself or others, damaging property, or destroying or interfering with evidence.

[522] [2003] 2 IR 1 at 4.

[523] This holding was followed in *People (DPP) v Christo* [2005] IECCA 3 where the accused had attended voluntarily at a garda station and was alleged to have made a statement on a voluntary basis without being arrested. *Cf. People (DPP) v McGing* (1985) 3 Frewen 18 at 29, where the Court of Criminal Appeal stated that it is "undesirable" and "contrary to normal Garda practice" for persons detained under s.30 of the Offences Against the State Act 1939 to be interviewed for lengthy periods by a single member and that it is "obviously desirable where it is practicable" for a ban garda to be physically present in an interview room while a female is being interrogated.

[524] Unreported, Court of Criminal Appeal, 22 November 1999.

[525] It should also be noted that reg.19(3) stipulates that a person in custody shall be provided with such meals as are necessary and, in any case, at least two light meals and one main meal in any 24-hour period.

[526] *People (DPP) v Connell* [1995] 1 IR 244 at 250; *People (DPP) v Reddan* [1995] 3 IR 560 at 566–567.

[527] In *People (DPP) v Murphy*, unreported, Court of Criminal Appeal, 12 July 2001, it was accepted by the prosecution that the failure to record what was described as "general chat" between the accused and a garda was a breach of regulation 12(11). *Cf. People (DPP) v McCowan* [2003] 4 IR 349, where reg.12(11) was not mentioned but the Court of Criminal Appeal was critical of the failure by the gardaí interviewing the accused to take sufficient notes of his assertions of innocence.

the names and ranks of the gardaí present.[528] The record is required to be made in the notebook of the garda concerned or in a separate document, to be as complete as possible and to be signed by the member making it.[529] If it is practicable to do so and the garda concerned is of the opinion that it will not interfere with the conduct of the interview, the record should be made while the interview is in progress or otherwise as soon as practicable afterwards.[530] The importance of compliance with these requirements, particularly the obligation to compile a record of the interview that is as complete as possible was emphasised by Hardiman J in *People (DPP) v Diver*[531] who said:

> "I wish to reiterate that the gardaí are not entitled to exercise total editorial control in recording what has been said. Nor are they entitled to cherry pick what is to be recorded. In this case, the omission of a series of denials is utterly unacceptable. It is not that the gardaí are required, when they are relying on written notes of an interview with an accused, to record what an interviewee has said verbatim. Regulation 12 requires that the record of the interview be 'as complete as practicable'. It must be a fair record of what was said and it is important to provide sufficient context to allow for an evaluation of what is said, especially where, as here, the accused was allegedly making ambiguous or inconclusive verbal statements and manifesting symptoms of distress. Audio visual recording is, of course, infinitely superior."

8–228   If, while being interviewed, an arrested person makes a complaint to a garda in relation to his or her treatment while in custody, the garda is obliged to bring it to the attention of the member in charge, if he or she is not present at the interview, and record it or cause it to be recorded in the record of the interview.[532]

3. Admissibility of Confessions Obtained in Breach of the Custody Regulations

8–229   The starting point for considering the admissibility of confessions obtained in breach of the Custody Regulations is s.7(3) of the Criminal Justice Act 1984 which provides as follows:

> "A failure on the part of any member of the Garda Síochána to observe any provision of the regulations shall not of itself render that person liable to any civil or criminal proceedings or itself affect the lawfulness of the custody of the detained person or the admissibility in evidence of any statement made by him."

8–230   One of the first cases to consider the application of s.7(3) was *DPP v Spratt*[533] where O'Hanlon J stated:

> "The phrase 'of itself' is obviously an important one in the construction of the statutory provisions, and I interpret the subsection as meaning that non-observance of the regulations is not to bring about automatically the exclusion from evidence of all that was done and said while the accused person was in custody. It appears to be left to the court of trial to adjudicate in every case as to the impact the non-compliance with the regulations should have on the case for the prosecution."[534]

---

[528] *Cf. People (DPP) v Smith*, unreported, Court of Criminal Appeal, 22 November 1999, where the failure to record the time at which a statement commenced and the time at which it finished was regarded as immaterial in circumstances where those times were established by other evidence.

[529] Regulation 12(11)(b) only imposed that requirement in the case of interviews that were not being electronically recorded but reg.4(4) of the Electronic Recording Regulations provides that, notwithstanding that an interview is electronically recorded, reg.12(11)(b) shall apply as if the interview was not electronically recorded.

[530] Regulation 12(11)(b)(ii).

[531] [2005] IESC 57 at [28], [2005] 3 IR 270 at 279–280.

[532] Regulation 12(10).

[533] [1995] 1 IR 585, [1995] 2 ILRM 117.

[534] [1995] 1 IR 585 at 591, [1995] 2 ILRM 117 at 122.

8–231   In *DPP (Lenihan) v McGuire*,[535] Kelly J endorsed the approach taken in *Spratt* and stated that:

> "there must be a causal link between failure to comply with the relevant regulations and whatever prejudice is alleged to have been suffered by the accused as a result thereof. The appropriate question to ask it is: if a breach of the regulations has taken place, was the accused prejudiced thereby?"[536]

8–232   These principles have since been applied in a number of cases and it was been emphasised that, where a breach of the Regulations is found, it is necessary for the trial judge to adjudicate on the impact that non-compliance with the Regulations has had on the case for the prosecution and whether the accused has been prejudiced by the breach.[537]

8–233   The application of s.7(3) in the specific context of confession evidence arose for consideration in *People (DPP) v Connell*.[538] The applicant was found guilty of murder and, on appeal, argued that an incriminating statement made by him should have been excluded because it had been taken in breach of the Custody Regulations. In particular, he had been interviewed on three occasions for a period in excess of the four-hour maximum set by reg.12(4) of the Regulations. There were also a number of omissions from the Custody Record. The Court of Criminal Appeal considered that the key to the interpretation of s.7(3) was the phrase "of itself". This meant that a statement could not be held inadmissible by the mere fact that it was taken in the course of an interview lasting more than four hours. It did, however, suggest that there could be factors other than the time factor which could render a statement inadmissible if the period exceeded four hours. Such factors were found to exist in the instant case in the fact that the applicant's request for a solicitor had not been complied with and the applicant's lack of sleep during the duration of his stay in the garda station (even though that lack of sleep was not the fault of the gardaí). Having regard to these factors, the Court held that the applicant's statement was inadmissible.

8–234   It is noteworthy that, although the Court in *Connell* described the numerous breaches of the Custody Regulations as "deplorable",[539] it did not rest its decision on the fact that there had been repeated breaches of the Custody Regulations. It could be argued that the multiple breaches of the Custody Regulations which indicated a policy of non-compliance, or at least a substantial lack of compliance, should be sufficient to provide the required extra factor to warrant exclusion. However, in *People (DPP) v O'Driscoll*,[540] the proposition that a trial judge would have to exercise his or her discretion to exclude a statement where there were multiple breaches of the Regulations was rejected. It is also questionable whether the mere fact that the applicant did not get any sleep during his stay at the garda station should be regarded as providing the extra factor. Where such a lack of sleep is not due in any way to fault on the part

---

[535] [1996] 3 IR 586.
[536] [1996] 3 IR 586 at 596. In that case, he took the view that it was extremely difficult to see how the failure complained of in that case, namely the failure of a garda to sign his name in the Station diary, could cause prejudice to the respondent.
[537] *DPP v Devlin*, unreported, High Court, 2 September 1998; *DPP v Cullen*, unreported, High Court, 7 February 2001; *DPP v Clark*, unreported, High Court, 31 May 2001; *DPP v Gillespie* [2011] IEHC 236.
[538] [1995] 1 IR 244.
[539] [1995] 1 IR 244 at 252.
[540] Unreported, Court of Criminal Appeal, *ex tempore*, 19 July 1999.

of the gardaí or is not linked to the breach of the Regulations, then it would seem somewhat at odds with the policy of the Regulations and s.7(3) to fasten on that as a factor weighing in favour of exclusion.[541]

8–235   The admissibility of inculpatory statements obtained following breaches of the Custody Regulations arose again in *People (DPP) v Darcy*.[542] The applicant had been detained under s.4 of the Criminal Justice Act 1984 in the early hours of a Saturday morning in connection with the murder of a youth. The gardaí, having established that the applicant was under 17, did not question him until an adult relative arrived at the station. However, he was then interviewed in breach of reg.12(3) which provides that not more than two gardaí should question an arrested person at any one time. In addition, there had not been detailed compliance with the requirements of reg.8(1) or 9(1)(a)(i). On appeal, it was contended that the trial judge should have exercised his discretion to exclude the statements. It was argued that the breach of reg.12(3) was particularly important in this case in view of the fact that the case against the applicant depended crucially on the admissions made by him while in custody. Also relevant were the facts that the applicant was a juvenile and that he was a person of low intelligence. However, the Court of Criminal Appeal was satisfied that, in the absence of a suggestion that the questioning of the applicant had been oppressive or unfair, this was clearly a case in which the trial judge could, in the exercise of his discretion, decide to admit the statements.[543] With regard to the breaches of regs 8(1) and 9(1)(a)(i), it was clear that the substance of the applicant's rights had been accorded to him since he was informed of his right to obtain a solicitor, the attendance of a responsible adult was secured as soon as practicable, that person was aware of the applicant's entitlement to legal advice and no interviewing was conducted until such time as he was present. The decision in *Darcy* was approved and a similar approach adopted in *People (DPP) v Casey*[544] where the Court of Criminal Appeal was also satisfied that, although there had been technical breaches of the Judges' Rules and the Custody Regulations, the substance of the accused's rights had been preserved.

8–236   The principles laid down in *Spratt* and *McGuire* were applied by the Court of Criminal Appeal in the context of a challenge to the admissibility of a confession in *People (DPP) v Murphy*.[545] The applicant argued that a confession made by him to gardaí whilst in custody should have been excluded because of a failure by the gardaí to keep a record of the entirety of the interview as required by reg.12(11) of the Regulations. It was common case that, prior to making the confession at issue, the applicant had engaged in what was termed "a general chat", none of which had been recorded. It is not alleged that anything of significance had occurred during this period and there had not been any evidence before the trial judge which would have warranted a conclusion that the absence of the record had prejudiced the position of the applicant. The Court was satisfied that "there should be a causal connection

---

[541] *Cf. People (DPP) v C* [2001] 3 IR 345 at 354, where the Court of Criminal Appeal rejected the submission advanced by the applicant that there was an equivalence between the situation where a detainee had suffered from a lack of sleep for reasons that had nothing to do with the investigating gardaí and circumstances where gardaí had deliberately deprived a detainee of sleep.

[542] Unreported, Court of Criminal Appeal, 29 July 1997.

[543] A similar approach was taken in *People (DPP) v Smith*, unreported, Court of Criminal Appeal, 22 November 1999 and *People (DPP) v O'Driscoll*, unreported, Court of Criminal Appeal, *ex tempore*, 19 July 1999.

[544] [2004] IECCA 49. See also *People (DPP) v Rattigan* [2013] IECCA 13 at [23].

[545] Unreported, Court of Criminal Appeal, 12 July 2001.

between the failure to comply with the relevant regulation and whatever prejudice is alleged to have been suffered by an accused".[546] The appropriate test was, therefore, (a) whether a breach of the Regulations had taken place, and (b) whether the accused had suffered prejudice as a result of the breach. However, the Court did enter the caveat that this test was "subject to the constitutional duty of the trial judge to ensure that the trial is fair and just".[547] In the instant case, there was a lacuna in the record but there was no evidence of any event occurring during that time to prejudice the applicant and there was no allegation of impropriety against the gardaí. The Court was, accordingly, satisfied that this lacuna was insufficient to render inadmissible the inculpatory statement of the applicant.

8–237 Although it deals with the admissibility of non-testimonial evidence obtained in breach of the Regulations, the decision of the Court of Criminal Appeal in *People (DPP) v McFadden*[548] should be noted. In that case, greater emphasis was laid on the importance of the provision that had been breached with Keane CJ stating:

> "It is understandable that the legislature provided that a failure to observe any provision of the regulations would not of itself affect the lawfulness of the custody of the detained person or the admissibility in evidence of any statements made by him. As one would expect, the regulations contain detailed requirements as to the treatment of persons in custody, including such matters as the accurate recording of a number of aspects of his detention in documentary form. A failure to observe the requirements of the regulations could clearly in some instances be of so trivial or inconsequential a nature as not to afford a sufficient ground for treating the detention of the person as unlawful or statements made by him inadmissible."[549]

8–238 These authorities were considered and an alternative test, focused on the impact of the breach of the Custody Regulations on the fairness of the trial, was put forward by Hardiman J when delivering the judgment of the Supreme Court in *People (DPP) v Diver*.[550] In that case, the appellant had been convicted of the murder of his wife. He had been arrested under s.4 of the Criminal Justice Act 1984 and a total of five interviews with him by gardaí had taken place, two of which were entirely unrecorded. Hardiman J rejected the explanation given for the failure to record those interviews, which was that taking of notes would have hindered the investigation, as one which was incapable of rational belief[551] and characterised the failure to record one of those interviews in the course of which the appellant made exculpatory statements as "a gross, deliberate and conscious breach"[552] of the Custody Regulations. There were a number of other breaches of the Custody Regulations including a failure to record in any of the interviews exculpatory statements by the appellant while recording any statements consistent with guilt. The learned judge emphasised the significance of these breaches:

> "I am of the opinion that the breaches of regulations in this case and in particular the total failure to record exculpatory statements and the failure to make any proper attempt to record the entire context of ambiguous statements which are nonetheless consistent with guilt, cannot be regarded as trivial or inconsequential. They are, on the contrary, grave, obvious and deliberate.... Written notes of what an accused says in custody provides a more reliable record of evidence to be tendered at a criminal trial than unaided recollection. This is not just in aid of the accused, but also in aid of the prosecution who are then in a position to tender

---

[546] Unreported, Court of Criminal Appeal, 12 July 2001 at 10.
[547] Unreported, Court of Criminal Appeal, 12 July 2001 at 10.
[548] [2003] 2 ILRM 201.
[549] [2003] 2 ILRM 201 at 208.
[550] [2005] IESC 57, [2005] 3 IR 270.
[551] [2005] IESC 57 at [27], [2005] 3 IR 270 at 279.
[552] [2005] IESC 57 at [16], [2005] 3 IR 270 at 276.

more reliable evidence to the jury. More importantly, it is of benefit for the conduct of the trial as a whole, reducing areas of controversy and providing clearer evidence for the trial judge and the jury of what an accused has said to the gardaí. It should also reduce the time spent by trial judges in resolving issues, in the absence of the jury, concerning breaches of the relevant regulations."[553]

8–239 He went on to identify the test to be applied to the admissibility of statements obtained in those circumstances as follows:

"Where there has been a breach of the regulations due to a failure to record 'so far as practicable' an interview with an accused, the task of the trial judge is to determine, whether in all the circumstances, the effect of the failure to observe the regulation has prejudiced the fairness of the trial of the accused other than by the fact of a breach of the regulations in themselves. The issue is not so much whether or not the breach of the regulations was of a 'trivial and inconsequential nature', although that is a factor to be taken into account, but whether the fairness of the trial of the accused would be prejudiced by the admission of statements made by him or her in respect of which the regulations were not followed. On a properly conducted trial or retrial it would be for the trial judge to determine the issue of admissibility on the criteria set out in this judgment. I wish to reiterate that the gardaí are not entitled to exercise editorial control over what is said. Nor are they entitled to cherry pick what is to be recorded. It is utterly unacceptable to omit denials. It is important to provide sufficient context to allow for an evaluation of what is said especially where, as here, the accused was allegedly making ambiguous or inconclusive verbal statements and manifesting symptoms of distress. All this is trite, because it has been said so often and it is said so often because gardaí have regularly avoided audio visual recording, made selective notes, and breached the clear and simple regulations for the treatment of persons in custody, apparently believing that such breaches will attract nothing worse than a judicial rebuke."[554]

8–240 It can be seen, therefore, that where there is a serious breach of the Custody Regulations which impacts on the fairness of the trial, this will lead to the exclusion of the statements obtained.

F. Questioning of Children

1. Introduction

8–241 Following some expressions of judicial concern in relation to the questioning of children by gardaí without a parent or other adult present to look after his or her interests,[555] a number of safeguards in relation to the treatment in custody and questioning of children were introduced by the Custody Regulations. These provisions remain in force but have been largely overtaken by the provisions of Part 6 of the Children Act 2001.[556]

2. The Custody Regulations

8–242 The Custody Regulations (as amended by s.70(2) of the Children Act 2001 and the Criminal Justice Act 1984 (Treatment of Persons in Custody in Garda Síochána

---

[553] [2005] IESC 57 at [27], [2005] 3 IR 270 at 279.
[554] [2005] IESC 57 at [29], [2005] 3 IR 270 at 280.
[555] See *DPP v F* (1980) 114 ILTR 110 at 112. See also *DPP v Patterson* (1979) 113 ILTR 6.
[556] See, generally, Drislane, "The Questioning of Child Suspects in Garda Siochana Stations" (2011) 1 ICLJ 10.

Stations) (Amendment) Regulations 2006[557]) contain a number of provisions which apply where children[558] are in custody and/or questioned:

(a) Under reg.8, the member in charge is required, in the case of an arrested person under the age of 18, to inform or cause him or her to be informed orally and furnish him or her with written notice that a parent or guardian (or, if he or she is married, his or her spouse) is being given requested to attend at the station without delay.

(b) Pursuant to reg.9, the member in charge is required to, as soon as practicable, inform or cause to be informed a parent, guardian or spouse of a person under the age of 18 that he or she is in custody in the station, in ordinary language of the offence or other matter in respect of which he or she has been arrested, and of his or her entitlement to consult a solicitor. The member in charge must also request the parent, guardian or spouse to attend at the station without delay.

(c) Regulation 13(1) stipulates that an arrested person under the age of 18 cannot be questioned in relation to an offence or asked to make a written statement unless a parent or guardian is present except in certain specified circumstances and with the authority of the member in charge.[559] Regulation 13(2) goes on to provide that, where an arrested person under 18 is to be questioned in relation to an offence in the absence of a parent or guardian, the member in charge must, unless it is not practicable to do so, arrange for the presence during questioning of: (a) the other parent or another guardian, (b) if the other parent or guardian is not readily available, or his or her presence is not appropriate,[560] an adult relative, or, (c) if the other parent or another guardian or an adult relative is not

---

[557] The amendments effected by s.70(2) of the Children Act 2001 initially rendered the provisions of the Custody Regulations internally inconsistent in that some of the provisions applied in the case of persons under 17 years and some in the case of persons under the age of 18 years but this was rectified by reg.3(a) of the Criminal Justice Act 1984 (Treatment of Persons in Custody in Garda Síochána Stations) (Amendment) Regulations 2006 (SI No. 641 of 2006) which substituted 18 years for 17 years throughout the Custody Regulations.

[558] Regulation 2(4) provides that, if and for so long as the member in charge has reasonable grounds for believing that the person in custody is not below the age of 18 years, the provisions of the Regulations shall apply as if he or she had attained that age. Pursuant to reg.22, the provisions of the Regulations relating to persons under the age of 18 apply, in addition to any other applicable provisions, in relation to a person in custody not below that age whom the member in charge suspects or knows to be mentally handicapped.

[559] That authority cannot be given unless: (a) it has not been possible to communicate with a parent or guardian in accordance with reg.9(1)(a); (b) no parent or guardian has attended at the station concerned within a reasonable time of being informed that the person was in custody and of being requested so to attend; (c) it is not practicable for a parent or guardian to attend within a reasonable time; or (d) the member in charge has reasonable grounds for believing that to delay questioning the person would involve a risk of injury to persons or serious loss of or damage to property, destruction of or interference with evidence, or escape of accomplices. In addition, a parent or guardian may be excluded from the questioning with the authority of the member in charge if: (i) the parent or guardian is the victim of, or has been arrested in respect of, the offence being investigated, (ii) the member in charge has reasonable grounds for suspecting him or her of complicity in the offence, or for believing that he or she would, if present during the questioning, be likely to obstruct the course of justice, or, while so present, his or her conduct has been such as to amount to an obstruction of justice.

[560] On the basis of the grounds set out in the proviso to reg.13(1).

readily available or the presence of the other parent or guardian is not appropriate,[561] some other responsible adult other than a garda.

(d) Where a request for the attendance of a solicitor is made during questioning by the parent, guardian, spouse or adult relative of an arrested person under 18 or another adult present, he or she shall not be asked to make a written statement in relation to an offence until a reasonable time for the attendance of the solicitor has elapsed.[562]

8–243 The admissibility of statements obtain in breach of the Custody Regulations will be dealt with in accordance with the principles outlined above.

3. Part 6 of the Children Act 2001

8–244 Part 6 of the Children Act 2001 places on a statutory footing (with some amendments) a number of the provisions contained in the Custody Regulations in relation to the treatment and questioning of children.[563] The main provisions of Part 6 so far as they relate to the questioning of children[564] are as follows:

(a) Section 55 imposes a general obligation on the gardaí with regard to the conduct of criminal investigations involving the commission of offences by children. It stipulates that, in any investigation relating to the commission or possible commission of an offence by children, the gardaí are required to act with due respect for the personal rights of the children and their dignity as human persons, for their vulnerability owing to their age and level of maturity and for the special needs of any of them who may be under a physical or mental disability, while complying with the obligation to prevent escapes from custody and continuing to act with diligence and determination in the investigation of crime and the protection and vindication of the personal rights of other persons.

(b) Section 56 imposes an obligation on the member in charge to ensure, as far as practicable, that any child, while detained in the station, shall not associate with an adult who is so detained and shall not be kept in a cell unless there is no other secure accommodation available.[565]

---

[561] On the basis of the grounds set out in the proviso to reg.13(1).

[562] Regulations 13(3) and 12(6). It should be noted that s.5B(1) of the Criminal Justice Act 1984 (as inserted by s.9 of the Criminal Justice Act 2011 but which has yet to be commenced), requires the Minister to make regulations in relation to access to a solicitor by persons detained in Garda Síochána stations and s.5B(2)(a) provides that the regulations may make different provision in relation to different classes of persons detained, thereby facilitating the making of bespoke provisions for children and other vulnerable persons.

[563] A child is defined in s.3(1) to mean a person under the age of 18. In *People (DPP) v Onumwere* [2007] IECCA 48 at [21], [2007] 3 IR 772 at 781–782, it was held that, for the purposes of the Act, age may be proved by various means including the statement by the witness of his own age and the opinion of a witness as to the age of another person. However, where age is an issue, stricter means of proof are appropriate and it may be proved by the admission of a party, by evidence of a witness who was present at the birth of the person concerned and by the production of a certificate of birth supplemented by evidence identifying the person whose birth is then certified by oral or written declarations.

[564] Under s.69, special provision is made for the application of Part 6 in the case of a child who is married.

[565] A contention that this section had not been complied with was rejected in *People (DPP) v Onumwere* [2007] IECCA 48 at [22], [2007] 3 IR 772 at 782.

(c) Section 57 provides that, where a child is arrested and brought to a garda station on suspicion of having committed an offence, the member in charge is required to inform the child or cause the child to be informed, in a manner and in language that is appropriate to the age and level of understanding of the child: (a) of the offence in respect of which he or she has been arrested, (b) that he or she is entitled to consult a solicitor and how this entitlement can be availed of, and (c) that the child's parent or guardian is being informed that the child is in custody in the station, given information in relation to the offence and the child's entitlement to consult a solicitor, and requested to attend at the station without delay.

(d) Section 58(1) stipulates that, where a child is arrested and brought to a garda station on suspicion of having committed an offence, the member in charge must, as soon as practicable inform a parent or guardian of the child, or cause him or her to be informed: (i) that the child is in custody in the station, (ii) in ordinary language of the nature of the offence in respect of which the child has been arrested, and (iii) that the child is entitled to consult a solicitor and as to how this entitlement can be availed of. The member in charge must also request the parent or guardian to attend at the station without delay. Under subs.(2), if the member in charge is unable to communicate with a parent or guardian of the child or the parent or guardian indicates that he or she cannot or will not attend at the station within a reasonable time, the member in charge is required to inform the child or cause the child to be informed without delay of that fact and of the child's entitlement to have an adult relative or other adult reasonably named by him or her given the information specified in subs.(1)(a) and requested to attend at the station without delay.[566]

(e) Where a garda has reasonable cause to believe that a child who is in custody in the station on suspicion of having committed an offence may be in need of care or protection, the member is required, as soon as practicable, to inform or cause to be informed the health board for the area in which the station is located and the health board is required to send a representative to the garda station as soon as practicable.[567]

(f) Section 60 deals with the notification of a solicitor and contains provisions which go further than those applicable in the case of an adult who has been arrested. If a child who is in custody or a parent, guardian, adult relative, any adult reasonably named by the child, or other adult (not being a garda) who is nominated by the member in charge[568] and present during the questioning of the child or the taking of a written statement, has asked for a solicitor, the member in charge is required to notify the solicitor or cause him or her to be notified as soon as practicable.[569] If the solicitor cannot be contacted within a reasonable time or is unwilling

---

[566] In *People (DPP) v Onumwere* [2007] IECCA 48, [2007] 3 IR 772, where gardaí had arranged for an adult to be present and the accused had been visited by his girlfriend who was an adult, the Court of Criminal Appeal rejected the contention that s.58 had not been complied with because the social worker assigned to him in the asylum process had not been contacted.

[567] Section 59(1). Section 131 of the Criminal Justice Act 2006 inserted a new subs.4 into s.59 providing that: "The Minister, with the agreement of the Minister for Health and Children, may issue guidelines in relation to the practical operation of this section."

[568] In accordance with s.61(1)(b).

[569] Section 60(1) and (3).

or unable to attend at the station, the child or adult who has asked for the solicitor must be so informed and given an opportunity to ask for another solicitor and the member in charge must notify or cause to be notified that other solicitor as soon as practicable.[570] If a request has been made by or on behalf of a child for a solicitor but without naming a particular solicitor, the member in charge is required to give the person making the request or cause him or her to be given the name of one or more solicitors whom the member in charge reasonably believes may be willing to attend at the station within a reasonable time. The provisions of s.60 are reinforced by s.61(5) which stipulates that, where a request has been made for a solicitor, the child cannot be asked to make a statement, either orally or in writing, in relation to the offence until a reasonable time for the attendance of the solicitor has elapsed.

(g) A child who has been detained in a garda station pursuant to any enactment cannot be questioned, or asked to make a written statement, in relation to an offence in respect of which he or she has been arrested except in the presence of a parent or guardian, an adult relative of the child, an adult reasonably named by the child, or another adult (not being a garda) nominated by the member in charge.[571]

8–245 The admissibility of statements taken otherwise that in compliance with the provisions of Part 6 is dealt with in s.66(2) which provides that:

> "Any failure on the part of any member of the Garda Síochána to observe any provision of the relevant sections shall not of itself render that member liable to any criminal or civil proceedings or of itself affect the lawfulness of the custody of a detained child or of the admissibility in evidence of any statement made by the child."

8–246 This provision is drafted in very similar terms to s.7(3) of the Criminal Justice Act 1984 and it would seem likely, therefore, that a similar approach to its application will be taken. However, given that the legislature has seen fit to the place the safeguards contained in Part 6 in primary legislation, it is arguable that the courts should not lightly excuse a failure to comply with them and should give due weight to the legislative intention to protect children. As can be seen from the decision in *People (DPP) v Onumwere*,[572] an important factor will be the age of the child concerned. In that case, the Court of Criminal Appeal was satisfied that there had not been any non-

---

[570] Section 60(2) and (3).

[571] Section 61(1). Under subs.(2), the member in charge may authorise the questioning of a child or the taking of a written statement in the absence of a parent, guardian, adult relative, an adult reasonably named by the child, or an adult (other than a garda) nominated by the member in charge, where the member has reasonable grounds for believing that to delay the questioning would involve a risk of death or injury to persons, serious loss of or damage to property, destruction of or interference with evidence, or the escape of accomplices. The member in charge also has power under subs. (3) to authorise the exclusion of such person during the questioning of the child or the taking of a written statement where: (a) the person is the victim of, or has been arrested in respect of, the offence being investigated, (b) the member in charge has reasonable grounds for suspecting the person of complicity in the offence, or (c) the member has reasonable grounds for believing that the person would, if present during the questioning or the taking of a written statement, be likely to obstruct the course of justice. Finally, under subs.(4), the member in charge may authorise the removal of such person during the questioning of the child or the taking of a written statement where the member in charge has reasonable grounds for believing that the conduct of the person is such as to amount to an obstruction of the course of justice.

[572] [2007] IECCA 48, [2007] 3 IR 772.

compliance with the provisions of Part 6 but indicated that, if it had been necessary to do so, the Court would have applied the provisions of subsection (2), specifically noting that the accused had been only been two months short of his eighteenth birthday at the time and had been living independently.

G. Electronic Recording Regulations

1. Introduction

8–247 The recording of interviews was first mooted in the report of the O'Briain Committee[573] and the audio-visual recording of interviews was strongly recommended by the Martin Committee.[574] High profile miscarriages of justice in the UK involving uncorroborated confessions, later found to have been compelled, altered or falsified, created impetus for legislation requiring such recording in this jurisdiction.[575] Section 27(1) of the Criminal Justice Act 1984 provided that the Minister for Justice could introduce regulations providing for the recording of interviews by electronic or other means. However, it was not until 1997 that such regulations, the Criminal Justice Act 1984 (Electronic Recording of Interviews) Regulations 1997[576] (the "Electronic Recording Regulations") were actually made.

8–248 As pointed out by the Martin Committee, the electronic recording of interviews has a number of advantages over traditional methods of note-taking by gardaí and represents a valuable safeguard for both accused persons and the gardaí. The provision of a complete contemporaneous record of interviews provides obvious benefits for arrested persons and is probably the best means of ensuring that the constitutional and legal rights of arrested persons are respected and that any inculpatory statements made by them are voluntary. In addition, the recording of interviews also has advantages from the viewpoint of the gardaí in terms of efficiency[577] and because it protects them from false claims of ill-treatment and oppression.[578] This point was made by Kearns J

---

[573] The O'Briain Committee, *Report of the Committee to Recommend Certain Safeguards for Persons in Custody and for Members of An Garda Síochána* (1978), para.67, recommended that feasibility studies be instituted in relation to the videotaping of interviews and that tape-recording of interviews be trialled on a widespread basis.

[574] *Report of the Committee to Enquire into Certain Aspects of Criminal Procedure* (1990), pp. 36.

[575] *People (DPP) v Murphy* [2005] IECCA 52 at [27], [2005] 4 IR 504 at 513.

[576] SI No. 74 of 1997. These have been amended by the Criminal Justice Act 1984 (Electronic Recording of Interviews) (Amendment) Regulations 2009 (SI No. 168 of 2009) and the Criminal Justice Act 1984 (Electronic Recording of Interviews) (Amendment) Regulations 2010 (SI No. 560 of 2010).

[577] *E.g.* the Western Australian Police Force Video Interview Monitoring Committee found that video recording of interviews enhanced police efficiency and reduced the time spent conducting interviews (see Hodge, "Video Recording Police Interviews" (1992) 19 (8) Brief 27 at 29). *Cf.* Geller, "Police Videotaping of Suspect Interrogations and Confessions: A Preliminary Examination of Issues and Practice" (Report to the National Institute of Justice, Washington DC, 1992), p.152, which gives details of a study for the US Department of Justice in 1992 of police departments wherein 97 per cent of all police departments found it useful on balance.

[578] See Dixon, Coleman & Bottomley, "Arrest and Detention" (1991) 141 NLJ 1639, where 91 per cent of police officers interviewed reported favourable or very favourable attitudes towards the recording of interviews because it produces unchallengeable evidence and reduced charges of malpractice. The Law Reform Commission of Canada concluded that recording of interrogation "…will not only assist the court and expedite the *voir dire*, but in a large measure it should protect

in *People (DPP) v Murphy*[579] who said that "it is An Garda Síochána who themselves are most put at risk by the failure to provide simple and basic electronic equipment which would protect them from the bringing of baseless allegations of ill treatment or other misbehaviour in or about the taking of confessions".[580] Thus, the electronic recording of interviews should serve to promote public confidence in the gardaí and the criminal justice system.[581]

8–249 The electronic recording of interviews also makes it much easier for courts to adjudicate upon the admissibility of confessions,[582] particularly as it is possible to see the demeanour of the accused while he or she was being questioned.[583] In circumstances where an accused denies having made an inculpatory statement at all or alleges that it should be excluded as involuntary or on some other basis, one of problems that invariably faces a court is that it has to make determinations of fact without a complete record of what took place in the course of the interviews of the accused. Its task in that regard is made more difficult by the fact that, quite often, there is a serious conflict of evidence between the accused and gardaí as to what took place.[584] However, in circumstances where there is a complete electronic record of interviews, those difficulties do not arise and the task of deciding the admissibility of inculpatory statements will be made much easier which should in turn lead to a decrease in the number of challenges to the admissibility of such statements.[585] This has been the experience in other jurisdictions where recording of interviews has been introduced.[586]

---

the police against unwarranted allegations of misconduct": "Questioning Suspects" (Working Paper No 32, 1984).

[579] [2005] IECCA 52 at [28], [2005] 4 IR 504 at 514.

[580] See to similar effect, *People (DPP) v Murphy* [2013] IECCA 1 at [57].

[581] *Cf. People (DPP) v Murphy*, unreported, Court of Criminal Appeal, 12 July 2001 at 11, where Denham J commented, in relation to a lacuna in the record of an interview with the accused, that: "the very fact of a lacuna and any uncertainty it may cause highlights the benefits of video recording interviews. The benefits from such recording accrue to the arrested person, the Gardaí and the community in that the process becomes more transparent". See Gearty, "Video Recording of Accused Persons in Custody" (2004) 9(2) BR 65.

[582] *R. v Oickle* [2000] 2 SCR 3 at 31. But see McConville and Mercell, "Recording the Interrogation: Have Police Got it Taped" [1983] Crim LR 158 at 160, on the practice of interrogating the witness until a confession is extracted, and then taping the confession.

[583] In *People (DPP) v Yu Jie* [2005] IECCA 95 at 5–6, McCracken J noted that a video recording has the advantage over a transcript in that it allows an assessment of the demeanour of the suspect. See also *People (DPP) v Murphy* [2013] IECCA 1 at [57]. However, concerns have been expressed in relation to what is referred to as "camera perspective bias" because the videorecording equipment is focused on the accused only: Lambert, "Confessions and Camera Perspective Bias" (2010) 15(6) BR 128.

[584] *Cf. People (DPP) v Ward*, unreported, Special Criminal Court, 27 November 1998, where very different versions of events were given by the accused and gardaí and the Court ultimately decided that inculpatory statements allegedly made by the accused should be excluded because the Court was not satisfied beyond reasonable doubt that the statements had actually been made.

[585] *People (DPP) v Murphy* [2005] IECCA 52 at [29], [2005] 4 IR 504 at 514.

[586] See the comments of Dawson J in *McKinney v R.* (1991) 171 CLR 468 at 491, and *State v Jiminez* (1989) 775 P 2d 694 at 696. In the *Report of Committee to Enquire into Certain Aspects of Criminal Procedure* (1990), p.35, reference is made to a Report prepared by Professor Alan Grant for the Law Reform Commission in Canada on a two-year pilot project involving audio-visual recording of suspects entitled *The Audio-Visual Taping of Police Interviews with Suspects and Accused by Halton Regional Police Force, Ontario, Canada*. According to that Report, with the audio-visual recording of interviews, the need for a "trial within a trial" disappeared entirely. *Cf.* Westling and Waye, "Videotaping Police Interrogations: Lessons from Australia" (1998) 25 Am J Crim L 493 at 542, and Jayne, "Empirical Experiences of Required Electronic Recording

8–250 In *People (DPP) v Murphy*,[587] Kearns J emphasised the considerable advantages from the electronic recording of interviews:

> "No sector of our society has a greater interest in maintaining high levels of public confidence in the propriety of police investigations than An Garda Síochána who, by the simple expedient of compliance with the regulations, can thereby provide a measure of protection for their members against dishonest attacks of this kind, if and when they are made. Indeed the regular "trial within a trial" as to the admissibility of confessions which presently arises in virtually every criminal case might well become a far less frequent event if electronic recording of interviews becomes the invariable or normal practice in all garda stations where suspects are interviewed. Any recording made should provide a clear picture or account of everything which transpires at interview. This should render futile many challenges or attacks which might otherwise be made on garda testimony during a criminal trial, reduce the length and costs of trials and contribute to the enhancement of public confidence in the system generally."

8–251 It is, therefore, not surprising that, as will be seen below, the courts are becoming increasingly intolerant of failures to electronically record interviews.

2. Outline of the Electronic Recording Regulations

(a) Obligation to electronically record interviews

8–252 The combined effect of regs 3[588] and 4(1) is to impose an obligation to electronically record[589] interviews, including the taking and reading back of statements, that take place in a garda station with persons detained under s.30 of the Offences Against the State Act 1939, s.4 of the Criminal Justice Act 1984, s.2 of the Criminal Justice (Drug Trafficking) Act 1996, s.42 of the Criminal Justice Act 1999, s.50 of the Criminal Justice Act 2007 and ss.16 or 17 of the Criminal Procedure Act 2010.[590] However, that requirement is diluted considerably by a series of caveats and exceptions contained in the Regulations.[591] The first, and perhaps, most important is that the Regulations only apply to stations where electronic recording equipment has been provided and installed.[592] In addition, pursuant to reg.4(3), an interview or part of an interview is not required to be electronically recorded where the equipment is: (i) unavailable due to a functional fault[593]; or (ii) the equipment is already in use

---

of Interviews and Interrogations on Investigator's Practices and Case Outcomes" (Forum Journal of Police Pursuits, January 2004), Table 7.

[587] [2005] IECCA 52 at [29], [2005] 4 IR 504 at 514.

[588] As amended by reg.4 of the Criminal Justice 1984 (Electronic Recording of Interviews) (Amendment) Regulations 2010 (SI No. 560 of 2010).

[589] Electronic recording is defined in reg.2(1) (as amended by reg.3 of the Criminal Justice 1984 (Electronic Recording of Interviews) (Amendment) Regulations 2010 (SI No. 560 of 2010)) to mean: "a recording on tape of (a) an oral communication, statement or utterance, or (b) a series of visual images which, when reproduced on tape, appear as a moving picture". A "tape" is, in turn, defined to include: "(a) a disc, magnetic tape, soundtrack or other device in which sound or sounds may be embodied for the purpose of being reproduced (with or without the aid of some other instrument) in audible form, and (b) a film, disc, magnetic tape or other device in which visual images may be embodied for the purpose of being reproduced (with or without the aid of some other instrument) in visual form".

[590] The obligation to electronically record an interview will not apply where a suspect attends a garda station and makes a statement without being arrested: *People (DPP) v Christo* [2005] IECCA 3.

[591] For a discussion of the application of this requirement in practice in other commonwealth jurisdictions, see Rowan, "Electronic Recording of Police Interviews in New Zealand" [1992] NZLJ 360.

[592] Regulation 3(1).

[593] The decision in *People (DPP) v Murphy* [2005] IECCA 52 at [36], [2005] 4 IR 504 at 516 indicates

at the time the interview is to commence, and the member in charge considers on reasonable grounds that the interview should not be delayed until the fault is rectified or the equipment becomes available[594]; or (iii) where the electronic recording of the interview is otherwise not practicable.[595]

8–253 Although the Regulations do not impose any obligation to bring an accused to a garda station where electronic recording facilities are available, if a suspect is interviewed in a garda station that does not have electronic recording equipment and this is relied on to excuse the failure to record interviews, gardaí will be required to justify the failure to bring the accused to a station with such equipment installed.[596] Explanations which have been accepted as satisfactory include operational and security reasons.[597] Similarly, the failure to electronically record an interview in a station that has the equipment installed will have to be justified. Where a satisfactory explanation is not forthcoming, then any inculpatory statements made by an accused may be ruled inadmissible on the basis that they have been unfairly obtained by reason of depriving the accused of an important procedural protection,[598] particularly if a conflict of fact arises as to what took place during the garda interviews.

8–254 In *People (DPP) v Kelly*[599] one of the factors taken into consideration by the Special Criminal Court in ruling inadmissible the contents of a number of interviews is that the gardaí could have brought the accused to a garda station where electronic recording equipment was available but did not do so. The Court accepted that there was no legal obligation to bring the accused to a garda station where such facilities were available but expressed grave reservations about the failure of gardaí to do so. Similar concerns about the failure to electronically record a statement were evident in *People (DPP) v Breen*[600] where the accused was alleged to have made verbal admissions, which were not contemporaneously noted, at a time after he was under physical restraint by gardaí and had been searched but before he was arrested. One of the factors relied on by the Court of Criminal Appeal in holding that those admissions should not have been admitted was that the statement had not been video recorded although it was conceded that this fact, taken on its own, would not render the evidence inadmissible.

8–255 *A fortiori*, if a court concludes that a suspect was brought to a garda station where electronic equipment has not been installed or was not available as a stratagem to

---

a healthy degree of scepticism towards claims that electronic recording equipment is unavailable due to a functional fault.

[594] See *People (DPP) v PA* [2008] IECCA 21 discussed below.

[595] Regulation 4(4) stipulates that: "Where an interview or part of an interview is not recorded for any of the reasons referred to in paragraph (3), the member in charge shall enter or cause to be entered in the custody record of the person to be interviewed a note setting out the fact that the interview was not electronically recorded and the reason."

[596] See *People (DPP) v Kelly*, Special Criminal Court, 26 November 2004 (transcript not available but this judgment is referred to in *People (DPP) v Murphy* [2005] IECCA 52 at [33]–[35], [2005] 4 IR 504 at 515–516) and *People (DPP) v Cunningham* [2007] IECCA 49.

[597] *People (DPP) v Holland*, unreported, Court of Criminal Appeal, *ex tempore*, 15 June 1998 (operational and security reasons); *People (DPP) v Cunningham* [2007] IECCA 49 (operational reasons).

[598] *Cf. per* Griffin J in *People (DPP) v Shaw* [1982] IR 1 at 61.

[599] Special Criminal Court, 26 November 2004 (transcript not available but this judgment is referred to in *People (DPP) v Murphy* [2005] IECCA 52 at [33]–[35], [2005] 4 IR 504 at 515–516).

[600] [2008] IECCA 136, [2009] 2 IR 262.

circumvent the obligation to electronically record interviews, this will almost certainly lead to the exclusion of any evidence of the contents of those interviews.[601]

(b) Conduct of electronically recorded interview

8–256   Before an interview which is to be electronically recorded commences, the member in charge must inform or cause to be informed the person to be interviewed orally and in ordinary language that the interview with him or her may be electronically recorded and that, where the interview is electronically recorded, he or she is entitled to receive a notice as to what is to happen to the tapes of that interview.[602] The member in charge must then give or cause to be given to the person a notice to that effect.[603]

8–257   The garda conducting the interview to be electronically recorded is required to set up the recording equipment in the sight of the person to be interviewed[604] and then, while the equipment is recording, to give details in relation to the interview[605] and to caution the person being interviewed as follows: "You are not obliged to say anything unless you wish to do so but whatever you say will be taken down in writing and may be given in evidence. As you are aware this interview is being taped and the tape may be used in evidence."[606]

8–258   Various rules and requirements with regard to the interruption or discontinuance of the electronic recording of interviews are laid down in regs 7 to 11.

8–259   At the conclusion of the interview, the garda conducting the interview must enquire of the person interviewed if there is anything further he or she wishes to say or to clarify and read back any notes or memoranda taken in the interview and enquire of the person interviewed if he or she wishes to make any alterations or additions.[607] He must then record the time, switch off the equipment, remove the tapes, seal one of the tapes with a master tape label and give it an identification number, and sign the master tape label and ask the person interviewed to sign it.[608] If the person interviewed refuses or is unable to sign the master tape label, the member in charge must be called to the interview room and asked to sign it.[609]

8–260   Section 57 of the Criminal Justice Act 2007 provides for the admissibility in evidence at the trial of a person of an electronic recording and/or a transcript of such

---

[601] See *People (DPP) v Holland*, unreported, Court of Criminal Appeal, *ex tempore*, 15 June 1998, where such an allegation was made and rejected on the facts but the Court indicated that, if proven, it would be a "serious matter".

[602] Regulation 5(1).

[603] Regulation 5(2).

[604] Regulation 6(1) requires the garda conducting the interview, before commencing same, to unwrap the required number of unused blank tapes, load the equipment with the tapes and set the equipment to record in the sight of the person to be interviewed.

[605] Regulation 6(2)(b) requires the garda conducting the interview to state: (i) the name and rank of that garda and the name and rank of any other gardaí present; (ii) the name and status of any other person present; (iii) the name of the person being interviewed; (iv) the date, time of commencement of the recording and the location of the station; and (v) that the person being interviewed has been given a notice pursuant to reg.5(2).

[606] Regulation 6(2)(a).

[607] Regulation 12(1).

[608] Regulation 12(1).

[609] Regulation 12(2).

a recording of the questioning of the person by the Garda Síochána in connection with the offence.

3. Non-Compliance with the Electronic Recording Regulations

8–261 The admissibility of statements taken otherwise than in compliance with the Electronic Recording Regulations is dealt with in s.27(4) of the Criminal Justice Act 1984 which provides as follows:

> "Any failure to comply with the provision of the regulations shall not by itself render a person liable to civil or criminal proceedings, and (without prejudice to the power of the court to exclude evidence at its discretion) shall not by itself render inadmissible in evidence anything said during such questioning."

8–262 This subsection is drafted in similar terms to s.7(3) of the 1984 Act dealing with breaches of the Custody Regulations. However, there is a significant difference in that, in a departure from the wording of s.7(3), the power to exclude evidence conferred by s.27(4) is stated to be without prejudice to the power of the court to exclude evidence at its discretion. This indicates that a court adjudicating on the effect of a breach of the Electronic Recording Regulations has a broader discretion than that available in respect of a breach of the Custody Regulations, which might be more readily exercised in favour of exclusion, especially in circumstances where there is a conflict of fact between the accused and gardaí which would have been resolved definitively by an electronic record of the interview.

8–263 An indication of the importance attributed to the audio-visual recording of interviews was given by Hardiman J, delivering the judgment of the Court of Criminal Appeal in *People (DPP) v Connolly*.[610] He pointed out that the audio-visual recording of interviews was now routine in most first world common law countries and was very critical of the delay in the widespread adoption of electronic recording in this jurisdiction saying that this had "ceased to be a mere oddity" and was "closely approaching the status of an anomaly".[611] He then went on to signal considerable judicial impatience with this situation:

> "The courts have been very patient, perhaps excessively patient, with delays in this regard. The time cannot be remote when we will hear a submission that, absent extraordinary circumstances (by which we do not mean that a particular garda station has no audio-visual machinery or that the audio-visual room was being painted), it is unacceptable to tender in evidence a statement which has not been so recorded."[612]

8–264 The Court of Criminal Appeal, having concurred with these comments in *People (DPP) v Christo*,[613] returned to this theme in *People (DPP) v Murphy*.[614] In that case, the accused had been arrested on suspicion of murder and brought to a garda station where electronic equipment had been installed but which was not operational when the accused had been arrested because of technical difficulties. The interviewing gardaí had also not been trained in its use with the result that the interviews with the accused were not recorded. The Court regarded the explanations proffered for the non-use of the equipment as unsatisfactory and noted that no entry had been made in the

---

[610] [2003] 2 IR 1.
[611] [2003] 2 IR 1 at 18.
[612] [2003] 2 IR 1 at 18.
[613] [2005] IECCA 3 at [16].
[614] [2005] IECCA 52, [2005] 4 IR 504.

custody record to account for the non-operation of the recording system on the day that the interviews took place. Ultimately, notwithstanding the non-compliances with the Electronic Recording Regulations, the Court decided to exercise its discretion under s.27(4) to hold that the failure to electronically record the interviews did not render inadmissible the admissions made by the accused. This conclusion was reached, in part, because these interviews had taken place prior to the handing down of the judgment in *Connolly* and, more importantly, because there had not been any significant contest at trial as to what was actually said by the accused. However, Kearns J, delivering the judgment of the Court, took the opportunity to lay down a marker as follows[615]:

"However, going forward and for the reasons already given, there should be a marked reluctance to excuse failures to comply with the requirements of the Criminal Justice Act 1984 (Electronic Recording of Interviews) Regulations 1997, other than those circumstances specified in the Regulations themselves. We feel, therefore, that in respect of station interviews from this point onwards, the court should only exercise its discretion under s.27(4) for very good reason."

8–265 The willingness of the courts to exclude the evidence of interviews which had not been recorded was reiterated in *Rattigan v DPP*[616] where Hardiman J stressed that "the recording of interviews in garda stations must be assiduously policed by the courts" and that non-recording should normally mean exclusion because it was only in this way that the courts could ensure that recording would be routine in practice.

8–266 Good reason to exercise the discretion conferred by s.27(4) was found to exist in *People (DPP) v PA*[617] where one of a series of interviews was not recorded because the equipment was in use at the time but the notes of the interview that had not been recorded had been put to the accused in a subsequent interview which had been recorded and he did not demur from same. The Court of Criminal Appeal accepted that the gardaí had been justified in conducting an interview even though the electronic recording equipment was unavailable in circumstances where there was only two hours of the period of detention left. Although the member in charge had failed, as he was required to by reg.4(4), to enter a note in the custody record of this fact and the reason, taking into account all of the circumstances including other allegations of impropriety made by the accused, the court was satisfied that the statement was admissable.

H. Breach of Fundamental Fairness

1. Introduction

8–267 At common law, a trial judge had a discretion to exclude a confession that had been unfairly obtained[618] and that discretion was given a constitutional grounding by Griffin J in *People (DPP) v Shaw*.[619] In that case, he posited a standard of fundamental fairness that had to be met before a confession could be admitted:

"Because our system of law is accusatorial and not inquisitorial, and because … our constitution postulates the observance of basic or fundamental fairness of procedures, the Judge presiding at a criminal trial should be astute to see that, although a statement may be technically voluntary, it should nevertheless be excluded if, by reason of the manner or of the circumstances in which

---

[615] [2005] IECCA 52 at [43], [2005] 4 IR 504 at 517.
[616] [2008] IESC 34 at [15]–[16], [2007] 2 IR 726 at 647.
[617] [2008] IECCA 21.
[618] *AG v Durnan (No.2)* [1934] IR 540 at 547; *R. v Sang* [1980] AC 402 at 437.
[619] [1982] IR 1.

it was obtained, it falls below the required standard of fairness. The reason for exclusion here is not so much the risk of an erroneous conviction as the recognition that the minimum standards must be observed in the administration of justice. Whether the objection to the statement be on constitutional or other grounds, the crucial test is whether it was obtained in compliance with basic or fundamental fairness and the trial Judge will have a discretion to exclude it 'where it appears to him that public policy, based on a balancing of interests, requires such exclusion'—*per* Kingsmill Moore J at p.161 of the report of *O'Brien's Case*."[620]

8–268   It is clear from this passage that the application of this test of fundamental fairness is independent of the voluntariness rule and other tests of admissibility and subsequent decisions have interpreted it as giving courts a broad residual discretion to be exercised whenever the a court concludes that the standard of fundamental fairness has not been met.[621] It should be noted in that regard that, although the test is formulated in terms of conferring a discretion on a trial judge, the element of judgment arises in determining whether a confession has been obtained in breach of the requirements of fundamental fairness—once that determination is made, then exclusion would seem to follow automatically.

8–269   One of the difficulties with applying the test of fundamental fairness is its inherent elasticity. The constitutionally prescribed minimum standards of fairness to which Griffin J referred in *Shaw* are not set out in the Constitution or any judicial decision and, thus, it is a matter for a trial judge in each case to make what is inevitably a subjective assessment of whether evidence has been obtained in a manner that is fundamentally unfair. In order to ensure some degree of consistency, it is submitted that judges should distinguish between circumstances where there is some element of unfairness in how a confession has been obtained and circumstances where the confession was obtained in a *fundamentally* unfair manner.

2. Application of the Test

8–270   The test of fundamental fairness was applied so as to supplement the Judges' Rules in *People (DPP) v Breen*.[622] While a search of the accused's farm for firearms and explosives was ongoing, the accused had become very agitated in the course of a conversation with a garda and intimated that he wished to say something but was afraid to do so. The garda asked the accused to tell him what was troubling him and the accused made some incriminating remarks. The Court of Criminal Appeal rejected the contention that the statements should have been excluded as having been taken in breach of r.2 of the Judges' Rules because the garda had not made up his mind to charge the accused and, thus, was not obliged to caution him. However, the Court took the view that, because the garda knew or ought to have known that the applicant was

---

[620] [1982] IR 1 at 61. As noted above, this test was proposed by Griffin J in *Shaw* as an alternative to the application of exclusionary rule in respect of unconstitutionally obtained evidence to confession evidence. However, in *People (DPP) v Lynch* [1982] IR 64 at 79, that approach was rejected by the Supreme Court with O'Higgins CJ stating that: "Once the Constitution has been violated for the purpose of securing a confession, the fruits of that violation must be excluded from evidence on that ground alone."

[621] See McGuckian, "Recent Developments in the Law Governing the Admissibility of Confessions in Ireland" (1999) 9 ICLJ 8 for a discussion of the shift of emphasis from the voluntariness test to the test of fundamental fairness. *Cf.* Clough, "The Exclusion of Voluntary Confessions: A Question of Fairness" (1997) UNSW LJ 25, and Schrager, "Recent Developments in the Law Relating to Confessions: England, Canada and Australia" (1981) 26 McGill LJ 435.

[622] Unreported, Court of Criminal Appeal, 13 March 1995.

on the threshold of admitting some involvement in a crime, he should not have been encouraged to make an admission without first cautioning him. It, therefore, held that the statements should have been excluded on the basis that the failure to administer a caution in the circumstances of the case violated the requirements of basic fairness.[623]

8–271   The decision in *Breen* was distinguished in *People (DPP) v O'Reilly*.[624] The wife of the accused had been murdered and a detailed statement was taken from him by Gardaí in his home at a time when he was a suspect but before an intention to charge him had been formed. It was argued, relying on *Breen*, that there had been a breach of his right to fundamental fairness and that he ought to have been cautioned before being invited to make a statement. However, the Court of Criminal Appeal considered that there was a stark contrast between the facts of that case and those of *Breen* given that the accused had not been agitated in any way at the time that the statement was taken and it had been given by him freely and voluntarily by way of a witness statement. Further, the statement was entirely exculpatory in its terms. The Court also rejected the proposition that the failure to give a caution could be equated to a want of fairness. Accordingly, the Court was satisfied that the statement had not been obtained in circumstances which fell below the required standard of fairness.

8–272   The test of fundamental fairness has been unsuccessfully invoked in a number of other cases[625] including *People (DPP) v C*.[626] One of the grounds on which the applicant sought leave to appeal was that certain statements made by him in custody should have been excluded as having been in obtained in breach of the standards of fundamental fairness in circumstances where the accused had only had approximately one hour's sleep in the previous 30 hours and had consumed a significant amount of alcohol. The accused had given evidence at the trial that he was extremely tired, hung-over and sore. The Court of Criminal Appeal accepted that, under the decision in *Shaw*, the trial judge had a discretion to exclude the applicant's statements but, as stated in that case, that discretion fell to be exercised in accordance with the facts of the particular case. In the instant case, the trial judge had accepted the evidence by the investigating gardaí and a doctor that the applicant was in a perfectly coherent condition at all stages and was unaffected by tiredness or alcohol consumption. The

---

[623]   *Cf. People (DPP) v Campbell*, unreported, Court of Criminal Appeal, 19 December 2003, where it was held that there was no unfairness in the procedures adopted by the gardaí in questioning the accused arising from the fact that, in some of the interviews, it had not been made clear to him that the normal caution did not apply to questioning under s.2 of the Offences Against the State (Amendment) Act 1998 which permits inferences to be drawn from the failure of a person when questioned to answer questions material to the investigation of the offence. It was held that the evidence of the contents of the interviews where this had been made clear was admissible.

[624]   [2009] IECCA 18.

[625]   See *DPP v Ryan* [2011] IECCA 6 (considered above) where the contention that inculpatory statements had been obtained by oppression was rejected as was the subsidiary argument that the trial judge had erred in failing to exclude the statements on the basis that there had been a breach of fundamental fairness in how they had been obtained. See also *People (DPP) v O'Callaghan* [2005] IECCA 72 (admission of inculpatory statements did not give rise to any fundamental unfairness by reason of the fact that the accused had acted on foot of advice by a solicitor to answer almost every question with the formula, "I don't remember. If I remember I'll tell you" and, therefore, had not given his own account of events) and *People (DPP) v Yu Jie* [2005] IECCA 95 (although not framed as a contention that there had been a breach of fundamental fairness, the suggestion that there had been impropriety in relation to the obtaining of an inculpatory statement by reason of the fact that the interpreter was a Chinese police officer which should have led to its exclusion was rejected).

[626]   [2001] 3 IR 345.

Court was satisfied that there was ample evidence before him to support his findings but indicated that, if the gardaí had deliberately deprived the accused of sleep, any statement obtained "would be excluded on the grounds of public policy and breach of fair procedures by the State by reason of the use of such methods independent of any question concerning the voluntariness of a statement".[627]

8–273 There are relatively few cases where a finding has been made that an inculpatory statement should be excluded on the basis that it has been obtained in a fundamentally unfair manner but a case where there was a clear failure to adhere to the requirements of fundamental fairness is *People (DPP) v Ward*.[628] The accused in that case had been arrested under s.30 of the Offences Against the State Act 1939 and questioned at Lucan garda station in relation to the murder of Veronica Guerin. He had been arrested under s.30 on a number of earlier occasions and gave evidence that he was well aware of the importance in his own interest of adopting a policy of total silence in the course of the interrogation and alleged that he had done so. On the second day of his detention, he was questioned by various teams of gardaí for the day but the evening interview was interrupted to allow a meeting with his partner, Vanessa Meehan, in a different interview room. She had also been arrested on the same day as the accused under s.30 and detained at another garda station. She did not ask to see the accused but nonetheless, on the following evening, she was brought to Lucan garda station. She gave evidence that she was told by the detectives that she could go home if she asked the accused where the gun was and that he could go home if he told them where it was. She said that she asked him and he denied having anything to do with the murder. After that meeting, the accused returned to the original interview room where it was alleged that he made the significant admission that he had disposed of the motorcycle and gun used in the murder. The next day, what the Court described as a "very disquieting episode" took place. Both the accused's mother and father had also been arrested under s.30. Although his mother did not ask to see him, nor he to see her, she was rushed to Lucan garda station in a squad car where she arrived just before the accused's extended period of detention was due to expire and was brought to see him almost immediately. This visit distressed the accused because of his concern for his mother and his father and it was alleged that after it, he made further admissions.

8–274 Dealing first with the visit of the accused's mother, the Court was satisfied that it was not "arranged for any humanitarian purpose but was a cynical ploy which it was hoped might break down the accused and cause him to make what was perceived to be a crucial admission regarding what had happened to the weapon".[629] As for the visit by Ms Meehan, the Court accepted her evidence that she was successfully subjected to grievous psychological pressure by garda officers to assist them in breaking down the accused. In the circumstances, and applying the test of fundamental fairness, the Court was satisfied that:

> "Both meetings amounted to a conscious and deliberate disregard of the accused's basic constitutional right to fair procedures and treatment while in custody. They constituted deliberate gross violations of the fundamental obligation which the interrogators and their superiors had of conducting their dealings with the accused in accordance with principles of basic fairness and justice."[630]

---

[627] [2001] 3 IR 345 at 354.

[628] Unreported, Special Criminal Court, 27 November 1998.

[629] Unreported, Special Criminal Court, 27 November 1998 at 13.

[630] Unreported, Special Criminal Court, 27 November 1998 at 14. The decision in *Ward* on this point

8–275 Thus, the Court was satisfied that, if they had actually been made (and this was a matter in respect of which the Court entertained some doubt), the inculpatory statements of the accused were inadmissible.

8–276 Although the test of fundamental fairness was not specifically invoked, it seems to have underpinned the decision in *People (DPP) v Murphy*[631] to exclude an admission that had been made by the accused when he had been alone with a garda inspector for a period of 1 hour and 15 minutes in connection with obtaining his signature on a document authorising the release of his medical records. The Court of Criminal Appeal was not satisfied that it was necessary or appropriate for the inspector to be alone with the accused for such a lengthy period and considered that there was substance to the suggestion that the inspector hoped that, if he remained in the accused's company long enough in the relaxed circumstances then obtaining, the accused might say something of an incriminating nature which he did. The Court was of the view that the accused was, in the circumstances, in a position of considerable vulnerability and that the actions of the inspector, possibly at an unconscious level, were tactically unfair and took advantage of that unusual level of vulnerability. Accordingly, the admissions made ought to have been excluded.

8–277 In *People (DPP) v Redmond*,[632] the test of fundamental fairness was also invoked to rule inadmissible tax returns made by the accused and the evidence of the accountant who had prepared them in circumstances where he considered that the accused had no option but to make those returns and obtain the assistance of the accountant to do so.

I. Corroboration of Confessions

1. Introduction

8–278 The traditional position at common law was that a person could be convicted solely on the basis of an uncorroborated confession.[633] There was no requirement either of corroboration,[634] or that the jury be given a warning as to the dangers of convicting on foot of an uncorroborated confession.[635] Such a warning could, of course, be given

---

was distinguished on the facts in *People (DPP) v Murphy* [2005] IECCA 52, [2005] 4 IR 504 where the accused had requested to see his girlfriend and no improper motive could be attributed to the gardaí and *People (DPP) v PA* [2008] IECCA 21 where the trial judge had found that the interview of the accused's mother and a visit by the accused's sister was not part of a cynical ploy by gardaí, a finding that was not disturbed on appeal. See also *People (DPP) v Kavanagh* [2009] IECCA 29 where the contention that a visit from a family member had undermined the will of the accused and was unfair was rejected.

[631] [2005] IECCA 52, [2005] 4 IR 504.

[632] Circuit Criminal Court (White J), November 2003 (transcript not available but the ruling is referred to in *CG v Appeal Commissioners* [2005] IEHC 121 at 26]–[27], [2005] 2 IR 472 at 480–482.

[633] *R. v McNicholl* [1917] 2 IR 557; *R. v Sullivan* (1887) 20 LR IR 550; *R. v Unkles* (1874) IR 8 CL 50; *R. v Wheeling* (1784) 1 Leach 311n. An exception existed with respect to homicide that "a party accused of homicide out not to be convicted on his own confession merely, without proof of finding of the dead body or evidence 'aliunde' that the party alleged to have been murdered is in fact dead" (*per* Fitzgerald J in *R. v Unkles* (1874) IR 8 CL 50 at 58). See also, *R. v Sullivan* (1887) 20 LR IR 570.

[634] *People (DPP) v Kavanagh* (1989) 3 Frewen 243.

[635] *People (DPP) v Kavanagh* (1989) 3 Frewen 243.

at the trial judge's discretion,[636] but it would appear that the only situation where such an instruction was required at common law was where it was sought to convict a person of murder or manslaughter solely on the basis of their confession without any direct or circumstantial proof of the *corpus delicti*.[637]

8–279   The contention that there should be a rule of practice that a judge should warn a jury that, whilst they were entitled to do so, it should ordinarily be considered unsafe to convict on the uncorroborated evidence of inculpatory statements made by an accused in custody was rejected by a majority of the Supreme Court in *People (DPP) v Quilligan (No.3)*.[638] Finlay CJ took the view that any such rule of practice would be overly broad and that the problems which arise in relation to uncorroborated confessions were not "amenable, as a matter of principle, to a general requirement for judicial warning in every case against the dangers of convicting on foot of the evidence contained in inculpatory statements, where it is not corroborated".[639] He pointed out that a trial judge could exercise his discretion to give a warning and it would be appropriate where uncorroborated verbal admissions were being relied upon "to specifically direct and warn a jury as to the difference in quality and, possibly, in persuasiveness of such admissions in general, as compared to written admissions signed by an accused person".[640] However, he felt that "the necessary flexibility of the charge of a trial judge to a jury in a criminal case, required for the attainment of justice, must permit of a wide discretion, having regard to the particular facts of each individual case."[641]

8–280   Although the Supreme Court in *Quilligan* declined to introduce a general corroboration requirement in respect of confessions, the Oireachtas, spurred on by a number of high profile cases involving miscarriages of justice which came to light in both Ireland and England in the late 1980s and early 1990s, did so in s.10 of the Criminal Procedure Act 1993[642] as part of a package of measures to address actual and potential miscarriages of justice.[643]

2. Section 10 of the Criminal Procedure Act 1993

8–281   Section 10 lays down a requirement of a mandatory corroboration warning in all cases tried on indictment in the following terms:

> "(1) Where at the trial of a person on indictment evidence is given of a confession made by

---

[636] See, *e.g. R. v Sykes* (1913) 8 Cr App R 233 at 237 (*per* Ridley J) (prudent to give the jury a warning because the case involved a high profile murder and "it might well be that a man under the influence of insanity or a morbid desire for notoriety would accuse himself of such a crime").

[637] *R. v McNicholl* [1917] 2 IR 557.

[638] [1993] 2 IR 305.

[639] [1993] 2 IR 305 at 331.

[640] [1993] 2 IR 305 at 331–332. *Cf. People (DPP) v Lynch* [1982] IR 64 at 81, where Walsh J indicated that he would have allowed the appeal against conviction on the basis of inculpatory statements made by the accused in circumstances where there were a number of facts that cast doubt on their veracity on the basis that the jury had been insufficiently directed as to the necessity to be satisfied that the statements were true before they acted on them.

[641] [1993] 2 IR 305 at 331.

[642] No.40 of 1993.

[643] See *per* Hardiman J in *Dunne v DPP* [2002] 2 IR 305 at 320, [2002] 2 ILRM 241 at 256, and *People (DPP) v Connolly* [2003] 2 IR 1 at 9–14, where the background to s.10 is set out. This approach had already been adopted in other commonwealth jurisdictions, *Cf.* Cato, "Electronic Recordings, uncorroborated confessions and the High Court of Australia" [1991] NZLJ 282.

that person and that evidence is not corroborated, the judge shall advise the jury to have due regard to the absence of corroboration.

(2) It shall not be necessary for a judge to use any particular form of words under this section."

8–282   The first question that arises in relation to s.10 is whether the warning it mandates is triggered by and relates to a lack of corroboration of the accused's guilt of the offence or a lack of corroboration of the making of the confession. An argument can be made that the mischief that the section is directed at is the fabrication of confessions and, thus, the warning is directed towards circumstances where there is no corroboration of the making of the confession.[644] This interpretation is supported by the wording used in subs.(1) which requires a warning when "evidence is given of a confession made ... and that evidence is not corroborated", *i.e.* the evidence that has to be corroborated is the evidence of the making of the confession. Such a requirement would give a significant evidential impetus to the use of audiovisual technology to record interviews.[645] However, the word "corroboration" is undoubtedly a term of art with a particular technical meaning, *i.e.* independent evidence that tends to implicate the accused in the commission of the offence.[646] Thus, the use of that term indicates that the section is directed towards the risk of a miscarriage of justice that arises when the only evidence against an accused is that of a confession or inculpatory statement made by him. In any event, this question has been settled in favour of the latter view by the decisions of the Court of Criminal Appeal in *People (DPP) v Connolly*[647] and *People (DPP) v Brazil*.[648]

8–283   In *Connolly*, the only evidence against the accused, who had been convicted of trespass and stealing, was an inculpatory statement made by him while in custody. On appeal, it was argued that the charge of the trial judge had failed to comply with s.10 of the Criminal Procedure Act 1993 in that it did not contain sufficiently strong or detailed advice to the jury on the weight to be given to the fact that the accused's statement was uncorroborated. Hardiman J, delivering the judgment of the Court of Criminal Appeal, examined the genesis of s.10 and commented that it could be inferred from its enactment that the legislature was of the view that juries might not be sufficiently aware of the need to have regard to the lack of corroboration in cases where the only evidence is an unsupported confession. The learned judge then went on to consider the meaning of the phrase "due regard" as used in s.10:

"The dictionary meaning of 'due' in this context includes proper, rightful or appropriate....To

---

[644] *Cf. People (DPP) v Ward*, unreported, Special Criminal Court, 27 November 1998, where one of the grounds upon which the Court decided to exclude a number of admissions allegedly made by the accused was that it was not satisfied beyond reasonable doubt that they had actually been made by him. *Cf.* Criminal Procedure Act 1993, s.10 (1993) 40 ICLSA 15 and Pattenden, "Should Confessions be Corroborated" (1991) 107 LQR 317.

[645] *Cf. McKinney v R.* (1991) 171 CLR 468, where a majority of the High Court of Australia held that, whenever police evidence of a confession statement allegedly made by an accused while in police custody is disputed and its making is not reliably corroborated, the judge should, as a matter of practice, warn the jury of convicting on the basis of that evidence alone. It is clear from the judgment of the majority that one of the main reasons for introducing that requirement was to provide an added incentive for the audiovisual recording of interviews. See further, Lightfoot and Mischin, "McKinney v The Queen" (1991) 21 W Aust LR 365.

[646] See *R. v Sheehan* (1826) Jebb CC 54 at 57, *R. v Baskerville* [1916] 2 KB 658 at 667 and, generally, Chap.4.

[647] [2003] 2 IR 1.

[648] Unreported, Court of Criminal Appeal, 22 March 2002.

render the statement 'having due regard to the absence of corroboration' intelligible at all to a lay audience, it must be explained in terms of the meaning of corroboration and the factual nature of the prosecution's case....[The section] is undoubtedly somewhat unspecific, because it is intended to leave a good deal of discretion to a trial judge to be exercised in accordance with the requirements of the individual case. Sub-section (2) makes it clear that a judge need not use any particular form of words. The phrase, with its necessarily generalised reference to 'due regard' cannot be explained or expounded to a jury without using words other than those of the section itself or precisely equivalent words. What is 'due' in any particular case will vary and some attempt must be made to suggest the considerations relevant in giving the absence of corroboration such regard as is 'due' on the facts of any particular case."[649]

8–284   He went on to elaborate on the required ingredients of the instruction to the jury:

"In particular, it seems to the court impossible meaningfully to advise that 'due regard' be paid to the absence of *corroboration* unless that term is properly, and not merely technically, explained. This will often, of course, be necessary in any event because in many cases there is evidence which could amount to corroboration if the jury accepted it. Because the judge cannot know in advance whether they will accept it or not, it will be necessary in such cases, even apart from s.10, to explain the meaning of corroboration in law. As a result of s.10, it will then be necessary to give the advice required by that section for the guidance of the jury if they do not accept the evidence said to constitute the corroboration. Accordingly, it is not unduly burdensome, in my view, to require that corroboration be explained. It is also necessary, I think, briefly and meaningfully to explain why it is natural to look for corroboration in serious cases and equally why, in some cases even the most diligent search will be unavailing. The facts of the individual case will suggest appropriate illustrations. Depending on the individual case, it may be desirable to say something about why corroboration would be desirable in confession cases especially. ... The form of words 'there have been a number of instances in the past where admissions have subsequently been proved to be unreliable' is neutral, in that it does not, quite correctly, attribute this wholly to malfeasance. It may not be necessary in every case and the circumstances of some cases may require a stronger warning."[650]

8–285   In that case, the Court concluded that the instruction given by the trial judge in purported compliance with s.10 was over-general and did not contain advice which was sufficiently explanatory of the term "due regard to the absence of corroboration". The Court went on to set out a possible but non-prescriptive direction which could have been given in the particular circumstances of the case. Although tailored to the particular facts before the Court, it is worth setting this out in full because it is likely to provide valuable guidance in future cases:

"This case stands or falls on the confession which the prosecution allege the accused made. Either you are satisfied beyond reasonable doubt that that confession is true and reliable, in which case you will convict, or you are not so satisfied in which case you will acquit. The law requires me to point out to you that there is no corroboration of the evidence of the confession. Corroboration means independent confirmation. In a case like this, it would mean some evidence independent of that of the gardaí who say they heard the accused confess, which you could fairly and reasonably regard as confirming the truth of the confession. There might have been forensic evidence placing the accused in the injured party's house, which would certainly confirm the truth of the alleged confession. He might have been found in possession of the stolen property or he might have been identified by some person as the robber. On the other hand, there are cases which of their nature make it hard to find corroboration. You must consider what sort of case this is from the point of view of corroboration. When you are considering whether you can feel sure that the statement is true and reliable beyond reasonable doubt, you must ask yourselves whether the absence of any corroboration or independent confirmation of the statement should reduce your trust in it to the point where you are not confident of its truth beyond reasonable doubt. Since the earliest times people faced with important decisions

---

[649] Unreported, Court of Criminal Appeal, 22 March 2002 at 15.
[650] Unreported, Court of Criminal Appeal, 22 March 2002 at 15–16 (emphasis in the original).

have sought to make their task easier by looking for independent confirmation of one view or another. It is very natural and prudent to do so, and very comforting if you find it. But if it is absent, the decision still has to be made. If it is absent where you would expect to find it, that fact in itself may affect the decision.

I am obliged to give you this warning because of a law passed by the Oireachtas in 1993 which says that I must advise you to give due regard to the absence of corroboration. It is essential that you do so. You must also bear in mind that, despite the absence of corroboration you are perfectly entitled to convict if you are indeed satisfied of the truth of the Defendant's confession beyond reasonable doubt. The law does not say that you cannot convict without corroboration, merely that you should specifically consider the absence of corroboration and what weight, if any, you should give to this factor. Once you do this, your decision is a matter for your own good sense and conscience."[651]

8–286 The guidance given by the Court in *Connolly* as to the required ingredients of the instruction is quite comprehensive but it appears, to use the words of Kingsmill Moore J in *People (AG) v Casey (No.2)*,[652] that the suggested direction is "not meant to be a stereotyped formula" or to prescribe the use of any particular form of words.[653] This was the view taken in *People (DPP) v Roche*[654] where criticisms made of the direction given by the trial judge pursuant to s.10 were rejected and it was held that a more detailed warning than that given had not been required. Referring to the decision in *Connolly*, Fennelly J stated that the "rather elaborate formula" in that case "was merely a suggestion and not mandatory". He pointed out that s.10 made it clear that to "lay down any general requirements would take away from that statutory provisions."[655]

8–287 One matter that is left unresolved in the aftermath of the decision in *Connolly* is the circumstances in which it is not necessary to give a warning. The judgment of Hardiman J in *Connolly* seems to indicate that a corroboration instruction pursuant to s.10 is required even where there is evidence that could amount to corroboration if the jury accepted it, because the trial judge cannot know in advance whether they will accept it or not. However, it appears from the wording of s.10 that the requirement to give an instruction to the jury as to the need to have due regard to the absence of corroboration only arises where the confession is not corroborated. If there is corroboration, no instruction is necessary. This was the view taken in *People (DPP) v Brazil*.[656] The applicant submitted that the trial judge should have warned the jury in accordance with s.10 in relation to inculpatory statements made by him in custody. However, that contention was rejected by the Court of Criminal Appeal on the basis that the jury were entitled to act upon the identification evidence in the case which had been properly left to them and, thus, the statements were not uncorroborated. A

---

[651] Unreported, Court of Criminal Appeal, 22 March 2002 at 16–17.

[652] [1963] IR 33 at 40.

[653] *People (DPP) v Murphy* [2005] IECCA 1 at [101], [2005] 2 IR 125 at 158. In the context of the direction required in respect of identification evidence, the courts have emphasised that no particular form of words is necessary provided that the trial judge addresses all relevant matters. The position was forcefully put by O'Flaherty J in *People (DPP) v Kavanagh,* unreported, Court of Criminal Appeal, *ex tempore,* 7 July 1997: "The Court rejects the idea that there should be a mechanical repetition of everything set forth in the *Casey* judgment. On the contrary, a judge should be accorded a wide discretion to express the warning in the way that he thinks best—having regard to the underlying rationale of the *Casey* decision."

[654] [2004] IECCA 24.

[655] [2004] IECCA 24 at 16. See also *People (DPP) v Keohane* [2010] IECCA 23 where, what was described as being a pithy warning, was held to be perfectly adequate in the particular circumstances of the case.

[656] Unreported, Court of Criminal Appeal, 22 March 2002.

similar approach was taken in *People (DPP) v Murphy*[657] where it was held that the trial judge would not have been under any duty to give a warning in accordance with s.10 if there was corroboration. The view was also taken that, even if a trial judge incorrectly identified as corroboration evidence which did not satisfy the legal definition thereof, a conviction would still stand even if a section 10 instruction was given provided that there was some corroborative evidence.[658]

8–288   The Court of Criminal Appeal went even further in *People (DPP) v O'Neill*.[659] In this case, the only evidence against the accused, apart from verbal admissions made by him, was forensic evidence that was only slightly supportive of the proposition that the accused had committed the offence. The trial judge gave the jury a warning pursuant to s.10 in the course of which he instructed the jurors on the meaning of corroboration in terms of the technical definition laid down in *R. v Baskerville*[660] and told them that the forensic evidence was capable of constituting corroboration. The Court of Criminal Appeal took the view that the trial judge had erred in instructing the jury that this evidence could amount to corroboration because it did not satisfy the requirement of implicating the accused in the commission of the offence. However, the jury were entitled to convict on the admissions of the accused even if uncorroborated and the Court was satisfied that they provided a satisfactory basis for the conviction. This approach appears to be somewhat more pragmatic than that applied in the case of the corroboration warning required in respect of accomplice testimony where a defect in the warning will result in the conviction being quashed unless the proviso can be applied.[661]

J. Miscellaneous Issues

1. Procedure for Challenging the Admissibility of a Confession

8–289   When it is sought to challenge the admissibility of a confession or inculpatory statement, the proper procedure is by way of *voir dire*.[662] On the hearing of the *voir dire* the trial judge will hear evidence tendered on behalf of the prosecution as to the voluntariness of the statement and any evidence called on behalf of the defence including the accused who can give evidence in a *voir dire* without compromising his right not to give evidence in the proceedings.[663] Having heard all the evidence and legal submissions by both counsel, the trial judge will then rule as to the admissibility of the confession.

---

[657] [2005] IECCA 1 at [102], [2005] 2 IR 125 at 159.

[658] See also *People (DPP) v MJ* [2014] IECCA 21 at [78] where a similar view appears to have been taken although on an *obiter* basis.

[659] Unreported, Court of Criminal Appeal, 28 January 2002.

[660] [1916] 2 KB 658.

[661] See *R. v McInnes* (1990) 90 Cr App R 99 at 103.

[662] *State v Treanor* [1924] 2 IR 193; *People (DPP) v Conroy* [1986] IR 460; *People (DPP) v Quilligan (No.3)* [1993] 2 IR 305.

[663] *R. v Mushtaq* [2005] UKHL 25 at [38], [2005] 1 WLR 1513 at 1528. In *Wong Kam-ming v R.* [1980] AC 247, [1979] 1 All ER 939, it was held that, on a *voir dire* as to the admissibility of a confession, the prosecution are not entitled to cross-examine the accused as to the truth of the statement because the sole issue on a *voir dire* is whether the statement has been made voluntarily and whether it was true or not was not relevant to that issue. There is no direct authority on the point in this jurisdiction but in *People (DPP) v Quilligan (No.3)* [1993] 2 IR 305 at 357, O'Flaherty J commented that the truth of a confession is not directly relevant at the *voir dire* stage.

8–290 If the trial judge rules the statement to be admissible, then the accused is entitled to traverse the same issues of fact that were covered during the *voir dire* and to challenge the voluntariness and truth of the confession before the jury with a view to attacking the weight to be attached to it.[664] The accused is, thus, entitled to cross-examine again all the witnesses who gave evidence during the *voir dire* although it should be noted that one of the disadvantages of the *voir dire* procedure is that those witnesses will be well prepared for the line of cross-examination involved.[665] In the case of a trial without a jury, the same basic principle applies except that it should not be necessary to traverse again matters that have to do exclusively with the admissibility of the confession.[666]

8–291 It was held in *People (DPP) v Quilligan (No.3)*,[667] that, where a trial judge rejects an allegation of involuntariness and decides to admit a confession and the voluntariness and truth of that confession are challenged again before the jury, the trial judge must direct the jury to have regard to all the evidence which is before it, including all the evidence suggesting that the statement has been obtained by unlawful or improper methods for the purpose of ascertaining whether they are satisfied beyond a reasonable doubt that the confession or incriminating statement is true and sufficient proof of the guilt of the accused.[668] Finlay CJ pointed out that a jury is not bound by a finding of fact made by a trial judge in the course of his ruling on the admissibility of a statement and it must be made clear to the jurors that their function, in having to be satisfied beyond a reasonable doubt as to the truth of a voluntary statement admitted into evidence, necessarily involves an examination by them of any allegations which are relevant to the question as to whether the statement was truly voluntary or not.[669] Finally, it should be made clear to the jury that if they have a reasonable doubt as to whether a statement was truly voluntarily given, that this would form a very solid ground for also entertaining a reasonable doubt as to whether it was true.[670]

8–292 It should be noted that, in *Wong Kam-ming v R.*,[671] it was held that, whether an accused's statement is excluded or admitted, the prosecution is not entitled as part of its case on the general issue to adduce evidence of the testimony given by the accused on the *voir dire* or, if the confession is excluded, to cross-examine the accused on his or her evidence given during the *voir dire*. However, if the impugned confession is admitted, and the accused gives evidence which is materially different to that given by him or her during the *voir dire*, cross-examination on the discrepancies between

---

[664] *People (AG) v Ainscough* [1960] IR 136 at 140; *People (DPP) v Conroy* [1986] IR 460 at 474; *People (DPP) v Quilligan (No.3)* [1993] 2 IR 305 at 357; *Finn v Convening Authority,* unreported, Courts-Martial Appeal Court, 11 June 1996 at 5–6. In *People (AG) v Ainscough* [1960] IR 136, the applicant's allegations that a confession made by him had been induced by a promise made to him by a detective were rejected and the statement was admitted. On appeal, the conviction of the applicant was quashed because of the failure of the trial judge to remind the accused, who was unrepresented, of his right to cross-examine the detective as to the circumstances of the taking of the statement in the presence of the jury. This failure of the accused to challenge the statement before the jury might have misled the jury as to the weight to be attached to the objection made to the admission of the statement.

[665] As acknowledged by Finlay CJ in *People (DPP) v Conroy* [1986] IR 460 at 472.

[666] *Finn v Convening Authority,* unreported, Courts-Martial Appeal Court, 11 June 1996 at 9.

[667] [1993] 2 IR 305.

[668] [1993] 2 IR 305 at 333 (*per* Finlay CJ).

[669] [1993] 2 IR 305 at 333 (*per* Finlay CJ) at 334.

[670] [1993] 2 IR 305 at 333 (*per* Finlay CJ) at 334.

[671] [1980] AC 247, [1979] 1 All ER 939.

his or her testimony on the *voir dire* and his or her testimony on the general issue is permissible.

2. Discretion to Exclude Inculpatory Statements made by an Accused

8–293   As noted in Chap.1, it is well established that a trial judge, as part of his or her function to ensure that an accused receives a fair trial, has a discretion to exclude evidence if, in his or her opinion, its probative value is outweighed by its prejudicial effect.[672] As can be seen from the decision in *People (DPP) v Carney*,[673] that discretion is potentially exercisable in respect of inculpatory statements made by an accused. However, the contention that the trial judge had erred in failing to exercise this discretion failed on the facts in that case because the Court of Criminal Appeal was satisfied that the statements admitted were probative and, although prejudicial to the accused, they were not so prejudicial as to outweigh their probative value.

3. Withdrawal of Confession from the Jury

8–294   A confession may be untrue and unreliable even where it is voluntary and, therefore, a trial judge has a discretion to withdraw a confession from the jury where he or she forms the view that it is not sufficiently reliable to ground a conviction.[674] However, the exercise of this discretion arises very infrequently because, if a trial judge has doubts about the reliability of a confession, it will usually be in circumstances where the confession is involuntary or grounds for the exercise of a discretion to exclude the confession under the Judges' Rules or the Custody Regulations arise.

8–295   A case where the view was taken on appeal that this discretion should have been exercised is *People (DPP) v. Quinn*.[675] The applicant had been tried with two others on a number of sexual offences and the case against him was based on two inculpatory statements made by him whilst in custody. The applicant was 13 years old at the time of the alleged offence but functioned at a very low intellectual level and had a mental age of only eight to nine years of age. He was interviewed in the presence of his mother but it appears that she was also a person of low intelligence. The Court of Criminal Appeal was "troubled" by the fact that there were a number of significant inconsistencies between the two statements. There were also inconsistencies between the first statement and the testimony of the complainant. In addition, the medical examination of the complainant did not afford any corroboration of the acts of assault described by the boy in his statement. No attempt had been made to hold an identification parade nor had any forensic samples been taken. Following a lengthy *voir dire*, the trial judge admitted the statements on the basis that they were voluntary

---

[672] See *People (AG) v O'Neill* [1964] Ir Jur Rep 1; *People (AG) v O'Brien* [1965] IR 142 at 159 (*per* Kingsmill Moore J*); *People (DPP) v Coddington*, unreported, Court of Criminal Appeal, 31 May 2001; *People (DPP) v Meleady (No.3)* [2001] 4 IR 16; *Blanchfield v Harnett* [2002] 3 IR 207 at 219; *People (DPP) v Murphy*, Court of Criminal Appeal, 8 July 2003; *People (DPP) v Flynn*, unreported, Court of Criminal Appeal, 30 July 2003; *People (DPP) v Carney* [2011] IECCA 53; *People (DPP) v Kearney* [2012] IECCA 1 at 8; *People (DPP) v Timmons* [2011] IECCA 13 at 18.

[673] [2011] IECCA 5 at 10–12.

[674] *People (DPP) v Murray* (1983) 2 Frewen 153; *People (DPP) v Quinn*, unreported, Court of Criminal Appeal, *ex tempore*, 23 March 1998; *People (DPP) v Coll*, unreported, Court of Criminal Appeal, 18 May 1998.

[675] Unreported, Court of Criminal Appeal, *ex tempore*, 23 March 1998.

and there had not been any significant breach of the Custody Regulations. However, the Court of Criminal Appeal took the view that, having regard to the contradictions in the complainant's evidence together with what it regarded as the "totally unreliable nature" of the confessions, the case should have been withdrawn from the jury and it proceeded to quash the conviction of the applicant for attempted rape as unsafe.[676]

4. Application of the Confession Rules to Exculpatory Statements

8–296 It might seem axiomatic that the rules regarding the admissibility of confessions should only be applied to inculpatory statements and should have no application to the admission of exculpatory statements made by an accused.[677] However, the dividing line between inculpatory and exculpatory statements is not always clear. As Kennedy CJ acknowledged in *AG v McCabe*,[678] "some statements, without being actually confessions, would be of so incriminating a character as to have the effect of implicating the accused like a confession or admission, and so to come for practical purposes under the latter category".[679]

8–297 Furthermore, it may be questioned whether any statement of the accused tendered by the prosecution can ever really be said to be wholly exculpatory. Indeed, if it were, it would seem to fall foul of the hearsay rule. In reality, when the prosecution tenders a statement which is ostensibly exculpatory, it does so in order to undermine the case for the defence or otherwise implicate the accused in the crime. A good example is furnished by *People (AG) v Fennell (No.1)*[680] where the accused, who was charged with murder, sought to exclude an exculpatory statement made by him. The reason why he sought to do so, and why the prosecution wished to adduce the statement in evidence, was that in it he stated that he had shot the deceased in self-defence but his defence at trial was that he was insane at the time of the shooting. Thus, the admissibility of a statement that is ostensibly exculpatory may fall to be tested on the same basis as a confession.

5. The Whole of a Confession is Admissible

8–298 When a statement of the accused[681] is put in evidence by the prosecution, then the whole of that statement is admissible and not just so much of it as is inculpatory.[682]

---

[676] See also *People (DPP) v Coll*, unreported, Court of Criminal Appeal, 18 May 1998, where it was held that a trial judge should have exercised his discretion not to admit an inculpatory statement were there was "intrinsic evidence" that the statement was not "the complete truth".

[677] *Cf. AG v McCabe* [1927] IR 129 at 133–134; *AG v O'Leary* [1926] IR 445 at 452, and *People (AG) v Murphy* [1947] IR 236 at 239.

[678] [1927] IR 129.

[679] [1927] IR 129 at 133. Where an issue arises as to whether a statement constitutes an admission on the part of an accused, this is decided having regard to all the circumstances surrounding the making of the statement: see *People (AG) v Sherlock* (1975) 1 Frewen 383; *People (DPP) v Pringle* (1981) 1 Frewen 57; *People (DPP) v Rose*, unreported, Court of Criminal Appeal, 21 February 2002.

[680] [1940] IR 445.

[681] *Cf. People (DPP) v Brazil*, unreported, Court of Criminal Appeal, 22 March 2002, where it was held that the trial judge had approached the admission of statements made by the applicant correctly by excluding so much of the interview notes as simply recorded the applicant as exercising his right to silence and directing that only those parts of the notes which recorded statements made which were either incriminatory or exculpatory of the applicant should go before the jury.

[682] *McCormack v DPP* [2007] IEHC 123 at [4], [2008] 1 ILRM 49 at 52–53; *People (DPP) v*

In *People (AG) v Crosby*[683] the Court of Criminal Appeal acknowledged that the original reason for the admission of the exculpatory balance of a mixed statement was to place an admission in context and give it its true significance. However, the Court held that, once admitted, the mixed statement was evidence of both exculpatory and incriminating facts stated therein.[684] This statement of the law was approved in *People (DPP) v Clarke*[685] and the relevant principles were summarised by O'Flaherty J as follows:

> "The true position in law … is that once a statement is put in evidence, as in this case by the prosecution, it then and thereby becomes evidence in the real sense of the word, not only against the person who made it but for him as to facts contained in it favourable to his defence, or case. A jury is not bound to accept such favourable facts as true, even if unrefuted by contrary evidence, but they should be told to receive, weigh and consider them as evidence."[686]

8–299 Thus, it is open to the jury to reject the portion of a mixed statement which is exculpatory and believe the portion which is inculpatory,[687] even if the exculpatory part is uncontradicted.[688] However, it is not necessary, and would be inappropriate, for a trial judge to attribute any particular probative value to or to take a view on the truth of the inculpatory and exculpatory parts of a mixed statement at the stage of an application for a direction because this is a matter for the jury after hearing the totality of the evidence.[689]

8–300 It should be noted that a trial judge, in his or her charge to the jury, is not prohibited from contrasting the inculpatory and exculpatory parts of the statement, and from commenting on the weight to be attached to them, so long as he or she does not give the jury the impression that the exculpatory parts are something less than evidence of the facts they state.[690] Thus, he or she can legitimately point out that the incriminating parts are more likely to be true as being against interest.[691] Conversely, if there are factors which bolster the creditworthiness of the exculpatory portions, such as the fact that the statement was made at an early stage, spontaneously, without legal advice and that the accused had not subsequently departed from it, then these should be pointed out to the jury.[692]

8–301 The position may be different in respect of a statement that is primarily

---

McCormack [2004] IECCA 42 at [10], [2004] 4 IR 333 at 339; *People (DPP) v Kenny*, unreported, Court of Criminal Appeal, 19 November 2002; *People (DPP) v Clarke* [1994] 3 IR 289 at 303, [1995] 1 ILRM 355 at 367; *People (AG) v Crosby* (1961) 1 Frewen 231 at 246; *People (AG) v Hannigan* [1941] IR 252 at 254; *R. v Gamble* [1989] NI 268 at 275; *R. v Sharp* (1987) 86 Cr App R 274 at 274–275, [1988] 1 All ER 65 at 71; *R. v Duncan* (1981) 73 Cr App R 359 at 365; *R. v Clewes* (1830) 4 C & P 221 at 226; *R. v Higgins* (1829) 3 C & P 603; *R. v Jones* (1827) 2 C & P 221.

[683] (1961) 1 Frewen 231.

[684] (1961) 1 Frewen 231 at 246. In the UK, it has been held that exculpatory parts of a mixed statement are not evidence of the facts stated therein: *R. v Pearce* (1979) 69 Cr App R 365; *Hamilton v R.* [2012] UKPC 37.

[685] [1995] 1 ILRM 355.

[686] [1995] 1 ILRM 355 at 303. This direction was endorsed as correct by Charleton J in *McCormack v DPP* [2007] IEHC 123 at [5], [2008] 1 ILRM 49 at 53. See also *People (DPP) v O'Reilly* [2009] IECCA 30 at [6]. The same position seems to obtain in England (see *R. v Duncan* (1981) 73 Cr App R 359 and *R. v Sharp* (1987) 86 Cr App R 274).

[687] *AG v Edwards* [1935] IR 500; *People (AG) v Hannigan* [1941] IR 252.

[688] *People (AG) v Crosby* (1961) 1 Frewen 231 at 243.

[689] *People (DPP) v Kenny*, unreported, Court of Criminal Appeal, 19 November 2002.

[690] *R. v Duncan* (1981) 73 Cr App R 359.

[691] *Cf. R. v Gamble* [1989] NI 268 at 275.

[692] *People (AG) v Clarke* [1994] 3 IR 289 at 368.

exculpatory. In *McCormack v DPP*,[693] one of the complaints made by the applicant in judicial review proceedings was that, by reason of the unstructured and chaotic nature of the garda interviews that had been conducted after he had been arrested on suspicion of larceny, he had been deprived of the opportunity to put his defence on video. Charleton J commented that there was a growing practice of arrested persons using the opportunity of being questioned by gardaí to make exculpatory statements for the purpose of having those put before the jury as part of the prosecution case. He held that this was not the purpose of such an interview and stated that the question of whether an entirely self-serving statement by an accused, that was repeated again and again, would be admissible as to every repetition by way of an exception to the rule against self-corroboration was a matter for the trial judge.

6. Admissibility of Exculpatory parts of Inadmissible Statement

8–302   In *People (DPP) v O'Neill*[694] the contention that the trial judge had erred by not admitting into evidence exculpatory portions of a statement which had been excluded as involuntary was rejected by the Court of Criminal Appeal which held that a statement could not be severed in this way. It was argued by the accused that the exculpatory portions ought to have been admitted because they were voluntarily obtained. However, the Court considered that such an approach would lead to undesirable results because a trial judge would be put in the impossible position of having to go through the statement line by line to decide which portions should be admitted. Further, an exculpatory statement would frequently be made in conjunction with an inculpatory statement so that to sever one from the other and admit the exculpatory statement only could lead to a very distorted picture being given to the jury. The Court acknowledged that there could be exceptional cases where the voluntariness of an interview might alter midstream so that the initial portion of an interview could be admitted but that was not the position in that case where the cause of involuntariness had affected the entire interview.

7. Editing of Statements

8–303   It is not uncommon that, either by agreement between the prosecution and the defence or by ruling of the trial judge, a statement made by an accused that is admissible is edited so as to exclude material that is irrelevant or prejudicial.[695] However, as pointed out in *People (DPP) v Rattigan*,[696] this is a practice that carries not only a risk of error but also the danger of presenting an incomplete and therefore inaccurate picture of an interview by removing evidence which may assist the jury in forming a picture of events. In that case, counsel for the prosecution had inadvertently read out a portion of an interview with the accused which the parties had agreed should be excised but the Court of Criminal Appeal agreed that the trial judge had been correct to refuse an application to discharge the jury on that basis.

---

[693] [2007] IEHC 123, [2008] 1 ILRM 49.
[694] [2007] IECCA 8, [2007] 4 IR 564.
[695] See *People (DPP) v O'Neill* [2007] IECCA 8 at [21], [2007] 4 IR 564 at 571.
[696] [2013] IECCA 13 at [23].

8. Confession is Not Evidence Against a Co-Accused

8–304   It is well established that an inculpatory statement is only evidence against the person who made it and is not evidence against a co-accused.[697] In *People (DPP) v Madden*,[698] O'Higgins CJ emphasised that:

> "Statements…which are alleged to have been made by certain of the defendants, and the recitation of the facts therein contained, must be treated as being admissible only in the case of the defendant who was alleged to have made them and are in no way explanatory of the conduct or action of any other defendant."[699]

8–305   In *R. v Donnelly*,[700] the Northern Ireland Court of Appeal emphasised that an admission which is admissible against one accused is inadmissible for all purposes against any co-accused. Hence, if that admission goes to bolster the credibility of a witness against the accused who made it, it cannot be used to bolster the credibility of that witness as against the other accused.

8–306   There is an obvious danger, where accused are being tried together,[701] that a jury might use a confession that implicates one accused as evidence against other co-accused. Therefore, the trial judge is required to give a clear warning to the jury that the confession is evidence only against the accused who made it and cannot be relied on as evidence against any co-accused.[702] Indeed, in *People (DPP) v McCarthy*,[703] McCarthy J stated that it is the duty of both counsel and the trial judge to advise the jury in those terms. However, if the confession does not implicate the other accused, then such a warning is not necessary as the risk that the jury will use it as evidence against them does not arise.[704]

9. Use of Confession as Proof of Facts Stated

8–307   An accused can only make an admission of a fact of which he or she could give admissible evidence.[705] Thus, a confession can only be used as proof of facts stated therein of which the accused has personal knowledge.[706] This principle has been applied, in particular, in the context of prosecutions for receiving stolen goods and it

---

[697] *People (DPP) v Madden* [1977] IR 336 at 341; *People (AG) v Keane* (1976) 110 ILTR 1; *R. v Graham* [1984] 18 NIJB 1; *R. v Clewes* (1830) 4 C & P 221 at 225; *R. v Daniel* [1973] Crim LR 627. *A fortiori*, an admission is not evidence against a person not charged in the proceedings: *People (DPP) v Ward*, unreported, Court of Criminal Appeal, 22 March 2002 at 7.

[698] [1977] IR 336.

[699] [1977] IR 336 at 341. See *contra R. v Hayter* [2005] 1 WLR 605 (analysed by McGourlay, "Is criminal practice impervious to logic: *R. v Hayter*" (2006) 10 E & P 126).

[700] [1986] 4 NIJB 32.

[701] The fact that a confession made by one accused implicates another is a well recognised basis for applications for separate trials: see *AG v Joyce* [1929] IR 526 at 537–538; *People (AG) v Murtagh* [1966] IR 361 at 363; *People (DPP) v Burke* (1986) 3 Frewen 92 at 93.

[702] *People (AG) v Sherlock* (1975) 1 Frewen 383 at 389; *People (DPP) v Burke* (1986) 3 Frewen 92 at 93–94; *People (DPP) v McCarthy*, unreported, Court of Criminal Appeal, 31 July 1992 at 12; *People (DPP) v Ferris*, unreported, Court of Criminal Appeal, *ex tempore*, 11 March 1997.

[703] Unreported, Court of Criminal Appeal, 31 July 1992 at 12.

[704] *People (DPP) v Palmer*, unreported, Court of Criminal Appeal, 22 March 2002. See also *People (DPP) v Ferris*, unreported, Court of Criminal Appeal, *ex tempore*, 11 March 1997, where the view was taken that, in circumstances where the inculpatory statement of one accused does not actually incriminate a co-accused, to give the warning might actually do more harm than good.

[705] *AG's Reference (No. 4 of 1979)* [1981] 1 WLR 667, [1981] 1 All ER 1193.

[706] *Comptroller of Customs v Western Electric Co Ltd* [1966] AC 367, [1965] 3 All ER 599; *Surujpaul v R.* [1958] 1 WLR 1050, [1958] 3 All ER 300.

has been held in a series of cases that where an accused admits, when questioned, that he or she believed goods to be stolen, this is not sufficient evidence to establish that the goods were actually stolen.[707]

8–308   The foregoing principles were applied by the Court of Criminal Appeal in *People (DPP) v McHugh*.[708] The accused had been convicted of handling money, the proceeds of drug trafficking, and one of the issues which arose on the appeal was whether the prosecution had tendered sufficient evidence to prove the fact the money in question was or represented the proceeds of drug trafficking. In order to prove this, the prosecution sought to rely, *inter alia*, on a statement made by the accused while in custody in which the accused had indicated his knowledge or belief that the money constituted the proceeds of drug trafficking. However, the Court accepted the submission made on behalf of the accused that this fact had to be proved by evidence of the same quality and character as any other fact and that admissions made in an inculpatory statement which were based on opinion or hearsay evidence were no more proof than if given in evidence by a witness for the prosecution:

> "The contents of a statement of admission made by the accused are admissible against him to prove any relevant fact. The statement is admissible because it tends to prove the truth of any fact about which the accused makes an inculpatory admission. Its value for that purpose is, nonetheless, dependent on its compliance with the normal rules of evidence. Where the statement deals with matters which are not within the knowledge of the person making it, it has no greater probative value than such evidence offered by any prosecution witness. A distinction must be made between matters in which the statement shows the accused to have been directly involved and those in respect of which he expresses an opinion or reports what he has been told."[709]

8–309   In that case, it was an essential ingredient of the offence charged that the property be shown to be, in whole or in part, or to represent, another person's proceeds of drug trafficking. However, the court was satisfied that the admission of the accused was not admissible evidence of this fact.

8–310   The decision in *McHugh* was followed but a different conclusion reached in *DPP v Buckley*[710] where an admission had been made by the accused that a substance recovered from his pocket was cannabis and the District Judge stated a case as to whether this was sufficient evidence of this fact in the absence of a certificate of analysis from the Garda Forensic Science Laboratory confirming that the substance was cannabis. Charleton J held that the qualities of cannabis were not so unusual that expert evidence as to its presence was required and an accused who admits a substance is cannabis can be, but not necessarily must be, relied on to know what he is talking about. Accordingly, when the prosecution adduced evidence of an admission by an accused that he was in possession of a controlled drug only without adducing in evidence a certificate of analysis to prove the nature of the substance, the issue for the judge was whether the circumstances showed that the accused could be relied on to have sufficient knowledge to allow that admission to be safely relied on.[711]

---

[707] See *R. v Porter* [1976] Crim LR 58; *R. v Marshall* [1977] Crim LR 106; *AG's Reference (No. 4 of 1979)* [1981] 1 WLR 667, [1981] 1 All ER 1193.

[708] [2002] 1 IR 352.

[709] [2002] 1 IR 352 at 361.

[710] [2007] IEHC 150, [2007] 3 IR 745.

[711] See also *Bird v Adams* [1972] Crim LR 174 and *R. v Chatwood* [1980] 1 WLR 874.

10. Evidence Derived from an Inadmissible Confession

8–311   In *R. v Warickshall*,[712] the accused had made a confession of receiving stolen property in the course of which she indicated where the property was to be found. Her confession was excluded as involuntary but the Court held that evidence of facts derived from an inadmissible confession could be given in evidence:

> "This principle respecting confessions has no application whatever as to the admission or rejection of facts, whether the knowledge of them is obtained in consequence of an extorted confession, or whether it arises from any other source; for a fact, if it exist at all, must exist invariably in the same manner, whether the confession from which it is derived be in other respects true or false. Facts thus obtained, however, must be fully and satisfactorily proved, without calling in the aid of any part of the confession from which they may have been derived … although confessions improperly obtained cannot be received in evidence, yet that any acts done afterwards might be given in evidence, notwithstanding they were done in consequence of such confession."[713]

8–312   Thus, facts discovered as a result of an inadmissible confession could be proved in evidence provided that this did not involve proof of any part of the confession. This remains the position in the UK where it has been held that there is no "fruit of the poisoned tree" doctrine. In *A v Secretary of State for the Home Department (No. 2)*[714] Lord Hoffmann stated:

> "As for the rule that we do not necessarily exclude the "fruit of the poisoned tree", but admit relevant evidence discovered in consequence of inadmissible confessions, this is the way we strike a necessary balance between preserving the integrity of the judicial process and the public interest in convicting the guilty."

8–313   However, even if real or other evidence obtained on foot of an inadmissible confession is, in principle, admissible, difficulties can arise in linking that evidence to the accused if no part of the confession can be proved in evidence. In order to address these difficulties, in some cases, the courts applied the reliability rationale that unpinned the voluntariness rule in order to hold that evidence could be given of such part of an inadmissible confession as was confirmed to be true by the discovery of subsequent facts.[715] For example, in *Wray v R.*,[716] evidence that an accused had led the police to the place in a swamp where he had disposed of a murder weapon was admitted although the main body of the confession admitting the murder was held to be inadmissible. However, the balance of authority in common law jurisdictions seems to be that no part of an inadmissible confession is admissible even where confirmed by subsequent facts.[717] Of particular note is the decision of the Privy Council in *Lam Chi-ming v R.*[718] where it was held that evidence of the police and of a video recording relating to the

---

[712] (1783) 1 Leach 263.
[713] (1783) 1 Leach 263 at 264–265.
[714] [2005] UKHL 71, [2006] 2 AC 221 at [88],
[715] *R. v Griffin* (1809) Russ & Ry 151; *R. v Gould* (1840) 9 Car & P 364; *R. v St. Lawrence* [1949] OR 215; *Wray v R.* [1971] SCR 272, (1970) 11 DLR (3d) 673. *Cf. R. v Barker* [1941] 2 KB 381, [1941] 3 All ER 33.
[716] [1971] SCR 272.
[717] *R. v Warickshall* (1783) 1 Leach 263; *R. v Berriman* (1854) 6 Cox CC 388; *Lam Chi-ming v R.* [1991] 2 AC 212, [1991] 3 All ER 173; *Chalmers v HM Advocate* 1954 JC 66; *R. v Beere* [1965] Qd R 370; *R. v Dally* [1990] 2 NZLR 184 at 192. See also, Black, "The Poisoned Tree: Inadmissible Confessions, Subsequent Facts and Reliability" [1991] 4 Cant LR 356.
[718] [1991] 2 AC 212, [1991] 3 All ER 173.

conduct of the appellants which led to the discovery of the murder weapon should not have been admitted since it was evidence of an inadmissible confession.[719]

8–314 There has been little consideration of this issue in this jurisdiction but the practice of the Irish courts was outlined by Walsh J in *People (AG) v O'Brien*,[720] as follows:

> "[I]n this country the practice in modern times has been to exclude every part of a confession which had been improperly obtained or induced irrespective of whether part of it at least could be shown by subsequent facts to have been true. It is also true to say that the practice has always been to admit in evidence facts, if they were relevant, which had been derived from the inadmissible statement or confession".

8–315 However, having pointed out that the voluntariness test was no longer based solely on concerns about the reliability of confessions but was also based, in part, on the principle that an accused should not be compelled to incriminate himself or herself, he went on to say that there was:

> "a consistent trend towards the concept that an accused person should not be unfairly or improperly induced to incriminate himself by way of confession which in itself directly incriminates him or which reveals the existence or the physical whereabouts of evidence which, when produced, would incriminate him."[721]

8–316 As pointed out in Chap.7, in the case of breaches of constitutional rights, the issue of derivative evidence in this jurisdiction is likely be dealt with by means of a causation inquiry which will exclude any evidence that would not have been obtained "but for" the breach of the accused's constitutional rights. An example of the application of this approach in the context of a confession that was obtained in breach of an accused's constitutional rights can be seen in the Canadian decision of *R. v Burlingham*.[722] The accused, who had been arrested in connection with a murder, made a number of incriminating statements to the police, took them to the murder scene and pointed out where he had disposed of the gun. He subsequently made an incriminating statement to his girlfriend. The confession was ruled inadmissible on the basis of a breach of the accused's right to counsel under s.10(b) of the Canadian Charter of Rights and Fundamental Freedoms and the evidence of the gun and of his girlfriend were also excluded on the basis that they were derivative evidence which would not have been obtained but for the incriminating statements made in violation of the accused's right to counsel.[723]

8–317 Given that, on the basis of the decision in *Re National Irish Bank*,[724] the voluntariness rule is now a constitutionally mandated ingredient of the guarantee of trial in due course of law in Art.38.1, a strong argument can be made, applying the protective principle, that any evidence discovered on foot of an involuntary confession should be excluded in order to fully vindicate the accused's right to a trial in due course of law. It is worth noting in that regard that, in *Re National Irish Bank*,[725] Barrington J stated that "what is objectionable under Art.38 of the Constitution is compelling a

---

[719] See also *Chalmers v HM Advocate* 1954 JC 66.
[720] [1965] IR 142 at 166.
[721] [1965] IR 142 at 166–167.
[722] [1995] 2 SCR 206, (1995) 124 DLR (4th) 7.
[723] See also *R. v Stillman* [1997] 1 SCR 607, (1997) 144 DLR (4th) 193, *R. v Grant* [2009] 2 SCR 353.
[724] [1999] 3 IR 145, [1999] 1 ILRM 321.
[725] [1999] 3 IR 145 at 188–189, [1999] 1 ILRM 321 at 360–361 (emphasis added).

person to confess and then convicting him *on the basis of* his compelled confession." Furthermore, if evidence of facts discovered as a consequence of an involuntary confession is admissible, this arguably creates an incentive for the executive to obtain involuntary confessions.[726]

8–318   The position is more complicated where a confession is excluded for a reason other than involuntariness. It might be expected that, if a confession is excluded as having been obtained in a fundamentally unfair manner, evidence discovered on foot of that confession will be admitted. However, in *People (DPP) v Murphy,*[727] where the Court of Criminal Appeal held that certain admissions ought to have been excluded on the basis that they were unfairly obtained, there was no suggestion that real evidence recovered on the basis of those admissions was inadmissible. With regard to derivative evidence obtained where there has been a breach of the Judges' Rules or the Custody Regulations, the decision in *People (DPP) v Buckley*[728] suggests that statements excluded by virtue of a breach of the Judges' Rules are not to be equated with statements excluded as involuntary. Thus, a different approach to the admissibility of derivative evidence may be taken.

---

[726] *Cf. per* Cory J in *R. v Hodgson* [1998] 2 SCR 449 at 464.
[727] [2005] IECCA 52 at [50]–[51], [2005] 4 IR 504 at 520.
[728] [1990] 1 IR 14.

CHAPTER 9

CHARACTER EVIDENCE

A. Introduction

9–01   In general, character evidence, meaning evidence of an individual's disposition, traits and characteristics, as well as his or her previous conduct,[1] is regarded as inadmissible because it is irrelevant to the facts at issue in criminal or civil proceedings.[2] However, there are a wide range of circumstances, examined in this chapter, where character evidence is admitted because it is relevant to the issues in proceedings or the credibility of a party or a witness. For ease of exposition, the chapter is divided into a number of sections which deal with the discrete circumstances where issues in relation to the admission of character evidence may arise.

B. Evidence of Good Character of the Accused

1. Introduction

9–02   The admission of evidence of the good character of an accused can be traced back to the seventeenth century[3] when it was allowed in capital cases "*in favorem vitae*".[4] Such evidence is now admissible in favour of the accused in any criminal proceedings and can be adduced by examination-in-chief of the accused or of witnesses called by the defence, or elicited on cross-examination of prosecution witnesses, a co-accused, or witnesses called by him or her.[5]

---

[1]   "Character in its wider sense is simply a compendious summary of a person's past actions, good and bad": Bryant, Lederman & Fuerst, *Sopinka, Lederman & Bryant: The Law of Evidence in Canada*, (4th edn, Lexis Nexis, 2014), p.609.

[2]   *People (DPP) v Ferris* [2008] 1 IR 1 at 6; *R. v Miller* [1952] 2 All ER 667 at 668.

[3]   The earliest example of evidence being admitted of an accused's good character seems to be *R. v Turner* (1664) 6 St Tr 565 and it was regularly admitted by the end of the eighteenth century (see, *e.g. R. v O'Connor* (1798) 27 St Tr 565).

[4]   *People (DPP) v Ferris* [2008] 1 IR 1 at 6 (*per* Fennelly J). See also *R. v Rowton* (1865) 10 Cox CC 25 at 30, [1861–73] All ER 549 at 552 (*per* Cockburn C.J.): "The allowing evidence of a prisoner's good character to be given has grown up from a desire to administer the law with mercy, as far as possible. It sprung up in a time when the law was, according to the common estimation of mankind, severer than it should have been."

[5]   See generally, Crinion "Adducing the Good Character of Prosecution Witnesses" [2010] Crim LR 570.

9–03   Where evidence of the good character of an accused is adduced, it not only bolsters his or her credibility[6] but can also be used to support the inference that the accused did not commit the offences charged.[7] As explained by Patteson J in *R. v Stannard*[8]:

> "the object of laying it before the jury is to induce them to believe, from the improbability that a person of good character should have conducted himself as alleged, that there is some mistake or misrepresentation in the evidence of the prosecution, and it is strictly evidence in the case."[9]

9–04   Thus, evidence of "previous good character lays the foundation of innocence"[10] and is generally led by the defence and put before the jury for the dual purpose of convincing them that the accused is unlikely to have committed the offences alleged and, further, to bolster the credibility of the accused if he or she gives evidence or made exculpatory pre-trial statements denying the commission of the offence.

2. Type of Good Character Evidence that is Admissible

9–05   The question as to the type of good character evidence that is admissible in favour of the accused was considered in *R. v Rowton*[11] where Cockburn CJ stated:

> "It is laid down in the books that a prisoner is entitled to give evidence as to his general character. What does that mean? Does it mean evidence as to his reputation amongst those to whom his conduct and position is known, or does it mean evidence of disposition? I think it means evidence of reputation only. I quite agree that what you want to get at, as bearing materially on the probability or improbability of the prisoner's guilt, is the tendency or disposition of his mind to commit the particular offence with which he stands charged; but no one ever heard of a question put deliberately to a witness called on behalf of a prisoner as to the prisoner's disposition of mind. The way, and the only way the law allows of your getting at the disposition and tendency of his mind is by evidence as to general character founded upon the knowledge of those who know anything about him and of his general conduct."[12]

9–06   This approach was approved in this jurisdiction in *People (DPP) v Ferris*[13] and, so, the only evidence of good character that may be adduced by witnesses called by the defence or elicited on cross-examination is evidence of the general reputation of the accused and not evidence of disposition. Also inadmissible is the opinion of a witness as to the character of an accused[14] although this rule is not always strictly adhered to in practice.[15] While a witness may add cogency to his or her testimony by outlining circumstances which show that he or she had a good opportunity of assessing the character of the accused, the evidence given must be of general reputation of good

---

[6]   *Per* Widgery CJ in *R. v Bellis* [1966] 1 WLR 234 at 236, [1966] 1 All ER 552n at 552: "possession of a good character is primarily a matter which goes to credibility". See also *R. v Boles* (1978) 43 CCC (2d) 414; *R. v Elmosri* (1984) 2 OAC 177, (1985) 23 CCC (3d) 503; *R. v Clarke* (1998) 18 CR (5th) 219.
[7]   *R. v Stannard* (1837) 7 C & P 673; *R. v Rowton* (1865) 10 Cox CC 25, [1861–73] All ER 549; *Salutin v R.* (1979) 11 CR (3d) 284; *R. v Boles* (1978) 43 CCC (2d) 414; *R. v Elmosri* (1984) 2 OAC 177, (1985) 23 CCC (3d) 503; *R. v Flis* (2006) 205 CCC (3d) 384.
[8]   (1837) 7 C & P 673.
[9]   (1837) 7 C & P 673 at 674.
[10] *Per* Cockburn CJ in *R. v Rowton* (1865) 10 Cox CC 25 at 30, [1861–73] All ER 549 at 552.
[11] (1865) 10 Cox CC 25, [1861–73] All ER 549.
[12] (1865) 10 Cox CC 25 at 29, [1861–73] All ER 549 at 551.
[13] [2008] 1 IR 1 at 9–10.
[14] *R. v Demyen (No.2)* (1976) 31 CCC (2d) 383, [1976] 5 WWR 324.
[15] See *R. v Redgrave* (1982) 74 Cr App R 10.

character and not an individual opinion on the part of the witness.[16] It follows logically that, in order to give evidence of good character, the witness must have some knowledge of the accused's standing in the community.[17]

9–07 It should be noted that there is authority that the limitation to evidence of general reputation does not apply to evidence of character given by the accused himself or herself.[18] This is because it is considered to be impossible for an accused to give evidence as to his or her own reputation, as he or she cannot reliably know what other persons in the community think of him or her when he or she is not present. Therefore, where an accused testifies as to his or her own good character, this will generally take the form of disposition evidence and he or she may give evidence of specific acts or instances tending to show that he or she has a good character.[19] However, a major disincentive to the accused giving any evidence of good character is that, by doing so, he or she will lose the protective shield afforded to him or her by s.1(f) of the Criminal Justice (Evidence) Act 1924 leaving himself or herself open to cross-examination as to his or her previous convictions and general bad character.[20]

3. Direction in Relation to Evidence of Good Character

9–08 There is a strong line of authority in the UK[21] and other Commonwealth jurisdictions[22] that, where evidence of the good character of the accused is adduced by the defence, the trial judge is required to give the jury a direction as to the use that can be made and the weight to be attached to this evidence. In *R. v Vye*,[23] it was held that two directions, generally referred to as the credibility and propensity directions,[24] are required to be given whenever evidence of good character of the accused is adduced:

> "(1) A direction as to the relevance of his good character to a defendant's credibility is to be given where he has testified or made pre-trial answers or statements. (2) A direction as to the relevance of his good character to the likelihood of his having committed the offence charged is to be given, whether or not he has testified, or made pre-trial answers or statements."[25]

---

[16] *R. v Rowton* (1865) 10 Cox CC 25 at 30, [1861–73] All ER 549 at 552 (*per* Cockburn CJ).

[17] *R. v Rowton* (1865) 10 Cox CC 25 at 30, [1861–73] All ER 549 at 552; *R. v Close* (1982) 68 CCC (2d) 105, (1982) 38 OR (2d) 453, (1982) 137 DLR (3d) 655 at 664. *Cf. R. v Demyen* [1976] 5 WWR 324, (1976) 31 CCC (2d) 383 and *R. v Grosse* (1983) 61 NSR (2d) 54, 9 CCC (3d) 465.

[18] *R. v Dunkley* (1926) 28 Cox CC 143 at 147–148, [1927] 1 KB 323, [1926] All ER 187; *R. v Close* (1982) 68 CCC (2d) 105, (1982) 38 OR (2d) 453, (1982) 137 DLR (3d) 655 at 663. See further, Munday, "What Constitutes A Good Character?" [1997] Crim LR 247 at 248.

[19] See, for example, *R v Samuel* (1956) 40 Cr App R 8; *R. v McNamara (No.1)* (1981) 56 CCC 193 at 348. See, *contra*, *R v Redgrave* (1982) 74 Cr App R 10 at 15.

[20] See section E below.

[21] See *R. v Vye* [1993] 1 WLR 471, [1993] 3 All ER 241; *R v Zoppola-Barrozza* [1994] CLR 833; *R v Durbin* [1995] 2 Cr App R 84; *R. v Aziz* [1996] AC 41 at 51, [1995] 3 All ER 149 at 156; *R v Martin* [2000] 2 Cr App R 42; *Teeluck v State of Trinidad and Tobago* [2005] 1 WLR 2421; *Gilbert v R* [2006] 1 WLR 2108; *R v D(P)* [2012] EWCA Crim 19, [2012] 1 Cr App R 33. See further Munday, "Directing Juries on the Defendant's Good Character" [1991] JCL 521.

[22] See *R. v Elmosri* (1984) 2 OAC 177, (1985) 23 CCC (3d) 503. In Australia, the giving of a direction as to good character is not mandatory (*R v Schmahl* [1965] VR 745 at 750; *Simic v R* (1980) 144 CLR 319 at 333; *R v Trimboli* (1979) SASR 577) but is considered desirable (*R v Trimboli* (1979) SASR 577) and should be given whenever it is asked for (*R v Thompson* [1966] QWN 47; *R v Williams* (1981) A Crim R 441; *R v Murphy* (1985) 4 NSWLR 42).

[23] [1993] 1 WLR 471, [1993] 3 All ER 241.

[24] *R. v Aziz* [1996] AC 41 at 47, [1995] 3 All ER 149 at 153.

[25] [1993] 1 WLR 471 at 479, [1993] 3 All ER 241 at 248. It was also held in *Vye* that an accused is

9–09   The decision in *Vye* was subsequently endorsed by the House of Lords in *R. v Aziz*[26] but a gloss was added that a trial judge is not required to give directions as to the good character of the accused where the claim to good character is spurious. This will obviously be the case where an accused has previous criminal convictions, but there are many other situations where a trial judge could take the view that an accused is not entitled to good character directions, as where he or she, though without previous convictions, has been shown to have been guilty of serious criminal behaviour similar to that charged against him or her. It was, therefore, held that a trial judge has a residual discretion to refuse to give character directions in respect of an accused without previous convictions if he or she considers it an insult to common sense to do so.[27] However, it was emphasised that this discretion is limited because, *prima facie*, the directions must be given and a trial judge would often be able to place a fair and balanced picture of the character of the accused before the jury by giving the credibility and propensity directions and then adding words of qualification concerning other proved or possible criminal conduct of the accused which emerged during the trial.[28] A helpful summary of the principles to be applied in deciding whether a direction should be given is to be found in the judgment of the Court of Appeal in *R v Gray*[29]:

> "(1) The primary rule is that a person of previous good character must be given a full direction covering both credibility and propensity. Where there are no further facts to complicate the position, such a direction is mandatory and should be unqualified (*Vye, Aziz*).
>
> (2) If a defendant has a previous conviction which, either because of its age or its nature, may entitle him to be treated as of effective good character, the trial judge has a discretion so to treat him, and if he does so the defendant is entitled to a *Vye* direction (passim); but
>
> (3) Where the previous conviction can only be regarded as irrelevant or of no significance in relation to the offence charged, that discretion ought to be exercised in favour of treating the defendant as of good character (*H, Durbin*, and, to the extent that it cited *H* with apparent approval, *Aziz*.) In such a case the defendant is again entitled to a *Vye* direction. It would seem to be consistent with principle (4) below that, where there is room for uncertainty as to how a defendant of effective good character should be treated, a judge would be entitled to give an appropriately modified *Vye* direction.
>
> (4) Where a defendant of previous good character, whether absolute or, we would suggest, effective, has been shown at trial, whether by admission or otherwise, to be guilty of criminal conduct, the *prima facie* rule of practice is to deal with this by qualifying a *Vye* direction rather than by withholding it *(Vye, Durbin, Aziz)*; but
>
> (5) In such a case, there remains a narrowly circumscribed residual discretion to withhold a good character direction in whole, or presumably in part, where it would make no sense, or would be meaningless or absurd or an insult to common sense, to do otherwise (*Zoppola-Barrazza* and *dicta* in *Durbin* and *Aziz*).
>
> (6) Approved examples of the exercise of such a residual discretion are not common. *Zoppola-Barrazza* is one. *Shaw* is another. Lord Steyn in *Aziz* appears to have considered that a person of previous good character who is shown beyond doubt to have been guilty of serious criminal behaviour similar to the offence charged would forfeit his right to any direction (at 53B). On the other hand Lord Taylor's manslaughter/murder example in *Vye* (which was cited again in *Durbin*) shows that even in the context of serious crime it may be crucial that a critical intent separates the admitted criminality from that charged.
>
> (7) A direction should never be misleading. Where therefore a defendant has withheld

---

entitled to good character directions even where he or she is tried with an accused of bad character who is not entitled to such directions.

[26]   [1996] AC 41, [1995] 3 All ER 149.

[27]   Lord Steyn took the view ([1996] AC 41 at 53, [1995] 3 All ER 149 at 158) that "a sensible criminal justice system should not compel a judge to go through the charade of giving directions in accordance with *R. v Vye* in a case where the defendant's claim to good character is spurious".

[28]   See also *R. v Durbin* [1995] 2 Cr App R 84 and *R. v Zoppola-Barranza* [1994] Crim LR 833.

[29]   [2004] EWCA Crim 1074, [2004] 2 Cr App R 30 at [57].

something of his record so that otherwise a trial judge is not in a position to refer to it, the defendant may forfeit the more ample, if qualified, direction which the judge might have been able to give (*Martin*)."

9–10　Subsequent cases have reiterated that it is important that a clear and positive direction is given that not only are the jury entitled to take the good character of the accused into account in assessing his or her credibility but also in determining whether the propensity of the accused to have committed the offences alleged.[30]

9–11　In Canada, the courts have adopted a similar approach and a failure on the part of the trial judge to direct the jury that good character evidence is relevant to the issue of guilt or innocence amounts to a misdirection[31] if that character evidence is relevant to the particular charge.[32]

9–12　There is little Irish authority on the point but the issue was briefly considered in *People (DPP) v McGovern*[33] where the trial judge had charged the jury in relation to the good character of the accused as follows:

"Now, you have had evidence in the case that the accused has no previous convictions. That means he is a person of good character, and you are entitled to take that into account in assessing him and assessing his evidence. You are entitled to take into account that he has been of good character in his life so far and to the present point of time, and take that into account in deciding what reliance to place on his evidence. He is of good character; that has been established in evidence."

9–13　The Court of Criminal Appeal rejected the contention that this charge was inadequate and considered that no further elaboration was required in the interests of justice.

C. Evidence of Bad Character of the Accused

1. Introduction

9–14　As a general rule, evidence of the bad character of an accused is inadmissible and the prosecution cannot adduce such evidence as a part of its case[34] or seek to elicit

---

[30]　See *R v Moustakim* [2008] EWCA Crim 3096; *R v D* [2012] EWCA Crim 19, [2012] 1 Cr App R 33; *R v M* [2009] 2 Cr App R 3, [2009] EWCA Crim 158. A more elaborate direction as to the relevance of good character to propensity may be required where the accused is tried for charges of historic sex abuse: *R v GJB* [2011] EWCA Crim 867.

[31]　*R. v Elmosri* (1984) 2 OAC 177, (1985) 23 CCC (3d) 503; *R. v Boles* (1978) 43 CCC (2d) 414, *R v Savion* (1980) 52 CCC (2d) 276; *R. v Logiacco* (1984) 11 CCC (3d) 374; *R. v Clarke* (1998) 18 C.R. (5th) 219.

[32]　See *R v S (RJ)* (1985) 19 CCC (3d) 115 (failure to give such an instruction did not amount to a misdirection in circumstances where the accused was charged with sexual offences and evidence was adduced that the accused had a reputation for honesty).

[33]　[2010] IECCA 79 at [10].

[34]　*DPP v Keogh* [1998] 1 ILRM 72 at 78; *King v Attorney General* [1981] IR 233 at 241–242; *Minister for Justice and Equality v Buckley* [2014] IEHC 321 at [45]; *R. v Rowton* (1865) 10 Cox CC 25, [1861–73] All ER 549; *R. v Butterwasser* [1948] 1 KB 4 at 6, [1947] 2 All ER 415 at 416; *R. v Harris* [1951] 1 KB 107 at 113, [1950] 2 All ER 816 at 818.

it by cross-examination of the accused or witnesses called on his or her behalf.[35] In *R. v Rowton*[36] Cockburn CJ explained that:

> "Although, logically speaking, it is quite clear that an antecedent bad character would form quite as reasonable a ground for the presumption and the probability of guilt as previous good character lays the foundation of innocence, yet you cannot, on the part of the prosecution, go into the evidence as to bad character."[37]

9–15 In *People (DPP) v Murphy*,[38] the Court of Criminal Appeal approved the following synopsis of the exclusionary rule in respect of evidence of bad character set out in *Halsbury*[39]:

> "As a general rule the jury should not be permitted to know of an accused's bad character. Thus the prosecution is debarred from tendering evidence to show that the accused is of bad character, or is guilty of criminal acts of the same nature as the offence charged, merely for the purpose of leading to the conclusion that the accused is a person likely from his criminal conduct or character to have committed the offence for which he is being tried."[40]

9–16 This exclusionary rule is subject to four exceptions.[41] The first is where the bad character of the accused is actually in issue in the case because it forms an ingredient of an offence or necessary proof in a case. The second is where the defence puts the character of the accused in issue by calling or eliciting evidence of his or her good character. Thirdly, evidence of acts of misconduct by an accused on occasions other than those the subject of the charges may be admitted in accordance with the principles outlined below. Fourthly, evidence of bad character may be admissible in certain circumstances under the provisions of s.1 of the Criminal Justice (Evidence) Act 1924 where an accused testifies in his or her own defence. The first two of these exceptions are dealt with in this section and the later two will be dealt with in succeeding sections.

2. Basis of the Exclusionary Rule

9–17 The exclusionary rule in respect of evidence of the bad character of an accused is predicated on its potential prejudicial effect on the tribunal of fact and, hence, on the fair trial of the accused.[42] This potential prejudice arises in a number of ways and its precise nature depends on the type of bad character evidence sought to be admitted. One danger is that, if the tribunal of fact is exposed to evidence of the bad character or previous convictions of an accused, it may convict the accused because of that

---

[35] *People (DPP) v D O'S* [2006] IESC 12 at [10], [2006] 3 IR 57 at 61, [2006] 2 ILRM 61 at 66. *R. v A (WA)* [1996] Man R (2d) 151, (1997) 112 CCC (3d) 83.

[36] (1865) 10 Cox CC 25, [1861–73] All ER 549.

[37] (1865) 10 Cox CC 25 at 30, [1861–73] All ER 549 at 552.

[38] [2005] IECCA 1 at [61], [2005] 2 IR 125 at 147.

[39] *Halsbury's Laws of England* (4th edn, 1990), vol.11(2), para.1074.

[40] This exclusionary rule was abolished in England and Wales by s.99 of the Criminal Justice Act 2003, Part 11 of which now governs the admission of evidence of bad character and provides for a liberal regime for adducing such evidence. See generally, Spencer, *Evidence of Bad Character* 2nd edn (Hart Publishing, 2009) and Redmayne, "The Ethics of Character Evidence" (2008) 61 Current Legal Problems 371.

[41] In *People (DPP) v McNeill* [2011] IESC 12 at [148], [2011] 2 IR 669 at 719, O'Donnell J expressed doubt as to whether there was, in fact, such a general exclusionary rule on the basis that the "exceptions are so numerous and wide-ranging as to raise doubts as to the existence of any general principle".

[42] *King v AG* [1981] IR 233 at 241; *People (AG) v Kirwan* [1943] IR 279 at 296; *Maxwell v DPP* [1935] AC 309 at 323, [1934] All ER 168 at 172; *DPP v Boardman* [1975] AC 421 at 451, [1974] 3 All ER 887 at 903; *DPP v Kilbourne* [1973] AC 729 at 756, [1973] 1 All ER 440 at 461.

evidence and not solely on the basis of the evidence adduced in the case before it.[43] Alternatively, the tribunal of fact may, consciously or unconsciously, discharge its duties less conscientiously because it believes that the consequences of a mistaken conviction are less serious because the accused is a person who "deserves" to be punished.

9–18   It is evident from the foregoing that the admission of evidence of bad character poses a serious threat to the fairness of a criminal trial. In particular, the admission of such evidence imperils the presumption of innocence[44] and the principle that an accused stands to be tried and convicted only in respect of the charges brought against him or her.[45] A strong argument can, therefore, be made that the exclusionary rule in respect of this evidence is underpinned by and, indeed, required by Art.38.1 and the guarantee of a trial in due course of law. This seems to have been the view of McWilliam J in *King v Attorney General*[46] who said:

> "One of the concepts of justice which the Courts have always accepted is that evidence of character or of previous convictions shall not be given at a criminal trial except at the instigation of the accused, as that could prejudice the fair trial of the issue of the guilt or innocence of the accused".[47]

9–19   This passage was quoted with approval in *DPP v Keogh*[48] where Kelly J, having referred to "the deep seated objection at common law to evidence of this type being adduced", expressed the view that "the adducing of such evidence would run counter to the basic concept of justice inherent in our legal system".[49]

3. Application of the Exclusionary Rule

9–20   Evidence that the accused has been convicted of criminal offences[50] or has served time in prison[51] or has a history of violence[52] clearly constitutes evidence of bad character so as to trigger the application of the exclusionary rule. Also excluded will be evidence of conduct that would be regarded as discreditable by a jury. In *People (DPP) v McGrath*,[53] it was held that evidence that the appellant, who had been convicted of the murder of her husband, had engaged in sexual liaisons with a number

---

43   There is some empirical research to suggest that a significant risk arises in this regard as discussed in Lloyd-Bostock, "The Effects on Juries of Hearing about the Defendant's Previous Criminal Record: A Simulation Study" [2000] Crim LR 734.

44   The linkage between the exclusionary rule and the presumption of innocence was made by McWilliam J in *King v Attorney General* [1981] IR 233 at 242, who referred with approval to the statement of O'Dálaigh CJ in *People (AG) v O'Callaghan* [1966] IR 501 at 509, that: "The Courts owe more than verbal respect to the principle that punishment begins after conviction, and that every man is deemed to be innocent until tried and duly found guilty." See also *People (DPP) v Murphy* [2005] IECCA 1 at [73], [2005] 2 IR 125 at 150 where Kearns J referred to the "significant erosion of the presumption of innocence" that could result from exposing the tribunal of fact to inadmissible evidence of bad character.

45   See *People (AG) v Kirwan* [1943] IR 279 at 296. *Cf.* ss.7, 9, 11(a) and (h) of the Canadian Charter of Fundamental Rights and Freedoms where this principle is enshrined.

46   [1981] IR 233.

47   [1981] IR 233 at 241–242.

48   [1998] 1 ILRM 72.

49   [1998] 1 ILRM 72 at 79. *Cf. DPP (Stratford) v O'Neill* [1998] 1 ILRM 221.

50   *People (DPP) v Murphy* [2005] IECCA 1 at [73], [2005] 2 IR 125 at 150.

51   See *People (DPP) v Reddan* [1995] 3 IR 560; *People (DPP) v Kelly* [2006] IECCA 2, [2006] 4 IR 273.

52   *People (DPP) v Doyle*, unreported, Court of Criminal Appeal, 22 March 2002.

53   [2013] IECCA 12.

of local men and had crushed up tablets which she gave to the deceased before dressing him in black tights and a skirt and calling the doctor to tell him that the deceased had gone mad should not have been admitted. This evidence, which was adduced by a co-accused, was evidence that tended to "blacken" the appellant's character and was clearly prejudicial.

9–21 In some cases, the question of whether particular evidence falls foul of the exclusionary rule will depend on the particular circumstances and the issues that arise. For example, in *People (AG) v Quinn*,[54] it was held that the suggestion that the accused was "generally known as a pretty tough man" was bad character evidence and inadmissible in circumstances where the accused had pleaded self-defence:

> "In a case such as this where the State case was that the accused unnecessarily hit another and a lighter man it would be very damaging to convey to the jury the impression that the accused had a reputation of being a truculent or aggressive person."[55]

9–22 Evidence will not necessarily be categorised as evidence of bad character simply because it portrays the accused in an unfavourable light. In *Attorney General v O'Leary*,[56] a distinction was drawn between evidence referring to the moral character, general reputation and disposition of the accused on the one hand, and evidence of the demeanour of the accused on the other. Only the former was to be regarded as evidence of bad character.

9–23 It should be noted that evidence of bad character is not limited to oral evidence given by a witness on oath. It was held in *People (AG) v Coleman*[57] that a document, which was an attempt to procure subornation of witnesses, was clearly evidence of bad character.

4. Inadvertent Disclosure of Evidence of Bad Character

9–24 The application of the exclusionary rule often arises for consideration in circumstances where evidence of the bad character of an accused is disclosed by inadvertence or unexpectedly in the course of a trial. The course to be taken where this occurs depends on the nature of the evidence disclosed and the degree of prejudice that may have been caused. In some instances, the view may be taken by the trial judge that any possible prejudice can be cured by appropriate directions to the jury[58] or, alternatively, that the accused would be best served if the matter was not mentioned and, thus, highlighted again.[59] In other cases, where there is a serious risk of an unfair trial because of the prejudice that has been caused, then the appropriate course of action is to discharge the jury.[60] However, the discharge of a jury has been variously

---

[54] [1965] IR 366.

[55] [1965] IR 366 at 383.

[56] [1926] IR 445.

[57] [1945] IR 237.

[58] See *People (DPP) v Doyle*, unreported, Court of Criminal Appeal, 22 March 2002 (evidence of previous acts of violence by the accused); *People (DPP) v Kavanagh*, unreported, Court of Criminal Appeal, *ex tempore*, 7 July 1997 (evidence of misconduct on other occasions).

[59] See *People (DPP) v Smith*, unreported, Court of Criminal Appeal, 16 November 1998; *People (DPP) v Kavanagh*, unreported, Court of Criminal Appeal, *ex tempore*, 7 July 1997; *People (DPP) v Kelly* [2006] IECCA 2 at [40], [2006] 4 IR 273 at 286.

[60] See *People (DPP) v Marley* [1985] ILRM 17 (evidence disclosed that the accused had previously been acquitted of murder); *People (DPP) v McGartland*, Court of Criminal Appeal, 20 January 2003 (evidence that the accused was known to gardaí).

characterised as "a very extreme remedy",[61] "an extreme step, to be taken only in exceptional circumstances"[62] and "a remedy of the very last resort".[63] A trial judge is afforded a broad discretion to deal with the inadvertent disclosure of evidence of bad character as he or she sees fit and, in general, an appellate court will be reluctant to interfere with the course adopted by him or her.[64]

9–25   The foregoing principles are applied differently in the case of a trial without a jury. It is assumed that judges, by their training and experience, are better able to exclude inadmissible prejudicial evidence from their minds in adjudicating upon the guilt of an accused and, thus, a judge may continue to hear a case even after being exposed to evidence of bad character that would have led to the discharge of a jury.[65]

5. Character of the Accused in Issue

9–26   The bad character of an accused will be admissible where it is directly in issue.[66] This will be the case at the sentencing stage when evidence may be given in relation to the previous convictions of an accused.[67] The convictions or some other aspect of the bad character of an accused may also be made an ingredient of an offence although it is clear from the decision in *King v Attorney General*[68] that to do so will give rise to significant constitutional difficulties.

6. Character of Accused Put in Issue by Defence

9–27   It would be inimical to the adjudicative function of the tribunal of fact if an accused could adduce evidence of good character and then shelter behind the exclusionary rule in relation to bad character to leave the tribunal of fact with a misleading impression as to his or her true character. As Cockburn CJ explained in *R. v Rowton*[69]:

---

[61]   *People (DPP) v Brophy* [1992] ILRM 709 at 716 (*per* O'Flaherty J).

[62]   *People (DPP) v O'Sullivan* [2013] IECCA 18 at [88] (*per* Fennelly J).

[63]   *Dawson v Irish Brokers' Association* [1998] IESC 39 at 6 (*per* O'Flaherty J). The passage from which this quote was taken was approved in the criminal context in *People (DPP) v Cleary* [2009] IECCA 142 at [8].

[64]   *People (DPP) v McGartland*, Court of Criminal Appeal, 20 January 2003 at 7; *R. v Docherty* [1999] 1 Cr App R 275 at 279. For examples of where convictions were quashed because of the inadvertent or unexpected disclosure of evidence of bad character, see *People (AG) v Goulding* (1964) Ir Jur Rep 54, *People (DPP) v Marley* [1985] ILRM 17 and *People (DPP) v McGartland*, Court of Criminal Appeal, 20 January 2003.

[65]   See, for example, *People (DPP) v McMahon* [1984] ILRM 461.

[66]   *Cf. Criminal Assets Bureau v PS* [2004] IEHC 351 at [25].

[67]   Section 18 of the Prevention of Crimes Act 1871 provides that: "A previous conviction may be proved in any legal proceeding whatever against any person by producing a record or extract of such conviction and by giving proof of the identity of the person against whom the conviction is sought to be proved with the person appearing in the record or extract of conviction to have been convicted." In practice, formal proof of convictions is generally not required and it suffices if a garda reads a printout of an accused's convictions. However, if an accused objects to this informal manner of proof, then formal evidence of the convictions must be adduced, generally by giving evidence of the relevant court orders: *State (Stanbridge) v Mahon* [1979] IR 214; *R. v Turner* (1924) 18 Cr App R 161 at 162.

[68]   [1981] IR 233. See also *DPP v Keogh* [1998] 1 ILRM 72 and *DPP (Stratford) v O'Neill* [1998] 1 ILRM 221.

[69]   (1865) 10 Cox CC 25, [1861–73] All ER 549.

"It has been put, that evidence in favour of the character of a person on his trial raises a collateral issue. I can hardly think that it is a collateral issue in the ordinary sense of the term; it is one of the pivots on which the jury are to find their verdict and take into their consideration with the evidence; and if the prisoner thinks proper to raise that issue as one of the elements for the consideration of the jury, nothing can be more unfair and unjust, and fatal to the proper administration of justice, than that the evidence should go to the jury altogether one-sided in its nature, and that the prisoner should have, on the consideration of his guilt or innocence, the advantage of an assumed unblemished character, when in point of fact, if his true character were known, it would be found to be just the reverse; and therefore that is a ground and a reasonable ground for not excluding it."[70]

9–28   Therefore, if the accused puts his or her character in issue by adducing or attempting to elicit from witnesses evidence of his or her good character, the prosecution is permitted to call evidence in rebuttal in order to show that he or she is a person of bad character.[71]

9–29   It should be noted that this exception only applies if an accused puts his or her character in issue as opposed to that of any other person involved in the proceedings. In *R. v Butterwasser*[72] the proposition that evidence of the bad character of an accused was admissible in rebuttal where an accused attacked the credibility of witnesses for the prosecution was rejected. Lord Goddard CJ pointed out that, by attacking the witnesses for the prosecution and suggesting they were unreliable, the accused was "not putting his character in issue", he was "putting their character in issue".[73] However, it should be noted that, if the accused decides to give evidence in his or her own defence, he or she may thereby open the door to cross-examination as to his or her character pursuant to s.1 of the Criminal Justice (Evidence) Act 1924.

(a) When rebutting evidence is admissible

9–30   Evidence of bad character in rebuttal is only admissible where an accused has called or elicited evidence of his or her good character. The question as to whether this threshold requirement is met is quite contextual and depends on a number of factors including the contents of the evidence given, the offences charged, the nature of the defence put forward by the accused and the likely impact of the evidence on the jury. So, for example, in *R. v de Vere*,[74] statements by an accused, who was charged with obtaining property by deception, that he was a man of substance and good repute was held to be evidence of good character. This opened the door to the introduction of rebutting evidence to the effect that he was not, in fact, a man of substantial means and had a number of previous convictions for fraud.[75]

---

[70]   (1865) 10 Cox CC 25 at 28–29, [1861–73] All ER 549 at 551.
[71]   *R. v Butterwasser* [1948] 1 KB 4 at 6, [1947] 2 All ER 415 at 416. There is authority in Canada to the effect that evidence of bad character may also be adduced where the credibility of the accused is crucial on the facts: *R. v Chambers* [1990] 2 SCR 1293, (1989) 47 CCC (3d) 503.
[72]   [1948] 1 KB 4, [1947] 2 All ER 415.
[73]   [1948] 1 KB 4 at 7, [1947] 2 All ER 415 at 416.
[74]   [1982] QB 75, [1981] 3 All ER 473.
[75]   See also *R. v Solomon* (1909) 2 Cr App R 80 (evidence as to the recent employment of the accused and its duration was not evidence of good character but a statement made by the accused to a police officer on arrest to the effect that he was a respectable man was).

(b) Type of rebutting evidence that is admissible

9–31   In *R. v Rowton*,[76] it was held that the same principles apply to the admission of evidence of bad character in rebuttal as to evidence of good character adduced on behalf of the accused:

> "...within what limits must the rebutting evidence be confined which is adduced to meet that evidence which the prisoner has brought forward? Now, I think that evidence must be of the same character and kept within the same limits; that while you can give evidence of general good character, so the evidence called to rebut it must be evidence of the same general description showing that the evidence which has been given to establish a good reputation on the one hand is not true because the man's reputation is bad."[77]

9–32   This approach was approved in this jurisdiction in *People (DPP) v Ferris*.[78] Thus, evidence of bad character in rebuttal is confined to evidence of general reputation (including evidence of previous convictions) and evidence cannot be given of particular acts or of the disposition of an accused to commit the offence charged. However, it should be noted that this limitation to evidence of general reputation does not apply where an accused gives evidence and is cross-examined as to his or her bad character pursuant to s.1 of the Criminal Justice (Evidence) Act 1924.[79]

9–33   The common law view was that the character of an accused is "indivisible"[80] and that an accused who puts his or her character in issue thereby exposes himself or herself to any evidence that tends to disprove the claim of good character.[81] In *R. v Winfield*,[82] Humphreys J declared that "there is no such thing known to our procedure as putting half a prisoner's character in issue and leaving out the other half". Thus, where the door is opened to the admission of evidence of bad character, such evidence is not restricted by any test of relevance to the charges at hand. So, for example, on the trial of a sexual offence, evidence may be led or elicited of previous convictions for offences involving dishonesty.[83]

(c) Purpose for which rebutting evidence of bad character may be used

9–34   Although evidence of good character may be introduced so as to suggest that the character of the accused is such that it is unlikely that he or she committed the offence charged,[84] evidence of bad character admitted in rebuttal may only be adduced in order to show that the accused is a person whose evidence might not be worthy of credit.[85] Given the obvious danger that a jury might not use the evidence solely for

---

[76]   (1865) 10 Cox CC 25, [1861–73] All ER 549.
[77]   (1865) 10 Cox CC 25 at 30–31, [1861–73] All ER 549 at 552. See also *R. v Butterwasser* [1948] 1 KB 4 at 6, [1947] 2 All ER 415 at 416, where Lord Goddard CJ referred with approval to the decision in *Rowton* and stated that evidence of bad character in rebuttal "must be evidence of general reputation and not dependent upon particular acts or actions".
[78]   [2008] 1 IR 1 at 9–10.
[79]   See *R. v Dunkley* (1926) 28 Cox CC 143, [1927] 1 KB 323, [1926] All ER 187; *R. v Close* (1982) 68 CCC (2d) 105, (1982) 38 OR (2d) 453, (1982) 137 DLR (3d) 655 at 663; *R. v McNamara (No.1)* (1981) 56 CCC (2d) 193 at 348.
[80]   *R. v Samuel* (1956) 40 Cr App R 8 at 11 (*per* Goddard LCJ).
[81]   *Stirland v DPP* [1944] AC 315 at 326–327, [1944] 2 All ER 13 at 18.
[82]   (1939) 27 Cr App R 139 at 141.
[83]   *R. v Winfield* (1939) 27 Cr App R 139 at 141. As to the position now in the UK under s.105 of the Criminal Justice Act 2006, see *R. v Renda* [2005] EWCA Crim 2826, [2006] 1 WLR 2498.
[84]   *R. v Stannard* (1837) 7 C & P 673 at 674–675.
[85]   *R. v Bond* [1966] IR 214 at 223; *People (DPP) v Ferris* [2008] 1 IR 1 at 10. *Cf. R. v Morin* [1988]

this limited purpose, a trial judge is under an obligation to explain to the jury that the evidence of bad character only goes to the credit of the accused and does not constitute evidence that he or she committed the offence charged.[86]

D. Misconduct Evidence

1. Introduction

9–35 As noted above, one of the exceptions to the general exclusionary rule in respect of evidence of bad character is that evidence of acts of misconduct by an accused on occasions other than those charged may be admitted in criminal proceedings[87] where the evidence is sufficiently relevant to an issue in the proceedings and the probative value of such evidence outweighs its prejudicial effect. The evidence admissible under this exception is often referred to as "similar fact evidence"[88] but this label is misleading because, as will be seen below, similarity is not necessarily the touchstone of admissibility.[89] Therefore, in the discussion which follows, it is proposed to use the shorthand term "misconduct evidence"[90] to describe the generic category of evidence which discloses acts of misconduct by an accused on occasions other than those charged.

2. Policy Basis for the Admission of Misconduct Evidence

9–36 The general prohibition against the admission of misconduct evidence is sometimes justified on the basis that "such evidence is simply irrelevant, because no number of similar offences in themselves can connect a person with a particular crime."[91] However, as will be seen below, misconduct evidence will sometimes be relevant, indeed highly relevant, to the issues in a case. The exclusion of such evidence

---

2 SCR 345 at 370.

[86] *R. v Bond* [1966] IR 214 at 223; *People (DPP) v Ferris* [2008] 1 IR 1 at 10; *Minister for Justice and Equality v Buckley* [2014] IEHC 321 at [45].

[87] The admission of such evidence in civil cases is generally determined on the basis of relevance but, in the case of trials before juries, may be excluded where its probative force is outweighed by its prejudicial effect: *Smyth v Tunney*, Supreme Court, 26 June 1992; *Sheehan v McMahon*, Supreme Court, 29 July 1993; *Hill v Cork Examiner* [2001] 4 IR 219; *Von Gordon v Helaba Dublin Landes Bank Hessen-Thuringen,* Supreme Court, 17 December 2003; *Condron v ACC Bank plc* [2012] IEHC 395 at [6], [2013] 1 ILRM 113 at 116; *Mood Music Publishing Co Ltd v De Wolfe Ltd* [1976] Ch 119; *O'Brien v Chief Constable of South Wales Police* [2005] UKHL 26, [2005] 2 AC 534; *Desmond v Bower* [2009] EWCA Civ 667, [2010] EMLR 5. See, further, Hutchinson, "Character Evidence in civil cases – Part 1" (2007) 25(1) ILT 10, Hutchinson, "Character Evidence in civil cases – Part 2" (2007) 25(2) ILT 27 and Munday, "Case Management, similar fact evidence in civil cases and a divided law of evidence" (2006) 10 E & P 81.

[88] But see *People (DPP) v BK* [2000] 2 IR 199 at 203, where the Court of Criminal Appeal altered the traditional terminology, applying the term "system evidence" to describe misconduct evidence which is admissible and the term, "similar fact evidence" to that which is not.

[89] See, for example, *R. v Straffen* [1952] 2 QB 911, [1952] 2 All ER 657 and *R. v Morris* [1983] 2 SCR 190, (1983) 7 CCC (3d) 97.

[90] This term was used by Denham J in the leading Supreme Court decision of *People (DPP) v McNeill* [2011] IESC 12, [2011] 2 IR 669.

[91] *B v DPP* [1997] 3 IR 140 at 152 (*per* Budd J). See also *Attorney General v Stevens* (1934) 1 Frewen 12 at 13; *People (AG) v Havlin* (1952) 1 Frewen 132 at 134; *R. v Miller* [1952] 2 All ER 667 at 668. See also *People (DPP) v Hayes* [2011] IECCA 65 at 7, where it was stated that propensity is generally not relevant in the course of a trial.

is, therefore, better explained by the threat which its admission poses to the fairness of the trial process.[92]

9-37 One of the principal dangers where the tribunal of fact is exposed to evidence of acts of misconduct by an accused is that it may proceed to convict the accused on the basis that he or she is a person of bad character who has a propensity to commit offences rather than on the basis of his or her guilt of the charges before it.[93] As explained by O'Donnell J in *People (DPP) v McNeill*[94]:

> "[T]his fundamental rule is not founded on logic but rather on policy. The forbidden reasoning is not something which a logician or a behavioural psychologist would necessarily reject. A police investigation which did not consider the criminal propensity of suspects would be rightly criticised. A school that employed a convicted, or indeed an alleged, child abuser would be regarded as culpably negligent. The reasoning is excluded therefore not because it does not have some value but rather because it is toxic to the forensic process of a fair trial. Evidence of propensity to commit an offence by reference, for example, to previous convictions for the same offence, infects and corrupts the careful process of the sifting of evidence by reference to the standard of proof required in criminal cases. In some cases it will overwhelm that process. It is evidence, or perhaps more correctly, reasoning which in every sense of the word is prejudicial. It deflects the jury from the task of considering the evidence to allow it to determine whether it is satisfied beyond a reasonable doubt that the accused did the act alleged and encourages it to conclude instead that he must have done it because he was proved to have done something wrong on another occasion."

9-38 Thus, the tribunal of fact may attribute a predictive quality to misconduct evidence and reason that, because the accused offended before, he or she is likely to have done on the occasion charged.

9-39 An allied concern is that the tribunal of fact, particularly a jury, will not properly consider or evaluate such evidence, giving it undeserved weight. In particular, where the allegation of misconduct relates to another complainant and is admitted on the basis that it would be an implausible coincidence if multiple groundless accusations were made against the accused, there is a risk the tribunal of fact may overestimate the likelihood of a coincidence.[95]

9-40 There is also a risk that the tribunal of fact may, consciously or unconsciously, discharge its duties less conscientiously, taking comfort from the fact that a court has previously found the accused to be guilty[96] or because it considers the consequences of a mistaken conviction are less serious because the accused is guilty of other acts of misconduct in any event. A related danger is that there may be a temptation for the tribunal of fact to punish the accused for the other acts of misconduct if they have previously gone unpunished. Alternatively, the jury may reason that, given his or her

---

[92] *King v AG* [1981] IR 233 at 241; *People (AG) v Kirwan* [1943] IR 279 at 296; *People (DPP) v McNeill* [2011] IESC 12 at [92]–[93], [2011] 2 IR 669 at 703; *Maxwell v DPP* [1935] AC 309 at 323, [1934] All ER 168 at 172; *DPP v Boardman* [1975] AC 421 at 451, [1974] 3 All ER 887 at 903; *DPP v Kilbourne* [1973] AC 729 at 756, [1973] 1 All ER 440 at 461. See further, Nair, "Prejudice and Irrelevance Revisited" [1993] Crim LR 432, Maher, "Developments in Bad Character Evidence: Undermining the Accused's Shield" (2007) 1 DULJ 57 and Kennedy, "Reform of the Exclusionary Rule in Relation to Evidence of Bad Character and Misconduct Evidence" (2014) 13 Hibernian LJ 98.

[93] *People (DPP) v C.C. (No.2)* [2012] IECCA 86 at [37].

[94] [2011] IESC 12 at [151], [2011] 2 IR 669 at 720 -721.

[95] [2011] IESC 12 at [153], [2011] 2 IR 669 at 721 (*per* O'Donnell J); *R. v Boardman* [1975] AC 421 at 456, [1974] 3 All ER 887 at 908 (*per* Lord Cross).

[96] [2011] IESC 12 at [151], [2011] 2 IR 669 at 720.

previous misconduct, an accused is likely to re-offend and may convict him or her on a preventative basis to prevent probable future offences even if unconvinced beyond a reasonable doubt of his or her guilt on the charge before it.

9–41   Finally, the admission of misconduct evidence may distract or confuse the tribunal of fact and thereby increase the risk of adjudicative error.[97] It will often be necessary for the tribunal of fact to determine whether an accused committed the alleged acts of misconduct and it may, consequently, concentrate unduly on deciding whether the accused committed those acts and insufficiently on the issue of the guilt or innocence of the accused in respect of the charges before it. The admission of such evidence may also create a risk of mechanistic decision making. This is because of the possibility that the tribunal of fact may extrapolate from its conclusion as to whether the accused is guilty of the misconduct alleged against him or her to that of the guilt or innocence of the accused in respect of the offence charged without an adequate consideration of the evidence in the case. In addition, the multiplicity of issues to which misconduct evidence gives rise, if admitted, may confuse the jury, prolong the trial and result in increased appeals because of the complexity of direction which the admission of this evidence often necessitates.

9–42   Given the foregoing difficulties attendant upon its admission, the question arises as to why misconduct evidence should ever be admitted. The answer, it is submitted, is to be found in the observation of O'Higgins CJ in *The Criminal Law Jurisdiction Bill, 1975*[98] that the phrase "due course of law" in Art.38.1 "requires a fair and just balance between the exercise of individual freedoms and the requirements of an ordered society".[99] Thus, while it is acknowledged that misconduct evidence presents a threat to the fair trial of the accused, and should generally be excluded, where such evidence is highly probative of guilt, it is admitted because to do otherwise could result in unmeritorious acquittals.

3. The Concept of Misconduct Evidence

9–43   The concept of misconduct evidence includes evidence that discloses the commission of a criminal offence by the accused[100] (whether or not the accused was convicted for same)[101] and evidence of possession by an accused of items which tend to show a criminal disposition.[102] It also extends to evidence of discreditable acts by an accused the disclosure of which could have a prejudicial effect on the tribunal of fact.[103] A good example of such conduct can be seen in *R. v Ball*[104] where a brother and

---

[97]   This risk was adverted to by O'Donnell J in *People (DPP) v McNeill* [2011] IESC 12 at [153], [2011] 2 IR 669 at 721–722.

[98]   [1977] IR 129.

[99]   [1977] IR 129 at 152.

[100]   In *People (DPP) v Timmons* [2011] IECCA 13 at 21, the Court rejected the proposition that misconduct evidence could only be admissible if it consisted of prior convictions.

[101]   Evidence of an offence in respect of which charges can no longer be brought is considered to be misconduct evidence: *R. v Shellaker* [1914] 1 KB 414 at 417.

[102]   *Thompson v R.* [1918] AC 221; *R. v Reading* [1966] 1 All ER 521 at 523; *R. v Mustafa* (1976) 65 Cr App R 26; *R. v Clarke* [1995] 1 Cr App R 425 at 435–434; *R. v Caccamo* [1976] 1 SCR 786, (1976) 54 DLR (3d) 685; *R. v A(J)* (1996) 112 CCC (3d) 528 at 536–537; *R. v Te One* [1976] 2 NZLR 510 at 515.

[103]   *B. v DPP* [1997] 3 IR 140 at 152; *R. v Ball* [1911] AC 47; *R. v Barrington* [1981] 1 All ER 1132; *R. v Robertson* (1987) 39 DLR (4th) 321.

[104]   [1911] AC 47.

sister were charged with incest and the prosecution tendered evidence to establish that they had committed incest prior to its criminalisation. Such conduct was repugnant to contemporary moral standards and would have had the inevitable effect of seriously prejudicing the jury against the accused. Its admissibility was, therefore, determined by reference to the test applicable to misconduct evidence.[105]

4. The Test for Admissibility

9–44   In the eighteenth and early nineteenth century, the general approach was that evidence would be excluded if it tended to disclose that the accused had been guilty of other offences similar to that with which he or she was charged.[106] Over time, that approach was diluted so that misconduct evidence was not excluded simply because it tended to disclose that an accused had committed offences of a similar kind. However, it was still impermissible for the prosecution to adduce such evidence for the purpose of inviting the jury to infer that the accused had a propensity to commit the offence with which he or she was charged. The most famous exposition of these principles is to be found in *Makin v Attorney-General for New South Wales*[107] where Lord Herschell stated:

> "It is undoubtedly not competent for the prosecution to adduce evidence tending to show that the accused has been guilty of criminal acts other than those covered by the indictment, for the purpose of leading to the conclusion that the accused is a person likely from his criminal conduct or character to have committed the offence for which he is being tried. On the other hand, the mere fact that the evidence adduced tends to show the commission of other crimes does not render it admissible if it be relevant to an issue before the jury, and it may be so relevant if it bears upon the question whether the acts alleged to constitute the crime charged in the indictment were designed or accidental, or to rebut a defence which would otherwise be open to the accused."[108]

9–45   The orthodox view of this passage is that it lays down two independent and mutually exclusive propositions covering the admissibility of misconduct evidence.[109] Misconduct evidence which is relevant only by way of an argument drawing upon the accused's bad character, i.e. evidence which invites the jury to reason from propensity to guilt, is inadmissible.[110] However, misconduct evidence which is relevant otherwise

---

[105] See also *R. v Barrington* [1981] 1 All ER 1132 (at the trial of the accused for indecent assault, evidence that he lured them into his house under the pretext of babysitting, showed them pornographic photographs and asked them to pose for photographs was treated as misconduct evidence even though there was no allegation that he had sexually assaulted them). *Cf. People (DPP) v Ramachchandran* [2000] 2 IR 307. The accused had been convicted of harassment contrary to s.10 of the Non-Fatal Offences Against the Person Act 1997 and it was held that evidence relating to the period prior to the coming into force of that section, which the Court viewed as prejudicial to the accused, should not have been admitted.

[106] See, e.g. *R. v Smith* (1827) 2 C & P 633 and the review of the early authorities in *R. v Bond* [1906] 2 KB 389. See further *R. v B (CR)* [1990] 1 SCR 717, (1990) 55 CCC (3d) 1, where McLachlin J reviewed the emergence of the inclusionary exception in England.

[107] [1894] AC 57.

[108] [1894] AC 57 at 65. This passage has been endorsed by the Irish courts on many occasions including: *Attorney General v Fleming* [1934] IR 166; *Attorney General v Joyce* [1929] IR 536; *People (AG) v Kirwan* [1943] IR 279; *People (AG) v Dempsey* [1961] IR 288; *People (DPP) v O'Sullivan* (1979) 2 Frewen 1 at 9; *People (DPP) v Wallace* (1982) 2 Frewen 125 at 129; *People (DPP) v McNeill* [2011] IESC 12, [2011] 2 IR 669 at 703 and 719.

[109] *Boardman v DPP* [1975] AC 421 at 451, [1974] 3 All ER 887 at 903 (*per* Lord Hailsham).

[110] As was succinctly stated by Lord Goddard CJ in *R. v Sims* [1946] KB 531 at 537, [1946] 1 All ER 697 at 700: "Evidence is not to be excluded merely because it tends to show the accused to be of a bad disposition, but only if it shows nothing more". *Cf. R. v Morris* [1983] 2 SCR 190 at 203, (1983) 7 CCC (3d) 97 at 106–107.

than via the accused's propensity is admissible. This orthodox view was expounded by Lord Hailsham in *R. v Boardman*[111]:

> "It is perhaps helpful to remind oneself that what is *not* to be admitted is a chain of reasoning and not necessarily a state of facts. If the inadmissible chain of reasoning be the *only* purpose for which the evidence is adduced as a matter of law, the evidence itself is not admissible. If there is some other relevant, probative purpose than the forbidden type of reasoning, the evidence is admitted, but should be made subject to a warning from the judge that the jury must eschew the forbidden reasoning."

9–46   The task for courts in the aftermath of *Makin* was to identify those situations where misconduct evidence could be said to be relevant otherwise than via the accused's bad disposition. This was not an easy task. Indeed, Lord Herschell had both prefaced and followed the passage set out above with a warning that the application of the principles set out therein would be difficult.

9–47   Faced with these difficulties, it is unsurprising that the courts took refuge in a categorical approach which simplified to a considerable degree the question of admission. The seeds of this formalism were to be found in *Makin* itself. Lord Herschell said that misconduct evidence was admissible where it was relevant to an issue before the jury, and it would be so relevant where it rebutted a defence which would otherwise be open to the accused such as that of accident. This seemed to indicate that there were a number of specific and identifiable issues in respect of which misconduct evidence would be admissible. The focus of subsequent case law was on identifying these issues and over time a number of categories emerged where misconduct evidence was admissible:

> (i)   where it was relevant to an issue before the jury such as intent[112] or to show that an article was adapted for the commission of an offence[113];
> (ii)   where it formed part of the res gestae[114];
> (iii)   to show whether the acts alleged to constitute the offence charged were designed or accidental[115]; and
> (iv)   to rebut a defence otherwise open to an accused,[116] such as innocent association.[117]

9–48   These categories acted as the touchstones of admissibility and if misconduct evidence could be brought within one of these categories, it was automatically admissible. However, in order to avoid the admission of such potentially prejudicial evidence where it was only of limited relevance to the issues in the proceedings, it was held that a trial judge retained a discretion to exclude such evidence if its probative value was outweighed by its prejudicial effect.[118]

---

[111]   [1975] AC 421 at 453, [1974] 3 All ER 887 at 905–906 (emphasis in original).
[112]   See *Attorney General v Fleming* [1934] IR 166; *People (AG) v Havlin* (1952) 1 Frewen 132 at 134; *Toppin v Feron* (1909) 43 ILTR 190. *Cf. R. v Quilter* (1913) 47 ILTR 264 (evidence not relevant to prove intention).
[113]   See *People (DPP) v Wallace* (1982) 2 Frewen 125.
[114]   See *Attorney General v McCabe* [1927] IR 129; *Attorney General v Joyce* [1929] IR 526; *Attorney General v Fleming* [1934] IR 166; *R. v Bond* [1906] 2 KB 389.
[115]   *Makin v Attorney-General for New South Wales* [1894] AC 57.
[116]   *People (AG) v Havlin* (1952) 1 Frewen 132 at 134.
[117]   *People (AG) v Dempsey* [1961] IR 288; *DPP v Boardman* [1975] AC 421 at 440, [1974] 3 All ER 887 at 894; *R. v Slender* [1938] 2 All ER 387 at 390; *Cf. R. v Smith* (1915) 11 Cr App R 229; *R. v Ball* [1911] AC 47.
[118]   *Noor Mohammed v R.* [1949] AC 182 at 192; *Harris v DPP* [1952] AC 694 at 707; *DPP v*

(a) Balancing Probative Force and Prejudicial Effect

9–49   The approach advocated in *Makin* led to a number of difficulties. First, the formalism of the categorical approach led to a mechanical approach to admissibility that obscured the difficulties raised by the admission of misconduct evidence and deflected attention from the real issues raised by such evidence. Secondly, and perhaps more fundamentally, it was asserted that the twin propositions laid down by Lord Herschell were misleading because, despite his assertion to the contrary, courts did sometimes admit evidence of misconduct in order to invite the tribunal of fact to reason from the propensity to guilt.[119] For these reasons, the *Makin* test was abandoned in most common law jurisdictions and replaced with a test which balances, in each individual case, the probative force of the misconduct evidence against the prejudicial effect attendant upon its admission.

9–50   The origins of the balancing test are to be found in the decision of the House of Lords in *DPP v Boardman*.[120] The appellant in that case was the headmaster of a boarding school for boys, and was charged with one count of buggery and two of incitement to buggery with pupils at his school. The count of buggery and one of the counts of incitement bore a number of similarities and, because of these, the trial judge held that the evidence on the two counts was mutually corroborative. The similarities were that both boys alleged that they had been woken up in the school dormitory, spoken to in a low voice, and invited to play the active part in the offence in the appellant's sitting room.

9–51   Although the Law Lords were unanimous in holding that the appeal should be dismissed, their judgments betrayed a marked lack of agreement about the status of the decision in *Makin* and the proper test to be applied to misconduct evidence. Three of the Lords heartily endorsed the approach of Lord Herschell. However, a radically different approach was adopted by Lords Wilberforce and Cross, neither of whom even mentioned *Makin*. Lord Cross rejected the idea that evidence could never be relevant solely via propensity, saying that circumstances could arise in which such evidence is so relevant that to exclude it would be an affront to common sense.[121] He took the view that the admission of misconduct evidence was a matter of law, not discretion, and, further, was a matter of degree. Lord Wilberforce agreed that the admission of misconduct evidence was a matter of degree and stated that, in each case, it is necessary to estimate (1) whether, and if so how strongly, the evidence tends to support, *i.e.* to make more credible, the evidence given as to the fact in question; (2) whether such evidence, if given, is likely to be prejudicial to the accused. These two judgments were subsequently taken to have established a test of admissibility based on the balancing of probative force and prejudicial effect.[122]

Boardman [1975] AC 421 at 453, [1974] 3 All ER 887 at 905.

[119] In *DPP v Boardman* [1975] AC 421 at 456, [1974] 3 All ER 887 at 908, Lord Cross instanced *R. v Straffen* [1952] 2 QB 911, [1952] 2 All ER 657 as an example of a case where misconduct evidence was adduced "to show that Straffen was a man likely to commit a murder of that particular kind".

[120] [1975] AC 421, [1974] 3 All ER 887.

[121] *Cf. R. v Lunt* (1987) 85 Cr App R 241 at 244; *R. v Robinson* (1953) 37 Cr App R 95 at 106; *R. v Bedford* (1991) 93 Cr App R 113 at 117.

[122] See the seminal article by Hoffman, "Similar Facts After Boardman" (1975) 91 LQR 193. See also Carter, "Forbidden Reasoning Permissible: Similar Fact Evidence After Boardman" (1985) 48 MLR 29; Mirfield, "Similar Facts–Makin Out?" [1987] Camb LJ 83; Acorn, "Similar Fact

9–52 All of the judgments in *Boardman* had placed emphasis on the striking similarities between the evidence of the complainants as an important factor in concluding that their evidence was cross-admissible. As a result, subsequent decisions of the Court of Appeal focused on the requirement of "striking similarity" as a proxy for the quantum of probative force required to outweigh the prejudicial effect of the admission of misconduct evidence.[123] However, this line of authority fell to be overruled by the House of Lords in *DPP v P*,[124] where the primacy of the balancing test was reasserted. The accused in that case had been convicted of the rape and incest of his two daughters. He appealed on the basis that the trial judge had erred in permitting the evidence of each daughter on the count concerning her to be admitted on the count concerning her sister. The decision of the Court of Appeal to allow his appeal on the ground that there had not been striking similarities between the girls' accounts of their father's behaviour towards them was reversed by the House of Lords. Lord Mackay, delivering the judgment of the House, stated that evidence of this type is admissible if its probative value outweighs its prejudicial effect. Applying that balancing test, it was held that evidence of an offence by the accused against one victim could be admitted at the trial of an alleged offence against another victim if the essential feature of the evidence which was to be admitted was that its probative force in support of the allegations was sufficiently great to make it just to admit the evidence. This was the case notwithstanding that it was prejudicial to the accused in tending to show that he was guilty of another crime.[125]

9–53 The test of balancing the probative force of misconduct evidence against its prejudicial effect subsequently achieved widespread acceptance in common law jurisdictions including Canada,[126] Australia,[127] and New Zealand[128] although, as noted below, it has since been superseded by legislative developments in the UK and New Zealand. However, approval of the test has not been unalloyed. It has proved difficult to apply in practice because of the relatively abstract level at which it is formulated[129]

Evidence and the Principle of Inductive Reasoning: Makin Sense" (1991) 11 OJLS 63; Zuckerman, "Similar Fact Evidence–The Unobservable Rule" (1987) 103 LQR 187.

[123] See *R. v Mansfield* [1978] 1 All ER 134 at 138–139; *R. v Scarrott* [1978] QB 1016 at 1020, [1978] 1 All ER 672 at 675; *R. v Lunt* (1987) 85 Cr App R 241 at 244; *R. v Beggs* (1990) 90 Cr App R 430 at 437; *R. v Butler* (1987) 84 Cr App R 12 at 13; *R. v Johannsen* (1977) 65 Cr App R 101 at 103; *R. v Clarke* (1978) 67 Cr App R 398 at 403; *R. v Shore* (1989) Cr App R 32 at 40.

[124] [1991] 2 AC 447, [1991] 3 All ER 337.

[125] See also *R. v Batt* [1994] Crim LR 592 at 593; *R. v Laidman* [1992] Crim LR 428 at 429; and *R. v Simpson* (1994) 99 Cr App R 48 at 53.

[126] See *Guay v R.* [1979] 1 SCR 18, (1979) 89 DLR (3d) 532; *Sweitzer v R.* [1982] 1 SCR 949, (1982) 137 DLR (3d) 702; *R. v B (CR)* [1990] 1 SCR 717; *R. v Seaboyer* [1991] 2 SCR 577, (1991) 83 DLR (4th) 193; *R. v Litchfield* [1993] 4 SCR 333, (1993) 86 CCC (3d) 97; *R. v B (FF)* [1993] 1 SCR 697; *R. v Lepage* [1995] 1 SCR 654, (1995) 95 CCC (3d) 385; *R. v Arp* (1998) 166 DLR (4th) 296 at 315.

[127] *R. v Hoch* [1988] 165 CLR 292; *Pfennig v The Queen* (1994–95) 182 CLR 461. See further, Bates, "Similar Facts and the Hallmark Doctrine in England and Australia" (1975) 39 JCL 283; Neasey J, "Similar Fact Reasoning and Propensity Reasoning" (1985) 9 Crim LJ 232.

[128] *R. v Te One* [1976] 2 NZLR 510 at 514; *R. v McLean* [1978] 2 NZLR 358; *R. v Anderson* [1978] 2 NZLR 363; *R. v Accused* [1988] 1 NZLR 573; *R. v M* [1999] 1 NZLR 315; *R. v Healy* [2007] 3 NZLR 850.

[129] See *R. v Anderson* [1978] 2 NZLR 363 at 365, where Woodhouse J commented that: "It has been said often enough that the principles are easier to state than to apply; and that it can be difficult to see where the line is to be drawn." See also *R. v Mustafa* (1976) 65 Cr App R 26 at 31, where Scarman LJ stated: "The principle is clear enough in general, the problem, as always, is the application of the principle to the particular circumstances of the case".

and the absence of any clearly identified factors to guide the application of the test has been the subject of justifiable criticism.[130] This may explain why, after initial enthusiasm, the test appears to have fallen out of favour in this jurisdiction.

(b) The Approach in this Jurisdiction

9–54 The *Makin* test of admissibility was approved and applied by the Court of Criminal Appeal in *Attorney General v Joyce and Walsh*[131] where Sullivan P held that:

> "the mere fact that evidence adduced tends to show the commission of other crimes does not render it inadmissible if it be relevant to an issue before the Court, and that it may be so relevant if it bears on the question whether the acts alleged to constitute the crime charged in the indictment were designed or accidental, or to rebut a defence that would be otherwise open to the accused…"[132]

9–55 The principles established in *Makin* subsequently received the imprimatur of the Supreme Court in *People (AG) v Kirwan*[133] with O'Byrne J stating that two propositions could be taken as established:

> "(1) That evidence that the accused has committed offences, other than that charged in the indictment preferred against him, is never admissible for the purpose of leading the jury to hold that the accused is likely, by reason of his criminal conduct or character, to have committed the crime in respect of which he is being tried; and
>
> (2) The mere fact that the evidence adduced tends to show the commission of other crimes does not render it inadmissible if it be relevant to some issue of fact which the jury is called upon to determine."[134]

9–56 He went on to say that:

> "As a corollary to, rather than a qualification upon, the foregoing rules, it must be taken as established that the trial Judge, in the exercise of his discretion, may refuse to admit evidence which is, strictly speaking, relevant to an issue before the jury if he considers that the evidence, if admitted, would probably have a prejudicial effect on the minds of the jury out of proportion to its true evidential value."[135]

9–57 That was the approach adopted by the Irish courts until the test of balancing the probative force and prejudicial effect was grafted on to the traditional approach by the Court of Criminal Appeal in *People (DPP) v BK*.[136] The appellant had been charged with a number of sexual offences against young boys which were alleged to have taken place in a residential home for children. At the commencement of the trial, counsel for the appellant applied to have each of the counts relating to different boys tried separately. The prosecution offered to withdraw the counts in relation to two of the boys and the trial continued against the appellant on four counts involving three separate individuals. Counts 1 and 2 charged him with indecent assault and buggery

---

[130] The English Law Commission recommended codifying the law as set out in *DPP v P*, but with the inclusion of statutory criteria to govern the application of the balancing test; Consultation Paper No. 141, Evidence in Criminal Proceedings: Previous Misconduct of a Defendant (HMSO, 1996) paras 9.45–9.57. *Cf.* Roberts, "All the Usual Suspects: A Critical Appraisal of Law Commission Consultation Paper No. 141" [1997] Crim LR 75; Redmayne, "The Law Commission's Character Convictions" (2002) 6 E & P 71.

[131] [1929] IR 526.

[132] [1929] IR 526 at 539.

[133] [1943] IR 279.

[134] [1943] IR 279 at 303.

[135] [1943] IR 279 at 304.

[136] [2000] 2 IR 199. See Gageby, "Multiple Complainant Trials: Severance and Cross-Admissibility" (2011) 3 ICLJ 59.

respectively against one boy. Counts 8 and 9 charged him with attempted buggery against two other boys. In the case of counts 1 and 2, the offences were alleged to have been committed in a dormitory at night and the complainant made allegations of lewd suggestions having been made to him during the day. With respect to counts 8 and 9, each of the boys gave evidence of sharing a bed with the appellant in a caravan in which the appellant and some of the boys stayed sometimes and waking up to find the appellant molesting him. The jury convicted him on counts 8 and 9 and one of the grounds of appeal was that the counts on the indictment which related to different persons should have been tried separately.

9–58 In considering this question, the Court accepted the submission made by the appellant that the effect of allowing the counts relating to different boys to be tried together would be, *de facto*, to provide corroboration of the charges against him where there was none in law.[137] It was, therefore, necessary to consider the principles governing the admission of misconduct evidence. The Court, in a judgment delivered by Barron J, engaged in a lengthy review of the authorities in the area (including the decisions of the House of Lords in *DPP v Boardman*[138] and *DPP v P*[139]) and distilled from them the following principles:

> "(1) The rules of evidence should not be allowed to offend common-sense.
> (2) So, where the probative value of the evidence outweighs its prejudicial effect, it may be admitted.
> (3) The categories of cases in which the evidence which can be so admitted is not closed.
> Such evidence is admitted in two main types of cases:
> (a) to establish that the same person committed each offence because of the particular feature common to each; or
> (b) where the charges are against one person only, to establish that offences were committed.
> In the latter case the evidence is admissible because:
> (a) there is the inherent probability of several persons making up exactly similar stories;
> (b) it shows a practice which would rebut accident, innocent explanation or denial."[140]

9–59 Applying those principles to the facts of the case, the Court was satisfied that counts 1 and 2 had been improperly joined with counts 8 and 9 because the evidence on counts 1 and 2 did not have the necessary nexus to justify being heard with counts 8 and 9. The Court was, however, satisfied that the evidence on counts 8 and 9 was cross-admissible.

9–60 Although the decision of the Court of Criminal Appeal in *BK* contained a clear endorsement of the balancing test, a vestige of the categorical approach remained in the distinction drawn by the Court between "system evidence" and "similar fact evidence":

> "On the one hand, there is system evidence which is so admissible; and, on the other hand, there is similar fact evidence, which is inadmissible. In the latter case, the reason is that, just because a person may have acted in a particular way on one occasion does not mean that such person acted in the same way on some other occasion. System evidence on the other hand is admissible because the manner in which a particular act has been done on one occasion suggests that it was also done on another occasion by the same person and with the same intent."[141]

9–61 The balancing test endorsed in *BK* was applied in a number of subsequent

---

[137] [2000] 2 IR 199 at 203. See also *Attorney General v Duffy* [1931] IR 144.
[138] [1975] AC 421, [1974] 3 All ER 887.
[139] [1991] 2 AC 447, [1991] 3 All ER 337.
[140] [2000] 2 IR 199 at 210–211.
[141] [2000] 2 IR 199 at 203.

decisions[142] and was considered in the first edition of this work to be the touchstone of the admissibility of misconduct evidence in this jurisdiction.[143]

9–62   However, that no longer appears to be the case following the decision of the Supreme Court in *People (DPP) v McNeill*.[144] The appellant in that case was alleged to have sexually abused the complainant over an eight year period. The prosecution proffered eight counts of sexual assault and rape against him but evidence was admitted of other alleged incidents of sexual abuse which were set out in the book of evidence. On appeal, the decision of the trial judge to admit that evidence was upheld by the Court of Criminal Appeal.[145] Having endorsed the decision in *BK* and applying the balancing test, it concluded that this constituted admissible "background evidence".[146] An appeal against that decision was dismissed by a majority of the Supreme Court but a very different approach to the admissibility of such evidence was adopted.

9–63   The leading judgment was delivered by Denham J who adopted the two propositions identified by O'Byrne J in *People (AG) v Kirwan*[147] which have been set out above and, in a passage with a clear echo of the opinion of Lord Herschell in *Makin*, she summarised the position as follows:

> "The general rule is that evidence that an accused has committed offences other than those charged on the indictment is not admissible for the purpose of leading a jury to hold that an accused is likely, by reason of his criminal conduct or character, to have committed the crime/s with which he is charged. However, the mere fact that the evidence adduced tends to show the commission of other alleged offences does not render it inadmissible if it is relevant and necessary to some issue of fact upon which the jury is required to determine."[148]

9–64   Accordingly, "background evidence" could be admitted, notwithstanding that it tended to show the commission of other offences, if its admission was necessary because it was "so closely and inextricably linked to the alleged offences and/or the relations between the relevant persons so as to form part of the body of evidence to render it coherent and comprehensible".[149] The test to be applied in that regard is whether "the background evidence is relevant and necessary".[150]

9–65   In his concurring judgment, O'Donnell J agreed that the correct position had been set out in *Makin* which had established that "evidence of previous bad character is inadmissible if introduced for a particular purpose; that of showing that such bad character alone makes it likely that the accused committed the offence for which he

---

[142] See *People (DPP) v Nevin* [2003] 3 IR 321; *People (DPP) v LG* [2003] 2 IR 517; *Condron v ACC Bank plc* [2012] IEHC 395 at [6], [2013] 1 ILRM 113 at 116.

[143] A view which was shared by the Court of Criminal Appeal in *People (DPP) v McNeill* [2007] IECCA 95 at [47].

[144] [2011] IESC 12, [2011] 2 IR 669. See Glynn "Admissibility of background evidence" (2011) 29(9) ILT 126.

[145] [2007] IECCA 95.

[146] The decision of the Court of Criminal Appeal was followed and applied in *People (DPP) v Baily* [2010] IECCA 25 where it was held that evidence of a portion of an interview of the accused by gardaí in which he admitted a sexual attraction to young boys and girls had been properly admitted as background evidence because its probative value outweighed any prejudicial effect that it might have had.

[147] [1943] IR 279.

[148] [2011] IESC 12 at [55], [2011] 2 IR 669 at 695.

[149] [2011] IESC 12 at [49], [2011] 2 IR 669 at 693.

[150] [2011] IESC 12 at [50], [2011] 2 IR 669 at 694.

is tried".[151] What was impermissible was "deciding on the guilt or innocence of the accused by a reasoning process that gives credence to the adage of giving a dog a bad name".[152] Thus, the key consideration was the purpose for which the evidence is adduced and "evidence which tends to show bad character on the part of the accused may nevertheless be adduced in a trial if it is adduced not for the purpose of proving guilt by propensity but rather for the purposes of tending to prove something that is an issue in the case".[153] He went on to examine the purpose for which the misconduct evidence had been adduced and he was satisfied that it had had not been adduced for the purpose of inviting the jury to consider that the applicant was guilty of the offences charged because of a predisposition to commit such offences. Indeed, he found it difficult to see how this could be so given that the credibility of the complainant was central and, if they believed her evidence about the other acts of abuse, they would also believe her evidence in relation to the offences charged and the accused would be convicted on that basis. Instead, the evidence had been admitted because it was an intrinsic part of the story necessary to understand the circumstances in which the complainant said that she had been abused over a protracted period by the appellant and he was satisfied that it was admissible for this purpose. The offences disclosed could potentially have been the subject of other counts in the indictment and, so, there was no prejudice to the accused.

9–66 In his dissenting judgment, Fennelly J reviewed the authorities and rejected the proposition, accepted by the Court of Criminal Appeal, that the decision in *People (DPP) v BK*[154] had established a balancing test of probative force and prejudicial effect. In his view, the Court of Criminal Appeal in that case had not intended any departure from the principles established in *Makin* and, while misconduct evidence was generally inadmissible, it could be admitted when the evidence was relevant as tending to prove the commission of the offence charged. He considered that it was only at the point where such evidence was established to be relevant that the question arose of the exercise of discretion on the part of a trial judge to exclude such evidence where its prejudicial effect outweighed its probative value.[155]

9–67 While the test of balancing probative value and prejudicial effect was not expressly disavowed in *McNeill*, it did not receive any support and O'Donnell J in the course of his judgment expressed "doubts about a balancing test where it is not very clear in advance what weight is being ascribed to factors which are not themselves measured in the same register".[156]

9–68 A notable feature of the judgments was the unanimity as to applicability of the rules as to admissibility propounded by Lord Herschell in *Makin* as adopted into Irish law in *Kirwan*.[157] It appears clear, therefore, that the Irish law in this area has reverted to the pre-*Boardman* position. Accordingly, it is suggested that the admissibility of

---

[151] [2011] IESC 12 at [149], [2011] 2 IR 669 at 719.

[152] [2011] IESC 12 at [151], [2011] 2 IR 669 at 720.

[153] [2011] IESC 12 at [151], [2011] 2 IR 669 at 721. A similar analysis is to be found in the judgment of the Court of Criminal Appeal in *People (DPP) v Morgan* [2011] IECCA 36 at [20].

[154] [2000] 2 IR 199.

[155] [2011] IESC 12 at [106]–[112], [2011] 2 IR 669 at 707–708.

[156] [2011] IESC 12 at [152], [2011] 2 IR 669 at 721.

[157] The principles laid down in *Makin* were also commended as "basic propositions of universal application" by Hardiman J in *People (DPP) v D O'S* [2006] IESC 12 at [33], [2006] 3 IR 57 at 68, [2006] 2 ILRM 61 at 71.

misconduct evidence now falls to be determined in accordance with the following principles:

(a) Misconduct evidence is not admissible for the purpose of inviting the jury to infer from it that the accused is a person who, by reason of his disposition or bad character, is likely to have committed the offences charged.

(b) Misconduct evidence can be admitted in evidence if (i) it is relevant to and sufficiently probative of an issue in the proceedings, (ii) its admission is necessary, and (iii) there is sufficient proof of the commission of the acts of misconduct.

(c) A trial judge has a discretion to exclude misconduct evidence which would otherwise be admissible if is probative force is outweighed by its prejudicial effect.

(d) In any case where misconduct evidence is admitted and there is a risk that the jury may draw the inference that the accused is likely, by reason of his other criminal conduct or character, to have committed the offences upon which he or she is charged, the trial judge should instruct the jury as to the limited purpose for which the evidence has been admitted and warn them not to draw such an inference.

5. Probative Force of Misconduct Evidence

9–69   In *People (DPP) v McNeill*,[158] Denham J stated that "the test to be applied is whether the evidence is relevant to some issue of fact which the jury have to decide". The decided cases have identified a number of instances where misconduct evidence may be relevant and have sufficient probative force in relation to the issues to be decided by the tribunal of fact otherwise than by way of an invitation to the jury to reason from propensity to guilt of the offences charged. It is of assistance to categorise these instances and that is done below, but it must be emphasised that these categories are not comprehensive or closed[159] and overlap to a considerable extent.

9–70   Before examining the various categories, it is important to emphasise that the relevance and probative value of misconduct evidence cannot be determined in the abstract but is crucially dependent on the other evidence in a case[160] and any change in the factual matrix may lead to a different result.[161] This can be illustrated by reference to the decision in *R. v Straffen*.[162] The accused had been convicted of the murder of a little girl called Linda. There were several peculiarities about the way in which she had been murdered. She had been killed by manual strangulation, no attempt had been made to conceal the body, there was no evidence of a struggle, no apparent motive, and she had not been sexually assaulted. The accused had been in the vicinity at the

---

[158] [2011] IESC 12 at [41], [2011] 2 IR 669 at 690.

[159] In *People (DPP) v McNeill* [2011] IESC 12 at [160], [2011] 2 IR 669 at 724, O'Donnell J said that it was "a mistake to seek to determine the admissibility of [misconduct] evidence only on the basis that it is, or is not, included in an identified sub-category sanctified by precedent". See also *People (DPP) v BK* [2000] 2 IR 199 at 207; *People (DPP) v D O'S* [2006] IESC 12 at [35], [2006] 3 IR 57 at 68, [2006] 2 ILRM 61 at 72 (*per* Hardiman J); *Harris v DPP* [1952] AC 694 at 705; *R. v Boardman* [1975] AC 421 at 452 and 457.

[160] *R. v Boardman* [1975] AC 421 at 457, [1974] 3 All ER 887 at 909 (*per* Lord Cross).

[161] See *R. v Brooks* (1991) 92 Cr App R 36 at 40.

[162] [1952] 2 QB 911, [1952] 2 All ER 657.

time of the killing and knew of the girl's death before being told about it by police. In order to prove that he was the perpetrator, evidence was led as to confessions by him to the murder of two other girls in very similar circumstances and, on appeal, it was held that the evidence had been correctly admitted. On the facts of *Straffen*, the probative force of this evidence derived from, and its admission of this evidence was justifiable on the basis of, the unlikelihood that a person who had been in the vicinity when Linda had been killed, was aware that she was dead, and who had killed two other girls in a very similar manner, had not also killed Linda. However, if the facts of the case had been different and no link had been established between the accused and the scene of the crime, then the misconduct evidence would not have had the same degree of probative force and is likely to have been excluded.[163] As Lord Hailsham observed in *Boardman*, "[w]hen there is nothing to connect the accused with a particular crime except bad character or similar crimes committed in the past, the probative value of the evidence is nil and the evidence is rejected on that ground".[164]

(a) Motive

9–71   Misconduct evidence that establishes motive to commit an offence will be regarded as relevant and having sufficient probative force to be admitted on the basis, articulated by Lord Atkinson in *R. v Ball*[165] that, "it is more probable that men are killed by those who have some motive for killing them than by those who have not."[166] In *Attorney General v Joyce and Walsh*[167] Sullivan P said that evidence could be admitted of "the existence of any motive likely to instigate the commission of the offence".

9–72   Thus, evidence of previous attempts by an accused to harm the person in respect of whom the offence is alleged to have been committed are admissible in order to establish that the accused bore malice towards that person and/or had a motive to harm the person.[168] In *Attorney General v Joyce and Walsh*[169] evidence was admitted, at the trial of the accused for murder, of an attempt by one of them to poison the deceased some years earlier.[170] Similarly, in *People (DPP) v Nevin*,[171] where the applicant had been convicted of the murder of her husband, the Court of Criminal Appeal was satisfied that:

> "evidence of attempts by the applicant to persuade witnesses to kill her husband, together with evidence as to her suggestions as to how his murder should be perpetrated, comprised evidence of extreme hostility and ill-will on the part of the applicant towards her husband and was accordingly, admissible in her trial on the charge of murder."[172]

---

[163]   *Cf.* the analysis of *R. v Ball* [1911] AC 47 by Hoffman, "Similar Facts After Boardman" (1975) 91 LQR 193.

[164]   [1975] AC 421 at 451, [1974] 3 All ER 887.

[165]   [1911] AC 47 at 68.

[166]   See *People (DPP) v Nevin* [2003] 3 IR 321 where misconduct evidence was admitted to prove motive.

[167]   [1929] IR 526 at 539.

[168]   See *Toppin v Feron* (1909) 43 ILTR 190; *Attorney General v Fleming* [1934] IR 166; *People (AG) v Havlin* (1952) 1 Frewen 132 at 134; *People (DPP) v Piotrowski* [2014] IECCA 17 at [10.3].

[169]   [1929] IR 526 at 539.

[170]   A similar conclusion was reached in *Attorney General v Fleming* [1934] IR 166 where evidence was admitted at the trial of the accused for the murder of his wife of a previous attempt to poison her.

[171]   [2003] 3 IR 321.

[172]   [2003] 3 IR 321 at 344.

(b) Rebuttal of a Defence

9–73   Misconduct evidence may be admitted where it negatives the possible availability of a defence that would otherwise be open to an accused[173] such as self-defence,[174] accident,[175] mistake[176] or innocent association.[177] So, in *R. v Ball*[178] where a brother and sister who lived together and shared a bed were charged with incest, evidence was admitted that they had previously lived as man and wife and had a child together in order to show that they shared a guilty passion and thereby rebut the defence of innocence association. Similarly, in *R. v Smith*[179] the accused was charged with the murder of his wife who had drowned in the bath. At his trial, evidence was adduced that he had entered into a bigamous marriage with the deceased and with two other woman who had also drowned in the bath and in each case, he had taken them to the doctor suggesting that they had suffered an epileptic fit and had benefited monetarily from their deaths. The evidence was admitted to show that the drowning of the deceased had been designed and not accidental.

(c) System Evidence

9–74   Misconduct evidence establishing the commission by an accused of offences (or discreditable acts) in similar circumstances to the offences charged establishing the use of a system or particular *modus operandi* by the accused may be highly probative of his or her guilt.[180] The most infamous example of such a case is *Makin v Attorney General for New South Wales*[181] where the accused had been found guilty of the murder of an infant whose body had been found buried in the back yard of their house. Evidence was given by the mother of the infant that she had given him to them and had paid a small sum of money to them on the basis of their representation that they would adopt and bring up the child as their own because they had lost their own child. It was held by the Privy Council that evidence had been properly admitted that other infants had been given by their mothers and payments made on the basis of similar representations and that the bodies of other infants had been found buried in the gardens of other houses where the accused had resided.

9–75   Another example involving discreditable acts rather than other offences can be seen in *R. v Barrington*[182] where the accused was charged with the indecent assault of three young girls. The prosecution case was that he had lured them into his house under the pretext of babysitting, showed them pornographic photographs, asked them to pose for photographs and indecently assaulted them. The evidence of three other young girls that they had also been lured into the house in this manner, shown photographs and

---

[173] *Makin v Attorney General for New South Wales* [1894] AC 57 at 65; *Attorney General v Joyce and Walsh* [1929] IR 526 at 539; *People (AG) v Havlin* (1952) 1 Frewen 132 at 134; *Condron v ACC Bank plc* [2012] IEHC 395 at [6], [2013] 1 ILRM 113 at 116.
[174] See *People (DPP) v Barnes* [2006] IECCA 130 at [96], [2007] 3 IR 130 at 159.
[175] *People (DPP) v McCurdy* [2012] IECCA 76 at [10].
[176] *R. v Seaman* (1978) 67 Cr App R 234 at 238–239.
[177] *People (AG) v Dempsey* [1961] IR 288; *R. v Ball* [1911] AC 47; *R. v Slender* [1938] 2 All ER 387 at 390; *DPP v Boardman* [1975] AC 421 at 440, [1974] 3 All ER 887 at 894.
[178] [1911] AC 47.
[179] (1915) 1 Cr App R 229.
[180] *People (DPP) v BK* [2000] 2 IR 199; *People (DPP) v McCurdy* [2012] IECCA 76 at [10].
[181] [1894] AC 57.
[182] [1981] 1 All ER 1132.

asked to pose in the nude, but had not been indecently assaulted, was admitted on the basis that the facts adduced in evidence were strikingly similar to the circumstances surrounding the alleged offences as set out in the evidence of the complainants.[183]

(d) Identity of Perpetrator

9–76 Misconduct evidence is admissible where it establishes the commission by the accused of offences with some special feature which is common to the offences charged and, thus, supports the inference that the accused was the perpetrator of the offences charged. A helpful exposition as to the nature of the signature or special feature that is required in order for misconduct evidence to be admissible on this basis is to be found in the judgment of Lord Salmon in *DPP v Boardman*[184]:

> "If, for example, A is charged with burglary at the house of B and it is shown that the burglar, whoever he was, entered B's house by a ground floor window, evidence against A that he had committed a long series of burglaries, in every case entering by a ground floor window, would be clearly inadmissible. This would show nothing from which a reasonable jury could infer anything except bad character and disposition to burgle. The fact of unique or striking similarity would be missing. There must be thousands of professional burglars who habitually enter through ground floor windows and the fact that B's house was entered in this way might well be a coincidence. Certainly it could not reasonably be regarded as evidence that A was the burglar. On the other hand, if, for example, A had a long series of convictions for burglary and in every case he had left a distinctive written mark or device behind him and he was then charged with a burglary in circumstances in which an exactly similar mark or device was found at the site of the burglary which he was alleged to have committed, the similarity between the burglary charged and those of which he had previously been convicted would be so uniquely or strikingly similar that evidence of the manner in which he had committed the previous burglaries would, in law, clearly be admissible against him."[185]

9–77 It is apparent from this passage that evidence will not be admissible on this basis where the similarities in issue are mere "stock in trade" similarities, common to many such offences. The courts require something more; something so unusual as to render it highly unlikely that the similarity between the misconduct evidence sought to be adduced and the offence charged could be a coincidence.

9–78 In a number of cases, the courts have singled out misconduct evidence which is admitted to prove the identity of a perpetrator as a special category that requires very high probative force.[186] In *People (DPP) v BK*,[187] Barron J stated that "[w]hen the identity of the perpetrator is unknown some special feature is necessary before evidence is admissible to establish that it was the same perpetrator in each case."

9–79 It is, however, important to point out that no particular degree of similarity is required[188] and a trial judge should not focus unduly on the idea of a signature or

---

[183] See also *R. v Robertson* (1987) 39 DLR (4th) 321.

[184] [1975] AC 421, [1974] 3 All ER 887.

[185] [1975] AC 421 at 426, [1974] 3 All ER 887 at 915. *Cf. R. v McGranaghan* [1995] 1 Cr App R 559 at 572.

[186] *People (DPP) v BK* [2000] 2 IR 199 at 209–210; *DPP v P* [1991] 2 AC 447 at 462, [1991] 3 All ER 337 at 348; *R. v Gurney* [1994] Crim LR 116 at 117; *R. v Johnson* [1995] Crim LR 53; *R. v Arp* (1998) 166 DLR (4th) 296 at 313. See generally, Pattenden, "Similar Fact Evidence and Proof of Identity" (1996) 112 LQR 446.

[187] [2000] 2 IR 199 at 209.

[188] In *R. v Ruiz* [1995] Crim LR 151, the Court of Appeal rejected the contention that "striking similarity" was essential for the admission of misconduct evidence where the issue was one of

unique feature. As noted above, the question of probative force is very contextual and, in circumstances where there is other evidence that establishes a link between an accused and the offence charged, a high degree of similarity between that offence and the misconduct evidence may not be required.

(e) Multiple Accusations

9–80   Logically, the fact that a number of different individuals make similar accusations against the same person strengthens the force of any individual allegation. As Lord Goddard observed in *R. v Sims*[189] "whereas the jury might think that one might be telling an untruth, three or four are hardly likely to tell the same untruth unless they were conspiring together." Thus, the relevance and probative force of this evidence derives from, and it can be admitted on the basis of, "the unlikelihood that the same person would himself be falsely accused on various occasions by different and independent individuals".[190] In *People (DPP) v C.C. (No.2)*,[191] O'Donnell J explained:

> "[I]f for example, the same person had lived in a number of different places and complainants had come forward independently and described in various degrees and detail offences containing perhaps a single distinctive element or signature, then any fact finder would be entitled to place considerable reliance on the fact that in the absence of deliberate collusion, it would be extremely unlikely that such witnesses could emerge by pure coincidence having the same mistaken or indeed false memory concerning the accused. The force of that reasoning is undeniable and explains why notwithstanding the risk, such evidence is admissible."

9–81   The assessment of probative force where there are multiple accusations was considered by the House of Lords in *DPP v P*.[192] In that case, the accused had been charged with sexual offences relating to the sexual abuse of his two daughters and the trial judge held that the evidence of the two girls was cross-admissible. Lord Mackay, delivering the decision of the House of Lords, rejected the contention that striking similarity was required before the evidence of complainants in sexual cases could be cross-admissible. He emphasised that the test of admissibility was whether the probative force of such evidence outweighed its prejudicial effect. Although such probative force could be derived from striking similarities in relation to the manner in which the crime had been committed, he took the view that there was no justification for restricting the circumstances in which there was sufficient probative force to cases where there was some striking similarity between the offences because probative force could arise in other ways.[193] The decision in *DPP v P* was referred to with approval by Budd J in *B v DPP*[194] who summarised the position as follows:

> "[T]he mere existence of multiple accusations of similar offences does not mean that the evidence will be admissible as it is still essential that there should be a sufficient degree of probative force to overcome the prejudicial force of such evidence. Whether the accounts of each of several complainants are corroborative and also the risk of collusion, either by conspiracy or where one witness has been unconsciously influenced by another, may well be relevant factors at the trial. It seems that the underlying principle is that the probative value

---

        identity. A similar conclusion has been reached in Canada: *R. v Arp* (1998) 166 DLR (4th) 296
        at 316.
[189]   [1946] KB 531 at 540, [1946] 1 All ER 697 at 701.
[190]   *Per* Budd J in *B v DPP* [1997] 3 IR 140 at 157 – 158.
[191]   [2012] IECCA 86 at [37].
[192]   [1991] 2 AC 447, [1991] 3 All ER 337.
[193]   See Mee, "Similar fact evidence: accusation = guilt?" (1991) 1 ICLJ 122 who has criticised the
        decision in *DPP v P* for abandoning the requirement of "striking similarity".
[194]   *B v DPP* [1997] 3 IR 140 at 157–158.

of multiple accusations may depend in part on their similarity, but also on the unlikelihood that the same person would find himself falsely accused on various occasions by different and independent individuals. The making of multiple accusations is a coincidence in itself, which has to be taken into account in deciding admissibility."

9–82 It can be seen, therefore, that the probative force of multiple accusations is not dependant upon any particular degree of similarity between the accusations. In circumstances where there are a large number of accusers, who have independently made allegations of a similar type of conduct against the accused, sufficient probative force might derive from the number of complainants alone without the need for their allegations to be very similar in substance. As the number of accusers falls, so the level of similarity required to maintain the required level of probative force based on the unlikelihood of coincidence rises until the point is reached at which there are only two accusers and the similarity must be very great indeed.[195]

9–83 Thus, "striking similarity is just one of the ways in which evidence may exhibit the exceptional degree of probative force required for admissibility, so that to insist upon it to an equal degree in all cases would be incorrect".[196] In addition, a trial judge must be careful not to attach too much weight to similarities between the circumstances of commission of the offences charged and the misconduct evidence that it is sought to adduce. This is because, particularly in sexual offences, what may appear to be unique features of the commission of offences may turn out to be the mere "stock in trade" of perpetrators of those offences.[197]

9–84 In order to have the required degree of probative force, it is important that the accusers are acting independently:

"The probative force is derived, if at all, from the circumstance that the facts testified to by the several witnesses bear to each other such a striking similarity that they must, when judged by experience and common sense, either all be true, or have arisen from a cause common to the witnesses or from pure coincidence."[198]

9–85 This was recognised by the Court of Criminal Appeal in *People (DPP) v C.C. (No.2)*[199] where O'Donnell J emphasised that the probative force of such evidence is entirely dependent on the independence of the complainants:

"Drawing conclusions from the possibility of events occurring by random, rather than simply assessing the evidence in relation to a particular incident, is permissible, but it is an exercise in logic and probability: in the absence of some connecting factor, it is highly unlikely that individual independent accounts of similar conduct could emerge and yet be mistaken. The greater the number of accounts the more remote the possibility of collective error. This is a powerful line of reasoning but its force is dependent on the exclusion of any possibility

---

[195] The equivalent passage from the first edition was quoted with approval by Hardiman J in *People (DPP) v McCurdy* [2012] IECCA 76 at [10]. *Cf. Boardman* [1975] AC 421 at 460, [1974] 3 All ER 887 at 911, where Lord Cross warned of the need to proceed with caution where there were only two accusers.

[196] *B v DPP* [1997] 3 IR 140 at 154 (*per* Budd J). See also *R. v Brooks* (1991) 92 Cr App R 36; *R. v Scarrott* [1978] QB 1016 at 1022, [1978] 1 All ER 672 at 676; *R. v Rance* (1975) 62 Cr App R 118 at 121; *R. v His En Feng* [1985] 1 NZLR 222 at 225.

[197] See *R. v Inder* (1978) 67 Cr App R 143 at 149; *Sutton v R.* (1983–84) 152 CLR 528 at 537; *R. v Holloway* [1980] 1 NZLR 315 at 319.

[198] *DPP v Boardman* [1975] AC 421 at 444, [1974] 3 All ER 887 at 897 (*per* Lord Wilberforce). See also *DPP v Kilbourne* [1973] AC 729 at 750, [1973] 1 All ER 440 at 456; *R. v Scarrott* [1978] QB 1016 at 1026–1027, [1978] 1 All ER 672 at 680; *R. v Wells* [1989] Crim LR 67 at 69; *R. v. Wright* [1994] Crim LR 55 at 55; *R. v Anderson* [1978] 2 NZLR 363 at 370–372.

[199] [2012] IECCA 86 at [37].

of connection between those giving the accounts, particularly when it is otherwise limited in verifiable detail. It is necessary to take into account the possibilities of suggestibility, contamination of evidence, copy cat evidence or collaboration, if only for the purposes of excluding them."

9–86   It is, therefore, very important that the risk of such a "cause common to the witnesses" such as collusion or contamination[200] can be discounted. It would seem logical that a trial judge would have to be satisfied that such a common cause did not exist before admitting evidence of multiple accusation. However, it was held by the House of Lords in *R. v H*[201] that contamination is not a factor to be taken into account in determining admissibility unless it is so blatant as to render the evidence totally unworthy of belief. Otherwise, the admissibility of the evidence should be determined on the basis that there is no contamination at all and the issue left to the jury. This approach was justified on the basis that in many, if not most cases, there is some danger of contamination, and it would be too stringent an approach to exclude evidence simply on that basis. Another reason advanced is that the question of contamination essentially involves an assessment of the credibility of witnesses, which is a jury function.

9–87   However, a different and, it is submitted, preferable approach was adopted by the High Court of Australia in *Hoch v R.*[202] Mason CJ explained that:

> "In cases where there is a possibility of joint concoction there is another rational view of the evidence. That rational view—*viz.* joint concoction—is inconsistent with the improbability of the complainants having concocted similar lies. It thus destroys the probative value of the evidence which is a condition precedent to its admissibility."[203]

9–88   The learned judge went on to formulate a test for the admissibility of misconduct evidence of multiple accusers based on whether such evidence was reasonably explicable on the basis of concoction. This was to be determined in light of common sense and experience, and the trial judge should consider whether the complainants had a sufficient relationship to each other, opportunity, and motive for concoction. If the evidence was reasonably explicable on the basis of concoction, then it would lack the probative force required to render it admissible. He made it clear that it is not necessary for the trial judge to decide whether there was in fact concoction; misconduct evidence should be excluded where the similarity "is capable of reasonable explanation on the basis of concoction."[204]

(f) Background Evidence

9–89   Misconduct evidence can be admitted where it is so inextricably bound up with the commission of the offences charged that its admission is necessary to contextualise the offences and/or to explain the relationship between the accused and other parties

---

[200] For a comprehensive discussion of the meaning of collusion/contamination, and the use of cross-admissible evidence as corroboration, see *R. v H* [1995] 2 AC 596 at 608–612, [1995] 2 All ER 865 at 873–877. *Cf. DPP v Boardman* [1975] AC 421 at 459, [1974] 3 All ER 887 at 910; *R. v Ananthanarayanan* [1994] 1 WLR 788 at 795–796, [1994] 2 All ER 847 at 854–855.

[201] [1995] 2 AC 596, [1995] 2 All ER 865. See also *DPP v Kilbourne* [1973] AC 729 at 750, [1973] 1 All ER 440 at 456; *R. v Johannsen* (1977) 65 Cr App R 101 at 103–104; *R. v Hunt* [1995] Crim LR 42.

[202] (1988) 165 CLR 292.

[203] (1988) 165 CLR 292 at 296.

[204] (1988) 165 CLR 292 at 297.

involved and thereby give the tribunal of fact a complete picture of the circumstances in which the offences occurred.[205] In *R. v Bond*,[206] Kennedy LJ explained:

> "The general rule cannot be applied where the facts which constitute distinct offences are at the same time part of the transaction which is the subject of the indictment. Evidence is necessarily admissible as to acts which are so closely and inextricably mixed up with the history of the guilty act itself as to form part of one chain of relevant circumstances, and so could not be excluded in the presentment of the case before the jury without the evidence being thereby rendered unintelligible."

9–90   So, in *Attorney General v Joyce*,[207] evidence was admitted at the trial of the accused for murder that, on a previous occasion, he had put guano into milk to be drunk by the deceased on the basis that this "formed part of one entire transaction...; it presented one aspect of the relations existing between the prisoners and the deceased..."[208]

9–91   The admission of evidence on this basis was reaffirmed in somewhat wider terms in *R. v Pettman*[209] where Purchas LJ stated:

> "Where it is necessary to place before the jury evidence of part of a continual background of history relevant to the offence charged in the indictment, and without the totality of which the account placed before the jury would be incomplete or incomprehensible, then the fact that the whole account involves including evidence establishing the commission of an offence with which the accused is not charged is not of itself a ground for excluding the evidence."

9–92   That decision was followed by the English Court of Appeal in *R. v M(T)*[210] where the somewhat misleading term, "background evidence",[211] was coined to describe evidence admissible on this basis.[212]

9–93   These authorities were considered and approved by the Supreme Court in *People (DPP) v McNeill*.[213] Denham J identified the circumstances in which "background evidence" would be admitted as follows:

> "Background evidence may be admitted to give a jury a relevant picture of the parties in the time prior to the offences charged. Background evidence may be admitted because if it were not admitted it would create an unreal situation. It arises in situations where if no background evidence was admitted, the evidence before the jury would be incomplete or incomprehensible. Background evidence is evidence which is so closely and inextricably linked to the alleged offences and/or the relations between the relevant persons so as to form part of the body of evidence to render it coherent and comprehensible."[214]

9–94   She went on to hold that such evidence would be admissible where it was

---

[205] See *Attorney General v McCabe* [1927] IR 129; *Attorney General v Joyce* [1929] IR 526; *Attorney General v Fleming* [1934] IR 166; *R. v Wylie* (1804) 1 B & P (NR) 92; *R. v Bond* [1906] 2 KB 389. Sometimes, such evidence is referred to as forming part of the *res gestae*: *People (DPP) v Mulligan* [2009] IECCA 24 at [2].

[206] [1906] 2 KB 389 at 400.

[207] [1929] IR 526.

[208] [1929] IR 526 at 540.

[209] Unreported, Court of Appeal, 2 May 1985.

[210] [2000] 1 WLR 421.

[211] This term seems to have been derived by the Court of Appeal in *R. v M(T)* [2000] 1 WLR 421 from a note by Professor Birch [1995] Crim LR 651.

[212] See also *People (DPP) v Baily* [2010] IECCA 25 where it was held that evidence of a portion of an interview of the accused by gardaí in which he admitted a sexual attraction to young boys and girls had been properly admitted as background evidence.

[213] [2011] IESC 12, [2011] 2 IR 669.

[214] [2011] IESC 12 at [49], [2011] 2 IR 669 at 693.

relevant and necessary and that the fact that it tended to show the commission of other crimes did not render it inadmissible. In that case where the prosecution had chosen to charge a number of specimen counts only, it was held that evidence establishing a continuum of sexual abuse of the complainant by the accused over a lengthy period had been properly admitted as background evidence. As O'Donnell J explained, it was admitted "because it is an intrinsic part of the story necessary to understand the circumstances in which the complainant says she was abused over a protracted period by the appellant".[215] If it were not admitted, then this could lead to the jury entertaining doubts about the credibility of the complainant arising from the fact that the evidence had been straitjacketed in relation to specified counts in ease of the accused. Further, for the reasons set out in his judgment, the risk of prejudice from its admission was considered to be small. While there good grounds for the admissibility of the evidence in the particular circumstances of that case,[216] there is considerable force to the criticism of Fennelly J in his dissenting judgment that such evidence could not properly be described as evidence as to the background to the offences as it constituted evidence of the commission of a large number of other offences.[217]

9–95   The concept of background evidence was also employed by the Court of Criminal Appeal in *People (DPP) v Morgan*[218] where it was held that documents which indicated that the accused had been operating a brothel on dates other than those charged had been properly admitted as background evidence to provide a complete account of the circumstances of the offences charged so as to make them comprehensible to the jury.[219]

6. Necessity for Admission

9–96   A fundamental question that must be addressed in every case where it is sought to admit misconduct evidence is whether it is necessary to do so.[220] In *People (AG) v Kirwan*,[221] Black J endorsed the statement of Bray J in *R. v Bond*,[222] that "bearing in mind the strong prejudice that would necessarily be created in the minds of the jury by evidence of this class … the greatest care ought to be taken to reject such evidence unless it is plainly necessary to prove something which is really in issue."[223] Similarly, in *People (AG) v Havlin*,[224] Davitt P rejected the contention that misconduct evidence was "admissible to rebut some subsidiary matter raised by the defence which was not clearly relevant to the issues whether the accused was or was not guilty of the offence charged." More recently, in *People (DPP) v McNeill*,[225] Denham J stated that

---

215 [2011] IESC 12 at [154], [2011] 2 IR 669 at 722.
216 Such "background" or "relationship" evidence has also been admitted in New Zealand (*R. v Underwood* [1999] Crim LR 227; *R. v Paniani,* unreported, New Zealand Court of Appeal, 18 March 1999) and Australia (*Roach v R.* (2011) 83 ALJR 588).
217 [2011] IESC 12 at [126]–[127], [2011] 2 IR 669 at 712.
218 [2011] IECCA 36.
219 See also *People (DPP) v Timmons* [2011] IECCA 13 where the English authorities on "background evidence" were approved and applied.
220 See Nair, "Similar Fact Evidence–Prejudice and Irrelevance Revisited" [1993] Crim LR 432.
221 [1943] IR 279.
222 [1906] 2 KB 389 at 417.
223 [1943] IR 279 at 309. See also *R. v Quilter* (1913) 67 ILTR 264 at 265 and *People (DPP) v Byrne* [1998] 2 IR 417 at 430.
224 (1952) 1 Frewen 132 at 134.
225 [2011] IESC 12 at [50], [2011] 2 IR 669 at 694.

misconduct evidence could only be admitted if it was necessary to do so and that it was not sufficient that it would helpful to the prosecution to admit the evidence. A trial judge should, therefore, be vigilant to ensure that the admission of misconduct evidence or the disclosure of misconduct on the part of an accused is really necessary for the determination of the issues in the case.[226]

9–97 A contention that the admission of misconduct evidence was not necessary failed on the facts in *People (DPP) v Wharrie*.[227] The appellant had been convicted of offences arising from the importation of a large quantity of drugs. At the trial, evidence was admitted that he had entered the State using a false passport with the name used on the false passport being connected by other evidence to the drugs and the other persons involved. On appeal, it was contended that this evidence ought not to have been admitted because it disclosed that the appellant had committed a falsehood and a criminal offence and that its admission was not necessary. However, in circumstances where a number of the other persons involved used false passports, the Court accepted that the prosecution had been entitled to lead evidence of the utilisation by the appellant of a false passport in order to establish a link between him and the drug importation. The purpose of introducing the evidence was to link various pieces of circumstantial evidence together and the Court was satisfied that the evidence was probative.

9–98 Particular difficulties have arisen as to when misconduct evidence can be adduced by the prosecution to rebut an anticipated defence. In *Thompson v R.*,[228] it was held that a defence had to be actually raised by an accused before misconduct evidence could be admitted to rebut it. Lord Sumner explained that:

> "Before an issue can be said to be raised, which would permit the introduction of such evidence so obviously prejudicial to the accused, it must have been raised in substance, if not in so many words, and the issue so raised must be one to which the prejudicial evidence is relevant. The prosecution cannot credit the accused with fancy defences in order to rebut them at the outset by some damning piece of prejudice."[229]

9–99 Subsequent English decisions have diluted the requirement that a defence must be raised by an accused, holding that it is permissible for the prosecution to adduce such evidence to rebut a defence that is reasonably open to, or it is anticipated may be raised by, an accused.[230] However, it is submitted that, having regard to the potential impact of the admission of misconduct evidence on the fairness of a trial, the better approach is that advocated by Black J in *People (AG) v Kirwan*,[231] who stated that misconduct evidence should not be admitted "unless the defence it is tendered to rebut is definitely put forward"[232] or is one which is raised in substance.[233]

---

[226] See *R. v Berry* (1986) 83 Cr App R 7 at 10, where it was held that misconduct evidence is not admissible to show intention at a trial where motive is not in issue.

[227] [2013] IECCA 20.

[228] [1918] AC 221.

[229] [1918] AC 221 at 232.

[230] See *Noor Mohammed v R.* [1949] AC 182, [1949] 1 All ER 365; *R. v Hall* [1952] 1 KB 302, [1952] 1 All ER 66; *Harris v DPP* [1952] AC 694 at 706, [1952] 1 All ER 1044 at 1047. A similar approach was adopted by a majority of the US Supreme Court in *Estelle v Maguire* (1991) 502 US 62.

[231] [1943] IR 279.

[232] [1943] IR 279 at 313.

[233] [1943] IR 279 at 316. The learned judge stated that a defence raised in substance would include a defence that the jury would inevitably raise themselves on the facts before them.

9–100   In some instances, it may be possible for misconduct evidence to be given in redacted form so that it is not necessary to reveal the misconduct or any details in relation thereto to the tribunal of fact. A good example of where this would have been possible is furnished by the facts of *People (AG) v Kirwan*.[234] The accused had been convicted of the murder of his brother, the dismembered body of whom had been found in a bog not far from where the accused and the deceased had lived. At the trial, evidence had been given by a prison warder that the accused had received training as a butcher while in prison, and by a prison doctor that the accused was familiar with a particular drug. Although the Supreme Court held that this evidence had been properly admitted as relevant to material issues before the jury, Black J took the view that the test of necessity had not been satisfied. He pointed out that the evidence of the prison warder as to the accused's anatomical knowledge and butchering skills could have been given without disclosing the fact that he was a prison warder. In his view, this evidence would not have given any less weight by the jury because he did not reveal his occupation. The same considerations applied to the evidence of the prison doctor, who could have given his evidence without revealing that he was a prison doctor as opposed to an ordinary doctor.

7. Whether Sufficient Proof of Commission of Acts of Misconduct

9–101   Obviously, the tribunal of fact can only rely upon misconduct evidence in its assessment of the guilt or innocence of an accused if it is satisfied that the acts of misconduct alleged were actually committed by the accused. Although this is primarily a question of fact for the tribunal of fact to determine, it also requires to be assessed by the trial judge in deciding whether the misconduct evidence should be admitted in the first instance. The test to be applied by the trial judge in that regard is not one of deciding whether there is satisfactory proof of the commission of the misconduct evidence, as this would be to usurp the role of the jury. Rather, it suffices that there is sufficient evidence from which a jury might reasonably conclude that the act of misconduct was committed by the accused.[235]

8. Discretion to Exclude Misconduct Evidence

9–102   In *People (AG) v Kirwan*,[236] O'Byrne J stated that: "the trial Judge, in the exercise of his discretion, may refuse to admit evidence which is, strictly speaking, relevant to an issue before the jury if he considers that the evidence, if admitted, would probably have a prejudical effect on the minds of the jury out of proportion to its true evidential value."[237] Thus, even if the trial judge is satisfied that misconduct evidence has sufficient probative force to be admitted, he or she has a discretion which should be exercised to exclude it if that probative force is outweighed by the risk of prejudice arising from its admission.[238]

9–103   The prejudicial effect of misconduct evidence relates to the degree to which "it tends to have some adverse effect upon a defendant beyond tending to prove the fact

---

[234] [1943] IR 279.
[235] *Attorney General v Fleming* [1934] IR 166 at 180.
[236] [1943] IR 279.
[237] [1943] IR 279 at 304.
[238] *People (DPP) v Piotrowski* [2014] IECCA 17 at [10.4].

or issue that justified its admission in evidence".[239] While this list is not exhaustive, it would appear that the most important factors which will bear on the degree of prejudice likely to be caused by the admission of a given item of misconduct evidence are: (i) the purpose for which the misconduct evidence is tendered; (ii) the similarity or otherwise of the misconduct evidence and the offences charged; (iii) the nature of the misconduct; and (iv) the relative gravity of the misconduct disclosed and the offence charged.

(a) The Purpose for which the misconduct evidence is tendered

9–104 The purpose for which the misconduct evidence is tendered is very important in assessing its prejudicial effect.[240] Where the relevance of the evidence derives from the jury accepting that the accused committed the acts of misconduct, the potential for prejudice is much greater than where evidence incidentally discloses misconduct on the part of the accused but does not derive its relevance from the misconduct aspect.[241]

(b) The similarity of the misconduct evidence and the offences charged

9–105 An important factor in assessing prejudicial effect is the similarity of the misconduct disclosed to the offences charged.[242] Where the misconduct evidence sought to be admitted discloses an offence similar to that charged, the risk of prejudice is very high because it will be very difficult, if not impossible, for the jury not to reason from the guilt of the accused in respect of the previous misconduct to his or her guilt on the offences charged.[243] As Kennedy J acknowledged in *R. v Bond*,[244] "[n]othing can so certainly be counted upon to make a prejudice against an accused person upon his trial as the disclosure to the jury of other misconduct of a kind similar to that which is the subject of the indictment". Conversely, where the misconduct evidence is not similar to the offences charged, this risk is correspondingly reduced.

(c) The nature of the misconduct

9–106 As noted above, one of the risks of prejudice associated with misconduct evidence is that a juror may wish to punish the accused for the misconduct and achieve that by convicting the accused of the offence charged. The quantum of this risk depends to some extent on how discreditable the misconduct disclosed is according to contemporary moral standards. Where the misconduct disclosed is "of a revolting character"[245] the risk of prejudice is great. A good example of a case where there was a high risk of prejudice on this basis is *R. v Ball*[246] where the misconduct evidence was of prior unpunished acts of incest between the two accused. Also significant is whether the accused has been convicted and sentenced in respect of the misconduct

---

[239] *US v Figueroa* (1980) 618 F 2d 934 (*per* Newman J).

[240] *Cf. Sweitzer v R.* [1982] 1 SCR 949, (1982) 137 DLR (3d) 702 at 706 and *R. v Paunovic* [1982] 1 NZLR 593 at 597.

[241] See, *e.g. People (AG) v Kirwan* [1943] IR 279 (evidence disclosed that accused had been in prison but not the offence for which he had been imprisoned).

[242] *Cf. People (DPP) v BK* [2000] 2 IR 199 at 203, where Barron J stated that the basic test to be applied was to ensure that the effect of "natural prejudice which will arise from the similarity of the allegation" is overborne by the probative effect of the evidence.

[243] *Cf. People (DPP) v BK* [2000] 2 IR 199 at 203.

[244] [1906] 2 KB 389 at 398.

[245] *R. v Bond* [1906] 2 KB 389 at 398 (*per* Kennedy J).

[246] [1911] AC 47.

because the risk of prejudice will be lessened where the accused has already been punished for the misconduct.

(d) The relative gravity of the misconduct disclosed and the offence charged

9–107   It is obvious that the potential for prejudice is related to the relative gravity of the misconduct disclosed and the offence charged.[247] So, in *People (DPP) v O'Sullivan*,[248] where the applicants were charged with murder and unedited inculpatory statements were adduced in evidence that disclosed the commission by them of larceny, the Court of Criminal Appeal was satisfied that no conceivable miscarriage of justice could have occurred. However, the result might have been different if the facts had been reversed because of the risk that the jury would reason that a person who had committed murder was eminently capable of committing larceny.

9. The Instruction to the Jury

9–108   Where misconduct evidence is admitted, a careful direction to the jury is required. The jury should be instructed as to the purpose for which that evidence was admitted, the requirement to be satisfied that the accused actually committed the alleged acts of misconduct before taking them into consideration, and the use that can be made of that evidence. In particular, the jury should be "informed as to the true purpose for which such evidence is admitted and warned of the danger of treating evidence of previous wrongdoing as itself proof of the wrongdoing charged".[249] Given the complexities that can arise, it is advisable for a trial judge to discuss this matter with counsel prior to the closing speeches.[250]

9–109   Helpful guidance as to the content of the direction required was given by Denham J in *People (DPP) v McNeil*.[251] Having endorsed the suggestion made by the Court of Criminal Appeal that the trial judge should inform the jury of the danger that the complainant's evidence in relation to the other offences was not truthful and that the commission of those offences did not prove that the accused was guilty of the offences charged, she went on to say:

> "It would be best practice for a trial judge, in most circumstances, to exercise his or her discretion, if admitting background evidence, to give a special warning to the jury as to the nature of the background evidence and of the issue to which it was relevant in the particular case. This would include a warning that such evidence is not admitted to prove, and may not be used to hold, that an accused is likely, by reason of his criminal conduct or character, to have committed the offences upon which he is charged. Rather, that such evidence is relevant to some specified issue of fact upon which the jury is required to determine. This should be particularised to the facts of a case, and may relate to issues such as consent or a relationship."[252]

9–110   In that case, the trial judge had not given such a direction but, having considered how the case had run at trial including, in particular, the restrained way in

---

[247] See *People (DPP) v O'Sullivan* (1979) 2 Frewen 1; *People (DPP) v Mulligan* [2009] IECCA 24 at [2]; *R. v D (LE)* [1989] 2 SCR 111, (1989) 50 CCC (3d) 142.
[248] (1979) 2 Frewen 1.
[249] *People (DPP) v McNeill* [2012] IESC 12 at [151], [2012] 2 IR 669 at 721 (*per* O'Donnell J).
[250] *People (DPP) v C.C. (No.2)* [2012] IECCA 86 at [36].
[251] [2011] IESC 12, [2011] 2 IR 669.
[252] [2011] IESC 12 at [44], [2011] 2 IR 669 at 692.

which it was treated, that the jury had clearly approached the counts individually, and the lack of any requisition, she concluded that verdict had not been unsafe.

9–111   The nature of the direction that should be given where there are a number of complainants and the trial judge rules that the evidence of a complainant on one count can be used as evidence and corroboration of the evidence of another complainant on another count were addressed by the Court of Criminal Appeal in *People (DPP) v C.C. (No.2)*.[253] O'Donnell J said that, where it is decided that the evidence of complainants is cross-admissible, not only should the jury be informed of this but also the reason why this is so. The jury should also be instructed of the risk that the multiplicity of complaints could be attributable to factors such as suggestibility, contamination or collaboration (related as appropriate to the facts of the case) and of the necessity to exclude these factors before using the evidence of one complainant as corroboration of the evidence of another complainant. He went on to say:

> "It was also important that the jury distinguish between two different processes of reasoning which may have been available to them. In the first place, if a jury concluded in relation to any one complainant that the case was compelling and that they were satisfied beyond any reasonable doubt of the guilt of the accused in relation to such incidents, then they could consider that it was now more likely that the account given by another complainant of a similar incident was true. However, it is also logically possible for a jury not to be satisfied beyond any reasonable doubt on the individual evidence relating to any *single* complainant or incident, but nevertheless to reach that point of being satisfied beyond reasonable doubt by virtue of the range of offences in respect of which evidence has been given, their interconnection, and the unlikelihood that the evidence in respect of each of the complaints is either the product of collusion or chance. But it is important that the jury should recognise which of these courses it is contemplating because it is obviously important to recognise, if indeed that is the case, that the jury is not satisfied beyond reasonable doubt on the individual evidence taken alone, and therefore the reliance being placed on the system evidence is that much greater."[254]

9–112   In that case, the trial judge had merely instructed the jury that the evidence of one complainant was admissible in relation to another and the Court concluded that the direction fell short of the level of detail required to give effective guidance to the jury on a central, and difficult, issue.

9–113   Useful guidance as to when a direction should be given to a jury consequent upon the admission of misconduct evidence and the content of that direction is also to be found in the decision of the New Zealand Supreme Court in *Mahomed v R*.[255] William Young J explained that what was described as a propensity evidence direction is required where the prosecution is: (a) relying on propensity reasoning and in doing so is invoking ideas about coincidence or probability; or (b) the evidence involves aspersions on the character of the appellant in respects not directly associated with the alleged offending; or (c) where, without it, there is a danger that the jury will not realise the relevance of the evidence in question or there is some particular risk of unfair prejudice associated with the evidence. However, a direction might not be required where the misconduct evidence was not led in reliance on coincidence or probability reasoning.

9–114   As to the content of a propensity evidence direction, William Young J was of

---

[253] [2012] IECCA 86 at [37]–[38].
[254] [2012] IECCA 86 at [38].
[255] [2011] NZSC 52, [2011] 3 NZLR 289 at [91]–[95]. See the case note by Pattenden at (2011) 15 E & P 361.

the view that there was no scope for a one size fits all direction. However, there were a number of matters that should be addressed. First, the trial judge should identify the evidence in question and explain why it has been led and the legitimate respects in which it might be taken into account by the jury. In most cases, the legitimate reasoning available to the jury will be based around coincidence or probability. That should be explained to the jury in simple and direct language addressed to the particular facts and what is said to be the implausible coincidence or how the evidence otherwise bears on the probability of the defendant being guilty. This is likely to require a discussion of the similarities involved in the conduct alleged. Where there are factors which may explain the postulated coincidence (for example, suggested collusion between the witnesses) that too should be addressed. Second, the judge should put the competing contentions of the parties in relation to the evidence. Third, the judge should caution the jury against reasoning processes which carry the risk of unfair prejudice associated with the propensity evidence. This should usually be along the lines that the fact that the defendant has or may have offended on other occasions does not establish guilt and that the only legitimate reasoning process available to the jury is the one which has been outlined.

10. Future Developments

9–115   When it examined the admission of bad character evidence, the Balance in the Criminal Law Review Group described this area as "difficult and complex"[256] and agreed with the assessment by the UK Criminal Law Review Revision Committee that this topic was by "far the most difficult of all the topics we have discussed".[257] Ultimately, it did not consider that any significant change or relaxation of the rules governing the admission of such evidence was warranted or justified as it was concerned about the potential impact on the fairness of the trial process and a possible increase in the risk of miscarriages of justice.[258] However, in *People (DPP) v McNeill*,[259] O'Donnell J suggested that this was an area that would benefit from a comprehensive review which would take account of the jurisprudence from other jurisdictions and consider the best contemporary learning in the field of psychology and sociology.[260] There is considerable merit to this suggestion and it is worth noting that the law in this area has been the subject of statutory intervention in England and Wales[261] (where the

---

[256] Balance in the Criminal Law Review Group, *Final Report* (2007), p.100.

[257] *11th Report Evidence* (General) (Cmnd 4991) (1972).

[258] Balance in the Criminal Law Review Group, *Final Report* (2007), pp.140–141.

[259] [2011] IESC 12 at [169], [2011] 2 IR 669 at 728.

[260] Some suggestions for reform are made by Kennedy, "Reform of the Exclusionary Rule in Relation to Evidence of Bad Character and Misconduct Evidence" (2014) 13 Hibernian LJ 98.

[261] Part 11 of the Criminal Justice Act 2003 significantly overhauled the law in relation to the admission of evidence of bad character. Such evidence, including evidence as to propensity, is admissible in a number of circumstances enumerated in s.101(1) commonly referred to as the gateways to admissibility. Part 11 implemented in part recommendations made by the Law Commission in its report, *Evidence of Bad Character in Criminal Proceedings* (Law Com No. 273, Cmnd 5257, 2011). For a detailed analysis of these provisions, see Spencer, *Evidence of Bad Character* 2nd edn (Hart Publishing, 2009) and Munday, *Evidence* 7th edn (Oxford University Press, 2013). See also Roberts, "All the Usual Suspects: a Critical Appraisal of the Law Commission Consultation Paper No. 141" [1997] Crim LR 93; McEwan, "Previous Misconduct at the Crossroads: Which Way Ahead?" [2002] Crim LR 180; Redmayne, "Recognising Propensity" [2011] Crim LR 117; Denyer, "Proving Bad Character" [2009] 8 Crim LR 562; Mirfield, "Character and Credibility" [2009] 3 Crim LR 135; Ormerod & Fortson, "Bad Character and Cross-admissibility" [2009] 5 Crim LR 313.

exclusionary rule against the admission of propensity evidence has been considerably diluted), New Zealand,[262] Australia[263] and the United States.[264]

E. Cross-Examination under the Criminal Justice (Evidence) Act 1924

1. Introduction

9–116   Section 1 of the Criminal Justice (Evidence) Act 1924, which reproduces s.1 of the Criminal Evidence Act 1898, effected a major change in the law by making an accused a competent witness in his or her own defence in all cases.[265] That change raised serious issues as to how an accused who chose to testify in his or her own defence should be treated and, in particular, the extent to which the prosecution should be allowed to ask questions with a view to eliciting evidence as to the commission of other offences or bad character.[266] It was recognised that, if an accused could be cross-examined as to other offences or his or her bad character, this would effectively preclude accused persons with a bad record from giving evidence and, thus, unfairly disadvantage them in putting forward their defence. However, if a blanket prohibition on such questioning was imposed, accused persons might seek to abuse that protection by attacking prosecution witnesses with impunity or asserting a good character that they did not possess.

9–117   Section 1(f) (as amended by s.33 of the Criminal Procedure Act 2010) contains a compromise whereby an accused is given the protection of what is generally referred to as a "shield"[267] against questioning about his or her convictions or bad character but this shield can be pierced in certain defined circumstances:

> "a person charged and called as a witness in pursuance of this Act shall not be asked, and if asked shall not be required to answer, any question tending to show that he has committed or been convicted of or been charged with an offence other than that wherewith he is then charged, or is of bad character, unless—

---

[262] Sections 40 to 43 of the Evidence Act 2006 which are based on the report of the New Zealand Law Commission, *Evidence: Reform of the Law* (NZLC R55) (1999). See further, *Mahomed v R.* [2011] NZSC 52.

[263] The statutory provisions at Federal and State level are discussed in Heydon, *Cross on Evidence* 9th Australian edn (LexisNexis Butterworths, 2013), pp.716–726.

[264] Rule 404 (b) of the Federal Rules of Evidence stipulates that: "Evidence of a crime, wrong, or other act is not admissible to prove a person's character in order to show that on a particular occasion the person acted in accordance with the character." However, it goes on to provide that: "This evidence may be admissible for another purpose, such as proving motive, opportunity, intent, preparation, plan, knowledge, identity, absence of mistake, or lack of accident." See Culberg "The Accused's Bad Character: Theory and Practice (2009) 84 Notre Dame Law Rev 1343.

[265] See *People (DPP) v Ferris* [2008] 1 IR 1 at 7, where Fennelly J stated that: "The Act of 1924… remedied the glaring injustice of depriving the accused of the right to swear to his own innocence."

[266] See the discussion of the background to s.1 of the Criminal Evidence Act 1898 in *Maxwell v DPP* [1935] AC 309 at 317, [1934] All ER 168 at 172.

[267] *People (DPP) v Ferris* [2008] 1 IR 1 at 8; *Maxwell v DPP* [1935] AC 309 at 314, [1934] All ER 168 at 172; *Jones v DPP* [1962] AC 635 at 682, [1962] 1 All ER 569 at 587. In *People (DPP) v Kelly*, unreported, Court of Criminal Appeal, *ex tempore*, 21 March 2002 at 5, Fennelly J said that s.1(f) had been "introduced as a protection which was designed to concentrate the mind of the court and the jury on the question of whether the accused person was guilty or not of the offence with which he was charged and not whether or not he was genuinely a bad character or had committed other offences on other occasions".

(i) the proof that he has committed or been convicted of such other evidence is admissible evidence to show that he is guilty of the offence wherewith he is then charged; or

(ii) he has personally or by his advocate asked questions of any witness with a view to establish his own good character, or has given evidence of his good character, or the nature or conduct of the defence is such as to involve imputations on the character of the person in respect of whom the offence was alleged to have been committed or the witnesses for the prosecution; or

(iii) he has given evidence against any other person charged with the same offence;

(iiia) the person has personally or by the person's advocate asked questions of any witness for the purpose of making, or the conduct of the defence is such as to involve, imputations on the character of a person in respect of whom the offence was alleged to have been committed and who is deceased or is so incapacitated as to be unable to give evidence"[268]

9–118   This section examines the nature and extent of the protection conferred by s.1(f) and the circumstances in which it may be lost together with some ancillary issues. As a preliminary matter, however, it is necessary to outline the relationship between ss.1(e) and 1(f) of the 1924 Act.

2. Relationship between Sections 1(e) and 1(f)

9–119   Section 1(e) of the 1924 Act provides that "a person charged and being a witness in pursuance of this Act may be asked any question in cross-examination notwithstanding that it would tend to criminate him as to the offence charged". It, thus, permits the prosecution to cross-examine an accused with a view to eliciting answers probative of his or her guilt. However, it is difficult to reconcile the ambit of that subsection with s.1(f) which contains a general prohibition on any questions as to the accused's previous convictions or character and, thus, excludes potentially incriminatory questions.

9–120   In reconciling these subsections, two possible interpretations of s.1(e) appear to be open.[269] The first is that the words "tend to criminate him as to the offence charged" renders admissible any evidence that tends to suggest the guilt of the accused including evidence of the accused's commission of other offences or bad character. However, were this interpretation to be adopted, the prohibition contained in s.1(f) would be deprived of all meaning. The second possible interpretation, and that ultimately adopted by the courts, is that s.1(e) bears a narrower meaning, referring only to evidence which tends to directly implicate the accused in the commission of the offence with which he is charged.

9–121   The relationship between subsections (e) and (f) was addressed in *Maxwell v DPP*[270] where a distinction was drawn by Viscount Sankey LC between questions as to matters probative of guilt, which were permitted pursuant to s.1(e), and matters outside and not directly relevant to the particular offence charged, which were prohibited by s.1(f).[271] The learned Judge took the view that s.1(f) is negative in form and, as such, is universal and absolute in its application, unless the exceptions come into play. He thus

---

[268] For a review of this section and suggestions for reform based on the provisions of Part 11 of the Criminal Justice Act 2003 in the UK, see Kennedy, "Reform of the Exclusionary Rule in Relation to Evidence of Bad Character and Misconduct Evidence" (2014) 13 Hibernian LJ 98.

[269] See *Jones v DPP* [1962] AC 635 at 663, [1962] 1 All ER 569 at 575 (*per* Lord Reid).

[270] [1935] AC 309, [1934] All ER 168.

[271] [1935] AC 309 at 317, [1934] All ER 168 at 172.

rejected the argument that s.1(e) renders admissible any evidence which is probative of guilt thereby overriding the prohibition contained in s.1(f). In his view, it did not follow "that when the absolute prohibition is superseded by a permission, that the permission is as absolute as the prohibition."[272]

9–122   The decision in *Maxwell* was followed in *Jones v DPP*[273] in which a majority of the House of Lords adopted a purposive approach and held that the English equivalent of s.1(e) permits only such questions as tend to directly incriminate the accused as to the offence charged, and does not permit questions which tend to do so indirectly. The view was taken that s.1(f) was intended to be a limit on the scope of s.1(e). Thus, the effect of the two provisions, taken together, is that an accused may be asked any question relevant to his guilt on the charge in issue provided that it is not prohibited by s.1(f), *i.e.* which does not relate to the commission by him or her of other offences or tend to show that he or she is of bad character. As Lord Reid explained:

> "This raises at once the question what is the proper construction of the words in proviso (e) 'tend to criminate him as to the offence charged'. Those words could mean tend to convince or persuade the jury that he is guilty, or they could have the narrower meaning—tend to connect him with the commission of the offence charged. If they have the former meaning there is at once an insoluble conflict between provisos (e) and (f). No line of questioning could be relevant unless it (or the answers to it) might tend to persuade the jury of the guilt of the accused. It is only permissible to bring in previous convictions or bad character if they are so relevant, so, unless proviso (f) is to be deprived of all content, it must prohibit some questions which would tend to criminate the accused of the offence charged if those words are used in the wider sense. But if they have the narrower meaning there is no such conflict. So the structure of the Act shows that they must have the narrower meaning."[274]

9–123   There is no Irish authority directly on the point but s.1(e) was considered by the Court of Criminal Appeal in *Attorney General v Murray*[275] where the view was taken that the 1924 Act did not place any restriction on the cross-examination of an accused who elected to give evidence, except that contained in s.1(f).[276]

3. The Prohibition in Section 1(f)

9–124   The prohibition contained in s.1(f) is absolute in that no questions falling within its terms may be asked, or if asked answered, unless and until one of the exceptions applies no matter how relevant the question is to the issues in the case.[277] A straightforward application of the prohibition can be seen in *Attorney General v Doyle*,[278] in which the applicants had been tried before the Special Criminal Court in respect of certain offences under the Emergency Powers Acts. The first named applicant challenged the admissibility of inculpatory statements made by him while in custody on the ground that they were involuntary. When giving evidence in relation to this issue, he was cross-examined in relation to a previous conviction, which he admitted, with the object of showing that he understood the nature and effect of a voluntary

---

[272] [1935] AC 309 at 318, [1934] All ER 168 at 173.
[273] [1962] AC 635, [1962] 1 All ER 569.
[274] [1962] AC 635 at 682–683, [1962] 1 All ER 569 at 574–575. See also *R. v Anderson* [1988] QB 678, [1988] 2 All ER 549 where the decisions in *Maxwell* and *Jones* were followed.
[275] [1926] IR 266.
[276] [1926] IR 266 at 282.
[277] *Jones v DPP* [1962] AC 635 at 663, [1962] 1 All ER 569 at 575 (*per* Lord Reid).
[278] (1943) 1 Frewen 39.

statement. This questioning was held to have violated the prohibition contained in s.1(f) and his conviction was set aside.[279]

9–125   It should be noted that s.1(f) protects an accused not only from being required to answer questions but also from being asked questions falling within the parameters of the section.[280] Accordingly, a trial judge should be vigilant so as to prevent such questions being put to the accused at all. The importance of this duty was emphasised in *R. v Ellis*,[281] where Bray J pointed out that the refusal to answer a question on the part of the accused can give rise to prejudice equal to, if not greater than, that which would arise from the answer:

> "The statute provides that the prisoner shall not be asked, and if asked shall not be required to answer, these questions. In our opinion, these words were intended to afford a double protection to the prisoner. The statute provides that the question shall not be asked. The reason of this is plain, because in most cases the mischief is done by the asking of the question. The jury naturally assume that no such question would be put unless there was foundation for it, and the more objection is made to it by the prisoner's counsel the stronger, to their minds, becomes that assumption. It is most damaging to the prisoner's case for his counsel to get up and argue that a question is inadmissible because it tends to show that the prisoner has committed another crime…It is the duty of the judge not to wait for any objection from the prisoner's counsel, but to stop such questions himself, and if by mischance the question be put, it is equally the clear duty of the judge to direct the jury to disregard it and not let it influence their minds."[282]

9–126   Thus, the trial judge is under an obligation to intervene before it becomes necessary for counsel for the accused to do so. In addition, if impermissible questions are asked, the judge has a duty to give a direction to the jury to counteract any prejudice caused by the accused's refusal to answer.

9–127   A number of issues arise from the wording of s.1(f) in relation to the application of the subsection and these are examined below as follows:

(a) the requirement that the accused be called as a witness;
(b) the limitation of the subsection to cross-examination;
(c) the meaning of the requirement of "tending to show"; and
(d) the questions prohibited by the subsection.

(a) Accused called as a witness

9–128   The first and, perhaps, most fundamental point to make about the prohibition contained in s.1(f) is that it only applies where an accused is "called as a witness". It cannot, therefore, be invoked as a basis for excluding a pre-trial statement made by an accused that discloses the commission of other offences or bad character.[283] If an accused does not give evidence, then the admission of evidence of his or her bad character and previous convictions is governed by the common law principles examined

---

[279] See also *People (AG) v Lehman (No.1)* [1947] IR 133; *People (AG) v Quinn* [1955] IR 367 at 383.
[280] See *Attorney General v Doyle* (1943) 1 Frewen 39 at 41, where it was held that a conviction may be set aside where an impermissible question is "asked, or asked and answered".
[281] [1910] 2 KB 746, [1908–10] All ER 488.
[282] [1910] 2 KB 746 at 763–764, [1908–10] All ER 488 at 494–495. Part of this passage was quoted with approval by the Court of Criminal Appeal in *People (DPP) v Kavanagh* [2008] IECCA 100.
[283] *People (DPP) v O'Sullivan* (1979) 2 Frewen 1.

in Section C above and satisfaction of any the exceptions contained in s.1(f) will not provide a basis for admitting such evidence.[284]

(b) Limitation of section 1(f) to cross-examination

9–129   Section 1(f) stipulates that an accused called as a witness "shall not be asked, and if asked shall not be required to answer" the questions specified in the subsection. In *Jones v DPP*,[285] it was held that this wording made it clear that the prohibition in s.1(f) only applies to the cross-examination of an accused and not examination-in-chief. Lord Reid explained:

> "It was suggested that [section 1(f)] applies to examination-in-chief as well as to cross-examination. I do not think so. The words 'shall not be required to answer' are quite inappropriate for examination-in-chief. The proviso is obviously intended to protect the accused. It does not prevent him from volunteering evidence, and does not in my view prevent his counsel from asking questions leading to disclosure of a previous conviction or bad character if such disclosure is thought to assist in his defence".[286]

9–130   This is clearly correct because the purpose of s.1(f) is to protect the accused from cross-examination as to other offences or his or her bad character and not to create an impediment to an accused making out a defence.

(c) Meaning of "tending to show"

9–131   Section 1(f) prohibits questions "tending to show" that an accused has committed or been convicted of, or been charged with another offence, or is of bad character. The interpretation of this phrase has been considered in a number of cases with the result that it has been construed as meaning "tending to show for the first time". In other words, the prohibition in s.1(f) only applies where the questions asked of an accused on cross-examination tend to suggest to the jury that he or she has committed a previous offence or is of bad character in circumstances where this has not previously been revealed.

9–132   The leading authority is *Jones v DPP*.[287] The appellant had been convicted of the murder of a girl guide. When arrested he had given a false alibi which he later retracted. He then gave a second alibi which was very similar to that given by him at his trial for the rape of another girl guide. In both cases, he stated that he had been with a prostitute and narrated a long conversation with his wife on the day after the night of the alibi which conversations corresponded almost word for word. At his trial on the murder charge, he elected to give evidence in his own defence and, in order to explain why he had initially given a false alibi, he stated that he had previously been "in trouble" with the police and did not want to be in trouble again. Counsel for the prosecution applied for and was granted leave to cross-examine the appellant as to the similarity of the second alibi to that previously advanced by the appellant when he was "in trouble" with the police with a view to showing it was not credible. The House

---

[284]   See *R. v Butterwasser* [1948] 1 KB 4 at 7, [1947] 2 All ER 415 at 416; *R. v De Vere* [1982] QB 75 at 80, [1981] 3 All ER 473 at 476. *Cf. People (DPP) v Ferris* [2008] 1 IR 1 at 10.

[285]   [1962] AC 635, [1962] 1 All ER 569.

[286]   [1962] AC 635 at 663, [1962] 1 All ER 569 at 575.

[287]   [1962] AC 635, [1962] 1 All ER 569. See also *R. v Ellis* [1910] 2 KB 746; [1908–10] All ER 488.

of Lords unanimously decided that the questions put to the appellant did not fall foul of the prohibition in s.1(f) but differed as to the reasons for reaching that conclusion.

9–133   Lord Reid adopted a purposive approach to s.1(f), taking the view that an accused does not require protection from the introduction of prejudicial evidence where such evidence has already been adduced and, therefore, any prejudice arising has already been caused. He concluded, therefore, that "show" must mean "reveal" as only the revelation of something new could cause such prejudice:

> "If the jury already knew that the accused has been charged with an offence, a question inferring that he had been charged would add nothing and it would be absurd to prohibit it."[288]

9–134   Viscount Simonds also focused on the impact of such evidence on the jury, stating:

> "As to the meaning of the words 'tend to show' I see no difficulty. It is not the intention of the question that matters but the effect of the question and presumably the possible answer. Nor is the word 'show' in its context ambiguous…in relation to the giving of oral evidence it can only mean 'make known'. The issue then is whether the challenged questions made known anything to the jury which they did not know before."[289]

9–135   Lord Denning, on the other hand, took a more literal approach and held that s.1(f) excluded any questions that tended to show that the accused had previously been charged with another offence:

> "I think that the questions tended to *show* that Jones had been charged with an offence, even though he had himself brought out the fact that he had been 'in trouble' before. It is one thing to confess to having been in trouble before. It is quite another to have it emphasised against you with devastating detail…It seems to me that questions which tend to reveal an offence, thus particularised, are directly within the prohibition in s.1 proviso (f) and are not rendered admissible by his own vague disclosure of some other offence."[290]

9–136   However, he went on to hold that the questions were admissible under s.1(e) on the basis that the questions were directly relevant to the offence charged because they tended to refute an explanation which the accused had given.

9–137   The decision of the majority in *Jones* was approved and applied in *R. v Anderson*.[291] The appellant, a member of the IRA, had been convicted of conspiracy to cause explosions. At the trial, the appellant had denied all knowledge of any conspiracy to cause explosions and explained the false identity papers and money found in her possession on the basis that she had been involved in an attempt to smuggle escaped IRA prisoners out of the country. The prosecution applied for and was granted leave to cross-examine her as to whether she was wanted by the police in Northern Ireland with a view to showing that, as a wanted person, it was unlikely that she would have been selected to help escaped prisoners or that she herself would have been willing to undertake such an expedition with the double risk of identification and arrest. Her appeal on the ground that the trial judge had erred in allowing this cross-examination failed. It was held that, by stating that she was involved in criminal activity by smuggling prisoners, the accused had already revealed the commission by her of other offences

---

[288] [1962] AC 635 at 664, [1962] 1 All ER 569 at 575.
[289] [1962] AC 635 at 659, [1962] 1 All ER 569 at 572–573.
[290] [1962] AC 635 at 667, [1962] 1 All ER 569 at 577 (emphasis in the original).
[291] [1988] QB 678, [1988] 2 All ER 549.

and, thus, there was no revelation involved in the evidence that she was wanted by the police in relation to an unspecified offence.[292]

9–138 A strong argument in favour of the interpretation of "tending to show" adopted in *Jones* and *Anderson* is that, if s.1(f) were construed so as to prohibit questions as to the accused's previous record in circumstances where the jury were already aware that he had been previously charged or convicted of an offence, it would be impossible for the prosecution to test any evidence given in that regard by the accused in examination-in-chief. An accused could, therefore, misrepresent the position in relation to an offence and the prosecution would not be afforded an opportunity to correct that by way of cross-examination.

(d) Prohibited Questions

9–139 Section 1(f) prohibits the asking of any question tending to show that the accused has committed or been convicted of or been charged with any offence other than that wherewith he is then charged, or is of bad character. Whether a question or line of questioning breaches that prohibition will depend on the particular circumstances of the case and the matters in issue. In *People (DPP) v Kelly*,[293] the accused had been convicted of a number of drug related offences. When arrested, the accused had in his possession a large sum of cash and he gave evidence that this money had been earned from trading in counterfeit goods. He was cross-examined at length about the sums of money that he had made from this trade and the fact that he had bought his house and other property for cash. One of the grounds of appeal was that this questioning had transgressed the prohibition in s.1(f) by tending to suggest that the application had committed or been convicted of another offence or that he was of bad character. The Court of Criminal Appeal noted that counsel for the prosecution had not explicitly suggested that the sums of money handled by the accused over the years constituted the proceeds of drug dealing rather than dealing in counterfeit goods but it was considered that this was the purpose of the questioning and tended to suggest to the jury that the accused had been engaged in dealing in illegal drugs. Accordingly, it was held that the questions contravened permissible bounds and the conviction was set aside.

4. Exceptions where the Prohibition in Section 1(f) does not Apply

9–140 Section 1(f) (as amended) provides that the prohibition contained therein does not apply or may be lost in four situations:

(a) where misconduct evidence is admissible;
(b) where an accused adduces or attempts to elicit evidence of his or her good character or casts imputations on the character of the person in respect of whom the offence was alleged to have been committed or witnesses for the prosecution;
(c) where an accused gives evidence against a co-accused; or
(d) where an accused cross-examines any witness for the purpose of making, or the conduct of the defence is such as to involve, imputations on the character of a person in respect of whom the offence was alleged to

---

[292] [1988] QB 678 at 687, [1988] 2 All ER 549 at 555.
[293] Unreported, Court of Criminal Appeal, *ex tempore*, 21 March 2002.

have been committed and who is deceased or so incapacitated as to be unable to give evidence.

9–141   Each of these exceptions will be examined below but, first, some preliminary points should be noted.

9–142   The first is that the exceptions to s.1(f) only permit the cross-examination of the accused in relation to other offences or his or her bad character and do not provide any basis for the admission of evidence of bad character by other witnesses that would not otherwise be admissible at common law. So, in *People (AG) v Havlin*,[294] where the conduct of the defence of the accused had been such as to involve imputations upon the character of the witnesses for the prosecution and to justify cross-examination in accordance with s.1(f)(ii), it was held that evidence given by a Garda suggesting that the accused had committed other offences should not have been admitted. The Court of Criminal Appeal was satisfied that there was no authority for the proposition that "such conduct of a case by the defence rendered relevant and admissible any evidence, other than that of the accused himself, as to his bad character".[295]

9–143   The second is that there is an important distinction between the exception provided for in s.1(f)(i) and those provided for in ss.1(f)(ii), 1(f)(iii) and 1(f)(iiia). The application of s.1(f)(i) is independent of the conduct of the defence and, thus, may apply without any particular action on the part of the defence whereas ss.1(f)(ii), 1(f)(iii) and 1(f)(iiia) deprive an accused of the benefit of the protection conferred by s.1(f) only where certain steps are taken by the accused. Another crucial difference is that, where questions are permissible pursuant to s.1(f)(i), any answers given by an accused may be used to prove guilt. By way of contrast, where questions are permitted pursuant to ss.1(f)(ii), 1(f)(iii) and 1(f)(iiia), any evidence adduced only goes to the credibility of the accused.

(a) Section 1(f)(i)

9–144   Section 1(f)(i) provides that an accused may be asked about the commission of other offences where "the proof that he has committed or been convicted of such other offence is admissible evidence to show that he is guilty of the offence wherewith he is then charged". In essence, this subsection permits an accused to be cross-examined about admissible misconduct evidence. However, it is important to point out that the subsection is limited in its application to evidence of the commission or conviction of other offences and, thus, will not apply where the accused has been charged but acquitted of an offence.[296] Neither, would it seem, will it apply where the misconduct evidence consists of discreditable but non-criminal acts.

9–145   In *Jones v DPP*,[297] Lord Morris rejected the proposition that, where misconduct evidence is admissible under s.1(f)(i), questions could only be put to the accused if, as part of the case for the prosecution, substantive evidence in regard to such other offence had already been given. Although he thought it undesirable for the matter to be first raised on cross-examination, he pointed out that the admission of an accused

---

[294] (1952) 1 Frewen 132.
[295] (1952) 1 Frewen 132 at 134 (*per* Davitt P).
[296] *R. v Cokar* [1960] 2 QB 207, [1960] 2 All ER 175.
[297] [1962] AC 635 at 685, [1962] 1 All ER 569 at 589.

when asked questions on cross-examination is proof and took the view that there is no essential requirement that proof should be given in any other way or at any earlier stage. The learned judge went on to say that, in practice, such a situation was unlikely to arise because it would be more effective and convenient to give such evidence as part of the prosecution case.

9–146   The application of this exception has, however, been largely rendered redundant by the decision of the House of Lords in *Jones*[298] as to the meaning of the phrase "tending to show". If, as is normally the case, the prosecution adduce misconduct evidence as part of its case in chief, then the prohibition in s.1(f) will have no application to the cross-examination of the accused in relation to that evidence, as questions put to him or her will not reveal the other offences to the tribunal of fact.

(b) Section 1(f)(ii)

9–147   Section 1(f)(ii) (as amended) actually contains two distinct though related exceptions:

> (i)   where an accused adduces or attempts to elicit evidence of his or her good character; and
>
> (ii) where an accused casts imputations on the character of the person in respect of whom the offence was alleged to have been committed or witnesses for the prosecution.

9–148   Each of these will be considered in turn and then the nature of the questioning permitted where the exception applies will be examined.

(i) Evidence of good character of accused

9–149   This exception is designed to prevent an accused abusing the protection conferred s.1(f) to mislead the jury in relation to his or her character. As Earl of Reading CJ explained in *R. v Wood*[299]:

> "… if the defendant endeavours to show that he is of good character when he is in fact of bad character, he presents a false view of the case, and the prosecution are not only entitled but bound to do what they can to prove to the jury that he ought not to be placed upon the high pedestal which he desires to occupy."[300]

9–150   There was a line of English authority to the effect that the word "character" as used in this exception bears a broader meaning than that which applies at common law so that an accused would forfeit the protection of s.1(f) and would be exposed to cross-examination on his or her entire record if he or she gave evidence as to his or her reputation *or* his or her disposition.[301] However, it was held in *People (DPP) v Ferris*[302] that the word "character" as used in s.1(f)(ii) should be given its common law meaning which is confined to evidence of general reputation.[303] Thus, an accused will

---

[298] [1962] AC 635, [1962] 1 All ER 569.
[299] [1920] 2 KB 179, [1920] All ER 137.
[300] [1920] 2 KB 179 at 182, [1920] All ER 137 at 138.
[301] See *R. v Dunkley* (1926) 28 Cox CC 143, [1927] 1 KB 323 at 329, [1926] All ER 187 at 190; *R. v Stirland* [1944] AC 315, [1944] 2 All ER 13; *Malindi v R.* [1967] AC 439 at 451, [1966] 3 All ER 285 at 291; *R. v Selvey* [1970] AC 304 at 333, [1968] 2 All ER 497 at 502.
[302] [2008] 1 IR 1 at 10. See *contra People (AG) v Coleman* [1945] IR 237.
[303] See *R. v Rowton* (1865) 10 Cox CC 25, [1861–73] All ER 549; *R. v Butterwasser* [1948] 1 KB 4, [1947] 2 All ER 415.

only forfeit the protection of s.1(f) where he or she has given, or by questions sought to elicit, evidence that he or she has a good character in the sense of general reputation.[304]

9–151   As originally enacted, the accused's shield could only be lost pursuant to s.1(f)(ii) where he gave evidence himself or herself of his or her good character or asked questions of prosecution witnesses which elicited such evidence. This led to the anomaly that, if evidence of good character was given by a defence witness, the accused could not be cross-examined on his or her criminal record[305] although rebuttal evidence could be adduced.[306] This has now been addressed by the amendment effected to s.1(f)(ii) by s.33(a)(i) of the Criminal Procedure Act 2010 which broadens the application of the exception from witnesses from the prosecution to any witness including those called by the defence.[307]

9–152   The question of whether an accused has sought to give or elicit evidence of his or her good character is decided by the trial judge, on the application of the prosecution, and depends on the nature of the evidence given in the context of the charge and the circumstances of the case.[308] It appears that the accused will only lose his shield if he adduces or seeks to elicit evidence that positively asserts a good character and it is not enough that the accused merely gives an impression that he or she is of good character by, for example, dressing well or giving evidence of a stable home life.[309]

9–153   It has been held that general questions put to the accused in examination-in-chief concerning the circumstances surrounding the alleged offences does not amount to evidence of good character, notwithstanding the fact that this may tend to show that the accused is innocent.[310] If it were otherwise, an accused would be severely hampered in testing the veracity and reliability of the evidence tendered against him.

9–154   An accused will also not be regarded as having asserted his or her good character if he or she attacks the character of a prosecution witness or another person not called as a witness. In *R. v Lee*,[311] the accused, who was charged with theft,

---

[304] A similar approach was taken in Canada in *R. v Close* (1982) 68 CCC (2d) 105, (1982) 38 OR (2d) 453, (1982) 137 DLR (3d) 655.

[305] *People (DPP) v Ferris* [2008] 1 IR 1 at 8; *R. v Redd* [1923] 1 KB 104 at 107, [1922] All ER 435 at 436.

[306] *R. v Rowton* (1865) 10 Cox CC 25 at 28–29, [1861–73] All ER 549 at 551; *R. v Butterwasser* [1948] 1 KB 4 at 6, [1947] 2 All ER 415 at 416.

[307] While the intention of the amendment to s.1(f)(ii) effected by s.33(a)(i), which gives effect to a recommendation of the Balance in the Criminal Law Review Group, *Final Report* (2007), p.115, is clear, it should be noted that s.33(a)(i) contains a drafting error in that it seeks to substitute the words "questions of any witness" for the words "questions for the witnesses for the prosecution" whereas the actual wording used in s.1(f)(ii) as originally enacted is "questions of the witnesses for the prosecution". It remains to be seen whether this error has the effect of undermining the efficacy of the amendment.

[308] For an example of where the accused was held to have led evidence of good character both through the evidence of the accused and by cross-examination of a prosecution witness so as to trigger the application of s.1(f)(ii), see *People (DPP) v Kavanagh* [2008] IECCA 100.

[309] See *R. v Coulman* (1927) 20 Cr App R 106 at 108. This is now dealt with in the UK by s.105 of the Criminal Justice Act 2003 which provides that where it appears to the court that a defendant, by means of his conduct (including appearance or dress), is seeking to give the court or jury an impression about himself that is false or misleading, the court may if appears just to do so, treat the defendant as being responsible for the making of an assertion which is apt to give that impression, thereby opening the door to the admission of evidence of bad character.

[310] *R. v Ellis* [1910] 2 KB 746 at 762, [1908–10] All ER 488 at 493.

[311] [1976] 1 WLR 71, [1976] 1 All ER 570.

contended that the theft could have been committed by two other persons, not called as witnesses. The defence cross-examined the victim of the alleged theft as to the previous convictions of these two persons for dishonesty and it was held that the judge had erred in concluding that, by means of that line of cross-examination, the accused was seeking to establish his own good character. The Court of Appeal held that the words used in s.1(f) should be given their ordinary and natural meaning and the accused could not be considered to have asked questions with a view to establishing his good character because it was not implicit in an accusation of dishonesty against a person that the accuser himself was honest.[312]

9–155   Having regard to the difficulties in judging whether an accused will be taken to have asserted good character, it is evident that counsel for the accused should exercise caution and restraint in questioning the accused and other witnesses in relation to any matter touching upon the character of the accused so as to avoid inadvertently opening the door to potentially very damaging evidence of the bad record of the accused.[313] Given the potentially serious consequences for an accused of losing his or her shield, it has been held that counsel for the prosecution should not ask questions of an accused in cross-examination with the object of eliciting answers which amount to evidence of his or her good character, thus, opening the door to questions as to his or her previous convictions and bad character.[314]

(ii) Imputations on the character of victim or prosecution witnesses

9–156   Section 1(f)(ii) (as amended) prevents an accused taking unfair advantage of the protection conferred on him by s.1 by providing that he or she will lose the shield from cross-examination as to other offences and bad character if "the nature or conduct of the defence is such as to involve imputations on the character of the person in respect of whom the offence was alleged to have been committed or the witnesses for the prosecution".[315] As originally enacted, imputations could be made with impunity on the character of the victim of the alleged offence if he or she did not give evidence for the prosecution but now this will result in the loss of the shield regardless of whether the victim gives evidence.

9–157   This subsection raises an obvious difficulty in that it will frequently be necessary for an accused to make imputations in relation to the character of witnesses for the prosecution in order to mount a proper defence. If this is sufficient to trigger the application of the exception and open the door to cross-examination on previous offences and bad character, an accused with a bad record will be placed in the invidious position of having to choose between forfeiting a line of defence or revealing that bad record to the jury.[316] In order to avoid this, the Irish courts endorsed the purposive approach developed in the older English authorities (although eschewed in later

---

[312] [1976] 1 WLR 71 at 73, [1976] 1 All ER 570 at 572.

[313] *Cf. per* Lord Hewart CJ in *R. v Baldwin* [1925] All ER 402 at 404, (1925) 18 Cr App R 175.

[314] *R. v Beecham* [1921] 3 KB 464; *R. v Baldwin* [1925] All ER 402 at 404, (1925) 18 Cr App R 175. *Cf. R. v Eidinow* (1932) 23 Cr App R 145 at 150.

[315] In *DS v HM Advocate* [2007] UKPC 1, [2007] HLRL 28, the Privy Council rejected the contention that a Scottish statutory provision which permitted evidence to be led of an accused's previous convictions for sex offences where he or she adduced evidence about the complainant's character or sex life was incompatible with Art.6 of the European Convention on Human Rights on the basis it undermined the right of a defendant to defend himself or herself.

[316] See McCormack, "Caught in a Quandary: The Accused With a Record" (1985) 3 ILT 43.

authorities) to the effect that an accused will not lose his or her shield if the imputations cast are necessary for the proper conduct of his or her defence.[317]

9–158   In *R. v Rouse*,[318] the accused, in answer to a question on cross-examination as to whether a prosecution witness's evidence was invented, stated that it was a lie and that the witness was a liar. Darling J held that this was not an imputation within the meaning of s.1(f)(ii) but a mere denial of the charge albeit it in emphatic terms. A similar approach was adopted in *R. v Turner*,[319] where the accused put forward the defence of consent to a charge of rape and gave evidence to the effect that the complainant had committed a gross indecency with him. It was held that the evidence was directed towards proof of consent and, although it made imputations on the character of the complainant, it did not deprive the accused of the protection given by s.1(f). The principle adopted in these authorities was summarised by Viscount Simon LC in *Stirland v DPP*,[320] as being that "an accused is not to be regarded as depriving himself of the protection of the section because the proper conduct of the defence necessitates the making of injurious reflections on the prosecutor or of his witnesses."[321]

9–159   However, a different approach, based on the literal meaning of s.1(f)(ii), was adopted in *R. v Hudson*,[322] where Lord Alverstone LCJ stated that the words used in s.1(f)(ii):

> "must receive their ordinary and natural interpretation, and that it is not legitimate to qualify them by adding or inserting the words 'unnecessarily', or 'unjustifiably', or 'for purposes other than that of developing the defence', or other similar words."[323]

9–160   In that case, the Court concluded that, where the defence accuses a prosecution witness of having committed the offence with which the accused is charged, the case came directly within s.1(f)(ii), and the accused could be cross-examined as to his character or his previous convictions.[324]

9–161   A choice between these two lines of authority fell to be made in *Selvey v DPP*[325] where the House of Lords adopted the literal interpretation of the subsection advocated by Lord Alverstone LCJ in *Hudson*. Although it was accepted that an emphatic denial of the prosecution case would not, of itself, be sufficient to trigger cross-examination under s.1(f)(ii), it was held that such cross-examination would be permitted if the nature and conduct of the defence involved imputations on a prosecution witness,

---

[317] *Attorney General v Campbell* (1928) 1 Frewen 1, (1928) 62 ILTR 30; *Attorney General v O'Shea* [1931] IR 713; *People (DPP) v McGrail* [1990] 1 IR 38. See generally, Newman, "Synthesising the Law of Evidence: The Probative Value/Prejudicial Effect Principle and McGrail" (1993) 3 ISLR 96.

[318] [1904] 1 KB 184.

[319] [1944] KB 463, [1944] 1 All ER 599.

[320] [1944] AC 315 at 317, [1944] 2 All ER 13 at 18.

[321] See also *R. v Grout* (1909) 26 TLR 60 at 60; *R. v Sheehan* (1908) 24 TLR 459 at 460; *R. v Turner* [1944] KB 463, [1944] 1 All ER 599; *R. v Martinelli* (1908) 10 WALR 33; *Hewitt v Lenthall* [1931] SASR 314.

[322] [1912] 2 KB 464.

[323] [1912] 2 KB 464 at 470–471. Cf. *R. v Bridgewater* [1905] 1 KB 131; *R. v Preston* [1909] 1 KB 568; *R. v Westfall* (1912) 7 Cr App R 176.

[324] [1912] 2 KB 464 at 470. See also *R. v Watson* (1913) 8 Cr App R 249 at 254.

[325] [1970] AC 304, [1968] 2 All ER 497.

notwithstanding that these imputations were a necessary part of the accused's answer to the charge.[326]

9–162   The application of s.1(f)(ii) was first considered in this jurisdiction in *Attorney General v Campbell*[327] where a literal approach to its interpretation was adopted. During the trial of the appellant on charges of conspiracy to steal and larceny, he alleged on cross-examination that a garda had coerced a witness into giving false evidence in order to convict him and that two other scrap dealers had conspired with the garda in order to exclude him from the scrap business. The trial judge was satisfied that these allegations constituted imputations within the meaning of s.1(f)(ii) and permitted the prosecution to adduce evidence of the conviction of the appellant for another offence. On appeal, Kennedy CJ, delivering the judgment of the Court of Criminal Appeal, regarded recourse to authority as unnecessary because the words of s.1(f)(ii) were to be construed in accordance with their "plain ordinary sense".[328] Although he emphasised that denial, however strong, of the prosecution case did not trigger the exception, he did not regard the case before him as an instance of denial. Instead, the charge of conspiracy levelled by the appellant involved a direct imputation on the character of at least three important witnesses for the prosecution. He concluded, therefore, that the trial judge had been correct in permitting the cross-examination of the accused in respect of his previous conviction. The decision in *Campbell* was subsequently distinguished in *Attorney General v O'Shea*,[329] where the Court of Criminal Appeal rejected the contention that a rigorous and searching cross-examination of witnesses called by the prosecution involved an imputation on the character of those witnesses.

9–163   The application of s.1(f)(ii) was also considered in *People (AG) v Coleman*.[330] The accused had been convicted of two counts of criminal abortion. During the trial, a number of allegations were levelled at the woman upon whom the abortion had been performed and her husband (who were witnesses for the prosecution) including an allegation that the husband had committed a similar offence himself. The trial judge had allowed cross-examination of the accused and, on appeal, one of the grounds raised was that the trial judge had erred in so ruling. The accused contended that the imputations made had been necessary for the proper conduct of his defence. However, Sullivan CJ, delivering the judgment of the Court of Criminal Appeal, pointed out that the imputation made was not that the husband had committed the offences charged against the accused but rather had committed a similar offence. Even if such evidence had been accepted by the jury, it would not necessarily have established a defence to the charges upon which the accused was being tried. The Court, therefore, took the view that the proper conduct of the defence did not necessitate the making of any of the imputations in question and the judge had been right to allow cross-examination.[331]

9–164   The proper construction of s.1(f)(ii) was definitively resolved in the landmark decision of *People (DPP) v McGrail*[332] where the Court of Criminal Appeal decisively rejected a literal interpretation of the subsection in favour of a purposive approach.

---

[326] See also *R. v Wignall* [1993] Crim LR 62; *R. v Manley* (1962) 46 Cr App R 235.
[327] (1928) 1 Frewen 1, (1928) 62 ILTR 30.
[328] (1928) 1 Frewen 1 at 4.
[329] [1931] IR 718.
[330] [1945] IR 237.
[331] See also *People (AG) v Coleman (No.2)* (1945) 1 Frewen 64.
[332] [1990] 1 IR 38. *Cf.* Newman, "Synthesising the Law of Evidence: The Probative Value/Prejudicial Effect Principle and McGrail" (1993) 3 ISLR 96.

The accused in that case had been tried and convicted of offences under the Firearms Act 1964. The prosecution alleged that he had been arrested while trying to escape from certain premises and that he had pointed out a place on the premises where some guns had been hidden. It was also alleged that the accused had made certain unsigned incriminating statements. During cross-examination, it was put to the garda witnesses that the accused had not made any of the incriminating statements and had not pointed out the hiding place of the guns and that the gardaí were trying to convict the accused by inventing false verbal statements and other incriminating evidence. The trial judge held that the conduct of the applicant's case involved imputations on the character of the prosecution witnesses and permitted cross-examination of the accused as to his previous convictions.

9–165 The judgment of the Court of Criminal Appeal was delivered by Hederman J who emphasised that an accused would be seriously hampered in making a defence if he or she could not cast necessary imputations on the character of prosecution witnesses:

> "Every criminal trial involves an imputation as to the character of somebody…. If the accused, either by giving evidence or through his counsel's cross-examination of the witnesses for the prosecution, suggests to them that they are not to be believed, that is also an imputation as to their character in as much as it is suggested that they are telling an untruth, if that is the way the matter is put to them. The defence may even require, in its efforts to rebut the prosecution case, to suggest to the witness and the court that in fact the real author of the crime, if it has been proved to have been committed, is not the accused but one or other, perhaps, of the witnesses for the prosecution. Such a course of conduct is inevitable if an accused person is not to be seriously hampered in the conduct of his defence. Any ruling otherwise would have the effect of inhibiting the conduct of the defence in that an accused person, who may have a criminal record, may be intimidated into abandoning an effort to put in issue the truth of the evidence of a prosecution witness lest his own character outside the facts of the trial be put in issue….It would be quite an intolerable situation if an accused person, in the conduct of the defence in cross-examining prosecution witnesses the veracity of whose evidence he was challenging, should be required to confine himself to suggesting a mistake or other innocent explanation to avoid the risk of having his own character put in issue."[333]

9–166 The learned judge rejected the literal interpretation of s.1(f)(ii) adopted in *Campbell* and by the English courts in *Hudson* and *Selvey* as incompatible with the requirements of fair procedures:

> "This court is of the view that the principles of fair procedures must apply. A procedure which inhibits an accused from challenging the veracity of the evidence against him at the risk of having his own previous character put in evidence is not a fair procedure."[334]

9–167 He thus concluded that s.1(f)(ii) had to be construed as applying only to imputations made that were independent of the facts of the particular case:

> "In the view of the court [s.1(f)(ii)] must be construed as applying only to imputations made on the character of the prosecutor or his witnesses independent of the facts of the particular case, as for example, when it is suggested that the witnesses are of such general ill-repute that they are persons who are not to be believed. To put to a prosecution witness that he fabricated the evidence he is giving, or that he and other witnesses for the prosecution combined together to fabricate evidence for the particular trial in question, may be necessary to enable the accused to establish his defence, if in fact his defence is that he made no such statement to one or more of the prosecution witnesses…. A distinction must be drawn between questions and suggestions which are reasonably necessary to establish either the prosecution case or the defence case, even if they do involve suggesting a falsehood on the part of the witness of one or the other

---

[333] [1990] 1 IR 38 at 48–49.
[334] [1990] 1 IR 38 at 51.

side, on one hand and, on the other hand, an imputation of bad character introduced by either side relating to matters unconnected with the proofs of the instant case."[335]

9–168   It is important to note that, even where an accused has cast imputations on the character of prosecution witnesses that are not considered necessary for the proper conduct of the defence, a trial judge has a discretion to disallow questioning in relation to other offences committed by an accused or his or her bad character so as to avoid any danger of unfairness.[336] The relevant principles were helpfully summarised by Ackner LJ in *R. v Burke*[337] as follows:

> "1.   The trial judge must weigh the prejudicial effect of the questions against the damage done by the attack on the prosecution's witnesses, and must generally exercise his discretion so as to secure a trial that is fair both to the prosecution and the defence...
>
> 2.   Cases must occur in which it would be unjust to admit evidence of a character gravely prejudicial to the accused, even though there may be some tenuous grounds for holding it technically admissible...the putting of the questions as to character of the accused person may be fraught with results which immeasurably outweigh the result of questions put by the defence and which make a fair trial of the accused almost impossible...
>
> 3.   In the ordinary and normal case the trial judge may feel that if the credit of the prosecutor or his witnesses had been attacked, it is only fair that the jury should have before them material on which they can form their judgment whether the accused person is any more worthy to be believed than those he has attacked. It is obviously unfair that the jury should be left in the dark about an accused person's character if the conduct of his defence has attacked the character of the prosecutor or the witnesses for the prosecution within the meaning of the section...
>
> 4.   In order to see if the conviction should be quashed, it is not enough that the court think it would have exercised its discretion differently. The Court will not interfere with the exercise of a discretion by a judge below unless he has erred in principle, or there is no material on which he could properly have arrived at his decision..."[338]

(iii) Notice Requirement

9–169   Section 33(b) of the Criminal Procedure Act 2010 Act introduced a notice requirement by inserting a new s.1A in the 1924 Act which stipulates that, where an accused intends to adduce evidence, personally or by his or her advocate, of a witness including the accused, that would involve imputations on the character of a prosecution witness, or evidence of the good character of the accused, at least 7 days notice to the prosecution or leave to adduce such evidence without giving that period of notice is required.

(iv) Rebuttal Evidence

9–170   If an accused leads or elicits evidence that involves imputations on the character of a prosecution witness or evidence of good character, s.1A(b) of the 1924 Act[339] provides that the prosecution can cross-examine the accused or ask any other

---

[335] [1990] 1 IR 38 at 49–50. This construction of s.1(f)(ii) was approved in the Balance in the Criminal Law Review Group, *Final Report* (2007), pp.117–118.

[336] *People (DPP) v McGrail* [1990] 2 IR 38 at 50. *cf. R. v Hudson* [1912] 2 KB 464; *Selvey v DPP* [1970] AC 304, [1968] 2 All ER 497; *R. v Burke* (1985) 82 Cr App R 156.

[337] (1985) 82 Cr App R 156.

[338] (1985) 82 Cr App R 156 at 161. See also *R. v Powell* (1986) 82 Cr App R 165 where these principles were endorsed.

[339] As inserted by s.33(b) of the Criminal Procedure Act 2010.

witness, questions that: (i) would show that the accused has been convicted of any offence other than the one wherewith he or she is then charged, or is of bad character, or (ii) would show that the person in respect of whom the offence was alleged to have been committed is of good character.

(c) Section 1(f)(iii)

9–171   Section 1(f)(iii) provides that an accused will lose his shield where "he has given evidence against any other person charged with the same offence". In *Attorney General v Joyce*,[340] Sullivan P characterised this exception as a right which was correlative to the right of an accused to give evidence under s.1. So, where an accused elects to exercise his or her right to give evidence, and such evidence is adverse to the interests of his or her co-accused, the co-accused has a right to cross-examine him or her.

9–172   In *Joyce*,[341] O'Sullivan P indicated that s.1(f)(iii) will only apply where an accused gives evidence *adverse* to a co-accused and this was also the view adopted by the House of Lords in *Murdoch v Taylor*.[342] It was held that "evidence against" a co-accused for the purpose of s.1(f)(iii) means evidence which supports the prosecution's case against the co-accused in a material respect or which undermines the defence of the co-accused.[343] Delivering the judgment of the majority, Lord Donovan emphasised that the test of whether evidence had been given against a co-accused was objective in nature and depended not on the intention of the questioner but rather on the effect on the jury:

> "The object of proviso (f)(iii) is clearly to confer a benefit on a co-accused. If evidence is given against him by another accused he may show, if he can, by reference to the latter's previous offences that his testimony is not worthy of belief. It is the effect of the evidence on the jury which is material and which may be lessened or dissipated by invoking the proviso. The effect on the jury is the same, whether the evidence be given in examination-in-chief or in cross-examination; and the desirability of the co-accused being able to meet it by cross-examination as to credit is of the same importance, however the evidence is given....
>
> The like considerations also lead me to reject the argument that proviso (f)(iii) refers only to evidence given by one accused against the other with hostile intent. Again it is the effect of the evidence on the minds of the jury which matters, not the state of mind of the person who gives it....In my opinion, the test to be applied in order to determine whether one accused has given evidence against his co-accused is objective and not subjective."[344]

9–173   The learned judge went on to consider the circumstances in which an accused would be regarded as having given evidence against a co-accused. At the one end of the scale was evidence which did no more than contradict something which a co-accused had said without further advancing the prosecution's case to any significant degree.[345] This was not the kind of evidence contemplated by the proviso. At the other end of the scale was evidence which, if the jury believed it, would establish the co-accused's guilt. The was obviously evidence against a co-accused but his Lordship was satisfied

---

[340] [1929] IR 526.

[341] [1929] IR 526 at 542.

[342] [1965] AC 574, [1965] 1 All ER 406.

[343] [1965] AC 574 at 592, [1965] 1 All ER 406 at 416.

[344] [1965] AC 574 at 590–591, [1965] 1 All ER 406 at 415.

[345] See also *R. v Bruce* [1975] 3 All ER 277, [1975] 1 WLR 1252; *R. v Hatton* (1976) 64 Cr App R 88; *R. v Davis* [1975] 1 All ER 233, [1975] 1 WLR 345; *R. v Varley* [1982] 2 All ER 519; *R. v Crawford* [1998] 1 Cr App R 338.

that the expression was not so confined and it was necessary to examine the particular piece of evidence in the light of the other evidence in the case.

9–174   In *People (DPP) v Kavanagh*,[346] it was held that the exception in s.1(f)(iii) did not apply even though the applicant gave evidence that her co-accused had committed the robberies with which they were jointly charged because they had entered guilty pleas before she gave evidence and had been sentenced.

9–175   In *Attorney General v Joyce*,[347] O'Sullivan P held that, unlike the position where an accused loses his shield pursuant to s.1(f)(ii), once an accused has given evidence against his co-accused within the meaning of s.1(f)(iii), a trial judge has no discretion not to allow the accused to be cross-examined:

> "...when it is the co-accused who seeks to exercise the right conferred by proviso (f)(iii) different considerations come into play. He seeks to defend himself; to say to the jury that the man who is giving evidence against him is unworthy of belief; and to support that assertion by proof of bad character. The right to do this cannot, in my opinion, be fettered in any way."[348]

(d) Section 1(f)(iiia)

9–176   Section 33(a) of the Criminal Procedure Act 2010 introduced this new subsection, the effect of which is that the accused's shield will be lost where the accused has personally or by his advocate, "asked questions of any witness for the purpose of making, or the conduct of the defence is such as to involve, imputations on the character of a person in respect of whom the offence was alleged to have been committed and who is deceased or so incapacitated as to be unable to give evidence".[349] In *People (DPP) v Dumbrell*,[350] Denham J explained that the purpose of this subsection "is to correct a potential imbalance in the trial process whereby an accused may attack the credibility of a victim through information on previous convictions". She also said that it had to be applied fairly by the trial court.

9–177   A notice requirement was introduced by s.1A of the 1924 Act (as inserted by s.33(b) of the 2010 Act) which stipulates that, where a person charged with an offence intends to adduce such evidence, at least 7 days notice to the prosecution or leave to adduce such evidence without giving that period of notice is required. If such evidence is led,[351] then s.1A(b) provides that the prosecution can cross-examine the accused or ask any other witness, questions that: (i) would show that the accused has been convicted of any offence other than the one wherewith he or she is then charged, or is of bad character, or (ii) would show that the person in respect of whom the offence was alleged to have been committed is of good character.

9–178   As can be seen from *People (DPP) v Dumbrell*,[352] in a case where there is

---

[346] [2008] IECCA 100.

[347] [1929] IR 526.

[348] [1929] IR 526 at 593, 416. See also *R. v Miller* [1952] 2 All ER 667 at 668–669.

[349] This implements a recommendation of the Balance in the Criminal Law Review Group, *Final Report* (2007), p.118, which regarded the then state of the law as anomalous.

[350] [2014] IECCA 22 at [63].

[351] As can be seen from *People (DPP) v Dumbrell* [2014] IECCA 22, an accused can give notice pursuant to s.1A but subsequently elect not to adduce such evidence in which case his or her shield will not be lost.

[352] [2014] IECCA 22.

more than one accused and imputations are cast on the character of the deceased or incapacitated victim of the offence by one of the accused only, the other accused can take such benefit as may thereby arise without losing their shield. In that case, the two appellants had been convicted of murder. In the course of the trial, the first appellant served notice pursuant of his intention to adduced evidence that would involve imputations on the character of the deceased victim, *viz.* that he had convictions for carrying knives. The trial judge having made it clear that this would lead to the first appellant losing his shield, he did not adduce that evidence but, in the course of cross-examination, the second named appellant gave unprompted evidence that the deceased had a large number of convictions including for carrying knifes and firearms. This led to the introduction into evidence of the convictions of the second appellant but not of the first appellant. The contention of the first appellant that his trial had been unfair because he did not have the facility to cross-examine the prosecution witnesses on that evidence was dismissed. The Court observed that he had obtained the benefit of that information going before the jury without him having to drop his shield and the lack of an opportunity to cross-examine prosecution witnesses on it was a consequence primarily of his decision that he did not want to drop his shield. Although it was not necessary to decide the issue, a query was raised as to whether it would have been open to the second appellant to cross-examine the prosecution witnesses as to the deceased's convictions without himself losing his shield.[353]

5. Questioning where the Shield has been Lost

9–179   If an accused loses his or her shield under s.1(f), then he or she can be asked "any question tending to show that he has committed or been convicted of or been charged with any offence other than that wherewith he is then charged, or is of bad character". However, there are still a number of restrictions that apply to such cross-examination. The first is that the questioning of the accused is subject to the test of relevance. This point was emphasised by Viscount Sankey LC in *Maxwell v DPP*[354] who stated:

> "But these instances all involve the crucial test of relevance. And in general no question as to whether a prisoner has been convicted or charged or acquitted should be asked or, if asked, allowed by the judge, who has a discretion under proviso (f), unless it helps to elucidate the particular issue which the jury is investigating, or goes to credibility, that is, tends to show that he is not to be believed on his oath…"

9–180   Applying the test of relevance, it was held in *Maxwell* that, even though the prohibition contained in s.1(f) extends to offences with which the accused had been charged, he or she could not be questioned about a charge of which he or she had been acquitted.[355] Viscount Sankey LC explained that:

> "The mere fact that a man has been charged with an offence is no proof that he committed the offence. Such a fact is, therefore, irrelevant; it goes neither to show that the prisoner did the acts for which he is actually being tried nor does it go to his credibility as a witness. Such

---

[353] [2014] IECCA 22 at [69]. Denham CJ said: "It is a factor for consideration as to whether it would be unfair to allow a situation whereby an accused, who has elected not to adduce evidence as to a deceased's victim's previous convictions by reason of an unwillingness to have his own previous convictions put in evidence, could subsequently benefit from a co-accused dropping his shield, and then proceed to cross-examine witnesses in relation to a deceased's previous convictions to demonstrate a proclivity for violence."

[354] [1935] AC 309 at 321, [1934] All ER 168 at 174.

[355] *Cf. People (AG) v Coleman* [1945] IR 237 at 251.

questions must, therefore, be excluded on the principle which is fundamental in the law of evidence as conceived in this country, especially in criminal cases, because, if allowed, they are likely to lead the minds of the jury astray into false issues; not merely do they tend to introduce suspicion as if it were evidence, but they tend to distract the jury from the true issue, namely, whether the prisoner in fact committed the offence on which he is actually standing his trial."[356]

9–181   This interpretation of s.1(f) was endorsed by Viscount Simon LC in *Stirland v DPP*.[357] Having considered the use of the word "charged" in s.1(f), he stated that it was plain that its meaning in the section was "accused before a court" and not merely "suspected or accused without prosecution". Therefore, where the accused denied that he had ever been charged previously, it was not permissible to question him as to whether he had been suspected by his previous employer of forgery in order to challenge the veracity of his denial. He went on to say:

> "Neither were [these questions] relevant as going to disprove good character: the most virtuous may be suspected, and an unproved accusation proves nothing against the accused. But the questions, while irrelevant both to the charge which was being tried and to the issue of good character, were calculated to injure the appellant in the eyes of the jury by suggesting that he had been in trouble before, and were, therefore, not fair to him. They should not have been put, and, if put, should have been disallowed."[358]

9–182   Thus, it is not disproof of good character that an accused has been suspected, or accused, of a previous crime. Questions in relation thereto can only be asked if the accused has sworn expressly to the contrary. This is because an accused may be cross-examined as to any evidence he himself has tendered in examination-in-chief, including statements as to his good record, with a view to testing his veracity or accuracy, or to showing that he is not to be believed on his oath.[359]

9–183   It should also be noted that there are restrictions as to how far questioning in relation to other offences may go. For example, in *People (AG) v Bond*,[360] it was held that counsel for the prosecution had gone further than he should, in cross-examining the accused as to his previous convictions, by asking questions directed not to his credibility but to the probability that the accused had committed the offence at trial. A useful summary of the relevant principles is to be found in the judgment of Gage J, delivering the judgment of the English Court of Appeal in *R. v McLeod*[361] as follows:

> "1.   The primary purpose of the cross-examination as to previous convictions and bad character of the accused is to show that he is not worthy of belief. It is not, and should not be, to show that he has a disposition to commit the type of offence with which he is charged...But the mere fact that the offences are of a similar type to that charged or because of their number and type have the incidental effect of suggesting a tendency or disposition to commit the offence charged will not make them improper...
>
> 2.   It is undesirable that there should be prolonged or extensive cross-examination relation to previous offences. This is because it will divert the jury from the principal

---

[356] [1935] AC 309 at 320, [1934] All ER 168 at 173–174. He held that an accused could only be questioned in relation to a charge "as a step in cross-examination leading to a question whether he was convicted on the charge, or in order to elicit some evidence as to statements made or evidence given by the prisoner in the course of the trial on a charge which failed, which tend to throw doubt on the evidence which he is actually giving, though this last class of case must be rare and permissible only with great safeguards." See also *R. v Doosti* (1985) 82 Cr App R 181.
[357] [1944] AC 315, [1944] 2 All ER 13.
[358] [1944] AC 315 at 324, [1944] 2 All ER 13 at 17.
[359] [1944] AC 315 at 324, [1944] 2 All ER 13 at 18.
[360] [1966] IR 214 at 222–223.
[361] [1995] 1 Cr App R 591.

issues in the case, which is the guilt of the accused of the instant offence, and not the details of earlier ones. Unless the earlier ones are admissible as similar fact evidence, prosecuting counsel should not seek to probe or emphasise similarities between the underlying facts of previous offences and the instant offence.

3. Similarities of defences which have been rejected by juries on previous occasions, for example false alibis or the defence that the incriminating substance has been planted and whether or not the accused pleaded guilty or was disbelieved having given evidence on oath, may be a legitimate matter for questions. These matters do not show a disposition to commit the offence in question; but they are clearly relevant to credibility.

4. Underlying facts that show particularly bad character over and above the bare facts of the case are not necessarily to be excluded. But the judge should be careful to balance the gravity of the attack on the prosecution with the degree of prejudice to the defendant which will result from the disclosure of the facts in question...

5. If objection is to be taken to a particular line of cross-examination about the underlying facts of a previous offence, it should be taken as soon as it is apparent to defence counsel that it is in danger of going too far. There is little point in taking it subsequently, since it will not normally be a ground for discharging the jury.

6. While it is the duty of the judge to keep cross-examination within proper bounds, if no objection is taken at the time it will be difficult thereafter to contend that the judge has wrongly exercised his discretion...."[362]

6. Direction to the Jury

9–184 Where an accused loses his shield pursuant to either s.1(f)(ii) or (iii), and evidence in relation to the commission by an accused of other offences or the bad character of an accused is admitted, a trial judge has a duty to ensure that no unfairness to the accused results by giving the jury a detailed direction as to the purpose for which that evidence has been admitted and the use that can be made of it by the jury.[363] In *People (AG) v Bond*,[364] the Court of Criminal Appeal accepted the submission that the trial judge had erred in that case by not instructing the jury that such evidence is generally inadmissible but was admitted by him in the case because the defence had attacked the character of witnesses for the prosecution. It was also held that he should have instructed the jury that it could only be used by them as going to the credibility of the accused and not as evidence of his having committed the offence for which he was being tried:

> "The way in which this evidence was to be used by the jury was vital to the interests of the applicant. It certainly necessitated a careful direction from the Judge as to why it was admitted, and as to how it was to be used; that it went to his credit only, and should on no account be used to show the probability of his guilt."[365]

9–185 Further directions may be required depending on the circumstances of the particular case. So, in *People (AG) v Coleman*,[366] where evidence had been admitted that the accused had, on previous occasions, been charged with but not convicted of similar offences, it is held to be essential that the jury were instructed that the accused must be regarded as innocent of those offences.

---

[362] [1995] 1 Cr App R 591 at 604–605.

[363] *People (AG) v Bond* [1966] IR 214; *R. v McLeod* [1995] 1 Cr App R 591 at 605.

[364] [1966] IR 214.

[365] [1966] IR 214 at 223 (*per* Haugh J). But see Munday, "Stepping Beyond the Bounds of Credibility" [1986] Crim LR 511 at 512, where he questions the efficacy of such a direction.

[366] [1945] IR 237 at 251.

F. Character of Witnesses in Criminal Cases

1. Evidence of the Good Character of a Witness

9–186 In general, it is impermissible for either the prosecution or the defence to adduce evidence of the good character of a witness called by them so as to bolster the credibility of that witness.[367] The rationale for this rule, which is sometimes referred to as the prohibition against "oath helping",[368] is that it is a matter for the jury to determine the credibility of witnesses and they are in as good as position to do so as another witness.[369]

9–187 Evidence of the good character of a witness is, however, admissible in rebuttal where the other party has adduced evidence of bad character to impeach the credibility of the witness.[370] In *Attorney General v O'Sullivan*[371] the accused, who had been convicted of attempted sodomy had tried, at the trial, to impeach the character of the complainant by suggesting that he had been expelled from a number of schools due to his bad character. It was held on appeal that the trial judge had properly allowed the prosecution to adduce evidence as to the general good character of the complainant to rebut the attack made.[372]

2. Evidence of the Bad Character of a Witness

9–188 Both the prosecution and the defence are free to ask questions of a witness called by the other side designed to impugn the credibility of a witness by eliciting evidence of his or her bad character.[373] However, it should be noted that, if a question relates only to the credit of a witness, then the cross-examiner is bound by the answer received and cannot call evidence to rebut it.[374] In *Harris v Tippett*,[375] Lawrence J explained the position as follows:

> "I will permit questions to be put to a witness as to any improper conduct of which he may have been guilty for the purpose of trying his credit; but, when the questions are irrelevant to the issue on the record, you cannot call witnesses to contradict the answers he gives."[376]

9–189 In *People (DPP) v Hayes*,[377] it was accepted by the Court of Criminal Appeal that an accused could cross-examine a witness on the basis that the witness rather than

---

[367] *R. v Turner* [1975] QB 834 at 842, [1975] 1 All ER 70 at 75; *R. v Marquard* [1993] 4 SCR 223, (1993) 108 DLR (4th) 47; *R. v AW* (1994) 94 CCC (3d) 441.

[368] *R. v Beland* (1987) 36 CCC (3d) 481, [1987] 2 SCR 398 at 408; *R. v Burns* [1994] 1 SCR 656 at 667.

[369] See *R. v Turner* [1975] QB 834 at 842, [1975] 1 All ER 70 at 74; *R. v Marquard* [1993] 4 SCR 223 at 248, (1993) 108 DLR (4th) 47 at 64; *R. v Burns* [1994] 1 SCR 656 at 667.

[370] *Attorney General v O'Sullivan* [1930] IR 552; *R. v Whelan* (1881) 14 Cox CC 595.

[371] [1930] IR 552.

[372] [1930] IR 552 at 558.

[373] There is also authority to the effect that it is open to a party to adduce evidence of the bad character of a witness called by that party where this is relevant to an issue in the proceedings: *R. v Ross* [2007] EWCA Crim 1457.

[374] See the discussion of the rule in relation to the finality of answers to collateral questions in Chap.3.

[375] (1811) 2 Camp. 637.

[376] (1811) 2 Camp. 637 at 638. In *R. v Dizaei* [2013] EWCA Crim 88, [2013] 1 WLR 2257, concerns were expressed about the potential for satellite litigation arising from the admission of evidence of the bad character of a witness. See further, Brewis et al "Bad character evidence and potential satellite litigation" (2013) 77(2) J Crim Law 110.

[377] [2011] IECCA 65 at [7].

the accused committed the offence in question. However, doubts were expressed as to whether it was not open to the accused to suggest that the witness had committed the offence because of a propensity to act in a particular way.

9–190   A trial judge exercises a general supervisory jurisdiction in relation to the cross-examination of witnesses and may disallow questions which he or she considers to be improper, vexatious or irrelevant to any matter at issue.[378] Guiding principles as to the exercise of that discretion in the specific context of questioning as to credit were laid down by Sankey LJ in *Hobbs v Tinling & Co. Ltd.*[379] as follows:

> "(i) such questions are proper if they are of such a nature that the truth of the imputation conveyed by them would seriously affect the opinion of the Court as to the credibility of the witness on the matter to which he testifies;
>
> (ii) such questions are improper if the imputation which they convey relates to matters so remote in time, or of such a character, that the truth of the imputation would not affect, or would affect in a slight degree, the opinion of the Court as to the credibility of the witness on the matter to which he testifies; and
>
> (iii) such questions are improper if there is a great disproportion between the importance of the imputation made against the witness's character and the importance of his evidence."

9–191   With regard to questioning as to previous convictions, this is governed by s.6 of the Criminal Procedure Act 1865 which provides that:

> "A witness may be questioned as to whether he has been convicted of any felony or misdemeanour, and upon being so questioned, if he either denies or does not admit the fact, or refuses to answer, it shall be lawful for the cross-examining party to prove such conviction."

9–192   Section 6 is broadly drafted and permits a witness to be cross-examined about a conviction for any offence whether or not such an offence is relevant to the issues in the case or the credibility of the witness.[380] However, any cross-examination in relation to previous convictions is also subject to the general supervisory discretion of a trial judge to disallow questions which are irrelevant, vexatious or oppressive.

3. Questioning of Complainants in Relation to their Previous Sexual History

9–193   At common law, evidence as to the previous sexual history of a complainant was admissible in accordance with the general test of relevance. In *People (DPP) v McGuinness*,[381] Kenny J explained the basis for the admission of such evidence as follows:

> "When the defence to a charge of rape is the assertion that the complainant consented to the sexual intercourse with the accused, the task of counsel for the defence is particularly difficult. The complainant will never admit that she consented, and counsel must seek to show that at the time of the offence her character and behaviour were such that she would be likely to have consented or that she has invented the evidence which she is giving. Both of these are extremely difficult to establish but counsel must try. He often seeks to do so by cross-examining the complainant about events in the past so that he can introduce doubts into the minds of the jurors about her character or her credibility and he may have to cover many aspects of her past life."[382]

---

[378] See the discussion of this supervisory jurisdiction in Chap.3.
[379] [1929] 1 KB 1 at 51.
[380] *Cf. Clifford v Clifford* [1961] 3 All ER 231 at 232, [1961] 1 WLR 1274 at 1276.
[381] [1978] IR 189.
[382] [1978] IR 189 at 190.

9–194 The learned judge went on to state that, in a rape case where the defence is consent, the judge is obliged to "allow unpleasant charges to be made against the complainant in connection with her past; he should not indicate to the jury that he disapproves of this being done".[383] However, the admission of such evidence was the subject of considerable criticism on the basis that it resulted in a situation where the complainant was effectively put on trial as to his or her character and it was contended that this contributed to a reluctance on the part of victims to report rape and other sexual offences.[384] Such criticisms led to the introduction of what are commonly known as "rape shield" provisions in many jurisdictions.[385]

9–195 The admission of evidence of sexual history and the cross-examination of a sexual complainant as to his or her sexual history is now governed by s.3 of the Criminal Law (Rape) Act 1981[386] (as amended by s.13 of the Criminal Law (Rape) (Amendment) Act 1990) which provides as follows:

> "(1) If at a trial any person is for the time being charged with a sexual assault offence[387] to which he pleads not guilty, then, except with the leave of the judge, no evidence shall be adduced and no question shall be asked in cross-examination at the trial, by or on behalf of any accused person at the trial, about any sexual experience (other than that to which the charge relates) of a complainant with any person....
> (2)(a) The judge shall not give leave in pursuance of subsection (1) for any evidence or question except on an application made to him, in the absence of the jury, by or on behalf of an accused person.
> (b) The judge shall give leave if, and only if, he is satisfied that it would be unfair to the accused person to refuse to allow the evidence to be adduced or the question to be asked, that is to say, if he is satisfied that, on the assumption that if the evidence or question was not allowed the jury might reasonably be satisfied beyond reasonable doubt that the accused person is guilty, the effect of allowing the evidence or question might reasonably be that they would not be so satisfied.[388]

---

[383] [1978] IR 189 at 191.

[384] Law Reform Commission, "Consultation Paper on Rape" (LRC 24–1987), para.31; *Report of the Task Force Against Women* (Stationery Office, Dublin, 1997), para.9.14. See further, Berger, "Man's Trial, Woman's Tribulation: Rape Cases in the Courtroom" (1977) 77 Colum L Rev 2; Giles, "The Admissibility of a Rape-Complainant's Previous Sexual Conduct: The Need for Legislative Reform" (1976) 11 New Eng L Rev 497; Temkin, "Sexual History Evidence–The Ravishment of Section 2" [1993] Crim LR 3; Temkin, "Towards a Modern Law of Rape" (1984) 45 MLR 399; Elliot, "Rape Complainants' Sexual Experience with Third Parties" [1984] Crim LR 4; Adler "The Relevance of Sexual History in Rape: Problems of Subjective Interpretation" [1985] Crim LR 769.

[385] Such provisions are to be found on the statute books in the UK (s.41 of the Youth Justice and Criminal Evidence Act 1999), Canada (ss.276 and 277 of the Canadian Criminal Code), Australia (see the synopsis of the statutory provisions in the various States to be found in Heydon, *Cross on Evidence* 9th edn (Lexis Nexis Butterworths Australia, 2013), at [19080]–[19090]) and New Zealand (s.44 of the Evidence Act 2006).

[386] As noted by the Court of Criminal Appeal in *People (DPP) v GK* [2006] IECCA 99 at [16], [2007] 2 IR 92 at 100, the provisions of s.3 of the 1981 Act clearly draw on the English antecedent of s.2 of the Sexual Offences (Amendment) Act 1976.

[387] A definition of "sexual assault offence" is given in s.1 of the Criminal Law (Rape) Act 1981 (as amended by s.12 of the Criminal Law (Rape) (Amendment) Act 1990. In *People (DPP) v GK* [2006] IECCA 99 at [13], [2007] 2 IR 92 at 99, it was pointed out that offences of unlawful carnal knowledge as defined in s.1(1) and s.2(1) of the Criminal Law Amendment Act 1935 do not appear to fall within the definition.

[388] It was noted in *People (DPP) v GK* [2006] IECCA 99 at [17], [2007] 2 IR 92 at 100, that the wording of this subsection draws heavily on the interpretation of s.2 of the English Sexual Offences (Amendment) Act 1976 in *R. v Lawrence* [1977] Crim LR 492 at 493.

(3) If, notwithstanding that the judge has given leave in accordance with this section for any evidence to be adduced or question to be asked in cross-examination, it appears to the judge that any question asked or proposed to be asked (whether in the course of so adducing evidence or of cross-examination) in reliance on the leave which he has given is not or may not be such as may properly be asked in accordance with that leave, he may direct that the question shall not be asked or, if asked, that it shall not be answered except in accordance with his leave given on a fresh application under this section." [389]

9–196 Notice of an intention to make an application under s.3 is required to be given to the prosecution by or on behalf of the accused before, or as soon as practicable after, the commencement of the trial for the offence concerned.[390] If an application is made under s.3, the complainant is entitled to be legally represented and heard in relation to the application[391] and the prosecution are required to so advise the complainant. An application under s.3 cannot be heard until those requirements have been complied with.[392]

9–197 In *People (DPP) v McDonagh*,[393] Finlay CJ commented on the operation of the section as follows:

"Upon the true construction of this section it would appear necessary for the Judge, in the absence of the jury, to hear all the necessary material which will permit him to reach, a conclusion either with regard to questioning or with regard to the tendering of evidence concerning sexual experience of a complainant with persons other than the accused, and that it is a matter for his discretion in what form that information would be put before him, whether by way of sworn testimony or by way of a proof of evidence. It is obviously desirable where it is practicable for a ruling to be made at an early stage in the trial on any such application. It may not, however, always be possible to rule it on one occasion only, and there is nothing inconsistent with the provisions of the section in a further or different application at a later

---

[389] For a detailed discussion of these provisions and the policy considerations, see O'Malley, *Sexual Offences,* 2nd edn (Dublin: Thomson Reuters Round Hall, 2013), Chap.18. See further, Leahy, "In Woman's Voice: A Feminist Analysis of Irish Rape Law" (2008) 26 ILT 203; Duffy, "'Balance' in the Criminal Justice System: Misrepresenting the Relationship between the Rights of Victims and Defendants" (2009) 19(1) ICLJ 2, Glynn "In the name of the victim: how the criminal justice system adequately protects the interests of victims" (2012) 30 ILT 152 and Counihan, "Rape Crisis Network Ireland Perspectives on Sexual Violence and the Criminal Justice System" (2013) 4 ICLJ 115.

[390] Section 4A(2) of the Criminal Law (Rape) Act 1981 (as inserted by s.34 of the Sex Offenders Act 2001). It was emphasised in *People (DPP) v Walsh* [2008] IECCA 111 that an application must be made in a timely manner, and either at the outset of the trial where the material contained in the Book of Evidence clearly suggests that such an application should properly be made, or in any event, not later than the end of the complainant's direct evidence although it was accepted that the interests of justice may require a late application to be granted in an appropriate case.

[391] Section 4A(1) of the Criminal Law (Rape) Act 1981 (as inserted by s.34 of the Sex Offenders Act 2001). The prosecution is required, as soon as practicable after the receipt by it of intention to make an application under s.3, to notify the complainant of the entitlement to be heard in relation to the application and to be legally represented for that purpose during the course of the application: s.4A(3).

[392] Section 4A(4) of the Criminal Law (Rape) Act 1981 (as inserted by s.34 of the Sex Offenders Act 2001) stipulates that the judge shall not hear the application without first being satisfied that these requirements have been complied with. If the period between the complainant being notified and the making of the application is not, in the judge's opinion, such as to have afforded the complainant a reasonable opportunity to arrange legal representation, the judge is required to postpone the hearing of the application (and, for this purpose, may adjourn the trial or proceeding concerned) for a period that the judge considers will afford the complainant such an opportunity: s.4A(5).

[393] Unreported, Court of Criminal Appeal, 24 July 1990 at 11.

stage in the trial or with the renewal of an application or the postponement of a decision on it. The grounds on which the learned trial judge shall exercise his discretion are very clearly set out at section 3(2)(b), and solely consist of the question as to whether he is satisfied that if the evidence or question was not allowed, the jury might reasonably be satisfied beyond a reasonable doubt that the accused person is guilty, whereas, the effect of allowing the evidence or question might reasonably be that they would not be so satisfied."

9–198   In *People (DPP) v Moloney*,[394] one of the grounds of appeal advanced by the applicant was that the trial judge had erred in not permitting cross-examination of the complainant on her previous sexual history. However, this submission was dismissed by the Court on the basis that cross-examination as to previous sexual history is primarily related to the question of consent which did not arise in the case where the complainant was 14 years of age. The view was also taken that the issue of consent could only arise where it is accepted that some form of sexual activity had taken place and here the accused denied that anything had ever happened. It might be noted that, while the Court is correct in asserting that, in the great majority of cases, previous sexual history will be relevant, if at all, to the issue of consent, such evidence can be admitted if sufficiently relevant to any issue in the case.[395]

9–199   The leading authority on the application of s.3 is the decision of the Court of Criminal Appeal in *People (DPP) v GK*.[396] Delivering the judgment of the Court, Kearns J noted that s.3 was drawn almost entirely from the corresponding English provision of s.2 of the Sexual Offences (Amendment) Act 1976 and referred with approval to the decision in *R. v Viola*[397] where it had been accepted that s.2 did not confer a discretion but required a trial judge to make a judgment on the facts of the particular case. As to how that judgment should be reached, it was held that the first question was whether the proposed questions are relevant according to the ordinary rules of evidence because, if not, they could not be allowed. He also referred with approval to a synopsis of the effect of s.2 to be found in *Archbold on Criminal Pleading Evidence and Practice*[398]:

"The section was clearly aimed primarily at excluding questions which went merely to credit and no more. If the proposed questions merely sought to establish that the complainant had sexual experience with other men to whom she was not married so as to suggest that, for that reason, she ought not to be believed on oath, the judge would exclude the questions or evidence. On the other hand, if the questions were relevant to an issue in the trial in the light of the way the case was being run—for example, consent as opposed merely to credit—they might as a general rule be admitted...

Questions which really do go to the issue of consent should, it is submitted, never be excluded under the Act of 1976. Questions which do not go to that issue and which relate to the complainant's previous sexual experience should be excluded, unless they are such as might reasonably lead the jury to take a different view of the complainant's evidence. Clearly, if the complainant has lied about her previous sexual experience, this is a matter which *may* affect the weight to be attached to her evidence. The mere fact that the complainant *has* previous sexual experience, however, is of no significance whatsoever. Suppose, in the instant case, that the truth was that the girl had previously had intercourse with her boyfriend, aged 15, on a number of occasions; if she had said in her witness statement that she was a virgin, or her evidence was given in such a way as to suggest that this was the case, it would obviously be right to permit cross-examination, as affecting the weight of her evidence. In the absence of such features, or any other particular feature, it is submitted that such questioning should not be permitted: the apparent suggestion in this case was that the eliciting of such information

---

[394] Unreported, Court of Criminal Appeal, 8 November 1999.
[395] See *R. v Viola* [1982] 3 All ER 73, [1982] 1 WLR 1138.
[396] [2006] IECCA 99, [2007] 2 IR 92.
[397] [1982] 1 WLR 1138.
[398] *Archbold on Criminal Pleading Evidence and Practice* (2000), paras 8–123.

would be relevant to the issue of consent. It is submitted that any such argument should be firmly resisted."

9–200   Kearns J acknowledged that the purpose and effect of s.3 was to significantly restrict the circumstances in which leave to cross-examine on previous sexual history would be granted:

> "Having regard to the severely restrictive terminology of the statutory provision, the court is of the view that, in general, a decision to refuse to allow cross-examination as to past sexual history may more readily be justified in most cases than the converse. Indeed the Act is quite explicit in so providing. Furthermore, the younger the age of a complainant, the less desirable it is to ever allow cross-examination which may well be extremely traumatic for a complainant of tender years. Where a form of questioning is allowed, it should be confined only to what is strictly necessary and should never be utilised as a form of character assassination of a complainant."[399]

9–201   However, it was held that the trial judge had erred in that case in refusing to grant the applicant, who was accused of a number of sexual offences involving the complainant while she was a young girl, leave to cross-examine the complainant on her sexual history with a number of boys on the basis that consent was not in issue in circumstances where the defence of the accused was that he had never had sexual relations with the complainant. The Court was satisfied that evidence as to the complainant's sexual history, which had been disclosed for the first time in a victim impact statement compiled after a re-trial, was potentially significant because of the manner in which it had emerged and gave rise to the possibility of some other motive for identifying the applicant as the only person with whom she had had sexual relations. It also served to undermine the probative force of the medical evidence relied on by the prosecution which, in the absence of any evidence of sexual activity with other persons, could only have been seen by the jury as providing significant corroboration of her evidence. The Court, therefore, concluded that the ruling not to permit "a limited and carefully monitored form of cross-examination of the complainant" was unfair to the accused in that her sexual history could have materially affected the jury's deliberations on whether to find him guilty.[400]

9–202   Subsequently, in *People (DPP) v TC*,[401] it was stated that the test established by *GK* was one of fairness and leave to cross-examine on sexual history should be granted if "it could have an important effect on the course of the trial, on the way counsel ran the case, on the cross-examination, and on the jury". This will not be the case and leave will not be granted where the questioning in relation to previous sexual history goes to the credibility of the complainant only.[402]

9–203   In *People (DPP) v Cronin*,[403] the sole issue on a charge of rape was consent.

---

[399] [2006] IECCA 99 at [25], [2007] 2 IR 92 at 103–104. *Cf. DC v DPP* [2005] IESC 77 at [31], [2005] 4 IR 281 at 296, where an application for relief by way of judicial review by the accused who was charged with rape on the basis that there had been a breach of the principles of natural and constitutional justice by Gardaí in failing to identify and make available witness statements of two specific individuals, one of whom might been intimate with the complainant on the night before the offences were alleged to have occurred was refused. It was held that to do this would be to introduce a back door to evade the policy laid down in s.3 of the Criminal Law (Rape) Act 1981.

[400] [2006] IECCA 99 at [29], [2007] 2 IR 92 at 105.

[401] [2009] IECCA 20 at [18].

[402] *People (DPP) v Walsh* [2008] IECCA 111.

[403] [2008] IECCA 94.

The trial judge refused to accede to an application for leave to cross-exa
complainant as to whether she had in place a contraceptive device on the oc
question on the basis that the complainant was more likely to have had consensual
sex if she was availing of contraception. The Court of Criminal Appeal accepted that,
where there is positive evidence or a strong suggestion of a particular state of affairs
in the prosecution case such as a suggestion of no previous sexual experience, then
cross-examination should be permitted. However, in that case it was held that the
trial judge had correctly refused to allow questioning of the complainant because the
question sought to be asked could not have been relevant to the issue of consent.

9–204   Where leave to cross-examine a complainant on his or her sexual history is
granted, then as was emphasised in *People (DPP) v Piotrowski*,[404] the trial judge has
an obligation to ensure that this is kept within the bounds of what is relevant to the
issues in the case and to disallow any questions and exclude any evidence sought to be
introduced through the cross-examination which is not sufficiently relevant to the issues.

9–205   There have been calls for an overhaul of this area.[405] However, having
regard to the guarantee of a trial in due course of law in art.38.1, and particularly the
entitlement of an accused to defend himself or herself, it appears that there would be
formidable constitutional difficulties to imposing a complete prohibition on questioning
in relation to the previous sexual conduct of a complainant. In *R. v A (No.2)*,[406] it was
held by the House of Lords that the equivalent provision in England and Wales, s.41
of the Youth Justice and Criminal Evidence Act 1999,[407] was not compatible with art.6
because it contained what amounted to a blanket exclusion of potentially relevant
evidence. However, a declaration of incompatibility was avoided by applying the
interpretative obligation provided for in s.3(1) of the Human Rights Act 1998 (UK)
so as to interpret s.41 in a manner that permitted evidence of logically relevant sexual
experiences between a complainant and an accused to be admitted. Subsequently, in
SN v Sweden,[408] the European Court of Human Rights accepted that certain measures
can be taken for the purpose of protecting the victim of a sexual offence while giving
evidence but subject to the proviso that such measures can be reconciled with an
adequate and effective exercise of the rights of the defence. Thus, there are limits to
any further statutory intervention in this area.

---

[404] [2014] IECCA 17 at [8.4] and [11.2].
[405] See the *Report of the Task Force on Violence Against Women* (Dublin: Stationery Office, 1997),
paras 9.14–9.17 and the Report of the Working Party on the Legal and Judicial Process for Victims
of Sexual and Other Crimes of Violence Against Women and Children (Dublin: National Women's
Council of Ireland, 1996) at 90. See also the Department of Justice, Equality and Law Reform,
"The Law on Sexual Offences: A Discussion Paper" (Dublin: Stationery Office, 1998), p.41.
[406] [2002] 1 AC 45, [2001] 3 All ER 1.
[407] Section 41 prohibits the giving of evidence and cross-examination of the complainant about any
sexual behaviour except with leave of the court. Leave may be given where (a) consent is in issue
and where the sexual behaviour of the complainant is alleged to have taken place at or about
the same time as the event which is the subject-matter of the charge against the accused, or (b)
where the sexual behaviour of the complainant to which the question relates is alleged to have
been in any respect so similar to the sexual behaviour which is shown by evidence to have taken
place as a part of the event which is the subject matter of the charge that, the similarity cannot
reasonably be explained as a coincidence.
[408] [2004] 39 EHRR 13 at [47].

CHAPTER 10

PRIVILEGE

A. Introduction

10–01   In general, a witness is bound to answer all relevant questions put to him or her,[1] and will be guilty of contempt of court if he or she refuses to do so. Indeed, it is well established that "the exercise of the judicial power carries with it the entitlement of a judge to compel the attendance of witnesses and, *a fortiori*, the answering of questions by witnesses."[2] As Walsh J stated in *Re Kevin O'Kelly*[3]: "[t]his is the ultimate safeguard of justice in the State, whether it be in pursuit of the guilty or the vindication of the innocent".[4]

10–02   However, there are a number of instances examined in this chapter where a party or person may enjoy a privilege from being compelled to answer a question or produce a document.[5] The recognition of such a privilege or immunity inevitably cuts down the amount of relevant evidence before the courts and, hence, impairs the administration of justice. However, there are certain situations in which it is considered that this impairment is outweighed by the damage that would otherwise be caused to some other objective which it is the policy of the courts to promote.[6] To paraphrase Finlay CJ in *Smurfit Paribas Bank Ltd v AAB Export Finance Ltd*,[7] a privilege may be "granted by the courts in instances which have been identified as securing an objective which in the public interest in the proper conduct of the administration of justice can be said to outweigh the disadvantage arising from the restriction of disclosure of all the facts."[8]

---

[1]   *Duchess of Kingston's Case* (1776) 20 St Tr 355 at 586.

[2]   *Heaney v Ireland* [1996] 1 IR 580 at 585, [1997] 1 ILRM 117 at 123 (*per* O'Flaherty J) (emphasis removed).

[3]   (1974) 108 ILTR 97 at 101.

[4]   See, to the same effect, *per* Walsh J in *Murphy v Dublin Corporation* [1972] IR 215 at 233.

[5]   Although the issue of privilege generally arises in the context of discovery, privileges apply equally to oral evidence and a witness can refuse to answer a question on the ground that the information sought to be elicited is privileged. See *SPUC v Grogan (No.3)* [1992] 2 IR 471, where Morris J refused to allow the defendants to call a senior adviser to the Attorney General to give evidence on the ground that the evidence sought to be elicited from him on certain questions was covered by legal professional privilege. See also *Duncan v Governor of Portlaoise Prison (No.2)* [1998] 1 IR 433 and *Burke v Central Independent Television Plc* [1994] 2 IR 61 at 79 (*per* Finlay CJ).

[6]   See *Skeffington v Rooney* [1997] 1 IR 22 at 32, [1997] 2 ILRM 56 at 66 and *Re Barings Plc* [1998] Ch 356 at 362, [1998] 1 All ER 673 at 678, *per* Scott VC.

[7]   [1990] 1 IR 469 at 477, [1990] ILRM 588 at 594.

[8]   See, to similar effect, *per* Keane J in *Skeffington v Rooney* [1997] 1 IR 22 at 32, [1997] 2 ILRM

10–03   Before going on to examine the various privileges that have been recognised by the courts, something should be said of the relationship between a "private" privilege and "public interest" privilege. Although the two have, traditionally, been treated as quite distinct, it is evident from the discussion below that each is ultimately grounded on a determination that the balance of public interest favours the recognition and upholding of the privilege.[9] The main difference between the two categories of privilege rests on the fact that, in the case of "private" privilege, the courts do not balance the conflicting policy interests on a case-by-case basis. Instead, the balancing of conflicting policy objectives occurs *ab initio* in determining whether to recognise and in setting the parameters of the particular privilege.[10] Thus, although not as immediately apparent, the courts are the ultimate arbiters of both the parameters and application of a "private" privilege.[11]

B. Legal Professional Privilege

1. Introduction

10–04   The origins of legal professional privilege can be traced back to the latter part of the sixteenth century but its policy and broad parameters were only settled in the nineteenth century when the various decisions of the common law and chancery courts were reconciled and the relationship of the privilege with the principles of discovery settled.[12]

10–05   Initial development of the privilege focused on communications between the client and lawyer for the purpose of giving or receiving legal advice. The privilege, which originally applied only to communications made to a barrister or solicitor after the commencement of litigation was, over time, extended to communications

---

56 at 66. *Cf. Three Rivers DC v Bank of England (No.6)* [2004] UKHL 48, [2005] 1 AC 610, at [35], where Lord Scott stated that: "Legal advice privilege should, in my opinion, be given a scope that reflects the policy reasons that justify its presence in our law."

[9]   See *Skeffington v Rooney* [1997] 1 IR 22 at 32, [1997] 2 ILRM 56 at 66, where Keane J did not draw any distinction between "private interest"' and "public interest" privilege but seemed to regard all privileges as resting ultimately on a judgment as to where the balance of public interest lies.

[10]   See *Fyffes Plc v DCC Plc* [2005] IESC 3, [2005] 1 IR 59, [2005] 1 ILRM 357, where Fennelly J considered the judgment of Finlay CJ in *Smurfit Paribas* and stated, at [23], that: "The then Chief Justice did not, in my view, by those words, mean to suggest that, in cases where reliance is placed on legal professional privilege in respect of documents the courts should balance the two considerations, as it were, on a case by case basis. He was referring to what the policy of the law should be." *Cf. Skeffington v Rooney* [1997] 1 IR 22 at 32, [1997] 2 ILRM 56 at 66.

[11]   *Smurfit Paribas Bank Ltd v AAB Export Finance Ltd* [1990] 1 IR 469 at 475, [1990] ILRM 588 at 592; *Skeffington v Rooney* [1997] 1 IR 22 at 32, [1997] 2 ILRM 56 at 66. *Cf.* the comments of Lord Taylor CJ in *R. v Derby Magistrates' Court, ex parte B* [1996] AC 487 at 508, [1995] 4 All ER 526 at 541: "Legal professional privilege and public interest immunity are as different in their origin as they are in their scope. Putting it another way, if a balancing exercise was ever required in the case of legal professional privilege, it was performed once and for all in the sixteenth century, and since then has applied across the board in every case, irrespective of the client's individual merits."

[12]   For a discussion of the history and development of the privilege, see the judgment of Lord Neuberger in *R. (Prudential Plc) v Special Comr of Income Tax* [2013] UKHL 1, [2013] 2 AC 185.

made in contemplation of litigation,[13] then to disputes where litigation was not yet contemplated[14] and, finally, to legal advice irrespective of whether litigation was contemplated or a dispute existed.[15]

10–06 Another strand of development related to communications with third parties in preparation for litigation and again, the process was one of gradual extension.[16] First, protection was afforded to information obtained by a solicitor from third parties for the purpose of litigation, and then to evidence gathered by agents employed by a solicitor for this purpose.[17] Next, privilege was extended to information gathered by the client at the request of the solicitor, and then to information volunteered by the client.[18] Finally, it was held that documents prepared by a client for the purpose of litigation, whether at the request of the solicitor or not, were privileged if prepared with the *bona fide* intention of being laid before the solicitor to obtain his or her advice and whether actually laid before him or not.[19]

10–07 By the last quarter of the nineteenth century, it was recognised that the effect of these two lines of authority had been to create two distinct privileges identified by Mellish LJ in *Anderson v Bank of British Columbia*,[20] as:

> "first, the privilege which protects a man from producing confidential communications made between him and his solicitor … [and], secondly, the privilege which entitles him to refuse to communicate evidence which he has obtained for the purpose of litigation."

10–08 The distinction between the two was copper-fastened by the decision in *Wheeler v Le Marchant*[21] which held that privilege did not apply to communications between a solicitor and third parties for the purpose of enabling the solicitor to give legal advice, and that third party communications were only protected from disclosure where they came into existence for the purposes of litigation which had commenced or was contemplated.

10–09 The existence of these two sub-categories of legal professional privilege, commonly termed "legal advice privilege" and "litigation privilege" respectively,[22] is now generally recognised,[23] though some uncertainty about their precise parameters

---

13 *Gainsford v Grammar* (1809) 2 Camp 9; *Williams v Mudie* (1824) 1 C & P 158.
14 *Clark v Clark* (1830) 1 Mo & Rob 3.
15 *Foster v Hall* (1831) 12 Pick 89; *Greenough v Gaskell* (1833) 1 My & K 98 at 101.
16 See the account of the development of the law given by Jessel M.R. in *Anderson v Bank of British Columbia* (1876) 2 Ch D 644 at 649–650.
17 See *Greenough v Gaskell* (1833) 1 My & K 98 at 103–104 and *Curling v Perring* (1835) 2 My & K 380 at 381.
18 See *Steele v Stewart* (1844) 1 Ph 471 and *Lafone v Falkland Islands Co.* (1857) 4 K & J 36.
19 *Southwark and Vauxhall Water Co. v Quick* (1878) 3 QBD 315. This decision was followed in *Worthington v Dublin, Wicklow and Wexford Railway Co.* (1888) 22 LR Ir 310 at 313.
20 (1876) 2 Ch D 644.
21 (1881) 18 Ch D 675 at 681.
22 See *Formica Ltd v Secretary of State acting by Export Credit Guarantee Department* [1995] 1 Lloyd's Rep 692 at 696; and *Highgrade Traders Ltd* [1984] BCLC 151 at 162 where this terminology was used. *Cf. Porter v Scott* [1979] NI 6, where Kelly J drew a distinction between legal professional privilege properly so called and lawyer's "work product" privilege.
23 In *Ahern v Mahon* [2008] IEHC 119 at [61], [2008] 4 IR 704 at 719, [2009] 1 ILRM 458 at 471, Kelly J explained that: "Legal professional privilege can be divided into two sub-classes. They are litigation privilege and legal advice privilege. Both are part of a single privilege." See also *Markey v Minister for Justice* [2011] IEHC 39 at [38], [2012] 1 IR 62 at 77.

and degree of overlap remains.[24] In particular, it is uncertain whether communications between a client and his or her legal adviser regarding litigation in being or anticipated are protected only by legal advice privilege or by both legal advice privilege and litigation privilege.[25] For the reasons articulated below, the better view is that communications between a client and his or legal adviser regarding litigation which are made for the purpose of giving or receiving legal advice are more properly protected by legal advice privilege alone, and that litigation privilege should be regarded as applying only to third party communications, work product and those communications between a client and his or her legal adviser regarding litigation which do not give or receive legal advice.[26]

10–10   The most recent expansion of the privilege has been the recognition by the courts that legal professional privilege may be invoked in the context of an inquisitorial process, such as a tribunal of inquiry.[27] It appears, however, that the entitlement of a party to assert legal professional privilege in this context may depend on his or her legal status at the tribunal, at least insofar as litigation privilege is concerned. In *Ahern v Mahon*,[28] Kelly J concluded that the applicant was a witness before a tribunal of inquiry whose conduct was under investigation, as a result of which he was entitled to the fundamental constitutional rights identified by the Supreme Court in *Re Haughey*.[29] He observed that these rights derive from the protection afforded by Art.40.3 of the

---

[24]   The explanation of the two sub-categories of privilege, and their interconnection, contained in the first edition of this text was cited with approval by Finlay Geoghegan J in *University College Cork v ESB* [2014] IEHC 135, at [26]. *Cf. Three Rivers District Council v Governor and Company of the Bank of England (No. 6)* [2004] UKHL 48, [2005] 1 AC 610, at [105] and *R. (Prudential Plc) v Special Comr of Income Tax* [2013] UKSC 1, [2013] 2 AC 185, at [18].

[25]   As O'Hanlon J in *Silver Hill Duckling Ltd v Minister for Agriculture* [1987] IR 289 appeared to contemplate.

[26]   This is the approach adopted in Canada (see Higgins, *Legal Professional Privilege for Corporations: A Guide to Four Major Common Law Jurisdictions*, (Oxford University Press, 2014), at [1.59]. See *Ahern v Mahon* [2008] IEHC 119 at [62], [2008] 4 IR 704 at 719, [2009] 1 ILRM 458 at [61] where Kelly J stated that: "Legal advice privilege protects a person and his legal advisor in respect of such advice whether proceedings are in being or contemplated or not." But see *Three Rivers DC v Bank of England (No. 6)* [2004] UKHL 48, [2005] 1 AC 610, at [27], where Lord Scott stated that: "...legal advice privilege has an undoubted relationship with litigation privilege. Legal advice is frequently sought or given in connection with current or contemplated litigation. But it may equally well be sought or given in circumstances and for purposes that have nothing to do with litigation. If it is sought or given in connection with litigation, then the advice would fall into both of the two categories. But it is long settled that a connection with litigation is not a necessary condition for privilege to be attracted ... On the other hand it has been held that litigation privilege can extend to communications between a lawyer or the lawyer's client and a third party or to any document brought into existence for the dominant purpose of being used in litigation. The connection between legal advice sought or given and the affording of privilege to the communication has thereby been cut."

[27]   *Ahern v Mahon* [2008] IEHC 119 at [88], [2008] 4 IR 704 at 723, [2009] 1 ILRM 458 at 475, *per* Kelly J; *Martin v Legal Aid Board* [2007] IEHC 76, [2007] 2 IR 759, at [37]. *Cf. Three Rivers DC v Bank of England (No. 6)* [2004] UKHL 48, [2005] 1 AC 610, where it was held that legal advice privilege extended to legal advice provided to someone whose conduct might be criticised by an inquiry. Lord Scott stated (at [44]) that this finding would extend to inquiries such as a coroner's inquest, a statutory inquiry under the Tribunals of Inquiry (Evidence) Act 1921 or an *ad hoc* inquiry. However, this decision suggests that litigation privilege will only be available where proceedings can be said to be "adversarial" in nature. *Cf. Re L (a minor) (Police Investigation: privilege)* [1997] AC 16. For a discussion of this issue, see Passmore, *Privilege*, 3rd edn (London: Sweet & Maxwell, 2013), [3-086] *et seq.*

[28]   [2008] IEHC 119, [2008] 4 IR 704, [2009] 1 ILRM 458.

[29]   [1971] IR 217, *per* O'Dalaigh CJ at 263.

Constitution to an individual, which includes the right to a good name, the right to fair procedures and the right to natural and constitutional justice. He went on to state that:[30]

> "It would, in my view, be anomalous and make little sense if a person to whom *In Re Haughey* rights applies could not assert an entitlement to litigation privilege. A person appearing before a tribunal of inquiry and to whom *In Re Haughey* rights apply is to be regarded as being in the same position as a party to High Court litigation and not a mere witness from the point of view of legal professional privilege."

10–11   It was held, therefore, that the labelling of the tribunal as inquisitorial rather than adversarial was not determinative, nor was the fact that the tribunal was not engaged in the administration of justice, as defined in *McDonald v Bord na gCon*[31]; the crucial issue was one of fairness.[32]

2. Legal Advice Privilege

10–12   Legal advice privilege entitles a client to refuse to disclose any communications with his or her lawyer made for the purpose of giving or receiving legal advice. Although that legal advice will often be sought in connection with litigation, the proximity or otherwise of litigation is irrelevant provided that the communications pass in the course of a professional legal relationship.[33]

(a) Policy of the privilege

10–13   Legal professional privilege began life as a privilege enjoyed by the lawyer based on consideration for his oath and honour.[34] However, the idea that the confidentiality of communications could be maintained on the basis of honour was subsequently rejected by the courts.[35] From the early eighteenth century onwards, a new theory began to emerge based on the desirability of protecting the inviolability of the lawyer/client relationship.[36] This rationale proceeds on the basis, articulated by Jessel MR in *Anderson v Bank of British Columbia*[37]:

> "[T]hat as, by reason of the complexity and difficulty of our law, litigation can only be properly conducted by professional men, it is absolutely necessary that a man, in order to prosecute his

---

[30]   [2008] IEHC 119 at [86], [2008] 4 IR 704 at 723, [2009] 1 ILRM 458 at 474.

[31]   [1965] IR 217.

[32]   [2008] IEHC 119 at [99], [2008] 4 IR 704 at 727, [2009] 1 ILRM 458 at 477. See also *O'Callaghan v Mahon* [2005] IESC 9, [2005] IEHC 265, [2006] 2 IR 32, where the Supreme Court held that the Tribunal was not entitled to assert confidentiality over documents where this would interfere with the right of a person against whom serious accusations were made at a tribunal to cross-examine his accuser.

[33]   *Ahern v Mahon* [2008] IEHC 119 at [62], [2008] 4 IR 704 at 719, [2009] 1 ILRM 458 at 471, *per* Kelly J; *Wheeler v Le Marchant* (1881) 17 Ch D 675 at 682; *Minter v Priest* [1929] 1 KB 655 at 675, [1930] AC 558, [1930] All ER 431. See *Great Atlantic Insurance v Home Insurance* [1981] 1 All ER 485, *per* Templeman LJ at 490: "The fact that litigation was not then contemplated was irrelevant. This appeal may serve a useful purpose if it reminds the profession that all communications between solicitor and client where the solicitor is acting as a solicitor are privileged subject to exceptions to prevent fraud and crime and to protect the client and that the privilege should only be waived with great caution."

[34]   See *Berd v Lovelace* (1577) Cary 62; *Dennis v Codrington* (1579) Cary 100 and, generally, Wigmore (3rd edn, Little Brown and Company, Boston, 1940), VIII, § 2290.

[35]   See *Duchess of Kingston's Case* (1776) 20 St Tr 355 at 586 and *Wilson v Rastall* (1792) 4 TR 753 at 758–789.

[36]   *Annesley v Earl of Anglesea* (1743) 17 How St Tr 1139 *per* Mounteney B. at 1225.

[37]   (1876) 2 Ch D 644 at 649.

rights or to defend himself from an improper claim, should have recourse to the assistance of professional lawyers, and it being so absolutely necessary, it is equally necessary, to use a vulgar phrase, that he should be able to make a clean breast of it to the gentleman with whom he consults with a view to the prosecution of his claim, or the substantiating his defence against the claims of others; that he should be able to place unrestricted and unbounded confidence in the professional agent, and that the communications he so makes to him should be kept secret, unless with his consent (for it is his privilege, and not the privilege of the confidential agent), that he should be enabled properly to conduct his litigation."[38]

10–14 In *Shell E & P Ireland Ltd v McGrath (No. 2)*,[39] where it was held that "the rationale for legal professional privilege is to ensure that a client may fully instruct his lawyer freely and openly safe in the knowledge that what he says to his lawyer in confidence will never be revealed without his consent", Smyth J observed that the privilege is that of the client and not the lawyer. He focused on the interest of the client in maintaining the privilege, stating that:

"The interest of the client in the maintenance of privilege is twofold:-
  (i) the client has an interest in maintaining the confidentiality of the privileged communication;
  (ii) even if the confidentiality is impaired or lost, the client has an interest in ensuring that the document is not used against him in proceedings."[40]

10–15 However, this rationale is not complete because it fails to explain why the private interests of the client in having effective legal representation should be allowed to trump the administration of justice and the truth-finding function of the courts. As Finlay CJ pointed out in *Smurfit Paribas Bank Ltd v AAB Export Finance Ltd*[41]:

"The existence of a privilege or exemption from disclosure for communications made between a person and his lawyer clearly constitutes a potential restriction and diminution of the full disclosure both prior to and during the course of legal proceedings which in the interests of the common good is desirable for the purpose of ascertaining the truth and rendering justice. Such privilege should, therefore … only be granted by the courts in instances which have been identified as securing an objective which in the public interest in the proper conduct of the administration of justice can be said to outweigh the disadvantage arising from the restriction of disclosure of all the facts."

10–16 In *Fyffes Plc v DCC Plc*,[42] McCracken J explained that, aside altogether from

---

[38] In *Smurfit Paribas Bank Ltd v AAB Export Finance Ltd* [1990] 1 IR 469 at 476, [1990] ILRM 588 at 593, Finlay CJ quoted this passage with approval which, he said, identified the "superior interest of the common good in the proper conduct of litigation which justified the immunity of communications from discovery in so far as they were made for the purpose of litigation as being the desirability in that good of the correct and efficient trial of actions by the courts". See also *Buckley v Incorporated Law Society* [1994] 2 IR 44 at 47, *Murphy v Kirwan* [1993] 3 IR 501 at 514, [1994] 1 ILRM 293 at 302, and *O'Brien v Personal Injuries Assessment Board (No. 3)* [2005] IEHC 100 at [65], [2007] 2 IR 1 at [25]. *Cf. R. v Derby Magistrates Court, Ex p B* [1996] AC 487 at 507–508; *B v Auckland District Law Society* [2003] 3 AC 736 at 757; *R. (Morgan Grenfell Ltd) v Special Comr* [2002] UKHL 21, [2003] 1 AC 563 at 607; *Three Rivers DC v Bank of England (No. 6)* [2004] UKHL 48, [2005] 1 AC 611 at 648; *Upjohn Co v United States* (1981) 449 US 383 at 389 and *Jones v Smith* [1999] 1 SCR 455 at 474–475.
[39] [2006] IEHC 409 at [14], [2007] 2 IR 574 at 580, [2007] 1 ILRM 544 at 551.
[40] [2006] IEHC 409 at [14], [2007] 2 IR 574 at 580, [2007] 1 ILRM 544 at 551.
[41] [1990] 1 IR 469 at 477, [1990] ILRM 588 at 594. See *Hansfield Developments v Irish Asphalt Ltd* [2009] IEHC 420 at [23], where McKechnie J stated that "[t]his rationale should not be seen as preferring a restrictive view of the preservation of privilege".
[42] [2005] IESC 3, [2005] 1 IR 59, [2005] 1 ILRM 357. *Cf. Keegan v Kilrane* [2011] IEHC 516 at [23], [2011] 3 IR 813 at 825, where Birmingham J stated that: "The doctrine of legal professional privilege exists so that clients can open up to their lawyers and be frank with them". See also *R. (Prudential Plc) v Special Comr of Income Tax* [2013] UKHL 1 at [39], [2003] 2 AC 185, where

protection of the client, legal professional privilege plays an important role in ensuring the proper administration of justice[43]:

> "The principle of privilege arising in the preparation or conduct of a case is based on the proper administration of justice. This requires that a litigant must be in a position to communicate freely with his or her legal advisors, and further must be entitled to obtain expert evidence from third parties to assist, not only in the preparation of the case, but in the assessment as to whether there is any case to be made ... it is important to remember at all times that privilege does not exist merely for the protection of a party, but also exists to ensure the proper administration of justice."

10–17 The protection conferred by the privilege is, therefore, attributable to the view of the courts that it ultimately aids the administration of justice. This accords with the older authorities, such as *Greenough v Gaskell*,[44] where Brougham LC opined that:

> "The foundation of this rule is not difficult to discover...it is out of regard to the interests of justice, which cannot be upholden, and to the administration of justice, which cannot go on without the aid of men skilled in jurisprudence, in the practice of the courts, and in those matters affecting rights and obligations which form the subject of all judicial proceedings. If the privilege did not exist at all, everyone would be thrown upon his own legal resources; deprived of all professional assistance, a man would not venture to consult any skilful person, or would only dare to tell his counsellor half his case."[45]

10–18 The various rationales identified above were considered by Laffoy J in *Martin v Legal Aid Board*.[46] Referring, in particular, to the judgment of Finlay CJ in *Smurfit Paribas*, she stated that:

> "What the judgment of Finlay CJ illustrates is that in this jurisdiction the existence and the definition of the parameters of legal professional privilege is predicated on there being a public interest requirement for it in the proper conduct of the administration of justice. It also identifies the nature of such requirement, which is the underlying rationale of the privilege—that the client should not be inhibited in the conduct of litigation or in obtaining legal advice by forced disclosure of communications and advice. Such inhibition might lead to the client not being 'able to make a clean breast of it' ... , or holding 'back half the truth' ... , or even tempt a client's counsel 'to forgo conscientiously investigating his own case' until 'the eve of or during the trial' ... , or constitute 'a prohibition upon professional advice and assistance' ... It is to obviate such outcomes, which would undermine the proper, fair and efficient administration of justice, that legal professional privilege exists and has been elevated beyond a mere rule of evidence to 'a fundamental condition on which the administration of justice as a whole rests'..."[47]

Lord Neuberger stated that legal advice privilege "is based on the need to ensure that a person can seek and obtain legal advice with candour and full disclosure, secure in the knowledge that the communications involved can never be used against that person."

[43] [2005] IESC 3 at [64], [2005] 1 IR 59 at [84], [2005] 1 ILRM 357 at 379. This dictum was cited with approval by McKechnie J in *Hansfield Developments v Irish Asphalt Ltd* [2009] IEHC 420 at [24].

[44] (1833) 1 My & K 98 at 103.

[45] This was described by the House of Lords as the first coherent characterisation of the rationale for the privilege in *R. (Prudential Plc) v Special Comr of Income Tax* [2013] UKHL 1 at [23], [2003] 2 AC 185. See also *Holmes v Baddeley* (1844) 1 Ph 476 at 480–481, 41 ER 713 at 715; *Lyell v Kennedy* (1884) 27 Ch D 1 at 18; *Kennedy v Lyell* (1883) 23 Ch D 387 at 404.

[46] [2007] IEHC 76 at [34], [2007] 2 IR 759, [2007] 1 ILRM 481.

[47] [2007] IEHC 76 at [34], [2007] 2 IR 759 at 775, [2007] 1 ILRM 481 at 494. The cases considered by Laffoy J included *R. v Derby Magistrates Court Ex p. B* [1995] 3 WLR 681 at 695, [1996] AC 487 at 507 (*per* Lord Taylor CJ), which was also cited with approval by McKechnie J in *Hansfield Developments v Irish Asphalt Ltd* [2009] IEHC 420 at [25]. See also *R. (Prudential Plc) v Special Comr of Income Tax* [2013] UKSC 1 at [21], [2013] 2 AC 185; *Three Rivers District Council v Bank of England (No. 6)* [2004] UKHL 48, [2004] 3 WLR 1274, [2005] 1 AC 610, at [31]; *Hobbs v Hobbs and Cousens* [1960] P 112 at 116–117, and *Balabel v Air India* [1988] Ch 317. *Cf.* the comments of Bingham LJ in *Ventouris v Mountain* [1991] 3 All ER 472 at 475: "The doctrine

10–19   The precise manner in which privilege is thought to promote the administration of justice is not specified in these decisions, but the following may be suggested. First, it can be argued that privilege is crucial to the effective functioning of our adversarial model of justice.[48] This relies heavily on the parties to seek out both the facts and the law that support their case and undermine that of their opponent. The likelihood that the court will reach the right result and justice will be done is intimately tied to the quality of those efforts which are, obviously, likely to be much better if the party is represented by a trained lawyer. For example, although cross-examination has been described by Wigmore[49] as the "greatest legal engine ever invented for the discovery of truth", its effectiveness is crucially dependent upon the forensic skills of the cross-examiner. Furthermore, many cases require legal argument and the citation of legal authorities and it is simply unrealistic to expect lay persons to have the requisite skill and knowledge in that regard. Secondly, the representation of the parties by persons with legal training and knowledge is likely to result in more efficient presentation and, hence, disposal of cases.[50] Thirdly, the involvement of a lawyer who is emotionally and financially detached from the underlying dispute aids a realistic appraisal of its prospects of success and its settlement or proper conduct if the matter comes to trial.[51] The foregoing considerations are underpinned and reinforced by the ethical obligations which barristers[52] and solicitors[53] owe to the court, ethical obligations which are not owed by lay clients and which clearly promote the administration of justice.[54]

10–20   Once it is accepted that it is desirable, in the interests of justice, that a client should be legally represented, then it necessarily follows that he or she should be enabled to make full and frank disclosure to the lawyer so that the foregoing benefits may be realised. In the absence of privilege, a client would be discouraged by the

---

of legal professional privilege is rooted in the public interest, which requires that hopeless and exaggerated claims and unsound and spurious defences be so far as possible discouraged, and civil disputes so far as possible settled without resort to judicial decision."

[48]   See *ESSO Australian Resources Ltd v Dawson* [1999] FCA 363 at [14], where the Federal Court of Australia opined that the absence of the privilege "would significantly undermine the proper functioning of the adversarial system of justice".

[49]   Wigmore, *Evidence*, 3rd edn (Boston: Little Brown and Company, 1940), Vol. V, § 1367.

[50]   See *Smurfit Paribas Bank Ltd v AAB Export Finance Ltd* [1990] 1 IR 469 at 476, [1990] ILRM 588 at 592–593.

[51]   *Cf.* the comments of Bingham LJ in *Ventouris v Mountain* [1991] 3 All ER 472 at 475: "The doctrine of legal professional privilege is rooted in the public interest, which requires that hopeless and exaggerated claims and unsound and spurious defences be so far as possible discouraged, and civil disputes so far as possible settled without resort to judicial decision."

[52]   Pursuant to § 5 of the Code of Conduct for the Bar of Ireland (adopted on 22 July 2013), a barrister is, *inter alia*, obliged to act at all times with courtesy to the court before which he or she is appearing and to use his or her endeavours in every case to avoid unnecessary expense and waste of the court's time. In addition, he or she must not knowingly deceive or mislead the court, must not coach a witness and must, in civil cases, ensure that the court is informed of any relevant decision on a point of law or any legislative provision of which he or she is aware immediately in point whether it is for or against his or her contention. See further *R. v O'Connell* (1844) 7 ILR 261.

[53]   In *IPLG v Fry*, unreported, High Court, Lardner J, 19 March 1992, it was held that a solicitor is an officer of the court and the court, thus, has an inherent jurisdiction to supervise a solicitor's conduct and to discipline him for misconduct. See further, P. O'Callaghan, *The Law on Solicitors in Ireland* (Dublin: Butterworths, 2000), § 1.06ff.

[54]   *Cf. New Victoria Hospital v Ryan* [1993] ICR 201 at 203, where Tucker J stated that the application of legal professional privilege "should be strictly confined to legal advisers such as solicitors and counsel, who are professionally qualified, who are members of professional bodies, who are subject to the rules and etiquette of their professions, and who owe a duty to the court".

possibility of future disclosure from consulting a lawyer and, even if he or she did, the natural temptation would be to hold back facts which he or she considered to be harmful to his or her case.[55] This might well lead a lawyer to advise that the client had a good case when, armed with all the relevant facts, he or she might have advised not to institute or to settle proceedings rather than fight a weak case.

10–21   The foregoing justifications all relate to the conduct of litigation and do not explain why privilege was extended to legal advice unconnected with litigation, but in *Greenough v Gaskell*[56] Brougham LC justified this extension on the basis that:

> "the protection would be insufficient, if it only included communications more or less connected with judicial proceedings; for a person oftentimes requires the aid of professional advice upon the subject of his rights and his liabilities, with no reference to any particular litigation, and without any other reference to litigation generally, than all human affairs have, in so far as every transaction may, by possibility, become the subject of judicial inquiry."[57]

10–22   In addition, he pointed out that conferring privilege on legal advice helps to avoid litigation:

> "If the privilege were confined to communications connected with suits begun, or intended, or expected, or apprehended, no one could safely adopt such precautions as might eventually render any proceedings successful, or all proceedings superfluous."[58]

10–23   This argument was taken up by Wigmore[59] who opined:

> "Now it cannot be denied that professional legal advice is as often needed for avoiding litigation as for carrying it on; still less can it be denied that the avowed ideal of the law, and the prudent custom of the profession, is to diminish litigation by so ordering the affairs of clients that litigation is not needed to correct their plight. It is a truism that much of litigation is due to the very failure of clients to seek legal advice until a resort to the Courts can be avoided. Thus the relation of client and legal adviser, and the freedom of entering into it, are of at least equal importance for matters that are still in the non-litigious stage; and the promotion of the relation in that stage tends to prevent its necessity in the further and less desirable stage".

10–24   In *Smurfit Paribas Bank Ltd v AAB Export Finance Ltd,*[60] Finlay CJ did not regard the case law as providing a satisfactory explanation for the expansion of privilege to legal advice but accepted that it was justified on the basis that:

> "Where a person seeks or obtains legal advice there are good reasons to believe that he

---

[55]   See *Keegan v Kilrane* [2011] IEHC 516 at [23], [2011] 3 IR 813 at 825, where Birmingham J stated that, "[t]he doctrine of legal professional privilege exists so that clients can open up to their lawyers and be frank with them". He held that objective bias arose in circumstances where the applicant was convicted various offences under the Road Traffic Acts by the respondent, a District Court judge, who refused to recuse himself, notwithstanding the fact that he had acted as a solicitor on behalf of the applicant in a number of previous proceedings in relation to similar offences.

[56]   (1833) 1 My & K 98. In *Wheeler v La Marchant* (1881) 17 Ch D 675 at 682, Jessel MR stated that legal advice privilege is "a rule established and maintained solely for the purpose of enabling a man to obtain legal advice with safety." He determined the scope of the rule by reference to the protection necessary to ensure that "legal advice may be obtained safely and sufficiently". Brett LJ stated (at 683) that the rule is one "which has been established on grounds of general or public policy".

[57]   (1833) 1 My & K 98 at 102. *Cf. Lawrence v Campbell* (1859) 4 Drew 485 at 489; *Wilson v Northampton and Banbury Junction Railway Co.* (1872) LR 14 Eq 477; *Minter v Priest* [1929] 1 KB 655 at 675, [1930] AC 558, [1930] All ER 431.

[58]   (1833) 1 My & K 98 at 103.

[59]   Wigmore, *Evidence*, 3rd edn (Boston: Little Brown and Company, 1940), VIII, § 2295.

[60]   [1990] 1 IR 469, [1990] ILRM 588.

necessarily enters the area of potential litigation. The necessity to obtain legal advice would in broad terms appear to envisage the possibility of a legal challenge or query as to the correctness or effectiveness of some step which a person is contemplating. Whether such query or challenge develops or not, it is clear that a person is then entering the area of possible litigation."[61]

10–25   Thus, the obtaining of legal advice was sufficiently linked to the conduct of litigation and the function of administering justice in the courts that the "public interest in the proper conduct of the administration of justice can be said to outweigh the disadvantage arising from the restriction of disclosure of all the facts".[62]

10–26   More recently, however, the House of Lords has sought to detach the justification for legal advice privilege from the conduct of litigation entirely, focusing instead on the importance of legal advice in a society based on the rule of law. In *Three Rivers DC v Bank of England*,[63] Lord Foscotte engaged in a comprehensive review of the authorities in which the rationale for legal advice privilege, as opposed to litigation privilege, has been considered, and concluded that:

> "None of these judicial *dicta* tie the justification for legal advice privilege to the conduct of litigation. They recognise that in the complex world in which we live there are a multitude of reasons why individuals, whether humble or powerful, or corporations, whether large or small, may need to seek the advice or assistance of lawyers in connection with their affairs; they recognise that the seeking and giving of this advice so that the clients may achieve an orderly arrangement of their affairs is strongly in the public interest; they recognise that in order for the advice to bring about that desirable result it is essential that the full and complete facts are placed before the lawyers who are to give it; and they recognise that unless the clients can be assured that what they tell their lawyers will not be disclosed by the lawyers without their (the clients') consent, there will be cases in which the requisite candour will be absent. It is obviously true that in very many cases clients would have no inhibitions in providing their lawyers with all the facts and information the lawyers might need whether or not there were the absolute assurance of non-disclosure that the present law of privilege provides. But the *dicta* to which I have referred all have in common the idea that it is necessary in our society, a society in which the restraining and controlling framework is built upon a belief in the rule of law, that communications between clients and lawyers, whereby the clients are hoping for the assistance of the lawyers' legal skills in the management of their ... affairs, should be secure against the possibility of any scrutiny from others, whether the police, the executive, business competitors, inquisitive busy-bodies or anyone else ... I, for my part, subscribe to this idea. It justifies, in my opinion, the retention of legal advice privilege in our law, notwithstanding that as a result cases may sometimes have to be decided in ignorance of relevant probative material."[64]

10–27   This view of the rationale for legal advice privilege was reaffirmed by the House of Lords in *R. (Prudential Plc) v Special Comr of Income Tax*,[65] where Lord Neuberger approached the task of determining the scope of legal advice privilege on the basis that it is justified by the "rule of law".

(b) Conditions required to establish privilege

10–28   In order to succeed in a claim of legal advice privilege, it is necessary to show that the document or information sought to be disclosed consists of a confidential

---

[61]   [1990] 1 IR 469 at 478, [1990] ILRM 588 at 594–595.
[62]   [1990] 1 IR 469 at 477, [1990] ILRM 588 at 594.
[63]   [2004] UKHL 48, [2005] 1 AC 610.
[64]   [2004] UKHL 48 at [34], [2005] 1 AC 610.
[65]   [2013] UKHL 1 at [21] and [26], [2003] 2 AC 185 at 216, *per* Lord Neuberger.

communication made in the course of a professional legal relationship for the purpose of giving or receiving legal advice.[66] Taking each of these elements in turn:

(i) Communication

10–29   The concept of "communication" is given a broad interpretation so as to bring within the scope of privilege all information which passes between the lawyer and client for the purpose of giving, receiving or formulating legal advice.[67] Thus, privilege will extend not only to written communications between a lawyer and client, but also to notes or memoranda of oral conversations,[68] documents generated by the lawyer in the course of formulating legal advice,[69] a solicitor's bill of costs,[70] copies of documents containing legal advice,[71] and documents which reproduce or incorporate legal advice.[72]

10–30   There are, however, a number of limitations on the concept of a "communication". First, privilege only applies to communications between the lawyer and client, and does not extend to communications between either the lawyer or client and third parties even though these relate to matters upon which the client has sought legal advice.[73] It is not necessary, however, that the communication passes directly between the lawyer and client. Law firms could not function without the use of agents such as secretaries and apprentices and a communication which is made to or by such an agent will be privileged on the same basis as if made to or by the lawyer.[74]

---

[66]   *R. (Prudential Plc) v Special Comr of Income Tax* [2013] UKSC 1 at [18], [2013] 2 AC 185 at 215; *Three Rivers District Council v Bank of England (No. 6)*[2004] UKHL 48 at [38], [2004] 3 WLR 1274, [2005] 1 AC 610; *Wheeler v La Marchant* (1881) 17 Ch D 675 at 681; *Minter v Priest* [1929] 1 KB 655, [1930] AC 558 at 568, [1930] All ER 431 at 434; *Great Atlantic Insurance v Home Insurance* [1981] All ER 485 at 490.

[67]   *Ochre Ridge Ltd v Cork Bonded Warehouses Ltd* [2004] IEHC 160 at [11]. *Stevens v Canada (Privy Council)* (1998) 161 DLR (4th) 85 at 100. *Cf. Descôteaux v Mierzwinski* [1982] 1 SCR 860 at 893, (1982) 141 DLR (3d) 590 at 618.

[68]   *Hurstridge Finance Ltd v Lismore Homes Ltd*, unreported, High Court, 15 February 1991 at 4.

[69]   *Pearce v Foster* (1885) 15 QBD 114 at 118; *Hurstridge Finance Ltd v Lismore Homes Ltd*, unreported, High Court, 15 February 1991 at 5 (notes made by solicitor for purpose of preparing draft letter held to be privileged).

[70]   *Chant v Brown* (1852) 9 Hare 790; *Stevens v Canada (Privy Council)* (1998) 161 DLR (4th) 85.

[71]   *Butler v Board of Trade* [1971] Ch 680 at 686, [1970] 3 All ER 593 at 596.

[72]   In *Bula Ltd v Crowley*, unreported, High Court, 8 March 1991, Murphy J rejected a distinction made in Syle & Hollander, *Documentary Evidence* 2nd edn (London: Longman, 1987), p.103, between a document which merely passes on legal advice within a firm or company which is privileged and a document which goes further in which case privilege is lost. He was unable to see how this precise boundary could be maintained and held that privilege applied to documents which "would of necessity disclose to a material extent confidential legal advice". *Cf. USP Strategies Plc v London General Holdings Limited* [2004] EWHC 373 and *Hansfield Developments v Irish Asphalt Ltd* [2009] IEHC 420 at [89].

[73]   *Kerry County Council v Liverpool Salvage Association* (1903) 38 ILTR 7 at 8; *Hurstridge Finance Ltd v Lismore Homes Ltd*, unreported, High Court, 15 February 1991 (privilege did not apply to notes of meetings with third parties which solicitors but not the client had attended); *Wheeler v Le Marchant* (1881) 17 Ch D 675 at 680–682; *Guardian Royal Exchange Assurance v Stuart* [1985] 1 NZLR 596 at 602. Privilege will, however, attach to a communication between a solicitor and client in which the solicitor relates information received by him from third parties (*Re Sarah C Getty Trust* [1985] QB 956, [1985] 2 All ER 809).

[74]   In *Wheeler v Le Marchant* (1881) 17 Ch D 675 at 682, Jessel MR said that a communication "is equally protected whether it is made by the client in person or is made by an agent on behalf of the client, and whether it is made to the solicitor in person or to a clerk or subordinate of the solicitor who acts in his place and under his direction." See also *Lyell v Kennedy* (1884) 27 Ch D 1 at 19;

10–31   The position in relation to clients is slightly more complicated and privilege will not extend to communications with every agent of the client, but only those who are employed or engaged for the purpose of obtaining or receiving legal advice on behalf of the client.[75] It should also be noted that a wide definition of "client" will be adopted so that a company can claim privilege in respect of communications that predate its incorporation.[76] Considerable confusion as to the extent to which the privilege will extend to employees of a company has been created by the decision of the Court of Appeal in *Three Rivers SC v Bank of England (No. 5)*,[77] where it was held that the definition of "client" for the purposes of legal advice privilege was limited to the officials appointed by the Bank to deal with communications with its solicitors in relation to the Bingham Inquiry (described as the Bank's Inquiry Unit) and did not extend to other employees of the Bank, however senior. As a result, documents prepared by employees of the Bank with the intention that they should be sent to the Bank's solicitors, and which were actually so sent, were treated as third party communications, as a result of which they were not covered by legal advice privilege.[78]

10–32   Secondly, the communication must owe its genesis to the professional legal relationship. It is, therefore, important to distinguish between documents created by the client for the purpose of submission to his or her lawyer in order to obtain legal advice (which are privileged),[79] and pre-existing documents created for a different purpose and submitted to a lawyer for his or her advice (which are not privileged).[80] Indeed, pre-existing documents enjoy no greater protection from disclosure in the hands of the solicitor than they would in the hands of the client.[81] *A fortiori*, privilege will not attach to copies of pre-existing documents which are made for the purpose of obtaining legal advice.[82]

Anderson v Bank of British Columbia (1876) 2 Ch D 644 at 649; *Hooper v Gumm* (1862) 2 J & H 602 at 606; *Reid v Langlois* (1849) 1 Mac & G 627 at 638–639; *Walker v Wildman* (1821) 6 Madd 47 at 47–48; *Steele v Stewart* (1844) 1 Phil 471 at 475; *Bunbury v Bunbury* (1839) 2 Beav 173 at 176.

[75] This statement of the law was cited with approval in *University College Cork v ESB* [2014] IEHC 135 at [47]. See also *Three Rivers DC v Bank of England (No.5)* [2003] QB 1556; *Wheeler v Le Marchant* (1881) 17 Ch D 675 at 684; *General Accident Assurance Co. v Chrusz* (1988) 37 OR (3d) 790; *Goodman & Carr v Minister of National Revenue* [1968] 2 OR 814, (1968) 70 DLR (2d) 670; *Mudgway v New Zealand Insurance Co. Ltd* [1988] 2 NZLR 283; *C-C Bottlers Ltd v Lion Nathan Ltd* [1993] 2 NZLR 445.

[76] *Ochre Ridge Ltd v Cork Bonded Warehouses Ltd* [2004] IEHC 160 at [11].

[77] [2003] QB 1556.

[78] The Bank was declined leave to appeal this aspect of the decision. In *Three Rivers DC v Bank of England (No. 6)* [2004] UKHL 48 at [118], [2005] 1 AC 610, Lord Carswell referred to this holding and stated, "I am not to be taken to have approved of the decision and would reserve my position as its correctness". However, in circumstances where this was not an issue in the appeal, it was not determined by the House of Lords. For a detailed discussion of the uncertainty this has created as a matter of English law, see Passmore, *Privilege* 3rd edn (London: Sweet & Maxwell, 2013), at [2-032] *et seq. Cf. National Westminster Bank Plc v Rabobank Nederland* [2006] EWHC 2332 (Comm).

[79] *Horgan v Murray* [1999] 1 ILRM 257; *Dunnes Stores Ltd v Smyth*, unreported, High Court, 24 July 1995; *M'Mahon v Great Northern Railway Co.* (1906) 40 ILTR 172 at 173.

[80] *Graham v Bogle* [1924] 1 IR 68 at 70; *Pearce v Foster* (1885) 15 QBD 114 at 118. *Cf. R. v Hayward* (1846) 2 C & K 234. But see *Sheehan v McMahon*, unreported, Supreme Court, 29 July 1993.

[81] *R. v Justice of the Peace for Peterborough, ex parte Hicks* [1978] 1 All ER 225 at 228, [1977] 1 WLR 1371 at 1374; *R. v King* [1983] 1 All ER 929 at 931, [1983] 1 WLR 411 at 414.

[82] *Tromso Sparebank v Beirne* [1989] ILRM 257; *Ochre Ridge Ltd v Cork Bonded Warehouses Ltd*

10–33   Thirdly, privilege only applies to facts communicated and not to every fact which a lawyer may learn in the course of his professional relationship with a client.[83] A distinction is, thus, drawn between facts communicated to a lawyer by the client and those which are patent to the senses.[84] In *Brown v Foster*,[85] Baron Martin stated that, "what passes between counsel and client ought not to be communicated, and is not admissible in evidence, but with respect to matters which the counsel sees with his own eyes, he cannot refuse to answer." In that case, it was held that counsel could give evidence as to whether a particular entry had been made in a book because this was not information communicated to him by the client but, rather, knowledge acquired by his own observation. Similarly, a lawyer may be required to give evidence as to whether a particular document was given to him by the client,[86] whether he saw the client execute a deed,[87] and whether handwriting is that of his client.[88]

(ii) Confidence

10–34   In order for a claim of privilege to succeed, it is a fundamental prerequisite that the communication passed was intended to pass in confidence.[89] Thus, in *Bord na gCon v Murphy*,[90] where a client made a statement to his solicitor of his version of events for the express purpose of corresponding with the complainant Board, it was held that the letter was not privileged and the solicitor could be required to disclose whether he had been instructed to write it and to make the statements contained therein because its contents were not intended to be confidential.[91]

10–35   The determination of whether a communication was intended to pass in confidence will depend on the circumstances in which the communication was made

---

[2004] IEHC 160 at [5]; *USP Strategies Plc v London General Holdings Ltd* [2004] EWHC 373 at [28].

[83]   *Dwyer v Collins* (1852) LR 7 Exch 639 at 645–646; *Bursill v Tanner* (1885) 16 QBD 1 at 5; *Commissioner of Taxation v Coombes* [1999] FCA 842, (1999) 164 ALR 131; *Coveney v Tannahill* (1841) 1 Hill 33 at 35 (NY).

[84]   *Sandford v Remington* (1793) 2 Ves Jun 189; *Greenough v Gaskell* (1833) 1 My & K 98 at 104; *Brown v Foster* (1857) 1 H & N 736; *Sawyer v Birchmore* (1837) 3 My & K 572; *Kennedy v Lyell* (1883) 23 Ch D 387 at 407; *Stevens v Canada (Privy Council)* (1998) 161 DLR (4th) 85.

[85]   (1857) 1 H & N 736 at 740.

[86]   *Dwyer v Collins* (1852) 7 Exch 639. But see *Madge v Thunder Bay (City)* (1990) 44 CPC (2d) 186.

[87]   *Duchess of Kingston's Case* (1776) 20 St Tr 355 at 613; *Sanford v Remington* (1793) 2 Ves Jr 189.

[88]   *Hurd v Moring* (1824) 1 C & P 372.

[89]   *Woori Bank v KDB Ireland Limited* [2005] IEHC 451 at [24]; *Three Rivers DC v Bank of England (No. 6)* [2004] UKHL 48 at [24], [2005] 1 AC 610; *Smurfit Paribas Bank Ltd v AAB Export Finance Ltd* [1990] 1 IR 469 at 473, [1990] ILRM 588 at 590 (*per* Costello J); *Webster v James Chapman & Co.* [1989] 3 All ER 939 at 944; *Ventouris v Mountain* [1991] 3 All ER 472 at 475; *Bursill v Tanner* (1885) 16 QBD 1 at 5; *R. v Dunbar* (1982) 138 DLR (3d) 221 at 244; *Zielinski v Gordon* (1982) 40 BCLR 165; *Federal Commissioner of Taxation v Coombes* [1999] FCA 842, (1999) 164 ALR 131.

[90]   [1970] IR 301.

[91]   See also *Buckley v Incorporated Law Society* [1994] 2 IR 44 at 48; *Murphy v Kirwan* [1993] 3 IR 501 at 514, [1994] 1 ILRM 293 at 302; *Conlon v Conlons Ltd* [1952] 2 All ER 462 (instructions given by client to his solicitor for the purpose of presenting an offer of settlement to the other side held not to be privileged); *Fraser v Sutherland* (1851) 2 Gr 442 (Can) (communications made to a solicitor which were intended to be and were put before the client's creditors as compromise proposal held not to be privileged).

including a consideration of any precautions taken to preserve the confidentiality of the communication. One factor which will militate strongly against an inference of confidentiality is the presence of a third party.[92] However, if the presence of the third party is reasonably necessary for the protection of the client's interests as where a relative or friend of the client is present, and it is clear from the circumstances that the communication was intended to pass in confidence, then privilege is likely to apply.[93]

(iii) Professional legal relationship

10–36   In order to ground privilege, the communication must be made to or by a lawyer[94] during the course of a professional legal relationship[95] or with the intention of establishing one.[96] The definition of lawyer for this purpose includes, obviously, solicitors and barristers[97] but also salaried in-house legal advisers,[98] foreign lawyers,[99]

---

[92]   *R. v Braham* [1976] VR 547; *Vanhorn v Commonwealth* (1931) 40 SW 2d 372; *People v Castiel* (1957) 315 P 2d 779.

[93]   See *Hansfield Developments v Irish Asphalt Ltd* [2009] IEHC 420 at [85] where it was held that the presence of a HomeBond representative at meetings between the plaintiffs and their legal advisers did not result in the loss of privilege in respect of the contemporaneous minutes of the meeting taken by the plaintiffs' legal advisers. *Cf. R. v Dunbar* (1982) 138 DLR (3d) 221 at 244.

[94]   *R. (Prudential Plc) v Special Comr of Income Tax* [2013] UKHL 1 at [29]–[30], [2003] 2 AC 185; *Slade v Tucker* (1880) 14 Ch D 824 at 828; *Wheeler v Le Marchant* (1881) 17 Ch D 675 at 681–682; *Minter v Priest* [1929] 1 KB 655, [1930] AC 558, [1930] All ER 431 at 581; *AG v Mulholland* [1963] 2 QB 477; and *D v National Society for the Prevention of Cruelty to Children* [1978] AC 171 at 243–244.

[95]   *Greenough v Gaskell* (1833) 1 My & K 98 at 101. It is immaterial whether the lawyer is remunerated for his advice (*Matters v State* (1930) 232 NW 781).

[96]   In *Minter v Priest* [1929] 1 KB 655, [1930] AC 558 at 568, [1930] All ER 431 at 434 (*per* Lord Buckmaster), it was held that a communication between a solicitor and client is privileged provided that the communication is such "as within a very wide and generous ambit of interpretation, must be fairly referable to the relationship". *Cf. Great Atlantic Insurance v Home Insurance* [1981] 1 All ER 485 at 489. It does not matter whether a professional legal relationship is actually established (*Shedd v Boland* [1942] OWN 316) but a communication to a lawyer who has declined or ceased to act is not privileged (*Doyle v Bergin* [2010] IEHC 531; *R. v Farley* (1846) 2 Cox CC 82; *R. v Schmidt* (1893) 11 NZLR 703).

[97]   In *R. (Prudential Plc) v Special Comr of Income Tax* [2013] UKHL 1 at [29], [2003] 2 AC 185, the House of Lords defined "members of the legal profession" as including, in England and Wales, members of the Bar, the Law Society, and the Chartered Institute of Legal Executives.

[98]   *R. (Prudential Plc) v Special Comr of Income Tax* [2013] UKHL 1 at [123], [2003] 2 AC 185; *Geraghty v Minister for Local Government* [1975] IR 300 at 312 endorsing the decision of the Court of Appeal to this effect in *Alfred Crompton Amusement Machines Ltd v Customs and Excise Commissioners (No.2)* [1972] 2 QB 102 at 109, [1972] 2 All ER 353 at 376. *Cf. Chancey v Dharmadi* (2007) 86 QR (3d) 602 (paralegals); *New Victoria Hospital v Ryan* [1993] ICR 201 at 202; *R. v Campbell* [1999] 1 SCR 565 at 601, (1999) 171 DLR (4th) 193 at 224–225; *IBM Canada Ltd v Xerox of Canada Ltd* [1978] 1 FC 513 at 516; *Attorney General for the Northern Territory v Kearney* (1985) 158 CLR 500 at 510. As a matter of European Community law, privilege is confined to communications from independent lawyers, i.e. lawyers who are not bound to the client by a relationship of employment: *AM & S Europe v Commission* [1982] ECR 1575, [1982] CMLR 264, [1983] QB 878, [1983] 1 All ER 705. This was recently reaffirmed in *Akzo Nobel Chemicals Ltd v Commission*, Case 550/07P, [2010] ECR I-08301. See Power, "In house lawyers and the European Court: The Akzo v Commission judgment" (2010) Irish Jurist 198. In Canada, this is assessed on a case by case basis, depending on the nature of the work carried out by the in-house counsel; *Pritchard v Ontario (Human Rights Commission)* (2004) SCC 31 at [20].

[99]   In *R. (Prudential Plc) v Special Comr of Income Tax* [2013] UKHL 1, [2003] 2 AC 185, at [45] and [123]; *Lawrence v Campbell* (1859) 4 Drew 485; *Macfarlan v Rolt* (1872) LR 14 Eq 580; *Re Duncan* [1968] P 306, [1968] 2 All ER 395; *Great Atlantic Insurance Co. v Home Insurance Co.*

and the Attorney General.[100] However, it does not include persons without a professional legal qualification who give legal advice,[101] or persons who have ceased to practise as a lawyer[102] or have been struck off,[103] on the basis that "privilege should be strictly confined to legal advisers such as solicitors and counsel, who are professionally qualified, who are members of professional bodies, who are subject to the rules and etiquette of their professions, and who owe a duty to the court".[104]

10–37 Nevertheless, because legal professional privilege exists for the benefit of the client, it will apply where the client does not know of the disability and reasonably believes the person to be a practising lawyer.[105] However, the onus is on the client to establish this,[106] and there should be reasonable grounds for the client's belief.[107]

10–38 The House of Lords has recently reaffirmed the general principle that legal advice privilege is confined to communications between a client and "a member of the legal profession". In *R. (Prudential Plc) v Special Comr of Income Tax*,[108] it was argued that legal advice privilege should extend to legal advice given by accountants in relation to a tax avoidance scheme. The House of Lords accepted that the communications were such that, had they been exchanged as between a client and a lawyer, they would undoubtedly have been subject to legal advice privilege. The Court declined, however, to extend legal advice privilege to communications in connection with advice given by professional persons other than lawyers, even where that advice was legal advice which the professional person was qualified to give.[109] In reaching this conclusion, Lords Neuberger, Mance and Reed all observed that, approaching the issue as a matter of principle or logic, and having regard to the rationale underpinning the privilege, there is a very strong argument for the extension of legal advice privilege to legal advice provided by a person suitably qualified to give that advice, whether that person is a member of the legal profession or some other profession whose activities include the

---

[1981] 2 All ER 485 at 490; *Mutual Life Assurance Co. of Canada v Canada (Deputy Attorney General)* (1989) 28 CPC (2d) 101 at 104.

[100] *Duncan v Governor of Portlaoise Prison (No.2)* [1998] 1 IR 433 at 442; *Quinlivan v Governor of Portlaoise Prison*, unreported, Supreme Court, 5 March 1997. Under Art.30 of the Constitution, the Attorney General is the legal advisor to the Government "in matters of law and legal opinion".

[101] *R. (Prudential Plc) v Special Comr of Income Tax* [2013] UKHL 1, [2003] 2 AC 185 (accountant); *New Victoria Hospital v Ryan* [1993] ICR 201 (personnel consultant); *Wilden Pump Engineering Co v Fusfeld* [1985] FSR 159 (patent agent); *In re Dormeuil Trade Mark* [1983] RPC 131 (trade mark agent); *R. v Umoh* (1986) 84 Cr App R 138 (prison officer acting as legal aid officer); *Lumonics Research Ltd v Gould* [1983] 2 FC 360 at 366 (patent agent); *Naujokat v Bratushesky* [1942] WWR 97, [1942] 2 DLR 721 (newspaper); *Schubkagel v Dierstein* (1890) 131 P 46 (law student).

[102] *Calley v Richards* (1854) 19 Beav 401.

[103] *Dadourian Group International v Simms* [2008] EWHC 1784 at [119]–[228].

[104] *New Victoria Hospital v Ryan* [1993] ICR 201 at 203 (*per* Tucker J). See also the *obiter* comment to the same effect by Gibbs CJ in *AG for the Northern Territory v Kearney* (1985) 158 CLR 500 at 510.

[105] *Dadourian Group International v Simms* [2008] EWHC 1784 at [122]–[128]; *Calley v Richards* (1854) 19 Beav 401; *Global Funds Management (NSW) Ltd v Rooney* (1994) 36 NSWLR 122; *R. v Choney* (1908) 17 Man R 467; *People v Barker* (1886) 60 Mich 277 at 27 NW 539; *State v Russell* (1892) 83 Wis 330 at 53 NW 441. But *cf. Feuerheerd v London General Omnibus Co.* [1918] 2 KB 565.

[106] *Dadourian Group International v Simms* [2008] EWHC 1784 at [122–128].

[107] *Global Funds Management (NSW) Ltd v Rooney* (1994) 36 NSWLR 122.

[108] *R. (Prudential Plc) v Special Comr of Income Tax* [2013] UKHL 1, [2003] 2 AC 185. *Cf. R. v Uljee* [1982] 1 NZLR 561.

[109] [2013] UKHL 1, [2003] 2 AC 185, at [51]–[52].

giving of legal advice.[110] Notwithstanding this, the House of Lords refused to extend the privilege on the basis that such an extension of the ambit of legal advice privilege would constitute a significant change in the law and raised questions of policy which should be left to Parliament.[111] The majority also expressed considerable concern that the consequences of such an extension of legal advice privilege are difficult to assess and "may lead to what is currently a clear and well understood principle becoming an unclear principle, involving uncertainty".[112]

10–39 The mere fact that the person making or receiving the communication is a lawyer is not sufficient to establish privilege; the communication must be made to or by the lawyer in his or her professional capacity.[113] Lamer J said in *Descôteaux v Mierzwinski*,[114] "the relationship must be a professional one at the exact moment of the communication". Thus, in *Smith v Daniell*,[115] it was held that a legal opinion obtained by the plaintiff from an eminent former Chancellor, Lord Westbury, was not privileged from disclosure because it was clear that he had given it as a friend rather than in discharge of any professional duty.[116] Similarly, in *Buckley v Incorporated Law Society*[117] correspondence between the complainants and the respondent society regarding the alleged misconduct of a solicitor was held not to be privileged because the complainants were not consulting the Law Society as a legal adviser. More recently, in *Doyle v Bergin*,[118] it was held that correspondence sent by a director of a company to another director, who happened to be a solicitor, was not privileged in circumstances where the solicitor had refused to accept instructions or to give advice in relation to the matter on the ground that a conflict of interest arose. Laffoy J concluded that the

---

[110] [2013] UKHL 1, [2003] 2 AC 185, *per* Lord Neuberger at [39], *per* Lord Mance at [79], *per* Lord Reed at [99]. See Loughrey, "An unsatisfactory stalemate: *R (on the application of Prudential Plc) v Special Commissioner for Income Tax*" (2014) 18 E & P 65.

[111] The Legal Services Regulation Bill, Part 7, contemplates the creation of multi-disciplinary practices in Ireland. It remains to be seen how the issues considered in *R. (Prudential Plc) v Special Comr of Income Tax* are addressed in this context. For a discussion of this, see Thanki, *The Law of Privilege* 2nd edn (Oxford University Press, 2011) at [1.49].

[112] [2013] UKHL 1, [2003] 2 AC 185, *per* Lord Neuberger at [52]. See also the comments of Lord Reed at [100] where he stated that: "the privilege must be capable of being relied upon if it is to serve its purpose of enabling clients and their legal advisers to communicate with each other with complete candour. It is therefore highly desirable that the privilege should, as far as possible, be based upon a principle which is clear, certain and readily understood. The existing common law principle meets those requirements. The variety of possible formulations of an extended common law principle, and the consequent scope for debate as to whether particular professional persons, in particular situations, would or would not fall within its scope, would detract from the certainty and clarity which presently exist." *Cf. Water Lilly & Co Ltd v Mackay* [2012] EWHC 649, where it was held that legal advice privilege did not extent to communications between a client and his claims consultant.

[113] *Per* Abbott CJ in *Bramwell v Lucas* (1824) 2 B & C 745 at 749. *Cf. Dunnes Stores Ltd v Smyth*, unreported, High Court, 24 July 1995; *Greenlaw v R.* (1838) 1 Beav 137 at 145; *Desborough v Rawlins* (1838) 3 My & Cr 515 at 521; *Minter v Priest* [1929] 1 KB 655, [1930] AC 558 at 568, [1930] All ER 431 at 434; *R. v Campbell* [1999] 1 SCR 565 at 601–602, (1999) 171 DLR (4th) 193 at 225; *Descôteaux v Mierzwinski* [1982] 1 SCR 860 at 872, (1982) 141 DLR (3d) 590 at 803; *Police v Mills* [1993] 2 NZLR 592 at 595.

[114] [1982] 1 SCR 860 at 872, (1982) 141 DLR (3d) 590 at 603.

[115] (1874) LR 18 Eq 649 at 654.

[116] See also *Rudd v Frank* (1889) 17 OR 758.

[117] [1994] 2 IR 44.

[118] [2010] IEHC 531 at [3.8].

communication was sent to the solicitor in his capacity as a director and officer of the company, rather than in his capacity as a lawyer.[119]

10–40 Problems can arise where a lawyer acts in a dual capacity, as can be seen from the discussion in *Somatra Ltd v Sinclair Roche & Temperley*.[120] An action for professional negligence had been taken by the plaintiff company against the defendant firm of solicitors. It was argued that privilege attached to communications between the managing partner of the firm and other partners of the firm concerning settlement discussions which the managing partner had held with the plaintiffs. However, the plaintiff argued that privilege did not attach because these communications had been made in his capacity as managing partner and not as a lawyer. The Court of Appeal held that privilege attached because, although the managing partner was in important respects acting in his capacity as such in trying to settle the plaintiff's claim, he was a lawyer and, thus, in position to give legal advice to the partnership. On balance, the court was prepared to accept the assertion made on affidavit that the managing partner in creating those documents had been exercising professional skill and judgment as a solicitor on behalf of the defendants.

10–41 The position of a solicitor and client in circumstances where the client is in receipt of legal aid in accordance with the Civil Legal Aid Act 1995 was considered by Laffoy J in *Martin v Legal Aid Board*,[121] where it was held that s.32(1) of the 1995 Act "puts the relationship between a solicitor and legally aided client, and the rights and privileges arising out of such relationship, on the same footing as that of a solicitor and non-legally aided client".[122] Accordingly, legal professional privilege applies to communications between a solicitor and a legally aided client in the ordinary manner, and the solicitor owes a duty of confidentiality to the legally aided client.[123] Furthermore, the umbrella of legal professional privilege extends to the Legal Aid Board and all of its members and authorised officers, as a result of which "there is a statutory embargo on privileged information which passes to an authorised officer of the [Board] ... being discovered."[124]

(iv) Legal advice

10–42 Not all communications that pass between a lawyer and client are privileged, only those made for the purpose of giving or receiving legal advice.[125] So, for

---

[119] [2010] IEHC 531 at [3.5].
[120] [2000] 2 Lloyd's Rep 673.
[121] [2007] IEHC 76, [2007] 2 IR 759, [2007] 1 ILRM 481.
[122] [2007] IEHC 76 at [23], [2007] 2 IR 759 at 770, [2007] 1 ILRM 481 at 490.
[123] Laffoy J concluded, however, that the rights and privileges arising out of the relationship of solicitor and legally aided client are subject to the provisions of s.32(2) of the 1995 Act, which mandates a solicitor to provide information to the Legal Aid Board, including information which would ordinarily be protected by legal professional privilege and client confidentiality, insofar as this is necessary to enable the Legal Aid Board to discharge its statutory functions under the Act [2007] IEHC 76 at [27], [2007] 2 IR 759 at 771, [2007] 1 ILRM 481 at 491.
[124] [2007] IEHC 76 at [39], [2007] 2 IR 759 at 777, [2007] 1 ILRM 481 at 496.
[125] *Three Rivers DC v Bank of England (No. 6)* [2004] UKHL 48 at [10], [2005] 1 AC 610; *National Maternity Hospital v Information Commissioner* [2007] IEHC 113 at [64], [2007] 3 IR 643; *Egan v O'Toole* [2005] IESC 53; *Doyle v Bergin* [2010] IEHC 531 at [3.3]; *Ochre Ridge Ltd v Cork Bonded Warehouses Ltd* [2004] IEHC 160; *Miley v Flood* [2001] 2 IR 50, [2001] 1 ILRM 489; *Smurfit Paribas Bank Ltd v AAB Export Finance Ltd* [1990] 1 IR 469, [1990] ILRM 588; *Calbeck v Boon* (1872) IR 7 CL 32 at 36–7; *Gillard v Bates* (1840) 6 M & W 548; *Re Cathcart,*

example, privilege does not attach to advice on business matters or conveyancing documents, but privilege may attach to correspondence associated with a conveyance or communications between a solicitor and client in respect of conveyancing transactions if they contain legal advice or are for the purpose of seeking or giving legal advice.[126] Privilege does not attach to communications from an opponent's solicitor, as such communication is hardly likely to convey legal advice.[127]

10–43   The distinction between communications seeking legal advice, which are privileged, and those seeking legal assistance, which are not exempt from disclosure, was drawn in the seminal decision of the Supreme Court in of *Smurfit Paribas Bank Ltd v AAB Export Finance Ltd.*[128] In *Smurfit*, the plaintiff sought disclosure of correspondence and instructions passing between the defendant and the solicitors then acting for it in relation to a charge taken by the defendant over the assets of a third party. The trial judge found that the documents in question did not request or contain any legal advice and were not, therefore, privileged, and this conclusion was upheld on appeal by the Supreme Court. Finlay CJ identified the basic principle to be applied in dealing with claims of legal advice privilege as follows:

> "The existence of a privilege or exemption from disclosure for communications made between a person and his lawyer clearly constitutes a potential restriction and diminution of the full disclosure both prior to and during the course of legal proceedings which in the interests of the common good is desirable for the purpose of ascertaining the truth and rendering justice. Such privilege should, therefore, in my view only be granted in instances which have been identified as securing an objective which in the public interest in the proper conduct of the administration of justice can be said to outweigh the disadvantage arising from the restriction of disclosure of all the facts."[129]

10–44   Having regard to the rationale for legal professional privilege, he was satisfied that legal advice satisfied this test but legal assistance did not because it was not "closely and proximately linked to the conduct of litigation and the function of administering justice in the courts"[130]:

> "There are many tasks carried out by a lawyer for his client and properly within the legal sphere, other than the giving of advice, which could not be said to contain any real relationship with the area of potential litigation. For such communications there does not appear to me to be any sufficient public interest or feature of the common good to be secured or protected which could justify an exemption from disclosure."[131]

---

ex parte Campbell (1870) 5 Ch App 703 at 705; *O'Rourke v Darbishire* [1920] AC 581 at 629, [1920] All ER 1 at 48; *Minter v Priest* [1929] 1 KB 655, [1930] AC 558 at 580–581, [1930] All ER 431 at 440; *Smith-Bird v Blower* [1939] 2 All ER 406; *Three Rivers District Council v Bank of England (No.6)* [2004] EWCA Civ 218, [2004] QB 916, [2004] 2 WLR 1065, [2004] 3 All ER 168; *Cf. R. v Bencardino* (1973) 2 OR (2d) 351 and *Federal Commissioner of Taxation v Coombes* [1999] FCA 842, (1999) 164 ALR 131.

126   *Ochre Ridge Ltd v Cork Bonded Warehouses Ltd* [2004] IEHC 160; *R. v Crown Court, ex parte Baines* [1987] 3 All ER 1025, [1988] 1 QB 579 at 587. In *Prendergast v McLoughlin* [2008] IEHC 296 at [23], [2010] 3 IR 445 at 453, Clarke J held that these general principles apply equally to equivalent documents which arise in the context of the making of a will.

127   *Ochre Ridge Ltd v Cork Bonded Warehouses Ltd* [2004] IEHC 160; *R. v Campbell* [1999] 1 SCR 565 at 602, (1999) 171 DLR (4th) 193 at 225.

128   [1990] 1 IR 469, [1990] ILRM 588.

129   [1990] 1 IR 469 at 477, [1990] ILRM 588 at 594.

130   [1990] 1 IR 469 at 478, [1990] ILRM 588 at 594. See the discussion of this aspect of the decision in *Martin v Legal Aid Board* [2007] IEHC 76 at [34]–[35], [2007] 2 IR 759 at 775, [2007] 1 ILRM 481 at 494.

131   [1990] 1 IR 469 at 478, [1990] ILRM 588 at 595. *Cf.* the Australian decision of *Federal Commissioner of Taxation v Coombes* [1999] FCA 842, (1999) 164 ALR 131, where it was stated

10–45 It has been accepted, however, that there may be circumstances where surrounding documents consulted for the purpose of drafting and for the purpose of obtaining legal advice, which include elements of legal assistance, may be privileged.[132] Furthermore, even if a client merely seeks legal assistance, this may entail the provision of legal advice because a solicitor's duty of care extends beyond the scope of the instructions given by the client and he or she is required "to consider not only what the client wishes him to do, but also the legal implications of the facts which the client brings to his attention."[133] In *Smurfit*, however, McCarthy J was explicit that it is only if such advice is in fact given that privilege will apply. He reasoned that public policy did not require that privilege extend to such communications unless they had, in fact, given rise to legal advice.[134]

10–46 The decision in *Smurfit* was followed in *Miley v Flood*[135] by Kelly J, who extracted from it the principle that a communication only attracts privilege if it seeks or contains legal advice and that the communication of any other information is not privileged. He therefore rejected the contention that privilege could be claimed in respect of the identity of a client on the basis that this was a "mere collateral fact"[136] unconnected with the receipt or provision of legal advice.[137] This conclusion was reaffirmed by the Supreme Court in *Cullen v Wicklow County Manager*,[138] where O'Donnell J held that "there are very few circumstances in which the identity of a client can be said to be privileged".[139] The decision of Kelly J in *Miley v Flood* was also followed by Moriarty J in *Inspector of Taxes v A Firm of Solicitors*,[140] where he ordered a firm of solicitors to divulge the identities and addresses of the persons who

---

that instructions to a lawyer to do a particular thing, *e.g.* to draft a legal document such as a will, would generally not be privileged because instructions to do something do not necessarily amount to a request for advice.

[132] *Ochre Ridge Ltd v Cork Bonded Warehouses Ltd* [2004] IEHC 160; *Prendergast v McLoughlin* [2008] IEHC 296, [2010] 3 IR 445, at [20]; *Hurstridge Finance Ltd v Lismore Homes Ltd*, unreported, High Court, 15 February 1991.

[133] *Per* Barron J in *McMullen v Farrell* [1993] 1 IR 123 at 143, [1992] ILRM 776 at 792. See *Prendergast v McLoughlin* [2008] IEHC 296 at [20], [2010] 3 IR 445 at 451–452; *Ochre Ridge Ltd v Cork Bonded Warehouses Ltd* [2004] IEHC 160 at [4], where this proposition was approved.

[134] [1990] 1 IR 469 at 480, [1990] ILRM 588 at 597. See, by way of example, *Hurstridge Finance Ltd v Lismore Homes Ltd* unreported, High Court, 15 February 1991. See also *R. v Crown Court, ex parte Baines* [1987] 3 All ER 1025, [1988] 1 QB 579, where it was held that communications between a solicitor and client giving legal advice in respect of a conveyancing transaction were privileged but records of a conveyancing transaction were not because they did not contain advice.

[135] [2001] 2 IR 50, [2001] 1 ILRM 489. See also *Buckley v Bough*, unreported, High Court, 2 July 2001.

[136] A phrase used by James LJ in *Re Cathcart, ex parte Campbell* (1870) 5 Ch App 703 at 705, referring to the address of a client.

[137] See also *Bursill v Tanner* (1885) 16 QBD 1; *A & D Logging Co. v Convair Logging Ltd* (1967) 63 DLR (2d) 618; *Cook v Leonard* [1954] VLR 591; *Southern Cross Commodities Pty Ltd v Crinis* [1984] VR 697. *Cf. United States v Mammoth Oil Co.* (1925) 56 OLR 635, [1925] 2 DLR 966; *Lavallee, Rackel and Heintz v Canada (AG)* (1998) 160 DLR (4th) 508 at 525; *Police v Mills* [1993] 2 NZLR 592. See, *contra*, Morrick, "Professional Privilege: the Client's Identity" (1980) 124 SJ 303.

[138] [2010] IESC 49 at [64], [2011] 1 IR 152 at 178. O'Donnell J noted that this was not a novel proposition, only recently identified, citing by way of example *Bursill v Tanner* (1885) 16 QBD 1. He stated that the only possible basis upon which identity might be privileged is if confidentiality of identity was specifically sought at the time instructions were being given.

[139] See also *Ochre Ridge Ltd v Cork Bonded Warehouses Ltd* [2004] IEHC 160.

[140] [2013] IEHC 67 at [10], [2013] 2 ILRM 1 at 5.

were the ultimate beneficiaries of transactions effected through bank accounts in the respondent firm's name, together with the relevant confirmatory documentation.[141]

10–47 A similar characterisation can be applied to facts such as the address of a client[142] and details of when the lawyer met the client.[143] Although these matters may well constitute important information for the purpose of establishing and maintaining a professional relationship between a solicitor and client, it is only in exceptional circumstances that they will be required by the solicitor in order to give legal advice. However, a lawyer will not be required to disclose information of this type if it is so intertwined with the legal advice given that the effect of revealing it would be to disclose the advice.[144]

10–48 The difficulties of distinguishing between legal advice and legal assistance were highlighted by Lavan J in *Ochre Ridge Ltd v Cork Bonded Warehouses Ltd*,[145] where he suggested that, in determining whether legal advice privilege applies to a communication, it is helpful to apply the test, which has found favour in the English authorities,[146] of whether the dominant purpose of the communication was the seeking or giving of legal advice.[147] This aspect of the decision was followed by McKechnie J in *Hansfield Developments v Irish Asphalt*,[148] where it was held that the dominant purpose test applies equally in this jurisdiction to both litigation privilege and legal advice privilege. It now appears to be established, therefore, that the dominant purpose test applies to determine whether a particular communication is to be characterised as legal advice or legal assistance. The role of the dominant purpose test in this context was explained by Clarke J in *Prendergast v McLoughlin*[149] as follows:

> "It is necessary to determine whether the dominant purpose of the communication concerned

---

[141] Moriarty J (at [10], 5) rejected the contention that client confidentiality precluded the disclosure of the information and documentation, observing that there are exceptions to the duty of confidentiality which arises between solicitor and client. *Cf. Walsh v National Irish Bank* [2008] 1 ILRM 56.

[142] *Re Cathcart, ex p. Campbell* (1870) 5 Ch App 703 at 705; *R. v Bell* (1980) 146 CLR LR 141.

[143] *R. v Manchester Crown Court, ex p. Rogers* [1999] 4 All ER 35 (solicitors ordered to produce any record or log which recorded the time of arrival of client at the solicitor's premises on a particular date). See also *Ochre Ridge Ltd v Cork Bonded Warehouses Ltd* [2004] IEHC 160 at [5].

[144] In *Ochre Ridge Ltd v Cork Bonded Warehouses Ltd* [2004] IEHC 160, Lavan J stated that: "A solicitor will not be required to disclose information as to the details of a client where it is so intertwined with the legal advice that the effect of revealing it would be to disclose the advice".*Cf. Miley v Flood* [2001] 2 IR 50, [2001] 1 ILRM 489; *Federal Commissioner of Taxation v Coombes* [1999] FCA 842, (1999) 164 ALR 131 and *Police v Mills* [1993] 2 NZLR 592. In *R. (Kelly) v Warley Magistrates Court* [2008] 1 WLR 2001, it was held that legal advice privilege includes the names, addresses and dates of birth of a party's potential witnesses where such information would reveal the fruits of legal advice (this information is also protected by litigation privilege provided that litigation is in reasonable contemplation).

[145] [2004] IEHC 160. In *Ochre Ridge*, Lavan J extracted 12 general principles from the decision of Finlay CJ in *Smurfit Paribas*, together with a number of other cases. These general principles were described by Clarke J as "of very considerable assistance in attempting to define the difficult boundary between legal advice and legal assistance" in *Prendergast v McLoughlin* [2008] IEHC 296 at [21], [2010] 3 IR 445 at 452.

[146] See *Three Rivers District Council v Bank of England (No.5)* [2003] QB 1556; *Three Rivers District Council v Bank of England (No.6)* [2004] EWCA Civ 218, [2004] QB 916, [2004] 3 All ER 168.

[147] [2004] IEHC 160 at [3].

[148] [2009] IEHC 420 at [28].

[149] [2008] IEHC 296 at [25], [2010] 3 IR 445 at 453; *University College Cork v ESB* [2014] IEHC 135 at [4].

is such that it relates to legal advice on the one hand, or legal assistance on the other. Where the dominant purpose is the obtaining of legal advice, then it seems to me that it is not appropriate to engage in a detailed analysis of the document concerned for the purposes of attempting to identify whether some minor aspects of the relevant document might not be properly characterised as being designed for the purposes of obtaining or giving legal advice."

10–49 He held that, when the dominant purpose of a communication was genuinely the giving or receiving of legal advice, then the entire communication will *prima facie* be privileged. However, where it is clear that the dominant purpose of the communication was for the purposes of obtaining legal assistance, privilege may not be claimed.[150]

10–50 In *Prendergast*, the plaintiff claimed that he was entitled to certain lands as a result of a promise made to him by the deceased and his brother. The defendant, a nephew of the deceased, asserted privilege over attendances taken by the solicitors for the deceased and his brother concerning the making of their respective wills, together with certain documents given to the solicitors for this purpose and a draft will. Clarke J held that documents produced for the purposes of giving instructions for the making of a will were not, by reason of that status alone, privileged.[151] However, there could be documents which pass between a client and solicitor in this context which are privileged, "where the dominant purpose of the document concerned is designed for the purposes of obtaining or giving legal advice connected with the making of a will, as opposed to legal assistance in the drawing of the will concerned."[152] This would be the case where legal advice was expressly requested, or where it was implicit in the nature of the instructions that the solicitor was under a duty to give legal advice arising out of the circumstances disclosed, rather than simply convert the client's instructions into a properly drafted will.[153]

10–51 The distinction between legal advice and legal assistance was also considered in *Moorview Developments v First Active plc*,[154] a case which arose out of the advance of commercial loans by the defendant to the plaintiff. Having considered the decision of Lavan J in *Ochre Ridge*, Clarke J extracted the following two general principles from the judgment: first, the fact that an individual document does not of itself convey legal advice or expressly seek legal advice does not necessarily prevent it from being part of a sequence of documents that is intimately connected with the seeking or giving of legal advice, so as to qualify for legal advice privilege; second, even where legal advice is not expressly sought, there may be circumstances where the solicitor owes the client a duty of care to give the client legal advice arising out of the solicitor's instructions in any event. Clarke J held that it logically follows from the decision in *Smurfit* that

---

[150] [2008] IEHC 296 at [26], [2010] 3 IR 445 at 455. Clarke J accepted, however, that in circumstances where the dominant purpose of a communication was to obtain legal assistance, but a subsidiary portion of the communication involves the seeking or giving of legal advice, the legal advice may be redacted.

[151] For a discussion of this aspect of the decision, see "No privilege in respect of instructions for will", (2010) 28(9) ILT 136. *Cf.* McCarthy, Case Comment, (2009) 14(1) CPLJ 32.

[152] [2008] IEHC 296 at [33], [2010] 3 IR 445 at 455.

[153] Clarke J disallowed the claim of privilege, and directed inspection of all of the documents, with the exception of two redacted passages recording the giving and receiving of legal advice; [2008] IEHC 296 at [31], [2010] 3 IR 445 at 454–455.

[154] Unreported, High Court, 3 July 2008 at 24. He was influenced in this regard by the fact that, in testamentary proceedings, it would not have been open to the defendant to decline to reveal the documents on grounds of privilege.

an account or description by a lawyer of a transaction which he carried out in the past is not subject to legal advice privilege unless it involves the giving of legal advice.[155] It was held, therefore, that a letter written by the plaintiff's solicitor, which recorded what was agreed as between the plaintiff and the bank at a particular meeting, and recorded representations and statements made by the parties at that meeting, was not subject to legal advice privilege.

10–52 The scope of legal advice privilege was considered by the House of Lords in the seminal decision of *Three Rivers DC v Bank of England (No 6)*,[156] where "legal advice" was defined as advice which "relates to the rights, liabilities, obligations or remedies of the client either under private law or under public law". Lord Scott cited the dictum of Taylor LJ in *Balabel v Air India*[157] with approval, where he stated that "legal advice is not confined to telling the client the law; it must include advice as to what should prudently and sensibly be done in the relevant legal context". He posited the following objective test to be applied in order to determine whether advice or assistance provided by a lawyer to a client falls within the scope of legal advice privilege:

> "If a solicitor becomes the client's 'man of business', and some solicitors do, responsible for advising the client on all matters of business, including investment policy, finance policy and other business matters, the advice may lack a relevant legal context. There is, in my opinion, no way of avoiding difficulty in deciding in marginal cases whether the seeking of advice from or the giving of advice by lawyers does or does not take place in a relevant legal context so as to attract legal advice privilege. In cases of doubt the judge called upon to make the decision should ask whether the advice relates to the rights, liabilities, obligations or remedies of the client either under private law or under public law. If it does not, then, in my opinion, legal advice privilege would not apply. If it does so relate then, in my opinion, the judge should ask himself whether the communication falls within the policy underlying the justification for legal advice privilege in our law. Is the occasion on which the communication takes place and is the purpose for which it takes place such as to make it reasonable to expect the privilege to apply? The criterion must, in my opinion, be an objective one."[158]

10–53 It was held that legal advice privilege also extended to what was described as "presentational advice", *i.e.* advice given to the Bank in relation to the presentation of factual information, including evidence and submissions, to a statutory inquiry for the purpose of convincing the inquiry that the discharge by the Bank of its public law obligations under the relevant legislation was not deserving of criticism.[159]

---

[155] Unreported, High Court, 3 July 2008 at 25.

[156] [2004] UKHL 48, [2004] 3 WLR 1274, [2005] 1 AC 610, *per* Lord Scott at [38]. This definition was cited with approval by the House of Lords in *R. (Prudential Plc) v Special Comr of Income Tax* [2013] UKSC 1, [2013] 2 AC 185, *per* Lord Neuberger at [19].

[157] [1988] 1 Ch 317 at 330.

[158] Lord Carswell held that, as a general principle, all communications between a solicitor and his client relating to a transaction in which the solicitor has been instructed for the purpose of obtaining legal advice will be privileged, notwithstanding that they do not contain advice on matters of law or construction, provided that they are directly related to the performance by the solicitor of his professional duty as adviser of his client" ([2004] UKHL 48, [2004] 3 WLR 1274, [2005] 1 AC 610, at [111]).

[159] [2004] UKHL 48, [2004] 3 WLR 1274, [2005] 1 AC 610, *per* Lord Scott at [43]. The House of Lords overturned the decision of the Court of Appeal that material prepared for the dominant purpose of putting relevant factual material before the inquiry in an orderly and attractive fashion was not prepared for the dominant purpose of taking legal advice on such material. Lord Scott concluded [at 44] that the skills involved in advising a client what evidence to place before the inquiry, and how to present the client and his story to the inquiry in the most favourable light, are "unquestionably legal skills being applied in a relevant legal context".

3. Litigation Privilege

10–54   Litigation privilege enables parties[160] to prepare for litigation without having to disclose those preparations in advance of the trial,[161] and only arises where proceedings are in existence or contemplation.[162] Traditionally, the privilege has been discussed in terms of the protection which it gives to communications with third parties but, as will become evident below, it also operates to confer a measure of protection on what may best be described as a lawyer's "work product",[163] *i.e.* documents and materials generated or compiled in preparation for litigation even though no element of communication can really be said to be involved.[164] As is the case in respect of legal advice privilege, confidentiality is an essential pre-requisite to a claim of litigation privilege.[165]

(a) Policy of the privilege

10–55   The extension of protection to communications with third parties was initially justified on the basis that such communications could not be disclosed without revealing the instructions of the client and the nature of the advice given by the legal adviser.[166] However, with the limitation of the ambit of protection to communications with third parties in contemplation of litigation,[167] the focus shifted to the role that the privilege plays in the adversarial system. In *Anderson v Bank of British Columbia*,[168] James LJ explained the cases on the basis "that as you have no right to see your adversary's brief, you have no right to see that which comes into existence merely as the materials for the brief".

10–56   Under the adversarial model, the quality of fact-finding is inextricably linked to the efforts of the parties to seek out evidence that supports their case. If both parties use their best endeavours, then the truth should out. The cloak of privilege is required

---

[160] In *Ahern v Mahon* [2008] IEHC 119 at [77], [2008] 4 IR 704 at 722, [2009] 1 ILRM 458 at 474, it was held that a witness to proceedings does not enjoy litigation privilege in respect of contact with third parties concerning their participation as a witness. Litigation privilege is confined to the parties to the litigation.

[161] Privilege will apply, not only to preparations to litigate a case, but also to those for the purpose of compromising it, because it is the policy of the courts to encourage settlement: *Horgan v Murray* [1999] 1 ILRM 257.

[162] *Ahern v Mahon* [2008] IEHC 119 at [62], [2008] 4 IR 704, [2009] 1 ILRM 458.

[163] To use the phrase adopted in the US: see *Hickman v Taylor* (1947) 329 US 495.

[164] In *Hansfield Developments v Irish Asphalt Ltd* [2009] IEHC 420 at [89], McKechnie J accepted that spreadsheets and charts created by the plaintiffs and their engineers were subject to litigation privilege in circumstances where they were created in furtherance of litigation. He observed that it would not be unusual, in complex litigation, for clients to produce summary documents for consideration by lawyers. It was further held that photographs may be subject to litigation privilege where the dominant purpose for their creation was litigation (at [64]). See also *Lyell v Kennedy* (1884) 27 Ch D 1 at 25–26.

[165] *Woori Bank v KDB Ireland Limited* [2005] IEHC 451 at [24]; *Shell E & P Ireland v McGrath (No. 2)* [2006] IEHC 409 at [28], [2007] 2 IR 574 at 585, [2007] 1 ILRM 544 at 555.

[166] *Anderson v Bank of British Columbia* (1876) 2 Ch D 644 at 649 (*per* Jessel MR). *Cf. Re Barings Plc* [1998] Ch 356 at 366, [1998] 1 All ER 673 at 681, where Scott VC reviewed the authorities and concluded that the only reason that privilege attached to documents brought into existence for the purposes of litigation is to keep inviolate communications between the client and his or her legal adviser.

[167] *Wheeler v Le Marchant* (1881) 17 Ch D 675.

[168] (1876) 2 Ch D 644 at 656.

to protect these efforts.[169] As O'Leary J explained in the Canadian decision of *Ottawa-Carleton (Regional Municipality) v Consumers' Gas Co.*:

> "The adversarial system is based on the assumption that if each side presents its case in the strongest light the court will be best able to determine the truth. Counsel must be free to make the fullest investigation and research without risking disclosure of his opinions, strategies and conclusions to opposing counsel. The invasion of privacy of counsel's trial preparation might well lead to counsel postponing research and other preparation until the eve of or during the trial, so as to avoid early disclosure of harmful information. The result would be counter-productive to the present goal that the early and thorough investigation by counsel will encourage an early settlement of the case. Indeed, if counsel knows he must turn over to the other side the fruits of his work, he may be tempted to forgo conscientiously investigating his own case in the hope he will obtain disclosure of the research, investigations and thought processes compiled in the trial brief of opposing counsel …".[170]

10–57 It is thus feared that the net effect of such a disincentive to the evidence-gathering efforts of the parties would be a diminution in the accuracy of fact-finding and ultimately of the quality of justice.

10–58 Another idea running through the case law is that the privacy of a lawyer in preparing for trial should be respected and if protection for pre-trial preparations was not given, inefficiencies would result. In *Hickman v Taylor*,[171] Murphy J opined that:

> "In performing his various duties … it is essential that a lawyer work with a certain degree of privacy, free from unnecessary intrusion by opposing parties and their counsel. Proper preparation of a client's case demands that he assemble information, sift what he considers to be the relevant from the irrelevant facts, prepare his legal theories and plan his strategy without undue and needless interference…This work is reflected, of course, in interviews, statements, memoranda, correspondence, briefs, mental impressions, personal beliefs, and countless other tangible and intangible ways—aptly though roughly termed by the Circuit Court of Appeals in this case as the 'work product of the lawyer'. Were such materials open to opposing counsel on mere demand, much of what is now put down in writing would remain unwritten. An attorney's thoughts, heretofore inviolate, would not be his own. Inefficiency, unfairness and sharp practices would invariably develop in the giving of legal advice and in the preparation of cases for trial. The effect on the legal profession would be demoralizing. And the interests of the clients and the cause of justice would be poorly served."

10–59 This idea fitted in with the traditional notion of "trial by ambush" whereby a litigant was, within certain limits, entitled to refuse to disclose the nature of his or her case until trial. As Lord Wilberforce put it in *Waugh v British Railways Board*,[172] "one side may not ask to see the proofs of the other side's witnesses or the opponent's brief or even know what witnesses will be called: he must wait until the card is played and cannot try to see it in the hand".

10–60 However, in more recent times, the courts have begun to question whether the availability of litigation privilege actually advances the administration of justice. In *Gallagher v Stanley*,[173] the Supreme Court was very critical of the "oak-like" attitude of the defendant hospital and its attempts to withhold innocuous documents. O'Flaherty

---

[169] In *Kennedy v Lyell* (1883) 23 Ch D 387 at 404, Cotton LJ cautioned "that no one is to be fettered in obtaining materials for his defence and, if for the purpose of his defence obtains evidence, the adverse party cannot ask to see it before the trial". See also *Lyell v Kennedy* (1884) 27 Ch D 1 at 18.

[170] (1990) 74 DLR (4th) 742 at 748.

[171] (1947) 329 US 495 at 510–511.

[172] [1980] AC 521 at 531, [1979] 2 All ER 1169 at 1172.

[173] [1998] 2 IR 267.

J stated that the purpose of legal professional privilege is "to aid the administration of justice; not to impede it" and "[i]n general, justice will be best served where there is the greatest candour and where all relevant documentary evidence is available."[174] Evident in the decision of the Supreme Court in *Gallagher v Stanley* was dissatisfaction on the part of the Court with the imperialist tendencies of litigation privilege in the hands of parties who wish to withhold probative material from disclosure. That, coupled with the policy consideration that as much relevant evidence as possible should be before the trial court, indicates that claims of litigation privilege will be subjected to rigorous examination.

10–61 This view was echoed in *Payne v Shovlin*,[175] where Kearns J stated that, "... it should be remembered that litigation privilege is itself an exception to the general principle that all relevant information should be before the court. The consequent need to construe this ... exception strictly has been recognised frequently by the Courts."[176]

10–62 The rationale for litigation privilege was recently considered by Finlay Geoghegan J in *University College Cork v ESB*,[177] where it was held that the maxim, "once privileged, always privileged" does not apply to litigation privilege, which attaches only in subsequent proceedings that are "closely related" to the original proceedings. Finlay Geoghegan J identified the objective of litigation privilege as "the creation of what has been referred to as a 'zone of privacy' in the interests of the efficacy of the adversarial system to permit a party in litigation to prepare its position without adversarial interference and without fear of premature disclosure".[178] It is clear from this decision that, in formulating the general principles governing litigation privilege, the courts will endeavour to do so in a manner which does not expand the scope of the privilege beyond what is necessary to achieve this objective.[179]

(b) Communications with third parties

10–63 Communications between either a client or his or her lawyer and third parties, such as potential witnesses or experts, are privileged where they are made in preparation for litigation which is, at the time of the communication, pending or reasonably apprehended.[180] Such communications may include documents emanating

---

[174] [1998] 2 IR 267 at 271. *Cf.* the comments of Lord Edmund-Davies in *Waugh v British Railways Board* [1980] AC 521 at 543, [1979] 2 All ER 1169 at 1182 that a court "should start from the basis that the public interest is, on balance, best served by rigidly confining within narrow limits the cases where material relevant to litigation may be lawfully withheld. Justice is better served by candour than suppression". See also *Grant v Downs* (1976) 135 CLR 674 at 686, where a plurality of the High Court of Australia criticised litigation privilege on the basis that it "detracts from the fairness of the trial by denying a party access to relevant documents or at least subjecting him to surprise".

[175] [2006] IESC 5 at [52], [2007] 1 IR 114 at 129, [2006] 2 ILRM 1 at 15.

[176] [2006] IESC 5 at [53], [2007] 1 IR 114 at 129, [2006] 2 ILRM 1 at 15.

[177] [2014] IEHC 135 at [4].

[178] Finlay Geoghegan J cited the decision of the Canadian Supreme Court in *Blank v Canada* [2006] SCC 39, [2006] 2 SCR 319 at [27], with approval where Fish J stated that the object of litigation privilege is "to ensure the efficacy of the adversarial process ... to achieve this purpose, parties to litigation, represented or not, must be left to prepare their contending positions in private, without adversarial interference and without fear of premature disclosure".

[179] *Cf. Three Rivers DC v Bank of England* [2004] UKHL 48 at [35], [2005] 1 AC 610.

[180] *Markey v Minister for Justice* [2011] IEHC 39 at [38], [2012] 1 IR 62 at 77–78. *Cf. Ahern v Mahon* [2008] IEHC 119 at [62], [2008] 4 IR 704 at 719, [2009] 1 ILRM 458 at 471.

from or prepared by third parties, provided they are prepared with the dominant purpose of use in existing or contemplated litigation.[181]

10–64 In *Hansfield Developments v Irish Asphalt Ltd*[182] an issue arose as to whether communications between a party to proceedings and a public relations firm could be subject to litigation privilege. McKechnie J held that this fell to be determined by the application of the "dominant purpose" test. He accepted that the public relations company was engaged because of the litigation, but pointed out that this did not necessarily mean that the dominant purpose of communications with them was the litigation; the focus of a public relations firm is the control of press and publicity. While McKechnie J did not hold that documents provided to a public relations company could *never* be privileged, or that the disclosure of documents to such a firm must implicitly be seen as a waiver of privilege, he expressed considerable doubt as to whether such communications could be said to be for the primary purpose of litigation.[183] Having considered the documents in issue, he concluded that there was nothing contained in them that would attract legal professional privilege.

(i) Communications with experts

10–65 An expert report which has come into existence for the dominant purpose of litigation is subject to litigation privilege.[184] Thus, an expert report, whether made for the purpose of enabling a party's legal advisers to give legal advice to their client or for discussion in a conference of a party's legal advisers, is privileged.[185] Privilege also attaches to draft expert reports produced for circulation amongst a party's advisers before a final report is prepared for exchange with the other side.[186]

10–66 The ambit of litigation privilege in the context of the commissioning of an independent expert was considered by Kelly J in *Ahern v Mahon*,[187] where he approved the following passage from *Passmore on Privilege*[188] as an accurate summary of the law in this jurisdiction:

> "Traditionally, whenever a professional third party has been engaged as an expert witness by or on behalf of a party to actual, pending or contemplated proceedings, litigation privilege has protected (i) confidential communications between any of the client, his solicitors or counsel and the expert, and (ii) the work of the expert prior to its disclosure or use in the litigation, so long as those communications or the expert's work are referable to the litigation concerned

---

[181] *Three Rivers v Governor and Company of the Bank of England (No. 5)* [2003] QB 1556 at 1561; *Hansfield Developments v Irish Asphalt Ltd* [2009] IEHC 420 at [29].

[182] [2009] IEHC 420 at [86].

[183] McKechnie J did, however, accept that the disclosure of documents to a public relations company for a limited and specific purpose, and on a confidential basis, may not give rise to a waiver of privilege [2009] IEHC 420 at [88]. He agreed, in this regard, with the analysis of the Australian courts in *Spotless Group Ltd v Premier Building & Consulting Group Pty Ltd* (2006) 16 VR 1 at 30, but emphasised that this would depend on the specific facts of each case.

[184] *Kincaid v Aer Lingus* [2003] 2 IR 314.

[185] *Jackson v Marley Davenport Ltd* [2004] 1 WLR 2926.

[186] *Payne v Shovlin* [2006] IESC 5 at [45], [2007] 1 IR 114 at 127, [2006] 2 ILRM 1 at 13; *Jackson v Marley Davenport Ltd* [2004] 1 WLR 2926; *Highland Fisheries Ltd v Lynk Electric Ltd* (1989) 63 DLR (4th) 493.

[187] [2008] IEHC 119 at [65], [2008] 4 IR 704 at 720, [2009] 1 ILRM 458 at 471.

[188] Passmore, *Privilege* 3rd edn (London: Sweet & Maxwell, 2013), para.3–160. The extract contained in the judgment was taken from the second edition (para.3–109), but the text is identical in the current edition.

and satisfy the dominant purpose test. This is so, whether the expert has been instructed with a view to assisting his client to understand, for example, the technical aspects of a claim, to assist in the preparation of a claim or its defence, or to provide expert evidence at the trial of the action."[189]

10–67 Kelly J considered it clear that "legal professional privilege extends to documents generated in connection with the instruction and retention of an expert witness, provided of course they are prepared for the purpose of the litigation".[190] He expressly stated, however, that the expert in question, when he came to give evidence, could legitimately be asked to give evidence as to the factual material which he used to form his opinion and the material instructions which were given to him.[191]

10–68 A significant exception to litigation privilege, insofar as expert reports are concerned, was created by RSC Ord.39, r.46(1), which applies to personal injuries proceedings and requires the parties to list and, subsequently, to exchange copies of all reports from expert witnesses intended to be called.[192] A party may withdraw reliance on an expert report which has been delivered, in which case "the same privilege (if any) which existed in relation to such report or statement shall be deemed to have always applied to it notwithstanding any exchange or delivery which may have taken place".[193] Privilege also applies to a report which was listed but not delivered, and in respect of which reliance is withdrawn.[194]

10–69 The scope of the exception provided for in Ord.39, r.46 has been considered in a number of cases. In *Payne v Shovlin*,[195] the Supreme Court held that Ord.39, r.46 extends to any report which contains any part of the substance of the evidence to be adduced by an expert, regardless of whether the preliminary report was subsumed in a more comprehensive final report furnished to the other side.[196] The extent to which a party to personal injuries proceedings may be required to disclose documents referred to in expert reports exchanged between the parties in accordance with RSC Ord.39, r.46(1) was considered by Finnegan P in *Doherty v North Western Health Board*.[197] The defendant sought disclosure of documents listed in the reports of two medical experts as document to which they had regard for the purpose of preparing the reports, which included correspondence and attendances emanating from the defendant's solicitor. The defendant contended that the documents fell within the definition of "report" in Ord.39, r.45(1)(c), which provides that a report "shall also include any maps, drawings, photographs, graphs, charts, calculations or other like matter referred to in any such report". Finnegan P rejected this contention, and held that this phrase must be construed *ejusdem generis* with the words preceding it. He was satisfied that the documents in

---

[189] For a detailed discussion of litigation privilege and expert witnesses, see Passmore, *Privilege* 3rd edn (London: Sweet & Maxwell, 2013), para.3–160 *et seq*.

[190] [2008] IEHC 119 at [66], [2008] 4 IR 704 at 720, [2009] 1 ILRM 458 at 471.

[191] [2008] IEHC 119 at [117], [2008] 4 IR 704 at 729–730, [2009] 1 ILRM 458 at 480.

[192] Inserted by SI No. 391 of 1998: Rules of the Superior Courts (No. 6) (Disclosure of Reports and Statements), 1998.

[193] Ord.39, r.46(6).

[194] *Kincaid v Aer Lingus* [2003] 2 IR 314.

[195] [2006] IESC 5, [2007] 1 IR 114, [2006] 2 ILRM 1.

[196] See also *Galvin v Murray* [2001] 1 IR 331, [2001] 2 ILRM 234, where it was held that Ord.39, r.46 is not limited to independent experts, and applies equally to employees or "in-house" experts.

[197] [2005] IEHC 404, [2006] 1 ILRM 282.

question not be considered as a like matter to a map, drawing, photograph, graph, chart or calculation.[198]

10–70 The litigation privilege which ordinarily attaches to expert reports is also displaced to some extent in proceedings in the Commercial List, where parties are required to deliver a signed statement outlining the essential elements of any expert evidence on which they intend to rely at trial.[199] It is also open to a judge, at the initial directions hearing, to direct any expert witnesses to consult with each other for the purposes of identifying the issues in respect of which they intend to give evidence and, where possible, reaching agreement on the evidence that they intend to give on those issues.[200]

10–71 The changes implemented by the disclosure rules in personal injuries actions[201] and the Commercial Court Rules[202] were considered by Finlay Geoghegan J in *University College Cork v ESB*,[203] where she observed that they "underline developments in the approach to disclosure for the fair but, perhaps, more efficient administration of justice in the adversarial system". The issue under consideration in that case was the duration of litigation privilege, and the court noted that the application of the maxim "once privileged, always privileged" to litigation privilege by the Irish Courts in *Quinlivan v Tuohy*[204] took place before these procedural changes were introduced. This was one of a number of factors which persuaded the court that a more restrictive approach should be adopted to the duration of litigation privilege in this jurisdiction, such that privilege only attaches in subsequent "closely related" proceedings.[205]

10–72 In criminal proceedings, s.34 of the Criminal Procedure Act 2010 requires an accused to obtain leave to call an expert witness or adduce expert evidence. In *Markey v Minister for Justice*,[206] Kearns J rejected the contention that s.34 interferes with litigation privilege, observing that legal professional privilege rarely arises as a contentious issue in the context of criminal prosecutions. Having considered the general principles governing litigation privilege, he cited the following extract from Archbold's *Criminal Pleading Evidence and Practice*[207] with approval:

> "Litigation privilege attaches to confidential communications between solicitors and expert witnesses but not to an expert's opinion based upon non-privileged material, nor to the non-privileged chattels or documents upon which the opinion was based.... Where the expert's opinion is, at least to a significant extent, based upon privileged material, the opinion itself is also privileged. Consequently the defence can object if the prosecution seek to elicit evidence from an expert who has been abandoned and not relied upon by the defence."

---

[198] Finnegan P noted, however, that at least some of the documents might require to be discovered on an order for discovery being made, and indicated that he was willing to peruse the documents with a view to determining whether or not they enjoyed privilege.

[199] RSC Ord.63A, r.22.

[200] RSC Ord.63A, r.6(1)(ix).

[201] Ord.39, rr.45 and 46, as inserted by SI No. 391 of 1998: Rules of the Superior Courts (No. 6) (Disclosure of Reports and Statements) 1998.

[202] RSC Ord.63A, r.22.

[203] [2014] IEHC 135 at [44].

[204] Unreported, High Court, 29 July 1992. The issue was also raised but not decided in *Breathnach v Ireland (No.3)* [1993] 2 IR 458.

[205] [2014] IEHC 135 at [46].

[206] [2011] IEHC 39, [2012] 1 IR 63.

[207] Archbold, *Criminal Pleading Evidence and Practice*, 59th edn (London: Sweet & Maxwell, 2011), p.1408, [12–11].

10–73   It was held that s.34 operates only in respect of reports which the defence wish to adduce in evidence. Accordingly, such litigation privilege as attaches to expert reports remains intact.[208]

(c) Proximity of Litigation

10–74   In determining whether a communication has come into being in preparation for litigation, the courts have generally focused on the proximity of litigation as the litmus test. Sufficient proximity obviously exists where litigation has commenced but beyond that the courts have struggled to find and apply a formulation which allows parties to make adequate preparations under cover of privilege for litigation which they reasonably anticipate may ensue but which does not result in the suppression of too much probative evidence. Various formulations, such as that litigation should be "apprehended", "contemplated" or "anticipated", have been put forward but none of them has an irreducible content.[209] The question is, at the end of the day, one of policy and the approach of the courts has been to try and reconcile the competing policy objectives by requiring that litigation be reasonably proximate. As a synthesis of the law in this area, it is difficult to improve upon the following statement by Barwick CJ in the Australian case of *Grant v Downs*:

> "[A] document which was produced or brought into existence either with the dominant purpose of its author, or of the person or authority under whose direction, whether particular or general, it was produced or brought into existence, of using it or its contents in order to obtain legal advice or to conduct or aid in the conduct of litigation, at the time of its production in reasonable prospect, should be privileged and excluded from inspection."[210]

10–75   This passage identifies the ingredients required for a successful claim of privilege, which will be examined in turn below. As is clear from its terms, the existence or contemplation of proceedings alone will not render a document subject to litigation privilege; it is also necessary to establish that the document in question was prepared for the dominant purpose of the litigation.[211]

(i) Reasonable prospect of litigation

10–76   The starting point of the modern case law[212] on this issue is the decision of

---

[208] [2011] IEHC 39 at [38], [2012] 1 IR 63 at 77. Kearns J noted that the criminal law system contains a number of legislative provisions which either require or encourage some measure of pre-trial disclosure by the defence, *e.g.* the requirement to give notice of an alibi (s.20 of the Criminal Justice Act 1984), the requirement for notice of an intention to adduce evidence as to the mental condition of an accused (s.19 of the Criminal Law (Insanity) Act 2006, and the requirement to obtain leave to call any other person to give evidence on behalf of an accused in a prosecution for membership of an unlawful organisation (s. 3(1) of the Offences Against the State (Amendment) Act 1998).

[209] In *Markey v Minister for Justice* [2011] IEHC 39 at [38], [2012] 1 IR 62 at 77, Kearns P stated that proceedings must be "contemplated" or "pending". In *Hansfield Developments v Irish Asphalt Ltd* [2009] IEHC 420 at [80], McKechnie J concluded that the date on which the plaintiffs decided to retain senior counsel could reasonably be taken as the date from which litigation was contemplated or threatened.

[210] (1976) 135 CLR 674 at 677. In *University College Cork v ESB* [2014] IEHC 135 at [4], Finlay Geoghegan J held that litigation must be "apprehended or threatened".

[211] *Markey v Minister for Justice* [2011] IEHC 39 at [38], [2012] 1 IR 62 at 77; *Ahern v Mahon* [2008] IEHC 119 at [66], [2008] 4 IR 704 at 720, [2009] 1 ILRM 458 at 471–472; *Hansfield Developments v Irish Asphalt Ltd* [2009] IEHC 90 at [8].

[212] The early Irish cases include: *Kerry County Council v Liverpool Salvage Association* (1904)

O'Hanlon J in *Silver Hill Duckling Ltd v Minister for Agriculture*.[213] The plaintiffs sought damages and compensation arising out of the slaughter of their flock of ducks following an outbreak of avian influenza. The defendants claimed privilege in respect of a number of documents on the ground, *inter alia*, that they had come into being in contemplation of and for the purpose of advising the Minister and his officers in relation to the plaintiff's claim. O'Hanlon J was satisfied that:

> "[a] sustainable claim [of legal professional privilege] may be made in respect of a wider category of documents than the conventional communications passing between a client and his legal adviser in contemplation of litigation...once litigation is apprehended or threatened, a party to such litigation is entitled to prepare his case, whether by means of communications passing between him and his legal advisers, or by means of communications passing between him and third parties, and to do so under the cloak of privilege."[214]

10–77 Applying these principles to the facts of the case, he was of the view that litigation between the parties could fairly be regarded as apprehended or threatened, and privilege thus applied from the point at which it became clear that there was such a large disparity between what the Department was offering in compensation and what the plaintiff was seeking, that it was apparent to both parties that the claim would ultimately have to be resolved by litigation.[215]

10–78 The learned judge took a similar approach in *PJ Carrigan Ltd v Norwich Union Fire Society Ltd*.[216] The defendant insurers had been notified by the plaintiffs of a claim in respect of their premises which had been destroyed by fire. They immediately commissioned a report from a firm of loss adjusters because they viewed the claim with some suspicion and wished to know whether any evidence available at the scene of the fire suggested that their suspicions were well-founded. O'Hanlon J accepted that the possibility of repudiating liability was a very real factor in the defendant's thinking from the time the claim was made by the plaintiffs and that, when commissioning the report, they were concerned to obtain not merely an evaluation of the claim in terms of financial loss, but also expert advice as to the circumstances in which the fire broke out. He was, therefore, satisfied that the report had been obtained in apprehension of

---

38 ILTR 7 (claim of litigation privilege failed because no litigation was then in contemplation); *M'Mahon v Great Northern Railway Co* (1906) 40 ILTR 172 (third party communications only protected where procured after litigation has commenced or in view of anticipated litigation); *Rushbrooke v O'Sullivan* [1926] IR 500 at 503 (*per* FitzGibbon J) ("documents prepared, not with a view to actual or threatened litigation, but with a view of ascertaining whether litigation should be initiated at some future time, are not entitled to the privilege given by the practice of the Court"); *Moroney v Great Southern Railway Ltd* [1933] LJ Ir 93 (routine report about the condition of a train engine which it was claimed had been prepared because the defendant apprehended litigation and in case it occurred held to be privileged).

[213] [1987] IR 289, [1987] ILRM 516.
[214] [1987] IR 289 at 291, [1987] ILRM 516 at 518–519.
[215] In reaching that conclusion, he followed the view of the Court of Appeal in *Alfred Crompton Amusement Machines Ltd v Customs and Excise Commissioners (No.2)* [1972] 2 QB 102, [1972] 2 All ER 353. See *United States of America v Philip Morris Inc* [2004] All ER (D) 448, where the Court of Appeal approved the statement of the trial judge that: "The requirement that litigation be reasonably in prospect is not in my view satisfied unless the party seeking to claim privilege can show that he was aware of circumstances which rendered litigation between himself and a particular person or class of persons a real likelihood rather than a mere possibility." [2003] EWHC 3028 at [46], [2003] All ER (D) 191. This dictum was cited with approval in *Rawlinson and Hunter Trustees v Akers* [2014] EWCA Civ 136 at [24]. *Cf. Westminster International BV v Dornoch Ltd* [2009] EWCA Civ 1323; *WXY v Gewanter* [2012] EWHC 1017.
[216] [1987] IR 618.

litigation because, even at that early stage, the defendants were contemplating the possibility of a showdown with the plaintiffs in which they might decide to repudiate liability under the policy and the plaintiffs in turn would then have to decide whether they were prepared to embark on litigation to enforce their claims under the policy.[217]

10–79   In *Gallagher v Stanley*,[218] this test was only considered in passing but O'Flaherty J emphasised that "it is essential that litigation should be reasonably apprehended at the least before a claim of privilege can be upheld".[219] That test was failed in *Irish Press Publications Ltd v Minister for Enterprise*,[220] where Carroll J rejected the claim of litigation privilege in circumstances where litigation "was mentioned only in the context of a possible option". The English authorities suggest that, where litigation has not been commenced at the time of the communication, "it has to be 'reasonably in prospect'; this does not require the prospect of litigation to be greater than 50 per cent, but it must be more than a mere possibility".[221]

10–80   It is clear from the authorities that, while a significant lapse in time between the date of the communication over which a claim of litigation privilege is asserted and the date on which proceedings ultimately commenced is a factor to be taken into account, it is not determinative.[222] In *Rhatigan v Eagle Star Life Assurance Company of Ireland Ltd*,[223] a claim of litigation privilege was asserted over correspondence between the defendant insurer and its reinsurer over a period of 16 months, all of which predated the letter containing the first intimation of litigation. The defendant had repudiated a life insurance policy on grounds of misrepresentation and non-disclosure in circumstances where the insurer entertained suspicions that there had been non-disclosure immediately following the notification of the claim. Cooke J held that the entitlement to claim privilege extends to communications brought into existence prior to the actual commencement of litigation, provided it is shown that litigation was contemplated or reasonably apprehended. Thus, an anticipatory request for general advice in relation to a claim not yet formulated or advanced could be the subject of a well founded claim to litigation privilege in subsequent proceedings. He concluded that, "…where the litigation in which the claim for privilege arises relates to a substantial benefit which has been repudiated under an insurance policy, the taking of the decision to repudiate is so likely to provoke litigation that the steps taken by the insurer towards making such a decision must necessarily be characterised as steps taken in apprehension of litigation."[224] Cooke J observed that, while the communications in issue were distant in point of time from the ultimate commencement of proceedings, it is the dominant purpose for which they were written which attracts the application

---

[217]   See also *Re Highgrade Traders* [1984] BCLC 151.

[218]   [1998] 2 IR 267 at 272.

[219]   See also *Martin v Legal Aid Board* [2007] IEHC 76 at [37], [2007] 2 IR 759 at 776. *Cf. Three Rivers District Council v Bank of England (No. 6)* [2004] UKHL 48, [2004] 3 WLR 1274, [2005] 1 AC 610.

[220]   [2002] 2 IR 110 at 114.

[221]   *Rawlinson and Hunter Trustees v Akers* [2014] EWCA Civ 136 at [13]; *United States of America v Philip Morris Inc* [2004] All ER (D) 448 at [67]–[68]; *Westminster International BV v Dornoch Ltd* [2009] All ER (D) 37 at [19]–[20].

[222]   But see *Rawlinson and Hunter Trustees v Akers* [2014] EWCA Civ 136 at [26], where Tomlinson LJ stated that the fact that proceedings still had not been commenced some two and a half years after a report had been produced considerably undermined the contention that litigation was "reasonably in prospect" when the report was commissioned.

[223]   [2013] IEHC 139.

[224]   [2013] IEHC 139 at [17].

of the principle.[225] He cited the decision of McCracken J in *Fyffes Plc v DCC Plc*[226] with approval, where it was held that the principle of privilege in the conduct of litigation extends, not only to the preparation of the case, but also to "the assessment as to whether there is any case to be made".

(ii) "Dominant purpose" test

10–81   Perhaps the most acute difficulties in this area have arisen with regard to situations where it is possible to identify more than one purpose or motive for a communication as, for example, where a company requires employees to complete an accident report form in the aftermath of an accident. If litigation subsequently ensues, the defendant will almost inevitably argue that the purpose of requiring the document to be completed was to brief the company's legal advisers in relation to the accident and to help the company to defend the claim. However, it may be possible to identify another purpose for the completion of the document such as accident prevention, which would bring it outside the protection of the privilege. The question as to whether the document should be privileged in those circumstances is crucial because it will frequently contain the most contemporaneous account of events and, again, policy considerations loom large.

10–82   One solution to the problem of multiple purposes, adopted in a series of English cases in the first half of the twentieth century, was to hold that a document need not be disclosed if one of the purposes for its creation (even if merely a subsidiary one) was that it be given to a solicitor for the purpose of advising on apprehended litigation.[227] Another approach which found favour with the High Court of Australia in *Grant v Downs*[228] was that a document should be disclosed unless the sole purpose for its genesis was apprehended litigation. However, in *Waugh v British Railways Board*,[229] the House of Lords rejected both of these extremes in favour of the intermediate approach adopted by Barwick CJ in his dissenting judgment in *Grant v Downs*[230] whereby a document will be protected by privilege if the dominant purpose for its creation is apprehended litigation.[231]

10–83   In *Waugh*, the plaintiff's husband, an employee of the defendant, was killed while working on the railways. She sought discovery of a standard accident report prepared two days after the accident. The House of Lords held that, in order to attract privilege, the dominant purpose for preparation of the reports must have been that of submission to a legal adviser for use in relation to anticipated or pending litigation. While this was undoubtedly one of the purposes of the reports, it was not the dominant one, another equally important purpose being to inform the Board about the cause of the accident in order that steps could be taken to avoid recurrence. Thus, privilege could not be claimed and discovery was ordered. Lord Wilberforce emphasised the policy background when he stated:

---

[225] [2013] IEHC 139 at [18].
[226] [2005] IESC 3 at [64], [2005] 1 IR 59 at 84, [2005] 1 ILRM 357 at 379.
[227] *Birmingham and Midland Motor Omnibus Co. Ltd v London and North Western Railway Co* [1913] 3 KB 850; *Ankin v London and North Eastern Railway Co* [1930] 1 KB 527, [1929] All ER 65; *Ogden v London Electric Railway Co* [1933] All ER 896.
[228] (1976) 135 CLR 674.
[229] [1980] AC 521, [1979] 2 All ER 1169.
[230] (1976) 135 CLR 674.
[231] See also *Neilson v Laugharne* [1981] QB 736; *Re Highgrade Traders Ltd* [1984] BCLC 151.

"It is clear that the due administration of justice strongly requires disclosure and production of this report: it was contemporary; it contained statements by witnesses on the spot; it would be not merely relevant evidence, but almost certainly the best evidence as to the cause of the accident. If one accepts that this important public interest can be overridden in order that the defendant may properly prepare his case, how close must the connection be between the preparation of the document and the anticipation of litigation? ... It appears to me that unless the purpose of submission to the legal adviser in view of litigation is at least the dominant purpose for which the relevant document was prepared, the reasons which require privilege to be extended to it cannot apply. On the other hand to hold that the purpose ... must be the sole purpose would, apart from difficulties of proof ... be too strict a requirement, and would confine the privilege too narrowly."[232]

10–84   The dominant purpose test was endorsed in this jurisdiction[233] by O'Hanlon J in *Silver Hill Duckling Ltd v Minister for Agriculture*,[234] and subsequently applied by Lynch J in *Davis v St Michael's House*.[235] The plaintiff, who was mentally handicapped, was injured in a fall in the defendant's school. The defendant claimed privilege in respect of an accident report form and a number of witness statements on the basis that these documents came into being in contemplation of possible proceedings. The defendant pointed out that it was obliged to notify its insurer of all accidents and, in addition to completing an accident report form, the defendant frequently obtained witness statements with a view to assessing the defendant's position in relation to any claim that might arise as a result of the accident. Lynch J identified the purpose of obtaining such documents as being to ensure that there was an accurate record of what happened from as many persons who may know something about it as possible so that in the event of a claim, the insurers would be forewarned and forearmed therewith for submission to their legal advisers, and witnesses would have a contemporary record of the events by which they would be able to refresh their memories at the trial of the action which could be many years later. He was, therefore, satisfied that the dominant purpose for which the documents came into being was in apprehension and/or anticipation of litigation and that the claim of privilege was valid.[236]

10–85   The dominant purpose test was endorsed by the Supreme Court in *Gallagher v Stanley*.[237] The infant plaintiff had a very difficult birth in the National Maternity

---

[232]   [1980] AC 521 at 531–532, [1979] 2 All ER 1169 at 1173–1174.

[233]   The dominant purpose test has also been approved in Canada (*Supercom of California v Sovereign General Insurance Co* (1998) 37 OR (3d) 597 at 605; *New West Construction Co v R.* [1980] 2 FC 44, (1980) 106 DLR (3d) 272; *Re Director of Investigation and Research and Shell Canada Ltd* (1975) 55 DLR (3d) 713) and New Zealand (*Guardian Royal Exchange Assurance v Stuart* [1985] 1 NZLR 596; *R. v Uljee* [1982] 1 NZLR 561). The dominant purpose test is applied in Australia under s.119 of the Evidence Act 1995, which reversed the decision in *Grant v Downs* (1976) 135 CLR 674 in relation to evidence adduced in court proceedings, and was extended to discovery and inspection of documents (which is governed by common law) in *Esso v Australia Resources Ltd v Commissioner of Taxation* (1999) 201 CLR 49 at 73.

[234]   [1987] IR 289, [1987] ILRM 516. McGovern J recently considered the development of the dominant purpose test, and affirmed it as the governing principle in this jurisdiction, in *Hansfield Developments v Irish Asphalt Ltd* [2009] IEHC 90 at [8]–[9]. See also the decision of McKechnie J in *Hansfield Developments v Irish Asphalt Ltd* [2009] IEHC 420 at [26], where he described *Waugh* as the "seminal case" for the test applicable to litigation privilege, and the decision of Kearns P in *Markey v Minister for Justice* [2011] IEHC 39 at [38], [2012] 1 IR 62.

[235]   Unreported, High Court, 25 November 1993.

[236]   See also *Andrews v Northern Ireland Railways Co. Ltd* [1992] NI 1. *Cf. Power City Ltd v Monahan*, unreported, High Court, 14 October 1996 (fax message from the solicitor of the defendants to their insurer's representatives made with a view to the insurers dealing with any response to made to letters from the plaintiff held to be privileged).

[237]   [1998] 2 IR 267. See also *Irish Press Publications Ltd v Minister for Enterprise and Employment*

Hospital, as a result of which he was severely disabled. Discovery was granted and the defendants claimed privilege in respect of certain documents on the basis that they were created in contemplation of litigation. The documents in question were statements made by nurses on duty the night of the birth. They had been requested to make these the following morning by the Matron of the hospital. In her affidavit, the Matron stated that she had requested the statements because she anticipated litigation and for the sole purpose of being furnished to the legal secretary of the hospital.

10–86 O'Flaherty J accepted that, in view of the increasingly litigious nature of society, apprehension of litigation was a consideration on the part of the Matron in requesting the statements but it was not the sole purpose. Instead, he was satisfied that the main concern of the Matron was that she should be in a position to account for the events of the night in question and how the staff under her control had conducted themselves, which information was required for the proper management and running of the hospital. He read the documents and this confirmed his belief that they were essentially straightforward accounts of events and conversations, and did not contain any element that should attract an entitlement to legal professional privilege. He observed that:

> "Both principles, full disclosure on the one hand and legal professional privilege on the other, are there to advance the cause of justice. Sometimes they may be on a collision course, but not, I think, here. This is not like a case where a client is expected to deal with his lawyer with the utmost disclosure so that the case will be properly presented. It is rather a case where both sides are entitled to know what exactly happened before and at the birth of the infant. After all the nurses are the mother and child's nurses as well as being hospital employees. I believe it is likely to help the course of the trial if these documents are made available to the plaintiff's advisers now and I do not see that the principle of legal professional privilege suffers in any way."[238]

10–87 In their concurring judgments, Lynch J and Barron J also endorsed the dominant purpose test. Lynch J pointed out that people often act for mixed motives and therefore the sole purpose test set too high a threshold for the application of privilege. The true test is that anticipation and/or contemplation of litigation should have been the dominant motive or reason. Barron J stressed that it was the court's view as to the purpose of the statements, not that of the hospital which was important. Bare assertion on the part of the hospital was not enough without anything to back it up. If there were good reasons why there was no need to take statements from the nurses in relation to hospital administration, this could have been put on affidavit.

10–88 It can be seen from the foregoing discussion of the cases that the conception and application of the dominant purpose test is strongly influenced by policy and lends itself to manipulation by the courts to achieve a desired result. A very obvious example of this can be seen in *Mark v Flexibox Ltd*.[239] While employed by the defendant, the plaintiff sought medical advice from a factory doctor about a rash and was referred to a consultant dermatologist who carried out tests. The plaintiff subsequently brought proceedings and sought discovery of the report of the results of these tests. The defendant argued that this was covered by litigation privilege because at the top of the report, there was the legend: "For the use of legal advisers in anticipation of

---

[2002] 4 IR 110 and *National Maternity Hospital v Information Commissioner* [2007] IEHC 113, [2007] 3 IR 643.

[238] [1998] 2 IR 267 at 273.

[239] [1988] NI 58.

litigation and for solicitors and counsel to advise." MacDermott LJ said that "the judicial determination of 'dominant purpose' is not concluded by protective headings or expressions of intent made by the maker of the document" and rejected the defendant's claim of privilege based on its awareness of the level of claims:

> "It may be … that this employer, like others, realises that employees in Northern Ireland tend to be litigious and thus an employer must always anticipate litigation and be vigilant in dealing with any situations which may be of relevance in subsequent litigation. If that is the point it is of such a sweepingly general nature as to be of little probative value when a judge is seeking to ascertain the 'dominant purpose' for which a particular document came into being."[240]

10–89 The learned judge went on to say that these matters are always questions of fact and degree and that:

> "… the claims of humanity must surely make the dominant purpose of any report upon the health of an employee who attends his factory doctor for advice (particularly where injuries have been sustained or are suspected) that of discovering what his state of health is and why he is ill or injured, if he is, so that he may be advised and measures to prevent recurrence may be discussed and, if possible, devised. For my part I think it will always be difficult for a defendant to satisfy the dominance test in this type of case."[241]

10–90 The policy underpinning the dominant purpose test was emphasised by McGovern J in *Hansfield Developments v Irish Asphalt*,[242] a case which concerned significant defects in newly constructed houses allegedly caused by quarry material containing a high level of pyrite. The documents over which a claim of litigation privilege was asserted were communications between the plaintiffs and HomeBond, an entity established by the State to provide structural defect cover for new homes.[243] Having considered the documents, McGovern J concluded that they were substantially concerned with how the pyrite issue should be addressed and investigated. While the communications dealt with issues such as how to address the defects in houses arising out of this problem, they were not specific to any litigation (although they could be said to be of relevance to apprehended claims). McGovern J agreed with the view expressed by Lord Wilberforce in the *Waugh* case, that it would be an excessive and unnecessary development to carry privilege protection further into cases where the purpose of preparing for litigation was secondary or equal with another purpose.[244] He was not satisfied that the documents in issue were created with the dominant purpose of preparing for litigation and concluded that this purpose, if it existed, was "secondary or equal" to another purpose; the working out between HomeBond and the plaintiffs

---

[240] [1988] NI 58 at 61. Peart J arrived at a similar conclusion in *Casey v Iarnrod Eireann* [2004] IEHC 117, where he accepted that the heading on a draft report—"in possible contemplation of litigation" —was a significant matter to take into account, but was not determinative. He referred to the possibility that the placing of such a heading on a document may be open to possible abuse, so as to attract privilege to an otherwise unprivileged document. *Cf. University College Cork v ESB* [2014] IEHC 135 at [14].

[241] [1988] NI 58 at 61.

[242] [2009] IEHC 90. The dominant purpose test was also applied by McKechnie J in a subsequent judgment delivered in the same proceedings ([2009] IEHC 420).

[243] In circumstances where HomeBond was not a party to the proceedings, the plaintiffs asserted that the documents were subject to common interest privilege. McGovern J concluded that the documents were not subject to litigation privilege, as a result of which it was unnecessary to reach a concluded view as to whether common interest privilege arose. However, he expressed the view, *obiter*, that the plaintiffs and HomeBond did not have a sufficient common interest ([2009] IEHC 90 at [12]).

[244] [2009] IEHC 90 at [14].

as to how they should address and investigate the issue of the involvement of pyrite in housing defects generally.

10–91 The assertion of litigation privilege was subjected to rigorous scrutiny in *University College Cork v ESB*,[245] where it was held that the document over which privilege is asserted "must have been created for the dominant purpose of the apprehended or threatened litigation; it is not sufficient that the document has two equal purposes, one of which is apprehended or threatened litigation". The claim arose out of a flood which the plaintiff contended was caused by the defendant. Finlay Geoghegan J rejected a claim of privilege asserted by the defendant over a number of emails and attached statements of fact circulated internally in the ESB. While she accepted that the defendant had established that a purpose of the preparation and transmission of the statements attached to the emails was apprehended or threatened litigation, she held that it was not the *dominant* purpose for which the statements were prepared. An additional purpose for the preparation of the statements was for use by representatives of the defendant who appeared before a Joint Oireachtas Committee on the Environment, Heritage and Local Government. It was held that this was, at a minimum, an equal purpose for the preparation and circulation of the statements.[246]

(iii) Purpose is determined objectively

10–92 The onus of establishing that, as a matter of probability, the dominant purpose for the creation of the document was apprehended or threatened litigation is borne by the party asserting privilege.[247] The dominant purpose test is an objective test to be applied by the court and, as such, does not depend solely on the motivation of the person who caused the document to be created.[248]

10–93 In *Woori Bank v KDB Ireland Limited*,[249] Finlay Geoghegan J refused to accept that the dominant purpose for the creation of two internal reports by the plaintiff bank was the litigation against the defendant, notwithstanding the inclusion of averments to this effect in the affidavits sworn on behalf of the plaintiff. She emphasised the objective nature of the dominant purpose test, stating that[250]:

> "...the purpose of the document is a matter for objective determination by the court in all the circumstances and does not only depend on the motivation of the person who caused the

---

[245] [2014] IEHC 135 at [4]. See also *Woori Bank and Hanvit LSP Finance Ltd v KDB Ireland Limited* [2005] IEHC 451.

[246] A second alternative purpose was also established in circumstances where there was evidence that it was the usual practice of the defendant to engage ESB International (ESBI) to prepare a report following a major flood event.

[247] *University College Cork v ESB* [2014] IEHC 135; *Rawlinson and Hunter Trustees v Akers* [2014] EWCA 136 at [13]; *West London Pipeline and Storage v Total UK* [2008] 2 CLC 258 at [50].

[248] See the decision of Carswell LJ in *Downey v Murray* [1988] NI 600 at 602–603, where he stated that, when assessing the dominant purpose of a communication, it "must be borne in mind that the important matter is the purpose, which is not necessarily the same as the intention of the person who composed it". This dictum was cited with approval in *Woori Bank & Hanvit LSP Finance Ltd v KDB Bank Ireland Limited* [2005] IEHC 451 at [6]. See also *University College Cork v ESB* [2014] IEHC 135 at [4].

[249] [2005] IEHC 451.

[250] [2005] IEHC 451 at [6]. See *Rawlinson and Hunter Trustees v Akers* [2014] EWCA 136 at [13], where the Court of Appeal stated that: "A mere claim in evidence before the court that the document was for a particular purpose will not be decisive". *Cf. Neilson v Laugharne* [1981] 1 All ER 829, *per* Lord Denning at 833 and *per* Oliver LJ at 837.

document to be created. Further that the court should not make a finding that the dominant purpose of a document is litigation based upon a bald assertion, even on affidavit, of such motivation or intention of the creator of the document."[251]

10–94   The circumstances surrounding the transactions, the subject matter of the proceedings, were investigated by the Board of Investigation and Audit (BAI) and the Financial Supervisory Services (FSS) in Korea. Having considered the affidavit evidence and having reviewed the documents in question, Finlay Geoghegan J accepted that the litigation was contemplated at the time the reports were prepared. However, she concluded that, in relation to the first report, at least an equal purpose for its creation was as an internal report for management or corporate governance purposes within the bank in respect of the meetings with the BAI inspector and the assessment of the options available to the bank in relation to the transactions the subject matter of the litigation.[252] In relation to the second report, she concluded that, at a minimum, an equal purpose for the creation of the document was to provide information and explanations to the FSS in relation to the transactions.[253]

10–95   A similar approach was adopted by the English Court of Appeal in *Rawlinson and Hunter Trustees v Akers*,[254] where Tomlinson LJ stated that:

"The court will look at 'purpose' from an objective standpoint, looking at all relevant evidence including evidence of subjective purpose... The evidence in support must be specific enough to show something of the deponent's analysis of the purpose for which the documents were created, and should refer to such contemporary material as is possible without disclosing the privileged material."[255]

The reports over which a claim of litigation privilege was asserted in *Rawlinson* were five reports commissioned by the joint liquidators of a company from a forensic accountancy firm. The joint liquidators contended that the reports were commissioned in order to assist them in the preparation of a defence and counterclaim in proceedings brought against the company, at the request of counsel in order to assist counsel in providing advice in relation to litigation strategy in the proceedings, and to enable the liquidators to obtain legal advice and brief counsel in relation to litigation which was contemplated against various potential defendants. However, the principal duty of the liquidators was to establish the assets and liabilities of the company and what steps (if any) were open to the liquidators to collect in the assets or to reduce or discharge the liabilities. Accordingly, there was an alternative purpose for the commissioning of the reports.[256] The Court of Appeal accepted that the purpose of establishing the financial position of the company did not necessarily have to be entirely independent of the need to take recovery proceedings. However, the onus was on the joint liquidators to establish that the dual purposes were *not* independent of one another, and that the dominant purpose was for use in the conduct of the litigation. Tomlinson LJ was critical of the evidence adduced in support of the claim of privilege, and observed that, "in circumstances which call for clarity and precision", the deponent "made no effort to grapple with the obvious need to establish which of dual or even multiple purposes was dominant is a plausible claim of privilege was to be made out".[257] It was held,

---

[251] See also *University College Cork v ESB* [2014] IEHC 135 at [4].
[252] [2014] IEHC 451 at [11].
[253] [2014] IEHC 451 at [12].
[254] [2014] EWCA 136, [2014] 2 BCLC 1 at [13].
[255] See also *West London Pipeline and Storage v Total UK* [2008] 2 CLC 258 at [53].
[256] *Cf Price Waterhouse v BCCI Holdings (Luxembourg) SA* [1992] BCLC 583 at 590–591 [54].
[257] [2014] EWCA Civ 136, [2014] 2 BCLC 1 at [22]. See *Rawlinson and Hunter Trustees SA v*

therefore, that the joint liquidators had failed to discharge the onus of establishing that the dominant purpose for the creation of the reports was the conduct of the litigation.[258]

10–96 During the course of his judgment in *Rawlinson*, Tomlinson LJ referred to the decision of Lord Carswell in *Three Rivers DC v Bank of England (No.5)*,[259] where he extracted the following statement of principle from the authorities:

> "... communications between parties or their solicitors and third parties for the purpose of obtaining information or advice in connection with existing or contemplated litigation are privileged, but only when the following conditions are satisfied: (a) litigation must be in progress or in contemplation; (b) the communications must have been made for the sole or dominant purpose of conducting that litigation; (c) the litigation must be adversarial, not investigative or inquisitorial."

Tomlinson J noted, in particular, the emphasis placed on "the conduct of the litigation as the dominant purpose which must be identified".[260] This suggests that the dominant purpose test may have been refined, so as to require the party asserting litigation privilege to establish that the document over which privilege is asserted was created for the dominant purpose of "the conduct of the litigation".

10–97 It is noteworthy that, in both *Woori Bank* and *Rawlinson*, the Court considered the question as to whether the documents had been provided by the party asserting privilege to its lawyers to be a significant one. In *Woori Bank*, Finlay Geoghegan J noted that, while a claim of litigation privilege was asserted in respect of a number of internal reports on the basis that they had been prepared for the purpose of assisting the Bank in the litigation, the reports had not been furnished by the Bank to its solicitors acting in the litigation prior to the swearing of the affidavit of discovery.[261] In *Rawlinson*, the Court of Appeal observed that the memorandum in issue was not provided to counsel for the purpose of obtaining advice and formulating draft particulars until nearly one year after it had been prepared, and no proceedings had issued.[262]

10–98 Insofar as the subjective intention of the person who caused the document to be created is a relevant factor for consideration, it is the motive of the person who procured the making of the communication rather than the person who made it which is determinative.[263] This can be seen in *Guinness Peat Properties Ltd v Fitzroy Robinson Partnership*.[264] The defendants wrote to their insurers, in accordance with the terms

---

Tchenguiz [2014] EWCA Civ 1129 at [20], a subsequent decision of the Court of Appeal in the same proceedings, where Moore Bick LJ stated that, where a document was prepared for more than one purpose, "it is essential not merely to assert that it was created for the dominant purpose of litigation, but that there may be material before the court from which it can see that that claim is well founded."

[258] *Cf Starbev GB Ltd v Interbrew Central European Holding BV* [2013] EWHC 4038. For examples of cases in which the court accepted that the dominant purpose for the creation of reports was litigation, see *Westminster International BV v Dornoch Ltd* [2009] EWCA Civ 1323 and *AXA Seguros SA v Allianz Insurance plc* [2011] EWHC 268 (Comm).

[259] [2003] QB 1556.

[260] [2014] EWCA 136, [2014] 2 BCLC1 at [14].

[261] *Woori Bank & Hanvit LSP Finance Ltd v KDB Bank Ireland Limited* [2005] IEHC 451 at [10]. The judge also considered the fact that the reports were held in the Bank's internal files to be significant.

[262] *Rawlinson and Hunter Trustees v Akers* [2014] EWCA 136 at [24].

[263] *M'Mahon v Great Northern Railway Co.* (1906) 40 ILTR 172 at 173; *Feuerheerd v London General Omnibus Co Ltd* [1918] 2 KB 565.

[264] [1987] 2 All ER 716.

of their professional indemnity policy, enclosing the notification of a claim by the first named plaintiffs and other relevant memoranda, and expressing their views on the merits of the claim. The plaintiffs argued that the defendants were not entitled to claim privilege for the letter because the dominant purpose for which it was written was to comply with the requirements of their indemnity policy, not for the purpose of obtaining legal advice or to assist in the conduct of litigation. However, it was held by the Court of Appeal that the dominant purpose for which a document was written does not necessarily fall to be determined by reference to the intention of the person who actually composed it. The dominant purpose of the communication had to be viewed objectively, particularly by reference to the intentions of the insurers who procured its genesis. Here the dominant purpose was to produce a letter of notification which would be used in order to obtain legal advice or to conduct or aid in the conduct of litigation which was at the time of its production in reasonable prospect.[265]

(d) Work product

10–99   The precise extent to which litigation privilege can be invoked so as to protect the "work product" of a lawyer preparing for litigation is unclear. However, it seems that some protection is afforded to the preparations of a lawyer for trial which do not fall under the umbrella of communications with third parties so as to enable him or her to prepare for litigation in privacy. Thus, privilege will attach to documents such as draft pleadings,[266] draft expert reports,[267] draft written legal submissions, internal memoranda and notes prepared by the lawyer.

10–100   However, it is important to note that privilege will not attach to documents which came into existence before litigation was contemplated[268] or copies of such documents[269] even if the documents were obtained by a party to litigation or his legal adviser for the purposes of the litigation.[270] In *Tromso Sparebank v Beirne*,[271] Costello J pointed out that the purpose of legal professional privilege was to enable a person to have recourse to his legal advisers in confidence and he did not agree that:

> "the interests of the litigant requires the privilege to be extended to copies of documents which came into existence prior to the contemplation of litigation, documents which are themselves

---

[265] See also *Andrews v Northern Ireland Railways Co Ltd* [1992] NI 1.

[266] *Argyle Brewery Pty Ltd v Darling Harbourside (Sydney) Pty Ltd* (1993) 120 ALR 537.

[267] *Payne v Shovlin* [2006] IESC 5, [2007] 1 IR 114, [2006] 2 ILRM 1 at 13; *Jackson v Marley Davenport Ltd* [2004] 1 WLR 2926; *Highland Fisheries Ltd v Lynk Electric Ltd* (1989) 63 DLR (4th) 493.

[268] *Ventouris v Mountain* [1991] 3 All ER 472.

[269] *Tromso Sparebank v Beirne* [1989] ILRM 257; *Lubrizol Corp v Esso Petroleum Co Ltd* [1992] 1 WLR 957.

[270] A possible exception may exist where documents or materials have been assembled by the application of professional skill and judgment by a lawyer and disclosure would betray the trend of his or her legal advice to the client (*Lyell v Kennedy* (1884) 27 Ch D 1; *Ventouris v Mountain* [1991] 3 All ER 472; *Dubai Bank Ltd v Galadari (No.7)* [1992] 1 All ER 658; *Ottawa-Carleton (Regional Municipality) v Consumers' Gas Co* (1990) 74 DLR (4th) 742; *Nickmar Pty Ltd v Preservatrice Skandia Insurance Ltd* (1985) 3 NSWLR 44). However, in *Bond v JN Taylor Holdings Ltd* (1991) 57 SASR 21 at 46, Debelle J argued with some force that this line of authority requires re-examination in the light of the modern law of discovery and the trend towards greater disclosure. Annotations made by a lawyer on a pre-existing document may also be privileged; *Vivan Imerman v Robert Tchenguiz* [2009] EWHC 2902.

[271] [1989] ILRM 257.

not privileged and which the other side could probably inspect as a result of third party discovery order and which they could have produced at the trial pursuant to a *subpoena duces tecum*."[272]

10–101   He went on to say that the rules of court should be construed so as to further the rules of justice and should not be interpreted so as to prevent a party inspecting documents which might assist its case in circumstances where this could not conceivably injure the interests of the other party.

10–102   In *MFM v PW*,[273] the issue arose as to whether privilege could be claimed in respect of notes taken by a solicitor of the evidence in previous proceedings. Legal professional privilege was claimed over the notes prepared by the solicitor for the plaintiff on the basis that they had been prepared in contemplation of legal proceedings. In an affidavit filed on behalf of the plaintiff, it was averred that the notes were prepared for the purpose of drawing the attention of certain points in the evidence to counsel and to the client and, further, that the notes were prepared specifically with the function of the solicitor in mind and assisted in its execution. Having reviewed the authorities,[274] Finnegan J regarded it as well settled that transcripts or solicitor's notes of proceedings and evidence are not privileged in a subsequent action. With regard to the question as to whether they were privileged in the action in which they were taken, he took the view that insofar as a solicitor's notes are of evidence and proceedings they are a record of what was *publici juris* and so are not entitled to privilege in the action in which they were taken. In circumstances where there was a note which was a mixture, being in part a note of proceedings and/or evidence and in part notes made by a solicitor for purpose of litigation, the practice of the courts had been to allow production with the latter parts covered up.[275] Thus, he indicated that he would examine the note of evidence taken to determine the extent to which it contained other material designed to assist the plaintiff in the prosecution of the action which should be covered up as privileged prior to inspection.

10–103   This decision was considered by Finlay Geoghegan J in *Woori Bank v KDB Ireland Limited*,[276] where the issue for determination was whether verbatim recordings of conversations between the plaintiff and third parties, which were not confidential, but which allegedly occurred as part of an exercise in gathering evidence for use in the litigation, were privileged. The court distinguished between the purpose for which the communications were recorded, and the purpose of the communication itself. While a communication may have been recorded because litigation was contemplated, it did not necessarily follow that the dominant purpose for the communication was for the purpose of litigation.[277]

10–104   It was argued in *Woori Bank* that the Irish courts should recognise a "materials for evidence" privilege, which exists as a separate basis of privilege from litigation privilege. Reliance was placed in this regard on Matthews and Malek, *Disclosure*,[278]

---

[272] [1989] ILRM 257 at 262.

[273] [2001] 3 IR 462.

[274] *Nordon v Defries* (1882) 8 QBD 508; *Lambert v Home* (1914) 3 KB 86; *Robson v Worswick* (1888) 33 Ch D 370.

[275] See *Ainsworth v Wilding* (1900) 2 Ch D 315.

[276] [2005] IEHC 451.

[277] [2005] IEHC 451 at [20].

[278] Matthews and Malek, *Disclosure*, 3rd edn (London: Sweet & Maxwell, 2007) at [11.53]. In considering whether the "materials for evidence" privilege can be said to exist today, however, the authors state that, "[t]he authorities are certainty meagre" at [11.57].

where the authors suggest that the existence of such a privilege is supported by Bray on *Discovery*.[279] In circumstances where it was held that confidentiality is an essential prerequisite to a claim of litigation privilege, as a result of which the claim of litigation privilege failed, it was unnecessary for the Court to reach a concluded view in this regard. Notwithstanding this, Finlay Geoghegan J stated that, even were such privilege to exist (which she expressly stated she was not holding), the limits of such an exception would have to be clearly defined.[280] She concluded that the plaintiffs had failed to identify any objective which, in accordance with the principles set out by the Supreme Court in *Smurfit*, would justify the extension of litigation privilege to non-confidential communications with third parties.[281]

(e) Communications with an adverse party

10–105   Litigation privilege operates to protect a party's case from disclosure to an adverse party and, therefore, by definition, communications with the other side will not attract privilege even where they are made in contemplation of litigation.[282] In *McKay v McKay*, Hutton LCJ explained that:

> "[A]s the basis of the privilege is that the communications which a party makes to his professional lawyer should be kept secret from the adverse party and that the adverse party cannot ask to see them before the trial it follows that the privilege cannot apply where the adverse party has himself supplied the information and is therefore aware of it. In such a case there is no need to keep the information secret from the opposing party because he already knows of it."[283]

10–106   Thus, in *Tobakin v Dublin Southern District Tramways Co*,[284] a statement obtained from the plaintiff by an inspector of the defendant company three days after the accident the subject-matter of the proceedings was held not to be privileged.[285] Similarly, in *Grant v Southwestern and County Properties*,[286] a claim of privilege in respect of a tape recording of a conversation between the plaintiffs and the second defendants, made by the second plaintiff because he contemplated that litigation between the parties might ensue and wished to be able to instruct his solicitors, was rejected.

10–107   It is often the case that a document such as an affidavit or written legal submissions will be prepared with the intention of being sent to or handed over to the other side either before or during proceedings. However, privilege will apply until such time as the document is actually handed over. In *Horgan v Murray*,[287] an issue

---

[279] Bray, *The Principles and Practice of Discovery*, (London: Reeves, 1884), p.407.
[280] Citing Matthews and Malek, *Disclosure*, 3rd edn (London: Sweet & Maxwell, 2007) at [11.58], where the authors state that: "In the absence of binding authority, it is submitted that the 'materials for evidence' privilege is justified, but that its limits must be clearly defined..."
[281] [2005] IEHC 451 at [26].
[282] *Tobakin v Dublin Southern District Tramways Co* [1905] 2 IR 58; *McKay v McKay* [1988] NI 611; *Grant v Southwestern and County Properties* [1975] 1 Ch 185; *Kennedy v Lyell* (1883) 23 Ch D 387 at 405; *Baker v London and South Western Railway Co.* (1867) LR 3 QB 91; *Flack v Pacific Press Ltd* (1970) 14 DLR (3d) 334.
[283] [1988] NI 611 at 617.
[284] [1905] 2 IR 58.
[285] In *Feuerheerd v London General Omnibus Co. Ltd* [1918] 2 KB 565, the English Court of Appeal refused to follow *Tobakin* but the Irish decision was followed in preference to that in *Feuerheerd* in *McKay v McKay* [1988] NI 611 and *Flack v Pacific Press Ltd* (1970) 14 DLR (3d) 334.
[286] [1975] 1 Ch 185.
[287] [1999] 1 ILRM 257.

was raised as to a memorandum which was prepared by the petitioner in the context of settlement negotiations and for the purpose of furnishing it to the respondents. However, relations between the parties deteriorated drastically and the petitioner decided not to hand over the document. O'Sullivan J rejected the contention of the respondents that because the dominant intention for the document coming into being was for the purpose of being handed over to the respondents, it was not privileged:

> "In the context of the 'to and fro conflicting elements' of negotiation, a document or memorandum may well be drafted by one of the parties who at the time of drafting intends to be handed over to the other but who subsequently changes his or her mind. I think it is unrealistic to require the production of such a document if the negotiations "go sour" because I still think that this document came into being for the purposes of litigation, albeit for the specific purpose being presented to the other side as part of an effort to avoid litigation by compromise."[288]

4. Criminal Prosecutions

10–108   The application of the principles of legal professional privilege to criminal prosecutions caused some difficulties in *Breathnach v Ireland (No.3)*.[289] The plaintiff had instituted civil proceedings against the State for various torts and breaches of his constitutional rights arising out of his unsuccessful prosecution for the Sallins train robbery. Discovery of communications between the gardaí and members of the DPP's office was ordered and the plaintiff brought a motion seeking inspection of various documents in respect of which privilege was claimed. Keane J rejected the claim of litigation privilege, pointing out that in every case where the commission of a crime is suspected, documentary material will be assembled by the gardaí, irrespective of whether a prosecution is ever initiated. The fact that the documents in question might be submitted to the DPP in order to obtain his decision as to whether a prosecution should be instituted could not possibly give that material the same status as a medical report obtained by a plaintiff in a personal injuries action solely for the purpose of his claim. Therefore, privilege did not attach. With regard to the claim of legal advice privilege, Keane J pointed out that the DPP does not stand in the relationship of client to any other lawyer. He is in a sense both lawyer and client because he decides whether or not to prosecute and then becomes one of the parties to the litigation. Despite this, Keane J held that the public policy underlying the legal advice category of privilege "applies equally to communications between the Director of Public Prosecutions and professional officers in his department, solicitors and counsel as to prosecutions by him which are in being or contemplated."[290]

10–109   It is somewhat unclear from the decision in *Breathnach* whether Keane J accepted or rejected the proposition that the DPP could claim legal advice privilege. In *Corbett v DPP*,[291] O'Sullivan J took the view that the effect of Keane J's judgment was that legal professional privilege did not apply to communications between the DPP and his professional officers and solicitors and counsel which were, instead, covered by public interest privilege. However, in *People (DPP) v Nevin*,[292] the principles laid

---

[288] [1999] 1 ILRM 257 at 260.
[289] [1993] 2 IR 458, [1992] ILRM 755. See also *Logue v Redmond* [1999] 2 ILRM 498.
[290] [1993] 2 IR 458 at 471, [1992] ILRM 755 at 765. *Cf. Evans v Chief Constable of Surrey* [1988] QB 588, [1989] 2 All ER 594.
[291] [1999] 2 IR 179 at 186–187.
[292] Unreported, Court of Criminal Appeal, 13 December 2001.

down by Keane J in *Breathnach* were applied so as to uphold a claim by the DPP of legal professional privilege in respect of a report that had been furnished to him by the gardaí for the purpose of seeking his legal advice and that of counsel. The better view seems to be that the DPP should be entitled to assert legal advice privilege where it can be established that a particular communication was made for the purpose of receiving or giving legal advice.

5. Exceptions to Legal Professional Privilege

10–110 Having regard to the importance of legal professional privilege to the administration of justice, the common law courts have, traditionally, set their face against any exceptions to it even where the information sought to be disclosed was of strong probative value. In *Williams v Quebrada Railway, Land and Copper Co*,[293] Kekewich J stressed that:

> "It is of the highest importance, in the first place, that the rule as to privilege of protection from production to an opponent of those communications which pass between a litigant, or an expectant or possible litigant, and his solicitor should not be in any way departed from. However hardly the rule may operate in some cases, long experience has shewn that it is essential to the due administration of justice that the privilege should be upheld."[294]

10–111 The argument against exceptions proceeds on the basis of the "chilling effect" of disclosure.[295] It is argued that the effective functioning of the lawyer/client relationship is crucially dependent upon the client being able to place unbounded confidence in his lawyer secure in the knowledge that whatever he says can never be disclosed without his consent. Thus, if disclosure were to be made, even in limited circumstances, this would fatally undermine the relationship because the absolute guarantee of confidentiality would now be hedged about with caveats. The inevitable result is that a client will be more circumspect in revealing information to his or her lawyer, thus, undermining the privilege.

10–112 However, in recent times there has been a greater recognition that the privilege is rooted in public policy and should, therefore, only be granted where the balance of advantage favours protection of confidentiality rather than disclosure.[296] As noted above, the Supreme Court held in *Smurfit Paribas Bank Ltd v AAB Export Finance Ltd*[297] that a balancing test ought to be applied in order to align the parameters

---

[293] [1895] 2 Ch 751 at 754.

[294] See also *Southwark and Vauxhall Water Co. v Quick* (1878) 3 QBD 315 at 317–318 *per* Cockburn CJ: "The relation between the client and his professional legal adviser is a confidential relation of such a nature that to my mind the maintenance of the privilege with regard to it is essential to the interests of justice and the well-being of society. Though it might occasionally happen that the removal of the privilege would assist in the elucidation of matters in dispute, I do not think that this occasional benefit justifies us in incurring the attendant risk." In *S v Safatsa* 1988 (1) SA 868 at 886, Botha JA stated that any claim to relaxation of the privilege must be approached with the greatest caution.

[295] See *R. v Derby Magistrates' Court, ex parte B* [1996] AC 487, [1995] 4 All ER 526; *R. (Morgan Grenfell Ltd) v Special Comr* [2002] UKHL 21, [2003] 1 AC 563 at 608.

[296] *Cf. Smith v Jones* [1999] 1 SCR 455 at 477. But see the comments of the House of Lords in *Three Rivers DC v Bank of England (No 6)* [2004] UKHL 48 at [24], [2005] 1 AC 610 at 646, *per* Lord Scott.

[297] [1990] 1 IR 469 at 477, [1990] ILRM 588 at 594.

of the privilege with the balance of public interest. To repeat again the salient passage from the judgment of Finlay CJ:

> "The existence of a privilege or exemption from disclosure for communications made between a person and his lawyer clearly constitutes a potential restriction and diminution of the full disclosure both prior to and during the course of legal proceedings which in the interests of the common good is desirable for the purpose of ascertaining the truth and rendering justice. Such privilege should, therefore, in my view, only be granted by the courts in instances which have been identified as securing an objective which in the public interest in the proper conduct of the administration of justice can be said to outweigh the disadvantage arising from the restriction of disclosure of all the facts."

10–113 It is clear, however, that Finlay CJ was not advocating the use of a balancing test in order to displace legal professional privilege on a case by case basis. This was explicitly clarified in the subsequent decision of the Supreme Court in *Fyffes Plc v DCC Plc*[298] where Fennelly J, referring to the dictum of Finlay CJ set out above, stated that:

> "The then Chief Justice did not, in my view, by those words, mean to suggest that, in cases where reliance is placed on legal professional privilege in respect of documents the courts should balance the two considerations, as it were, on a case by case basis. He was referring to what the policy of the law should be. In my view, whether or not documents are privileged will be determined by the application of these principles to the facts of the case. Once it is found to exist, there is no judicial discretion to displace it."

10–114 Similar comments were made by the House of Lords in *Three Rivers DC v Bank of England (No 6)*,[299] where the Court rejected the contention that such a balancing exercise falls to be carried out as a matter of English law[300]:

> "...if a communication or document qualifies for legal professional privilege, the privilege is absolute. It cannot be overridden by some supposedly greater public interest. It can be waived by the person, the client, entitled to it and it can be overridden by statute ... but it is otherwise absolute. There is no balancing exercise that has to be carried out... The Supreme Court of Canada has held that legal professional privilege although of great importance is not absolute and can be set aside if a sufficiently compelling public interest for doing so, such as public safety, can be shown... But no other common law jurisdiction has, so far as I am aware, developed the law of privilege in this way. Certainly in this country legal professional privilege, if it is attracted by a particular communication between lawyer and client or attaches be to a particular document, cannot be set aside on the ground that some other higher public interest requires that to be done."[301]

10–115 The question as to whether the court enjoys a residual discretion to override legal professional privilege where the interests of justice so require was considered in this jurisdiction in *McGrath v Athlone Institute of Technology*,[302] where Hogan J concluded that it does not. He emphasised the fundamental importance of the privilege and, in particular, the important interplay between the privilege and the right to legal advice, stating[303]:

> "It is true that there is an exception of long standing to the effect that the privilege cannot

---

[298] [2005] IESC 3 at [23], [2005] 1 IR 59 at 67, [2005] 1 ILRM 357 at 364. See also *R. (Morgan Grenfell Ltd) v Special Comr* [2002] UKHL 21, [2003] 1 AC 563 at 608, where Lord Hoffman stated that legal professional privilege "does not involve such a balancing of interests. It is absolute and based not merely upon the general right to privacy but also upon the right of access to justice."

[299] [2004] UKHL 48, [2005] 1 AC 610 at 646.

[300] [2004] UKHL 48 at [24], [2005] 1 AC 610 at 646, *per* Lord Scott.

[301] See also *R. (Prudential Plc) v Special Comr of Income Tax* [2013] UKSC 1, [2013] 2 AC 185.

[302] [2011] IEHC 254.

[303] [2011] IEHC 254 at [9].

be used to mask a crime... but beyond this any further exceptions would gnaw at the core and essence of the right to take legal advice. In a free and democratic society based on the rule of law, the right of the citizen to take such advice is, of course, fundamental. If the court enjoyed a free ranging jurisdiction to override such advice, this would be tantamount, as the US Supreme Court has observed, to 'a prohibition upon professional advice and assistance' ... I cannot accept that this Court could carve another wide-ranging exception to the scope of legal professional privilege without undermining the fundamental right to seek legal advice itself."

10–116   It is submitted that, notwithstanding the "chilling effect" referred to above, exceptions should be made to legal professional privilege where the balance of public interest in disclosure clearly outweighs that in the maintenance of privilege. As O'Flaherty J said in *Gallagher v Stanley*,[304] the purpose of legal professional privilege "is to aid the administration of justice, not to impede it". However, it is clear from *Fyffes Plc v DCC Plc* and *McGrath v Athlone Institute of Technology* that any such developments in the law will have to occur by way of the principled recognition of defined exceptions, rather than on a case by case basis.

10–117   It is possible to identify from the case law, four categories of case where courts are or may be prepared to pierce privilege: (i) communications in furtherance of conduct which is criminal, fraudulent or injurious to the interests of justice; (ii) proceedings involving the welfare of children; (iii) testamentary dispositions; and (iv) where the innocence of an accused is at stake. Each of these is examined in turn.

(a) Communications in furtherance of conduct which is criminal, fraudulent, or injurious to the interests of justice

10–118   It has long been established that legal privilege cannot be invoked to protect from disclosure communications in furtherance of a criminal or fraudulent purpose.[305] Subsequent decisions have broadened the exception to include fraudulent conduct and conduct injurious to the interests of justice, but the courts have refused to extend it to conduct which is merely tortious and does not include any element of moral turpitude.

10–119   Initially, the courts adopted a definitional approach to hold that privilege could not attach to a communication in furtherance of criminal conduct on the basis that such a communication could not be said to pass in the course of a professional legal relationship because it is no part of a lawyer's professional occupation to facilitate the commission of a crime or fraud.[306] In addition, it was argued that the necessary

---

[304] [1998] 2 IR 267 at 271. These comments were cited with approval by Peart J in *Casey v Iarnrod Eireann* [2004] IEHC 117.

[305] *Annesley v Earl of Anglesea* (1743) 17 How St Tr 1229; *Kelly v Jackson* (1849) 1 Ir Jur 233; *R. v Cox and Railton* (1884) 14 QBD 153; *Bullivant v AG for Victoria* [1901] AC 196 at 201 (*per* Earl of Halsbury LC); *R. v Smith* (1915) 84 LJ KB 2153; *Barclays Bank Plc v Eustice* [1995] 1 WLR 1238 at 1249, [1995] 4 All ER 511; *BBGP Managing General Partner Limited v Babcock & Brown Global Partners* [2010] EWHC 2176, [2011] 2 WLR 496; *C v C (Privilege)* [2006] EWHC (Fam), [2008] 1 FLR 115.

[306] See *Follett v Jefferyes* (1850) 1 Sim NS 3 at 17, where Lord Cranworth VC stated that it was "not accurate to speak of cases of fraud contrived by the client and solicitor in concert together, as cases of *exception* to the general rule. They are cases not coming within the rule itself; for the rule does not apply at all which passes between a client and his solicitor, but only to what passes between them in professional confidence; and no Court can permit it to be said that the contriving of a fraud can form part of the professional occupation of an attorney or solicitor". See also *Russell v Jackson* (1851) 9 Hare 387 at 392; and *R. v Cox* (1884) 14 QBD 153 at 165–166. *Cf. AG for the Northern Territory v Kearney* (1985) 158 CLR 500 at 514.

ingredient of confidentiality was lacking because there could not be a confidence as to the disclosure of iniquity.[307] However, the impetus for the development of this exception in the last century has been a recognition that the rationale for privilege cannot be extended to such communications. As Stephen J explained in *R. v Cox and Railton*:

> "[t]he reason on which the rule is said to rest cannot include the case of communications criminal, in themselves or intended to further any criminal purpose, for the protection of such communications, cannot possibly be otherwise than injurious to the interests of justice and to those of the administration of justice".[308]

10–120 It is this test, whether applying privilege would be injurious to the administration of justice, which justifies the exception and establishes its parameters.

(i) Communications in furtherance of crime or fraud

10–121 One of the earliest cases to refuse to apply the privilege to criminal conduct was *Annesley v Earl of Anglesea*.[309] The plaintiff brought ejectment proceedings in respect of land in County Meath against his uncle, the defendant, who he alleged had contrived to have him kidnapped and sold into slavery in America so that he could inherit the family estates when the plaintiff's father died. After returning to England from America, the plaintiff accidentally shot and killed a gamekeeper and was acquitted of his murder. However, the defendant then engaged a solicitor to start a private prosecution for murder saying that he would be willing to give £10,000 if he could get the plaintiff hanged. Mounteney B in the Irish Court of Exchequer said that this declaration was not privileged because it was:

> "The declaration now offered to be proved is of that nature, and so highly criminal, that, in my opinion, mankind is interested in the discovery; and whoever it was made to, attorney or not attorney, lies under an obligation to society in general, prior and superior to any obligation he can lie under to a particular individual, to make it known."[310]

10–122 Later cases extended the exception to fraudulent conduct.[311] In *Williams v Quebrada Railway, Land and Copper Co,*[312] the exception was applied in circumstances where a claim was made that a charge had been entered into by a company with the intention of defeating the holders of floating debentures. Kekewich J held that the exception was applicable to civil as well as criminal cases and said that:

> "where there is anything of an underhand nature or approaching to fraud, especially in commercial matters where there should be the veriest good faith, the whole transaction should be ripped up and disclosed in all its nakedness to the light of the Court".

---

[307] In *Gartside v Outram* (1856) 26 LJ Ch 113 at 114, Page Wood VC stated: "The true doctrine is that there is no confidence as to the disclosure of iniquity. You cannot make me the confidant of a crime or a fraud, and be entitled to close up my lips upon any secret which you have the audacity to disclose to me relating to any fraudulent intention on your part. Such a confidence cannot exist." *Cf. Annesley v Earl of Anglesea* (1743) 17 How St Tr 1139 at 1242.

[308] (1884) 14 QBD 153 at 167.

[309] (1743) 17 How St Tr 1139.

[310] (1743) 17 How St Tr 1139 at 1243. A subsequent example can be seen in *People (AG) v Coleman* [1945] IR 237, where the Court of Criminal Appeal upheld the view of the trial judge that privilege did not apply to a note written by the accused which sought to procure the subornation of witnesses because it contemplated and suggested the commission of a crime.

[311] *Cf. Barclays Bank Plc v Eustice* [1995] 1 WLR 1238 at 1249, [1995] 4 All ER 511; *BBGP Managing General Partner Limited v Babcock & Brown Global Partners* [2010] EWHC 2176, [2011] 2 WLR 496; *C v C (Privilege)* [2006] EWHC (Fam), [2008] 1 FLR 115.

[312] [1895] 2 Ch 751 at 754–755.

10–123 Subsequently, in *Crescent Farm Sports v Sterling Offices*,[313] Goff J clarified that "fraud in this connection is not limited to the tort of deceit, and includes all forms of fraud and dishonesty, such as fraudulent breach of trust, fraudulent conspiracy, trickery and sham contrivances."[314]

10–124 Privilege will not automatically be pierced merely because a client consults a lawyer before committing a crime or fraud.[315] In order for this to occur, it must be shown that the communication in question was made in preparation for or in furtherance of a criminal or fraudulent purpose.[316] However, complicity or knowledge on the part of the lawyer is not required and privilege will be set aside if a client seeks legal advice intended to facilitate him or her in the commission of a crime or a fraud even though the legal adviser is entirely ignorant of that purpose.[317]

(ii) Conduct injurious to the interests of justice

10–125 The courts have drawn on the policy foundation of legal privilege to broaden the scope of the exception beyond criminal and fraudulent conduct to include conduct injurious to the interests of justice.[318] The leading case in this jurisdiction is the decision of the Supreme Court in *Murphy v Kirwan*.[319] The plaintiff sought specific performance of an agreement but his claim was dismissed. The defendant had counterclaimed that the proceedings were vexatious, frivolous and an abuse of the process of the court and sought discovery of legal advice obtained by the plaintiff relating to the specific performance claim up to the date of the trial. A majority of the Supreme Court was satisfied that privilege could be pierced. Taking a purposive approach, Finlay CJ stated that:

> "the essence of the matter is that professional privilege cannot and must not be applied so as to be injurious to the interests of justice and to those in the administration of justice where persons have been guilty of conduct of moral turpitude or of dishonest conduct, even though it may not be fraud."[320]

10–126 With regard to the allegation at hand, that the plaintiff had abused the processes of the court, he was satisfied that:

---

[313] [1972] Ch 553 at 565.

[314] See *Gamlen Chemical Co (UK) Ltd v Rochem Ltd* [1983] RPC 1, where the exception was applied to allegations of conspiracy by former employees to breach their duty and confidence to a company.

[315] *R. v Campbell* [1999] 1 SCR 565, (1999) 171 DLR (4th) 193.

[316] Thus, if the communication does not actually further that purpose as where a lawyer issues an unsolicited warning of the consequences of persisting in a certain course of conduct, privilege will not be lost: *Butler v Board of Trade* [1971] Ch 680, [1970] 3 All ER 593. *Cf. R. v Snaresbrook Crown Court, ex parte DPP* [1988] QB 532, [1988] 1 All ER 315.

[317] *R. v Cox and Railton* (1884) 14 QBD 153 at 165–166; *R. v Orton* (1873) 18 Digest (Rep.) 4116. In *Tichborne v Lushington* (1872) 22 Digest (Rep.) 409, Bovill CJ justified this approach on the basis that "if any such privilege should be contended for or existed, it would work most grievous hardship on an attorney who, after he had been consulted upon what subsequently appeared a most manifest crime and fraud, would have his lips closed, and might place himself in the very serious position of being suspected to be a party to the fraud, and without his having an opportunity of exculpating himself".

[318] *Murphy v Kirwan* [1993] 3 IR 501, [1994] 1 ILRM 293; *AG for the Northern Territory v Kearney* (1985) 158 CLR 500; *Police v Mills* [1993] 2 NZLR 592.

[319] [1993] 3 IR 501, [1994] 1 ILRM 293.

[320] [1993] 3 IR 501 at 511, [1994] 1 ILRM 293 at 300.

"Nothing could be more injurious to the administration of justice nor to the interests of justice than that a person should falsely and maliciously bring an action, and should abuse for an ulterior or improper purpose the processes of the court."[321]

10–127 The scope of this exception arose again for consideration in *Bula Ltd v Crowley (No.2)*.[322] The plaintiffs brought proceedings claiming, *inter alia*, that the first named defendant had been negligent in failing to follow certain legal advice obtained by him in the course of carrying out his duties as receiver of the first named plaintiff. The plaintiffs sought discovery of documents containing this legal advice arguing that privilege did not protect from disclosure documents containing or seeking legal advice where the question whether, and in what terms, such advice was sought or received was in issue. Alternatively, it was argued that the court has a discretion to view the legal advices and, in the light of those advices and of the allegations made, it should, if it is satisfied that that is the essential ground on which that part of the plaintiff's claim rested, exercise a discretion exempting the documents from privilege.

10–128 This contention was rejected by the Supreme Court which held, following *Murphy v Kirwan*[323] that the exemption under this head was restricted to conduct which contained an element of fraud, dishonesty or moral turpitude and did not extend to allegations of tortious conduct. Finlay CJ said that the extension of the exception to "any case where it was proved that the nature of the legal advice obtained by a party was clearly relevant to an issue as to the commission of a tort would be inconsistent with the principles" he had set out in *Murphy v Kirwan* and was of the view that acceptance of the plaintiff's argument would involve "a massive undermining ... of the important confidence in relation to communications between lawyers and their clients which is a fundamental part of our system of justice".[324] For this reason, the Court also rejected the further submission made by the plaintiffs that a court should inspect documents and order their disclosure if it finds them to be highly relevant to the issues in an action. While relevance was a necessary precondition to the application of the exception, it was not sufficient.[325]

10–129 It is clear from these decisions that the exception will only be applied where the conduct complained of is injurious to the interests of justice and this will be the case only if it involves some degree of moral turpitude. Sufficient moral turpitude will generally not be found where the allegations of tortious conduct or breach of contract are made. However, sufficient moral turpitude will exist where legal advice is sought

---

[321] [1993] 3 IR 501 at 511, [1994] 1 ILRM 293 at 300. *Cf. Police v Mills* [1993] 2 NZLR 592 at 600 (privilege would be pierced if it could be shown that client had consulted lawyer for the improper purpose of seeking to cloak with privilege information regarding a criminal offence which the lawyer had obtained outside of the professional relationship).

[322] [1994] 2 IR 54, [1994] 1 ILRM 495.

[323] [1993] 3 IR 501, [1994] 1 ILRM 293.

[324] [1994] 2 IR 54 at 59, [1994] 1 ILRM 495 at 498. The decision of the Supreme Court on this point was followed by Smyth J in *Shell E&P Ireland Ltd v McGrath (No.2)* [2006] IEHC 409, [2007] 2 IR 574, [2007] 1 ILRM 544 at [21].

[325] This exception was adverted to by the Supreme Court in *Fyffes Plc v DCC Plc* [2005] IESC 3 at [24], [2005] 1 IR 59 at 67, [2005] 1 ILRM 357 at [364], where Fennelly J observed that, while the law attaches significant value and accords a high degree of protection to the principle of legal professional privilege, "[i]t can, of course, be lost if it is clear that it is being used as a cloak to cover fraud".

with the intention of defeating the legal rights and entitlements of a person.[326] The dividing line between the two can be hard to draw.

10–130   In *Crescent Farm (Sidcup) Sports Ltd v Sterling Offices Ltd*,[327] it was held that the tort of inducing a breach of contract was not within the ambit of the exception. Goff J said that:

> "parties must be at liberty to take advice as to the ambit of their contractual obligations and liabilities in tort and what liability they will incur whether in contract or tort by a proposed course of action without thereby in every case losing professional privilege".[328]

10–131   However, *Crescent Farm* was distinguished by the High Court of Australia in *AG for the Northern Territory v Kearney*.[329] At issue were communications made for the purpose of giving and receiving legal advice which came into existence in connection with a scheme by the Administrator of the Northern Territory to make regulations with the object of defeating potential aboriginal land claims. It was held that these communications were not privileged because it:

> "would be contrary to the public interest which the privilege is designed to secure—the better administration of justice—to allow it to be used to protect communications made to further a deliberate abuse of statutory power and by that abuse to prevent others from exercising their rights under the law".[330]

10–132   The difficulties which arise in respect of borderline cases where some degree of moral turpitude has occurred is apparent from *McMullen v Giles J. Kennedy & Co*,[331] a case with a protracted history.[332] The plaintiff sued his solicitors for professional negligence arising out of a settlement agreement. Senior counsel for the plaintiff in the original proceedings was the principal witness for the defendant solicitors and accepted responsibility in relation to the wording of the settlement agreement. The defendant acted as solicitor for the plaintiff's former solicitors in the professional negligence proceedings. Having been unsuccessful in the professional negligence proceedings, the plaintiff issued a second set of proceedings against the senior counsel, in which he was unsuccessful. During the hearing, however, a letter from the defendant to his client, the insurer of the plaintiff's former solicitors, was inadvertently disclosed to the plaintiff. The letter recorded a without prejudice conversation between the defendant and Senior Counsel, during which the defendant, who was aware that Senior Counsel was acting for the plaintiff in another case and might still have some influence over him, indicated that the insurer wished to join him as a defendant to the proceedings but that the defendant was not keen to do so. The letter stated that the objective of this was to provide "an opportunity and incentive" to counsel to "dissuade" the claimant. The plaintiff appealed both sets of proceedings to the Supreme Court, which refused to admit the letter as new evidence in the appeal.[333]

---

[326] *Crawford v Treacy* [1999] 2 IR 171 at 177; *Barclays Bank Plc v Eustice* [1995] 1 WLR 1238, [1995] 4 All ER 511.

[327] [1972] Ch 553.

[328] [1972] Ch 553 at 565.

[329] [1985] 158 CLR 500.

[330] [1985] 158 CLR 500 at 515 (*per* Gibbs CJ).

[331] [2007] IEHC 263, [2008] IESC 69.

[332] This case arose out of the events the subject matter of the decisions of the Supreme Court in *McMullen v Carty*, unreported, Supreme Court, 27 January 1998, and *McMullen v Clancy (No. 2)* [2005] IESC 10, [2005] 2 IR 445, which are considered elsewhere in this Chapter.

[333] See *McMullen v Clancy (No. 2)* [2005] IESC 10, [2005] 2 IR 445.

10–133 The plaintiff then instituted a third set of proceedings against the defendant, in which he alleged that he had improperly sought to influence the outcome of the plaintiff's negligence action against his former solicitors by influencing counsel to give evidence in their defence and to accept in evidence that he was responsible for the error in the settlement agreement. An order for discovery was made and the defendant asserted a claim of privilege in respect of a number of documents on the basis that they were privileged communications prepared for the purpose of the plaintiff's proceedings against his former solicitors, in which proceedings the plaintiff's former solicitors (and their insurer) were the defendant's clients. In the High Court,[334] Murphy J refused to order disclosure of these documents, concluding that the exception in respect of communications "injurious to the interests of justice" did not apply. This decision was reversed on appeal by the Supreme Court,[335] where Macken J held that the allegations made by the plaintiff "could be classified as seeking to suborn the witness ... for the purposes of ensuring that he gave particular evidence, which was false, and highly disadvantageous to the appellant". Essentially, the plaintiff contended that, given the terms of the letter, there were grounds for believing that counsel gave false evidence, in light of the threat made to him of otherwise being sued. Macken J observed that the exception in respect of communications which are injurious to the interests of justice does not apply to allegations of simple tortious conduct, but held that the allegations made by the plaintiff in this case were not so limited[336]:

> "The exemption was restricted to conduct which contained an element of fraud, dishonesty or moral turpitude. Here the allegation on its face is clearly a very serious one indeed, made against an officer of the court and allegedly constituting an attempt to persuade a counsel to give evidence, in order to 'buy off' a possible or likely claim against that very counsel, falling into the category of moral turpitude, if it were true. It would in my view be injurious to the interest of justice to permit legal professional privilege to be applied in such circumstances, so as to prevent proper disclosure. That said, however, it is only in such unusual circumstances that I am prepared to make an exceptional order, which in ordinary course could not be made, having regard to the importance attaching to the principle of legal professional privilege."[337]

10–134 The Supreme Court did not, however, consider it appropriate that the documents of which the plaintiff sought disclosure should be disclosed to him. Having considered the authorities,[338] Macken J concluded that the correct approach was for the court, having inspected the documents in question, to review their contents and to come to a decision as to whether or not they included any relevant material which should be disclosed.[339]

---

[334] [2007] IEHC 263.

[335] [2008] IESC 69. The appeal was upheld by a 2:1 majority (Macken and Kearns JJ), Fennelly J dissenting.

[336] [2008] IESC 69 at [11] of the judgment of Macken J.

[337] Fennelly J, dissenting, accepted that the letter suggested "improper behaviour" on the part of the defendant solicitor, but stated that the misbehaviour appeared to consist in seeking to induce counsel to persuade the plaintiff to withdraw his claim against his former solicitors by threatening him with the possibility of being joined himself as a party to the action. There was no evidence of an attempt to influence counsel as to the content of the evidence he would give at the hearing of the action: [2008] IESC 69 at [29].

[338] *Murphy v Corporation of Dublin* [1972] IR 215; *Logue v Redmond* [1999] 1 ILRM 498; *McDonald v RTÉ* [2001] 1 IR 355; *Bula Limited v Tara Mines Limited (No.5)* [1994] 1 IR 487, [1991] 1 IR 217.

[339] If the court concluded that any of the documents should be disclosed, it was held that it would then be necessary to permit the plaintiff's former solicitors, in whom the privilege may vest, to be heard. Fennelly J (dissenting) held that, as "the privilege belongs to the former clients, not the solicitor" and the solicitors in question were not on notice of the application, the "Court should

10–135   Another recent example of a case in which sufficient moral turpitude to bring the case within the exception was found to exist is *Doyle v Bergin*,[340] where the respondent sought to claim privilege over an email and memorandum sent by him to the petitioner in proceedings instituted pursuant to s.205 of the Companies Act 1963. Both the applicant and the petitioner were directors of a company. The petitioner was a solicitor by profession. The email and attached memorandum informed the petitioner that the respondent had appropriated funds from the company, failed to disclose income to the Revenue Commissioners, and concluded a settlement with the Revenue Commissioners which was funded by the company. Having considered the documents in question, Laffoy J concluded that the email and attachment were not privileged, as the necessary ingredients for legal advice privilege were not present.[341] Notwithstanding this conclusion, she proceeded to hold that[342]:

> "What the respondent is attempting to do in this case, by reliance on the principle of legal professional privilege, to adopt the terminology used by Fennelly J in *Fyffes Plc v DCC Plc* is to use it in s.205 proceedings 'as a cloak' to cover his acknowledged appropriation to his own use of the company's money and effectively nullify the petitioner's cause of action in respect of that action. To allow the respondent to achieve that objective would be to allow legal professional privilege, which Kelly J in *Miley v Flood* ... characterised as 'a fundamental condition on which the administration of justice as a whole rests', to have the effect of undermining the proper conduct of the administration of justice in the public interest."

10–136   Having considered the decision of Finlay CJ in *Murphy v Kirwan*, she concluded that the allegation which formed the basis of the petitioner's claim of oppression within the meaning of s.205—the acknowledged appropriation by the respondent of the assets of the company for his own use—must be "an allegation of a type of moral turpitude or dishonest conduct which precludes the application of the general rule in relation to legal professional privilege".[343]

The Standard of Proof

10–137   The standard of proof which must be met by a party in order to bring himself or herself within the scope of this exception was addressed in *Murphy v Kirwan*,[344] where it was held that it suffices that a person's allegations are supported to an extent that they are, in the view of the court, viable and plausible.[345] Finlay CJ said that where the claim was one for malicious prosecution or abuse of the processes of the court, to require a person to prove an allegation as a matter of probability would make it impossible to obtain an order of discovery necessary for the fair trial of the action.[346]

---

not make any order impinging on the rights of those parties without hearing them", ([2008] IEHC 69 at [25]).

[340]   [2010] IEHC 531.

[341]   [2010] IEHC 531 at [3.5]–[3.7]. Laffoy J concluded that the petitioner received the documents in his capacity as director and officer, rather than as solicitor for the company, and the documents did not include any request for legal advice, either by the respondent or the company.

[342]   [2010] IEHC 531 at [3.9].

[343]   [2010] IEHC 531 at [3.10].

[344]   [1993] 3 IR 501, [1994] 1 ILRM 293.

[345]   [1993] 3 IR 501 at 512, [1994] 1 ILRM 293. *Cf. Quinlivan v Governor of Mountjoy Prison*, unreported, High Court, 23 January 1997 (appeal dismissed by Supreme Court, 5 March 1997) where Kelly J dismissed as "extravagant speculation" with no evidence to support it, the submission of the applicant that the claim of legal professional privilege made by the notice parties was vitiated because of an alleged conspiracy between the Director of Public Prosecutions, the Minister for Justice and the Attorney General.

[346]   He also specified that it would be necessary for the party making the claim of an abuse of process

Although the comments of the Chief Justice were directed solely to where allegations of malicious prosecution or abuse of process are made, there is no reason in principle why a different standard of proof should apply to allegations made within this category of exception. Therefore, it would seem that unlike the position in England, a *prima facie* case will not be required.[347]

10–138 One instance where a higher standard of proof may be required is where the allegation of fraud relates to the actual conduct of the proceedings themselves. In *Chandler v Church*[348] the plaintiffs sought discovery of communications between the defendant and his solicitors on the basis that he had obtained their assistance to mount an allegedly bogus defence. The plaintiffs submitted *prima facie* evidence to support their allegation. However, Hoffman J held that disclosure at an interlocutory stage based on evidence of fraud in the very proceedings in which disclosure is sought carries a far greater risk of injury to the party against whom discovery is sought, should he turn out to have been innocent, than disclosure of advice concerning an earlier transaction. On the facts, the risk of injustice to the defendant in being required to reveal communications with his lawyers for the purpose of his defence, together with the damage to the public interest which the violation of such confidences would cause, outweighed the risk of injustice to the plaintiffs.[349] That is not to say that such an application would never succeed but the courts will be have to be completely satisfied of the merits of the allegations made before granting the application. Otherwise, a party would only have to make an allegation of fraud in order to gain access to an opponent's brief.

10–139 This risk was also adverted to by Clarke J in *Moorview Developments Ltd v First Active plc*.[350] It was not alleged, in that case, that the defendant's legal advisers were involved in the fraud. However, it was suggested that certain transactions put in place by the defendant's legal advisers formed part of the alleged fraudulent activity. Referring to the decision of Finlay CJ in *Murphy v Kirwan*, Clarke J noted that the Chief Justice held in that case that the allegations of fraud "should be supported to an extent that they are, in the view of the court, viable and plausible". He stated that "a very high status indeed is accorded to legal professional privilege", as a result of which "it is only in rare and exceptional cases that a countervailing factor which will outweigh the requirement to preserve legal professional privilege will be found to exist".[351] Clarke J concluded that it would be an inappropriate and impermissible intrusion into legal

---

to establish either that the claim has failed in its entirety or that is bound to do so and that the failure of the claim was not derived from the resolution by the trial court of a conflict of evidence with regard to the primary facts or from a special legal defence raised by the defendant such as the Statute of Frauds.

[347] See *O'Rourke v Darbishire* [1920] AC 581, [1920] All ER 1 (which was cited with approval by Egan J in his dissent in *Murphy v Kirwan* [1993] 3 IR 501, [1994] 1 ILRM 293 on this point); *Butler v Board of Trade* [1973] 3 All ER 593 at 598 (*per* Goff J) ("what has to be shown *prima facie* is not merely that there is a *bona fide* and reasonably tenable charge of crime or fraud but a *prima facie* case that the communications in question were made in preparation for or in furtherance or as part of it.")

[348] [1987] NLJR 451.

[349] See also *R. v Crown Court at Snaresbrook, ex p. DPP* [1988] 1 All ER 315; *Francis & Francis (a firm) v Central Criminal Court* [1988] 3 All ER 775; *Owners and/or Demise Chartered of the Deredger Kamal XXVI v Owners of the Ship Arelia* [2010] EWHC 2531 (Comm); *BBGP Managing General Partner Limited v Babcock & Brown Global Partners* [2010] EWHC 2176, [2011] 2 WLR 496.

[350] Unreported, High Court, 21 December 2007.

[351] Unreported, High Court, 21 December 2007 at 14.

professional privilege if a party who alleged fraud and produced some evidence to back up that claim, but only to a very low threshold, was allowed to gain access to the other party's legal advice. While he stopped short of adopting the standard of "a very strong *prima facie* case of fraud" articulated by Longmore LJ in *Kuwait Airways v Iraqi Airways (No. 6)*,[352] he held that "a significant onus rests upon a party, who wishes to displace an otherwise legitimate claim to legal professional privilege on the basis of an allegation of fraud, to establish by cogent evidence that he has a real, viable and sustainable claim in that regard".[353] The policy reasons underpinning this conclusion were explained as follows:

> "...there are sound reasons of precedent and policy for taking the view that a court should impose a significant threshold, at least in cases where the fraud which is alleged to have displaced legal professional privilege is the same fraud which is at the heart of the proceedings. To take any other course would run the risk of either allowing unmeritorious parties, who had no more than a bare colourable case in fraud, to have carte blanch to examine their opponent's legal advice or would require the court to enter into a detailed analysis, at an interlocutory stage, of the strength of the very case that will have to be determined at trial. Neither of these courses of action is desirable."[354]

(b) Proceedings involving the welfare of children

10–140   There is a strong vein of authority to the effect that the rules of evidence should not be applied with the same vigour in inquisitorial proceedings involving the welfare of children because the rules of evidence which were laid down in an adversarial context are not appropriate where there is no *lis inter partes*.[355] Thus, in *TL v VL*,[356] McGuinness J held that legal professional privilege could be pierced in proceedings concerning the welfare of children. She surveyed the English decisions and followed that of the Court of Appeal in *Oxfordshire County Council v M*[357] where it held that proceedings under the Children Act 1989 (UK) are not adversarial and the court's duty is to investigate and to seek to achieve a result which is the interests of the welfare of the child or children the subject of the proceedings. Such proceedings are not similar to ordinary adversarial litigation, in which the doctrine of professional privilege applies, but fall into a special category where the court is bound to undertake all necessary steps to arrive at an appropriate result in the paramount interests of the welfare of the child. Accordingly, the court has power to override legal professional privilege and order disclosure of a privileged communication. She was of the opinion that these principles could be applied equally to proceedings in this jurisdiction governed by s.3 of the Guardianship of Infants Act 1964, which requires a court to have regard to the welfare of the child as the paramount consideration. Indeed, the statutory duty of the court in this regard was strengthened by the well established constitutional right of the child to have its welfare promoted and protected by the court. Although it was not necessary for the purposes of her decision, the learned judge cited with approval

---

[352] [2005] EWCA Civ 286, [2005] 1 WLR 2734. It was held, in that case, that where fraud is not one of the issues in the action, a *prima facie* case of fraud may be enough.

[353] Unreported, High Court, Clarke J, 21 December 2007, at 23. Clarke J stated that this standard is significantly higher than the threshold articulated in *Barry v Buckey* [1981] IR 306, and applied by the courts on an application to strike out proceedings as frivolous, vexatious and bound to fail.

[354] Unreported, High Court, 21 December 2007 at 22.

[355] See, in relation to the rule against hearsay, *Eastern Health Board v MK* [1999] 2 IR 99 (also reported *sub nom. In the Matter of MK, SK and WK* [1999] 2 ILRM 321).

[356] [1996] IFLR 126.

[357] [1994] 2 All ER 269.

a number of English decisions to the effect that, not only were legal representatives in possession of material relevant to the determination but contrary to the interests of their client unable to resist disclosure by reliance on legal professional privilege, they have a positive duty to disclose it to the other parties and to the court.[358]

10–141 McGuinness J did, however, emphasise a number of limitations. First, the English decisions referred solely to medical and expert reports and clearly such reports are the type of material which would normally require to be disclosed in this context. She said that the same considerations do not necessarily apply to other matters normally covered by legal professional privilege, and in each case "the desirability of disclosure must on the facts of the case be weighed against the desirability of maintaining the privilege and a decision taken in the light of the interests of the child concerned."[359] She went on to accept that the power to override privilege in such cases should "be exercised only rarely and only when the court is satisfied that it is necessary".[360] She ultimately decided not to order discovery of the document at issue because she did not think that the material was of such a nature that the interests of the child required that it be disclosed by way of discovery.

(c) Testamentary dispositions

10–142 In general, the fact that a client is dead does not affect the existence of legal professional privilege[361] which will inure for the benefit of his or her successors in title.[362] However, a possible exception may exist in respect of testamentary dispositions, the parameters of which are far from clear.

10–143 The starting point in this area is the decision in *Russell v Jackson*[363] where it was contended that a gift of the residue of the testator's estate to the executors was made upon a secret trust for the founding of a socialist school in Birmingham. In order to establish this fact, it was sought to examine by interrogatories the solicitor who had drawn up the will as to the circumstances surrounding this alleged secret trust. He refused to answer the interrogatories on the ground of privilege. On the facts, Turner VC held that privilege could not be set up by the executor against the next of kin claiming against the estate because both were claiming under the testator. However, he also advanced the view that in the case of testamentary dispositions, the rationale for the privilege did not apply:

> "The disclosure in such cases can affect no right or interest of the client. The apprehension of it can present no impediment to the full statement of his case to his solicitor. ... In the cases of testamentary dispositions the very foundation on which the rule proceeds seem to be wanting; and in the absence, therefore, of any illegal purpose entertained by the testator there does not appear to be any ground for applying it...Another view of the case is that the protection which the rule gives is the protection of the client; and it cannot, I think, be said to

---

[358] See *Re R. (A Minor) (Disclosure of Privileged Material)* [1993] 4 All ER 702; *Essex County Council v R.* [1993] 2 FLR 826; *Re H(D) (A Minor) (Child Abuse)* [1994] 1 FLR 679.

[359] [1996] IFLR 126 at 137.

[360] [1996] IFLR 126 at 137.

[361] *Bullivant v AG for Victoria* [1901] AC 196.

[362] In *Swidler & Berlin v United States* (1998) 524 US 399, Rehnquist CJ justified this on the basis that posthumous disclosure might be feared by a client as much as disclosure during his or her lifetime and, thus, maintaining the confidentiality of communications after death would help to foster full and frank communication between client and counsel.

[363] (1851) 9 Hare 387 at 392.

be for the protection of the client that evidence should be rejected, the effect of which would be to prove a trust created by him, and to destroy a claim to take beneficially by parties who have accepted that trust."[364]

10–144   This passage was cited with approval by the Ontario Court of Appeal in *Stewart v Walker*,[365] where Moss CJO explained that:

"The nature of the case precludes the question of privilege from arising. The reason on which the rule is founded is the safeguarding of the interests of the client, or those claiming under him when they are in conflict with the claims of third persons not claiming, or assuming to claim under him. And that is not this case, where the question is as to what testamentary dispositions, if any, were made by the client."[366]

10–145   It can be seen that this line of authority is predicated on the recognition that where a dispute arises about a testamentary disposition, the client has no recognisable interest in the maintenance of privilege. On the contrary, the concern of the deceased client is that his or her instructions and intentions would be carried into effect and there would have been no "chilling effect" on the solicitor/client relationship if the client had been aware that privileged communications could be disclosed after his or her death.

10–146   Another vein of authority has focused on the partially inquisitorial role of the courts in probate matters. In *Re Fuld's Estate (No.2)*,[367] Scarman J drew a distinction with regard to the application of legal privilege between the inquisitorial function of a court in relation to the execution of a will and its role in an adversarial dispute:

"[T]here can be in a probate case an apparent clash or conflict between the right of the court to know everything that its witness knows or has said about execution, and the right of a party to claim privilege for communications passing between that witness and himself or his solicitor for the purpose of collecting evidence for the hearing. If there be such a conflict, I have no doubt that it must be resolved in favour of the court. Strictly, however, there is no conflict because the court in its inquisitorial capacity is seeking the truth as to execution. The parties upon the issue of execution are assisting the court in its search for the truth."[368]

10–147   These strands of authority were considered by O'Sullivan J in *Crawford v Treacy*.[369] The case concerned a probate dispute. The first defendant sought to establish that she was the lawful wife of the deceased and was thus entitled to a share of his estate in accordance with the provisions of Part IX of the Succession Act 1965. The plaintiffs, who were the executors of the deceased's estate, brought an application seeking directions of the court. In the course of discovery, an affidavit was sworn by the first named plaintiff claiming legal professional privilege in respect of a number of documents relating to the preparation of the will and a separation agreement.

10–148   Having been requested to do so, O'Sullivan J examined the documents in dispute and concluded that some of them were privileged. He then went on to consider the submissions of the first named defendant that even if privilege attached to the documents, discovery should be ordered by reason of the application of two

---

[364]   (1851) 9 Hare 387 at 392.

[365]   (1903) 6 OLR 495 at 497.

[366]   In *Re Ott* [1972] 2 O.R. 5, [1972] O.J. No 1693 (Ont. Supr. Ct.), it was emphasised that it was in the interests of justice that privilege not be invoked as otherwise it would be impossible to ascertain the true intention of the testator. *Cf. Gartside v Sheffield, Young & Ellis* [1983] NZLR 37.

[367]   [1965] P 405, [1965] 2 All ER 657.

[368]   [1965] P 405 at 410, [1965] 2 All ER 657 at 659.

[369]   [1999] 2 IR 171.

exceptions to the general rule. The first was stated to arise out of the consideration that the proceedings were not truly inter partes but rather proceedings brought by the executors of the will for directions. It was submitted that the court's primary concern was the ascertainment of the truth rather than the protection of the interests of one of the parties and that this concern was paramount over such interests of the deceased as might be protected by the claim to privilege. It was further submitted that it would be anomalous if privilege were to apply such that the plaintiffs would be in possession of more information than the court itself. Reliance was placed in this regard on the decisions in *Russell v Jackson* and *Re Fuld's Estate (No.2)*.

10–149   O'Sullivan J distinguished these cases on the basis that in both, justice clearly required production of the documents or evidence. In *Russell*, there was a question not only of a secret trust but a breach of the law. In *Fuld*, the court was concerned with establishing a central fact in relation to the execution of a will. With regard to the instant case, he pointed out that the document sought related to advice and that the facts upon which that advice was given would be known to the court independently from incidental recitals in the documents passing between solicitor, counsel and the deceased. Having considered the documents, he did not think that the truth could only be discovered by ordering disclosure of the documents. The outcome of the application for directions would not, in his view, be dependent upon or influenced by production of those documents to the court. He concluded that the interests of justice did not necessitate disclosure of the privileged documents.

(d) Innocence of the accused

10–150   The question has not yet arisen in this jurisdiction as to whether privilege may be pierced where disclosure of a privileged communication is sought in order to prove the innocence of an accused. It is clear that public interest immunity will yield to the interest of a defendant in proving his innocence[370] and it would seem as if private privilege, which ultimately rests on public policy, should also yield. This was indeed the view taken by Caulfield J who approached the matter free from the constraints of authority in *R. v Barton*:

> "If there are documents in the possession or control of a solicitor which, on production, help to further the defence of an accused man, then in my judgment no privilege attaches. I cannot conceive that our law would permit a solicitor or other person to screen from a jury information which, if disclosed to the jury, would perhaps enable a man either to establish his innocence or to resist an allegation made by the Crown."[371]

10–151   This decision was approved in *R v Ataou*,[372] where the Court of Appeal held that where a defendant sought to pierce privilege claimed by a client or solicitor, he bore the burden of showing on the balance of probabilities that the claim for privilege could not be sustained because there was no ground on which the client could any longer reasonably be regarded as having a recognisable interest in asserting the privilege, and the legitimate interest of the defendant in seeking to breach the privilege outweighed that of the client in seeking to maintain it. French J stated that:

> "the resolution of the problem in each individual case involves balancing the competing

---

[370] *Director of Consumer Affairs v Sugar Distributors Ltd* [1991] 2 IR 225 at 229; *Goodman International v Hamilton (No.3)* [1993] 3 IR 320 at 327.
[371] [1972] 2 All ER 1192 at 1194.
[372] [1988] 2 All ER 321.

interests of the public in the due and orderly administration of justice, on the one hand, and of the public and the accused, in ensuring that all evidence supportive of his case is before the court, on the other hand".[373]

10–152   However, this line of authority was overturned by the House of Lords in *R. v Derby Magistrates' Court, ex parte B*.[374] The appellant had been arrested on suspicion of having murdered a girl. He admitted being solely responsible for the murder but later changed his story and stated that his stepfather had killed the girl and that he had taken part under duress. He was tried and acquitted of the girl's murder and was subsequently called as a witness by the prosecution at the committal proceedings of his stepfather on a charge of murdering the girl. Counsel for the stepfather sought to cross-examine him on the instructions which he had given to his solicitors during the period between his first account and his second account. The appellant refused to waive privilege and an application was made for a witness summons directing the solicitor to produce certain privileged documents.

10–153   The House of Lords took the view that *Ataou* had been incorrectly decided and that it was impermissible to engage in such a balancing exercise which cut across the fundamental principle of "once privileged, always privileged" unless the client chose to waive privilege. Lord Taylor CJ observed that legal professional privilege is much more than an ordinary rule of evidence but is a fundamental condition on which the administration of justice as a whole rests, and rejected the proposition that there could be exceptions to it:

> "[T]he drawback to that approach is that once any exception to the general rule is allowed, the client's confidence is necessarily lost. The solicitor, instead of being able to tell his client that anything which the client might say would never in any circumstances be revealed without his consent, would have to qualify his assurance. He would have to tell the client that his confidence might be broken if in some future case the court were to hold that he no longer had 'any recognisable interest' in asserting his privilege. One can see at once that the purpose of the privilege would thereby be undermined."[375]

10–154   Lord Lloyd said that there could not be a balancing exercise because:

> "the courts have for many years regarded legal professional privilege as the predominant public interest. A balancing exercise is not required in individual cases, because the balance must always come down in favour of upholding the privilege, unless, of course, the privilege is waived."[376]

10–155   He also rejected the idea that privilege could be set aside where the client could be shown to have no recognisable interest in maintaining it.

> "If the client had to be told that his communications were only confidential so long as he had 'a recognisable interest' in preserving the confidentiality, and that some court on some future occasion might decide that he no longer had any such recognisable interest, the basis of the confidence would be destroyed or at least undermined. There may be cases where the principle will work hardship on a third party seeking to assert his innocence. But in the overall interests of the administration of justice it is better that the principle should be preserved intact."[377]

10–156   Lord Nicholls pointed to the practical difficulties of any balancing test and the impossibility of setting satisfactory parameters to it. He characterised the

---

[373] [1988] 2 All ER 321 at 326.
[374] [1996] AC 487, [1995] 4 All ER 526. See also *Carter v Northmore Hale Davey & Leake* (1995) 183 CLR 121.
[375] *R. v Derby Magistrates' Court, ex parte B* [1996] AC 487 at 508, [1995] 4 All ER 526 at 541.
[376] [1996] AC 487 at 509, [1995] 4 All ER 526 at 542.
[377] [1996] AC 487 at 509–510, [1995] 4 All ER 526 at 543.

prospect of a balancing exercise as "a veritable will-o'-the wisp". He was attracted to the argument that the client could not assert privilege where he had no recognisable interest in maintaining it, *i.e.* where no rational person would regard himself as having any continuing interest in protecting the privilege. However, the point did not arise for decision as this test was not satisfied in the instant case where he was likely to be accused in the upcoming murder trial of having committed the murder.

10–157 The Canadian courts have taken a different and, it is submitted, preferable approach.[378] In *R. v Dunbar*,[379] Martin JA took the view that:

> "No rule of policy requires the continued existence of the privilege in criminal cases when the person claiming the privilege no longer has any interest to protect, and when maintaining the privilege might screen from the jury information which would assist an accused."[380]

10–158 This decision has been approved by the Supreme Court of Canada in a number of decisions, where it has been held that legal professional privilege may have to give way to the constitutional right of an accused to make full answer and defence to a criminal charge.[381] In *Smith v Jones*,[382] the Supreme Court disavowed the approach in *Derby Magistrates'* pointing out that the privilege in Canada is subject to certain well defined and limited exceptions which are not closed and could be expanded in the future.

6. Duration of Legal Professional Privilege

10–159 In keeping with the policy behind legal advice privilege, "the law has considered it the wisest policy to encourage and sanction this confidence, by requiring that on such facts the mouth of the attorney shall be forever sealed".[383] Therefore, the general rule as stated by Lindley MR in *Calcraft v Guest*[384] is "once privileged always privileged",[385] and legal advice privilege will continue after the lawyer/client relationship has ended[386] and even after the death of the client.[387] This general rule was recently reaffirmed in *University College Cork v ESB*,[388] where it was held that legal advice privilege "is permanent in duration and, unless waived, lasts forever". This is

---

[378] See also s.62(7) of the Evidence Act 2006 in New Zealand, which provides that, subject to the privilege against self-incrimination, a judge may disallow a claim of legal professional privilege conferred under the Act in respect of a communication or information if the judge if of the opinion that such evidence is necessary to enable the defendant in a criminal proceeding to present an effective defence. See Mathieson, *Cross on Evidence*, 9th edn (New Zealand: Lexis Nexis, 2013) at [284].

[379] (1983) 138 DLR (3d) 221.

[380] (1983) 138 DLR (3d) 221 at 252.

[381] *R. v McClure* [2001] 1 SCR 445; *R. v Seaboyer* [1991] 2 SCR 577 at 607; *A(LL) v B(A)* [1995] 4 SCR 536 at 577; *Smith v Jones* [1999] 1 SCR 455 at 477–478, (1999) 169 DLR (4th) 385 at 391; *R. v Campbell* [1999] 1 SCR 565 at 610–611, (1999) 171 DLR (4th) 193 at 231–232.

[382] [1999] 1 SCR 455, (1999) 169 DLR (4th) 385.

[383] *Per* Shaw CJ in *Hatton v Robinson* (1833) 14 Pick 416 at 422. See also *Wilson v Rastall* (1792) 4 Term Rep 753 at 759 (*per* Buller J) ("the privilege ... never ceased at any period of time ... it is not sufficient to say that the cause is at an end; the mouth of such person is closed forever").

[384] [1898] 1 QB 759.

[385] [1898] 1 QB 759 at 761. See also *Bullock v Corry* (1878) 3 QBD 356; *Pearce v Foster* (1885) 15 QBD 114 at 118; *Mann v American Automobile Insurance Co* (1938) 52 BCR 460, [1938] 2 DLR 261.

[386] *Cholmondeley v Clinton* (1815) 19 Ves Jun 261 at 268; *Bell v Smith* [1968] SCR 664, (1968) 68 DLR (2d) 751.

[387] *Russell v Jackson* (1851) 9 Hare 387; *Gartside v Sheffield, Young & Ellis* [1983] NZLR 37.

[388] [2014] IEHC 135 at [32].

justified on the basis that disclosure at any point in the future could potentially harm the interests of the client and would have a chilling effect on communications with his or her lawyer.[389]

10–160   The question as to whether the maxim of "once privileged always privileged" applies equally to communications protected by litigation privilege has proved more controversial. In *Bullock v Corry*,[390] the plaintiffs brought proceedings against the defendants for failing to unload cargo at a certain port. It was held that the defendants were not entitled to inspection of the papers in the plaintiff's possession relating to a previous action brought against them by the ship-owner, including correspondence between them and their solicitor and between their solicitor and other persons, because those papers would have been privileged from discovery in the former action and the fact that such action had terminated did not deprive them of their privilege. Cockburn CJ said:

> "The privilege which attaches by the invariable practice of our courts to communications between solicitor and client ought to be carefully preserved. In my opinion, the rule is, once privilege, always privileged. This will apply, *a fortiori*, where the succeeding action is substantially the same as that in which the documents were used."[391]

10–161   That decision was followed in *Pearce v Foster*,[392] where Brett MR said that "if a document is once so privileged, the fact that it is another action in which it is being inquired about will not destroy the privilege".[393]

10–162   This question was considered in this jurisdiction is *Quinlivan v Tuohy*.[394] The plaintiff instituted proceedings claiming damages for personal injuries arising out of a car accident. She had been involved in a previous accident in which she had suffered similar injuries and the defendants sought disclosure of two medical reports prepared in connection with proceedings arising out of that accident. The plaintiff argued that privilege continued to subsist in these reports and Barron J agreed. He regarded the issue as settled by authority and followed *Bord na Mona v Sisk*,[395] in which Costello J had approved the holding in *The Aegis Blaze*.[396] In that case, the English Court of Appeal held that privilege could be claimed in respect of a surveyor's report prepared for the purpose of earlier proceedings and refused to impose a requirement that the subject-matter of the two actions be identical or substantially the same or that the parties to the two actions should be the same. Barron J, therefore, held that the reports were privileged and "that it would be to the Plaintiff's detriment and contrary to the principles from which the privilege was granted in the first place to allow this report now to be seen by the Defendants".[397]

10–163   In *Quinlivan*, Barron J declared that, even in the absence of authority, he would still have regarded the public interest as requiring the maintenance of privilege.

---

[389] *Porter v Scott* [1979] NI 6 at 16–17.

[390] (1878) 3 QBD 356.

[391] (1878) 3 QBD 356 at 358.

[392] (1885) 15 QBD 114 at 118.

[393] This appears to remain the position in England. See Passmore, *Privilege*, 3rd edn (London: Sweet & Maxwell, 2013), at [6-104] *et seq*.

[394] Unreported, High Court, 29 July 1992. The issue was also raised but not decided in *Breathnach v Ireland (No.3)* [1993] 2 IR 458.

[395] [1990] 1 IR 85.

[396] [1986] 1 Lloyd's Rep 203.

[397] Unreported, High Court, 29 July 1992 at 3.

However, an alternative approach was adopted by Kelly J in *Porter v Scott*,[398] where he distinguished between legal advice privilege and litigation privilege and held that the maxim "once privileged always privileged" applied to the former, but not to the latter, unless the subject-matter of the proceedings was the same:

> "There is sound public policy in applying this rule 'once privileged always privileged' to strict legal privilege, *i.e.* lawyer/client communications. What a client reveals to his lawyer for professional purposes should not only be secret but is intended to remain permanently so or at least until the client decides otherwise. To reduce or qualify the permanency of this secret would be to inhibit free and unreserved communication and this is essential to our system of law. The element of permanency does not seem to pervade communications made in contemplation of litigation. Such communications are not generally intended to remain unrevealed—indeed more often than not it is intended that they should be revealed at the appropriate time in one form or another during the course of legal proceedings. They come into existence for the precise and limited purpose of use in contemplated litigation and I do not see on any grounds of public policy or otherwise why they should remain clothed with privilege when the proceedings for which they were made have been disposed and abandoned."[399]

10–164 An approach similar to that adopted in *Porter v Scott* was taken in a decision which does not seem to have been drawn to the attention of Barron J in *Quinlivan*. In *Kerry County Council v Liverpool Salvage Association*[400] the plaintiffs sued the defendants for having caused an obstruction of Valentia harbour by depositing a wreck there. The defendants, who had been employed by an insurance company to salvage the vessel, resisted disclosure of certain correspondence on the ground that it was privileged. It was argued that this correspondence had come into being in connection with an anticipated claim by the ship-owner against the insurance company, and was therefore privileged, and that this privilege subsisted in these subsequent proceedings. The claim of privilege was rejected by the Court of Appeal on the ground that the correspondence would not have been privileged in the first action. However, two members of the Court did go on to deal, *obiter*, with the plaintiff's invocation of the maxim "once privileged, always privileged". Fitzgibbon LJ distinguished between legal advice privilege and litigation privilege. In relation to the latter, he said that the person claiming privilege must "show some connection between the parties, or the subject-matter, or both".[401] Holmes LJ was also of the opinion that privilege would not extend "to all cases, whatever might be the change of subject-matter or of parties".[402]

10–165 The duration of litigation privilege was considered by Laffoy J in *Martin v Legal Aid Board*,[403] who distinguished between legal professional privilege, which ceases to operate as a protective mechanism when the litigation comes to an end, and the duty of confidentiality, which endures.

10–166 More recently, in *University College Cork v ESB*,[404] Finlay Geoghegan J declined to follow the approach adopted in *Quinlivan*, preferring instead the approach

---

[398] [1979] NI 6.

[399] [1979] NI 6 at 16. The Canadian courts have also distinguished between those communications protected by legal advice privilege and those protected by litigation privilege and held that litigation privilege ends with the litigation for which the communications were prepared (*Meaney v Busby* (1977) 15 OR (2d) 71; *Boulianne v Flynn* [1970] 3 OR 84).

[400] (1904) 38 ILTR 7.

[401] (1904) 38 ILTR 7 at 8.

[402] (1904) 38 ILTR 7 at 8.

[403] [2007] IEHC 76 at [36], [2007] 2 IR 759 at 776.

[404] [2014] IEHC 135.

adopted by the Supreme Court of Canada in *Blank v Canada*,[405] where it was held that litigation privilege comes to an end, absent closely related proceedings, upon the termination of the litigation that gave rise to the privilege.[406] She observed that there was no consideration in either *Quinlivan* and *Bord na Mona* of the purpose of litigation privilege, as opposed to legal advice privilege, and held that the duration of litigation privilege should be reconsidered in light of the general principles set out by the Supreme Court decision in *Smurfit*.[407]

10–167   Having considered the decision of the Supreme Court of Canada in *Blank v Canada*, where a distinction was drawn between the policy considerations underlying litigation privilege and legal advice privilege, Finlay Geoghegan J concluded that the analysis, reasoning and conclusions arrived at by the Canadian Supreme Court are consistent with the judgments handed down by the Supreme Court in *Smurfit*.[408] She cited the following dictum of Fish J with approval, where he explained the rationale for the conclusion that litigation privilege is "neither absolute in scope, nor permanent in duration"[409]:

> "Though conceptually distinct, litigation privilege and legal advice privilege serve a common cause: The secure and effective administration of justice according to law. And they are complementary and not competing in their operation. But treating litigation privilege and legal advice privilege as two branches of the same tree tends to obscure the true nature of both.
>
> Unlike the solicitor-client privilege, the litigation privilege arises and operates *even in the absence of a solicitor-client relationship*, and it applies indiscriminately to all litigants, whether or not they are represented by counsel ... In short, the litigation privilege and the solicitor-client privilege are driven by different policy considerations and generate different legal consequences.
>
> The purpose of the litigation privilege ... is to create a 'zone of privacy' in relation to pending or apprehended litigation. Once the litigation has ended, the privilege to which it gave rise has lost its specific and concrete purpose - and therefore its justification. But to borrow a phrase, the litigation is not over until it is over: It cannot be said to have 'terminated', in any meaningful sense of that term, where litigants or related parties remain locked in what is essentially the same legal combat.
>
> Except where such related litigation persists, there is no need and no reason to protect from discovery anything that would have been subject to compellable disclosure but for the pending or apprehended proceedings which provided its shield. Where the litigation has indeed ended, there is little room for concern lest opposing counsel or their clients argue their case 'on wits borrowed from the adversary'..."

---

[405] [2006] SCC 39, [2006] 2 SCR 319.

[406] See also *Liquor Control Board of Ontario v Lifford Wine Agencies Ltd* (2005) 76 OR (3d) 401; *General Accident Assurance Co v Chrusz* (1999) 45 OR (3d) 321; *Ontario (Attorney General) v Ontario (Information and Privacy Commission, Inquiry Officer)* (2002) 62 OR (3d) 167; *Boulianne v Flynn* [1970] 3 OR 84; *Wujda v Smith* (1974) 49 DLR (3d) 476; *Meaney v Busby* (1977) 15 OR (2d) 71; *Canada Southern Petroleum Ltd v Amoco Canada Petroleum Co* (1995) 176 AR 134.

[407] The decisions in *Quinlivan* and *Bord na Mona* placed reliance on the decision of the English Court of Appeal in *The Aegis Blaze* [1986] 1 Lloyd's Rep 203. Finlay Geoghegan J observed that this decision did not distinguish between the policy underlying litigation privilege, as distinct from legal advice privilege. Accordingly, notwithstanding the authorities opened to the Court to the effect that it remains the case in England and Wales that the maxim "once privileged, always privileged" applies to both legal advice and litigation privilege, she preferred the Canadian approach: [2014] IEHC 135 at [40].

[408] Finlay Geoghegan J also concluded that the approach of the Canadian Supreme Court in *Blank v Canada* is consistent with that adopted by the High Court of Northern Ireland in *Porter v Scott* [1979] NI 6 as well as the *obiter* comments of Fitzgibbon J in *Kerry County Council v Liverpool Salvage Association* (1904) 38 ILTR 7.

[409] *Blank v Canada* [2006] SCC 39 at [31]–[35], [2006] 2 SCR 319.

10–168 Finlay Geoghegan J identified the objective of litigation privilege as "the creation of what has been referred to as a 'zone of privacy' in the interests of the efficacy of the adversarial system to permit a party in litigation to prepare its position without adversarial interference and without fear of premature disclosure",[410] and held that this objective does not require litigation privilege to automatically continue beyond the final termination of either the litigation or closely related litigation. Applying the balancing test provided for in *Smurfit*, she held that:

> "Where the second proceedings are not closely related to the first proceedings, there is no objective of the proper conduct of the administration of justice which can be said to outweigh the disadvantage arising from the restriction of all the facts."[411]

10–169 In *University College Cork v ESB*, the document in respect of which litigation privilege was asserted was an expert report prepared for the purpose of drafting a defence to Circuit Court proceedings in 1990. Finlay Geoghegan J was not satisfied that there was a substantive or close connection between the plaintiff's claim in the proceedings arising out of a flood in 2009, and the claim made by an unconnected person in Circuit Court proceedings arising out of a flood in 1990. It was held, therefore, that the defendant was not entitled to claim litigation privilege in respect of the report.[412]

10–170 It remains to be seen whether the Supreme Court will affirm the "closely related" test articulated in *University College Cork v ESB*. Having regard to the admonition of Finlay CJ in *Smurfit Paribas Bank Ltd v AAB Export Finance Ltd*,[413] that the parameters of privilege should only be drawn as broadly as necessary to advance the advantages secured by it, a strong argument can be made that the balance of public interest is against maintaining litigation privilege in subsequent proceedings. It is submitted, therefore, that the approach adopted in *University College Cork v ESB* is the correct approach, and that the application of litigation privilege should be limited to the proceedings for which they came into being, unless there is a close connection between the subsequent proceedings and the original proceedings which gave rise to the privilege.

7. Assertion of Privilege

10–171 Privilege belongs to the client,[414] not the lawyer.[415] Therefore, the decision as to whether to assert privilege is one for the client to make, although the lawyer is

---

[410] [2014] IEHC 135 at [46].

[411] [2014] IEHC 135 at [46]. The judge emphasised that this conclusion applies only to litigation privilege.

[412] [2014] IEHC 135 at [48].

[413] [1990] 1 IR 469 at 477, [1990] ILRM 488 at 594.

[414] Or to the client's successors in title: *Chant v Brown* (1849) 7 Hare 79; *Re Konigsberg* [1989] 3 All ER 289 (trustee in bankruptcy); *Geffen v Goodman Estate* [1991] 2 SCR 353, (1991) 81 DLR (4th) 211.

[415] *McMullen v Giles J Kennedy & Co* [2007] IEHC 263 at [13] of the judgment, [2008] IESC 69 at [23]. *Gallagher v Stanley* [1998] 2 IR 267 at 271; *McMullen v Carty*, unreported, Supreme Court, 27 January 1998 at 9; *Breathnach v Ireland (No.3)* [1993] 2 IR 458 at 471; *Wilson v Rastall* (1792) 4 Term Rep 753 at 759; *Wright v Mayer* (1801) 6 Ves Jr 281; *Minter v Priest* [1929] 1 KB 655, [1930] AC 558 at 579, [1930] All ER 431 at 439; *Schneider v Leigh* [1955] 2 All ER 173; *Geffen v Goodman Estate* [1991] 2 SCR 353, (1991) 81 DLR (4th) 211; *R. v Craig* [1975] 1 NZLR 597 at 598. In *Ventouris v Mountain* [1991] 3 All ER 472 at 475, Bingham LJ criticised the term "legal professional privilege" as "unhappy" because it falsely suggested a privilege enjoyed by the legal profession rather than the client. This aspect of the decision was cited with approval by

under a duty to tell the client that he or she can claim privilege[416] and to assert it on his or her behalf unless otherwise instructed.[417] In *McMullen v Giles J. Kennedy & Co*,[418] Murphy J cited the following extracts from *Halsbury's Laws of England*[419] as an accurate statement of the principles which apply in this jurisdiction:

> "The effect of the privilege is that neither the client, nor the solicitor without his consent, can be compelled to disclose the communications in the course of legal proceedings. The privilege is the client's, not the solicitor's, and accordingly the client may restrain the solicitor from making disclosure or may waive the privilege. Until the client has waived the privilege it is the solicitor's duty, if he is requested to make disclosure, to claim the privilege."

10–172   In *McMullen v Carty*,[420] Lynch J stressed that "[a] lawyer, whether solicitor or barrister, is under a duty not to communicate to any third party information entrusted to him by or on behalf of his client" and there is authority to the effect that, if a lawyer attempts to give evidence in breach of this duty, a court can of its own motion intervene to protect the interests of the client.[421] In subsequent proceedings arising out of the same events, *McMullen v Clancy (No. 2)*,[422] it was held that a lawyer called to give evidence against a former client in relation to matters covered by legal professional privilege should raise the issue of privilege, even in circumstances where it is clear that the privilege has been waived by the client.[423]

10–173   The fact that a claim of privilege can properly be asserted in respect of a document does not exempt it from the discovery process; all relevant documents over which privilege is claimed must be listed in Part II of the First Schedule to an affidavit of discovery.[424] While, in the ordinary course, an order for discovery is made and the party making discovery then asserts a claim of privilege over those documents listed

---

the House of Lords in *R. (Prudential Plc) v Special Comr of Income Tax* [2013] UKSC 1 at [22], [2013] 2 AC 185.

[416] *R. v Barton* [1972] 2 All ER 1192 at 1194; *Re Cross* [1981] 2 NZLR 673 at 677.

[417] *Bell v Smith* [1968] SCR 664, (1968) 68 DLR (2d) 751; *R. v Craig* [1975] 1 NZLR 597 at 598. Cf. *McMullen v Carty* unreported, Supreme Court, 27 January 1998. But see the comments of O'Donnell J in *Cullen v Wicklow County Manager* [2010] IESC 49 at [66], [2011] 1 IR 152, delivering the judgment of the Supreme Court, where he stated that a solicitor could not properly raise a claim of privilege without instructions. For a discussion of the duties owed by both solicitors and counsel to the Court in respect of discovery, see *Law Society of Ireland v Walker* [2007] 3 IR 581.

[418] [2007] IEHC 263 at [13] (reversed on appeal by the Supreme Court [2008] IESC 69).

[419] *Halsbury's Laws of England*, 4th edn (London: Butterworths, 1973) Vol. 44 at [74].

[420] Unreported, Supreme Court, 27 January 1998.

[421] *Beer v Ward* (1821) Jacob 77; *Stevens v Canada (Privy Council)* [1998] 4 FC 89, (1998) 161 DLR (4th) 85; *Geffen v Goodman Estate* [1991] 2 SCR 353 at 383–384, (1991) 81 DLR (4th) 211 at 232; *Bell v Smith* [1968] SCR 664, (1968) 68 DLR (2d) 751.

[422] [2005] IESC 10 at [60], [2005] 2 IR 445: (*per* McGuinness J in the High Court at 457; *per* Fennelly J in the Supreme Court at 468).

[423] The High Court rejected the contention that the relationship between a barrister instructed by a solicitor and a client is a fiduciary relationship (*per* McGuinness J at 460). The Supreme Court upheld the finding that no fiduciary relationship existed in this case, but observed that such a relationship could arise if a barrister came into possession of valudable confidential infromation in the course of the relationship and took advantage of it to his personal benefit (*per* Fennelly J at 469, [65]).

[424] *Keating v Radio Telefís Éireann* [2013] IESC 22 at [45]; *Bula Ltd (in receivership) v Crowley* [1991] 1 IR 220, [1990] ILRM 756; *Spring Grove Services Ltd v O'Callaghan* [2000] IEHC 62. See Delany and McGrath, *Civil Procedure in the Superior Courts*, 3rd edn (Dublin: Roundhall, 2012), Chap.10 section J, para.10–189 *et seq.*

in the privileged schedule,[425] it has been that, where discovery is sought of documents which are *prima facie* exempt from production as privileged documents, then the court should not make an order for discovery unless it is satisfied on proof that for some special reason that exemption must be lifted.[426] In *Irish Bank Resolution Corporation Ltd v Quinn*,[427] however, Kelly J made an Order requiring the defendants to attend for cross-examination and to make disclosure of documents, including documents in the possession of the defendants' former solicitors, notwithstanding the assertion of the defendants that legal professional privilege attached to these documents. He held that the assertion of legal privilege was not a basis for refusing to make the order sought in circumstances where it was otherwise justified, and stated that the question of privilege could be addressed during the course of the cross-examination. This issue was also considered by the Supreme Court in *Keating v Radio Telefís Éireann*,[428] where McKechnie J identified the applicable principles as follows:

> "…there is also no doubt but that on a discovery motion the court has an inherent jurisdiction to refuse the application on the basis that its entire purpose, namely access to relevant evidence capable of aiding or defeating a particular claim, can never be achieved in the face of a privilege plea which inevitably must succeed. Before holding however that the normal process can be abridged in this way and that privilege can ground a refusal for a discovery order as distinct from an inspection order, the court will have to be satisfied that such plea permits of no other possible result. For if it should or might, the court will not refuse to grant a discovery order on such grounds. To view the situation otherwise would be to conflate distinct steps in a two-tier process which involve addressing different questions and determining different issues. Accordingly, when the matter is raised at this stage of the process, the first enquiry must be to determine whether success on the plea is unavoidable. It is only if it is, that an affidavit as to documents will not be required."[429]

10–174   Where a claim of privilege is challenged, the onus is on the party asserting privilege to establish that the documents or materials are privileged.[430] However, once the party claiming privilege has discharged this onus, it falls on the party challenging the assertion of privilege to do so by evidence.[431] While a court may be satisfied simply from a description of a document that it is privileged, the court has such powers as are

---

[425] But see *Haughey v Moriarty* [1998] IEHC 6, where it was held that, in circumstances where a claim of privilege will almost certainly be challenged, a court may exceptionally, in the interests of expediency, adjudicate on the issue of privilege when dealing with the question of discovery.

[426] *Bula Ltd (in receivership) v Tara Mines* [1994] 1 IR 494 at 498 (where the documents were created in the course of the proceedings in which discovery was sought). In *Croke v Waterford Crystal Ltd* [2009] IEHC 158 at [11]–[13]. Birmingham J extended this principle to documents which, while not created in the course of the proceedings before the court, were nonetheless of a category that were *prima facie* privileged. But see *Doherty v North Western Health Board* [2005] IEHC 404, [2006] 1 ILRM 282, where Finnegan P suggested (*obiter*) that an order for discovery could be made in respect of documents, which included correspondence and attendances emanating from the defendant's solicitor.

[427] [2012] IEHC 510 at [71].

[428] [2013] IESC 22 at [46].

[429] This case concerned public interest privilege. However, the principles set out by McKechnie J appear to relate to all claims of privilege, including legal professional privilege. In *Thema International Fund Plc v HSBC Institutional Trust Services (Ireland)* [2011] IEHC 485 at [3.2], Clarke J stated that it is common in practice for claims of privilege to be determined before discovery is ordered where to do otherwise might lead to an entirely redundant exercise, *e.g.* a party being required to make discovery of documentation which is manifestly privileged. See also *Tir na nOg Projects Ireland Limited v Kerry County Council* [2008] IEHC 48 at [2.4].

[430] *University College Cork v ESB* [2014] IEHC 135 at [4]; *Ochre Ridge Limited v Cork Bonded Warehouses Limited* [2004] IEHC 160; *Irish Haemophilia Society v Lindsay* [2011] IEHC 240; *Waugh v British Railways Board* [1980] AC 521 at 541, [1979] 2 All ER 1169 at 1181.

[431] *Ochre Ridge Limited v Cork Bonded Warehouses Limited* [2004] IEHC 160; *Irish Haemophilia*

necessary to examine any relevant documents, irrespective of the wishes of the parties, in order to determine whether any communication is privileged from disclosure.[432] In practice, the court will often inspect documents in order to determine whether they are privileged.[433]

10–175 Where clients jointly retain a lawyer, privilege cannot be claimed *inter se* in respect of communications passing between either of them and the solicitor, but will be maintained against third parties unless waived jointly.[434] The courts have also recognised a species of legal professional privilege, termed "common interest privilege", where a joint retainer does not exist but nevertheless a person has a common interest with the client in the subject-matter of the privileged communication.

10–176 Privilege cannot, however, be invoked by persons who are strangers to the lawyer/client relationship. Thus, in *Schneider v Leigh*,[435] it was held that a doctor who had carried out an examination and written a medical report at the request of a defendant company could not assert litigation privilege in respect of that report in subsequent proceedings for libel taken against him. Similarly, in *R. v Jack*[436] it was held that the accused, who was charged with the murder of his wife, could not assert privilege on her behalf in respect of a conversation which she had had with her lawyer shortly before her death.

8. Waiver of Privilege

10–177 Privilege may be waived expressly or impliedly[437] and, again, the decision as to whether privilege is waived is that of the client.[438] In general, a lawyer does not have authority to waive privilege and cannot do so without the express consent of his or her client.[439] However, he or she may be regarded as having implied authority to waive privilege in the course of proceedings in accordance with the general principle that a lawyer has ostensible authority to conduct proceedings on behalf of the client as

---

Society v Lindsay [2001] IEHC 240. See Delany and McGrath, *Civil Procedure in the Superior Courts* 3rd edn (Dublin: Round Hall, 2012), Chap.10, section J, para.10–194.

[432] *Smurfit Paribas Bank Ltd v AAB Export Finance Ltd* [1990] 1 IR 469 at 480, [1990] ILRM 588 at 597 (*per* McCarthy J). In exceptional cases, the court may order the cross-examination of a deponent in relation to a claim of privilege (*Duncan v Governor of Portlaoise Prison* [1997] 1 IR 588 at 573, [1997] 2 ILRM 296 at 309).

[433] See, by way of example, *Hansfield Developments v Irish Asphalt* [2009] IEHC 90 and *Hansfield Developments v Irish Asphalt* [2009] IEHC 420. *Cf. Doherty v North Western Health Board* [2005] IEHC 404, [2006] 1 ILRM 282, where Finnegan P indicated that he was willing to peruse the documents with a view to determining whether or not they enjoyed privilege. However, it may not be appropriate for the trial judge to do so; see *Moorview Developments v First Active plc*, unreported, High Court, 3 July 2008 at 39.

[434] *The Sagheera* [1997] 1 Lloyd's Rep 160; *Re Konigsberg* [1989] 3 All ER 289; *R. v Dunbar* (1982) 138 DLR (3d) 221.

[435] [1955] 2 All ER 173.

[436] (1992) 70 CCC (3d) 67.

[437] *Fyffes Plc v DCC Plc* [2005] IESC 3 at [25], [2005] 1 IR 59 at 67, [2005] 1 ILRM 357 at 364; *McMullen v Carty*, unreported, Supreme Court, 27 January 1998 at 9.

[438] *Gallagher v Stanley* [1998] 2 IR 267 at 271; *McMullen v Carty*, unreported, Supreme Court, 27 January 1998 at 9; *Breathnach v Ireland (No.3)* [1993] 2 IR 458 at 471; *Century Insurance Office Ltd v Falloon* [1971] NI 234 at 235; *Minter v Priest* [1929] 1 KB 655, [1930] AC 558, 579, [1930] All ER 431 at 439.

[439] *McMullen v Carty*, unreported, Supreme Court, 27 January 1998 at 9; *Porter v Scott* [1979] NI 6 at 17.

he or she thinks fit.[440] Privilege will be taken to have been waived where a privileged document or its contents are disclosed by a lawyer to an adverse party, unless it is expressly reserved.[441]

(a) Partial or selective waiver

10–178   Although privilege may be waived in whole or in part, a person intending to make a partial waiver only may, nonetheless, be taken to have impliedly waived privilege in the whole of a document where unfairness might result from partial disclosure.[442] Thus, in *Great Atlantic Insurance v Home Insurance*,[443] it was held that the introduction of part of a document into evidence waived privilege in relation to the whole document, as a party is not entitled to disclose only those parts of a document that are to his advantage. As a practical matter, this means that "if a document is privileged then privilege must be asserted, if at all, to the whole document unless the document deals with separate subject matters so that the document can in effect be divided into two separate and distinct documents each of which is complete."[444]

10–179   Similarly, although waiver of privilege in one of a series of communications will not, generally, be construed as waiver of privilege in all,[445] a party will not be permitted to waive privilege in such a partial and selective manner that unfairness or misunderstanding may result.[446] The rule was stated as follows by the Court of Appeal in *Paragon Finance v Freshfields*,[447] where Bingham CJ stated that:

> "A client expressly waives his legal professional privilege when he elects to disclose communications which the privilege would entitle him not to disclose. Where the disclosure is partial, issues may arise on the scope of the waiver. Practical difficulties occur in determining such issues ... But the law is clear. While there is no rule that a party who waives privilege in relation to one communication is taken to waive privilege in relation to all, a party may not waive privilege in such a partial and selective manner that unfairness or misunderstanding may result."

---

[440] *Great Atlantic Insurance Co v Home Insurance Co* [1981] 2 All ER 485; *Causton v Mann Egerton* [1974] 1 WLR 162 at 167; *Porter v Scott* [1979] NI 6 at 17.

[441] *Porter v Scott* [1979] NI 6; *Caldbeck v Boon* (1872) IR 7 CL 32. Privilege will be lost at the point when the document is handed over and it is not necessary that the document actually be opened in court (*Porter v Scott*).

[442] *Great Atlantic Insurance Co. v Home Insurance Co* [1981] 2 All ER 485; *AG for the Northern Territory v Maurice* (1986) 161 CLR 475; *Argyle Brewery Pty Ltd v Darling Harbourside (Sydney) Pty Ltd* (1993) 120 ALR 537; *Equiticorp Industries Group Ltd v Hawkins* [1990] 2 NZLR 175.

[443] [1981] 2 All ER 485.

[444] [1981] 2 All ER 485 at 490. But see *Hansfield Developments v Irish Asphalt Ltd* [2009] IEHC 420 at [77], where McKechnie J upheld a claim of common interest privilege and held that partial disclosure did not give rise to any unfairness in circumstances where documents were heavily redacted, in order to black out sections of the documents which were subject to privilege. See also *Prendergast v McLoughlin* [2008] IEHC 296, [2010] 3 IR 445, where Clarke J held that, where it was clear that the dominant purpose of a document was the obtaining of legal assistance rather than legal advice, privilege should not be asserted, but the party making discovery is entitled to redact any subsidiary portion of the document which involves the seeking or giving of legal advice.

[445] See, *contra*, *Smith v Smith* [1958] OWN 135.

[446] *Hellard v Irwin & Mitchell* [2012] All ER (D) 71; *Nea Karteria Maritime Co Limited v Atlantic and Great Lakes Steamship Corporation and Cape Breton Development Corporation and Others* (No.2) [1981] Comm LR 138, *Paragon Finance Plc v Freshfields* [1999] 1 WLR 1183 at 1188; *R. v Secretary of State for Transport, ex parte Factortame* (1997) 9 Admin LR 591 at 598.

[447] [1999] 1 WLR 1183 at 1188.

10–180   The rationale for this rule was explained in similar terms by Clarke J in *Moorview Developments v First Active plc,*[448] where he stated that "a serious risk of injustice would exist if a party were entitled to cherry pick some but not all out of a connected series of privileged documents for disclosure".

10–181   In *Hansfield Developments v Irish Asphalt,*[449] it was accepted that a party may waive privilege over documents by virtue of the selective disclosure of documents of a similar type. Having reviewed the authorities, both here and in other common law jurisdictions, McKechnie J held that[450]:

> "It is ... clear that a party may not make selective disclosure with regards to a group of documents of a similar nature. The question which arises in this case is whether the documents over which the plaintiffs still claim privilege are of such a similar nature to the ones which they have produced or expressly waived privilege over that this might give rise to unfairness by presenting a partisan or biased view of their case to the Court and the other party."

10–182   In that case, documents over which a claim of common interest privilege had been asserted were disclosed on foot of a written judgment of McGovern J, in which he concluded that communications between the plaintiffs and a third party (HomeBond) were not privileged.[451] However, the plaintiffs maintained a claim of privilege over a number of documents falling within this category of documents. McKechnie J accepted that there were justifiable differences between the disclosed documents and those over which privilege was maintained in circumstances where the latter were comprised of drafts which involved consultation by the plaintiffs with their legal advisors during a series of meetings which, unlike the documents produced for inspection, were never sent to any other party. He also accepted that the disclosure was not such that, as a result of its partial or selective nature, would mislead the court.[452]

(b) Deployment of privileged materials in litigation

10–183   In a series of decisions, the Irish courts have considered the extent to which privilege will be taken to be waived where privileged material is deployed in proceedings.[453] In *Hannigan v DPP,*[454] Hardiman J held that the status of a document, from the point of view of privilege or immunity from disclosure, changes once it has been referred to in pleadings or affidavits. He adopted the following statement of this general rule in Matthews & Malek, *Discovery*:

---

[448] [2009] IEHC 214 at [3.14].
[449] [2009] IEHC 420 at [55].
[450] [2009] IEHC 420 at [61].
[451] [2009] IEHC 90. See *British American Tobacco (Investments) Ltd v United States of America* [2004] All ER (D) 605 at [36]–[37], where it was held that partial or selective disclosure could not be said to have occurred in circumstances where documents were disclosed by a party under compulsion, as a result of which no election to disclose was made, either partial or comprehensive.
[452] [2009] IEHC 420 at [85].
[453] The English courts adopt the same approach. *Paragon Finance Plc v Freshfields* [1999] 1 WLR 1183 at 1188; *R. v Secretary of State for Transport, ex parte Factortame* (1997) 9 Admin LR 591 at 598; *Great Atlantic Insurance v Home Insurance* [1981] 1 All ER 485 at 492; *Nea Karteria Maritime Co Ltd v Atlantic and Great Lakes Steamship Corp (No.2)* [1981] Com LR 138 at 139; *Burnell v British Transport Commission* [1955] 3 All ER 822, [1956] 1 QB 187 at 190. For an example of a case where the English courts concluded that privileged material had not been deployed, see *Digicel (St. Lucia) v Cable and Wireless Plc* [2009] All ER (D) 44.
[454] [2001] IESC 10, [2001] 1 IR 378 (*sub nom. TH v DPP* [2002] 1 ILRM 48) (public interest privilege in document waived in circumstances where it was summarised in an affidavit), at 383.

"The general rule is that where privileged material is deployed in court in an interlocutory application, privilege in that and any associated material is waived."[455]

10–184   Hardiman J observed that the basis of this rule is discussed in *Nea Karteria Maritime Company Ltd v Atlantic and Great Lakes Steamships Corporation (No. 2)*,[456] where its rationale was explained by Mustill J as follows:

"the principle underlying the rule of practice ... is that, where a party is deploying in court material which would otherwise be privileged, the opposite party and the court must have an opportunity of satisfying themselves that what the party has chosen to release from privilege represents the whole of the material relevant to the issue in question. To allow an individual item to be plucked out of context would be to risk injustice through its real weight or meaning being misunderstood."[457]

10–185   The document in issue in *Hannigan v DPP* was a letter, which was referred to in an affidavit. Hardiman J concluded that, in circumstances where the contents of the letter were summarised and it was relied upon as evidence of the intention of the DPP as of the date on which it was written, the document had been deployed and, as a result, privilege had been waived.

10–186   The cases show that the question as to whether a document has deployed tends to be very fact-specific. In general terms, however, reference to the contents of a privileged communication in a pleading or affidavit will waive privilege, whereas mere reference to its existence will not do so.[458] Thus, in *Egan v O'Toole*,[459] the Supreme Court upheld the finding of the High Court that documents to which reference were made in an affidavit were not deployed, as they were merely referred to in the narrative of events. A similar conclusion was arrived at by Kelly J in *Ahern v Mahon*,[460] where the deployment relied upon was a statement read into the record of the public hearings of the Mahon Tribunal, in which the applicant made reference in general terms to "banking evidence" and "banking documentation" considered by an expert witness. Kelly J observed that the bank statements to which reference was made had been circulated by the tribunal itself, and that two written reports had been prepared by the expert in question. In light of this, he concluded that the statements made by the applicant

---

[455] Hardiman J adopted this statement of the law from Matthews and Malek, *Discovery*, 1st edn (London: Sweet & Maxwell, 1992) at para.9.15. For the discussion of deployment in the current edition, see Matthews and Malek, *Disclosure*, 4th edn (London: Sweet & Maxwell, 2012) at [16.21].

[456] [1981] Com LR 139.

[457] The current edition of Matthews and Malek, *Disclosure*, 4th edn (London: Sweet & Maxwell, 2012), at [16.21] identifies the general rule in relation to deployment by reference to this dictum. The authors go on to state that: "The key word here is 'deploying'. A mere reference to a privileged document in an affidavit does not of itself amount to a waiver of privilege and this is so even if the document is being relied on for some purpose, for reliance itself is not the test. Instead, the test is whether the *contents* of the document are being relied on, rather than its *effect*." Matthews and Malek, *Disclosure*, 4th edn (London: Sweet & Maxwell, 2012) at [16.21].

[458] *Egan v O'Toole* [2005] IESC 53; *Tromso Sparebank v Beirne* [1989] ILRM 257; *Buttes Gas & Oil Co v Hammer (No.3)* [1981] QB 223, [1980] 3 All ER 475; *Tate & Lyle International Ltd v Government Trading Corp* [1984] LS Gaz R 3341; *Lac La Ronge Indian Board v Canada* (1996) 6 CPC (4th) 110. *Cf. R. v Campbell* [1999] 1 SCR 565, (1999) 171 DLR (4th) 193. This is consistent with the position as set out in the Rules of the Superior Courts. Ord.31, r.15 makes provision for a party to be required to produce for inspection a document referred to in its pleadings, but that party is entitled to object to its production (Ord.31, r.17).

[459] [2005] IESC 53.

[460] [2008] IEHC 119 at [114], [2008] 4 IR 704 at 729, [2009] 1 ILRM 458 at 480.

did not amount to deployment, so as to waive litigation privilege in communications between the applicant's lawyers and the expert witness in question.

10–187   The circumstances in which a party may lose privilege as a result of the deployment or partial disclosure of documents was considered by the Supreme Court in *Fyffes Plc v DCC Plc*,[461] where Fennelly J referred to the "well-established rule regarding privilege", that "a party who seeks to deploy his privileged documents by partially disclosing them or summarising their effect so as to gain an advantage over his opponent in the action in which they are privileged, runs a serious risk of losing the privilege." The issue in that case, however, was not the deployment of the documents in the civil proceedings before the Court, but rather the partial disclosure of the documents to a third party for use in a criminal investigation.

10–188   In *Shell E & P Ireland v McGrath (No. 2)*,[462] attendance dockets were inadvertently included in a book of inter partes correspondence in an exhibit to an affidavit. Disjointed excerpts from the attendances were then published in the *Irish Times*. The defendants contended that the attendance dockets had been deployed by the plaintiff, as a result of which privilege had been waived. Smyth J concluded that there was an inadvertent disclosure of the attendance dockets, which was patent to any recipient having any knowledge of legal procedure. He accepted that neither the plaintiff nor its solicitor was aware as to how the material came into the possession of the *Irish Times*. In these circumstances, he concluded that there was no question that the attendance dockets were deployed by either the plaintiff or its solicitors. However, Smyth J accepted that, "[i]f a client discloses a privilege communication deliberately to the public or a significant part of it confidentiality and consequently the entitlement to claim privilege would be lost and the party could well be taken as having waived the privilege." [463]

10–189   The question of waiver through deployment was considered again by Clarke J in *Byrne v Shannon Foynes Port Company*,[464] a case in which a large volume of documents over which privilege could have been claimed were disclosed in the non-privileged schedule to the affidavit of discovery in error. Clarke J concluded that the first defendant had waived privilege in the documents, as a result of which an issue arose as to whether the plaintiffs were entitled to disclosure of additional documentation in respect of which privilege was claimed and which might be said to be connected to the documents disclosed. It was held that, where a document is deployed in an interlocutory application or at trial, the party concerned will be taken to have waived privilege to that document, and also to any other documents which are connected to the document in question in such a manner that it would be unjust to allow the document in question to be deployed without also disclosing the content of the other documentation concerned.[465] However, the document in question must be "deployed"; mere reference to a privileged document in an affidavit does not of itself amount to a waiver of privilege, even if the document referred to is being relied on for

---

[461] [2005] IESC 3 at [40], [2005] 1 IR 59 at 72, [2005] 1 ILRM 357 at 368–369.
[462] [2006] IEHC 409, [2007] 2 IR 574, [2007] 1 ILRM 544.
[463] [2006] IEHC 409 at [28], [2007] 2 IR 574 at 585, [2007] 1 ILRM 544 at 555.
[464] [2007] IEHC 315, [2008] 1 IR 814, [2008] 1 ILRM 529.
[465] [2007] IEHC 315 at [41], [2008] 1 IR 814 at 826, [2008] 1 ILRM 529 at 541.

some purpose.[466] Clarke J identified the test as whether the contents of the document are being relied upon[467]:

"… the test is as to whether the party concerned has placed reliance on the content of the document concerned. It does not seem to me that the mere disclosure of the existence of the document without claiming privilege in respect of it in an affidavit of discovery can be said to amount to the placing of reliance on the document in the proceedings so as to, properly speaking, suggest that the document has been deployed. Obviously, if the document is relied on as to its contents in an interlocutory application, or *a fortiori*, at trial, then it follows that it has been deployed."

10–190 He proceeded to consider the extent to which a party may be required to disclose other documents which are connected to the document or documents over which privilege has been waived. Clarke J. rejected the contention that the fact that one or more privileged documents are deployed necessarily leads to the conclusion that all other privileged documents in the hands of the party concerned must be taken to have privilege waived, stating[468]:

"It cannot be said that the mere fact that one privileged document was disclosed and relied on would make it unjust to permit the party concerned to maintain a claim of privilege in respect of wholly unconnected documents. The test, in my view, must be as to whether there is a sufficient *nexus* between the document deployed and the document or documents whose disclosure is sought, so as to render it unjust to permit the one to be deployed without disclosing the content of the others."

10–191 In circumstances where no reliance had been placed by the first defendant on any of the documents over which privilege had been waived, it was held that the documents had not been deployed.[469] However, Clarke J stated that, in circumstances where documents over which privilege could have been claimed are disclosed in the affidavit of discovery without claiming privilege, but are not deployed, the question as to whether the disclosing party intends to rely on the documents should be clarified in order that the court may consider whether further discovery is required.[470]

10–192 The general principle that a party may, by its pleadings or by deployment in court, waive privilege over a document, was confirmed by the Supreme Court in *Redfern v O'Mahony*,[471] where Finnegan J stated that[472]:

"Where a party deploys in court material which would otherwise be privileged the other party and the court must have an opportunity of satisfying themselves that what the party has chosen to release from privilege represents the whole of the material relevant to the issue in question. To allow an individual item to be plucked out of context would be to risk injustice through its real weight or meaning being misunderstood."

---

[466] [2007] IEHC 315 at [39], [2008] 1 IR 814 at 826, [2008] 1 ILRM 529 at 540. Citing *Marubeni Corporation v Alafouzos* [1988] CLY 2841.

[467] [2007] IEHC 315 at [40], [2008] 1 IR 814 at 826, [2008] 1 ILRM 529 at 540.

[468] [2007] IEHC 315 at [42], [2008] 1 IR 814 at 827, [2008] 1 ILRM 529 at 541.

[469] See *Moorview Developments v First Active plc*, unreported, High Court, 3 July 2008 at [6], where Clarke J affirmed the general principle that the inclusion of a document over which privilege could have been claimed in an affidavit of discovery does not, of itself, amount to such deployment of the documents in the course of the proceedings as would entitle the other party to seek disclosure of further connection documents. *Cf. Ryanair Limited v Murrays Europcar Ltd* [2009] IEHC 306.

[470] *Moorview Developments v First Active plc*, unreported, High Court, 3 July 2008 at [55]. Clarke J stated that it is not appropriate for this question to be left over to the trial of the action; the question as to whether the disclosing party intends to rely on the documents should be clarified as soon as their existence is disclosed without a claim of privilege.

[471] [2009] IESC 18, [2009] 3 IR 583.

[472] [2009] IESC 18 at [28], [2009] 3 IR 583 at 595.

10-193 It was held, however, that deployment will only arise where the contents and effect of the legal advice are disclosed; it does not arise where only the fact that legal advice was obtained in relied upon.[473]

10-194 In *Ryanair Ltd v Murrays Europcar Ltd*,[474] Cooke J followed the decision of Clarke J in *Byrne v Shannon Foynes*, where it was held that a mere reference to a privileged document is not sufficient to treat it as deployed, even if some reliance is placed on it. He concluded that the test in this regard is whether the party concerned has placed some reliance on the *content* of the document concerned.[475] It was held that the plaintiff had not deployed an expert report to which reference was made in an affidavit, notwithstanding the fact that the affidavit stated that the report was strongly supportive of the plaintiffs' case. The affidavit referred to the existence of strong supportive evidence from an expert in order to rebut the accusation that the plaintiffs' claim was obstructive or vexatious. Cooke J concluded, therefore, that the report was merely referred to in corroboration of the plaintiff's intention to prosecute the claim, as a result of which privilege had not been waived.

(c) Limited disclosure

10-195 As seen above, the protection afforded by privilege is predicated on confidentiality[476] and, therefore, if a client discloses a privileged communication to the public or a significant part of it, confidentiality and the consequent entitlement to claim privilege will be lost and a party will be taken to have waived privilege.[477] However, more limited disclosure to persons not including the adverse party may not be taken as waiver. It has, thus, been held that privilege will not be lost where the communication is disseminated to third parties who share a common interest in the subject-matter of the communication with the client,[478] or even where a copy is sent to or shown to a third party for a limited and specific purpose unconnected to the prosecution of the proceedings.[479]

---

[473] [2009] IESC 18 at [33], [2009] 3 IR 583 at 596.

[474] [2009] IEHC 306.

[475] [2009] IEHC 306 at [7].

[476] See *Woori Bank v KDB Ireland Ltd* [2005] IEHC 451 at [24], where it was held that confidentiality is an essential prerequisite to a claim of litigation privilege.

[477] *Bula Ltd v Crowley*, unreported, High Court, 8 March 1991; *Chandris Lines Ltd v Wilson & Horton Ltd* [1981] 2 NZLR 600.

[478] *Bula Ltd v Crowley*, unreported, High Court, Murphy J, 8 March 1991; *Buttes Gas and Oil Co v Hammer (No.3)* [1981] QB 223, [1980] 3 All ER 475; *Gotha City v Sotheby's* [1998] 1 WLR 114.

[479] *Woori Bank v KDB Ireland Limited* [2005] IEHC 451, at [15]; *Hansfield Developments v Irish Asphalt* [2009] IEHC 420 at [40]; *Fyffes v DCC Plc* [2005] IESC 3 at [40]–[42], [2005] 1 IR 59 at 72–73, [2005] 1 ILRM 357 at 369; *B v Auckland District Law Society* [2003] UKPC 38, [2003] 2 AC 736 (disclosure of privileged documents in an investigation into a complaint to the Law Society); *Wilson v Liquid Packaging Ltd* [1979] NI 165 at 169 (copy of a witness statement which had come into being in anticipation of litigation had been sent to the plaintiffs' MP to see whether the plaintiffs could obtain redress by political means rather than by litigation); *British Coal Corp v Dennis Rye Ltd (No.2)* [1988] 3 All ER 816 and *Downey v Murray* [1988] NI 600 (documents disclosed in accordance with party's duty to assist in the prosecution of criminal proceedings); *Goldman v Hesper* [1988] 1 WLR 1238 at 1245 (disclosure of privileged documents in the course of taxation of costs); *Harbour Inn Seafood Ltd v Switzerland General Insurance Co Ltd* [1990] 2 NZLR 381 at 384; *C-C Bottlers Ltd v Lion Nathan Ltd* [1993] 2 NZLR 445. *Cf. Berezovsky v Hine* [2011] EWCA Civ 1089.

10–196   *A fortiori*, privilege will continue to subsist where the communication is disclosed on the condition that confidentiality be maintained.[480] Thus, in *Downey v Murray*,[481] a copy of a statement made by the plaintiff had been sent to the police subject to the condition that it would not form part of any police report or be communicated to any other person. It was held that the plaintiff was entitled to claim privilege for the document because the effect of sending a copy of the document to the police was not a general waiver. The plaintiff's solicitors were entitled to impose a condition on the use of the copy statement and the waiver of the privilege was limited to the purposes specified by them.

10–197   The Supreme Court emphatically rejected the contention that any disclosure of privileged materials to a third party will automatically result in a loss of privilege in *Fyffes Plc v DCC Plc*,[482] which concerned the disclosure by the defendants of privileged expert reports to the Stock Exchange with a view to persuading the DPP not to prosecute them for insider trading. The reports were made available for review on a confidential basis by way of a "confidential data room", and remained physically in the possession of and under the control of the defendants. It was agreed by the Stock Exchange that, once it had communicated its views to the DPP, any notes made during the review would be destroyed. Fennelly J rejected the contention that, in order to avoid the loss of the privilege, any communication to a third party had to be made in pursuance of a public duty.[483] Having considered the decision of the Australian courts in *Goldberg v Ng*,[484] where Clarke J denied the existence of any "universal rule that the disclosure of documents produced for the sole purpose of seeking legal advice or litigation to a stranger to that litigation constitutes a waiver of the privilege in that document", Fennelly J stated[485]:

> "I am quite satisfied that this is a correct statement of the law and that it undermines the first basic proposition advanced on behalf of the plaintiff. In the absence of a general principle that communication to any third party will lose the privilege unless it is made in pursuit of some public duty, no legal basis has been advanced for its loss in the circumstances of the present case, when disclosure was made for a particular purpose and subject to express conditions as to confidentiality."

10–198   In *Fyffes*, the Supreme Court was invited to follow a line of Australian authority commencing with *Goldberg v Ng*,[486] which established a principle that a claim to privilege might be disallowed where a party had made voluntary disclosure of privileged documents (otherwise than in the proceedings in which the claim of privilege is asserted) in circumstances where it would be unfair to deprive the opposing party

---

[480]   *Woori Bank v KDB Ireland Limited* [2005] IEHC 451 at [15]; *Goldberg v Ng* (1994) 33 NSWLR 639 at 651. See *Fyffes v DCC Plc* [2005] IESC 3 at [40], [2005] 1 IR 59, [2005] 1 ILRM 357, where Fennelly J stated that, in considering whether partial disclosure of a document to a third party gives rise to a loss of privilege, stipulations of confidentiality will be a material factor, and will negative all cases of express waiver and most cases of implied waiver.

[481]   [1988] NI 600. Cited with approval in *Woori Bank v KDB Ireland Limited* [2005] IEHC 451.

[482]   [2005] IESC 3 at [28], [2005] 1 IR 59 at 68, [2005] 1 ILRM 357 at 365.

[483]   [2005] IESC 3 at [29], [2005] 1 IR 59 at 69, [2005] 1 ILRM 357 at 365. He considered *British Coal Corp v Dennis Rye Ltd (No.2)* [1988] 3 All ER 816 and *Downey v Murray* [1988] NI 600, both cases in which documents were disclosed to a prosecuting authority, and concluded that they did not lay down any general principle that, in order for the privilege to remain intact, the communication had to be to a public body in pursuance of a public duty.

[484]   (1994) 33 NSWLR 639 at 676.

[485]   [2005] IESC 3 at [29], [2005] 1 IR 59, [2005] 1 ILRM 357.

[486]   (1994) 33 NSWLR 639 at 676.

in the litigation of equal access to them. Commenting on this development in the law, Fennelly J observed that[487]:

"Up to this point in time and, apart for the Australian jurisprudence, it seems clear that the circumstances in which privilege is lost are limited to the effects of some voluntary act of the person claiming it. An extreme instance is fraudulent behaviour. More commonly, the voluntary act is considered as amounting to waiver. It is probable that the application of waiver proceeds from some notion of fairness, but it is certainly not the same thing. As will be seen, even in the Australian case, fairness comes into play only when there has been some voluntary act of disclosure."

10–199   Fennelly J did not accept that a claim to privilege could be disallowed merely on grounds of unfairness.[488] Having considered the case law from other common law jurisdictions in relation to partial or selective waiver of privilege,[489] and the decision of the Supreme Court in *Hannigan v DPP*[490], he summarised the principles which govern the loss of privilege through disclosure in this jurisdiction as follows:[491]

"I would conclude ... that the well-established rule regarding privilege, whether including a notion of fairness or not, goes no further than the proposition that a party who seeks to deploy his privileged documents by partially disclosing them or summarising their effect so as to gain an advantage over his opponent in the action in which they are privileged, runs a serious risk of losing the privilege. I do not deny that the partial disclosure which has that effect might, in some circumstances, be made to a third party, but it would have to be for the purpose of gaining an advantage in that action. I would add that express stipulations of confidentiality, such as in the present case, will necessarily be a material factor. They will obviously negative any claim of express waiver and most cases of implied waiver."

10–200   Fennelly J stated that, while the civil proceedings and the criminal investigations concerned precisely the same subject matter and the basis of liability in both flowed from the same provision of the Companies Act 1990, the criminal and civil proceedings were entirely distinct. The decision of the DPP in relation to the institution of criminal proceedings would not have any effect on the civil proceedings, and it was not an advantage which gave rise to any disadvantage on the part of the plaintiff in the civil action. It was held, therefore, that there had been no implied or imputed waiver of privilege on the part of the defendants.

10–201   McCracken J arrived at the same conclusion, but focused in particular on the policy considerations underpinning the privilege, stating that, "in considering the question of waiver it is important to remember at all times that privilege does not exist merely for the protection of a party, but also exists to ensure the proper administration of justice". He observed that there may be many situations in which it is desirable, or even mandatory, that privileged documents be disclosed to a third party for a limited purpose, and stated that[492]:

"If such disclosures are to be governed solely or primarily by a concept of fairness ... each case is going to be looked at subjectively according to its own particular facts without any

---

[487] [2005] IESC 3 at [31], [2005] 1 IR 59 at 69, [2005] 1 ILRM 357 at 366.
[488] See also *Redfern v O'Mahony* [2009] IESC 18 at [29], [2009] 3 IR 583; *Farm Assist (in liquidation) v Secretary of State for the Environment, Food and Rural Affairs* [2008] All ER (D) 124 at [48]; and *Paragon Finance v Freshfields* [1999] 1 WLR 1183, 1194.
[489] Wigmore, *Evidence in Trials at Common Law* (Boston: Little, Brown, 1961) Vol.8, para.2327; *Attorney General (N.T.) v Maurice* (1986) 69 ALR 31; and *Great Atlantic Insurance Co. v Home Insurance Co.* [1981]2 All ER 485.
[490] [2001] 1 IESC 10, [2001] 1 IR 378.
[491] [2005] IESC 3 at [40], [2005] 1 IR 59 at 72, [2005] 1 ILRM 357 at 368–369.
[492] [2005] IESC 3 at [65], [2005] 1 IR 59 at 84, [2005] 1 ILRM 357 at 379.

particular regard to a general rule. In my view this is highly undesirable. While one cannot lay down absolute rules in matters such as this, it is essential that there should be as great a degree of certainty as possible, so that parties can reasonably foresee the result of actions of disclosure taken by them. Were that not so, it is possible that serious injustices could occur because a party might fail to make a disclosure due to the fear that it might lose the benefit of a legal privilege to which it was entitled."

10–202   McCracken J did not, however, rule out the possibility that there may be cases in which the question of fairness may arise, in which case "the general rule that a disclosure for a limited purpose does not amount to a waiver may have to give way where a serious injustice might result."[493]

10–203   The question of limited disclosure was considered again by the Supreme Court in *Redfern v O'Mahony*,[494] where the Court confirmed that there is no universal rule that the disclosure of privileged documents to a third party constitutes a waiver of privilege; privilege will not be lost where there is limited disclosure for a particular purpose, or to parties with a common interest. The issue for determination in that case was whether the plaintiff had waived privilege over counsel's opinion, which had been shared with the board of the management company of the shopping centre and the solicitor for South Dublin County Council. It was accepted that disclosure to the management company would potentially constitute disclosure to all of the lessees in the shopping centre, and that each member of South Dublin County Council could request sight of the opinion. Accordingly, the disclosure represented a very wide disclosure. Finnegan J, delivering judgment for the Supreme Court, accepted that privilege may be waived by disclosure and stated that, if a document comes into the public domain, privilege will be lost. He concluded, however, that the disclosure which had taken place was limited and was to parties having a common interest with the plaintiff in the proposed development of the car park, stating that "[s]uch disclosure does not evince an intention to waive privilege".[495] It was held, therefore, that the plaintiff had not waived privileged, notwithstanding the relatively wide disclosure which had taken place.

10–204   The principles identified by the Supreme Court in *Redfern* and *Fyffes* were applied by McKechnie J in *Hansfield Developments v Irish Asphalt Ltd*,[496] where he held that, when waiver by disclosure is in issue, the factors to be considered by the Court include the intention with which a document was supplied, the purpose and breadth of disclosure, and the relationship between the issuer and the recipient.[497] There is no general rule that any disclosure to a third party will lead to a loss of privilege; "whilst disclosure can defeat privilege it is not bound to do so".[498] One of the issues which arose for consideration in *Hansfield Developments v Irish Asphalt Ltd* was the extent to which the provision of documents to a public relations firm gave rise to a waiver of privilege. McKechnie J held that, where documents are provided to a public relations

---

[493]   [2005] IESC 3 at [66], [2005] 1 IR 59 at 85, [2005] 1 ILRM 357 at 379.
[494]   [2009] IESC 18, [2009] 3 IR 583.
[495]   [2009] 3 IR 583 at [17], [2009] IESC 18 at 590.
[496]   [2009] IEHC 420 at [38]–[40].
[497]   [2009] IEHC 420 at [38].
[498]   [2009] IEHC 420 at [39]. See *British American Tobacco (Investments) Ltd v United States of America* [2004] All ER (D) 605 at [34]–[35], where it was held that limited disclosure in accordance with a foreign consent order did not give rise to a waiver of privilege. The court concluded that, while the order was described as a consent order, the plaintiff had in fact objected. It was held that there an element of compulsion, as a result of which the plaintiff had not voluntarily expressly or impliedly waived privilege.

company for a limited and specific purpose, and on the understanding that they are being provided on a confidential basis, their disclosure will not necessarily give rise to a waiver of privilege. However, whether the communications are privileged, or whether their disclosure will give rise to a waiver of privilege, will turn on the specific facts of each case.[499]

10–205 The same general principle was extracted from *Fyffes Plc v DCC Plc* by Laffoy J in *Martin v Legal Aid Board*,[500] where it was held that the disclosure of documentation to a third party for a limited purpose did not constitute a general waiver of the privilege. She concluded that the disclosure of privileged information by solicitors to authorised officers of the Legal Aid Board for the limited purpose of enabling the Board to discharge its statutory functions could not result in the loss of legal professional privilege.[501]

10–206 Similarly in *Woori Bank v KDB Ireland Limited*,[502] Finlay Geoghegan J held that the disclosure of privileged information for the purposes of making a criminal complaint in another jurisdiction did not give rise to a waiver of privilege. The documents over which a claim of litigation privilege was asserted had been disclosed by the plaintiff to the Public Prosecutor's Office ("PPO") in Korea, where the plaintiff laid a criminal complaint against an employee of the defendant arising out of the transactions the subject matter of the proceedings. While the documents had been requested by the PPO, the plaintiff was not under a legal obligation, as a matter of Korean law, to disclose them. However, it was in its interests to do so, as certain adverse consequences may have followed if the request was refused. Having considered the Supreme Court decision in *Fyffes Plc v DCC Plc*, Finlay Geoghegan J held that the existence or absence of a legal obligation was not determinative in considering whether such disclosure as had occurred had given rise to a waiver of privilege.[503] A far more significant factor was the extent to which steps were taken to preserve the confidentiality of the documents when they were submitted to the PPO.

10–207 In *Woori Bank*, the defendant contended that the purpose of the plaintiff in making the criminal complaint in Korea was to gain an advantage over the defendant in the Irish proceedings. It was further contended that the plaintiff was seeking to rely, in the Irish proceedings, on an admission made by an employee of the defendant in the criminal proceedings in Korea. On the basis of the evidence before the Court, it was held that the partial disclosure of the documents to the PPO in Korea was not made for the purpose of gaining an advantage in the Irish proceedings, as a result of which such limited disclosure as had occurred did not give rise to a waiver of the privilege. Finlay Geoghegan J observed, however, that the matter might be reopened in the event that the plaintiff sought to rely on the alleged admission obtained in the criminal proceedings.[504]

---

[499] Adopting the analysis of the Australian courts in *Spotless Group Ltd v Premier Building & Consulting Group Pty Ltd* (2006) 16 VR 1. McKechnie J concluded that the documents in issue in this case were not created for the dominant purpose of litigation, as a result of which they were not subject to litigation privilege and the question of waiver did not arise. [2009] IEHC 420 at [88]–[89].
[500] [2007] IEHC 76, [2007] 2 IR 759.
[501] [2007] IEHC 76 at [42], [2007] 2 IR 759 at 779.
[502] [2005] IEHC 451.
[503] [2005] IEHC 451 at [14].
[504] [2005] IEHC 451 at [19].

(e) Communications put in issue by the client

10–208 Considerations of fairness dictate that if a client puts the contents of privileged communications in issue, then he or she will be taken to have impliedly waived privilege to the extent necessary for a fair disposition of the issue. Thus, implied waiver will occur where a client pleads that he or she acted in good faith reliance on particular legal advice,[505] where he or she disputes the authority of his or her legal advisers to enter into a settlement agreement on his or her behalf,[506] or where he or she sues his or her legal advisers.[507]

10–209 The principles applicable where solicitors and/or barristers are being sued were reviewed in *McMullen v Carty*.[508] The appellant instituted proceedings against the respondent firm of solicitors for negligence arising out of the conduct and disposal of previous proceedings brought by him. At the trial in the High Court, evidence was given by the senior counsel briefed by the respondents in the previous proceedings, and on appeal it was contended by the appellant that this evidence had been given in breach of legal professional privilege. Lynch J, delivering the judgment of the Supreme Court, explained the basis of the waiver as follows:

> "When a client sues his solicitor for damages for alleged negligence arising out of the conduct of previous litigation against third parties and especially as in this case arising out of the settlement of such previous litigation the client thereby puts in issue all the communications as between the solicitor and the client and the barrister and the client and also as between the barrister and the solicitor relevant to the settlement of the case and thereby impliedly waives the privilege of confidentiality. … It would be manifestly unjust and wrong if the solicitor was precluded by the rule of confidentiality from making his case before the court."[509]

10–210 He went on to say that the same principles applied where the barrister was sued and where the solicitor alone was sued. Thus, the Senior Counsel in question had not breached legal professional privilege (which had been impliedly waived) by giving evidence against the client.[510] It can be seen, therefore, that it is the fact that

---

[505] *R. v Campbell* [1999] 1 SCR 565, (1999) 171 DLR (4th) 193.

[506] *Century Insurance Office Ltd v Falloon* [1971] NI 234; *Conlon v Conlons Ltd* [1952] 2 All ER 462; *Newman v Nemes* (1979) 8 CPC 229.

[507] *Fyffes Plc v DCC Plc* [2005] IESC 3 at [25], [2005] 1 IR 59 at 68, [2005] 1 ILRM 357 at 364; *McMullen v Carty,* unreported, Supreme Court, 27 January 1998. Implied waiver will not occur in circumstances where the client puts together a team to advise on a transaction which includes lawyers and other professionals such as accountants and subsequently sues the accountants but not the lawyers: *Nederlandse Reassurantie Groep Holding NV v Bacon & Woodrow* [1995] 1 All ER 976. As to the extent of the waiver, see *Paragon Finance Plc v Freshfields* [1999] 1 WLR 1183, where it was held that the waiver extended to communications between the client and its former solicitors, whom it was suing, but not to communications with the client's current solicitors. In *Lillicrap v Nalder & Son* [1993] 1 All ER 724, it was held that, where a client alleges negligence in relation to one of a number of related transactions, the implied waiver may extend to the whole series of transactions.

[508] Unreported, Supreme Court, 27 January 1998.

[509] Unreported, Supreme Court, 27 January 1998 at 9–10. This conclusion was affirmed by both the High Court and the Supreme Court in *McMullen v Clancy (No. 2)* [2005] IESC 10, [2005] 2 IR 445.

[510] Note that § 3.4(c) of the Code of Conduct for the Bar of Ireland (22 July 2013)which deals with the obligation of confidentiality owed by a barrister to a client provides that: "When an accusation is made by the lay client against his solicitor a barrister is still bound to maintain secrecy as to matters coming to his knowledge as counsel and may not give a statement or give evidence concerning such matters without the consent of the lay client." In *McMullen v Clancy (No. 2)* [2005] IESC 10, [2005] 2 IR 445, it was held that the Code of Conduct is not justiciable.

advices are put in issue rather than the identity of the party sued that is determinative. If a solicitor being sued could not put in evidence communications with the barrister briefed by him or her, that would severely impair his or her ability to defend himself or herself and injustice could result.[511]

10–211   In *Cullen v Wicklow County Manager*,[512] the Supreme Court observed that there is no obligation on a party to disclose the legal advice they received. However, in circumstances where a party seeks to be excused from responsibility for certain conduct on the basis that they acted upon legal advice, it is entirely unsatisfactory for that party to provide only partial and selective disclosure of that advice.[513]

10–212   The Supreme Court considered the extent to which privilege may be waived where a party puts their state of mind in issue in *Redfern v O'Mahony*,[514] where the defendants relied upon the fact that legal advice was obtained in relation to a particular agreement, as well as the terms of the agreement itself, in order to establish the absence of an intention to procure a breach of contract or to interfere with the plaintiff's contractual relations. However, the defendants did not disclose the legal advice sought or given. The Supreme Court reviewed a number of Australian cases, in which it was held that, where a party relies in his pleadings on his state of mind, and it would be unfair to permit that party to maintain privilege in respect of communications passing between that party and his legal advisers which must bear upon the existence of that state of mind, privilege may be lost.[515] Finnegan J accepted that, in circumstances where a client institutes professional negligence proceedings against his solicitor, a waiver of privilege arises to prevent unfairness.[516] He went on to note that legal professional privilege may also be lost on the basis of unfairness where there is partial disclosure or deployment of legal advice. Subject to these exceptions, however, he concluded that there is no general principle, as a matter of English law, that unfairness will result in implied waiver of privilege.

10–213   Finnegan J referred in this regard to the decision of Ramsey J in *Farm Assist (in liquidation) v Secretary of State for the Environment, Food and Rural Affairs*,[517]

Accordingly, a breach of this provision will render a barrister susceptible to disciplinary action, but is not actionable in proceedings.

[511]   *Cf. Nederlandse Reassurantie Groep Holding NV v Bacon & Woodrow* [1995] 1 All ER 976.

[512]   [2010] IESC 49 at [35], [2011] 1 IR 152 at 166-167, *per* O'Donnell J.

[513]   *Cf. Barry v Flood* [2013] IEHC 171 at [52], where the applicant sought to explain his delay in instituting judicial review proceedings on the basis of legal advice, but only partially waived privilege and did not disclose the advice in full. O'Malley J stated that, "[i]f the decision is to be laid at the door of his legal advisors one might have thought that proper evidence should be given as to the full contents of those advices." See also *Moorview Developments v First Active plc*, unreported, High Court, 3 July 2008, *per* Clarke J at [35]. By way of contrast, see *Marshall v Arklow Town Council* [2004] IEHC 249, [2004] 4 IR 92.

[514]   [2009] IESC 18, [2009] 3 IR 583.

[515]   *Hong Kong Bank of Australia Ltd v Murphy* [1993] 2 VR 419; *Telstra Corporation v B.T. Australasia Pty Ltd* (1998) 156 ALR 634; *Liquorland (Australia) Pty Ltd v Anghie* [2003] VSC 73; *Wardrope v Dunne* [1996] 1 Qd R 224.

[516]   However, he stated that: "The loss of privilege by the mere instigation of proceedings is limited to negligence actions instituted by a client against his solicitor: it is based on unfairness. The privilege attached to transactions with other solicitors, however closely related or relevant, is not affected." [2009] IESC 18 at [27], [2009] 3 IR 583 at 595. See *Paragon Finance Plc v Freshfields* [1999] 1 WLR 1183; *Nederlandse Reassuratic Groep Holding N.V. v Bacon and Woodrow (a firm)* [1995] 1 All ER 976; *McMullen v Carty*, unreported, Supreme Court, 27 January 1998.

[517]   [2008] All ER (D) 124, *per* Ramsey J at [48]. Reliance was also placed on *Paragon Finance v*

where it was held that there is no general implied waiver of privilege merely because a state of mind or certain actions are put in issue. Ramsey J held that the test for waiver in English law is not based on general principles of fairness or relevance:

> "...the underlying reasoning in the Australian and United States authorities referred to in *Hayes v Dowding*[518] was that of fairness. That however is not a test which is applied generally in English law when deciding whether there has been an implied waiver of privilege. Whilst there might be an implied waiver in proceedings between a client and solicitor because of unfairness that does not mean that wherever there is unfairness there will always be an implied waiver of privilege".

10–214   This decision was followed by the Supreme Court, which declined to adopt the Australian approach. It was held, therefore, that there is no general proposition, as a matter of Irish law, that privilege may be lost where the court may be misled if a document is not available, or where a party in his pleadings relies upon his state of mind, as a result of which it would be unfair to permit that party to maintain privilege.[519]

9. Privileged Communications Disclosed by Inadvertence or Misconduct

10–215   The traditional common law approach was that disclosure of privileged communications, whether by inadvertence or misconduct, resulted in the loss of the privilege, and evidence of the privileged communications whether original or secondary was admissible. This approach was closely linked to that adopted in respect of illegally obtained evidence and, in *Calcraft v Guest*,[520] Lindley MR endorsed a passage from the judgment of Parke B in *Lloyd v Mostyn*[521] to the effect that:

> "Where an attorney instrusted confidentially with a document communicates the contents of it, or suffers another to take a copy, surely the secondary evidence so obtained may be produced. Suppose the instrument were even stolen, and a correct copy taken, would it not be reasonable to admit it?"

10–216   However, some measure of protection was restored by the decision in *Lord Ashburton v Pape*[522] which held that the admissibility in evidence of copies of privileged communications did not affect the jurisdiction of the court to protect the underlying confidence where those copies had been obtained surreptitiously. Thus, in that case an injunction was granted to restrain the defendant from using copies of privileged correspondence between the plaintiff and his solicitors that he had obtained by trick.

10–217   A number of attempts to reconcile those two decisions were made[523] and in *Guinness Peat Properties Ltd v Fitzroy Robinson Partnership*,[524] Slade LJ synthesised

---

> *Freshfields* [1999] 1 WLR 1183 at 1194, where Lord Bingham CL stated that, "fairness is not the touchstone by which it is determined whether a client has or has not impliedly waived his privilege."

[518] [1996] PNLR 57.
[519] [2009] IESC 18 at [33], [2009] 3 IR 583 at 597.
[520] [1898] 1 QB 759.
[521] (1842) 10 M & W 478 at 481–482.
[522] [1913] 2 Ch 469.
[523] See *Goddard v Nationwide Building Society* [1986] 3 All ER 264, [1986] 3 WLR 734; *Re Briamore Manufacturing Ltd* [1986] 3 All ER 132; *Guinness Peat Properties Ltd v Fitzroy Robinson Partnership* [1987] 1 WLR 1027, [1987] 2 All ER 716; *English & American Insurance Co. Ltd v Smith* [1988] FSR 232; *Webster v James Chapman & Co* [1989] 3 All ER 939; *Derby & Co v Weldon (No. 8)* [1991] 1 WLR 73; *Pizzey v Ford Motor Co Ltd*, [1994] PIQR 15, TLR, 8 March 1993; *IBM Corp. v Phoenix International (Computers) Ltd* [1995] 1 All ER 413.
[524] [1987] 1 WLR 1027, [1987] 2 All ER 716.

the English position as follows.[525] The general rule is that once the other party has inspected a document protected by privilege, it is too late for the first party to correct the mistake by applying for injunctive relief. However, if the other party has either (a) procured inspection of the relevant document by fraud, or (b) on inspection realised that he has been permitted to see the document only by reason of an obvious mistake,[526] the court has power to grant an injunction, provided there are no other circumstances which would make it unjust to grant relief.[527] In such cases, the court should ordinarily grant the injunction unless it can properly be refused having regard to the general principles governing the grant of a discretionary remedy.[528] However, the party seeking to restrain the use of the privileged documents must do so before the other party has adduced the confidential communication in evidence or otherwise relied on it at trial.[529]

10–218 In England, the Civil Procedure Rules now provide that, where a party inadvertently allows a privileged document to be inspected, the party who has inspected the document may use it or its contents only with the permission of the court.[530] There is no longer a need, therefore, to seek an injunction to prevent the use of inadvertently disclosed documents. The principles which govern the exercise of the court's jurisdiction to permit the use of documents which have been disclosed through inadvertence are substantially the same as those on which the court formerly exercised its discretion to grant relief by way of injunction.[531] It is clear from the more recent authorities, however, that where a party has disclosed privileged documents by mistake, it will generally be too late for that party to claim privilege in order to attempt to correct the mistake. Moreover, even where documents have been disclosed as a result

---

[525] See also *Al-Fayed v Metropolitan Police Comr* [2002] EWCA Civ 780, *per* Clarke LJ at [16], and *Breeze v John Stacey & Sons Ltd*, unreported, Court of Appeal, 21 June 1999.

[526] As to whether disclosure has occurred as the result of an obvious mistake, see *IBM Corp. v Phoenix International (Computers) Ltd* [1995] 1 All ER 413. In *MMI Research Ltd v Cellxion Ltd* [2007] All ER (D) 142, it was held that it is not sufficient that the mistake is obvious after further inquiries. But see *contra, Moorview Developments v First Active plc*, unreported, High Court, Clarke J, 3 July 2008 at [15].

[527] *Al-Fayed v Metropolitan Police Comr* [2002] EWCA Civ 780; *Goddard v Nationwide Building Society* [1986] 3 All ER 264; *English & American Insurance Co Ltd v Smith* [1988] FSR 232 and *Derby & Co v Weldon (No. 8)* [1991] 1 WLR 73.

[528] *Cf. Webster v James Chapman & Co* [1989] 3 All ER 939 where Scott J stated that the Court was required to exercise its discretion by balancing the legitimate interests of the plaintiff in seeking to keep the confidential information suppressed and the legitimate interests of the defendant in seeking to make use of it and, in carrying out this exercise, the manner in which the privileged document came into the possession of the other side, the issues in the action, the relevance of the document and all the other circumstances will have to be taken into account.

[529] *Goddard v Nationwide Building Society* [1986] 3 All ER 264, [1986] 3 WLR 734; *English & American Insurance Co Ltd v Herbert Smith* [1988] FSR 232; *Great Atlantic Insurance v Home Insurance* [1981] 1 All ER 485 at 491–492 (where it was held that remedial action during the trial may be possible, but that once the evidence had been introduced into the trial record as a result of mistake on the part of the party asserting privilege, the court could not "put the clock back" and "undo what has been done"). The High Court appeared to accept that this was the position in *Shell E & P Ireland Ltd v McGrath (No. 2)* [2006] IEHC 409 at [32], [2007] 2 IR 574, [2007] 1 ILRM 544.

[530] CPR 30.20.

[531] *Rawlinson and Hunter Trustees SA v Tchenguiz* [2014] EWCA Civ 1129 at [11]; *Al-Fayed v Commissioner of Police for the Metropolis* [2002] EWCA Civ 780 at [18]. See also Lord Mackay of Clashfern (ed.) *Halsbury's Laws of England, Civil Procedure* Vol.12, 5th edn (London: Lexis Nexis, 2009), at [551] and Matthews and Malek, *Disclosure*, 4th edn (London: Sweet & Maxwell, 2012) at [16.19]–[16.20].

of an obvious mistake, the court may refuse to restrain the use of the documents if it concludes that it would not be inequitable or unjust to do so.[532]

10–219   A more protectionist approach has been adopted in other common law jurisdictions, such as Australia,[533] New Zealand[534] and Canada.[535] While this alternative approach has, to some extent, been considered by the Irish courts, the principles ultimately applied in order to determine whether privilege has been waived through inadvertent disclosure are those identified in the English decisions considered above.

10–220   The first case in which the jurisdiction of the Court to grant an Order restraining the use of privileged documents disclosed through inadvertence was considered by the Irish courts was *Shell E & P Ireland v McGrath (No. 2)*,[536] where attendance dockets were inadvertently included in inter partes correspondence exhibited to an affidavit and disjointed excerpts from the attendances were then published in a newspaper. Neither the plaintiff nor its solicitors engaged with the newspaper, and the plaintiff claimed privilege over the attendances. Smyth J considered the rationale for the privilege, and concluded that[537]:

> "The free flow of information a client is entitled to convey to his legal advisors to be properly and fully advised would clearly be impaired if the client is to run the risk that his confidence will not be honoured, or if inadvertently or improperly divulged would be used against him/ her at trial."

10–221   In the absence of any Irish authority prescribing the procedure which should

---

[532] *Rawlinson and Hunter Trustees SA v Tchenguiz* [2014] EWCA Civ 1129 at [11], citing *Al-Fayed v Commissioner of Police for the Metropolis* [2002] EWCA Civ 780 at [16]–[18], with approval.

[533] In *Expense Reduction Analysts Group Pty Ltd v Armstrong Strategic Management and Marketing Pty Ltd* [2013] HCA 46 at [45], the High Court of Australia declined to follow the English authorities requiring the mistake as a result of which disclosure has occurred to be obvious to a reasonable solicitor and held that, where a privileged document is inadvertently disclosed, the court should ordinarily permit the correction of that mistake and order the return of the document if the party receiving it refuses to do so. Section 122 of the Australian Uniform Evidence Act was introduced to address the uncertainty surrounding this issue, and introduced a requirement that the client disclose the privileged material "knowingly and voluntarily". Section 122 of the Evidence Act 2008 (Vic) was considered in *QUBE Logistics (Vic) Pty Ltd v Wimmera Container Line Pty Ltd* [2013] VSC 695. See also Stephen Odgers, *Uniform Evidence Law* 10th edn (Sydney: Thomson Reuters Australia, 2012) [1.3.11080].

[534] In *R. v Uljee* [1982] 1 NZLR 561, the New Zealand Court of Appeal declined to follow *Calcraft v Guest* [1898] 1 QB 759, preferring to approach the question on the basis of principle. But see *National Insurance Co Ltd v Whirlybird* [1994] 2 NZLR 513 and *Spicers Paper (NZ) Ltd v Whitcalls Group Ltd* [1996] 1 NZLR 513, where the principles set out in the *Guinness Peat Properties v Fitzroy Robinson* [1987] 1 WLR 1027, [1987] 2 All ER 716 were applied.

[535] A more protectionist approach to legal professional privilege is adopted in Canada, where the courts generally take the view that inadvertent disclosure does not result in a waiver of privilege: *Descoteaux v Mierwinski* [1982] 1 SCR 860 at 875; *Kennedy v McKenzie* [2005] OJ No. 2060; *Chapelstone Developments Inc v Canada* [2004] NBJ No. 450; *Aviaco International Leasing Inc v Boeing Canada Inc* [2000] OJ No. 2420; *Elliott v Toronto (City)* (2001) 54 OR (3d) 472; *Anderson Exploration Ltd v Pan-Alberta Gas Ltd* [1998] 10 WWR 633; *Airst v Airst* (1998) 37 OR (3d) 654; *Stevens v Prime Minister* (1997) 144 DLR (4th) 353; *Bernado v Deathe* [1991] OJ No. 862 (Gen Div); *Somerville Belkin Industries Ltd v Brocklesby Transport* (1985) 5 CPC (2d) 239. In the US, Federal Rule of Evidence 502 provides that inadvertent disclosure does not operate as a waiver, provided that the privilege holder took reasonable steps to prevent disclosure and rectify the error. See *McCormick on Evidence*, 7th edn (Thomson Reuters Westlaw, 2013) at § 88, pp.572–573.

[536] [2006] IEHC 409, [2007] 2 IR 574, [2007] 1 ILRM 544.

[537] [2006] IEHC 409 at [15], [2007] 2 IR 574 at 580, [2007] 1 ILRM 544 at 552.

be adopted where a privileged document has been disclosed by inadvertence, he considered the approach adopted in England and in other common law jurisdictions, such as Canada and Australia. While he concluded that, on the facts of the case before him, the plaintiff was entitled to an order restraining the defendants from using the privileged documents regardless of which approach was adopted, Smyth J expressed the view that the more protective approach adopted in Canada and Australia is the more correct approach.[538]

10–222 Smyth J rejected the contention that it was too late to restore the status quo in circumstances where the document had been circulated, on the basis that the document had not been circulated to the public. The defendants also sought to contend that the plaintiff had failed to move expeditiously to reassert its claim of privilege. Again, however, this contention was rejected by Smyth J, who was satisfied that, when the plaintiff and its solicitor had an apprehension as to who had received copies of the documents, and the use to which they might be put, the plaintiff had immediately asserted the privilege. Referring to the jurisdiction to restrain the use of privileged material disclosed through inadvertence, he held that "the focus of the remedy is not simply the protection of the confidentiality of the communication, but on restraining its use".[539]

10–223 Having considered the relevant English authorities, Smyth J concluded that the court should adopt an objective test in determining whether it ought to have been evident to the recipient solicitor that the privileged documents had been disclosed through mistake. In this regard, he cited the following passage from the judgment of Aldous J in *IBM Corp. v Phoenix International (Computers) Ltd*[540] with approval:

> "The court must adopt the mantle of the reasonable solicitor. The evidence of what a solicitor thought at the time can be relevant. However, the decision is for the Court. The Court must decide whether it is satisfied, on the balance of probabilities, that the reasonable solicitor would have realised that privilege had not been waived."

10–224 Thus, Smyth J formulated the question the court must ask itself as "whether in the light of the evidence and the surrounding circumstances it had been proved on the balance of probabilities that the disclosure of the document would be seen by the reasonable solicitor to have been disclosed by mistake".[541] He was satisfied on the balance of probabilities that a reasonable solicitor would have realised that the attendance dockets had come to him in error, and that the information was privileged and contained legal advice. In reaching this conclusion, he emphasised "the very important interest that is served by privilege and its important role in the administration of justice", which render it appropriate to adopt a protective approach to privilege in circumstances where documents are disclosed inadvertently.[542]

10–225 The principles which determine whether privilege has been waived in circumstances where documents are discovered though inadvertence or mistake were considered again by Clarke J in *Byrne v Shannon Foynes Port Company*,[543] where it was held that the inclusion by mistake of a privileged document in a schedule to

---

[538] [2006] IEHC 409 at [29], [2007] 2 IR 574 at 585, [2007] 1 ILRM 544 at 556.
[539] [2006] IEHC 409 at [32], [2007] 2 IR 574 at 587, [2007] 1 ILRM 544 at 557.
[540] [1995] 1 All ER 413 at 424.
[541] [2006] IEHC 409 at [36], [2007] 2 IR 574 at 589, [2007] 1 ILRM 544 at 559.
[542] [2006] IEHC 409 at [38], [2007] 2 IR 574 at 589, [2007] 1 ILRM 544 at 559–560.
[543] [2007] IEHC 315, [2008] 1 IR 814, [2008] 1 ILRM 529.

an affidavit of discovery in respect of which no claim for privilege is made will not be treated as a waiver of privilege.[544] If a document is mistakenly included in the first part of the First Schedule of an affidavit of discovery, therefore, the court will ordinarily permit the amendment of the schedule at any time before inspection has taken place.[545] After inspection has taken place or copies of the document have been provided, however, the general rule is that the privilege has been lost.[546] It was held, however, that this position is not absolute. Clarke J adopted the following extract from Matthews and Malek, *Disclosure*,[547] as an accurate statement of the principles which govern the jurisdiction to restrain the use of a privileged document:

> "Thus where such circumstances occur in the context of an inspection of documents, such as procuring inspection of the relevant document by fraud, or realising the mistake on inspection but saying nothing, the court will in effect allow the mistake to be corrected, and refuse to permit the opposing party to use the privileged document. The test is in two stages:
>> (1) Was it evident to the solicitor seeing privileged documents that a mistake had been made?
>> (2) If not, would it have been obvious to the hypothetical reasonable solicitor that disclosure had occurred as a result of a mistake? …[548]
>
> [I]f the answer to either question is 'yes', then, [under the CPR], the court would normally restrain the solicitor if he did not give the documents back, and might restrain him from acting further if he had read the documents and it was impossible for the advantage to be removed in any other way."

10–226   Having considered the decision in *Shell E & P Ireland Ltd v McGrath (No. 2)*,[549] he concluded that the test to be applied is a two step test[550]:

> "Firstly, the court must consider whether the solicitor seeing the document or documents concerned realised that a mistake had been made. Secondly, and perhaps most importantly on the basis of the authorities, the court must put itself in the position of a reasonable solicitor and consider whether, on the balance of probabilities, such solicitor would have taken the disclosure to have been as a result of a mistake."[551]

10–227   It was accepted that it was not evident to the plaintiff's solicitor that a mistake

---

[544] [2007] IEHC 315 at [15], [2008] 1 IR 814 at 820, [2008] 1 ILRM 529 at 535. The authorities cited in support of this conclusion were *Re Briamore Manufacturing Limited* [1986] 1 WLR 1429 and *Guinness Peat Ltd Ltd v Fitzroy Robinson* [1987] 1 WLR 1027, [1987] 2 All ER 716.

[545] But see *Fyffes Plc v DCC Plc* [2005] IESC 3 at [25], [2005] 1 IR 59, [2005] 1 ILRM 357, where Fennelly J stated that the inclusion of potentially privileged documents in the non-privileged schedule to the affidavit may give rise to an implied waiver of privilege.

[546] [2007] IEHC 315 at [16], [2008] 1 IR 814 at 820, [2008] 1 ILRM 529 at 535. *Re. Briamore Manufacturing Limited* [1986] 1 WLR 1429; *Guinness Peat Ltd Ltd v Fitzroy Robinson* [1987] 1 WLR 1027, [1987] 2 All ER 716; *Pizzey v Ford Motor Co. Ltd*, [1994] PIQR 15, TLR, 8 March 1993.

[547] The extract is taken from Matthews and Malek, *Disclosure*, 3rd edn (London: Sweet & Maxwell, 2007), p.400. This text remains in the current edition. Matthews and Malek, *Disclosure*, 4th edn (London: Sweet & Maxwell, 2012) at [16.20].

[548] The omitted text states that: "A relevant factor under (2) will be if the solicitor gave detailed consideration to the question and honestly concludes that there was no mistake. This will tend to show that it would not be obvious to the reasonable solicitor that a mistake had been made." Matthews and Malek, *Disclosure*, 4th edn (London: Sweet & Maxwell, 2012) at [16.20]. See *Al-Fayed v Commissioner of Police for the Metropolis* [2002] EWCA Civ 780.

[549] [2006] IEHC 409, [2007] 2 IR 574, [2007] 1 ILRM 544.

[550] [2007] IEHC 315 at [21], [2008] 1 IR 814 at 822, [2008] 1 ILRM 529 at 536.

[551] The English authorities suggest that, where the Court concludes that either limb of this test is satisfied, relief will also be granted where there are no other circumstances which would make it unjust or inequitable to grant relief. See *Rawlinson and Hunter Trustees SA v Tchenguiz* [2014] EWCA Civ 1129 at [11] and *Al-Fayed v Commissioner of Police for the Metropolis* [2002] EWCA Civ 780 at [16]–[18].

had been made by the defendants' solicitor. Accordingly, the case turned on whether, objectively speaking, it would have been obvious that the inclusion of the relevant documents in the file supplied had occurred as a result of a mistake. It was held that, notwithstanding the objective nature of this inquiry, the explanation provided as to how the mistake occurred is relevant and must be assessed; if there is an obvious explanation for the mistake (which should have been obvious to a receiving solicitor) then the objective test would be met and the documents would have to be returned. However, if there is no satisfactory explanation for the mistake, then it follows that the thinking of the hypothetical objective solicitor would necessarily have been influenced by that absence.[552] Ultimately, Clarke J concluded that, on the balance of probabilities, a hypothetical receiving solicitor would not have concluded that the absence of a claim to privilege over the documents in issue was due to an error. He was influenced, in this regard, by the sheer volume of documents in respect of which privilege could have been, and was not, claimed. In addition, privilege had been claimed in respect of some, but not all, of what appeared to be sequences of documentation. Clarke J observed that an objective and hypothetical solicitor would have been unlikely to conclude that so many fundamental errors could have occurred through inadvertence. He noted that the case was one in which the *bona fides* or reasonableness of the first defendant was in issue, as a result of which there could have been a basis for electing to disclose privileged documentation.[553] It was held, therefore, that the defendants were not entitled to claim privilege in respect of the documents which had been disclosed.[554]

10–228 The principles governing the loss of privilege through inadvertent disclosure were considered again by Clarke J in *Moorview Developments v First Active plc*,[555] where a particular document was included as part of a bundle of documents listed in the First Part of the First Schedule to the affidavit, and was also individually listed in the Second Part of the First Schedule. In applying the test set out in *Byrne v Shannon Foynes*, Clarke J had particular regard to the volume of documentation discovered in the proceedings, observing that the test must be seen against the possibility that, in very complex litigation with a large volume of documentation, errors on all sides can occur.[556] In that case, the solicitors for the defendant had not noticed that the document had been included in both the First and Second Parts of the First Schedule to the affidavit of discovery, and the document had been handed over to the solicitors for the defendant

---

[552] [2007] IEHC 315 at [28], [2008] 1 IR 814 at 823, [2008] 1 ILRM 529 at 537–538. In *Al-Fayed v Commissioner of Police for the Metropolis* [2002] EWCA Civ 780 at [16]–[18], Clarke LJ held that, where a solicitor gives a detailed consideration to the question whether the documents have been made available for inspection by mistake and honestly concludes that they have not, that fact will be a relevant (and in many cases an important) pointer to the conclusion that it would not be obvious to a reasonable solicitor that a mistake had been made, but is not conclusive; the decision remains a matter for the court. This principle was cited with approval in *Rawlinson and Hunter Trustees SA v Tchenguiz* [2014] EWCA Civ 1129 at [11].

[553] See also *Moorview Developments v First Active plc*, unreported, High Court, 3 July 2008 at [4]–[5], where Clarke J concluded that it would not have been clear to a hypothetical, reasonable solicitor that the failure to claim privilege in respect of a variety of documents included in the various affidavits of discovery sworn in the proceedings could have occurred as a result of mistake. Again, he was influenced by his conclusion that there were a number of bases upon which, in the context of that particular case, it could have been assumed that the plaintiff might wish to rely on the fact that legal advice had been given in respect of certain matters.

[554] [2007] IEHC 315 at [36]–[37], [2008] 1 IR 814 at 825, [2008] 1 ILRM 529 at 539.

[555] Unreported, High Court, 3 July 2008.

[556] Unreported, High Court, 3 July 2008 at [13]. See the comments of the Canadian Supreme Court in *Canadian Bearings Ltd v Celanese Canada Inc* [2006] 2 SCR 189.

together with all of the other documentation discovered by the plaintiffs. It was held, however, that the hypothetical solicitor, had he applied his mind to this discrepancy, would have seen the inclusion of the letter in that documentation as an error.[557]

10–229 The two-step test formulated by Clarke J in *Byrne v Shannon Foynes* was applied by Hogan J in *McGrath v Athlone Institute of Technology*,[558] a case which involved the disclosure of legal advice to a third party, who then relayed the contents of the advice to the plaintiff. Hogan J concluded that it was perfectly clear that the disclosure took place in error, and did not attach any significance to the fact that the party to whom the privileged document was inadvertently disclosed was not a solicitor.[559] An equally protective approach was adopted by Clarke J in *Tir na nOg Projects Ireland Ltd v County Council of Kerry*,[560] where it was held that it is immaterial whether the inadvertent disclosure occurred in the context of the exchange of documents as part of court proceedings:

> "The underlying test which the court must apply is as to whether a reasonable person would objectively view any privilege that might have attached to the document as having being waived in the light of the circumstances in which the document had come to the other sides attention. Those circumstances are, therefore, material in that they may affect the proper judgment as to whether, objectively speaking, a party might legitimately take the privilege to have been waived. The circumstances do not, however, affect the test."

10–230 It was held, however, that privilege in the document had been waived in circumstances where it had been placed on the public planning file for a considerable period of time.

10–231 As noted above, a more protective approach to the privilege has been adopted in Canada,[561] where the courts generally take the view that inadvertent disclosure does not result in a waiver of privilege.[562] Accordingly, as regards the grant of injunctive relief, it is irrelevant whether the mistake should have been apparent to the recipient of the documents.[563] The Canadian courts have also emphasised that privilege is not lost where the inadvertently disclosed documents are relevant or prove particularly useful to the receiving party.[564] Having considered the English case law discussed above, the Manitoba Court of Appeal summarised the position as follows in *Metcalfe v Metcalfe*[565]:

---

[557] Unreported, High Court, 3 July 2008 at [15]–[17]. Clarke J appeared to accept that it was sufficient if, had further inquiries been made, the mistake would have been obvious. But see *contra MMI Research Ltd v Cellxion Ltd* [2007] All ER (D) 142.

[558] [2011] IEHC 254.

[559] [2011] IEHC 254 at [7].

[560] [2008] IEHC 48 at [4.4].

[561] *Descoteaux v Mierwinski* [1982] 1 SCR 860 at 875. See generally Bryant, Fuerst and Hederman, *Sopinka, Lederman & Bryant: The Law of Evidence in Canada* 4th edn (Lexis Nexis, 2014) at §14.159 *et seq.*

[562] *Kennedy v McKenzie* [2005] OJ No. 2060; *Chapelstone Developments Inc v Canada* [2004] NBJ No. 450; *Aviaco International Leasing Inc v Boeing Canada Inc* [2000] OJ No. 2420; *Elliott v Toronto (City)* (2001) 54 OR (3d) 472; *Anderson Exploration Ltd v Pan-Alberta Gas Ltd* [1998] 10 WWR 633; *Airst v Airst* (1998) 37 OR (3d) 654; *Stevens v Prime Minister* (1997) 144 DLR (4th) 353; *Bernado v Deathe* [1991] OJ No. 862 (Gen Div); *Somerville Belkin Industries Ltd v Brocklesby Transport* (1985) 5 CPC (2d) 239.

[563] *Fording Coal Ltd v Steamworkers of America* (1999) 70 BCLR. (3rd) 74; *Somerville Belkin Industries v Brocklesby Transport* (1985) 65 BCLR 260; *Otting v Elkford* (1992) 70 BCLR (2d) 202; *Tilley v Hails* (1993) 12 OR (3d) 306.

[564] *Chan v Dynasty Executive Suites Ltd* [2006] OJ No. 2877 at [23]; *Nova Growth Corp v Kepinski* [2001] OJ No. 5993 at [23].

[565] (2001) 198 DLR (4th) 318.

"The Canadian position does not generally adhere to the English position. In Canada, generally, an opposing party is restrained from using inadvertently released privileged materials whether the mistake was obvious or not. Many of the Canadian cases start with the principle that the privilege belongs to the client and that an inadvertent release does not constitute a true waiver of the privilege. In Canada, the inadvertent disclosure of privileged material will be restrained on the basis "of the proper administration of justice" or "in the interests of justice", not merely on the basis of whether the mistake would have been obvious to the opposing side."[566]

10–232 Indeed, the Canadian courts have gone considerably further than simply restraining the use of privileged documents disclosed through inadvertence.[567] In *Canadian Bearings Ltd v Celanese Canada Inc*,[568] the Supreme Court of Canada confirmed that a court may make such orders as are considered necessary to remedy the disclosure, including an order disqualifying the lawyers who received the privileged communications. The Supreme Court acknowledged that a disqualification order of this type gives rise to a conflict between two conflicting values; solicitor-client privilege and the right to select counsel of one's choice[569]:

"The conflict must be resolved ... on the basis that no one has the right to be represented by counsel who has had access to relevant solicitor-client confidences in circumstances where such access ought to have been anticipated and, without great difficulty, avoided and where such counsel has failed to rebut the presumption of a resulting risk of prejudice ..."

10–233 The rationale for the expansive protection afforded to the privilege in Canada was explained by the Supreme Court as follows[570]:

"Whether through advertence or advertence the problem is that solicitor-client information has wound up in the wrong hands. Even granting that solicitor-client privilege is an umbrella that covers confidences of differing centrality and importance, such possession by the opposing party affects the integrity of the administration of justice. Parties should be free to litigate their disputes without fear that their opponent has obtained an unfair insight into secrets disclosed in confidence to their legal advisors. The defendant's witnesses ought not to have to worry in the course of being cross-examined that the cross-examiner's questions are prompted by information that had earlier been passed in confidence to the defendant's solicitors. Such a possibility destroys the level playing field and creates a serious risk to the integrity of the administration of justice. To prevent such a danger from arising, the courts must act "swiftly and decisively" as the Divisional Court emphasized. Remedial action in cases such as this is intended to be curative not punitive."

10–234 The Supreme Court held that, once an opposing firm of solicitors is shown to have received confidential information attributable to a solicitor and client relationship relevant to the matter at hand, a risk of prejudice will be presumed to flow from an opponent's access to solicitor-client confidence, unless the receiving solicitors can show "that the public represented by the reasonably informed person would be satisfied that no use of confidential information would occur".[571] In cases of inadvertent disclosure,

---

[566] See also *McPherson v Institute of Chartered Accountants* [1989] 2 WWR 649 and *Double-E Inc v Positive Action Tool Western Ltd* [1989] 1 FC 163.

[567] The reliefs granted in this regard include an injunction restraining the use of privilege documents (*Aviaco International Leasing Inc v Boeing Canada Inc*, [2000] OJ No. 2420) and an order expunging documents from the record (*Tilley v Hails* (1993) 12 OR (3d) 306). In *Canadian Bearings Ltd v Celanese Canada Inc* [2006] 2 SCR 189, the Supreme Court observed that, in cases of inadvertent disclosure, the remedy is often an order requiring the document to be deleted or returned and a direction that no use is to be made of it.

[568] [2006] 2 SCR 189. See also *Nova Growth Corp. v Kepinski,* [2001] OJ No. 5993 and *Chan v Dynasty Executive Suites Ltd* [2006] OJ No. 2877.

[569] [2006] 2 SCR 189 at [2].

[570] [2006] 2 SCR 189 at [34].

[571] This principle was first established in *MacDonald Estate v Martin* [1990] 3 SCR 1235 at

therefore, the onus is on the receiving solicitor to rebut the presumption of a risk of prejudice.[572] However, disqualification is not automatic.[573] The task of the Court is to determine whether the integrity of the justice system, viewed objectively, requires removal of counsel in order to address the violation of privilege, or whether a less drastic remedy would be effective. The Supreme Court accepted that the right of a party to continue to be represented by counsel of its choice is an important element of the adversarial system of litigation and that mistakes will be made, particularly in commercial litigation where large volumes of documentation are exchanged.[574] The following non-exhaustive list of factors was identified for consideration in the exercise of this discretion: (i) how the documents came into the possession of the plaintiff or its counsel; (ii) what the plaintiff and its counsel did upon recognition that the documents were potentially subject to solicitor-client privilege; (iii) the extent of review made of the privileged material[575]; (iv) the contents of the solicitor-client communications and the degree to which they are prejudicial; (v) the stage of the litigation; and (vi) the potential effectiveness of a firewall or other precautionary steps to avoid mischief.[576]

10–235 To date, the more protectionist approach adopted in Canada and Australia has not found favour with either the English courts or the courts in this jurisdiction. The recent judgment of Longmore LJ in *Rawlinson and Hunter Trustees SA v Tchenguiz*,[577] however, suggests that this is a matter which may be revisited. While he accepted that the Court of Appeal was bound to follow *Al-Fayed v Commissioner of Police for the Metropolis*,[578] and hold that privilege had been waived in circumstances where the mistake which resulted in the disclosure of privileged documents was not one which would have been obvious to a reasonable solicitor, Longmore LJ expressed his regret that this was the case. He referred to the recent decision of the Australian High Court in *Expense Reduction Analysts Group Pty Ltd v Armstrong Strategic Management and Marketing Pty Ltd*,[579] where it was held that, where a privileged document is inadvertently disclosed, the court should ordinarily permit the correction of that mistake

---

1260–1262, which concerned a solicitor moving from one firm to another. Only where there is "clear and convincing evidence" to the contrary will the presumption be rebutted: "*A fortiori* undertakings and conclusory statements in affidavits without more" will not suffice.

[572] [2006] 2 SCR 189 at [54]. The Supreme Court accepted that the receiving solicitors had not set out to obtain access to, or to gain some advantage from, privileged material. Rather, this occurred through carelessness during a search carried out on foot of an Anton Pillar Order. The Court stated that the order was not intended to be punitive, but "[t]he protection of solicitor-client privileges is a matter of high importance".

[573] [2006] 2 SCR 189 at [56]. A disqualification order was refused in *Coulumbe v Beard* (1993) 16 OR (3d) 627 (Gen Div). See also *Nova Growth Corp. v Kepinski* [2001] OJ No. 5993 (SCJ). For an example of a case in which a disqualification order was made, see *Chan v Dynasty Executive Suites Ltd* [2006] OJ No. 2877 and *Grenzservice Speditions Ges.m.b.H. v Jans* (1995) 15 BCLR (3d) 370.

[574] Similar comments were made by Clarke J in *Moorview Developments v First Active plc*, unreported, High Court, 3 July 2008 at [13]: "… in the context of the enormous discovery in a case such as this it is perhaps inevitable that some errors will occur and that the application of the test needs to be seen against such a background, *i.e.* the possibility that in very complex litigation with a large volume of documentation errors on all sides can occur."

[575] The Supreme Court agreed with the submission of the Canadian Bar Association that the receiving solicitor should promptly return the inadvertently disclosed privileged material and advise the adversary if the extent to which those materials have been reviewed: [2006] 2 SCR 189 at [62].

[576] [2006] 2 SCR 189 at [59].
[577] [2014] EWCA Civ 1129 at [48]–[52].
[578] [2002] EWCA Civ 780.
[579] [2013] HCA 46.

and order the return of the document, and stated that, "[i]f the Supreme Court were ever to be presented with a case of the inadvertent disclosure of privileged documents, it is not impossible that the simpler Australian approach would commend itself."[580]

10. Common Interest Privilege

10–236   Where clients jointly retain a lawyer, privilege cannot be claimed *inter se* in respect of communications passing between either of them and the solicitor, but will be maintained against third parties unless waived jointly.[581] The courts have also recognised a species of legal professional privilege, termed "common interest privilege", where a joint retainer does not exist but, nevertheless, a person has a common interest with the client in the subject-matter of the privileged communication.[582]

10–237   In *Hansfield Developments v Irish Asphalt Ltd*,[583] McKechnie J observed that common interest privilege does not constitute a *sui generis* category of privilege; rather, it preserves legal professional privilege where a third party recipient or creator of a communication has a common interest in the subject of the privilege with the primary holder thereof.[584] Thus, common interest privilege essentially involves the determination of whether there has been a waiver of privilege through disclosure to a third party.[585]

10–238   Common interest privilege cannot be claimed as between the client and the person with the common interest in respect of communications which came into being during the currency of the common interest, but it can be asserted against any person who does not share the common interest.[586] Examples of persons with a common interest can, depending on the circumstances, include partners, a company and its shareholders, companies with a group of companies or related companies,[587] a trustee and cestui que trust, a lessor and lessee, principal and agent, a husband and

---

[580] *Rawlinson and Hunter Trustees SA v Tchenguiz* [2014] EWCA Civ 1129 at [52].

[581] *R. (Ford) v Financial Services Authority* [2011] EWHC 2583 (Admin), [2012] 1 All ER 1238; *Love v Fawcett* [2011] IEHC 1686; *The Sagheera* [1997] 1 Lloyd's Rep 160; *Re Konigsberg* [1989] 3 All ER 289; *R. v Dunbar* (1982) 138 DLR (3d) 221. For a discussion of joint interest, see Abrahamson, Dwyer & Fitzpatrick, *Discovery and Disclosure*, 2nd edn (Dublin: Thomson Reuters Round Hall, 2013) at [40].

[582] *Ochre Ridge Limited v Cork Bonded Warehouses* Limited [2004] IEHC 160; *Bula Ltd v Crowley*, unreported, High Court, 8 March 1991; *Svenska Handelsbanken v Sun Alliance & London Insurance Plc* [1995] 2 Lloyd's Rep 84; *Buttes Gas and Oil Co v Hammer (No.3)* [1981] QB 223, [1980] 3 All ER 475; *CIA Barca de Panama SA v George Wimpey & Co Ltd* [1980] 1 Lloyd's Rep 598; *Leif Heogh & Co A/S v Petrolsea Inc (The World Era) (No.2)* [1993] 1 Lloyd's Rep 363; *Supercom of California Ltd v Sovereign General Insurance Co* (1998) 37 OR (3d.) 597. *Cf. Lee v South West Thames Regional Health Authority* [1985] 1 WLR 845.

[583] [2009] IEHC 420 at [35].

[584] See *WXY v Gewanter* [2012] EWHC 1071 (QB) at [30], where Parkes QC stated that, "common interest privilege is not a free-standing head of privilege but is parasitic on orthodox legal privilege".

[585] *Hansfield Developments v Irish Asphalt Ltd* [2009] IEHC 420, *per* McKechnie J at [55]. See also *Dadourian Group International Inc v Simms* [2008] EWHC (Ch) 1784 at [88].

[586] *CIA Barca de Panama SA v George Wimpey & Co Ltd* [1980] 1 Lloyd's Rep 598; *Talbot v Marshfield* (1865) 2 Dr & Sm 549; *Ontario (AG) v Ballard Estate* (1994) 119 DLR (4th) 750; *Platt v Buck* (1902) 41 DLR 421.

[587] *Moorview Developments v First Active plc* [2008] IEHC 274 at [6.13], [2009] 2 IR 788, [2009] 2 ILRM 262.

wife, insurer and insured,[588] and insurer and reinsurer.[589] It has been held that, even if differences arise between the parties, this will not automatically preclude common interest privilege arising.[590] However, common interest privilege may not arise if the parties are potential adversaries, or are acting from purely selfish motives.[591]

10–239   In *Moorview Developments v First Active plc*,[592] Clarke J held that common interest privilege arises in relation to documents or materials which would be the subject of either legal advice or litigation privilege in the hands of one person or body, but where the relevant materials are given to a third party who may be said to have a common interest in either the legal advice or the litigation concerned. It was held, therefore, that two questions arise for consideration where a claim of common interest privilege is asserted[593]:

> "The first is as to whether the documents would, in the hands of a single party, have the benefit of privilege in the first place. If not, then no question of common interest privilege could arise. If, however, the materials pass that first test but have been released by one party to a second party then it follows that it is also necessary to ask whether the release was on foot of a common interest in either the relevant litigation or advice. If so then the documents will remain privileged, notwithstanding their release, by virtue of the doctrine of common interest. If not, then the release may be taken to be a waiver of any privilege which would otherwise have attached to the documents concerned."[594]

10–240   Clarke J concluded that the documents and materials in question, which related to negotiations which took place as between co-defendants, were subject to without prejudice privilege. Notwithstanding this finding, however, he proceeded to consider the extent to which the material in question might also attract common interest privilege. Clarke J noted that, in practice, there is likely to be an overlap between the circumstances in which co-defendants may be able to rely on both without prejudice privilege and common interest privilege in the context of litigation[595]; in many cases,

---

[588] *Guinness Peat Property Ltd v Fitzroy Robinson Partnership* [1987] 1 WLR 1027; *Winterthur Insurance Company and the National Insurance & Guarantee Corporation Ltd v AG (Manchester) Ltd (in liquidation)* [2006] EWHC 839 (Comm).

[589] *Winterthur Insurance Company and the National Insurance & Guarantee Corporation Ltd v AG (Manchester) Ltd (in liquidation)* [2006] EWHC 839 (Comm) at [78], citing *Guinness Peat Property Ltd v Fitzroy Robinson Partnership* [1987] 1 WLR 1027 and *Commercial Union v Mander* [1996] 1 Lloyd's Rep 640. *Cf. Rhatigan v Eagle Star Life Assurance Company of Ireland Ltd* [2013] IEHC 139.

[590] *Hansfield Developments v Irish Asphalt Ltd* [2009] IEHC 420 at [49]; *Leif Heogh & Co A/S v Petrolsea Inc (The World Era) (No.2)* [1993] 1 Lloyd's Rep 363 at 366; *Svenska Handelsbanken v Sun Alliance and London Insurance Plc* [1995] 2 Lloyd's Rep 84 at 86.

[591] *Hansfield Developments v Irish Asphalt Ltd* [2009] IEHC 420 at [50]. The authority cited in support of this conclusion is *Todd v Novotny* [1999] WASC 22.

[592] *Moorview Developments v First Active plc* [2008] IEHC 274 at [6.13], [2009] 2 IR 788, [2009] 2 ILRM 262.

[593] [2008] IEHC 274 at [6.13], [2009] 2 IR 788 at 821, [2009] 2 ILRM 262 at 292. This two step test was applied by McGovern J in *Hansfield Developments v Irish Asphalt Ltd* [2009] IEHC 90, where he did not consider it necessary to reach a concluded view as to whether the plaintiff and Homebond had a common interest in circumstances where he held that the documents in question were not prepared for the dominant purpose of preparing for litigation, as a result of which they were not privileged.

[594] This statement of the law was cited with approval by both McGovern J and McKechnie J in the High Court in *Hansfield Developments v Irish Asphalt Ltd* [2009] IEHC 90 at [11], [2009] IEHC 420 at [41]. This authority does not appear to have been opened to the Supreme Court in *Redfern v O'Mahony* [2009] 3 IR 583, [2009] IESC 18.

[595] See, for example, *Hansfield Developments v Irish Asphalt Ltd* [2009] IEHC 90 at [16], where a

the defendants will have a potential common interest in defeating the plaintiff's claim, while also wishing to resolve those issues which arise between them as defendants.[596] Clarke J concluded that the negotiations which took place between the defendants attracted common interest privilege.[597]

10–241   The Supreme Court adopted a broad approach to common interest privilege in *Redfern Ltd v O'Mahony*,[598] a case in which the plaintiff sought specific performance of a joint venture agreement for the development of a car park. The issue for determination was whether the plaintiff had waived privilege over counsel's opinion, which had been shared with the board of the management company of the shopping centre and the solicitor for South Dublin County Council. The management company was a party to the joint venture agreement, and it was contemplated that South Dublin County Council would dispose of lands to the plaintiff with a view to the development of the car park. Notwithstanding the relatively wide disclosure which had taken place, it was held that the plaintiff had not waived privilege, as that there was limited disclosure to parties having a common interest with the plaintiff in the proposed development of the car park.[599]

10–242   The existence of common interest privilege was recognised by the English Court of Appeal in *Buttes Gas & Oil Co. v Hammer (No. 3)*,[600] in which case Brightman LJ appeared to suggest that common interest privilege would arise where two parties share a common interest and a common solicitor.[601] Subsequently, in *Bank of Nova Scotia v Hellenic Mutual War Risks Association (Bermuda), 'The Good Luck'*,[602] it was held that it would suffice for the parties to establish the existence of a common interest

---

claim for common interest privilege failed, but McGovern J accepted that one of the documents in issue was subject to "without prejudice" privilege.

[596] See *WXY v Gewanter* [2012] EWHC 1071 (QB) at [31], where Parkes QC accepted that, where defendants have a common interest in the defence of litigation, it followed that each of them might assert privilege in any communication between them which either: (a) consisted of or set out any confidential information between the defendants and their respective lawyers made for the purpose of giving or obtaining legal advice or assistance (*i.e.* where the original document was subject to legal advice privilege), or (b) was a document which came into existence once litigation was in reasonable prospect for the sole or dominant purpose of giving or receiving legal advice, or collecting information for use in the litigation (*i.e.* where the document was subject to litigation privilege in the hands of at least one defendant). It was further accepted that the second category would include communications between the defendants in which they discussed the nature or merits of the claimant's claim, their tactics in the litigation, or where one defendant passed to another information or evidence which he had acquired for the defence of the proceedings.

[597] [2008] IEHC 274 at [6.14], [2009] 2 IR 788 at 821–822, [2009] 2 ILRM 262 at 293. He observed, however, that an internal memorandum generated by the parent company of the first defendant, which related to the proposed terms of settlement as between the first defendant and the third defendant and was prepared for the purpose of securing approval for the proposed settlement agreement, might not attract common interest privilege, "not being a document which is concerned with the mutual interests of the parties in defending the plaintiff's claim".

[598] [2009] 3 IR 583, [2009] IESC 18.

[599] [2009] IESC 18 at [17], [2009] 3 IR 583 at 590.

[600] [1981] QB 223, [1980] 3 All ER 475.

[601] [1980] All ER 475 at 502. There was some difficulty applying this general principle to the facts of the case under consideration, given that litigation was anticipated from 2 April 1970 and the common firm of solicitors was not instructed by the parties until June 1970 and October 1970 respectively. Further, in 1979, one of the parties changed to another firm of solicitors. Lord Denning concluded that this did not matter (at 476), and Donaldson LJ adverted to the difficulty but upheld the claim of common interest privilege nonetheless (at 490).

[602] [1992] Lloyd's Rep.540 at 542.

so close that they could, had they chosen to do so, have used the same solicitor. In *Winterthur Insurance Company and the National Insurance & Guarantee Corporation Ltd v AG (Manchester) Ltd (in liquidation)*,[603] Aikens J observed that the English courts had refused to be prescriptive about the circumstances in which two parties will have a sufficient "common interest" in the communications under consideration, focusing instead on the particular facts of each individual case. More recent English authority suggests that it is not necessary for the parties to establish that they could have instructed the same solicitor, if they so wished, in order for common interest privilege to arise.[604] However, there appears to some ongoing uncertainty in this regard.[605]

10–243   This issue was considered in *Hansfield Developments v Irish Asphalt Ltd*,[606] where the court considered the nature of the relationship or connection required in order to ground an assertion of common interest privilege. McKechnie J rejected the contention that there is a requirement that the parties either have the same solicitor, or that their interests are sufficiently close that they could be represented by the same solicitor, before common interest privilege can arise. He held that, in considering whether there is a sufficient common interest between the parties, the court must consider whether the party to whom the documents have been disclosed has a sufficiently close interest in the subject matter of the primary privilege, *i.e.* in the proceedings, if litigation privilege applies, or in the advice if legal advice privilege applies.[607] Having engaged in a comprehensive review of the authorities, McKechnie J articulated the test for common interest privilege as follows:

> "... the Court must first determine by normal standards whether the documents would be privileged in the hands of the party transmitting the information, assuming that no disclosure had in fact been made. If it is found that the documents would be so privileged, then the court must ask whether the relationship between the parties was sufficiently close that the transmission of documents should *not* be held to amount to an implied waiver of the privilege. In considering this the Court should take into account the relationship between the parties, as well as the nature and purpose of the disclosure and whether there could be held to be an objective intention to waive privilege on the part of the holder. Privilege should not be overborne lightly, and therefore the ultimate question must be whether it is reasonable in the

---

[603] [2006] EWHC 839 (Comm) at [78]. See also *Formica Ltd v Secretary of State* [1995] 1 Lloyd's Rep 692 at 699, where Coleman J stated that, "the essential question in each case is whether the nature of their mutual interest in the context of their relationship is such that the party to which the documents are passed receives them subject to a duty of confidentiality which the law will protect in the interests of justice".

[604] *Svenska Handelsbanken v Sun Alliance and London Insurance Plc* [1995] 2 Lloyd's Rep 84 at 86; *Penny v Monatgu Private Equity LLP* [2010] EWHC 2354 (Ch) at [13]. See the discussion in Passmore, *Privilege*, 3rd edn (London: Sweet & Maxwell, 2013), at [6-074]. But see Matthews and Malek, *Disclosure*, 4th edn (London: Sweet & Maxwell, 2012), which states that it is not necessary for the parties to be represented by the same solicitor, "as long as their interests are close enough to be able to do so".

[605] In *Dadourian Group Int Inc v Simms* [2008] EWHC (Ch) 1784, [2008] All ER (D) 343 at [89], Patten J stated that parties must share a common solicitor for common interest privilege to arise. This dictum was considered by Lewison J in *Penny v Monatgu Private Equity LLP* [2010] EWHC 2354 (Ch) at [13], who concluded nonetheless that a common solicitor is not an essential requirement. The approach adopted in *Dadourian Group Int Inc v Simms* was described as 'too restrictive' by McKechnie J in *Hansfield Developments v Irish Asphalt Ltd* [2009] IEHC 420 at [47].

[606] [2009] IEHC 420. The question of common interest privilege was also considered by McGovern J in an earlier written decision handed down in the same case, *Hansfield Developments v Irish Asphalt Ltd* [2009] IEHC 90.

[607] [2009] IEHC 420 at [38]. He appeared to accept that such an interest should be legal, rather than of a commercial or economic nature.

circumstances to conclude that there was an implied waiver of the privilege. If such an implied waiver cannot be found, the Court should not otherwise interfere."[608]

10–244   Referring to what he described as the "putative common solicitor test", McKechnie J concluded that such a restrictive approach had been implicitly rejected by the High Court in *Moorview Developments v First Active plc*,[609] and by the Supreme Court in *Redfern Ltd v O'Mahony*,[610] given that it could not be suggested in either of those cases that the parties were, or could have been, served by the same solicitors. Thus, while the question as to whether the parties could be represented by the same solicitor is a relevant factor to be taken into account in deciding whether the relationship between the parties is sufficiently close for common interest privilege to arise, it is in no way determinative.[611]

11. Status of the Privilege

10–245   The traditional common law view of legal professional privilege was that it was merely a rule of evidence, the application of which was tied to the curial context. However, decisions in England,[612] Canada,[613] Australia,[614] and New Zealand[615] have taken the view that the privilege is more than a rule of evidence and have ascribed to it a substantive content which is capable of application in pre-trial and non-curial contexts.[616]

10–246   The Canadian courts have, perhaps, gone the furthest in that regard. Dickson J, delivering the judgment of the Supreme Court of Canada in *Solosky v Canada*,[617] described the right to communicate in confidence with one's legal adviser as "a fundamental civil and legal right, founded upon the unique relationship of solicitor

---

[608] [2009] IEHC 420 at [53] (emphasis in the original).

[609] [2009] 2 IR 788, [2009] 2 ILRM 262, [2008] IEHC 274.

[610] [2009] 3 IR 583, [2009] IESC 18.

[611] [2009] IEHC 420 at [54]. See the discussion in Passmore, *Privilege*, 3rd edn (London: Sweet & Maxwell, 2013) at [6-074] fn.92, where the decisions of the Irish courts in *Moorview Developments v First Active plc* [2009] 2 IR 788, [2009] 2 ILRM 262, [2008] IEHC 274; *Redfern Ltd v O'Mahony* [2009] 3 IR 583, [2009] IESC 18 and *Hansfield Developments v Irish Asphalt Ltd* [2009] IEHC 420 are cited in support of the contention that the ability to instruct the same solicitor is no longer an essential requirement.

[612] See *R. v Derby Magistrates' Court, ex parte B* [1996] AC 487 at 507, [1995] 4 All ER 526 at 540–541 and *General Mediterranean Holdings SA v Patel* [1999] 3 All ER 673, [2000] 1 WLR 272.

[613] In *R. v McClure* [2001] SCC 14 at [17], [2001] 1 SCR 445, it was held that solicitor-client privilege is "part of and fundamental to the Canadian legal system". See also *Smith v Jones* [1999] 1 SCR 455; *Stevens v Canada (Privy Council)* (1998) 161 DLR (4th) 85; *Descôteaux v Mierzwinski* [1982] 1 SCR 860, (1982) 141 DLR (3d) 590; *Solosky v Canada* [1980] 1 SCR 821, (1980) 105 DLR (3d) 745; *Re Director of Investigation and Research and Canada Safeway Ltd* (1972) 26 DLR (3d) 745.

[614] See *Daniels Corpn International Pty Ltd v Australian Competition and Consumer Commission* (2002) 213 CLR 543 at 563; *ESSO Australia Resources Ltd v Dawson* [1999] FCA 363, (1999) 162 ALR 79; *Carter v Northmore Hale Davy & Leake* (1995) 183 CLR 121; *Baker v Campbell* (1983) 153 CLR 52.

[615] *Rosenberg v Jaine* [1983] NZLR 1.

[616] *Cf. United States v Zolin* (1989) 491 US 544, 109 S Ct 2619.

[617] (1980) 105 DLR (3d) 745 at 760.

and client".[618] Subsequently, in *Smith v Jones*,[619] Cory J stated that legal professional privilege was "an element that is both integral and extremely important to the functioning of the legal system" and "the highest privilege recognised by the courts".[620]

10–247 In *Miley v Flood*,[621] Kelly J referred with approval to those developments and reiterated the view previously taken by him in *Duncan v Governor of Portlaoise Prison*[622] that: "Legal professional privilege is more than a mere rule of evidence. It is a fundamental condition on which the administration of justice as a whole rests."[623] These comments echo those of Hamilton CJ in *Quinlivan v Governor of Portlaoise Prison*,[624] that the privilege has "always been regarded by the courts as absolutely essential and of paramount importance in the administration of justice", and Finlay CJ in *Bula Ltd v Crowley (No. 2)*,[625] who referred to "the important confidence in relation to communications between lawyers and their clients which is a fundamental part of our system of justice and is considered in all the authorities to be a major contributor to the proper administration of justice."[626]

10–248 It now appears to be accepted that legal professional privilege has a constitutional foundation.[627] In *Martin v Legal Aid Board*,[628] the issue under

---

[618] In *Domican v AXA Insurance Ltd* [2007] IEHC 14, [2007] 2 IR 682 at [37], it was held that a party's entitlement to have access to the courts, and to have the benefit of legal assistance in so doing, carries with it an entitlement to restrain any action which would amount to a material or significant interference with such party's relationship between himself and his legal advisors in the context of litigation or potential litigation. See also *O'Brien v Personal Injuries Assessment Board* [2005] IEHC 100, [2007] 2 IR 1.

[619] [1999] 1 SCR 455 at 474–475.

[620] See also *Comr of Inland Revenue v West Walker* [1954] NZLR 191, where it was held that legal professional privilege is not merely a rule of evidence, but a substantive right founded on an important public policy.

[621] [2001] 2 IR 50 at 65, [2001] 1 ILRM 489 at 504.

[622] [1997] 1 IR 558 at 575, [1997] 2 ILRM 296 at 311 (quoting in both cases the statement to that effect of Lord Taylor CJ in *R. v Derby Magistrates' Court, ex parte B* [1996] AC 487 at 507, [1995] 4 All ER 526 at 540–541). See also *Dadourian Group International Inc v Simms* [2008] EWCA 1748 (Ch) and *Irish Haemophilia Society Ltd v Lindsay* [2011] IEHC 240.

[623] Referring to this dictum, Clarke J stated in *Moorview Developments v First Active plc*, unreported, High Court, 16 December 2007 at 14, that "a very high status indeed is accorded to legal professional privilege". See also *Ahern v Mahon* [2008] IEHC 119 at [59], [2008] 4 IR 704, [2009] 1 ILRM 458, where it was held that legal professional privilege is fundamental to the administration of justice and is protected by art.6 of the European Convention on Human Rights. See also *Doyle v Bergin* [2010] IEHC 531 and *Martin v Legal Aid Board* [2007] IEHC 76, [2007] 2 IR 759.

[624] Unreported, Supreme Court, 5 March 1997.

[625] [1994] 2 IR 54 at 59.

[626] See *AGAO v Minister for Justice* [2006] IEHC 251 at [28], [2007] 2 IR 492 at 499, where it was held that the right of access to a lawyer is a fundamental one. In *Hansfield Developments v Irish Asphalt* [2009] IEHC 420 at [24]–[25], McKechnie J cited a series of cases in which the fundamental importance of legal professional privilege (encompassing both litigation privilege and legal advice privilege) to the administration of justice was acknowledged.

[627] This possibility was adverted to in the first edition of this work, at [10-109], which noted that it could be argued that the right to communicate in confidence with a legal adviser is protected in the civil context by Art.40.3 as a facet of the right of access to the courts (*Macauley v Minister for Posts and Telegraphs* [1966] IR 345; *R. v Campbell* [1999] 1 SCR 565 at 601, (1999) 171 DLR (4th) 193 at 224) and in the criminal context by the right to legal representation (*State (Healy) v Donoghue* [1976] IR 325).

[628] [2007] IEHC 76 at [20], [2007] 2 IR 759 at [769].

consideration was the constitutionality of a provision of the Civil Legal Aid Act 2005,[629] which required the solicitors of legally aided clients to provide information to the Legal Aid Board, notwithstanding the duty of confidentiality owed by the solicitor to the client and regardless of whether the information was subject to legal professional privilege. The plaintiff contended that legal professional privilege is constitutionally protected as a dimension of the protection of the administration of justice (Art.34.1), the right to legal assistance (Arts 38.1 and 40.3) and the right of access to the courts (Art.40.3.1). During the course of her decision, Laffoy J referred to "the acknowledged constitutional protection which attaches to legal professional privilege as a dimension of the protection afforded by Article 34".[630] However, in circumstances where she concluded that s.32(2) of the 1995 Act would neither override nor interfere with the application of legal professional privilege, she did not proceed to consider the nature of the "constitutional dimension" which legal professional privilege has.[631]

10–249   These developments are in line with the approach adopted by the House of Lords in a series of cases commencing with *R. v Derby Magistrates' Court, ex parte B*,[632] where Lord Taylor made the following statement, which has been repeatedly adopted by the Irish courts[633]:

> "The client must be sure that what he tells his lawyer in confidence will never be revealed without his consent. Legal professional privilege is thus much more than an ordinary rule of evidence, limited in its application to the facts of a particular case. It is a fundamental condition on which the administration of justice as a whole rests."

10–250   This decision was cited with approval by the House of Lords in *R. (Morgan Grenfell & Co Ltd) v Special Comr of Income Tax*,[634] where it was held that legal professional privilege was a fundamental human right that could be overridden only by express words or necessary implication.[635] Lord Hoffman stated that legal professional privilege "is a fundamental human right long established in the common law", and "a necessary corollary of the right of any person to obtain skilled advice about the law".[636]

---

[629] Section 32(2) of the Civil Legal Aid Act 1995.

[630] [2007] IEHC 76 at [28], [2007] 2 IR 759. The State parties made no admission that legal professional pirvilege was protected by the Constitution, but did acknowledge that the privilege has a constitutional dimension.

[631] The arguments of counsel for the defendants are summarized in the judgment of Laffoy J (at [63]). Counsel accepted that it is clear from the authorities that the privilege is regarded as part of, and is fundamental to, the administration of justice and, to that extent, is subject to the Constitution. However, he pointed to the policy underlying the privilege, from which it is clear that its purpose is the furtherance of the administration of justice. It was argued that, even accepting that legal professional privilege is a constitutional right which can be asserted by an individual citizen (which was not conceded), such right cannot be greater than is required for the purposes of protecting or furthering the administration of justice.

[632] [1996] AC 487 at 507. See also *General Mediterranean Holdings SA v Patel* [1999] 3 All ER 673, [2000] 1 WLR 272.

[633] See, by way of example, *Miley v Flood* [2001] 2 IR 50 at 65, [2001] 1 ILRM 489 at 504; *Duncan v Governor of Portlaoise Prison* [1997] 1 IR 558 at 575, [1997] 2 ILRM 296 at 311; *Moorview Developments v First Active plc*, unreported, High Court, 16 December 2007 at 14; *Ahern v Mahon* [2008] IEHC 119, [2008] 4 IR 704, [2009] 1 ILRM 458; *Doyle v Bergin* [2010] IEHC 531; and *Martin v Legal Aid Board* [2007] IEHC 76, [2007] 2 IR 759.

[634] [2002] UKHL 21, [2003] 1 AC 563.

[635] *Cf. Bowman v Fell* [2005] 1 WLR 3083. But see *McE v Prison Service of Northern Ireland* [2009] 1 AC 908, where it was held that a statute providing for the surveillance of communications between persons in custody and their legal advisers was sufficiently explicit to override privilege. It was held, however, that the surveillance which had taken place was unlawful.

[636] [2002] UKHL 21, [2003] 1 AC 563 at 606–607. This aspect of the decision has been affirmed

He rejected the contention that legal professional privilege requires a balancing of interests, stating that the privilege "is absolute and based not merely upon the general right to privacy but also upon the right of access to justice."[637]

10–251 It is also well established that legal professional privilege is protected by the European Convention on Human Rights.[638] The principal source of this protection is art.6 of the European Convention on Human Rights, which guarantees the right to fair trial. In *Niemitez v Germany*,[639] the European Court of Human Rights stated that "where a lawyer is involved, an encroachment on professional secrecy may have repercussions on the proper administration of justice and hence on the rights guaranteed by article 6".[640] In addition, confidential communications passing between a lawyer and client are protected under art.8, which guarantees the privacy of correspondence.[641] In *Campbell v United Kingdom*,[642] the Court held that it is in the public interest "that any person who wishes to consult a lawyer should be free to do so under conditions which favour the full and uninhibited discussion"[643] and, therefore, correspondence with a solicitor is privileged under art.8.

10–252 European decisions in this area assumed additional significance with the incorporation of the Convention into domestic law by the European Convention on Human Rights Act 2003. This was adverted to by Lavan J in *Ochre Ridge Ltd v Cork Bonded Warehouses Ltd*[644] where, having referred to the dictum of Kelly J in *Miley v Flood* to the effect that legal professional privilege is more than a mere rule of evidence and "a fundamental notion on which the administration of justice rests", he stated that "[t]he fact that legal professional privilege is also protected by article 8 of

---

by the House of Lords in *Three Rivers DC v Bank of England (No. 6)* [2004] UKHL 48, [2005] 1 AC 610 and *R. (Prudential Plc) v Special Comr of Income Tax* [2013] UKHL 1, [2003] 2 AC 185.

[637] [2002] UKHL 21, [2003] 1 AC 563 at 608.

[638] *Ahern v Mahon* [2008] IEHC 119 at [60], [2008] 4 IR 704 at 719, [2009] 1 ILRM 458 at 471; *Miley v Flood* [2001] 2 IR 50 at 69, [2001] 1 ILRM 489 at 506; *R. (Morgan Grenfell Ltd) v Special Comr* [2002] UKHL 21, [2003] 1 AC 563 at 607. This possibility was adverted to in the first edition of this work at [10-109]. However, some doubt was expressed in this regard, given the comments of Advocate-General Warner in *AM & S Europe Ltd v Commission* [1983] 1 All ER 705 at 721, who pointed out that legal professional privilege was not expressly protected in the Convention or in the constitution of any member state and that while it was a right that was generally recognised, he did not think that it was a fundamental human right.

[639] (1992) 16 EHRR 97.

[640] Previously, in *S. v Switzerland* (1992) 14 EHRR 670, it had been held that the ability to communicate in confidence with a lawyer of one's choice without those communications being intercepted was one of the basic requirements of a fair trial in a democratic society and was protected by art.6(3)(c) of the Convention which guarantees the right of a defendant to obtain legal assistance in criminal trials.

[641] But see *Domican v AXA Insurance Ltd* [2007] IEHC 14, [2007] 2 IR 682, at [38] where Clarke J held that the practice of the defendant to copy correspondence sent to the plaintiff's solicitor directly to the plaintiff, despite the plaintiff's solicitors informing the defendant that the plaintiff did not wish to receive any direct correspondence, did not amount to a significant or material interference in the solicitor/client relationship. Clarke J further held that this did not amount to a breach of the constitutional right to privacy or the right to privacy, as guaranteed by the European Convention on Human Rights.

[642] [1993] 15 EHRR 137. See also *Foxley v United Kingdom* (2000) 31 EHRR 637.

[643] [1993] 15 EHRR 137 at 160.

[644] [2004] IEHC 160.

the European Convention of Human Rights, now part of Irish law, must be considered in this regard".[645]

C. Without Prejudice Privilege

1. Basis of the Privilege

10–253   The privilege granted in respect of communications in furtherance of settlement, commonly referred to as without prejudice privilege, rests on two bases; public policy and convention.[646] The primary justification for the rule is the public policy "of encouraging litigants to settle their differences rather than litigate them to a finish".[647] As Keane J explained in *Greencore Group Plc v Murphy*,[648] it is in the public interest that:

> "parties should be encouraged as far as possible to settle their disputes without recourse to litigation and should not be discouraged by the knowledge that anything that is said in the course of negotiations may be used in the course of proceedings."[649]

10–254   The privilege thus promotes the settlement of disputes by enabling parties to discuss their dispute and the relative strengths and weakness of their cases with complete candour, secure in the knowledge that anything said in the course of the negotiations cannot be used to their prejudice in the course of the proceedings. In the absence of such a privilege any concession made in the course of settlement negotiations, or even the fact that an offer of compromise was made, would be admissible as an admission and "[i]f this were permitted, the effect would be that no attempt to compromise a dispute could ever be made".[650] Therefore, although the privilege results in the exclusion of relevant evidence, any disadvantage to the administration of justice occasioned thereby is far outweighed by the advantages flowing from the settlements that are thereby facilitated. For this reason, the courts have generally given it an expansive application[651] and in

---

[645]   The European Court of Justice has also confirmed that the privilege is part of Community law—
AM&S Europe Ltd v Commission of the European Communities (Case 155/79) [1983] QB 878.

[646]   *Oceanbulk Shipping and Trading SA v TMT Asia Ltd* [2011] 1 AC 662 at 675 [24]; *Ofulue v Bossert* [2009] 1 AC 990 at 998, [2009] 2 WLR 749 at 754 (*per* Lord Hope), at 1013 at 769 (*per* Lord Walker) and 1021 at 777 (*per* Lord Neuberger); *Cutts v Head* [1984] Ch 290 at 313–314, [1984] 1 All ER 597 at 611; *Forster v Friedland*, unreported, Court of Appeal, 10 November 1992; *Unilever Plc v Proctor & Gamble Co.* [2000] 1 WLR 2436 at 2448–2449, [2001] 1 All ER 783 at 796.

[647]   *Rush & Tompkins v Greater London Council* [1989] AC 1280 at 1299, [1988] 3 All ER 737 at 739 (*per* Lord Griffiths); *Oceanbulk Shipping and Trading SA v TMT Asia Ltd* [2011] 1 AC 662 at 674 [19] (*per* Lord Clarke). See also *Moorview Developments v First Active plc* [2009] 2 IR 788 at 819, [2008] IEHC 274 at [6.7]; *Ryan v Connolly* [2001] 2 ILRM 174 at 181; *Greencore Group Plc v Murphy* [1995] 3 IR 520 at 525, [1996] 1 ILRM 210 at 216; *Quinlivan v Tuohy*, unreported, High Court, 29 July 1992 at 4; *Cutts v Head* [1984] Ch 290 at 306, [1984] 1 All ER 597 at 605–606; *Tomlin v Standard Telephones and Cables Ltd* [1969] 3 All ER 201 at 205; *I Waxman and Sons Ltd v Texaco Canada Ltd* [1968] 1 OR 642 at 656, (1968) 67 DLR (2d) 295 at 309; *Field v Commissioner for Railways for New South Wales* (1957) 99 CLR 285 at 291; *Cedenco Foods v State Insurance* [1996] 3 NZLR 205 at 210.

[648]   [1995] 3 IR 520 at 525, [1996] 1 ILRM 210 at 216.

[649]   [1995] 3 IR 520 at 525, [1996] 1 ILRM 210 at 216. See, to the same effect, *per* Keane CJ in *Ryan v Connolly* [2001] 2 ILRM 174 at 181.

[650]   *Per* Romilly MR in *Jones v Foxall* (1852) 15 Beav 388 at 396.

[651]   In *I Waxman and Sons Ltd v Texaco Canada Ltd* [1968] OR 642 at 656, (1968) 67 DLR (2d) 295 at 309, Fraser J said that it was "in the public interest that it not be given a restrictive application".

Dixons Stores Group Ltd v Thames Television Plc,[652] Drake J noted that "the modern tendency has been to enlarge the cloak under which negotiations may be conducted without prejudice".

10–255 This public policy justification is reinforced by the convention or implied agreement that when parties embark on settlement negotiations on a without prejudice basis they do so on the understanding that the contents of those discussions will not be used to the prejudice of either party.[653] There is a line of authority to the effect that the convention justification is separate from and may operate to modify or even expand the application of the public policy justification.[654] However, more recent decisions have emphasised that, while the express or implied agreement of the parties does form part of the justification for the rule, it is a privilege which is based on public policy. In *Ofulue v Bossert*,[655] Lord Rodgers identified *Rush & Tompkins Ltd v Greater London Council*[656] as an "important" decision because it establishes that, not only the parties to the without prejudice communication, but also third parties, are prevented from making use of its contents:

> "This in turn shows that, while part of the justification for excluding reference to what was said is to be found in the understanding of the parties to the relevant correspondence or negotiations, the rule is actually a privilege which forms part of the general law of evidence and is based on public policy. So, unless the parties make some agreement to narrow or broaden its effect, the scope of the privilege is a matter of general law and is not based on the supposed boundaries of a notional agreement between the parties."[657]

10–256 In *Oceanbulk Shipping and Trading SA v TMT Asia Ltd*,[658] the UK Supreme Court observed that the approach to without prejudice negotiations and their effect has undergone significant development over the years. The rule initially focused on the case where the negotiations between two parties were regarded as without prejudice to the position of each of the parties if the negotiations failed, and the essential purpose of the rule was to ensure that, if the dispute proceeded, neither party could rely on admissions made by the other in the course of negotiations. The underlying rationale of the rule was that the parties would be more likely to speak frankly if nothing they said could subsequently be relied upon and, as a result, would be more likely to settle the dispute. Lord Clarke stated, however, that "[i]t is now well settled that the rule is not limited to such a case".[659] The rule is based both on public policy and on the express or implied agreement of the parties that communications made during negotiations

---

[652] [1993] 1 All ER 349 at 351.

[653] *Cutts v Head* [1984] Ch 290 at 313–314, [1984] 1 All ER 597 at 611; *South Shropshire District Council v Amos* [1987] 1 All ER 340 at 343; *Muller v Linsley* (1994) 139 SJ LB 43.

[654] See *Hodgkinson & Corby Ltd v Wards Mobility Services Ltd* (1997) 24 FSR 178 at 190. *Cf. Muller v Linsley* (1994) 139 SJ LB 43. In *Unilever Plc v Proctor and Gamble* [2000] 1 WLR 2436 at 2445, [2001] 1 All ER 783 at 792, Walker LJ identified the express or implied agreement of the parties as the basis for the recognition by the court of the exception to the privilege for an offer made "without prejudice save as to costs" and stated that: "[t]here seems to be no reason in principle why parties to without prejudice negotiations should not expressly or impliedly agree to vary the application of the public policy rule in other respects, either by extending or by limiting its reach."

[655] [2009] 1 AC 990, [2009] 2 WLR 749.

[656] [1989] AC 1280.

[657] [2009] 1 AC 990 at 1008, [2009] 2 WLR 749 at 764. *Rush & Tompkins Ltd v Greater London Council* was also identified as an important decision by Lord Clarke in *Oceanbulk Shipping and Trading SA v TMT Asia Ltd* [2011] 1 AC 662 at 675.

[658] [2011] 1 AC 662, [2010] 3 WLR 1424.

[659] [2011] 1 AC 662 at 675, [2010] 3 WLR 1424 at 1432.

should not be admissible in evidence, and is not limited to admissions but extends much more widely to the content of discussions such as occurred in the case under consideration. Lord Clarke concluded, therefore, that: "[t]he without prejudice rule is now very much wider than it was historically. Moreover, its judicial importance has been judicially stressed on many occasions..."[660]

10–257 It would seem that in this jurisdiction, due to constitutional considerations, the contractual justification must be considered to be subsidiary to the public policy justification and could not be invoked to justify the application or extension of the privilege beyond the parameters supported by public policy.

2. Conditions for Establishing the Privilege

10–258 In order for a claim of privilege to succeed, the party claiming it must establish that the communication in question was made: (i) in a *bona fide* attempt to settle a dispute between the parties; and (ii) with the intention that, if negotiations failed, it could not be disclosed without the consent of the parties. These two tests can be seen to be closely related to the twin rationales identified above, which also influence how they are applied.[661]

(a) Bona fide attempt to settle dispute

10–259 The party seeking to assert privilege must show that at the time the communication was made, a dispute existed between the parties in respect of which legal proceedings had commenced or were contemplated[662] and the communication was made in a genuine attempt to further negotiations to settle that dispute.[663]

10–260 The fact that a communication concerns a dispute between parties is not sufficient to confer privilege—it must be made in furtherance of the settlement of the dispute. This is clear from the decision of Costello J in *O'Flanagan v Ray-Ger Ltd.*[664] The defendant objected to the admission of a letter written by its solicitor and headed "without prejudice" which contained an admission that the defendant held disputed property in trust for the plaintiff. The learned judge heard evidence from both the plaintiff and defendant about the circumstances surrounding the genesis of the letter. He noted that the plaintiff had not threatened legal proceedings and that her main concern was to ascertain from the defendant's solicitor what the true position was about her property. He concluded that the letter was admissible because it was not an

---

[660] [2011] 1 AC 662 at 676, [2010] 3 WLR 1424 at 1433–1434.

[661] In *Muller v Linsley* (1994) 139 SJ LB 43, Hoffmann LJ noted a trend towards a more rationale-based analysis of the privilege.

[662] It is not necessary that proceedings have commenced: *Rush & Tompkins Ltd v Greater London Council* [1988] 1 All ER 549 at 554 (*per* Balcombe LJ); *Warren v Gray Goose Stage Ltd* [1937] 1 WWR 465 at 472. In *Moorview Developments Ltd v First Active plc* [2009] 2 IR 788 at 818, [2008] IEHC 274 at [6.6], Clarke J accepted that negotiations as between the first and third defendants to the proceedings were conducted in contemplation of potential litigation in circumstances where the third defendant had indicated his intention to seek an indemnity or contribution from the first defendant in without prejudice correspondence. Proceedings had been commenced by the plaintiff against the defendant.

[663] This passage was cited with apparent approval by Murphy J in *O'Connor v P. Elliott & Co Ltd* [2010] IEHC 167 at [12].

[664] Unreported, High Court, 28 April 1983 at 14.

offer to settle a dispute but a statement as to the rights of the plaintiff and her husband in relation to certain property.[665]

10–261 In *O'Flanagan*, Costello J approved the statement in *Re Daintrey, ex parte Holt*,[666] that the privilege "has no application unless some person is in dispute or negotiation with another, and terms are offered for the settlement of the dispute or negotiation" and there is Commonwealth authority to the effect that privilege only applies to communications which contain terms for settlement.[667] The balance of authority indicates, however, that it is not necessary for a communication to contain terms[668] and privilege extends to all communications that are part of the negotiation process, including a document which merely seeks to initiate settlement discussions,[669] provided that it indicates a clear willingness to negotiate.[670] Privilege will not, however, apply to a communication made not as part of but after negotiations have concluded unsuccessfully[671] unless reference is made to the contents of the previous "without prejudice" communication.[672]

10–262 Although the designation by a party of a communication as "without prejudice" is a *prima facie* indication that the communication is in furtherance of settlement negotiations,[673] those words "possess no magic properties"[674] and will not be regarded as conclusive.[675] As Hoffman LJ emphasised in *Forster v Friedland*,[676] "whatever the parties may stipulate, the rule covers only those communications which are genuinely aimed at a settlement to avoid litigation". The propensity of parties, and particularly their solicitors, to mis-characterise their communications as being without prejudice has been the subject of adverse judicial comment.[677] A court will

---

[665] *Cf. Buckinghamshire County Council v Moran* [1990] Ch 623, [1989] 2 All ER 225 and *William Allan Real Estate Co v Robichaud* (1987) 37 BLR 286.

[666] [1893] 2 QB 116 at 119 (*per* Vaughan Williams J).

[667] *Drabinsky v Maclean-Hunter Ltd* (1980) 28 OR (2d) 23, 108 DLR (3d) 391; *Lamoureux v Smit* (1982) 40 BCLR 151; *Cedenco Foods v State Insurance* [1996] 3 NZLR 205 at 211.

[668] *South Shropshire District Council v Amos* [1987] 1 All ER 340 at 344; *Pirie v Wyld* (1886) 11 OR 422 (privilege applies to all communications fairly made for the purpose of expressing the writer's views on the matter of litigation or dispute as well as overtures for settlement or compromise).

[669] *South Shropshire District Council v Amos* [1987] 1 All ER 340 at 344; *Phillips v Rodgers* (1988) 62 Atla LR (2d) 146.

[670] In *Buckinghamshire County Council v Moran* [1990] Ch 623 at 634, [1989] 2 All ER 225 at 231, Slade LJ said that the public policy on which the privilege rests does not "justify giving protection to a letter which does not unequivocally indicate the writer's willingness to negotiate". In that case privilege was held not to apply to a letter marked "without prejudice" which contained an assertion of the defendant's rights rather than an indication of any willingness to negotiate.

[671] *Holland v McGill*, unreported, High Court, 16 March 1990; *Dixons Stores Group Ltd v Thames Television Plc* [1993] 1 All ER 349 at 351.

[672] *Somatra Ltd v Sinclair Roche & Temperley* [2000] 2 Lloyd's Rep 673 at 681.

[673] *South Shropshire District Council v Amos* [1987] 1 All ER 340 at 344.

[674] *O'Flanagan v Ray-Ger Ltd*, High Court, 28 April 1983 at 13.

[675] *Ryan v Connolly* [2001] 2 ILRM 174 at 181; *South Shropshire District Council v Amos* [1987] 1 All ER 340 at 344; *Dixons Stores Group Ltd v Thames Television Plc* [1993] 1 All ER 349 at 351; *Forster v Friedland*, unreported, Court of Appeal, 10 November 1992; *Cote v Rooney* [1982] 137 DLR (3d) 371 at 374.

[676] Unreported, Court of Appeal, 10 November 1992.

[677] In *Christie v Odeon (Ireland) Ltd* (1958) 92 ILTR 106 at 109, Kingsmill Moore J remarked that the use of the phrase "without prejudice" had "become quite indiscriminate in legal correspondence" and that "it would be to close one's eyes to all experience of the way correspondence is conducted between solicitors to suggest that all or even the majority of letters so headed have to do with attempts at settlement of the case". *Cf. Tomlin v Standard Telephones and Cables Ltd* [1969]

not, therefore, hesitate to examine a communication in order to ascertain whether it actually owes its genesis to an attempt to compromise a dispute.[678]

10–263 Indeed, the "without prejudice" tag is sometimes used by parties or their solicitors in an attempt to cloak from disclosure and absolve of legal consequence communications which have little or nothing to do with the settlement of disputes. This has prompted the courts to emphasise that privilege will only apply to communications made in a genuine[679] or *bona fide*[680] attempt to negotiate a settlement. As Walker LJ cautioned in *Unilever Plc v Proctor and Gamble Co*,[681] "without prejudice" is not a label which can be used indiscriminately so as to immunise an act from its normal consequences where there is no genuine dispute or negotiation. A good example of the attempted misuse of the privilege can be seen in *Kooltrade Ltd v XTS Ltd*.[682] The claimants sought to restrain threats of proceedings for patent infringement made by the defendants in connection with the importation of buggies for children by the claimants into the UK. One of these threats was allegedly contained in a letter marked "without prejudice" which had been sent to Tesco Home Shopping Ltd (the claimant's principal customer) and copied to the claimants. Pumfrey J held that letter was not privileged and could be admitted as an actionable threat because there were not, at the material time, any relevant negotiations taking place between the parties. Moreover, the letter had not been sent to the claimant but to Tesco and he inferred that it had nothing whatsoever to do with negotiation and everything to do with making the claimant's position with Tesco as difficult as possible.[683]

10–264 A more recent example of a case in which the court went behind the designation of communications as "without prejudice" is *O'Connor v P. Elliott & Co Ltd*,[684] where an issue arose as to whether two letters constituted a memorandum of an agreement for the sale of land for the purposes of the Statute of Frauds, notwithstanding the fact that they were marked "without prejudice". The parties had entered into a development agreement, in accordance with which the plaintiff agreed that he would not object to the grant of planning permission in respect of an adjoining property, on the basis that both properties would be redeveloped by the defendant. A dispute arose and the defendant indicated that it no longer intended to honour the original development agreement, at which point the plaintiff indicated that his original

---

3 All ER 201 at 205, where Ormrod J referred to instances of letters being headed "without prejudice" "in the most absurd circumstances". See also *Ofulue v Bossert* [2010] 1 AC 990 at 996, [2009] 2 WLR 749 at 752, where Lord Hope of Craighead stated that: "Sometimes letters get headed 'without privilege' in the most absurd circumstances... But where the letters are not headed 'without prejudice' unnecessarily or meaninglessly ... the court should be very slow to lift the umbrella unless the case for doing so is absolutely plain" (citing Ormrod J in *Tomlinson v Standard Telephones & Cables Ltd* [1969] 1 WLR 1378 at 1384 with approval).

[678] *Ryan v Connolly* [2001] 2 ILRM 174 at 181.

[679] *Rush & Tompkins Ltd v Greater London Council* [1989] AC 1280 at 1299, [1988] 3 All ER 737 at 740.

[680] *Dixons Stores Group Ltd v Thames Television Plc* [1993] 1 All ER 349 at 351; *I Waxman and Sons Ltd v Texaco Canada Ltd* [1968] 1 OR 642 at 644, (1968) 67 DLR (2d) 295 at 297.

[681] [2000] 1 WLR 2436 at 2448, [2001] 1 All ER 783 at 795.

[682] [2001] FSR 158.

[683] See also *In re Daintrey, ex parte Holt* [1893] 2 QB 116, where it was held that a written notice sent by a debtor to one of his creditors that he has suspended or was about to suspend payment of his debts was admissible to prove an act of bankruptcy upon the hearing of a bankruptcy petition even though expressed to be "without prejudice".

[684] [2010] IEHC 167.

forbearance in declining to object to the development works might be reversed and action taken accordingly. A meeting was held between the parties, during which an oral agreement for the sale of the plaintiff's property to the defendant was concluded. Correspondence subsequently exchanged between the parties in relation to the terms of the agreement was headed "without prejudice", rather than "subject to contract". The plaintiff contended that the correspondence was admissible on the basis that the communications were not sent in the context of a dispute or negotiations for the settlement of a dispute. Having considered the authorities, including *Unilever*, Murphy J confirmed that "[t]he use of the phrase 'without prejudice' should not inadvertently immunise acts from their normal legal consequences".[685] He concluded that, at the time the letters were sent, the essential elements of the deal had been agreed between the parties and agreement had also been reached in relation to compensation for disturbance. It was held, therefore, that the correspondence was not protected by the privilege, as there was no genuine dispute or negotiation to settle a dispute at the time it was sent.

10–265 It is important to note, however, that the stipulation of *bona fides* is directed towards ensuring that communications actually involve an attempt to resolve the parties' differences and does not import any general requirement of good faith.[686] This is evident from *WH Smith Ltd v Colman*[687] in which the plaintiff sought a variety of reliefs against the defendant arising from his opportunistic registration and subsequent offer for sale of the domain name WHSmith.com. After proceedings had been issued, the defendant wrote a letter to the Chairman of the plaintiff headed "without prejudice" which contained a plea to settle amicably. The trial judge concluded that the letter was not privileged because he was not satisfied of the *bona fides* of the defendant and did not regard the letter as a genuine offer to negotiate a settlement. However, Walker LJ in the Court of Appeal said that whatever doubts there were about the merits of the defendant's case and his *bona fides*, his letter indicated that he was negotiating for a settlement in order to avoid litigation and, therefore, the letter was privileged.

10–266 Furthermore, the courts are unconcerned with the substance of the settlement proposals or the nature of the compromise sought to be brokered. Thus, in *Forster v Friedland*,[688] it was held that the trial judge had erred in holding that privilege did not apply because there was no real dispute as to the legal issues and the purpose of the negotiations was simply to gain time. Hoffman LJ stated that there was no basis in authority or principle for limiting the rule to negotiations aimed at resolving the legal issues between the parties. Provided that the negotiations are genuinely aimed at settlement and the avoidance of litigation, "the nature of the proposals put forward or the character of the arguments used to support them, are irrelevant".

(b) Intention that the communication would not be disclosed

10–267 Settlement negotiations are not always conducted with the intention that any offers made should not subsequently be disclosed. Sometimes, a party will for tactical or other reasons, make an offer to compromise proceedings in "open" correspondence or negotiations. If that is the case, then the contents of those negotiations will be liable

---

[685] [2010] IEHC 167 at [14].
[686] *Alizadeh v Nikbin*, unreported, Court of Appeal, 25 February 1993; *The Times*, 19 March 1993.
[687] [2001] FSR 91.
[688] Unreported, Court of Appeal, 10 November 1992.

to production and admission in evidence in accordance with general principles.[689] Therefore, it is essential to establish whether the communication at issue was made with the express or implied intention that it would not be disclosed if negotiations failed.

10–268   The universal means of evincing such an intention is to preface or head the communication "without prejudice" and the use of this phrase will constitute *prima facie* evidence of the author's intention that privilege apply.[690] However, it is not necessary that a communication be so described if the court is satisfied from an examination of the contents of the communication and the surrounding circumstances that the parties intended that the contents of their settlement negotiations would not be disclosed.[691] A court will generally be willing to infer the existence of such an intention where it finds that a communication was in furtherance of settlement negotiations[692] but will not do so it if finds evidence that it was intended to be open.[693]

10–269   If a communication is made to the other side which is expressed to be "without prejudice", then, in general, any answer to it will also be privileged even if not expressed to be "without prejudice".[694] However, one party cannot force another to negotiate under the cloak of privilege if the other party does not wish to do so and, therefore, an answer to a "without prejudice" letter will not be privileged if it is clearly written on an "open" basis (as where it is so headed).[695] Where negotiations have commenced on a "without prejudice" basis, the courts will generally find that any subsequent communications were intended to be privileged[696] unless they find very clear evidence of an intention to change the character of the negotiations to "open".[697] Conversely, negotiations which commenced on an "open" basis may be found to have

---

[689] *Dixons Stores Group Ltd v Thames Television Plc* [1993] 1 All ER 349 at 351–352.

[690] *South Shropshire District Council v Amos* [1987] 1 All ER 340 at 344; *Kirk v Tompkins* (1992) 86 DLR (4th) 759 at 766–767. It is not necessary that the words be used to head the document; it will suffice if they appear in the main body: *Cory v Bretton* (1830) 4 C & P 462.

[691] *Greencore Group Plc v Murphy* [1995] 3 IR 520 at 525, [1996] 1 ILRM 201 at 216; *Rush & Tompkins Ltd v Greater London Council* [1989] AC 1280 at 1299, [1988] 3 All ER 737 at 740; *Rodgers v Rodgers* (1964) 114 CLR 608 at 614; *R. v Secord* [1992] 3 NZLR 570 at 572.

[692] See *Cheddar Valley Engineering Ltd v Chaddlewood Homes Ltd* [1992] 4 All ER 942 at 945 (communications in furtherance of settlement negotiations are *prima facie* privileged even if not headed "without prejudice"); *Forster v Friedland*, unreported, Court of Appeal, 10 November 1992 (fact that a communication is aimed at settlement may be strong indication of an intention that it should be "without prejudice"). Cf. *William Allan Real Estate Co. v Robichaud* (1987) 37 BLR 286 (privilege arises if the communication is made for the purpose of effecting a settlement without any need for proof of intention).

[693] *Forster v Friedland*, unreported, Court of Appeal, 10 November 1992. See, *e.g. Podovinikoff v Montgomery* (1984) 58 BCLR 204, 14 DLR (4th) 716, where the British Columbia Court of Appeal reached the conclusion that privilege did not apply to letters which were not marked "without prejudice" because the author was an experienced loss-adjuster and the court, therefore, inferred that the decision not to mark them without prejudice was conscious.

[694] *Christie v Odeon (Ireland) Ltd* (1958) 92 ILTR 106 at 109; *Paddock v Forrester* (1842) 3 Man & G 903; *Dixons Stores Group Ltd v Thames Television Plc* [1993] 1 All ER 349 at 351.

[695] *Marron v Louth County Council* (1938) 72 ILTR 101 at 103.

[696] *Bord na Mona v John Sisk and Son Ltd* [1990] 1 IR 85 at 88; *Denovan v Lee* (1990) 40 CPC (2d) 54.

[697] *Cheddar Valley Engineering Ltd v Chaddlewood Homes Ltd* [1992] 4 All ER 942 at 945 (the test is whether the change was made in circumstances as would have brought it home to the mind of a reasonable man in the position of the recipient).

changed to "without prejudice" basis at a later point and any communications from that point onwards will be protected.[698]

10–270   The position can be less clear in relation to settlement meetings or discussions. In the event that the parties have entered into "without prejudice" discussions with a view to compromising their differences, the privilege will cover whatever is said in the course of the discussion, including admissions; it is not ordinarily permissible to isolate some parts of the discussion and treat them as falling outside of the protection.[699] However, there is nothing to prevent the parties from agreeing that some communications are "without prejudice", whereas others are not. In *R. v K*,[700] the parties had agreed that part of a meeting was to be conducted "on the record" or on an open basis, with the balance of the meeting to be held on a "without prejudice" basis. The Court of Appeal held that, in these circumstances, the privilege did not afford any protection to statements made during the part of the meeting that was not held on a "without prejudice" basis.

3. Ambit of the Privilege

10–271   A fundamental question, in respect of which there was some uncertainty, is the precise ambit of the privilege and, in particular, whether it applies only to admissions as to liability made in the course of settlement negotiations, or whether it applies more broadly to prevent evidence being given of anything said in the course of settlement negotiations. Support for both approaches could be found in the case law and the authorities on this issue were not easy to reconcile. More recent authority, however, suggests that the privilege applies broadly, so as to exclude evidence of any statements made in the course of without prejudice negotiations.[701]

10–272   The narrower view was justified by reference to the genesis of the privilege, which evolved to protect parties from being prejudiced by any admission made in the course of settlement negotiations.[702] It followed that the application of the privilege was confined to circumstances where it was sought to admit a without prejudice communication as an admission of liability at the trial of the action.[703] This viewpoint was, perhaps, best articulated by Hoffmann LJ in *Muller v Linsley*[704]:

> "If one analyses the relationship between the without prejudice rule and the other rules of evidence, it seems to me that the privilege operates as an exception to the general rule on admissions (which can itself be regarded as an exception to the rule against hearsay) that the statement or conduct of a party is always admissible against him to prove any fact which is

---

[698] *Marron v Louth County Council* (1938) 72 ILTR 101; *South Shropshire District Council v Amos* [1987] 1 All ER 340.

[699] *R. v K* [2009] EWCA Crim 1640 at [49], citing *Unilever Plc v Proctor & Gamble* [2000] 1 WLR 2436, [2001] 1 All ER 784 with approval.

[700] [2009] EWCA Crim 1640 at [48]–[49].

[701] *Moorview Developments Ltd v First Active plc* [2008] IEHC 274 at [6.11], [2009] 2 IR 788 at 820.

[702] See *Waldridge v Kennison* (1794) 1 Esp 143 and *Jones v Foxall* (1852) 15 Beav 388 at 397.

[703] *Marron v Louth County Council* (1938) 72 ILTR 101 at 103; *Christie v Odeon (Ireland) Ltd* (1958) 92 ILTR 106 at 109; *Rush & Tompkins Ltd v Greater London Council* [1989] AC 1280 at 1299–1300, [1988] 3 All ER 737 at 740; *Muller v Linsley* (1994) 139 SJ LB 43; *Dora v Simper*, unreported, Court of Appeal, 15 March 1999; *Field v Commissioner for Railways for New South Wales* (1957) 99 CLR 285 at 291; *Cedenco Foods Ltd v State Insurance Ltd* [1996] 3 NZLR 205 at 210–211.

[704] [1996] PNLR 74 at 79, (1994) 139 SJ LB 43.

thereby expressly or impliedly asserted or admitted. The public policy aspect of the rule is not in my judgment concerned with the admissibility of statements which are relevant otherwise than as admissions, *i.e.* independently of the truth of the facts alleged to have been admitted."[705]

10–273   According to this theory, the privilege does not, therefore, prevent the admission of without prejudice communications where the relevance of the communication lies in the fact that it was made, rather than in the truth of any fact asserted therein; for example, where it is admitted to explain delay,[706] apparent acquiescence, or laches,[707] or to ascertain whether a party in settling a claim acted reasonably to mitigate his or her loss.[708] Applying similar reasoning, it has been held that the privilege does not apply to objective facts ascertained in the course of settlement negotiations,[709] communications which are relevant as facts independently of the merits of the case,[710] and statements made which do not relate to the negotiations such as statements as to future conduct.[711]

10–274   Other cases have, however, taken a broader view based on the public policy and convention rationales outlined above and have applied the privilege so as to protect a party from being prejudiced in any way by anything said in the course of settlement negotiations.[712] An early example of this approach can be seen in *Walker v Wilsher*[713] where Lindley LJ said that the words "without prejudice" meant "without prejudice to the position of the writer of the letter if the terms he proposes are not accepted". It was held that without prejudice communications could not be taken into consideration on the issue of costs and Bowen LJ justified this conclusion by reference to the justifications for the rule:

"In my opinion it would be a bad thing and lead to serious consequences if the Courts allowed

---

[705] See also *Bradford & Bingley v Rashid* [2006] 1 WLR 2066 at 2072–2073. However, this decision should be treated with caution, in light of the recent decision of the House of Lords in *Ofulue v Bossert* [2009] 1 AC 990, [2009] 2 WLR 749.

[706] *Marron v Louth County Council* (1938) 72 ILTR 101 at 103; *Family Housing Association (Manchester) Ltd v Michael Hyde and Partners* [1993] 1 WLR 354 at 363; *Jones v Foxall* (1852) 15 Beav 388 at 397; *Schetky v Cochrane* (1917) 24 BCR 496; *Cedenco Foods v State Insurance* [1996] 3 NZLR 205 at 210–211.

[707] *Walker v Wilsher* (1889) 23 QBD 335 at 338.

[708] *Muller v Linsley* (1994) 139 SJ LB 43.

[709] *Field v Commissioner for Railways for New South Wales* (1957) 99 CLR 285 at 291.

[710] In *Rush & Tompkins Ltd v Greater London Council* [1989] AC 1280 at 1300, [1988] 3 All ER 737 at 740, Lord Griffiths regarded the "exceptional" case of *Waldridge v Kennison* (1794) 1 Esp 143 in which without prejudice communications were admitted as proof of handwriting as authority for the proposition that the admission of an "independent fact" in no way connected with the merits of the case is admissible even if made in the course of negotiations for a settlement. This holding was applied in *McDowell v Hirschfield Lipson & Rumney* [1992] 2 FLR 126 at 132 where without prejudice correspondence was admitted on the issue of whether severance of a joint tenancy had taken place. See also *Tenstat Pty Ltd v Permanent Trustee Australia Ltd* (1992) 28 NSWLR 625 (without prejudice communications admitted to show notice of the exercise of an option).

[711] *Greencore Group Plc v Murphy* [1995] 3 IR 520 at 526, [1996] 1 ILRM 210 at 217; *Holland v McGill*, unreported, High Court, 16 March 1990 at 8.

[712] See *Walker v Wilsher* (1889) 23 QBD 335 at 337; *Simaan General Contracting Co v Pilkington Glass Ltd* [1987] 1 All ER 345 at 348; *Unilever Plc v Proctor & Gamble* [2000] 1 WLR 2436, [2001] 1 All ER 784. But *cf. Cutts v Head* [1984] Ch 290 at 306, [1984] 1 All ER 597 at 605–606 where Oliver LJ took the view that the public policy justification "essentially rests on the desirability of preventing statements or offers made in the course of negotiations for settlement being brought before the court of trial as admissions on the question of liability".

[713] (1889) 23 QBD 335 at 337.

the action of litigants, on letters written to them without prejudice, to be given in evidence against them or to be used as material for depriving them of costs. It is most important that the door should not be shut against compromises, as would certainly be the case if letters written without prejudice and suggesting methods of compromise were liable to be read without when a question of costs arose. The agreement that the letter is without prejudice ought, I think, to be carried out in its full integrity."[714]

10–275 The broader view was endorsed by the Court of Appeal in *Unilever Plc v Proctor & Gamble*.[715] The claimant instituted proceedings seeking a declaration of non-infringement of the defendant's patent and sought to admit evidence of a claim of right and threat to bring enforcement proceedings made by the defendant during a without prejudice meeting between the parties. The defendant applied to strike out the proceedings as an abuse of process on the basis that the statement in question was privileged. However, the claimant, relying on the old decision of *Kurtz & Co v Spence and Sons*,[716] argued that without prejudice privilege was confined in its application to admissions and did not extend to statements of the type at issue. Walker LJ, who delivered the leading judgment in the Court of Appeal, stated that the privilege "has a wide and compelling effect"[717] and took the view that:

"One party's advocate should not be able to subject the other party to speculative cross-examination on matters disclosed or discussed in without prejudice negotiations simply because those matters do not amount to admissions."[718]

10–276 Turning to the issue before the court, he refused to follow the decision in *Kurtz* and, instead, advocated a broader approach in line with the more modern authorities:

"Whatever difficulties there are in a complete reconciliation of [the modern] cases, they make clear that the without prejudice rule is founded partly in public policy and partly in the agreement of the parties. They show that the protection of admissions against interest is the most important practical effect of the rule. But to dissect out identifiable admissions and withhold protection from the rest of without prejudice communications (except for special reason) would not only create huge practical difficulties but would be contrary to the underlying objection of giving protection to the parties, in the words of Lord Griffiths in *Rush & Tompkins Ltd v Greater London Council*[719]: 'to speak freely about all issues in the litigation both factual and legal when seeking compromise and, for the purpose of establishing a basis of compromise, admitting certain facts.' Parties cannot speak freely at a without prejudice meeting if they must constantly monitor every sentence, with lawyers or patent agents sitting at their shoulders as minders."[720]

---

[714] (1889) 23 QBD 335 at 339. But see *Cutts v Head* [1984] Ch 290 at 306, [1984] 1 All ER 597 at 605, where Oliver LJ propounded the narrower view that the privilege is confined to admissions of liability only and acknowledged that the decision in *Walker v Wilsher* could not be explained by this theory because at the point where the issue of costs came to be determined, there were not further issues of fact to be determined on which admissions could be relevant. He went on to say that the decision could not be said to rest on public policy because, contrary to the view of Bowen LJ, it would not encourage settlements: "As a practical matter, a consciousness of a risk as to costs if reasonable offers are refused can only encourage settlement, whilst, on the other hand, it is hard to imagine anything more calculated to encourage obstinacy and unreasonableness than the comfortable knowledge that a litigant can refuse with impunity whatever may be offered to him even if it is as much as or more than everything to which he is entitled in the action". Therefore, he held that the decision was grounded on the conventional rationale for the privilege.
[715] [2000] 1 WLR 2436, [2001] 1 All ER 783.
[716] (1888) 5 RPC 161.
[717] [2000] 1 WLR 2436 at 2443, [2001] 1 All ER 783 at 791.
[718] [2000] 1 WLR 2436 at 2446, [2001] 1 All ER 783 at 793.
[719] [1989] AC 1280 at 1300, [1988] 3 All ER 737 at 740.
[720] [2000] 1 WLR 2436 at 2449, [2001] 1 All ER 783 at 796.

10–277   He, therefore, concluded that the trial judge had been right to conclude that it was an abuse of process for the plaintiff to be allowed to plead anything that was said at the meeting either as a threat or as a claim of right.

10–278   It is submitted that, ultimately, the question is one of policy and the parameters of the privilege should be dictated by the balance of public interest. In general, the balance of public interest will favour giving an expansive interpretation to the privilege. The privilege achieves its objective of promoting settlements by guaranteeing non-disclosure of the contents of the negotiations. This guarantee fosters the candour which is critical to the settlement process and which is undermined by disclosure for any purpose. It is only where parties can be sure that they can speak their minds and give their views in confidence that nothing said can be used to their prejudice and that the necessary candour can be forthcoming. Thus, the privilege should be applied to exclude evidence of without prejudice negotiations except where it can be clearly shown that greater damage to the interests of justice would be effected by non-admission than by disclosure.[721]

10–279   A broad interpretation of the ambit of the privilege was adopted by the High Court in *Moorview Developments Ltd v First Active plc*,[722] where Clarke J concluded that it is unnecessary, in the context of negotiations which seek to resolve existing or potential litigation, for a party asserting privilege to identify that admissions against interest had been made in the course of the negotiations; the entirety of the without prejudice negotiations is privileged. He emphasised the public interest objectives of the privilege, stating[723]:

> "The overriding principle is that a very heavy weight indeed needs to be attached to without prejudice privilege. The only circumstances where, therefore, evidence of without prejudice negotiations can be admitted is where ... 'it can be clearly shown that greater damage to the interests of justice would be affected by non-admission than by disclosure'. The exceptions to the general rule can be seen as deriving from that principle. For example the whole purpose behind the privilege is to encourage negotiation and settlement of litigation. That purpose would hardly be achieved if parties were precluded from leading evidence as to, at least, aspects of the negotiations, in circumstances where it was contended that the negotiations had achieved the desired end of settling the litigation.
>
> I am, therefore, satisfied that it is unnecessary, in the context of negotiations which seek to resolve existing or potential litigation, for a party asserting privilege to identify that admissions against interest had been made in the course of those negotiations."

10–280   It was held, therefore, that the criticism by the plaintiff of the failure on the part of the defendants to identify admissions against interest in the without prejudice communication in issue was "misplaced" and "based on a mistaken view as to the law of this jurisdiction in that regard". Thus, while evidence of the agreement concluded as between the defendants was admissible, evidence of all of the negotiations which took place between the first and third defendants and their representatives in respect of the agreement were inadmissible.

10–281   The broader view was also preferred by the House of Lords in *Ofulue v*

---

[721] This passage was approved as an accurate statement of the law in this jurisdiction by Clarke J in *Moorview Developments Ltd v First Active plc* [2008] IEHC 274 at [6.10], [2009] 2 IR 788 at 820.

[722] [2008] IEHC 274 at [6.11], [2009] 2 IR 788 at 817–820.

[723] [2008] IEHC 274 at [6.11]–[6.12], [2009] 2 IR 788 at 820.

Bossert,[724] where it was held that the privilege extended to an acknowledgement contained in a without prejudice offer made in previous proceedings, notwithstanding the fact that the acknowledgement was an agreed fact in those proceedings. The claimants, who were the registered owners of property in which the defendant resided, commenced possession proceedings in 1987, in which the defendant and her father counterclaimed for a lease. In circumstances where the claimants failed to pursue the possession proceedings, they were stayed automatically and, subsequently, struck out. The claimants then issued new possession proceedings, in which the defendant contended that the property had passed to her by way of adverse possession. During the course of the original proceedings, the defendant and her father made a without prejudice offer to purchase the property, which was refused by the claimants. The claimants sought to admit evidence of the without prejudice offer to purchase the property, as an acknowledgement of the claimants' title to the property.

10–282   The House of Lords accepted that the offer to purchase the property constituted an acknowledgement of the claimants' title. However, it was held that, in circumstances the offer had been made with the genuine intention of seeking to settle the earlier proceedings and the issue which had been raised in those proceedings remained unresolved, the without prejudice rule continued to apply.[725] Lord Neuberger, with whom the majority agreed, held that, save perhaps where it is wholly unconnected with the issues between the parties, a statement in without prejudice settlement negotiations should not be admissible in evidence, other than in exceptional circumstances.[726] He rejected the contention that the statement was admissible because it was relied on to establish that an acknowledgement of title was made, rather than to prove the truth of the statement, stating that "the distinction between an acknowledgement and an admission is not one which can be easily drawn ... at least in the context of identifying exceptions to the without prejudice rule".[727]

10–283   Lord Hope referred to the comments made by the Court of Appeal in *Unilever Plc v Proctor & Gamble*,[728] to the effect that the application of the privilege to admissions only would cause huge practical difficulties and would be contrary to the underlying objective of the rule, and observed that "[t]hese comments show that this is not a situation in which arguments that resort to procedural or linguistic technicalities are appropriate".[729] He suggested that the public policy underpinning the privilege should determine its limits:

> "The essence of [the rule] lies in the nature of the protection that is given to parties when they are attempting to negotiate a compromise. It is the ability to speak freely that indicates where the limits of the rule should lie. Far from being mechanistic, the rule is generous in its application. It recognises that unseen dangers may lurk behind things said or written during this period, and it removes the inhibiting effect that this may have in the interests of promoting attempts to achieve a settlement. It is not to be defeated by other considerations of public

---

[724] [2009] 1 AC 990, [2009] 2 WLR 749.
[725] Lord Hope noted that the without prejudice offer to purchase the lands could not have been made without the acknowledgement of title. Accordingly, the acknowledgement could not be said to be unconnected with, or fall outside the area of, the offer to compromise; it was a necessary part of it: [2009] 1 AC 990 at 999, [2009] 2 WLR 749 at 755.
[726] [2009] 1 AC 990 at 1022, [2009] 2 WLR 749 at 778.
[727] [2009] 1 AC 990 at 1023, [2009] 2 WLR 749 at 779.
[728] [2000] 1 WLR 2436, [2001] 1 All ER 783.
[729] [2009] 1 AC 990 at 998, [2009] 2 WLR 749 at 754.

policy which may emerge later, such as those suggested in this case, that would deny them that protection."[730]

10–284   Thus, it was held that, where correspondence is written "without prejudice" during negotiations conducted with a view to a compromise, the protection of the rule will be given to the communication unless the party seeking to admit it in evidence can show that there is a good reason for not doing so.[731]

10–285   As noted above, a communication may be admissible by way of an exception where the court is satisfied that greater damage to the interests of justice would result from its non-admission than disclosure. This was the conclusion reached in *Ryan v Connolly*.[732] The plaintiff instituted proceedings seeking damages for personal injury against the defendant more than three years after the date of the accident in question, but argued that the defendant was estopped from relying on the provisions of the Statute of Limitations 1957 (as amended). In order to establish this plea, the plaintiff sought to rely on statements made by the defendant in "without prejudice" correspondence exchanged between the parties which, it was argued, induced him to refrain from issuing proceedings within time. Keane CJ, delivering the Supreme Court judgment, emphasised the importance of without prejudice privilege and the public interest underpinning it out went on to say that:

> "The rule, however, although firmly based on considerations of public policy, should not be applied in so inflexible a manner as to produce injustice. Thus, where a party invites the court to look at 'without prejudice' correspondence, not for the purpose of holding his opponent to admissions made in the course of negotiations, but simply in order to demonstrate why a particular course had been taken, the public policy considerations may not be relevant. It would be unthinkable that the attachment of the 'without prejudice' label to a letter which expressly and unequivocally stated that no point under the Statute of Limitations would be taken if the initiation of the proceedings was deferred pending negotiations, would oblige a court to decide, if the issue arose, that no action of the defendant had induced the plaintiff to refrain from issuing proceedings."[733]

10–286   The Chief Justice, therefore, concluded that the court was entitled to look at the "without prejudice" correspondence for the purpose of determining whether the defendants were estopped from maintaining their plea that the proceedings were statute barred and, having done so, he was satisfied that they were not so precluded.[734]

10–287   Similarly, in *Oceanbulk Shipping and Trading SA v TMT'Asia Ltd*,[735] although the UK Supreme Court emphasised that privilege has a wide and compelling effect, it confirmed that exceptions to it are permitted where the justice of the case so requires. In that case, it was held that without prejudice communications were admissible in

---

[730] [2009] 1 AC 990 at 999, [2009] 2 WLR 749 at 755–756.
[731] [2009] 1 AC 990 at 997, [2009] 2 WLR 749 at 752–753.
[732] [2001] 2 ILRM 174.
[733] [2001] 2 ILRM 174 at 181. See also *Murphy v Grealis* (2006) IEHC 22, where the defendant initially sought to invoke the privilege, but subsequently accepted that no reliance would be placed on it. MacMenamin J. considered that the initial invocation of "without prejudice" privilege by the defendant suggested, in and of itself, that the parties had been involved in bona fide attempts to negotiate a settlement of the proceedings. This decision was upheld on appeal by the Supreme Court ([2009] IESC 9, [2009] 3 IR 366).
[734] See also *Family Housing Association (Manchester) Ltd v Michael Hyde and Pattners* [1993] 1 WLR 354 at 362–363, where it was held that without prejudice correspondence could be opened on an application to dismiss proceedings for want of prosecution.
[735] [2011] 1 AC 662.

evidence, by way of an exception to the privilege, as part of the factual matrix for the purpose of the construction of a settlement agreement and on the issue of estoppel.[736]

4. Effect of the Privilege

10–288   The privilege is the joint privilege of the parties to the settlement negotiations[737] and, if negotiations fail, a privileged communication may only be disclosed to the court with the consent of each of the parties.[738] However, if negotiations succeed the reason for non-disclosure ceases and the fact of the compromise is admissible.[739]

10–289   The privilege may, of course, be expressly waived by the parties but, in addition, a party may, by his or her conduct, impliedly waive privilege. Thus, if a party deploys privileged material in support of its case on the merits of the action, whether at the trial or on any interlocutory application, the other party will also be entitled to refer to the contents of those without prejudice communications to advance its case.[740]

10–290   In general, without prejudice communications will remain inadmissible in any subsequent litigation connected with the same subject-matter, whether between the same or different parties.[741] This is because it would discourage settlements if a party believed that admissions made in settlement negotiations in other proceedings could be used against him or her in other, perhaps, more important proceedings.[742] In *Rush & Tompkins Ltd v Greater London Council*,[743] it was held that public policy also required that without prejudice communications should be privileged from production as against persons not involved in the settlement negotiations, including other parties to the litigation. Lord Griffiths adverted to the possibility of one party taking up an unreasonably intransigent attitude and opined that it would "place a serious fetter on negotiations between other parties if they knew that everything that passed between them would ultimately have to be revealed to one obdurate litigant".[744]

10–291   This decision was distinguished in *Gnitrow Ltd v Cape Plc*[745] where the defendant, in an action for indemnity or contribution brought against it by the plaintiff, sought disclosure of the terms of a without prejudice agreement reached with another

---

[736] Cf. Zuckerman, "Without prejudice interpretation – with prejudice negotiations: *Oceanbulk Shipping and Trading SA v TMT Asia Ltd*' (2011) 15 E & P 232.

[737] *Cutts v Head* [1984] Ch 290 at 314, [1984] 1 All ER 597 at 611 (*per* Fox LJ) (the expression "without prejudice" "must be read as creating a situation of mutuality which enables both sides to take advantage of the 'without prejudice' protection"). Protection also extends to the parties' solicitors (*La Roche v Armstrong* [1922] 1 KB 485 at 489 (*per* Lush J).

[738] *Marron v Louth County Council* (1938) 72 ILTR 101 at 103; *Dixons Stores Group Ltd v Thames Televisions Plc* [1993] 1 All ER 349 at 351; *Walker v Wilsher* (1889) 23 QBD 335 at 339.

[739] *Moorview Developments Ltd v First Active plc* [2008] IEHC 274 at [6.12], [2009] 2 IR 788 at 820–821; *Quinlivan v Tuohy*, unreported, High Court, 29 July 1992.

[740] *Somatra Ltd v Sinclair Roche & Temperley* [2000] 2 Lloyd's Rep 673.

[741] *Greencore Group Plc v Murphy* [1995] 3 IR 520 at 525, [1996] 1 ILRM 210 at 216; *Bord na Móna v John Sisk and Son Ltd* [1990] 1 IR 85 at 88–89; *Rush & Tompkins Ltd v Greater London Council* [1989] AC 1280 at 1301, [1988] 3 All ER 737 at 741; *David J Instance Ltd v Denny Bros Printing Ltd* [2000] FSR 869 at 879–880; *I Waxman & Sons Ltd v Texaco Canada Ltd* (1968) 67 DLR (2d.) 295 at 309.

[742] *Rush & Tompkins Ltd v Greater London Council* [1989] AC 1280 at 1301, [1988] 3 All ER 737 at 741.

[743] [1989] AC 1280, [1988] 3 All ER 737.

[744] [1989] AC 1280 at 1305, [1988] 3 All ER 737 at 744.

[745] [2000] 3 All ER 763.

potential defendant. It was held by Court of Appeal that privilege did not attach to the agreement because the mischief identified by Lord Griffiths did not exist. However, Pill LJ confined his conclusion to the situation where a claimant has settled for a fixed sum a specific claim against him and seeks only an indemnity or contribution with respect to the sum paid by him. He acknowledged that the circumstances would be different, for example, if a claimant in an action for damages for personal injuries were to settle with one of two defendants. It could be a severe disincentive to negotiations generally if, by declining to negotiate, a party could routinely claim the advantage of knowing what other parties have agreed before condescending to negotiate for himself.

10–292   In *Ofulue v Bossert*,[746] the facts of which are outlined above, the House of Lords held that the privilege may continue to protect without prejudice communications from disclosure after the action which the parties were trying to settle when they entered into the negotiations has been struck out. This conclusion was explained by Lord Hope on the basis that: "[t]he public policy grounds for the rule would be contradicted if the protection were not available in fresh proceedings to replace those which were struck out".[747] In the same case, Lord Rodger noted that the purpose of the privilege is to prevent the use of anything said in without prejudice negotiations as evidence, but stated that:

> "its rationale appears to be wider: it is that parties and their representatives who are trying to settle disputes should be able to negotiate openly, without having to worry that what they say may be used against them subsequently, whether in the current dispute or in some different situation".[748]

10–293   It was held that the principles which govern the admissibility in subsequent proceedings, of a statement made in without prejudice negotiations to settle earlier proceedings, should be the same as those which would govern its admissibility in the earlier proceedings.[749] Thus, the Court extended the privilege to negotiations which took place in connection with earlier proceedings involving an issue that was still unresolved.

10–294   The Irish courts have held that the privilege protects without prejudice negotiations between two or more defendants, which result in a settlement agreement as between the defendants but do not result in the compromise of the proceedings as between the plaintiff and the defendants. In *Moorview Developments Ltd v First Active plc*,[750] an internal memorandum generated by the parent company of the first defendant, which related to the proposed terms of settlement as between the first defendant and the third defendant, came to the attention of the plaintiff through inadvertence. The memorandum was prepared for the purpose of securing approval for the proposed settlement agreement and, as such, it recorded the thinking of the first defendant and its parent company in relation to the proposed settlement, as well as certain other arrangements entered into in relation to the conduct of the proceedings. The first and third defendants asserted that the memorandum was covered by without prejudice privilege. Clarke J accepted that the negotiations (and proposed agreement) the subject matter of the memorandum were conducted at a time when potential litigation was contemplated as between the first and third defendants. Having considered the public policy underpinning the privilege, he concluded that the privilege extended to

---

[746] [2009] 1 AC 990, [2009] 2 WLR 749.
[747] [2009] 1 AC 990 at 999, [2009] 2 WLR 749 at 755.
[748] [2009] 1 AC 990 at 1010, [2009] 2 WLR 749 at 766.
[749] [2009] 1 AC 990 at 1020–1021, [2009] 2 WLR 749 at 776.
[750] [2008] IEHC 274 at [6.11], [2009] 2 IR 788 at 817–820.

the entirety of the negotiations between the first and third defendants, including the memorandum.[751]

10–295   The extent to which statements made in the course of "without prejudice" communications in civil proceedings are admissible against a party in subsequent criminal proceedings was considered by the English Court of Appeal in *R. v K*.[752] The statements in question were made during meetings held on a without prejudice basis with a view to negotiating the settlement of family law proceedings, and disclosed the existence of various accounts and investment portfolios in Switzerland and Liechtenstein. The admissions tended to implicate the defendant in tax evasion and the Crown sought to rely upon them in subsequent criminal proceedings. The trial judge held that the statements were not admissible in the criminal law proceedings. This decision was reversed by the Court of Appeal, which concluded that the public interest in prosecuting crime is sufficient to outweigh the public interest in the settlement of disputes and, accordingly, admissions made in the course of 'without prejudice' negotiations are not inadmissible simply by virtue of the circumstances in which they are made.[753]

5. Exceptions to the Privilege

10–296   Apart from the instances, discussed in the foregoing section, where the courts have found the privilege not to apply, there are a number of recognised circumstances in which the courts will pierce the veil of privilege in the interests of justice.[754] The "most important" instances in which the privilege does not apply were identified by Walker LJ in *Unilever v Proctor and Gamble*[755] in a statement of the law which has been cited with approval in a series of subsequent cases, both in England and in this jurisdiction.[756]

10–297   Thus, "without prejudice" communications are admissible if a question arises as to whether they have resulted in a concluded agreement,[757] whether a settlement document reflects what was actually agreed between the parties,[758] and where

---

[751] [2008] IEHC 274 at [6.12], [2009] 2 IR 788 at 817–820.

[752] [2009] EWCA Crim 1640.

[753] [2009] EWCA Crim 1640 at [72].

[754] *Rush & Tompkins Ltd v Greater London Council* [1989] AC 1280 at 1300, [1988] 3 All ER 737 at 740.

[755] [2000] 1 WLR 2436 at 2444–2445, [2001] 1 All ER 784 at 791–792.

[756] See, for example, *Meath County Council v Irish Shell Ltd* [2006] IEHC 391 and *Oceanbulk Shipping SA v TMT Ltd* [2011] 1 AC 662 at 677–678 [31]–[32].

[757] *Moorview Developments Ltd v First Active plc* [2008] IEHC 274 at [6.7], [2009] 2 IR 788 at 819; *Admiral Management Services Ltd v Para-Protect Europe Limited* [2002] 2 WLR 2722 at 2742; *Tomlin v Standard Telephones and Cables Ltd* [1969] 3 All ER 201 at 203; *Walker v Wilsher* (1889) 23 QBD 335 at 337; *Pearlman v National Life Assurance Co of Canada* (1917) 39 OLR 141 at 142; *Butler v Countrywide Finance Ltd* (1992) 5 PRNZ 447. *Cf. Hunnisett v Owens*, unreported, High Court, 15 May 1992, where without prejudice correspondence was opened where a dispute arose as to whether the plaintiff's claim had been settled as a result of negotiations between the parties. In *Meath County Council v Irish Shell Ltd* [2006] IEHC 391, evidence of without prejudice communications was admitted in an action for specific performance of an agreement concluded following settlement negotiations between the parties (see also *Thermo King Ireland Ltd v Burke* [2005] IEHC 401).

[758] *Admiral Management Services Ltd v Para-Protect Europe Limited* [2002] 2 WLR 2722, cited with apparent approval in *Meath County Council v Irish Shell Ltd* [2006] IEHC 391 at [19]; *Allison v KPMG* (1994) 8 PRNZ 128. *Cf. Mespil Ltd v Capaldi* [1986] ILRM 373 where evidence of

rectification of a settlement agreement is sought.[759] Without prejudice communications are also admissible if a question arises as to whether they give rise to an estoppel.[760] In addition, without prejudice communications may be admitted to explain delay or apparent acquiescence,[761] or to ascertain whether a party in settling a claim acted reasonably to mitigate his or her loss.[762]

10–298   Evidence of the negotiations is also admissible to show that an agreement apparently concluded between the parties during the negotiations should be set aside on the ground of misrepresentation, fraud or undue influence.[763] Similarly, evidence of without prejudice negotiations may also be admitted if the exclusion of the evidence would act as a cloak for perjury, blackmail or other "unambiguous impropriety".[764]

10–299   The jurisdiction of the courts to recognise new exceptions to the rule where justice so requires it, and the principles governing the exercise of this jurisdiction, have been considered by the House of Lords and the English Supreme Court in two recent decisions. In *Ofulue v Bossert*,[765] the House of Lords accepted that it was open to the courts to recognise new exceptions to the privilege where justice so required, but concluded that reasons of legal and practical certainty made it inappropriate to create a further exception so as to allow for evidence of "independent" admissions. The issue for determination was whether a without prejudice offer by the defendant to purchase the claimants property in previous proceedings was admissible as evidence of an acknowledgement of the claimants' title for the purposes of the Limitation Act 1980. The claimant argued that the acknowledgement could be viewed as "a fact" independently of any admission contained in the without prejudice offer. In support of this contention, the claimant argued that the communication was relied upon in order to establish the fact that there was an acknowledgement of title within the 12 year period, and not to establish the truth of the admission (that the claimant was the owner of the property).

---

without prejudice communications was given where there was a disagreement as to what had actually been agreed.
[759] *Oceanbulk Shipping SA v TMT Ltd* [2011] 1 AC 662 at 679; *Meath County Council v Irish Shell Ltd* [2006] IEHC 391 at [22]; *Admiral Management Services Ltd v Para-Protect Europe Limited* [2002] 2 WLR 2722 at 2742.
[760] *Hodgkinson & Corby Ltd v Wards Mobility Services Ltd* [1997] FSR 178 at 190–191, cited with approval by Walker LJ in *Unilever Plc v Proctor and Gamble* [2000] 1 WLR 2436 at 2444, [2001] 1 All ER 783 at 792.
[761] *Walker v Wilsher* (1889) 23 QBD 335 at 338. It was held that, in that case, that the evidence of without prejudice communications admitted on this basis may be limited to the fact that such communications were made and the dates on which they were made. However, in *Unilever Plc v Proctor and Gamble* [2000] 1 WLR 2436 at 2444–2445, [2001] 1 All ER 784 at 792, Walker LJ recognised the admission of evidence to explain delay or apparent acquiescence as a recognised exception to the privilege, and stated that more substantive evidence may be admissible as an exception to the privilege in the event that this is required in order give the court "a fair picture of the rights and wrongs of the delay".
[762] *Muller v Linsley* (1994) 139 SJ LB 43, cited with approval by Walker LJ in *Unilever Plc v Proctor and Gamble* [2000] 1 WLR 2436 at 2444, [2001] 1 All ER 783 at 792.
[763] *Underwood v Cox* (1912) 4 DLR 66, cited with approval by Walker LJ in *Unilever Plc v Proctor and Gamble* [2000] 1 WLR 2436 at 2444, [2001] 1 All ER 784 at 792.
[764] *Forster v Friedland*, unreported, Court of Appeal (Civil Division), 10 November 1992; *Finch v Wilson*, unreported, 8 May 1987; *Harwick Jersey International Ltd v Caplan*, The Times, 11 March 1998; *Fazil-Alizadeh v Nikbin*, unreported, 25 February 1993; Court of Appeal (Civil Division).
[765] [2009] 1 AC 990, [2009] 2 WLR 749.

10–300   Lord Neuberger, with whom the majority agreed,[766] rejected the contention that the offer to compromise was admissible because it was relied upon to establish the fact that an acknowledgement of title had occurred, rather than as evidence of the truth of the admission. Referring to the statement of Lord Hoffman in *Muller v Linsley*,[767] that "the public policy aspect of the rule is not ... concerned with the admissibility of statements which are relevant otherwise than as admissions, *i.e.* independently of the truth of the facts alleged to have been admitted", Lord Neuberger stated that this "is a distinction which is too subtle to apply in practice", and the application of which would often risk falling foul of the problem identified by Robert Walker LJ in the *Unilever* case.[768] In addition, this distinction also appears to be limited to the public policy reason for the privilege, and does not consider the contractual justification.

10–301   In *Ofulue*, all of the members of the House of Lords accepted that it is open to the court to create further exceptions to the privilege. However, the majority concluded that it would be inappropriate, for reasons of legal and practical certainty, to do so in respect of an "independent fact" lying outside the area of the offer to compromise. This conclusion, which was firmly based upon the public policy behind the rule, was explained as follows by Lord Rodgers[769]:

> "Undoubtedly, it would be possible to carve out an exception along those lines. The question is whether creating such an exception would be consistent with the overall policy behind the rule... In my view there must indeed be a significant danger that allowing in evidence of admissions of 'independent facts' would undermine the effectiveness of the rule as an encouragement to parties to speak freely when negotiating a compromise of their dispute. As was said many years ago,
>> 'If the proper basis of the rule is privilege, is there any logical theory under which the court can, by methods akin to chemistry, analyze a compromise conversation so as to precipitate one element of it as an offer of settlement and the other as an independent statement of fact? Would not the layman entering into a compromise negotiation be shocked if he were informed that certain sentences of his conversation could be used against him and other sentences could not?'[770]"

10–302   A similar approach was adopted by Lord Walker, who stated that, as a matter of principle, the without prejudice rule should not be restricted unless justice clearly demands it.[771] He noted that the without prejudice rule has developed "vigorously" and held that, while there are exceptions to the rule where the justice of the case requires it, the recognised exceptions should not "whittle down the protection given to the parties to speak freely".[772]

10–303   The scope of the exceptions to the without prejudice rule were considered again by the UK Supreme Court in *Oceanbulk Shipping and Trading SA v TMT Asia Ltd*,[773] which concerned a dispute between the parties in relation to the proper

---

[766] While there was only one dissenting judgment, from Lord Scott, written judgments were delivered by Lord Hope, Lord Walker, Lord Rodgers and Lord Neuberger. Lords Hope, Walker and Rodgers agreed with Lord Neuberger, but wished to make a number of observations in relation to what they considered to be a "troublesome" issue.

[767] [1996] PNLR 74 at 79, (1994) 139 SJ LB 43.

[768] [2009] 1 AC 990 at 1023, [2009] 2 WLR 749 at 779.

[769] [2009] 1 AC 990 at 1008–1009, [2009] 2 WLR 749 at 764–765.

[770] John E Tracy, "Evidence—Admissibility of Statements of Fact made During Negotiation for Compromise" [1935–1936] 34 Mich L Rev 524 at 529.

[771] [2009] 1 AC 990 at 1013, [2009] 2 WLR 749 at 769.

[772] [2009] 1 AC 990 at 1013 at 1014, [2009] 2 WLR 749 at 769–770.

[773] [2011] 1 AC 662.

interpretation of a written settlement agreement. The communications included an email sent without prejudice and assertions made during without prejudice meetings. The trial judge concluded that the evidence was potentially of significant probative value and might possibly be crucial upon an issue of construction that was central to the proceedings. It was held that without prejudice communications were admissible in evidence, by way of an exception to the privilege, as part of the factual matrix for the purpose of the construction of a settlement agreement and on the issue of estoppel.

10–304   Lord Clarke stated that the authorities show that, because of the importance of the without prejudice rule, its boundaries should not be lightly eroded. Having considered the established exceptions to the rule, he observed that evidence of without prejudice communications is admissible in order to establish whether an agreement has been concluded, to resolve the issue of what that agreement was, and in circumstances where a party is seeking rectification of a settlement agreement.[774] He distinguished between two "entirely distinct" questions: the first, whether the evidence a party seeks to admit forms part of the factual matrix and, as a result, is admissible as an aid to interpretation; the second, whether, in circumstances where the pre-contractual negotiations are without prejudice, evidence of the negotiations is admissible as an aid to construction of a settlement agreement. He concluded that there was no reason why the ordinary principles governing contractual interpretation should not apply to a settlement agreement concluded following without prejudice negotiations, stating[775]:

> "The language should be construed in the same way and the question posed by Lord Hoffmann should be the same, namely what a reasonable person having all the background knowledge which would have been available to the parties would have understood them to be using the language in the contract to mean. That background knowledge may well include objective facts communicated by one party to the other in the course of the negotiations. As I see it, the process of interpretation should in principle be the same, whether the negotiations were without prejudice or not. In both cases the evidence is admitted in order to enable the court to make an objective assessment of the parties' intentions."

10–305   Lord Clarke held that the recognition of an exception to the without privilege rule in respect of negotiations which form part of the factual matrix does not undermine the public policy underpinning the rule, which is to encourage parties to speak freely and, thus, to promote settlement. On the contrary, if a party to negotiation is aware that, in the event of a dispute about what a settlement agreement means, objective facts which emerge during negotiations will be admitted in order to assist the court to interpret the agreement in accordance with the parties' true intentions, settlement is likely to be encouraged rather than discouraged.[776] He concluded that the recognition of an exception in respect of statements which form part of the factual matrix was the only way in which the modern principles of construction of contracts could properly be respected, and observed that there is no sensible distinction between this exception and the exceptions already recognised in respect of rectification, the admission of evidence in order to determine whether an agreement has been concluded, and the admission of evidence in order to ascertain the terms of the agreement which has been concluded.

(a) Illegality and "unambiguous impropriety"

10–306   As we have seen, the privilege is founded on public policy and, therefore,

---

[774] [2011] 1 AC 662 at 679, [2010] 3 WLR 1424 at 1436.
[775] [2011] 1 AC 662 at 681, [2010] 3 WLR 1424 at 1438.
[776] [2011] 1 AC 662 at 681, [2010] 3 WLR 1424 at 1438.

cannot be used in a way to further ends which are contrary to public policy. Thus, parties will not be permitted to use privilege as a cloak for illegality or impropriety as where threats are made in the course of settlement negotiations. For example, in *Greenwood v Fitts*,[777] it was held that privilege did not apply in circumstances where the defendant told the plaintiffs in the course of without prejudice negotiations that unless they withdrew their claim for fraudulent misrepresentation he would give perjured evidence and bribe other witnesses to perjure themselves, and further, that if they nevertheless succeeded, he would leave the jurisdiction rather than pay damages. Shepherd JA said that the privilege "was never intended to give protection to this sort of thing."[778] Neither will parties be permitted to assert privilege where to do so would result in the court being deceived or misled.[779]

10–307   The scope of this exception has been considered in a series of cases involving the surreptitious recording of settlement meetings by one of the participants, the transcripts of which were later sought to be admitted on the basis that they disclosed impropriety on the part of the other party. In the first of these, *Hawick Jersey Ltd v Caplan*,[780] an analogy was drawn with the crime/fraud exception to legal professional privilege and the transcripts were admitted because they contained *prima facie* evidence that the transaction the subject-matter of the proceedings had not taken place as alleged and that the plaintiffs were bringing the proceedings in order to put pressure on the defendants to settle other proceedings. Subsequently, in *Forster v Friedland*,[781] Hoffmann LJ in the Court of Appeal rejected as dangerous the analogies sought to be drawn with the crime/fraud exception to legal professional privilege. He said that: "[i]f there is any analogy between the without prejudice rule and legal professional privilege, it is with advice as to the conduct of the litigation rather than advice as to a transaction which becomes the subject matter of litigation." He stressed the high threshold to be met before privilege could be pierced:

> "I accept that a party, whether plaintiff or defendant, cannot use the without prejudice rule as a cloak for blackmail ... but the value of the without prejudice rule would be seriously impaired if its protection could be removed by anything less than unambiguous impropriety. The rule is designed to encourage parties to express themselves freely and without inhibition. I think it is quite wrong for tape recorded words of a layman, who has used colourful or even exaggerated language, to be picked over in order to support an argument that he intends to raise defences which he does not really believe to be true."[782]

10–308   On the facts, he was satisfied that there had not been any blackmail. The plaintiff argued that the tapes disclosed that the first defendant was threatening to advance what he knew to be a sham defence, namely, that there had been no agreement. However, the learned judge took the view that the tapes merely amounted to a restatement by the first defendant of his position that there had been no legally binding agreement.

---

[777] (1961) 29 DLR (2d) 260.

[778] (1961) 29 DLR (2d) 260 at 269. *See also Underwood v Cox* (1912) 26 OLR 303, [1912] 4 DLR 66 and *Dora v Simper*, unreported, Court of Appeal, 15 March 1999 (statements of defendants that they would transfer their assets so as to avoid the effect of any judgment obtained held to be capable of establishing the unambiguous impropriety required to set aside privilege).

[779] *McFadden v Snow* (1951) 69 WN (NSW) 8 at 10; *Pitts v Adney* [1961] NSWR 535 at 539; *JA McBeath Nominees Pty Ltd v Jenkins Development Corporation Pty Ltd* [1992] 2 Qd R 121.

[780] Unreported, Queen's Bench Division, 26 February 1988, *The Times*, 11 March 1988.

[781] Unreported, Court of Appeal, 10 November 1992.

[782] Unreported, Court of Appeal, 10 November 1992.

10–309   In *Alizadeh v Nikbin*,[783] the test of "unambiguous impropriety" was applied and the claim of privilege was upheld because although the transcripts disclosed evidence of impropriety, that evidence was not unambiguous. Brown LJ explained why a high threshold in cases of this kind was desirable:

> "There are in my judgment powerful policy reasons for admitting in evidence as exceptions to the without prejudice rule only the very clearest of cases. Unless this highly beneficial rule is most scrupulously and jealously protected, it will all too readily become eroded. Not least requiring of rigorous scrutiny will be claims for admissibility of evidence advanced by those (such as the first defendant here) who have procured their evidence by clandestine methods and who are likely to have participated in discussions with half a mind at least to their litigious rather than their settlement advantages. That distorted approach to negotiation to my mind is itself to be discourages, militating, as inevitably it must, against the prospects of successful settlement."

10–310   The unambiguous impropriety test has been considered in a number of recent decisions which demonstrate its stringency.[784] In *WH Smith Ltd v Colman*,[785] the Court of Appeal held that it did not apply on the facts, with Walker LJ emphasising that the privilege "is not to be set aside simply because a party making a without prejudice communications appears to be putting forward an implausible or inconsistent case or to be facing an uphill struggle if the litigation continues." Neither was the test satisfied in *Kooltrade Ltd v XTS Ltd*,[786] where Pumfrey J took the view that a threat of infringement proceedings in circumstances where the person did not have a patent or design right was not "so grave and unambiguous an impropriety as would justify invasion of the without prejudice privilege if otherwise the privilege were available."[787]

10–311   In *Ofulue v Bossert*,[788] the House of Lords rejected the contention that the offer to purchase the property ought to be admissible as an exception to the privilege, on the basis that the defendant had engaged in impropriety; Lord Walker observed that the defendant's "switch from claiming to be a tenant to claiming to be a squatter may be unattractive, but it did not amount to 'unambiguous impropriety'."

6. Calderbank Letter

10–312   As noted above, without prejudice communications are inadmissible on the issue of costs[789] but in *Calderbank v Calderbank*,[790] Scarman LJ suggested that a letter could be written on a without prejudice basis but with a reservation on the part of the writer of the right to refer to it on the issue of costs. This suggestion was made in the context of and confined to matrimonial proceedings relating to finances in order to overcome the disadvantages accruing from the lack of a lodgement procedure but was quickly taken up by practitioners who started to employ and rely on "Calderbank letters" in other contexts. In *Cutts v Head*,[791] the Court of Appeal endorsed the use of such letters in all cases where the subject-matter is something more than a simple

---

[783] Unreported, Court of Appeal, 25 February 1993, *The Times,* 19 March 1993.
[784] See Casey, "'Without Prejudice Privilege' and 'Unambiguous Impropriety'" (2004) (8) ILT 122.
[785] Unreported, Court of Appeal, 20 March 2000.
[786] [2001] FSR 158 at 164.
[787] See also *Savings and Investment Bank Ltd v Fincken* [2003] EWCA Civ 1630, [2004] 1 WLR 667, [2004] 1 All ER 1125; *Berry Trade Ltd v Moussawi* (2003) 147 SJLB 625.
[788] [2009] 1 AC 990 at 1013, [2009] 2 WLR 749 at 769.
[789] *Walker v Wilsher* (1889) 23 QBD 335 at 339.
[790] [1976] Fam 93, [1975] 3 All ER 333.
[791] [1984] Ch 290, [1984] 1 All ER 597.

money claim in respect of which a payment into court would be the appropriate way of proceeding. The court took the view that a Calderbank letter would promote the settlement of actions because of the parties' consciousness of a potential costs penalty if a reasonable offer was refused.[792] So far as the conventional rationale for the privilege was concerned, this had been modified by the widespread practice of the courts to give effect to the reservation contained in the letter.[793]

10–313   The efficacy of offers without prejudice save as to costs is now underpinned by Ord.99, r.1A, which was inserted by the Rules of the Superior Courts (Costs) 2008 Order[794] and provides that an offer in writing to settle proceedings can be taken into account when a court is exercising its discretion in relation to costs.[795]

D. Public Interest Privilege

1. Introduction

10–314   While, as explained above, all privileges are ultimately founded on the public interest, this is much more evident in the case of public interest privilege because, as will be seen below, a claim of public interest privilege will only be upheld after an individualised adjudication and finding that the balance of public interest favours the claim.

10–315   Before proceeding to examine the cases in this area, some explanation should be given of the nomenclature used. The expression "public interest privilege" has gained judicial currency[796] at the expense of the older phrase "executive privilege",[797] reflecting the fact that the privilege is not confined in its application to the executive functions of the State but is available whenever the balance of public interest favours non-disclosure. In England, the term "public interest immunity" is now favoured,[798]

---

[792]   Oliver LJ said ([1984] Ch 290 at 306, [1984] 1 All ER 597 at 605) that: "As a practical matter, a consciousness of a risk as to costs if reasonable offers are refused can only encourage settlement, whilst, on the other hand, it is hard to imagine anything more calculated to encourage obstinacy and unreasonableness than the comfortable knowledge that a litigant can refuse with impunity whatever may be offered to him even if it is as much as or more than everything to which he is entitled in the action."

[793]   This exception to the privilege was recognised by Walker LJ in *Unilever v Proctor and Gamble* [2000] 1 WLR 2436 at 2445, [2001] 1 All ER 784 at 792–793. In this jurisdiction, the admissibility of a 'Calderbank' offer was considered by Laffoy J in *Murnaghan v Markland Holdings Limited* [2004] IEHC 406 at [3]–[5], [2004] 4 IR 537 at 539–541, where she concluded that the offer under consideration could have no bearing on the question of costs on the basis that it came too late in the day, and it lacked certainty.

[794]   SI No. 12 of 2008.

[795]   Ord.99, r.1A(2) expressly provides that an "offer in writing" includes an offer in writing made without prejudice save as to the issue of costs. It should be noted, however, that in accordance with Ord.11, r.1A, the High Court is not entitled to consider an offer in writing to settle an action in respect of a claim or a counterclaim if a lodgment or tender offer in lieu of a lodgment could have been made in accordance with Ord.22.

[796]   See, *e.g. McDonald v RTÉ* [2001] 1 IR 355, [2001] 2 ILRM 1; *Hughes v Commissioner of An Garda Síochána*, unreported, High Court, *ex tempore*, 20 January 1998.

[797]   In *Murphy v Dublin Corporation* [1972] IR 215 at 239, Walsh J said that he used it "for want of a better term".

[798]   See, *e.g. R. v Whittle* [1997] 1 Cr App R 166; *Lonrho Plc v Fayed (No.4)* [1994] QB 775, [1994] 1 All ER 870; *Makanjuola v Commissioner of Police of the Metropolis* [1992] 3 All ER 617. In *Rogers v Secretary of State for the Homes Department* [1973] AC 388 at 400, [1972] 2 All ER

principally on the basis that the term "privilege" is only applicable to a claim which can be waived and public interest immunity, where it is found to apply, cannot be waived by the executive or any person.[799] However, as discussed below, the Irish courts have rejected the proposition that a claim of non-disclosure based on the public interest cannot be waived.[800] Thus, it is submitted that the term "public interest privilege" more accurately reflects the nature of the claim in this jurisdiction.[801]

2. Public Interest Privilege

10–316   At common law, the Crown enjoyed a prerogative, known as "Crown privilege" to refuse to produce documents or even to disclose their existence. If a Minister, or a senior civil servant on his behalf, certified or swore an affidavit to the effect that disclosure of the documents sought would be prejudicial to the public interest, that was conclusive of the matter and a court could not examine the documents or otherwise go behind that certificate.[802]

10–317   That privilege was carried over into the law of the Free State in *Leen v President of the Executive Council*,[803] where it was placed on the more republican footing of the public interest. Meredith J rejected the contention that the privilege could only be claimed by the Crown stating:

> "I can see nothing … in the authorities on this privilege in respect of discovery to suggest that the rule of law which has always been in force, and which has to be administered as heretofore under the Constitution of the Irish Free State, is dependent upon the magic of any particular nomenclature. On the contrary, it appears to me to be broadbased upon the public interest. … The principle has roots in the general conception of State interests and the functions of Courts of Justice, which make it independent of the particular type of constitution under which the body of law which recognises that principle is administered."[804]

10–318   This privilege retained the incidents of the old Crown privilege and, therefore, once a claim of privilege was made in the appropriate form, it had to be accepted by the courts without any further inquiry.[805] However, it became evident over the course of the

---

1057 at 1060, Lord Reid criticised the older term "Crown privilege": "I think that the expression is wrong and may be misleading. There is no question of any privilege in the ordinary sense of the word. The real question is whether the public interest requires that the letter shall not be produced and whether that public interest is so strong as to override the ordinary right and interest of a litigant that he shall be able to lay before a court of justice all relevant evidence." The term "public interest immunity" is also favoured in Australia: see *Attorney General for the Northern Territory v Kearney* (1985) 158 CLR 500 at 510, in which Gibbs J referred to "what used to be called 'crown privilege', and is now often called 'public interest immunity'".

[799] *Rogers v Secretary of State for the Home Department* [1973] AC 388 at 407, [1972] 2 All ER 1057 at 1066 (*per* Lord Simon); *Air Canada v Secretary of State for Trade (No.2)* [1983] 2 AC 394 at 436, [1983] 1 All ER 910 at 917.

[800] *Egan v O'Toole* [2005] IESC 53 (on appeal from a decision of Kelly J, unreported, High Court, 15 June 2004); *McDonald v RTÉ* [2001] 1 IR 355, [2001] 2 ILRM 1; *Hannigan v DPP* [2001] 1 IR 378 (*sub nom. TH v DPP* [2002] 2 ILRM 48).

[801] But *cf. Murphy v Dublin Corporation* [1972] IR 215 at 224, where Kenny J said that the word "privilege" was inaccurate to describe the claim being made. See also Casey, "Inadmissibility of Evidence on Grounds of Public Interest" (1977) DULJ 11.

[802] See *Duncan v Cammell Laird & Co Ltd* [1942] AC 624, [1942] 1 All ER 587.

[803] [1926] IR 456.

[804] [1926] IR 456 at 463.

[805] *Leen v President of the Executive Council* [1926] IR 456; *Smith v Commissioners of Public Works* [1936] Ir Jur Rep 67; *Malone v O'Hanlon* [1938] Ir Jur Rep 8; *Kenny v Minister for Defence* [1942] Ir Jur Rep 81; *O'Leary v Minister for Industry and Commerce* [1966] IR 676.

next half-century that the cloak of privilege was being abused to the extent that some of the claims made were judicially criticised as "grotesque" and "evidence not of any care for the public interest but of a remarkable elasticity of conscience".[806] It was not surprising therefore that in the landmark decision of *Murphy v Dublin Corporation*[807] the Supreme Court undertook a radical overhaul of this area.

10–319 In *Murphy* the plaintiff sought production of the report of an inspector relating to a compulsory purchase order, which was resisted by the Minister for Local Government on the grounds that its production would be contrary to public policy and the public interest. Walsh J, with whom the other members of the Court concurred, rejected the proposition that it was for the executive to decide whether documents were to be produced. He pointed out that:

> "[u]nder the Constitution the administration of justice is committed solely to the judiciary in the exercise of their powers in the courts set up under the Constitution. Power to compel the attendance of witnesses and the production of evidence is an inherent part of the judicial power of government of the State and is the ultimate safeguard of justice in the State. The proper exercise of the functions of the three powers of government set up under the Constitution, namely, the legislative, the executive and the judicial is in the public interest. There may be occasions when the different aspects of the public interest 'pull in contrary directions'. ... If the conflict arises during the exercise of the judicial power then, in my view, it is the judicial power which will decide which public interest shall prevail."[808]

10–320 Applying those principles to the claim of "executive privilege" made by the Minister, he said:

> "Where documents come into existence in the course of carrying out of the executive powers of the State, their production may be adverse to the public interest in one sphere of government in particular circumstances. On the other hand, their non-production may be adverse to the public interest in the administration of justice. As such documents may be anywhere in the range from the trivial to the vitally important, somebody or some authority must decide which course is calculated to do the least injury to the public interest, namely, the production of the document or the possibility of the denial of right in the administration of justice. It is self evident that this is a matter which falls into the sphere of the judicial power for determination. In a particular case the court may be able to determine this matter having regard to the evidence available on the subject and without examining the document in question, but in other cases it may be necessary as the court may think, to produce the document to the court itself for the purpose of inspecting it and making the decision having regard to the conflicting claims made with reference to the document."[809]

10–321 He made it clear that the court would not always decide that the interest of the litigant should prevail. However, once the court was satisfied that the document is relevant, the burden of satisfying the court that it should not be produced lies upon the party making the claim and a particularised objection would have to be made in respect of each document. He thus rejected the idea that there were any documents which could be withheld from production on the grounds that they belonged to a certain class of documents:

> "Having regard to the nature of the powers of the courts in these matters, it seems clear to me that there can be no documents which may be withheld from production simply because they belong to a particular class of documents. Each document must be decided upon having regard to the considerations which apply to that particular document and its contents. To grant

---

[806] *Per* Kenny J in *Murphy v Dublin Corporation* [1972] IR 215 at 226.
[807] [1972] IR 215.
[808] [1972] IR 215 at 233.
[809] [1972] IR 215 at 234–235.

or withhold the production of a document simply by reason of the class to which it belongs would be to regard all documents as being of equal importance notwithstanding that they may not be."[810]

10–322   An attempt to partially overrule *Murphy* was rejected by the Supreme Court in *Ambiorix Ltd v Minister for the Environment (No.1)*.[811] The defendants argued that documents emanating from a senior level of the Civil Service relating to the formulation of policy or proposals for legislation and intended for the ultimate consideration of Ministers should be absolutely immune from production and inspection.[812] However, the Supreme Court was unanimous in rejecting this contention, which Finlay CJ said suffered from the fundamental flaw of ignoring the constitutional origin of the decision in *Murphy*.[813] McCarthy J took a similar view, describing discovery as a constitutionally guaranteed fair procedure, and said that to depart from the decision in *Murphy* would "lessen or impair judicial sovereignty in the administration of justice".[814] The Chief Justice also pointed out the practical difficulties for plaintiffs which would flow from accepting the submission of the defendants. It would, for example, prevent plaintiffs from challenging a decision made by the Government or a Minister on the grounds that it was made without taking relevant material into account or in reliance on irrelevant material.[815]

10–323   In the course of his judgment, Finlay CJ codified the principles which had been laid down in *Murphy* as follows[816]:

> "1.   Under the Constitution the administration of justice is committed solely to the judiciary by the exercise of their powers in the courts set up under the Constitution.
> 2.   Power to compel the production of evidence (which, of course, includes a power to compel the production of documents) is an inherent part of the judicial power and is part of the ultimate safeguard of justice in the State.
> 3.   Where a conflict arises during the exercise of the judicial power between the aspect of public interest involved in the confidentiality or exemption from documents pertaining to the exercise of the executive powers of the State, it is the judicial power which will decide which public interest shall prevail.[817]

---

[810]   [1972] IR 215 at 235. A striking example of this can be seen in *Ambiorix v Minister for the Environment (No.1)* [1992] 1 IR 277, [1992] ILRM 209, where a class claim in respect of a certain category of documents was rejected by the trial judge who proceeded to examine the documents and concluded that the public interest involved in their production clearly outweighed any harm to the executive that might arise from disclosing them. On appeal, Finlay CJ noted (at 285: 214) that it had not been suggested "that consideration of the individual documents as distinct from a consideration of the nature and character of the documents involved could lead to any other conclusion".

[811]   [1992] 1 IR 277, [1992] ILRM 209.

[812]   In *Geraghty v Minister for Local Government* [1975] IR 300, a class claim in respect of communications between the Minister or his parliamentary secretary and civil servants had been rejected on the basis of the decision in *Murphy*.

[813]   [1972] IR 215.

[814]   [1992] 1 IR 277 at 289, [1992] ILRM 209 at 217.

[815]   Citing the judgment of McCarthy J in *O'Keefe v An Bord Pleanála* [1993] 1 IR 39, [1992] ILRM 237, who pointed out that capacity of an individual to challenge the decision of an administrative body depended on his or her right to avail of the procedures of interrogatories and discovery.

[816]   [1992] 1 IR 277 at 283, [1992] ILRM 209 at 213. He stressed that these principles were re-stated "by way of summary, but not by way of expansion or qualification".

[817]   *Cf. Taylor v Shannon Explosives Ltd*, unreported, High Court, 13 March 2003, where it was held that, in circumstances where the Minister for Justice wished to rely on public interest privilege as a basis for withholding information in relation to an application for a licence under the Explosives Act 1875, it was necessary for him to apply to court for approval to do so.

4. The duty of the judicial power to make that decision does not mean that there is any priority or preference for the production of evidence over other public interests, such as the security of the State or the efficient discharge of the functions of the executive organ of the Government.
5. It is for the judicial power to choose the evidence upon which it might act in any individual case in order to reach that decision."

10–324 He went on to say that these principles led to a number of practical conclusions where a claim of public interest privilege was made:

"(a) The Executive cannot prevent the judicial power from examining documents which are relevant to an issue in a civil trial for the purpose of deciding whether they must be produced.
(b) There is no obligation on the judicial power to examine any particular document before deciding that it is exempt from production, and it can and will in many instances uphold a claim of privilege in respect of a document merely on the basis of a description of its nature and contents which it (the judicial power) accepts.
(c) There cannot, accordingly, be a generally applicable class or category of documents exempted from production by reason of the rank in the public service of the person creating them, or of the position of the individual or body intended to use them."

10–325 The principles set out in *Murphy* and *Ambiorix* were affirmed by the Supreme Court in *Keating v Radio Telefís Eireann*,[818] where McKechnie J stated that, "as a result of this constitutional position, which is mandated by the separation of powers and which permits of no exception, it is for the courts to resolve, in a justiciable setting, any conflict or tension which may arise as between the public interest in the administration of justice, and the public interest which is advanced as a ground for non-disclosure of documents on the other". It was held, therefore, that "neither the Executive nor any other person can arrogate to themselves" the power to decide that documents are subject to public interest privilege.[819] Thus, where a claim of public interest is asserted, the interest relied upon must be formulated by reference to the issues in question and must be particularised in such a way that the court can properly adjudicate the issue.[820]

10–326 In *Keating*, the Revenue Commissioners appealed an order for non-party discovery, which required it to make discovery of documents relating to information gathering and surveillance carried out by the Revenue with the gardaí in connection with the enforcement of drug legislation. The order was made in defamation proceedings instituted by the plaintiff against RTÉ in respect of a Prime Time programme, which portrayed the plaintiff as a drug dealer and member of a criminal gang. The plaintiff contended that he was acting at all times as an agent of the gardaí. Both the gardaí and the Revenue confirmed that the plaintiff was a member of the witness protection programme. The Revenue contended that, in circumstances where public interest privilege would be asserted, and where that claim would most likely be upheld by the courts, an order for non-party discovery should not have been granted. The Supreme Court emphatically rejected this contention, holding that the sole decision maker where

---

[818] [2013] IESC 22.
[819] [2013] IESC 22 at [37]. *Cf. McLoughlin v Aviva Insurance* [2011] IESC 42 *per* Denham J at [11]; *AP v Minister for Justice and Equality* [2014] IEHC 17.
[820] *Cf. MacAodhain v Eire* [2010] IEHC 40 at [27], [2012] 1 IR 430 at 440, where Clarke J refused to accept that there was a general public interest immunity which applied to documents relating to the appointment of a District Court judge, and stated that any claim of public interest asserted in respect of specific documents would have to be "raised in the appropriate way in the affidavit of discovery and backed up with appropriate evidence in that affidavit."

a claim of public interest privilege is asserted is the judicial power.[821] McKechnie J stated that, absent any detailed information as to how Revenue would formulate a claim to privilege in respect of such documents as they might have, he was far from satisfied that the claim to privilege would inevitably succeed. It was held, therefore, that Revenue was required to make discovery, and that any issues of privilege which arose could be dealt with in the ordinary manner.[822]

3. The Balancing Test

10–327   The effect of the decisions in *Murphy, Ambiorix* and *Keating* has been to establish a balancing test. In each case where a claim of public interest privilege is made, the court is required to balance the public interest in the proper administration of justice against the public interest put forward for non-disclosure in order to decide which is the superior public interest in the circumstances of the case.[823] It was emphasised in these decisions that the courts would not approach the application of this test with any preconceived notion of where the balance should lie and would not automatically favour the administration of justice over the competing public interest. However, as will be evident from the decisions examined below, the rejection of class claims and the requirement that a particularised reason be advanced for the non-disclosure of each individual document has, in practical terms, weighted the test in favour of disclosure.

(a) The public interest in the proper administration of justice

10–328   The public interest in the proper administration of justice requires that a court should have all relevant evidence before it because this will help to ensure that justice is done and that the risk of adjudicative error is minimised. This public interest is closely allied to the interests of an individual litigant who avails of his or her constitutionally protected right of access to the courts[824] in order to vindicate his or her constitutional and legal rights.[825] In order for this right of access to be effective, a litigant must be afforded access to any documentation that helps to support his or

---

[821]   McKechnie J held that this position could only be departed from if the extreme situation postulated in *Murphy*, or one of equal gravity, came to pass. He referred, in this regard, to the judgment of Walsh J in *Murphy*, where he adverted to the possibility that there may be a case in which the head of State of an appropriate member of the Executive expressed the opinion that the mere disclosure of the existence of a document could, in and of itself, be a threat to the security of the State. However, McKechnie J stated (*obiter*) that, even in such a situation, a balancing test would have to be carried out ([2003] IESC 22 at [42]).

[822]   *Cf. Cunningham v President of the Circuit Court* [2006] IESC 51 at [32], [2006] 3 IR 541 at 551, where the Supreme Court made an order for discovery against the DPP but held that he "had the fullest entitlement to claim privilege over any document, over all documents, or over any portion of any document as he may be advised or think fit".

[823]   *Livingstone v Minister for Justice* [2004] IEHC 58 at [6]; *Skeffington v Rooney* [1997] 1 IR 22 at 32, [1997] 2 ILRM 56 at 66; *Burke v Central Independent Television Plc* [1994] 2 IR 61 at 79; *Breathnach v Ireland (No.3)* [1993] 2 IR 458 at 469, [1992] ILRM 755 at 763; *Incorporated Law Society v Minister for Justice* [1987] ILRM 42 at 44; *Hunt v Roscommon VEC*, unreported, High Court, 1 March 1981 at 3.

[824]   See *Macauley v Minister for Posts and Telegraphs* [1966] IR 345.

[825]   In *Gormley v Ireland* [1993] 2 IR 75 at 78, Murphy J said that there had to be weighed against the grounds for forward for non-disclosure, "the conflicting interest of the litigant to have access to such documents as may be necessary to enable him to prosecute fairly and properly his actions in the courts set up under the Constitution".

her case, or undermines that of his or her opponent. The withholding of any relevant material inevitably impairs his or her ability to make out a case.[826]

10–329 It follows from the foregoing that the most important indicator of the weight of the public interest in the proper administration of justice is the relevance of the information sought to the issues in the case, and this has been used as a proxy in many cases for an assessment of this public interest.[827] For example, in *Breathnach v Ireland (No.3)*,[828] Keane J, having referred to the principles laid down in *Compagnie Financiére du Pacifique v The Peruvian Guano Co*,[829] stated that, in considering the public interest in the administration of justice, "it is necessary to determine to what extent, if any, the relevant documents may advance the plaintiff's case or damage the defendant's case or fairly lead to an enquiry which may have either of those consequences".[830] In criminal proceedings, a document "will fulfil this test for relevance if it may fairly lead to a train of inquiry which may have either of these consequences"[831]; reliance is not the test for refusing disclosure.[832]

10–330 A court is likely to hold that the public interest in the administration of justice will trump the competing public interest where the documents sought are crucial or very relevant to the litigant's case.[833] Conversely, if the documents sought would be of some relevance but are not of vital importance, the balance may well lie in favour of non-disclosure.[834] So, for example, in *Hughes v Commissioner of An Garda Síochána*,[835] Laffoy J ordered disclosure of documents which she considered to be centrally germane to the issues in the proceedings, but refused to order disclosure of others which only had a marginal relevance.

---

[826] *Cf.* the comments of Finlay CJ in *Ambiorix Ltd v Minister for the Environment (No.1)* [1992] 1 IR 277 at 285, [1992] ILRM 209 at 214. It is clear from the decision of the Supreme Court in *O'Callaghan v Mahon* [2005] IEHC 265, [2005] IESC 9, [2006] 2 IR 32 that this applies with equal force to the ability of a person against whom accusations are made in a statutory public tribunal to defend their good name.

[827] See, for example, the decision of the Supreme Court in *O'Callaghan v Mahon* [2005] IEHC 265, [2005] IESC 9, [2006] 2 IR 32.

[828] [1993] 2 IR 458, [1992] ILRM 755.

[829] (1882) 11 QBD 55 at 63.

[830] [1993] 2 IR 458 at 469, [1992] ILRM 755 at 763. This test was applied in *A.P. v Minister for Justice and Equality* [2014] IEHC 17 at [24]. See to the same effect *Hughes v Commissioner of An Garda Síochána*, unreported, High Court, *ex tempore*, 20 January 1998; *Logue v Redmond* [1999] 2 ILRM 498 at 507; *Corbett v DPP* [1999] 2 IR 179 at 189.

[831] *McNibb v Minister for Justice, Equality and Law Reform* [2013] IEHC 238, *per* O'Malley J at [28]; *Traynor v Delahunt* [2008] IEHC 272 at [19], [2009] 1 IR 605 at 611; *Director of Public Prosecutions v Special Criminal Court* [1999] 1 IR 60.

[832] *Traynor v Delahunt* [2008] IEHC 272 at [10], [2009] 1 IR 605 at 610.

[833] See *AP v Minister for Justice and Equality* [2014] IEHC 17 at [20] and [25]; *O'Callaghan v Mahon* [2005] IEHC 265, [2005] IESC 9, [2006] 2 IR 32; *Hughes v Commissioner of An Garda Síochána*, unreported, High Court, *ex tempore*, 20 January 1998 and *Logue v Redmond* [1999] 2 ILRM 498 at 508. *Cf. Ahern v Minister for Industry and Commerce*, unreported, High Court, Lardner J, 11 March 1988, where Lardner J refused to uphold a claim of privilege in circumstances where he was satisfied that the documents in question would be important evidence in the case.

[834] See *Hughes v Commissioner of An Garda Síochána*, unreported, *ex tempore*, 20 January 1998 and *Gormley v Ireland* [1993] 2 IR 75 at 80, where Murphy J refused to order the disclosure of "highly confidential material, the disclosure of which might be significantly detrimental to the public interest" because although the documents "might be of some value to the plaintiff in the conduct of his case", they were "in no sense fundamental to it".

[835] Unreported, High Court, Laffoy J, *ex tempore*, 20 January 1998.

10–331   The availability of alternative evidence will mitigate against disclosure. An example of this is provided by *Leech v Independent Newspapers*,[836] where O'Neill J was not satisfied that the public interest in the administration of justice would be defeated by the non-disclosure of the workings of an *ad hoc* public inquiry in circumstances where the defendants had available to them "considerable resources of evidence", including the report recording the findings of the inquiry.[837] He was further influenced by the fact that the inquiry took place after the newspaper reports the subject matter of the defamation proceedings were written, and expressed the view that, "[i]n reality, the defendant is being denied what may be described as a windfall resulting from the holding of the inquiry, a factor which adds some slight additional weight in the balance against granting the discovery sought".[838]

10–332   Another factor to be considered is the nature of the litigant's case and the interests sought to be protected. In *Cahalane v Revenue Commissioners*,[839] McCracken J laid considerable stress on the fact that the plaintiff was seeking to vindicate a basic constitutional right, the right to earn a livelihood. For this reason, the public interest in the administration of justice in the case was of great importance and he ordered discovery of most of the documents sought.

10–333   It is clear from the decision of the Supreme Court in *O'Callaghan v Mahon*[840] that the right of a person against whom serious accusations are made in a statutory tribunal to vindicate their good name is an interest which will be afforded considerable weight. The Supreme Court held that, in circumstances where the assertion of public interest immunity interfered with the right of the applicant to cross-examine his accuser, one of the rights enumerated in *In Re Haughey*,[841] the tribunal was not entitled to maintain confidentiality over the documents in issue.[842]

10–334   These principles are further attenuated when the innocence of a person is at stake because there is an overriding public interest in ensuring that an innocent person is not convicted. Therefore, if an accused can establish that certain documentation is, or may be, relevant to the question of his innocence; then this facet of the public interest will trump that in favour of non-disclosure.[843]

---

[836] [2009] IEHC 259, [2009] 3 IR 766.
[837] [2009] IEHC 259 at [15], [2009] 3 IR 766 at 772.
[838] [2009] IEHC 259 at [16], [2009] 3 IR 766 at 773.
[839] Unreported, High Court, 14 May 1999.
[840] [2005] IEHC 265, [2005] IESC 9, [2006] 2 IR 32.
[841] [1971] IR 217.
[842] *Cf. AP v Minister for Justice and Equality* [2014] IEHC 17 at [25], which concerned an application for judicial review of the refusal of an application for naturalisation. O'Malley J ordered disclosure of one of the documents, observing that, "In the normal course, this is a document which the court would expect to be furnished as a matter of fair procedures..."
[843] In *Wong v Minister for Justice*, unreported, High Court, 16 March 1993, Denham J declined to order production of two confidential documents but she stated that if the documents aided the applicant and their was a prosecution pending, then the court might consider the balance differently. *Cf. Traynor v Delahunt* [2008] IEHC 272, [2009] 1 IR 605, [2009] 1 ILRM 113. See also *Director of Consumer Affairs v Sugar Distributors Ltd* [1991] 1 IR 225, [1991] ILRM 395 and *Goodman International v Hamilton (No.3)* [1993] 3 IR 320 dealing with informer privilege.

(b) The public interest in non-disclosure

10–335   The categories of public interest in favour of non-disclosure are not closed[844] and hence, are not capable or exhaustive or comprehensive categorisation. However, a consideration of the decided cases discloses four main categories which have been identified to date: (i) national security; (ii) international relations; (iii) the proper functioning of the public service; and (iv) the prevention and detection of crime. Before examining these categories, two general observations can be made. First, in order for a claim of privilege to succeed, it is essential to show that the communication in question was brought into being in circumstances of confidentiality and, where this factor is lacking, a claim of privilege will fail *ab initio*.[845] Secondly, in keeping with the decision in *Murphy*, the Irish courts have taken a resolute stand against any attempts to establish class claims whether directly or by recourse to generic arguments which would apply equally to all documents within a certain class.[846] Thus, in order for a claim of privilege to succeed, it must be particularised and the party asserting privilege must identify the damage to the public interest in question which will accrue from disclosure of each individual document.[847]

(i) National security

10–336   In *Murphy*,[848] Walsh J identified national security as one of the vital interests of the State, and it is axiomatic that the public has an interest in the security of the State. Indeed, there may be cases involving the security of the State where even the disclosure of the existence of a document should not be allowed.[849] This does not mean, however, that a claim based on national security will automatically succeed and the courts, consistent with the principles established in *Murphy*, will scrutinise such a claim to ascertain if it is properly made out.

10–337   This is evident from *Gormley v Ireland*,[850] where the plaintiff civil servant sought discovery of documents concerning his internment pursuant to the Offences Against the State Act 1939 and the treatment by the Government of civil servants who had been interned. Production of these documents was resisted on the basis that their disclosure would be injurious to the interests of national security. Adjudicating

---

[844] *Per* Keane J in *Skeffington v Rooney* [1997] 1 IR 22 at 32, [1997] 2 ILRM 56 at 66 (citing *D v NSPCC* [1978] AC 171 at 230, [1977] 1 All ER 589 at 605 (*per* Lord Hailsham)).

[845] See *Skeffington v Rooney* [1997] 1 IR 22, [1997] 2 ILRM 56 and *PMPS Ltd v PMPA Insurance Plc* [1990] 1 IR 284.

[846] See *Traynor v Delahunt* [2008] IEHC 272 at [26], [2009] 1 IR 605, [2009] 1 ILRM 113; *MacAodhain v Eire* [2010] IEHC 40 at [27], [2012] 1 IR 430 at 440; *Breathnach v Ireland (No.3)* [1993] 2 IR 458, [1992] ILRM 755; *W v Ireland (No.1)* [1997] 2 IR 132 (*sub nom Walker v Ireland* [1997] 1 ILRM 363); *Incorporated Law Society v Minister for Justice* [1987] ILRM 42 at 44.

[847] See, e.g. *MacAodhain v Eire* [2010] IEHC 40 at [27], [2012] 1 IR 430 at 440; *W v Ireland (No.1)* [1997] 2 IR 132 (*sub nom Walker v Ireland* [1997] 1 ILRM 363).

[848] [1972] IR 215 at 234.

[849] *Murphy v Dublin Corporation* [1972] IR 215 at 234; *Breathnach v Ireland (No.3)* [1993] 2 IR 458 at 469, [1992] ILRM 755 at 763. But see the comments of McKechnie J in *Keating v Radio Telefis Éireann* [2013] IESC 22 at [42], where he considered this aspect of the decision in *Murphy* and stated (*obiter*) that, even in a situation where the head of State of an appropriate member of the Executive expressed the opinion that the mere disclosure of the existence of a document could in and of itself be a threat to the security of the State, a balancing test would have to be carried out.

[850] [1993] 2 IR 75.

on this claim, Murphy J stated that, notwithstanding the involvement of the Offences Against the State Act 1939, he was not satisfied that all of the documents in respect of which privilege was claimed involved national security. On balance, he decided that production of some of the documents should be ordered even though they were "unquestionably confidential, sensitive documents" recording for the greater part submissions and advices by senior civil servants to Ministers and the Government.

10–338   A claim of public interest security based on national security was considered in *AP v Minister for Justice and Equality*,[851] which concerned an application for judicial review of the respondent's decision to refuse to grant a certificate of naturalisation to the applicant. The Minister contended that rigorous checks are carried out in respect of applications for certificates of naturalisation, which involve requests for information from external agencies, including intelligence and security agencies. It was further contended that this information is received on a confidential basis and relates to matters of national security and that, were the Respondent to disclose the existence of such documents and identify the reason for the refusal to disclose as being related to the security or defence of the State, international relations, or the existence of a confidential source, this would compromise the interests of the State. Having considered the decision of Walsh J in *Murphy*,[852] O'Malley J concluded that the privilege claimed was not primarily concerned with a threat to the 'safety of the State'. She stated that the use of confidential information or intelligence reports has been an accepted tool in the administration of justice in this jurisdiction for many years, particularly in the investigation and prosecution of organised crime and counter-terrorism, and observed that its use in the criminal law "is subject to a degree of scrutiny consistent with a fair trial". It is clear, therefore, "that it is possible to formulate and scrutinise a reason for an opinion whilst protecting the confidentiality of its source from disclosure."[853]

(ii) International relations

10–339   There is an obvious public interest in fostering good international relations and in protecting the confidentiality of any document, the disclosure of which might endanger relations with other countries or international organisations.[854] Thus, in *O'Mahony v Minister for Defence*,[855] Barrington J had little difficulty in accepting that privilege could be claimed in respect of the report of a UNIFIL inquiry into an incident in which an Irish soldier had been killed. This report had been given to the Irish government in circumstances of confidentiality and he accepted, as quite reasonable, the view of the government that it was obliged to maintain confidentiality in the report.[856]

---

[851] [2014] IEHC 17. This category of public interest privilege was also invoked in *O'Neill v An Taoiseach* [2009] IEHC 119, where Murphy J identified the general principles, but did not consider it necessary to determine this issue in circumstances where he concluded that the disclosure of the material in issue was subject to a statutory privilege.

[852] O'Malley J noted that this matter was also 'touched upon' by McKechnie J in *Keating v Radio Telefís Éireann* [2014] IEHC 17 at [21]–[22].

[853] [2014] IEHC 17 at [23].

[854] *Cf. AG v Simpson* [1959] IR 105 at 112, where Davitt P thought it clear that there must be privilege must apply to documents containing state secrets, the disclosure of which might endanger diplomatic relations or international peace.

[855] Unreported, High Court, *ex tempore*, 27 June 1989.

[856] Followed on this point by O'Hanlon J in *O'Brien v Ireland* [1995] 1 IR 568, [1995] 1 ILRM 22 who also relied on the provisions of s.9 of the Diplomatic Relations and Immunities Act 1967.

10–340   The public interest in maintaining the confidentiality of inter-state communications was discussed in *W v Ireland (No.1)*.[857] The case arose out of the delay in extraditing a Catholic priest to Northern Ireland to face charges of sexual offences against minors. The plaintiff, who was one of the alleged victims, claimed that she had suffered personal injury, including psychiatric injury and mental distress, by reason of a negligent delay on the part of the Attorney General's office in processing the extradition request. Discovery was granted but the defendants claimed privilege in respect of a number of documents on the basis that they were supplied to the Irish Attorney General by the Attorney General for the UK and Northern Ireland on a confidential basis for the limited purpose of allowing the Irish Attorney General to decide whether to back the warrants for extradition. It was contended that disclosure of such documents would be prejudicial to the proper and effective operation of the extradition arrangements between the two States and that if the claim of privilege was not upheld, the free flow of information and consequently the effective operation of the extradition procedure would be seriously inhibited.

10–341   This was the first case in which the principles applicable to communications between sovereign states had arisen and in the absence of direct Irish authority on the point, Geoghegan J had recourse to the English decision of *Buttes Gas and Oil Co. v Hammer (No.3)*.[858] In that case, the Court of Appeal had refused to subscribe to the proposition that an absolute public interest privilege attached to confidential communications between states. Having regard to the provisions of the Irish Constitution, Geoghegan J said that there was an even stronger case in this jurisdiction for not countenancing any form of absolute privilege in relation to communications passing between sovereign states. He accepted that, as a general rule, documents in connection with an extradition request would be assumed by both states to be confidential and that there was a public interest in the State maintaining that confidentiality as far as possible.

10–342   However, having read the documents, he came to the conclusion that the balance of public interest lay in favour of disclosure. In arriving at this view, he attached importance to four factors: (i) the criminal proceeding to which the action related had long been disposed of; (ii) the State had failed to discharge the onus on it of establishing that there was a greater public interest in non-disclosure; (iii) there was no evidence before the Court of any objection by the office of the Attorney General of Northern Ireland to the production of the documents; and (iv) while it would be understandable that both this State and the UK would want, as a matter of principle, to maintain the role of confidentiality in relation to such documentation, it was difficult to see any particular reason why the government of the UK would be concerned about the production of the particular documents sought to be produced in the case.

10–343   The objections raised in *Egan v O'Toole*[859] were very similar to those considered by Geoghegan J in *W v Ireland (No. 1)*. However, there were a number of features which differentiated this case from the *W* case. In the first place, this was not a case in which the criminal proceedings against the person whose extradition was being sought had long being disposed of; the plaintiff and his co-accused were

---

[857] [1997] 2 IR 132 (*sub nom. Walker v Ireland* [1997] 1 ILRM 363).
[858] [1981] QB 223, [1980] 3 All ER 475.
[859] [2005] IESC 53. The Supreme Court upheld the decision of Kelly J in the High Court, unreported, 15 June 2004.

awaiting trial. Second, the State addressed the issue of public interest and did not merely assert confidentiality. Third, unlike the *W* case, there was evidence on affidavit of a specific objection by the UK authorities to the disclosure of the documents on the basis that they were of a confidential nature. In the High Court, Kelly J concluded that these differentiating features caused a recalibration of the balance of the public interest, and upheld the claim to privilege in respect of the documents. This decision was upheld by the Supreme Court on appeal where Denham J, delivering judgment for the court, stated that:

> "In determining whether or not to order production of communications which were claimed to be privileged the court must balance the public interest in maintaining the confidentiality of documents furnished in the extradition request against the public interest in all the relevant evidence being before the court for the purposes of litigation. In carrying out this balancing act it may be necessary for the court to inspect the documents in issue."

10–344 The Supreme Court also upheld the decision of Kelly J not to order disclosure of confidential communications between members of An Garda Síochána and the Devon and Cornwall Constabulary for the extradition of the plaintiff. The State argued that there was a public interest in withholding the production of these communications on the grounds that they were confidential communications that had passed between sovereign states. Kelly J concluded, that the plaintiff had failed to show that, on balance, the public interest favoured production of these documents.

10–345 The European Court of Human Rights has recognised that the protection of the public interest warrants a refusal of access to documents relating to investigations carried out by the Commission which may lead to infringement proceedings against a member state for an alleged failure to properly transpose a Directive into national law.[860] This public interest privilege was applied by Kelly J in *Sweetman v An Board Pleanala*,[861] where he described it as "a form of public interest confidentiality" which preserves documents relating to such investigations from public disclosure.

(iii) Proper functioning of the public service

10–346 In *Murphy*,[862] it was held that a claim of "executive privilege" could only be made where the exercise of the executive functions of the State was at issue. However, this limitation was an undesirable accretion to the principles laid down therein and has been quietly dropped from the jurisprudence in this area.[863] It is now clear that a claim of privilege may be maintained on the broader ground that disclosure of the information sought would be detrimental to the public interest in the proper functioning of the public service.[864]

---

[860] *World Wide Fund for Nature v Commission of the European Communities* [1997] ECR II-00313, Case T-105/95 at [63]; *Petrie & Ors v Commission of the European Community* [2001] ECR II-3677, Case T-191/99.

[861] [2009] IEHC 174 at [20].

[862] [1972] IR 215 at 237–238. See also *Geraghty v Minister for Local Government* [1975] IR 300 at 312 (*per* Griffin J).

[863] The first indication that immunity would extend beyond the narrow confines of executive functions came in *Geraghty v Minister for Local Government* [1975] IR 300. In the High Court, Kenny J excluded from disclosure a document which was written by one civil servant to another and was, he said, clearly intended to be confidential. His conclusion in this regard was upheld without comment by the Supreme Court even though it purported to faithfully apply the decision in *Murphy*.

[864] *Skeffington v Rooney* [1997] 1 IR 22 at 32, [1997] 2 ILRM 56 at 66; *Director of Consumer Affairs*

10–347 There is no precise definition as to what constitutes the public service but it extends beyond central government,[865] to include local authorities[866] and persons or bodies which perform important statutory functions in the public interest.[867] For example, in *Skeffington v Rooney*,[868] it was held that public interest privilege could be claimed by the Garda Síochána Complaints Board in an appropriate case. Keane J stressed the policy considerations underpinning the Garda Síochána (Complaints) Act 1986 which had established the Board[869] and said that, in determining the claim of privilege made by the Board, "there must be weighed against the public interest in the disclosure of the documents relating to the complaint to the Board, the public interest in ensuring that the statutory functions of the Board are not frustrated."[870] Again, in *Haughey v Moriarty*,[871] Geoghegan J took the view that "the efficient discharge of the functions of a tribunal established by the resolution of each House of the Oireachtas would normally ... override the conflicting public interest in the right to adduce evidence".

10–348 One decision which seems to be at variance with this line of authority is *Buckley v Incorporated Law Society*,[872] where Costello J held that the Law Society could not claim public interest privilege because it was not part of the public service, even though he acknowledged that it carries out important statutory duties in the public interest. This decision may have been prompted by a desire to limit the potential ambit of the privilege but if so, such a desire seems misplaced. Such a limitation may have made sense at a time when a Ministerial certificate was accepted without question, but does not do so now when claims of privilege are subject to scrutiny by the courts. Rather than adopting an *a priori* limitation on the bodies that can claim privilege, it is submitted that it would be better for the courts to adopt a broad approach to the question of whether a body is part of the public service and then decide the claim of privilege on its merits.

10–349 Claims that disclosure of documentation would undermine the proper functioning of the public service are based on the "candour argument". This proceeds on the basis that free and candid communication between persons in the public service

---

v *Sugar Distributors Ltd* [1991] 1 IR 225 at 227; *Incorporated Law Society v Minister for Justice* [1987] ILRM 42 at 44.

[865] *Per* Lord Edmund-Davies in *D. v NSPCC* [1978] AC 171 at 245, [1977] 1 All ER 589 at 618, quoted with approval by Geoghegan J in *Goodman International v Hamilton (No.3)* [1993] 3 IR 320 at 328.

[866] *Conway v Rimmer* [1968] AC 910, [1968] 1 All ER 874; *Campbell v Tameside Metropolitan Borough Council* [1982] QB 1065, [1982] 2 All ER 791.

[867] *Skeffington v Rooney* [1997] 1 IR 22, [1997] 2 ILRM 56 (Garda Síochána Complaints Board); *Haughey v Moriarty*, unreported, High Court, 20 January 1998 (tribunal of inquiry); *Fitzpatrick v Independent Newspapers* [1988] IR 132 (Bord na gCon); *PMPS Ltd v PMPA Insurance Plc* [1990] 1 IR 284 (Registrar of Friendly Societies); *State (Williams) v Army Pensions Board* [1983] IR 308 at 313 (Army Pensions Board).

[868] [1997] 1 IR 22, [1997] 2 ILRM 56.

[869] He pointed out ([1997] 1 IR 22 at 30, [1997] 2 ILRM 56 at 64) that: "The establishment of procedures designed to ensure that complaints of misconduct against members of the garda may be the subject of an investigation under the supervision of an independent body is not only of value in protecting the rights of individual citizens who complain of misconduct. It can also play an important part in maintaining and enhancing the confidence of the public in the Garda Síochána."

[870] [1999] 1 IR 22 at 35–36, [1997] 2 ILRM 56 at 69.

[871] Unreported, High Court, Geoghegan J, 20 January 1998.

[872] [1994] 2 IR 44.

is essential and the possibility that such communications could be disclosed will have a "chilling effect".[873] It is further argued that the efficiency of the public service will be adversely affected because officials will tend, where possible, to communicate orally instead of in writing in order to obviate the possibility of disclosure.[874] Apart from the lack of empirical data to support this argument, it is undermined considerably by the provisions of the Freedom of Information Act 1997 pursuant to which many such communications are liable to disclosure. Furthermore, a major difficulty with this argument is that it requires the recognition of a class claim because it is only where a blanket immunity from disclosure is conferred that the desired candour will be fostered. However, as we have seen, the concept of class claims was roundly rejected by the Supreme Court in *Murphy*.

10–350 It was for this reason that the candour argument was rejected by Murphy J in *Bula Ltd. v Tara Mines Ltd.*[875] The Minister for Energy sought to resist the production of a number of documents, virtually all of which related to advice given by senior civil servants to Ministers and submissions by Ministers to the Government based on such advice. It was argued on behalf of the Minister that it was undesirable in the public interest that these documents should be disclosed because such disclosure would tend to inhibit civil servants in providing proper and candid advice to the executive. However, Murphy J pointed out that it was the possibility rather than the reality of disclosure which would tend to cause a deterioration in the scope and quality of advice available to a Minister. As a result of the decision in *Geraghty v Minister for Local Government*,[876] all administrators had to be conscious of the fact that no absolute privilege attaches to documents containing advice to Ministers and therefore, these hypothesised ill-effects must have occurred already.[877]

10–351 Of course, some weight must be given to the candour argument because the "chilling effect" on communication within the public service will bear a correlation to the perceived risk of disclosure; the more often disclosure is ordered, the greater the likelihood that candour will be undermined. However, this risk is of its nature small and unquantifiable in respect of an individual case. It is, therefore, likely to cede to the interests of the plaintiff in prosecuting his litigation, at least where some injustice to the plaintiff might accrue by refusing disclosure. Thus, claims of privilege based on the proper functioning of the public service have generally been unsuccessful.[878]

---

[873] See the grounds for privilege put forward in *Incorporated Law Society v Minister for Justice* [1987] ILRM 42 at 43.

[874] See the grounds for privilege put forward in *Hunt v Roscommon VEC*, unreported, High Court, 1 May 1981 at 6; *Incorporated Law Society v The Minister for Justice* [1987] ILRM 42 at 43 and *Ambiorix v Minister for Environment (No.1)* [1992] 1 IR 277 at 281, [1992] ILRM 209 at 211.

[875] Unreported, High Court, 25 July 1991.

[876] [1975] IR 300.

[877] See also *Hunt v Roscommon VEC*, unreported, High Court, 1 May 1981, where the candour argument was given short shrift by McWilliam J relying on *Conway v Rimmer* [1968] AC 910, [1968] 1 All ER 874 and *Burmah Oil Co v Bank of England* [1980] AC 1090, [1979] 3 All ER 700 and *cf.* the comment of McCarthy J in *Ambiorix Ltd v Minister for the Environment (No.1)* [1992] 1 IR 277 at 287, [1992] ILRM 209 at 216, that the progeny of *Murphy* gave an empirical answer to the candour argument.

[878] See *Geraghty v Minister for Local Government* [1975] IR 300; *Hunt v Roscommon VEC*, unreported, High Court, 1 May 1981; *Folens v Minister for Education* [1981] ILRM 121; *Incorporated Law Society of Ireland v Minister for Justice* [1987] ILRM 42; *Ahern v Minister for Industry and Commerce*, unreported, High Court, Lardner J, 4 March 1988; *Ambiorix Ltd*

10–352 This bias in favour of disclosure is illustrated by the decision in *Incorporated Law Society v Minister for Justice*[879] where a claim of privilege was made on the ground of that production of the documents sought would be detrimental to the proper functioning of the public service. Murphy J identified the function of the court as being to determine, first, whether the production of the documents at issue would be detrimental to the efficiency of the public service and, second, whether such prejudice outweighed the interest of the plaintiffs in their claim to have justice administered by the court. Applying this balancing test, he acknowledged that the possibility of future discovery of documentation could have an inhibiting effect on the manner in which advice would be transmitted and recorded within the public service. The danger attendant upon this possibility was accentuated in the instant case because the documentation in question included correspondence passing between Ministers. However, he was satisfied that there was nothing in the documentation that had any *special* potential for damage to the proper administration of the public service.[880] On the other hand, although he found it difficult to evaluate the benefits which would flow to the plaintiff from the disclosure of the documents, he was of opinion that to deny the plaintiffs access to the documentation would be to impose some measure of injustice on them and "that injustice is almost necessarily greater than the potential damage to the public service".[881]

10–353 The public interest in maintaining the confidentiality of material given to *ad hoc* tribunals was considered in *Leech v Independent Newspapers*,[882] where O'Neill J refused to order the disclosure of documentation relating to the workings of the inquiry into the awarding of public relations consultancy contracts by the Office of Public Works and the Department of the Environment, Heritage and Local Government to the plaintiff. The Taoiseach appointed the former chairman of the Revenue Commissioners to conduct the inquiry and a report of his findings was prepared for the Dáil. O'Neill J accepted that the obligation of confidentiality to the individuals who participated in the inquiry could not, of itself, outweigh the public interest in full disclosure being made. However, he adopted the statement of Lord Hailsham in *D v NSPCC*,[883] which was quoted by Geoghegan J in *Goodman International v Hamilton (No. 3)*,[884] that "[t]here are ... cases when confidentiality is itself a public interest..." He accepted the argument that, in this case, confidentiality underpinned the other public interest in the effectiveness and viability of *ad hoc* tribunals, which were described as "a useful if not essential tool in public administration".[885] O'Neill J stated that confidentiality is essential in order for *ad hoc* tribunals to work, as the possibility that material given to such a public inquiry was capable of disclosure would deter persons with relevant

---

v Minister for the Environment (No.1) [1992] 1 IR 277, [1992] ILRM 209; *Gormley v Ireland* [1993] 2 IR 75; *Skeffington v Rooney* [1994] 1 IR 480 (HC).

[879] [1987] ILRM 42.

[880] An important factor in reaching this conclusion was the fact that the documentation showed "a degree of expertise and involvement by the Ministers concerned ... which is more likely to advance the interests of the public service than to damage it" ([1987] ILRM 42 at 44). However, if the converse was the case, *i.e.* the documentation showed a lack of expertise, then because of the great relevance which the documents would have to the plaintiff's case, the test would also be weighted in favour of disclosure.

[881] [1987] ILRM 42 at 44.

[882] [2009] IEHC 259, [2009] 3 IR 766.

[883] [1978] AC 171, [1977] 1 All ER 589.

[884] [1993] 3 IR 320.

[885] [2009] IEHC 259 at [6.2], [2009] 3 IR 766.

evidence from co-operating with the inquiry. Furthermore, in circumstances where such an inquiry does not have legal powers to compel the attendance of witnesses or the production of documents, the inquiry would fail as an effective method of establishing the truth absent such co-operation.[886]

10–354   The decision of O'Neill J in *Leech v Independent Newspapers* was considered by Clarke J in *MacAodhain v Éire*,[887] where he rejected the contention that it amounted to a finding that there are certain categories of document which are immune from disclosure:

> "It is not that the documents involved in the inquiry in question in *Leech* are in a category which are immune from disclosure. Rather it is that the public interest which outweighed disclosure on the facts of *Leech* was in permitting persons to deal with an inquiry of the type concerned on a confidential basis rather than that the information contained in the documents themselves was itself such that its disclosure would be contrary to the public interest."[888]

10–355   The issue in this case was the extent to which the government complied with s.71 of the Courts of Justice Act 1924, which requires that, insofar as may be practicable having regard to all relevant circumstances, a District Court judge assigned to an area where the Irish language is in general use shall possess such a knowledge of the Irish language as would enable him to dispense with the assistance of an interpreter when evidence is given in that language. Clarke J made an order for the discovery of any documents taken into account by the government in considering the provisions of s.71 when making the appointment. He concluded that the respondents had failed to establish that there was any necessary public interest which precluded disclosure, given the limited form of the information sought. The applicant did not seek disclosure of all documents relevant to the nomination of the District Court judge or any other judge; rather, the documents sought were limited to those which were relevant to the specific question of whether the government complied with its obligations under s.71.[889] Clarke J stated it remained open to the respondents to raise a claim of public interest privilege is respect of any specific materials contained in the documents if it could be asserted that the disclosure of that information might be contrary to the public interest, but refused to accept that there was any "general public interest immunity which could preclude discovery of documents of the type sought in this case".[890]

10–356   The entitlement of a tribunal to refuse disclosure on foot of an "understanding of confidentiality" between the tribunal and third parties and witnesses who provide information to the tribunal was considered in *O'Callaghan v Mahon*,[891] where the applicant was a businessman against whom serious allegations were made by a witness at the tribunal set up to investigate irregularities in the planning process (the Mahon Tribunal). Before the witness gave evidence, the applicant was provided with a statement of the evidence he proposed to give. During the oral hearing, however, the notice party raised a number of serious allegations against the applicant, which

---

[886] O'Neill J rejected the contention that a plaintiff should not be permitted to benefit from public interest privilege, stating that the interest in ensuring the effectiveness and viability of *ad hoc* public inquiries was a public interest which could not be defeated merely because a person such as the plaintiff derived a collateral benefit from it; [2009] IEHC 259 at [6.3], [2009] 3 IR 766.

[887] [2012] 1 IR 430 at 439.

[888] *Cf. McLoughlin v Aviva Insurance* [2011] IESC 42 at [6], *per* O'Donnell J.

[889] Clarke J observed, however, that he could "well see that there might be a legitimate public interest in preventing the disclosure of any wider category of documents". [2012] 1 IR 430 at 439 [26].

[890] [2012] 1 IR 430 at 439.

[891] [2005] IESC 9, [2006] 2 IR 32.

had not been included in the statement of evidence. The applicant sought disclosure of all prior statements made by the notice party to the tribunal so that he could be cross-examined in relation to inconsistencies between his prior statements and his oral evidence. The tribunal ruled that the applicant was not entitled to disclosure of these statements, as they had been furnished to the tribunal in confidence, and contended that the courts should refrain from interfering with this decision on the basis that the tribunal was master of its own procedures.

10–357 The Supreme Court held that, in circumstances where the assertion of public interest privilege interfered with the right of the applicant to cross-examine his accuser, the tribunal was not entitled to maintain confidentiality over the documents in issue. Commenting on the "understanding of confidentiality" relied upon by to the tribunal, Geoghegan J stated that a tribunal of inquiry cannot possibly ensure absolute confidentiality relating to information which might turn out to be highly relevant to matters to it was investigating. Any such confidentiality must necessarily be limited to information which is not used during an oral hearing. Furthermore, if confidential information becomes essential for the purposes of a cross-examination pursuant to the rights enumerated in *In Re Haughey*, then the tribunal is not entitled to maintain confidentiality.[892]

(iv) Cabinet discussions

10–358 The principles which govern disclosure of cabinet discussions[893] were considered in *Attorney General v Hamilton (No.1)*.[894] The Chairman of a tribunal of inquiry set up to investigate allegations of fraud and malpractice in the beef industry (commonly known as the "Beef Tribunal") sought to question a former Government Minister about whether a particular decision had been taken by the Government at a Cabinet meeting. However, a majority of the Supreme Court acceded to the contention that absolute confidentiality attached to cabinet discussions pursuant to the collective responsibility provisions of Art.28.4.2. In reaching this decision, the majority distinguished *Murphy* and *Ambiorix* on the basis that they were concerned with the exercise of the judicial power, whereas the Tribunal was set up pursuant to the legislative power.

10–359 The decision in *Hamilton* expressly left open the question as to whether a similar constitutional immunity would apply if the issue arose in the context of the administration of justice.[895] However, the view was subsequently taken by O'Hanlon J in *O'Brien v Ireland*[896] that, given its constitutional foundation, the effect of the decision was to create an absolute prohibition on the disclosure of the contents and details of cabinet discussions with no scope for a balancing by the courts of the competing public interests involved.[897]

---

[892] [2005] IESC 9 at [124], [2006] 2 IR 32 at 81–82.
[893] For a more comprehensive discussion, see Hogan and Morgan, *Administrative Law in Ireland* 3rd edn (Dublin: Round Hall Sweet & Maxwell, 1998), pp.939–942 and Hogan, "The Cabinet Confidentiality Case of 1992" (1993) 8 Irish Political Studies 131.
[894] [1993] 2 IR 250, [1993] ILRM 81.
[895] [1993] 2 IR 250 at 271, [1993] ILRM 81 at 99.
[896] [1995] 1 ILRM 22.
[897] See also *Lang v Government of Ireland*, unreported, High Court, 7 July 1993 but compare the view of Keane J in *Skeffington v Rooney* [1997] 1 IR 22 at 32, [1997] 2 ILRM 56 at 66, that the decision in *Hamilton* offered an apparent rather than a real exception to the principles established

10–360   The issue is now governed by the provisions of Art.28.4.3, which was inserted by constitutional referendum in 1997. This Article provides, *inter alia*, that the confidentiality of cabinet discussions must be respected except where the High Court determines that disclosure should be made in respect of a particular matter in the interests of the administration of justice. It would appear from the decision in *Irish Press Publications Ltd v Minister for Enterprise*[898] that the effect of that amendment is that the principles laid down in *Murphy* and *Ambiorix* apply, *mutatis mutandis*, to cabinet discussions. In that case, Carroll J was satisfied, applying those principles, that the administration of justice would not be compromised in any way or the plaintiffs unjustly disadvantaged by upholding the defendants' claim to privilege on the ground of cabinet confidentiality. Interestingly, she applied the distinction drawn by Finlay CJ in *Attorney General v Hamilton (No.1)*[899] between documents which set out the decisions made at cabinet and those which record or reveal the discussions made. She, thus, ordered to be produced for inspection a letter setting out a Government decision taken at cabinet. However, she refused to order production of documents which had been circulated in advance of the cabinet meeting and formed the basis of discussion at that meeting because, when compared with the actual Government decision, they would disclose elements of the cabinet discussion.

10–361   Article 28.4.3 was considered briefly by Clarke J in *Mac Aodhain v Éire*,[900] where it was held that, in circumstances where the issue for determination in the proceedings was the extent to which the government had complied with a specific statutory obligation, it would not be appropriate to take any general view to the effect that discovery of government level documentation ought not to be disclosed simply because such disclosure might involve the disclosure of documents prepared for government meetings. Given the limited scope of the discovery sought, Clarke J held that it was appropriate having regard to the provisions of Art.28.4.3. He observed, however, that, "[q]uestions which might concern the merits of appointing one judge or another judge or in allocating one judge or another judge to a particular district or circuit would, it seems to me, fall into a different category such that any materials disclosing the debate at cabinet as to the merits of any particular appointment or allocation might well not be properly disclosable."[901]

10–362   The scope of the protection afforded to cabinet confidentiality by Art.28.4.3 in the context of statutory provisions conferring an entitlement on members of the public to the disclosure of information has been considered by the courts in a number of cases. In *Minister for Education v Information Commissioner*,[902] an issue arose as to whether the Minister was required to disclose a draft memorandum prepared for the purpose of discussions at cabinet in relation to the contribution of religious congregations to the residential institutions redress scheme in accordance with the Freedom of Information Act 1997. The draft memorandum was not, in fact, submitted to the cabinet. The Information Commissioner concluded that the draft memorandum

---

by *Murphy* and *Ambiorix* because the evidence was not sought in the course of any proceedings in courts and, in any event, the immunity against disclosure rested on the particular constitutional position of the government.
[898]   [2002] 4 IR 110.
[899]   [1993] 2 IR 250, [1993] ILRM 81.
[900]   [2010] IEHC 40, [2012] 1 IR 430.
[901]   [2010] IEHC 40 at [28], [2012] 1 IR 430 at 440.
[902]   [2008] IEHC 279, [2009] 1 IR 588.

did not fall within the exception provided for in s.19(1) of the 1997 Act, in respect of a record which "has been, or is proposed to be, submitted to the Government for their consideration by a Minister of the Government or the Attorney General and was created for that purpose". This decision was overturned on appeal by the High Court, where it was held that the draft memorandum was prepared and created for the purpose of submission to the government and, as such, fell within the scope of s.19(1). In arriving at this conclusion, McGovern J expressed the view that, if a document containing the advice of a Minister to the Government on an issue such as this could be disclosed merely because it was not ultimately submitted to cabinet, it would totally undermine the position of the Minister concerned, and would have serious implications for Government. He adopted the following dictum of Finlay CJ in *Attorney General v Hamilton (No.1)*[903] where, having recounted the obligations imposed on the Government by Art.28.4.1 and Art.28.4.2, he stated that:

> "These obligations involve some obvious, necessary, consequential duties.
> The first of those relevant to the issues arising in this appeal is the necessity for full, free and frank discussions between members of the Government prior to the making of decisions, something which would appear to be an inevitable adjunct to the obligation to meet collectively and to act collectively.
> The obligation to act collectively must, of necessity, involve the making of a single decision on any issue, whether it is arrived at unanimously or by a majority.
> The obligation to accept collective responsibility for decisions and, presumably, for acts of government as well, involves, as a necessity, the non-disclosure of different or dissenting views held by the members of the Government prior to the making of decisions."[904]

10–363   In *An Taoiseach v The Commissioner for Environmental Information*,[905] the issue for determination was the entitlement of the applicant to refuse to disclose environmental information in accordance with the EC (Access to Information on the Environment) Regulations 2007.[906] It was held that the Taoiseach was entitled to refuse to disclose information which included a reference to discussions at government meetings, notwithstanding the absence of any express exclusion in the Directive underpinning the Regulations in favour of cabinet confidentiality. In arriving at this conclusion, O'Neill J emphasised the public interest underpinning cabinet confidentiality:

> "... meetings of the government are the occasions when as provided for in Art.28.4.2 of the Constitution the members of the government come together to act as a collective authority, collectively responsible for all departments of State. Meetings of the government are the constitutionally mandated means or system of communication between its members for the purpose of discharging their collective responsibility. These meetings and their records are required by the Constitution to be private and confidential unless otherwise directed by the High Court under Art [28.4.3] of the Constitution. Whereas many aspects of the functions of the government are essentially public and external in nature, meetings of the government are quintessentially private and internal to the overall functions of the government."[907]

---

[903] [1993] 2 IR 250, [1993] ILRM 81.
[904] [1993] 2 IR 250 at 266, [1993] ILRM 81 at 95.
[905] [2010] IEHC 241.
[906] SI No. 133 of 2007. The Regulations transposed Directive 2003/4/EC of the European Parliament and of the Council of 28 January 2003 on Public Access to Environmental Information into Irish law. Article 10(2) of the Regulations provides for an express exclusion in respect of cabinet confidentilaity. However, there is no express exclusion in respect of government meetings in the Directive. O'Neill J held that government meetings and the records of same fell within the definition of "internal communications of a public authority" within the meaning of art.9 of the Directive, which outlines discretionary grounds on which a public authority may refuse to make environmental information available.
[907] [2010] IEHC 241 at [9.6].

(v) Prevention and detection of crime

10–364   The public clearly has an interest in the prevention and detection of crime and it may, therefore, be in the public interest to protect the confidentiality of certain communications in order to facilitate this aim. The leading decision on the application of this head of public interest privilege is *Breathnach v Ireland (No.3)*.[908] The plaintiff had been convicted of the Sallins train robbery and subsequently brought civil proceedings against the State and named gardaí seeking damages for various torts and breach of his constitutional rights. In order to prosecute these proceedings, the plaintiff sought discovery from the DPP of all communications between the investigating gardaí concerning the arrest, detention and interrogation of the plaintiff. Privilege was claimed in respect of these documents on a number of grounds including the following: (i) that the documents were brought into existence for the purpose of communicating with the DPP in relation to matters relevant to the exercise of his functions; (ii) that the communications were made by members of the gardaí in circumstances where they held a reasonable belief that the communications were, and would remain, confidential; (iii) that it was necessary to maintain the confidentiality of such communications in order to ensure full disclosure by the gardaí of any fact considered to be of relevance to the DPP in the discharge of his office; and (iv) that the documents might make reference to the opinion of gardaí as to the involvement in the offence of the accused or others who were not charged and their opinion as to whether these persons are members of particular organisations.

10–365   In dealing with these contentions, Keane J began by reiterating his conclusion in *State (Hanley) v Holly*,[909] that a class claim in respect of communications between one member of the gardaí and another in the course of their duties was unsustainable having regard to the principles laid down in *Murphy*.[910] As regards the specific grounds put forward by the defendants, he pointed out that virtually all of the grounds stated would apply equally to any other criminal prosecution. Therefore, if the court were to accept these contentions without considering any countervailing considerations or inspecting the documents, it would follow that a similar course would have to be adopted in every case where those objections were raised and this was not in accordance with the constitutional position as laid down in the case law. He went on to elaborate on the proper approach to apply:

> "[T]he court, as I understand the law, is required to balance the public interest in the proper administration of justice against the public interest reflected in the grounds put forward for non-disclosure in the present case. The public interest in the prevention and prosecution of crime must be put in the scales on the one side. It is only where the first public interest outweighs the second public interest that an inspection should be undertaken or disclosure should be ordered."[911]

10–366   In considering the first public interest, it was necessary to determine to what extent, if any, the relevant documents might advance the plaintiff's case or damage

---

[908] [1993] 2 IR 458, [1992] ILRM 755. See also *Logue v Redmond* [1992] 2 ILRM 498; *Corbett v DPP* [1999] 2 IR 179; *Cahalane v Revenue Commissioners*, unreported, High Court, 14 May 1999; and *McDonald v RTÉ* [2001] 1 IR 355, [2001] 2 ILRM 1, where the principles laid down in *Breathnach* are approved and applied.

[909] [1984] ILRM 149. In *Hanley*, he had overruled an earlier decision of a divisional High Court in *Attorney General v Simpson* [1959] IR 105, which had held that a class privilege attached to communications between gardaí in the course of their duties.

[910] [1972] IR 215.

[911] [1993] 2 IR 458 at 469, [1992] ILRM 755 at 763.

the defendant's case. In considering the second public interest, the factors identified by the defendants had to be given due weight.[912] Of these, the most important was the desirability of free communication between the gardaí and the DPP. The extent to which that freedom of communication might be inhibited by the knowledge that the documents furnished to the DPP might subsequently be disclosed in court proceedings was clearly a matter which had to be taken into consideration in determining whether the public interest in the particular case required their production. Drawing a distinction between civil and criminal cases, he said:

> "In civil proceedings, the desirability of preserving confidentiality in the case of communications between members of the executive has been significantly eroded as a factor proper to be taken into account by the courts… However, different considerations would appear to apply to communications between gardaí and the Director of Public Prosecutions, where the public interest in the prevention and prosecution of crime must be given due weight. It would be clearly unacceptable if in every case where a person was acquitted of a criminal charge, he could, by instituting proceedings for wrongful arrest or malicious prosecution, embark on a fishing expedition though all the files of the gardaí relating to the case. The circumstances of the particular case must determine, in the light of the constitutional principles to which I have referred, whether an inspection should be undertaken by the court and whether, as a result of that inspection, production of any of the documents should be ordered."[913]

10–367 Weighing up these factors in the circumstances of the case, he pointed out that the plaintiff's claim included one for damages for malicious prosecution. He was of the opinion that the disputed documentation might well furnish evidence which would be of significance in establishing a want of reasonable cause for the prosecution. Therefore, he was satisfied that the public interest in the administration of justice outweighed the general desirability of preserving the confidentiality of such documents and he examined them in order to decide whether they should be produced.

10–368 The principles laid down in *Breathnach* were approved and applied in *People (DPP) v Nevin*.[914] The applicant had been convicted of the murder of her husband and brought a motion seeking disclosure of certain documents from the DPP in aid of her appeal. The DPP was willing to disclose some of the documents but claimed public interest privilege in respect of a report which analysed the documents on the basis that it had been furnished in circumstances where it was in the interest of the State that the gardaí furnishing same should be entitled to make a full and frank analysis in confidence and that the public interest in the maintenance of this confidentiality outweighed any potential interest that the applicant might have in relation thereto. The DPP also claimed public interest privilege in respect of a certain list drawn up by the gardaí on the basis that it would disclose the methodology of the garda and would lead to the publication of the names of parties who were entitled to the presumption of innocence. The Court of Criminal Appeal held that the DPP's claim of legal professional privilege in respect of the documents was well-founded but went on to make it clear that, even if it were not, the court would have held that the claim of confidentiality by the DPP should be upheld, as the arguments for non-disclosure outweighed the arguments for disclosure.[915]

---

[912] See also *Logue v Redmond* [1999] 2 ILRM 498 at 507.
[913] [1993] 2 IR 458 at 472–473, [1992] ILRM 755 at 766.
[914] Unreported, Court of Criminal Appeal, 13 December 2001.
[915] Unreported, Court of Criminal Appeal, 13 December 2001 at 4. In *H(T) v DPP* [2004] IEHC 76 at [83], it was held that "it is important that the D.P.P. should be personally responsible for raising the plea of public interest immunity". Accordingly, the affidavit grounding such a plea should expressly state that the pleas of privilege and public interest immunity were made on behalf of and on instructions of the Director of Public Prosecutions.

Applying the principles set out by Keane J in *Breathnach* in weighing the competing interests, the court found that there was nothing in the documents which could in any way advance the appellant's appeal, attaching significance to the fact that nothing contained therein tended to contradict anything in the affidavit sworn by a member of the gardaí in response to the motion for disclosure.

10–369 Subsequently, in *Nevin v DPP*,[916] the applicant sought an order quashing her conviction on the basis that a new or newly discovered fact showed that there had been a miscarriage of justice in relation to the conviction.[917] One of the newly discovered facts relied upon in support of the application was the existence of a "Suspect Antecedent Form" completed by the gardaí, which suggested that one of the chief witnesses may himself have been a suspect. This form was published in a tabloid newspaper. It transpired that similar forms had been filled out in respect of a large number of people during the investigation, and that they were used by the gardaí to record basic information in relation to persons who came up during their enquiries and were not known to the gardaí, regardless of whether the person was a suspect or not. Hardiman J observed that any criminal investigation will generate documentation, much of which will relate to lines of investigation that run into the sand or exclude persons who were suspected but are found to be innocent. It is clearly most important that investigators are allowed to exchange working papers of this type with one another. It was held, therefore, that "it would be contrary to the public interest, and would tend to handicap any major policy inquiry" if the working papers of investigators were required to be disclosed.[918]

10–370 The principles laid down in *Breathnach* were also applied in *Livingstone v Minister for Justice*.[919] The plaintiffs brought civil proceedings claiming damages for a number of torts allegedly committed by members of the gardaí in the course of a murder investigation in which the first named plaintiff had been identified as a suspect in the murder of his wife. In order to prosecute the proceedings, discovery of various categories of documents relating to the criminal investigation was sought. Having reviewed the authorities, Murphy J pointed out that there was no blanket ban against ordering the discovery of garda files or documents relating to a criminal investigation and that garda communications were not, as a class, privileged. Thus, each case has to be decided on its own facts and it was necessary to weigh the competing interests. Having done so, he ordered the discovery of some of the documents sought but refused to order discovery of documents that would hamper the criminal investigation into the murder of the deceased or prejudice any possible prosecution.[920]

---

[916] [2010] IECCA 106.

[917] In accordance with s.2 of the Criminal Procedure Act 1993.

[918] [2010] IECCA 106 at [56]. Hardiman J held that the same principle applies to the disclosure of the working papers of the defence lawyers, observing that it would be 'outrageous' if these had to be disclosed to the prosecution.

[919] [2004] IEHC 58. *Cf. Cunningham v President of the Circuit Court* [2006] IESC 51, [2006] 3 IR 541, where the Supreme Court made an order for discovery against the Director of Public Prosecutions in circumstances where the applicant sought relief by way of judicial review proceedings on grounds of delay. Macken J held that the DPP was fully entitled to raise a claim of privilege over some or all of the documents discovered, but rejected the contention that an order for discovery should not be made in the first place because of the DPP's 'special position'.

[920] *Cf. McNibb v Minister for Justice, Equality and Law Reform* [2013] IEHC 238, where O'Malley J ordered discovery of a Garda Operational Plan, Duty Roster and a report from the Chief Superintendent to the Gardaí, subject to redaction.

10–371   The public interest in the prevention and detection of crime was recognised by the Supreme Court in *McLoughlin v Aviva Insurance*,[921] where Denham J cited the following dictum of Lord Reid in *Conway v Rimmer*[922] with approval:

> "The police are carrying on an unending war with criminals many of whom are today highly intelligent. So it is essential that there should be no disclosure of anything which might give any useful information to those who organise criminal activities. And it would generally be wrong to require disclosure in a civil case of anything which might be material in a pending prosecution: but after a verdict has been given or it has been decided to take no proceedings there is not the same need for secrecy."

10–372   The Gardaí asserted privilege in civil proceedings in respect of material which was *bona fide* required for the purposes of an ongoing investigation, which might result in criminal proceedings. The Supreme Court accepted that, as a general rule, documents material to an ongoing criminal investigation by An Garda Siochana should not be required to be disclosed in civil proceedings.[923] However, the necessity for the privilege abates after the criminal trial concludes or a decision has been taken by the Director of Public Prosecutions not to prosecute. Denham CJ observed, therefore, that this public interest privilege "exists only for a limited amount of time".[924] Given the limited temporal scope of the privilege, the Supreme Court concluded that it was not necessary to carry out a balancing test; the disputed items were privileged until such time as a decision had been made by the DPP whether to prosecute.[925] As regards the scope of the privilege, it was held that it extends to all documents which are material to a criminal investigation, regardless of whether the documents or items of evidence were created by the prosecuting authorities.[926]

10–373   In criminal proceedings, particular weight will be given to the right to a fair trial when concludding the balancing exercise. In *Traynor v Delahunt*,[927] McMahon J cited the dictum of Keane J in *Breathnach* with approval, and held that it is not open to the DPP to claim public interest privilege in respect of documents emanating from the Garda Complaints Board merely because they belong to a particular class.[928]

---

[921] [2011] IESC 42 at [12], *per* Denham CJ.

[922] [1968] AC 910 at 953, [1968] 1 All ER 874.

[923] [2011] IESC 42 at [12] *per* Denham CJ, at [3] *per* O'Donnell J.

[924] [2011] IESC 42 at [13], *per* Denham CJ.

[925] [2011] IESC 42 at [22]–[23], *per* Denham CJ. O'Donnell J observed (at [5]) that, in circumstances where the DPP does not seek a stay on civil proceedings but asserts public interest privilege, "the parties to the litigation have the choice whether to proceed without the material in the same way as a party might proceed having failed in the challenge to legal professional privilege, or they can wait until the issue of public interest immunity falls away either by the disclosure of the material in criminal proceedings, or by a decision not to prosecute."

[926] [2011] IESC 42 at [20] *per* Denham CJ, at [4] *per* O'Donnell J. Denham CJ defined documents material to a criminal investigation as including documents created, sought, obtained for and relevant to a criminal investigation by a prosecutor.

[927] [2008] IEHC 272 at [26], [2009] 1 IR 605 at 613–614, [2009] 1 ILRM 113 at 120.

[928] Referring to *Breathnach*, McMahon J stated that: "If the balancing exercise is what should be undertaken where civil litigants seek disclosure of material accumulated in a failed criminal prosecution, how much more appropriate is it that a similar weighing process should be undertaken in the present case where the applicant's reputation and freedom are at stake and where she is entitled to a fair trial under the Constitution?" [2008] IEHC 272 at [27], [2009] 1 IR 605 at 614, [2009] 1 ILRM 113 at 121. *Cf. Dodd v Director of Public Prosecutions* [2007] IEHC 97.

4. Determination of a Claim of Privilege

10–374   In *Murphy v Dublin Corporation*,[929] it was held that once a particular document is established to be relevant, the burden of satisfying the court that it should be privileged from production lies upon the party making the claim of privilege. In this regard, it is essential that the affidavit of discovery be sworn in the proper form, such that the documents in respect of which privilege are claimed are listed individually and the grounds on which privilege is claimed particularised.[930] In *O'Brien v Minister for Defence*,[931] where this had not been done and a general claim of privilege had been made in respect of bundles of documents and files, the Supreme Court stated that it was unable to assess whether a claim of public interest privilege could be maintained.[932] This was recently reaffirmed by the Supreme Court in *Keating v Radio Telefís Éireann*,[933] where it was held that "the nature of the asserted privilege and of the document the subject thereof, must be sufficiently particularised so as to permit the court to evaluate the claim. Generalised, non-specific details will not suffice".[934]

10–375   In any case where a claim of privilege is made, the court has the power to examine the documents[935] and will generally do so before upholding the claim.[936] However, there is no requirement to examine the documents and the court may uphold a claim merely on the basis of a description of the nature and contents of the document.[937]

---

[929] [1972] IR 215 at 235.

[930] In accordance with the principles laid down by the Supreme Court in *Bula Ltd v Tara Mines Ltd (No.4)* [1991] 1 IR 217; *Bula Ltd v Crowley* [1991] 1 IR 220, [1990] ILRM 756; and *O'Brien v Minister for Defence* [1998] 2 ILRM 156. See *Corbett v DPP* [1999] 2 IR 179 at 188–189, where a dispute arose as to whether a claim of public interest privilege had been competently raised.

[931] [1998] 2 ILRM 156.

[932] See also *Hunt v Roscommon VEC*, unreported, High Court, 1 May 1981, where McWilliam J refused to remedy the deficiencies in the affidavit claiming privilege by examining the disputed documents. The learned judge criticised the failure to particularise the grounds on which privilege was claimed in respect of each document and said that "to ask the Court to examine all these documents under the circumstances of this case seems to me to be getting very close to asking the Court to prepare the parts of the affidavit of discovery."

[933] [2013] IESC 22 at [45].

[934] *Cf. Mac Aodhain v Éire* [2010] IEHC 40 at [27], [2012] 1 IR 430 at 440 *per* Clarke J. But see *Sweetman v An Bord Pleanala* [2009] IEHC 174 at [21], where it was held that, where it is clear that documents are protected from disclosure by public interest privilege, the court may refuse to order discovery in order to avoid the additional expense and costs which would be incurred were the respondent required to swear an affidavit of discovery and assert privilege.

[935] *Kennedy v DPP* [2012] IESC 34 at [3.2] Clarke J stated: "It is ... well established that, in an appropriate case, in seeking to exercise that balance, a judge may review documents or materials concerned so as to form an opinion on the weight to be attached to the confidentiality asserted on behalf of the executive and to balance that weight against the importance of the relevant materials to the issues which are likely to arise at trial". See also *Murphy v Dublin Corporation* [1972] IR 215 at 235; *Ambiorix Ltd v Minister for the Environment (No.1)* [1992] 1 IR 277 at 283, [1992] ILRM 209 at 213.

[936] In *Corbett v DPP* [1999] 2 IR 179 at 189, O'Sullivan J took the view that once a *prima facie* claim of privilege has been established, then the courts should proceed to examine the documents to ascertain whether the claim is properly founded.

[937] *McNibb v Minister for Justice, Equality and Law Reform* [2013] IEHC 238 at [21]; *McLaughlin v Aviva Insurance* [2011] IESC 42, *per* O'Donnell J at [6]; *Murphy v Dublin Corporation* [1972] IR 215 at 235; *Ambiorix Ltd v Minister for the Environment (No.1)* [1992] 1 IR 277 at 283, [1992] ILRM 209 at 213; *Skeffington v Rooney* [1997] 1 IR 22 at 35, [1997] 2 ILRM 56 at 69; *Casey v Iarnrod Éireann* [2004] IEHC 117. In *Breathnach v Ireland (No.3)* [1993] 2 IR 458 at 469, [1992] ILRM 755 at 764, Keane J held that the burden of satisfying the court that it should not proceed to examine the documents lies upon the person seeking to withhold the documents. But

Conversely, if the court is satisfied that a *prima facie* claim of privilege has not been made out, it is not required to inspect the documents to vouchsafe that conclusion.[938] In *McDonald v RTÉ*,[939] Murphy J sounded a cautionary note in relation to the examination of documents, stating that although this procedure will generally be the best method for adjudicating on a claim of privilege, there are circumstances where it will not be. In particular, there were cases where the examination of documents by a judge without any information as to the significance of particular documents or any explanation as to how they might benefit one party or embarrass the other could lead to an injustice.

10–376 The practice which has developed in respect of the implementation of the principles set out in *Murphy* and *Ambiorix* was considered by McKechnie J in *Keating v Radio Telefís Eireann*,[940] where he identified the following guiding principles[941]:

> (i) "in general, where competing interests conflict the court will examine the text of the disputed document and determine where the superior interest rests: it will carry out this enquiry on a case-by-case basis[942];
>
> (ii) this exercise may not always be necessary. On rare occasions, it may be possible for the court to come to a decision solely by reference to the description of the document as set out in the affidavit; that is, without recourse to an examination of the particular text of the document itself ... [943];
>
> (iii) in all cases however (and this is the crucial point) it will be for the examining court to both make the decision and to decide on what material is necessary for that purpose; and finally
>
> (iv) in performing this exercise, no presumption of priority exists as between conflicting interests."[944]

10–377 In some cases where the public interest is finely balanced or even weighted in favour of non-disclosure, the courts have edited the documents and ordered partial disclosure.[945] This enables the courts to place the maximum amount of information possible before the party seeking disclosure while at the same time paying due attention

---

see *Burke v Minister for Justice*, Supreme Court, *ex tempore*, 18 July 2002 at 4, where Keane CJ stated that, "the court of trial must itself inspect the documents for the purpose of ascertaining whether the public interest relied on for their non-production by the State authorities outweighs the public interest in the administration of justice".

[938] *McLaughlin v Aviva Insurance* [2011] IESC 42 at [6] *per* O'Donnell J; See also *Hunt v Roscommon VEC*, unreported, High Court, 1 May 1981; *Skeffington v Rooney* [1997] 1 IR 22, [1997] 2 ILRM 56; *Casey v Iarnrod Eireann* [2004] IEHC 117.

[939] [2001] 1 IR 355, [2001] 2 ILRM 1.

[940] [2013] IESC 22.

[941] These general principles were cited in full and applied by O'Malley J in *McNibb v Minister for Justice, Equality and Law Reform* [2013] IEHC 238 at [24]. She noted that the Supreme Court was concerned in *Keating* with an application for discovery, but held that the analysis of McKechnie J applies equally to the determination of a claim of public interest privilege (at [27]).

[942] See, by way of example, *A.P. v Minister for Justice and Equality* [2014] IEHC 17 at [4], where the Court examined the three documents over which a claim of public interest privilege was asserted.

[943] But see *McLaughlin v Aviva Insurance (Europe) Public Limited Company* [2011] IESC 42 at [6] *per* O'Donnell J, where he stated that: "The Court is free to inspect the items if it considers it either appropriate or necessary to do so, and is not bound to accept the Commissioner's claim. However, the Courts have repeatedly made it clear that the fact that the court may inspect material does not mean that the court must do so to verify any claim for privilege, if the nature of the claim is obvious from the description of the document."

[944] [2013] IESC 22 at [36].

[945] See, *e.g. A.P. v Minister for Justice and Equality* [2014] IEHC 17 at [26]–[27]; *Gormley v Ireland* [1993] 2 IR 75 at 79; *Wong v Minister for Justice*, unreported, High Court, 16 March 1993 and *Bula Ltd v Tara Mines Ltd*, unreported, High Court, Murphy J, 25 July 1991.

to the countervailing public interest. Thus, in *Bula Ltd v Tara Mines Ltd*,[946] where the Minister for Energy was anxious that the form in which certain Cabinet documents are cast should not be disclosed, disclosure of the documents was ordered but the Minister's concerns were addressed by the pasting over of parts of the documents.[947]

10–378   The requirement for caution in relation to the procedures adopted in respect of the inspection of documents over which a claim of public interest privileged is claimed is apparent from the decision of the European Court of Human Rights in *Edwards and Lewis v DPP*,[948] where it was held that there had been a violation of art.6.1[949] in circumstances where the trial judge inspected documents over which a claim of public interest privilege was asserted and upheld the claim of privilege, as a result of which the defendant was denied access to the documents. The defence alleged entrapment and contended that the material over which public interest privilege was asserted was relevant to this issue. The Court stated that:

> "It is in any event a fundamental aspect of the right to a fair trial that criminal proceedings, including the elements of such proceedings which relate to procedure, should be adversarial and that there should be equality of arms between the prosecution and defence. The right to an adversarial trial means, in a criminal case, that both prosecution and defence must be given the opportunity to have knowledge of and comment on the observations filed and the evidence adduced by the other party... In addition, art.6 § 1 requires that the prosecution authorities should disclose to the defence all material evidence in their possession for or against the accused...
>
> The entitlement to disclosure of relevant evidence is not, however, an absolute right. In any criminal proceedings there may be competing interests, such as national security or the need to protect witnesses at risk of reprisals or keep secret police methods of investigation of crime, which must be weighed against the rights of the accused. In some cases it may be necessary to withhold certain evidence from the defence so as to preserve the fundamental rights of another individual or to safeguard an important public interest. Nonetheless, only such measures restricting the rights of the defence which are strictly necessary are permissible under art.6 § 1. Furthermore, in order to ensure that the accused receives a fair trial, any difficulties caused to the defence by a limitation on its rights must be sufficiently counterbalanced by the procedures followed by the judicial authorities."

10–379   The European Court of Human Rights concluded that it was not possible for the defence representatives to argue the case on entrapment in full before the judge because the defence was denied access to the evidence. The Court also pointed out that, in each case, the judge who subsequently rejected the defence submissions on entrapment had seen prosecution evidence which might have been relevant to the issue.

10–380   The decision in *Edwards and Lewis v UK* was considered by the Supreme Court in *Kennedy v DPP*,[950] where an issue arose as to whether it was appropriate for the trial judge to inspect documents over which a claim of public interest privilege was asserted, while retaining seisin over the substantive judicial review proceedings. The applicant objected to the inspection of the documents by the trial judge and submitted, in reliance on *Edwards v UK*, that the documents should have been inspected by a judge other than the trial judge. Notwithstanding this, the trial judge proceeded to inspect the documents and upheld the claim of public interest privilege on a number of grounds, including the fact that the documents were "highly prejudicial" to the applicant and

---

[946] Unreported, High Court, 25 July 1991.
[947] See also *Wong v Minister for Justice*, unreported, High Court, 16 March 1993.
[948] (2005) 40 EHRR 24.
[949] While the European Court of Human Rights granted a declaration of violation of art.6 rights, it held that this violation did not entail that the applicants were wrongly convicted.
[950] [2012] IESC 34.

could only damage his case.[951] The trial judge stated that he would not take any of the documentation into account in his consideration of the application for judicial review, and proceeded to hear the substantive judicial review proceedings, in which he refused to grant the reliefs sought by the applicant.

10–381 The Supreme Court rejected the contention that the procedure adopted by the trial judge was unfair, or inconsistent with the decision of the European Court of Human Rights in *Edwards*. Denham J stated that "[t]he procedure of inspection of documents by a court of trial is a very useful one and is often very much in the interest of the party challenging the privilege claimed".[952] She distinguished the decision in *Edwards* on the basis that it concerned a criminal trial, whereas the proceedings before the Court were civil proceedings arising on foot of an application for judicial review.

10–382 In a concurring judgment, Clarke J engaged in a detailed analysis of the procedures governing the inspection of documents over which a claim of public interest privilege is asserted and observed that, in many cases, the trial judge will have a much better understanding of the potential importance of the documents to the issues which are likely to arise during the case, as a result of which he or she may be better placed to carry out the balancing exercise required where a claim of public interest privilege is asserted. However, he accepted that there is a possibility that the trial judge may, in reviewing the materials, become aware of matters which have not been established in evidence and which, in the event that disclosure is not directed, will not be available to the other parties to the litigation.[953] It was held, therefore, that the decision as to whether it is appropriate that documents or materials over which a claim of public interest privilege is asserted should be conducted by the trial judge or another judge is one which must be considered on a case by case basis.[954]

10–383 Another technique which had been used in some cases was to order disclosure but restrict inspection of documents to the lawyers of the party seeking disclosure upon their undertaking not to reveal the contents to anyone without the leave of the court.[955] However, the Supreme Court in *Burke v Central Independent Television Plc*[956] cast doubt on the propriety of this practice. Finlay CJ said that this would result in the lawyers for the plaintiffs having access to a number of documents which might well be significant and weighty tools to be used in cross-examination of witnesses adduced on behalf of the defendant and be unable to use such documents or explain to their clients their failure to use them. He opined that this would constitute an unprecedented

---

[951] The Supreme Court rejected the contention that this gave rise to objective bias on the part of the trial judge. However, the Court was heavily influenced in this regard by the fact that, following the determination of the claim of public interest privilege and prior to the hearing of the substantive judicial review proceedings, the applicant did not request that the trial judge recuse himself.

[952] [2012] IESC 34 at [35].

[953] [2012] IESC 34 at [3.3]–[3.4] *per* Clarke J.

[954] Clarke J stated that, while there is nothing wrong in principle with the trial judge looking at documents for the purpose of determining whether a claim of public interest privilege should be upheld, there may be cases where, having done so, the trial judge realises that a potential and significant prejudice has occurred, which warrants the trial judge declining to hear the case further. It was strongly recommended, therefore, that the inspection of documents over which a claim of public interest privilege is asserted should take place in advance of the hearing date, so that another trial judge can be assigned to the case if necessary.

[955] *Ambiorix Ltd v Minister for the Environment (No.1)* [1992] 1 IR 277 at 286, [1992] ILRM 209 at 215; *Gormley v Ireland* [1993] 2 IR 75 at 80.

[956] [1994] 2 IR 61, [1994] 2 ILRM 161.

and wholly undesirable breach of the duty which counsel owe to their client and an interference in the trust which should exist between a client and his or her lawyers.[957]

5. Assertion and Waiver of Claim

10–384   Because of its nature, public interest privilege does not fit easily within the conceptual framework of a privilege which requires that a privilege exist for the benefit of an identified person or persons who can choose to assert it or waive it as they see fit. Public interest privilege exists to further the public interest and, therefore, in so far as a holder of the privilege can be identified, it is the public as a whole. For this reason, the view has been taken that it can be invoked by any party to litigation or, if no objection is otherwise taken, the issue can and should be raised by the court of its own motion in an appropriate case.[958]

10–385   A controversial question is whether the privilege may be waived. In England, the view has been taken that because it involves an adjudication of where the balance of public interest lies, the doctrine of waiver has no application.[959] However, the Irish courts have taken a different approach and in two Supreme Court decisions, *Hannigan v DPP*[960] and *McDonald v RTÉ*,[961] it was held that privilege may be waived. Thus, in *Hannigan*, it was held that privilege had been waived in respect of a document which had been summarised in an affidavit. Hardiman J said that the deployment of the document for litigious purposes was inconsistent with an assertion of the harmful effects following from its disclosure and it was just and equitable that the appellant should have access to it.[962]

10–386   In *Egan v O'Toole*,[963] the Supreme Court upheld the decision of Kelly J in the High Court that documents to which reference was made in an affidavit sworn in rendition proceedings in accordance with the Extradition Act 1965 (as amended) had not been deployed, as a result of which privilege had not been waived. Kelly J concluded that the documents were merely referred to in the narrative of events set out in affidavit, as a result of which they did not come within the scope of Ord.31, r.15. He also had regard to the claim of confidentiality maintained by the English police in respect of the documents and observed that there was no entitlement to disclosure of such documents in England.[964]

---

[957]   See also *DPP v Special Criminal Court* [1999] 1 IR 60 at 84–88 and *R. v Davis* [1993] 1 IR 613 at 616.

[958]   *AG v Simpson* [1959] IR 105, 133; *Duncan v Cammell Laird & Co Ltd* [1942] AC 624, [1942] 1 All ER 587.

[959]   *Rogers v Secretary of State for the Home Department* [1973] AC 388 at 407, [1972] 2 All ER 1057 at 1066; *Air Canada v Secretary of State for Trade* [1983] 2 AC 394 at 436, [1983] 1 All ER 910 at 917.

[960]   [2001] 1 IR 378, *sub nom. TH v DPP* [2002] 1 ILRM 48.

[961]   [2001] 1 IR 355, [2001] 2 ILRM 1.

[962]   *Cf. Cunningham v President of the Circuit Court* [2006] IESC 51, [2006] 3 IR 541 at 550, where Macken J cited this decision with approval in the context of an application for discovery against the Director of Public Prosecutions. See also *Hughes v Commissioner of An Garda Síochána*, unreported, High Court, *ex tempore*, 20 January 1998 where Laffoy J rejected as unsustainable a claim of public interest privilege in respect of documents relating to matters which had been aired in court in earlier proceedings.

[963]   [2005] IESC 53 (on appeal from a decision of Kelly J, unreported, High Court, 15 June 2004).

[964]   In the High Court, Kelly J stated: "It would be anomalous if the plaintiff were entitled to production of such a document in this jurisdiction when it was not open to him to demand its inspection

E. Miscellaneous Privileges

10–387   Wigmore has suggested four conditions which must be satisfied before a privilege can be recognised in respect of a given relationship⁹⁶⁵:

(1)   The communications must originate in a confidence that they will not be disclosed;

(2)   This element of confidentiality must be essential to the full and satisfactory maintenance of the relation between the parties;

(3)   The relation must be one which in the opinion of the community ought to be sedulously fostered; and

(4)   The injury that would inure to the relation by the disclosure of the communications must be greater than the benefit thereby gained for the correct disposal of the litigation.

10–388   It is evident that these factors are satisfied with regard to the established categories of privilege such as legal professional privilege and without prejudice privilege and they also underpin the miscellany of privileges which are discussed below.⁹⁶⁶

1. Informer Privilege

10–389   It has long been recognised⁹⁶⁷ that privilege can be claimed in respect of the identities of informers and documents from which their identities can be established.⁹⁶⁸ Surrounding evidence which would be likely to, or might tend to, disclose the identity of the informer may also be protected by the privilege.⁹⁶⁹ It is founded on the two interlinking justifications that, first, disclosure of the identities of informants might well place them in physical danger⁹⁷⁰ and, second, if privilege is not granted, the flow

---

in England, although the position might have been different had the defendant deployed the documents in these proceedings". This dictum was cited with apparent approval by the Supreme Court.

⁹⁶⁵ Wigmore, *Evidence* 3rd edn (Boston: Little Brown and Company, 1940), VIII, § 2285.

⁹⁶⁶ At present, a privilege for psychotherapy is not recognised as a matter of Irish law. The possibility of the recognition of such a privilege was, however, adverted to in *G. O'R v DPP* [2011] IEHC 368 at [17], [2011] 1 IR 193 at 203 where Charleton J considered an article by Simon O'Leary, "A Privilege for Psychotherapy? Part 2" (2007) 12(2) BR 76. Charleton J stated that the court had no view on this issue, as it was not a matter which fell to be determined in the case under consideration. However, he described the reasoning of the author as "both sensible and correct". *Cf. Jaffee v Redmond* (1996) 518 US 1.

⁹⁶⁷ *R. v Hardy* (1794) 24 St Tr 199; *Attorney General v Briant* (1846) 15 M & W 169 at 185. One of the earliest examples of its successful invocation in Ireland is to be found in *R. v Smith O'Brien* (1848) 7 St Tr NS 123 at 126, where, at the trial of William Smith O'Brien for treason arising out of the Young Irelander's rebellion, the court refused to compel a witness to disclose the identity of a person who had given him certain information.

⁹⁶⁸ In *Re. Sean Dunne, a Bankrupt* [2014] IEHC 285 at [13]; *P.B. v A.F.* [2012] IEHC 428 at [6.12]; *Clarke v Governor of Cloverhill Prison* [2011] IEHC 199 at [26], [2011] 2 IR 743 at 750; *Millstream Recycling Limited v Tierney* [2010] IEHC 55; *Buckley v Incorporated Law Society of Ireland* [1994] 2 IR 44; *Director of Consumer Affairs v Sugar Distributors Ltd* [1991] 1 IR 225, [1991] ILRM 395; *Ward v Special Criminal Court* [1998] 2 ILRM 493; *People (DPP) v McGinley* [1998] 2 IR 408 at 415; *McKeon v DPP*, unreported, Supreme Court, 12 October 1995; *Marks v Beyfus* (1890) 25 QBD 494; *D v NSPCC* [1978] AC 171, [1977] 1 All ER 589. In addition, in *People (DPP) v Eccles* (1986) 3 Frewen 36 at 63, and *People (DPP) v Reddan* [1995] 3 IR 560 at 571–572, it was held that a garda witness could refuse to identify an informant as garda or civilian on the basis that it would be dangerous to do so. *Cf. R. v Basi* [2009] 3 SCR 389.

⁹⁶⁹ *People (DPP) v Kelly* [2006] IESC 20 at [10], [2006] 3 IR 115 *per* Geoghegan J.

⁹⁷⁰ *Millstream Recycling Limited v Tierney* [2010] IEHC 55 at [39]–[44]; *Ward v Special Criminal*

of information from them would dry up.[971] Both of these policy considerations were adverted to by the Court of Appeal in *People (DPP) v Fitzpatrick*,[972] where O'Donnell J explained that:

> "Normally, either the identity of the informant, or the manner in which information has been gathered by investigating authorities, is of little possible relevance to any case, since such information is itself not adduced in evidence. On the other hand, even apparently innocuous pieces of information about informants, or the method by which investigating authorities obtain information about criminal activities, may be of considerable value to the intelligence gathering operations of organisations involved in criminality, particularly paramilitary crime. Accordingly, courts throughout the world approach the question of informer's privilege with considerable, and appropriate, sensitivity."

10–390 Although, this privilege is sometimes regarded as a discrete example of public interest privilege,[973] it is better regarded as a distinct category of privilege because, except where the "innocence at stake" exception is at issue, its application does not involve any case by case balancing exercise.[974]

10–391 While the courts have upheld a claim of public interest privilege in order to protect the integrity of the Witness Protection Programme and the identity of witnesses admitted to the programme, this must be balanced with "the need to ensure that defending counsel had access to information necessary to enable him to effectively cross-examine the protected witness with respect to any benefits or favours that he may have received..."[975]

(a) Informers protected by the privilege

10–392 The traditional view of the privilege was that it was grounded on the public interest in the prevention and detection of crime[976] and, therefore, only applied to

---

Court [1998] 2 ILRM 493; *R. v Smith O'Brien* (1848) 7 St Tr NS 123; *R. v Hennessy* (1978) 68 Cr App R 419; *Cf. Burke v Central Independent Television* [1994] 2 IR 61.
[971] *Cf. AG v Simpson* [1959] IR 105 at 125; *D v NSPCC* [1978] AC 171 at 218, [1977] 1 All ER 589 at 595 (*per* Lord Diplock).
[972] [2012] IECCA 74 at [20].
[973] *Cf. Director of Consumer Affairs v Sugar Distributors Ltd* [1991] 1 IR 225 at 227, [1991] ILRM 395 at 397; *Buckley v Incorporated Law Society of Ireland* [1994] 2 IR 44 at 49; *Breathnach v Ireland* [1993] 2 IR 458 at 469, [1992] ILRM 755 at 763.
[974] As far back as *Marks v Beyfus* (1890) 25 QBD 494 at 498, Esher MR declared that "this rule of public policy is not a matter of discretion; it is a rule of law, and as such should be applied by the judge at the trial, who should not treat it as a matter of discretion whether he should tell the witness to answer or not". *Cf. Millstream Recycling Limited v Tierney* [2010] IEHC 55 at [39]–[44]; *Ward v Special Criminal Court* [1998] 2 ILRM 493 at 504 and *D v NSPCC* [1978] AC 171 at 218, [1977] 1 All ER 589 at 595 (*per* Lord Diplock). *Cf. R. v Basi* [2009] 3 SCR 389, where the Supreme Court of Canada held that informer privilege only yields where innocence is at stake; the privilege is not amenable to any sort of public interest balancing.
[975] *DPP v Ryan* [2011] IECCA 6 at [21]; *People (DPP) v Gilligan* [2006] 1 IR 107. See Chap.6 where the issue of whether a trial is rendered unfair by reasons of the use of belief evidence in circumstances where a claim of informer privilege is asserted in respect of the material on which the belief is based is considered. *Cf. People (DPP) v O'Kelly* [2006] IESC 20, [2006] 3 IR 115, [2006] 2 ILRM 321; *People (DPP) v Matthews* [2006] IECCA 103, [2007] 2 IR 169; *People (DPP) v Binead* [2006] IECCA 374, [2007] 1 IR 374; *People (DPP) v Birney* [2006] IECCA 58, [2007] 1 IR 337; *People (DPP) v O'Donohue* [2007] IECCA 97, [2008] 2 IR 193; *People (DPP) v Kelly* [2007] IECCA 110; *People (DPP) v Bullman* [2009] IECCA 84; *People (DPP) v Donnelly* [2012] IECCA 78; *Redmond v Ireland* [2009] 2 ILRM 419.
[976] See *Ward v Special Criminal Court* [1998] 2 ILRM 493 at 504; *Buckley v Incorporated Law*

police or prison[977] informants.[978] However, the range of informants protected by the privilege has been greatly expanded and it now appears as if privilege will extend to all communications between informers and bodies with law enforcement functions and powers.[979]

10–393   The landmark case in this regard is the decision of the House of Lords in *D v NSPCC*[980] where privilege was conferred on communications by informers to the defendant society concerning alleged abuse of children. Lord Diplock justified the extension of privilege from police informers to NSPCC informers on the basis that the public interest served by preserving the anonymity of both classes of informers is analogous. The NSPCC was an organisation authorised by statute to bring legal proceedings for the welfare of children and the public interest in the effective exercise of its functions in this regard was as weighty as that in respect of police informers.[981]

10–394   This decision was followed in *Director of Consumer Affairs v Sugar Distributors Ltd*,[982] where Costello J held that privilege applied to the contents of a complaint made by a company to the Director that the defendant had breached restrictive practices legislation:

> "[T]he Oireachtas has conferred on the Director important law enforcement functions. I am satisfied that it is in the public interest that the court should protect the effective functioning by the Director of his statutory powers. I am further satisfied that to enable him to exercise his powers effectively he must be able to assure complainants that information given to him (and, indeed, in certain circumstances the names of the complainants) will be treated in confidence and not disclosed as otherwise complaints may not be forthcoming and breaches of ministerial orders are likely to go undetected."[983]

10–395   He subsequently distinguished this decision in *Buckley v The Incorporated Law Society of Ireland*,[984] where privilege was claimed by the Law Society in respect of complaints of misconduct made to it. Costello J pointed to what he regarded as a crucial distinction between the duties of the Law Society and those of the Director of

---

Society of Ireland [1994] 2 IR 44 at 49; *Director of Consumer Affairs v Sugar Distributors Ltd* [1991] 1 IR 225 at 227, [1991] ILRM 395 at 397.

[977]   *State (Comerford) v Governor of Mountjoy Prison* [1981] ILRM 86.

[978]   For examples of cases in which the exception was applied in respect of police informants, see *McKeon v Director of Public Prosecutions*, unreported, Supreme Court, 12 October 1995, and *Clarke v Governor of Cloverhill Prison* [2011] IEHC 199 at [26], [2011] 2 IR 743 at 750.

[979]   In *P.B. v A.F.* [2012] IEHC 428 at [6.12], it was held that the privilege extended to information provided to An Garda Síochána on which reliance was placed in proceedings under the Proceeds of Crime Act 1996 (as amended).

[980]   [1978] AC 171, [1977] 1 All ER 589.

[981]   See also *Rogers v Secretary of State for the Home Department; Gaming Board of Great Britain v Rogers* [1972] 2 All ER 1057, [1973] AC 388, where the court extended the principle to persons from whom the Gaming Board received information for the purpose of the exercise of their statutory functions.

[982]   [1991] 1 IR 225, [1991] ILRM 395.

[983]   [1991] 1 IR 225 at 228, [1991] ILRM 395 at 399. See *Foley v Bowden* [2003] 2 IR 607, where the High Court refused to make an order for the examination of a witness in accordance with RSC Ord.42, r.36 on the basis that this might result in the disclosure of a participant in a witness protection scheme. The Supreme Court reversed this decision, holding that it would be open to the witness to object to the production of any document whose disclosure would not be in the public interest. The Supreme Court held, however, that an order of the type sought should not be granted in other circumstances where it would necessarily imperil the successful implementation of the witness protection scheme in the future.

[984]   [1994] 2 IR 44.

Consumer Affairs, in that the Director was concerned to investigate possible breaches of the criminal law, whereas the defendant was concerned with allegations of professional misconduct. The fact that, in some cases, the misconduct might involve breaches of the criminal law did not alter the fundamental nature of the defendant's statutory duties. He, therefore, had to consider whether informer privilege should be extended to complaints made to the Law Society and he did so by balancing the competing public interests.[985] The exemption from disclosure of documents would clearly constitute a potential restriction and diminution of the full disclosure which was desirable for the purpose of ascertaining the truth and rendering justice in civil proceedings. However, it was argued by the defendant that if it is known that documents relating to complaints to the defendant might be disclosed at some future time, persons with legitimate complaints might be discouraged by the fear of public disclosure of their private affairs from coming forward, thus reducing the effectiveness of the defendant's supervisory role. Costello J was in no doubt as to where the balance lay. It was a demonstrable probability that if inspection was refused this would result in the frustration of the court's duty to ascertain the truth and do justice between the parties. This probability outweighed what he considered to be a small risk that complainants would be deterred from approaching the defendants.[986]

10–396   The decision in *D v NSPCC*[987] was also relied upon by Geoghegan J in *Goodman International v Hamilton (No.3)*.[988] This case arose out of the decision by the respondent, who was Chairman of the Tribunal of Inquiry into the Beef Industry, that a number of TDs could rely on informer privilege to protect the identity of their sources.[989] Geoghegan J relied on the principle enunciated by Lord Edmund-Davies in D v NSPCC[990] that, where a confidential relationship exists and disclosure would be in breach of some ethical or social value involving the public interest, the court has a discretion to uphold a refusal to disclose relevant evidence provided it considers that, on balance, the public interest would be better served by excluding such evidence. He opined that most Irish people would regard it as important that matters of actual or potential public concern may be confidentially brought to the attention of elected national public representatives without fear of the confidence being broken. Therefore, having regard to the all the circumstances of the case,[991] the balance lay in favour of non-disclosure.

---

[985] Applying the test laid down by Finlay CJ in *Smurfit Paribas Bank Ltd v AAB Export Finance Ltd* [1990] 1 IR 469 at 477, [1990] ILRM 588 at 594.

[986] But see *Buckley v Law Society (No. 2)* [1984] 3 All ER 313, [1984] 1 WLR 1101, where the court refused to order inspection, holding that the public interest in protecting the identity of persons who had given information to the Law Society, which had enabled it to intervene in a case of suspected dishonesty, was greater than the public interest in disclosure of all relevant documents to the solicitor.

[987] [1978] AC 171, [1977] 1 All ER 589.

[988] [1993] 3 IR 320.

[989] It should be noted that reliance on common law privilege may not be necessary because it was held in *Howlin v Morris* [2006] 2 IR 321, [2004] 2 ILRM 53 that TDs will, in certain circumstances, be entitled to invoke on parliamentary privilege under Art.15 of the Constitution to refuse to disclose their sources or any communications with them.

[990] [1978] AC 171 at 245, [1977] 1 All ER 589 at 618.

[991] These circumstances included the fact that informants reasonably believed that their identity would be protected by constitutional privilege pursuant to Art.15 and the fact that the respondent had at all times made it clear that hearsay evidence would not be admitted to undermine the good names of the applicants.

10–397   The decision of the Supreme Court in *Skeffington v Rooney*⁹⁹² may indicate that the courts will take an even broader approach in the future and recognise informer privilege where it is essential to the proper functioning of a statutory body. In that case, Keane J seemed to take the view that informer privilege could apply to the identity of informants and the substance of complaints made to the Garda Síochána Complaints Board. It might be noted though that, in that case, the Court stressed the importance of the functions of the Board and, even though that Board has no law enforcement powers as such, if a complaint is made which the Board is of opinion may constitute an offence committed by the garda concerned, it must refer the matter to the DPP.

10–398   Informer privilege has also been extended to the source of information relied upon by the Official Assignee in seeking a warrant under s.28 of the Bankruptcy Act 1988,⁹⁹³ as well as the source of information provided to the Dental Council, on foot of which an inquiry into professional misconduct was initiated.⁹⁹⁴

(b) The "Innocence at Stake" Exception

10–399   Almost as old as informer privilege itself is the recognition that it is subject to what O'Flaherty J in *Ward v Special Criminal Court*⁹⁹⁵ termed the "innocence at stake" exception which was described as follows by Esher MR in *Marks v Beyfus*:

> "[I]f upon the trial of a prisoner the judge should be of opinion that the disclosure of the name of the informant is necessary or right in order to show the prisoner's innocence, then one public policy is in conflict with another public policy, and that which says that an innocent man is not to be condemned when his innocence can be proved is the policy that must prevail."⁹⁹⁶

10–400   A similar view was taken by Costello J in *Director of Consumer Affairs v Sugar Distributors Ltd.*⁹⁹⁷ He said that where a claim of informer privilege is made, the court should examine the documents and permit inspection where it "concludes that the documents might tend to show that the defendant had not committed the wrongful acts alleged against him".⁹⁹⁸

10–401   The innocence at stake exception was considered by the Supreme Court in *Howlin v Morris*,⁹⁹⁹ which arose out of the garda investigation into allegations of Garda misconduct regarding the McBrearty family in Donegal. The applicant stated that he had received information from an unidentified source that a garda who was under investigation was in a position to blackmail two assistant garda commissioners

---

⁹⁹² [1997] 1 IR 22 at 36, [1997] 2 ILRM 56 at 69.

⁹⁹³ *Re Sean Dunne, a bankrupt* [2014] IEHC 285 at [13]. Section 28 of the Bankruptcy Act 1988 (as amended) provides for a search warrant to be issued "where it appears to the Court that there is reason to believe that any other property of the bankrupt is concealed in any house, building, room or other place not belonging to the bankrupt".

⁹⁹⁴ *Al-Sukhun v The Dental Council* [2011] IEHC 533 at [16]. The emails were not submitted in evidence before the Fitness to Practice Committee and did not form part of the case against the applicant. However, the inqquiry appeared to have been initiated following receipt of the emails and the applicant expressed concern that the author of the emails may have had contact or connection with some of the witnesses.

⁹⁹⁵ [1998] 2 ILRM 493 at 501. See, further, O'Connor, "The Privilege of Non-Disclosure and Informers" (1980) 15 Ir Jur 111.

⁹⁹⁶ (1890) 25 QBD 494 at 498. *Cf.* the opinion of Dixon J in *AG v Simpson* [1959] IR 105 at 141, that this proposition is based on a non sequitur.

⁹⁹⁷ [1991] 2 IR 225. See also *Goodman International v Hamilton (No.3)* [1993] 3 IR 320 at 327.

⁹⁹⁸ [1991] 2 IR 225 at 229.

⁹⁹⁹ [2005] IESC 85, [2006] 2 IR 321.

and that the internal garda investigation was compromised. The informant also alleged that a large number of convictions had been achieved by "planting" evidence, and that two assistant commissioners of An Garda Siochana were aware of this. The applicant met with the Minister for Justice and discussed the allegations with him, and made statements in the Dáil regarding garda activity in Donegal. While he met with the gardaí, he refused to disclose the name of his informant. The Tribunal of Inquiry into Complaints Concerning some Gardaí in the Donegal Division requested that the applicant make discovery of all documents relating to the information received by him in respect of the allegations. The applicant claimed that the documents were privileged under Art.15.10 of the Constitution. The Supreme Court held that the "innocence at stake" exception applied, as a result of which disclosure would have been required, even if the private papers were privileged in accordance with Art.15.10. Hardiman J stated that the innocence at stake exception applies to an investigation into corruption in the same manner as it applies to a criminal trial, and observed that, in circumstances where the allegations made raised the prospect that people had been "framed" and thereby wrongfully convicted of criminal offences, this presented an "innocence at stake" situation in an acute form.[1000]

10–402   The decision in *Howlin v Morris* was followed by the Court of Criminal Appeal in *People (DPP) v Donnelly*,[1001] where O'Donnell J stated the general principles governing the innocence at stake exception as follows:

> "The so called informer's privilege is not something which can be claimed as a right by any garda witness. First, it must be established that the circumstances are such as to give rise to a valid claim for privilege. Second, the privilege itself is not absolute. From the time when it was formulated in cases such as *Marks v. Beyfus* ... it was recognised that it was subject to an innocence at stake exception. This point was, in any event, confirmed by the Supreme Court in *Howlin v. Morris*... It follows from this that in an appropriate case the privilege can be challenged and, if necessary, the court can inspect any documents or other materials."

10–403   It is clear, however, from the decision of the Court of Appeal in *People (DPP) v Fitzpatrick*[1002] that the innocence at stake exception must be applied with caution. O'Donnell J observed that, in those cases in which where the court concludes that the disclosure of information in relation to the identity of an informer is necessary because the innocence of the accused is at stake, the prosecution will often decide to abandon the case, rather than incur the risk to the individual informer and the damage to the investigative process that disclosure might entail. As a result, issues of disclosure are frequently pursued as a tactic on the part of the defence. He stated that:

> "For these reasons courts have always emphasised that the matter must be approached with considerable sensitivity, delicacy and precision, and that, in the words of McLachlan J in *R. v Leipert* [1997] 2 LRC 260, disclosure cannot trump privilege. It is important, therefore, that this sometimes difficult issue is addressed only when it is necessary and essential on the facts of the case, and then in a focussed and, where necessary, nuanced fashion."[1003]

10–404   In circumstances where the issue of disclosure was not raised until after the trial had commenced, and then in a very "broad and indiscriminate way", it was held that there had been no challenge to the claim of informer privilege asserted by the prosecution, and the Court was not requested to apply the innocence at stake exception.

[1000] [2005] IESC 85, [2006] 2 IR 321 *per* Hardiman J (at [67], 372) and Geoghegan J (at [98], 387–388).
[1001] [2012] IECCA 78 at [31].
[1002] [2012] IECCA 74.
[1003] [2012] IECCA 74 at [41].

10–405 Where a claim of informer privilege is challenged on the basis that the "innocence at stake" exception applies, the Court has a discretion whether to examine the documents in dispute.[1004] There is, however, no obligation on the court to do so.[1005]

2. Journalistic Privilege

10–406 It is now well established in this jurisdiction that journalists enjoy a right to refuse to disclose their sources.[1006] For ease of reference, and in circumstances where the term is deployed in the authorities, the entitlement of journalists to refuse to disclose their source is referred to as 'journalistic privilege' throughout this section. However, while this right is generally referred to as 'journalistic privilege', it is not strictly correct to describe it as a discrete 'privilege'. This was explained by Hogan J in *Cornec v Morrice*[1007]:

> "While I have thus far loosely spoken of a journalistic privilege, there is, in fact, *in strictness*, no such thing. The protection is rather the high value which the law places on the dissemination of information and public debate. Journalists are central to that entire process, a point expressly recognised by Art.40.6.1§.i of the Constitution itself when it recognises 'their rightful liberty of expression' on the part of the press, albeit counter balanced by the stipulation that this rightful liberty shall not be used to undermine 'public order or morality or the authority of the State'."

10–407 He observed that "the constitutional right in question would be meaningless if the law could not (or would not) protect the *general right* of journalists to protect their sources".[1008] The policy considerations underpinning journalistic privilege were explained as follows by the High Court in *Mahon v Keena*[1009]:

> "Going hand in hand with this, is the critical importance of a free press as an essential organ in a democratic society. An essential feature of the operation of a free press is the availability of sources of information. Without sources of information journalists will be unable to keep

---

[1004] *Cf. Ward v Special Criminal Court* [1998] 2 ILRM 493, where the application of informer privilege and the "innocence at stake" exception was considered by the Supreme Court in the criminal context. The Court stressed that prosecution counsel, who have an overall responsibility to ensure that a trial is fair and just, play a crucial role in the application of the privilege and owe a duty to disclose any possible source of evidence that may help the defence. If a doubt arises as to whether a particular document should be disclosed, then it is a matter for the trial judge to decide having, if necessary examined the documents. This aspect of the decision was confirmed by the Supreme Court in the *People (DPP) v McKevitt* [2008] IESC 51 at [14], [2009] 1 IR 525 at 531–532.

[1005] *People (DPP) v McKevitt* [2008] IESC 51 at [19], [2009] 1 IR 525 at 533; *Ward v Special Criminal Court* [1999] 1 IR 60, [1998] 2 ILRM 493 at 87–88. But see *Millstream Recycling Limited v Tierney* [2010] IEHC 55, where it was held that, if a serious issue were to arise, the appropriate procedure would be to ask the judge to privately inspect the documents in the presence of a high ranking Garda officer under the strictest security.

[1006] *Re Kevin O'Kelly* (1974) 109 ILTR 97; *Mahon v Keena* [2009] IESC 64, [2010] 1 IR 336; *Walsh v News Group Newspapers Ltd* [2012] IEHC 353; *Cornec v Morrice* [2012] IEHC 376, [2012] 1 IR 805. But see *Gray v Minister for Justice* [2007] IEHC 52 at [60], [2007] 2 IR 654 at 665, where Quirke J described journalistic privilege as a 'questionable privilege'.

[1007] [2012] IEHC 376 at [42], [2012] 1 IR 805 at 818.

[1008] Hogan J also identified the policy underpinning the privilege by reference to the Constitution: "... the public interest in ensuring that journalists can protect their sources remains very high, since journalism is central to the free flow of information which is essential in a free society. This is all underscored and tacitly complemented by the entire constitutional edifice, such as the democratic nature of the State (Art.5); the accountability of the executive branch to the Dáil (Art.28.4.1§) and the provisions in relation to elections and referenda."

[1009] [2007] IEHC 348 at [30], in a passage cited with approval by the Supreme Court ([2009] IESC 64 at [31], [2010] 1 IR 336 at 348).

society informed on matters which are or should be of public interest. Thus there is a very great public interest in the cultivation of and protection of journalistic sources of information as an essential feature of a free and effective press."[1010]

10–408   It is clear, however, that the right of a journalist to protect their sources is not absolute or inviolable, and the Court is required to balance the competing public interests at play where a claim of journalistic privilege is asserted.[1011] In carrying out this balancing exercise, the court is required to weigh the public interest in the freedom of the press against the countervailing interests which require disclosure, which vary from case to case. For example, the public interest in disclosure is obviously less compelling in commercial proceedings than it would be in criminal proceedings where the potential innocence of a third party is at stake,[1012] or where the requirement for disclosure is the production of evidence of a serious crime.[1013]

10–409   In general, however, a court will only require a journalist to reveal his or her sources if the necessity for disclosure is "convincingly established".[1014] This test originates in the case law of the European Court of Human Rights interpreting art.10 of the European Convention of Human Rights,[1015] the incorporation of which into domestic law[1016] marked a significant development in the law in this area.[1017] The right to freedom of expression is protected by art.10(1) of the Convention. This right is not, however, absolute and art.10(2) goes on to provide that:

"The exercise of these freedoms, since it carries with it duties and responsibilities, may be subject to such formalities, conditions, restrictions or penalties as are prescribed by law and are necessary in a democratic society, in the interests of national security, territorial integrity or public safety, for the prevention of disorder or crime, for the protection of health or morals, for

---

[1010] See also *Walsh v News Group Newspapers Ltd* [2012] IEHC 353 at [20], [2012] 3 IR 136 at 146. The decision of O'Neill J in that case suggests that journalistic privilege may will protect what he described as "improper journalism", referred to allegations that the defendant newspaper had offered financial inducements to members of the public to obtain information. However, in circumstances where he concluded that the privilege did not apply for other reasons, it was not necessary to determine this issue.

[1011] *Re Kevin O'Kelly* (1974) 109 ILTR 97 at 101; *Mahon v Keena* [2009] IESC 64, [2010] 1 IR 336 at 363; *Cornec v Morrice* [2012] IEHC 376, [2012] 1 IR 805 at 819.

[1012] *Cornec v Morrice* [2012] IEHC 376 at [49], [2012] 1 IR 804 at 821.

[1013] The example given by the European Court of Human Rights in *Goodwin v United Kingdom* (1996) 22 EHRR 123 of a case in which there would be a pressing need for disclosure.

[1014] *Mahon v Keena* [2009] IESC 64 at [80], [2010] 1 IR 336 at 360; *Cornec v Morrice* [2012] IEHC 376 at [60], [2012]1 IR 804 at 824.

[1015] Prior to the incorporation of the Convention into domestic law, it was already established that the courts would only order the disclosure by a journalist of their sources where this was necessary. See *People (DPP) v Nevin* [2003] 3 IR 321, where cross-examination of journalists in relation to articles written by them had been permitted during the trial of the applicant, but the trial judge declined to order the journalists to reveal their sources on the basis that such evidence would be irrelevant. The Court of Criminal Appeal held that the trial judge had properly exercised her discretion, pointing out that, although the concept of journalistic privilege was unknown to the law, it was the practice, in this and other common law jurisdictions, that a trial judge would exercise a certain element of discretion in ruling as to whether a journalist had to answer a question about his or her sources. Thus, the judge was entitled to satisfy herself that the answer to such a question was properly relevant to the matters to be tried and that the interests of justice required that an answer to be given.

[1016] By the European Convention on Human Rights Act 2003.

[1017] See *Walsh v News Group Newspapers Ltd* [2012] IEHC 353 at [15], [2012] 3 IR 136 at 144, where O'Neill J stated: "Journalistic privilege is now firmly established in our legal jurisprudence, largely resulting from art.10 of the European Convention on Human Rights 1950..."

the protection of the reputation or rights of others, for preventing the disclosure of information received in confidence, or for maintaining the authority and impartiality of the judiciary."

10–410   In *Goodwin v United Kingdom*,[1018] a case which concerned an order directing a journalist to disclose a source, it was held by the European Court of Human Rights that:

"Protection of journalistic sources is one of the basic conditions for press freedom, as is reflected in the laws and the professional codes of conduct in a number of Contracting States and is affirmed in several international instruments on journalistic freedoms. Without such protection, sources may be deterred from assisting the press in informing the public on matters of public interest. As a result the vital public watchdog role of the press may be undermined and the ability of the press to provide accurate and reliable information may be adversely affected. Having regard to the importance of the protection of journalistic sources for press freedom in a democratic society and the potentially chilling effect an order of source disclosure has on the exercise of that freedom, such a measure cannot be compatible with art.10 of the Convention unless it is justified by an overriding requirement in the public interest."

10–411   The significance of art.10 of the Convention in circumstances where a claim of journalistic privilege is asserted is apparent from the decisions of both the Divisional High Court[1019] and the Supreme Court in *Mahon v Keena*.[1020] Having considered the cases in which the European Court of Human Rights has been called on to assess restrictions or penalties imposed on the right to freedom of expression by member states in accordance with art.10(2),[1021] the Supreme Court summarised the approach of the Court as follows[1022]:

"The European Court of Human Rights has been at pains to emphasise that the right to freedom of expression is not unlimited. It usually states, as in the above passage, that the press must not 'overstep certain bounds'. The court has said that 'art.10 does not ... guarantee a wholly unrestricted freedom of expression even with respect to press coverage of matters of serious public concern'. For example, it may be necessary, depending on the circumstances, to balance an individual's right to private and family life guaranteed by art.8 of the Convention. Member states have a 'certain margin of appreciation in assessing whether' there is a need for a restriction.

Nonetheless, the court constantly emphasises the value of a free press as one of the essential foundations of a democratic society, that the press generates and promotes political debate, informs the public in time of elections, scrutinises the behaviour of governments and public officials and, for these reasons, that persons in public life must expect to be subjected to disclosure about their financial and other affairs, to criticism and to less favourable treatment

---

[1018] (1996) 22 EHRR 123 at 143. For a comprehensive discussion of the relevant decisions of the European Court of Human Rights, see *Mahon v Keena* [2007] IEHC 348; [2009] IESC 64, [2010] 1 IR 336, [2009] 2 ILRM 373.

[1019] [2007] IEHC 348. Having considered the decisions of the European Court of Human Rights in relation to art.10, the High Court stated that: "These cases ... illustrate, on the part of the European Court of Human Rights, a stalwart defence of freedom of expression, and a trend of strictly construing potential interferences with that right that might claim justification under the variety of justifiable interferences set out in art.10(2). This approach by the European Court of Human Rights is particularly evident in cases involving publications relating to political matters. There was no reported case opened to us in which the European Court of Human Rights has upheld an order of a domestic court ordering the disclosure of a journalistic source." This passage of the High Court judgment was described by Geoghegan J as "an important passage" ([2009] IESC 64 at [31], [2010] 1 IR 336 at 348).

[1020] [2009] IESC 64, [2010] 1 IR 336. See McMahon, "*Journalists Privilege in light of Mahon v Keena*" (2010) 28(6) ILT 90.

[1021] *Lingens v Austria* (1986) 8 EHRR 407; *Castells v Spain* (1992) 14 EHRR 445; *Fressoz and Roire v France* (2001) 31 EHRR 28; *Tromso v Norway* (1999) 29 EHRR 125; *Goodwin v United Kingdom* (1996) 22 EHRR 123; *Radio Twist AS v Slovakia* [2006] ECHR 1129.

[1022] [2009] IESC 64 at [71]–[72], [2010] 1 IR 336 at 358.

than those in private life. Generally, therefore, restrictions on freedom of expression must be justified by an 'overriding requirement in the public interest'."

10–412   Referring to the decision of the European Court of Human Rights in *Goodwin*, Fennelly J noted that the Court laid emphasis on the need for any restriction on freedom of expression to be "convincingly established", and stated that the "national margin for appreciation is circumscribed by the interest of democratic society in ensuring and maintaining a free press". Accordingly, any limitation placed on the confidentiality of journalistic sources calls for "the most careful scrutiny by the court".[1023]

10–413   In *Mahon v Keena*, a confidential letter from the tribunal of inquiry established to investigate irregularities in the planning process to a witness was sent anonymously to a journalist. The contents of the letter, which contained information in relation to certain payments alleged to have been made to then Taoiseach, was published in the body of an article in the *Irish Times*. In circumstances where the witness to whom the letter had been sent was adamant that he was not the source of the letter, the tribunal initiated an investigation of the 'leak' of confidential information. The journalist and his editor appeared before the Tribunal but refused to answer any questions which might result in the disclosure of the source of the letter and indicated that they had destroyed all documents in their possession concerning the story in order to protect their sources. The defendants contended that there was a strong public interest in disclosure, given that it suggested that the Taoiseach had received money from businessmen while he was Minister for Finance. The High Court, heavily influenced by the reprehensible conduct of the defendants in destroying the documents, made an order for disclosure.[1024] This decision was reversed on appeal by the Supreme Court, which held that the great weight attached by the High Court to the reprehensible conduct of the defendants caused it to adopt an erroneous approach to the balancing exercise required by the decision of the European Court of Human Rights in *Goodwin v The United Kingdom*.[1025]

10–414   The requirement that the necessity for disclosure must be "convincingly established" was applied by Hogan J in *Cornec v Morrice*,[1026] where he stated that "[t]he protection of journalistic sources is, subject to appropriate exceptions, regarded as a core value protected by art.10 of the Convention".[1027] Having engaged in a comparison between the language of Art.40.6 of the Constitution and art.10 of the Convention, he concluded that:

> "… the overlap between the two documents with regard to the role of the media is virtually a complete one, even if allowance is made for the fact that, unlike Art.40.6.1§, the text of art10 of the European Convention on Human Rights does not actually seek to confer on the media a special or privileged position in terms of public debate or in criticism of government policy. In both cases, the approach is the same: has the case for the restriction on or overriding journalistic privilege … been convincingly established?"[1028]

10–415   An issue arose in *Cornec* as to whether the entitlement to assert journalistic privilege is restricted to a journalist, in the strict sense of the term, in circumstances where the deposition of an investigative journalist and a former theologian who

---

[1023] [2009] IESC 64 at [80], [2010] 1 IR 336 at 360 (discussing the decision of the ECHR in *Goodwin v United Kingdom* (1996) 22 EHRR 123).
[1024] [2007] IEHC 348.
[1025] [2009] IESC 64 at [99], [2010] 1 IR 336 at 365.
[1026] [2012] IEHC 376, [2012] 1 IR 804.
[1027] [2012] IEHC 376 at [47], [2012] 1 IR 804 at 820.
[1028] [2012] IEHC 376 at [49], [2012] 1 IR 804 at 821.

specialised in the investigation of cults was sought. Hogan J observed that "the traditional distinction between journalists and lay people has broken down in recent decades, not least with the rise of social media".[1029] He concluded that the activities of the former theologian, in chronicling the activities of religious cults, fell squarely within the "education of public opinion" envisaged by Art.40.6.1 and, as such, there was a high constitutional value in ensuring that his right to voice his views in relation to the actions of religious cults was protected. In a passage which may have significant implications for the scope of the privilege, Hogan J stated that: "A person who blogs on an internet site can just as readily constitute an 'organ of public opinion' as those which were more familiar in 1937 and which are mentioned (but only as examples) in Art.40.6.1§, namely, the radio, the press and the cinema."[1030]

10–416   The ambit or scope of journalistic privilege is a matter with which the courts have had to grapple in a number of cases. The principal question which arises is whether the privilege is limited to the identity of the source, or also extends to the information provided by the source. In *Cornec v Morrice*,[1031] Hogan J held that there is no *ex ante* distinction between the protection of the source, on the one hand, and the contents of what the source disclosed, on the other. In that case, there was considerable circumstantial evidence available, which tended to identify the journalist's sources and an argument was advanced to the effect that, once a source has been identified, the privilege lapses. The disclosure sought was directed to communications between the journalist and her sources, as well as the identity of the sources. However, it was held that the public interest in protecting a journalist from compelled disclosure is equally high where the contents of what the source said is in issue, rather than the identity of the source, "since the exploration of the contents of any discussions with the source also has the ability significantly to hamper the exercise of freedom by the journalist in question."[1032] This is consistent with the decision of O'Neill J in *Walsh v News Group Newspapers*,[1033] where he stated that:

> "... the interest which is identified as protected by journalistic privilege is the proper functioning of journalism, namely, that there is a free flow of information from the public to journalists which is not inhibited or *'chilled'* by the prospect that the source will be disclosed. Implicit in all of this is that the risk to the proper functioning of journalism is disclosure or identification of the person supplying the information. Ordinarily, information supplied will end up published; thus, *per se*, it could not be said that the content of the information enjoyed privilege from disclosure. If, however, the content of the information which, necessarily, was not published, could lead to the identification of the source, then it would seem to me that it too must enjoy the privilege from disclosure, as otherwise, the overall purpose of the privilege would fail."

10–417   As regards the approach to be adopted where the source is anonymous, it is clear from the decision of the Supreme Court in *Mahon v Keena*[1034] that, while it is a relevant consideration, it is not determinative. It was argued in that case that, in circumstances where the source is anonymous, journalistic privilege either does not arise at all or is to be afforded very little weight, as the professional obligation to protect a source from disclosure cannot arise. The Supreme Court accepted that there is a

---

[1029] [2012] IEHC 376 at [65], [2012] 1 IR 804 at 825.

[1030] [2012] IEHC 376 at [66], [2012] 1 IR 804 at 825. See Carolan, "The Implications of Media Fragmentation and Contemporary Democratic for 'Journalistic Privilege' and the Protections of Sources" (2013) 49 Irish Jurist 182.

[1031] [2012] IEHC 376, [2012] 1 IR 804.

[1032] [2012] IEHC 376 at [61], [2012]1 IR 804 at 824.

[1033] [2012] IEHC 353 at [20], [2012] 3 IR 136 at 146.

[1034] [2009] IESC 64, [2010] 1 IR 336.

difference between a source whose identity is known to the journalist and a completely anonymous source, and that "greater weight" will attach to the privilege where the source is known.[1035] The court considered, however, that there remained an interest that was worthy of protection. Fennelly J noted that disclosure of the letter sent to the journalist by an anonymous source was sought by the tribunal in order to investigate, by way of the examination of the letter, whether the leak came from within the tribunal or from an external source. The principal issue the tribunal wished to determine was whether the letter had the tribunal's letterhead on it and whether it was signed. Fennelly J held that, insofar as the anonymity of the source weakens the journalistic privilege, it also weakens the case for disclosure; where the source is known to the journalist, there will be a concrete benefit from disclosure. Where, on the other hand, the source is anonymous, the benefit from disclosure is "speculative at best".[1036]

10–418 Journalistic privilege will not protect the identity of a source in circumstances where this was openly disclosed in the article or broadcast in question. This is apparent from the decision of the Court of Criminal Appeal in *Re Kevin O'Kelly*,[1037] where it rejected a claim of privilege in respect of the identity of a journalist's source in circumstances where the identity of the source was disclosed during the interview.[1038] It was further held, in *Walsh v News Group Newspapers*,[1039] that journalistic privilege may not be asserted in respect of communications between a journalist and a party who is not a source and whose identity has been disclosed. This case concerned an article published in *The Sun* newspapers which alleged that the plaintiff was being investigated by An Garda Síochána regarding a claim that he had indecently or sexually assaulted a man. It subsequently transpired that the allegations were false. The plaintiff alleged that the story was procured by financial inducements offered by the defendant to the complainant and that the defendant had misrepresented that it had obtained the story from An Garda Síochána. The defendant sought to assert journalistic privilege but suggested on affidavit that the complainant was not the source of the article. Given that the complainant's identity was known, and it was not contended that he was the journalistic source, O'Neill J held that the only basis upon which journalistic privilege could arise would be if it were shown that the disclosure of the content of the communications between the defendant and the complainant could lead to the disclosure of another source, either in respect of the story the subject matter of the article or other investigations conducted by the defendant's journalists.

10–419 It is also clear from the decision in *Walsh v News Group Newspapers* that journalistic privilege cannot be availed of in order to shelter evidence of the commission of a criminal offence.[1040] In that case, a claim of journalistic privilege was asserted in respect of communications between the defendant and members of An Garda Síochána.

[1035] [2009] IESC 64 at [95], [2010] 1 IR 336 at 364.

[1036] [2009] IESC 64 at [98], [2010] 1 IR 336 at 365.

[1037] (1974) 109 ILTR 97.

[1038] See the analysis of this decision by Hogan J in *Cornec v Morrice* [2012] IEHC 376, [2012] 1 IR 805 at 817, where he stated that it has been "not fully understood" and appeared to suggest that it is a decision which can be confined to its own particular facts.

[1039] [2012] IEHC, [2012] 3 IR 136.

[1040] An issue arose in that case as to whether journalistic privilege may be availed of where financial inducements have been offered by a newspaper to members of the public in order to obtain information. O'Neill J appeared to suggest that it could not, but did not reach any concluded view on this issue, as he determined that the privilege did not arise ([2012] IEHC at [21], [2012] 3 IR 136 at 146).

The documents sought were relevant in order to establish the plaintiff's claim that the defendant had misrepresented that the source of the story was An Garda Síochána. Furthermore, in the event that a member of An Garda Síochána was the source, such disclosure would be a criminal offence in accordance with s.62(2)(g)(ii) of the Garda Síochána Act 2005. It was held that, in circumstances where the privilege is asserted to shelter the commission of a crime, the overwhelming public interest in the detection and prosecution of crime outweighs the public interest in the proper functioning of journalism.[1041]

10–420   A claim to journalistic privilege may succeed as a variation of informer privilege where disclosure of the identity of the source would put that person's life and/or bodily integrity at risk. In *Burke v Central Independent Television Plc*,[1042] the plaintiffs had instituted proceedings against the defendant for libel arising out of a television programme broadcast by the defendant in which it was alleged that certain premises were being used as the financial nerve centre of the IRA. The defendant objected to the disclosure of documents which would, or would be likely to, lead to the identification of its sources of information on the ground, *inter alia*, that the life and safety of those sources would be put at risk if their identities became known. In the Supreme Court, Finlay CJ identified the two conflicting public interests in the case. On the one hand, there is the public interest in protecting Irish citizens from the risk of death or bodily injury at the hands of terrorists. On the other, there is the public interest in the administration of justice which requires that the plaintiffs should be entitled to the discovery which they are seeking if that is necessary for the protection and vindication of their constitutional right to their good names. Implicitly applying the theory of a hierarchy of constitutional rights, he was satisfied that the constitutional right of individual citizens to the protection of their life and bodily integrity must of necessity take precedence over the right of citizens to the protection and vindication of their good name and, therefore, upheld the claim of privilege.

3. Communications with Spiritual Advisers

10–421   The generally accepted view is that, prior to the Reformation, the common law recognised a sacerdotal privilege whereby a priest could not be compelled to reveal what had been communicated to him by a penitent in confession.[1043] The position in the aftermath of the Reformation in England was unclear but in *Wheeler v Le Marchant*,[1044] Jessel MR declared that communications "made to a priest in the confessional on matters perhaps considered by the penitent to be more important even than his life or his fortune are not protected". In Ireland, there was some authority which went the other way with *obiter dicta* in *In Re Keller*[1045] and *Tannian v Synott*[1046] recognising the existence of a sacerdotal privilege but refusing to extend it further to confidential communications between a priest and parishioner.

[1041] [2012] IEHC at [28], [2012] 3 IR 136 at 159–150. O'Neill J adverted to the possibility that, in the event that such disclosure by a member of An Garda Síochána had taken place, this might have the effect of discouraging victims of sexual assaults to give evidence or report such offences.
[1042] [1994] 2 IR 61, [1994] 2 ILRM 161.
[1043] See Callahan, "Historical Inquiry into the Priest-Penitent Privilege" (1976) 36 Jurist 328.
[1044] (1881) 17 Ch D 675 at 681. See also *Anderson v Bank of British Columbia* (1876) 2 Ch D 644 at 651.
[1045] (1887) 22 LR Ir 158.
[1046] (1903) 37 ILTSJ 275.

10–422   It was against that background that Gavan Duffy J delivered his judgment in *Cook v Carroll*.[1047] The issue in the case was whether a priest who refused to testify in an action for seduction as to the contents of a conversation he had had with the defendant and the plaintiff's daughter at his house was guilty of contempt. Gavan Duffy J availed of the opportunity to repudiate the common law position as stated in *Wheeler v Le Marchant*.[1048] He referred to Art.44.1.2 of the then recently adopted Bunreacht na hÉireann wherein the State recognised the special position of the Catholic Church as the guardian of the faith professed by the great majority of the citizens and stated:

> "In a State where nine out of every ten citizens to-day are Catholics and on a matter closely touching the religious outlook of the people, it would be intolerable that the common law, as expounded after the Reformation in a Protestant land, should be taken to bind a nation which persistently repudiated the Reformation as heresy. When, as a measure of necessary convenience, we allowed the common law generally to continue in force, we meant to include all the common law in harmony with the national spirit. We never contemplated the maintenance of any construction of the common law affected by sectarian background."[1049]

10–423   In the absence of binding authority, he approached the issue as a matter of first principle by reference to the conditions laid down by Wigmore[1050] for the recognition of privileges (which are set out above).[1051] He found those conditions to be satisfied and held that communications made in confidence to a priest, in private consultation between him and his parishioners were privileged and that such privilege could not be waived by a party thereto without the consent of the priest.

10–424   The nature and application of this privilege was clarified by Geoghegan J in *Johnston v Church of Scientology*.[1052] The plaintiff alleged, *inter alia*, that she had been "brainwashed" by the defendants. An order for discovery was granted and the defendants sought to resist the disclosure of certain "counselling notes" on the basis of sacerdotal privilege. These counselling notes were generated during "spiritual practices" of scientology called "auditing" and "training". The defendant explained that auditing and training were conducted on a one to one confidential basis and it was claimed that for an auditor to disclose any of the communications he had with the other person, even if that person was to waive any privilege in respect of them, would be so fundamentally contrary to the beliefs and tenets of the Church of Scientology as to render him liable to eternal damnation.

10–425   Although Geoghegan J criticised the decision of Gavan Duffy J in *Cook v Carroll* on the basis that it proceeded on the erroneous view that there were constitutional and legal effects arising from the then "so-called" special position of the Catholic Church, he took the view that "as matter of common sense and justice, it was reasonable for the courts to revive what Gavan Duffy J says was the pre-reformation common law protecting the seal of the confessional even against waiver by the penitent". However, this absolute and unwaivable sacerdotal privilege which attached to the "priest penitent relationship in the confessional" was *sui iuris* and could not be successfully invoked by the defendants in the circumstances of the instant case. He rejected the analogy which they sought to make between the teachings of Scientology

---

[1047] [1945] IR 515.
[1048] (1881) 17 Ch D 675 at 681.
[1049] [1945] IR 515 at 519.
[1050] Wigmore, *Evidence* 3rd edn (Boston: Little Brown and Company, 1940), VIII, § 2285.
[1051] At [10–179].
[1052] Unreported, High Court, 30 April 1999.

and the seal of confessional. He pointed out that no evidence had been adduced that it was part of the doctrines of the Scientology that any disclosure of what transpired in auditing or training sessions led to some kind of eternal punishment. Moreover, the question as to whether the Church of Scientology even constituted a religion remained controversial.

10–426   Geoghegan J also accepted that there could be a broader counselling privilege which would apply to counselling by a parish priest of a parishioner. However, this could be waived by the person being counselled and here the plaintiff had waived any privilege which was alleged to exist.

10–427   The decision of Geoghegan J sets the law in this area on a course of more rational development. As recognised by the learned judge, there are two separate privileges which may apply to communications between a spiritual adviser and a parishioner: (i) sacerdotal privilege, and (ii) a privilege in respect of communications between a spiritual advisor and parishioner made for the purpose of giving or receiving spiritual guidance. It is important to distinguish between the two because their nature and incidents are quite distinct. In particular, the identity of the holders of the privilege is different in respect of each privilege.

10–428   Amongst the arguments in favour of sacerdotal privilege is that there are very strong ethical obligations with serious consequences imposed on ministers of a wide variety of religions not to reveal confessional communications. For example, the Canon Law of the Catholic Church states that the sacramental seal of confession is inviolable. Because of this, priests and ministers will face civil or penal sanctions rather than submit to any attempt to compel disclosure of such communications. There is, therefore, a strong argument to be made that the priest or minister is the ultimate holder or at least a co-holder of sacerdotal privilege because waiver by the penitent will still not relieve the priest or minister of his ethical and religious obligations to protect the secrecy of the confessional.

10–429   Quite different considerations attach, however, to any sort of counselling privilege which is recognised in respect of communications between a priest or minister and a parishioner. Such privilege exists primarily to protect the interests of the parishioner and to promote his or her ability to make frank disclosure in order to obtain spiritual guidance. Therefore, such privilege should be capable of being waived by the parishioner.

4. Marital Privilege

10–430   In Art.41.3.1 of the Constitution, the state pledges itself "to guard with special care the institution of marriage, on which the family is founded, and to protect it against attack" and this Article may be invoked to justify the recognition of privilege in circumstances where it advances this objective.

(a) Marriage counsellors

10–431   In *ER v JR*,[1053] Carroll J considered a claim of privilege made in respect of communications made to a priest who acted as a marriage counsellor in his capacity as

---

[1053] [1981] ILRM 125.

such. She applied the four conditions for the recognition of a privilege articulated by Wigmore (which are set out above), to determine whether privilege should be granted. Taking the first two conditions, she was satisfied that:

> "The nature of the relationship is such that a priest acting as marriage counsellor will be consulted by a spouse or spouses in order to get advice in connection with difficulties in their marriage. I consider that confidentiality is an essential element in that relationship. I can imagine nothing less conducive to frank and open discussion between priest and spouses, possibly leading to admissions to faults and failings on both sides, then the possibility that total confidentiality will not be observed."[1054]

10–432 Turning to the third requirement that "the relation must be one which in the opinion of the community ought to be sedulously fostered", she adverted to Art.41 and opined that "[t]he provision of confidential marriage counselling which may help a married couple over a difficulty in their marriage is protection of the most practical kind for the family and should be fostered."[1055] Finally, she was also satisfied that the fourth requirement was met on the basis that "any benefit which could be gained in litigation by having the evidence available does not outweigh the possible injury to the relationship if disclosure can be compelled".[1056] She further specified that the privilege belonged to the spouses and could only be waived by both.[1057]

10–433 An important factor in *ER v JR* was that the counsellor was also a priest and Carroll J reserved the question as to whether privilege could arise where the counsellor was not a minister of religion. However, given the grounding of the privilege in Art.41 rather than Art.44 and the strong public policy in protecting and promoting the institution of marriage, it is difficult to see why this factor should be determinative and in *Johnston v Church of Scientology*,[1058] Geoghegan J took the view that the privilege in respect of marriage counselling should be available on a secular basis.

(b) Marital privacy

10–434 A privilege may also exist in respect of communications, the disclosure of which would injure marital privacy. Spouses formerly enjoyed a statutorily conferred[1059] privilege not to disclose any communications made by the other spouse during the subsistence of the marriage both in civil[1060] and criminal[1061] proceedings. This privilege was abolished by s.3 of the Criminal Evidence Act 1992[1062] but s.26 of that Act contains a saver in respect of marital privacy.[1063] Therefore, it would seem that privilege can be claimed where necessary to protect marital privacy.[1064]

[1054] [1981] ILRM 125 at 126.
[1055] [1981] ILRM 125 at 126.
[1056] [1981] ILRM 125 at 126.
[1057] Following the decision of *Pais v Pais* [1970] P 119, [1970] 2 All ER 491 in this regard.
[1058] Unreported, High Court, 30 April 1999.
[1059] In *Shenton v Tyler* [1939] Ch 620, it was held by the Court of Appeal that no equivalent protection existed at common law.
[1060] Section 3 of the Evidence (Amendment) Act 1853.
[1061] Section 1(d) of the Criminal Justice (Evidence) Act 1924.
[1062] Implementing the recommendation of the Law Reform Commission in its *Report on the Competence and Compellability of Spouses as Prosecution Witnesses*, at p.27.
[1063] See also s.112 of the Civil Partnership and Certain Rights and Obligations of Cohabitants Act 2010.
[1064] Marital privacy was considered by the European Court of Justice in *Van der Heijden v the Netherlands*, Judgment of the Grand Chamber, 3 April 2012, [2012] ECHR 588, (2013) 57 EHRR

5. Parliamentary Privilege

(a) Official documents and private papers

10–435   The provisions of Art.15 of the Constitution confer a number of privileges and immunities on the Houses of the Oireachtas and their members.[1065] In particular, Art.15.10[1066] provides that: "Each House … shall have power to ensure freedom of debate, to protect its official documents and the private papers of its members, and to protect itself and its members against any person or persons interfering with, molesting or attempting to corrupt its members in the exercise of their duties."[1067] This power to protect the papers of private members is enabling in nature and, as such, the relevant House must extend such protection to the private papers of its member before these are privileged.[1068] In recognition of this, a resolution was passed by the Dáil on 6 July 2001 conferring this power on the Committee on Procedure and Privileges on behalf of the Dáil.

10–436   What exactly is required on the part of the Committee to extend such protection to the private papers of a member was examined in *Howlin v Morris*.[1069] This case involved a challenge to an order for discovery made by the Morris Tribunal. In the High Court, Kearns J held that the private papers of a member could be designated privileged and rendered altogether immune from discovery, provided the Committee had exercised their power to do so.[1070] Having regard to the principle of the separation of powers, he held that the courts would not lightly or without very good reason interfere with or query the procedures whereby the Oireachtas had asserted its wishes and intentions in relation to the internal matters concerning its own members. On the facts of the case before him, he was satisfied that the plaintiff could successfully invoke Art.15.10 as a ground for resisting discovery of his private papers including his telephone records, and proceeded to quash the order. However, he held that, in order to be privileged, the papers in question must have been generated or received by members in connection with the performance of their functions under the constitution.[1071]

13, where it was held that the imprisonment of the applicant for failing to testify against her life partner did not constitute a violation of Art.8. However, the applicant had not formally registered her union in accordance with national law.

[1065] For a discussion of the combined effect of Arts 15.10, 15.12 and 15.13, see the joint judgment of Clarke and O'Donnell JJ in *Callely v Moylan* [2014] IESC 26 at [56].

[1066] Article 15.10 is identical to Art.20 of the Constitution of Saorstát Eireann 1922.

[1067] In both *Howlin v Morris* [2005] IESC 85 at [40], [2006] 2 IR 321 at 364, and *Callely v Moylan* [2011] IEHC 2 at [46], [2011] 1 IR 676 at 701, it was held that the approach to the interpretation of Art.15.10 should be a literal and strict one.

[1068] *Howlin v Morris* [2003] IEHC 55, [2006] 2 IR 321, [2004] 2 ILRM 53.

[1069] [2003] IEHC 55, [2006] 2 IR 321, [2004] 2 ILRM 53.

[1070] The Committee had authorised the parliamentary legal adviser to instruct counsel on behalf of Dáil Éireann to apply for representation at the Tribunal, and to make submissions concerning the powers and privileges of Dáil Eireann and its members. A similar authorisation was given in respect of the Seanad. Counsel according made an application for representation before the Tribunal, and asserted that the appropriate way of exercising the power conferred by Art.15.10 was to appear and make representations regarding the scope of the relevant constitutional provision. The Chairman of the Tribunal accepted the validity of the delegation of the power to the Committee, but ruled that the means adopted by the Committee was not a valid exercise of the power.

[1071] A wide interpretation of what may constitute "private papers" was taken, as in this case the "papers" actually consisted of documentary records of telephone conversations. In circumstances where this interpretation was accepted by the parties, the Supreme Court did not engage in any detailed consideration of this issue. However, Geoghegan J stated that the question of what exactly is

10–437   This decision was reversed on appeal by the Supreme Court,[1072] which held that, whatever powers the committee may have been given to protect the private papers of members, those powers had not been validly exercised. The reasoning on which this conclusion was based was articulated as follows by Geoghegan J, with whom the other members of the court agreed:

> "Article 15.10 does not envisage some kind of *ad hoc* exercise of a power to impose a privilege whether by a formal motion ... or otherwise. In my view, it is a misreading of Art.15.10 to suggest that it is divided into two quite separate sections, one involving the House making its own rules and standing orders and the other conferring various powers on the House. As I see it, what was envisaged was that the nature and scope of these powers would be formally enacted in rules or standing orders and they would then automatically apply in particular situations. Neither House in this instance had made any rules or standing orders relating to the private papers of its members. Accordingly, there was no entitlement for the second notice party to instruct its counsel to plead any kind of privilege before the tribunal."[1073]

10–438   Having reached this conclusion, it was unnecessary for the court to reach a concluded view as to whether the power to "protect" would encompass privilege as against third parties in court or tribunal proceedings. Notwithstanding this, Geoghegan J proceeded to express the view, with which Murray CJ and Denham J concurred, that[1074]:

> "...since there were no words included in Art.15.10 equivalent to the words included in Art.15.12 and Art.15.13 clearly indicating absolute privilege or even any express words indicating a qualified privilege, there is not nor is there the potentiality to create any constitutional privilege under Art.15.10 that can be pleaded against a third party or stranger in ordinary court proceedings or against a tribunal in tribunal proceedings.
>
> Still less of course is there anything in Art.15.10 to suggest a self executing privilege...[1075] The most that can be said is that Art.15.10 does seem to assume that, independently of the terms of Art.15.10 itself, the freedom of debate, the protection of official documents and the protection of private papers of members were all natural to the efficiency and efficacy of a house of parliament. The main purpose of Art.15.10 is to dispense with the necessity for legislation to secure these freedoms and protections by allowing each House to make its own separate rules relating to them... Effectively, Art.15.10 is allowing each House to make its own laws in this connection."[1076]

10–439   Geoghegan J expressly reserved his position as to whether, in the event that there was a privilege attaching to the "private papers" of a member within the meaning of Art.15.10, that individual member would be entitled to raise the privilege before a court tribunal. He observed, however, that there is a significant difference between the power to create the privilege in the first instance, and the subsequent availing of it before a court or tribunal, and stated that he was "by no means convinced that in such a situation a member could assert the privilege".[1077]

---

meant by "private papers" may have to be considered in a future case ([2005] IESC 85 at [76] and [96], [2006] 2 IR 321 at 375).

[1072] [2005] IESC 85, [2006] 2 IR 321.

[1073] [2005] IESC 85, [2006] 2 IR 321 at 386.

[1074] [2005] IESC 85, [2006] 2 IR 321 at 387.

[1075] The term 'self executing' was used in argument in respect of Arts 15.12 and 15.13, which are fully effective in and of themselves to confer privilege. See the judgment of Hardiman J at [2014] IESC 85 at [42], [2006] 2 IR 321 at 364.

[1076] The Supreme Court held that the only kind of privilege which could conceivably have been pleaded by the applicant was the so-called common law privilege, which is not a privilege in the strict sense, but rather public interest privilege. The court concluded that the applicant had already carried out the balancing test required where a claim of public interest privilege is asserted, and upheld his conclusion that the public interest favoured disclosure.

[1077] [2005] IESC 85 at [94], [2006] 2 IR 321 at 386–387. These passages were cited with approval by O'Neill J in *Callely v Moylan* [2011] IEHC 2 at [42], [2011] 1 IR 676 at 702, which concerned the

(b) Official reports and parliamentary utterances subsequently published

10–440   Article 15.12 of the Constitution provides that: "All official reports and publications of the Oireachtas or of either House thereof, and utterances made in either house wherever published shall be privileged".[1078] It was held by the Supreme Court in *AG v Hamilton (No 2)*[1079] that the effect of Art.15.12 is that an official publication or an utterance made in either House cannot form the subject-matter of *any* form of legal proceeding, whether in a defamation context or not, and regardless of where it was published.[1080] This is of particular importance, as it prevents the loss of privilege by the re-publication of any statement made in the Dáil, regardless of form.[1081]

(c) Non-amenability

10–441   Article 15.13 further provides that the members of each House of the Oireachtas "shall not, in respect of any utterance in either House, be amenable to any court or any authority other than the House itself".[1082] The scope of the protection afforded by these Constitutional provisions came under scrutiny in *AG v Hamilton*

---

investigation by the Committee on Member's Interest of Seanad Éireann in accordance with the Ethics in Public Office Act 1995 and the Standards in Public Office Act 2001 into claims that the applicant had misrepresented his normal place of residence for the purpose of claiming expenses. O'Neill J rejected the contention that the matters sought to be litigated were non-justiciable and made an order of certiorari quashing the determination of the Committee and the resolution of the Seanad. This decision was reversed by the Supreme Court on appeal ([2014] IESC 26). The Supreme Court did not, however, consider the extent to which, in circumstances where the requisite rule or standing order has been passed by a House of the Oireachtas, Art.15.10 gives rise to a constitutional privilege which Art.15.10 can be raised against a third party or stranger in proceedings before a court or tribunal.

[1078] Article 15.12 is identical to Art.19 of the Constitution of Saorstát Éireann 1922.

[1079] [1993] 3 IR 227.

[1080] [1993] 3 IR 227 at 302 *per* Denham J, at 268 *per* Finlay CJ. See *Callely v Moylan* [2014] IESC 26 at [52], where Clarke and O'Donnell JJ stated, in a joint judgment, that: "... it has been held that the privilege conferred by Art.15.12 is an extensive one and is not limited to privilege from defamation. The Irish text makes it clear that privilege here means privilege from *any legal proceedings* (táid saor ar chúrsaí dlí cibé áit a bhfoilsítear) and as observed by Finlay CJ in *The Attorney General v Hamilton (No.2)* [1993] 3 IR 227 at 268 in rejecting an argument that the privilege in Art.15.12 was limited to defamation: '[The relevant subsections of Art.15] very clearly indicate that there are a great variety of legal proceedings which could follow upon the making of an utterance over and above a claim for damages for defamation, were it not for the privilege and immunity granted by these articles'." They expressed the view that the report of the Committee on Member's Interest of Seanad Éireann into claims that the applicant had misrepresented his normal place of residence for the purpose of claiming expenses was entitled to privilege under Art.15.2.

[1081] [1993] 3 IR 227 at 268 (*per* Finlay CJ).

[1082] Article 15.13 repeats, with minor amendments, Art.18 of the Constitution of Saorstát Eireann 1922. The amendments slightly extend the scope of privilege in relation to utterances in the House (*Howlin v Morris* [2005] IESC 85 at [71], [2006] 2 IR 321 *per* Geoghegan J). This branch of parliamentary privilege can be traced back to art.9 of the Bill of Rights 1689 and, to some extent, the earlier common law. Under the heading "freedom of speech", art.9 provides that: "the freedom of speech and debates or proceedings in Parliament ought not to be impeached or questioned in any court or place out of Parliament." For a discussion of the history of this privilege, see *AG v Hamilton (No. 2)* [1993] 3 IR 227 and *Ahern v Mahon* [2008] IEHC 119, [2008] 4 IR 704, [2009] 1 ILRM 458. But see *Callely v Moylan* [2011] IEHC 2 at [39], [2011] 1 IR 676 at 696, where O'Neill J stated: "It is well settled that the source of parliamentary privileges and powers is now solely to be found in the Constitution itself."

(No 2)[1083] in circumstances where TDs had furnished statements of evidence to the Beef Tribunal in which they repeated and clarified certain statements made by them in the Dáil. In the Supreme Court, it was held that the dual speaking of the words did not destroy the privilege,[1084] and that the TDs could not be questioned as regards the sources of the allegations contained in the statements as this would, in effect, be to compel them to answer questions as to the Dáil utterances.

10–442 The decision in *Hamilton (No.2)* was applied in *Howlin v Morris*,[1085] in which Kearns J stated that, where Dáil utterances are repeated outside the house, the issue is to be determined by inquiring whether the statements were factually the same as the utterances made in the Dáil. If so, the jurisdiction of the court is ousted and both the statement and the sources of information upon which it was founded are privileged, as to seek to go behind the statement is to seek to go behind the Dáil utterance. However, he made it clear that Art.15.13 only confers an absolute privilege where the statements under inquiry are first made in Dáil Éireann. Here, the statements were first made in a meeting with the Minister for Justice. The utterances in the Dáil merely commented on the failure of the Minister to act on foot of these statements. As such, the information was first given expression in circumstances where no privilege attached, and the deputy was amenable to questioning. This aspect of the decision was upheld on appeal by the Supreme Court.[1086]

10–443 A more nuanced argument in favour of disclosure was advanced in *Ahern v Mahon*,[1087] which concerned statements made by the applicant in the Dáil in relation to loans provided to him in the early 1990s, in respect of which the applicant had provided information to the tribunal during its inquiries and had also made statements to the media. The tribunal accepted that it could not question the applicant in relation to the statements made in the Dáil or call into question their veracity or motivation. It wished, however, to draw the applicant's attention to inconsistencies between the statements made in the Dáil and statements made by the Applicant outside of it (including the statement to the media and such evidence as was given by the applicant before the tribunal). In circumstances where neither the decisions in *AG v Hamilton (No. 2)* nor *Howlin* were precisely on point, Kelly J considered the decision of the Privy Council in *Prebble v Television New Zealand Ltd*,[1088] where it was held that the defendants in a libel action were not entitled to refer to statements made by the plaintiff in Parliament in support of a plea of justification, to the effect that the plaintiff made statements in parliament calculated to mislead it or which were otherwise improperly motivated. Kelly J adopted the following dictum of Lord Browne Wilkinson[1089]:

> "There are three such issues in play in these cases: first, the need to ensure that the legislature can exercise its powers freely on behalf of its electors, with access to all relevant information;

[1083] [1993] 3 IR 227.

[1084] *Per* Finlay CJ (at 272–273) and Blayney J (at 297). O'Flaherty J (at 292) reached a similar conclusion, holding that the tribunal was inextricably involved with the applicant's utterances in the Dáil, and that the furnishing of statements should not be employed to circumvent the constitutional privilege. He considered that, in reality, these individuals were being questioned as regards utterances made in the Dáil.

[1085] [2003] IEHC 55, [2006] 2 IR 321, [2004] 2 ILRM 53.

[1086] *Howlin v Morris* [2005] IESC 85 at [73], [2006] 2 IR 321 at 374 *per* Geoghegan J.

[1087] [2008] 4 IR 708. *Cf.* Higgins, "Parliamentary Privilege and Free Speech in the Oireachtas", (2010) DULJ 94.

[1088] [1995] 1 AC 321.

[1089] [1995] 1 AC 321 at 336.

second, the need to protect freedom of speech generally; third, the interests of justice in ensuring that all relevant evidence is available to the courts. Their Lordships are of the view that the law has been long settled that, of these three public interests, the first must prevail."[1090]

10–444   He observed that the Privy Council was unequivocal in its finding that "parties to litigation, by whomsoever commenced, cannot bring into question anything said or done in the House by suggesting (whether by direct evidence, cross-examination, inference or submission) that the actions or words were inspired by improper motives or were untrue or misleading. Such matters lie entirely within the jurisdiction of the House..."[1091] Kelly J stated that the position is no different in respect of a tribunal of inquiry, and held that Art.15.13 "protects a member of the national parliament from both direct and indirect attempts to make such person amenable to anybody other than the Houses themselves in respect of any utterance made in such Houses".[1092] He concluded that, were the Tribunal to draw the applicant's attention to inconsistencies between the statements made by him in parliament and statements made by him outside of it, this "may incorporate a suggestion that the words spoken in parliament were untrue or misleading", which was impermissible.[1093]

6. Statutory Privilege

10–445   The decisions in *Murphy*[1094] and *Ambiorix*,[1095] which emphasised that the question of whether documents were privileged from production was a matter solely for the judicial power, might seem to cast some doubt as to the competence of the Oireachtas to create statutory privileges. However, in *O'Brien v Ireland*[1096] O'Hanlon J stated, that notwithstanding the absoluteness of the language used, neither decision:

> "...was intended to convey that the power of the legislature to intervene and confer the privilege of exemption from production on specified categories of documentary or other evidence was curtailed or restricted in any way, save insofar as any legislation enacted must not conflict with the overriding provisions of the Constitution".

10–446   That conclusion was endorsed by the Supreme Court in *Skeffington v Rooney*[1097] and it would appear, therefore, that it is open to the Oireachtas to create a statutory privilege in respect of a specified category of documentation within the parameters set by the Constitution. Furthermore, such a statutory privilege will supersede any common law privilege which might otherwise have been applicable.[1098]

[1090] Cited at [2008] IEHC 119 at [33], [2008] 4 IR 704 at 713.

[1091] [1995] 1 AC 321 at 337.

[1092] [2008] IEHC 119 at [36], [2008] 4 IR 704 at 714. See the joint judgment of Clarke and O'Donnell JJ in *Callely v Moylan* [2014] IESC 26 at [53], where they stated that members of the Oireachtas are not amenable to any court or authority other than the House itself for utterances made; "This is an individual privilege in addition to the privilege attached to the utterance itself wherever published, pursuant to Art.15.12. It is clear that, in the words of Art.18 of the 1922 Constitution from which this provision is drawn, a member shall not 'in respect of any utterance in either House, be amenable to any action or proceeding in any Court other than the House itself'."

[1093] [2008] IEHC 119 at [37], [2008] 4 IR 704 at 714. It was held, however, that the Tribunal could record the statements made in the Dáil in its report. While it could not suggest that the statement was untrue or misleading, it would be for the reader of the report to draw his own conclusions.

[1094] [1972] IR 215.

[1095] [1992] 1 IR 277, [1992] ILRM 209.

[1096] [1995] 1 ILRM 22 at 29.

[1097] [1997] 1 IR 22 at 36–37, [1997] 2 ILRM 56 at 70–71.

[1098] *PB v AL* [1996] 1 ILRM 154 at 158; *SM v GM* [1985] ILRM 186 at 187.

10–447 Where a claim of statutory privilege is made, it is a question of statutory interpretation as to whether a privilege has been created and what communications and persons/bodies are protected by it.[1099] Among the legislative provisions that have been held to create statutory privileges are s.8 of the Adoption Act 1976,[1100] s.16 of the Central Bank Act 1989,[1101] s.9 of the Diplomatic Relations and Immunities Act 1967,[1102] art.11(2) of the Defence Forces Regulations 1982,[1103] s.27 of the Commission to Inquire into Child Abuse Act 2000,[1104] and s.11 of the Commissioner of Investigations Act 2004.[1105] However, a claim that s.12 of the Garda Síochána (Complaints) Act 1986 had created a privilege from disclosure failed in *Skeffington v Rooney*[1106] and it would appear from that decision that clear evidence of a legislative intention to create a privilege is required.[1107]

7. Confidentiality

10–448 It will be evident from the discussion of the various privileges above that a fundamental prerequisite for a privilege from disclosure to arise is that the communication must be confidential in nature.[1108] However, the corollary does not follow, and the mere fact that a communication came into being in the course of a confidential relationship and/or was intended to pass in confidence will not clothe it with privilege.[1109] In *Re Kevin O'Kelly*,[1110] Walsh J emphasised that:

[1099] See, *e.g. SM v GM* [1985] ILRM 186 at 188 and *O'Brien v Minister for Defence* [1998] 2 ILRM 156 at 159.

[1100] See *SM v GM* [1985] ILRM 186; *PB v AL* [1996] 1 ILRM 154; *DC v DM* [1999] 2 IR 150.

[1101] See *Cully v Northern Bank Finance Corp Ltd* [1984] ILRM 683, where O'Hanlon J held that the predecessor to s.16, s.31 of the Central Bank Act 1942, created a statutory privilege in favour of information and documents coming into the possession or control of officers of the Central Bank.

[1102] See *O'Brien v Ireland* [1995] 1 IR 568, [1995] 1 ILRM 22.

[1103] See *O'Brien v Minister for Defence* [1998] 2 ILRM 156 (decision of O'Hanlon J in the High Court reported *sub nom O'Brien v Ireland* [1995] 1 IR 568, [1995] 1 ILRM 22); *O'Mahony v Minister for Defence*, unreported, High Court, 27 June 1989.

[1104] *MB v Commission to Inquire into Child Abuse* [2007] IEHC 376, [2008] 3 IR 541.

[1105] *O'Neill v An Taoiseach* [2009] IEHC 119 at [16].

[1106] [1997] 1 IR 22 at 37, [1997] 2 ILRM 56 at 71. *Cf. Traynor v Delahunt* [2008] IEHC 272 at [31], [2009] 1 IR 605, [2009] 1 ILRM 113.

[1107] See *Miggin (a minor) v HSE* [2010] 4 IR 338 and *Buckley v Bough*, unreported, High Court, 2 July 2001, where it was held that transcripts of proceedings before the Fitness to Practice Committee do not bear privilege, notwithstanding the implied statutory discretion to hold the proceedings in camera.

[1108] If the ingredient of confidentiality is lacking as where a communication is overheard by a third party, privilege will not arise: see *Smurfit Paribas Bank Ltd v AAB Export Finance Ltd* [1990] 1 IR 469 at 473, [1990] ILRM 588 at 590 (legal professional privilege); *People (AG) v Coleman* [1945] IR 237 at 248 (marital privilege).

[1109] *Cf. McNibb v Minister for Justice, Equality and Law Reform* [2013] IEHC 238 at [26]; *Keating v Radio Telefís Éireann* [2013] IESC 22 at [48]; *Miley v Flood* [2001] 2 IR 50, [2001] 1 ILRM 489; *Cooper Flynn v RTÉ* [2000] 3 IR 344 at 351, [2001] 1 ILRM 208 at 217; *Johnston v Church of Scientology*, unreported, High Court, 30 April 1999; *Skeffington v Rooney* [1997] 1 IR 22 at 35, [1997] 2 ILRM 56 at 69; *Burke v Central Independent Television Plc* [1994] 2 IR 261; *In re Kevin O'Kelly* (1974) 108 ILTR 97 at 101; *Duchess of Kingston's Case* (1776) 20 St Tr 355 at 586; *Greenlaw v R.* (1838) 1 Beav 137 at 145; *Wheeler v Le Marchant* (1881) 17 Ch D 675 at 681. It may, however, be a material consideration to bear in mind where public interest privilege is asserted. See *O'Callaghan v Mahon* [2005] IESC 9 at [83], [2005] IEHC 265, [2006] 2 IR 32; *Alfred Crompton Amusement Machines Ltd v Customs and Excise Commissioners* [1974] AC 405.

[1110] [1974] 108 ILTR 97 at 101.

"The fact that a communication was made under terms of expressed confidence or implied confidence does not create a privilege against disclosure. So far as the administration of justice is concerned the public has a right to every man's evidence except for those persons protected by a constitutional or other established and recognised privilege."

10–449 As noted by the House of Lords in *Three Rivers DC v Bank of England (No 6)*,[1111] given the public interest in the admission of all relevant evidence in both civil and criminal proceedings, the interests of justice will usually require the disclosure of confidential communications.[1112] Referring to the distinction between the special privilege afforded to communications between a lawyer and client, Lord Scott stated that[1113]:

"In relation to all other confidential communications, whether between doctor and patient, accountant and client, husband and wife, parent and child, priest and penitent, the common law recognises the confidentiality of the communication, will protect the confidentiality up to a point, but declines to allow the communication the absolute protection allowed to communications between lawyer and client giving or seeking legal advice. In relation to all these other confidential communications the law requires the public interest in the preservation of confidences and the private interest of the parties in maintaining the confidentiality of their communications to be balanced against the administration of justice reasons for requiring disclosure of the confidential material. There is a strong public interest that in criminal cases the innocent should be acquitted and the guilty convicted, that in civil cases the claimant should succeed if he is entitled to do so and should fail if he is not, that every trial should be a fair trial and that to provide the best chance of these desiderata being achieved all relevant material should be available to be taken into account. These are the administration of justice reasons to be placed in the balance. They will usually prevail."

10–450 This is the case, regardless of whether the obligation of confidentiality arises from statute or in some other manner.[1114] Thus, the courts have rejected claims of privilege in respect of communications passing between a doctor and patient,[1115] a banker and customer,[1116] and accountant and client,[1117] an agent and principal,[1118] and a probation officer and probationer.[1119] Neither can a privilege from disclosure be created by a contractual stipulation that information is not to be disclosed.[1120]

[1111] [2004] UKHL 48, [2004] 3 WLR 1274, [2005] 1 AC 610.

[1112] *Cf. Traynor v Delahunt* [2008] IEHC 272, [2009] 1 IR 605, [2009] 1 ILRM 113.

[1113] [2004] UKHL 48 at [28], [2004] 3 WLR 1274, [2005] 1 AC 610, *per* Lord Scott.

[1114] *Skeffington v Rooney* [1997] 1 IR 22 at 35, [1997] 2 ILRM 56 at 69; *Carlton v Director of Public Prosecutions (No. 2)* [2000] 3 IR 269 at 279–280; *Gamble v The Garda Siochana Complaints Board* [2004] IEHC 364. See also *Eastern Health Board v Fitness to Practice Committee* [1998] 3 IR 399 and *Miggin (A minor) v HSE* [2010] 4 IR 338, where it was held that a statutory imperative that proceedings of a particular nature be held in private (in camera) does not imply that there is an absolute embargo on the disclosure of evidence in all circumstances.

[1115] *Brady v Haughton* [2006] 1 IR 1; *Miley v Flood* [2001] 2 IR 50, [2001] 1 ILRM 489; *Duchess of Kingston's Case* (1776) 20 St Tr 355; *R. v Gibbons* (1823) 1 C & P 97; *Wheeler v Le Marchant* (1881) 17 Ch D 675 at 681; *Anderson v Bank of British Columbia* (1876) 2 Ch D 644 at 651; *Campbell v Tameside Metropolitan Borough Council* [1982] QB 1065, [1982] 2 All ER 791. *Cf. WW v PB*, unreported, High Court, Barr J, 18 March 1999 where a claim of privilege in respect of the plaintiff's medical, psychiatric and counselling records and reports was rejected in circumstances where the plaintiff instituted proceedings alleging that the defendant had sexually assaulted him.

[1116] *Cooper Flynn v RTÉ* [2000] 3 IR 344 at 351, [2001] 1 ILRM 208 at 217; *Loyd v Freshfield* (1826) 2 C & P 325.

[1117] *Chantrey Martin & Co v Martin* [1953] 2 QB 286, [1953] 2 All ER 691.

[1118] *Kerry County Council v Liverpool Salvage Association* [1905] 2 IR 38 at 44; *Anderson v Bank of British Columbia* (1876) 2 Ch D 644 at 648; *Slade v Tucker* (1880) 14 Ch D 824 at 827.

[1119] *R. v Umoh* (1986) 84 Cr App R 138; *R. v Walker* (1992) 74 CCC (3d) 97.

[1120] *Johnston v Church of Scientology*, unreported, High Court, 30 April 1999; *Federal Commissioner*

10–451 The distinction between "confidential information" and privileged information was emphasised by McMahon J in *Traynor v Delahunt*,[1121] where it was held that privilege, when it applies, is an absolute right, whereas confidentiality is merely a factor the courts will take into account when balancing the interests. McMahon J cited the following dictum of Hardiman J in *O'Callaghan v Mahon* with approval, where he stated that:

> "... one must first look closely at the precise scope and nature of the claim to confidentiality advanced, and determine whether the disputed material is indeed confidential. One must then consider whether such degree of confidentiality as may be found to exist is or is not outweighed by the public interest, based fundamentally on constitutional considerations, in according fair procedures to the applicant in the circumstances in which they are claimed."[1122]

10–452 He rejected the contention that the obligation on the Director of Public Prosecutions to preserve the confidentiality of information sent to the Director by the Garda Siochana Complaints Board precluded the disclosure of relevant and material documents to the accused in a criminal trial. It was held that it was for the trial judge to examine the documents in question and to engage in a balancing exercise as to whether they should be disclosed or withheld.[1123]

10–453 As is clear from the decision in *Cooper Flynn v RTÉ*,[1124] the courts recognise that there is a public interest in maintaining the confidentiality of certain communications.[1125] Thus, although confidentiality will not provide a sufficient basis, of itself, to resist the disclosure of information, it is a factor which will be taken into account and will influence the court in deciding whether to order a witness to answer questions or whether to order the discovery, production or inspection of documents.[1126] In addition, if an order for the disclosure of confidential information is made, the courts will, where possible, take steps to ameliorate the effects of disclosure by, for example, ordering disclosure in redacted form only or limit it to a party's legal advisers.

(a) Solicitor and Client

10–454 The scope of the duty of confidentiality owed by a solicitor to a client, aside altogether from legal professional privilege, and the circumstances in which it may be overridden, were considered by Moriarty J in *Inspector of Taxes v A Firm of*

---

of *Taxation v Coombes* [1999] FCA 842, (1999) 164 ALR 131; *Southern Cross Commodities Pty Ltd v Crinis* [1984] VR 697.

[1121] [2008] IEHC 272 at [31], [2009] 1 IR 605 at 615, [2009] 1 ILRM 113 at 122.

[1122] [2005] IESC 9 at [89], [2006] 2 IR 32 at 71.

[1123] [2008] IEHC 272 at [33], [2009] 1 IR 605 at 616, [2009] 1 ILRM 113 at 122–123. McMahon J placed particular emphasis on the important of fair procedures and the right of an accused to a fair trial.

[1124] [2001] 1 ILRM 208 at 217.

[1125] See *Brady v Haughton* [2006] 1 IR 1 at 87, where Geoghegan J stated that there is no legal privilege between doctor and patient, but observed that: "Even in the case of a relationship which does not give rise to a legal privilege in the strict sense, a court may have regard to the confidentiality rights of a party in considering whether it is absolutely necessary that such evidence be given."

[1126] See *Independent Newspapers (Ireland) Ltd v Murphy* [2006] 3 IR 566, where Clarke J held that the courts should only order discovery of confidential documents such as instructions to lawyers (which are not subject to legal professional privilege) where the interests of justice require an order for discovery to be made. See also *Brady v Houghton* [2006] 1 IR 1 at 87; *Cooper Flynn v RTÉ* [2000] 3 IR 344 at 351, [2001] 1 ILRM 208 at 217–218; *Wallace Smith Trust Co Ltd v Deloitte Haskins & Sells* [1996] 4 All ER 403 at 417; *Science Research Council v Nassé* [1980] AC 1028 at 1089, [1979] 3 All ER 673 at 699.

Solicitors,[1127] where he ordered a firm of solicitors to divulge the identities and addresses of the persons who were the ultimate beneficiaries of 19 transactions effected through bank accounts in the respondent firm's name between 2005 and 2007, together with the relevant confirmatory documentation. Having rejected the contention that legal professional privilege precluded the disclosure of the identity of the clients,[1128] he proceeded to consider the extent to which client confidentiality precluded or exempted the furnishing of that information and documentation. Moriarty J referred to the decision of McKechnie J in *Walsh v National Irish Bank,*[1129] a case which concerned the duty of confidentiality between a banker and customer, where it was held that there are a number of exceptions to the duty of confidentiality. These include situations in which disclosure is under compulsion of law, or where there is a duty to the public to disclose. It was further held that these exceptions are not mutually dependent and must give way, where the circumstances so demand, to the overriding duty of disclosure in the public interest. An example of this would be attempt to undercover fraud or detect crime.[1130] Moriarty J concluded that, in the case before him, confidentiality was outweighed by the overriding public interest of ensuring that the lengthy Revenue investigation in relation to offshore accounts was brought to finality and taxes properly due addressed and discharged. He concluded that, "[n]o duty of confidentiality is absolute, and the present circumstances amply justify it being overridden".[1131]

10–455 The importance of the distinction between the duty of confidence owed by a solicitor to a client, on the one hand, and legal professional privilege, on the other, was emphasised by Laffoy J in *Martin v Legal Aid Board.*[1132] The issue under consideration in that case was the constitutionality of a provision of the Civil Legal Aid Act 2005,[1133] which required the solicitors of legally aided clients to provide information to the Legal Aid Board, notwithstanding the duty of confidentiality owed by the solicitor to the client and regardless of whether the information was subject to legal professional privilege. She accepted the submission of counsel for the defendants that, while the foundation of both concepts is confidentiality of communication within the relationship of the solicitor and client, legal professional privilege requires the fulfilment of criteria which go beyond those required to establish the duty of confidentiality. Laffoy J described the practical implications of this distinction as follows[1134]:

> "Where, in the ordinary relationship, the solicitor discloses information in breach of his duty of confidentiality, the client can recover damages from him or, in the case of an anticipated breach, he can obtain an injunction to restrain the breach. The solicitor may also incur a disciplinary sanction imposed by the Law Society or the High Court under the Solicitors' Code. However, even though information communicated by a client to his solicitor in the ordinary relationship may have privileged status, that does not seem to me to be a sound basis for concluding that there is a constitutional imperative that every communication which a client makes to a solicitor in confidence should be protected from disclosure."

10–456 It was held that, while legal professional privilege ceased to operate as a

---

[1127] [2013] IEHC 67 at [10], [2013] 2 ILRM 1 at 4.
[1128] Applying the decision of Kelly J in *Miley v Flood Miley v Flood* [2001] 2 IR 50, [2001] 1 ILRM 489.
[1129] [2008] 2 ILRM 56.
[1130] [2008] 2 ILRM 56 at 68.
[1131] [2013] IEHC 67 at [10], [2013] 2 ILRM 1 at 4.
[1132] [2007] IEHC 76, [2007] 2 IR 759, [2007] 1 ILRM 481.
[1133] Section 32(2) of the Civil Legal Aid Act 1995.
[1134] [2007] IEHC 76 at [30], [2007] 2 IR 759 at 772–773, [2007] 1 ILRM 481 at 492.

protective mechanism for a client when litigation ceased, the duty of confidentiality toward a client endured.

CHAPTER 11

SELF-INCRIMINATION

A. Introduction

11–01   The exact origins and course of development of the right not to be compelled to incriminate oneself are not free from doubt or controversy but the orthodox account, which has achieved widespread judicial acceptance,[1] is that of Wigmore.[2] He traces the origins of the right to abuses by the English ecclesiastical courts, most notably the Court of High Commission and the Court of Star Chamber, in the administration of the oath *ex officio, i.e.* inquisitorial oath. This oath, which replaced the oath of compurgation, pledged the accused to answer honestly and was followed by a process of judicial questioning. The main difficulty with the oath, especially as employed in the zealous pursuit of heretics, was that it was not preceded by a proper presentation of charges against the accused. Thus, a person could be called before these courts and subjected to a searching examination under oath without notice of the precise charge against him or her. These courts often used the lack of particularity as an excuse to embark upon an untrammelled investigation into the life of the accused in the hope that the commission of an offence would be revealed.

---

[1]   See, *e.g.* the judgments of Walsh J in *Saunders v United Kingdom* (1996) 23 EHRR 313 at 344, 345 and Wilson J in *Thomson Newspapers Ltd v Canada (Director of Investigation and Research, Restrictive Trade Practices Commission)* [1990] 1 SCR 425 and McLachlin J in *R. v Hebert* [1990] 2 SCR 151.

[2]   Wigmore, *Evidence* (3rd edn, 1940), Vol. VIII, §2250. See also L. Herman, "The Unexplored Relationship Between the Privilege Against Compulsory Self-Incrimination and the Involuntary Confession Rule (Part I)" (1992) 53 Ohio St LJ 101. However, Wigmore's account has been challenged and it has been suggested that the development of the privilege is linked to the advent of defence counsel and the adversarial model of trial (see Langbein, "The Historical Origins of the Privilege Against Self-incrimination at Common Law" (1994) 92 Mich Law Rev 1047 and Moglen, "Taking the Fifth: Reconsidering the Origins of the Constitutional Privilege against Self-incrimination" (1994) 92 Mich Law Rev 1086). See also Cotton, "The Judicial Use of History in Decisions About the Privilege Against Self Incrimination" (2009) 13 *Legal History* 175. A detailed and insightful review of the historical record by McInerney, "The privilege against self-incrimination from early origins to Judge's Rules: challenging the orthodox view" (2014) 18 E & P 101, which analyses separately the development of the three discrete sub-rights identified below, also casts doubt on the consensus view.

11–02   As is clear from the watershed case of Lilburn's trial,[3] the reaction against these abuses initially focused on the procedural deficiencies in the administration of the oath and the lack of notice of charges rather than the compulsion to answer questions. However, in the seventeenth century, in the aftermath of Lilburn's trial and the abolition of the Courts of Star Chamber and High Commission, a general principle began to emerge at common law that a person was not bound to incriminate himself or herself on any charge (whether properly instituted or not) in any court. Similar abuses by magistrates interrogating accused persons before trial prompted the emergence of a right to silence and caution at the pre-trial stage.[4] This extension has been justified on the basis that, if an accused did not enjoy a right to silence at the pre-trial investigative stage, the immunity from testifying at trial would be "illusory".[5] Finally, the right not to incriminate oneself was extended to witnesses in civil cases and, later, to persons questioned in any proceedings. Again, the rationale was that the immunity from testifying at trial "would be of very little use or value if a man could be compelled to tell all to the authorities before a trial".[6]

11–03   It can be seen, therefore, that the result of the development of the right not to be compelled to incriminate oneself, as encapsulated in the principle *nemo tenetur se ipsum accusare*, is a number of distinct though connected rights which are generally grouped together under the umbrella term of "the privilege against self-incrimination" or, sometimes, "the right to silence". In *R. v Director of the Serious Fraud Office, ex p. Smith*,[7] Lord Mustill identified a "disparate group of immunities" encompassed within the "right to silence" as follows:

> "(1) a general immunity, possessed by all persons and bodies, from being compelled on pain of punishment to answer questions posed by other persons or bodies;
>
> (2) a general immunity, possessed by all persons and bodies, from being compelled on pain of punishment to answer questions the answers to which may incriminate them;
>
> (3) a specific immunity, possessed by all persons under suspicion of criminal responsibility whilst being interviewed by police officers or others in similar positions of authority, from being compelled on pain of punishment to answer questions of any kind;
>
> (4) a specific immunity, possessed by accused persons undergoing trial, from being compelled to give evidence, and from being compelled to answer questions put to them in the dock;
>
> (5) a specific immunity, possessed by persons who have been charged with a criminal offence, from having questions material to the offence addressed to them by police officers or persons in a similar position of authority;
>
> (6) a specific immunity (at least in certain circumstances, which it is unnecessary to explore), possessed by accused persons undergoing trial, from having adverse comment made on any failure (a) to answer questions before the trial, or (b) to give evidence at the trial."[8]

---

3   (1637–1645) 3 How St Tr 1315.
4   *R. v Director of Serious Fraud Office, ex p Smith* [1993] AC 1 at 31, [1992] 3 All ER 456 at 464 (*per* Lord Mustill).
5   *R. v Hebert* [1990] 2 SCR 151 at 174 (*per* McLachlin J). *Cf.* Zuckerman. "Trial by Unfair Means—The Report of the Working Group on the Right of Silence" [1989] Crim LR 855.
6   *Saunders v UK* (1996) 23 EHRR 313 at 345 (*per* Walsh J).
7   [1993] AC 1, [1992] 1 All ER 456.
8   [1993] AC 1 at 30, 31, [1992] 1 All ER 456 at 463, 464. This "helpful analysis" was quoted by Costello J (as he then was) in *Heaney v Ireland* [1994] 3 IR 593 at 601, 602, [1994] 2 ILRM 420 at 427 and, again, by Kearns J in *Dunnes Stores Ireland Company v Ryan* [2002] 2 IR 60 at 115.

11–04   Of these diverse manifestations of the general right not to incriminate oneself, three main sub-rights can be identified: (1) the right of an accused person not be to compelled to give evidence at his trial (which will be referred to in this chapter as the "right not to give evidence"); (2) the right of a criminal suspect not to answer questions (which will be referred to as the "right to silence"); and (3) the privilege enjoyed by witnesses and other persons subject to questioning in any form of proceedings not to answer questions which may tend to incriminate them, (which will be referred to as the "privilege against self-incrimination"). It has to be acknowledged that this terminology does not coincide with that used in some of the cases but it is submitted that its adoption assists in an understanding of the discrete issues that arise in relation to the different aspects of the general right not to incriminate oneself.

B. Rationale of the Right not to Incriminate Oneself

11–05   Although the genesis of the right not to incriminate oneself is largely attributable to historical circumstance, judges and commentators have advanced a number of rationales for its continued vitality.[9] The first point to be made about these is no one theory can adequately explain the current ambit and formulation of the right but the influence of each can be seen to underlie it to a greater or lesser extent. The second point, drawing on the first, is that, as emphasised by Lord Mustill in *R. v Director of Serious Fraud Office, ex p. Smith*,[10] the justifications for the various sub-rights will not necessarily coincide. Thirdly, it is convenient to divide the rationales into two categories: (i) substantive rationales whereby the right is justified by reference to substantive rights and principles; and (ii) non-substantive rights and principles.[11] This is because the substantive rationales focus primarily (though not exclusively) on the compulsion of evidence rather than its use at trial whereas the non-substantive rationales concentrate on the consequences of the use of compelled evidence at trial.

1. Substantive Rationales

11–06   It can be argued that the right not to incriminate oneself is grounded in a number of substantive rights and values including (a) personal autonomy and the dignity of the individual, (b) the right to privacy, and (c) freedom of expression. The common thread running through each of these rationales is that, because substantive rights are involved, a breach will occur, if at all, at the point when a person is compelled to answer and, irrespective of whether the answer is subsequently tendered in evidence.[12]

---

[9]   See generally, Dennis, "Instrumental Protection, Human Right or Functional Necessity? Reassessing the Privilege Against Self-Incrimination" (1995) 54 CLJ 342 and Redmayne, "Rethinking the privilege against self-incrimination" (2007) 27(2) Oxford Journal of Legal Studies 209.

[10]   [1993] AC 1 at 30, [1992] 1 All ER 456 at 463.

[11]   *Cf.* Choo, *The Privilege Against Self-Incrimination and Criminal Justice*, (Hart Publishing, 2013) who categorises the rationales for the privilege as either epistemic (related to the promotion of accurate fact finding) or non-epistemic in nature and Roberts and Zuckerman, *Criminal Evidence*, 2nd edn (Oxford: Oxford University Press, 2010), at pp.547–563 who identify three types of rationale: intrinsic rationales (hardship, dilemma and privacy), conceptualist rationales (adversarial procedure, the presumption of innocence and fair trial) and instrumental rationales (promoting fact-finding and protecting the innocent).

[12]   See *Pyneboard Pty Ltd v Trade Practices Commission* (1982) 152 CLR 328 at 346, 45 ALR 609 (*per* Murphy J).

These rationales are not concerned as such with the fairness of any subsequent trial which falls, instead, to be examined by reference to Art.38.1 of the Constitution and the non-substantive rationales set out below. That is not to say, however, that these rationales cannot lead to the conclusion that compelled answers should be excluded from evidence. In *People (DPP) v Kenny*,[13] a vindication theory for the exclusionary rule in respect of unconstitutionally obtained evidence was propounded whereby a person should be put in the position, in so far as possible, as he or she would have been in if his or her rights had not been breached. In order to do that, and to ensure that a person is not disadvantaged by the breach of his or her rights, it is necessary to exclude any incriminating statements made.

(a) Personal autonomy

11–07 This rationale proceeds on the basis that the dignity and freedom of the individual are core constitutional values[14] and, as recognised by the South African Constitutional Court in *Ferreira v Levin*,[15] these values are infringed where a person is compelled to incriminate himself because of the restriction placed on the choices open to the individual by reason of the compulsion.[16] Thus, the right not to incriminate oneself protects the personal autonomy or will of a person by respecting their freedom of choice: a person can choose to co-operate with the State and to incriminate himself or herself but cannot be forced to do so. As McLachlin J explained in *R. v Stillman*,[17] the various manifestations of the right not to be compelled to incriminate oneself:

> "... rest on the premise that a suspect cannot be coerced to give evidence against himself or herself. The suspect has the right to *choose* whether to make a statement or not. The right to choose whether or not to make a statement which may be used in evidence against oneself is a right that lies at the heart of the principle against self-incrimination."[18]

11–08 This rationale has, in recent years, emerged as the primary substantive rationale underpinning the right not to incriminate oneself. According to Shanley J in *Re National Irish Bank*,[19] the right is "first and foremost, concerned with respecting the will of an accused person to remain silent" echoing the view of the European Court of Human

---

13   [1990] 2 IR 110, [1990] ILRM 569.
14   The Preamble to the Constitution identifies as an objective of the Constitution, the promotion of the common good, with due observance of prudence, justice and charity, "so that the dignity and freedom of the individual may be assured". *Cf. Ferreira v Levin* 1996 (1) SA 984 at 1013, 1014, where Ackermann J characterised the rights of human dignity and freedom as core rights that were fundamental to the South African Constitution.
15   1996 (1) BCLR 1, 1996 (1) SA 984 at 1018, 1019 (*per* Ackermann J). See also *S. v Thebus* (2003) (2) SACR 319 at [54].
16   See also *EPA v Swalcliffe Ltd* [2004] IEHC 190 at [40], [2004] 2 IR 549 at 562, [2005] 1 ILRM 120 at 133, where Kearns J linked the privilege against self-incrimination to the value placed by society upon personal autonomy and dignity and *Pyneboard Pty. Ltd v Trade Practices Commission* (1982) 152 CLR 328 at 346, 45 ALR 609, where Murphy J stated that the privilege against self-incrimination was "based on the desire to protect personal freedom and human dignity".
17   [1997] 1 SCR 607.
18   [1997] 1 SCR 607 at 706. See also. *per* McLachlin J in *R. v Hebert* [1990] 2 SCR 151 at 180. A similar emphasis on the element of choice is apparent in the judgment of Costello J in *Heaney v Ireland* [1994] 3 IR 593 at 604, [1994] 2 ILRM 420 at 429: "The law does not prohibit a suspect from confessing to a crime—nor does it prohibit the questioning of a suspect in custody. It provides, however, that a suspect should not be required to answer questions on pain of punishment should he not wish to do so; that he is free to remain silent should he so choose and that he should be informed of his right to do so."
19   [1999] 3 IR 145 at 153, [1999] 1 ILRM 321 at 329.

Rights in *Saunders v United Kingdom*[20] that: "The right not to incriminate oneself is primarily concerned ... with respecting the will of an accused person to remain silent."[21] As Walsh J explained in *Saunders*:

> "Persons are always free to incriminate themselves if in doing so they are exercising their own will; but that it essentially different from a person being compelled in any criminal case to be a witness against himself."[22]

11–09 The importance of protecting the personal autonomy of persons has also been linked to more general concerns as to the inroads on personal freedom and abuses of power that would follow if the state could compel persons to incriminate themselves. In *Thomson Newspapers Ltd v Canada (Director of Investigation and Research, Restrictive Trade Practices Commission)*,[23] Wilson J opined that the rights not to testify and the privilege against self-incrimination were:

> "... prompted by a concern that the privacy and personal autonomy and dignity of the individual be respected by the state. The state must have some justification for interfering with the individual and cannot rely on the individual to produce the justification out of his own mouth. Were it otherwise, our justice system would be on a slippery slope towards the creation of a police state."[24]

11–10 Viewed in this way, the right not to incriminate oneself can be regarded as a protection of personal freedom and bulwark against overweening state power.[25]

(b) Privacy

11–11 It is evident that the right not to incriminate oneself also plays an important role in protecting the constitutionally protected right to privacy.[26] In *Re National Irish Bank*,[27] Shanley J endorsed the view of Lord Mustill in *R. v Director of Serious Fraud Office, ex p Smith*,[28] that the right "is a simple reflection of the common view that one person should so far as possible be entitled to tell another person to mind his own business."[29] Again, in *R. v Amway Corp*,[30] Sopinka J identified the dominant principle for the privilege against self-incrimination as being "to protect the individual against the affront to dignity and privacy inherent in a practice which enables the prosecution to force the person charged to supply the evidence out of his or her own mouth."

---

[20] (1996) 23 EHRR 313 at 337.
[21] See also *Heaney v Ireland* (2001) 33 EHRR 12 at [40].
[22] (1996) 23 EHRR 313 at 344.
[23] [1990] 1 SCR 425.
[24] [1990] 1 SCR 425 at 480.
[25] *Cf. per* McLachlin J in *R. v Hebert* [1990] 2 SCR 151 at 174, who traced the genesis of the right not to incriminate oneself to: "an abhorrence of the interrogation practised by the old ecclesiastical courts and the Star Chamber and the notion which grew out of that abhorrence that the citizen involved in the criminal process must be given procedural protections against the overweening power of the state".
[26] See *Kennedy v Ireland* [1987] IR 587, [1988] ILRM 472; *X v Flynn*, unreported, High Court, 19 May 1994; *O'T v B* [1998] 2 IR 321; *Hanahoe v Hussey* [1998] 3 IR 69.
[27] [1999] 3 IR 145 at 153, [1999] 1 ILRM 321 at 329.
[28] [1993] AC 1 at 31, [1992] 3 All ER 456 at 464.
[29] The linkage between the right and the value placed by society upon individual privacy was also made by Kearns J in *EPA v Swalcliffe Ltd* [2004] IEHC 190 at [40], [2004] 2 IR 549 at 562, [2005] 1 ILRM 120 at 133.
[30] [1989] 1 SCR 21 at 40.

(c) Freedom of expression

11–12   As will be seen below, in *Heaney v Ireland*,[31] the Supreme Court employed the concept of correlative rights to identify a constitutional grounding for the right to silence in the guarantee of freedom of expression contained in Art.40.6.1°.[32] In doing so, the court ignored a line of authority to the effect that this guarantee is restricted to the protection of convictions and opinions and does not extend to the dissemination of factual information.[33] The communication of such information is, instead, protected by an unenumerated right contained in Art.40.3.[34] Leaving aside the question of the proper locus for the protection of the right to communicate, it seems logical to hold that it carries with it a corollary right not to communicate which is promoted by a right not to incriminate oneself.

2. Non-Substantive Rationales

11–13   Although, as noted, the substantive rationales examined above can be employed by means of a vindication theory to justify the exclusion of evidence obtained in breach of the right not to incriminate oneself, the use which can be made of compelled statements also falls to be examined by reference to a number of non-substantive rationales. These are not concerned with compulsion *per se* but rather with the impact of the admission of compelled statements at trial.[35] It is possible to identify three such non-substantive rationales, each of which will be examined in turn: (a) the presumption of innocence; (b) the prevention of miscarriages of justice; and (c) fairness.

(a) Presumption of innocence

11–14   A close linkage between the right not to incriminate oneself and the presumption of innocence (which is a constitutionally mandated ingredient of a fair trial in this jurisdiction)[36] has been recognised in a number of cases.[37] In *Sorby v The Commonweath*,[38] Gibbs CJ explained that:

> "It is a cardinal principle of our system of justice that the Crown must prove the guilt of an accused person, and the protection which that principle affords to the liberty of the individual will be weakened if power exists to compel a suspected person to confess his guilt."[39]

11–15   Because of the historical genesis of the right to incriminate oneself, the relationship with the presumption of innocence is particularly close in the case of the

---

[31]   [1996] 1 IR 580, [1997] 1 ILRM 117.
[32]   [1996] 1 IR 580 at 585, [1997] 1 ILRM 117 at 123.
[33]   *AG v Paperlink* [1984] ILRM 373; *Kearney v Minister for Justice* [1986] IR 116; *Oblique Financial Services Ltd v Promise Production Co. Ltd* [1994] 1 ILRM 74.
[34]   *AG v Paperlink* [1984] ILRM 373.
[35]   *Cf.* O'Connor and Cooney, "Criminal Due Process, the Pre-Trial Stage and Self-Incrimination" (1980) Ir Jur 219.
[36]   See *O'Leary v AG* [1993] 1 IR 102 at 107, [1991] ILRM 454 at 458, 459, [1995] 1 IR 254 at 259, [1995] ILRM 259 at 267; *People (DPP) v D O'T* [2003] 4 IR 286 at 290.
[37]   See *Heaney v Ireland* [1994] 3 IR 593 at 604, [1994] 2 ILRM 420 at 430; *People (DPP) v P(P) M* [2010] IECCA 61 at 5; *Saunders v United Kingdom* (1996) 23 EHRR 329 at 337; *Thomson Newspapers Ltd v Canada (Director of Investigation and Research, Restrictive Trade Practices Commission)* [1990] 1 SCR 425 at 479, 480; *Sorby v The Commonwealth* (1983) 152 CLR 281 at 294.
[38]   (1983) 152 CLR 281.
[39]   (1983) 152 CLR 281 at 294.

discrete sub-right of an accused not to testify. This was recognised by the European Court of Human Rights in *Saunders v United Kingdom*[40]:

> "The right not to incriminate oneself, in particular, presupposes that the prosecution in a criminal case seek to prove their case against the accused without resort to evidence obtained through methods of coercion or oppression in defiance of the will of the accused. In this sense the right is closely linked to the presumption of innocence contained in Article 6(2) of the Convention."[41]

11–16 The right not to give evidence thus reinforces the adversarial nature of the criminal trial by preventing it acquiring an inquisitorial character through any form of compelled questioning either at the instance of the judge or the prosecution.

(b) Prevention of miscarriages of justice

11–17 One of most enduring justifications for the right to silence is that it protects the innocent[42] and helps to avoid miscarriages of justice by preventing the extraction by police of untrue confessions.[43] The importance of this factor in the development of the right to silence was acknowledged by Costello J in *Heaney v Ireland*[44] and was also identified in *Murray v United Kingdom*,[45] where the European Court of Human Rights said that, by "providing the accused with protection against improper compulsion" the right not to give evidence and the right to silence "contribute to avoiding miscarriages of justice and to securing the aim of art.6."[46]

11–18 Apart from directly helping to prevent miscarriages of justice, certain instrumental benefits are thought to flow from the right to silence. The first is that it helps to protect the integrity of the criminal justice system by preventing the abuse by the police of their powers and the ill-treatment of suspects in custody.[47] The second is that it reduces the reliance of the police on confessions and encourages the police

---

[40] (1996) 23 EHRR 313.

[41] (1996) 23 EHRR 313 at 337. See also *Heaney v Ireland* (2001) 33 EHRR 12 at [40].

[42] See *per* Byles J in *Barlett v Lewis* (1862) 12 CBNS 249 at 265: "The rule was intended for the protection of the innocent, and not for that of the guilty."

[43] *Heaney v Ireland* [1994] 3 IR 593 at 604, [1994] 2 ILRM 420 at 431; *EPA v Swalcliffe Ltd* [2004] IEHC 190 at [40], [2004] 2 IR 549 at 562, [2005] 1 ILRM 120 at 133; *AT & T Istel Ltd v Tully* [1993] AC 45 at 53, [1992] 3 All ER 523 at 530.

[44] [1994] 3 IR 593 at 604, [1994] 2 ILRM 420 at 431.

[45] (1996) 22 EHRR 29.

[46] (1996) 22 EHRR 29 at 60. See to the same effect: *Saunders v United Kingdom* (1996) 23 EHRR 313 at 337.

[47] This argument was strongly advanced by Wigmore, *Evidence* (3rd ed., 1940), Vol. VIII, §2251, p.309: "The real objection is that *any system of administration which permits the prosecution to trust habitually to compulsory self-disclosure as a source of proof must itself suffer morally thereby*. The inclination develops to rely mainly upon such evidence, and to be satisfied with an incomplete investigation of the other sources. The exercise of the power to extract answers begets a forgetfulness of the just limitations of that power. The simple and peaceful process of questioning breeds a readiness to resort to bullying and to physical force and torture. If there is a right to an answer, there soon seems to be a right to the expected answer— that is, to a confession of guilt. Thus the legitimate use grows into the unjust abuse; ultimately, the innocent are jeopardized by the encroachments of a bad system. Such seems to have been the course of experience in those legal systems where the privilege was not recognised." See to similar effect *Validity of Section 92(4) of the Vehicles Act 1957 [Sask]* [1958] SCR 608 at 619; *S. v Thebus* (2003) (2) SACR 319 at [55].

to obtain non-testimonial evidence, which is likely to be more reliable, to support a conviction.[48]

11–19   Although this rationale is primarily advanced to justify the right to silence, it also has some application to the right not to give evidence because it has been argued that this sub-right protects those accused persons who, though innocent, would be bad witnesses and might convict themselves because of a bad performance in the witness box.[49]

(c) Fairness

11–20   As a reaction against the abuses of the inquisitorial procedures of the Court of Star Chamber and the High Commission, a view gained currency that it was unfair to compel a man to convict himself out of his own mouth.[50] This view was adverted to by Shanley J in *Re National Irish Bank*[51] who identified as one of the justifications for the right not to incriminate oneself that "the prospect of an accused's guilt being extracted or established solely on his own testimony ... was offensive to the common law's latter day sense of 'fair play'".[52]

11–21   A modern variation on this theme is the argument that the right protects the accused from "cruel choices". This justification was articulated in *Murphy v Waterfront Commission*[53] by Goldberg J who said, in the context of right not to give evidence, that the privilege against self-incrimination reflected "our unwillingness to subject those suspected of crime to the cruel trilemma of self-accusation, perjury or contempt". The same idea is to be found in the judgment of Lord Mustill in *R. v Director of the Serious Fraud Office, ex p. Smith*[54] who referred to the instinct of the common law "that it is contrary to fair play to put the accused in a position where he is exposed to punishment whatever he does. If he answers, he may condemn himself out of his own mouth; if he refuses he may be punished for his refusal".[55] This theory was, however, rejected by Martens J in trenchant terms in his dissenting opinion in *Saunders v United Kingdom*[56]:

> "I pass over—as in my view defective—such 'rationales' as that these immunities prevent a suspect from being subjected to '*cruel* choices', or that it is *unethical* to compel somebody to

---

[48]   The incentives for police to over-rely on confessions were vividly summarised in the anecdotal tale recited by Sir James Fitzjames Stephens, *History of the Criminal Law* Vol. I, (London: Macmillan & Co., 1883), p.342, where he relates the explanation of a police officer in India as to why torture was sometimes applied to prisoners: "There is a great deal of laziness in it. It is far pleasanter to sit comfortably in the shade rubbing red pepper into a poor devil's eyes than to go about in the sun hunting up evidence."

[49]   See Charleton and McDermott, "Constitutional Aspects of Non-Jury Courts" (2000) 6 BR 141 at 143.

[50]   *Cf.* Gilbert, *The Law of Evidence* (Dublin, 1794), who argued that the privilege against self-incrimination followed "the law of nature, which commands every man to endeavour his own preservation" (quoted by O'Flaherty J in *Heaney v Ireland* [1996] 1 IR 580 at 588, [1997] 1 ILRM 117 at 126).

[51]   [1999] 3 IR 145 at 153, 154, [1999] 1 ILRM 321 at 329.

[52]   Bentham, *Rationale of Judicial Evidence*, b. IX, pt. IV, c. III (Bowring's ed., vol. VII, pp.452ff) pilloried two early versions of this theory which he termed "the old woman's reason" and the "fox-hunter's reason" as misguided concessions to the guilty.

[53]   (1964) 378 US 52 at 55.

[54]   [1993] AC 1, [1992] 1 All ER 456.

[55]   [1993] AC 1 at 32, [1992] 1 All ER 456 at 465.

[56]   (1996) 23 EHRR 313 at [9], n.74.

collaborate in bringing about his own doom. Such 'rationales' cannot justify the immunities under discussion since they obviously presuppose that the suspect is guilty, for an innocent suspect would not be subject to such choices nor bring about his own ruin by answering questions truthfully! Innocent suspects are, therefore, not treated cruelly or ethically, whilst guilty suspects should not complain that society does not allow them to escape conviction by refusing to answer questions or otherwise hiding evidence."[57]

11–22   This argument is compelling and it is, therefore, somewhat surprising that the cruel choices argument stills maintains currency at the highest judicial level and received an uncritical judicial airing in *Re National Irish Bank*.[58]

C. Development of the Right

1. Introduction

11–23   Once established, the right not to incriminate oneself very quickly came to be viewed as a cardinal principle of the common law and the principle of *nemo tenetur se ipsum accusare* was variously described as "one of the most sacred principles in the law",[59] and "a maxim of our law as settled, as important, and as wise as almost any other in it".[60] It, thus, became very firmly entrenched at common law as a fundamental right[61] and it is not surprising therefore, that the right has been afforded protection in the constitutions of a number of common law countries[62] and international conventions.[63]

11–24   Most importantly, the right has been held by European Court of Human Rights

---

[57]   See, to the same effect, the comments of Dennis, "Instrumental Protection, Human Right or Functional Necessity? Reassessing the Privilege Against Self-Incrimination" (1995) 54 CLJ 342 at 359, that: "An innocent suspect would, at least in theory, have nothing to lose by answering questions truthfully. There is therefore no cruelty involved in requiring the innocent suspect to speak. Once the true nature of the premise is recognised the argument loses much of its claim to moral force. It becomes difficult to accept that the interest of a guilty person in escaping conviction by not disclosing evidence of the crime is worthy of official legal protection."

[58]   [1999] 1 ILRM 321 at 329 (*per* Shanley J), [1999] 1 ILRM 343 at 350, 351 (*per* Barrington J).

[59]   *Re Worrall, ex parte Cossens* (1820) Buck 531 at 540 (*per* Lord Eldon).

[60]   *R. v Scott* (1856) 7 Cox CC 164 at 171 (*per* Coleridge J).

[61]   See *Pyneboard Pty v Trade Practices Commission* (1982) 152 CLR 328 at 345, 45 ALR 609 at 621 and *Sorby v The Commonwealth* (1983) 152 CLR 281 at 311, 312; 46 ALR 237 at 260, where the right not to incriminate oneself was treated as a common law right.

[62]   See the Fifth Amendment to the United States Constitution (no person "shall be compelled in any criminal case to be a witness against himself"); s.11(c) of the Canadian Charter of Rights and Freedoms which confers on an accused person, the right "not to be compelled to be a witness in proceedings against that person in respect of the offence" and s.7 which protects the right to silence as a principle of fundamental justice (see *R. v Hebert* [1990] 2 SCR 151); and s.25(d) of the New Zealand Bill of Rights which specifies as one of the minimum rights of a person charged with an offence, in relation to the determination of the charge, "[t]he right not to be compelled to be a witness or to confess guilt". For a discussion of the right not to incriminate oneself in Canadian law, see Watson, "Talking About the Right to Remain Silent" (1991) 34 Crim LQ 106 and Ratushny, *Self-Incrimination in the Canadian Criminal Process* (Toronto: Carswell, 1979).

[63]   See art.14(3)(g) of the International Covenant for the Protection of Civil and Political Rights and art. 8(2)(g) of the American Convention on Human Rights.

to be protected under art.6 of European Convention of Human Rights,[64] with the Court explaining in *Murray v United Kingdom*,[65] that:

> "Although not specifically mentioned in Article 6 of the Convention, there can be no doubt that the right to remain silent under police questioning and the privilege against self-incrimination are generally recognised standards which lie at the heart of the notion of fair procedure under Article 6. By providing the accused with protection against improper compulsion by the authorities these immunities contribute to avoiding miscarriages of justice and to securing the aim of Article 6."[66]

11–25   As will be seen below, the jurisprudence of the European Court of Human Rights has had an influence on the Irish case law in this area and since the enactment of the European Convention on Human Rights Act 2003, that influence has grown.

2. Jurisprudence of the Irish and European Courts

11–26   The constitutional basis and parameters of the right not to incriminate oneself has been developed in a series of cases and it is, perhaps, helpful to discuss these in tandem with the relevant European case law.

(a) The right to silence

11–27   The seminal case in relation to the constitutional basis for the right not to incriminate oneself and, more particularly, the right to silence, is *Heaney v Ireland*.[67] The plaintiffs had been arrested under s.30 of the Offences Against the State Act 1939. While in custody, they were asked to account for their movements pursuant to s.52 of the Offences Against the State Act 1939. This section provides that, where a person is detained under s.30 of the Act, a member of the Garda Síochána may demand a full account of that person's movements and actions during any specified period and all information in his possession in relation to the commission or intended commission by another person of any offence under any section of the Act or any scheduled offence. Under s.52(2), it is an offence to fail or refuse to give an account or information when requested to do so, and the plaintiffs, having refused to provide such an account, were convicted of an offence. They subsequently issued proceedings challenging the constitutionality of s.52 on the basis, *inter alia*, that it infringed their right to silence.

11–28   In the High Court, Costello J, after reviewing the decisions of the House of Lords in *R. v Director of Serious Fraud Office, ex parte Smith*[68] and *AT & T Istel Ltd*

---

[64]   See *Funke v France* (1993) 16 EHRR 297 at 326; *Murray v United Kingdom* (1996) 22 EHRR 29 at 60; *Saunders v United Kingdom* (1997) 23 EHRR 313 at 337; *Heaney v Ireland* (2001) 33 EHRR 12 at [40]; *Quinn v Ireland* [2000] ECHR 690.

[65]   (1996) 22 EHRR 29.

[66]   (1996) 22 EHRR 29 at 60. See to similar effect, *Saunders v United Kingdom* (1996) 23 EHRR 313 at 337; *Serves v France* [1997] ECHR 82; *Heaney v Ireland* (2001) 33 EHRR 12 at [40]; *JB v Switzerland* [2001] ECHR 324; *Allan v United Kingdom* [2002] ECHR 702 at [44]. One small point of distinction is that in *Murray*, the Court referred to the twin rights of the right to silence and the privilege against self-incrimination but in subsequent cases has referred to the rights to silence and not to incriminate oneself. The latter equates to what is described in this chapter as the right not to give evidence.

[67]   [1994] 3 IR 593, [1994] 2 ILRM 420 (HC), [1996] 1 IR 580, [1997] 1 ILRM 117 (SC). The issue of the constitutional status of the right had previously been raised but not decided in *Re McAllister* [1973] IR 238 at 242, 243 and *People (DPP) v Quilligan (No.3)* [1993] 2 IR 305 at 323.

[68]   [1993] AC 1, [1992] 3 All ER 456.

v Tully,[69] reached the following conclusions about the nature and ambit of the right to silence existing at common law[70]:

> "(1) The right to silence can arise in a variety of different circumstances. The nature and scope of the right and the reasons why it was conferred by law can differ in significant ways and will depend on the circumstances in which it is conferred and exercised.
>
> (2) The right to silence can properly be referred to as an immunity or a privilege against self-incrimination. This immunity has also been termed by the Supreme Court "the right to protection against self-incrimination".[71]
>
> (3) When a person is arrested as a suspect and subsequently charged with an offence two discrete immunities are conferred by the common law. The common law recognises (a) the immunity against self-incrimination of a suspect and, (b) the immunity against self-incrimination of an accused person during his trial...
>
> (4) The common law immunity against self-incrimination also exists in favour of a person who is subject to interrogation by a person in authority other than a police officer...
>
> (5) Parliament has, apart from the provisions of s.52 of the Act of 1939, limited the exercise of these common law immunities."

11–29 The learned judge then went on to consider the submission of the plaintiff that these common law immunities were constitutionally entrenched rights protected, in particular, by Art.38.1. His task in this regard was identified as being to decide whether they were "basic concepts of justice" protected by that article.[72] He considered first the immunity of an accused at his trial not to be obliged to give evidence or adduce evidence and not to be questioned against his will (described in this chapter as the right not to give evidence). Having regard to its lineage as a long established principle of the common law and its protection on the international plane, he was satisfied that:

> "the concept is such a long-standing one and so widely accepted as basic to the rules under which criminal trials are to be conducted that it should properly be regarded as one of those which comes within the terms of the guarantee of a fair trial contained in Article 38, section 1".[73]

11–30 Turning next to the right to silence enjoyed by a suspect in custody, he rejected the submission that this could not be protected by Art.38.1 which was restricted, in the ambit of its protection, to the *trial* of persons on criminal charges. He noted that the fairness of a trial may be compromised by what has happened prior to it and stated that "if the right to silence of a suspect can properly be regarded as a basic requirement for our system of criminal justice then it would be protected by this Article".[74] Although this immunity was of much later origin, it was nonetheless constitutionally protected in comparable legal systems and had been recognised by the European Court of Human Rights in *Funke v France*.[75] He was, thus, satisfied that the immunity conferred on suspects was also protected by Art.38.1.

11–31 This right was not, however, absolute and in assessing the constitutional validity of s.52, the learned judge employed the test of proportionality laid down by the Supreme Court of Canada in *Chaulk v R*.[76] Thus, the objective of the impugned provision

---

[69] [1993] AC 45, [1992] 3 All ER 523.
[70] [1994] 3 IR 593 at 603–604, [1994] 2 ILRM 420 at 428–429.
[71] *People (DPP) v Quilligan (No.3)* [1993] 2 IR 305 at 323.
[72] [1994] 3 IR 593 at 605, [1994] 2 ILRM 420 at 430.
[73] [1994] 3 IR 593 at 606, [1994] 2 ILRM 420 at 430.
[74] [1994] 3 IR 593 at 606, [1994] 2 ILRM 420 at 431.
[75] (1993) 16 EHRR 297 at 326.
[76] [1990] 3 SCR 1303 at 1335–1336.

had to be of sufficient importance to warrant overriding a constitutionally protected right relating to pressing and substantial concerns in a free and democratic society and the means chosen had to pass a proportionality test, *viz.* (a) be rationally connected to the objective and not be arbitrary, unfair or based on irrational considerations; (b) impair the right as little as possible; and (c) be such that their effects on rights are proportional to the objective.[77]

11–32 Dealing first with the object of s.52, Costello J noted that the section is only operable when Part V of the 1939 Act is in force which requires a proclamation to the effect that the Government is satisfied that the ordinary courts are inadequate to secure the effective administration of justice and the preservation of public peace and order. It was clear from a consideration of 1939 Act that s.52 was designed to assist the police in their investigation into serious crimes of a subversive nature involving the security of the State. This object was one for which a legislature in a democratic state was entitled to legislate and thus, the first limb of the proportionality test was satisfied. Turning to the second limb, he was satisfied that the section was based on rational considerations and this left for consideration the issues as to whether it impaired the suspect's rights as little as possible and whether its effects were proportional to the objective which the section sought to achieve.

11–33 The learned judge had earlier identified the purpose of the right to silence enjoyed by a suspect as being to avoid the risk of untrue confessions being obtained from him or her whilst in police custody, and while a provision which requires a suspect to give information under pain of punishment if he or she refuses to do so undoubtedly increased that risk, he pointed out that a number of other protections were afforded to persons arrested under s.30[78] which minimised that risk. Having regard to these protections and the object of s.52, which was the investigation and punishment of serious subversive crime, he concluded that "the restriction on the right to silence imposed by the section cannot be regarded as excessive and that it is proportionate to the objective which it is designed to achieve".[79]

11–34 After dismissing submissions that s.52 infringed the presumption of innocence and imposed an inquisitorial trial in breach of the plaintiff's right to an adversarial trial,[80] the learned judge went on to reject the contention that the right to silence was an unspecified personal right within the meaning of Art.40.3.1 on the basis that it was not one of the "personal rights" protected by the article but rather "one of those fundamental civil rights arising from a free democratic society established by the Constitution which obtains protection elsewhere".[81] It is, thus, evident that Costello J, in deciding to elevate the right not to incriminate oneself to constitutional status, was primarily impelled by the non-substantive rationales—hence the focus on the prevent of miscarriages of justice and the grounding of the right in Art.38.1.

11–35 Although the Supreme Court upheld the conclusion that s.52 was

---

[77] [1994] 3 IR 593 at at 608–609, [1994] 2 ILRM 420 at 432–433.
[78] These had been summarised by Finlay CJ in *People (DPP) v Quilligan (No.3)* [1993] 2 IR 305 at 321.
[79] [1994] 3 IR 593 at 610, [1994] 2 ILRM 420 at 434.
[80] He pointed out (at 611, 434) that, although the right not to give evidence enjoyed by an accused at his trial is based on the rejection of an inquisitorial type of trial, the right to silence of a suspect in custody is derived from different principles.
[81] [1994] 3 IR 593 at 611–612, [1994] 2 ILRM 420 at 435.

constitutional,[82] a very different approach was taken both in relation to the locus of the right to silence and the extent of permissible statutory interference with it.[83] Starting with the constitutional foundation of the right, O'Flaherty J, delivering a judgment with which the other members of the Court concurred, expressly reserved his opinion in relation to the question of whether Art.38 was applicable in this type of case. He accepted that what happens in the pre-trial period may have an adverse effect on the due course of a trial but took the view that nothing touching on the due course of a trial arose as a result of the failure to answer questions because that failure constituted a separate and distinct offence. Instead, drawing on the idea of correlative rights adopted in *Education Company of Ireland Ltd v Fitzpatrick (No.2)*,[84] he preferred to rest the decision of the Court on "the proposition that the right to silence is but a corollary to the freedom of expression that is conferred by Article 40".[85]

11–36 The learned judge went on to draw a distinction "between the absolute entitlement to silence as against the entitlement to remain silent when to answer would give rise to self-incrimination".[86] He took the view that, where a person was "totally innocent of any wrongdoing as regards his movements, it would require a strong attachment to one's apparent constitutional rights not to give such an account when asked pursuant to statutory requirement".[87] He thus identified the issue before the Court as being one of whether there was "an encroachment against the right not to have to say anything that might afford evidence that is self-incriminating".[88]

11–37 In considering this issue, he drew attention to the qualifying language in Art.40 which states that the guarantee of freedom of expression is subject to public order and morality, which restrictions also applied to the correlative right to silence. Therefore, in his view, the State is entitled to encroach on the right of the citizen to remain silent in pursuit of its entitlement to maintain peace and order. The question for the consideration of the Court was whether the power given to the Garda Síochána by the section was proportionate to the objects to be achieved by the legislation, *i.e.* a test of proportionality had to be applied. In answering this question, the learned judge drew attention to the exceptional nature of s.52 which was contained in Part V of the Act:

> "It is in this context that the problem which arises in the present case falls to be resolved. On the one hand, constitutional rights must be construed in such a way as to give life and reality to what is being guaranteed. On the other hand, the interest of the State in maintaining public order must be respected and protected. We must, therefore, ask ourselves whether the restriction which s.52 places on the right to silence is any greater than is necessary having

---

[82] [1996] 1 IR 580, [1997] 1 ILRM 117.

[83] For a scathing critique of the decision of the Supreme Court in *Heaney* and its "crude ends-means analysis", see Hogan, "Constitutional Law—The Right to Silence after *National Irish Banks* and *Finnerty*" (1999) 21 DULJ 176.

[84] [1961] IR 345.

[85] [1996] 1 IR 580 at 585, [1997] 1 ILRM 117 at 123. It should be noted that, by designating Art.40.6.1°.i as the locus of the right to silence, the court appears to have ignored a line of authority to the effect that the guarantee of free expression contained in that article is restricted to the protection of convictions and opinions and does not extend to the dissemination of factual information (see *AG v Paperlink* [1984] ILRM 373; *Kearney v Minister for Justice* [1986] IR 116; *Oblique Financial Services Ltd v Promise Production Co. Ltd* [1994] 1 ILRM 74). It was held by Costello J (as he then was) in *Paperlink* that the right to communicate factual information is, instead, protected by Art.40.3.1.

[86] [1996] 1 IR 580 at 586, [1997] 1 ILRM 117 at 124.

[87] [1996] 1 IR 580 at 586, [1997] 1 ILRM 117 at 124.

[88] [1996] 1 IR 580 at 586, [1997] 1 ILRM 117 at 124.

regard to the disorder against which the State is attempting to protect the public...the State is entitled to encroach on the right of the citizen to remain silent in pursuit of its entitlement to maintain public peace and order. Of course, in this pursuit the constitutional rights of the citizen must be affected as little as possible. As already stated, the innocent person has nothing to fear from giving an account of his or her movements, even though on grounds of principle, or in the assertion of constitutional rights, such a person may wish to take a stand. However, the Court holds that the *prima facie* entitlement of citizens to take such a stand must yield to the right of the State to protect itself. *A fortiori*, the entitlement of those with something relevant to disclose concerning the commission of a crime to remain mute must be regarded as of a lesser order."[89]

11–38 The Court, therefore, concluded that there was a proper proportionality in s.52 between any infringement of the citizen's rights with the entitlement of the State to protect itself and the section was constitutional.[90]

11–39 One of the most notable features of the decision of the Supreme Court in *Heaney* was, undoubtedly, the lack of enthusiasm displayed by the Court for the right to silence. In his judgment, O'Flaherty J quoted the dictum of Lord Mustill in *R. v Director of Serious Fraud Office, ex p. Smith*,[91] that "statutory interference with the right is almost as old as the right itself" and proceeded to catalogue, without any apparent doubt as to their constitutional validity, a number of statutory provisions which evinced "a legislative intent to abrogate, to various extents, the right to silence, in a myriad of contrasting circumstances".[92] Thus, in an apparent reversal of the normal order of constitutional adjudication, legislative encroachment set the parameters of a right rather than the other way around. The source of this disenchantment with the right is not difficult to identify as, in a number of passages in the judgment, O'Flaherty J echoed the Benthamite view that the right to silence is one which benefits only the guilty.

11–40 The decision in *Heaney* is, in any event, of little precedential value given the subsequent decision of the European Court of Human Rights in *Heaney v Ireland*[93] that the conviction of the applicants for failure to comply with s.52 constituted a breach of art.6 of the European Convention on Human Rights. In *Heaney*, the contention advanced by the State that s.52 did not violate the Convention because of the range of protections open to a person arrested under that provision was rejected by the Court because none of these served to reduce the degree of compulsion imposed by s.52 or the choice presented thereby which was to provide the information requested or face a term of imprisonment. The Court also rejected the submission that s.52 was a reasonable measure on the basis that, following the decision in *Re National Irish Bank*,[94] a statement made pursuant to the section could not be admitted in evidence against the author and derivative evidence could only be admitted if the trial judge considered it fair and equitable to do so. The Court pointed out that the legal position

---

[89] [1996] 1 IR 580 at 589–590, [1997] 1 ILRM 117 at 127–128. *Cf. Gilligan v Criminal Assets Bureau* [1998] 3 IR 185 at 230, where McGuinness J criticised a submission put forward by the respondent on the basis that it was a sophisticated version of the "the innocent have nothing to fear" argument which she regarded as being insufficient to offset a threat to the privilege against self-incrimination.

[90] See also *Markey v Minister for Justice* [2011] IEHC 39 at [42]–[44], [2012] 1 IR 62 at 79–80 where Kearns P reiterated that the right to silence is not absolute and that legislative modification is permissible provided that it is proportionate.

[91] [1993] AC 1 at 40, [1992] 3 All ER 456 at 472.

[92] [1996] 1 IR 580 at 588, [1997] 1 ILRM 117 at 126.

[93] (2001) 33 EHRR 12. See also *Quinn v Ireland* [2000] ECHR 690.

[94] [1999] 3 IR 145, [1999] 1 ILRM 321.

with regard to the admissibility of statements made in response to a demand under s.52 was uncertain at the time that the applicants were questioned[95] and the applicants had been given conflicting information. The Court, therefore, concluded that:

> "... the 'degree of compulsion', imposed on the applicants by the application of section 52 of the 1939 Act with a view to compelling them to provide information relating to charges against them under that Act, in effect, destroyed the very essence of their privilege against self-incrimination and their right to remain silent."[96]

11–41   The Court went on to consider the contention advanced by the State that s.52 was a proportionate response to the subsisting terrorist and security threat and reflected the need to ensure the proper administration of justice and the maintenance of public peace and order. It concluded that these considerations could not "justify a provision which extinguishes the very essence of the applicants' rights to silence and against self-incrimination guaranteed by Article 6(1) of the Convention".[97] In addition, given the close link identified between the right to silence and the presumption of innocence guaranteed by art.6(2), the Court found that this had also been violated.

11–42   Influenced, perhaps, by the jurisprudence of the European Court of Human Rights, greater solicitude for the right to silence was displayed by Kearns P in *Dokie v DPP*.[98] He held that s.12 of the Immigration Act 2004, which created an offence for a non-national to fail to give a satisfactory explanation for his inability to produce a passport or document establishing identity, breached the right not to incriminate oneself because silence in the face of a demand would amount to a failure to provide a satisfactory explanation and, thus, would become part of the commission of the offence.

11–43   However, it should be noted that not every compulsion to provide information, even on pain of criminal penalty, will result in a violation of art.6. In *O'Halloran and Francis v United Kingdom*,[99] the applicants were the owners of vehicles which had been caught speeding by speed cameras. In order to establish that the applicants were the drivers at the material times, the police invoked s.172 of the UK Road Traffic Act 1988 which requires the registered keeper of a vehicle or any other person to provide the police with information relating the identity of the driver of the vehicle on an occasion when the driver allegedly committed an offence. It is an offence not to provide this information when requested to do so and the applicants contended that this constituted a violation of their right to remain silent and the privilege against self-incrimination. However, the Grand Chamber rejected the contention that any direct compulsion to provide incriminating evidence will automatically result in a violation:

> "The applicants contended that the right to remain silent and the right not to incriminate oneself are absolute rights and that to apply any form of direct compulsion to require an accused person to make incriminatory statements against his will of itself destroys the very essence of that right. The Court is unable to accept this. It is true, as pointed out by the applicants, that in all the cases to date in which "direct compulsion" was applied to require an actual or potential suspect to provide information which contributed, or might have contributed, to his conviction, the Court has found a violation of the applicant's privilege against self-incrimination. It does not, however, follow that any direct compulsion will automatically result in a violation. While the right to a fair trial under Article 6 is an unqualified right, what constitutes a fair

---

[95]   It should be noted that the decision in *People (DPP) v McGowan* [1979] IR 45 indicated that such statements were admissible.
[96]   (2001) 33 EHRR 1 at [55].
[97]   (2001) 33 EHRR 1 at [58].
[98]   [2010] IEHC 110 at [38], [2011] 1 IR 805 at 820.
[99]   [2007] ECHR 544, (2007) 46 EHRR 397.

trial cannot be the subject of a single unvarying rule but must depend on the circumstances of the particular case."[100]

11–44   In the circumstances of the case and having regard, in particular, to the regulatory regime in issue including the nature of the offence, the limited nature of the information sought and the purpose for which it could be used, the Court considered that the essence of the applicants' right to remain silent and their privilege against self-incrimination has not been destroyed so that there was no violation of Art.6(1).[101]

(b) Inferences from silence

11–45   The constitutionality of provisions permitting inferences to be drawn from the exercise of the right to silence was considered in *Rock v Ireland*.[102] The case involved a challenge to ss.18 and 19 of the Criminal Justice Act 1984 which allow inferences to be drawn at trial from the failure of an accused to account for certain objects, substances or marks, or his or her presence at a particular place. Unsurprisingly, at the hearing before the Supreme Court,[103] the State placed heavy reliance on the decision in *Heaney*. However, Hamilton CJ, delivering the judgment of the Supreme Court, stated that *Heaney* did not automatically dispose of the issues raised. He highlighted two significant differences between s.52 and ss.18 and 19. First, as emphasised by the Supreme Court in *Heaney*, Part V of the 1939 Act contains exceptional provisions which are intended to deal with circumstances where there is an extraordinary threat to public order, and perhaps even to the security of the State. In contrast, the 1984 Act was a piece of ordinary criminal legislation. Second, although an accused is liable to imprisonment for up to six months for failure to comply with s.52, no adverse inferences could be drawn at his trial. However, failure to comply with ss.18 or 19 could lead to the drawing of an inference which, in turn, could result in an accused being convicted of an offence (carrying a sentence of anything from five years to life) in circumstances where there might otherwise have been insufficient evidence. He was, therefore, of the view that the consequences of non-compliance with ss.18 and 19 were potentially more serious than those of non-compliance with s.52.

11–46   In assessing the constitutionality of the sections, Hamilton CJ stated that the question to be considered by the Court was whether the restrictions which the impugned sections placed on the privilege were any greater than necessary to enable the State to fulfil its constitutional obligation and, in his view, they were not:

> "It is the opinion of this Court that, in enacting sections 18 and 19 of the 1984 Act, the legislature was seeking to balance the individual's right to avoid self-incrimination with the right and duty of the State to defend and protect the life, person and property of all its citizens. In this situation, the function of the Court is not to decide whether a perfect balance has been achieved, but merely to decide whether, in restricting individual constitutional rights, the legislature have acted within the range of what is permissible. In this instance, the Court finds

---

[100] [2007] ECHR 544, (2007) 46 EHRR 397 at [53].

[101] See also *Krumphloz v Austria* [2010] ECHR 341 where the decision in *O'Halloran and Francis* was distinguished. See, generally, Birdling, "Self-incrimination goes to Starusbourg: *O'Halloran and Francis v United Kingdom* (2008) 12 E & P 58; Spencer, "Curbing Speed and Limiting the Right to Silence" [2007] CLJ 531. Burns, "Good to Talk?" (2007) 157 NLJ 1454.

[102] [1997] 3 IR 484, [1998] 2 ILRM 35.

[103] The constitutionality of the sections had been upheld by Murphy J in the High Court (unreported, High Court, 10 November 1995) in a judgment that was delivered between that of the High Court and Supreme Court in *Heaney*.

they have done so, and must accordingly uphold the constitutional validity of the impugned statutory provisions."[104]

11–47   While Hamilton CJ accepted that the sections could lead to the conviction of an accused of a serious offence in circumstances where he or she might otherwise have been acquitted, there were two important limiting factors at work. Firstly, he pointed out that an inference could not form the basis for a conviction in the absence of other evidence. Secondly, he stated that an inference adverse to the accused could only be drawn where the court deemed it proper to do so.

11–48   The decision in *Rock* provides little guidance as to the circumstances in which it is permissible for the legislature to permit inferences to be drawn from the exercise of the right to silence. It is surprising that there was no consideration by the Court of the decision of the European Court of Human Rights on this issue in *Murray v United Kingdom*.[105] The applicant in that case had been convicted on the basis of inferences drawn by the trial judge under arts 4 and 6 of the Criminal Evidence (Northern Ireland) Order 1988 from the fact that he had not given evidence at his trial and he had refused to account for his presence at a particular place when requested to do so. He contended that he had thereby been deprived of a fair trial contrary to art.6 of the Convention but this contention was rejected by the European Court of Human Rights. The Court identified the issue before it as being whether the right not to give evidence and the right to silence were absolute rights or whether the exercise of those rights could, in any circumstances be used against an accused and stated:

> "On the one hand, it is self-evident that it is incompatible with the immunities under consideration to base a conviction solely or mainly on the accused's silence or on a refusal to answer questions or to give evidence himself. On the other hand, the Court deems it equally obvious that these immunities cannot and should not prevent that the accused's silence, in situations which clearly call for an explanation from him, being taken into account in assessing the persuasiveness of the evidence adduced by the prosecution."[106]

11–49   The Court was thus of the opinion that the right not to give evidence and the right to silence were not absolute and it did not accept "that an accused's decision to remain silent throughout criminal proceedings should necessarily have no implications when the trial court seeks to evaluate the evidence against him".[107] The Court declined, however, to lay down definitive guidelines as to the circumstances in which adverse inferences could be drawn from silence stating:

> "Whether the drawing of adverse inferences from an accused's silence infringes Article 6 is a matter to be determined in the light of all the circumstances of the case, having particular regard to the situations where inferences may be drawn, the weight attached to them by the national courts in their assessment of the evidence and the degree of compulsion inherent in the situation."[108]

11–50   The Court acknowledged that the threat of the drawing of inferences involves a "certain level of indirect compulsion". However, the Court pointed out that the

---

[104] [1997] 3 IR 484 at 501, [1998] 2 ILRM 35 at 50. Even though the learned Chief Justice set out the test of proportionality that had been applied by Costello J in *Heaney v Ireland* [1994] 3 IR 593, it appears that the Court's conclusion was based, not on the application of that test, but rather on the application of the principles laid down in *Tuohy v Courtney* [1994] 3 IR 1 at 47, with regard to the balancing of competing rights which were also quoted with approval in his judgment.
[105] (1996) 22 EHRR 29.
[106] (1996) 22 EHRR 29 at 60.
[107] (1996) 22 EHRR 29 at 61.
[108] (1996) 22 EHRR 29.

applicant had, in fact, remained silent and distinguished the case from that of *Funke v France*[109] where the bringing of criminal proceedings to compel that applicant to provide information exerted such a degree of compulsion as to destroy the very essence of the right not to incriminate oneself.

(c) The privilege against self-incrimination

11–51   The right not to incriminate oneself, this time in its manifestation as the privilege against self-incrimination, was considered in *Re National Irish Bank*.[110] In that case, company inspectors appointed to investigate the affairs of National Irish Bank sought directions that persons (whether natural or legal) were not entitled to refuse to answer questions put by the Inspectors or to refuse to provide documents on the grounds that the answers or documents might tend to incriminate them. The relevant statutory provisions were s.10 of the Companies Act 1990 which placed a duty on officers and agents of a company being investigated and other persons in possession of relevant information to co-operate with the inspectors and to produce documents and answer questions and s.18 which provided that an answer given by a person could "be used in evidence against him".[111]

11–52   The first question was whether, as a matter of statutory interpretation, s.10 abrogated the privilege against self-incrimination and, having examined the statutory scheme and purpose of Part II of the 1990 Act, its legislative history and the case law, Shanley J in the High Court concluded that it did:

> "I am satisfied that I cannot construe Section 10 of the Act as preserving the privilege against self-incrimination: to do so would require a qualification on the duty imposed by the Act such that the duty to answer applied *save where the giving of such answers would tend to incriminate the witness.* No such saver appears in Section 10. It seems to me clear that, had the Oireachtas intended to save the privilege, it could easily have done so. I am satisfied therefore that as a matter of statutory interpretation a witness may not refuse to answer questions on the grounds that his answers might tend to incriminate him and that Section 10 has the effect of impliedly abrogating the right against self-incrimination."[112]

11–53   The learned judge then turned to the issue of whether the section constituted a proportional restriction of the privilege in accordance with the principles laid down in *Heaney*. He took the view that the restriction which the impugned sections placed on the privilege was not any greater than necessary to enable the State to fulfil its constitutional obligations:

> "It is, of course, a legitimate objective of the State, and entirely in the public interest, to lay bare frauds and dishonest stratagems, and where the only means of effectively achieving such an objective is to provide an investigative procedure without a right to silence (as in the instant case) then one can properly assert that the restrictions imposed by s.10 on the right to

---

[109] (1993) 16 EHRR 297. See also *Heaney v Ireland* (2001) 33 EHRR 12.

[110] [1999] 3 IR 145, [1999] 1 ILRM 321. For a discussion of this and earlier decisions, see McGuckian, "Confessions and the Constitution" (2004) 26 DULJ 272.

[111] See Redmond, "The Privilege Against Self-Incrimination in the Context of the 1990 Companies Act" (1992) 2 ICLJ 118, for a discussion of the approach adopted by the English courts in respect of comparable provisions, and Middleton, "Legislation Comment: The Corporations Legislation (Evidence) Amendment Act 1992 (Cth)" (1993) 17 Crim LJ 339 for a discussion of the Australian approach.

[112] [1999] 3 IR 145 at 162, [1999] 1 ILRM 321 at 337 (emphasis in the original).

silence are no greater than is necessary to enable the State to fulfil its constitutional obligations of ensuring equality before the law and of protecting the property rights of every citizen."[113]

11–54 The conclusion that s.10 was a proportional restriction on the right to silence was endorsed by the Supreme Court. Consistent with the decision in *Heaney*, Barrington J, delivering the judgment of Court, drew a distinction between the protection afforded by Art.40.6.1 and that afforded by Art.38.1 on the basis that the former applied to the obtaining of statements while the latter was applied to their use at trial. The appellant had also sought to rely on Art.40.3 but, as far as Barrington J was concerned, this merely reinforced the protection conferred by these articles. He proceeded, therefore, to deal with the question of whether s.10 impermissibly abridged the privilege against self-incrimination protected by Art.40.6.1° (as reinforced by Art.40.3). He referred to the decision in *Heaney* and observed that, while the investigation of commercial fraud may often be a much less serious matter than the matters that were under investigation in that case, it was, nevertheless, potentially a matter of great importance in modern society. He also referred to *Saunders v United Kingdom*[114] where the European Court of Human Rights had characterised the equivalent powers of Inspectors in the UK as essentially investigative in nature and declined to extend the guarantees set forth in art.6(1) of the Convention to the exercise of those powers on the basis that it "would in practice unduly hamper the effective regulation in the public interest of complex financial and commercial activities".[115] He was likewise of the view that, "if there are grounds for believing that there is malpractice or illegality in the operation of the banking system, it is essential, in the public interest, that the public authorities should have power to find out what is going on".[116] He thus concluded that the powers given to the inspectors under s.10 were no greater than the public interest required and, accordingly, interviewees were not entitled to refuse to answer questions properly put to them.

11–55 In the High Court, Shanley J had declined to go any further and deal with the issue of the admissibility of answers compelled under s.10 and evidence derived therefrom at any subsequent criminal trial. Barrington J acknowledged that the question of admissibility of evidence in the course of a criminal trial is primarily a matter for the trial judge[117] and he did not wish to pre-empt that decision. Nevertheless he thought, the inspectors having sought guidance in relation to the matter, that it was appropriate to address this issue which, in accordance with the distinction drawn earlier between the protection afforded by Arts 40.6.1 and 38.1, fell to be dealt with under Art.38.1.

11–56 The learned judge referred again to the decision in *Saunders* where it had been held that the use of compelled answers given in reply to questions put by the inspectors at a subsequent criminal trial had violated the applicant's right to a fair trial under art.6(1) of the Convention:

> "[T]he general requirements of fairness contained in Article 6, including the right not to incriminate oneself, apply to criminal proceedings in respect of all types of criminal offences without distinction, from the most simple to the most complex. The public interest cannot be invoked to justify the use of answers compulsorily obtained in a non-judicial investigation to incriminate the accused during the trial proceedings…Moreover the fact that statements were

---

[113] [1999] 3 IR 145 at 166, [1999] 1 ILRM 321 at 341 (emphasis in the original).
[114] (1996) 23 EHRR 313.
[115] (1996) 23 EHRR 313 at 337.
[116] [1999] 3 IR 145 at 180, [1999] 1 ILRM 321 at 353.
[117] See *O'C v Smith*, unreported, Supreme Court, 24 January 1997.

made by the applicant prior to his being charged does not prevent their later use in criminal proceedings from constituting an infringement of the right."[118]

11–57   A similar conclusion had also been reached by the South African Constitutional Court in *Ferreira v Levin*.[119]

11–58   Barrington J pointed out that it is a fundamental rule at common law that a confession is not admissible unless it is voluntary[120] and, after reviewing the relevant Irish case law dealing with the admissibility of statements obtained by statutory compulsion,[121] he was satisfied that the better view was that the admission of a compelled statement would constitute a breach of the guarantee of a trial in due course of law in Art.38.1:

> "It appears to me that the better opinion is that a trial in due course of law requires that any confession admitted against an accused person in a criminal trial should be a voluntary confession and that any trial at which an alleged confession other than a voluntary confession were admitted in evidence against the accused person would not be a trial in due course of law within the meaning of Article 38 of the Constitution and that it is immaterial whether the compulsion or inducement used to extract the confession came from the executive or from the legislature."[122]

11–59   Applying that conclusion and the presumption of constitutionality[123] to the interpretation of s.18, he was satisfied that the better interpretation of the section was that it did not authorise the admission of compelled incriminating statements.[124] However, he acknowledged that the question of whether a confession was voluntary was one of fact which was to be decided, in the first instance, by the trial judge.

11–60   The decision in *Re National Irish Bank* was subsequently considered by Kearns J in *Dunnes Stores Ireland Company v Ryan*[125] in the context of a challenge to the constitutionality of another provision of the Companies Act 1990, s.19. This section empowers the Minister for Enterprise, Trade and Employment, or an authorised officer appointed by him or her, to give directions and to require the production of books and documents by companies and other persons and to require explanations in relation to them in certain circumstances. Under subs.(5), it is an offence not to produce books or documents or provide an explanation and, further, under subs.(6), it was provided that a statement made by a person in compliance with a requirement imposed by virtue of the section could "be used in evidence against him".

11–61   In dealing with the contentions advanced as to the constitutionality of the section, the learned judge pointed out that it was, first, necessary to identify the precise aspect of the right not to be compelled to incriminate oneself that was in issue. He quoted with approval from the judgment of Lord Mustill in *R. v Director of Serious*

---

[118] (1996) 23 EHRR 31 at 340.
[119] 1996 (1) BCLR 1, 1996 (1) SA 984.
[120] *People (AG) v Cummins* [1972] IR 312 at 322.
[121] See also *People (AG) v Gilbert* [1973] IR 383, *People (DPP) v Madden* [1977] IR 336, and *People (DPP) v McGowan* [1979] IR 45.
[122] [1999] 3 IR 145 at 186–187, [1999] 1 ILRM 321 at 359.
[123] See *East Donegal Co-Operative Ltd v AG* [1970] IR 317.
[124] In *Quinn v O'Leary* [2004] IEHC 232 at [90], [2004] 3 IR 128 at 162, O Caoimh J reached the unsurprisingly conclusion that, applying this reasoning, a statement made in response to a request pursuant to s.52 of the Offences Against the State Act 1939 would not admissible unless the court was satisfied that it was voluntary.
[125] [2002] 2 IR 60.

Fraud Office, ex p. Smith[126] and took the view that the list of immunities enumerated by his Lordship indicated "a hierarchy of different situations in which the requirement not to infringe the right has a greater or lesser degree of importance".[127] He bolstered this conclusion by reference to the judgment of Sachs J in *Ferreira v Levin*[128] who had stated:

> "In my view, the breach of the long-standing right not to compelled to incriminate oneself out of one's own mouth would, in any context, raise a question of constitutional freedom. At the same time, the absence of an explicitly stated generalised right against self-incrimination in the Constitution, indicates that the operation of the principle outside of a trial situation is weaker than within. The privilege against self incrimination should therefore neither be reduced to a restricted immunity confined to the trial situation, nor be enlarged so as to become an absolute right to be used on all occasions. Its application depends on time, place and context. The closer to a trial situation, the more powerful the principle; the more remote from a trial, the weaker it will be."

11–62   He pointed out that, in the case before him, there was no suggestion of a trial nor was there a suspect who had been arrested and thus he was of the view that the case was at the lower end of the spectrum.

11–63   Dealing, first, with the constitutionality of subs.(5), the learned judge identified a number of factors which weighed in favour of its constitutionality. He noted that the objective of s.19 was to obtain sight of books and documents and, given the objective reality of the existence of this information, the requirement for protection was less compelling. It was also necessary to have regard to the strong public interest in good corporate governance which had been identified previously in *Re National Irish Bank*. Further, he accepted the point made by counsel for the respondents that those who enjoy the benefits of incorporation must also accept the concomitant duties and obligations of incorporation. Taking all of these considerations into account, he was satisfied that s.19(5) did not fail the proportionality test as laid down by the Supreme Court in *Heaney*:

> "The compulsion to produce books and documents is completely unobjectionable and the requirement to answer questions of a fairly limited nature under s.19 does not, in my view, constitute an infringement of Article 40 of the Constitution of sufficient substance to warrant condemning the section when weighed in the balance with the countervailing public interest in good corporate governance."[129]

11–64   Turning then to the question of the constitutionality of subs.(6), Kearns J took the view that the effect of the section was that:

> "The examinee is obliged, on pain of punishment for a refusal, to answer questions or provide explanations which may be incriminating and which may be used in subsequent criminal proceedings against him."[130]

11–65   He referred to the judgment of Barrington J in the Supreme Court in *Re National Irish Bank* where the issue of admissibility was determined to revolve around the question of voluntariness and expressed some degree of dissatisfaction with the degree of uncertainty which this approach created:

> "This approach essentially 'parks' any issue as to later use or admissibility raised under s.10,

---

[126] [1993] AC 1, [1992] 3 All ER 456.
[127] [2002] 2 IR 60 at 116.
[128] 1996 (1) BCLR 1 at 272, 1996 (1) SA 984.
[129] [2002] 2 IR 60 at 119.
[130] [2002] 2 IR 60 at 119.

leaving it to be dealt with on a case by case basis. This approach inevitably means that the use or admissibility of incriminatory material is not determined by any objective standard, but remains an essentially subjective test going to whether the will of the witness was overborne in the particular circumstances. It would appear to displace the objective test of self-incrimination at common law."[131]

11–66 The learned judge went on to draw a distinction between s.19 and s.10 of the Companies Act 1990 on the basis that, under s.10, a person who was unwilling or refused to answer had the opportunity of having the reasonableness of that refusal tested as an issue by the court whereas a person interviewed under s.19 had no such scope for dissent because failure to answer automatically led to the commission of an offence. On that basis, he distinguished the decision in *Re National Irish Bank*:

> "Can it be said that there is any scope for 'voluntariness' with regard to the answering of questions in this framework? In my view there is not ... the fact that any answer given may be used in later proceedings can only constitute a further pressure on the interviewee to keep silent, so that his only 'choice' is between a conviction on refusal, and self-incrimination in the context of a later prosecution on making answer."[132]

11–67 He, therefore, concluded that, by not immunising answers given from later use in criminal proceedings, s.19(6) infringed the minimum invasion test enunciated by Costello J in *Heaney*.

11–68 This decision is somewhat difficult to square with that in *Re National Irish Bank*. Although the learned judge is correct that there was a greater degree of compulsion involved in s.19 in comparison to s.10 and this cast doubt on whether an explanation or statement furnished pursuant to the section could ever be regarded as voluntary and, thus, admissible, this did not lead inexorably or even logically to a finding that s.19(6) was unconstitutional. This is because the core of the holding in *Re National Irish Bank* on this point was that an involuntary confession is inadmissible and s.18 (which dealt with the admissibility of statements made pursuant to s.10) was interpreted as not authorising the admission of involuntary statements. It is difficult to see why the same reasoning was not applied in *Dunnes Stores* and the conclusion reached, applying the presumption of constitutionality, that s.19(6) was constitutional even if, as a practical matter, the circumstances in which a statement obtained pursuant to s.19 would be found to be voluntary would be very rare.

3. Parameters of the Right not to Incriminate Oneself

11–69 Some tentative conclusions in relation to the constitutional basis and parameters of the right not to incriminate oneself can be drawn from the case law discussed above. The first is that, although there is considerable confusion because of the different nomenclature used in the various decisions, there has been implicit recognition that the general right not to incriminate oneself encompasses three distinct sub-rights, namely: (1) the right not to give evidence enjoyed by an accused person in a criminal trial; (2) the right to silence enjoyed by a suspect when questioned by gardaí; and (3) the privilege against self-incrimination enjoyed by witnesses in criminal and civil proceedings and also by persons who appear before non-judicial tribunals or are questioned by persons with investigative powers.

---

[131] [2002] 2 IR 60 at 121.
[132] [2002] 2 IR 60 at 122.

11–70 Secondly, in analysing any statutory infringement upon the right not to incriminate oneself, it is very important to distinguish between these discrete sub-rights because the constitutional basis and the degree of abridgement that is constitutionally permissible depends on which sub-right is involved. In general terms, there appears to be a sliding scale in the protection of the right depending on the proximity of a criminal trial with the right not to give evidence at one end of the scale and the privilege against self-incrimination at the other end.

11–71 It is apparent from the case law examined above that the right not to give evidence is considered to be a core ingredient of the right to a fair trial protected by Art.38.1 of the Constitution and art.6(1) of the Convention respectively. As such, the scope for legislative abridgement of this right is very limited. This is evident from the comments of Barrington J in *Re National Irish Bank*[133] that it was doubtful if the principle of proportionality had any useful application in this context because a criminal trial was either conducted "in due course of law" or not. However, while a provision that compelled an accused to testify or imposed a sanction upon him or her for not testifying would, undoubtedly, be considered to violate Art.38.1 of the Constitution and art.6(1) of the Convention, it appears that a statutory provision that allowed the tribunal of fact to draw certain limited inferences from the failure of an accused to testify may not do so.[134]

11–72 Turning next to the right to silence enjoyed by a suspect who is questioned by gardaí, here again the scope for statutory curtailment is somewhat limited. As seen above, the Supreme Court in *Heaney* upheld the constitutionality of s.52 of the Offences Against the State Act 1939 on the basis that it was a proportional interference with the right to silence although this decision is of doubtful precedential status having regard to the decision of the European Court of Human Rights in *Heaney v Ireland*[135] coupled with the incorporation of the European Convention on Human Rights into domestic law. However, it appears from the decisions in *Rock v Ireland*[136] and *Murray v United Kingdom*[137] that legislation may provide for inferences to be drawn, in certain circumstances, from the failure of an accused to answer questions or account for certain matters when questioned by gardaí or other agents of the executive before trial.[138]

11–73 Finally, with regard to the privilege against self-incrimination, it appears that the constitutionality of any statutory provisions requiring persons to answer questions or furnish particular information will fall to be decided on the basis of whether they involve a proportionate restriction of the substantive constitutional rights of the person affected including, in particular, the right not to communicate, but also the rights to personal autonomy and privacy. It is apparent from the decisions in *Heaney* and *Re National Irish Bank,* that the test of proportionality will not be difficult to satisfy if a legitimate and substantial public interest can be identified. However, due to the constitutionalised voluntariness test, it will be much more difficult to have such answers admitted in

---

[133] [1999] 3 IR 145 at 180, [1999] 1 ILRM 321 at 353.
[134] See *Murray v United Kingdom* (1996) 22 EHRR 29 at 60–61. *Cf. Rock v Ireland* [1997] 3 IR 484, [1998] 2 ILRM 35.
[135] (2001) 33 EHRR 12.
[136] [1997] 3 IR 484, [1998] 2 ILRM 35.
[137] (1996) 22 EHRR 29 at 60–61.
[138] But *cf. People (DPP) v Bourke Waste Removal Ltd* [2010] IEHC 122 at [35], [2011] 1 ILRM 126 at 146 where McKechnie J held that an adverse inference for the purpose of deciding on an application for costs could not be drawn from the exercise by an accused of his right to silence.

evidence. Indeed, Barrington J's judgment clearly suggests that there is an *absolute* rule, grounded in Art.38.1, against the admission of compelled statements. If this is so, then it would appear that the net effect of the decision is that the Oireachtas may readily abridge the privilege against self-incrimination but if the statute in question does not make provision for the sterilisation of any compelled answers,[139] that result will effectively be achieved by the application of the voluntariness test. On the basis of the decision in *Saunders v United Kingdom*,[140] it appears that the result under the Convention will be similar.

D. Right not to Give Evidence

1. Introduction

11–74   As seen above, the right of a person not to be compelled to give evidence or answer questions at his or her trial developed in reaction to the abuses of the Courts of Star Chamber and High Commission. The origin and nature of this right were explained as follows by Costello J in *Heaney v Ireland*:

> "An *accused's immunity* was developed from the objections taken by the common law courts to the abuses arising from court procedures involving the judicial interrogation of accused persons. As a result an accused cannot be compelled to adduce evidence on his own behalf and is entitled to remain silent during it, and not to be questioned either by the prosecution or the presiding judge."[141]

11–75   This right was given statutory recognition in the Criminal Justice (Evidence) Act 1924. Section 1 of that Act made an accused a competent but not compellable witness for the defence with para.(a) specifically providing that "a person so charged shall not be called as a witness in pursuance of this Act except upon his own application".

2. Comment by the Prosecution

11–76   The proscription on compulsion of the accused to give evidence in para.(a) of s.1 of the Criminal Justice (Evidence) Act 1924 is reinforced by para.(b) which stipulates that "the failure of any person charged with an offence, or of the wife or husband, as the case may be, of the person so charged, to give evidence shall not be made the subject of any comment by the prosecution".[142] In *People (DPP) v P(P)M*,[143] Macken J, delivering the judgment of the Court of Criminal Appeal, explained that:

> "The object of s.1(b) of the Act of 1924, especially in its time context, was to prevent the prosecution, directly or indirectly, from negating the right to silence and the presumption of innocence from which it flows, by inveighing against an accused's failure to give evidence in his own defence (itself a relatively new right in 1924)."

11–77   Having regard to its purpose, she emphasised the importance of adherence to this prohibition:

> "The terms of the statutory provision in s.1(b) recited at the commencement of this judgment are very clear. The reasons for it are equally abundantly clear. As mentioned above, the applicant

---

[139] See, *e.g.* s.254(4) of the Companies Act 1963 and s.21(4) of the Bankruptcy Act 1988.
[140] (1996) 23 EHRR 313. *Cf. JB v Switzerland* [2001] ECHR 324.
[141] [1994] 3 IR 593 at 604, [1994] 2 ILRM 420 at 429.
[142] *Cf. R. v Miller* (1999) 131 CCC (3d) 141 dealing with the equivalent Canadian provision.
[143] [2010] IECCA 61 at [5].

carries with him at all times the constitutional right to be presumed innocent until proven guilty beyond reasonable doubt. The onus of doing so rests at all times on the prosecution and does not shift to the accused, who is not obliged to establish his innocence. That being so, the parties engaged in a trial must be extremely careful not to suggest or infer in any way, or pass comment, or make statements, from which an adverse inference might be drawn by the jury which could affect that presumption of innocence. Because the presumption of innocence exists, and because no burden transfers to the accused to establish his innocence, the fact that he does not give evidence, as he is not obliged to, cannot be a basis from which any inference can be drawn."[144]

11–78   In that case, the prosecution justified a comment on the failure of the accused to give evidence in relation to a particular matter on the basis that cross-examination of prosecution witnesses had taken place on the premise that evidence would be called on that issue from the accused but he was not, in fact, called. However, that justification was rejected with the Court making it clear that any statements by counsel for the accused or the manner in which cross-examination was conducted was not a reason for breaching the clear prohibition in s.1(b).

11–79   When dealing with the consequences of the breach of s.1(b), the Court followed the approach adopted in earlier cases[145] that this could be remedied by the charge of the trial judge. As to whether this was the case:

"It seems to the Court that that exercise must depend, to some extent at least, on the nature of the alleged failure to comply with the section of the Act, the context in which such failure arises, and the precise nature of the judge's charge or recharge in relation to same. However, the nature of the wording of the section is such that, if a contravention occurs, and if it is to be remedied in the charge, as appears to be capable of being done according to case law, nevertheless in seeking to do so and save in unusual circumstances not arising in this case, the trial judge should do so in clear, certain, and wholly unambiguous terms, having regard nevertheless for the undoubted disadvantage which may also arise for a defence when such a remedial charge must be given."[146]

11–80   Having considered the terms of the judge's charge and recharge, the Court was not satisfied that it was directed sufficiently to the offending words so as to cure the infringement of s.1(b) and this ground of appeal succeeded.

3. Inferences from Failure to Give Evidence

11–81   In *People (DPP) v Finnerty*,[147] Keane J regarded it as beyond dispute that:

"the exercise by an accused person of his right not to give evidence in his own defence cannot lead to any inferences adverse to him being drawn by the court and that, in the case of the trial by jury, the jury must be expressly so advised by the trial judge."[148]

---

[144] [2010] IECCA 61 at [9]. She went on to note that, even where the burden of proof in respect of a particular defence shifted to the accused, he was not obliged to give evidence himself.

[145] See *People (DPP) v Maples*, unreported, Court of Criminal Appeal, 30 March 1992.

[146] [2010] IECCA 61 at [10]–[11].

[147] [1999] 4 IR 364, [2000] 1 ILRM 191.

[148] [1999] 4 IR 364 at 376, [2000] 1 ILRM 191 at 203. *Cf.* the earlier authorities of *People (AG) v Travers* [1956] IR 110 (conviction overturned on the basis that the trial judge told the jury that it was his duty to refer to the applicant's failure to give evidence and that they could take into account the fact that he had not gone into the witness box); *People (AG) v Reynolds* (1958) 1 Frewen 184 (objection to comments of trial judge in his charge on failure of the accused to give evidence and to clear up matters of doubtful incriminating effect dismissed); *People (AG) v Sykes* [1958] IR 355 (comments of trial judge on failure of accused to explain certain incriminating material found on his trousers could not have misled the jury into thinking that there was an onus on the accused to do so). See further, Palmer, "Silence in Court—The Evidential Significance

11–82   Thus, if an accused decides to exercise his or her right not to give evidence, a trial judge is required to point out to the jury that an accused is not obliged to give evidence and to counter any temptation that they might have to draw adverse inferences from his failure to testify by instructing them that they are not entitled to do so.[149] It was held by the Court of Criminal Appeal in *People (DPP) v White*[150] that no particular form of words is required and, in that case, a direction to the jury that they should not hold it against the accused that he had exercised his right to silence was held to provide the mandated explanation "in a very clear and express format" which would be understood by a jury of ordinary people of reasonable intelligence.[151]

11–83   The trial judge must be careful not to instruct the jury in terms which suggests that there is any sort of onus on the accused to provide an explanation of his conduct or that they are entitled to take the lack of an explanation from the accused in respect of incriminating facts into account in deciding whether to convict. In *People (DPP) v Coddington*,[152] the applicant had been convicted of possession of a controlled drug, cannabis, for the purpose of supply. One of the main planks of the prosecution case against him was evidence of the finding of a large sum of cash hidden in two locations at his residence. The trial judge, in his charge, commented that the jury were being invited by the defence to speculate as to the explanation for the money being there in circumstances where they had heard no evidence from the accused in relation to the matter. His charge was criticised by the Court of Criminal Appeal on the basis that it suggested to the jury that there was some onus on the accused to provide evidence of an innocent explanation for the presence of the money, and further, that an adverse inference should be drawn from the failure of the accused to give evidence in respect of a possible innocent explanation for the finding of the money. This, however, was clearly impermissible having regard to the principles laid down in *Finnerty*. Murray J, delivering the judgment of the Court, reiterated that:

> "[w]hile the trial judge may remind the jury of the fact that the accused had, as was his right,

---

of an Accused's Person's Failure to Testify" (1995) 18 UNSWLJ 130; Henchliffe, "The Silent Accused at Trial—Consequences of an Accused's Failure to Give Evidence in Australia" (1996) 19 U Queens LJ 137; and Gibson, "Adverse Judicial Comment" [1992] NZLJ 347.

[149] See also *People (DPP) v Hardiman* [2011] IECCA 69 (trial judge had discharged his obligation by warning the jury that they should be very careful about coming to any conclusion based on the failure of the accused to give an explanation); *People (DPP) v MK* [2005] IECCA 93 at [15], [2005] 3 IR 423 at 431 (charge of the trial judge was not inadequate by reason of his failure to tell the jury that they should not draw any adverse inference from the exercise by the accused of his right not to give evidence in circumstances where he informed the jury that the accused had a right of silence and they were not to take any consequence from his exercise of that right). *Cf. People (DPP) v Lavery*, unreported, Court of Criminal Appeal, *ex tempore*, 19 March 2002 (conviction was not quashed even though the Court accepted that it would have been better if the trial judge had not made reference in charge to a matter in respect of which the jury would have liked to have heard the evidence of the accused and if he had stated specifically that no inference should be drawn from the failure of the accused to give evidence in circumstances where he had emphasised that the accused did not have to give evidence and did not need to prove anything).

[150] [2011] IECCA 78 at [36]–[37].

[151] In *People (DPP) v MJ* [2014] IECCA 21, the trial judge had informed them that there was no obligation on an accused to give evidence and that he had an absolute right to remain silent. The contention that the jury could have misunderstood this direction as referring to his right to remain silent while in garda custody rather than his right not to give evidence was summarily rejected by the Court of Criminal Appeal which regarded any distinction between the phrase "the right to remain silent" and that of "the right not to give evidence" as more philosophical than practical.

[152] Unreported, Court of Criminal Appeal, 31 May 2001.

not given evidence in the trial, they had to be expressly instructed not to draw any inference from the exercise of that right."[153]

11–84 However, a trial judge is not totally precluded from commenting on the exercise by an accused of his or her right to silence provided that he or she does so fairly.[154] So, for example, the trial judge is entitled to point out to the jury that a defence put forward by the accused has not been substantiated in evidence. In *People (DPP) v Brazil*,[155] the trial judge had instructed the jury that the fact that the applicant had not given evidence was not proof of his guilt but pointed out that counsel could not give evidence on his behalf. Thus, although counsel for the applicant had told the jury that the applicant denied making certain inculpatory statements when interviewed by gardaí, the only evidence in relation to those statements was that of the gardaí and, in considering the explanation offered by counsel for the applicant, the jury was entitled to bear in mind that the applicant had not given evidence. This charge was impugned on the basis that the jury might have been left under the impression that they were entitled to use the fact that the applicant had not given evidence against him but, Keane CJ, delivering the judgment of the Court of Criminal Appeal, dismissed this contention:

> "In drawing the jury's attention to the fact that they were to decide this matter solely on the evidence that they had heard in court, while at the same time emphasising to them that it was the defendant's right not to give evidence and that they should not draw any inference adverse to him simply because he did not give evidence, the trial judge was doing no more than stating what the law is and the court is satisfied that the jury could not have been in any way misled by that statement."[156]

11–85 Indeed, he ventured the opinion that it would have been remiss of the trial judge not to instruct the jury to confine themselves to the evidence before them lest they were under the mistaken impression that they could give weight to the explanation that they had been told the applicant would have given had he given evidence.[157]

11–86 Furthermore, it is open to the tribunal of fact to have regard to the fact that the prosecution evidence in relation to certain issues has not been contradicted by the accused in deciding whether to convict. In *People (DPP) v Foley*,[158] the Court of Criminal Appeal rejected the submission that the applicant had been penalised because he had not given evidence on the basis that, if proper recognition were given to his entitlement not to give evidence, then his acquittal should have followed. Budd J explained that:

> "What the 'right to silence' amounts to is that an accused is entitled in the first instance to call on the prosecution to prove its case. *Prima facie*, his situation is that he does not have to give an explanation or give evidence. But if proof of guilt is forthcoming—if circumstances

---

[153] Unreported, Court of Criminal Appeal, 31 May 2001 at 8. In *People (DPP) v White* [2011] IECCA 78 at 37, it was observed that the reference to "any inference" in this passage was clearly intended to be a reference to adverse inferences.

[154] See *People (AG) v Reynolds* (1958) 1 Frewen 184 (trial judge entitled to comment on failure to give evidence provided that the comments are not unfair or to convey to a jury that there is an onus on an accused to prove his innocence); *People (DPP) v Connolly* [2003] 2 IR 1 at 5–6 (no inhibition on trial judge commenting on the accused's failure to give evidence so long as he does so fairly); *People (AG) v Travers* [1956] IR 110 at 114 (judge has a discretion as to whether to comment on the failure to give evidence "which should be discretely exercised").

[155] Unreported, Court of Criminal Appeal, 22 March 2002.

[156] Unreported, Court of Criminal Appeal, 22 March 2002 at 11–12.

[157] See also *People (DPP) v Connolly* [2003] 2 IR 1 at 5–6, where the decision in *Brazil* was approved and applied.

[158] [1995] 1 IR 267.

are laid before the court of trial that point to the guilt of the accused—then an accused must attempt to rebut the prosecution case by evidence or else suffer the consequences."[159]

11–87   Thus, it appears that, although the tribunal of fact cannot draw any adverse inferences from the failure of an accused to give evidence, it is something that may affect the weight to be attached to the evidence that has been adduced in the case. Nonetheless, it is important to remember that the legal burden remains on the prosecution to establish the guilt of the accused beyond a reasonable doubt and inferences drawn from the failure to give evidence should not be used to strengthen the prosecution case if it falls short of that standard.[160]

4. Waiver of the Right not to Give Evidence

11–88   As explained below, a witness who gives evidence in criminal proceedings enjoys a privilege against self-incrimination, *i.e.* he or she has a right "to refuse to answer a question ... when to do so would in the opinion of a court tend to expose such an individual to a real risk of criminal prosecution or penalty".[161] However, it would obviously create an anomalous situation if an accused could decide to give evidence setting out his or her defence and a favourable version of events but could invoke the privilege against self-incrimination so as to avoid any questions on cross-examination that would tend to incriminate him or her or show that he or she was guilty of the offence for which he or she was being tried. Therefore, s.1(e) of the Criminal Justice Act 1924 expressly provides that:

> "a person charged and being a witness in pursuance of this Act may be asked any question in cross-examination notwithstanding that it would tend to criminate him as to the offence charged".

11–89   This provision was considered in *Attorney General v Murray*[162] and it was held that the accused in that case, who had elected to give evidence, could be asked any question in the course of cross-examination that might tend to incriminate him as to the offence charged and that there was no restriction on such cross-examination except that contained in s.1(f) of the 1924 Act.[163] However, it should be noted that, in *Jones v DPP*,[164] a majority of the House of Lords held that the English equivalent of s.1(e) permits only such questions as tend directly to incriminate the accused as to the offence charged and does not permit questions which tend to do so indirectly.[165]

11–90   It appears that, if an accused is charged with more than one offence, it is not open to him or her to waive his or her right not to give evidence in respect of one offence only and retain its protection in respect of other offences. In *People (AG) v Reynolds*[166] the applicant had been convicted of one count of obtaining money by false pretences and one count of fraudulent conversion of property. The trial judge had allowed the defence to call the accused to give evidence in relation to the false pretences charge only and not to be cross-examined so as to incriminate himself on

---

[159] [1995] 1 IR 267 at 292.
[160] *R. v Noble* [1997] 1 SCR 874 at 921–923 (*per* Sopinka J).
[161] *Re National Irish Bank* [1999] 3 IR 145 at 153, [1999] 1 ILRM 321 at 329 (*per* Shanley J).
[162] [1926] IR 266.
[163] For a discussion of the restrictions on cross-examination imposed by s.1(f), see Chap.9.
[164] [1962] AC 635, [1962] 1 All ER 569.
[165] See also *Maxwell v DPP* [1935] AC 309, [1934] All ER 168 and for a general discussion, see Chap.9.
[166] (1958) 1 Frewen 184.

the fraudulent conversion charge. The Court of Criminal Appeal described this course of action as "unprecedented" and expressed the opinion that "the interests of justice were not served by this extraordinary and in our view incorrect procedure adopted by the trial Judge at the persuasion of applicant's counsel".[167]

E. Right to Silence

1. Introduction

11–91   As outlined above, the right to silence[168] developed in order to protect the right of an accused not to give evidence on the basis that, if an accused did not enjoy a right to silence at the pre-trial investigative stage, the immunity from testifying at trial would be "illusory".[169] The right to silence was of particular importance at a time when accused persons were incompetent witnesses on their own behalf in criminal trials, thus raising the spectre of a person being convicted on the basis of an alleged incriminating statement which they did not have the opportunity to rebut or challenge by giving evidence at the trial.[170] However, even after this disability had been removed, it was still considered to be an important safeguard against abuses by the police and unreliable confessions. Indeed, it is evident that there is a strong link between the right to silence and the voluntariness test,[171] one which has been strengthened by the holding in *Re National Irish Bank*[172] that Art.38.1 requires the exclusion of involuntary confessions.

2. Informing an Accused of the Right to Silence

11–92   A desire to ensure that a suspect was aware of his or her right to silence gave rise to the practice of administering a caution to the effect that he or she was not obliged to answer any questions but that whatever the person said would be taken down in writing and might be given in evidence. That practice later became formalised in the Judges' Rules which require a suspect to be cautioned before being questioned if he or she is in custody or a garda has made up his mind to charge him or her.[173] The purpose of the caution was explained by Murnaghan J in *Attorney General v Durnan (No.2)*[174] as follows:

> "The proper caution will bring home to the mind of the accused when he has been charged that he need not make any statement; but, on the other hand, that, if he does volunteer a statement, it may be used in evidence at his trial. This caution enshrines the result of long experience and it is no idle formula. The first part in substance warns the accused that on an occasion

---

[167] (1958) 1 Frewen 184 at 188 (*per* Maguire CJ).

[168] See generally, Daly, "Is Silence Golden? The Legislative and Judicial Treatment of Pre-trial silence in Ireland" (2009) DULJ 35; Coen, "The Decline of Due Process and the Right to Silence's Demise" (2008) 1 ICLJ 10; Jackson, "Re-conceptualizing the right to silence as an effective fair trial standard" (2009) 58 ICLQ 835.

[169] *R. v Hebert* [1990] 2 SCR 151 at 174 (*per* McLachlin J).

[170] See *R. v Director of Serious Fraud Office, ex p Smith* [1993] AC 1 at 32, [1992] 3 All ER 456 at 465, (*per* Lord Mustill); *Heaney v Ireland* [1996] 1 IR 580 at 589, [1997] 1 ILRM 117 at 126 (*per* O'Flaherty J).

[171] See *R. v Hebert* [1990] 2 SCR 151 at 173, (1990) 57 CCC (3d) 1 at 32 (*per* McLachlin J).

[172] [1999] 3 IR 145, [1999] 1 ILRM 321.

[173] See rules 2 to 5 of the Judges' Rules which are discussed in Chap. 8, section D.

[174] [1934] IR 540.

when it might reasonably be expected that some answer should be made the law does not require any answer; while the second part of the caution warns the accused that if he makes any statement it should be no glib or untrue excuse, and further, it being a principle that the prosecution must prove the guilt of the accused, it gives a warning that admissions made at the time may be used to prove the guilt of the accused."[175]

11–93   More succinctly, in *People (DPP) v Bowes*,[176] Fennelly J explained that: "The object of the usual caution is to inform the suspect that he is not obliged to answer any questions."

11–94   As noted above, it was held by the Supreme Court in *Heaney v Ireland*[177] that the right to silence is constitutionally protected by the guarantee of freedom of expression in Art.40.6.1°. One question raised by that decision that has yet to be addressed is whether the recognition of a constitutional foundation for the right to silence has had the effect of constitutionalising the requirement to give a caution. In *People (DPP) v Lynch*[178] Walsh J explained the justification for giving the caution as follows:

> "Generally speaking, nobody is obliged to answer any questions and, if one were to assume that everybody knows that that is the law, there would be no need for the warning: but practical experience has shown that there is a need for such a warning."[179]

11–95   It would be difficult to justify the courts taking an approach that was less protective of a suspect's interests now that the right to silence has constitutional status and, thus, a strong argument can be made that gardaí are required to inform a suspect that he or she has a right to silence.[180] If this concomitant right were to be recognised, it would have significant repercussions because, as matters stand, a failure to give a caution merely gives rise to a discretion to exclude any confession obtained thereafter[181] whereas a breach of the right to silence would, arguably, give rise to the application of the exclusionary rule as formulated in *People (DPP) v Kenny*[182] which would very likely result in the exclusion of a confession if a caution had not been given.

3. Exercise of the Right to Silence

11–96   If a suspect, having been informed of the right to silence, decides to exercise it, the question arises as to whether the gardaí are entitled to question the suspect. In *People (DPP) v Yu Jie*[183] the accused indicated on a number of occasions during an interview that he did not wish to answer any more questions but gardaí continued to

---

[175] [1934] IR 540 at 548.
[176] [2004] IECCA 44 at [31], [2004] 4 IR 223 at 238.
[177] [1996] 1 IR 580, [1997] 1 ILRM 117.
[178] [1982] IR 64, [1981] ILRM 389.
[179] [1982] IR 64 at 86, [1981] ILRM 389 at 400. *Cf. Travers v Ryan* [1985] ILRM 343, where it was held that the advice of a father to his minor son not to speak to gardaí was not an obstruction of justice.
[180] *Cf. Miranda v Arizona* (1966) 384 US 436 where it was held by the US Supreme Court that police officers were obliged to inform a suspect of his right to remain silent. However, it should be noted that it has been held in Canada that police are not under such an obligation: *R. v Farrell* (1992) 76 CCC (3d) 201; *R. v Smith* (1996) 105 CCC (3d) 58, 19.
[181] *McCarrick v Leavy* [1964] IR 225 at 236–238; *People (AG) v Cummins* [1972] IR 312 at 322–323; *People (DPP) v Buck* [2002] 2 IR 268 at 277.
[182] [1990] 2 IR 110.
[183] [2005] IECCA 95.

question him. The Court of Criminal Appeal rejected the contention that they had thereby breached his right to silence, with McCracken J stating:

> "A person may be held in custody and interviewed by the gardaí for the purpose of investigating a crime. The law protects any such person from self-incrimination by providing that there is a right to silence, and a person under questioning is not bound to answer any question, subject to a very few exceptions which are not relevant in the present case. However, there is no authority whatever for the proposition put forward on behalf of the Applicant that the questioning should have ceased when he indicated that he did not want to answer any more questions."[184]

11–97 When this issue was revisited by the Court of Criminal Appeal on an application for a certificate for leave to appeal to the Supreme Court,[185] it considered that this issue had been decided by the Supreme Court previously in *Lavery v Member in Charge, Carrickmacross Garda Station*[186] where it had been held that gardaí were entitled to interrogate a suspect and there was no entitlement to have a solicitor present during questioning. McCracken J also expressed the view that, if the contention that questioning had to cease was correct, it "would render nugatory" the provisions of s.4 of the Criminal Justice Act 1984, the purpose of which was the detention of suspects so that they could be interrogated and questioned.[187]

11–98 A similar conclusion was reached by the Canadian Supreme Court in *R. v Singh*.[188] Charron J, delivering the judgment of the majority, rejected the proposition that police must cease questioning when a detainee asserts his or her right to silence:

> "What the common law recognises is the individual's right to *remain* silent. This does not mean, however, that a person has the right *not to be spoken to* by state authorities. The importance of police questioning in the fulfilment of their investigative role cannot be doubted. One can readily appreciate that the police could hardly investigate crime without putting questions to persons from whom it is thought that useful information may be obtained. The person suspected of having committed the crime being investigated is no exception. Indeed, if the suspect in fact committed the crime, he or she is likely the person who has the most information to offer about the incident. Therefore, the common law also recognises the importance of police interrogation in the investigation of crime."[189]

11–99 However, there was more merit to the contention advanced in *Yu Jie* than allowed by the Court of Criminal Appeal. Authority for such a proposition is to be found in the decision of the US Supreme Court in *Miranda v Arizona*[190] where a majority of the Court, in an opinion delivered by Warren CJ, held:

> "If the individual indicates in any manner, at any time prior to or during questioning, that he wishes to remain silent, the interrogation must cease. At this point, he has shown that he intends to exercise his Fifth Amendment privilege; any statement taken after the person invokes his privilege cannot be other than the product of compulsion, subtle or otherwise. Without the right to cut off questioning, the setting of in-custody interrogation operates on the individual to overcome free choice in producing a statement after the privilege has been once invoked."[191]

11–100 Having regard to the recent decision of the Supreme Court in *People (DPP) v Gormley and White*,[192] where it was held that, when a suspect requests access to a

---

[184] [2005] IECCA 95 at [4].
[185] [2005] IECCA 137.
[186] [1999] 2 IR 390.
[187] [2005] IECCA 137 at [3].
[188] [2007] 3 SCR 405.
[189] [2007] 3 SCR 405 at [28].
[190] (1966) 384 US 436.
[191] (1966) 384 US 436 at 473–474.
[192] [2014] IESC 17, [2014] 1 ILRM 377. See, further Chap.8.

solicitor, questioning has to cease until such access is afforded, it can be argued that, similarly, when a suspect exercises his or her right to silence, that decision should be respected by gardaí who should not continue to question a suspect in an effort to get him or her to answer questions notwithstanding his or her expressed desire not to do so.

4. Inferences from the Exercise of the Right to Silence at Common Law

11–101   It is now well established that, except where statutory provision is made in that regard, inferences adverse to an accused may not be drawn from the exercise by an accused of his or her right to silence. Furthermore, he or she may not be cross-examined as to the reasons why the right was exercised or why facts relied upon in defence of the charges were not mentioned, nor may these matters be the subject of adverse comment by the judge when instructing the jury.

11–102   The leading authority is the decision of the Supreme Court in *People (DPP) v Finnerty*.[193] At the trial of the applicant on a charge of rape, counsel for the applicant cross-examined the complainant at considerable length and put a detailed exculpatory account of the incident which, he said, the applicant would give in evidence. Counsel for the prosecution was then granted liberty to prove that no such account had been given by the applicant during the period of his detention under s.4 of the Criminal Justice Act 1984 and that the applicant had maintained silence throughout. The applicant was also cross-examined as to his answers to questions put to him by the gardaí during his detention. The Court of Criminal Appeal held that there had not been any breach of the applicant's right to silence but certified a point of law of exceptional public importance as to whether (i) it was permissible for the prosecution to elicit from members of the Garda Síochána who interviewed the applicant that he had declined to say anything in relation to the complainant's accusations, and (ii) to cross-examine the applicant when he gave detailed evidence of his version of events on the night in question as to why he did not give that account when interviewed by the gardaí.

11–103   Delivering the judgment of the Supreme Court, Keane J (as he then was) pointed out that, at common law, a suspect enjoyed a right, subsequently enshrined in the Judges' Rules, to refuse to answer any questions at a defined stage of a criminal investigation and that the police were under an obligation to inform him or her of that right by means of the traditional caution. He considered next whether the Criminal Justice Act 1984 had altered this position and concluded that it had not.

11–104   The learned judge was of the view that the 1984 Act did not modify, in any way, the right of a suspect to refuse to answer questions or his or her entitlement under the Judges' Rules to be reminded of that right before any questioning begins. Therefore, even though there was no express requirement in the Criminal Justice Act 1984 or the Custody Regulations[194] to give a caution, he thought it clear that it should be given.[195] He fortified this conclusion by a consideration of the legislative

---

[193] [1999] 4 IR 364, [2000] 1 ILRM 191. *Cf.* the earlier authorities of *AG v Fleming* [1934] IR 166; *AG v Durnan (No.2)* [1934] IR 540; *People (AG) v Duggan* [1958] IR 116; *People (AG) v Saunders* [1958] IR 355; *People (DPP) v Maples*, unreported, Court of Criminal Appeal, 26 February 1996.

[194] The Criminal Justice Act 1984 (Treatment of Persons in Custody in Garda Síochána Stations) Regulations 1987 (SI No. 119 of 1987). See, generally, Chap.8, section E.

[195] Relying on the judgment of Walsh J in *People (DPP) v Quilligan* [1986] IR 495 at 508, [1987] ILRM 606 at 623, dealing with s.30 of the Offences Against the State Act 1939.

intention as manifested in the provisions of the 1984 Act. He pointed out that ss.18 and 19 (examined below) permitted the drawing of adverse inferences from the failure or refusal of a person arrested to account for the presence of certain objects in his or her possession or his or her presence at a particular place. Also notable was the lack of any general provision allowing inferences to be drawn along the lines of s.34 of the English Criminal Justice and Public Order Act 1994. He took the view that, had the Oireachtas intended to abridge the right of silence by allowing inferences to be drawn, it would have expressly so legislated and the absence of such a provision led "to the inevitable conclusion that no such general abridgement of the right of silence was intended to be effected where a person declined to answer questions put to him by the gardaí" when detained under s.4 of the 1984 Act.[196]

11–105   A consideration of the constitutional position also supported this conclusion. The right of suspects to remain silent in custody had been held to be a constitutional right in *Heaney v Ireland*[197] and the provisions of the 1984 Act had to be construed accordingly. Therefore, absent any express statutory provisions entitling a tribunal of fact to draw inferences from the silence of a suspect when questioned, it followed that this right was left unaffected by the 1984 Act save in those instances falling within the ambit of ss.18 and 19.

11–106   Having failed to discern any legislative intention in the 1984 Act to modify the common law or constitutional right to silence, he evinced little difficulty in concluding that it would be seriously undermined if juries were permitted to draw inferences from its exercise:

> "That right would, of course, be significantly eroded if at the subsequent trial of the person concerned the jury could be invited to draw inferences adverse to him from his failure to reply to those questions and, specifically, to his failure to give the questioning gardaí an account similar to that subsequently given by him in evidence. It would also render virtually meaningless the caution required to be given to him under the Judges' Rules.
>   It must also be borne in mind that it is a usual practice for solicitors to advise their clients while they are in custody, not to answer any questions put to them by the gardaí, if they consider that it would not be in their interests to do so. However, if the jury could be invited to draw inferences from the failure to reply to such questions, the result would be that persons in custody would have to be advised by solicitors that, notwithstanding the terms of the caution, it might be inimical to their client's interests not to make a full statement to the gardaí, thereby eroding further the right to silence recognised at common law."[198]

11–107   Two reasons why allowing the drawing of inferences would impermissibly undermine the right to silence can be identified in these paragraphs. The first is that, having regard to its terms, the caution can be construed as containing an implicit promise that the silence of a suspect will not be used in evidence against him or her. Having given the defendant that impression, it would be unfair to admit evidence of his or her silence in reliance on the caution. As Cory J put it in *R. v Chambers*[199]:

> "... it would be a snare and a delusion to caution the accused that he need not say anything in response to a police officer's question but nonetheless put in evidence that the accused clearly exercised his right and remained silent in the face of a question which suggested his guilt."[200]

---

[196]   [1999] 4 IR 364 at 379, [2000] 1 ILRM 191 at 206.
[197]   [1996] 1 IR 580, [1997] 1 ILRM 117.
[198]   [1999] 4 IR 364 at 379, [2000] 1 ILRM 191 at 206.
[199]   [1990] 2 SCR 1293.
[200]   [1990] 2 SCR 1293 at 1316. See also *R. v Robertson* (1975) 21 CCC (2d) 385 at 400 and *R. v Noble* [1997] 1 SCR 874 at 918–919.

11–108   The second reason is that, allowing comment on, or inferences to be drawn from, the exercise of the right to silence is, adopting the words of Douglas J in *Griffin v California*[201] to impose a penalty for exercising a constitutional privilege which "cuts down on the privilege by making its assertion costly". To these two reasons may be added a third, which is that to use silence as a basis for inferences is to treat it as communicative of guilt and as Sopinka J stated in *R. v Noble*[202]:

> "Just as a person's words should not be conscripted and used against him or her by the state, it is equally inimical to the dignity of the accused to use his or her silence to assist in grounding a belief in guilt beyond a reasonable doubt. To use silence in this manner is to treat it as communicative evidence of guilt ... and is contrary to the underlying purpose of the right to silence."[203]

11–109   When applying his conclusions in relation to the 1984 Act to the facts of the case, Keane J took the opportunity to lay down principles for guidance in future cases:

> "The principles applicable in a case such as the present where a defendant while detained under the provisions of the 1984 Act has refused to answer questions put to him[204] can be stated as follows:
> (1)   Where nothing of probative value has emerged as a result of such a detention but it is thought desirable that the court should be aware that the defendant was so detained, the court should be simply informed that he was so detained but that nothing of probative value emerged.[205]
> (2)   Under no circumstances should any cross-examination by the prosecution as to the refusal of the defendant during the course of his detention to answer any questions be permitted.
> (3)   In the case of a trial before a jury, the trial judge in his charge should, in general, make no reference to the fact that the defendant refused to answer questions during the course of his detention."[206]

11–110   Although the decision in *Finnerty* was ostensibly confined to the position of persons detained under s.4 of the 1984 Act, the principles laid down therein are, obviously, of much broader application and confirm the position previously established in the case law that it is impermissible for the tribunal of fact to draw inferences from, or for the trial judge to comment adversely on, the exercise by an accused of his or her right to silence.[207] The principles laid down therein have since been applied in a number of cases and appeals allowed where they have not been adhered to.[208]

---

[201] (1965) 380 US 609 at 614.

[202] [1997] 1 SCR 874.

[203] [1997] 1 SCR 874 at 920.

[204] It was held in *People (DPP) v Bowes* [2004] IECCA 44 at [24], [2004] 4 IR 223 at 226 that an accused does not exercise his right to silence and the principles laid down in *Finnerty* do not apply where, rather than remaining silent in response to questions, the accused has given an answer even if this does not amount to a clear admission.

[205] Where an accused has exercised his right of silence in respect of some of the questions asked but not others and evidence is adduced of the answers given, the formula that nothing of probative value emerged in the balance of the interview should be used: *People (DPP) v Bowes* [2004] IECCA 44 at [24], [2004] 4 IR 223 at 226.

[206] [1999] 4 IR 364 at 381, [2000] 1 ILRM 191 at 208.

[207] See *People (AG) v Quinn* [1955] IR 57 where the direction of the trial judge that the jury could take into account in support of the evidence of the complainant the fact that the applicant made no statement when charged, on the basis that an innocent man would have taken a different course of action, was held by the Court of Criminal Appeal to be "utterly wrong". *Cf.* Hogan, "The Right to Silence after *National Irish Bank* and *Finnerty*" (1999) 21 DULJ 176.

[208] See *People (DPP) v McCowan* [2003] 4 IR 349; *People (DPP) v McDermott*, unreported, Court of Criminal Appeal, 17 June 2002; *DPP v Roibu* [2012] IEHC 421.

11–111   In *People (DPP) v O'Reilly*[209] it was contended that the first of the principles laid down by Keane J in *Finnerty* had been breached in circumstances where a number of memoranda of interviews with the accused were admitted into evidence which had been edited so as excise material which was irrelevant or inadmissible. Given that details were given of the start and end time of the interviews, it was argued that it would be obvious to the jury that they were only being given a memorandum of a portion of the interview and this inevitably conveyed to the jury that the accused had exercised his right to silence during the interviews. However, the Court of Criminal Appeal, in a judgment delivered by Murray CJ, held that it was not the law that evidence from which it might be inferred that an accused exercised his right to silence should be excluded from the jury for that reason alone. It was noted that it would be impossible in many circumstances, such as where an accused failed to give evidence, to prevent matters coming before a jury from which they might infer that the accused exercised his right to silence. It was for this reason that a trial judge instructed the jury that an accused's failure to give evidence could not lead to any inference adverse to him being drawn by it. The Court distinguished the decision in *Finnerty* as being based on very different factual circumstances because the prosecution in the case before it had not invited the jury to infer that the accused had exercised his right to silence or to suggest that inferences should be drawn from the exercise of the right to silence and the jury had not been left under the impression that they were entitled to do so. On the contrary, the trial judge had given careful directions to the jury including a specific direction that what they had heard in evidence with regard to interviews with the applicant were his answers to relevant questions and that anything else that might have occurred was irrelevant and not of evidential value. Accordingly, the Court was satisfied that the trial judge had been correct to admit evidence of the portions of the interviews including the start and end times of the interviews which provided a framework for the evidence and was not prejudicial to the accused.[210]

5. Statutory Provisions Permitting Inferences to be Drawn from the Exercise of the Right to Silence

11–112   Statutory provision for inferences to be drawn from the exercise by a suspect of his or her right to silence[211] was first made in ss.18 and 19 of the Criminal Justice Act 1984 which permitted inferences to be drawn from the failure of an accused to account for an object, substance or mark or his or her presence in a particular place respectively. As noted above, the constitutionality of those provisions was upheld in *Rock v Ireland*.[212] Section 7 of the Criminal Justice (Drug Trafficking) Act 1996[213]

---

[209] [2009] IECCA 18.

[210] See also *People (DPP) v Kearney* [2009] IECCA 112 where the decision in *O'Reilly* was followed and it was held that the trial judge had correctly admitted evidence that there had been a number of interviews with the accused from which nothing of evidential value had arisen.

[211] See generally, Pattenden, "Inferences from Silence" [1995] Crim LR 602; Jackson, "Interpreting the Silence Provisions: The Northern Ireland Cases" [1995] Crim LR 587; Jackson, "The Right to Silence: Judicial Responses to Parliamentary Encroachment" (1994) 57 MLR 270; Thomas, "The So-Called Right to Silence" (1991) 14 NZULR 299; Stone, "Calling a Spade a Spade: the Embarrassing Truth about the Right to Silence" (1998) 2 CLJ 17; and Ayer, "The Fifth Amendment and the Inference of Guilt from Silence: *Griffin v California* after Fifteen Years" (1980) 78 Mich LR 841.

[212] [1997] 3 IR 484, [1998] 2 ILRM 35.

[213] See Ryan, "The Criminal Justice (Drug Trafficking) Act 1996: Decline and Fall of the Right to Silence?" (1997) 7 ICLJ 22; Ní Raifeartaigh, "The Criminal Justice System and Drug Related

introduced provision for inferences to be drawn in proceedings for a drug trafficking offence where an accused failed to mention any fact relied on in his or her defence in those proceedings, being a fact which in the circumstances existing at the time he or she could reasonably have been expected to mention. Similar provision was made in respect of scheduled offences for the purposes of Part V of the Offences Against the State Acts 1939 by s.5 Offences Against the State (Amendment) Act 1998. In addition, s.2 of that Act permitted inferences to be drawn from the failure by a person charged with membership of an unlawful organisation to answer any question material to the investigation of the offence. These statutory provisions were significantly overhauled by the Criminal Justice Act 2007[214] to broaden their application[215] and to introduce a number of safeguards in order to render their operation compatible with the jurisprudence of the European Court of Human Rights as to when inferences may be drawn consistent with the guarantee of a fair trial in art.6(1) of the European Convention on Human Rights.[216] This array of provisions permitting inferences to be drawn was added to in 2009[217] by the insertion of s.72A of the Criminal Justice Act 2006 which deals specifically with prosecutions relating to organised crime. The various statutory provisions will first be outlined and then some issues common to their operation will be discussed.

(a) Section 18 of the Criminal Justice Act 1984

11–113   Section 18(1) of the Criminal Justice Act 1984 ("the 1984 Act") (as substituted by s.28 of the Criminal Justice Act 2007[218]) provides as follows:

> (1)   Where in any proceedings against a person for an arrestable offence[219] evidence is given that the accused–
>
>   (a)   at any time before he or she was charged with the offence, on being questioned by a member of the Garda Síochána in relation to the offence, or
>
>   (b)   when being charged with the offence or informed by a member of the Garda Síochána that he or she might be prosecuted for it,[220]

Offending: Some Thoughts on Procedural Reforms" (1998) 4 (1) BR 15; and Keane, "Detention Without Charge and the Criminal Justice (Drug Trafficking) Act 1996" (1997) 7 ICLJ 1.

[214] The changes effected by the Criminal Justice Act 2007 are based, in part, on recommendations made in the *Final Report of the Balance in the Criminal Law Group* (2007), p.92. See, generally, McGillicuddy, "Restrictions on the Right to Silence under the Criminal Justice Act 2007 – Part 1" (2008) 18(3) ICLJ 77 and McGillicuddy, "Restrictions on the Right to Silence under the Criminal Justice Act 2007 – Part 2" (2008) 18(4) ICLJ 112.

[215] Although the obvious purpose of the amendments effected by the Criminal Justice Act 2007 was to improve the operation of the various provisions, in *People (DPP) v Fitzpatrick* [2012] IECCA 74 at [40], O'Donnell J was critical of the quality of the draftsmanship of s.18 which he did not regard as easy to interpret "as a coherent whole", commenting that "it may be that the section is the product of an eclectic process of amendment, rather than a product of one overall coherent approach". He suggested (at [43]) that there "is a case for the streamlining of the Act so that it operates in a coherent and comprehensible way".

[216] See *Murray v United Kingdom* (1996) 22 EHRR 29; *Condron v United Kingdom* (2001) 31 EHRR 1; *Averill v United Kingdom* (2001) 31 EHRR 36.

[217] By s.9 of the Criminal Justice (Amendment) Act 2009.

[218] Transitional provisions are contained in ss.28(2) and (3) of the 2007 Act.

[219] Subsection (9) provides that "arrestable offence" has the same meaning as in s.2 of the Criminal Law Act 1997 (as amended by s.8 of the Criminal Justice Act 2006).

[220] One of the significant changes in the amended s.18 is that there is no longer a requirement that a suspect have been arrested in order for it to apply. Thus, as noted by O'Donnell J in *People (DPP) v Fitzpatrick* [2012] IECCA 74 at [40], a suspect does not have to be in custody and the section can, in theory, be invoked where a suspect is questioned by gardaí in public.

was requested by the member to account for any object, substance or mark, or any mark on any such object, that was-

(i) on his or her person,

(ii) in or on his or her clothing or footwear,[221]

(iii) otherwise in his possession, or

(iv) in any place in which he or she was during any specified period,

and which the member reasonably believes may be attributable to the participation of the accused in the commission of the offence and the member informed the accused that he or she so believes, and the accused failed or refused to give an account, being an account which in the circumstances at the time clearly called for an explanation from him or her when so questioned, charged or informed,[222] as the case may be, then, the court, in determining whether a charge should be dismissed under Part IA of the Criminal Procedure Act 1967[223] or whether there is a case to answer and the court (or, subject to the judge's directions, the jury) in determining whether the accused is guilty of the offence charged (or of any other offence of which he or she could lawfully be convicted on that charge) may draw such inferences from the failure or refusal as appear proper;[224] and the failure or refusal may, on the basis of such inferences, be treated as, or as capable of amounting to, corroboration of any evidence in relation to which the failure or refusal is material."[225]

11–114 The section contains a number of important safeguards in relation to the drawing of inferences. First, subs.(2) stipulates that a person cannot be convicted of an offence solely or mainly on the basis of an inference drawn from a failure or refusal to account for a matter to which subs.(1) relates. Secondly, subs.(3) provides that subs. (1) will not have effect unless the accused was told in ordinary language when being questioned, charged or informed, as the case may be, what the effect of the failure or refusal to account for a matter to which the subsection applies might be and the accused was afforded a reasonable opportunity to consult a solicitor before such failure or refusal occurred. Thirdly, subs.(6) stipulates that the section will not apply in relation to questioning by a member of the Garda Síochána unless it is recorded by electronic or similar means or the person consents in writing to it not being so recorded.[226]

---

[221] Subsection (7) provides that subs.(1) applies to the condition of clothing or footwear as it applies to a substance or mark thereon.

[222] In *People (DPP) v Fitzpatrick* [2012] IECCA 74 at [40], O'Donnell J expressed the view that the syntax of this subsection had gone awry where it spoke of the failure or refusal to "give an account, being an account which in the circumstances at the time clearly called for an explanation from him or her when so questioned, charged or informed".

[223] Subsection (8) provides that references in subs.(1) to evidence will, in relation to a hearing of an application under Part IA of the Criminal Procedure Act 1967 for the dismissal of a charge, be taken to include a statement of the evidence to be given by a witness at the trial.

[224] Subsection (5) stipulates that the court (or, subject to the judge's directions, the jury) is required, for the purposes of drawing an inference under the section to have regard to whenever, if appropriate, the account of the matter was first given by the accused.

[225] Subsection (4) contains a saver that nothing in the section shall, in any proceedings: "(a) prejudice the admissibility in evidence of the silence or other reaction of the accused in the face of anything said in his or her presence relating to the conduct in respect of which he or she is charged in so far as evidence thereof would be admissible apart from this section, (b) be taken to preclude the drawing of any inference from the silence or other reaction of the accused which could properly be drawn apart from this section, or (c) be taken to preclude the drawing of any inference from a failure or refusal to account for the presence of an object, substance or mark or for the condition of clothing or footwear which could properly be drawn apart from this section." Thus, the section does not curtail or affect the admissibility of admissions by conduct including admissions made by way of acceptance of accusations admissible by way of an exception to the hearsay rule (see further Chap.5).

[226] The electronic recording of interviews is discussed in Chap.8, section G.

(b) Section 19 of the Criminal Justice Act 1984

11–115 Section 19 of the 1984 Act (as substituted by s.29 of the Criminal Justice Act 2007) is drafted in very similar terms to s.18 and permits inferences to be drawn in proceedings against a person for an arrestable offence in circumstances where the accused "was requested by the member to account for his or her presence at a particular place at or about the time the offence is alleged to have been committed, and the member reasonably believes that the presence of the accused at that place and at that time may be attributable to his or her participation in the commission of the offence" and fails or refuses to account, being an account which in the circumstances at the time clearly called for an explanation from him or her.

(c) Section 19A of the Criminal Justice Act 1984

11–116 Section 19A of the Criminal Justice Act 1984 (as inserted by s.30 of the Criminal Justice Act 2007[227]), which replaces s.7 of the Criminal Justice (Drug Trafficking) Act 1996[228] and s.5 of the Offences Against the State (Amendment) Act 1998[229] with a provision of more general application, provides as follows:

> "Where in any proceedings against a person for an arrestable offence evidence is given that the accused—
>
> > (a) at any time before he or she was charged with the offence, on being questioned by a member of the Garda Síochána in relation to the offence, or
> >
> > (b) when being charged with the offence or informed by a member of the Garda Síochána that he or she might be prosecuted for it,
>
> failed to mention any fact relied on in his or her defence in those proceedings, being a fact which in the circumstances existing at the time clearly called for an explanation from him or her when so questioned, charged or informed, as the case may be, then, the court, in determining whether a charge should be dismissed under Part IA of the Criminal Procedure Act 1967[230] or whether there is a case to answer and the court (or, subject to the judge's directions, the jury) in determining whether the accused is guilty of the offence charged (or of any other offence of which he or she could lawfully be convicted on that charge) may draw such inferences from the failure as appear proper;[231] and the failure may, on the basis of such inferences, be treated as, or as capable of amounting to, corroboration of any evidence in relation to which the failure is material."[232]

---

[227] Transitional provisions are contained in subs.(7).

[228] See Ryan, "The Criminal Justice (Drug Trafficking) Act 1996: Decline and Fall of the Right to Silence?" (1997) 7 ICLJ 22; Ní Raifeartaigh, "The Criminal Justice System and Drug Related Offending: Some Thoughts on Procedural Reforms" (1998) 4 (1) BR 15; and Keane, "Detention Without Charge and the Criminal Justice (Drug Trafficking) Act 1996" (1997) 7 ICLJ 1.

[229] Those sections are repealed by s.3 and Sch.1 to the Criminal Justice Act 2007.

[230] Subsection (8) provides that references in subs.(1) to evidence will, in relation to a hearing of an application under Part IA of the Criminal Procedure Act 1967 for the dismissal of a charge, be taken to include a statement of the evidence to be given by a witness at the trial.

[231] Subsection (5) stipulates that the court (or, subject to the judge's directions, the jury) is required, for the purposes of drawing an inference under the section to have regard to when the account of the matter was first given by the accused.

[232] Subsection (4) contains a saver that nothing in the section shall, in any proceedings: "(a) prejudice the admissibility in evidence of the silence or other reaction of the accused in the face of anything said in his or her presence relating to the conduct in respect of which he or she is charged in so far as evidence thereof would be admissible apart from this section, (b) be taken to preclude the drawing of any inference from the silence or other reaction of the accused which could properly be drawn apart from this section, or (c) be taken to preclude the drawing of any inference from a failure or refusal to account for the presence of an object, substance or mark or for the condition of clothing or footwear which could properly be drawn apart from this section." Thus, the section does not curtail or affect the admissibility of admissions by conduct including admissions made

11–117 This section contains the same safeguards as apply to ss.18 and 19. Thus, subs. (2) stipulates that a person cannot be convicted of an offence solely or mainly on an inference drawn from a failure to mention a fact to which subs.(1) relates. Subsection (3) provides that subs.(1) will not have effect unless the accused was told in ordinary language when being questioned, charged or informed, as the case may be, what the effect of the failure to mention a fact to which the subsection applies might be and the accused was afforded a reasonable opportunity to consult a solicitor before such failure occurred. Subsection (6) stipulates that the section will not apply in relation to questioning by a member of the Garda Síochána unless it is recorded by electronic or similar means or the person consents in writing to it not being so recorded.[233]

(d) Section 2 of the Offences Against the State (Amendment) Act 1998

11–118 Section 2(1) of the Offences Against the State (Amendment) Act 1998[234] (as amended by s.31 of the Criminal Justice Act 2007[235]) provides that:

> "Where in any proceedings against a person for an offence under section 21 of the Act of 1939[236] evidence is given that the accused at any time before he or she was charged with the offence, on being questioned by a member of the Garda Síochána in relation to the offence, failed to answer[237] any question material to the investigation of the offence,[238] then the court in determining whether a charge should be dismissed under Part IA of the Criminal Procedure Act 1967[239] or whether there is a case to answer and the court (or subject to the judge's directions, the jury) in determining whether the accused is guilty of the offence may draw such inferences from the failure as appear proper;[240] and the failure may, on the basis of such inferences, be treated as, or as capable of amounting to, corroboration of any evidence in relation to the offence, but a person shall not be convicted of the offence solely or mainly on an inference drawn from such a failure."[241]

11–119 Subsection (2) provides that subs.(1) will not have effect unless the accused

---

by way of acceptance of accusations admissible by way of an exception to the hearing rule (see further Chap.5).

[233] The electronic recording of interviews is discussed in Chap.8, section G.

[234] See the Report of the Committee to Review the Offences Against the State Acts 1939–1998 and Related Matters (Dublin 2002), Chap.8, for a discussion of the operation of this provision and the now repealed s.5.

[235] Transitional provisions are contained in s.31(2) of the 2007 Act.

[236] This section creates the offence of membership of an unlawful organisation.

[237] Subsection (4)(b) provides that "references to a failure to answer include references to the giving of an answer that is false or misleading and references to the silence or other reaction of the accused shall be construed accordingly".

[238] Subsection (4)(a) provides that "references to any question material to the investigation include references to any question requesting the accused to give a full account of his or her movements, action, activities or associations during any specified period".

[239] Subsection (3C) provides that references in subs.(1) to evidence will, in relation to a hearing of an application under Part IA of the Criminal Procedure Act 1967 for the dismissal of a charge, be taken to include a statement of the evidence to be given by a witness at the trial.

[240] Subsection (3A) stipulates that the court (or, subject to the judge's directions, the jury) is required, for the purposes of drawing an inference under the section to have regard to whenever, if appropriate, an answer to the question concerned was first given by the accused.

[241] Subsection (3) contains a saver for the position at common law by stipulating that nothing in the section shall, in any proceedings "(a) prejudice the admissibility in evidence of the silence or other reaction of the accused in the face of anything said in his or her presence relating to the conduct in respect of which he or she is charged, in so far as evidence thereof would be admissible apart from this section, or (b) be taken to preclude the drawing of any inference from the silence or other reaction of the accused which could be properly drawn apart from this section". See, further, Chap.5, section D.

was told in ordinary language when being questioned what the effect of such a failure might be and was afforded a reasonable opportunity to consult a solicitor before such a failure occurred. It is, thus, necessary for the garda questioning the accused to make it clear that the usual caution, if it has been given, does not apply and inferences can be drawn if the accused declines to answer.

11–120 Subsection (3B) stipulates that the section will not apply in relation to questioning by a member of the Garda Síochána unless it is recorded by electronic or similar means or the person consents in writing to it not being so recorded.[242]

(e) Section 72A of the Criminal Justice Act 2006

11–121 Section 72A of the Criminal Justice Act 2006 was inserted by s.9 of the Criminal Justice (Amendment) Act 2009 as part of a package of measures directed at organised crime. Subsection (1) provides that:

> "Where in any proceedings against a person for an offence under this Part[243] evidence is given that the defendant at any time before he or she was charged with the offence, on being questioned by a member of An Garda Síochána in relation to the offence, failed to answer[244] any question material to the investigation of the offence,[245] then the court in determining whether a charge should be dismissed under Part IA of the Criminal Procedure Act 1967[246] or whether there is a case to answer and the court (or subject to the judge's directions, the jury) in determining whether the defendant is guilty of the offence may draw such inferences from the failure as appear proper;[247] and the failure may, on the basis of such inferences, be treated as, or as capable of amounting to, corroboration of any evidence in relation to the offence, but a person shall not be convicted of the offence solely or mainly on an inference drawn from such a failure."[248]

11–122 This section contains the same safeguards as are found in the other statutory provisions discussed above. Subsection (2) stipulates that subs.(1) will not have effect unless the accused was told in ordinary language when being questioned what the effect of such a failure might be and the accused was afforded a reasonable opportunity to consult a solicitor before such failure occurred. Subsection (5) further stipulates that the section will not apply in relation to questioning by a member of the Garda Síochána

---

[242] The electronic recording of interviews is discussed in Chap.8, section G.

[243] Part 7 of the Criminal Justice Act 2006 which contains offences relating to organised crime.

[244] Subsection (8) provides that "references to a failure to answer include references to the giving of an answer that is false or misleading and references to the silence or other reaction of the accused shall be construed accordingly".

[245] A detailed list of questions that are "material to the investigation of the offence" is provided in subs.(7).

[246] Subsection (6) provides that references in subs.(1) to evidence will, in relation to a hearing of an application under Part IA of the Criminal Procedure Act 1967 for the dismissal of a charge, be taken to include a statement of the evidence to be given by a witness at the trial.

[247] Subsection (4) stipulates that the court (or, subject to the judge's directions, the jury) is required, for the purposes of drawing an inference under the section to have regard to when the account of the matter was first given by the accused.

[248] Subsection (3) contains a saver for the position at common law by stipulating that nothing in the section shall, in any proceedings "(a) prejudice the admissibility in evidence of the silence or other reaction of the accused in the face of anything said in his or her presence relating to the conduct in respect of which he or she is charged, in so far as evidence thereof would be admissible apart from this section, or (b) be taken to preclude the drawing of any inference from the silence or other reaction of the accused which could be properly drawn apart from this section". See, further, Chap.5, section D.

unless it is recorded by electronic or similar means or the person consents in writing to it not being so recorded.[249]

(f) Explanation of the Effect of the Failure or Refusal

11–123 In *Murray v United Kingdom,*[250] one of the safeguards contained in the relevant UK legislation permitting inferences to be drawn was that, before inferences could be drawn, an appropriate warning was required to have been given to the accused as to the legal effects of maintaining silence. Unsurprisingly, therefore, each of the statutory provisions was regarded by the European Court of Human Rights as important in reaching the conclusion that there had not been a breach of art.6 of the Convention in the particular circumstances of that case. This requirement stipulates that inferences cannot be drawn in accordance therewith unless the accused was told in ordinary language what the effect of the failure or refusal to provide an account or the failure to mention a fact might be.

11–124 It follows that, where a person is questioned by gardaí and it is anticipated that reliance may subsequently be placed on any of these statutory provisions, the usual caution should not be administered as it would convey the misleading impression that the person is entitled to stay silent and there will be no adverse consequences for doing so.[251] If the usual caution is given and there could have been any confusion on the part of the accused as to the consequences of failing to answer questions, then the court of trial is unlikely to draw any inferences from the silence of the accused[252] although a contention that inferences should not have been drawn on this basis was rejected on the facts in *People (DPP) v Bolger (No.2).*[253] In practical terms, the best way to ensure that there is a proper explanation of the effect of a failure or refusal to account or mention a fact and that such confusion does not arise is for gardaí to hold a separate interview with a suspect which commences with the required explanation.

11–125 Care in the formulation of the terms of the caution or warning given to a suspect is required and a bespoke caution is required for each of the statutory provisions. In *People (DPP) v Bowes,*[254] Fennelly J was critical of the terms of the cautions given by gardaí to the accused upon the invocation of s.7 of the Drug Trafficking Act 1996:

> "The warning required by the section must draw the attention of the suspect to the danger of not mentioning any *fact* upon which he will or is likely to rely in his defence. The first version of the warning given, relating to "failure to answer some questions", clearly does not satisfy that requirement. The second formulation mentioned "failure to mention any fact which you may rely on in your defence" is closer to what is needed. However, it was given at a very late stage in the questioning and certainly long after the items of evidence were shown to the accused. In any event, for the reason already given, it does not relate to any *fact* of the sort covered by the section."[255]

---

[249] The electronic recording of interviews is discussed in Chap.8, section G.
[250] (1996) 22 EHRR 29.
[251] *Cf. People (DPP) v Finnerty* [1999] 4 IR 364 at 379, [2000] 1 ILRM 191 at 206.
[252] *Cf. People (DPP) v Campbell,* unreported, Court of Criminal Appeal, 19 December 2003.
[253] [2014] IECCA 1.
[254] [2004] IECCA 44 at [32], [2004] 4 IR 223 at 238. See Ennis, "'Confidential Information' and the Right to Silence" (2005) 15(2) ICLJ 31.
[255] [2004] IECCA 44 at [37], [2004] 4 IR 223 at 239. The form of the warnings used should be contrasted with the caution mandated in the UK in similar circumstances by para.10.5 of Code C of the Revised Code of Practice for the Detention, Treatment and Questioning of Persons by Police Officers (May 2014) that: "You do not have to say anything. But it may harm your defence

11–126   A contention that the Special Criminal Court had erred in drawing inferences from the failure of the accused to answer questions because gardaí had failed to adequately explain the operation of ss.2 and 5 of the 1998 Act and the interaction between them failed in *People (DPP) v Matthews*.[256] The Court of Criminal Appeal was satisfied that the trial court had not erred in its assessment of the memorandum of interviews or the videorecordings of same and that it had been entitled to draw inferences from the failure of the accused to answer questions and from lies given by the accused:

> "It is clear from the transcripts that the accused knew full well precisely what he was being asked, its significance, and the various legal consequences which might well arise were he to be charged in due course with the offences of which he was in fact, charged, where he had not responded to questions poses. Nor is there any error of law established by the accused as to the inferences actually drawn by the trial court in the course of its judgment from the responses actually given by him."[257]

11–127   Section 32 of the Criminal Justice Act 2007 confers on the Minister for Justice the power to make regulations providing for the administration of cautions by members of the Garda Síochána to persons in relation to offences and, pursuant to subs.(3), those Regulations may provide for different forms of caution to be administered to a person in different circumstances and in different classes of case thus permitting a bespoke caution to be prescribed for use when these statutory provisions are invoked.[258] Even though the Court of Criminal Appeal in *People (DPP) v Fitzpatrick*[259] suggested that the question of the appropriate caution should be reviewed, no such regulations have yet been made.

(g) Reasonable Opportunity to Consult with a Solicitor

11–128   Given that statutory provisions which allow for the drawing of inferences from the exercise of the right to silence constitute significant encroachments on that right, legal advice as to whether to invoke the right to silence or to answer questions is of particular importance. In *Murray v United Kingdom*,[260] although the European Court of Human Rights held that the drawing of inferences under the relevant provisions of the Criminal Evidence (Northern Ireland) Order 1988 did not breach art.6 of the Convention, it found that there had been a breach of the concept of fairness enshrined in art.6 because the applicant had been denied access to a solicitor for the first 48 hours of his detention. It emphasised the importance of access to legal advice in the context of a statutory regime that permits inferences to be drawn from the exercise of the right to silence:

> "The Court is of opinion that the scheme contained in the Order is such that it is of paramount importance for the rights of the defence that an accused has access to a lawyer at the initial stages of police interrogation. It observes in this context that, under the Order, at the beginning

---

if you do not mention when questioned something which you later rely on in Court. Anything you do say may be given in evidence."
[256] [2006] IECCA 103, [2007] 2 IR 169.
[257] [2006] IECCA 103 at [22], [2007] 2 IR 169 at 179.
[258] The *Final Report of the Balance in the Criminal Law Group* (2007), p.34, regarded it as unsatisfactory that the Judges' Rules and the traditional caution has not been revised to take into account the inference drawing statutory provisions as they then stood and considered that the form of caution should be updated.
[259] [2012] IECCA 74 at [44].
[260] (1996) 22 EHRR 29.

of police interrogation, an accused is confronted with a fundamental dilemma relating to his defence. If he chooses to remain silent, adverse inferences may be drawn against him in accordance with the provisions of the Order. On the other hand, if the accused opts to break his silence during the course of interrogation, he runs the risk of prejudicing his defence without necessarily removing the possibility of inferences being drawn against him."[261]

11–129 The decision in *Murray* was subsequently applied in *Averill v United Kingdom*[262] which was also concerned with the drawing of inferences under the Criminal Evidence (Northern Ireland) Order 1988. In that case, the applicant had been denied access to a lawyer during the first 24 hours of his detention and the Court regarded this as a significant factor to be taken into account in deciding whether it was proper to draw inferences from the silence of the applicant:

> "For the Court, considerable caution is required when attaching weight to the fact that a person, arrested, as in this case, in connection with a serious criminal offence and having been denied access to a lawyer during the first 24 hours of his interrogation, does not provide detailed responses when confronted with incriminating evidence against him. Nor is the need for caution removed simply because an accused is eventually allowed to see his solicitor but continues to refuse to answer questions. It cannot be excluded that the accused's continued silence is based on, for example, *bona fide* advice received from his lawyer. Due regard must be given to such considerations by the fact-finding tribunal when confronted with the possible application of Articles 3 and 5 of the 1988 Order."[263]

11–130 In *Condron v United Kingdom*[264] the applicants had been afforded access to a solicitor who was present during the interviews and this was regarded by the European Court of Human Rights as a particularly important factor in deciding whether their trial had been unfair because of the inferences drawn against them:

> "It must also be observed that the applicant's solicitor was present throughout the whole of their interviews and was able to advise them not to volunteer any answers to the questions put to them. The fact that an accused person who is questioned under caution is assured access to legal advice, and in the applicants' case the physical presence of a solicitor during police interview, must be considered a particularly important safeguard for dispelling any compulsion to speak which may be inherent in the terms of the caution."[265]

11–131 The Court went on to reiterate the importance of the presence or absence of a lawyer and legal advice when deciding whether and what inferences can be drawn:

> "For the Court, particular caution is required when a court of trial seeks to attach weight to the fact that a person who is arrested in connection with a criminal offence and who has not been given access to a lawyer does not provide detailed responses when confronted with questions the answers to which may be incriminating. At the same time, the very fact that an accused is advised by his lawyer to maintain his silence must also be given appropriate weight by the domestic court. There may be good reason why such advice may be given."[266]

11–132 In order to ensure that the statutory provisions for the drawing of inferences are compatible with art.6 of the Convention in the light of these decisions, each of the sections specifically provides that it will not have effect unless the accused was afforded a reasonable opportunity to consult a solicitor before the failure to account or mention a fact or answer a material question occurred.

---

[261] (1996) 22 EHRR 29 at 67.
[262] (2001) 31 EHRR 839.
[263] (2001) 31 EHRR 839 at 853–854.
[264] (2001) 21 EHRR 1.
[265] (2001) 21 EHRR 1 at 21.
[266] (2001) 21 EHRR 1 at 21. See also *Beckles v United Kingdom* (2003) 36 EHRR 162; *Adetoro v United Kingdom* [2010] ECHR 609.

11–133   The question as to nature of the consultation required arose for consideration in *People (DPP) v Fitzpatrick.*[267] One of the grounds of appeal was that, although it was accepted that the first appellant had been given ample access to his solicitor during his detention, complaint was made that, once s.18 had been invoked, he was not given a specific opportunity of consulting with his solicitor so that subs.(3)(b) had not been complied with. O'Donnell J, delivering the judgment of the Court, considered it clear that this subsection was "intended to act as a significant safeguard". Adopting a purposive approach to its interpretation, he rejected the contention that it was sufficient if there has been access to a solicitor prior to the invocation of s.18:

> "Looked at functionally, however, the section seems to envisage the opportunity of consultation at or around the same time as the request for an account. If the reasonable opportunity to consult a solicitor cannot be interpreted literally to mean an opportunity on any occasion (and it is conceded, correctly, that it cannot) it is difficult to see how it could be intended that the opportunity should be given before a s.18 or s.19 request is invoked, and without knowledge that they are likely to be invoked. The whole structure of subs. (3) seems to imply that the opportunity for consultation under subs. 3(b) should be given at or around the same time as the explanation in ordinary language required under subs. (3)(a), since both provisions are contained in the same subsection and linked by the conjunction "and". Since subs (3)(a) can only occur just before, or just after, the making of a request for an account under s. 18, then it should follow that subs. (3)(b) must occur within the same timescale, and be similarly linked to the making of the request for an account. Again, this makes some sense. It is for the member of the gardaí to inform the accused in ordinary language as to the general effect of a failure or refusal, and it is for the solicitor to advise the accused as to the potential impact in the particular circumstances of his own case. Accordingly, an approach to the language of the section in the context of the section as a whole suggests that the opportunity must be given to consult in relation to a s.18 request. That normally means that an opportunity be given after the section is invoked, but it might also be satisfied by an opportunity to consult when the gardaí have informed the accused and his solicitor that the section may be invoked... Finally, the formulation of the provision which refers to a reasonable opportunity to *consult*, as opposed to the phrase then commonly used which refers to the right of reasonable *access*, suggests the section requires more than a general opportunity of speaking to a solicitor. It implies that the solicitor can be consulted for advice, which suggests that the matter in respect of which advice is to be given is the s.18 request. That advice cannot be given unless the client and solicitor know and are informed that the section has been, or is likely to be invoked. On this approach, it would not be sufficient to prove that the reasonable opportunity to consult a solicitor arose before the request was made and when neither the appellant nor his solicitor necessarily knew that the section was likely to be invoked. If the reasonable opportunity to consult provided for under subs. (3)(b) must be linked in time to the invocation of s.18 and the making of a request thereunder, then there is no reason why it should not be linked in purpose aswell."[268]

11–134   He considered that this conclusion was reinforced by the constitutional and Convention jurisprudence on the right to silence. Given that the subsection was intended "to act as a safeguard in respect of a provision which operates as a significant interference with the suspect's right to silence" and the provisions for the drawing of inferences marked a significant departure from the position as communicated in the usual caution, he thought that it was entirely appropriate that legal advice should be available to a suspect in relation to the position once such a provision had been invoked.

11–135   This conclusion is consistent with the decision of the Supreme Court in *People (DPP) v Gormley and White*,[269] that the constitutional right to a solicitor

---

267   [2012] IECCA 74.
268   [2012] IECCA 74 at [41].
269   [2014] IESC 17, [2014] 1 ILRM 377.

necessarily carries with it an entitlement not to be interrogated after such access is requested and after such access is obtained. In that case, Clarke J observed that:

"[T]here can be little doubt but that advice on the immediate events which often occur on the arrest of a suspect (such as questioning) is one of the most important aspects of the advice which any suspect is likely to require as a matter of urgency. There would be little point in giving constitutional recognition to a right of access to a lawyer while in custody if one of the principal purposes of that custody in many cases, being the questioning of the relevant suspect, could continue prior to legal advice being obtained."[270]

11–136   Similarly, there would be little point in holding that the requirement to afford a suspect a reasonable opportunity to consult a solicitor was satisfied by access before the invocation of ss.18 or 19.

11–137   It should be noted that, if an adequate explanation is given by gardaí of the operation of subs.(1) and reasonable access to a solicitor is afforded, then inferences may be drawn even if the suspect is given incorrect or inadequate legal advice from his or her solicitor because the solicitor is entirely independent of the State which cannot be held responsible for the content of that advice or any shortcomings in it.[271]

(h) Reliance on Legal Advice as a Justification for Silence

11–138   In *Condron v United Kingdom*[272] the European Court of Human Rights accepted that reliance on legal advice could be a good reason for remaining silent and that this explanation had to be given appropriate weight.[273] However, if legal advice was accepted as a justification for the exercise of the right to silence in every case, it would effectively neuter provisions permitting the drawing of inferences. Therefore, the English courts have sought to distinguish between situations where an accused, for good reason, relied on legal advice to remain silent and circumstances where claimed reliance on such advice is an attempt to disguise the inability of the accused when questioned to provide a plausible exculpatory account. In *R. v Betts*,[274] Kay LJ addressed the decision in *Condron* and said:

"In the light of the judgment in *Condron v United Kingdom* it is not the quality of the decision but the genuineness of the decision that matters. If it is a plausible explanation that the reason for not mentioning facts is that the particular appellant acted on the advice of his solicitor and not because he had no or no satisfactory answer to give then no inference can be drawn.

That conclusion does not give a licence to a guilty person to shield behind the advice of his solicitor. The adequacy of the explanation advanced may well be relevant as to whether or not the advice was truly the reason for not mentioning the facts. A person, who is anxious not to answer questions because he has no or no adequate explanation to offer, gains no protection from his lawyer's advice because that advice is no more than a convenient way of disguising his true motivation for not mentioning facts."

11–139   The approach adopted in *Betts* was endorsed in *R. v Hoare*[275] where the Court of Appeal reiterated that:

---

[270] [2014] IESC 17 at [9.2], [2014] 1 ILRM 377 at 402.
[271] *People (DPP) v Birney* [2006] IECCA 58 at [98]–[99], [2007] 1 IR 337 at 367–368.
[272] (2001) 21 EHRR 1.
[273] See also *Beckles v United Kingdom* (2003) 36 EHRR 162; *Adetoro v United Kingdom* [2010] ECHR 609 at [51].
[274] [2001] EWCA Crim 224, [2001] 2 Cr App R 257 at [53]–[54]. See, generally, Daly, "Silence and Solicitors: Lessons Learned from England and Wales?" (2007) 17(2) ICLJ 2.
[275] [2004] EWCA Crim 784, [2005] 1 WLR 1804.

"even where a solicitor has in good faith advised silence and a defendant has genuinely relied on it in the sense that he accepted it and believed that he was entitled to follow it, a jury may still draw an adverse inference if it is sure that the true reason for his silence is that he had no or no satisfactory explanation consistent with innocence to give."[276]

11–140   Auld LJ went on to explain:

"It is not the purpose of section 34 to exclude a jury from drawing an adverse inference against a defendant because he genuinely or reasonably believes that, regardless of his guilt or innocence, he is entitled to take advantage of that advice to impede the prosecution case against him. In such a case the advice is not truly the reason for not mentioning the facts. The section 34 inference is concerned with flushing out innocence at an early stage or supporting other evidence of guilt at a later stage, not simply with whether a guilty defendant is entitled, or genuinely or reasonably believes that he is entitled, to rely on legal rights of which his solicitor has advised him. Legal entitlement is one thing. An accused's reason for exercising it is another. His belief in his entitlement may be genuine, but it does not follow that his reason for exercising it is – a distinction with which Professor Di Birch in her commentary in the Criminal Law Review in Howell appears not to have grappled, in asserting that the question must surely be 'has the suspect genuinely relied on his solicitor's advice'

The question in the end, which is for the jury, is whether regardless of advice, genuinely given and genuinely accepted, an accused has remained silent not because of that advice but because had no or no satisfactory explanation to give. For this purpose, but only for this purpose, section 34 in its provision for the drawing of an adverse inference, qualifies a defendant's right to silence. However, it is still for the prosecution to prove its case, section 38(3) of the 1994 Act ensures that a finding of a case to answer or a conviction shall not be based solely on such an inference."[277]

11–141   If an accused seeks to rely on legal advice as a justification for silence, then this may raise difficult questions as to whether, and the extent to which, he has waived legal professional privilege in relation to the communications with his solicitor and some of the complexities arising in that regard were explored in *R. v Seaton*.[278]

(i) Electronic Recording of Questioning

11–142   As noted in Chap.8, art.4(1) of the Criminal Justice Act 1984 (Electronic Recording of Interviews) Regulations 1997[279] imposes an obligation to electronically record the interviews that take place with persons detained under s.4 of the Criminal Justice Act 1984, s.30 of the Offences Against the State Act 1939 and s.2 of the Criminal Justice (Drug Trafficking) Act 1996. This obligation is reinforced by the stipulation in each of ss.18, 19 and 19A of the Criminal Justice Act 1984 and s.2 of the Offences Against the State (Amendment) Act 1998 that they do not apply in relation to the questioning of a person unless it is recorded by electronic or similar means or the person consents in writing to it not being so recorded. While this is an important and welcome safeguard, it should be noted that the drawing of inferences where there has been a failure to electronically record the statements of an accused is not ruled out entirely because this requirement only applies where a person is being questioned by gardaí and inferences may also be drawn on the basis of a failure to account or to mention a fact when a person is charged with an offence or informed by a garda that he or she might be prosecuted for it.

---

[276] [2004] EWCA Crim 784, [2005] 1 WLR 1804 at [51].
[277] [2004] EWCA Crim 784, [2005] 1 WLR 1804 at [54]–[55]. See also *R. v Beckles* [2004] EWCA Crim 2766, [2005] 1 WLR 2829, [2005] 1 All ER 705; *R. v Bresa* [2005] EWCA Crim 1414, [2006] Crim LR 179; *R. v Armstrong* [2009] EWCA Crim 643.
[278] [2010] EWCA Crim 1980, [2011] 1 WLR 623.
[279] SI No. 74 of 1997.

(j) Failure to Account, to Mention Facts and to Answer Material Questions

11–143   Although there are structural similarities between ss.18, 19 and 19A of the 1984 Act (dealing with a failure or refusal of an accused to give an account or to mention a fact relied on in his or her defence respectively) on the one hand and s.2 of the 1998 Act and s.72A of the 2006 Act (dealing with a failure to answer material questions) on the other, there are some important differences in the purpose and wording of the sections which bear significantly on their scope of application.

11–144   One important point of distinction is that it is expressly stipulated in both s.2 of the 1998 Act and s.72A of the 2006 Act that "references to a failure to answer include references to the giving of an answer that is false or misleading and references to the silence or other reaction of the defendant shall be construed accordingly".[280] That stipulation is notably missing from the other sections and this has important consequences in terms of the entitlement to draw adverse inferences from false and misleading answers.

11–145   In *People (DPP) v Bullman*,[281] the accused, when questioned about certain incriminating text messages sent to and from a phone in his possession, answered that he could not remember sending or receiving them. The Court of Criminal Appeal was satisfied that the Special Criminal Court had been entitled to draw inferences from those answers pursuant to s.2 of the 1998 Act on the basis that the answers were not truthful and that this amounted to a failure to answer material questions.[282] A different conclusion was reached in *People (DPP) v Devlin*[283] where the Special Criminal Court had drawn inferences pursuant to s.18 of the 1984 Act by reason of the failure of the accused, who was charged with possession of an explosive device, to account for his possession of certain items. The accused had actually given an explanation for his possession of those items and it was held by the Court of Criminal Appeal that the answer given, whether it was regarded as satisfactory or not, was an answer and did not amount to a failure or refusal to account:

> "It is not at all clear, on the evidence, that the appellant *failed to account* for the two most important items. Section 18, subject to observation of the procedures it lays down, permits evidence to be given of the *'failure or refusal'* of a person to account for, *inter alia,* an object that was *'in or on his or her clothing or footware'* or *'otherwise in his or her possession...'* The provision does not apply where an account of any kind has been given."[284]

11–146   Another important point of distinction arises between the scope of application of ss.18 and 19 which are directed towards a failure to account for specified matters and s.2 of the 1998 Act and s.72A of the 2006 Act which deal, more broadly, with a failure to answer material questions. In *People (DPP) v Donnelly*,[285] the appellants were convicted by the Special Criminal Court of membership of an unlawful organisation having been stopped at a checkpoint in the early morning in a car not owned by any of them which contained an imitation firearm, cable ties, gloves, duct tape, bin liners and a black beanie hat. When asked to account for their movements and for the items found in the car, the accused refused to respond although two of them made a

---

[280] Section 2(4)(b) of the Offences Against the State (Amendment) Act 1998 and s.72A(8) of the Criminal Justice Act 2006.
[281] [2009] IECCA 84.
[282] [2009] IECCA 84 at [15].
[283] [2012] IECCA 70.
[284] [2012] IECCA 70 at [38].
[285] [2012] IECCA 78 at [32].

very short statement denying guilt. The Court of Criminal Appeal distinguished the decision in *Devlin* having regard to the different wording of s.18 of the 1984 Act which permitted inferences to be drawn from a failure to account, and s.2 of the 1998 Act, which permitted inferences to be drawn from a failure to answer any question. It held that the test to be applied was not whether an account was given but rather whether the accused had failed to answer any material question. Here, the accused had failed to answer virtually every question and had simply made a short statement in the course of one of the interviews denying his guilt which was characterised as a "small island of volubility in an ocean of silence". In those circumstances, it was held that the Special Criminal Court had been entitled to find the accused, notwithstanding his short volunteered statement, had failed to answer questions material to the investigation of the events and that the court was fully entitled to draw the inferences which it did and to conclude that the failure of the accused to answer questions was capable of amounting to corroboration of other evidence in the case.

11–147 Finally, it should be noted that there is a significant difference between the operation of s.19A and the other provisions. Section 19A only applies if an accused seeks to rely, in his or her defence of the proceedings, on a fact that was not previously mentioned when the accused was questioned, cautioned or informed of the risk of prosecution. While the decision as to whether the other statutory provisions are invoked is a matter for the prosecution, the accused can, by tailoring the defence mounted, control whether s.19A is triggered.

(k) The Drawing of Inferences

11–148 The decision of the Supreme Court in *Rock v Ireland*,[286] which upheld the constitutionality of ss.18 and 19 of the Criminal Justice Act 1984, provided little guidance as to when it was appropriate to draw inferences and what inferences could be drawn. Hamilton CJ confined his observations to stating that it is clear from these sections that a court is entitled, but not obliged, to draw such inferences as appear proper and:

> "In deciding what inferences may properly be drawn from the accused person's failure or refusal, the court is obliged to act in accordance with the principles of constitutional justice and having regard to an accused person's entitlement to a fair trial must be regarded as being under a constitutional obligation to ensure that no improper or unfair inferences are drawn or permitted to be drawn from such failure or refusal."[287]

11–149 Little further insight was provided by the example given by the learned Chief Justice of an improper inference which was where the prejudicial effect of the inference would outweigh its probative value as evidence.[288] However, some helpful guidance as to the circumstances in which it is permissible to draw inferences from silence can be obtained from an examination of the jurisprudence of the European Court of Human Rights.

11–150 In *Murray v United Kingdom*,[289] the European Court of Human Rights observed that it was only "common sense inferences which the judge considers proper, in the light of the evidence against the accused, that [could] be drawn under

---

[286] [1997] 3 IR 484, [1998] 2 ILRM 35.
[287] [1997] 3 IR 484 at 497, [1998] 2 ILRM 35 at 47.
[288] [1997] 3 IR 484 at 501, [1998] 2 ILRM 35 at 50.
[289] (1996) 22 EHRR 29.

the Order."[290] Having reviewed the evidence in the case, the Court concluded that the drawing of inferences against the applicant from his refusal to provide an explanation for certain matters at arrest, during questioning and at trial, was a matter of common sense and could not be regarded as unfair or unreasonable in the circumstances.

11–151 In *Averill v United Kingdom*[291] the European Court of Human Rights returned to this issue and expressed the view that:

> "the extent to which adverse inferences can be drawn from an accused's failure to respond to police questioning must be necessarily limited. While it may no doubt be expected in most cases that innocent persons would be willing to co-operate with the police in explaining that they were not involved in any suspected crime, there may be reasons why in a specific case an innocent person would not be prepared to do so. In particular, an innocent person may not wish to make any statement before he has had an opportunity to consult a lawyer."[292]

11–152 The Court took the view that the trial judge had not exceeded the limits of fairness in drawing adverse inferences against the accused. In reaching that conclusion, it took into account a number of factors. First, the decision to draw adverse inferences was only one of the elements taken into account by the trial judge in finding that the charges had been proved beyond a reasonable doubt. Second, given that the accused had been arrested near the scene of the offence, the presence of incriminating fibres on his hair and clothing called for an explanation by him and his failure to provide an explanation when questioned could, as a matter of common sense, allow the drawing of an adverse inference that he had no explanation and was guilty. Third, the applicant did not contend that he stayed silent on the strength of legal advice.

11–153 The type of adverse inferences that can be drawn, consistent with the guarantee of a fair trial contained in art.6(1) of the Convention, was also considered in *Condron v United Kingdom*.[293] The applicants were convicted of drug offences and argued that their trial had been unfair because of the directions given by the trial judge to the jury in relation to drawing inferences from their silence when questioned; in accordance with the provisions of s.34 of the Criminal Justice and Public Order Act 1994. Both applicants were heroin addicts and their solicitor had formed the view that they were unfit to be interviewed. He therefore advised them to maintain silence and they failed to mention facts that they later relied on as part of their defence when giving evidence at the trial. The Court went on to reiterate the importance of the presence or absence of a lawyer and legal advice when deciding whether and what inferences can be drawn:

> "For the Court, particular caution is required when a court of trial seeks to attach weight to the fact that a person who is arrested in connection with a criminal offence and who has not been given access to a lawyer does not provide detailed responses when confronted with questions the answers to which may be incriminating. At the same time, the very fact that an accused is advised by his lawyer to maintain his silence must also be given appropriate weight by the domestic court. There may be good reason why such advice may be given."[294]

11–154 In that case, the Court concluded that the direction given by the trial judge in relation to the applicants' silence failed to respect the balance required to be drawn between the right to silence and the circumstances in which an adverse inference may

---

[290] (1996) 22 EHRR 29 at 62.
[291] (2001) 31 EHRR 839.
[292] (2001) 31 EHRR 839 at 853.
[293] (2001) 21 EHRR 1.
[294] (2001) 21 EHRR 1 at 21.

be drawn from silence. The applicants had put forward an explanation for their failure to mention certain facts relied on by them in their evidence at trial which had been confirmed by their solicitor. Although the trial judge had brought this explanation to the attention of the jury, he did so in terms which left the jury at liberty to draw an adverse inference notwithstanding that it was satisfied as to the plausibility of the explanation:

> "In the Court's opinion, as a matter of fairness, the jury should have been directed that if it was satisfied that the applicants' silence at the police interview could not sensibly be attributed to their having no answer or none that would stand up to cross-examination it should not draw an adverse inference."[295]

11–155   The Court regarded it as imperative that, where the trier of fact is a jury, it is properly advised on how to address the issue of the silence of an accused.

11–156   In *People (DPP) v Donnelly*[296] (the facts of which have been set out above), it was held that the court can only draw an inference that appears "proper" which means "one that follows logically from the questions asked and the refusal in the particular case".[297] It was also noted that, even in such a case, the court is not obliged to draw any such inference. O'Donnell J went on to observe that:

> "the objections to the drawing of inferences from the silence of an accused while in garda custody have rarely been with the logic or common sense of such inferences. Most people would regard a refusal to answer questions as to the movements of a person in circumstances which in the words of the European Court of Human Rights "call out for explanation", (such as those in the present case) as itself at least suggestive of guilt."[298]

11–157   Inferences pursuant to s.2 of the 1998 Act were found to have been correctly drawn by the Special Criminal Court in *People (DPP) v Binéad*[299] where the accused, who were charged with membership of an unlawful organisation, had reacted with "stony silence" to the questioning by gardaí. Those inferences, when taken together with belief evidence given by a Chief Superintendent pursuant to s.3(2) of the Offences Against the State (Amendment) Act 1972 and other evidence, was found to be sufficient to establish the offence beyond a reasonable doubt.

11–158   Inferences were also held to have been correctly drawn pursuant to ss.18, 19 and 19A of the 1984 Act in *People (DPP) v Bolger*[300] in circumstances where (a) the accused was advised by the gardaí that they intended to invoke the statutory provisions, (b) the accused had consulted with his solicitor, (c) the garda explained the sections of the statute to him in layman's language, (d) the accused indicated that he understood the caution, (e) the accused engaged with the gardaí, and (f) this was recorded on videotape.

11–159   The distinction between the drawing of inferences from the exercise of the right to silence and the admission of evidence of the invocation of the right to silence simpliciter was highlighted in *People (DPP) v Bowes*.[301] Fennelly J noted that the

---

[295] (2001) 21 EHRR 1 at 22.

[296] [2012] IECCA 78 at [32].

[297] See also *People (DPP) v Bullman* [2009] IECCA 84 at [11], where it was held, following the decision in *Murray v United Kingdom* (1996) 22 EHRR 29, that a trial judge "may only draw such inferences and such degree of inferences, as may be proper".

[298] [2012] IECCA 78 at [34].

[299] [2006] IECCA 374, [2007] 1 IR 374.

[300] [2013] IECCA 6 at [49].

[301] [2004] IECCA 44 at [32], [2004] 4 IR 223 at 238.

statutory provision at issue, s.7 of the Drug Trafficking Act 1996, had qualified the right to silence but that a suspect was, in principle, free to remain silent although his exercise of the right could, subject to compliance with the requirements of the section, become part of the evidence. However, he entered the important caveat that:

> "The section does not relate to silence generally. In particular, it does not relate to the fact that the accused, in response to garda questioning, exercised his right to remain silent and declined to answer any questions. There must be an identifiable fact relied on by the defence *at the trial* which the accused "could reasonably have been expected to mention…when questioned."[302]

11–160 Accordingly, it was held that the prosecution should not have commented when opening the case that the accused had no comment to make when shown various items in garda custody because it did not yet know what facts would be relied on by the defence. The section did not justify any prosecution reliance on failure by an accused person to comment. He emphasised that the section does not permit general silence to be admitted into evidence.

11–161 It should be noted that one matter that is required by each of the statutory provisions to be taken into account in deciding what inference should be drawn is when the account was first given, the fact was first mentioned, or the answer to the material question was first given by the accused.

(l) The Use of Inferences as Corroboration

11–162 In *People (DPP) v Devlin*,[303] the Court of Criminal Appeal held that a failure or refusal to account, as the case may be, must be such as is "capable of amounting to … corroboration of any evidence in relation to which the failure or refusal is material." Thus, in accordance with the decision in *People (DPP) v Gilligan*,[304] the evidence had to be such as tended to implicate the accused in the commission of the offence. However, in *People (DPP) v Donnelly*,[305] the Court of Criminal Appeal, in a judgment delivered by O'Donnell J, differed from *Devlin* in relation to the question of corroboration, stating:

> "Finally, it is perhaps appropriate to observe that a question may arise as to the meaning of 'corroboration' in statutory provisions such as s.2 of the Offences Against the State Act 1998 and s. 18 of the Criminal Justice Act 1984. It does not appear to this Court that the reference to such evidence being 'capable of amounting to corroboration' amounts to a requirement that such evidence be capable of satisfying the test for corroborative evidence before it can be accepted. On the contrary, such evidence is deemed by statute to be capable of amounting to corroboration, so that in such cases where corroboration is required as a matter of law or practice, it is capable of being supplied by inferences being drawn pursuant to the relevant statutory provisions."[306]

11–163 The Court further held that the Special Criminal Court had been entitled to treat the failure to answer questions as capable of amounting to corroboration of the belief evidence of a garda superintendent that had been admitted pursuant to s.3(2) of the Offences Against the State (Amendment) Act 1972:

> "Under the section it is specifically provided that the failure to answer questions may, on the basis of the inferences to be drawn, be treated as corroboration. However, this is not a case in

---

[302] [2004] IECCA 44 at [34], [2004] 4 IR 223 at 238.
[303] [2012] IECCA 70.
[304] [2005] IESC 78, [2006] 1 IR 107.
[305] [2012] IECCA 78 at [32].
[306] [2012] IECCA 78 at [38].

which there was evidence which required corroboration in the strict sense in which that term is used in the law of evidence. It appears the section uses the term in the more general sense of other evidence of guilt, which by virtue of the section may amount to corroboration, where that is required by law. Furthermore, it is perhaps important to point out that it is not the failure to answer questions which itself amounts to corroboration or indeed is itself evidence. Rather, the failure to answer questions material to the offence permits the court (but does not require it) to draw inferences from such failure as appear proper. It is those inferences which provide the basis on which the failure may amount to the type of corroboration contemplated by the section. Accordingly, any fact finder faced with s.2 must first consider whether there has been a <u>failure</u> to answer questions material to the investigation of the offence, and thereafter what <u>inferences</u> may be drawn from such failure as a matter of logic. An inference of guilt is not an inevitable consequence of a failure to answer. In some cases one inference may be that the accused did not understand either the import of the question or the consequences of a failure. In another situation, a refusal to answer questions may be indicative of a desire to avoid disclosing matters shameful and reprehensible, though perhaps not illegal. In still other cases, one inference might be that it is a desire to avoid disclosing a matter which is illegal, albeit not the illegality with which the person is being taxed. A further possible inference is that a suspect has already given a comprehensive account and does not see any merit in repetition."[307]

11–164   In that case, the Court of Criminal Appeal was satisfied that the Special Criminal Court had been entitled to conclude that the only possible inference from the sequence of events and the manner in which the accused had responded (or, more accurately, failed to respond) to questions in a number of interviews, which refusal was complete and comprehensive, was that they were members of an unlawful organisation, thus corroborating the belief evidence of the Chief Superintendent.

(m) Inferences Cannot be the Sole or Main Basis for Conviction

11–165   As noted above, in *Murray v United Kingdom*,[308] the European Court of Human Rights held that the right to silence was not absolute and that it should not prevent the accused's silence, in situations which clearly call for an explanation from him, being taken into account in assessing the persuasiveness of the evidence adduced by the prosecution. However, the Court regarded it as self-evident that it is incompatible with the right to silence to base a conviction solely or mainly on the accused's silence or refusal to answer questions.[309] Accordingly, each of the statutory provisions stipulates that a person cannot be convicted of an offence "solely or mainly on an inference" drawn from a failure or refusal to account, mention a fact or answer a material question as the case may be.

(n) Instruction to the Jury

11–166   In a series of cases, the European Court of Human Rights has emphasised the need for a careful instruction by the trial judge to the jury where reliance is placed on a statutory provision permitting inferences to be drawn from silence.

11–167   In *Condron v United Kingdom*,[310] discussed above, the Court concluded that the direction given by the trial judge in relation to the applicants' silence failed to respect the balance required to be drawn between the right to silence and the circumstances in which an adverse inference may be drawn from silence. The applicants had put

---

[307] [2012] IECCA 78 at [40].
[308] (1996) 22 EHRR 29.
[309] (1996) 22 EHRR 29 at 60.
[310] (2001) 21 EHRR 1.

forward an explanation for their failure to mention certain facts relied on by them in their evidence at trial which had been confirmed by their solicitor and although the trial judge had drawn this explanation to the attention of the jury, he did so in terms which left the jury at liberty to draw an adverse inference notwithstanding that it was satisfied as to the plausibility of the explanation:

> "In the Court's opinion, as a matter of fairness, the jury should have been directed that if it was satisfied that the applicants' silence at the police interview could not sensibly be attributed to their having no answer or none that would stand up to cross-examination it should not draw an adverse inference."[311]

11–168 The Court regarded it as imperative that, where the trier of fact is a jury, it is properly advised on how to address the issue of the silence of an accused.

11–169 The importance of properly directing the jury as to their entitlement to draw inferences particularly in circumstances where the accused has given an explanation for exercising his or her right to silence was reiterated in *Beckles v United Kingdom*.[312] In that case, the applicant gave evidence at this trial that he did not respond to police questioning because he had been advised by his solicitor not to do so and had indicated a willingness to disclose the contents of that advice. In the course of his charge, the trial judge instructed the jury that the applicant had a right to silence, that the applicant's failure to reply to police questioning could not of itself prove guilt, that it was for the jury to decide whether it was fair and proper to draw inferences and that, if they thought the applicant had given a good reason for his silence, then it should not be held against him. However, he also told them that there was "no independent evidence" of what the solicitor said at the police station without mentioning his willingness to disclose the details of that advice of other circumstances consistent with this explanation. In the circumstances, the Court concluded that the direction was deficient:

> "For the Court, these are all matters which go to the plausibility of the applicant's explanation and which, as a matter of fairness, should have been built into the direction in order to allow the jury to consider fully whether the applicant's reason for his silence was a genuine one, or whether, on the contrary, his silence was in effect consistent only with guilt and his reliance on legal advice to stay silent merely a convenient self-serving excuse…
>
> Nevertheless, the Court considers that the trial judge failed to give appropriate weight in his direction to the applicant's explanation for his silence at the police interview and left the jury at liberty to draw an adverse inference from the applicant's silence notwithstanding that it may have been satisfied as to the plausibility of the explanation given by him (c.f. the above-mentioned *Condron* judgment, § 61). Quite apart from the fact that the trial judge had undermined the value of the applicant's explanation by referring to the lack of independent evidence as to what was said by the solicitor and by omitting to mention that the applicant was willing to give his version of the incident to the police before he spoke to his solicitor, it is also to be noted that he invited the jury to reflect on whether the applicant's reason for his silence was "a good one" without also emphasising that it must be consistent only with guilt.
>
> In the Court's opinion, the jury should have been reminded of all of the relevant background considerations referred to above and directed that if it was satisfied that the applicant's silence at the police interview could not sensibly be attributed to his having no answer or none that would be stand up to police questioning it should not draw an adverse inference (c.f. § 61 of the above-mentioned *Condron* judgment)."[313]

---

[311] (2001) 21 EHRR 1 at 22.
[312] [2002] ECHR 661, (2003) 36 EHRR 162.
[313] [2002] ECHR 661, (2003) 36 EHRR 162 at [62]–[64].

11–170   The Court considered that "it was crucial that the jury was properly directed on this matter" and, accordingly, found that there had been a breach of art.6(1).[314]

11–171   Thus, it would appear that, in any case where any of ss.18, 19 and 19A of the Criminal Justice Act 1984 or s.2 of the Offences Against the State (Amendment) Act 1998 are invoked, and a jury is invited to draw adverse inferences from a failure or refusal of the accused to account, mention a fact or answer a material question as the case may be, the jury should be given detailed instructions as to the operation of the provisions, what inferences they are entitled to draw and how they should approach any explanation offered by or on behalf of the accused for the failure or refusal to account, mention a fact or answer a material question including, in particular, reliance on legal advice as a reason for maintaining silence.

11–172   Very useful guidance as to the contents of the direction that should be given where the prosecution relies on s.19A in particular can be found in the specimen direction issued by the Judicial Studies Board in the UK in relation to s.34 of the Criminal Justice and Public Order Act 1994 as follows[315]:

"1.   Before his interview(s) the defendant was cautioned. He was first told that he need not say anything. It was therefore his right to remain silent. However, he was also told that it might harm his defence if he did not mention when questioned something which he later relied on in court; and that anything he did say might be given in evidence.

2.   As part of his defence, the defendant has relied upon *(here specify the facts to which this direction applies)*. But [the prosecution say][he admits] that he failed to mention these facts when he was interviewed about the offence(s). [If you are sure that is so, this/This] failure may count against him. This is because you may draw the conclusion from his failure that he [had no answer then/had no answer that he then believed would stand up to scrutiny/has since invented his account/has since tailored his account to fit the prosecution's case/*(here refer to any other reasonable inferences contended for)*]. If you do draw that conclusion, you must not convict him wholly or mainly on the strength of it; but you may take it into account as some additional support for the prosecution's case and when deciding whether his [evidence/ case] about these facts is true.

3.   However, you may draw such a conclusion against him only if you think it is a fair and proper conclusion, and you are satisfied about three things: first, that when he was interviewed he could reasonably have been expected to mention the facts on which he now relies; second, that the only sensible explanation for his failure to do so is that he had no answer at the time or none that would stand up to scrutiny; third, that apart from his failure to mention those facts, the prosecution's case against him is so strong that it clearly calls for an answer by him.

4.   *(Add, if appropriate:)* The defence invite you not to draw any conclusion from the defendant's silence, on the basis of the following evidence (here set out the evidence). If you [accept this evidence and] think this amounts to a reason why you should not draw any conclusion from his silence, do not do so. Otherwise, subject to what I have said, you may do so.

5.   *(Where legal advice to remain silent is relied upon, add the following to or instead of paragraph 4 as appropriate:)* The defendant has given evidence that he did not answer questions on the advice of his solicitor/legal representative. If you accept the evidence that he was so advised, this is obviously an important consideration:

---

[314]   See also *Adetoro v United Kingdom* [2010] ECHR 609 where, even though the charge of the trial judge was found to be deficient in that he had failed to advise the jury that no inferences could be drawn unless they were satisfied that the reason for the applicant's silence was that he had no answer to the questions asked or none that would stand up to cross-examination, the Court, nonetheless, concluded that the trial had not been unfair.

[315]   Judicial Studies Board, *Crown Court Bench Book* (March 2010), Appendix 2.

but it does not automatically prevent you from drawing any conclusion from his silence. Bear in mind that a person given legal advice has the choice whether to accept or reject it; and that the defendant was warned that any failure to mention facts which he relied on at his trial might harm his defence. Take into account also *(here set out any circumstances relevant to the particular case, which may include the age of the defendant, the nature of and/or reasons for the advice given, and the complexity or otherwise of the facts on which the defendant has relied at the trial).* Having done so, decide whether the defendant could reasonably have been expected to mention the facts on which he now relies. If, for example, you considered that he had or may have had an answer to give, but genuinely and reasonably relied on the legal advice to remain silent, you should not draw any conclusion against him. But if, for example, you were sure that the defendant remained silent not because of the legal advice but because he had no answer or no satisfactory answer to give, and merely latched onto the legal advice as a convenient shield behind which to hide, you would be entitled to draw a conclusion against him, subject to the direction I have given you."

F. Privilege Against Self-Incrimination

1. Introduction

11–173   In *Re National Irish Bank*,[316] Shanley J stated that the privilege against self-incrimination "has always encapsulated a right in the individual to refuse to answer a question or produce a document when to do so would in the opinion of a court tend to expose such an individual to a real risk of criminal prosecution or penalty."[317] This formulation identifies the major elements of the privilege[318] which will be examined in detail below.

2. Criminal Prosecution

11–174   The precise categories of adverse consequences that will ground the exercise of the privilege in this jurisdiction are uncertain. The privilege can certainly be asserted where there is a risk of prosecution for, and conviction of, a criminal offence although a degree of uncertainty exists as to whether the offence is required to have been committed within the jurisdiction.[319] It also seems to be reasonably settled that it is not available

---

[316] [1999] 3 IR 145, [1999] 1 ILRM 321.

[317] [1999] 3 IR 145 at 153, [1999] 1 ILRM 321 at 329. *Cf. Blunt v Park Lane Hotel* [1942] 2 KB 253 at 257, [1942] 2 All ER 187 at 189, where Goddard LJ gave what is probably the best known formulation of the privilege: "The rule is that no-one is bound to answer any question if the answer thereto would, in the opinion of the judge, have a tendency to expose [him] to any criminal charge, penalty or forfeiture which the judge regards as reasonably likely to be preferred or sued for." *Cf. Sorby v Commonwealth* (1983) 152 CLR 281, 46 ALR 237 and *Accident Insurance Mutual Holdings Ltd v McFadden* (1993) 31 NSWLR 412.

[318] See, generally, Leonowicz, "The Privilege against Self-incrimination – Part 1" (2005) 23(4) ILT 55; Leonowicz, "The Privilege against Self-incrimination – Part 2" (2005) 23(5) ILT 77.

[319] This question was left open by Ó Dálaigh CJ in *State (Magee) v O'Rourke* [1971] IR 205 but he seemed to agree with the thrust of the English cases that, in general, it cannot be invoked in such circumstances (see *King of the Two Sicilies v Willcox* (1851) 1 Sim NS 301; *United States v Rae* (1868) 3 Ch App 79; *Re Atherton* [1912] 2 KB 251 at 255).

where a witness would merely be exposed to civil liability[320] including ecclesiastical punishment or censure,[321] bankruptcy proceedings[322] or disciplinary proceedings.[323]

11–175   However, it is less clear whether the privilege can be invoked to avoid a risk of the imposition of penalties or forfeiture. In *Re National Irish Bank*,[324] Shanley J took the view that the privilege could also be invoked where a person would be exposed to the risk of the imposition of a penalty and there is a strong body of English authority that supports the application of the privilege to penalties[325] including penalties for civil contempt[326] and penalties under European Law.[327] There is also authority for the proposition that the privilege is available to avoid a risk of forfeiture[328] even though this is a civil rather than a criminal remedy.[329] These extensions of the privilege were strongly criticised by Murphy J in *Pyneboard Pty Ltd v Trade Practices Commission*[330]:

> "It is an absurd state of the law if a witness, in a civil or criminal trial, can lawfully refuse to answer because the answer may tend to expose him or her…to forfeiture of a lease, or to a civil action for penalties, but may not refuse if the exposure is to some other civil loss, such as an action for damages, even punitive damages. In so far as such absurdity has been introduced or maintained by judicial decision … it can and should be erased by judicial decision."[331]

11–176   It is submitted that this reasoning is persuasive and that the Irish courts, who are unconstrained by authority, should not extend the privilege beyond its core application to criminal offences.

3. Risk of Prosecution

11–177   A witness can only rely on the privilege as a ground for refusing to answer a question if to do so would, in the opinion of the court, tend to expose the person to a real risk of prosecution.[332] It is not enough for a witness to simply assert a risk of

---

[320] *R. v Viscount Melville* (1806) 29 St Tr 549; *McClure v Backstein* (1987) 17 CPC (2d) 242; *R. v Amway Corp* [1989] 1 SCR 21.

[321] Historically, the privilege was available in respect of ecclesiastical punishments and censure but this aspect of the privilege was regarded as obsolete in *Blunt v Park Lane Hotel Ltd* [1942] 2 KB 253, [1942] 2 All ER 187 and, in *Pyneboard Pty Ltd v Trade Practices Commission* (1982) 152 CLR 329 at 345, 45 ALR 609, Murphy J took the view that such an extension of the privilege did not form part of the common law of Australia.

[322] *Re XY, ex parte Haes* [1902] 1 KB 98. *Cf. Re Ginsberg* (1917) 40 OLR 136, 38 DLR 261.

[323] *Re Fang and College of Physicians and Surgeons of Alberta* (1985) 25 DLR (4th) 632; *Re Johnstone and Law Society of British Columbia* (1987) 40 DLR (4th) 550; *Re Prousky and the Law Society of Upper Canada* (1987) 41 DLR (4th) 565.

[324] [1999] 3 IR 145, [1999] 1 ILRM 321.

[325] See *Earl of Mexborough v Whitwood UDC* [1897] 2 QBD 111 at 114–115.

[326] *Bhimmji v Chatwani (No.3)* [1992] 4 All ER 912, [1992] 1 WLR 1158. However, the privilege cannot be asserted in a second set of contempt proceedings on the basis that it would expose the party to a penalty in the first set of proceedings: *Crest Homes Plc v Marks* [1987] AC 829 at 859; [1987] 2 All ER 1074 at 1082.

[327] *Rio Tinto Zinc Corp v Westinghouse Electric Corp* [1978] AC 547, [1978] 1 All ER 434.

[328] See *Blunt v Park Lane Hotel* [1942] 2 KB 253 at 257, [1942] 2 All ER 187 at 189. However, it should be noted that the application of the privilege to forfeiture has been abolished in civil proceedings in England by s.16(1)(a) of the Civil Evidence Act 1968.

[329] See *AG v Southern Industrial Trust Ltd* (1957) 94 ILTR 161 and *Gilligan v Criminal Assets Bureau* [1998] 3 IR 185 at 223.

[330] (1982) 152 CLR 328, 45 ALR 609.

[331] (1983) 152 CLR 328 at 346.

[332] *De Gortari v Smithwick* [2001] 1 ILRM 354 at 370; *Re National Irish Bank* [1999] 3 IR 145 at 153, [1999] 1 ILRM 321 at 329 (*per* Shanley J); *R. v Boyes* (1861) 1 B & S 311 at 329–330;

prosecution because it is ultimately a matter for the court, not the witness, to decide as to whether a real risk of prosecution exists.[333] The nature of the risk required was explained by Denning MR in *Rio Tinto Zinc Corp v Westinghouse Electric Corp*[334]:

> "It is not necessary for [the witness] to show that proceedings are likely to be taken against him, or would probably be taken against him. It may be improbable that they will be taken, but nevertheless, if there is some risk of their being taken—a real and appreciable risk—as distinct from a remote or insubstantial risk, then he should not be made to answer or to disclose the documents."[335]

11–178   Thus, a witness will not be permitted to rely on the privilege if the court concludes that the risk of prosecution is remote because prosecutions of the particular type are rare[336] or non-existent because the witness has already been convicted of the offence.[337]

11–179   It also appears from the authorities that, in addition to the requirement of a realistic possibility of a prosecution, the information which is sought from the witness must be such as to materially increase the risk of prosecution. So, for example, in *Kelly v Colhoun*,[338] which involved civil proceedings for libel and conspiracy, a claim of privilege by the first defendant in respect of the production of the original document in which the libel had been published was rejected. Murphy J held that, in circumstances where the first defendant had admitted that he had published the document, its production for inspection could not increase the risk of criminal proceedings against him.[339] However, privilege will apply even if the prosecuting authorities have evidence upon which to base a prosecution if the information sought could strengthen the prosecution's case and materially increase the risk of a prosecution.[340]

4. Tendency to Incriminate the Witness

11–180   In order to invoke the privilege, the witness must establish, to the satisfaction of the court, "that there are reasonable grounds to fear that the answer will tend to

---

Sociedade Nacional de Combustiveis de Angola UEE v Lundqvist [1991] 2 QB 310, [1990] 3 All ER 283.

[333] *De Gortari v Smithwick* [2001] 1 ILRM 354 at 370; *Re National Irish Bank* [1999] 3 IR 145 at 153, [1999] 1 ILRM 321 at 329 (*per* Shanley J); *Kelly v Colhoun* [1899] 2 IR 199 at 205; *R. v Boyes* (1861) 1 B & S 311; *Re Reynolds* (1882) 20 Ch D 294 at 300; *Rio Tinto Zinc Corp v Westinghouse Electric Corp* [1978] AC 547 at 574; [1977] 3 All ER 717 at 721 (*per* Denning MR); *Singh v R* [2010] NZLR 161 at [31]. See, *contra*, *Murray v "The Northern Whig" Ltd* (1911) 46 ILTR 77.

[334] [1978] AC 547, [1977] 3 All ER 717.

[335] [1978] AC 547 at 574, [1977] 3 All ER 717 at 722. *Cf. per* Cockburn CJ in *R. v Boyes* (1861) 1 B & S 311 at 330–331: "the Court must see, from the circumstances of the case and the nature of the evidence which the witness is called to give, that there is reasonable ground to apprehend danger to the witness from his being called to answer ... the danger to be apprehended must be real and appreciable with reference to the ordinary operation of law in the ordinary course of things—not a danger of an imaginary and unsubstantial character".

[336] *Cf. R. v Boyes* (1861) 1 B & S 311 at 331 (no instance of impeachment by House of Commons had ever occurred).

[337] *Hutch v Dublin Corporation* [1993] 3 IR 551 at 565 (*per* Egan J).

[338] [1899] 2 IR 199.

[339] See also *Khan v Khan* [1982] 2 All ER 60 (claim of privilege did not succeed in circumstances where the witness had been manifestly dishonest and the evidence against him was already so strong that the answers sought did not materially increase the risk of a prosecution for theft).

[340] *Rio Tinto Zinc Corp v Westinghouse Electric Corp* [1978] AC 547, [1978] 1 All ER 434.

incriminate him or her" and "could be used against him in criminal proceedings".[341] This will not be the case if the danger of incrimination has already arisen in advance of answering.[342] However, a witness will generally be afforded considerable latitude if he or she contends that the answer to a particular question would tend to incriminate him or her[343] and, in *Rio Tinto Zinc Corp v Westinghouse Electric Corp*,[344] Lord Denning MR stated that a witness should not be compelled to go into detail because that may involve his or her disclosing the very matter which he or she does not wish to reveal.

11–181 It is important to note that a witness will be permitted to invoke the privilege not only where the information sought would directly incriminate him or her but also where it would do so indirectly.[345] Otherwise, it would, as explained by Lord Tenterden CJ in *R. v Slaney*,[346] be easy to circumvent the protection conferred by the privilege:

> "You cannot only not compel a witness to answer that which will criminate him, but that which tends to criminate him: and the reason is this, that the party would go from one question to another; and though no question might be asked, the answer of which would directly criminate the witness, yet they would get enough from him whereon to found a charge against him."[347]

11–182 In addition, a witness will be entitled to rely on the privilege where the information sought might lead to a line of enquiry which would or might furnish a link in the chain of evidence required for a prosecution.[348]

5. Persons on whose Behalf the Privilege can be Claimed

11–183 As noted, the privilege against self-incrimination is a manifestation of the right of a person not to be compelled to incriminate oneself and it follows logically that it can only be claimed by the person at risk of prosecution and not by any other person on his or her behalf.[349] It has, thus, been held that a person cannot rely on the privilege to refuse to answer questions or produce documents on the basis that to do so would tend to incriminate another person.[350]

11–184 The question of whether a director or agent of a company can invoke the privilege to refuse to answer questions on the basis that it would tend to incriminate the company has not been addressed in this jurisdiction but the balance of authority

---

[341] *De Gortari v Smithwick* [2001] 1 ILRM 354 at 365 and 370 (*per* McGuinness J).
[342] *R. v Khan* [2007] EWCA Crim 2331 at [31].
[343] *R. v Boyes* 1861) 1 B & S 311 at 330.
[344] [1978] AC 547 at 574, [1977] 3 All ER 717 at 721.
[345] *R. v Slaney* (1832) 5 C & P 213 at 214; *R. v Boyes* 1861) 1 B & S 311 at 330; *Saunders v United Kingdom* (1996) 23 EHRR 313 at 338–339.
[346] (1832) 5 C & P 213.
[347] (1832) 5 C & P 213 at 214.
[348] *Saunders v United Kingdom* (1996) 23 EHRR 313 at 345 (*per* Walsh J); *Sociedade Nacional de Combustiveis de Angola UEE v Lundqvist* [1991] 2 QB 310 at 331, [1990] 3 All ER 283 at 297 (*per* Beldam LJ).
[349] *Rio Tinto Zinc Corporation v Westinghouse Electric Corporation* [1978] AC 547 at 637, [1978] 1 All ER 434 at 465 (*per* Lord Diplock); *Pyneboard Pty. Ltd v Trade Practices Commission* (1983) 152 CLR 328 at 346; *Singh v R* [2010] NZLR 161.
[350] *Ex p Reynolds* (1882) 20 Ch D 294; *R. v Minihane* (1921) 16 Cr App R 38.

in other jurisdictions is that privilege cannot be invoked by an artificial legal person[351] or by a person on its behalf.[352]

6. Proceedings in which Privilege can be Claimed

11–185   The privilege is given a broad application in civil and criminal proceedings and can be invoked, not only in the course of trial but also at an interlocutory stage to refuse the production or inspection of documents that have been discovered[353] and to refuse to answer interrogatories.[354] It has also been held to apply in the context of Anton Piller orders,[355] and Mareva injunctions.[356]

11–186   Although there has been a reluctance in some jurisdictions to extend the privilege to extra-judicial proceedings,[357] Shanley J in *Re National Irish Bank*,[358] ascribed a very wide application to the privilege saying that it was "one which is vested in witnesses before Courts and in all persons subjected to investigations whether they be formal investigations or not."[359] However, the extra-judicial application of the privilege is not unlimited and it appears that it will not apply where information is required to be provided in a non-adversarial context pursuant to general regulatory requirements.[360]

7. Informing a Witness of the Privilege

11–187   The privilege is not "self-executing" and must be invoked by a witness.[361]

---

[351] *R. v Amway Corp* [1989] 1 SCR 21; *Pyneboard Pty Ltd v Trade Practices Commission* (1982) 152 CLR 328 at 346, 45 ALR 609 (*per* Murphy J); *EPA v Caltex Refining Co. Pty Ltd* (1993) 178 CLR 477; *Baltimore & Ohio Railroad Co. v Interstate Commerce Commission* (1911) 221 US 612 at 622; *United States v White* (1944) 322 US 694 at 701; *George Campbell Painting Corp v Reid* (1968) 392 US 286. But see, *contra*, *Triplex Safety Glass Co. Ltd v Lancegaye Safety Glass (1934) Ltd* [1939] 2 KB 395, [1939] 2 All ER 613; *Rio Tinto Zinc Corp v Westinghouse Electric Corp* [1978] AC 547, [1978] 1 All ER 434; *Pear and Apple Marketing Board v Master & Sons Ltd* [1986] 1 NZLR 191. See, generally, O'Neill, "The Right to Silence and the Company" (2004) Ir Jur 111, who reviews the authorities and argues that companies enjoy a right to silence.

[352] *Pyneboard Pty Ltd v Trade Practices Commission* (1982) 152 CLR 328 at 347, 45 ALR 609 (*per* Murphy J.); *United States v White* (1944) 322 US 694 at 699, 700; *Wilson v United States* (1911) 221 US 361 at 384–385; *Kensington International v Congo* [2007] 2 Lloyds Rep 382 at [47].

[353] *Istel Ltd v Tully* [1993] AC 45 at 53, [1992] 3 All ER 523 at 530.

[354] See *Murray v "The Northern Whig" Ltd* (1911) 46 ILTR 77.

[355] *Rank Film Distributors Ltd v Video Information Centre* [1982] AC 380, [1981] 1 All ER 434. *Cf. Microsoft Corporation v Bright Point Ireland Limited* [2001] 1 ILRM 540.

[356] *Sociedade Nacional de Combustiveis de Angola UEE v Lundqvist* [1990] 3 All ER 283.

[357] See *Pyneboard Pty Ltd v Trade Practices Commission* (1983) 152 CLR 329 where a majority of the High Court of Australia took the view that the privilege is not inherently capable of application in non-judicial proceedings. *Cf. Saunders v United Kingdom* (1996) 23 EHRR 313 at 337, where a majority of the European Court of Human Rights declined to extend the guarantees set forth in art.6(1), including the right not to incriminate oneself, to the exercise of investigative powers by company inspectors on the basis that it "would in practice unduly hamper the effective regulation in the public interest of complex financial and commercial activities".

[358] [1999] 3 IR 145, [1999] 1 ILRM 321.

[359] [1999] 3 IR 145 at 153, [1999] 1 ILRM 321 at 329. *Cf. Lefkowitz v Turley* (1973) 414 US 70 at 77, where White J stated that: "The [Fifth] Amendment not only protects the individual from being involuntarily called as witness against himself in a criminal prosecution but also privileges him not to answer official questions put to him in any other proceeding, civil or criminal, formal or informal, where the answers might tend to incriminate him in future criminal proceedings."

[360] *Cf. EPA v Swalcliffe Ltd* [2004] IEHC 190, [2004] 2 IR 549, [2005] 1 ILRM 120.

[361] *Salinas v Texas* (2013) 133 S Ct 2174 at 2178.

At common law, the position was that there was no obligation on a judge to inform a witness of his or her entitlement to invoke the privilege to refuse to answer a question[362] but he or she had a discretion to do so.[363] However, following the recognition of the privilege as a constitutionally protected aspect of the right not to incriminate oneself in *Re National Irish Bank*,[364] the better view would seem to be that a trial judge should, where appropriate, inform a witness that he or she can refuse to answer on the basis of the privilege.

8. Substituted Protection

11–188   It is common for statutes that abrogate the privilege against self-incrimination to provide a form of substituted protection by placing limitations on the use that may be made of any answers given, generally in the form of a blanket prohibition on the use of such answers in any subsequent criminal proceedings except for perjury or a cognate offence.[365] However, even where a statutory provision requiring the disclosure of information does not contain such a prohibition, the courts have indicated a willingness to achieve a similar result by requiring, as a condition of making certain orders requiring the disclosure of information, an undertaking from the relevant prosecution authority not to use that information in the course of a criminal prosecution against the person ordered to make the disclosure. In *State (Williams) v DPP*,[366] O'Hanlon J explained that:

> "Some statutory exceptions have been created to the rule that a witness is not bound to answer questions where the answers may incriminate him. These exceptions arise in the case of statutes absolving from penal consequences persons who make a full discovery of what they know in inquiries instituted under certain statutes, and a person thus protected cannot refuse to answer a question on the ground that it would incriminate him. ... The situation where an undertaking is given by the DPP not to rely on answers given by a witness to found a prosecution against him appears to me to be analogous to the exceptions thus created by statute. The privilege is given to the witness to ensure that he will not be compelled to put himself in jeopardy by the evidence he may give, and where this element of jeopardy is removed then the basis for the privilege may well disappear along with it."[367]

11–189   The undertaking in that case had been volunteered by the Director of Public Prosecutions but was required by Moriarty J as a condition of the making a disclosure order in *M v D*.[368] In that case, the applicant sought an order requiring the respondent

---

[362]   *R. v Shanahan* (1912) 46 ILTR 254; *R. v Coote* (1873) LR 4 PC 599.
[363]   For an example of where this was exercised in favour of informing the witness, see *Wexford Timber Co. v Wexford Corporation* (1952) 88 ILTR 137.
[364]   [1999] 3 IR 145, [1999] 1 ILRM 321.
[365]   See, e.g. s.245(6) of the Companies Act 1963 (as substituted by s.126 of the Companies Act 1990) and s.44 of the Company Law Enforcement Act 2001); s.5 of the Tribunals of Inquiry (Evidence) (Amendment) Act 1979 (considered in *White v Morris* [2005] IEHC 391, [2007] 4 IR 445); s.21(4) of the Bankruptcy Act 1988; s.19 of the Companies Act 1990 (as substituted by s.29 of the Company Law Enforcement Act 2001); s.12 of the Committees of the Houses of the Oireachtas (Compellability, Privileges and Immunities of Witnesses) Act 1997; s.5 of the Comptroller and Auditor General and Committees of the Houses of Oireachtas (Special Provisions) Act 1998. The failure to provide such substituted protection was one of the factors that led Kearns P to conclude in *Dokie v DPP* [2010] IEHC 110 at [38], [2011] 1 IR 805 at 820 that s.12 of the Immigration Act 2004 which created an offence for a non-national to fail to give a satisfactory explanation for the inability to produce a passport or document establishing identity breached the right not to incriminate oneself.
[366]   [1983] ILRM 285.
[367]   [1983] ILRM 285 at 289.
[368]   [1998] 3 IR 175.

to file an affidavit under s.9 of the Proceeds of Crime Act 1996 which empowers the court to make an order directing a respondent to file an affidavit specifying the property of which he or she is in possession or control and/or the income, and the sources of income, of the respondent during the period specified in the order. This application was resisted on the ground that the relief sought would infringe the respondent's privilege against self-incrimination. However, Moriarty J took the view, applying the decisions of the Court of Appeal in *Re O (Restraint Order: Disclosure of Assets)*[369] and the House of Lords in *AT & T Istel Ltd v Tully*,[370] that any possible prejudice to the respondent could be averted by requiring the Director of Public Prosecutions to furnish an undertaking not to make use of the material divulged as a result of the disclosure order as evidence in any prosecution of the person required to make the disclosure.

11–190   Subsequently, in *Gilligan v Criminal Assets Bureau*,[371] McGuinness J said that, in order to minimise any encroachment on constitutional rights and in order to operate the procedures under the Proceeds of Crime Act 1996 in accordance with constitutional justice, a court would have to take particular care in deciding whether to make an order under s.9 requiring disclosure. In view of the very close nexus between the personnel of Criminal Assets Bureau and the gardaí, she opined that the type of undertaking sought in *M v D* would be essential in virtually every case where an order under s.9 is granted.[372] However, she acknowledged that, even if such an undertaking was required, there might well be difficulty in operating it in a secure and watertight manner.

11–191   Furthermore, as noted above, it was held in *Re National Irish Bank*[373] that the guarantee in Art.38.1 of a trial in due course of law requires the exclusion of involuntary confessions and the admission of a compelled statement would constitute a breach of that guarantee. Thus, even if there is no specific provision sterilising the use of an incriminating statement obtained through the use of statutory powers of compulsion, the application of the voluntariness test will provide an effective form of substitute protection.

9. Use of Derivative Evidence

11–192   In *Re National Irish Bank*,[374] Barrington J addressed the issue of the admissibility of derivative evidence, *i.e.* evidence obtained on foot of compelled answers as follows:

> "In the course of submissions the question arose of what would be the position of evidence discovered by the Inspectors as a result of information uncovered by them following the exercise by them of their powers under s.10. It is proper therefore to make clear what is

---

[369] [1991] 2 QB 520, [1991] 1 All ER 330.
[370] [1993] AC 45, [1992] 3 All ER 523.
[371] [1998] 3 IR 185.
[372] *Cf. Carroll v Law Society* [2003] 1 IR 284, [2000] 1 ILRM 161, where an issue was raised as to the possible infringement of the applicant's privilege against self-incrimination in circumstances where the respondent had instituted disciplinary proceedings into allegations of misconduct against him that involved criminal offences which the respondent was empowered to prosecute. Although McGuinness J declined to make an order, she directed the respondent's attention to the need to maintain a clear line of division between the disciplinary inquiry and any aspect of the respondent's role as prosecutor.
[373] [1999] 3 IR 145, [1999] 1 ILRM 321.
[374] [1999] 3 IR 145; [1999] 1 ILRM 321.

objectionable under Article 38 of the Constitution is compelling a person to confess and then convicting him on the basis of his compelled confession. ... The Inspectors have the powers to demand answers under section 10. These answers are in no way tainted and further information which the Inspectors may discover as a result of these answers is not tainted either. The case of *The People v O'Brien* [1965] IR 142, which deals with evidence obtained in breach of the accused's constitutional rights has no bearing on the present case. In the final analysis however, it will be for the trial judge to decide whether, in all the circumstances of the case, it would be just or fair to admit any particular piece of evidence, including any evidence obtained as a result or in consequence of the compelled confession."[375]

11–193   Thus, it appears that, provided that any statutory abridgement of the privilege against self-incrimination is proportional and, thus, constitutional, evidence discovered on foot of a compelled statement will, in principle, be admissible although a trial judge will have a discretion to exclude it if it would be unfair to admit it.[376]

G. Regulatory Requirements to Provide Information

11–194   Although it was held in *Re National Irish Bank*[377] that it is immaterial whether the compulsion or inducement used to extract an incriminating statement comes from the Executive or from the Legislature, it is clear that not all information provided pursuant to a statutory requirement will involve an abridgement of the right not to incriminate oneself and, more particularly, of the right to silence. In particular, no breach of the right will occur in circumstances where a person is required to provide information in a non-adversarial context pursuant to a generally applicable regulatory regime.

11–195   In *EPA v Swalcliffe Ltd*,[378] the accused had been charged with a number of offences under the Waste Management Act 1996 (the "1996 Act") and objected to the admission of records required to be kept pursuant to the conditions of a waste licence granted by the prosecutor and a waste licence audit report compiled, on the basis that the records were involuntary confessions by the accused. However, Kearns J was satisfied that there was no element of compulsion and that the right not to incriminate oneself was not involved at all in the case. He accepted the submission advanced by counsel for the prosecutor that:

> "In applying for a waste licence, the accused must be taken as having freely accepted the conditions attaching to the licence, which formed part of the entire package under the regulatory scheme. It was the accuseds' own free choice to participate in the particular activity and at the time they chose to do so they were well aware of their record keeping obligations and of the penalties for non-compliance with the requirements of the 1996 Act."[379]

---

[375] [1999] 3 IR 145 at 188; [1999] 1 ILRM 321 at 360–361.

[376] This approach is similar to that adopted by the South African Constitutional Court in *Ferreira v Levin* 1996 (1) BCLR 1, 1996 (1) SA 984 and advocated by La Forest J in *Thomson Newspapers Ltd v Canada (Director of Investigation and Research, Restrictive Trade Practices Commission)* [1990] 1 SCR 425, (1990) 67 DLR (4th) 161. For a comprehensive discussion of the various possible approaches to derivative evidence, see *Thomson Newspapers* and *R. v S (RJ)* [1995] 1 SCR 451, (1995) 121 DLR (4th) 589. *Cf.* the approach in the United States (see *Kastigar v United States* (1972) 406 US 441) and Australia (see *Pyneboard Pty Ltd v Trade Practises Commission* (1982) 152 CLR 328), 45 ALR 609.

[377] [1999] 3 IR 145, [1999] 1 ILRM 321.

[378] [2004] IEHC 190, [2004] 2 IR 549, [2005] 1 ILRM 120.

[379] [2004] IEHC 190 at [41], [2004] 2 IR 549 at 562, [2005] 1 ILRM 120 at 133.

11–196   He followed the decision of the Supreme Court of Canada in *R. v Fitzpatrick*[380] which he regarded as being on "all-fours" with the case before him. In that case, the accused had made daily "hail" reports of his catch by radio and had recorded daily fishing logs of his estimated catch as required by the relevant fishing regulations. He was charged with overfishing and the hail reports and fishing logs were sought to be introduced in evidence. La Forest J, having reviewed the purposes and concerns underlying the principle against self-incrimination, identified four main factors that militated against the conclusion that it applied[381]:

(1) the lack of real coercion by the State in obtaining the statement;
(2) the lack of an adversarial relationship between the accused and the State at the time the statements were obtained;
(3) the absence of an increased risk of unreliable confessions as a result of the statutory compulsion; and
(4) the absence of an increased risk of abuses of power by the State as a result of the statutory compulsion.

11–197   Applying those principles to the case before him, Kearns J stressed the importance of context in assessing the rights of the accused and stated:

"In my view none of the purposes or concerns which underlie the principle against self-incrimination are meaningfully brought into play in the circumstance of this particular case. Firstly, it cannot be said that there is any real coercion by the state in obtaining the information contained in the records. Secondly, there was no adversarial relationship between the accused and the state at the time the material was obtained. I do not see any increased risk of 'unreliable confessions' as a result of the statutory compulsion, nor do I perceive any increased risk of abuses of power by the State as a result of the statutory compulsion."[382]

11–198   In the instant case, he took the view that neither the waste licence audit report nor the waste records could not properly be characterised as "confessions" for the purposes of the involuntariness test. Furthermore, even if he was mistaken in that view, he was of the opinion that any limitation on the right to silence arising by the use of such material in criminal proceedings was proportionate and reasonable and within the parameters laid down in *Heaney v Ireland*.[383]

H. Concurrent Civil and Criminal Proceedings

11–199   It is well established that a court has a discretion to adjourn or grant a stay of civil proceedings where criminal proceedings in relation to the same subject matter are pending against the same person and there is a real risk of prejudice or injustice if the civil proceedings go ahead.[384] Such a risk may arise where the continued prosecution

---

[380] [1995] 4 SCR 154.
[381] See Bryant, Lederman & Fuerst, *Sopinho, Lederman & Bryant: The Law of Evidence in Canada* 4th edn (Canada: Lexis Nexis, 2014) §8.272.
[382] [2004] IEHC 190 at [43], [2004] 2 IR 549 at 562, [2005] 1 ILRM 120 at 133.
[383] [1996] 1 IR 580, [1997] 1 ILRM 117.
[384] See *Dillon v Dunnes Stores* [1966] IR 397; *O'Flynn v Mid-Western Health Board* [1991] 2 IR 223 at 236; *CG v Appeal Commissioners* [2005] IEHC 121, [2005] 2 IR 472; *Wicklow County Council v O'Reilly* [2006] IEHC 273, [2006] 3 IR 623; *Moore v Moore* [2010] IEHC 263; *Jefferson Ltd v Bhetcha* [1979] 1 WLR 898; *R. v Institute of Chartered Accountants of England and Wales, ex p. Brindle* [1994] BCC 297; *R. v Panel on Takeover and Mergers, ex p. Fayed* [1992] BCLC 938.

of the civil proceedings could undermine the accused's right not to incriminate himself or herself.

11–200   In *CG v Appeal Commissioners*,[385] the applicant sought to quash the decision of the respondent refusing to adjourn his appeal against income tax assessments raised by the Revenue Commissioners. This application had been made on the basis that there were criminal charges pending against him for failure to make tax returns in respect of the same years as were the subject of the income tax appeal. On the particular facts of the case, Finlay Geoghegan J was satisfied that the applicant had failed to establish a real risk of prejudice because there was no evidence to suggest that the applicant would be required to give evidence of an incriminating nature at the hearing of the tax appeal. Furthermore, even if any evidence of a self-incriminating nature was given by the applicant, she held that it would be a matter for the trial judge at the criminal trial to determine whether it would be in breach of the applicant's rights under Art.38.1 to admit such evidence against him. She therefore dismissed the application.[386]

11–201   The interaction between criminal and civil proceedings and the potential for interference with the right of an accused/defendant not to incriminate himself or herself was revisited by Clarke J in *Wicklow County Council v O'Reilly*.[387] The plaintiff council sought various reliefs against the defendants pursuant to s.58 of the Waste Management Act 1996 arising from the alleged unlawful disposal of waste. A number of the defendants brought an application seeking to stay the civil proceedings on the basis that criminal charges arising from the disposal of the waste had also been brought against the tenth defendant. One of the grounds of alleged prejudice was that the continued prosecution of the civil proceedings would necessarily amount to a denial of the tenth defendant's right to silence because of the requirement for it to put affidavit evidence before the court in the civil proceedings in order to properly defend them. However, Clarke J distinguished the circumstances from those in *Re National Irish Bank*[388] where persons were required, under pain of criminal penalty, to answer questions posed by inspectors appointed under the provisions of the Companies Act 1990. He took the view that any compulsion was less onerous than that in *Re National Irish Bank* because the defendants could not be compelled to "confess" to any wrongdoing and, if guilty of wrongdoing, would not have to admit this on affidavit. He acknowledged that the defendants might be at a significant disadvantage if they did not put forward such evidence as they thought appropriate in order to defend the civil proceedings, particularly if they wished to mount a defence that involved expressly or implicitly accepting the validity of at least part of the case made against them. However, he noted that a defendant who filed an affidavit which was wholly exculpatory would not be at any disadvantage in the criminal process whereas a defendant who filed an affidavit making a "confession" would be most unlikely to suffer any disadvantage by not filing the affidavit. He concluded that, having regard to the public interest in the enforcement of environmental protection which was underpinned by the State's obligations pursuant to Council Directive 75/442/EEC dealing with waste:

> "the limited form of interference with the right to silence by indirect means which applies in circumstances where a party may, as a matter of practice, though not as a matter of legal obligation, be required to file an affidavit in defence to an application for an order under s.58

---

[385]   [2005] IEHC 121, [2005] 2 IR 472.
[386]   This decision was followed by Laffoy J in *Moore v Moore* [2010] IEHC 263.
[387]   [2006] IEHC 273, [2006] 3 IR 623.
[388]   [1999] 3 IR 145, [1999] 1 ILRM 321.

amounts, in general terms, to a proportionate interference with the right to silence for the purposes of securing the objectives of the Act of 1996, even where a criminal prosecution is in being."[389]

11–202 He considered that the taking of any different view would mean that the price which the public interest would have to pay for the invocation of the criminal jurisdiction under the Waste Management Acts would be a significant deferral of what might otherwise be the entitlement of the public (through the relevant statutory agencies), to have appropriate remedial works carried out in a timely fashion. However, he did not rule out the possibility that it might be necessary to revisit the question and the balancing of rights at a subsequent stage in the proceedings in light of discovery ordered and whether oral evidence was to be tendered.

11–203 *A fortiori*, if criminal proceedings have not commenced, a breach of the right not to incriminate oneself will not occur and civil proceedings will not be stayed merely because the possibility of such proceedings acts as a disincentive to a defendant giving evidence to defend those proceedings.[390]

I. Documents and Non-Testimonial Evidence

11–204 In *Re National Irish Bank*,[391] Shanley J indicated that the privilege against self-incrimination encompassed not only an entitlement to refuse to answer questions but also to refuse to produce documents. This is consistent with the English authority at the time which held that privilege extended to pre-existing documents[392] but can be contrasted with the position in the United States where the privilege only applies to testimonial communications and not to pre-existing incriminating documents[393] or non-testimonial evidence.[394] In *Schmerber v California*,[395] Brennan J in the US Supreme Court observed that the Fifth Amendment to the US Constitution "protects an accused only from being compelled to testify against himself, or otherwise provide the State with evidence of a testimonial or communicative nature"[396] so that "the privilege is a bar against compelling 'communications' or 'testimony', but that compulsion which makes a suspect or accused the source of 'real or physical evidence' does not violate it".[397] Thus, it was held the Fifth Amendment offered no protection against compulsion to provide non-testimonial evidence such as fingerprints, photographs, participation

---

[389] [2006] IEHC 273 at [46], [2006] 3 IR 623 at 638.
[390] See *Director of Corporate Enforcement v Rogers* [2005] IEHC 443.
[391] [1999] 3 IR 145 at 153, [1999] 1 ILRM 321 at 329.
[392] See, *e.g. Tate Access Floors Inc v Boswell* [1990] 3 All ER 303. The position is not so clear now following the decision in *C Plc v P* [2007] EWCA Civ 493, [2007] 3 WLR 437. See further, Moules "The privilege against self-incrimination and real evidence" (2007) 66(3) CLJ 528; Ng "Privilege against self-incrimination in independent evidence: *C Plc v P (Attorney-General intervening)*" (2008) 12(2) E & P 150, Zuckerman, "Editors Note: The Privilege Against Self-incrimination may not Confer a Right to Refuse Disclosure of Incriminating Documents that came into Existence Independently of the Disclosure Order" (2007) 26 CJQ 395.
[393] *Fisher v United States* (1976) 425 US 391.
[394] *Schmerber v California* (1966) 384 US 757.
[395] (1966) 384 US 757.
[396] (1966) 384 US 757 at 761.
[397] (1966) 384 US 757 at 764.

in identity parades or the provision of blood samples.[398] In *Fisher v United States*,[399] the Supreme Court introduced the "act of production" doctrine whereby the privilege may not bar the state from compelling the production of incriminating material from the accused as long as the process involved does not compel the accused to *create* an incriminating testimonial response by complying with the state's order.

11–205   A similar approach was adopted by the European Court of Human Rights in *Saunders v United Kingdom*[400] where it was held that:

> "The right not to incriminate oneself is primarily concerned, however, with respecting the will of an accused to remain silent. As commonly understood in the legal systems of the Contracting Parties to the Convention and elsewhere, it does not extend to the use in criminal proceedings of material which may be obtained from the accused through the use of compulsory powers but which has an existence independent of the will of the suspect such as, *inter alia*, documents acquired pursuant to a warrant, breath, blood and urine samples and bodily tissue for the purpose of DNA testing."[401]

11–206   However, it should be noted that right not to incriminate oneself can, in limited circumstances encompass real evidence. In *Jalloh v Germany*,[402] a suspected drug dealer, who had swallowed what was believed to be a package containing drugs, had been forcibly administered emetics to precipitate the regurgitation of it in circumstances that were considered to violate the guarantee in art.3 against inhuman and degrading treatment. Although the Grand Chamber accepted that the right not to incriminate oneself "is commonly understood in the Contracting States and elsewhere to be primarily concerned with respecting the will of the defendant to remain silent in the face of questioning and not to be compelled to provide a statement",[403] it nonetheless held that it was engaged in the particular circumstances of the case. Although the drugs hidden in the applicant's body fell into the category of material having an existence independent of the will of the applicant, that real evidence had been retrieved in defiance of the applicant's will and the degree of force used differed significantly from the degree of compulsion normally required to obtain the types of material referred to in *Saunders*. Indeed, it had been obtained by a means of a procedure which the court found had violated art.3. In determining whether the applicant's right not to incriminate himself had been violated, the court had regard to "the nature and degree of compulsion used to obtain the evidence; the weight of the public interest in the investigation and punishment of the offence at issue; the existence of any relevant safeguards in the procedure; and the use to which any material so obtained is put".[404] Unsurprisingly, given its conclusion that there had been a breach of art.3, the court proceeded to find that there had also been a breach of art.6(1).

11–207   There are *dicta* in a number of decisions in this jurisdiction in relation to

---

[398] See, for example, *People v Slavin* 1 NY 3d 392, 807 NE 2d 259 (privilege against self-incrimination not violated by admission of photographs of tattoos on the accused's body).
[399] (1976) 425 US 391.
[400] (1996) 23 EHRR 313.
[401] (1996) 23 EHRR 313 at 337, 338. See also *Boyce v Ireland* (2013) 56 EHRR SE11 at [50] where the European Court of Human Rights, in an admissibility decision, affirmed that the privilege against self-incrimination "does not apply to blood or other physical or objective specimens used in forensic analysis".
[402] [2006] ECHR 721, (2007) 44 EHRR 667.
[403] [2006] ECHR 721, (2007) 44 EHRR 667 at [110].
[404] [2006] ECHR 721, (2007) 44 EHRR 667 at [117].

requiring accused persons to undertake tests[405] and the taking of samples from an accused[406] that suggested the possible recognition by the Irish courts of a broad right not to be compelled to incriminate oneself that extends to non-testimonial evidence. However, there are other authorities where a clear distinction between verbal admissions and incriminating real evidence such as fingerprints has been drawn.[407] In *Curtin v Dáil Éireann*,[408] the distinction drawn in *Schmerber v California* and *Saunders* between requiring a person to make a statement or give evidence that may tend to incriminate him and requiring him to produce a document or other physical item was endorsed by the Supreme Court, albeit it on an *obiter* basis.

11–208   That the right not to incriminate oneself does not extend to items of real evidence was confirmed by the Supreme Court in *People (DPP) v Gormley and White*.[409] In the second of the two appeals under consideration, an issue arose as to the admissibility of forensic samples that had been obtained after the accused had requested access to a solicitor but before that access had been afforded to him. Clarke J noted that a key difference between inculpatory statements and real evidence obtained such as forensic samples is that the results of forensic testing are objective and do not depend on the will or a suspect. Accordingly, he did not consider that the right not to incriminate oneself was involved and concluded that there was no constitutional impediment to the admission of such evidence:

> "On that basis, at the level of principle, I am not satisfied that the mere fact that otherwise lawful forensic sampling is properly taken prior to the attendance of a legal adviser renders any subsequent trial, at which reliance is placed on the results of tests arising out of that forensic material, unfair. It remains, of course, the case that the suspect is entitled to reasonable access to a lawyer. The authorities in whose custody the suspect is held are required to take reasonable steps to facilitate such access. What consequences may flow, in respect of the admissibility of forensic evidence taken from a suspect where such reasonable steps are not taken, is a matter to be decided in a case where those circumstances arise. However, I am not satisfied that there is any fair trial constitutional prohibition on the taking, without prior legal advice, of a sample in a minimally intrusive way which is justified in law.
>
> In those circumstances, I am not satisfied that the "due course of law" provisions of

---

[405] See *Sullivan v Robinson* [1954] IR 161 (voluntariness test and other rules in relation to confessions applied where accused required to undertake test to determine whether he was drunk).

[406] See *DPP v McGarrigle* [1996] 1 ILRM 271 at 273 (Finlay CJ stated that the statutory obligation to provide a blood or urine specimen was a "significant though not unique exception to the general principles of our criminal code which protect accused persons against involuntary self-incrimination"); *DPP v Elliot* [1997] 2 ILRM 156 at 159 (McCracken J recognised that there was a general principle that a person is not obliged to incriminate himself but it was not an absolute principle and could be abridged by legislation requiring specimens of blood or urine to be taken); *DPP v McDonagh* [2008] IESC 57 at [30], [2009] 1 IR 767 at 779 (Denham J referred to the right of an accused not to incriminate himself in the context of breath sample) and *People (DPP) v Boyce* [2008] IESC 62 at [53], [2009] 2 IR 124 at 139, [2009] 1 ILRM 253 at 265 (Denham J referred to s.3 of the Criminal Justice (Forensic Evidence) Act 1990, which provides for inferences to be drawn from the refusal of an accused to give a sample, as creating "an exception to the rule that a suspect ought not to be obliged to provide evidence that may incriminate him").

[407] See *People (AG) v McGrath* (1964) 99 ILTR 59, *People (DPP) v Walsh* [1980] IR 294 at 309; *People (DPP) v Costigan* [2006] IECCA 51 at [32], [2007] 4 IR 511 at 521. In *Walsh*, it was held that no form of caution was required to be given prior to obtaining fingerprints but in *People (DPP) v Cleary* [2005] IECCA 51 at [46], [2005] 2 IR 189 at 204–205, it was held that a suspect should be given a tailored caution prior to a request to take fingerprints. The decision in *Costigan* is authority to the effect that an informed consent is required which requires that the suspect be informed of his entitlement to withhold consent.

[408] [2006] IESC 14 at [155]–[156], [2006] 2 IR 556 at 634, 635.

[409] [2014] IESC 17, [2014] 1 ILRM 377.

Bunreacht na hÉireann preclude the taking of objective forensic samples from a suspect while that suspect is in custody, after the relevant suspect has requested legal advice and before the relevant legal advice becomes available. That general statement is subject, of course, to the requirement that there be a legal basis for the taking of the sample concerned and that any conditions or procedures specified in the statute conferring that legal basis have been complied with. The methods adopted must also be minimally obtrusive."[410]

11–209   He did acknowledge that the position might be different where a suspect had genuine legal choices available in relation to the taking of the samples (other than a choice to refuse to give the sample and commit a criminal offence) so that it would be reasonably necessary for the suspect concerned to have access to legal advice before making any such choices. However, this exception is not meant to suggest that the right not to incriminate oneself applies in those circumstances, merely that the Art.38.1 guarantee of a trial in due course of law may be engaged and real evidence excluded on that basis where such choices exist and the accused has been deprived of legal advice as to how to exercise them.

11–210   Clarke J also rejected the contention that the admission of such evidence gave rise to a breach of the rights of the accused under art.6(1) of the European Convention on Human Rights. Having reviewed the relevant jurisprudence of the European Court of Human Rights including *Saunders* and *Jalloh* and said that he was not satisfied that:

> "the jurisprudence of the ECtHR leads to a conclusion that the taking of objective forensic samples without the benefit of legal advice amounts to a breach of the right against self-incrimination and, thus, to an unfair trial if evidence obtained from the taking of such samples is materially relied on. This is so at least in cases where, as here, any samples are taken in an unobtrusive way."[411]

11–211   This conclusion undoubtedly copperfastened his view as to the Irish position in relation to the matter.

---

[410] [2014] IESC 17 at [10.3], [2014] 1 ILRM 377 at 407.
[411] [2014] IESC 17 at [10.2], [2014] 1 ILRM 377 at 409.

CHAPTER 12

DOCUMENTARY, REAL AND ELECTRONIC EVIDENCE

A. Documentary Evidence

1. Introduction

12–01   Having regard to the central feature of orality in our justice system,[1] there is a clear preference for the oral evidence of witnesses, where available, over any form of documentary substitute.[2] However, oral evidence as to the subject-matter of a document is not always available and documentary evidence often provides essential proof of matters at issue in proceedings.

12–02   Documentary evidence is, of course, subject to the general rules of admissibility. Of particular importance in this regard is the hearsay rule which serves to exclude any document which it is sought to rely upon as evidence of the truth of its contents unless an exception to that rule is applicable[3] and the opinion evidence rule which generally serves to exclude any expressions of opinion by non-experts.[4] Apart from these general rules of admissibility, there are two specific rules at common law relating to the proof of documents and their receivability in evidence which must be satisfied before a party can rely on the contents of a document: (a) the party must prove the contents of the document; and (b) in some instances, the party must prove that the document was properly executed.[5] It is important not to conflate the rules of admissibility and the rules as to receivability of documentary evidence. In *The Leopardstown Club Limited v Templeville Developments Limited*,[6] Edwards J drew a clear and correct distinction between the general rules of admissibility that apply to all evidence including documentary evidence and the specific rules as to the receivability

---

[1]   See *Phonographic Performance Ltd v Cody* [1998] 2 ILRM 21 at 26, and *Mapp v Gilhooley* [1991] 2 IR 253 at 262.

[2]   See *Curran v Finn*, unreported, Supreme Court, 20 May 1999, where the trial judge had misunderstood the notation used on medical treatment notes admitted by consent of the parties and, as a result, attributed to the plaintiff symptoms that she was not in fact suffering from. Murphy J stated that the facts of the case "underscore[d] the dangers and difficulties or examining or analysing documents provided on discovery or put in evidence by agreement without sworn testimony of the author and his explanation of the records made by him".

[3]   See Chap.5.

[4]   See Chap.6.

[5]   See *The Leopardstown Club Limited v Templeville Developments Limited* [2010] IEHC 152 at [5.17]–[5.20].

[6]   [2010] IEHC 152 at [5.17]–[5.20] and [5.45].

of documentary evidence. He further noted that issues of admissibility do not arise for consideration at all if a document is not receivable in evidence and a document that is receivable in evidence may or may not be admissible in evidence.

12–03   As will be seen below, the legislative trend is towards more liberal admission of documentary evidence. There are numerous statutory provisions, some of which are examined below, which relax the rules in relation to the receivability in evidence in documents, and it is becoming increasingly common for statutory provisions to not only abrogate those requirements but also the hearsay rule by providing that a document will be admissible without further proof if specified conditions are satisfied.[7] The Law Reform Commission has examined the rules and principles governing the admission of documentary evidence, in its various forms, in its *Consultation Paper on Documentary and Electronic Evidence*[8] and it has provisionally recommended the adoption of an inclusionary approach to the admissibility of both manual and electronic documentary evidence, subject to a number of safeguards and the continuance of the discretion of the court to exclude the evidence.[9]

2. Concept of "Document"

12–04   The traditional definition of a "document" is that propounded in *R. v Daye*[10] by Darling J, who said that:

> "any written thing capable of being evidence is properly described as a document and…it is immaterial on what the writing may be inscribed. It might be inscribed on paper, as is the common case now; but the common case once was that it was not on paper, but on parchment; and long before that it was on stone, marble, on clay, and it might be, and often was, on metal."

12–05   However, this definition, which focused on the concept of writing, has been overtaken by technological developments and the courts are now willing to treat as a document any item from which information may be derived. In *McCarthy v O'Flynn*,[11] Kenny J pointed out that, etymologically, the word "document" is derived from the Latin word "documentum" which is turn comes from the verb "docere". He held, therefore, that a document "is something which teaches or gives information or a lesson or an example for instruction"[12] and includes "anything which, if adduced in evidence at the hearing of the proceedings, would be put in, or become annexed to the court file of the proceedings".[13] Applying that expansive approach, it has been held that the concept of "document" includes photographs,[14] maps,[15] X-rays,[16] facsimile

---

7   See, for example, s.37 of the Extradition Act 1965 (as inserted by s.17 of the Extradition (European Union Conventions) Act 2001) which was considered in *Attorney General v Pratkunas* [2009] IESC 34, [2009] 2 ILRM 1.
8   LRC CP 57–2009.
9   LRC CP 57–2009 at [5.19].
10   [1908] 2 KB 333 at 340.
11   [1979] IR 127.
12   [1979] IR 127 at 131. See also *Hill v R.* [1945] KB 329 at 334 and *Grant v South Western Properties* [1975] Ch 185. *Cf. Keane v An Bord Pleanála* [1997] 1 IR 184 at 194–196, where the authorities were reviewed by Murphy J. The Canadian courts have adopted a similar approach: see *Reichmann v Toronto Life Publishing Co.* (1988) 66 OR (2d) 65.
13   [1979] IR 127 at 129. This dictum was approved and applied by Budd J in *Clifford v Minister for Education and Science* [2005] IEHC 288 at [27].
14   *R. v Hayes* [1920] 1 KB 250 at 251.
15   *R. v Hayes* [1920] 1 KB 250 at 251.
16   *McCarthy v O'Flynn* [1979] IR 127.

transmissions,[17] audio tape recordings,[18] film recordings,[19] electronic information stored on a computer,[20] and microfiche.[21]

12–06 There has also been significant statutory intervention in this area. In criminal cases, s.2 of the Criminal Evidence Act 1992[22] defines "document" as including: (i) a map, plan, graph, drawing or photograph, and (ii) a reproduction in permanent legible form, by a computer or other means (including enlarging), of information in non-legible form.[23] Section 2 goes on to define "information" as including "any representation of fact, whether in words, or otherwise" and "information in non-legible form" as including "information on microfilm, microfiche, magnetic tape or disk". While there is no equivalent definition in the civil sphere, the provisions of the Electronic Commerce Act 2000, which are discussed below, should also be noted. The Law Reform Commission has recommended the enactment of a wide and technologically neutral definition of "document" which would encompass both traditional hard copy documents and electronic and automated information and would be applicable in both criminal and civil proceedings.[24]

3. Proof of Contents of Documents

12–07 At common law, the "best evidence rule" sought to reduce the risks of fabrication and inaccuracy by requiring a party to adduce the best evidence available of facts in issue having regard to the nature of the case.[25] Over time this rule has been fallen into disuse and has no continuing vitality in Irish law as an independent rule of admissibility.[26] However, one remaining vestige of its application is to be found in the

---

[17]   *Hastie & Jenkenson v McMahon* [1990] 1 WLR 1575 at 1583, [1991] All ER 255 at 262, 263.

[18]   *Clifford v Minister for Education and Science* [2005] IEHC 288 at [27];*Grant v Southwestern and County Properties Ltd* [1975] Ch 185, [1974] 2 All ER 465; *Tide Shore Loggin Co. v Commonwealth Insurance Co.* (1979) 13 BCLR 316, (1979) 100 DLR (3d) 112; *R. v Swartz* [1979] 2 SCR 256, (1979) 93 DLR (3d) 161.

[19]   *Senior v Holdsworth, Ex p. Independent Television News Ltd* [1976] QB 23, [1976] 2 All ER 1009.

[20]   *Clifford v Minister for Education and Science* [2005] IEHC 288 at [27]; *Dome Telecom v Eircom* [2007] IESC 59 at [13], [2008] 2 IR 726 at 736–737; *Derby v Weldon (No 9)* [1991] 1 WLR 652 at 658, [1991] 2 All ER 901 at 906; *cf. Tecoglas Inc v Domglas Inc* (1985) 19 DLR 738; *R. v Cordell* (1982) 39 AR 281. In *Prism Hospital Softward Ltd v Hospital Medical Records Institution* [1992] 2 WWR 157, (1991) 62 BCLR (2d) 393, it was held that a file which had been deleted but remained recoverable from a computer constituted a document.

[21]   *R. v Sanghi* (1971) 3 NSR 70, 6 CCC 123.

[22]   See also the definition of document in s.1 of the Criminal Justice Surveillance Act 2009: "'document' includes (a) any book, record or other written or printed material in any form, and (b) any recording, including any data or information stored, maintained or preserved electronically or otherwise than in legible form"

[23]   It should also be noted that s.30 of the 1992 Act defines document to include "a film, sound recording or video-recording".

[24]   In its *Consultation Paper on Documentary and Electronic Evidence* (LRC CP 57–2009) at [1.33], the Law Reform Commission provisionally recommended that "document" should be defined for the purposes of the law of evidence as "anything in which information of any description is recorded".

[25]   The best known formulation of the rule is to be found in *Omychund v Barker* (1744) 1 Atk 21, 26 ER 15, where Lord Hardwicke observed that "the judges and sages of the law have laid it down that there is but one general rule of evidence, the best that the nature of the case will admit". See also *Ford v Hopkins* (1701) 1 Salk 283, 90 ER 964.

[26]   *Hussey v Twomey* [2009] IESC 1 at [31], [2009] 3 IR 293 at 306, *sub nom. Hussey v MIBI* [2009] 1 ILRM 321 at 332, 333; *Martin v Quinn* [1980] IR 244 at 249 (*per* Henchy J). The best

primary evidence rule[27] which stipulates that a party who seeks to adduce evidence of and rely upon the contents of a document must adduce primary evidence thereof.[28] In most cases, this means that the original of the document rather than a copy or oral evidence of its contents must be produced. The rationale for the rule is to protect against the risk of error or fraud that arose if the original was not produced.[29]

12–08 The primary evidence rule (which is often referred to in this context as the best evidence rule), and the main exceptions thereto, were summarised as follows by O'Flaherty J in *Primor Plc v Stokes Kennedy Crowley*[30]:

> "The best evidence rule operates in this sphere to the extent that the party seeking to rely on the contents of a document must adduce primary evidence of those contents, *i.e.* the original document in question. The contents of a document may be proved by secondary evidence if the original has been destroyed or cannot be found after due search. Similarly, such contents may be proved by secondary evidence if production of the original is physically or legally impossible."[31]

12–09 A number of qualifications to the primary evidence rule should be noted. Firstly, if the party seeks to prove a fact and the document in question is merely one (or even the best) way by which that fact can be proven, then the primary evidence rule will not apply and oral evidence as to the existence of that fact will not be regarded as secondary evidence.[32] Secondly, it does not apply where a document is adduced as real evidence rather than as testimonial evidence or original evidence[33] as where it is sought to prove the fact of a document's existence rather than its contents.[34] Thirdly, the courts have declined to extend it to "non-written" documents[35] such as audio tapes,[36] video

---

evidence rule is also considered redundant in the UK: *Kajala v Noble* (1982) 75 Cr App R 149 and *Masquerade Music v Springsteen* [2001] EWCA Civ 563.

27 See the comments of Lord Denning M.R. in *Garton v Hunter* [1969] QB 37 at 44: "the old rule has gone by the board long ago. The only remaining instance of it that I know is that if the original document is available in one's hands, one must produce it. One cannot give secondary evidence by producing a copy". See also *Kajala v Noble* (1982) 75 Cr App R 149 at 152 (*per* Ackner LJ); *Martin v Quinn* [1980] IR 244 at 249 (*per* Henchy J) and *The Leopardstown Club Limited v Templeville Developments Limited* [2010] IEHC 152 at [5.17] (*per* Edwards J).

28 *Martin v Quinn* [1980] IR 244 at 248; *Primor plc v Stokes Kennedy Crowley* [1996] 2 IR 459 at 518; *Fitzpatrick v DPP* [2007] IEHC 383 at [8]; *Slatterie v Pooley* (1840) 6 M & W 664 at 447.

29 The Law Reform Commission, *Consultation Paper on Documentary and Electronic Evidence* (LRC CP 57–2009), at [2.25].

30 [1996] 2 IR 459.

31 [1996] 2 IR 459 at 518. This passage was quoted with approval and applied by O'Neill J in *Fitzpatrick v DPP* [2007] IEHC 383 and *Weir v DPP* [2008] IEHC 268 and by Edwards J in *The Leopardstown Club Limited v Templeville Developments Limited* [2010] IEHC 152 at [5.18]. The Law Reform Commission in its *Consultation Paper on Documentary and Electronic Evidence* (LRC CP 57–2009) at [2.152]–[2.153] has provisionally recommended the abolition of the best evidence rule so far as it applies to documents and its replacement with a rule that documentary evidence is, in general, admissible in civil and criminal proceedings where the court is satisfied as to its relevance and necessity.

32 See, for example, *AG v Kyle* [1933] IR 15 at 18 (proof that premises were insured); *Martin v Quinn* [1980] IR 244 at 249 (proof that medical practitioner was registered) *People (DPP) v O'Reilly* [2009] IECCA 18 at [29]–[30] (proof of existence of licence).

33 *The Leopardstown Club Limited v Templeville Developments Limited* [2010] IEHC 152 at [5.18].

34 *AG v Kyle* [1933] IR 15 at 18; *R. v Holy Trinity, Kingston Upon Hill (Inhabitants)* (1827) 7 B & C 611 at 614; *R. v Elworthy* (1867) LR 1 CCR 103; *Pelrine v Arron* (1969) 3 DLR (3d) 713 at 724.

35 In *Commissioner for Railways (NSW) v Young* (1962) 106 CLR 535 at 544, Dixon J said that "the rule excluding secondary evidence did not go beyond writing and include physical objects".

36 *Butwera v DPP (Vic.)* (1987) 164 CLR 180 at 195.

recordings[37] and photographs.[38] Fourthly, there are a number of exceptions, examined below, which permit secondary evidence, usually in the form of copies of the original, to be admitted in evidence. Fifthly, the rule is routinely ignored in civil cases and secondary evidence of the contents of documents, particularly by means of photocopies, is often admitted by the express or tacit agreement of the parties.[39] Finally, it has been largely abrogated in criminal cases by s.30 of the Criminal Evidence Act 1992 and in civil cases concerning the welfare of children by s.26 of the Children Act 1997.

(a) Primary evidence of contents of document

12–10   There are three categories of primary evidence of the contents of a document: (i) the original of the document; (ii) copies of enrolled documents; and (iii) admissions. Obviously, the best species of primary evidence is the original of a document.

(i) Original of a document

12–11   The best or most satisfactory form of primary evidence is clearly the original document itself and, if the original is produced, secondary evidence is inadmissible.[40] In most cases, the identification of the original document should not give rise to controversy. However, this can be problematic in certain circumstances, *e.g.* where duplicates or counterparts of a document are produced. Where a document is produced in duplicate and signed by each of the parties to it, each duplicate is an original.[41] In the case of counterparts, a counterpart is regarded as the original against the individual who signed it.[42] The decision as to whether a document is a duplicate or counterpart is for the court and is decided by reference to the intention of the parties at the time the document was created.

(ii) Copies of enrolled documents

12–12   An enrolled copy of a document is a copy of a private document which has been officially filed in a court or public office. Such documents are usually required to be enrolled by law and are filed in a public registry. Where a copy of an enrolled document is issued by the court or office that has lawful custody of the original, it is treated by the courts as an original. For example, the probate copy of a will is treated as primary evidence of the contents.[43]

---

[37]   *Kajala v Noble* (1983) 75 Cr App R 149 at 152–153; *Taylor v Chief Constable of Cheshire* [1986] 1 WLR 1479 at 1483.

[38]   *R. v Dodson* (1984) 79 Cr App Rep 220.

[39]   *Cf. Mapp v Gilhooley* [1991] 2 IR 253 at 262, where Finlay CJ stated that this practice does not constitute an exception to the general principle that, for the purpose of trials in either civil or criminal cases, *viva voce* evidence must be given on oath or affirmation.

[40]   *Mulhearn v Cleary* [1930] IR 649 at 682.

[41]   *Forbes v Samuel* [1913] 3 KB 706 at 722; *Hood v Cronkite* (1869) 29 UCQB 98 at 111; *Kingborne v Montreal Telegraph Co.* (1859) 18 UCQB 60 at 66; *Buckley v Macken* [1961] NZLR 46.

[42]   *Doe d West v Davis* (1806) 7 East 363.

[43]   *In re Harrison* (1885) 30 Ch D 390 at 394. A court may, however, insist on inspecting the original if there is a query which cannot be resolved by inspecting the copy: *Cecil v Battie Wrightson* [1920] 2 Ch 330 at 339.

(iii) Admissions

12–13   An informal admission as to the contents of a document by a party to litigation constitutes primary evidence of the contents and is admissible in evidence against him or her.[44] For example, in *AG v Kyle*,[45] an informal admission made by the accused to a civic guard was held admissible as proof that he had taken out an insurance policy in circumstances where the policy itself was unavailable.

(b) Secondary evidence of contents of documents

12–14   Secondary evidence of a document generally takes the form of a copy, and where it is sought to admit in evidence a copy of a document, proof is required that it is a true copy of the original.[46] It should be noted that the general rule is that "there are no degrees of secondary evidence".[47] Thus, it is immaterial whether the copy sought to be adduce in evidence is a copy of the original or a copy of a copy[48]—this is a factor which goes only to the weight to be attached to the evidence.

12–15   In general, secondary evidence of the contents of a document may also be given by means of oral testimony even if a copy of the document is available. However, there are a number of exceptions. Firstly, the contents of a will that has been admitted to probate may not be proved by oral evidence if the original will or a probate copy exists. Secondly, judicial documents may only be proved by office copies and bankers' books by examined copies. Thirdly, certain public documents may only be proved by oral evidence where specified categories of copies are not available.

12–16   There are a number of well established exceptions to the primary evidence rule where secondary evidence of the contents of a document can be given[49]: (i) when there is a failure by an opposing party to produce the original after service of a notice to produce; (ii) when a third party lawfully refuses to produce the document; (iii) if the original has been lost or destroyed; (iv) if the production of the original is impossible or inconvenient; (v) public documents; and (vi) bankers' books. The common thread running through the various exceptions is that the party adducing the documentary evidence is unable, through no fault of their own, to produce the original.[50]

(i) Failure to produce after service of notice to produce

12–17   If the opponent of a party has the original of a document in his or her possession, this presents an obvious difficulty to that party in complying with the primary evidence rule. To surmount this difficulty, it is open to a party to serve a notice to produce documents[51] on his or her opponent and, if he or she fails to produce the

---

[44]   *Slatterie v Pooley* (1840) 6 M & W 664 at 668.

[45]   [1933] IR 15.

[46]   *R. v Collins* (1960) 44 Cr App R 170; *R. v Betterest Vinyl Manufacturing Ltd* (1989) 42 BCLR 198, [1990] 2 WWR 751.

[47]   *Doe d Gilbert v Ross* (1840) 7 M & W 102 at 106 (*per* Lord Abinger CB); *R. v Wayte* (1982) 76 Cr App R 110 at 116; *Butwera v DPP* (1987) 164 CLR 180.

[48]   *Lafone v Griffin* (1909) 25 TLR 308 at 309; *R. v Collins* (1960) 44 Cr App R 170 at 174.

[49]   The equivalent passage in the first edition listing these exceptions was approved by O'Neill J in *Weir v DPP* [2008] IEHC 268 at [11]–[12].

[50]   *Cf. R. v Wayte* (1982) 76 Cr App R 110 at 116.

[51]   See Ord.32, r.8 and Appendix C, Form 16 of the Rules of the Superior Courts.

original of a document, the party who served the notice may adduce secondary evidence of the contents of that document.[52] However, it should be noted that the mere fact that an original document is in the possession of an opponent is not sufficient to justify the admission of secondary evidence of its contents; service of a notice to produce is an essential prerequisite.[53]

(ii) The lawful refusal of a third party to produce a document

12–18   This exception arises where the original document is in the power or possession of a third party who is lawfully entitled to refuse to produce it, *e.g.* where the document is privileged from production or the individual in question is outside the jurisdiction of the court. However, in order for secondary evidence of the document to be admissible, the refusal to produce the document must be lawful because if it is unlawful, production can be compelled by issuing a *subpoena duces tecum*[54] and/or instituting proceedings for contempt.

(iii) Where the original document is lost or destroyed

12–19   Where it is established to the satisfaction of the court that an original document has been lost or destroyed, secondary evidence of the contents of the original may be admitted[55] even if it has been destroyed by the party seeking to adduce the document in evidence.[56] However, the party seeking to adduce the secondary evidence must demonstrate that a pro*per se*arch was conducted and outline the steps taken to try and locate the document.[57] This exception to the primary evidence rule was helpfully summarised by Randall QC (sitting as a deputy judge of the High Court) in *Park Lane Ventures Ltd v Locke*[58] as follows:

> "In essence, to act on secondary evidence I must be satisfied that the document existed, that it has been lost or destroyed (*i.e.* the original document or 'primary evidence' is not available), and that a reasonable explanation for this has been given. For this purpose I must judge whether a sufficient search has been made, and do so according to the particular circumstances of the case."[59]

12–20   The court must also be satisfied on the evidence adduced that the original document was properly executed by all the parties and that the contents were the same as those of the copy produced. It follows that, where an original document has been damaged and reconstructed, secondary evidence of the contents of the original may

---

[52]   *Re JPR* (1970) 74 ILTR 11 at 14; *AG v Kyle* [1933] IR 15 at 18; *R. v Collins* (1960) 44 Cr App R 170 at 173; *Hayball v Shepherd* (1866) 25 UCQB 536; *Morgan v Babcock and Wilcox Ltd* (1929) 43 CLR 163; *R. v Governor of Pentonville Prison, ex parte Osman* [1939] 3 All ER 701 at 728.

[53]   *Owner v Beehive Spinning Co. Ltd* [1914] KB 105 at 108; *R. v Morgan* [1925] 1 KB 752.

[54]   See Ord.39, rr.25–34 and Appendix D, Form 3 of the Rules of the Superior Courts.

[55]   *In the Goods of McQuillan* [1954] Ir Jur Rep 10 at 12; *Fitzpatrick v DPP* [2007] IEHC 383 at [8]; *R. v Wayte* (1982) 76 Cr App Rep 110; *Public Prosecution Service v Duddy* [2008] NICA 18; *R. v Swartz* (1977) 37 CCC 409 at 410–412; *R. v Thompson* [2001] 1 NZLR 129.

[56]   *Post Office Counters v Mahida* [2003] EWCA Civ 1583.

[57]   *Staples v Young* [1908] 1 IR 135 at 151; *McDonald v Royal Bank of Canada* [1934] 1 WWR 732 at 741; *Lilwall v Stockford* [1934] 3 WWR 746 at 749. It is a matter for the trial judge to decide whether sufficient efforts to locate the original of the document have been made: *Arowolo v DPP* [2013] EWHC (Admin) 1671 at [17].

[58]   [2006] EWHC 1578 (Ch) at [28].

[59]   See also *Random House UK Ltd v Allason* [2008] EWHC 2854 (Ch) at [46] and *R. v Cassell* (1998) 45 NSWLR 325 at 337 (tape recording).

only be given by the individual responsible for the reconstruction as otherwise it will not be possible for the tribunal of fact to reach a conclusion as to how reliable the secondary evidence of the contents is.[60]

12–21 This exception is particularly important in the context of documents of title because it is not uncommon for deeds to be lost or damaged over time. In the case of registered land, the memorial in the Registry of Deeds usually suffices as secondary evidence.[61] In *Nally v Nally*,[62] a copy of an original deed was held to be admissible as evidence of the contents of the original in circumstances where the original deed was shown to have been lost even though it had never been stamped as required by law.[63]

(iv) Production of original impossible or inconvenient

12–22 Secondary evidence of the contents of a document is admissible where the production of the original is impossible, in the sense that it is physically impossible to produce it in court,[64] *e.g.* where the document consists of an inscription on a building or tombstone.[65] In *Owner v Bee Hive Spinning Co Ltd*,[66] the document in question was a notice setting out mealtimes in a factory that was required, by statute, to remain fixed to the wall. Ridley J reaffirmed the principle that where the production of the original is impossible, or highly inconvenient, secondary evidence is admissible.[67]

(v) Public documents

12–23 The exception that secondary evidence of documents could be adduced where production of the original was physically impossible was extended at common law to permit the reception of secondary evidence of the contents of public documents[68] because of the degree of inconvenience involved in the production of the originals.[69] Proof of the contents of public documents by means of secondary evidence is now provided for by a number of statutory provisions which provide for the admission

---

[60]   *People (DPP) v Marley* [1985] ILRM 17.

[61]   *In Re Harding's Estate* (1860) Ch App 29 at 32 (the memorial coupled with evidence of uninterrupted receipt of the rent charge was admissible as secondary evidence of the creation and subsistence of said rentcharge).

[62]   [1953] IR 19 at 21.

[63]   See also *London & County Banking Company v Radcliffe* (1880) 6 App Cas 722 at 730.

[64]   *Fitzpatrick v DPP* [2007] IEHC 383 at [8].

[65]   See *Mortimer v M'Callan* (1840) 6 M & W 58 at 68.

[66]   [1914] KB 105.

[67]   [1914] KB 105 at 108.

[68]   The Law Reform Commission in its *Consultation Paper on Documentary and Electronic Evidence* (LRC CP 57–2009), at [1.41] has provisionally recommended that a "public document" should be defined as "a document retained in a depository or register relating to a matter of public interest whether of concern to sectional interests or to the community as a whole, compiled under a public duty and which is amenable to public inspection". It also provisionally recommended (at [3.82]) that such a public document should be presumed to be admissible as proof of its contents subject to any contrary evidence as to its authenticity but (at [3.94]) that there should be no presumption of due execution of private documents.

[69]   See *Mortimer v M'Callan* (1840) 6 M & W 58 (books of the Bank of England).

of examined copies,[70] certified copies,[71] office copies[72] or Stationery Office copies[73] as appropriate. Specific statutory provision is made for proof of the proceedings of either House of the Oireachtas,[74] the passing of a resolution by either House of the Oireachtas,[75] the treaties governing the European Communities, acts adopted by an institution of the European Communities and judgments and orders of the European Court of Justice,[76] proclamations, treaties and Acts of State of foreign countries,[77] county and other boundaries in ordnance maps,[78] the vesting of land in the Land Commission,[79] documents registered in the Companies Office,[80] entries in the register of pharmacists[81] and entries in the register of births, the register of stillbirths, the register of adoptions, the register of deaths, the register of marriages, the register of decrees of divorce and the register of decrees of nullity.[82] In addition, s.14 of the Evidence Act 1851 contains

---

[70] An examined copy is a copy proved by the oral evidence of a person who has examined the original to correspond to the original.

[71] A certified copy is a copy certified by an official with custody of the original to be an accurate copy.

[72] An office copy is a copy of a judicial document prepared by a court official with custody of the original and authenticated with the seal of the court.

[73] A Stationery Office copy is a copy printed under the superintendence or authority of and published by the Stationery Office: see ss.1 and 5 of the Documentary Evidence Act 1925. Section 2 of the Documentary Evidence Act 1868 originally provided for proof of a proclamation, order or regulation by production of either a copy of the *Gazette* in which it was published or a copy printed by the government printer. This was amended by s.2 of the Documentary Evidence Act 1882 so as to render documents printed by the Stationary Office receivable in evidence. Section 4 of the 1882 Act specifically applied these provisions to Ireland.

[74] Section 2 of the Documentary Evidence Act 1925 provides that *prima facie* evidence of the Journal of the proceedings of either House of the Oireachtas may be given by the production of a copy of such Journal printed under the superintendence or authority of and published by the Stationery Office.

[75] Section 11 of the Criminal Evidence Act 1992 provides that, in any criminal proceedings, evidence of the passing of a resolution by either House of the Oireachtas, whether before or after the commencement of the section, may be given by the production of a copy of the Journal of the proceedings of that House relating to the resolution and purporting to have been published by the Stationery Office.

[76] See the European Communities (Judicial Notice and Documentary Evidence) Regulations 1972 (SI No. 341 of 1972).

[77] Section 7 of the Evidence Act 1851.

[78] The County Boundaries (Ireland) Act 1872 provides that every a copy of any ordnance map made under that Act or the Survey (Ireland) Acts 1854–1859 and purporting to be duly certified as a true copy shall be conclusive evidence of the original map for all purposes. See the discussion of these provisions in *Brown v Donegal County Council* [1980] IR 132. See also s.6(5) of the Curragh of Kildare Act 1961 which makes provision for the admission in evidence of certified copies of a deposited map of the Curragh and was considered in *Minister for Defence v Buckley* [1978] IR 314.

[79] Section 40 of the Land Act 1923. See *Nugent v McGuinness* [1948] IR 419 at 421.

[80] Section 370(3) of the Companies Act 1963 (as inserted by s.62 of the Company Law Enforcement Act 2001). It was held in *Director of Corporate Enforcement v Bailey* [2007] IEHC 365, [2008] 2 ILRM 13 at 45, that the certification of copies of documents registered in the Companies Office which are admitted pursuant to this section does not improve the admissibility of the original document and the copy will not be admissible if the original would not.

[81] Section 23 of the Pharmacy Act 2007.

[82] Section 13(4) of the Civil Registration Act 2004 provides that evidence of an entry in one of these registers, and of the facts stated therein, may be given by the production of a document purporting to be a legible copy of the entry and to be certified to be a true copy by an An tÁrd Chláraitheoir, a person authorised in that behalf by an An tÁrd Chláraitheoir, a Superintendent Registrar, an authorised officer of a registrar. As to the retrospective effect of this subsection, see *DPP v McDermott* [2005] IEHC 132, [2005] 3 IR 378 (dealing with s.30A of the Registration of

a catch-all provision whereby certified or examined copies may be used to prove the contents of documents of such a public nature that they are admissible in evidence if produced from proper custody if no other statute provides for proof of the contents of such document by means of a copy.[83]

12–24   The Documentary Evidence 1925 contains a number of very important provisions regarding proof of the contents of primary and secondary legislation. Section 2 provides that *prima facie* evidence of an Act of the Oireachtas may be given by the production of a copy of such Act printed under the superintendence or authority of and published by the Stationery Office.[84] Section 4 further provides that *prima facie* evidence of any rules,[85] orders, regulations or byelaws made by the Government, Ministers or statutory bodies may be given by the production of a copy of the *Iris Oifigiúil* purporting to contain same or by the production of a copy of such rules, orders, regulations,[86] or byelaws printed under the superintendence or authority of and published by the Stationery Office.[87] Section 5 contains a presumption that every copy of an Act of the Oireachtas, proclamation, order, rule, regulation, by-law, or other official document which purports to be published by the authority of the Stationery Office is presumed, until the contrary is proven, to have been printed under the superintendence and authority of and to have been published by the Stationery Office.

12–25   Sections 2 and 4 were considered by the Supreme Court in *DPP v Collins*,[88] where Henchy J noted that it was not necessary to prove the specified documents in evidence and production of same was sufficient:

> "In both cases it is the *production* of the specified version that enables the court to treat that version as *prima facie* evidence of the document. Thus it is that the courts routinely act on the Stationery Office version of a piece of delegated legislation (such as the Rules of Courts) no less than they act on the Stationery Act version of a statute. They do so under the enabling powers bestowed on them by the 1925 Act, and it makes no difference whether the case is

---

Births and Deaths Act 1863). The provisions of s.68 of the Act (which are discussed in Chap.5) should also be noted. See also s.5(5) of the Criminal Evidence Act 1992 which provides that, where a document purports to be a birth certificate issued pursuant to the Births and Deaths Registration Acts 1863 to 1987 and a person is named therein as father or mother of the person to whose birth the certificate relates, the document shall be admissible in any criminal proceedings as evidence of the relationship indicated therein.

[83] See also s.1 of the Evidence Act 1845 which provides that where a statute provides for proof of a document by a certified, sealed or stamped copy, the copy, provided that it purports to be signed, sealed or stamped is admissible without proof of the sign, seal or stamp. Section 8 of the Documentary Act 1925 provides that the Evidence Acts 1868, 1882 and 1845 do not apply to documents to which the 1925 Act applies. However, where the 1925 Act does not apply they continue in force.

[84] See also s.5 of the Statute Law (Restatement) Act 2002 which applies the provisions of the Documentary Evidence Act 1925 to Restatements as if they were Acts of the Oireachtas. It should also be noted that s.13 of the Interpretation Act 2005 provides that an Act of the Oireachtas is a public document and is required to be judicially noticed.

[85] In *Tangney v District Justice for Kerry* [1928] IR 358 at 375, it was held that the District Court Rules were rules made by a Minister within the meaning of the 1925 Act and, therefore, a copy of the Rules printed by the Stationary Office was *prima facie* evidence that the Rules had been validly made.

[86] See *O'Conghaile v Wallace* [1938] IR 526 at 541.

[87] In *Mitchell v Member in Charge, Terenure Garda Station* [2013] IEHC 221 at [5]–[6], it was held by Hogan J that resolutions by the Houses of the Oireachtas fall outside the scope of s.4 because s.4(1) is confined to "rules, orders, regulations or bye-laws" and does not extend to resolutions and the Oireachtas is not a body specified in s.4(2).

[88] [1981] ILRM 447.

civil or criminal, or, if criminal, whether the piece of delegated legislation in question has created the offence charged."[89]

12–26 Given that s.13 of the Interpretation Act 2005, which requires judicial notice to be taken of Acts of the Oireachtas, is confined in its application to primary legislation, the failure by the prosecution to prove the contents of subordinate legislation in accordance with the provisions of the Documentary Evidence Act will generally prove fatal to a criminal prosecution because it will raise a doubt as to the existence of and precise ingredients of the offence.[90] However, judicial notice may be taken of statutory instruments when they are "so notorious, well established, embedded in judicial decisions, and susceptible of incontrovertible proof, [that] a judge could not but take judicial notice of their making".[91]

(vi) Bankers' Books

12–27 The Bankers' Books Evidence Acts 1879 and 1959[92] (as amended by s.131 of the Central Bank Act 1989 and s.126 of the Building Societies Act 1989) provide for the admissibility of copies of entries from the books and records of a bank[93] against any person[94] as *prima facie* evidence of their contents in any proceedings.[95] If a book or record can be proven utilising the provisions of the Act, then an officer of the bank is not compellable to produce that book or record or to appear as a witness to prove the matters therein recorded except by order of a judge made for special cause.[96]

12–28 At a time when banks recorded transactions by way of handwritten entries in books, the purpose of allowing proof of such entries by secondary evidence was to avoid the inconvenience that resulted from requiring a bank official to bring the original books of the bank to court which were not then available to the bank to make entries therein.[97] Given that bank records are no longer maintained by way of handwritten entries in books, the modern day purpose of these provisions is to provide a convenient means of proving information contained in bank records and avoid the necessity of requiring a bank official to attend, most likely on foot of a *subpoena duces tecum*, to give

---

[89] [1981] ILRM 447 at 450.

[90] *People (AG) v Kennedy* [1946] IR 517 at 521; *People (AG) v Griffin* [1974] IR 416 at 419; *DPP v Collins* [1981] ILRM 447 at 450; *People (DPP) v Cleary* [2005] IECCA 51 at [33], [2005] 2 IR 189 at 201; *Kelly v Dempsey* [2010] IEHC 336.

[91] *DPP v Collins* [1981] ILRM 447, 451. See further, Chap.13.

[92] See, generally, Dunne and Davies, "The Bankers' Books Evidence Acts 1879 and 1959" (1997) 2 (7) BR 297. The Law Reform Commission in its *Consultation Paper on Documentary and Electronic Evidence* (LRC CP 57–2009), at [4.162] provisionally recommended the retention of the Bankers' Book Evidence Act 1879 (as amended) with its application extended to all credit institutions.

[93] The concept of "bank" and "banker" are defined in s.9 of the 1879 Act (as amended by s.2 of the Bankers' Books Evidence (Amendment) Act 1959 and s.126 of the Building Societies Act 1989).

[94] *Harding v Williams* (1880) 14 Ch D 197 at 199.

[95] Section 3 of the Bankers' Books Evidence Act 1879.

[96] Section 6. As noted by O'Malley J in *Ulster Bank Ireland Ltd v Dermody* [2014] IEHC 140 at [19], until amended by s.131 of the Central Bank Act 1989, s.6 only applied to legal proceedings to which the bank was not itself a party.

[97] *Bank of Scotland plc v Stapleton* [2012] IEHC 549 at [9]; *JB O'C v PCD* [1985] IR 265 at 274; *Larkins v National Union of Mineworkers* [1985] IR 671 at 695.

such evidence.[98] Although the provisions can be availed of by a bank in order to prove bank records in any proceedings,[99] this is not the primary purpose of the legislation.[100]

12–29   The application of the these Acts turns on the concept of "bankers' books" which are defined in s.9 of the 1879 Act (as amended[101]) to include any records used in the ordinary business of a bank, or used in the transfer department of a bank acting as registrar of securities, whether comprised in bound volume, loose-leaf binders or other loose-leaf ledger sheets, pages, folios, or cards, or kept on microfilm,[102] magnetic tape or in any non-legible form (by the use of electronics or otherwise)[103] which is capable of being reproduced in a permanent legible form together with documents in manuscript, documents which are typed, printed, stencilled or created by any other mechanical or partly mechanical process in use from time to time and documents which are produced by any photographic or photostatic process.[104] It was held by Murphy J in *Volkering v Haughton*[105] that this definition of bankers' books is wide enough to include correspondence from a customer to a bank relating to an account with has been retained and forms part of the records of the bank.[106]

12–30   In order for an entry in a bankers' book to be admitted in evidence, it must be proved by the person seeking to admit the copy that, at the time of the making of the entry, the book was one of the ordinary books of the bank,[107] the entry was made in the usual and ordinary course of business, and the book is in the custody or control of the bank.[108] In accordance with s.4 of Bankers' Books Evidence Act 1879, such evidence must be given by a partner or officer[109] of the bank (orally or by affidavit)

---

[98]   *Moorview Developments Ltd v First Active plc* [2010] IEHC 275 at [4.8]; *Walsh v National Irish Bank Ltd* [2013] IESC 2 at [7.5]. See also *JB O'C v PCD* [1985] IR 265 at 274.

[99]   *Ulster Bank Ireland Ltd v Dermody* [2014] IEHC 140 at [48].

[100]   *Moorview Developments Ltd v First Active plc* [2010] IEHC 275 at [4.8]; *Bank of Ireland v Keehan* [2013] IEHC 631.

[101]   By s.2 of the Bankers' Books Evidence (Amendment) Act 1959 and s.131 of the Central Bank Act 1989.

[102]   In *Wheatley v Commissioner of Police of British Virgin Islands* [2006] UKPC 24 at [13], [2006] 1 WLR 1683, 1692 it was accepted that copies of cheques drawn by customers and recorded on microfilm fell within the definition of "bankers' books".

[103]   Where computer printouts are relied upon, it is necessary to prove that the computer accurately records the relevant data and was operating correctly: *R. v Chow* (1991) 68 CCC 190.

[104]   *Cf. Williams v Williams* [1988] 1 QB 161 (addition of cheque or credit slip to the bundles of such documents retained by a bank could not be regarded as making an entry in the records of the bank) and *Barker v Wilson* [1980] 1 WLR 884, [1980] 2 All ER 81 (entry in bankers' books included any form of permanent record kept by the bank by means made available by modern technology including records on microfilm).

[105]   [2005] IEHC 240, [2010] 1 IR 417.

[106]   He did not follow the narrower view of Murphy J in *JB O'C v PCD* [1985] IR 265, a decision which predated the amendment to s.9 effected by s.131 of the Central Bank Act 1989, that the concept of bankers' books did not extend to items of correspondence because the removal of those documents would not inconvenience the business of a bank. He also distinguished English cases including *R. v Dadson* (1983) 77 Cr App R 91 on the basis that the definition of bankers' books in s.9 (as amended) is wider than the amended definition in the UK.

[107]   See *Permanent TSB v Beades* [2014] IEHC 81 at [21] where McGovern J was satisfied that the description of documents in an affidavit as "books, documents and records of the Plaintiff bank" was sufficient to establish that they were "bankers' books" for the purpose of the 1897 Act.

[108]   Section 4 of the Bankers' Books Evidence Act 1879. Such proof may be given by a partner or officer of the bank orally or by affidavit.

[109]   An employee of the bank will be considered to an officer for the purposes of the Acts: *Ulster Bank Ireland Ltd v Dermody* [2014] IEHC 140 at [50].

and it was held in *Bank of Scotland Plc v Stapleton*[110] that delegation in this regard is not permissible so that such evidence cannot be given by a person who is not a partner or officer of the bank even if authorised by the bank to do so and even if that person has direct access to the records of the bank.[111] *A fortiori*, the Acts cannot be invoked if the person giving evidence is not an employee and therefore not an officer of the bank in question.[112]

12–31   It must also be proved by evidence given orally or on affidavit by a person who has examined the original entry and the copy that the copy of the entry in the bankers' book is an accurate copy.[113] However, such evidence does not have to given by a partner or official in the bank.[114]

4. Proof of Copies in Criminal Proceedings

12–32   Section 30 of the Criminal Evidence Act 1992 greatly simplifies and relaxes the common law rules with regard to the admission of documentary evidence by making copies of documents "freely admissible"[115] in criminal proceedings. Subsection (1) provides that, where information contained in a document[116] is admissible in evidence in criminal proceedings, "the information may be given in evidence, whether or not the document is still in existence, by producing a copy of the document, or of the material part of it, authenticated in such manner as the court may approve". It is immaterial, in that regard, how many removes there are between the copy and the original, or by what means (which may include facsimile transmission) the copy produced or any intermediate copy was made.[117] It is also immaterial that the quality of the copies is poor if they have been sufficiently authenticated.[118]

12–33   It should be noted that s.2(2) of the 1992 Act provides that nothing in s.30

---

[110] [2012] IEHC 549 at [15].

[111] In *Permanent TSB v Beades* [2014] IEHC 81, McGovern J rejected a contention that the plaintiff bank had failed to establish that the deponents of affidavits, who described their functions within the bank but did not expressly state they were officers of the bank, were in fact officers of the bank.

[112] *Ulster Bank Ireland Ltd v Dermody* [2014] IEHC 140 at [52]. In *Ulster Bank Ireland Ltd v Kavanagh* [2014] IEHC 299, Baker J refused to give the decision in *Dermody* retrospective effect so as to set aside a judgment obtained before that decision was handed down.

[113] Section 5 of the Bankers' Books Evidence Act 1879 as originally enacted required proof that the copy had been examined with the original entry and was correct. Section 5 (as substituted by s.131 of the Central Bank Act 1989) now provides that a copy of an entry in a bankers' book cannot be received in evidence unless it is proved that: (a) in the case where the copy sought to be received in evidence has been reproduced in a legible form directly by either or both mechanical and electronic means from a bankers' book maintained in non-legible form, it has been so reproduced; (b) in the case where the copy sought to be received in evidence has been made (either directly or indirectly) from a copy to which paragraph (a) of the section would apply, the copy sought to be so received has been examined with a copy so reproduced and is a correct copy and the copy so reproduced is a copy to which paragraph (a) would apply if it were sought to have it received in evidence; and (c) in any other case, the copy has been examined with the original entry and is correct. Under s.5(2), proof that the foregoing requirements have been met can be only be given by the categories of persons specified therein and may be given either orally or on affidavit.

[114] *Bank of Scotland plc v Stapleton* [2012] IEHC 549 at [12]; *R. v Albutt* (1911) 6 Cr App R 55.

[115] *Per* Hardiman J in *McFarlane v DPP* [2006] IESC 11 at [29], [2007] 1 IR 134 at 146.

[116] Document is defined in s.30(3) as including a film, sound recording or video-recording.

[117] Subsection (2).

[118] See *Public Prosecution Service v Duddy* [2008] NICA 18 dealing with an equivalent provision in art.30 of the Criminal Justice (Evidence) (Northern Ireland) Order 2004.

shall prejudice the admissibility in evidence in any criminal proceedings of information contained in a document that would otherwise be admissible. The converse also applies and s.30 cannot be relied on to render admissible a copy of a document if the original would not be admissible on the basis that it is hearsay or otherwise.[119]

12–34　The application of s.30 arose for consideration in *Carey v Hussey*.[120] The applicant had been prosecuted for a domestic violence offence arising out of an alleged breach of a safety order. When the matter came on for hearing, the prosecution sought to adduce in evidence a photocopy of the original safety order. However, the applicant objected on the basis that the photocopy was not admissible and that the only admissible evidence of the making of such an order was the production of either the original order or a certified copy of same. Kearns J stated that s.30 confers a very wide discretion on a judge to accept copies, be they photocopies or facsimile copies, as admissible evidence. It was a matter for the judge to determine the manner in which he or she would deem a copy of a document to be duly authenticated. Thus, in the instant case, the District Judge was perfectly entitled to accept a photocopy as adequate proof of the order.[121]

5. Proof of Copies in Proceedings Concerning the Welfare of Children and Persons with a Mental Disability

12–35　Section 26 of the Children Act 1997, which applies to civil proceedings under Part III of that Act concerning the welfare of a child or a person with a mental disability, contains provisions very similar to those of s.30 of the Criminal Evidence Act 1992.[122] Subsection (1) provides that, where information contained in a document[123] is admissible in evidence in proceedings concerning the welfare of a child, "the information may be given in evidence, whether or not the document is still in existence, by producing a copy of the document, or of the material part of it, authenticated in such manner as the court may approve". It is immaterial, in that regard, how many removes there are between the copy and the original, or by what means (which may include facsimile transmission) the copy produced or any intermediate copy was made.[124]

6. Proof of Due Execution

12–36　As a general rule, proof of due execution of a document is required for its admission in evidence in either civil or criminal proceedings.[125] This generally involves proving that it was written or signed by the person by whom it purports to have been written or signed.[126] However, in most cases, proof of due execution of documents is

---

[119] *Cf. Director of Corporate Enforcement v Bailey* [2007] IEHC 365, [2008] 2 ILRM 13 at 45.
[120] [2000] 2 ILRM 401.
[121] See also *Fitzpatrick v DPP* [2007] IEHC 383 at [9].
[122] See s.20 of the 1997 Act. Under that section, the provisions of Part III relating to children are applied, with necessary modifications, to civil proceedings concerning the welfare of a person who is of full age but who has a mental disability to such an extent that it is not reasonably possible for the person to live independently.
[123] "Document" is defined in s.26(3) as including a sound recording and a video-recording.
[124] Subsection (2).
[125] See *The Leopardstown Club Limited v Templeville Developments Limited* [2010] IEHC 152 at [5.19] for a detailed discussion of this requirement. *Cf. Walker v Leonach* [2012] IEHC 24 at [111].
[126] It should be noted that where a document is required to be signed, it is not necessary that the

presumed or excused by a combination of common law presumptions and statutory provisions.

(a) Dispensing with the requirement for proof of due execution

12–37   At common law, there is a presumption of due execution where a document is 30 years old and comes from proper custody.[127] The concept of "proper custody" means that the document has been kept in a place in which one might reasonably and naturally expect to find it, having regard to the nature of the document and the circumstances of the case.[128] It is also presumed that the document was made on the date on which it purports to have been made.[129] Proof of due execution is also dispensed with where a party, on whom a notice to produce documents has been served, refuses to produce the original.[130]

12–38   In the case of public documents, the requirement for proof of due execution is generally dispensed with by the statutory provisions (considered above) that provide for proof of the contents of those documents by secondary evidence. In addition, the maxim of *omnia praesumuntur rite et solemniter esse acta* gives rise to a rebuttable presumption that a public document has been properly executed on production of an admissible copy. This presumption has been applied so as to uphold the validity of signatures applied by rubber stamp unless it is shown that it was not affixed by the person whose signature it purports to be.[131]

(b) Proof of handwriting or signature

12–39   Where it is required to be proved, the handwriting or signature of the author of a document may be proved in a variety of ways. Firstly, oral evidence may be given by the author of the document to the effect that he or she wrote and/or signed it, or by another person who witnessed the writing or signing of the document. Alternatively, the execution of the writing or signature of the document may be proved by an admissible hearsay statement of the author or a witness.

---

signature be legible provided that it is shown to be the authentic signature of the signatory: *DPP v Collins* [1981] ILRM 447.

[127] *Donegall v Templemore* (1858) 9 ICLR 374 at 404; *Miller v Wheatley* (1890) 25 LR Ir 144 at 161; *Permanent Trustee Co. of NSW v Fels* [1918] AC 879. In *Doe d Oldham v Wolley* (1828) 8 B & C 22 at 24, the court held that the presumption is equally applicable to a will.

[128] *Murphy on Evidence*, 8th edn (Oxford: Oxford University Press, 2003), p.670, para.19.16. See *Doe d. Jacobs v Phillips* (1845) 8 QB 158 and *Thompson v Bennett* (1872) 22 UCCP 393.

[129] *Anderson v Weston* (1840) 6 Bing NC 296; *Dillon v Grange* (1941) 64 CLR 253. In the case of a deed which is over 20 years old, there is a presumption that it was duly made and executed on the date it bears and duly sealed (s.2(2) of the Vendor and Purchaser Act 1874). There is also a presumption that any alterations on the face of the deed were made prior to execution (*Doe d Tatum v Catomore* (1851) 16 QB 745). That presumption does not apply in the case of wills and there is, instead, an onus on a person who seeks to derive an advantage from an alteration in a will to adduce some evidence to establish that the alteration was made before the will was executed (*In the Goods of Benn* [1938] IR 313; *In the Estate of Myles* [1993] ILRM 34).

[130] *Jones v Jones* (1841) 9 M & W 75.

[131] *People (DPP) v McCormack* [1984] IR 177; *State (McCarthy) v Governor of Mountjoy Prison* [1997] 2 ILRM 361. In *McCarthy*, Ó Dálaigh CJ endorsed the view expressed by Boville CJ in *Bennett v Brumfitt* (1867) LR 3 CP 28, that there is no distinction in principle between using a pen or pencil and using a stamp where the impression is put upon the paper by the proper hand of the party signing.

12–40   Secondly, opinion evidence may be given by a person who, although not a witness to the execution of the document, is acquainted with the handwriting of the person in question.[132] Obviously, the weight to be attached to such opinion evidence will vary according to the circumstances, in particular, the extent to which the witness is familiar with the handwriting of the alleged author.

12–41   Finally, handwriting or a signature may be proved by the comparison of the disputed document in question (or a photocopy thereof[133]) with another document which is proved or admitted to have been written by the person in question.[134] The admissibility of such evidence is provided for in s.8 of the Criminal Procedure Act 1865:

> "Comparison of a disputed writing with any writing proved to the satisfaction of the judge to be genuine shall be permitted to be made by witnesses; and such writings, and the evidence of witnesses respecting the same, may be submitted to the court and jury as evidence of the genuineness or otherwise of the writing in dispute."[135]

12–42   Section 8 does not specify that a comparison of handwriting can only be made by an expert witness, and, to date, the Irish courts have not imposed any such restriction.[136] However, the English courts have held that the jury should not engage in a comparison of samples of handwriting without the assistance of an expert witness[137] and, further, should be warned of the dangers of doing so.[138]

12–43   Although s.8 applies to both civil and criminal proceedings, the standard of proof which must be met differs accordingly. In civil proceedings it will suffice if the court is satisfied as to the genuineness of the specimen of handwriting on a balance of probabilities. However, in a criminal case, this must be proved beyond a reasonable doubt.[139]

---

[132] *Doe d Mudd v Suckermore* (1837) 5 Ad & El 703 at 705. See also *People (DPP) v Malocco*, unreported, Court of Criminal Appeal, 23 May 1996; *Pitre v R.* [1933] SCR 69, [1933] 1 DLR 417. For a discussion of the dangers of such evidence, see *Summer v Booth* [1974] 2 NSWLR 174.

[133] *Lockheed-Arabia Corp v Owen* [1993] 3 All ER 641 at 647; *Grayden v R.* [1989] WAR 208 at 211–213. *Cf. Hartzell v US* (1934) 72 F 2d 569 at 583, where it was held that photographic comparisons of handwriting samples are admissible. See Katz, "Expert and Photographic Evidence of Authorship of Unavailable Disputed Writings" (1991) Aust Bar Rev 153.

[134] It has been held in Australia that the control document can be proved to be the handwriting of the person in question by expert evidence: *Hannes v DPP (Cth) (No.2)* (2006) 165 A Crim R 151.

[135] See *People (DPP) v Malocco*, unreported, Court of Criminal Appeal, 23 May 1996, where Keane J stated that s.8 "is intended to provide a machinery for the determination of the authenticity of a disputed writing, requiring as a precondition that the trial judge should satisfy himself that a genuine specimen of the disputed handwriting has been proved, before allowing witnesses to give evidence as to the genuineness or otherwise of the disputed writing". In *People (DPP) v Barnes* [2006] IECCA 165 at [96], [2007] 3 IR 130 at 159, it was stated that this method of proving a signature was "not ideal".

[136] *Cf. AG v Kyle* [1933] IR 15 (employee of insurance company permitted to give comparison evidence). See also *R. v Stephens* [1999] 3 NZLR 81 (witness may be either an expert, or someone familiar with the handwriting of the accused).

[137] *R. v Rickard* (1918) 13 Cr App R 140; *R. v Tilley* [1961] 1 WLR 1309 at 1312.

[138] *R. v O'Sullivan* [1969] 1 WLR 497 at 503, [1969] 2 All ER 237 at 242. A warning is also required in New Zealand (see *R. v AB* [1974] 2 NZLR 425).

[139] *R. v Ewing* [1983] 2 All ER 645 at 653, [1983] QB 1039 at 1047; *Blythe v Blythe* [1966] AC 643 at 673. The Australian Court of Criminal Appeal declined to follow *Ewing* in *R. v Browne-Kerr* [1990] VR 78. However, the courts in New Zealand have also adopted the standard of proof beyond a reasonable doubt (see *R. v Sim* [1987] 1 NZLR 356).

(c) Proof of attestation

12–44   On occasion, proof of due execution may require evidence of attestation. For example, this is often necessary where it is sought to prove wills and other testamentary documents. The attestation of a will may be proved by the oral evidence of one of the attesting witnesses if available. Where it is sought to adduce other evidence of attestation, it must be established that all of the attesting witnesses are dead, insane, outside the jurisdiction, or untraceable. However, strict compliance with this rule is not required in practice where a grant of probate has been obtained.

(d) Stamping of documents

12–45   Any transfer or lease of land which is subject to a requirement of stamping is inadmissible in evidence, other than in criminal proceedings or civil proceedings by the Revenue Commissioners to recover stamp duty, unless it is duly stamped.[140]

7. Admission of Documents by Agreement in Civil Cases

12–46   In the vast majority of civil cases, with judicial encouragement if required, it is agreed by parties that, unless an issue is taken with the authenticity of a particular document, all documents which are discovered in the proceedings are admissible without proof of their contents or execution. As Clarke J observed in *Moorview Developments Ltd v First Active plc*[141]: "It would be unreal, in modern litigation, to require a plaintiff to prove documentation which had ... been discovered on oath by a defendant or defendants." A party who refuses to agree to proceed on this basis is likely to be visited with some form of adverse costs order arising from the inevitable extension in the length of the trial that will thereby result unless there is a good reason for adopting this position.[142]

12–47   Documents that are agreed to be admitted on this basis are still subject to the rules of evidence governing admissibility including, most importantly, the hearsay rule and so will not be admissible in order to prove the truth of their contents unless an exception to the hearsay rule applies. In order to surmount this difficulty, in cases that feature large numbers of documents, particularly those that have been admitted to the Commercial List or Competition List or are case managed as if they had been so admitted, the agreement between the parties generally goes further and it is agreed that documents are admissible on what has become known as the *Bula/Fyffes* basis.[143] Where this is agreed, the documents the subject of the agreement (usually the discovered documents and/or the documents compiled in core books) are also admitted as *prima facie* evidence of the truth of their contents as against the party who created the original of the document in question. However, documents, the originals of which were created

---

[140]   Section 12(3) of the Stamp Duties Consolidation Act 1999 (as amended by s.101 of the Finance Act 2007). See also *Slatterie v Pooley* (1840) 6 M & W 664 at 664 and *Anakin Pty Ltd v Chatswood BBQ King Pty Ltd* (2008) 250 AKR 620.

[141]   [2008] IEHC 211 at [3.4].

[142]   The imposition of a costs sanction on a party who unreasonably insisted on original documents being proved in evidence was canvassed by the Singapore Court of Appeal in *Jet Holdings Ltd v Cooper Cameron (Singapore) Ptd Ltd* [2006] SGCA 20 at [50].

[143]   See *Moorview Developments Ltd v First Active plc* [2008] IEHC 211 at [3.4]–[3.8] and [2009] IEHC 214 at [3.1], referring to *Bula Ltd (Receivership) v Tara Mines Ltd* [1997] IEHC 202 and *Fyffes v DCC* [2005] IEHC 477.

by any other party to the proceedings or a non-party, are not so admitted. Such an agreement, which will result in significant savings in time at a hearing, recognises the reality that, frequently, the documents created by a party will be admissible as an admission by way of an exception to the hearsay rule in any event.

12–48   As can be seen from *Moorview Developments Ltd v First Active plc*,[144] an agreement to admit documents on the *Bula/Fyffes* basis can lead to some practical difficulties. As Clarke J noted in that case:

> Without such an admission, any document which a party wished to establish would need to be proved in the ordinary way. The document would, therefore, be the subject of some reference by a relevant witness. If anyone wanted to say anything about the document then that witness, or indeed any other witness, could be asked about it. Any other related documents which, it might be said, placed the document under consideration in context, could also be referred to. At a minimum the fact that some reliance was being placed on the document concerned would be obvious to each of the parties, and indeed, the court.[145]

12–49   He went on to say that the fundamental issue in this regard was to ensure fairness:

> Where a party makes a concession to the effect that its documents can be admitted on the *Bula/Fyffes* basis, then it seems to me that basic fairness requires that an opposing party wishing to place reliance on any such document or documents needs to make some reference to the document concerned, and to the interpretation which it is sought to place on that document, so as to give the party whose document it is an opportunity to know the case against it that is being made in reliance on the document or documents concerned, and to challenge that case if it should wish to do so. It seems to me, therefore, that at the level of principle it would amount to an unfair procedure if a party were to allow the evidence to close without making any reference to a particular document, but then to rely on that document as evidence whether in closing submissions or, in the case, as here, of an application for a non-suit, in submissions at the close of the plaintiff's case. To take a contrary view would lead to a real possibility of injustice.[146]

12–50   He entered the caveat that there should not be an over rigid application of this principle and he identified some of the complications that could arise.[147] First, a document might form part of a series of connected documents in which case it could be regarded as being in evidence where other connected documents had been referred to and where, in all the circumstances, it would not be unfair to regard the document concerned as being before the court. Secondly, if it was clear, either from submissions or evidence given by a witness, that reliance was being placed upon a particular document or category of documents which were readily identifiable then, even if not specifically mentioned, the court should lean in favour of allowing reliance to be placed on the document. Therefore, he took the view that, as a matter of general principle, the court should take a broad view as to whether it could properly be said that the opposing party ought to have reasonably understood that the document in question was being relied on. Only where the court was satisfied that an opposing party could not reasonably have apprehended that reliance was being placed upon a particular document for a particular purpose, should the court exclude that document from its consideration.[148]

12–51   The learned judge went on to express concern about the potential unfairness

---

[144] [2009] IEHC 214.
[145] [2009] IEHC 214 at [3.5].
[146] [2009] IEHC 214 at [3.6].
[147] [2009] IEHC 214 at [3.8]–[3.9].
[148] [2009] IEHC 214 at [3.10].

that could arise if a party was entitled to selectively rely on documents that had been admitted on the *Bula/Fyffes* basis without an opposing party being entitled to refer to connected documents:

> "It seems to me that it would, therefore, always be open to a party whose documents have been relied on by its opponent on the *Bula/Fyffes* basis to refer to any connected documents. It is important to emphasise the reason why this is so. In the ordinary way the party who has produced the documents concerned in discovery will not be able to place any reliance on those documents without calling a relevant witness to prove them. Where parties proceed on the basis of *Bula/Fyffes*, then that party's own documents will not, of course, be capable of being admitted in evidence against its opponent. In the ordinary way, therefore, such documents can only be admitted if proved.
>
> However, it would seem to me to be a clear abuse of the *Bula/Fyffes* model if a party were permitted to cherry pick those of its opponent's documents on which it wished to place reliance, and refrain from putting in evidence other connected documents. Such a practice could lead to significant procedural unfairness and would be a recipe for unjust results. While a party placing reliance on a *Bula/Fyffes* concession is not obliged to place any of its opponent's documents before the court, it seems to me that if it does so it must, in like manner to a party waiving privilege, also accept that all other connected documents can properly be referred to without being proved."[149]

12–52   He also expressed the view that, any party wishing to place reliance on documents on the basis of a concession along *Bula/Fyffes* lines ought, prior to the close of the evidence, make clear that reliance is being placed on the document or set of documents in question, so as to place its opponent on fair notice in a timely fashion of the fact and nature of the reliance being placed on the relevant document or documents.

8. Tendering a Document in Evidence

12–53   In *The Leopardstown Club Limited v Templeville Developments Limited,*[150] Edwards J addressed the question of when a document is to be regarded as having been tendered in evidence and said:

> "At its most basic a document is an inanimate object incapable of offering itself in evidence. Neither mere allusion to the document, nor the mere physical production of the document, has of itself the effect of tendering it in evidence. A document is tendered in evidence by a party if, by virtue of his conduct, that party is to be regarded as seeking to rely upon the document in evidence in its own right, whether as real, original or testimonial evidence, and the relevant document is physically present in court and is before, or is in the hands of, a witness who is being questioned about it."

12–54   Of course, a witness cannot be questioned about a document unless the requirements in relation to receivability have been satisfied (or waived) and the document is admissible in evidence either as testimonial, original or real evidence.

B. Real Evidence

1. Introduction

12–55   In general terms, real evidence is evidence that the tribunal of fact "can

---

[149] [2009] IEHC 214 at [3.13]–[3.14].
[150] [2010] IEHC 152 at [5.51].

scrutinise or examine for itself".[151] The forms of real evidence are quite diverse and include: (a) material objects; (b) the appearance of persons and animals; (c) the demeanour of a witness; (d) documents where tendered in evidence as a material object; (e) tape-recordings, films and photographs; (f) records generated by computer systems; and (g) views and demonstrations.

2. Forms of Real Evidence

(a) Material objects

12–56   A material object is any object, the existence, appearance or condition of which is relevant to the issues in a case. Common examples include the alleged murder weapon in a murder case, stolen goods in a prosecution for receiving stolen goods and the product in a products liability case. In general, such objects are produced in court for inspection and examination by the tribunal of fact.[152] However, where it is not possible or practical to produce the actual object, secondary evidence of it may be adduced.[153] This may take the form of photographs[154] or films of the object or the oral evidence of someone who has seen it.[155]

12–57   Where the material object is not produced for inspection, this may affect the weight attached to it by the tribunal of fact.[156] Further, where the nature of the object is such that expert evidence is required in order to assess it, the jury should be directed not to rely upon their own inexpert conclusions while inspecting it.[157]

(b) The appearance of persons and animals

12–58   Where the physical appearance or characteristics of a person or animal are relevant, this may amount to real evidence.[158] For example, in a personal injuries action, the nature and extent of injuries suffered by a plaintiff are relevant and may be shown to or inspected by the tribunal of fact.[159] As regards animals, their production may be required to assess characteristics such as temperament.[160] In a criminal case, the fingerprints of an accused constitute real evidence.[161]

---

[151] *Per* Edwards J in *The Leopardstown Club Limited v Templeville Developments Limited* [2010] IEHC 152 at [5.12].

[152] Whether the jury are permitted to take such objects into the jury room with them for inspection is a matter of judicial discretion: *R. v Wright* [1993] Crim LR 607 at 608.

[153] *Hocking v Ahlquist Bros Ltd* [1944] KB 120 at 124.

[154] *McFarlane v DPP* [2006] IESC 11 at [31], [2007] 1 IR 134 at 147.

[155] In *McFarlane v DPP* [2006] IESC 11 at [30], [2007] 1 IR 134 at 146, *McCormack v DPP* [2007] IEHC 123, [2008] 1 ILRM 49 at 56 and *Toohey v DPP* [2007] IEHC 64 at [8], the equivalent paragraph in the first edition was quoted with approval.

[156] *R. v Francis* (1874) LR 2 CCR 128 at 133.

[157] *R. v Tilley* [1961] 1 WLR 1309 at 1312 (samples of handwriting).

[158] *R. v Murphy* [1990] NI 306.

[159] See *Sornberger v Canadian Pacific Railway Co.* [1987] OAR 263 at 270. *Cf. Cullen v Clarke* [1963] IR 368 at 377 (trial judge entitled to take into account his observation of the condition of injured person and any visible injury and disability in deciding whether person suffered from total incapacity to work for the purpose of Workmen's Compensation Act 1934).

[160] *Line v Taylor* (1862) 3 F & F 731 at 732, 733.

[161] *People (AG) v Lawlor* [1955–56] Ir Jur Rep 38 at 42.

(c) The demeanour of a witness

12–59   The demeanour of a witness while giving evidence is real evidence which can be taken into consideration by the tribunal of fact in assessing the credibility of the witness and may be a factor of decisive importance in some cases.[162]

(d) Documents where tendered in evidence as a material object

12–60   As explained by Edwards J in *The Leopardstown Club Limited v Templeville Developments Limited*[163]: "If a document is tendered in evidence as a material object, regardless of the words contained in it, for instance to show the bare fact of its existence, the substance of which it is made (whether parchment or paper) or the condition that it is in (whether crumpled or torn or perhaps in the case of stolen banknotes stained with dye), it constitutes real evidence". Thus, a stolen document will constitute real evidence in a prosecution for theft of that document.[164] Similarly, a document may be admitted as real evidence where it establishes a link between a person and a place[165] or between persons,[166] that a person was in possession of particular information at a particular time,[167] or that a person was involved in a particular activity.[168] Where handwriting or a signature is disputed, a document containing the disputed handwriting or signature or a sample of handwriting constitutes real evidence.[169]

(e) Tape recordings, films and photographs

12–61   It has been held that photographs,[170] tape recordings,[171] and video evidence[172] are admissible as items of real evidence. However, before such evidence can be admitted, it must be authenticated.[173] In the case of photographs, this may involve oral evidence from both the person who took the photograph and the person who developed it. Where photographs have been taken using a digital camera, these may be excluded where the provenance of same including the date on which they were taken is not established in evidence.[174] In the case of videos and tape recordings, the circumstances in which the recording was made must be set out, and all of those persons with access

---

[162] For a general discussion of demeanour of witnesses as real evidence, see *R. v Murphy* [1990] NI 306.

[163] [2010] IEHC 152 at [5.12].

[164] *Cf. Hamilton v Al Fayed*, unreported, English Court of Appeal, 21 December 2000.

[165] See, for example, *R. v Lydon* [1987] Crim LR 407.

[166] See, for example, *People (DPP) v Timmons* [2011] IECCA 13 (text messages constituted real evidence of conspiracy); *R. v Owens* [2006] EWCA Crim 2206.

[167] See, for example, *R. v Romeo* (1982) 30 SASR 243.

[168] See, for example, *People (DPP) v Morgan* [2011] IECCA 36.

[169] *Cf. People (AG) v Lawlor* [1955–56] Ir Jur Rep 38 at 42.

[170] *Wicklow County Council v Jessup* [2011] IEHC 81 at [2.14]; *People (DPP) v Foley* [2006] IECCA 72 at [6], 2007] 2 IR 486 at 490; *R. v Tolson* (1864) 4 F & F 103 at 104.

[171] *People v Prunty* [1986] ILRM 716 at 719–720; *R. v Senat* (1968) 52 Cr App R 282 at 286–287; *R. v Maqsud Ali* [1966] 1 QB 688 at 701, [1965] 2 All ER 464.

[172] *People (DPP) v Maguire* [1995] 2 IR 286; *Braddish v DPP* [2002] 1 IR 151; *People (DPP) v Foley* [2006] IECCA 72 at [6], [2007] 2 IR 486 at 490; *People (DPP) v Larkin* [2008] IECCA 138 at 10. For a discussion of the principles regarding the admission and use of video evidence, see Chap.4, section F.

[173] See generally McFarlane, "Photographic Evidence: Its Probative Value at Trial and the Judicial Discretion to Exclude it from Evidence" (1974) 16 CLQ 149; Wiebe, "Regarding Digital Images: Determining Admissibility Standards" (2000) Man LJ 61.

[174] *Burke v Fulham* [2010] IEHC 448 at [39]–[41].

to it thereafter identified. The trial judge must make some inquiry as to the history of the tapes, and their nature and condition.[175] The trial judge has a discretion as to whether the jury can be provided with a transcript of a tape recording.[176] However, where a recording is of good quality and comprehensible by the tribunal of fact, it should normally be played in court rather than transcribed.[177]

12–62　　The general approach of the courts to this category of real evidence has been quite facilitative of its admission on the basis that it approximates to eyewitness testimony and, in the case of video evidence, may provide a court with the best possible evidence of the commission of an offence.[178] As stated by Hardiman J in *Dunne v DPP*,[179] video evidence "can have very dramatic effect in appropriate cases." The traditional view was that this category of evidence was quite reliable because there was little danger of fabrication or mistake.[180] However, in light of increasingly sophisticated digital technology capable of substantially altering photographic and other images, this assumption may no longer hold good.

(f) Records Generated by Computer Systems

12–63　　Records generated by computer systems mechanically without human intervention are admissible as real evidence.[181] Before such evidence can be admitted, evidence has to be adduced as to the function and operation of the computer system in question.[182] A common example of such evidence is printouts of the records of

---

[175] In *R. v Robson* [1972] 1 WLR 651 at 654 it was held that a party seeking to rely on the evidence must give the history of the video or tape from the time of recording up until its production in court in order to exclude the possibility that it may have been interfered with. In *R. v Stevenson* [1971] 1 WLR 1 at 3, 4, it was held that, where there is some doubt as regards interference, the court should exclude the evidence.

[176] *R. v Rampling* [1987] Crim LR 823 at 823. See also *R. v Maqsud Ali* [1966] 1 QB 688, [1965] 2 All ER 464 in which the jury had to be supplied with a transcript of a tape recording of a conversation in Punjabi.

[177] *Butwera v DPP (Vic)* (1987) 164 CLR 180 at 195.

[178] See *Dunne v DPP* [2002] 2 IR 307 at 311, [2002] 2 ILRM 241 at 247; *Braddish v DPP* [2001] 3 IR 127 at 135. See also *R. v Maqsud Ali* [1966] 1 QB 668 at 701, [1965] 2 All ER 464 and *R. v Clare* [1995] 2 Cr App R 333 at 339.

[179] [2002] 2 IR 307 at 311, [2002] 2 ILRM 241 at 247.

[180] See *Sapporo Maru (Owners) v Statue of Liberty (Owners), The Statue of Liberty* [1968] 1 WLR 739 at 740.

[181] *People (DPP) v Murphy* [2005] IECCA 1 at [78]–[84], [2005] 2 IR 125 at 151–153; *People (DPP) v Meehan* [2006] IECCA 104 at [31]–[32], [2006] 3 IR 468 at 480 (mobile telephone records); *Sapporo Maru (Owners) v Statue of Liberty (Owners), The Statue of Liberty* [1968] 1 WLR 739 at 740 (film of radar echoes); *R. v Spiby* (1990) 91 Cr App R 186 (telephone records); *R. v Wood* (1982) 76 Cr App R 23 (computer analysis of metals); *Castle v Cross* [1984] 1 WLR 1372; (print out from intoximeter); *R. v Governor of Brixton Prison, ex parte Levin* [1997] AC 741, [1997] 3 WLR 117 (records of transfer of funds); *R. v Minors* [1989] 1 WLR 441, [1989] 2 All ER 208 (bank records); *State of Louisiana v Armstead* (1983) 432 So 2d 837 at 839 (trace records). Where the data recorded in the computer system have been inputed by a person, then the print out will amount to a hearsay statement and inadmissible if relied on to prove the information recorded unless it falls within the scope of an exception to the hearsay rule: *Myers v DPP* [1965] AC 1001, [1964] 3 WLR 145; *R. v Coventry Justices, ex parte Bullard* (1992) 95 Cr App Rep 175.

[182] *People (DPP) v Murphy* [2005] IECCA 1 at [84], [2005] 2 IR 125 at 153; *People (DPP) v Meehan* [2006] IECCA 104 at [33], [2006] 3 IR 468 at 480; *R. v Cochrane* [1993] Crim LR 48.

telephone calls generated by the computer systems of mobile telephone companies.[183] Another example is the print out from a breath test apparatus.[184]

(g) Views and demonstrations

12–64   A view is a category of real evidence that is regarded as analogous to the admission of a material object for the inspection and examination of the tribunal of fact.[185] It generally takes the form of an out of court inspection by the tribunal of fact[186] of the *locus in quo*[187] but may involve an inspection of some other form of real evidence which cannot be brought to court for inspection without considerable inconvenience.[188] A demonstration or recreation of events may also take place.[189] As with material objects, secondary evidence of a view is admissible, such as photographs or a video of a location.[190] The view may also be attended by a witness who has given evidence so long as he or she is available to be recalled for cross-examination.[191]

12–65   In *People (DPP) v Maguire*,[192] it was emphasised that a view can be used by a tribunal of fact for a limited purpose only, which is to assess the credibility of evidence given by witnesses. Thus, it is not for the jury to decide, on the basis of a view, whether some action was or was not possible but, rather, to decide whether the evidence of a witness that it was or was not should be accepted as credible.[193] This should be made clear to the jury by means of an appropriate instruction.[194]

12–66   Given that, of its very nature, a view takes place outside of the confines of the courtroom, it is important to ensure that fair procedures are observed. Although judges sometimes conduct views on their own, the better view is that, in every case, civil or criminal, the parties should be informed in advance of the intention to conduct a view and given the opportunity to attend with their legal advisors.[195] Otherwise, there

---

[183] See *People (DPP) v Murphy* [2005] IECCA 1, [2005] 2 IR 125; *People (DPP) v Meehan* [2006] IECCA 104, [2006] 3 IR 468; *R. v McDonald* [2011] EWCA Crim 2933 at [42].

[184] *PPS v Duddy* [2008] NICA 18, [2009] NI 19 at [29].

[185] *Goold v Evans & Co.* [1951] 2 TLR 1189 at 1191; *R. v Karamat* [1956] AC 256, [1956] 1 All ER 415.

[186] Where the tribunal of fact consists of a jury, it is not sufficient for one juror to attend and report back to the others: *R. v Gurney* [1976] Crim LR 567 at 568.

[187] See *McAllister v Dunnes Stores*, unreported, High Court, 5 February 1987, where the judge viewed the scene of an accident.

[188] See *Buckingham v Daily News* [1956] 2 QB 534, [1956] 2 All ER 904, where a view was held to inspect a piece of machinery.

[189] See *Molumby v Kearns*, unreported, High Court, 19 January 1999, where the trial judge, O'Sullivan J, visited a premises, the subject matter of a nuisance action, and a demonstration was held of some of the activities complained of.

[190] See, *e.g. AG v Joyce* [1929] IR 526 at 541, where a photograph showing a dummy in the location where the deceased's body had been found was admitted in a murder trial in order to illustrate and render intelligible the evidence of witness as to where the body had been discovered. It might be noted that the Canadian courts will refuse admission of photographic or video evidence where it is so inflammatory in nature that its prejudicial effect is likely to outweigh its probative value: *Draper v Jacklyn* [1970] SCR 92, (1970) 9 DLR (3d) 264. See Gardner, "Explanations and Illustrations: Demonstrative Evidence in the Criminal Courtroom" (1996) 38 CLQ 425 at 440.

[191] *R. v Karamat* [1956] AC 256, [1956] 1 All ER 415; *R. v Martin* (1872) LR 1 CCR 378.

[192] [1995] 2 IR 286.

[193] [1995] 2 IR 286 at 290. For an example of the correct approach to be adopted, see *Browne v Dowie* (1959) 93 ILTR 179 at 183, 184.

[194] [1995] 2 IR 286 at 290.

[195] *Cf. Goold v Evans & Co.* [1951] 2 TLR 1189; *Parry v Boyle* (1986) 83 Cr App R 310 and *Gibbons*

is a danger that the tribunal of fact may reach a conclusion on the basis of something observed during the view (which might be erroneous) without giving the parties an adequate opportunity to comment upon same and, perhaps, call relevant evidence. If a party, having been given an adequate opportunity to do so, declines to attend, this will not affect the admissibility of the evidence of the view.[196] While a view is being held, nothing should be said by either party unless the judge asks for an explanation or demonstration.[197]

3. The Duty to Seek Out and Preserve Evidence

12–67 Although it is an area which falls outside the scope of this chapter, it should be noted that it is well established that there is a duty on the gardaí to seek out and preserve real evidence such as video evidence in advance of trial.[198]

C. Electronic Evidence

1. Introduction

12–68 To date, the Irish courts have not recognised electronic evidence as a distinct category of evidence requiring separate consideration or safeguards.[199] Instead, it is treated simply as a variety of documentary evidence,[200] or sometimes as real evidence,[201] and problems such as what constitutes the original of a document produced on a computer[202] have been dealt with within that framework. However, with the

---

v DPP, unreported, Queen's Bench Division, 12 December 2000.

[196] *R. v Karamat* [1956] AC 256, [1956] 1 All ER 415.

[197] *Goold v Evans & Co.* [1951] 2 TLR 1189 at 1191.

[198] See *Murphy v DPP* [1989] ILRM 71; *Braddish v DPP* [2001] 3 IR 127, [2002] 1 ILRM 151; *Dunne v DPP* [2002] 2 IR 306, [2002] 2 ILRM 241; *Bowes v DPP* [2003] 2 IR 25, [2002] 2 ILRM 241; *Connolly v DPP* [2003] 4 IR 121; *Scully v DPP* [2005] IESC 11, [2005] 2 ILRM 203; *McFarlane v DPP* [2006] IESC 11, [2007] 1 IR 134; *Savage v DPP* [2008] IESC 39, [2009] 1 IR 185; *Ludlow v DPP* [2008] IESC 54, [2009] 1 IR 640; *Byrne v DPP* [2010] IESC 213, [2011] 1 IR 346; *Wall v DPP* [2013] IESC 56, [2014] 2 ILRM 1. See also Birmingham, "The Obligation to Seek Out and Preserve Evidence" (2004) 9 BR 86 and Heffernan, *Evidence in Criminal Trials* (Bloomsbury, 2014) at 683–698. A similar duty to preserve evidence has been recognised by the Canadian Supreme Court in *R. v Egger* [1993] 2 SCR 451 at 472, the extent of which increases in direct proportion to the relevance of the evidence concerned: *R. v La* [1997] 2 SCR 680 at 691. See also *R. v Maghdoori* [2008] ONCJ 129, 161 CRR (2d) 157 and *R. v Leung* [2008] ONCJ 110, 171 CRR (2d) 300.

[199] The issues and difficulties that can arise with electronic evidence and the legislative intervention required are addressed by the Law Reform Commission in its *Consultation Paper on Documentary and Electronic Evidence* (LRC CP 57–2009). One of its provisional recommendations (at [2.213]) is that "the rules of evidence concerning the need to produce an original of an electronic or automated document be interpreted to mean presenting a reproduction in legible form (including a printout) or a copy or derivative of an electronic document". See, generally, Mason, *Electronic Evidence*, (3rd edn, LexisNexis 2012) (Chap.14 of which deals specifically with Ireland and was written by Ruth Cannon and Catherine Dawson).

[200] As noted above, "document" is defined in s.2 of the Criminal Evidence Act 1992 to include "a reproduction in permanent legible form, by a computer or other means (including enlarging), of information in non-legible form".

[201] See [12–63] above.

[202] In *Derby v Weldon (No.9)* [1991] 1 WLR 652 at 658, [1991] 2 All ER 901 at 906, it was held that the original of a document produced on a computer is the file saved on the computer rather than a document printed therefrom. See also *Prism Hospital Software Ltd v Hosp Medical Records*

increasing importance of electronic evidence in civil and criminal cases and a growing recognition of the specific dangers of unreliability posed by such evidence, it can be expected that, at some point, guidelines regarding the admission and use of electronic evidence will have to provided by legislation or judicial decisions.[203] The issues and difficulties that can arise with electronic evidence and the legislative intervention required are addressed by the Law Reform Commission in its *Consultation Paper on Documentary and Electronic Evidence*.[204] One of its provisional recommendations is that "the rules of evidence concerning the need to produce an original of an electronic or automated document be interpreted to mean presenting a reproduction in legible form (including a printout) or a copy or derivative of an electronic document".[205] It was also provisionally recommended the adoption of an inclusionary approach to the admissibility of electronic documentary evidence, subject to a number of safeguards and the continuance of the discretion of the court to exclude the evidence.[206]

2. Electronic Commerce Act 2000

12–69   The Electronic Commerce Act 2000[207] (the "2000 Act") is a wide-ranging piece of legislation that is designed to reflect and anticipate technological developments by providing for the legal recognition of electronic contracts, electronic writing, electronic signatures and original information in electronic form as well as the admissibility of evidence in relation to such matters.[208]

(a) Legal equivalence of electronic information and signatures

12–70   One of the main objectives of the 2000 Act is to accord electronic information and electronic signatures the legal status of their traditional written counterparts. A pivotal provision is s.2(2) which stipulates that:

> "In the application of this Act, 'writing', where used in any other Act or instrument under an Act (and whether or not qualified by reference to it being or being required to be under the hand of the writer or similar expression) shall be construed as including electronic modes of representing or reproducing words in visible form, and cognate words shall be similarly construed."

12–71   That subsection is reinforced by Part 2 of the Act which contains a number of provisions dealing with the legal recognition of electronic communications and information in electronic form. Section 9 provides that information "shall not be denied legal effect, validity or enforceability solely on the grounds that it is wholly or partly in electronic form, whether as an electronic communication or otherwise". Section

---

Institution [1992] 2 WWR 157, (1991) 62 BCLR (2d) 393, (1991) 40 CPR (3d) 97 where it was accepted that a recovered file on a computer was a document. For a discussion of this issue, see *R. v Walsh* (1980) 53 CCC 568.

[203] See, generally, Lambert, "The Search for Elusive Electrons" [2001] 1(1) JSIJ 23; Newman, "Evidential Issues" (2000) Law Society CLE Seminar; Woods, "Email as Evidence: Will it Stand up in Court?" (1998) 92 (10) LSG 16; Tapper, "Evanescent Evidence" (1993) 1(1) IJLIT 35; Quinn, "Computer Evidence In Criminal Proceedings: Farewell to the ill-fated s.69 of the Police and Criminal Evidence Act 1984" (2001) 5 E & P 174.

[204] (LRC CP 57–2009).

[205] (LRC CP 57–2009) at [2.213].

[206] (LRC CP 57–2009) at [5.19].

[207] The Act implements the Electronic Signatures Directive (1999/93/EC) and the Electronic Commerce Directive (2000/13/EC).

[208] For an overview of the Act, see Murray, "The Electronic Commerce Bill" (2001) 11 ILT 174.

13 goes on deal with the validity of electronic signatures and provides that, if by law or otherwise, the signature of a person or public body is required or permitted, then, in the circumstances specified in the section, an electronic signature may be used.[209]

12–72   There are also a number of provisions dealing with the storage and supply of information in electronic form as an equivalent to writing. Section 12 provides that, if by law or otherwise, a person or public body is required or permitted to give information in writing, the person or public body may give the information in electronic form, whether as an electronic communication or otherwise. Section 17 goes on to provide that, if by law or otherwise, a person or public body is required or permitted to present or retain information in its original form, then, subject to certain safeguards specified in subs.(2), the information may be presented or retained in electronic form.[210]

(b) Admissibility of electronic information

12–73   Section 22 of the 2000 Act ensures that, while electronic evidence still has to meet the thresholds of admissibility faced by all documentary evidence, its evidential value is no longer in doubt simply by virtue of its electronic form. It is worth setting out the provisions of s.22 in full:

> "In any legal proceedings, nothing in the application of the rules of evidence shall apply so as to deny the admissibility in evidence of—
>> (a) an electronic communication, an electronic form of a document, an electronic contract, or writing in electronic form—
>>> (i) on the sole ground that it is an electronic communication, an electronic form of a document, an electronic contract, or writing in electronic form, or
>>> (ii) if it is the best evidence that the person or public body adducing it could reasonably be expected to obtain, on the grounds that it is not in its original form, or
>> (b) an electronic signature—
>>> (i) on the sole ground that the signature is in electronic form, or is not an advanced electronic signature,[211] or is not based on a qualified certificate,[212] or is not based on a qualified certificate issued by an accredited certification service provider,[213] or is not created by a secure signature creation device,[214] or
>>> (ii) if it is the best evidence that the person or public body adducing it could reasonably be expected to obtain, on the grounds that it is not in its original form."

---

[209] Section 14 deals with requirements for signatures to be witnessed and s.16 deals with requirements for documents to be executed under seal.

[210] *Cf. DPP v McKeown* [1997] 2 Cr App R 155.

[211] An "advanced electronic signature" is defined in s.2 of the Act as meaning an electronic signature: "(a) uniquely linked to the signatory, (b) capable of identifying the signatory, (c) created using means that are capable of being maintained by the signatory under his, her or its sole control, and (d) linked to the data to which it relates in such a manner that any subsequent change of the data is detectable".

[212] A "qualified certificate" is defined in s.2 of the Act as meaning "a certificate which meets the requirements set out in Annex I and is provided by a certification service provider who fulfils the requirements set out in Annex II".

[213] A "certification service provider" is defined in s.2 of the Act as meaning "a person or public body who issues certificates or provides other services related to electronic signatures".

[214] A "signature creation device" is defined in s.2 of the Act as meaning "a device, such as configured software or hardware used to generate signature verification data" and "signature verification data" is defined as meaning "data, such as codes, passwords, algorithms or public cryptographic keys, used for the purposes of verifying an electronic signature".

12–74   The importance and scope of s.22 is apparent from the breadth of the definitions given in s.2 of the Act.[215] Firstly, "electronic" is defined as including "electrical, digital, magnetic, optical, electromagnetic, biometric, photonic and any other form of related technology" and "information" is defined as including "data, all forms of writing and other text, images (including maps and cartographic material), sound, codes, computer programmes, software, databases and speech". This definition should be sufficiently broad to ensure the continued application of the Act regardless of advances in information technology. Secondly, "legal proceedings" are defined as meaning "civil or criminal proceedings, and includes proceedings before a court, tribunal, appellate body of competent jurisdiction or any other body or individual charged with determining legal rights or obligations". It can be seen from the foregoing definitions, that s.22 will be of importance and potential application in a wide range of proceedings and contexts.

12–75   However, s.22 is open to criticism on the basis that it does not include any safeguards with regard to the admission of electronic evidence.[216] Electronic evidence may raise significant reliability issues because of the ease with which electronic information can be altered or tampered with by persons with access to the particular computer or even by persons with no access to a computer by means of computer viruses, worms etc.[217] The degree of risk in that regard is dependent upon a multitude of factors, including the number of persons with access to the particular computer, the adequacy of security protections taken and the availability of the computer for inspection by the party against whom the evidence is being tendered.

12–76   In order to explain and highlight these problems, expert evidence may be required. However, one of the shortcomings of s.22 is the absence of any requirement of advance notice of the use of electronic evidence.[218] This potentially places a defendant at a disadvantage where he or she is unaware that particular evidence is to be tendered in electronic format as he or she is unlikely to be in a position to tender expert rebuttal evidence.

12–77   A question also arises as to whether, given the potential problems of unreliability, a trial judge will be required to give a cautionary instruction to the jury in cases whether a prosecution is wholly or substantially dependant upon the veracity and reliability of electronic evidence. Much will depend on the facts of the individual case and the defence of the accused but it seems likely that there will be cases where a trial judge will be required to give a warning to the jury in discharge of his duty

---

[215] However, it should be noted that s.10 provides that the Act does not affect laws in relation to wills and testamentary instruments, trusts or enduring powers of attorney, property, affidavits or declarations, or rules and procedures of courts and tribunals. Section 11 also excludes laws relating to taxation, the Companies Acts, the Criminal Evidence Act 1992 and the Consumer Credit Act 1995.

[216] For a discussion of the potential problems with electronic evidence, see Sopinka, "It looks great, but can you use it? Admissibility Issues with Respect to Computer-Generated Evidence", Can Bar Assoc (Ontario) CLE Toronto, November 1997.

[217] See Nicoll, "Should Computers be Trusted? Hearsay and Authentication with Special Reference to Electronic Commerce" [1999] JBL 332; Lambert, "The Search for Elusive Electrons: Getting a Sense for Electronic Evidence" (2001) 1(1) JSIJ 23.

[218] See Newman, "Evidential Issues" (2000) Law Society CLE Seminar and Lambert, "The Search for Elusive Electrons: Getting a Sense for Electronic Evidence" (2001) 1(1) JSIJ 23 at 44, 45.

to put the defence case fairly and adequately and to avoid the danger of an innocent person being convicted.[219]

---

[219] See *People (AG) v Casey (No.2)* [1963] IR 33 at 37, 38 and, generally, Chap.4, section G.

CHAPTER 13

FACTS NOT REQUIRING PROOF

A. Introduction

13–01   In general, a court can only make a finding of fact if evidence in relation to the existence or non-existence of that fact has been adduced by the parties to the proceedings before it. However, there are some circumstances, examined in this chapter, where facts may be taken as established even though no evidence in respect of them has been adduced. The first is where a party makes a formal admission as to the existence of a fact, which has the effect that his or her opponent is relieved of the obligation to prove that fact because it will be taken to exist by the tribunal of fact. The second is where the tribunal of fact takes judicial notice of the existence of notorious or indisputable facts, thus dispensing with the necessity to prove their existence. Another instance where a party may be relieved of the obligation to prove a fact is where he or she benefits from the operation of a presumption. However, presumptions will not be considered further here as they have already been examined in Chapter 2, section D.

B. Formal Admissions

1. Introduction

13–02   A party in either criminal or civil proceedings can make a formal admission as to a fact which relieves his or her opponent from having to prove that fact.[1] A formal admission is distinguishable from an informal admission[2] in that it is one made after proceedings have commenced for cost or other tactical considerations and has the effect of narrowing the issues in the proceedings, whereas an informal admission is simply admissible as evidence of the facts admitted. Furthermore, unless it is withdrawn, a formal admission is conclusive against the party that has made it, as opposed to an informal admission which a party may deny or seek to explain away.

2. Criminal Cases

13–03   Dispensing with the requirement of proof by formal admission in criminal

---

[1]   *Yager v R.* (1977) 51 ALJR 361 at 371 (*per* Gibbs CJ); *Urquhart v Butterfield* (1887) 37 Ch D 357 at 369 (*per* Cotton LJ).
[2]   Considered in Chap.5, section D.

proceedings is governed by s.22 of the Criminal Justice Act 1984.[3] Subsection (1) provides:

> "any fact of which oral evidence may be given in oral proceedings may be admitted for the purpose of those proceedings[4] by or on behalf of the prosecution or the accused, and the admission by any party of such fact under this section shall as against that party be conclusive evidence in those proceedings of the fact admitted."[5]

13–04   Subsection (2) goes on to provide that an admission may be made before or at the hearing but, if made otherwise than in court, it must be made in writing and signed[6] by the person making it.[7] In order to protect accused persons, certain restrictions are placed on their ability to make formal admissions. If an admission is made on behalf of an accused who is an individual, it must be made by his or her counsel or solicitor and, if made at any stage before the hearing, it must be approved by his or her counsel or solicitor either at the time it was made or subsequently.[8] An admission made under the section may, with the leave of the court, be withdrawn in the proceedings for the purpose of which it is made or any subsequent criminal proceedings relating to the same matter.[9]

13–05   In *People (DPP) v Piotrowski*,[10] where a number of formal admissions were made on behalf of the accused, the Court of Criminal Appeal rejected the contention that the trial judge had erred in failing to explain in his charge to the jury the nature and legal basis of those admissions thereby creating a risk that the jury were confused as to the precise terms of those admissions. The Court considered that the legal status of the admissions did not differ from a common sense understanding of them and that it would not have added anything to explain to the jury that they were conclusive evidence against the accused.

3. Civil Cases

13–06   Formal admissions are most commonly made in civil proceedings during the exchange of pleadings when a party either expressly admits a fact alleged in the pleadings of his or her opponent[11] or admits it implicitly by failing to controvert the

---

3   Similar provision for formal admission of specific facts is made in s.10 of the Criminal Justice Act 1967 in the UK, s.655 of the Canadian Criminal Code, RSC 1985, s.9 of the New Zealand Evidence Act 2006 and s.184 of the Evidence Act 1995 (Cth) in Australia.
4   Subsection (3) provides that an admission under the section for the purpose of proceedings relating to any matter shall be treated as an admission for the purpose of any subsequent criminal proceedings relating to that matter including any appeal or retrial.
5   For examples of the application of s.22, see: *People (DPP) v Bambrick*, unreported, Court of Criminal Appeal, 8 March 1999, [1999] 2 ILRM 71 (s.22 was availed of by counsel for the appellant to make lengthy formal admissions of fact); *McKenna v Commissioner of An Garda Síochána* [1993] 3 IR 543 at 550 (the plaintiff's solicitor made an offer to furnish an admission in writing under s.22 if the gardai returned one of the plaintiff's machines); *Flynn v DPP*, unreported, High Court, 7 October 1997 (prosecution offered to make admissions pursuant to s.22 to alleviate prejudice suffered by reason of death of witness in context of allegation of prosecutorial delay).
6   Subsection (2) contains a rebuttable presumption that a signature is to be taken to be that of the person whose signature it appears to be unless the contrary is shown.
7   If the admission is made by a body corporate, it must be signed by a director or manager, or the secretary or clerk, or some other similar officer of the body corporate.
8   Section 22(2).
9   Section 22(4).
10   [2014] IECCA 17.
11   Order 32, r.1 of the Rules of the Superior Courts provides that any party to a cause or matter may

fact.[12] A party may also make an admission in writing either in response to a notice to admit facts[13] or otherwise.[14] A party, or a solicitor or a barrister on his or her behalf, may also make a formal admission of facts in court thereby dispensing with the requirement for proof of those facts.[15] The effect of such an admission is that evidence is not required to prove the admitted fact and, further, evidence may not be adduced to contradict or qualify it.[16] However, it has been held that a court is not bound to accept and act on an admitted fact which it is inconsistent with the other facts established or is inherently incredible.[17]

13–07 In general, a formal admission may be withdrawn at any stage of proceedings except where the circumstances are such as to give rise to an estoppel[18] or where the withdrawal of the admission would amount to an abuse of process or obstruct the just disposal of the proceedings.[19] In *Braybrook v Basildon & Thurrock University NHS Trust*,[20] Sumner J identified a number of factors that would be taken into consideration in deciding whether leave to withdraw an admission would be granted: (a) the reasons and justification for the application which must be made in good faith; (b) the balance of prejudice to the parties; (c) whether any party has been the author of any prejudice they may suffer; (d) the prospects of success of any issue arising from the withdrawal of an admission; (e) the public interest, in avoiding where possible satellite litigation, disproportionate use of court resources and the impact of any strategic manoeuvring. He also emphasised that the nearer any application is to a final hearing the less chance of success it will have even if the party making the application can establish clear prejudice.[21]

13–08 An admission made in a civil case may be relied on in a subsequent civil case[22] unless it is withdrawn. In *Tchenguiz v Director of the Serious Fraud Office*,[23] leave to withdraw an admission of trespass made in earlier related proceedings, which was sought on the basis that the defendant's new legal team took a different view as to its liability in that regard, was granted with Eder J commenting: "absent irremediable prejudice, the overriding objective demands or at least points strongly in favour of the

---

give notice, by his pleading, that he admits the truth of the whole or any part of the case of any other party.

[12] RSC Ord.19, r.13 provides that: "Every allegation of fact in any pleading, not being a petition, if not denied specifically or by necessary implication, or stated to be not admitted in the pleading of the opposite party, shall be taken to be admitted, except as against an infant, or person of unsound mind."

[13] See RSC Ord.32, r.4.

[14] RSC Ord.32, r.1 provides that any party to a cause or matter may give notice in writing that he admits the truth of the whole or any part of the case of any other party.

[15] See, *e.g. Urquhart v Butterfield* (1887) 37 Ch D 357 at 369, where Cotton LJ stated that the admission of counsel should have been accepted without question and that the trial judge had erred in considering the matter in respect of which the admission had been made.

[16] *ACCC v Bridgestone Corp* (2010) 186 FCR 214 at [12]–[16].

[17] *Minister for the Environment, Heritage and the Arts v PGP Developments Pty Ltd* (2010) 183 FCR 10 at [35].

[18] *H Clark (Doncaster) Ltd v Wilkinson* [1965] Ch 694 at 703.

[19] *Walley v Stoke on Trent City Council* [2006] EWCA Civ 1137, [2007] 1 WLR 352.

[20] [2004] EWHC 3352 (QB) at [45].

[21] These criteria were endorsed by the Court of Appeal in *Sowerby v Charleton* [2005] EWCA Civ 1610, [2006] 1 WLR 568 and a revised version is now to be found in rule 14.1(5) of the Civil Procedure Rules.

[22] *Hoy Mobile Pry Ltd v Allphones Retail Pty Ltd* (2008) 167 FCR 314 at [18].

[23] [2013] EWHC 1578 (QB) at [59].

court arriving at a decision which is correct in law rather than on a foundation based upon an admission which may be incorrect as a matter of law ...".

C. Judicial Notice

1. Introduction

13–09   The truth or existence of certain matters may be accepted by a court without the necessity for proof pursuant to the doctrine of judicial notice.[24] A succinct explanation of the operation of this doctrine is to be found in the judgment of Lavan J in *Greene v Minister for Defence*[25]:

> "Judicial notice refers to facts which a Judge can be called upon to receive, and to act upon, either from his general knowledge of them, or from enquiries to be made by himself for his own information from sources to which it is proper for him to refer. ... Judicial notice is therefore a means of establishing rather than providing a fact. ... The Court is entitled to act upon such facts as if they were given in evidence before the Court by a competent witness in the ordinary way. That does not, of course, mean that the Court is bound to accept that evidence any more than it is bound to accept any other evidence which may be put before it. The doctrine of judicial notice concerns itself with the method of establishing facts rather than the weighing of conflicting evidence."[26]

13–10   Matters of which judicial notice may be taken are traditionally regarded as falling into two categories: (1) facts which are so notorious or well-known that they are not reasonably disputable; and (2) facts which are capable of immediate and accurate demonstration by having resort to readily accessible sources of indisputable accuracy. In addition, judicial notice is required to be taken of certain matters specified by statute. Each of these categories will be dealt with separately below and the related issue of the use by a judge or jury of general and personal knowledge will also be examined.

2. Facts Which are not Reasonably Disputable

13–11   In *Bank of Ireland v Keehan*[27] Ryan J said that "courts have to take judicial notice of the obvious and commonplace facts and circumstances of ordinary life". This limb of the judicial notice rests upon "foundations of common sense, experience, and convenience".[28] To require proof of facts about which there is no serious dispute[29] would be a waste of both time and resources. It might also bring the administration of justice into disrepute if the court refused to take cognisance of such facts.[30] In addition, the general nature of such facts may make it difficult to conclusively prove or disprove

---

[24]   See, generally, Manchester, "Judicial Notice and Personal Knowledge" (1979) 42 MLR 22, Nokes, "The Limits of Judicial Notice" (1958) 74 LQR 59 and Davis "Judicial Notice" (1955) 55 Colum LR 945.

[25]   [1998] 4 IR 464.

[26]   [1998] 4 IR 464 at 484. This extract is taken from the defendant's submissions in relation to the definition of judicial notice which were quoted with apparent approval by Lavan J.

[27]   [2013] IEHC 631 at [24].

[28]   *Per* Davitt J in *State (Taylor) v Circuit Court Judge for Wicklow* [1951] IR 311.

[29]   *Cf. Reference Re Alberta Statutes* [1938] SCR 100 at 128, where Duff CJ defined such facts as "facts which are known to intelligent persons generally" and *Australian Communist Party v The Commonwealth* (1951) 83 CLR 1 at 196, where Dixon J referred to such facts as the knowledge of "educated men".

[30]   *DPP v Collins* [1981] ILRM 447 at 451 (*per* Henchy J).

them in the ordinary way.[31] Another reason sometimes advanced is that the taking of judicial notice promotes consistency of findings in relation to matters of fact where such consistency is desirable.[32] However, if there is a possibility of inconsistency of findings, this would seem to indicate that the matter in question is reasonably disputable and, therefore, *prima facie* does not fall within the parameters of judicial notice unless the court decides on policy grounds that it should.

13–12   Facts that have been considered to be sufficiently notorious or well-known that judicial notice could be taken of them are diverse and include: the administrative counties which comprise the State and the cities and towns that are in the State[33]; matters relating to the courts system and administration of justice in this jurisdiction[34] and other jurisdictions[35]; economic conditions[36]; commercial practices[37]; the prices

---

[31] *Australian Communist Party v Commonwealth* (1951) 83 CLR 1 at 256.

[32] See *R. v Simpson* [1983] 3 All ER 789 at 793 (*per* Lord Lane CJ).

[33] *People (DPP) v McGeough* [1978] IR 384 at 385. However, Walsh J stated that the courts did not have judicial knowledge as to whether any particular farmhouse or yard was within or without the State and this had to be properly proved in evidence. See also *State (Gilsenan) v McMorrow* [1978] IR 360 at 369 (courts are bound to take judicial notice of the expression "Northern Ireland" as connoting that part of the island which is outside the functioning jurisdiction of the State).

[34] Judicial notice has been taken of the fact that there is a system of District Courts established by the Oireachtas reasonably available for ordinary and special sittings throughout the country and year (*Attorney General v Wallace,* unreported, High Court, 18 June 1996), that many of the persons concerned in the administration of justice are not competent to conduct the business of the courts in the Irish language (*Attorney General v Joyce* [1929] IR 526 at 531–532), that there is a requirement for a 20 minute observation period when using an intoxilyser (*DPP (Curran) v Foley* [2006] IEHC 11 at [19], [2006] 3 IR 334 at 339), of the reasons for delay on the part of complainants in reporting sexual abuse offences (*K(S) v DPP* [2007] IEHC 45), that convicted sex offenders may continue to pose a risk to the community after their release from prison (*Murray v Newsgroup Newspapers Ltd* [2010] IEHC 248 at [75], [2011] 2 IR 156 at 195), that memory of events diminishes with the passage of time and the ageing process (*Murray v Commission to Inquire into Child Abuse* [2004] 2 IR 222 at 256), that a notary public is a person empowered to administer oaths (*Attorney General v Q* [2006] IEHC 414), that video link evidence requires a very high level of prior organisation (*Health Service Executive v W* [2013] IESC 38 at [36]), the role of Senior Counsel (*McMullen v Kennedy* [2012] IEHC 28 at [36]), and that solicitors and counsel are required by the rules of their respective professionals to have professional indemnity insurance (*Irish Hereford Breed Society Ltd v Ross* [2006] IEHC 76).

[35] Judicial notice has been taken of the fact that most European states have a civil law system (*Minister for Justice, Equality and Law Reform v Altaravicius* [2006] IEHC 270, [2007] 2 IR 265), that criminal trials in England are conducted in a broadly similar fashion to criminal trials in this jurisdiction (*Carne v O'Toole* [2005] IESC 22) and that tort lawyers in the United States have a reputation for seeking and pursuing deep pockets with both imagination and determination (*McCaughey v Anglo Irish Bank Corporation Ltd* [2011] IEHC 546 at 88).

[36] Judicial notice has been taken of the fact that there was a serious economic crisis after September 2008 (*McKenzie v Minister for Finance* [2010] IEHC 461 at [5.2]), that there was a collapse of the national economy around 2008 followed by a protracted financial downturn with adverse financial consequences (*Director of Corporate Enforcement v Walsh* [2014] IEHC 365 at [3]), that there was a general downturn in the economy that had caused hardship (*Wicklow County Council v Jessup* [2011] IEHC 81 at [6.30]), that there was a property price crash after 2007 (*Bank of Scotland Plc v Shovlin* [2012] IEHC 35 at [14]), and that the property market was moribund in 2009 (*Re Vantive Holdings* [2009] IESC 68 at [25], [2010] 2 ILRM 156 at 176).

[37] Judicial notice has been taken of the fact that building societies are very reluctant to lend money to persons without an income (*Northern Bank Ltd v Henry* [1981] IR 1 at 7), that large pension schemes are frequently managed by professional trustees on a fee paying basis with a view to making a profit (*Cadbury Ireland Pension Trust Ltd v Revenue Commissioners* [2007] IEHC 179 at [70], [2007] 4 IR 334 at 361, [2008] 1 ILRM 296 at 320), that companies including banks maintain computer records (*Bank of Ireland v Keehan* [2013] IEHC 631 at [24]), and that a postcard is an

of goods and services[38]; nomenclature and characteristics of controlled substances,[39] proscribed terrorist organisations,[40] the context and purpose of the insertion of Art.40.3.3 protecting the right to life of the unborn into the Constitution[41] and the essentials of the Islamic marriage ceremony.[42] Matters which have not been considered so notorious and well-known that judicial notice should be taken of them include the relative levels of interest rates.[43]

13-13   The categorisation of facts as notorious may change over time. Thus, in *Whaley v Carlisle*[44] which was decided in 1866, judicial notice was taken of who had been foreign minister in 1802. Such a fact may have been notorious in 1866 but could hardly be so regarded today.

13-14   It appears that certain customs or business practices may fulfil the requirement of notoriety.[45] In *State (Taylor) v Circuit Judge for Wicklow*[46] Davitt P, referred with approval to *Halsbury*,[47] where three stages in the establishment of a custom or usage were identified. The first stage is when the usage must be proved by evidence with certainty and precision. The second stage is when the court has become to some degree familiar with the usage and slight evidence is required to establish it. The final stage is when the court takes judicial notice of the usage and proof is not required.

13-15   Although, they must ordinarily be proved in accordance with the provisions of s.4(1) of the Documentary Evidence Act 1925,[48] statutory instruments may be judicially noticed when they are "so notorious, well established, embedded in judicial decisions,

---

open document, the writing on which is visible to every person through whose hands it passes (*Robinson v Jones* (1879) 4 LR Ir 391 at 395, 396; *Huth v Huth* [1915] 3 KB 32).

38   Judicial notice has been taken of the price of cattle during a particular period (*Waters v Cruickshank* [1967] IR 378 at 384) and rental levels in Dublin (*McCann v Morrissey* [2013] IEHC 288).

39   Judicial notice has been taken that heroin is a highly addictive drug (*People (DPP) v Byrne* [2012] IECCA 72 at [20]), that marihuana is an alternative name for cannabis and LSD is a popular name and acronym for the drug Lysergide (*Minister for Justice, Equality and Law Reform v Wicinski* [2011] IEHC 169 at 11) and that cocaine hydrochloride is a kind of cocaine (*AG (Cayman Islands) v Roberts* [2002] 1 WLR 1842 at [36]).

40   *R. v Z* [2005] UKHL 35, [2005] 2 AC 645.

41   *Roche v Roche* [2009] IESC 82 at [209]–[210], [2010] 2 IR 321 at 390, [2010] 2 ILRM 411 at 455.

42   *Aslam v Minister for Justice, Equality and Law Reform* [2011] IEHC 512 at [26].

43   Judicial notice was not taken that an interest rate of 12per cent was set at a penal level (*Cussens v Brosnan* [2008] IEHC 169 at [47]) or that the mortgage interest rates charged by a particular lender are out of kilter with those charged by other lenders (*Secured Property Loans Ltd v Floyd* [2011] IEHC 189 at [36], [2011] 2 IR 652 at 667). However, in *Ulrich v. Treasury Solicitor* [2005] 1 All ER 1059 at [9]–[10] judicial notice was taken of the assessment of what a capital sum would have earned in past periods and its value compared to wages of those periods which was conducted by reference to the information obtainable from statutes and law reports of that period.

44   (1866) 17 ICLR 792.

45   See, *e.g. Brandao v Barnett* (1846) 12 Cl & Fin 787 (banker's lien); *George v Davies* [1911] 2 KB 445 (domestic servant might terminate her employment within the first month of her engagement by less than a full month's notice); *Davey v Harrow Corp.* [1958] 1 QB 60 at 69, [1957] 2 All ER 305 at 307 (line on ordnance survey map delineating a boundary hedge indicates the centre of the hedge).

46   [1951] IR 311 at 321.

47   *Halsbury's Laws of England*, 4th edn (London: Butterworths, 1973) at p.63.

48   *People (AG) v Kennedy* [1946] IR 517; *People (AG) v Griffin* [1974] IR 416. See, further, Chap.12, section A.

and susceptible of incontrovertible proof, [that] a judge could not but take judicial notice of their making".[49] An example of such a statutory instrument is furnished by *State (Taylor) v Circuit Judge of Wicklow*.[50] The prosecutor in that case had been convicted of attempting to drive a mechanically propelled vehicle in a public place while drunk, contrary to s.30 of the Road Traffic Act 1933. On appeal to the Circuit Court, he contended that the prosecution were not entitled to succeed in the absence of proof that Part III of the Act (which contained s.30) had been brought into force. This submission was rejected, the Circuit Court judge holding that he was entitled to take judicial notice of the fact that the Act was in force at the material time. His conclusion in this regard was upheld by Davitt P in the High Court. He held that the judge was permitted to make use of his knowledge and experience as a judge to take judicial notice of the fact that the Road Traffic Act, which he had been administering for years, was in force at the material time.

13–16   The decision in *Taylor* was approved and followed by the Supreme Court in *DPP v Collins*.[51] The defendant in that case had been convicted in the District Court of an offence under s.49 of the Road Traffic Act 1961 (as inserted by s.10 of the Road Traffic (Amendment) Act 1978). A question arose as to whether the prosecution had to prove certain regulations made under the 1978 Act, in accordance with the provisions of s.4(1) of the Documentary Evidence Act 1925. Henchy J, delivering the opinion of the Supreme Court, said that the procedure laid down by s.4(1) did not curb the inherent power of a court to treat certain matters as worthy of judicial notice. The particular regulations in question were so well known to members of the bench that if "a judge were to hold that the prosecution must fail for want of proof of the Regulations, such self-induced judicial blindness would bring the administration of the law into disrepute".[52]

13–17   However, it appears that judicial notice cannot be taken of regulations that have to be proven because they create the offence prosecuted.[53]

13–18   Although the English courts have taken judicial notice of foreign patent law,[54] it was held by the New Zealand Court of Appeal in *Mokbel v The Queen*[55] that "[o]nly rarely, however, will foreign laws be so well-known that their contents are 'notorious'." so that judicial notice of them can be taken.

3. Facts Capable of Immediate and Accurate Demonstration

13–19   There are some facts which, although not immediately within the judge's knowledge, are indisputable and can be ascertained from sources to which it is proper for the judge to refer.[56] These include authoritative texts, dictionaries, almanacs, reference

---

[49] *DPP v Collins* [1981] ILRM 447 at 451.

[50] [1951] IR 311.

[51] [1981] ILRM 447.

[52] [1981] ILRM 447 at 451. See also *Minister for Justice v Bartold* [2012] IEHC 108 (statutory instrument designating Poland as a designated state for the purposes of the European Arrest Warrant Act 2003).

[53] *DPP v Collins* [1981] ILRM 447 at 450; *People (DPP) v Cleary* [2005] IECCA 51, [2005] 2 IR 189; *Kelly v Dempsey* [2010] IEHC 336 (Misuse of Drugs Regulations).

[54] *Oxonica Energy Ltd v Neuftec Ltd* [2008] EWHC 2177 (Pat) at [12].

[55] [2013] VSCA 118 at [26].

[56] *Norrie v NSW Registrar of Births, Deaths and Marriages* [2013] NSWCA 145 at [94].

works, and certificates from various officials. Facts which it has been held may be proved in this way include official or political matters,[57] historical facts,[58] geographical facts,[59] population figures[60] and the day of the week upon which a particular date fell.[61]

13–20   An interesting example of this category of judicial notice can be seen in *Mitchell v Member in Charge, Terenure Garda Station.*[62] The validity of the applicant's detention depended on whether s.10 of the Offences Against the State (Amended) Act 1998 had been continued in force by a resolution passed by each House of the Oireachtas. In the course of an application in the District Court to extend the period of detention, it was contended that the detention should not be continued because there had been a failure to prove that the requisite resolutions had been passed. The District Judge rose and consulted the Oireachtas website from which he was able to ascertain that the resolutions had been passed and proceeded to take judicial notice of this fact. On an Art.40 inquiry into the legality of the detention of the applicant, Hogan J considered that the consultation by the District Judge of the Oireachtas website was the equivalent of inspecting a public document containing this information and, once he had done so, he was then perfectly aware that the resolutions had been passed and could take judicial notice of this fact.[63]

4. Judicial Notice Required to be Taken by Statute

13–21   There are a number of statutory provisions that require judicial notice to be taken of specified matters.[64] The most notable example is s.13 of the Interpretation Act 2005 which provides that every Act of the Oireachtas shall be judicially noticed. Other examples are to be found in: art.4 of the European Communities (Judicial Notice and Documentary Evidence) Regulations 1972,[65] ss.4(1) and 11(1) of the Jurisdiction of Courts (Maritime Conventions) Act 1989,[66] s.6 of the Child Abduction and Enforcement

---

[57]   *Cf. R. v Bottrill, ex p. Kuechenmeister* [1947] KB 41, [1946] 2 All ER 434; *Duff Development Co v Government of Kelantan* [1924] AC 797, [1924] All ER 1; *Re Chateau Gai Wines Ltd v Canada (AG)* (1971) 14 DLR 411; *Bradley v Commonwealth of Australia* (1973) 128 CLR 557.

[58]   *State (O'Connor) v Ó Caomhanaigh* [1963] IR 112 at 141; *Bemis v Minister for Arts, Heritage, Gaeltacht and the Islands* [2005] IEHC 207; *DPP v Independent Newspapers (Ireland) Ltd* [2008] IESC 8 at [43], [2008] 4 IR 88 at 102, [2008] 2 ILRM 161 at 174; *Read v Bishop of Lincoln* [1892] AC 644; *Monarch S.S. Co Ltd v Karlshamns of Oljefabriker* [1949] AC 196 at 234, [1949] 1 All ER 1 at 20; *R. v Bartleman* (1984) 12 DLR (4th) 73 at 77; *R. v Nikal* (1996) 133 DLR (4th) 658 at 669.

[59]   *K v Refugee Appeals Tribunal* [2008] IEHC 294 at [18].

[60]   *Oloo-Omee v Refugee Appeals Tribunal* [2012] IEHC 455 at [22].

[61]   *R. v Dyer* (1703) 6 Mod 41; *Hoyle v Lord Cornwallis* (1720) 1 Str 387.

[62]   [2013] IEHC 221.

[63]   See also *Minister for Justice and Equality v Kiernowicz* [2014] IEHC 270 at [13] where Murphy J, on an application for an order pursuant to s. 16 of the European Arrest Warrant Act 2003 directing that the Respondent be surrendered to such person as is duly authorised by the issuing state to receive him, checked the Polish Framework Decision on the European e-justice portal and took judicial notice of it.

[64]   One instance of where a statutory provision stipulates that judicial notice is *not* to be taken of a matter is to be found in s.1(g) of the Interpretation Act 1937 which contains a prohibition on judicial notice being taken of the marginal notes at the side of a statutory provision. See, further, *Cork County Council v Whillock* [1993] 1 IR 231 at 235.

[65]   SI No.341 of 1972. Article 4 requires judicial notice to be taken of the treaties governing the European Communities of the Official Journal and of any decision of, or expression of opinion by, the European Court on any question in respect of which that Court has jurisdiction.

[66]   Section 4(1) requires judicial notice to be taken of the Brussels Convention on the Arrest of

of Custody Orders Act, 1991,[67] s.3 of the Civil Liability (Assessment of Hearing Injury) Act 1998,[68] s.18 of the Jurisdiction of Courts and Enforcement of Judgments Act 1998,[69] s.2(2) of the Protection of Children (Hague Convention) Act 2000,[70] s.5 of the Statute Law (Restatement) Act 2002,[71] s.4 of the European Convention on Human Rights Act 2003[72] and s.8 of the Arbitration Act 2010.[73]

5. General Knowledge

13–22 Judicial notice provides a formalised system for taking into account matters which have not been proved in evidence. However, apart from formally taking judicial notice of a matter, the courts are often willing to act consciously, or unconsciously on the basis of their general knowledge.[74] Thus, in *People (AG) v Moore*[75] the Court of Criminal Appeal declared that it did not require any expert scientific testimony to enable it to conclude that driving ability could be seriously impaired by alcohol. The Court believed that the "tendency of alcohol to affect adversely a persons [*sic*] faculties generally, and, in particular, his judgment of time, speeds and distances, as well as his ability to exercise functions requiring skill in performance, is ... a matter of common knowledge".[76] Similarly, in *McMullen v Farrell*,[77] Barron J stated that when

---

Seagoing Ships and s.11(1) requires judicial notice to be taken of the Brussels Convention on Certain Rules Concerning Civil Jurisdiction in Matters of Collision.

[67] Section 6 requires judicial notice to be taken of the Convention on the Civil Aspects of International Child Abduction, signed at the Hague on 25 October 1980 (commonly known as the Hague Convention).

[68] Section 3 requires judicial notice to be taken of the Report to the Minister for Health and Children by an Expert Hearing Group, published by the Department of Health and Children on 9 April 1998, entitled "Hearing Disability Assessment" (also known as the "Green Book") in all proceedings before a court claiming damages for personal injury arising from a hearing injury. See *Greene v Minister for Defence* [1998] 4 IR 464.

[69] Section 18 requires judicial notice to be taken of the Lugano Convention (the Convention on jurisdiction and the enforcement of judgments in civil and commercial matters, signed at Lugano on 16 September 1988).

[70] Section 2(2) requires judicial notice to be taken of the Hague Convention (the Convention on jurisdiction, applicable law, recognition, enforcement and co-operation in respect of parental responsibility and measures for the protection of children, signed at the Hague on 19 October 1996).

[71] Section 5 provides that judicial notice shall be taken of a restatement.

[72] Section 4 requires that judicial notice be taken of the provisions of the European Convention on Human Rights and of (a) any declaration, decision, advisory opinion or judgment of the European Court of Human Rights, (b) any decision or opinion of the European Commission of Human Rights, (c) any decision of the Committee of Members established under the Statute of the Council of Europe, and a court is required, when interpreting and applying the Convention provisions, to take due account of the principles laid down by those declarations, decisions, advisory opinions, opinions and judgments. It was held in *Byrne v Dublin City Council* [2009] IEHC 122 at [23], that, although a court was required to take judicial notice of such decisions etc, it was not bound by them.

[73] Section 8 requires judicial notice to be taken of the *travaux préparatoires* of the United Nations Commission on International Trade Law and its working group relating to the preparation of the Model Law which is given the force of law in the State and applied to arbitrations by s.6.

[74] See the comments of Murray CJ in *Roche v Roche* [2009] IESC 82, [2010] 2 IR 321 at 350, [2010] 2 ILRM 411 at 419.

[75] [1964] Ir Jur Rep 6.

[76] [1964] Ir Jur Rep 6 at 12. See also *McCartney v. R* (2006) 31 WAR 416 at [150], where it was held that medical evidence was not needed to establish that having a person of equal or greater weight sitting or lying on one's chest or abdomen can be an impediment to breathing.

[77] [1993] 1 IR 123 at 141, [1992] ILRM 776 at 791.

dealing with an allegation of negligence against a solicitor, "the court is in a different position from cases of other professional negligence because the court has of itself its own factual knowledge of how litigation is conducted." In these cases, the general knowledge on which the court was relying was evident but, in many other cases, it will be an unacknowledged factor in the determination of the tribunal of fact.

13–23   The right of judges and juries to apply their general knowledge and powers of reasoning to the determination of the issues which come before them was regarded by Davitt J in *State (Taylor) v Circuit Judge for Wicklow*⁷⁸ as "unquestioned".⁷⁹ This also seems to have been the view of Holmes LJ in *Byrne v Londonderry Tramway Co*⁸⁰ who stated:

> "Judges and jurors must bring to the consideration of the questions they are called on to decide their knowledge of the common affairs of life, and it is not necessary on the trial of an action to give formal evidence of matters with which men of ordinary intelligence are acquainted."⁸¹

13–24   Such common knowledge may legitimately be confined to the locality in question where the court is one of limited and local jurisdiction, *i.e.* the District and Circuit Courts. In *Dougal v Mahon*,⁸² the applicant sought an order of certiorari quashing his convictions for offences under the Road Traffic Acts on the basis, *inter alia*, that the respondent District Justice had made use of his own personal knowledge that a certain car-park was a public place in refusing an application for a direction by the defence on the ground that this element of the offence had not been proved. Commenting on this contention, Gannon J was of the opinion that:

> "in relation to such matters, obviously of notorious public knowledge, he was entitled to and properly could take account of his own knowledge of the place, unless some factor became apparent which could give rise to a doubt about the reliability of his knowledge".⁸³

6. Personal Knowledge

13–25   While it is permissible, and indeed inevitable, that the tribunal of fact will take general knowledge into account in discharging its functions, the matter is otherwise where a member of the tribunal of fact possesses personal knowledge relevant to the facts in issue.⁸⁴ The general position, as laid down by Johnson J in *R. v Justices of Antrim*,⁸⁵ is that a member of the tribunal of fact cannot rely, directly or indirectly on facts within his or her own particular or private knowledge in contradiction of the

---

⁷⁸   [1951] IR 311.
⁷⁹   [1951] IR 311 at 320. See also *R. v Justices of Antrim* [1895] 2 IR 603 at 651 (*per* Johnson J).
⁸⁰   [1902] 2 IR 457.
⁸¹   [1902] 2 IR 457 at 480.
⁸²   Unreported, High Court, 2 December 1988.
⁸³   Unreported, High Court, 2 December 1988 at 13. See also *Keane v Mount Vernon Colliery Co Ltd* [1933] AC 309; *Ingram v Percival* [1969] 1 QB 548, [1968] 3 All ER 657; *Paul v DPP* (1989) 90 Cr App R 173. *Cf. Reynolds v Llanelly Associated Tinplate Co Ltd* [1948] 1 All ER 140 where Lord Greene MR said that whereas the use of knowledge of matters within the common knowledge of everyone in a district is permissible, it is improper to draw on knowledge of a particular or highly specialised nature.
⁸⁴   See, generally, Tunkel, "When may a judge use personal knowledge?" (1997) NLJ (Supp.) 168, and Manchester, "Judicial Notice and Personal Knowledge" (1979) 42 MLR 22. See *R. v Potts* (1982) 36 OR (2d) 195 at 203, 134 DLR (3d) 227; *Denton v Auckland City* [1969] NZLR 256; *Turner v Allison* [1971] NZLR 833 at 849; and *Hayman v Forbes* (1975) 13 SASR 225 at 234, for a discussion of the distinction between general and personal knowledge.
⁸⁵   [1895] 2 IR 603.

evidence adduced.[86] Where a person has such knowledge, he or she ought to be sworn as a witness and having given evidence should take no further part in the proceedings.[87]

13–26 In England, it has been held that it is permissible for a juror to draw on special knowledge of the circumstances forming the background to a case in considering, weighing up and assessing the evidence adduced. Thus, in *Wetherall v Harrison*[88] it was held that in deciding whether the defendant had a reasonable excuse for failure to give a blood sample, the justices could draw on their war-time experiences of the fear that inoculations create in certain individuals. The difficulty of drawing a line between personal knowledge which goes merely to the evaluation of evidence and that which goes to the facts in issue is acute. Having regard to this difficulty and to the right of an accused to a trial based solely on admissible evidence, it is submitted that *Wetherall* should not be followed in this jurisdiction and that juries should not be permitted to make use of any personal knowledge of a particularised nature.[89] Of course, the difficulties of preventing jurors from relying on such knowledge are formidable.

13–27 *A fortiori*, a judge should not rely on such evidence and where he or she possesses knowledge of a particular kind which may bear on his or her evaluation of the evidence, it would seem that fair procedures would require the judge to draw this knowledge to the attention of the affected party and allow him or her the opportunity to call evidence to rebut or explain it.

---

[86] See also *State (Taylor) v Circuit Court Judge for Wicklow* [1951] IR 311 at 322 (*per* Davitt J). *Cf. R. v Field (Justices), ex p. White* (1895) 64 LJMC 158.
[87] *R. v Justices of Antrim* [1895] 2 IR 603 at 651–652 (*per* Johnson J). *Cf. R. v Blick* (1966) 50 Cr App R 280.
[88] [1976] QB 773, [1976] 1 All ER 241. *Cf. R. v S.(R.D.)* [1997] 3 SCR 484, 151 DLR (4th) 193.
[89] *Cf. Mangano v Farleigh Nettheim Pty Ltd* (1965) 65 SR (NSW) 228, where it was held that a warning should be given to a juror with special knowledge.

INDEX